AMERICAN LITERATURE SERIES

HARRY HAYDEN CLARK, *General Editor*

AMERICAN PLAYS

SELECTED AND EDITED WITH CRITICAL INTRODUCTIONS AND BIBLIOGRAPHIES

BY

ALLAN GATES HALLINE

DEPARTMENT OF ENGLISH, UNIVERSITY OF WISCONSIN

AMERICAN BOOK COMPANY

NEW YORK · CINCINNATI · CHICAGO · BOSTON · ATLANTA

Halline's American Plays
W. P. I

Made in U. S. A.

PREFACE

The aim of the present volume of plays is to give the reader an adequate picture of the development of American drama by means of a group of representative plays, together with a series of introductions designed to indicate the work of the dramatist as a whole and to analyze his selected play in particular. A distinct effort has been made to define the thought of the plays and to show their reflection of the same philosophical currents which conditioned the major writings in other fields; it will thus be seen that our drama is more closely integrated with our literature as a whole than has been commonly supposed. Since drama is a social art, we may assume that the character of a nation's theatre is, like Ruskin's architecture, a clue to the character of its people. Commentary on the purely dramatic aspects of the plays has been subordinated in favor of philosophical interpretation and literary kinship; but this does not mean that the plays were chosen with this in mind—they were chosen first of all as drama: practically all of them were distinct theatrical successes in their day, and there is only one for which no record of production exists. It will be seen, in fact, that some of the plays contain principally action, little reflection; but an attempt has been made to define underlying attitudes and to orient the plays culturally. In cases where the dramatic propriety of the utterances of characters in the plays may raise questions as to the author's own ideas, the utterances of the characters have been interpreted with reference to the author's ideas expressed in letters or other undramatic writing.

The approach to American literature so trenchantly set forth in *The Reinterpretation of American Literature*, edited by Norman Foerster, applies to drama as well as to other literary *genres*. A consideration of the plays will reveal that Puritanism is reflected, in one manner or another, in such plays as *Superstition*, *Icebound*, and *The Field God;* that Romanticism is distinctly felt in *The Gladiator*, *Bianca Visconti*, *Francesca da Rimini*, and *Madame Sand;* that the Frontier is pictured in *Horizon* and *The Danites in the Sierras;* and that Realism appears and later comes to full strength in such plays as *Horizon*, *The Henrietta*, *The New York Idea*, *Icebound*, and *The Field God*. It is interesting to note that nationalism is strongest in those plays nearest the Revolution: *The Contrast*, *André*, and *The Bucktails;* it is to occur again in *Fashion*. From another point of view, *The Contrast* may be regarded as a comedy of manners, as indeed may *The Bucktails*, *Fashion*, and *The New York Idea*. The drama of ideas is illustrated in *You and I*,

The Field God, and *The Great God Brown*, with the expressionistic technique fully developed in the latter.

The following have kindly given permission to reprint quotations from the sources indicated: E. S. Bradley, from his *George Henry Boker: Poet and Patriot;* Columbia University Press, from Bronson Howard's *The Autobiography of a Play;* Dodd, Mead and Company, from Burns Mantle's *American Playwrights of Today;* E. P. Dutton & Co., Inc., from Montrose J. Moses's *Representative American Dramatists;* Harper & Brothers, from S. Marion Tucker's *Modern American and British Plays;* Alfred A. Knopf, Inc., from Elizabeth Shepley Sergeant's *Fire Under the Andes;* Little, Brown & Company, from Montrose J. Moses's Introduction to *The Detour;* C. M. Morrison, Editor, from a letter from Eugene O'Neill in the *Philadelphia Public Ledger* (January 22, 1922); Paul H. Musser, from his *James Nelson Barker;* Arthur Hobson Quinn, from his *A History of the American Drama from the Beginning to the Civil War*, *A History of the American Drama from the Civil War to the Present Day*, and *Representative American Plays.*

Acknowledgments to copyright owners appear with the individual plays. I should like to express particular gratitude to Clement E. Foust for his permission to use his version of *The Gladiator* as text for this collection.

Professor Arthur Hobson Quinn's excellent work in the field of American Drama has been indispensable in the preparation of this volume, as the multiplicity of references to his writings will testify. The extensive researches of Montrose J. Moses have also proved of immense value.

To Professor Harry Hayden Clark of the University of Wisconsin I am deeply indebted for stimulating suggestions and advice; he has done much to shape the approach to this study.

A. G. H.

CONTENTS

THE CONTRAST

By Royall Tyler

ROYALL TYLER

[1757–1826]

ROYALL TYLER, a justice of the Vermont Supreme Court, is remembered chiefly as the author of *The Contrast;* however, he was so eager to disclaim authorship of his first play that he delivered over the copyright to the actor Wignell.

Born July 18, 1757, in Boston, William Clark (later Royall) Tyler enjoyed the advantages of a cultured family, his father having been a graduate of Harvard. After preparation in a local Latin school, the son also attended Harvard, where he was known as a gay and brilliant student, graduating as valedictorian of his class in the historic year of 1776.[1]

He served in the War for Independence and was later sent to New York by Governor Bowdoin to assist in the suppression of Shays's rebellion.[2] It was only a few weeks after his arrival in New York that Tyler wrote *The Contrast*, which was produced on April 16 and 18, 1787, and also on the 12th of the following month; the play was revived, chiefly for historic reasons, in 1894, in 1912, and again in 1917.

In 1779 Tyler had received an M.A. degree from Harvard and was admitted to the bar in Vermont. He became a Justice of the Supreme Court of that state in 1801 and served as Chief Justice from 1807 to 1812. His death occurred August 18, 1826.

Tyler was a wit and a gifted conversationalist; he numbered many prominent people among his large circle of acquaintances, some of his close friends being Col. John Trumbull, Christopher Gore, Rufus King, William Eustice, Aaron Dexter, and the Adams and Quincy families. Among the patrons for *The Contrast* were Washington and four cabinet members.[3]

Tyler's other productions include *May-Day in Town, or New York in an Uproar*, performed May 19, 1787, and *A Georgia Spec, or Land in the Moon*, performed about ten years later. These two plays have not survived, though the first, an opera, met with "unusual success," [4] and the second, a satire on land speculation, was well received.[5] Existing in manuscript form are four plays:

[1] In fact, his abilities must have been especially outstanding, for Yale College gave him a B.A. degree at the same time he received one from Harvard.

[2] For Tyler's correspondence during this period see *Brattleboro, Windham County, Vermont,* by Henry Burnham, ed. by Abby Maria Hemenway. Brattleboro: 1880. The important source of information regarding Tyler is: Helen Tyler Brown and Frederick Tupper's *Grandmother Tyler's Book: the Recollections of Mary Palmer Tyler* (Mrs. Royall Tyler), *1775–1866*. New York: 1925.

[3] For a further account of personalities see Ellis, H. M., "Joseph Dennie and his Circle," *Bulletin of the University of Texas,* no. 40, July 15, 1915.

[4] Burnham, *op. cit.*, p. 93.

[5] Quinn, Arthur H., *A History of the American Drama from the Beginning to the Civil War.* New York: 1923, p. 71.

The Island of Barrataria, based on *Don Quixote; The Origin of the Feast of Purim, or The Destinies of Haman and Mordecai; Joseph and His Brethren;* and *The Judgment of Solomon*, the three latter being religious plays.[1]

In addition Tyler wrote a novel, *The Algerine Captive* (1797) which is partly based on the capture of a relative by the Algerian pirates. His minor works include a series of letters, *Yankey in London*, and a *Comic Grammar*.

Critics of the American drama have tended to regard the introduction of Jonathan, the native Yankee, as the significant aspect of *The Contrast*. In his *History of the American Theatre* Dunlap says of the play: "It is extremely deficient in plot, dialogue, or incident, but has some marking in the characters, and in that of Jonathan, played by Wignell, a degree of humour, and knowledge of what is termed Yankee dialect. . . ." Jonathan "was the principal character, perhaps, strictly speaking, the only character." Montrose J. Moses says: "The only native product, as I have said, is Jonathan . . ." and ". . . the only interest that could attach itself to this comedy for the theatre-going audience of today would be in the presentment according to the customs and manners of the time." [2] In the introduction to the play in *Representative American Plays*, Quinn comments: "It is our first comedy, and while its central theme is the contrast between native worth and affectation of foreign manners it is of especial significance as introducing to our stage in the character of 'Jonathan' the shrewd, yet uncultivated type of New England farmer which has since become known as the 'Stage Yankee.' " But striking as this character is and despite the many imitations which followed,[3] there are two difficulties in accepting this evaluation of the play: first, recent investigation has uncovered a possible source from which Tyler *might* have taken his Jonathan (this question is discussed further later); second, there is reason to believe that the significant aspect of the play is the question of nationalism, arising from the situation which gives the play its title. When Tyler's friends were urging him to try writing a play, they suggested that it be "strictly national in plot and characters"; [4] the Prologue begins its nationalistic plea thus:

"Exult, each patriot heart!—this night is shewn
A piece, which we may fairly call our own."

Not only is the theme of native worth versus foreign affectation stated in the play itself, but it appears almost at the opening and provides the final, conclusive note of the play. Tyler also appears to be strongly nationalistic elsewhere, as in the preface to *The Algerine Captive* which deplores the fact that the widely-read

[1] For brief commentaries on the contents of these plays, consult Quinn, *op. cit.*, pp. 71–73.

[2] *Representative Plays by American Dramatists*, p. 437. Moses also speaks of "Jonathan, the first stage Yankee," p. 436.

[3] These include: Robinson's *The Yorker's Stratagem*, Barker's *Tears and Smiles*, Lindsley's *Love and Friendship*, Paulding's *The Bucktails, or Americans in England*, Woodworth's *Forest Rose*.

[4] *Brattleboro*, p. 93.

current novels were not of American manufacture, and as also in his strongly nationalistic speech delivered to the Shays rebellionists.

The Contrast is an outgrowth of the period in which it was written. The nationalistic forces which had brought about the Revolution and carried it to a successful conclusion were now struggling to consolidate themselves in some permanent form; the concept of national unity reached its culmination in the drafting of the Constitution. This, coincidentally enough, was in 1787. Close as it is to the Revolution, *The Contrast* exhibits little of the belligerent spirit; it is neither wrathful nor malicious; it is scarcely anti-Anglican; but it is essentially nationalistic; the assumption which lies back of its central attitudes is the intrinsic worth of American as opposed to European culture; it is in its own sphere a spiritual Declaration of Independence. In the words of Manly: "But, if our country has its errors in common with other countries, I am proud to say America—I mean the United States—has displayed virtues and achievements which modern nations may admire, but of which they have seldom set us the example." [1] It is not, however, possible to regard this nationalism either as relentlessly felt or as perfectly applied in view of the fact that Tyler fashions part of his play after a foreign model, Sheridan's *School for Scandal;* but even though Tyler made a well-nigh necessary [2] concession with respect to the means he employed, yet his nationalistic intent is not therefore invalidated.

Other nationalistic currents find expression in the play, e.g., the contemporary reverence for Washington, the high esteem for Lafayette, the movement for confidence in the federal currency, the agitation for aid to the disabled veterans. Suggested by the foregoing and in view of Manly's strictures on the Grecians, who divided and fell, the nationalism of the play appears to be Federalistic; like other plays of the period, particularly *André* by Dunlap, *The Contrast* reflects, in a mild way, the philosophy of the Hamiltonian Federalists with respect to strong union. John T. Buckingham also points out that "The complexion of the political articles was purely federalistic." [3]

Since Jonathan has been traditionally spoken of as the conspicuous contribution of the play, it must not be casually supposed that he furnishes the contrast to Dimple; obviously, Manly is the proponent of the American view. A second misconception should be guarded against: that of not taking Manly seriously (cf. the Prologue). Though the modern temper and modern drama shun the obviously moralistic, yet in 1787 the theatregoer was more receptive to sentiment and the technique of the drama was less highly developed than it is today.

We have, then, inner moral worth and essential respect of others as it reveals

[1] Act IV, sc. 1., p. 32.

[2] Tyler had seen few plays, had received no instruction in dramatic writing, and composed *The Contrast* in a period of three weeks while on a visit to New York.

[3] *Specimens of Newspaper Literature*, II, 203.

itself in opposition to external accomplishment of manners and comparative disregard of one's fellow-men—especially fellow-women.[1] Though the nationalism of the play is not malevolent, as has been pointed out, yet little care is taken to distinguish the variety from the species, i.e., the offensive pseudo-Chesterfieldian from the European. That such inattention is dramatic rather than malicious is suggested by the presence of Jonathan himself, who is as ridiculous as Dimple is odious.[2] But inattention it remains, and one thus tends to regard *The Contrast* as a nationalistic document rather than a completely disinterested evaluation of Anglo-American cultural relationships.

Tyler gives the first dramatic presentation of the concept of American cultural self-consciousness and self-sufficiency which developed over and above the antagonism to foreign culture incidental to the more comprehensive, more intense spirit of hostility that lay back of the Revolution itself.[3] The "Hartford Wits" consciously strove to create an American literature that would be commensurate in scope and elevation with the masterpieces of the old world. In his preface to *The Conquest of Canaan* Dwight expresses this ambition for a national literature, and though his *Greenfield Hill* purports to imitate a different English poet in each part, yet the scene and subject are American; Barlow's *Vision of Columbus* and his *Columbiad* are designedly concerned with America. In 1788 Freneau protests against the incursions of foreign culture in his poem *Literary Importation.* The ambition on the part of American writers to achieve a national culture is not merely a burst of enthusiasm induced by the Revolution, but it establishes itself as a conditioning factor in nineteenth-century thought; it is to appear as theory in Emerson's *American Scholar* and in its applied form in Whitman's *Leaves of Grass.*

The narrower subject of dandyism suggested to Tyler by Sheridan's *School for Scandal* likewise finds treatment by other American writers: Franklin in *The Way to Wealth*, Crèvecœur in *What is an American?* and Freneau in *The Bergen Planter.*[4]

In *The Contrast* not only do we see the reception accorded to a particular type of foreign culture, but we glimpse other aspects of contemporary American society as well, particularly that of New York. Though in no sense a comprehensive or thorough study of social life, yet Tyler's play contains representations, at once suggestive in detail and authentic in import, of current dress, entertain-

[1] That Tyler himself was sensitive to moral distinctions is suggested by the fact that he hesitated to go into the ministry because, as he says, "a consciousness of having lived too gay a life in my youth, made me tremble lest I should in some way bring disgrace upon the sacred cause." (*Brattleboro*, p. 95.)

[2] Cf. also the slurs which Charlotte casts on her brother's unfashionable uniform.

[3] See, for example, Dwight's war song, *Columbia.*

[4] For other American plays including the beau, see Reed, P. I., "The Realistic Presentation of American Characters in Native American Plays prior to Eighteen Seventy," *Ohio State University Bulletin*, XXII, no. 26 (May, 1918).

ment, manners, sentiments, morals, and character. So prevalent is sentiment that Herbert R. Brown regards the drama as "fundamentally sentimental." [1] He shows Maria and Manly particularly in this light: Maria reads "Sir Charles Grandison, Clarissa Harlow, Shenstone, and the Sentimental Journey." [2] There is much truth in this description of the play, but to view it wholly from this standpoint would be to overlook the effective anti-sentimentalism of Charlotte [3] and to undervalue the genuine nationalism of Manly.

The extent of Tyler's originality in character study and plot invention will have to be determined with reference to the possible sources of the play. As already noted, it has generally been held that Tyler presented for the first time the Yankee character Jonathan with his rustic language and stupidities, but Marston Balch recently called attention to an Irish play,[4] performed just a year before *The Contrast*, in which there is a Yankee "Jonathan" with many of the characteristics exhibited by Tyler's Jonathan. However, since the Irish play was not published until after the production of *The Contrast*, it is quite improbable that Tyler ever had any direct knowledge of the piece, and the way still lies open for Tyler's own originality in the creation of Jonathan. It is possible, to be sure, that an unknown play or novel furnished the prototype for both dramatists; but until additional evidence is available, no more definite conclusions can be drawn.

According to his own statement Tyler made some use of Sheridan's *School for Scandal*, the play which so shocked Jonathan during his visit in New York. More than likely Tyler received from Sheridan suggestions for the fop, for the rules of behavior, and for the flippant, gossipy, charming Charlotte; but the bulk of the play yet remains Tyler's own. With respect to the origin of the song *Alknomook*, it has been pointed out that although Freneau includes it in the *American Museum* [5] and Mrs. Hunter in her collection in 1806, yet a parallel of the song appears in a Dublin play, *New Spain; or, Love in May*, produced in 1740.[6]

It is remarkable that a man so little trained dramatically as Tyler should write a play so sharp in its characterization, so effective in dramatic presentation, and so significant culturally.

The text of *The Contrast* follows the Wignell edition of 1790.

[1] Brown, Herbert R., "Sensibility in Eighteenth Century American Drama," *American Literature*, IV, 57 (March, 1932).

[2] Act I, sc. 1, p. 12.

[3] Though Brown points out that even Charlotte swings to sentimentalism at the very end, it must be remembered that it is only at the end; throughout the play she is ridiculing sentiment.

[4] *A Match for a Widow, or The Frolics of Fancy*, by Captain Joseph Atkinson, 1786. See "Jonathan the First," *Modern Language Notes*, XLVI, 281–288 (May, 1931).

[5] *American Museum*, I, 77. But Freneau never included it in his own poems.

[6] Cf. Moses' *Representative Plays by American Dramatists*, I. T. J. McKee concluded, however, that the song was Tyler's own composition. See Introduction to *The Contrast*, Dunlap Society Publications, 1–3, 1887, p. x.

PROLOGUE

WRITTEN BY A YOUNG GENTLEMAN OF NEW-YORK, AND SPOKEN BY MR. WIGNELL

EXULT, each patriot heart!—this night is shewn
A piece, which we may fairly call our own;
Where the proud titles of "My Lord! Your Grace!"
To humble *Mr.* and plain *Sir* give place.
Our Author pictures not from foreign climes
The fashions or the follies of the times;
But has confin'd the subject of his work
To the gay scenes—the circles of New-York.
On native themes his Muse displays her pow'rs;
If ours the faults, the virtues too are ours.
Why should our thoughts to distant countries roam,
When each refinement may be found at home?
Who travels now to ape the rich or great,
To deck an equipage and roll in state;
To court the graces, or to dance with ease,
Or by hypocrisy to strive to please?
Our free-born ancestors such arts despis'd;
Genuine sincerity alone they priz'd;
Their minds, with honest emulation fir'd;
To solid good—not ornament—aspir'd;
Or, if ambition rous'd a bolder flame,
Stern virtue throve, where indolence was shame.

But modern youths, with imitative sense,
Deem taste in dress the proof of excellence;
And spurn the meanness of your homespun arts,
Since homespun habits would obscure their parts;
Whilst all, which aims at splendor and parade,
Must come from Europe, *and be ready made.*
Strange! we should thus our native worth disclaim,
And check the progress of our rising fame.
Yet *one*, whilst imitation bears the sway,
Aspires to nobler heights, and points the way.
Be rous'd, my friends! his bold example view;
Let your own Bards be proud to copy *you!*
Should rigid critics reprobate our play,
At least the patriotic heart will say,
"Glorious our fall, since in a noble cause.
The bold *attempt alone* demands applause."
Still may the wisdom of the Comic Muse
Exalt your merits, or your faults accuse.
But think not, 'tis her aim to be severe;—
We all are mortals, and as mortals err.

If candor pleases, we are truly blest;
Vice trembles, when compell'd to stand confess'd.
Let not light Censure on your faults offend,
Which aims not to expose them, but amend.
Thus does our Author to your candor trust;
Conscious, the *free* are generous, as just.

CHARACTERS

	New-York	Maryland
Col. Manly	Mr. *Henry*	Mr. *Hallam*
Dimple	Mr. *Hallam*	Mr. *Harper*
Van Rough	Mr. *Morris*	Mr. *Morris*
Jessamy	Mr. *Harper*	Mr. *Biddle*
Jonathan	Mr. *Wignell*	Mr. *Wignell*
Charlotte	Mrs. *Morris*	Mrs. *Morris*
Maria	Mrs. *Harper*	Mrs. *Harper*
Letitia	Mrs. *Kenna*	Mrs. *Williamson*
Jenny	Miss *Tuke*	Miss *W. Tuke*

Servants

Scene, New-York

THE CONTRAST

ACT I

SCENE I. *An Apartment at* CHARLOTTE'S

CHARLOTTE *and* LETITIA *discovered*

LETITIA. And so, Charlotte, you really think the pocket-hoop unbecoming.

CHARLOTTE. No, I don't say so. It may be very becoming to saunter round the house of a rainy day; to visit my grand-mamma, or to go to Quakers' meeting: but to swim in a minuet, with the eyes of fifty well-dressed beaux upon me, to trip it in the Mall, or walk on the battery, give me the luxurious, jaunty, flowing, bell-hoop. It would have delighted you to have seen me the last evening, my charming girl! I was dangling o'er the battery with Billy Dimple; a knot of young fellows were upon the platform; as I passed them I faultered with one of the most bewitching false steps you ever saw, and then recovered myself with such a pretty confusion, flirting my hoop to discover a jet black shoe and brilliant buckle. Gad! how my little heart thrilled to hear the confused raptures of—"*Demme, Jack, whàt a delicate foot!*" "*Ha! General, what a well-turned—*"

LETITIA. Fie! fie! Charlotte [*Stopping her mouth.*], I protest you are quite a libertine.

CHARLOTTE. Why, my dear little prude, are we not all such libertines? Do you think, when I sat tortured two hours under the hands of my friseur, and an hour more at my toilet, that I had any thoughts of my aunt Susan, or my cousin Betsey? though they are both allowed to be critical judges of dress.

LETITIA. Why, who should we dress to please, but those who are judges of its merit?

CHARLOTTE. Why, a creature who does not know *Buffon* from *Souflee*—Man!—my Letitia—Man! for whom we dress, walk, dance, talk, lisp, languish, and smile. Does not the grave Spectator assure us that even our much bepraised diffidence, modesty, and blushes are all directed to make ourselves good wives and mothers as fast as we can? Why, I'll undertake with one flirt of this hoop to bring more beaux to my feet in one week than the grave Maria, and her sentimental circle, can do, by sighing sentiment till their hairs are grey.

LETITIA. Well, I won't argue with you; you always out-talk me; let us change the subject. I hear that Mr. Dimple and Maria are soon to be married.

CHARLOTTE. You hear true. I was consulted in the choice of the wedding clothes. She is to be married in a delicate white sattin, and has a monstrous pretty brocaded lutestring for the second day. It would have done you good to have seen with what an affected indifference the dear sentimentalist turned over a thousand pretty things, just as if her heart did not palpitate with her approaching happiness, and at last made her choice and arranged her dress with such apathy as if she did not know that plain white sattin and a simple blond lace whould shew her clear skin and dark hair to the greatest advantage.

LETITIA. But they say her indifference to dress, and even to the gentleman himself, is not entirely affected.

CHARLOTTE. How?

LETITIA. It is whispered that if Maria gives her hand to Mr. Dimple, it will be without her heart.

CHARLOTTE. Though the giving the heart is one of the last of all laughable considerations in the marriage of a girl of spirit, yet I should like to hear what antiquated notions the dear little piece of old-fashioned prudery has got in her head.

LETITIA. Why, you know that old Mr. John-Richard-Robert-Jacob-Isaac-Abraham-Cornelius Van Dumpling, Billy Dimple's father (for he has thought fit to soften his name, as well as manners, during his English tour), was the most intimate friend of Maria's father. The old folks, about a year before Mr. Van Dumpling's death, proposed this match: the young folks were accordingly introduced, and told they must love one another. Billy was then a good-natured, decent-dressing young fellow, with a little dash of the coxcomb, such as our young fellows of fortune usually have. At this time, I really believe she thought she loved him; and had they then been married, I doubt not they might have jogged on, to the end of the chapter, a good kind of a sing-song lack-a-daysaical life, as other honest married folks do.

CHARLOTTE. Why did they not then marry?

LETITIA. Upon the death of his father, Billy went to England to see the world and rub off a little of the patroon rust. During his absence, Maria, like a good girl, to keep herself constant to her *nown true-love*, avoided company, and betook herself, for her amusement, to her books, and her dear Billy's letters. But, alas! how many ways has the mischievous demon of inconstancy of stealing into a woman's heart! Her love was destroyed by the very means she took to support it.

CHARLOTTE. How?—Oh! I have it—some likely young beau found the way to her study.

LETITIA. Be patient, Charlotte; your head so runs upon beaux. Why, she read Sir Charles Grandison, Clarissa Harlow, Shenstone, and the Sentimental Journey; and between whiles, as I said, Billy's letters. But, as her taste improved, her love declined. The contrast was so striking betwixt the good sense of her books and the flimsiness of her love-letters, that she discovered she had unthinkingly engaged her hand without her heart; and then the whole transaction, managed by the old folks, now appeared so unsentimental, and looked so like bargaining for a bale of goods, that she found she ought to have rejected, according to every rule of romance, even the man of her choice, if imposed upon her in that manner. Clary Harlow would have scorned such a match.

CHARLOTTE. Well, how was it on Mr. Dimple's return? Did he meet a more favorable reception than his letters?

LETITIA. Much the same. She spoke of him with respect abroad, and with contempt in her closet. She watched his conduct and conversation, and found that he had by travelling acquired the wickedness of Lovelace without his wit, and the politeness of Sir Charles Grandison without his generosity. The ruddy youth, who washed his face at the cistern every morning, and swore and looked eternal love and constancy, was now metamorphosed into a flippant, palid, polite beau, who devotes the morning to his toilet, reads a few pages of Chesterfield's letters, and then minces out, to put the infamous principles in practice upon every woman he meets.

CHARLOTTE. But, if she is so apt at conjuring up these sentimental bugbears, why does she not discard him at once?

LETITIA. Why, she thinks her word too sacred to be trifled with. Besides, her father, who has a great respect for the memory of his deceased friend, is ever telling her how he shall renew his years in their union, and repeating the dying injunctions of old Van Dumpling.

CHARLOTTE. A mighty pretty story! And so you would make me believe that the sensible Maria would give up Dumpling manor, and the all-accomplished Dimple as a husband, for the absurd, ridiculous reason, forsooth, because she despises and abhors him. Just as if a lady could not be privileged to spend a man's fortune, ride in his carriage, be called after his name, and call him her *nown dear lovee* when she wants money, without loving and respecting the great he-creature. Oh! my dear girl, you are a monstrous prude.

LETITIA. I don't say what I would do; I only intimate how I suppose she wishes to act.

CHARLOTTE. No, no, no! A fig for sentiment. If she breaks, or wishes to break, with Mr. Dimple, depend upon it, she has some other man in her eye. A woman rarely discards one lover until she is sure of another. Letitia little thinks what a clue I have to Dimple's conduct. The generous man submits to render himself disgusting to Maria, in order that she may leave him at liberty to address me. I must change the subject.

[*Aside, and rings a bell.*]

Enter SERVANT

CHARLOTTE. Frank, order the horses to.—Talking of marriage, did you hear that Sally Bloomsbury is going to be married next week to Mr. Indigo, the rich Carolinian?

LETITIA. Sally Bloomsbury married!—why, she is not yet in her teens.

CHARLOTTE. I do not know how that is, but you may depend upon it, 'tis a done affair. I have it from the best authority. There is my aunt Wyerly's Hannah. You know Hannah; though a black, she is a wench that was never caught in a lie in her life. Now, Hannah has a brother who courts Sarah, Mrs. Catgut the milliner's girl, and she told Hannah's brother, and Hannah, who, as I said before, is a girl of undoubted veracity, told it directly to me, that Mrs. Catgut was making a new cap for Miss Bloomsbury, which, as it was very dressy, it is very probable is designed for a wedding cap. Now, as she is to be married, who can it be to but to Mr. Indigo? Why, there is no other gentleman that visits at her papa's.

LETITIA. Say not a word more, Charlotte. Your intelligence is so direct and well grounded, it is almost a pity that it is not a piece of scandal.

CHARLOTTE. Oh! I am the pink of prudence. Though I cannot charge myself with ever having discredited a tea-party by my silence, yet I take care never to report any thing of my acquaintance, especially if it is to their credit,—*discredit*, I mean,—until I have searched to the bottom of it. It is true, there is infinite pleasure in this charitable pursuit. Oh! how delicious to go and condole with the friends of some backsliding sister, or to retire with some old dowager or maiden aunt of the family, who love scandal so well that they cannot forbear gratifying their appetite at the expense of the reputation of their nearest relations! And then to return full fraught with a rich collection of circumstances, to retail to the next circle of our acquaintance under the strongest injunctions of secrecy,—ha, ha, ha!—interlarding the melancholy tale with so many doleful shakes of the head, and more doleful "Ah! who would have thought it! so amiable, so prudent a young lady, as we all thought her, what a monstrous pity! well, I have nothing to charge myself with; I acted the part of a friend, I warned her of the principles of that rake, I told her what would be the consequence; I told her so, I told her so."—Ha, ha, ha!

LETITIA. Ha, ha, ha! Well, but, Charlotte, you don't tell me what you think of Miss Bloomsbury's match.

CHARLOTTE. Think! why, I think it is probable she cried for a plaything, and they have given her a husband. Well, well, well, the puling chit shall not be deprived of her plaything: 'tis only exchanging London dolls for American babies.—Apropos, of babies, have you heard what Mrs. Affable's high-flying notions of delicacy have come to?

LETITIA. Who, she that was Miss Lovely?

CHARLOTTE. The same; she married Bob Affable of Schenectady. Don't you remember?

Enter SERVANT

SERVANT. Madam, the carriage is ready.

LETITIA. Shall we go to the stores first, or visiting?

CHARLOTTE. I should think it rather too early to visit, especially Mrs. Prim; you know she is so particular.

LETITIA. Well, but what of Mrs. Affable?

CHARLOTTE. Oh, I'll tell you as we go; come, come, let us hasten. I hear Mrs. Catgut has some of the prettiest caps arrived you ever saw. I shall die if I have not the first sight of them. [*Exeunt.*

SCENE 2. *A Room in* VAN ROUGH'S *House*

MARIA *sitting disconsolate at a Table, with Books, etc.*

SONG

I.

The sun sets in night, and the stars shun the day;
But glory remains when their lights fade away!
Begin, ye tormentors! your threats are in vain,
For the son of Alknomook shall never complain.

2.

Remember the arrows he shot from his bow;
Remember your chiefs by his hatchet laid low:
Why so slow?—do you wait till I shrink from the pain?
No—the son of Alknomook will never complain.

3.

Remember the wood where in ambush we lay,
And the scalps which we bore from your nation away:
Now the flame rises fast, you exult in my pain;
But the son of Alknomook can never complain.

4.

I go to the land where my father is gone;
His ghost shall rejoice in the fame of his son:
Death comes like a friend, he relieves me from pain;
And thy son, Oh Alknomook! has scorn'd to complain.

There is something in this song which ever calls forth my affections. The manly virtue of courage, that fortitude which steels the heart against the keenest misfortunes, which interweaves the laurel of glory amidst the instruments of torture and death, displays something so noble, so exalted, that in despite of the prejudices of education I cannot but admire it, even in a savage. The prepossession which our sex is supposed to entertain for the character of a soldier is, I know, a standing piece of raillery among the wits. A cockade, a lapell'd coat, and a feather, they will tell you, are irresistible by a female heart. Let it be so. Who is it that considers the helpless situation of our sex, that does not see that we each moment stand in need of a protector, and that a brave one too? Formed of the more delicate materials of nature, endowed only with the softer passions, incapable, from our ignorance of the world, to guard against the wiles of mankind, our security for happiness often depends upon their generosity and courage. Alas! how little of the former do we find! How inconsistent! that man should be leagued to destroy that honor upon which solely rests his respect and esteem. Ten thousand temptations allure us, ten thousand passions betray us; yet the smallest deviation from the path of rectitude is followed by the contempt and insult of man, and the more remorseless pity of woman; years of penitence and tears cannot wash away the stain, nor a life of virtue obliterate its remembrance. Reputation is the life of woman; yet courage to protect it is masculine and disgusting; and the only safe asylum a woman of delicacy can find is in the arms of a man of honor. How naturally, then, should we love the brave and the generous; how gratefully should we bless the arm raised for our protection, when nerv'd by virtue and directed by honor! Heaven grant that the man with whom I may be connected—may be connected! Whither has my imagination transported me—whither does it now lead me? Am I not indissolubly engaged, by every obligation of honor which my own consent and my father's approbation can give, to a man who can never share my affections, and whom a few days hence it will be criminal for me to disapprove—to disapprove! would to heaven that were all—to despise. For, can the most frivolous manners, actuated by the most depraved heart, meet, or merit, anything but contempt from every woman of delicacy and sentiment?

[VAN ROUGH *without*. Mary!]

Ha! my father's voice—Sir!—

Enter VAN ROUGH

VAN ROUGH. What, Mary, always singing doleful ditties, and moping over these plaguy books.

MARIA. I hope, Sir, that it is not criminal to improve my mind with books, or to divert my melancholy with singing, at my leisure hours.

VAN ROUGH. Why, I don't know that, child; I don't know that. They us'd to say, when I was a young man, that if a woman knew how to make a pudding, and to keep herself out of fire and water, she knew enough for a wife. Now, what good have these books done you? have they not made you melancholy? as you call it. Pray, what right has a girl of your age to be in the dumps? haven't you everything your heart can wish; an't you going to be married to a young man of great fortune; an't you going to have the quit-rent of twenty miles square?

MARIA. One-hundredth part of the land, and

a lease for life of the heart of a man I could love, would satisfy me.

Van Rough. Pho, pho, pho! child; nonsense, downright nonsense, child. This comes of your reading your story-books; your Charles Grandisons, your Sentimental Journals, and your Robinson Crusoes, and such other trumpery. No, no, no! child; it is money makes the mare go; keep your eye upon the main chance, Mary.

Maria. Marriage, Sir, is, indeed, a very serious affair.

Van Rough. You are right, child; you are right. I am sure I found it so, to my cost.

Maria. I mean, Sir, that as marriage is a portion for life, and so intimately involves our happiness, we cannot be too considerate in the choice of our companion.

Van Rough. Right, child; very right. A young woman should be very sober when she is making her choice, but when she has once made it, as you have done, I don't see why she should not be as merry as a grig; I am sure she has reason enough to be so. Solomon says that "there is a time to laugh, and a time to weep." Now, a time for a young woman to laugh is when she has made sure of a good rich husband. Now, a time to cry, according to you, Mary, is when she is making choice of him; but I should think that a young woman's time to cry was when she despaired of *getting* one. Why, there was your mother, now: to be sure, when I popp'd the question to her she did look a little silly; but when she had once looked down on her apron-strings, as all modest young women us'd to do, and drawled out ye-s, she was as brisk and as merry as a bee.

Maria. My honored mother, Sir, had no motive to melancholy; she married the man of her choice.

Van Rough. The man of her choice! And pray, Mary, an't you going to marry the man of your choice—what trumpery notion is this? It is these vile books. [*Throwing them away.*] I'd have you to know, Mary, if you won't make young Van Dumpling the man of *your* choice, you shall marry him as the man of *my* choice.

Maria. You terrify me, Sir. Indeed, Sir, I am all submission. My will is yours.

Van Rough. Why, that is the way your mother us'd to talk. "My will is yours, my dear Mr. Van Rough, my will is yours"; but she took special care to have her own way, though, for all that.

Maria. Do not reflect upon my mother's memory, Sir—

Van Rough. Why not, Mary, why not? She kept me from speaking my mind all her *life*, and do you think she shall henpeck me now she is *dead* too? Come, come; don't go to sniveling; be a good girl, and mind the main chance. I'll see you well settled in the world.

Maria. I do not doubt your love, Sir, and it is my duty to obey you. I will endeavor to make my duty and inclination go hand in hand.

Van Rough. Well, well, Mary; do you be a good girl, mind the main chance, and never mind inclination. Why, do you know that I have been down in the cellar this very morning to examine a pipe of Madeira which I purchased the week you were born, and mean to tap on your wedding day?—That pipe cost me fifty pounds sterling. It was well worth sixty pounds; but I over-reach'd Ben Bulkhead, the supercargo. I'll tell you the whole story. You must know that—

Enter Servant

Servant. Sir, Mr. Transfer, the broker, is below. [*Exit.*

Van Rough. Well, Mary, I must go. Remember, and be a good girl, and mind the main chance. [*Exit.*

Maria [*alone*]. How deplorable is my situation! How distressing for a daughter to find her heart militating with her filial duty! I know my father loves me tenderly; why then do I reluctantly obey him? Heaven knows! with what reluctance I should oppose the will of a parent, or set an example of filial disobedience; at a parent's command, I could wed awkwardness and deformity. Were the heart of my husband good, I would so magnify his good qualities with the eye of conjugal affection, that the defects of his person and manners should be lost in the emanation of his virtues. At a father's command, I could embrace poverty. Were the poor man my husband, I would learn resignation to my lot; I would enliven our frugal meal with good humor, and chase away misfortune from our cottage with a smile. At a father's command, I could almost submit to what every female heart knows to be the most mortifying, to marry a weak man, and blush at my husband's folly in every company I visited. But to marry a depraved wretch, whose only virtue is a polished exterior; who is actuated by the unmanly ambition of conquering the defenceless; whose heart, insensible to the emotions of patriotism, dilates at the plaudits of every unthinking girl; whose laurels are the sighs and tears of the miserable victims of his specious behavior,—can he, who has no regard for the peace and happiness of other families, ever have a due regard for the peace and happiness of his own? Would to heaven that my father were not so hasty in his temper! Surely, if I were to state my reasons for declining this match, he would not compel me to marry a man, whom, though my lips may solemnly promise to honor, I find my heart must ever despise.

[*Exit.*

END OF THE FIRST ACT

ACT II

Scene 1

Enter Charlotte *and* Letitia

Charlotte [*at entering*]. Betty, take those things out of the carriage and carry them to my chamber; see that you don't tumble them. My dear, I protest, I think it was the homeliest of the whole. I declare I was almost tempted to return and change it.

Letitia. Why would you take it?

Charlotte. Didn't Mrs. Catgut say it was the most fashionable?

Letitia. But, my dear, it will never fit becomingly on you.

Charlotte. I know that; but did not you hear Mrs. Catgut say it was fashionable?

Letitia. Did you see that sweet airy cap with the white sprig?

Charlotte. Yes, and I longed to take it; but, my dear, what could I do? Did not Mrs. Catgut say it was the most fashionable; and if I had not taken it, was not that awkward gawky, Sally Slender, ready to purchase it immediately?

Letitia. Did you observe how she tumbled over the things at the next shop, and then went off without purchasing anything, nor even thanking the poor man for his trouble? But, of all the awkward creatures, did you see Miss Blouze endeavoring to thrust her unmerciful arm into those small kid gloves?

Charlotte. Ha, ha, ha, ha!

Letitia. Then did you take notice with what an affected warmth of friendship she and Miss Wasp met? when all their acquaintance know how much pleasure they take in abusing each other in every company.

Charlotte. Lud! Letitia, is that so extraordinary? Why, my dear, I hope you are not going to turn sentimentalist. Scandal, you know, is but amusing ourselves with the faults, foibles, follies, and reputations of our friends; indeed, I don't know why we should have friends, if we are not at liberty to make use of them. But no person is so ignorant of the world as to suppose, because I amuse myself with a lady's faults, that I am obliged to quarrel with her person every time we meet: believe me, my dear, we should have very few acquaintance at that rate.

Servant *enters and delivers a letter to* Charlotte, *and*— [*Exit.*

Charlotte. You'll excuse me, my dear.

[*Opens and reads to herself.*]

Letitia. Oh, quite excusable.

Charlotte. As I hope to be married, my brother Henry is in the city.

Letitia. What, your brother, Colonel Manly?

Charlotte. Yes, my dear; the only brother I have in the world.

Letitia. Was he never in this city?

Charlotte. Never nearer than Harlem Heights, where he lay with his regiment.

Letitia. What sort of a being is this brother of yours? If he is as chatty, as pretty, as sprightly as you, half the belles in the city will be pulling caps for him.

CHARLOTTE. My brother is the very counterpart and reverse of me: I am gay, he is grave; I am airy, he is solid; I am ever selecting the most pleasing objects for my laughter, he has a tear for every pitiful one. And thus, whilst he is plucking the briars and thorns from the path of the unfortunate, I am strewing my own path with roses.

LETITIA. My sweet friend, not quite so poetical, and a little more particular.

CHARLOTTE. Hands off, Letitia. I feel the rage of simile upon me; I can't talk to you in any other way. My brother has a heart replete with the noblest sentiments, but then, it is like—it is like—Oh! you provoking girl, you have deranged all my ideas—it is like—Oh! I have it—his heart is like an old maiden lady's bandbox; it contains many costly things, arranged with the most scrupulous nicety, yet the misfortune is that they are too delicate, costly, and antiquated for common use.

LETITIA. By what I can pick out of your flowery description, your brother is no beau.

CHARLOTTE. No, indeed; he makes no pretension to the character. He'd ride, or rather fly, an hundred miles to relieve a distressed object, or to do a gallant act in the service of his country; but should you drop your fan or bouquet in his presence, it is ten to one that some beau at the farther end of the room would have the honor of presenting it to you before he had observed that it fell. I'll tell you one of his antiquated, anti-gallant notions. He said once in my presence, in a room full of company,—would you believe it?—in a large circle of ladies, that the best evidence a gentleman could give a young lady of his respect and affection was to endeavor in a friendly manner to rectify her foibles. I protest I was crimson to the eyes, upon reflecting that I was known as his sister.

LETITIA. Insupportable creature! tell a lady of her faults! if he is so grave, I fear I have no chance of captivating him.

CHARLOTTE. His conversation is like a rich, old-fashioned brocade,—it will stand alone; every sentence is a sentiment. Now you may judge what a time I had with him, in my twelve months' visit to my father. He read me such lectures, out of pure brotherly affection, against the extremes of fashion, dress, flirting, and coquetry, and all the other dear things which he knows I doat upon, that I protest his conversation made me as melancholy as if I had been at church; and heaven knows, though I never prayed to go there but on one occasion, yet I would have exchanged his conversation for a psalm and a sermon. Church is rather melancholy, to be sure; but then I can ogle the beaux, and be regaled with "here endeth the first lesson," but his brotherly *here*, you would think had no end. You captivate him! Why, my dear, he would as soon fall in love with a box of Italian flowers. There is Maria, now, if she were not engaged, she might do something. Oh! how I should like to see that pair of penserosos together, looking as grave as two sailors' wives of a stormy night, with a flow of sentiment meandering through their conversation like purling streams in modern poetry.

LETITIA. Oh! my dear fanciful—

CHARLOTTE. Hush! I hear some person coming through the entry.

Enter SERVANT

SERVANT. Madam, there's a gentleman below who calls himself Colonel Manly; do you chuse to be at home?

CHARLOTTE. Shew him in. [*Exit* SERVANT.] Now for a sober face.

Enter COLONEL MANLY

MANLY. My dear Charlotte, I am happy that I once more enfold you within the arms of fraternal affection. I know you are going to ask (amiable impatience!) how our parents do,—the venerable pair transmit you their blessing by me. They totter on the verge of a well-spent life, and wish only to see their children settled in the world, to depart in peace.

CHARLOTTE. I am very happy to hear that they are well. [*Coolly.*] Brother, will you give me leave to introduce you to our uncle's ward, one of my most intimate friends?

MANLY [*saluting Letitia*]. I ought to regard your friends as my own.

CHARLOTTE. Come, Letitia, do give us a little dash of your vivacity; my brother is so sentimental and so grave, that I protest he'll give us the vapors.

MANLY. Though sentiment and gravity, I know, are banished the polite world, yet I hoped they might find some countenance in the meeting of such near connections as brother and sister.

CHARLOTTE. Positively, brother, if you go one step further in this strain, you will set me crying, and that, you know, would spoil my eyes; and then I should never get the husband which our good papa and mamma have so kindly wished me—never be established in the world.

MANLY. Forgive me, my sister,—I am no enemy to mirth; I love your sprightliness; and I hope it will one day enliven the hours of some worthy man; but when I mention the respectable authors of my existence,—the cherishers and protectors of my helpless infancy, whose hearts glow with such fondness and attachment that they would willingly lay down their lives for my welfare,—you will excuse me if I am so unfashionable as to speak of them with some degree of respect and reverence.

CHARLOTTE. Well, well, brother; if you won't be gay, we'll not differ; I will be as grave as you wish. [*Affects gravity.*] And so, brother, you have come to the city to exchange some of your commutation notes for a little pleasure?

MANLY. Indeed you are mistaken; my errand is not of amusement, but business; and as I neither drink nor game, my expenses will be so trivial, I shall have no occasion to sell my notes.

CHARLOTTE. Then you won't have occasion to do a very good thing. Why, here was the Vermont General—he came down some time since, sold all his musty notes at one stroke, and then laid the cash out in trinkets for his dear Fanny. I want a dozen pretty things myself; have you got the notes with you?

MANLY. I shall be ever willing to contribute, as far as it is in my power, to adorn or in any way to please my sister; yet I hope I shall never be obliged for this to sell my notes. I may be romantic, but I preserve them as a sacred deposit. Their full amount is justly due to me, but as embarrassments, the natural consequences of a long war, disable my country from supporting its credit, I shall wait with patience until it is rich enough to discharge them. If that is not in my day, they shall be transmitted as an honorable certificate to posterity, that I have humbly imitated our illustrious WASHINGTON, in having exposed my health and life in the service of my country, without reaping any other reward than the glory of conquering in so arduous a contest.

CHARLOTTE. Well said heroics. Why, my dear Henry, you have such a lofty way of saying things, that I protest I almost tremble at the thought of introducing you to the polite circles in the city. The belles would think you were a player run mad, with your head filled with old scraps of tragedy; and as to the beaux, they might admire, because they would not understand you. But, however, I must, I believe, introduce you to two or three ladies of my acquaintance.

LETITIA. And that will make him acquainted with thirty or forty beaux.

CHARLOTTE. Oh! brother, you don't know what a fund of happiness you have in store.

MANLY. I fear, sister, I have not refinement sufficient to enjoy it.

CHARLOTTE. Oh! you cannot fail being pleased.

LETITIA. Our ladies are so delicate and dressy.

CHARLOTTE. And our beaux so dressy and delicate.

LETITIA. Our ladies chat and flirt so agreeably.

CHARLOTTE. And our beaux simper and bow so gracefully.

LETITIA. With their hair so trim and neat.

CHARLOTTE. And their faces so soft and sleek.

LETITIA. Their buckles so tonish and bright.

CHARLOTTE. And their hands so slender and white.

LETITIA. I vow, Charlotte, we are quite poetical.

CHARLOTTE. And then, brother, the faces of the beaux are of such a lily-white hue! None of that horrid robustness of constitution, that vulgar corn-fed glow of health, which can only serve to alarm an unmarried lady with apprehension, and prove a melancholy memento to a married one, that she can never hope for the happiness of being a widow. I will say this to the credit of our city beaux, that such is the delicacy of their complexion, dress, and address, that, even had I no reliance upon the honor of the dear Adonises, I would trust myself in any possible situation with them, without the least apprehensions of rudeness.

MANLY. Sister Charlotte!

CHARLOTTE. Now, now, now, brother [*Interrupting him.*], now don't go to spoil my mirth with a dash of your gravity; I am so glad to see you, I am in tiptop spirits. Oh! that you could be with us at a little snug party. There is Billy Simper, Jack Chaffé, and Colonel Van Titter, Miss Promonade, and the two Miss Tambours, sometimes make a party, with some other ladies, in a side-box at the play. Everything is conducted with such decorum. First we bow round to the company in general, then to each one in particular, then we have so many inquiries after each other's health, and we are so happy to meet each other, and it is so many ages since we last had that pleasure, and if a married lady is in company, we have such a sweet dissertation upon her son Bobby's chin-cough; then the curtain rises, then our sensibility is all awake, and then, by the mere force of apprehension, we torture some harmless expression into a double meaning, which the poor author never dreamt of, and then we have recourse to our fans, and then we blush, and then the gentlemen jog one another, peep under the fan, and make the prettiest remarks; and then we giggle and they simper, and they giggle and we simper, and then the curtain drops, and then for nuts and oranges, and then we bow, and it's pray, Ma'am, take it, and pray, Sir, keep it, and oh! not for the world, Sir; and then the curtain rises again, and then we blush and giggle and simper and bow all over again. Oh! the sentimental charms of a side-box conversation! [*All laugh.*]

MANLY. Well, sister, I join heartily with you in the laugh; for, in my opinion, it is as justifiable to laugh at folly as it is reprehensible to ridicule misfortune.

CHARLOTTE. Well, but, brother, positively I can't introduce you in these clothes: why, your coat looks as if it were calculated for the vulgar purpose of keeping yourself comfortable.

MANLY. This coat was my regimental coat in the late war. The public tumults of our state have induced me to buckle on the sword in support of that government which I once fought to establish. I can only say, sister, that there was a time when this coat was respectable, and some people even thought that those men who had endured so many winter campaigns in the service of their country, without bread, clothing, or pay, at least deserved that the poverty of their appearance should not be ridiculed.

CHARLOTTE. We agree in opinion entirely, brother, though it would not have done for me to have said it: it is the coat makes the man respectable. In the time of the war, when we were almost frightened to death, why, your coat was respectable, that is, fashionable; now another kind of coat is fashionable, that is, respectable. And pray direct the taylor to make yours the height of the fashion.

MANLY. Though it is of little consequence to me of what shape my coat is, yet, as to the height of the fashion, there you will please to excuse me, sister. You know my sentiments on that subject. I have often lamented the advantage which the French have over us in that particular. In Paris, the fashions have their dawnings, their routine, and declensions, and depend as much upon the caprice of the day as in other countries; but there every lady assumes a right to deviate from the general *ton* as far as will be of advantage to her own appearance. In America, the cry is, what is the fashion? and we follow it indiscriminately, because it is so.

CHARLOTTE. Therefore it is, that when large hoops are in fashion, we often see many a plump girl lost in the immensity of a hoop-petticoat, whose want of height and *en-bon-point* would never have been remarked in any other dress. When the high head-dress is the mode, how then do we see a lofty cushion, with a profusion of gauze, feathers, and ribband, supported by a face no bigger than an apple! whilst a broad, full-faced lady, who really would have appeared tolerably handsome in a large head-dress, looks with her smart chapeau as masculine as a soldier.

MANLY. But remember, my dear sister, and I wish all my fair country-women would recollect, that the only excuse a young lady can have for going extravagantly into a fashion is because it makes her look extravagantly handsome.—Ladies, I must wish you a good morning.

CHARLOTTE. But, brother, you are going to make home with us.

MANLY. Indeed I cannot. I have seen my uncle and explained that matter.

CHARLOTTE. Come and dine with us, then. We have a family dinner about half-past four o'clock.

MANLY. I am engaged to dine with the Spanish ambassador. I was introduced to him by an old brother officer; and instead of freezing me with a cold card of compliment to dine with him ten days hence, he, with the true old Castilian frankness, in a friendly manner, asked me to dine with him today —an honor I could not refuse. Sister, adieu —Madam, your most obedient— [*Exit.*

CHARLOTTE. I will wait upon you to the door, brother; I have something particular to say to you. [*Exit.*

LETITIA [*alone*]. What a pair!—She the pink of flirtation, he the essence of everything that is *outré* and gloomy.—I think I have completely deceived Charlotte by my manner of speaking of Mr. Dimple; she's too much the friend of Maria to be confided in. He is certainly rendering himself disagreeable to Maria, in order to break with her and proffer his hand to me. This is what the delicate fellow hinted in our last conversation. [*Exit.*

SCENE 2. *The Mall*

Enter JESSAMY

JESSAMY. Positively this Mall is a very pretty place. I hope the cits won't ruin it by repairs. To be sure, it won't do to speak of in the same day with Ranelagh or Vauxhall; however, it's a fine place for a young fellow to display his person to advantage. Indeed, nothing is lost here; the girls have taste, and I am very happy to find they have adopted the elegant London fashion of looking back, after a genteel fellow like me has passed them.—Ah! who comes here? This, by his awkwardness, must be the Yankee colonel's servant. I'll accost him.

Enter JONATHAN

JESSAMY. Votre très-humble serviteur, Monsieur. I understand Colonel Manly, the Yankee officer, has the honor of your services.

JONATHAN. Sir!—

JESSAMY. I say, Sir, I understand that Colonel Manly has the honor of having you for a servant.

JONATHAN. Servant! Sir, do you take me for a neger,—I am Colonel Manly's waiter.

JESSAMY. A true Yankee distinction, egad, without a difference. Why, Sir, do you not perform all the offices of a servant? do you not even blacken his boots?

JONATHAN. Yes; I do grease them a bit sometimes; but I am a true blue son of liberty, for all that. Father said I should come as Colonel Manly's waiter, to see the world, and all that; but no man shall master me. My father has as good a farm as the colonel.

JESSAMY. Well, Sir, we will not quarrel about terms upon the eve of an acquaintance from which I promise myself so much satisfaction;—therefore, sans ceremonie—

JONATHAN. What?—

JESSAMY. I say I am extremely happy to see Colonel Manly's waiter.

JONATHAN. Well, and I vow, too, I am pretty considerably glad to see you; but what the dogs need of all this outlandish lingo? Who may you be, Sir, if I may be so bold?

JESSAMY. I have the honor to be Mr. Dimple's servant, or, if you please, waiter. We lodge under the same roof, and should be glad of the honor of your acquaintance.

JONATHAN. You a waiter! by the living jingo, you look so topping, I took you for one of the agents to Congress.

JESSAMY. The brute has discernment, notwithstanding his appearance.—Give me leave to say I wonder then at your familiarity.

JONATHAN. Why, as to the matter of that, Mr. —; pray, what's your name?

JESSAMY. Jessamy, at your service.

JONATHAN. Why, I swear we don't make any great matter of distinction in our state between quality and other folks.

JESSAMY. This is, indeed, a levelling principle.—I hope, Mr. Jonathan, you have not taken part with the insurgents.

JONATHAN. Why, since General Shays has sneaked off and given us the bag to hold, I don't care to give my opinion; but you'll promise not to tell—put your ear this way —you won't tell?—I vow I did think the sturgeons were right.

JESSAMY. I thought, Mr. Jonathan, you Massachusetts men always argued with a gun in your hand. Why didn't you join them?

JONATHAN. Why, the colonel is one of those folks called the Shin—Shin—dang it all, I can't speak them lignum vitæ words—you know who I mean—there is a company of them—they wear a china goose at their button-hole—a kind of gilt thing.—Now the colonel told father and brother,—you must know there are, let me see—there is Elnathan, Silas, and Barnabas, Tabitha—no, no, she's a she—tarnation, now I have it—there's Elnathan, Silas, Barnabas, Jonathan, that's I—seven of us, six went into the wars, and I staid at home to take care of mother. Colonel said that it was a burning shame for the true blue Bunker Hill sons of liberty, who had fought Governor Hutchinson, Lord North, and the Devil, to have any hand in kicking up a cursed dust against a government which we had, every mother's son of us, a hand in making.

JESSAMY. Bravo!—Well, have you been abroad in the city since your arrival? What have you seen that is curious and entertaining?

JONATHAN. Oh! I have seen a power of fine sights. I went to see two marble-stone men and a leaden horse that stands out in doors in all weathers; and when I came where they was, one had got no head, and t'other wern't there. They said as how the leaden man was a damn'd tory, and that he took wit in his anger and rode off in the time of the troubles.

JESSAMY. But this was not the end of your excursion?

JONATHAN. Oh, no; I went to a place they call Holy Ground. Now I counted this was a place where folks go to meeting; so I put my hymn-book in my pocket, and walked softly and grave as a minister; and when I came there, the dogs a bit of a meeting-house could I see. At last I spied a young gentlewoman standing by one of the seats which they have here at the doors. I took her to be the deacon's daughter, and she looked so kind, and so obliging, that I thought I would go and ask her the way to lecture, and—would you think it?—she called me dear, and sweeting, and honey, just as if we were married: by the living jingo, I had a month's mind to buss her.

JESSAMY. Well, but how did it end?

JONATHAN. Why, as I was standing talking with her, a parcel of sailor men and boys got around me, the snarl-headed curs fell a-kicking and cursing of me at such a tarnal rate, that I vow I was glad to take to my heels and split home, right off, tail on end, like a stream of chalk.

JESSAMY. Why, my dear friend, you are not acquainted with the city; that girl you saw was a—[*Whispers.*]

JONATHAN. Mercy on my soul! was that young woman a harlot!—Well! if this is New-York Holy Ground, what must the Holy-day Ground be!

JESSAMY. Well, you should not judge of the city too rashly. We have a number of elegant, fine girls here that make a man's leisure hours pass very agreeably. I would esteem it an honor to announce you to some of them.—Gad! that announce is a select word; I wonder where I picked it up.

JONATHAN. I don't want to know them.

JESSAMY. Come, come, my dear friend, I see that I must assume the honor of being the director of your amusements. Nature has given us passions, and youth and opportunity stimulate to gratify them. It is no shame, my dear Blueskin, for a man to amuse himself with a little gallantry.

JONATHAN. Girl huntry! I don't altogether understand. I never played at that game. I know how to play hunt the squirrel, but I can't play anything with the girls; I am as good as married.

JESSAMY. Vulgar, horrid brute! Married, and above a hundred miles from his wife, and thinks that an objection to his making love to every woman he meets! He never can have read, no, he never can have been in a room with a volume of the divine Chesterfield.—So you are married?

JONATHAN. No, I don't say so; I said I was as good as married, a kind of promise.

JESSAMY. As good as married!—

JONATHAN. Why, yes; there's Tabitha Wymen, the deacon's daughter, at home; she and I have been courting a great while, and folks say as how we are to be married; and so I broke a piece of money with her when we parted, and she promised not to spark it with Solomon Dyer while I am gone. You wou'dn't have me false to my true-love, would you?

JESSAMY. May be you have another reason for constancy; possibly the young lady has a fortune? Ha! Mr. Jonathan, the solid charms: the chains of love are never so binding as when the links are made of gold.

JONATHAN. Why, as to fortune, I must needs say her father is pretty dumb rich; he went representative for our town last year. He will give her—let me see—four times seven is—seven times four—nought and carry one,—he will give her twenty acres of land—somewhat rocky though—a Bible, and a cow.

JESSAMY. Twenty acres of rock, a Bible, and a cow! Why, my dear Mr. Jonathan, we have servant-maids, or, as you would more elegantly express it, waitresses, in this city, who collect more in one year from their mistresses' cast clothes.

JONATHAN. You don't say so!—

JESSAMY. Yes, and I'll introduce you to one of them. There is a little lump of flesh and delicacy that lives at next door, waitress to Miss Maria; we often see her on the stoop.

JONATHAN. But are you sure she would be courted by me?

JESSAMY. Never doubt it; remember a faint heart never—blisters on my tongue—I was going to be guilty of a vile proverb; flat against the authority of Chesterfield. I say there can be no doubt that the brilliancy of your merit will secure you a favorable reception.

JONATHAN. Well, but what must I say to her?

JESSAMY. Say to her! why, my dear friend, though I admire your profound knowledge on every other subject, yet, you will pardon my saying that your want of opportunity has made the female heart escape the poignancy of your penetration. Say to her! Why, when a man goes a-courting, and hopes for success, he must begin with doing, and not saying.

JONATHAN. Well, what must I do?

JESSAMY. Why, when you are introduced you must make five or six elegant bows.

JONATHAN. Six elegant bows! I understand that; six, you say? Well—

JESSAMY. Then you must press and kiss her hand; then press and kiss, and so on to her lips and cheeks; then talk as much as you can about hearts, darts, flames, nectar, and ambrosia—the more incoherent the better.

JONATHAN. Well, but suppose she should be angry with I?

JESSAMY. Why, if she should pretend—please to observe, Mr. Jonathan—if she should pretend to be offended, you must—But I'll tell you how my master acted in such a case: He was seated by a young lady of eighteen upon a sofa, plucking with a wanton hand the blooming sweets of youth and beauty. When the lady thought it necessary to check his ardor, she called up a frown upon her lovely face, so irresistibly alluring, that it would have warmed the frozen bosom of age; remember, said she, putting her delicate arm upon his, remember your character and my honor. My master instantly dropped upon his knees, with eyes swimming with love, cheeks glowing with desire, and in the gentlest modulation of voice he said: My dear Caroline, in a few months our hands will be indissolubly united at the altar; our hearts I feel are already so; the favors you now grant as evidence of your affection are favors indeed; yet, when the ceremony is once past, what will now be received with rapture will then be attributed to duty.

JONATHAN. Well, and what was the consequence?

JESSAMY. The consequence!—Ah! forgive me, my dear friend, but you New England gentlemen have such a laudable curiosity of seeing the bottom of everything;—why, to be honest, I confess I saw the blooming cherub of a consequence smiling in its angelic mother's arms, about ten months afterwards.

JONATHAN. Well, if I follow all your plans, make them six bows, and all that, shall I have such little cherubim consequences?

JESSAMY. Undoubtedly.—What are you musing upon?

JONATHAN. You say you'll certainly make me acquainted?—Why, I was thinking then how I should contrive to pass this broken piece of silver—won't it buy a sugar-dram?

JESSAMY. What is that, the love-token from the deacon's daughter?—You come on bravely. But I must hasten to my master. Adieu, my dear friend.

JONATHAN. Stay, Mr. Jessamy—must I buss her when I am introduced to her?

JESSAMY. I told you, you must kiss her.

JONATHAN. Well, but must I buss her?

JESSAMY. Why kiss and buss, and buss and kiss, is all one.

JONATHAN. Oh! my dear friend, though you have a profound knowledge of all, a pugnancy of tribulation, you don't know everything. [*Exit.*

JESSAMY [*alone*]. Well, certainly I improve; my master could not have insinuated himself with more address into the heart of a man he despised. Now will this blundering dog sicken Jenny with his nauseous pawings, until she flies into my arms for very ease. How sweet will the contrast be between the blundering Jonathan and the courtly and accomplished Jessamy!

END OF THE SECOND ACT

ACT III

SCENE I. DIMPLE'S *Room*

DIMPLE *discovered at a Toilet, Reading*

"Women have in general but one object, which is their beauty." Very true, my lord; positively very true. "Nature has hardly formed a woman ugly enough to be insensible to flattery upon her person." Extremely just, my lord; every day's delightful experience confirms this. "If her face is so shocking that she must, in some degree, be conscious of it, her figure and air, she thinks, make ample amends for it." The sallow Miss Wan is a proof of this. Upon my telling the distasteful wretch, the other day, that her countenance spoke the pensive language of sentiment, and that Lady Wortley Montague declared that if the ladies were arrayed in the garb of innocence, the face would be the last part which would be admired, as Monsieur Milton expresses it, she grinn'd horribly a ghastly smile. "If her figure is deformed, she thinks her face counterbalances it."

Enter JESSAMY *with letters*

DIMPLE. Where got you these, Jessamy?

JESSAMY. Sir, the English packet is arrived.

DIMPLE [*opens and reads a letter enclosing notes*].

"Sir,

"I have drawn bills on you in favor of Messrs. Van Cash and Co. as per margin. I have taken up your note to Col. Piquet, and discharged your debts to my Lord Lurcher and Sir Harry Rook. I herewith enclose you copies of the bills, which I have no doubt will be immediately honored. On failure, I shall empower some lawyer in your country to recover the amounts.

"I am, Sir,

"Your most humble servant,

"JOHN HAZARD."

Now, did not my lord expressly say that it was unbecoming a well-bred man to be in a passion, I confess I should be ruffled. [*Reads.*] "There is no accident so unfortunate, which a wise man may not turn to his advantage; nor any accident so fortunate, which a fool will not turn to his disadvantage." True, my lord; but how advantage can be derived from this I can't see. Chesterfield himself, who made, however, the worst practice of the most excellent precepts, was never in so embarrassing a situation. I love the person of Charlotte, and it is necessary I should command the fortune of Letitia. As to Maria!—I doubt not by my *sang-froid* behavior I shall compel her to decline the match; but the blame must not fall upon me. A prudent man, as my lord says, should take all the credit of a good action to himself, and throw the discredit of a bad one upon others. I must break with Maria, marry Letitia, and as for Charlotte—why, Charlotte must be a companion to my wife.—Here, Jessamy!

Enter JESSAMY. DIMPLE *folds and seals two letters*

DIMPLE. Here, Jessamy, take this letter to my love. [*Gives one.*]

JESSAMY. To which of your honor's loves? —Oh! [*Reading.*] to Miss Letitia, your honor's rich love.

DIMPLE. And this [*Delivers another.*] to Miss Charlotte Manly. See that you deliver them privately.

JESSAMY. Yes, your honor. [*Going.*]

DIMPLE. Jessamy, who are these strange lodgers that came to the house last night?

JESSAMY. Why, the master is a Yankee colonel; I have not seen much of him; but the man is the most unpolished animal your honor ever disgraced your eyes by looking upon. I have had one of the most *outré* conversations with him!—He really has a most prodigious effect upon my risibility.

DIMPLE. I ought, according to every rule of Chesterfield, to wait on him and insinuate myself into his good graces.—Jessamy, wait on the colonel with my compliments, and if he is disengaged I will do myself the honor of paying him my respects.—Some ignorant, unpolished boor—

JESSAMY *goes off and returns*

JESSAMY. Sir, the colonel is gone out, and Jonathan his servant says that he is gone to stretch his legs upon the Mall.—Stretch his legs! what an indelicacy of diction!

DIMPLE. Very well. Reach me my hat and sword. I'll accost him there, in my way to Letitia's, as by accident; pretend to be struck by his person and address, and endeavor to steal into his confidence. Jessamy, I have no business for you at present. [*Exit.*

JESSAMY [*taking up the book*]. My master and I obtain our knowledge from the same source;—though, gad! I think myself much the prettier fellow of the two. [*Surveying himself in the glass.*] That was a brilliant thought, to insinuate that I folded my master's letters for him; the folding is so neat, that it does honor to the operator. I once intended to have insinuated that I wrote his letters too; but that was before I saw them; it won't do now; no honor there, positively. —"Nothing looks more vulgar [*Reading affectedly.*], ordinary, and illiberal than ugly, uneven, and ragged nails; the ends of which should be kept even and clean, not tipped with black, and cut in small segments of circles."—Segments of circles! surely my lord did not consider that he wrote for the beaux. Segments of circles; what a crabbed term! Now I dare answer that my master, with all his learning, does not know that this means, according to the present mode, let the nails grow long, and then cut them off even at top. [*Laughing without.*] Ha! that's Jenny's titter. I protest I despair of ever teaching that girl to laugh; she has something so execrably natural in her laugh, that I declare it absolutely discomposes my nerves. How came she into our house! [*Calls.*] Jenny!

Enter JENNY

JESSAMY. Prythee, Jenny, don't spoil your fine face with laughing.

JENNY. Why, mustn't I laugh, Mr. Jessamy?

JESSAMY. You may smile, but, as my lord says, nothing can authorise a laugh.

JENNY. Well, but I can't help laughing.—Have you seen him, Mr. Jessamy? ha, ha, ha!

JESSAMY. Seen whom?

JENNY. Why, Jonathan, the New England colonel's servant. Do you know he was at the play last night, and the stupid creature don't know where he has been. He would not go to a play for the world; he thinks it was a show, as he calls it.

JESSAMY. As ignorant and unpolished as he is, do you know, Miss Jenny, that I propose to introduce him to the honor of your acquaintance?

JENNY. Introduce him to me! for what?

JESSAMY. Why, my lovely girl, that you may take him under your protection, as Madame Ramboulliet did young Stanhope; that you may, by your plastic hand, mould this uncouth cub into a gentleman. He is to make love to you.

JENNY. Make love to me!—

JESSAMY. Yes, Mistress Jenny, make love to you; and, I doubt not, when he shall become *domesticated* in your kitchen, that this boor, under your auspices, will soon become *un aimable petit Jonathan.*

JENNY. I must say, Mr. Jessamy, if he copies after me, he will be vastly, monstrously polite.

JESSAMY. Stay here one moment, and I will call him.—Jonathan!—Mr. Jonathan!— [*Calls.*]

JONATHAN [*within*]. Holla! there.—[*Enters.*] You promise to stand by me—six bows you say. [*Bows.*]

JESSAMY. Mrs. Jenny, I have the honor of presenting Mr. Jonathan, Colonel Manly's waiter, to you. I am extremely happy that I have it in my power to make two worthy people acquainted with each other's merits.

JENNY. So, Mr. Jonathan, I hear you were at the play last night.

JONATHAN. At the play! why, did you think I went to the devil's drawing-room?

JENNY. The devil's drawing-room!

JONATHAN. Yes; why, an't cards and dice the devil's device, and the play-house the shop where the devil hangs out the vanities of the world upon the tenter-hooks of temptation? I believe you have not heard how they were acting the old boy one night, and the wicked one came among them sure enough, and went right off in a storm, and carried one quarter of the play-house with him. Oh! no, no, no! you won't catch me at a play-house, I warrant you.

JENNY. Well, Mr. Jonathan, though I don't scruple your veracity, I have some reasons for believing you were there: pray, where were you about six o'clock?

JONATHAN. Why, I went to see one Mr. Morrison, the *hocus pocus* man; they said as how he could eat a case knife.

JENNY. Well, and how did you find the place?

JONATHAN. As I was going about here and there, to and again, to find it, I saw a great crowd of folks going into a long entry that had lantherns over the door; so I asked a man whether that was not the place where they played *hocus pocus?* He was a very civil, kind man, though he did speak like the Hessians; he lifted up his eyes and said, "They play *hocus pocus* tricks enough there, Got knows, mine friend."

JENNY. Well—

JONATHAN. So I went right in, and they shewed me away, clean up to the garret, just like meeting-house gallery. And so I saw a power of topping folks, all sitting round in little cabbins, just like father's corn-cribs; and then there was such a squeaking with the fiddles, and such a tarnal blaze with the lights, my head was near turned. At last the people that sat near me set up such a hissing—hiss—like so many mad cats; and then they went thump, thump, thump, just like our Peleg threshing wheat, and stampt away, just like the nation; and called out for one Mr. Langolee,—I suppose he helps act the tricks.

JENNY. Well, and what did you do all this time?

JONATHAN. Gor, I—I liked the fun, and so I thumpt away, and hiss'd as lustily as the best of 'em. One sailor-looking man that sat by me, seeing me stamp, and knowing I was a cute fellow, because I could make a roaring noise, clapt me on the shoulder and said, "You are a d——d hearty cock, smite my timbers!" I told him so I was, but I thought he need not swear so, and make use of such naughty words.

JESSAMY. The savage!—Well, and did you see the man with his tricks?

JONATHAN. Why, I vow, as I was looking out for him, they lifted up a great green cloth and let us look right into the next neighbor's house. Have you a good many houses in New-York made so in that 'ere way?

JENNY. Not many; but did you see the family?

JONATHAN. Yes, swamp it; I see'd the family.

JENNY. Well, and how did you like them?

JONATHAN. Why, I vow they were pretty much like other families;—there was a poor, good-natured, curse of a husband, and a sad rantipole of a wife.

JENNY. But did you see no other folks?

JONATHAN. Yes. There was one youngster; they called him Mr. Joseph; he talked as sober and as pious as a minister; but, like some ministers that I know, he was a sly tike in his heart for all that. He was going to ask a young woman to spark it with him, and—the Lord have mercy on my soul!—she was another man's wife.

JESSAMY. The Wabash!

JENNY. And did you see any more folks?

JONATHAN. Why, they came on as thick as mustard. For my part, I thought the house was haunted. There was a soldier fellow, who talked about his row de dow, dow, and courted a young woman; but, of all the cute folk I saw, I liked one little fellow—

JENNY. Aye! who was he?

JONATHAN. Why, he had red hair, and a little round plump face like mine, only not altogether so handsome. His name was—Darby;—that was his baptizing name; his other name I forgot. Oh! it was Wig—Wag—Wag-all, Darby Wag-all,—pray, do you know him?—I should like to take a sling with him, or a drap of cyder with a pepper-pod in it, to make it warm and comfortable.

JENNY. I can't say I have that pleasure.

JONATHAN. I wish you did; he is a cute fellow. But there was one thing I didn't like in that Mr. Darby; and that was, he was afraid of some of them 'ere shooting irons, such as your troopers wear on training days. Now, I'm a true born Yankee American son of liberty, and I never was afraid of a gun yet in all my life.

JENNY. Well, Mr. Jonathan, you were certainly at the play-house.

JONATHAN. I at the play-house!—Why didn't I see the play then?

JENNY. Why, the people you saw were players.

JONATHAN. Mercy on my soul! did I see the wicked players?—Mayhap that 'ere Darby that I liked so was the old serpent himself, and had his cloven foot in his pocket. Why, I vow, now I come to think on't, the candles seemed to burn blue, and I am sure where I sat it smelt tarnally of brimstone.

JESSAMY. Well, Mr. Jonathan, from your account, which I confess is very accurate, you must have been at the play-house.

JONATHAN. Why, I vow, I began to smell a rat. When I came away, I went to the man for my money again; you want your money? says he; yes, says I; for what? says he; why, says I, no man shall jocky me out of my money; I paid my money to see sights, and the dogs a bit of a sight have I seen, unless you call listening to people's private business a sight. Why, says he, it is the School for Scandalization.—The School for Scandalization!—Oh! ho! no wonder you New-York folks are so cute at it, when you go to school to learn it; and so I jogged off.

JESSAMY. My dear Jenny, my master's business drags me from you; would to heaven I knew no other servitude than to your charms.

JONATHAN. Well, but don't go; you won't leave me so—

JESSAMY. Excuse me.—Remember the cash. [*Aside to him, and—Exit.*

JENNY. Mr. Jonathan, won't you please to sit down? Mr. Jessamy tells me you wanted to have some conversation with me. [*Having brought forward two chairs, they sit.*]

JONATHAN. Ma'am!—

JENNY. Sir!—

JONATHAN. Ma'am!—

JENNY. Pray, how do you like the city, Sir?

JONATHAN. Ma'am!—

JENNY. I say, Sir, how do you like New-York?

JONATHAN. Ma'am!—

JENNY. The stupid creature! but I must pass some little time with him, if it is only to endeavor to learn whether it was his master that made such an abrupt entrance into our house, and my young mistress's heart, this morning. [*Aside.*] As you don't seem to like to talk, Mr. Jonathan—do you sing?

JONATHAN. Gor, I—I am glad she asked that, for I forgot what Mr. Jessamy bid me say, and I dare as well be hanged as act what he bid me do, I'm so ashamed. [*Aside.*] Yes, Ma'am, I can sing—I can sing Mear, Old Hundred, and Bangor.

JENNY. Oh! I don't mean psalm tunes. Have you no little song to please the ladies, such as Roslin Castle, or the Maid of the Mill?

JONATHAN. Why, all my tunes [are] go to meeting tunes, save one, and I count you won't altogether like that 'ere.

JENNY. What is it called?

JONATHAN. I am sure you have heard folks talk about it; it is called Yankee Doodle.

JENNY. Oh! it is the tune I am fond of; and if I know anything of my mistress, she would be glad to dance to it. Pray, sing!

JONATHAN [*sings*].

Father and I went up to camp,
Along with Captain Goodwin;
And there we saw the men and boys,
As thick as hasty-pudding.
Yankee doodle do, etc.

And there we saw a swamping gun,
Big as log of maple,
On a little deuced cart,
A load for father's cattle.
Yankee doodle do, etc.

And every time they fired it off
It took a horn of powder,
It made a noise—like father's gun,
Only a nation louder.
Yankee doodle do, etc.

There was a man in our town,
His name was—

No, no, that won't do. Now, if I was with Tabitha Wymen and Jemima Cawley down at father Chase's, I shouldn't mind singing this all out before them—you would be affronted if I was to sing that, though that's a lucky thought; if you should be affronted, I have something dang'd cute, which Jessamy told me to say to you.

JENNY. Is that all! I assure you I like it of all things.

JONATHAN. No, no; I can sing more; some other time, when you and I are better acquainted, I'll sing the whole of it—no, no—that's a fib—I can't sing but a hundred and ninety verses; our Tabitha at home can sing it all.—[*Sings.*]

Marblehead's a rocky place,
And Cape-Cod is sandy;
Charlestown is burnt down,
Boston is the dandy.
Yankee doodle, doodle do, etc.

I vow, my own town song has put me into such topping spirits that I believe I'll begin to do a little, as Jessamy says we must when we go a-courting.—[*Runs and kisses her.*] Burning rivers! cooling flames! red-hot roses! pig-nuts! hasty-pudding and ambrosia!

JENNY. What means this freedom? you insulting wretch. [*Strikes him.*]

JONATHAN. Are you affronted?

JENNY. Affronted! with what looks shall I express my anger?

JONATHAN. Looks! why as to the matter of looks, you look as cross as a witch.

JENNY. Have you no feeling for the delicacy of my sex?

JONATHAN. Feeling! Gor, I—I feel the delicacy of your sex pretty smartly [*Rubbing his cheek.*], though, I vow, I thought when you city ladies courted and married, and all that, you put feeling out of the question. But I want to know whether you are really affronted, or only pretend to be so? 'Cause, if you are certainly right down affronted, I am at the end of my tether; Jessamy didn't tell me what to say to you.

JENNY. Pretend to be affronted!

JONATHAN. Aye, aye, if you only pretend, you shall hear how I'll go to work to make cherubim consequences. [*Runs up to her.*]

JENNY. Begone, you brute!

JONATHAN. That looks like mad; but I won't lose my speech. My dearest Jenny—your name is Jenny, I think?—My dearest Jenny, though I have the highest esteem for the sweet favors you have just now granted me—Gor, that's a fib, though; but Jessamy says it is not wicked to tell lies to the women. [*Aside.*] I say, though I have the highest esteem for the favors you have just now granted me, yet you will consider that, as soon as the dissolvable knot is tied, they will no longer be favors, but only matters of duty and matters of course.

JENNY. Marry you! you audacious monster! get out of my sight, or, rather, let me fly from you. [*Exit hastily.*

JONATHAN. Gor! she's gone off in a swinging passion, before I had time to think of consequences. If this is the way with your city ladies, give me the twenty acres of rock, the Bible, the cow, and Tabitha, and a little peaceable bundling.

SCENE 2. *The Mall*

Enter MANLY

MANLY. It must be so, Montague! and it is not all the tribe of Mandevilles that shall convince me that a nation, to become great, must first become dissipated. Luxury is surely the bane of a nation: Luxury! which enervates both soul and body, by opening a thousand new sources of enjoyment, opens, also, a thousand new sources of contention and want: Luxury! which renders a people weak at home, and accessible to bribery, corruption, and force from abroad. When the Grecian states knew no other tools than the axe and the saw, the Grecians were a great, a free, and a happy people. The kings of Greece devoted their lives to the service of their country, and her senators knew no other superiority over their fellow-citizens than a glorious pre-eminence in danger and virtue. They exhibited to the world a noble spectacle,—a number of independent states united by a similarity of language, sentiment, manners, common interest, and common consent, in one grand mutual league of protection. And, thus united, long might they have continued the cherishers of art and sciences, the protectors of the oppressed, the scourge of tyrants, and the safe asylum of liberty. But when foreign gold, and still more pernicious foreign luxury, had crept among them, they sapped the vitals of their virtue. The virtues of their ancestors were only found in their writings. Envy and suspicion, the vices of little minds, possessed them. The various states engendered jealousies of each other; and, more unfortunately, growing jealous of their great federal council, the Amphictyons, they forgot that their common safety had existed, and would exist, in giving them an honorable extensive prerogative. The common good was lost in the pursuit of private interest; and that people who, by uniting, might have stood against the world in arms, by dividing, crumbled into ruin;—their name is now only known in the page of the historian, and what they once were is all we have left to admire. Oh! that America! Oh! that my country, would, in this her day, learn the things which belong to her peace!

Enter DIMPLE

DIMPLE. You are Colonel Manly, I presume?

MANLY. At your service, Sir.

DIMPLE. My name is Dimple, Sir. I have the honor to be a lodger in the same house with you, and, hearing you were in the Mall, came hither to take the liberty of joining you.

MANLY. You are very obliging, Sir.

DIMPLE. As I understand you are a stranger here, Sir, I have taken the liberty to introduce myself to your acquaintance, as possibly I may have it in my power to point out some things in this city worthy your notice.

MANLY. An attention to strangers is worthy a liberal mind, and must ever be gratefully received. But to a soldier, who has no fixed abode, such attentions are particularly pleasing.

DIMPLE. Sir, there is no character so respectable as that of a soldier. And, indeed, when we reflect how much we owe to those brave men who have suffered so much in the service of their country, and secured to us those inestimable blessings that we now enjoy, our liberty and independence, they demand every attention which gratitude can pay. For my own part, I never meet an officer, but I embrace him as my friend, nor a private in distress, but I insensibly extend my charity to him.—I have hit the Bumkin off very tolerably. [*Aside.*]

MANLY. Give me your hand, Sir! I do not proffer this hand to everybody; but you steal into my heart. I hope I am as insensible to flattery as most men; but I declare (it may be my weak side) that I never hear the name of soldier mentioned with respect, but I experience a thrill of pleasure which I never feel on any other occasion.

DIMPLE. Will you give me leave, my dear Colonel, to confer an obligation on myself, by shewing you some civilities during your stay here, and giving a similar opportunity to some of my friends?

MANLY. Sir, I thank you; but I believe my stay in this city will be very short.

DIMPLE. I can introduce you to some men of excellent sense, in whose company you will esteem yourself happy; and, by way of amusement, to some fine girls, who will listen to your soft things with pleasure.

MANLY. Sir, I should be proud of the honor of being acquainted with those gentlemen;—but, as for the ladies, I don't understand you.

DIMPLE. Why, Sir, I need not tell you, that when a young gentleman is alone with a young lady he must say some soft things to her fair cheek—indeed, the lady will expect it. To be sure, there is not much pleasure when a man of the world and a finished coquette meet, who perfectly know each other; but how delicious is it to excite the emotions of joy, hope, expectation, and delight in the bosom of a lovely girl who believes every tittle of what you say to be serious!

MANLY. Serious, Sir! In my opinion, the man who, under pretensions of marriage, can plant thorns in the bosom of an innocent, unsuspecting girl is more detestable than a common robber, in the same proportion as private violence is more despicable than open force, and money of less value than happiness.

DIMPLE. How he awes me by the superiority of his sentiments. [*Aside.*] As you say, Sir, a gentleman should be cautious how he mentions marriage.

MANLY. Cautious, Sir! No person more approves of an intercourse between the sexes than I do. Female conversation softens our manners, whilst our discourse, from the superiority of our literary advantages, improves their minds. But, in our young country, where there is no such thing as gallantry, when a gentleman speaks of love to a lady, whether he mentions marriage or not, she ought to conclude either that he meant to insult her or that his intentions are the most serious and honorable. How mean, how cruel, is it, by a thousand tender assiduities, to win the affections of an amiable girl, and, though you leave her virtue unspotted, to betray her into the appearance of so many tender partialities, that every man of delicacy would suppress his inclination towards her, by supposing her heart engaged! Can any man, for the trivial gratification of his leisure hours, affect the happiness of a whole life! His not having spoken of marriage may add to his perfidy, but can be no excuse for his conduct.

DIMPLE. Sir, I admire your sentiments;—they are mine. The light observations that fell from me were only a principle of the tongue; they came not from the heart; my practice has ever disapproved these principles.

MANLY. I believe you, Sir. I should with reluctance suppose that those pernicious sentiments could find admittance into the heart of a gentleman.

DIMPLE. I am now, Sir, going to visit a family, where, if you please, I will have the honor of introducing you. Mr. Manly's ward, Miss Letitia, is a young lady of immense fortune; and his niece, Miss Charlotte Manly, is a young lady of great sprightliness and beauty.

MANLY. That gentleman, Sir, is my uncle, and Miss Manly my sister.

DIMPLE. The devil she is! [*Aside.*] Miss Manly your sister, Sir? I rejoice to hear it, and feel a double pleasure in being known to you.—Plague on him! I wish he was at Boston again, with all my soul. [*Aside.*]

MANLY. Come, Sir, will you go?

DIMPLE. I will follow you in a moment, Sir. [*Exit* MANLY.] Plague on it! this is unlucky. A fighting brother is a cursed appendage to a fine girl. Egad! I just stopped in time; had he not discovered himself, in two minutes more I should have told him how well I was with his sister. Indeed, I cannot see the satisfaction of an intrigue, if one can't have the pleasure of communicating it to our friends. [*Exit.*

END OF THE THIRD ACT

ACT IV

SCENE I. CHARLOTTE'S *Apartment*

CHARLOTTE *leading in* MARIA

CHARLOTTE. This is so kind, my sweet friend, to come to see me at this moment. I declare, if I were going to be married in a few days, as you are, I should scarce have found time to visit my friends.

MARIA. Do you think, then, that there is an impropriety in it?—How should you dispose of your time?

CHARLOTTE. Why, I should be shut up in my chamber; and my head would so run upon—upon—upon the solemn ceremony that I was to pass through!—I declare, it would take me above two hours merely to learn that little monosyllable—*Yes*. Ah! my dear, your sentimental imagination does not conceive what that little tiny word implies.

MARIA. Spare me your raillery, my sweet friend; I should love your agreeable vivacity at any other time.

CHARLOTTE. Why, this is the very time to amuse you. You grieve me to see you look so unhappy.

MARIA. Have I not reason to look so?

CHARLOTTE. What new grief distresses you?

MARIA. Oh! how sweet it is, when the heart is borne down with misfortune, to recline and repose on the bosom of friendship! Heaven knows that, although it is improper for a young lady to praise a gentleman, yet I have ever concealed Mr. Dimple's foibles, and spoke of him as of one whose reputation I expected would be linked with mine; but his late conduct towards me has turned my coolness into contempt. He behaves as if he meant to insult and disgust me; whilst my father, in the last conversation on the subject of our marriage, spoke of it as a matter which lay near his heart, and in which he would not bear contradiction.

CHARLOTTE. This works well; oh! the generous Dimple. I'll endeavor to excite her to discharge him. [*Aside*.] But, my dear friend, your happiness depends on yourself. Why don't you discard him? Though the match has been of long standing, I would not be forced to make myself miserable; no parent in the world should oblige me to marry the man I did not like.

MARIA. Oh! my dear, you never lived with your parents, and do not know what influence a father's frowns have upon a daughter's heart. Besides, what have I to allege against Mr. Dimple, to justify myself to the world? He carries himself so smoothly, that every one would impute the blame to me, and call me capricious.

CHARLOTTE. And call her capricious! Did ever such an objection start into the heart of woman? For my part, I wish I had fifty lovers to discard, for no other reason than because I did not fancy them. My dear Maria, you will forgive me; I know your candor and confidence in me; but I have at times, I confess, been led to suppose that some other gentleman was the cause of your aversion to Mr. Dimple.

MARIA. No, my sweet friend, you may be assured, that though I have seen many gentlemen I could prefer to Mr. Dimple, yet I never saw one that I thought I could give my hand to, until this morning.

CHARLOTTE. This morning!

MARIA. Yes; one of the strangest accidents in the world. The odious Dimple, after disgusting me with his conversation, had just left me, when a gentleman, who, it seems, boards in the same house with him, saw him coming out of our door, and, the houses looking very much alike, he came into our house instead of his lodgings; nor did he discover his mistake until he got into the parlor, where I was; he then bowed so gracefully, made such a genteel apology, and looked so manly and noble!—

CHARLOTTE. I see some folks, though it is so great an impropriety, can praise a gentleman, when he happens to be the man of their fancy. [*Aside*.]

MARIA. I don't know how it was,—I hope he did not think me indelicate,—but I asked him, I believe, to sit down, or pointed to a chair. He sat down, and, instead of having recourse to observations upon the weather, or hackneyed criticisms upon the theatre, he entered readily into a conversation worthy a man of sense to speak, and a lady of delicacy and sentiment to hear. He was not strictly handsome, but he spoke the language of sentiment, and his eyes looked tenderness and honor.

CHARLOTTE. Oh! [*Eagerly.*] you sentimental, grave girls, when your hearts are once touched, beat us rattles a bar's length. And so you are quite in love with this he-angel?

MARIA. In love with him! How can you rattle so, Charlotte? am I not going to be miserable? [*Sighs.*] In love with a gentleman I never saw but one hour in my life, and don't know his name! No; I only wished that the man I shall marry may look, and talk, and act, just like him. Besides, my dear, he is a married man.

CHARLOTTE. Why, that was good-natured—he told you so, I suppose, in mere charity, to prevent you falling in love with him?

MARIA. He didn't tell me so; [*Peevishly.*] he looked as if he was married.

CHARLOTTE. How, my dear; did he look sheepish?

MARIA. I am sure he has a susceptible heart, and the ladies of his acquaintance must be very stupid not to—

CHARLOTTE. Hush! I hear some person coming.

Enter LETITIA

LETITIA. My dear Maria, I am happy to see you. Lud! what a pity it is that you have purchased your wedding clothes.

MARIA. I think so. [*Sighing.*]

LETITIA. Why, my dear, there is the sweetest parcel of silks come over you ever saw! Nancy Brilliant has a full suit come; she sent over her measure, and it fits her to a hair; it is immensely dressy, and made for a court-hoop. I thought they said the large hoops were going out of fashion.

CHARLOTTE. Did you see the hat? Is it a fact that the deep laces round the border is still the fashion?

DIMPLE [*within*]. Upon my honor, Sir!

MARIA. Ha! Dimple's voice! My dear, I must take leave of you. There are some things necessary to be done at our house. Can't I go through the other room?

Enter DIMPLE *and* MANLY

DIMPLE. Ladies, your most obedient.

CHARLOTTE. Miss Van Rough, shall I present my brother Henry to you? Colonel Manly, Maria,—Miss Van Rough, brother.

MARIA. Her brother! [*Turns and sees* MANLY.] Oh! my heart! the very gentleman I have been praising.

MANLY. The same amiable girl I saw this morning!

CHARLOTTE. Why, you look as if you were acquainted.

MANLY. I unintentionally intruded into this lady's presence this morning, for which she was so good as to promise me her forgiveness.

CHARLOTTE. Oh! ho! is that the case! Have these two penserosos been together? Were they Henry's eyes that looked so tenderly? [*Aside.*] And so you promised to pardon him? and could you be so good-natured? have you really forgiven him? I beg you would do it for my sake. [*Whispering loud to* MARIA.] But, my dear, as you are in such haste, it would be cruel to detain you; I can show you the way through the other room.

MARIA. Spare me, my sprightly friend.

MANLY. The lady does not, I hope, intend to deprive us of the pleasure of her company so soon.

CHARLOTTE. She has only a mantua-maker who waits for her at home. But, as I am to give my opinion of the dress, I think she cannot go yet. We were talking of the fashions when you came in, but I suppose the subject must be changed to something of more importance now. Mr. Dimple, will you favor us with an account of the public entertainments?

DIMPLE. Why, really, Miss Manly, you could not have asked me a question more *mal-apropos.* For my part, I must confess that, to a man who has travelled, there is nothing that is worthy the name of amusement to be found in this city.

CHARLOTTE. Except visiting the ladies.

DIMPLE. Pardon me, Madam; that is the avocation of a man of taste. But for amusement, I positively know of nothing that can be called so, unless you dignify with that title the hopping once a fortnight to the sound of two or three squeaking fiddles, and the clattering of the old tavern windows, or sitting to see the miserable mummers, whom you call actors, murder comedy and make a farce of tragedy.

MANLY. Do you never attend the theatre, Sir?

DIMPLE. I was tortured there once.

CHARLOTTE. Pray, Mr. Dimple, was it a tragedy or a comedy?

DIMPLE. Faith, Madam, I cannot tell; for I sat with my back to the stage all the time, admiring a much better actress than any there—a lady who played the fine woman to perfection; though, by the laugh of the horrid creatures round me, I suppose it was comedy. Yet, on second thoughts, it might be some hero in a tragedy, dying so comically as to set the whole house in an uproar. Colonel, I presume you have been in Europe?

MANLY. Indeed, Sir, I was never ten leagues from the continent.

DIMPLE. Believe me, Colonel, you have an immense pleasure to come; and when you shall have seen the brilliant exhibitions of Europe, you will learn to despise the amusements of this country as much as I do.

MANLY. Therefore I do not wish to see them; for I can never esteem that knowledge valuable which tends to give me a distaste for my native country.

DIMPLE. Well, Colonel, though you have not travelled, you have read.

MANLY. I have, a little; and by it have discovered that there is a laudable partiality which ignorant, untravelled men entertain for everything that belongs to their native country. I call it laudable; it injures no one; adds to their own happiness; and, when extended, becomes the noble principle of patriotism. Travelled gentlemen rise superior, in their own opinion, to this; but if the contempt which they contract for their country is the most valuable acquisition of their travels, I am far from thinking that their time and money are well spent.

MARIA. What noble sentiments!

CHARLOTTE. Let my brother set out where he will in the fields of conversation, he is sure to end his tour in the temple of gravity.

MANLY. Forgive me, my sister. I love my country; it has its foibles undoubtedly;—some foreigners will with pleasure remark them—but such remarks fall very ungracefully from the lips of her citizens.

DIMPLE. You are perfectly in the right, Colonel—America has her faults.

MANLY. Yes, Sir; and we, her children, should blush for them in private, and endeavor, as individuals, to reform them. But, if our country has its errors in common with other countries, I am proud to say America—I mean the United States—has displayed virtues and achievements which modern nations may admire, but of which they have seldom set us the example.

CHARLOTTE. But, brother, we must introduce you to some of our gay folks, and let you see the city, such as it is. Mr. Dimple is known to almost every family in town; he will doubtless take a pleasure in introducing you.

DIMPLE. I shall esteem every service I can render your brother an honor.

MANLY. I fear the business I am upon will take up all my time, and my family will be anxious to hear from me.

MARIA. His family! but what is it to me that he is married! [*Aside.*] Pray, how did you leave your lady, Sir?

CHARLOTTE. My brother is not married [*Observing her anxiety.*]; it is only an odd way he has of expressing himself. Pray, brother, is this business, which you make your continual excuse, a secret?

MANLY. No, sister; I came hither to solicit the honorable Congress, that a number of my brave old soldiers may be put upon the pension-list, who were, at first, not judged to be so materially wounded as to need the public assistance. My sister says true [*To* MARIA.]: I call my late soldiers my family. Those who were not in the field in the late glorious contest, and those who were, have their respective merits; but, I confess, my old brother-soldiers are dearer to me than the former description. Friendships made in adversity are lasting; our countrymen may forget us, but that is no reason why we should forget one another. But I must leave you; my time of engagement approaches.

CHARLOTTE. Well, but, brother, if you will

go, will you please to conduct my fair friend home? You live in the same street—I was to have gone with her myself—[*Aside.*] A lucky thought.

MARIA. I am obliged to your sister, Sir, and was just intending to go. [*Going.*]

MANLY. I shall attend her with pleasure. [*Exit with* MARIA, *followed by* DIMPLE *and* CHARLOTTE.]

MARIA. Now, pray, don't betray me to your brother.

CHARLOTTE [*just as she sees him make a motion to take his leave*]. One word with you, brother, if you please. [*Follows them out.*]

Manent, DIMPLE *and* LETITIA

DIMPLE. You received the billet I sent you, I presume?

LETITIA. Hush!—Yes.

DIMPLE. When shall I pay my respects to you?

LETITIA. At eight I shall be unengaged.

Re-enter CHARLOTTE

DIMPLE. Did my lovely angel receive my billet? [*To* CHARLOTTE.]

CHARLOTTE. Yes.

DIMPLE. What hour shall I expect with impatience?

CHARLOTTE. At eight I shall be at home unengaged.

DIMPLE. Unfortunate! I have a horrid engagement of business at that hour. Can't you finish your visit earlier and let six be the happy hour?

CHARLOTTE. You know your influence over me. [*Exeunt severally.*

SCENE 2. VAN ROUGH'S *House*

VAN ROUGH [*alone*]. It cannot possibly be true! The son of my old friend can't have acted so unadvisedly. Seventeen thousand pounds! in bills! Mr. Transfer must have been mistaken. He always appeared so prudent, and talked so well upon money matters, and even assured me that he intended to change his dress for a suit of clothes which would not cost so much, and look more substantial, as soon as he married. No, no, no! it can't be; it cannot be. But, however, I must look out sharp. I did not care what his principles or his actions were, so long as he minded the main chance. Seventeen thousand pounds! If he had lost it in trade, why, the best men may have ill-luck; but to game it away, as Transfer says —why, at this rate, his whole estate may go in one night, and, what is ten times worse, mine into the bargain. No, no; Mary is right. Leave women to look out in these matters; for all they look as if they didn't know a journal from a ledger, when their interest is concerned they know what's what; they mind the main chance as well as the best of us. I wonder Mary did not tell me she knew of his spending his money so foolishly. Seventeen thousand pounds! Why, if my daughter was standing up to be married, I would forbid the banns, if I found it was to a man who did not mind the main chance.—Hush! I hear somebody coming. 'Tis Mary's voice; a man with her too! I shouldn't be surprised if this should be the other string to her bow. Aye, aye, let them alone; women understand the main chance.—Though, i' faith, I'll listen a little. [*Retires into a closet.*]

MANLY *leading in* MARIA

MANLY. I hope you will excuse my speaking upon so important a subject so abruptly; but, the moment I entered your room, you struck me as the lady whom I had long loved in imagination, and never hoped to see.

MARIA. Indeed, Sir, I have been led to hear more upon this subject than I ought.

MANLY. Do you, then, disapprove my suit, Madam, or the abruptness of my introducing it? If the latter, my peculiar situation, being obliged to leave the city in a few days, will, I hope, be my excuse; if the former, I will retire, for I am sure I would not give a moment's inquietude to her whom I could devote my life to please. I am not so indelicate as to seek your immediate approbation; permit me only to be near you, and by a thousand tender assiduities to endeavor to excite a grateful return.

MARIA. I have a father, whom I would die to make happy; he will disapprove—

MANLY. Do you think me so ungenerous as to seek a place in your esteem without his consent? You must—you ever ought to consider that man as unworthy of you who seeks an interest in your heart contrary to a father's approbation. A young lady should reflect that the loss of a lover may be supplied, but nothing can compensate for the loss of a parent's affection. Yet, why do you suppose your father would disapprove? In our country, the affections are not sacrificed to riches or family aggrandizement: should you approve, my family is decent, and my rank honorable.

MARIA. You distress me, Sir.

MANLY. Then I will sincerely beg your excuse for obtruding so disagreeable a subject, and retire. [*Going.*]

MARIA. Stay, Sir! your generosity and good opinion of me deserve a return; but why must I declare what, for these few hours, I have scarce suffered myself to think?—I am—

MANLY. What?

MARIA. Engaged, Sir; and, in a few days, to be married to the gentleman you saw at your sister's.

MANLY. Engaged to be married! And have I been basely invading the rights of another? Why have you permitted this? Is this the return for the partiality I declared for you?

MARIA. You distress me, Sir. What would you have me say? You are too generous to wish the truth. Ought I to say that I dared not suffer myself to think of my engagement, and that I am going to give my hand without my heart? Would you have me confess a partiality for you? If so, your triumph is complete, and can be only more so when days of misery with the man I cannot love will make me think of him whom I could prefer.

MANLY [*after a pause*]. We are both unhappy; but it is your duty to obey your parent—mine to obey my honor. Let us, therefore, both follow the path of rectitude; and of this we may be assured, that if we are not happy, we shall, at least, deserve to be so. Adieu! I dare not trust myself longer with you. [*Exeunt severally.*

END OF THE FOURTH ACT

ACT V

SCENE I. DIMPLE'S *Lodgings*

JESSAMY *meeting* JONATHAN

JESSAMY. Well, Mr. Jonathan, what success with the fair?

JONATHAN. Why, such a tarnal cross tike you never saw! You would have counted she had lived upon crab-apples and vinegar for a fortnight. But what the rattle makes you look so tarnation glum?

JESSAMY. I was thinking, Mr. Jonathan, what could be the reason of her carrying herself so coolly to you.

JONATHAN. Coolly, do you call it? Why, I vow, she was fire-hot angry: may be it was because I buss'd her.

JESSAMY. No, no, Mr. Jonathan; there must be some other cause; I never yet knew a lady angry at being kissed.

JONATHAN. Well, if it is not the young woman's bashfulness, I vow I can't conceive why she shouldn't like me.

JESSAMY. May be it is because you have not the Graces, Mr. Jonathan.

JONATHAN. Grace! Why, does the young woman expect I must be converted before I court her?

JESSAMY. I mean graces of person: for instance, my lord tells us that we must cut off our nails even at top, in small segments of circles—though you won't understand that; in the next place, you must regulate your laugh.

JONATHAN. Maple-log seize it! don't I laugh natural?

JESSAMY. That's the very fault, Mr. Jonathan. Besides, you absolutely misplace it. I was told by a friend of mine that you laughed outright at the play the other night, when you ought only to have tittered.

JONATHAN. Gor! I—what does one go to see fun for if they can't laugh?

JESSAMY. You may laugh; but you must laugh by rule.

JONATHAN. Swamp it—laugh by rule! Well, I should like that tarnally.

JESSAMY. Why, you know, Mr. Jonathan, that to dance, a lady to play with her fan, or a gentleman with his cane, and all other natural motions, are regulated by art. My master has composed an immensely pretty gamut, by which any lady or gentleman, with a few years' close application, may learn to laugh as gracefully as if they were born and bred to it.

JONATHAN. Mercy on my soul! A gamut for laughing—just like fa, la, sol?

JESSAMY. Yes. It comprises every possible display of jocularity, from an *affettuoso* smile to a *piano* titter, or full chorus *fortissimo* ha, ha, ha! My master employs his leisure hours in marking out the plays, like a cathedral chanting-book, that the ignorant may know where to laugh: and that pit, box, and gallery may keep time together, and not have a snigger in one part of the house, a broad grin in the other, and a d——d grum look in the third. How delightful to see the audience all smile together, then look on their books, then twist their mouths into an agreeable simper, then altogether shake the house with a general ha, ha, ha! loud as a full chorus of Handel's at an Abbey commemoration.

JONATHAN. Ha, ha, ha! that's dang'd cute, I swear.

JESSAMY. The gentlemen, you see, will laugh the tenor; the ladies will play the countertenor; the beaux will squeak the treble; and our jolly friends in the gallery a thorough bass, ho, ho, ho!

JONATHAN. Well, can't you let me see that gamut?

JESSAMY. Oh! yes, Mr. Jonathan; here it is. [*Takes out a book.*] Oh! no, this is only a titter with its variations. Ah, here it is. [*Takes out another.*] Now, you must know, Mr. Jonathan, this is a piece written by Ben Jonson, which I have set to my master's gamut. The places where you must smile, look grave, or laugh outright, are marked below the line. Now look over me. "There was a certain man"—now you must smile.

JONATHAN. Well, read it again; I warrant I'll mind my eye.

JESSAMY. "There was a certain man, who had a sad scolding wife,"—now you must laugh.

JONATHAN. Tarnation! That's no laughing matter, though.

JESSAMY. "And she lay sick a-dying";—now you must titter.

JONATHAN. What, snigger when the good woman's a-dying! Gor, I—

JESSAMY. Yes, the notes say you must—"and she asked her husband leave to make a will,"—now you must begin to look grave;—"and her husband said"—

JONATHAN. Ay, what did her husband say? Something dang'd cute, I reckon.

JESSAMY. "And her husband said, you have had your will all your lifetime, and would you have it after you are dead, too?"

JONATHAN. Ho, ho, ho! There the old man was even with her; he was up to the notch—ha, ha, ha!

JESSAMY. But, Mr. Jonathan, you must not laugh so. Why you ought to have tittered *piano*, and you have laughed *fortissimo*. Look here; you see these marks, A, B, C, and so on; these are the references to the other part of the book. Let us turn to it, and you will see the directions how to manage the muscles. This [*Turns over.*] was note D you blundered at.—You must purse the mouth into a smile, then titter, discovering the lower part of the three front upper teeth.

JONATHAN. How? read it again.

JESSAMY. "There was a certain man"—very well!—"who had a sad scolding wife,"—why don't you laugh?

JONATHAN. Now, that scolding wife sticks in my gizzard so pluckily that I can't laugh for the blood and nowns of me. Let me look grave here, and I'll laugh your belly full, where the old creature's a-dying.

JESSAMY. "And she asked her husband"—[*Bell rings.*] My master's bell! he's returned, I fear.—Here, Mr. Jonathan, take this gamut; and I make no doubt but with a few years' close application, you may be able to smile gracefully. [*Exeunt severally.*

SCENE 2. CHARLOTTE'S *Apartment*

Enter MANLY

MANLY. What, no one at home? How unfortunate to meet the only lady my heart was ever moved by, to find her engaged to another, and confessing her partiality for me! Yet engaged to a man who, by her intimation, and his libertine conversation with me, I fear, does not merit her. Aye! there's the sting; for, were I assured that Maria was happy, my heart is not so selfish but that it would dilate in knowing it, even though it were with another. But to know she is unhappy!—I must drive these thoughts from me. Charlotte has some books; and this is what I believe she calls her little library. [*Enters a closet.*]

Enter DIMPLE *leading* LETITIA

LETITIA. And will you pretend to say now, Mr. Dimple, that you propose to break with Maria? Are not the banns published? Are not the clothes purchased? Are not the friends invited? In short, is it not a done affair?

DIMPLE. Believe me, my dear Letitia, I would not marry her.

LETITIA. Why have you not broke with her before this, as you all along deluded me by saying you would?

DIMPLE. Because I was in hopes she would, ere this, have broke with me.

LETITIA. You could not expect it.

DIMPLE. Nay, but be calm a moment; 'twas from my regard to you that I did not discard her.

LETITIA. Regard to me!

DIMPLE. Yes; I have done everything in my power to break with her, but the foolish girl is so fond of me that nothing can accomplish it. Besides, how can I offer her my hand when my heart is indissolubly engaged to you?

LETITIA. There may be reason in this; but why so attentive to Miss Manly?

DIMPLE. Attentive to Miss Manly! For heaven's sake, if you have no better opinion of my constancy, pay not so ill a compliment to my taste.

LETITIA. Did I not see you whisper her today?

DIMPLE. Possibly I might—but something of so very trifling a nature that I have already forgot what it was.

LETITIA. I believe she has not forgot it.

DIMPLE. My dear creature, how can you for a moment suppose I should have any serious thoughts of that trifling, gay, flighty coquette, that disagreeable—

Enter CHARLOTTE

DIMPLE. My dear Miss Manly, I rejoice to see you; there is a charm in your conversation that always marks your entrance into company as fortunate.

LETITIA. Where have you been, my dear?

CHARLOTTE. Why, I have been about to twenty shops, turning over pretty things, and so have left twenty visits unpaid. I wish you would step into the carriage and whisk round, make my apology, and leave my cards where our friends are not at home; that, you know, will serve as a visit. Come, do go.

LETITIA. So anxious to get me out! but I'll watch you. [*Aside.*] Oh! yes, I'll go; I want a little exercise. Positively [DIMPLE *offering to accompany her.*], Mr. Dimple, you shall not go; why, half my visits are cake and caudle visits; it won't do, you know, for you to go. [*Exit, but returns to the door in the back scene and listens.*]

DIMPLE. This attachment of your brother to Maria is fortunate.

CHARLOTTE. How did you come to the knowledge of it?

DIMPLE. I read it in their eyes.

CHARLOTTE. And I had it from her mouth. It would have amused you to have seen her! She, that thought it so great an impropriety to praise a gentleman that she could not bring out one word in your favor, found a redundancy to praise him.

DIMPLE. I have done everything in my power to assist his passion there: your delicacy, my dearest girl, would be shocked at half the instances of neglect and misbehavior.

CHARLOTTE. I don't know how I should bear neglect; but Mr. Dimple must misbehave himself indeed, to forfeit my good opinion.

DIMPLE. Your good opinion, my angel, is the pride and pleasure of my heart; and if the most respectful tenderness for you, and an utter indifference for all your sex besides, can make me worthy of your esteem, I shall richly merit it.

CHARLOTTE. All my sex besides, Mr. Dimple!—you forgot your tête-à-tête with Letitia.

DIMPLE. How can you, my lovely angel, cast a thought on that insipid, wry-mouthed, ugly creature!

CHARLOTTE. But her fortune may have charms?

DIMPLE. Not to a heart like mine. The man, who has been blessed with the good opinion of my Charlotte, must despise the allurements of fortune.

CHARLOTTE. I am satisfied.

DIMPLE. Let us think no more on the odious subject, but devote the present hour to happiness.

CHARLOTTE. Can I be happy when I see the man I prefer going to be married to another?

DIMPLE. Have I not already satisfied my charming angel, that I can never think of marrying the puling Maria? But, even if it were so, could that be any bar to our happiness? for, as the poet sings,

"Love, free as air, at sight of human ties,
Spreads his light wings, and in a moment flies."

Come, then, my charming angel! why delay our bliss? The present moment is ours; the next is in the hand of fate. [*Kissing her.*]

CHARLOTTE. Begone, Sir! By your delusions you had almost lulled my honor asleep.

DIMPLE. Let me lull the demon to sleep again with kisses. [*He struggles with her; she screams.*]

Enter MANLY

MANLY. Turn, villain! and defend yourself.—[*Draws.*]

VAN ROUGH *enters and beats down their swords*

VAN ROUGH. Is the devil in you? are you going to murder one another? [*Holding* DIMPLE.]

DIMPLE. Hold him, hold him,—I can command my passion.

Enter JONATHAN

JONATHAN. What the rattle ails you? Is the old one in you? Let the colonel alone, can't you? I feel chock-full of fight,—do you want to kill the colonel?—

MANLY. Be still, Jonathan; the gentleman does not want to hurt me.

JONATHAN. Gor! I—I wish he did; I'd shew him Yankee boys play, pretty quick.—Don't you see you have frightened the young woman into the *hystrikes?*

VAN ROUGH. Pray, some of you explain this; what has been the occasion of all this racket?

MANLY. That gentleman can explain it to you; it will be a very diverting story for an intended father-in-law to hear.

VAN ROUGH. How was this matter, Mr. Van Dumpling?

DIMPLE. Sir,—upon my honor,—all I know is, that I was talking to this young lady, and this gentleman broke in on us in a very extraordinary manner.

VAN ROUGH. Why, all this is nothing to the purpose; can you explain it, Miss? [*To* CHARLOTTE.]

Enter LETITIA *through the back scene*

LETITIA. I can explain it to that gentleman's confusion. Though long betrothed to your daughter [*To* VAN ROUGH.], yet, allured by my fortune, it seems (with shame do I speak it) he has privately paid his addresses to me. I was drawn in to listen to him by his assuring me that the match was made by his father without his consent, and that he proposed to break with Maria, whether he married me or not. But, whatever were his intentions respecting your daughter, Sir, even to me he was false; for he has repeated the same story, with some cruel reflections upon my person, to Miss Manly.

JONATHAN. What a tarnal curse!

LETITIA. Nor is this all, Miss Manly. When he was with me this very morning, he made the same ungenerous reflections upon the weakness of your mind as he has so recently done upon the defects of my person.

JONATHAN. What a tarnal curse and damn, too!

DIMPLE. Ha! since I have lost Letitia, I believe I had as good make it up with Maria. Mr. Van Rough, at present I cannot enter into particulars; but, I believe, I can explain everything to your satisfaction in private.

VAN ROUGH. There is another matter, Mr. Van Dumpling, which I would have you explain. Pray, Sir, have Messrs. Van Cash & Co. presented you those bills for acceptance?

DIMPLE. The deuce! Has he heard of those

bills! Nay, then, all's up with Maria, too; but an affair of this sort can never prejudice me among the ladies; they will rather long to know what the dear creature possesses to make him so agreeable. [*Aside.*] Sir, you'll hear from me. [*To* MANLY.]

MANLY. And you from me, Sir.—

DIMPLE. Sir, you wear a sword.—

MANLY. Yes, Sir. This sword was presented to me by that brave Gallic hero, the Marquis De La Fayette. I have drawn it in the service of my country, and in private life, on the only occasion where a man is justified in drawing his sword, in defence of a lady's honor. I have fought too many battles in the service of my country to dread the imputation of cowardice. Death from a man of honor would be a glory you do not merit; you shall live to bear the insult of man and the contempt of that sex whose general smiles afforded you all your happiness.

DIMPLE. You won't meet me, Sir? Then I'll post you for a coward.

MANLY. I'll venture that, Sir. The reputation of my life does not depend upon the breath of a Mr. Dimple. I would have you to know, however, Sir, that I have a cane to chastise the insolence of a scoundrel, and a sword and the good laws of my country to protect me from the attempts of an assassin.—

DIMPLE. Mighty well! Very fine, indeed! Ladies and gentlemen, I take my leave; and you will please to observe in the case of my deportment the contrast between a gentleman who has read Chesterfield and received the polish of Europe and an unpolished, untravelled American. [*Exit.*

Enter MARIA

MARIA. Is he indeed gone?—

LETITIA. I hope, never to return.

VAN ROUGH. I am glad I heard of those bills; though its plaguy unlucky; I hoped to see Mary married before I died.

MANLY. Will you permit a gentleman, Sir, to offer himself as a suitor to your daughter? Though a stranger to you, he is not altogether so to her, or unknown in this city. You may find a son-in-law of more fortune, but you can never meet with one who is richer in love for her, or respect for you.

VAN ROUGH. Why, Mary, you have not let this gentleman make love to you without my leave?

MANLY. I did not say, Sir—

MARIA. Say, Sir!—I—the gentleman, to be sure, met me accidentally.

VAN ROUGH. Ha, ha, ha! Mark me, Mary; young folks think old folks to be fools; but old folks know young folks to be fools. Why, I knew all about this affair. This was only a cunning way I had to bring it about. Hark ye! I was in the closet when you and he were at our house. [*Turns to the company.*] I heard that little baggage say she loved her old father, and would die to make him happy! Oh! how I loved the little baggage! And you talked very prudently, young man. I have inquired into your character, and find you to be a man of punctuality and mind the main chance. And so, as you love Mary and Mary loves you, you shall have my consent immediately to be married. I'll settle my fortune on you, and go and live with you the remainder of my life.

MANLY. Sir, I hope—

VAN ROUGH. Come, come, no fine speeches; mind the main chance, young man, and you and I shall always agree.

LETITIA. I sincerely wish you joy [*Advancing to* MARIA.]; and hope your pardon for my conduct.

MARIA. I thank you for your congratulations, and hope we shall at once forget the wretch who has given us so much disquiet, and the trouble that he has occasioned.

CHARLOTTE. And I, my dear Maria,—how shall I look up to you for forgiveness? I, who, in the practice of the meanest arts, have violated the most sacred rights of friendship? I can never forgive myself, or hope charity from the world; but, I confess, I have much to hope from such a brother; and I am happy that I may soon say, such a sister.

MARIA. My dear, you distress me; you have all my love.

MANLY. And mine.

CHARLOTTE. If repentance can entitle me to forgiveness, I have already much merit; for

I despise the littleness of my past conduct. I now find that the heart of any worthy man cannot be gained by invidious attacks upon the rights and characters of others;—by countenancing the addresses of a thousand;—or that the finest assemblage of features, the greatest taste in dress, the genteelest address, or the most brilliant wit, cannot eventually secure a coquette from contempt and ridicule.

MANLY. And I have learned that probity, virtue, honor, though they should not have received the polish of Europe, will secure to an honest American the good graces of his fair countrywomen, and, I hope, the applause of THE PUBLIC.

THE END

ANDRÉ

By William Dunlap

WILLIAM DUNLAP
[1766–1839]

William Dunlap was born of Irish parentage February 19, 1766, at Perth Amboy, New Jersey. He was early interested in drama, reading Shakespeare at the age of ten and attending a performance of *The Beaux' Stratagem* in New York in 1777; it was not long before he had written several dramatic sketches based in part on the Arabian Nights.

Another talent of Dunlap's, painting, appeared early in life, and at sixteen he was a professional portraitist. In 1784 his father sent him to London to study painting under the famous Benjamin West, but it appears that the stage and the society of fashionable young men held such a charm for Dunlap that his father, skeptical of how much painting his son was learning, called him home in 1787.

In this year the success of *The Contrast*, together with his own memories of the English stage, inspired Dunlap to write a play; the result was a comedy, *The Modest Soldier; or, Love in New York*, written in 1788, but never produced. Dunlap's first play to be produced was *The Father* (1789); it was a success and determined Dunlap upon a career of playwriting. From this time on until 1828, when his last play, *A Trip to Niagara*, appeared, he wrote prolifically, though a majority of his productions were adaptations or translations from foreign sources, chiefly from the successful German playwright Kotzebue.

In addition to his plays Dunlap wrote *A History of the American Theatre*, *A History of the Rise and Progress of the Arts of Design in the United States*, *A History of New York*, and numerous biographical accounts. His death in 1839 brought to a close a life devoted to art, letters, and the theatre.

Dunlap's plays fall naturally into two groups: those which are chiefly of his own composition and those which are translations from foreign sources. The first group of plays is in some measure derivative, for Dunlap wrote scarcely a play which was not suggested by or based on some other play, novel, or historical incident. He altered, developed, or added to the original in a degree sufficient to justify his being called the author of the final product; but he did not synthesize his materials with that force of imagination which results in the creation of something new. What originality Dunlap did bring to his work was largely from 1787 to 1799, for increasingly burdensome duties as a theatrical producer and the comparative ease of adapting another's work induced him more and more to resort to translation of popular foreign plays, particularly those of Kotzebue, from whom he translated at least a dozen plays.

Among Dunlap's original productions it is possible to distinguish several different types. His first play, *The Modest Soldier; or, Love in New York*, has been lost; his second play, *The Father; or, American Shandyism*, belongs distinctly to the sentimental school.[1] It concerns the separation and subsequent reunion of father and son, complicated by a drawing-room seducer who is trying to capture the son's betrothed for himself. The villain is exposed in his roguery and virtue is triumphant. *The Italian Father*, in its tearful feelings and perfect devotions, is also of the sentimental group. It is based largely on Dekker's *The Honest Whore* and shows the unsuccessful temptation of a daughter and her unwavering loyalty to husband and father. Other sentimental dramas of Dunlap's are *Sterne's Maria* and *The Natural Daughter*.

Dunlap's first tragedy, *Leicester*, was written in 1790; in its exaggerated and lachrymal emotion, in its amorous intrigue, and in its explicit moralizing, it is related to the sentimental drama; in its villainous plots and murders, it is suggestive of the Elizabethan tragedy of blood. Though the figure of Leicester's wife, Matilda, urging her lover to murder, is suggestive of Lady Macbeth, Dunlap points out that there is more resemblance to Clytemnestra; the Shakespearean influence, however, is clearly present in addition to the murder instigated by Matilda: the victim is stabbed in his sleep and after the crime Matilda tries to quiet the fears of the murderer. There appears also in *Leicester* the idea of fatalism:

> "there is a dread fatality
> Attends the human race, hurtling them down
> The precipice of guilt to deep destruction." [2]

This theme is to recur in *André*.

Another type of play which Dunlap experimented with and succeeded in is the Gothic. In *Fontainville Abbey* a Marquis, who is a fratricide, plots to win his niece to his lust and later to murder her. La Motte, who had earlier robbed the Marquis, is led to assist in these plots in order to dissuade the Marquis from pressing the robbery charge. From this proposed course of crime La Motte is turned back by the sharp promptings of his conscience. He confesses his former guilt to the court and in view of his repentance is forgiven. The Marquis is led to execution.

The settings and atmosphere of the play are completely Gothic: thunder-storms, ruined castles, dark, damp corridors, flickering lights, rumbling sounds—all these, together with fear, horror, murder, are the materials out of which Gothic romances are constructed. Thus we see how closely identified Dunlap was with various literary currents. *Fontainville Abbey* is based on Mrs. Radcliffe's *Romance of the Forest;* other plays of Dunlap belonging to this late eighteenth-century

[1] See T. McDowell, "Sensibility in the 18th Century American Novel," *Studies in Philology*, XXIV, 383–402 (July, 1927).

[2] *Leicester*, Act II, sc. 1.

horror-romance are *Ribbemont; or, the Feudal Baron* and *The Man of Fortitude; or, the Knight's Adventure*, the latter based on Godwin's *Caleb Williams* and Schiller's *Die Räuber*. There is good reason to believe that Dunlap introduced Gothic romance to America, his first works preceding Brown's by four years.[1] That Dunlap considered himself something of an experimenter is suggested by the epilogue to *Fontainville Abbey* in which Cupid appears to complain that he is being neglected by the author for other interests:

"Twice has the author, who, in *my* despite,
You've honored with applause this very night,
Dar'd without me to form a tragic plan. . . ."

The dramatist's answer is:

"Too long has love usurp'd the boards:
The tragic scene a wider scope affords:
Each passion in its turn the mind should move.'

Diversified as the foregoing plays are, it is possible to observe at the center of practically all of them a consistent, definite, and integrated point of view toward the values of life as they took shape in the mind of Dunlap. In *The Father* it appears that the only happiness is in virtue and that he who is guilty of selfishness, duplicity, betrayal, must renounce these before he can expect contentment of mind. Elwina in *Leicester* says:

"Guilt, sirs, is ever ready!
It is a whirlpool, drawing heedless mortals
Near and more near—then, plunging them to death."

Or:

"Let native fortitude and conscientious virtue
Assert their rights, and thou may'st brave all storms." [2]

We learn from *Fontainville Abbey* that peace

"never flies that place however poor;
Where virtue dwells an inmate." [3]

In *The Italian Father* the happy man is "he that in truth and virtue puts his trust." Also, "Man is not man until passion dies."

That this explicit moralizing is not to be regarded simply as a feature of sentimental literature, that it is, indeed, an expression of Dunlap's own views, integrated with his basic thinking on the drama, is clear when one bears in mind his *History of the American Theatre*. Among his numerous reflections on the drama in general, we find the following: "Such a history will tend to mark the growth and improvement of our country, and may be eminently subservient to the cause of

[1] Coad, Oral Sumner, *William Dunlap*. New York, The Dunlap Society, 1927, p. 153. See also, same author, "The Gothic Element in American Literature before 1835," *Journal of English and Germanic Philology*, XXIV, 72–93 (January, 1925).

[2] *Leicester*, Act I, sc. 1.

[3] *Fontainville Abbey*, Act II.

morals, whether the theatre as it exists is so or not."[1] "Believing as we do that the stage might be made subservient to the moral improvement of man, and that its productions in very many instances have enlightened the mind and improved the heart, we shall not conceal the important truth that those persons who have made acting the business of their lives have been in an uncommon degree the slaves of their passions."[2]

It has been pointed out in the comments on *The Contrast* that the period following the Revolution was one in which the nation strove intensely to consolidate itself as a political unit, to put into definite and permanent form its ideals of commonwealth; as a part of this preoccupation with government and national unity, we saw that the desire for independence, culturally as well as politically, lay behind much that was written at the time, much that belonged not simply to applied literature but to *belles lettres*. It was felt to be time for a cultural as well as a political secession from Europe.

Now, international though his borrowings and adaptations may be, and open-minded as many of his judgments are, yet Dunlap reflects, and in a conspicuous way, the nationalistic currents of the time. This is the case with his play having the enemy title *André;* dealing as it does, in many ways sympathetically, with the tragedy of this British officer and spy, yet the play is a piece of strong nationalism, crowded with patriotic actions and utterances. Perhaps most striking in this respect is the figure of Washington, dominating the action at nearly every point, and portrayed with the greatest respect and veneration, to be seen particularly in the forgiving calm with which he receives Bland's impetuous renunciation of the cockade.

There are explicit declarations of patriotic feeling:

> "O patriotism!
> Thou wondrous principle of godlike action!
>
> * * *
>
> 'Tis this alone which saves thee, O my country!
> And, till that spirit flies these western shores,
> No power on earth shall crush thee."[3]

Bland is particularly concerned with liberty—for his country as well as for André.

> "O grant that thus may fall
> All those who seek to bring this land to woe!
> All those, who . . . seek to shake
> The Tree of Liberty, or stop its growth."[4]

[1] *History of the American Theatre*, p. 2.

[2] *Ibid.*, p. 95.

[3] Act I, sc. [2], p. 55. Cf. also Act III, sc. [3], p. 65:

> ". . . tho' all-powerful Europe league against us
> And pour in arms her legions on our shores;
> Who is so dull would doubt their shameful flight?
> Who doubt our safety, and our glorious triumph?"

[4] Act I, sc. [1], p. 54.

Seward hopes for an independence and isolation that is complete, not only politically and culturally, but in every other respect:

"O, would to heaven
That in midway between these sever'd worlds
Rose barriers, all impassable to man,
Cutting off intercourse, till either side
Had lost all memory of the other!" [1]

It has been seen that the nationalism of *The Contrast* was in a certain measure open-minded; the nationalism of *André* is even more so. Strong as the patriotic utterances are, yet the title character of the play, enemy of America, is portrayed in a decidedly sympathetic light: Bland has been won to André by the latter's mercy while Bland was a British prisoner; André tries to dissuade Bland from desertion, for "thy country's woes are full"; André despises his own "curs'd disguise" when he was a spy; he accepts his death penalty heroically, and generously refuses to blame America for taking his life:

"Thy country for my death incurs no blame."

The plight of the rejected suitor, in which André reveals himself, arouses sympathy, and the subsequent cutting short of reawakened hope is a scene of genuine pathos. The devotion of Bland alone tends to arouse a kindred feeling in the reader or spectator. Then, too, it must not be overlooked that the British finally released the elder Bland, whom they had threatened to kill if André were not freed. André suffered the death penalty, though as a spy, to be sure. The concluding speech of the play, by M'Donald, though urging that "every child be taught to lisp the tale" of our struggle for independence, that we still "abhor the motives" of those who oppressed us, nevertheless counsels that we

"Never let memory of the sire's offence
Descend upon the son."

M'Donald further says that America should look to "Europe's knowledge" and her "blest science."

It appears, then, that nationalism with Dunlap is a strong interest, but one which does not exclude others nor prevent him from realizing the full value of foreign culture; this latter can hardly be said of Tyler. It appears further that the nationalism of *André* is Federalistic, as it is in *The Contrast*. "How all-resistless is a union'd people," says Seward; the utterances of Washington are naturally consonant with this view. The philosophical concept of man's natural evil or weakness which lies behind the Federalistic view finds decided expression in the play: for Melville it is "man, the murderer," who is responsible for war; Washington counsels M'Donald to "ever keep in mind that man is frail"; and the

[1] Act II, sc. [2], p. 59.

captive André thus explains his fear: "Frail nature shrinks." Passion is something that cannot be relied upon:

> "How passion
> Mars thee! . . . passion sometimes sways
> My older frame, through former uncheck'd habit;
> But when I see the havoc which it makes
> In others, I can shun the snare accurst." [1]

In view of man's naturally weak or evil character, it is necessary to achieve some kind of control or discipline which will properly shape one's course of life: Washington explains that his men owe their present safety

> "To that good discipline which they observe,
> The discipline of men to order train'd
> Who know its value, and in whom 'tis virtue;
> To that prompt hardihood with which they meet
> Or toil or danger, poverty, or death." [2]

It is to "enlighten'd judgment" or reason that man is to look for this control:

> "I hope my every act
> Has been the offspring of deliberate judgment."

Washington speaks of the

> "tide of passion struggling still with Reason's
> Fair and favorable gale." [3]

André reproves himself for having "dared act against" his "reason."

We are not to understand by the foregoing that the feelings, or the heart, are to be entirely suppressed or neglected—in fact, "Man owes to man all love,"—but it does mean that they are to be directed. With proper control of the feelings by the judgment, there results an ideal balance, one which M'Donald finds in Washington:

> ". . . first among men;
> By nature, or by early habit, grac'd
> With that blest quality which gives due force
> To every faculty, and keeps the mind
> In healthful equipoise, ready for action." [4]

Opposed to these views is that of the youth Bland, strongly suggestive of Hotspur, who places his confidence in feeling: he takes exception to M'Donald's principles:

> "Rather perversion monstrous of all good
> Is thy accurs'd, detestable opinion.
> Cold-blooded reasoners, such as thee, would blast
> All warm affection; asunder sever
> Every social tie of humanized man.
> Curst be thy sophisms, cunningly contriv'd." [5]

[1] Act IV, sc. [1], p. 67.
[2] Act I, sc. [2], p. 55.
[3] Act I, sc. [2], p. 57.
[4] Act I, sc. [2], p. 57.
[5] Act IV, sc. [1], p. 67.

But Bland's emotional outbursts are in the main ineffectual and in the end he comes to see that he "was again the sport of erring passion."

The concept of judgment or reason controlling our impulses involves the question as to how far the individual has within himself the power of determining his own fate. The inevitability of war despite man's efforts at peace is suggested by Melville:

> "In vain the enlighten'd friends of suffering man
> Point out, of war, the folly, guilt, and madness.
> Still, age succeeds to age, and war to war." [1]

Washington feels the importance of a single event in determining the lives of many:

> "But the destiny of millions, millions
> Yet unborn, depends upon the rigor
> Of this moment." [2]

Nor can Washington pardon when he desires to:

> "[I] . . . feel the strong wish to use such blessed power;
> Yet know that circumstances strong as fate
> Forbid to obey the impulse." [3]

M'Donald says of rebellion:

> "Rises not man forever 'gainst oppression?
> It is the law of life; he can't avoid it." [4]

But the above commentary of M'Donald's cannot be interpreted as conclusive, for on other occasions he suggests that Lady Fortune cannot be held accountable for man's failures. He further asserts his faith in man's ability to reshape the course of his life:

> "Say to thyself: 'I *am* not what I *was;*
> I am not *now* the instrument of vice;
> I'm changed; I am a man; Virtue's firm friend;
> Sever'd forever from my former self;
> No link, but in remembrance salutary.'" [5]

Since, however, Dunlap's primary interest was the production of a play, and since he was not engaged in developing philosophical concepts, it would be inappropriate to press the search for a nice dovetailing of the above two tendencies with respect to the will. Perhaps a coalition of major inevitabilities and a limited will, though a denial of modern determinism, corresponds to "common sense" views frequently held by the average thinker. Perhaps the unresolved problems in the play suggest the unresolved problems in life.

The text of *André* is based on the 1798 edition.

[1] Act I, sc. 1, p. 53.
[2] Act III, sc. [2], p. 62.
[3] Act V, sc. [2], p. 72.
[4] Act I, sc. [2], p. 56.
[5] Act V, sc. [1], p. 71.

PROLOGUE

SPOKEN BY MR. MARTIN

A NATIVE Bard, a native scene displays,
And claims your candor for his daring lays:
Daring, so soon, in mimic scenes to shew,
What each remembers as a real woe.
Who has forgot when gallant ANDRÉ died?
A name by Fate to Sorrow's self allied.
Who has forgot, when o'er the untimely bier,
Contending armies paus'd, to drop a tear.

Our Poet builds upon a fact tonight;
Yet claims, in building, every Poet's right;
To choose, embellish, lop, or add, or blend,
Fiction with truth, as best may suit his end;
Which, he avows, is pleasure to impart,
And move the passions but to mend the heart.

O, may no party spirit blast his views,
Or turn to ill the meanings of the Muse:
She sings of wrongs long past, Men as they were,
To instruct, without reproach, the Men that are;
Then judge the Story by the genius shown,
And praise, or damn it, for its worth alone.

CHARACTERS

GENERAL, dress, American staff uniform, blue, faced with buff, large gold epaulets, cocked hat, with the black and white cockade, indicating the union with France, buff waistcoat and breeches, boots........................Mr. Hallam

M'DONALD, a man of forty years of age, uniform nearly the same as the first.....Mr. Tyler

SEWARD, a man of thirty years of age, staff uniform.......................Mr. Martin

ANDRÉ, a man of twenty-nine years of age, full British uniform after the first scene..Mr. Hodgkinson

BLAND, a youthful but military figure, in the uniform of a Captain of horse—dress, a short blue coat, faced with red, and trimmed with gold lace, two small epaulets, a white waistcoat, leather breeches, boots and spurs; over the coat, crossing the chest from the right shoulder, a broad buff belt, to which is suspended a manageable hussar sword; a horseman's helmet on the head, decorated as usual, and the union cockade affixed.............Mr. Cooper

MELVILLE, a man of middle age, and grave deportment; his dress a Captain's uniform when on duty; a blue coat, with red facings, gold epaulet, white waistcoat and breeches, boots and cocked hat, with the union cockade..Mr. Williamson

BRITISH OFFICER..Mr. Hogg

AMERICAN OFFICER...Mr. Miller

CHILDREN..............................Master Stockwell and Miss Hogg

AMERICAN SERGEANT...Mr. Seymour

AMERICAN OFFICERS and SOLDIERS, &c.

MRS. BLAND..Mrs. Melmoth

HONORA...Mrs. Johnson

SCENE, *the Village of Tappan, Encampment, and adjoining country*

TIME, *ten hours*

ANDRÉ

ACT I

SCENE I, *A Wood seen by star-light; an Encampment at a distance appearing between the trees.*

Enter MELVILLE

MELVILLE. The solemn hour, "when night and morning meet,"
Mysterious time, to superstition dear,
And superstition's guides, now passes by;
Deathlike in solitude. The sentinels,
In drowsy tones, from post to post send on
The signal of the passing hour. "All's well,"
Sounds through the camp. Alas, all is not well;
Else, why stand I, a man, the friend of man,
At midnight's depth, deck'd in this murderous guise,
The habiliment of death, the badge of dire
Necessitous coercion. 'Tis not well.
—In vain the enlighten'd friends of suffering man
Point out, of war, the folly, guilt, and madness.
Still, age succeeds to age, and war to war;
And man, the murderer, marshals out his hosts
In all the gaiety of festive pomp,
To spread around him death and desolation.
How long! how long!——
—Methinks I hear the tread of feet this way.
My meditating mood may work me woe.
[*Draws.*]
Stand, whoso'er thou art. Answer. Who's there?

Enter BLAND

BLAND. A friend.

MELVILLE. Advance and give the countersign.

BLAND. Hudson.

MELVILLE. What, Bland!

BLAND. Melville, my friend, you *here?*

MELVILLE. And *well*, my brave young friend. But why do you,
At this dead hour of night, approach the camp
On foot, and thus alone?

BLAND. I have but now
Dismounted; and from yon sequester'd cot,
Whose lonely taper through the crannied wall
Sheds its faint beams and twinkles midst the trees,
Have I, adventurous, grop'd my darksome way.
My servant and my horses, spent with toil,
There wait till morn.

MELVILLE. Why waited not yourself?

BLAND. Anxious to know the truth of those reports
Which, from the many mouths of busy Fame,
Still, as I pass'd, struck varying on my ear,
Each making th' other void. Nor does delay
The color of my hasteful business suit.
I bring dispatches for our great Commander;
And hasted hither with design to wait
His rising, or awake him with the sun.

MELVILLE. You will not need the last, for the blest sun
Ne'er rises on his slumbers; by the dawn
We see him mounted gaily in the field,
Or find him wrapt in meditation deep,
Planning the welfare of our war-worn land.

BLAND. Prosper, kind heaven! and recompense his cares.

MELVILLE. You're from the South, if I presume aright?

BLAND. I am; and, Melville, I am fraught with news.
The South teems with events—convulsing ones.
The Briton, there, plays at no mimic war;
With gallant face he moves, and gallantly is met.
Brave spirits, rous'd by glory, throng our camp;
The hardy hunter, skill'd to fell the deer,
Or start the sluggish bear from covert rude;

And not a clown that comes, but from his youth
Is trained to pour from far the leaden death,
To climb the steep, to struggle with the stream,
To labor firmly under scorching skies,
And bear, unshrinking, winter's roughest blast.
This, and that heaven-inspir'd enthusiasm
Which ever animates the patriot's breast,
Shall far outweigh the lack of discipline.

MELVILLE. Justice is ours; what shall prevail against her?

BLAND. But as I past along, many strange tales
And monstrous rumors have my ears assail'd:
That Arnold had prov'd false; but he was ta'en
And hung, or to be hung—I know not what.
Another told that all our army, with their
Much-lov'd Chief, sold and betray'd, were captur'd.
But as I nearer drew, at yonder cot
'Twas said that Arnold, traitor like, had fled;
And that a Briton, tried and prov'd a spy,
Was, on this day, as such, to suffer death.

MELVILLE. As you drew near, plain truth advanced to meet you.
'Tis even as you heard, my brave young friend.
Never had people on a single throw
More interest at stake; when he who held
For us the die prov'd false and play'd us foul.
But for a circumstance of that nice kind,
Of cause so microscopic that the tongues
Of inattentive men call it the effect
Of chance, we must have lost the glorious game.

BLAND. Blest, blest be heaven! whatever was the cause!

MELVILLE. The blow ere this had fallen that would have bruis'd
The tender plant which we have striven to rear,
Crush'd to the dust, no more to bless this soil.

BLAND. What warded off the blow?

MELVILLE. The brave young man, who this day dies, was seiz'd
Within our bounds, in rustic garb disguis'd.
He offer'd bribes to tempt the band that seiz'd him;
But the rough farmer, for his country arm'd,
That soil defending which his ploughshare turn'd,
Those laws his father chose and he approv'd,
Cannot, as mercenary soldiers may,
Be brib'd to sell the public weal for gold.

BLAND. 'Tis well. Just Heaven! O grant that thus may fall
All those who seek to bring this land to woe!
All those, who, or by open force, or dark
And secret machinations, seek to shake
The Tree of Liberty, or stop its growth,
In any soil where thou hast pleased to plant it.

MELVILLE. Yet not a heart but pities and would save him;
For all confirm that he is brave and virtuous,
Known, but till now, the darling child of Honor.

BLAND [*contemptuously*]. And how is call'd this—honorable spy?

MELVILLE. André's his name.

BLAND [*much agitated*]. André!

MELVILLE. Aye, Major André.

BLAND. André! O no, my friend, you're sure deceiv'd—
I'll pawn my life, my ever sacred fame,
My General's favor, or a soldier's honor,
That gallant André never yet put on
The guise of falsehood. O, it cannot be!

MELVILLE. How might I be deceiv'd? I've heard him, seen him,
And what I tell, I tell from well-prov'd knowledge;
No second tale-bearer, who heard the news.

BLAND. Pardon me, Melville. O, that well-known name,
So link'd with circumstances infamous!—
My friend must pardon me. Thou wilt not blame
When I shall tell what cause I have to love him;
What cause to think him nothing more the pupil
Of Honor stern, than sweet Humanity.
Rememberest thou, when cover'd o'er with wounds

And left upon the field, I fell the prey
Of Britain? To a loathsome prison-ship
Confin'd, soon had I sunk, victim of death,
A death of aggravated miseries;
But, by benevolence urg'd, this best of men,
This gallant youth, then favor'd, high in power,
Sought out the pit obscene of foul disease,
Where I and many a suffering soldier lay,
And, like an angel, seeking good for man,
Restor'd us light and partial liberty.
Me he mark'd out his own. He nurst and cur'd,
He lov'd and made his friend. I liv'd by him,
And in my heart he liv'd, till, when exchang'd,
Duty and honor call'd me from my friend.
Judge how my heart is tortur'd.—Gracious Heaven,
Thus, thus to meet him on the brink of death—
A death so infamous. Heav'n grant my prayer. [*Kneels.*]
That I may save him, O, inspire my heart
With thoughts, my tongue with words that move to pity! [*Rises.*]
Quick, Melville, show me where my André lies.

MELVILLE. Good wishes go with you.

BLAND. I'll save my friend! [*Exeunt.*

SCENE [2], *the Encampment by star-light*

Enter the GENERAL, M'DONALD, *and* SEWARD

GENERAL. 'Tis well. Each sentinel upon his post
Stands firm, and meets me at the bayonet's point;
While in his tent the weary soldier lies,
The sweet reward of wholesome toil enjoying;
Resting secure as erst within his cot
He careless slept, his rural labor o'er;
Ere Britons dar'd to violate those laws,
Those boasted laws by which themselves are govern'd,
And strove to make their fellow-subjects slaves.

SEWARD. They know to whom they owe their present safety.

GENERAL. I hope they know that to themselves they owe it;
To that good discipline which they observe,
The discipline of men to order train'd
Who know its value, and in whom 'tis virtue;
To that prompt hardihood with which they meet
Or toil or danger, poverty or death.
Mankind who know not whence that spirit springs,
Which holds at bay all Britain's boasted power,
Gaze on their deeds astonish'd. See the youth
Start from his plough and straightway play the hero;
Unmurmuring bear such toils as veterans shun;
Rest all content upon the dampsome earth;
Follow undaunted to the deathful charge;
Or, when occasion asks, lead to the breach,
Fearless of all the unusual din of war,
His former peaceful mates. O patriotism!
Thou wondrous principle of godlike action!
Wherever liberty is found, there reigns
The love of country. Now the self-same spirit
Which fill'd the breast of great Leonidas
Swells in the hearts of thousands on these plains,
Thousands who never heard the hero's tale.
'Tis this alone which saves thee, O my country!
And, till that spirit flies these western shores,
No power on earth shall crush thee.

SEWARD. 'Tis wondrous!
The men of other climes from this shall see
How easy 'tis to shake oppression off;
How all-resistless is a union'd people;
And hence, from our success (which, by my soul,
I feel as much secur'd as though our foes
Were now within their floating prisons hous'd,
And their proud prows all pointing to the east),
Shall other nations break their galling fetters,
And re-assume the dignity of man.

M'DONALD. Are other nations in that happy state,
That, having broke Coercion's iron yoke,
They can submit to Order's gentle voice,
And walk on earth self-ruled? I much do fear it.
As to ourselves, in truth, I nothing see,
In all the wondrous deeds which we perform,
But plain effects from causes full as plain.
Rises not man forever 'gainst oppression?
It is the law of life; he can't avoid it.
But when the love of property unites
With sense of injuries past and dread of future,
Is it then wonderful that he should brave
A lesser evil to avoid a greater?

GENERAL [*sportively*]. 'Tis hard, quite hard, we may not please ourselves,
By our great deeds ascribing to our virtue.

SEWARD. M'Donald never spares to lash our pride.

M'DONALD. In truth I know of naught to make you proud.
I think there's none within the camp that draws
With better will his sword than does M'Donald.
I have a home to guard. My son is—butcher'd—

SEWARD. Hast thou no nobler motives for thy arms
Than love of property and thirst of vengeance?

M'DONALD. Yes, my good Seward, and yet nothing wondrous.
I love this country for the sake of man.
My parents, and I thank them, cross'd the seas,
And made me native of fair Nature's world,
With room to grow and thrive in. I have thriven;
And feel my mind unshackled, free, expanding,
Grasping with ken unbounded mighty thoughts,
At which, if chance my mother had, good dame,
In Scotia, our revered parent soil,
Given me to see the day, I should have shrunk
Affrighted. Now, I see in this new world
A resting spot for man, if he can stand
Firm in his place, while Europe howls around him,
And all unsettled as the thoughts of vice,
Each nation in its turn threats him with feeble malice.
One trial, now, we prove; and I have met it.

GENERAL. And met it like a man, my brave M'Donald.

M'DONALD. I hope so; and I hope my every act
Has been the offspring of deliberate judgment;
Yet feeling seconds reason's cool resolves.
O! I could hate, if I did not more pity
These bands of mercenary Europeans,
So wanting in the common sense of nature,
As, without shame, to sell themselves for pelf
To aid the cause of darkness; murder man—
Without inquiry murder, and yet call
Their trade the trade of honor—high-soul'd honor—
Yet honor shall accord in act with falsehood.
O that proud man should e'er descend to play
The tempter's part, and lure men to their ruin!
Deceit and honor badly pair together.

SEWARD. You have much shew of reason; yet, methinks
What you suggest of one, whom fickle Fortune,
In her changeling mood, hath hurl'd, unpitying,
From her topmost height to lowest misery,
Tastes not of charity. André, I mean.

M'DONALD. I mean him, too; sunk by misdeed, not fortune.
Fortune and chance; O, most convenient words!
Man runs the wild career of blind ambition,
Plunges in vice, takes falsehood for his buoy,
And when he feels the waves of ruin o'er him,
Curses, "in good set terms," poor Lady Fortune.

GENERAL [*sportively to* SEWARD]. His mood is all untoward; let us leave him.

Tho' he may think that he is bound to rail,
We are not bound to hear him. [*To* M'DONALD.] Grant you that?

M'DONALD. O, freely, freely! You I never rail on.

GENERAL. No thanks for that; you've courtesy for office.

M'DONALD. You slander me.

GENERAL. Slander that would not wound.
Worthy M'Donald, though it suits full well
The virtuous man to frown on all misdeeds,
Yet ever keep in mind that man is frail;
His tide of passion struggling still with Reason's
Fair and favorable gale, and adverse
Driving his unstable bark upon the
Rocks of error. Should he sink thus shipwreck'd,
Sure, it is not Virtue's voice that triumphs
In his ruin. I must seek rest. Adieu!

[*Exeunt* GENERAL *and* SEWARD.

M'DONALD. Both good and great thou art; first among men;
By nature, or by early habit, grac'd
With that blest quality which gives due force
To every faculty, and keeps the mind
In healthful equipoise, ready for action;
Invaluable temperance—by all
To be acquired, yet scarcely known to any.

[*Exit.*

END OF THE FIRST ACT

ACT II

SCENE [I], *a Prison*

ANDRÉ *discovered, in a pensive posture, sitting at a table; a book by him and candles; his dress neglected, his hair dishevelled: he rises and comes forward.*

ANDRÉ. Kind Heaven be thank'd for that I stand alone
In this sad hour of life's brief pilgrimage!
Single in misery; no one else involving,
In grief, in shame, and ruin. 'Tis my comfort.
Thou, my thrice honor'd sire, in peace went'st down
Unto the tomb, nor knew to blush, nor knew
A pang for me. And thou, revered matron,
Could'st bless thy child, and yield thy breath in peace!
No wife shall weep, no child lament my loss.
Thus may I consolation find in what
Was once my woe. I little thought to joy
In not possessing, as I erst possest,
Thy love, Honora! André's death, perhaps,
May cause a cloud pass o'er thy lovely face;
The pearly tear may steal from either eye;
For thou mayest feel a transient pang, nor wrong
A husband's rights: more than a transient pang
O mayest thou never feel! The morn draws nigh
To light me to my shame. Frail nature shrinks—
And *is* Death then so fearful? I have brav'd
Him, fearless, in the field, and steel'd my breast
Against his thousand horrors; but his cool,
His sure approach, requires a fortitude
Which naught but conscious rectitude can give. [*Retires, and sits leaning.*]

Enter BLAND, *unperceived by* ANDRÉ

BLAND. And is that André? O, how changed! Alas!
Where is that martial fire, that generous warmth,
Which glow'd his manly countenance throughout,
And gave to every look, to every act,
The tone of high chivalrous animation?—
André, my friend, look up!

ANDRÉ. Who calls *me* friend?

BLAND. Young Arthur Bland.

ANDRÉ [*rising*]. That name sounds like a friend's. [*With emotion.*]
I have inquired for thee—wish'd much to see thee—
I prythee take no note of these fool's tears—
My heart was full—and seeing thee—

BLAND [*embracing him*]. O André!
I have but now arrived from the South—
Nor heard—till now—of this—I cannot speak;
Is this a place?—O, thus to find my friend!

ANDRÉ. Still dost thou call me friend? I, who dared act

Against my reason, my declared opinion;
Against my conscience and a soldier's fame?
Oft in the generous heat of glowing youth,
Oft have I said how fully I despis'd
All bribery base, all treacherous tricks in war:
Rather my blood should bathe these hostile shores,
And have it said, "He died a gallant soldier,"
Than with my country's gold encourage treason,
And thereby purchase gratitude and fame.

BLAND. Still mayest thou say it, for thy heart's the same.

ANDRÉ. Still is my heart the same, still may I say it;
But now my deeds will rise against my words;
And should I dare to talk of honest truth,
Frank undissembling probity and faith,
Memory would crimson o'er my burning cheek,
And actions retrospected choke the tale.
Still is my heart the same. But there has past
A day, an hour, which ne'er can be recall'd.
Unhappy man! Tho' all thy life pass pure;
Mark'd by benevolence thy every deed;
The out-spread map, which shows the way thou'st trod,
Without one devious track or doubtful line;
It all avails thee naught, if in one hour,
One hapless hour, thy feet are led astray;—
Thy happy deeds all blotted from remembrance;
Cancel'd the record of thy former good.
Is it not hard, my friend? Is't not unjust?

BLAND. Not every record cancel'd—O, there are hearts
Where Virtue's image, when 'tis once engraved,
Can never know erasure.

ANDRÉ. Generous Bland! [*Takes his hand.*]
The hour draws nigh which ends my life's sad story.
I should be firm—

BLAND. By heaven, thou shalt not die!
Thou dost not sure deserve it. Betray'd, perhaps—
Condemn'd without due circumstance made known?
Thou didst not mean to tempt our officers?
Betray our yeoman soldiers to destruction?
Silent! Nay, then 'twas from a duteous wish
To serve the cause thou wast in honor bound—

ANDRÉ. Kind is my Bland, who to his generous heart
Still finds excuses for his erring friend.
Attentive hear and judge me.—
Pleas'd with the honors daily shower'd upon me,
I glow'd with martial heat my name to raise
Above the vulgar herd, who live to die,
And die to be forgotten. Thus I stood,
When avarice or ambition Arnold tempted,
His country, fame, and honor to betray,
Linking his name to infamy eternal.
In confidence it was to me propos'd
To plan with him the means which should ensure
Thy country's downfall. Nothing then I saw
But confidential favor in the service,
My country's glory, and my mounting fame;
Forgot my former purity of thought,
And high-ton'd honor's scruples disregarded.

BLAND. It was thy duty so to serve thy country.

ANDRÉ. Nay, nay; be cautious ever to admit
That duty can beget dissimulation.
On ground, unoccupied by either part,
Neutral esteem'd, I landed, and was met.
But ere my conference was with Arnold clos'd,
The day began to dawn; I then was told
That till the night I must my safety seek
In close concealment. Within your posts convey'd,
I found myself involved in unthought dangers.
Night came. I sought the vessel which had borne
Me to the fatal spot; but she was gone.
Retreat that way cut off, again I sought
Concealment with the traitors of your army.
Arnold now granted passes, and I doff'd
My martial garb, and put on curs'd disguise.
Thus in a peasant's form I pass'd your posts;

And when, as I conceiv'd, my danger o'er,
Was stopt and seiz'd by some returning scouts.
So did ambition lead me, step by step,
To treat with traitors, and encourage treason;
And then, bewilder'd in the guilty scene,
To quit my martial designating badges,
Deny my name, and sink into the spy.

BLAND. Thou didst no more than was a soldier's duty,
To serve the part on which he drew his sword.
Thou shalt not die for this. Straight will I fly—
I surely shall prevail—

ANDRÉ. It is in vain.
All has been tried. Each friendly argument—

BLAND. All has not yet been tried. The powerful voice
Of friendship in thy cause has not been heard.
My General favors *me*, and loves my father—
My gallant father, would that he were here!
But he, perhaps, now wants an André's care,
To cheer his hours—perhaps now languishes
Amidst those horrors whence thou sav'd'st his son.
The present moment claims my thought. André,
I fly to save thee!

ANDRÉ. Bland, it is in vain.
But, hold—there is a service thou may'st do me.

BLAND. Speak it.

ANDRÉ. O, think, and as a soldier think,
How I must die—the *manner* of my death—
Like the base ruffian, or the midnight thief,
Ta'en in the act of stealing from the poor,
To be turn'd off the felon's—murderer's cart,
A mid-air spectacle to gaping clowns;—
To run a short, an envied course of glory,
And end it on a gibbet.—

BLAND. Damnation!

ANDRÉ. Such is my doom. O, have the manner changed,
And of mere death I'll think not. Dost thou think—?
Perhaps thou canst gain *that?*—

BLAND [*almost in a phrenzy*]. Thou shalt not die.

ANDRÉ. Let me, O, let me die a soldier's death,
While friendly clouds of smoke shroud from all eyes
My last convulsive pangs, and I'm content.

BLAND [*with increasing emotion*]. Thou shalt not die! Curse on the laws of war!
If worth like thine must thus be sacrificed
To policy so cruel and unjust,
I will forswear my country and her service;
I'll hie me to the Briton, and with fire,
And sword, and every instrument of death
Or devastation, join in the work of war!
What! shall worth weigh for naught? I will avenge thee!

ANDRÉ. Hold, hold, my friend! thy country's woes are full.
What! wouldst thou make me cause another traitor?
No more of this; and, if I die, believe me,
Thy country for my death incurs no blame.
Restrain thy ardor—but ceaselessly entreat
That André may at least die as he lived,
A soldier.

BLAND. By heaven! thou shalt not die!

[BLAND *rushes off;* ANDRÉ *looks after him with an expression of love and gratitude, then retires up the stage. Scene closes.*]

SCENE [2], *the* GENERAL'S *Quarters*

Enter M'DONALD *and* SEWARD, *in conversation*

M'DONALD [*coming forward*]. Three thousand miles the Atlantic wave rolls on,
Which bathed Columbia's shores, ere, on the strand
Of Europe, or of Africa, their continents,
Or sea-girt isles, it chafes.

SEWARD. O, would to heaven
That in midway between these sever'd worlds
Rose barriers, all impassable to man,
Cutting off intercourse, till either side
Had lost all memory of the other!

M'DONALD. What spur now goads thy warm imagination?

SEWARD. Then might, perhaps, one land on earth be found,

Free from th' extremes of poverty and riches;
Where ne'er a scepter'd tyrant should be known,
Or tyrant lordling, curses of creation;—
Where the faint shrieks of woe-exhausted age,
Raving, in feeble madness, o'er the corse
Of a polluted daughter, stained by lust
Of viand-pampered luxury, might ne'er be heard;
Where the blasted form of much abused
Beauty, by villany seduced, by knowledge
All unguarded, might ne'er be viewed, flitting
Obscene, 'tween lamp and lamp, i' th' midnight street
Of all-defiling city; where the child—

M'DONALD. Hold! Shroud thy raven imagination.
Torture not me with images so curst!

SEWARD. Soon shall our foes, inglorious, fly these shores.
Peace shall again return. Then Europe's ports
Shall pour a herd upon us, far more fell
Than those, her mercenary sons, who now
Threaten our sore chastisement.

M'DONALD. Prophet of ill,
From Europe shall enriching commerce flow,
And many an ill attendant; but from thence
Shall likewise flow blest science. Europe's knowledge,
By sharp experience bought, we should appropriate;
Striving thus to leap from that simplicity,
With ignorance curst, to that simplicity,
By knowledge blest; unknown the gulph between.

SEWARD. Mere theoretic dreaming.

M'DONALD. Blest wisdom
Seems, from out the chaos of the social world,
Where good and ill in strange commixture float,
To rise, by strong necessity impell'd;
Starting, like Love divine, from womb of Night,
Illuming all, to order all reducing;
And showing by its bright and noontide blaze
That happiness alone proceeds from justice.

SEWARD. Dreams, dreams! Man can know naught but ill on earth.

M'DONALD. I'll to my bed, for I have watch'd all night;
And may my sleep give pleasing repetition
Of these my waking dreams! Virtue's incentives. [*Exit.*

SEWARD. Folly's chimeras rather: guides to error.

Enter BLAND, *preceded by a* SERGEANT

SERGEANT. Pacquets for the General. [*Exit.*

BLAND. Seward, my friend!

SEWARD. Captain, I'm glad to see the hue of health
Sit on a visage from the sallow South.

BLAND. The lustihood of youth hath yet defied
The parching sun, and chilling dew of even.
The General—Seward—?

SEWARD. I will lead you to him.

BLAND. Seward, I must make bold. Leave us together,
When occasion offers. 'Twill be friendly.

SEWARD. I will not cross your purpose. [*Exeunt.*

SCENE [3], *a Chamber*

Enter MRS. BLAND

MRS. BLAND. Yes, ever be this day a festival
In my domestic calendar. This morn
Will see my husband free. Even now, perhaps,
Ere yet Aurora flies the eastern hills,
Shunning the sultry sun, my Bland embarks.
Already, on the Hudson's dancing wave,
He chides the sluggish rowers, or supplicates
For gales propitious; that his eager arms
May clasp his wife, may bless his little ones.
O, how the tide of joy makes my heart bound,
Glowing with high and ardent expectation!

Enter two CHILDREN

FIRST CHILD. Here we are, Mamma, up, and dress'd already.

MRS. BLAND. And why were ye so early?

FIRST CHILD. Why, did not you tell us that Papa was to be home today?

MRS. BLAND. I said, perhaps.

SECOND CHILD [*disappointed*]. Perhaps!

FIRST CHILD. I don't like perhaps's.

SECOND CHILD. No, nor I neither; nor "may-be-so's."

MRS. BLAND. We make not certainties, my pretty loves;
I do not like "perhaps's" more than you do.

SECOND CHILD. O! don't say so, Mamma! for I'm sure I hardly ever ask you anything but you answer me with "may be so," "perhaps," or "very likely." "Mamma, shall I go to the camp tomorrow, and see the General?" "May be so, my dear." Hang "may be so," say I!

MRS. BLAND. Well said, Sir Pertness!

FIRST CHILD. But I am sure, Mamma, you said that, today, Papa would have his liberty.

MRS. BLAND. So your dear father, by his letters, told me.

SECOND CHILD. Why, then, *I am sure* he will be here today. When he can come *to us*, I'm sure he will not stay among those strange Englishmen and Hessians. I often wish'd that I had wings to fly, for then I would soon be with him.

MRS. BLAND. Dear boy!

Enter SERVANT, *and gives a letter to* MRS. BLAND

SERVANT. An express, Madam, from New-York to Head-quarters, in passing, delivered this.

SECOND CHILD. Papa's coming home today, John. [*Exeunt* SERVANT *and* CHILDREN.

MRS. BLAND. What fears assail me! O, I did not want
A letter now! [*She reads in great agitation, exclaiming, while her eyes are fixed on the paper:*] My husband doomed to die! Retaliation!
[*She looks forward with wildness, consternation, and horror.*]
To die, if André dies! *He* dies today!
My husband to be murdered! And today!
Today, if André dies! Retaliation!
O curst contrivance! Madness relieve me!
Burst, burst, my brain! Yet—André is not dead;
My husband lives. [*Looks at the letter.*] "One man has power."
I fly to save the father of my children!
[*Rushes out.*

END OF THE SECOND ACT

ACT III

SCENE [1], *the* GENERAL'S *Quarters*

The GENERAL *and* BLAND *come forward*

GENERAL [*papers in his hand*]. Captain, you are noted here with honorable
Praises. Depend upon that countenance
From me, which you have prov'd yourself so richly
Meriting. Both for your father's virtues
And your own, your country owes you honor—
The sole return the poor can make for service.

BLAND. If from my country aught I've merited,
Or gain'd the approbation of her champion,
At any other time I should not dare,
Presumptuously, to show my sense of it;
But now my tongue, all shameless, dares to name
The boon, the precious recompense, I wish,
Which, granted, pays all service, past or future,
O'erpays the utmost I can e'er achieve.

GENERAL. Brief, my young friend, briefly, your purpose.

BLAND. If I have done my duty as a soldier;
If I have brav'd all dangers for my country;
If my brave father has deserved aught;
Call all to mind—and cancel all—but grant
My one request—mine, and humanity's.

GENERAL. Be less profuse of words, and name your wish;
If fit, its fitness is the best assurance
That not in vain you sue; but, if unjust,
Thy merits, nor the merits of thy race,
Cannot its nature alter, nor my mind,
From its determined opposition change.

BLAND. You hold the fate of my most lov'd of friends;
As gallant soldier as e'er faced a foe,
Bless'd with each polish'd gift of social life,
And every virtue of humanity.

To me, a savior from the pit of death,
To me, and many more, my countrymen.
Oh, could my words portray him what he is!
Bring to your mind the blessings of his deeds,
While thro' the fever-heated, loathsome holds
Of floating hulks, dungeons obscene, where ne'er
The dewy breeze of morn, or evening's coolness,
Breath'd on our parching skins, he pass'd along,
Diffusing blessings; still his power exerting,
To alleviate the woes which ruthless war,
Perhaps thro' dire necessity, heap'd on us;
Surely the scene would move you to forget
His late intent—tho' only serving then
As duty prompted—and turn the rigor
Of War's iron law from him, the best of men,
Meant only for the worst.

GENERAL. Captain, no more.

BLAND. If André lives, the prisoner finds a friend;
Else helpless and forlorn—
All men will bless the act, and bless thee for it.

GENERAL. Think'st thou thy country would not curse the man
Who, by a clemency ill-tim'd, ill-judg'd,
Encourag'd treason? That *pride* encourag'd,
Which, by denying us the rights of nations,
Hath caus'd those ills which thou hast now portray'd?
Our prisoners, brave and generous peasantry,
As rebels have been treated, not as men.
'Tis mine, brave yeomen, to assert your rights;
'Tis mine to teach the foe, that, though array'd
In rude simplicity, ye yet are men,
And rank among the foremost. Oft their scouts,
The very refuse of the English arms,
Unquestion'd, have our countrymen consign'd
To death, when captur'd, mocking their agonies.

BLAND. Curse them! [*Checking himself.*] Yet, let not censure fall on André.
O, there are Englishmen as brave, as good,
As ever land on earth might call its own;
And gallant André is among the best!

GENERAL. Since they have hurl'd war on us, we must show
That by the laws of war we will abide;
And have the power to bring their acts for trial
To that tribunal, eminent 'mongst men,
Erected by the policy of nations,
To stem the flood of ills, which else fell war
Would pour, uncheck'd, upon the sickening world,
Sweeping away all trace of civil life.

BLAND. To pardon him would not encourage ill.
His case is singular; his station high;
His qualities admired; his virtues lov'd.

GENERAL. No more, my good young friend: it is in vain.
The men entrusted with thy country's rights
Have weigh'd, attentive, every circumstance.
An individual's virtue is by them
As highly prized as it can be by thee.
I know the virtues of this man and love them.
But the destiny of millions, millions
Yet unborn, depends upon the rigor
Of this moment. The haughty Briton laughs
To scorn our armies and our councils. Mercy,
Humanity, call loudly, that we make
Our now despised power be felt, vindictive.
Millions demand the death of this young man.
My injur'd country, he his forfeit life
Must yield, to shield thy lacerated breast
From torture. [*To* BLAND.] Thy merits are not overlook'd.
Promotion shall immediately attend thee.

BLAND [*with contemptuous irony*]. Pardon me, sir, I never shall deserve it.
[*With increasing heat.*] The country that forgets to reverence virtue;
That makes no difference 'twixt the sordid wretch
Who, for reward, risks treason's penalty,

And him unfortunate, whose duteous service
Is, by mere accident, so chang'd in form
As to assume guilt's semblance, I serve not:
Scorn to serve. I have a soldier's honor,
But 'tis in union with a freeman's judgment,
And when I act, both prompt. Thus from my helm
I tear what once I proudly thought the badge
Of virtuous fellowship. [*Tears the cockade from his helmet.*] My sword I keep. [*Puts on his helmet.*]
Would, André, thou hadst never put thine off.
Then hadst thou through opposers' hearts made way
To liberty, or bravely pierc'd thine own!
[*Exit.*

GENERAL. Rash, headstrong, maddening boy!
Had not this action past without a witness,
Duty would ask that thou shouldst rue thy folly—
But, for the motive, be the deed forgotten.
[*Exit.*

SCENE [2], *a Village*

At a distance some tents. In front muskets, drums, and other indications of soldiers' quarters.

Enter MRS. BLAND *and* CHILDREN, *attended by* MELVILLE

MELVILLE. The General's doors to you are ever open.
But why, my worthy friend, this agitation?
Our colonel, your husband—

MRS. BLAND [*in tears, gives him the letter*]. Read, Melville.

FIRST CHILD. Do not cry, Mamma, for I'm sure if Papa said he would come home today, he will come yet; for he always does what he says he will.

MRS. BLAND. He cannot come, dear love; they will not let him.

SECOND CHILD. Why, then, they told him lies. O, fye upon them!

MELVILLE [*returning the letter*]. Fear nothing, Madam, 'tis an empty threat:
A trick of policy. They dare not do it.

MRS. BLAND. Alas, alas! what dares not power to do?
What art of reasoning, or what magic words,
Can still the storm of fears these lines have raised?
The wife's, the mother's fears? Ye innocents,
Unconscious on the brink of what a perilous
Precipice ye stand, unknowing that today
Ye are cast down the gulph, poor babes, ye weep
From sympathy. Children of sorrow, nurst,
Nurtur'd, 'midst camps and arms; unknowing man,
But as man's fell destroyer; must ye now,
To crown your piteous fate, be fatherless?
O, lead me, lead me to him! Let me kneel,
Let these, my children, kneel, till André, pardon'd,
Ensures to me a husband, them a father.

MELVILLE. Madam, duty forbids further attendance.
I am on guard today. But see your son;
To him I leave your guidance. Good wishes
Prosper you. [*Exit* MELVILLE.

Enter BLAND

MRS. BLAND. My Arthur, O my Arthur!

BLAND. My mother! [*Embracing her.*]

MRS. BLAND. My son, I have been wishing
For you—[*Bursts into tears, unable to proceed.*]

BLAND. But whence this grief, these tears, my mother?
Why are these little cheeks bedew'd with sorrow?
[*He kisses the children, who exclaim,* Brother, brother!]
Have I done aught to cause a mother's sadness?

MRS. BLAND. No, my brave boy! I oft have fear'd, but never
Sorrow'd for thee.

BLAND. High praise! Then bless me, Madam;
For I have pass'd through many a bustling scene
Since I have seen a father or a mother.

MRS. BLAND. Bless thee, my boy! O, bless him, bless him, Heaven!
Render him worthy to support these babes,
So soon, perhaps, all fatherless—dependent.

BLAND. What mean'st thou, Madam? Why these tears?

MRS. BLAND. Thy father—

BLAND. A prisoner of war—I long have known it—
But made so without blemish to his honor,
And soon exchang'd, returns unto his friends,
To guard these little ones, and point and lead
To virtue and to glory.

MRS. BLAND. Never, never!
His life, a sacrifice to André's manes,
Must soon be offer'd. Even now, endungeon'd,
Like a vile felon, on the earth he lies,
His death expecting. André's execution
Gives signal for the murder of thy father—
André now dies!

BLAND [*despairingly*]. My father and my friend!

MRS. BLAND. There is but one on earth can save my husband—
But one can pardon André.

BLAND. Haste, my mother!
Thou wilt prevail. Take with thee in each hand
An unoffending child of him thou weep'st.
Save—save them both! This way—haste—lean on me. [*Exeunt.*

SCENE [3], *the* GENERAL'S *Quarters*

Enter the GENERAL *and* M'DONALD

GENERAL. *Here* have I intimation from the foe,
That still they deem the spy we have condemn'd,
Merely a captive; by the laws of arms
From death protected; and retaliation,
As they term it, threaten, if we our purpose hold.
Bland is the victim they have singled out,
Hoping his threaten'd death will André save.

M'DONALD. If I were Bland I boldly might advise
My General how to act. Free, and in safety,
I will now suppose my counsel needless.

Enter an AMERICAN OFFICER

OFFICER. Another flag hath from the foe arrived,
And craves admittance.

GENERAL. Conduct it hither. [*Exit* OFFICER.
Let us, unwearied hear, unbias'd judge,
Whate'er against our martial court's decision,
Our enemies can bring.

Enter BRITISH OFFICER, *conducted by the* AMERICAN OFFICER

GENERAL. You are welcome, sir.
What further says Sir Henry?

BRITISH OFFICER. This from him.
He calls on you to think what weighty woes
You now are busy bringing on your country.
He bids me say, that if your sentence reach
The prisoner's life—prisoner of arms he deems him,
And no spy—on him alone it falls not.
He bids me loud proclaim it, and declare,
If this brave officer, by cruel mockery
Of war's stern law, and justice' feign'd pretence,
Be murder'd; the sequel of our strife, bloody,
Unsparing and remorseless, *you* will make.
Think of the many captives in our power.
Already one is mark'd; for André mark'd;—
And when his death, unparallel'd in war,
The signal gives, then Colonel Bland must die.

GENERAL. 'Tis well, sir; bear this message in return.
Sir Henry Clinton knows the laws of arms:
He is a soldier, and, I think, a brave one.
The prisoners he retains he must account for.
Perhaps the reckoning's near. I, likewise, am
A soldier; entrusted by my country.
What I shall judge most for that country's good,
That shall I do. When doubtful, I consult
My country's friends; never her enemies.
In André's case there are no doubts; 'tis clear:
Sir Henry Clinton knows it.

BRITISH OFFICER. Weigh consequences.

GENERAL. In strict regard to consequence I act;
And much should doubt to call that action right,
Howe'er specious, whose apparent end

Was misery to man. That brave officer
Whose death you threaten, for himself drew not
His sword—his country's wrongs arous'd his mind;
Her good alone his aim; and if his fall
Can further fire that country to resistance,
He will, with smiles, yield up his glorious life,
And count his death a gain; and tho' Columbians
Will lament his fall, they will lament in blood. [GENERAL *walks up the stage.*]

M'DONALD. Hear this, hear this, mankind!

BRITISH OFFICER. Thus am I answered?

Enter a SERGEANT *with a letter*

SERGEANT. Express from Colonel Bland.
[*Delivers it and exit.*

GENERAL. With your permission. [*Opens it.*]

BRITISH OFFICER. Your pleasure, sir. It may my mission further.

M'DONALD. O Bland, my countryman, surely I know thee!

GENERAL. 'Tis short; I will put form aside, and read it. [*Reads.*] "Excuse me, my Commander, for having a moment doubted your virtue; but you love me. If you waver, let this confirm you. My wife and children, to you and my country. Do *your* duty." Report this to your General.

BRITISH OFFICER. I shall, sir.
[*Bows, and exit with* AMERICAN OFFICER.

GENERAL. O Bland, my countryman!
[*Exit, with emotion.*

M'DONALD. Triumph of virtue!
Like him and thee, still be Americans.
Then, tho' all-powerful Europe league against us,
And pour in arms her legions on our shores;
Who is so dull would doubt their shameful flight?
Who doubt our safety, and our glorious triumph?

SCENE [4], *the Prison*

Enter BLAND

BLAND. Lingering, I come to crush the bud of hope
My breath has, flattering, to existence warmed.
Hard is the task to friendship! hard to say
To the lov'd object, there remains no hope,
No consolation for thee; thou *must* die
The worst of deaths, no circumstance abated.

Enter ANDRÉ, *in his uniform, and dress'd*

ANDRÉ. Is there that state on earth which friendship cannot cheer?

BLAND. Little *I* bring to cheer thee, André.

ANDRÉ. I understand. 'Tis well. 'Twill soon be past.
Yet, 'twas not much I asked. A soldier's death,
A trifling change of form.

BLAND. Of that I spoke not.
By vehemence of passion hurried on,
I pleaded for thy precious life alone;
The which denied, my indignation barr'd
All further parley. But strong solicitation
Now is urg'd to gain the wish'd-for favor.

ANDRÉ. What is 't o'clock?

BLAND. 'Tis past the stroke of nine.

ANDRÉ. Why, then, 'tis almost o'er. But to be hung—
Is there no way to escape that infamy?
What then *is* infamy?—no matter—no matter.

BLAND. Our General hath received another flag.

ANDRÉ. Soliciting for me?

BLAND. On thy behalf.

ANDRÉ. I have been ever favor'd.

BLAND. Threat'nings, now;
No more solicitations. Harsh, indeed,
The import of the message; harsh, indeed.

ANDRÉ. I am sorry for it. Would that I were dead,
And all was well with those I leave behind.

BLAND. Such a threat! Is it not enough, just Heaven,
That I must lose this man? Yet there was left
One for my soul to rest on. But, to know
That the same blow deprives them both of life—

ANDRÉ. What mean'st thou, Bland? Surely my General
Threats not retaliation. In vengeance
Dooms not some better man to die for me?

BLAND. The best of men.

ANDRÉ. Thou hast a father, captive—
I dare not ask—

BLAND. That father dies for thee.

ANDRÉ. Gracious Heaven, how woes are heap'd upon me!
What! cannot one, so trifling in life's scene,
Fall, without drawing such a ponderous ruin?
Leave me, my friend, awhile—I yet have life—
A little space of life—let me exert it
To prevent injustice; from death to save
Thy father, thee to save from utter desolation.

BLAND. What mean'st thou, André?

ANDRÉ. Seek thou the messenger
Who brought this threat. I will my last entreaty
Send by him. My General, sure, will grant it.

BLAND. To the last thyself! [*Exit.*

ANDRÉ. If, at this moment,
When the pangs of death already touch me,
Firmly my mind against injustice strives,
And the last impulse to my vital powers
Is given by anxious wishes to redeem
My fellow-men from pain; surely my end,
Howe'er accomplish'd, is not infamous.
[*Exit.*

END OF THE THIRD ACT

ACT IV

SCENE [1], *the Encampment*

Enter M'DONALD *and* BLAND

BLAND. It doth in truth appear, that as a—spy—
Detested word!—brave André must be view'd.
His sentence he confesses strictly just.
Yet sure, a deed of mercy from *thy* hand,
Could never lead to ill. By such an act,
The stern and blood-stain'd brow of War
Would be disarm'd of half its gorgon horrors;
More humanized customs be induced;
And all the race of civilized man
Be blest in the example. Be it thy suit:
'Twill well become thy character and station.

M'DONALD. Trust me, young friend, I am alone the judge
Of what becomes my character and station;
And having judg'd that this young Briton's death,
Even though attended by thy father's murder,
Is necessary, in these times accurs'd,
When every thought of man is ting'd with blood,
I will not stir my finger to redeem them.
Nay, much I wonder, Bland, having so oft
The reasons for this necessary rigor
Enforced upon thee, thou wilt still persist
In vain solicitations. Imitate
Thy father!

BLAND. My father knew not André.
I know his value; owe to him my life;
And gratitude, that first, that best of virtues,—
Without the which man sinks beneath the brute,—
Binds me in ties indissoluble to him.

M'DONALD. That man-created virtue blinds thy reason.
Man owes to man all love; when exercised,
He does no more than duty. Gratitude,
That selfish rule of action, which commands
That we our preference make of men,
Not for their worth, but that they did *us* service,
Misleading reason, casting in the way
Of justice stumbling-blocks, cannot be virtue.

BLAND. Detested sophistry! 'Twas André sav'd me.

M'DONALD. He sav'd thy life, and thou art grateful for it.
How self intrudes, delusive, on man's thoughts.
He sav'd thy life, yet strove to damn thy country;
Doom'd millions to the haughty Briton's yoke;
The best and foremost in the cause of virtue
To death, by sword, by prison, or the halter;
His sacrifice now stands the only bar
Between the wanton cruelties of war
And our much-suffering soldiers; yet when weigh'd
With gratitude, for that he sav'd *thy* life,

These things prove gossamer, and balance air;—
Perversion monstrous of man's moral sense!

BLAND. Rather perversion monstrous of all good
Is thy accurs'd, detestable opinion.
Cold-blooded reasoners, such as thee, would blast
All warm affection; asunder sever
Every social tie of humanized man.
Curst be thy sophisms, cunningly contriv'd
The callous coldness of thy heart to cover,
And screen thee from the brave man's detestation!

M'DONALD. Boy, boy!

BLAND. Thou knowest that André's not a spy.

M'DONALD. I know him one. Thou hast acknowledg'd it.

BLAND. Thou liest!

M'DONALD. Shame on thy ruffian tongue! How passion
Mars thee! I pity thee. Thou canst not harm,
By words intemperate, a virtuous man.
I pity thee; for passion sometimes sways
My older frame, through former uncheck'd habit;
But when I see the havoc which it makes
In others, I can shun the snare accurst,
And nothing feel but pity.

BLAND [*indignantly*]. Pity me! [*Approaches him, and speaks in an under voice.*]
Thou canst be cool, yet, trust me, *passion* sways thee.
Fear does not warm the blood, yet 'tis a *passion.*
Hast thou no feeling? I have call'd thee liar!

M'DONALD. If thou could'st make me one, I then might grieve.

BLAND. Thy coolness goes to freezing; thou'rt a coward!

M'DONALD. Thou knowest thou tell'st a falsehood.

BLAND. Thou shalt know
None with impunity speaks thus of me.
That to rouse thy courage! [*Touches him gently with his open hand, in crossing him.* M'DONALD *looks at him unmoved.*] Dost thou not yet feel?

M'DONALD. For *thee* I feel. And, tho' another's acts
Cast no dishonor on the worthy man,
I still feel for thy father. Yet, remember,
I may not, haply, ever be thus guarded;
I may not always the distinction make,
However just, between the blow intended
To provoke, and one that's meant to injure.

BLAND. Hast thou no sense of honor?

M'DONALD. Truly, yes:
For I am honor's votary. Honor, with me,
Is worth; 'tis truth; 'tis virtue; 'tis a thing
So high pre-eminent, that a boy's breath,
Or brute's, or madman's blow can never reach it.
My honor is so much, so truly mine,
That none hath power to wound it, save myself.

BLAND. I will proclaim thee through the camp a coward.

M'DONALD. Think better of it! Proclaim not thine own shame.

BLAND. I'll brand thee—damnation! [*Exit.*

M'DONALD. O passion, passion!
A man who values fame far more than life;
A brave young man; in many things a good;
Utters vile falsehood; adds injury to insult;
Striving with blood to seal such foul injustice;
And all from impulse of unbridled feeling. [*Pause.*]
Here comes the mother of this headstrong boy,
Severely rack'd. What shall allay her torture?
For common consolation, *here*, is insult.

Enter MRS. BLAND *and* CHILDREN

MRS. BLAND. O my good friend!

M'DONALD [*taking her hand*]. I know thy cause of sorrow.
Art thou now from our Commander?

MRS. BLAND [*drying her tears and assuming dignity*]. I am.
But vain is my entreaty. All unmov'd
He hears my words, he sees my desperate sorrow.
Fain would I blame his conduct—but I cannot.
Strictly examin'd, with intent to mark
The error which so fatal proves to *me*,

My scrutiny but ends in admiration.
Thus when the prophet from the hills of Moab
Look'd down upon the chosen race of Heaven,
With fell intent to curse, ere yet he spake,
Truth all resistless, emanation bright
From great Adonai, fill'd his froward mind,
And chang'd the curses of his heart to blessings.

M'DONALD. Thou payest high praise to virtue. Whither now?

MRS. BLAND. I still must hover round this spot, until
My doom is known.

M'DONALD. Then to my quarters, lady;
There shall my mate give comfort and refreshment:
One of your sex can best your sorrows soothe. [*Exeunt.*

SCENE [2], *the Prison*

Enter BLAND

BLAND. Where'er I look, cold desolation meets me.
My father—André—and self-condemnation.
Why seek I André now? Am *I* a man
To soothe the sorrows of a suffering friend?
The weather-cock of passion! fool inebriate!
Who could with ruffian hand strive to provoke
Hoar wisdom to intemperance! who could lie!
Aye, swagger, lie, and brag!—Liar! Damnation!
O, let me steal away and hide my head,
Nor view a man, condemned to harshest death,
Whose words and actions, when by mine compar'd,
Show white as innocence and bright as truth.
I now would shun him, but that his shorten'd
Thread of life gives me no line to play with.
He comes with smiles, and all the air of triumph,
While *I* am sinking with remorse and shame;
Yet *he* is doom'd to death, and *I* am free.

Enter ANDRÉ

ANDRÉ. Welcome, my Bland! Cheerly, a welcome hither!
I feel assurance that my last request
Will not be slighted. Safely thy father
Shall return to thee. [*Holding out a paper.*] See what employment
For a dying man. Take thou these verses;
And, after my decease, send them to her
Whose name is woven in them; whose image
Hath controul'd my destiny. Such tokens
Are rather out of date. Fashions
There are in love as in all else; they change
As variously. A gallant knight, erewhile,
Of Cœur de Lion's day, would, dying, send
His heart home to its mistress; degenerate
Soldier, I send but some blotted paper.

BLAND. If 'twould not damp thy present cheerfulness,
I would require the meaning of thy words.
I ne'er till now did hear of André's mistress.

ANDRÉ. Mine is a story of that common kind,
So often told, with scanty variation,
That the pall'd ear loaths the repeated tale.
Each young romancer chuses for his theme
The woes of youthful hearts, by the cold hand
Of frosty age, arm'd with parental power,
Asunder torn. But I long since have ceas'd
To mourn; well satisfied that she I love,
Happy in holy union with another,
Shares not my wayward fortunes. Nor would I
Now these tokens send, remembrance to awaken,
But that I know her happy; and the happy
Can think on misery and share it not.

BLAND [*agitated*]. Some one approaches.

ANDRÉ. Why, 'tis near the time!
But tell me, Bland, say,—is the manner chang'd?

BLAND. I hope it, but I yet have no assurance.

ANDRÉ. Well, well!

HONORA [*without*]. I must see him.

ANDRÉ. Whose voice was that?
My senses! Do I dream? [*Leans on* BLAND.]

Enter HONORA

HONORA. Where is he?

ANDRÉ. 'Tis she!

[*Starts from* BLAND *and advances towards* HONORA; *she rushes into his arms.*]

HONORA. It is enough! He lives, and *I* shall save him. [*She faints in the arms of* ANDRÉ.]

ANDRÉ. She sinks—assist me, Bland! O, save her, save her! [*Places her in a chair and looks tenderly on her.*]
Yet, why should she awake from that sweet sleep!
Why should she ope her eyes—[*Wildly.*]—to see me hung!
What does she here? Stand off—[*Tenderly.*]—and let her die.
How pale she looks! How worn that tender frame!—
She has known sorrow! Who could injure her?

BLAND. She revives—André—soft, bend her forward.

[ANDRÉ *kneels and supports her.*]

HONORA. André—!

ANDRÉ. Lov'd excellence!

HONORA. Yes, it is André!
[*Rises and looks at him.*]
No more deceived by visionary forms,
By him supported—[*Leans on him.*]

ANDRÉ. Why is this?
Thou dost look pale, Honora—sick and wan—
Languid thy fainting limbs—

HONORA. All will be well.
But was it kind to leave me as thou did'st?
So rashly to desert thy vow-link'd wife?

ANDRÉ. When made another's both by vows and laws—

HONORA [*quitting his support*]. What meanest thou?

ANDRÉ. Did'st thou not marry him?

HONORA. Marry!

ANDRÉ. Did'st thou not give thy hand away
From me?

HONORA. O, never, never.

ANDRÉ. Not married?

HONORA. To none but thee, and but in will to thee.

ANDRÉ. O blind, blind wretch! Thy father told me—

HONORA. Thou wast deceived. They hurried me away,
Spreading false rumors to remove thy love—
[*Tenderly.*] Thou did'st too soon believe them.

ANDRÉ. Thy father—
How could I but believe Honora's father?
And he did tell me so. I reverenc'd age,
Yet knew age was not virtue. I believed
His snowy locks, and yet they did deceive me.
I have destroy'd myself and thee!—Alas,
Ill-fated maid, why did'st thou not forget me?
Hast thou rude seas and hostile shores explor'd
For this? To see my death? Witness my shame?

HONORA. I come to bless thee, André, and shall do it.
I bear such offers from thy kind Commander
As must prevail to save thee. Thus the daughter
May repair the ills her cruel sire inflicted.
My father, dying, gave me cause to think
That arts were us'd to drive thee from thy home;
But what those arts I knew not. An heiress left,
Of years mature, with power and liberty,
I straight resolv'd to seek thee o'er the seas.
A long-known friend, who came to join her lord,
Yielded protection and lov'd fellowship.—
Indeed, when I did hear of thy estate,
It almost kill'd me;—I was weak before—

ANDRÉ. 'Tis I have murder'd thee!

HONORA. All shall be well.
Thy General heard of me, and instant form'd
The plan of this my visit. I am strong,
Compar'd with what I was. Hope strengthens me;
Nay, even solicitude supports me now;
And when thou shalt be safe, *thou* wilt support me.

ANDRÉ. Support thee!—O Heaven! What!—and *must* I die?
Die!—and leave her *thus*—suffering—unprotected!

Enter MELVILLE *and* GUARD

MELVILLE. I am sorry that my duty should require
Service, at which my heart revolts; but, sir,
Our soldiers wait in arms. All is prepar'd—

HONORA. To death! Impossible! Has my delay,
Then, murder'd him? A momentary respite—

MELVILLE. Lady, I have no power.

BLAND. Melville, my friend,
This lady bears dispatches of high import,
Touching this business; should they arrive too late—

HONORA. For pity's sake, and heaven's, conduct me to him;
And wait the issue of our conference.
O, 'twould be murder of the blackest dye,
Sin execrable, not to break thy orders—
Inhuman, thou art not.

MELVILLE. Lady, thou say'st true;
For rather would I lose my rank in arms,
And stand cashier'd for lack of discipline,
Than gain 'mongst military men all praise,
Wanting the touch of sweet humanity.

HONORA. Thou grantest my request?

MELVILLE. Lady, I do.
Retire! [*Soldiers go out.*

BLAND. I know not what excuse, to martial men,
Thou canst advance for this; but to thy heart
Thou wilt need none, good Melville.

ANDRÉ. O Honora!

HONORA. Cheer up, I feel assur'd. Hope wings my flight,
To bring thee tidings of much joy to come.

[*Exit* HONORA, *with* BLAND *and* MELVILLE.

ANDRÉ. Eternal blessings on thee, matchless woman!—
If Death now comes, he finds the veriest coward
That e'er he dealt withal. I cannot think
Of dying. Void of fortitude, each thought
Clings to the world—the world that holds
Honora! [*Exit.*

END OF THE FOURTH ACT

ACT V

SCENE [1], *the Encampment*

Enter BLAND

BLAND. SUSPENSE—uncertainty—man's bane and solace!
How racking now to me! My mother comes.
Forgive me, O my father, if in this war,
This wasting conflict of my 'wildering passions,
Memory of thee holds here a second place!
M'Donald comes with her. I would not meet him;
Yet I *will* do it. Summon up some courage—
Confess my fault, and gain, if not *his* love,
At least the approbation of *my* judgment.

Enter MRS. BLAND *and* CHILDREN, *with* M'DONALD

BLAND. Say, Madam, is there no change of counsel,
Or new determination?

MRS. BLAND. *Naught new*, my son.
The tale of misery is told unheard.
The widow's and the orphans' sighs
Fly up, unnoted by the eye of man,
And mingle, undistinguish'd, with the winds.
My friend [*To* M'DONALD.], attend thy duties. I must away.

SECOND CHILD. You need not cry, Mamma, the General will do it, I am sure, for I saw him cry. He turn'd away his head from *you*, but I saw it.

MRS. BLAND. Poor thing! Come, let us home and weep. Alas!
I can no more, for war hath made men rocks.
[*Exeunt* MRS. BLAND *and* CHILDREN.

BLAND. Colonel, I used thee ill this morning.

M'DONALD. No!
Thyself thou used'st most vilely, I remember.

BLAND. Myself sustained the injury, most true;
But the intent of what I said and did
Was ill to thee alone; I'm sorry for it.
See'st thou these blushes? They proceed from warmth
As honest as the heart of man e'er felt;
But not with shame unmingled, while I force

This tongue, debased, to own it slander'd thee,
And utter'd—I could curse it—utter'd falsehood.
Howe'er misled by passion, still my mind
Retains that sense of honest rectitude
Which makes the memory of an evil deed
A troublesome companion. I was wrong.

M'DONALD. Why, now, this glads me; for thou *now* art right.
O, may thy tongue, henceforward, utter naught
But Truth's sweet precepts, in fair Virtue's cause!
Give me thy hand. [*Takes his hand.*] Ne'er may it grasp a sword
But in defence of justice.

BLAND. Yet, erewhile,
A few short hours scarce past, when this vile hand
Attempted on *thee* insult; and was raised
Against thy honor; ready to be raised
Against thy life. If this my deep remorse—

M'DONALD. No more, no more! 'Tis past. Remember it
But as thou would'st the action of another,
By thy enlighten'd judgment much condemn'd;
And serving as a beacon in the storms
Thy passions yet may raise. Remorse is vice;
Guard thee against its influence debasing.
Say to thyself: "I *am* not what I *was;*
I am not *now* the instrument of vice;
I'm changed; I am a man; Virtue's firm friend;
Sever'd forever from my former self;
No link, but in remembrance salutary."

BLAND.[1] Noble M'Donald, truth and honor's champion!
Yet think not strange that my intemperance wrong'd thee:
Good as thou art! for, would'st thou, can'st thou, think it?
My tongue, unbridled, hath the same offence,
With action violent, and boisterous tone,
Hurl'd on that glorious man, whose pious labors
Shield from every ill his grateful country.
That man, whom friends to adoration love,
And enemies revere. Yes, M'Donald,
Even in the presence of the first of men
Did I abjure the service of my country,
And reft my helmet of that glorious badge
Which graces even the brow of Washington.
How shall I see him more?

M'DONALD. Alive himself to every generous impulse,
He hath excused the impetuous warmth of youth,
In expectation that thy fiery soul,
Chasten'd by time and reason, will receive
The stamp indelible of godlike virtue.
To me, in trust, he gave this badge disclaim'd,
With power, when thou should'st see thy wrongful error,
From him, to reinstate it in thy helm,
And thee in his high favor.
[*Gives the cockade.*]

BLAND [*takes the cockade and replaces it*]. Shall I speak my thoughts of thee and him?
No! let my actions henceforth show what thou
And he have made me. Ne'er shall my helmet
Lack again its proudest, noblest ornament,
Until my country knows the rest of peace,
Or Bland the peace of death! [*Exit.*

---

[1] The three speeches which follow were inserted after the first night of the play instead of the original lines which were hissed by the audience when the actor playing the part of Bland tore off his American cockade and threw it down. The original passage reads as follows:

BLAND. How all men tower above me!
M'DONALD. Nay, not so.
Above what once thou wast, some few do rise;
None above what thou art.
BLAND. It shall be so.
M'DONALD. It is so.
BLAND. Then to prove it.
For I must yet a trial undergo,
That will require a consciousness of virtue.
[*Exit.*

M'DONALD. O, what a temper doth in man reside!
How capable of yet unthought perfection!
[*Exit.*

SCENE [2], *the* GENERAL'S *Quarters*

Enter GENERAL *and* SEWARD

GENERAL. Ask her, my friend, to send by thee her pacquets. [*Exit* SEWARD.
O, what keen struggles must I undergo!
Unbless'd estate! to have the power to pardon;
The court's stern sentence to remit;—give life;—
Feel the strong wish to use such blessed power;
Yet know that circumstances strong as fate
Forbid to obey the impulse. O, I feel
That man should never shed the blood of man!

Enter SEWARD

SEWARD. Naught can the lovely suitor satisfy,
But conference with thee, and much I fear
Refusal would cause madness.

GENERAL. Yet to admit,
To hear, be tortur'd, and refuse at last—

SEWARD. Sure never man such spectacle of sorrow
Saw before. Motionless the rough-hewn soldiers
Silent view her, or walk aside and weep.

GENERAL [*after a pause*]. Admit her. [SEWARD *goes out.*] O, for the art, the precious art,
To reconcile the sufferer to his sorrows!

[HONORA *rushes in, and throws herself wildly on her knees before him; he endeavors to raise her.*]

HONORA. Nay, nay, here is my place, or here, or lower,
Unless thou grant'st his life. All forms away!
Thus will I clasp thy knees, thus cling to thee—
I am his wife—'tis I have ruin'd him—
O, save him! Give him to me! Let us cross
The mighty seas, far, far—ne'er to offend again—

[*The* GENERAL *turns away, and hides his eyes with his hand.*]

Enter SEWARD *and an* OFFICER

GENERAL. Seward, support her; my heart is torn in twain.

[HONORA, *as if exhausted, suffers herself to be raised, and leans on* SEWARD.]

OFFICER. This moment, sir, a messenger arrived
With well confirm'd and mournful information,
That gallant Hastings, by the lawless scouts
Of Britain taken, after cruel mockery
With show of trial and of condemnation,
On the next tree was hung.

HONORA [*wildly*]. O, it is false!

GENERAL. Why, why, my country, did I hesitate? [*Exit.*

[HONORA *sinks, faints, and is borne off by* SEWARD *and* OFFICER.]

SCENE [3], *the Prison*

ANDRÉ *meeting* BLAND

ANDRÉ. How speeds Honora? [*Pause.*] Art thou silent, Bland?
Why, then, I know my task. The mind of man,
If not by vice debas'd, debilitated,
Or by disease of body quite unton'd,
Hath o'er its thoughts a power—energy divine.
Of fortitude the source and every virtue—
A godlike power, which e'en o'er circumstance
Its sov'reignty exerts. Now from my thoughts,
Honora! Yet she is left alone—expos'd—

BLAND. O, André, spurn me, strike me to the earth;
For what a wretch am I in André's mind,
That he can think he leaves his love alone,
And I retaining life!

ANDRÉ. Forgive me, Bland,
My thoughts glanc'd not on thee. Imagination
Pictur'd only, then, her orphan state, helpless;
Her weak and grief-exhausted frame. Alas!
This blow will kill her.

BLAND [*kneeling*]. Here do I myself
Devote, my fortune consecrate, to thee,

To thy remembrance, and Honora's service.
ANDRÉ. Enough! Let me not see her more—nor think of her—
Farewell, farewell, sweet image! Now for death.
BLAND. Yet that thou should'st the felon's fate fulfil—
Damnation! My blood boils. Indignation
Makes the current of my life course wildly
Through its round and maddens each emotion.
ANDRÉ. Come, come, it matters not.
BLAND. I do remember,
When a boy at school, in our allotted tasks,
We, by our puny acts, strove to pourtray
The giant thoughts of Otway. I was Pierre.
O, thou art Pierre's reality—a soldier,
On whose manly brow sits fortitude enamor'd;
A Mars, abhorring vice, yet doom'd to die
A death of infamy; thy corse expos'd
To vulgar gaze—halter'd—distorted—oh—
[*Pauses, and then adds in a low hollow voice:*]
Pierre had a friend to save him from such shame—
And so hast thou.
ANDRÉ. No more, as thou dost love me.
BLAND. I have a sword, and arm, that never fail'd me.
ANDRÉ. Bland, such an act would justly thee involve,
And leave that helpless one thou sworest to guard
Expos'd to every ill. O, think not of it!
BLAND. If thou wilt not my aid—take it thyself. [*Draws and offers his sword.*]
ANDRÉ. No, men will say that cowardice did urge me.
In my mind's weakness, I did wish to shun
That mode of death which error represented
Infamous: now let me rise superior;
And with a fortitude too true to start
From mere appearances, show your country
That she, in me, destroys a man who might
Have liv'd to virtue.
BLAND [*sheathing his sword*]. I will not think more of it;
I was again the sport of erring passion.
ANDRÉ. Go thou and guide Honora from this spot.
HONORA [*entering*]. Who shall oppose his wife? I will have way!
They, cruel, would have kept me from thee, André.
Say, am I not thy wife? Wilt thou deny me?
Indeed I am not dress'd in bridal trim.
But I have travelled far:—rough was the road—
Rugged and rough—that must excuse my dress.
[*Seeing* ANDRÉ'S *distress.*] Thou art not glad to see me.
ANDRÉ. Break my heart!
HONORA. Indeed, I feel not much in spirits. I wept but now.

Enter MELVILLE *and* GUARD

BLAND [*to* MELVILLE]. Say nothing.
ANDRÉ. I am ready.
HONORA [*seeing the* GUARD]. Are *they* here?
Here again—the *same*—but they shall not harm me.
I am with *thee*, my André—I am safe—
And *thou* art safe with me. Is it not so? [*Clinging to him.*]

Enter MRS. BLAND

MRS. BLAND. Where is this lovely victim?
BLAND. Thanks, my mother.
MRS. BLAND. M'Donald sent me hither. My woes are past.
Thy father, by the foe released, already
Is in safety. This be forgotten now;
And every thought be turn'd to this sad scene.
Come, lady, home with me.
HONORA. Go home with thee?
Art thou my André's mother? We will home
And rest, for thou art weary—very weary. [*Leans on* MRS. BLAND.]
[ANDRÉ *retires to the* GUARD, *and goes off with them, looking on her to the last, and with an action of extreme tenderness takes leave of her.* MELVILLE *and* BLAND *accompany him.*]
HONORA. Now we will go. Come, love! Where is he?
All gone!—I do remember—I awake—
They have him. Murder! Help! O, save him! save him! [HONORA *attempts to follow, but falls.* MRS. BLAND *kneels to assist her. Scene closes.*]

SCENE [4], *the Encampment*

Procession to the execution of ANDRÉ. *First enter Pioneers—Detachment of Infantry—Military Band of Music—Infantry. The Music having passed off, enter* ANDRÉ *between* MELVILLE *and* AMERICAN OFFICER; *they sorrowful, he cheerfully conversing as he passes over the stage.*

ANDRÉ. It may in me be merely prejudice,
The effect of young opinion deep engraved
Upon the tender mind by care parental;
But I must think your country has mistook
Her interests. Believe me, but for this I should
Not willingly have drawn a sword against her. [*They bow their heads in silence.*]
Opinion must, nay, ought to sway our actions;
Therefore—

[*Having crossed the stage, he goes out as still conversing with them. Another detachment of Infantry, with muffled and craped drums, closes the procession; as soon as they are off—*

SCENE [5]

draws and discovers the distant view of the Encampment.]

[*Procession enters in same order as before, proceeds up the stage, and goes off on the opposite side.*]

Enter M'DONALD, *leading* BLAND, *who looks wildly back*

BLAND. I dare not *thee* resist. Yet why, O why
Thus hurry me away?—
M'DONALD. Would'st thou behold—
BLAND. O, name it not!
M'DONALD. Or would'st thou, by thy looks
And gestures wild, o'erthrow that manly calmness
Which, or assumed or felt, so well becomes thy friend?
BLAND. What means that cannon's sound?
M'DONALD [*after a pause*]. Signal of death
Appointed. André, thy friend, is now no more.
BLAND. Farewell, farewell, brave spirit! O! let my countrymen,
Henceforward when the cruelties of war
Arise in their remembrance; when their ready
Speech would pour forth torrents in their foe's dispraise,
Think on this act accurst, and lock complaint in silence.
[BLAND *throws himself on the earth.*]
M'DONALD. Such are the dictates of the heart, not head.
O, may the children of Columbia still
Be taught by every teacher of mankind,
Each circumstance of calculative gain,
Or wounded pride, which prompted our oppressors;
May every child be taught to lisp the tale;
And may, in times to come, no foreign force,
No European influence, tempt to misstate,
Or awe the tongue of eloquence to silence.
Still may our children's children deep abhor
The motives, doubly deep detest the actors;
Ever remembering that the race who plann'd,
Who acquiesced, or did the deeds abhor'd,
Has pass'd from off the earth; and, in its stead,
Stand men who challenge love or detestation
But from their proper, individual deeds.
Never let memory of the sire's offence
Descend upon the son.

CURTAIN DROPS

THE BUCKTAILS; OR, AMERICANS IN ENGLAND

By James Kirke Paulding

JAMES KIRKE PAULDING

[1778–1860]

JAMES KIRKE PAULDING's birth during the American struggle for independence seems to have been of significance in determining the strongly nationalistic and anti-British views he entertained throughout life. His biographer relates that the figure of his aged grandfather, rendered insane by a British attack, made a strong impression on the boy's mind; and "When to all this is added the fact that he grew up in a district reeking with tales of British, Hessian, or Tory atrocities, none can wonder that he imbibed a lasting prejudice against England and every thing English." [1]

Paulding was born August 22, 1778, in New York State. After a youth of comparative quiet and solitude, spent amid country scenes, he went to New York City, where he formed significant friendships with Washington Irving, Henry Brevoort, Jr., and Gouverneur Kemble. From his association with Irving grew the important *Salmagundi* papers that marked the literary debut of both writers. Paulding held important naval posts in Washington and New York, and in 1838 his long services in this field were rewarded with the Secretaryship of the Navy. Apparently his nationalistic views were of service to him politically, for Madison noted these aspects of his character when Paulding first went to Washington in 1815. Unlike the travelled Irving, Paulding never went abroad; after leaving the Secretaryship of the Navy in 1841, he retired to rural Hyde Park, where he resided until his death on April 6, 1860.

There are few other American writers whose ideas turned so persistently upon the pole of nationalism as Paulding's. His *Diverting History of John Bull and Brother Jonathan* (1812) is an allegorical anti-British account of the historical relations between England and America; *John Bull in America; or, the New Munchausen* (1825) represents an English traveller with distorted prejudices who gives his observations on this country: the book grows directly out of the widespread indignation aroused by the numerous hostile accounts of America published by British travellers, some of whom are purported never to have crossed the ocean.[2] *The United States and England* is a reply to the criticism of Inchiquin's

[1] Paulding, William I., *The Literary Life of James K. Paulding.* New York: 1867, p. 25. See also Amos Herold's *James Kirke Paulding, Versatile American* (New York: 1926).

[2] This discussion was of great importance during the early part of the century, and the foremost magazines of the two countries were protagonists in the affray. For an able account of these magazines see Cairns, William B., *British Criticisms of American Writings, 1783–1815,* in *University of Wisconsin Studies in Language and Literature,* no. 1. Madison: 1918. Extracts from the hostile

Letters contained in the *Quarterly Review* for January, 1814; and *The Lay of the Scottish Fiddle* is a poetic parody on Scott. Paulding's lost *Lion of the West*, "the first drama to introduce a raw and uncouth frontiersman [Wildfire] as its leading character,"[1] had a long run here and in England.

The foregoing writings, most of them not drama, are mentioned here because they define the channel of thought through which ran many of Paulding's ideas and which shaped his play *The Bucktails; or, Americans in England.* But this play overflowed the limits of nationalism, as did his clever prose satire, *The Merry Tales of the Three Wise Men of Gotham*, and spread to aspects of thought and feeling universal in their scope and application. This we shall see more clearly as we study the play; but let us first consider its less universal currents.

In view of the fact that *The Bucktails* "was written shortly after the conclusion of the late war with England,"[2] there is little wonder that the nationalism of the play is especially strong. The title satirizes the Englishman's view of Americans as primitives, and we soon see the Britishers describing their recent countrymen as people who "wear copper rings in their noses—eat raw meat—paint one-half their faces red and the other black—and are positively half naked." An American visiting in England, Jane Warfield, avows: "I shall never marry out of my own dear country"; and her sister, married to a London merchant, is apparently an unsuccessful internationalist: she thinks that her countrywomen "will only find solid respectability and lasting happiness among the friends of their youth in the land of their birth."[3] In the beggar scene at the conclusion of the play, royalty is satirized for its pretense, its taxation, and its robbery; blood, rank, and nobility are ridiculed in the person of Lord Noland and deflated by Henry, who believes that man is by necessity democratic: "Man can't remove one step from man—his nature fixes him." The descent of power is pictured in an amusing light by Jane: "What! the hereditary legislator, who, according to the law of England, inherits wisdom as a fox does instinct?"[4] As a corollary, though not applicable to England alone, the society scene is represented as demoralizing in contrast to the "sacred quiet of a calm evening—the repose of a country scene—": "It is at midnight balls and masquerades, where lascivious music assails the senses—where dazzling lights confound the imagination, and wines and costly viands pamper the heated appetites. It is there that virtue melts like wax, and female purity is most successfully assailed."[5] Country walks, on the other hand, are conducive to mutual understanding and happy marriages.

---

accounts of English travellers may be found in the introduction to *John Bull in America*, pp. 149–168 of *The Bulls and the Jonathans*, by James K. Paulding, ed. by William I. Paulding. New York: 1867.

[1] See N. F. Adkins, "James K. Paulding's *Lion of the West*," *American Literature*, III, 249–258 (Nov., 1931), for all that is known of this play.

[2] Preface to *American Comedies*, J. K. Paulding and William I. Paulding. Philadelphia: 1847.

[3] Act I, sc. 1, p. 85.

[4] Act I, sc. 1, p. 84.

[5] Act III, sc. 2, p. 96.

The striking aspect of *The Bucktails*, however, is that its satire reaches beyond nationalism to types of character found in any civilized country; though these characters happen to be Englishmen in the play, they are satirized for their personal qualities, not for their national idiosyncrasies. It is here that Paulding's commentary strikes the note of universality. This may readily be tested by noting that today, when relations with England are amicable, there is less appeal in the nationalistic theme than in the caricature of the individuals. We may note this same universality in *The Merry Tales of the Three Wise Men of Gotham;* in the introduction to this Paulding himself says that the locality of Gotham belongs to all nations—"whether in the New or the Old World is of little consequence."

First among those in *The Bucktails* whose foibles are amusingly brought to light is the antiquarian, Mr. Obsolete, who values nothing that has happened since the deluge and who could become interested in the present only 6,000 years hence; he hates news (foreshadowing Thoreau?), he objects to anyone turning over a new leaf, and his idea of complimenting a young lady is to tell her that her dimple is "exactly the shape of the old Saxon letter C!" He finally follows his daughter to America, but only under the conviction that it is the land of "unexplored antiquities." The overzealous humanitarian and reformer, who thrives on pity for the misfortunes of others, is satirized in the person of Miss Obsolete; she is as extreme in her attachments and prejudices as her brother is in his: a potential lover may appeal to the eternal feminine in Miss Obsolete, "but a wooden leg, or a man just going to be turned off, is to my mind a thousand times more interesting." [1] This same view toward the reformer is reflected in Paulding's *Wise Men of Gotham;* the discourse of the first wise man on "The Man Machine" shows reformers to be somewhat ineffectual against "the circumstances" and the "counteracting principles"; at the conclusion of the discourse, it is necessary to leave the earth and look elsewhere to realize the "perfectibility of man."

The scientist, or perhaps pseudo-scientist, fares no better than the antiquarian or the humanitarian. A medical man is spoken of as a "great man-killer"; indeed his "picture will one day be hung up in the medical college." [2] Professor Sniggersdorf's new planet and Sir Humphrey Davidoff's gas lamps are ridiculed, and there is related the account of Dr. Burdock who caught a fatal cold while "sitting up all night in his garden to hear a mandrake scream." This latter incident is strongly suggestive of the way Swift, in "Laputa," might have pictured Bacon's famous demise. There are also strong reminiscences of "Laputa" in the experiments and analyses of the professor who "erected the most stupendous science of modern times upon the wagging of a mastiff's tail." [3]

[1] Act I, sc. 2, p. 87.

[2] Act V, sc. 8, p. 112. In the discourse by the third wise man, an ailing person remarks: "I have not money to pay a doctor, and it would mortify my pride to be killed for nothing." (*Wise Men of Gotham*, p. 215.) Paulding did not consult a physician in his last illness.

[3] *Wise Men of Gotham*, p. 181. The third wise

In fact, the whole satire on science recalls Swift's attack on the virtuosi of his day, and it is entirely possible that the seventeenth century English satirist had a share in forming the technique which was subsequently turned upon his own country.[1] A few Shakespearean traces are found [2] and the English "comedy of humours" is suggested by the tenacity with which the characters cling to their idiosyncrasies: Obsolete is always the antiquarian; the Admiral, the seaman; Sir Kit, the book collector; and so on. It is curious but human psychology—taking with one hand and striking with the other.

Despite the satiric temper in the play, it contains much contemporary sentimentalism (a combination of qualities found also in Tyler's *The Contrast* and Mrs. Mowatt's *Fashion*, both of which are related to *The Bucktails* in their nationalistic feeling against foreign cultures). Aside from the protestations of loyalty, sentimentalism appears in Henry's willingness to lay his heart at the feet of the fair sex, and also in Frank's insistence on filial devotion: "She that forgets her duty to a parent will never learn it for a husband." [3] The romantic interest in nature finds expression in these two youths: in Henry's enthusiasm for moonlight in the country and in Frank's praise of America for "her waving woods, her boundless fields. . . ." Henry, however, becomes the realist in his commentary on women's relative interest in the city and country: ". . . the most inveterate town lady loves the country—when she's in a crowd—and the most ardent votary of rural shades adores a crowd—when she's alone in the country." It is in such passages as these, and in the numerous poignant thrusts at eccentricity that Paulding rises from the local to the universal; it is in its transcending of nationalism that *The Bucktails* becomes significant drama.

The present text of the play follows the original edition, included in *American Comedies*, by J. K. Paulding and William Irving Paulding. Carey and Hart, Philadelphia: 1847.

---

man states that "there were so many people running after science, that there were not sciences enough for them to run after." (*Ibid.*, p. 173.)

[1] In the preface to *John Bull in America* Paulding refers directly to Swift: "The character of these travels being that of a severe and inflexible truth, a title was chosen in direct antithesis, partly in sportive imitation of the facetious philosopher Lucian, who gave the name of 'A True Story' to one of the most improbable fictions of antiquity; and partly in allusion to Dr. Jonathan Swift, who in like manner disguised one of the gravest of satires under the mask of 'A Tale of a Tub,' than which nothing can be more opposite to its real character." (*The Bulls and the Jonathans*, p. 172.) Paulding's technique of satire is uncannily like that of Swift: he refers to his *John Bull in America* as "a work of incomparable veracity under the garb of a work of fiction" (it being, of course, exactly the opposite), and he solemnly goes about adducing evidence as to its probable author. He has utmost faith that the three Wise Men of Gotham did experience the wonders they relate, but he is inclined to doubt that they really put to sea in a bowl.

Paulding, to be sure, confesses his indebtedness to Goldsmith's *Citizen of the World:* "I read it, I believe, twenty times at least, and if I have any taste or style, I owe them to that charming work of the most delightful of all English writers." But the strong flavor of Swift remains.

[2] "'Look, my lord, it comes—angels and ministers!'" ". . . 'lay on, Macduff.' Now will I peach most villainously." (Act II, sc. 3.)

[3] Act V, sc. 1, p. 105.

DRAMATIS PERSONÆ

Henry Tudor, a young American on visit to England
Frank Tudor, his brother
Obsolete, an Antiquary
Noland, a profligate Lord
Sir Christopher, a Physician
Admiral Gunwale, a Yellow Admiral
Major Longbow, retired on half-pay
Threadneedle, a Banker
Paddy Whack, servant to Noland
Rust, servant to Obsolete
Jonathan Peabody, servant to the Tudors
Bamfylde Moore Carew, king of the Beggars and Crows
Fortune Teller
Little Billy and Rogues

Mrs. Carlton, wife to a young American Merchant in London
Jane Warfield, her sister,—an Heiress
Miss Obsolete, sister to the Antiquary
Mary Obsolete, his daughter

Scene, *Bath*, *in England*

THE BUCKTAILS; OR, AMERICANS IN ENGLAND

ACT I

SCENE I. *A Parlor*

MRS. CARLTON *and* JANE *at their needles*

JANE. Heigh ho! sister.

MRS. CARLTON. Well, Jane, translate that sigh into English. Is it for a husband, or what?

JANE. In plain English, then, I am tired of England, and Bath in particular, which is like a belle who has seen her best days, and given place to other rivals in the *beau monde*. It is little better than an Invalid Hospital now. I'm right down home-sick.

MRS. CARLTON. So then, Jane, you would leave me alone in a land of strangers, where, of all others, strangers, without rank or wealth to throw away, are least at home—would you, Jane?

JANE. No, dearest sister.—You were a mother to me when I had no other; my guide when I most wanted one—and [*Kissing her.*] I will never leave thee or forsake thee.

MRS. CARLTON. Not even for a husband, Jane? But what have you to complain of here? We live in one of the most beautiful cities in the world, in spite of all you may say to the contrary; we have health and competency—I have an affectionate husband and you a host of admirers, of such infinite variety of character, that you may pass your whole life in the charming perplexity of not knowing which to choose.

JANE. Yes, a delightful variety, indeed! The tower does not contain a rarer collection of animals, and the best of it is, they are so disinterested! I dare say not one of them has an eye to the hundred thousand pounds my prudent uncle left me in the funds here, because, poor man, he couldn't trust his own country! Tell me now, sister, on your conscience, is there one among them that will pass muster in any court of Cupid in all Christendom?

MRS. CARLTON. The admiral—for instance.

JANE. He! why, he's so asthmatic that he wants breath to tell his exploits, which is a sore pity, since everybody else has forgot them. Then his limbs are scatter'd over the four seas, and the worst of it is, that nobody knows in what battles he lost them. Then he is continually boasting of the flag of England, flying triumphantly in every sea, which might have done well enough before the time of Perry and Decatur. No—no, sister, if I ever marry a sailor, it shall be one of our own sprightly young heroes, that have risen by their own merit instead of the merits of those below them. Then he's so old—

MRS. CARLTON. Well, Jane, your tongue runs finely! What say you to the gallant Major?

JANE. What! the valiant *Cid* of the peninsula? —he that drinks nothing but gunpowder tea for breakfast—who has bled whole kingdoms—whose conquests would make a geography larger than Pinkerton's! He was made a knight-companion of [the] Bath, in the last batch, but he shall never be my night companion, I promise you.

MRS. CARLTON. No! Well, then, what think you of the little banker, Threadneedle?

JANE. Lord, sister! he should have been a tailor by his name; and, to say the truth, I think by his nature too.

MRS. CARLTON. How so?

JANE. Why, he worships the goose, and, according to his own account, has invented more fashions than a score of tailors. Then he's such a simpleton,—I don't believe he has wit enough to make a marriage lawful.

MRS. CARLTON. At this rate you'll never get a husband. What have you to say to the antiquary, and the member of ever so many societies?

JANE. What! Mr. Obsolete and Sir Christopher? Eh! [*Shivers.*] Why, sister, would you have me become an unsuccessful rival to a dry parchment manuscript, a rare copy in black letter, or an old Saxon inscription? One of them, I am positively assured, broke the heart of his wife, because the poor woman cut up a sheet of old parchment, with some fragments of unknown letters upon it, to cover her pots of sweetmeats.

MRS. CARLTON. O, that's one of Carlton's jokes.

JANE. Upon my honor, I believe every word of it. It was no longer ago than yesterday that Mr. Obsolete, after looking me in the face a whole quarter of an hour with such intensity that I actually thought he was admiring my beauty, and gave him one of my best smiles,—would you believe it,—he assured me the dimple in my cheek was exactly the shape of the old Saxon letter C! That ever I should live to be coupled with an old Saxon parchment! Why, he'd barter me away before the honeymoon for a rare book of old ballads, and be in ecstasies with his bargain.

MRS. CARLTON. Jane! Jane! If you go on at this rate, I shall set you down for an old maid. Why, Mr. Obsolete is consulted by the connoisseurs for his knowledge of all sorts of old things.

JANE. Say no more, dear sister. That's a sure sign he'd care little for young things. He'll hate me for not having been born in the time of King Bladud. My youth will be a perpetual reproach to one who is such an admirer of old things; he shuts his doors against new brooms in defiance of the proverb.

MRS. CARLTON. But you know every year would obviate his objection to your youth; and then how delightful to have a husband that would love you the better, the older you grew.

JANE. True, sister. But I shouldn't like to wait till I grow old to be loved by my husband. Besides, I should never grow old enough to rival Signior Belzoni's Mummy. I am told he goes to London once a month to ogle it, and has been detected making downright love.

MRS. CARLTON. Well, even this is better than some husbands, who don't confine themselves to making love to mummies, I promise you. You'd better consider.

JANE. Dear sister, say no more. I should stand no chance against the mummy, or even the dead mermaid, lately brought from the Indies. Why, he don't value a newspaper till it's a century old, and hates everything not rusted with age to such a degree, that he'll never forgive me for being young, and born in a new world.

MRS. CARLTON. I believe we've got through the list, with the exception of my Lord. Is not he a distinguished person?

JANE. What! the hereditary legislator, who, according to the law of England, inherits wisdom as a fox does instinct? Distinguished! Notorious, you mean, sister. With talents to be respectable, he is a nuisance in that society whose laws he violates, and whose rules he thinks himself privileged to despise. I am sure, rather than be overlooked, he would play the merry-Andrew at a fair, or run away to Gretna Green, with an old apple-woman, to be talked of one day.

MRS. CARLTON. Now, Jane, you are coming out with what Carlton calls your Bucktail notions. I wish he were back from London to keep you in order.

JANE. I don't care—I've no patience with these degenerate men, who abuse the advantages which birth and fortune throw in their way. His lordship has attempted to rival every boxer, stage coachman, and pedestrian of note, for the last twenty years, and failing in this noble species of ambition, is now indebted to his follies and absurdities for the notice of mankind. But let us leave this subject. I shall never marry out of my own dear country.

MRS. CARLTON. You are right, Jane. Women, and especially American women, should never marry to go abroad, or go abroad to be married. In this country the distinctions in society rest upon other foundations than those of mere education, morals or manners. Rank and title everywhere take precedence, and condemn strangers without either, to the society of vulgar riches, thriving haberdashers, yellow admirals, card-playing dowagers and tattling spinsters, who think they honor us by winning our money and taking away our reputations. Take my word for it, Jane; though chance, or caprice, or novelty, may give a momentary *éclat* to one of our strolling countrywomen, they will only find solid respectability and lasting happiness among the friends of their youth in the land of their birth. But come, let us get our bonnets and take advantage of this fine English day—for I see the sun almost shines. [*Exeunt.*

SCENE 2. *The Antiquary's Room*

OBSOLETE *and* RUST

RUST. Have you heard the news, sir?

OBSOLETE. News? How often have I commanded you never to use that detestable word in my presence? What care I for news, marry? Knowest thou not, most precious Rust of Antiquity, that I feel no interest whatever in what has taken place since the deluge, and that unless I were assured of living some six thousand years hence, the events of the present time would be utterly indifferent?

RUST. But, sir—

OBSOLETE. Most venerable Rust, shut thy juvenile mouth, unless, like another Herculaneum, thou couldst yield up therefrom some precious obliterated manuscript, or invaluable fragment of stone jug, out of which an unknown person drank some two thousand years ago.

RUST. But, sir—the mummy is expected tomorrow—and the two Mr. Tudors from the new world have arrived. They left this letter while you were out.

OBSOLETE. The expected arrival of the mummy, most venerable Rust, makes some amends for the actual arrival of the youths from America. Young men—new world—bad, both bad. I hate young men, and above all, I hate new worlds. Why, I'm told there is nothing to be found there to puzzle a learned inquirer, or confound the ingenuity of antiquaries.—Everything is new and detestable; and the very rocks, they say, were made but yesterday. But where is Miss Obsolete? She's certainly neither very young nor very new, for by Cox-body she carries her nativity beyond all record, and the time of her birth is as great a mystery as the building of the Pyramids. Then as for novelty, she has read me the same lecture every day for the last thirty years.

RUST. Miss Obsolete is gone to jail, sir.

OBSOLETE. The D—l she has! Pray, was it on an action of debt, assault and battery, or *Scan-mag?* [1]

RUST. No, sir—She's gone to comfort the unfortunate man that murdered his wife the other day, and teach him to become a good husband. After that, she's going to the alehouse, where there is a deal of immorality to correct. From thence she goes to the Bridewell, to reform some compunctious ladies who are willing to be good if they are well paid for it. From the Bridewell she goes to the hospital, where—

OBSOLETE. Where I wish they would shut her up, with all my heart. Why, the woman is like to become a precious helpmate in my house, by keeping such worshipful company. Marry, I expect nothing else but she will bring home all the plagues of Egypt in her train one of these days.

RUST. I think she will reform the world in good sooth, sir.

OBSOLETE. Reform a fiddlestick! She'd better set about reforming herself. Why, she don't care a fig about her niece, and I verily believe it is because she has never been in Bridewell, or committed a *faux-pas.* —As for me—'sfoot! I am become perfectly indifferent to her, for lack of the irresistible attraction of some incurable disease that qualifies me for the hospital, or some interesting crime that qualifies me for the gallows. I begin to fear she will one day or other elope with some heroic highwayman, or wooden-legged Adonis of a beggar, and deprive me of her fortune merely because I am neither a cripple nor a culprit.

RUST. Of a truth, sir, she hath a tender heart.

[1] *Scan-mag.:* abbreviation of *scandalum magnatum*—in English law a defamatory speech or writing against a public official. Formerly considered a very serious offense.

OBSOLETE. That's more than I know. People that require the most high-seasoned dishes have not the most delicate appetites. I am strongly inclined to think the sympathies of those who can only be excited by high-wrought scenes of guilt and misery, are not of the finest kind. Feelings that can only be awakened by the undeserving, are not exactly to my taste.

RUST. But, sir, they say misery loves company.

OBSOLETE. Ay, and Miss Obsolete loves misery; so they are well met. But where is the letter you spoke of? [RUST *gives the letter.*] Ah! parchment, as I live! This looks something like antiquity. Primeval was always a man smacking of olden time.—Rust, go and inquire if Miss Obsolete has returned—I want to consult her about giving a dinner to these moderns. Let me see. [*Reads.*]

WORTHY SIR:

Thine of the 25th came safe to hand. I think this new world must be somewhat older than you suppose, for I have detected several large masses of primitive rocks in various parts. But of this anon. I commend to your old English hospitality, two youngsters, at whose father's house I have been entertained for the last two months, during which I was confined by a tertian ague. They come abroad to be civilized, and are somewhat tinctured with radical notions; but you will be kind to them for their hospitality to your old friend. You need not be afraid they will borrow money of you, for they are rich for this country.

ADAM PRIMEVAL.

P.S.—I have lately heard of a real mummy found in a cave in Kentucky. Does not this indicate an Egyptian origin?

Enter MISS OBSOLETE

MISS OBSOLETE. My dear Mr. Obsolete, I'm in such spirits! I've just come from seeing—

OBSOLETE [*not noticing her*]. A mummy! a mummy! found in a cave in Kentucky!

MISS OBSOLETE. A mummy found in a cave in Kentucky! A fool's head from—Pray, brother, where was you born? But as I was saying, I've seen the most edifying example of—

OBSOLETE. O—ay—yes—I know what your edifying sights are, my good sister—but pray spare me at this moment—some penitent culprit, or—But I'm just now going to visit two youngsters from America. They brought a letter from your cousin Primeval. So we must give them a dinner, you know. They come from the wilds fresh as an unlick'd cub, I suppose, so we'll give them a good stuffing, and let them run. Good-by, sister—Tell Mary to beware of their claws.

MISS OBSOLETE. Claws! Why, you don't mean to trust your daughter with these wild men, brother?

OBSOLETE. O, never fear; I shall invite a sufficient number of civilized men to keep them in order. I mean to bid them tomorrow—a short notice is good policy, you know—They may be engaged, you know—and if not, it looks as if one were eager to see them at one's house, you know.

MISS OBSOLETE. Lord, brother, what shall we do with these aboriginals? I have been assured they wear copper rings in their noses—eat raw meat—paint one-half their faces red and the other black—and are positively half naked. I hope you're only in jest about the dinner.

OBSOLETE. Not I, indeed, marry, I never joke—I can't find that the antediluvians were given to jesting, and therefore hold it as a modern abomination. But suppose they do wear copper rings in their noses, we'll set that off against those in your ears.—Touching the raw meat, our rare roast beef will serve instead;—as to painting, that is all the rage among our most fashionable young men—and the fine ladies will keep their nakedness in countenance.

MISS OBSOLETE. But how in the name of wonder shall we make them understand without an interpreter?

OBSOLETE. O, don't be uneasy about that. I dare say they've brought one with them, and if not, they are very expert at signs.

MISS OBSOLETE. Well—well, if it must be, it must. I wish it was any other day, for I am engaged so delightfully tomorrow—the morning I was to spend at Bridewell—the evening at the Penitentiary—But I suppose I must send an apology to Mrs. Toogood. (*Heigho!*) [*Going out, she returns.*] Pray, brother, is either of these aboriginals crippled?

OBSOLETE. No, thank my stars—at least I believe not—So there's no danger they should prove too interesting.

[*Exit* OBSOLETE.

MISS OBSOLETE *rings, and enter* RUST

MISS OBSOLETE. Call your young lady. I must write a note of apology to Mrs. Toogood, and say I can't go with her to Bridewell. [*Writes.*]

Enter MARY

MARY. Did you want me, aunt?

MISS OBSOLETE. Yes—to tell you we are to have company tomorrow to dinner.

MARY. The old set, I suppose; the admiral and his crew. In sober sadness, aunt, I'm sick to death of these tiresome people, and do so long for something new, that I'm almost tempted sometimes—to accompany you to the Penitentiary.

MISS OBSOLETE. Well, child, you're like to have something new tomorrow. Two young American aboriginals are to dine with us.

MARY. Well, aunt, anything for novelty. I am amused with my father's little whims, and the odd things he sometimes brings home with him. I should like to see a new species of men, for I am tired of the old.

MISS OBSOLETE. And I am out of all patience. We shall be the laughing-stock of all the *ton* here, with two such out of the way animals in our train. What will my Lord Bamboozle and Lady Kitty say to us?

MARY. Never mind what they say, aunt; if it amuses my father, I am content.

MISS OBSOLETE. Why, I expect to see him bring home the Italian Signior's mummy to dinner one of these days. I verily believe there's nothing, not even his sister, daughter, or money, he wouldn't part with for this precious antique. He told me the other day in ecstasy, that it was certainly three thousand years old. For my part, I almost wish I were three thousand years old, and then I might stand a chance for his admiration.

MARY. It's more than I do, aunt, I promise you. I wouldn't be a year older to please all the lovers of antiquity in the world. I wouldn't exchange the delicious hopes, and darling dreams, nay, even the little disappointments of youth, for all the reliques of the catacombs. I hate mummies, and feel a hundred times more curiosity to see these living representatives of the new world, than all the dry bones and parched skins of upper or lower Egypt.

MISS OBSOLETE. Well, well, every one to their taste. But a wooden leg, or a man just going to be turned off, is to my mind a thousand times more interesting.

MARY. My dear aunt, commend me to a two-legg'd savage in preference.

MISS OBSOLETE. On my conscience, niece, I begin to believe you have serious designs upon these copper-colored people. Why, would you cross the seas; live in a wigwam; eat raw meat, never see a rout, or taste peaches at two guineas a-piece? Would you forsake the divine Corinthians, and carry a pappoose at your back through a wilderness without beginning or end, while your husband was hunting beaver, or taking scalps?—Mercy upon us!

MARY. Why, I don't know, aunt, what despair may bring me to. I am so sick of the desperate monotony of this fashionable life; and so tired of the natural or artificial inanity of the present race of beaux, that I almost think I could be tempted to marry anything in the shape of a healthy, sprightly young fellow, whose soul was not completely evaporated, and whose frame would not fall into chaos at the shock of a cotillion. Alas! by the time they are twenty they have worn out their sensibilities, and all the rest of their lives is spent in search of—sensation. In truth, aunt, there is a great scarcity of passable men at present since the invention of loose pantaloons. I fear we shall never see a goodly leg in a handsome silk stocking again.

MISS OBSOLETE. Poor girl! she's far gone in romance! But I know you're only jesting. So pray let us go and prepare for this great war-feast. We must muster all our tinsel and feathers, for I have heard the aboriginals are desperately fond of finery. Suppose you paint your face half red and half white—you would then be sure of a conquest.

MARY. Nay, aunt—they shall have fair play. I'll not board them under false colors. I hope, at least, there are still English *women* that can conquer under their own flag. So come, let's prepare. [*Exeunt.*

END OF ACT FIRST

ACT II

SCENE I. LORD NOLAND'S *Lodgings*

LORD NOLAND *and the* ADMIRAL

ADMIRAL. As I was telling you, my lord, we gave three cheers, and prepared all hands for boarding, when—

NOLAND. I tell you what, admiral, if you board me with that story again, I'll bear away, and leave you to fight your battles by yourself, which is but a dull business. I hate fighting, except at boxing matches—and harkee, admiral—d'ye see this inimitable tie? There's little Threadneedle, and a hundred others, would resign a grove of laurels, only to be able to reach the happy folds of this cravat. What's the use of a man risking his limbs in search of honor, when he can gain it by tying his neckcloth—hey, Bully?

ADMIRAL. My lord, let me ask you one question. What would you give to have lost this leg, like me, in the service of your country?

NOLAND. What would I give? Why, faith, I'd give all I was ever worth in the world to have it back again.

ADMIRAL. Hem! [*Biting his lips.*] Your lordship's notions are not peculiar.

NOLAND. Take notice, admiral, if I hadn't been born to honor, honor would never have been born to me. Honor! what's modern honor but a pledge at the gaming table—a fiddlestick to make music at the expense of other's heart-strings—a tavern bully that pays his debts by cudgeling his landlord, tempting his wife, and kicking duns that have the insolence to ask for money?

ADMIRAL. Your lordship seems to hold honor rather cheap.

NOLAND. Yes—'Tis amazing how little we that inherit honor from a long line of ancestors, value this idol to which you soldiers sacrifice life and limb. For my part, my noble progenitors and myself have had such a surfeit of it, that, as respects my own particular, I'd rather at this present moment have a little profit, than the first place at the coronation, though I got the basin and towel for my pains. Apropos—talking of profit—you dine at Obsolete's today.

ADMIRAL. Yes—are the rest of our rivals to be there?

NOLAND. I'll be bound. Obsolete can't make a party without the old set. He hates all new things, you know, and especially new faces.

ADMIRAL. Have you heard the occasion of this feast?

NOLAND. O, some antediluvian era, I suppose. Probably the birth-day of Noah, or Lot's wife, for he hates all modern anniversaries. But here comes our learned Sir Kit, the physician, who has been dubbed a knight, not like the major, for killing his majesty's enemies, but his liege subjects. These tattling fellows know everything—I dare say he can tell us all about it.

Enter SIR CHRISTOPHER, *the* MAJOR *and* THREADNEEDLE

NOLAND. What news, Sir Kit?

SIR KIT. Great news, my lord. Professor Sniggersdorf has discovered a new planet in Virgo.

NOLAND. No! why, I thought there was no breeding of planets in that quarter. It must be illegitimate. What else?

SIR KIT. Sir Humphrey Davidoff has just announced to the world a method of turning night into day, by means of a perpetual gas lamp.

NOLAND. And if he does, there will be worse things brought to light in London than the Lame Devil ever showed to the scholar of Spain. I hope he'll let me know when he sets about it, for hang me if I have not serious objections to his plan. What will become of the devotees at Shockford's? 'Tis a breach of privilege thus to interfere with a nobleman's privacy. What more, Sir Kit?

SIR KIT. Poor Doctor Burdock died yesterday of a cold he caught sitting up all night in his garden to hear a mandrake scream. The society is inconsolable.

NOLAND. Alas! poor doctor—he's gone the way of all his patients.

SIR KIT. Yes—[*Sighing.*] But what was I saying?

NOLAND. I can't say—but for a hundred I'll tell what you were thinking about. A lady whose name begins with a W.—Hey, Sir Kit?

SIR KIT. Why, where do you expect to go when you die? Your lordship is akin to the witches. Indeed, I was just then thinking of my lovely duodecimo, Miss Warfield.

NOLAND. You mean you are thinking of her hundred thousand pounds, Sir Kit?

SIR KIT. My lord, I scorn your insinuations. My affection for Miss Warfield is identified with my love of books. There is to be a great sale of precious black letter jewels at Fonthill, all unique, and unless I marry the pretty Jane, I can't purchase the treasures. Ergo, it is not avarice, but a refined literary taste that causes me to covet her fortune.

NOLAND. Most logical King Kit! most disinterested scholar!

ADMIRAL. But for all this, by Neptune, I'll have her.

MAJOR. By Mars, no! 'Tis I am hers, and she shall be mine.

THREADNEEDLE. By Plutus, no! Credit and paper-money against the field—'tis I that must and shall. We bankers rule the world!

NOLAND. By my Nobility, my little Threadand-needle, honor hereditary wins the day. I inherit from mine ancestors an estate—at least I did inherit it—which is gone, and a privilege to precede ye commoners on all occasions, which, as I could neither spend in dice, nor drinking, I still retain. Therefore, get thee behind me, ye Sathans, for 'tis I that must make this Joan a lady.

Enter OBSOLETE *in a great hurry*

OBSOLETE. It's come—she's come—he's come—Huzza—It's come—she's come—they're come!

LORD NOLAND. Who—who—for a hundred pounds! I bet the King from Ireland.

SIR KIT. And I the Pope from Rome.

ADMIRAL. And I the D—l from London.

THREADNEEDLE. And I, the Duchess of Matchem, and her three desperate graces. Take care of yourselves, gents.

OBSOLETE. You're out—you're all out—So pay me the hundred, and do what you never did before.—Thus shall we have a modern miracle to confound all those radicals and unbelievers who despair of ever seeing your money.

NOLAND. That's a hit at you, Sir Kit.

SIR KIT. Nay, thank fortune for once, I'm no lord.—Your lordship takes precedence on this occasion.

NOLAND. But what mean you, most sphinxlike Obsolete? Thou art as mysteriously intricate this morning as an Egyptian hieroglyphic, or a prime minister's speech.

OBSOLETE. The mummy! the mummy! is come—the divine mummy, whose beautiful brown complexion and lack-lustre eyes, surpass all the roses and diamonds of all the living beauties in Christendom.

NOLAND. Very well—note that down, Sir Kit. I shall not fail to tell Miss Warfield what a compliment you've just paid her.

OBSOLETE. Nay, fair play, my lord—no peaching.—But apropos—you all dine with me today, to meet—

NOLAND. The mummy? I declare off.

OBSOLETE. Pshaw! no—The young Aborigines—the two lads from the uninteresting new world, which will never be fit to live in till its temples are in ruins and its cities like unto Babylon.

NOLAND. Hast seen them, good Obsolete? What do they look like? Have they rings in their noses—eh?

SIR KIT. Their faces painted?

ADMIRAL. Their heads crowned with feathers?

THREADNEEDLE. Their feet cased in moccasins?

NOLAND. Do they wear a necklace of scalps?

OBSOLETE. I can't say—I didn't see them, but left a note of invitation which they accepted last evening. I have asked Miss Warfield to keep my daughter in countenance.

The sly boots laughed heartily, and I suspect has some joke to play off on the occasion. But I must positively pay my respects to the mummy before dinner. So adieu, gentlemen. Remember six is the hour. [*Exit* OBSOLETE.

THREADNEEDLE. I say, my lord, don't forget that we are to quiz the Aborigines. We'll have brave sport, i' faith. But good morning—I must go and see my horses.

MAJOR. And I my old uncle, upon pain of being disinherited.

[*Exeunt* THREADNEEDLE, *the* ADMIRAL, MAJOR *and* SIR KIT.]

NOLAND. And I must go and invent excuses for pacifying my duns, "horrible monsters, hated by Gods and men." [*Exit.*

SCENE 2. *The Street*

JONATHAN PEABODY, *gaping about, whistling Yankee Doodle*

JONATHAN. What tarnal comical creturs these towns are. I'll be darned but I guess I've lost my way, though I chalked the corners of the streets as I went along. I snore, I think the young fellows must have lost their gumption to send me with a note in this plaguy place. O, here comes a gentleman will maybe tell me where I am.

Enter a fat hackney COACHMAN

JONATHAN. I say, you mister with the long whip, can you tell me the way home?

COACHMAN. The way home? You must tell me where you live first.

JONATHAN. By gum, that's jist what I want you to tell me, I swow.

COACHMAN. What! you don't know where you live? Why, what a pretty kiddy you must be. Where was you born? maybe you can tell me that?

JONATHAN. Can't, indeed—it's so long ago, I've no notion on't.

COACHMAN. This fellow is a real bumpkin—I'll quiz him. What's your name, friend?

JONATHAN. Name? Why, darnation, how should I know? Do you think I stood my own godfather?

COACHMAN. The fellow's a perfect natural. Maybe you can tell who owns the house you stay at, friend.

JONATHAN. O, yes! the man that lives in it, I partly guess.

COACHMAN. A bright guess—who lives in it, then?

JONATHAN. He that owns it, like as not.

COACHMAN. O, then I think I can put you in the way. You must first go to the North Parade; then to the South Parade—then to the Park out of town, and thence to the well, where you will find an old man by the name of King Bladud.—He'll tell you all about it, if you can only get an answer, for he's a crusty old piece of timber.

JONATHAN. Thank ye, thank ye, friend—[*Going, he turns about.*] I say, do you drive a hackney coach?

COACHMAN. Ay, that I do—it's just at hand. Shall I give you a cast?

JONATHAN. Any horses to it?

COACHMAN. Horses!—Why, to be sure.—Two spanking bays.

JONATHAN [*going, returns again*]. O—I forgot.—What may your name be, mister?

COACHMAN. Bitefig, at your service.

JONATHAN. Bitefig! That's a 'tarnal droll name. Well, then, Mister Bitefig, I heard a gentleman at the Pump asking for you jist now. He wants a coach to take him to Lunnon right off. Run as if heaven and earth were coming together, for he's in a tarnashun haste.

COACHMAN. To London! Zounds, I mustn't lose the job. Good-by, friend; don't forget King Bladud. [*Exit.*

JONATHAN [*laughing in a dry manner*]. My service to you, Mr. Bitefig. I think I'm partly even with that jockey and his King Bladud. If he finds any gentleman at the Pump going to Lunnon in a hackney coach, I'll give him leave to tell me on't. But, by zounds! here's one of my marks—now I shall find my way home without asking of King Bladud, I partly guess.

[*Exit—whistling Yankee Doodle.*

SCENE 3. OBSOLETE'S *House*

OBSOLETE, MISS OBSOLETE, JANE *and* MARY

JANE. Well, Mary, don't your heart flutter at the thought of seeing these wild men of the forests, these Bucktails, as Miss Obsolete calls them?

MARY [*smiling*]. Why, I confess to a little trepidation. I hope they'll treat us to the war-whoop and buffalo-dance after dinner.

MISS OBSOLETE. I'm sure it's more than I do. I tremble already like a patient in a charming fit of the ague. I hope, brother, you'll not give them too much liquor, for they say they are apt to scalp one another in drink. But I think I hear the bell. Mercy upon us! they're coming! [*Runs behind a great chair.*]

Enter LORD NOLAND, ADMIRAL, MAJOR, SIR KIT *and* THREADNEEDLE

NOLAND. Benign Miss Warfield, and you the elder and the younger grace, I worship you. [*Bowing.*]

ADMIRAL. And I.

SIR KIT. And I.

MAJOR. And I.

THREADNEEDLE. I say ditto to my lord.

JANE. In the name of all the graces I thank—my lord, knight, admiral, major, and ditto to Mr. Threadneedle. [*Courtesies to each.*] Who shall say the age is wanting in chivalry or piety, when here are five gallant knights ready to worship even a heathen deity.

NOLAND. Nay, madam, if thus you treat your votaries, your shrine will be deserted, even though you joined the wit of Minerva to the beauty of Venus.

OBSOLETE. My lord grows classical. That speech certainly found a wrong mouth. It belongs to the most erudite Sir Christopher.

NOLAND. What, my adorer of ancient mummyhood, is it war between us? *Allons*—"lay on, Macduff." Now will I peach most villainously, and repeat word for word, that gallant speech you made at my levee this blessed morning.

OBSOLETE [*aside to him*]. For Heaven's sake, my lord! I entreat you by the antiquity of thine ancestors to be as silent as the head of your great great grandsire.

JANE. O, tell us, by all means, my lord. If there was ever a poor damsel died of a curiosity of the heart, it will be me, if I don't instantly hear the story.

OMNES, *except* MARY. By all means—the story—the story!

NOLAND. Well, though bound by my nobility to despise the will of the majority, I yield this once, that I may be greatly revenged. You will be pleased, or rather you will be displeased, to know, Miss Warfield—

Enter RUST, *trembling*

RUST. Madam–b–b–b–the Aboriginals are come–B–b–b–they–they–

[MISS OBSOLETE *again gets behind the great chair, and* RUST *behind her.*]

OBSOLETE [*alarmed*]. Why, what is the blockhead frightened at! He shivers like a poplar leaf.

RUST. S–s–sir–I've never been steady since the last earthquake we encountered at the foot of Mount Ætna.

Enter HENRY *and* FRANK TUDOR. MISS OBSOLETE *remains behind the chair*—OBSOLETE *eyes them with a sort of alarmed curiosity, and forgets to pay the ordinary civilities,* MISS OBSOLETE *ventures to peep out, and exclaims aside*—NOLAND *and the others laugh at* MR. *and* MISS OBSOLETE.

MISS OBSOLETE [*aside*]. Why, as I live, they are dressed, and look like absolute Christians! If they only had wooden legs, like the admiral, they'd be an ornament to the hospital.

MARY [*apart to* JANE]. For Heaven's sake, Jane, say something—I am so ashamed at this reception, my feet are grown fast to the floor. Speak, dear Jane—or be dumb forever.

JANE [*laughing*]. Well, rather than incur the penalty: Gentlemen [*To the* TUDORS.], to convince you that you have not been invited to dine at an asylum of the deaf and dumb, I am urged to present you to this good silent company, who are so delighted to see you that they have forgot to bid you welcome. As a countrywoman, permit me to present you to Miss Obsolete, who will please to come out of her hiding-place. I assure you, madam, there's no danger. [*Laughs.*]

MISS OBSOLETE. I believe I may venture.—[*Comes partly forward, then retires again in a fright.*]

HENRY [*apart to* FRANK]. What can all this mean, Frank? I begin to be angry.—Could I suppose there was any intention—

FRANK. Pooh, pooh, brother—'tis nothing but the old English hospitality we've heard so much about.

JANE. Mr. Obsolete [*Apart.*]—Mr. Obsolete, if you don't instantly find the use of your tongue, and do the honors of the house, I'll cast you from the list of my beaux into outer darkness.

OBSOLETE. I go, most lovely, and yet to go am loth. But such a threat would make a Cicero of me, though mum as a mummy. I go—and yet I do not go, for at this moment I am dumbfounded. Beseech thee, mistress Jane, to set my sister Miss Obsolete at them; she hath a never-failing stream of speech, whereas just now I labor under a great drought of ideas.

JANE. Well, this is politeness! Miss Obsolete, pray try and supply the deficiencies of your brother.

MISS OBSOLETE. Why, what can I do? I don't understand Choctaw, nor Chickasaw, nor Potawottomy, nor any of the polite aboriginal tongues—and as for English, there's no use in talking to them, I suppose.

JANE. It's enough to provoke a saint—though I can't help laughing. Go, then, madam, and try what signs will do.

FRANK [*to* HENRY]. "Look, my lord, it comes—angels and ministers!"

HENRY. Hush! she's going to enter into a treaty of peace with us. See—she is plucking the olive branch.

MISS OBSOLETE *advances cautiously from behind her chair, followed by* RUST—*She plucks a branch from a flower pot in the room—motions them to sit down, and attempts a conversation by signs.* FRANK, LORD NOLAND *and the guests laugh aside—while* HENRY *exhibits signs of angry impatience.*

HENRY. What mummery is this? [*Advancing.*] Pray, gentlemen, who of all this good company represents our hospitable entertainer?

LORD NOLAND. Faith, these seem a pair of downright gentlemen after all.—For the honor of old England, I'll welcome them myself—[*Advances.*] Permit me, sir, to answer that question, in behalf of a certain gentleman whose wits seem a little out at the elbow just now. This is Mr. Obsolete, who is struck dumb with the pleasure of seeing you. I am called Lord Noland, and if I might be permitted to act as his substitute, I would offer you my hand, and say you're welcome to England.

HENRY. I thank you, my lord; and to say the truth, I felt a little mortified that Mr. Obsolete did not inquire at least about an old friend of his I left at my father's.

FRANK. And I felt, and do still feel very angry with these young ladies, whom I can't forgive under the price of hearing their voices once at least before I die.

[*Bows to* MARY *and* JANE.]

MARY [*apart to* JANE]. Speak, Jane! The woman is dead within me.

JANE. Speak, Jane! why, you little blushing thing. I begin to believe you have already been struck with an arrow from the quiver of one of these Aborigines, who, you know, are very expert at the bow. Pray, gentlemen, are the ladies of your country fond of rural life? I know you can talk of that if nothing else. [*To* MARY.]

HENRY. Those who live in the cities, madam—those who reside in the country are not so fond of retirement. It is easy, however, to give them what taste we please, in this respect, since the most inveterate town lady loves the country—when she's in a crowd—and the most ardent votary of rural shades adores a crowd—when she's alone in the country.

JANE. I should hope, Mr. Tudor, it did not require to be placed at one extreme, in order to admire the other.

HENRY. Perhaps not in all cases, madam. Yet I have very often found, that the ladies who talked most about the charms of rural life, were most often to be seen at public places; and that the most sincere votaries of the repose of the country, were apt to say the least on the subject.

JANE. You don't mean to insinuate that we women talk most of what we think the least?

HENRY. Not among yourselves, madam.

[*Bowing.*]

MARY [*speaking eagerly*]. I'm sure—I'm sure—[*Retires confused, and blushing.*]

FRANK [*aside*]. They say I'm one of the most

impudent fellows in the world—and I believe it, for it can be nothing but the force of contrast that draws my heart towards that little flower of blushing modesty. See how her blood goes and comes of errands from her face to her heart!

OBSOLETE [*after a deep sigh*]. I begin to breathe again. Pray, Mr. Tudor, are you of the family of Owen Tudor, who married our Queen Katherine?

FRANK [*to* HENRY]. Bravo! an ox spoke once at Rome, and so did an ass in Judea!

HENRY. I fancy not, sir. I remember my grandfather—but who his grandfather was, is more than appears in our family tree.

OBSOLETE. Perhaps by going to the Herald's office you may trace out the descent. Should we meet in London during the winter, I shall be happy to aid your inquiries.

HENRY. I thank you, sir. But I believe I shall not trouble you. I mean not to detract from the advantages of birth and title, but in America, we lay little claim to such distinctions. Those who left this country to settle mine, forgot their pedigrees in toils and dangers; and those of their descendants, who rely upon the mere identity of names to prove their claim to noble blood, only make themselves ridiculous.

NOLAND. Then I presume, sir, there's no distinction between the cobler and the king, and the son of a cobler and a king?

HENRY. The law makes none, and that's sufficient. We are taught to consider a king, and the son of a king, as much the subject of our thoughts and judgment, as the beggar that goes in rags. Man can't remove one step from man—his nature fixes him.

NOLAND [*apart*]. Why, Sir Kit, this smells of the radical!

SIR KIT. The very radical heat and moisture of democracy, my lord. We must have them at the Alien office. They are certainly of the mischievous sect of the Bucktails, we've read about.

Enter RUST

RUST. Dinner waits, sir.

OBSOLETE. My lord, be pleased to hand Miss Obsolete.

NOLAND [*aside*]. The fiend take my nobility this time, however. O, for the glorious system of equality!

OBSOLETE. Sir Christopher—my daughter's hand. I shall escort Miss Warfield.

FRANK [*aside*]. Shall I venture? I will—I'll cross that Sir Kit were he twenty knights of Bath or Garter. May it please you, madam. [*Takes* MARY'S *hand and leads her out.*]

SIR KIT. A Bucktail! a real Bucktail! Why, he don't comprehend the first rudiments of etiquette, the very corner-stone and cement of society—a Bucktail—I say again a Bucktail! [*Exit.*

RUST [*walking behind* FRANK, *scrutinizing him closely*]. I don't see the bucktail, after all. [*Exit.*

END OF ACT SECOND

ACT III

SCENE I. *A Servants' Hall* [1]

RUST, JONATHAN, *and* PADDY WHACK

RUST. Then you make a point of dining out with your master?

JONATHAN. I've no master, I calculate.

RUST. No! I beg pardon, I thought you served the young aboriginal gentlemen?

JONATHAN. May be, so I do—but serving a man don't make him my master, by a darn'd sight.

RUST. The dickons it don't! How do you make that out, Master Peabody?

JONATHAN. Mr. Tudor pays me a salary for taking care of him, I calculate—but I don't see how one white man can be the master of another.

PADDY. Be quiet now, Master Rust—I take the jontleman. By my soul, I believe he's what they call a governor: such as go beyond sea to take care of the young sprigs of nobility, till they come to years of discretion to spend their estates.

JONATHAN. I guess you're half right, my daddy.

PADDY. Daddy!—Half? Faith, that's pretty near the mark for a rough guess. So I drink

[1] This scene may be curtailed in the performance. It is partly introduced to give the company time for dinner. [*Note in 1847 edition.*]

to our better acquaintance, mister half governor. But as there are two of these aboriginals, won't you recommend me to take care of the other? I warrant you I'll civilize him—I'll give him the polish of a potatoe.

JONATHAN. I'll see about it, I guess.

PADDY. You guess? Can't you be sure of it now?

JONATHAN. I reckon not.

PADDY. Do you mean to insult me, Governor Peabody? If you do, you'll maybe reckon without your host. I'm a peaceable man, everybody knows, and never fight except for a frolic; but when a man talks about reckoning, it always puts me in mind of a long score at a tavern, and brings on low spirits. My sarvice to you, Mr. Rust— [*Drinks.*]

RUST. Master Whack, quiet thy clack. Governor Peabody, I see, don't like to commit himself. Yes and no are dangerous little words, and all great men avoid them as much as possible.

PADDY. Excuse me, Master Rust, but I've a leaning towards becoming a great man myself, and don't like to be put off with reckonings and may-be-sos.

RUST. Well, then, why don't you give the Governor some account of yourself, Mr. Whack, that he may see and judge of your character and qualifications.

PADDY. Agreed, Master Rust. You shall hear as pretty a piece of biography as ever you saw in a dictionary.

RUST. Make haste, then, for I think I hear a stir above. We shall be wanted presently.

JONATHAN. Ay, begin—with your ugly mouth.

PADDY. Ugly mouth! I'll spoil your mouth if you go to reflect on my beauty. [*Squares up to him.*]

JONATHAN. Your ugly mouth—as the saying is—'tis an old saying in my country.

PADDY. O! if it's only an old saying—I'm pacified.

JONATHAN. Begin, then—with your ugly mouth.

PADDY. What! [*Squares up again.*]

JONATHAN. As the saying is, Mister Whack.

PADDY. O, ay—I forgot—as the saying is. So here goes. I was born, though perhaps you wouldn't believe it, in old Ireland.

JONATHAN. I guessed as much, I swow.

PADDY. You did! you knowing aboriginal. My parents, as I am in duty bound to suspect, were honest, but as to their industry, I can't say as much for that. My father was a lord—

RUST. A lord!

JONATHAN. Lord a mercy upon us—you don't say so—with your ugly mouth?

PADDY. Ugly! O, ay—But Mister Governor, I'll take it as a particular favor, if you just forgot that same old saying.

JONATHAN. Well—well—go on—with your —hem!

PADDY. My father was a lord, I say—for he did everything like a lord. He ate and drank like a lord—spent his time like a lord, in gaming and horse-racing—and his money like a lord, faster than he got it. If this isn't being a lord, I don't know what is.

RUST. It's better than a certificate from the Herald's office. But I hear the bell—excuse me a little. [*Exit.*

JONATHAN. As sure as two-pence, I cussnotcher.

PADDY. As sure as two-pence! Why in the Divil's name is two-pence surer than onepence, or a half-pence, Governor Peabody?

JONATHAN. It's likely—maybe so, Mr. Whack.—But don't you know, guyhang it, if there be two of anything, one can swear for the other—whereas a single thing has nobody to stand up for it. Two-pence is therefore twice as much to be relied upon as a single penny.

PADDY. I'm satisfied. Pacify me with a good reason, and I'm as reasonable as any man that walks upon four legs. Now for my edification.

JONATHAN. Never say a word about that, Mr. Whack—with your ugly—hem! Anybody may see with their two eyes you've been well brought up.

PADDY. With two eyes? What the Divil d'ye mean with two eyes, Governor Peabody? Why didn't you say with half an eye, and that would have been a pretty compliment?

JONATHAN. No offence, Mister Whack. I mentioned two eyes for the same reason I did the two-pence; that one might swear for the other to your education, which I calculate must have been liberal.

PADDY. Faith, you may say that—with your ugly mouth—as the saying is. It was at other people's expense—if that ain't liberal, I don't know what is.

JONATHAN. Very liberal, I snore. But tell us now how you got over to England. You didn't come by land, I guess?

PADDY. Land! What a Judy for a Governor! I came in the royal squadron, as one of the King's *suites*.

JONATHAN. What, did the King carry you on his back? That's playing comical.

PADDY. On his back—pooh! To be one of the King's *suit*, is to come in his train, honey.

JONATHAN. Wrapt up in the tail of his robe, I calculate.

PADDY. Wrapt up in the skin of a potatoe! Why, botheration, governor, if I don't believe—Why, 'sblood! Why, a man in the King's suite, means one that belongs to the King.

JONATHAN. O—ay—I guess—He's a slave, like one of our niggers.

PADDY [*jumping up*]. I'll tell you what, Governor Peabody, if you mean to insult me, with your caparison betwixt a courtier and a nager, you've got the wrong sow by the ear.

JONATHAN. Sow—you mean boar, I calculate. Maybe this is one of your bulls, Mr. Whack?

PADDY. Bull, boar or sow, governor, it's well for you that you're my patron, or by the faith of my pagan ancestors, I'd—

JONATHAN. Never mind what you'd do. I'll take your word for it, Mr. Whack.

PADDY. Take my word—you'll wait till I give it, won't you? But take care you don't get a great knock before the word comes—for it's always a word and a blow with me, honey; and faith, the blow may come first.

JONATHAN. Mr. Whack, I'll be darn'd if that wouldn't be a greater bull than the other.

PADDY. Wait, now—till I make out whether that's a reflection or not.

JONATHAN. No, I thank you—I'm in a hurry just now, and must go and take care of the young squires. Day, day. I'll not fail to speak a good word for you, as sure as two-pence. [*Exit* JONATHAN.

PADDY. By the powers, that chap bothers me now. It takes all my sagacity to tell whether he is making a fool of me, or I of him, or whether he is a great fool, and I another.

Enter RUST

RUST. Mr. Whack, your master wants you to go on a message.

PADDY. Very well, but I reckon I've no master, as that tundering Yankee says. Yet I'll obey him to show my good breeding, honey. [*Exeunt* RUST *and* PADDY.

SCENE 2. *A Drawing-Room*

Enter MISS OBSOLETE, JANE, MARY, FRANK *and* HENRY, *as from dinner*

JANE. I'm sorry for you, Mr. Tudor; you'll be *cut* by all the fashionable Corinthians, for preferring the ladies to the bottle. You see all our admirers remain true to their allegiance.

HENRY. Faith, Miss Warfield, I cannot help it. I must submit to the penalty, for I never yet hesitated between the two, though I fear in preferring the company of the ladies to that of the bottle, I only exchange a headache for a heartache.

MARY [*to* FRANK]. Is it not the custom in your country to sit long after dinner?

FRANK. Why, yes—that is, among old bachelors, who must either drink or sleep—and reverend young city beaux, who couple women and wine, as people do fire and faggots, to keep their fancy warm.

JANE. But seriously, gentlemen—I'm afraid you've made too great a sacrifice. Pray, return to the dining-room. We poor souls will try to kill time, by canvassing the last new fashions, or perhaps the merits of the gentlemen at the dinner table.

FRANK. I'll not trust my character in such jeopardy. In truth, my brother and I are no great champions at the bottle. We have been used to amuse ourselves after dinner with rural sports and exercises, that kept up our spirits without the aid of wine.

HENRY [*to* MISS OBSOLETE]. Madam, suppose

we take advantage of this fine evening to stroll into the country for a little exercise? May we expect the honor of your company, madam?

MISS OBSOLETE [*alarmed*]. What! mercy upon us! Stroll into the country by moonlight, with a couple of young fellows! [*Bridling.*]—I assure you, Mr. Tudor, I can't think of exposing my reputation by such imprudence. Moonlight walks alone in the country! Mercy upon us, what a rake! [*Aside.*]

HENRY. I beg pardon, madam. If I have asked anything improper, I hope you'll place it to the account of my country breeding.

MISS OBSOLETE. No impropriety in young ladies like us, walking by moonlight in the country with young fellows! [*Tossing her head.*] I promise you, sir, I for one will not expose myself to such scandalous imputations. I wonder what my Lord Bamboozle and Lady Kitty would say to it?

FRANK. Bless me, brother, explain yourself. The old lady will cry out rape and murder directly. [*Aside.*]

HENRY. 'Tis the custom of my country, madam.

MISS OBSOLETE. The custom of your country! Mercy upon us! What profligates these Bucktails are—[*Aside.*] Are you really serious, sir, in telling me that the young ladies are allowed such unseemly liberties?

HENRY. Quite serious, madam, I assure you.

MISS OBSOLETE. What! do they stroll about the fields with the young fellows?

HENRY. Yes. [*Shrugs his shoulders.*]

MISS OBSOLETE. And in the woods, too?

HENRY. Yes. [*Shrugs.*]

MISS OBSOLETE. And walk arm in arm?

HENRY. Yes, sometimes. [*Shrugs.*]

MISS OBSOLETE [*holding up her hands*]. And what is the consequence of all this?

HENRY. Mutual affection—and happy marriages.

MISS OBSOLETE. Hem—Well, I declare, I should have expected something very different. [*Sighs.*]

HENRY. Why so, my dear madam? 'Tis not the light of the moon, the sacred quiet of a calm evening—the repose of a country scene—nor the pure beauties of nature—nor the innocent intercourse of a lonely walk, that inflame the senses, or corrupt the heart. It is at midnight balls and masquerades, where lascivious music assails the senses—where dazzling lights confound the imagination, and wines and costly viands pamper the heated appetites. It is there that virtue melts like wax, and female purity is most successfully assailed.

MISS OBSOLETE. It may be so, sir. But may I ask what sort of wives these strolling moonlight damsels make?

HENRY. The best in the world, madam. The daily intercourse which is permitted enables them to choose with better judgment; and the freedom of choice, to consult their hearts. They do not marry to come out into the gay world, but to retire from it. Here, marriage frees the bird from its cage, where it has been all its life confined; and can it be wondered at, that just escaped from its prison, the charm of new-born liberty sometimes tempts it into the fowler's net, or the sportsman's lure?

MISS OBSOLETE. Did ever body hear such strange doctrines?—I suppose these are what they call Yankee notions! [*Aside.*] The American mothers must be strange people, Mr. Tudor.

HENRY. They seem to be somewhat different from those of Europe, who appear to consider their daughters as tradesmen do their wares. They keep them bright and clean till they are disposed of, and then let them take their chance afterwards.

Enter NOLAND, SIR KIT, OBSOLETE, *and the* ADMIRAL, *as from table. The* ADMIRAL *fuddled* [1]*—the rest somewhat gay.*

NOLAND. Ha, ha! I'faith, the admiral is half seas over. His brain is like the ocean, always rolling. How goes it with thee, Sir Kit?

SIR KIT. O! Cookery—cookery, that kills more than war, pestilence and famine, and would destroy the whole human race—if—if—

NOLAND. If physic didn't lend its aid in dispatching some of them—hey, Kit?

[1] The admiral must not be made as drunk as a beast, as is too often the case. [*Note in 1847 edition.*]

ADMIRAL [*sings*]. "There's a sweet little cherub that sits up aloft"—

JANE. Ah—that's me, admiral.—Come, now, is it not? In wine there's truth, they say. Speak, wreck of a great sea-monster! [*Aside.*]

ADMIRAL [*flourishing his crutch*]. Huzza—boys—board 'em—board the Yankees—[*Sings.*] "Britannia rules the waves"—Where's the Major, and little needle and thread? I think I punished 'em—[*Sings.*] "Rule Britannia"—Pray Mr. T-Tudor, what was the name of the Yankee frigate captured by the Shannon? [*To* FRANK.]

FRANK. O—the Guerrière.

ADMIRAL. Pshaw! no.

FRANK. The Macedonian?

ADMIRAL. D—n it, sir, no.

FRANK. The Java?

ADMIRAL. 'Sblood—no.

FRANK. Perhaps you mean the Wasp?

ADMIRAL. Hem—no—[*Faintly.*]

FRANK. The Frolic?

ADMIRAL. What an ignoramus this is—I mean—I mean [*Sings.*] "Britannia rules the waves."

FRANK. Ay—and the winds, too, I suppose—like another Lapland witch.

NOLAND. Faith, I believe the Bucktail is quizzing the admiral. [*To* SIR KIT.]

ADMIRAL. "Why, sailors, why should we be melancholy boys?" Wine, rosy wine forever.

NOLAND [*apart to the* ADMIRAL]. Whisky—whisky, admiral—'Tis a distillation from tongues and hearts, you know, and, according to the Indian doctrine, makes a man talk like an angel, and fight like Satan. Now's your time—Give Miss Warfield a broadside, and she'll strike directly.

ADMIRAL. D'ye think so? Then, faith, here's at her. I've the tongues of ten *parliamentary orators* in my throat.

NOLAND [*aside*]. Of ten donkeys, more likely. But bray away, admiral.

The ADMIRAL *bustles up to* MISS OBSOLETE, *and mistakes her for* JANE.

ADMIRAL. Divine lady—most lovely Amphitrite, that sails round the world in a cockle shell—shall we be spliced?

MISS OBSOLETE [*fanning violently*]. Spliced!—what does the shocking sea-serpent mean?

FRANK. He takes you for a rope's end, madam.

ADMIRAL [*discovering his mistake, wheels round and comes back as before to* MISS OBSOLETE]. Divine Miss Warfield—translucent creature—shall Neptune and Amphitrite couple?

NOLAND. Gad a mercy! what a race of mermaids and sea-monsters shall we have? Why, the man must see more than double to make such a blunder!—To her again, admiral—Your eloquence would silence an equinoctial gale. [*Aside.*] To her again, my hero.

ADMIRAL. Never fear me. I'll get to windward of her.—Divine Miss Warfield [*To* MISS OBSOLETE.]—do you—What shall I say?—Do you believe in the great New England sea-serpent?

MISS OBSOLETE [*in a passion*]. Yes, sir—and in all other sea-monsters, since I had the honor of your acquaintance.

NOLAND. Egad, admiral, that broadside would sink a double-decker.—Strike or run.

ADMIRAL. Not I, faith—you shall see now how I'll take her betwixt wind and water. Hem—Madam, I don't wonder at your believing in serpents—you inherit that from grandmother Eve. Hem—I think I had her there, my bully!

NOLAND. Well said, lord high admiral! There spoke the claret. O generous, inspiring wine, henceforth I'll adore thee—thou hast drawn wit from a sea-calf. [*Aside.*]

[ADMIRAL, *wheeling round, and accidentally, at length, addressing* MISS WARFIELD.]

ADMIRAL [*sings*]. "Rule Britannia, Britannia."—Divine Miss Warfield, say but Y-y-yes—and I'll undertake the labors of Hercules; I'll perform impossibilities.

JANE. Well, admiral, on one condition I am thine. Get the command of a British ship, and bring me in an American of equal force, and you shall command me for life.

NOLAND. Egad, admiral, this beats the labors of Hercules put together. What sayest thou, my bully Hector? Faith, the very idea has sober'd him. [*Aside.*]

ADMIRAL. Why, you know—I'm on the invalid list.

JANE. And yet dare pretend to a sprightly young damsel, with a hundred thousand pounds in her pocket! Good invalid, depart in peace. I don't mean to enlist in that *corps*, I assure you. I hereby protest, unless I can meet with one of your countrymen that can do this feat, I'll never marry an Englishman.

ADMIRAL. Then may you become a leader of legions of apes in—Hem! Good evening, madam. "Rule Britannia," &c. [*They laugh.*]
[*Exit* ADMIRAL.

NOLAND. Do any of this good company attend the Rooms tonight?

JANE. My sister is alone this evening. Her husband is gone to London, and I shall keep her company. Mr. Tudor [*To* HENRY.], pray ask me to permit you the honor of seeing me to the carriage—will you?

HENRY. You have the start of me, madam. 'Twas just what I was thinking of. [*Bows.*]

MISS OBSOLETE. And I must just step over to Mrs. Toogood.

OBSOLETE. And I must go and bid the mummy good night.

During the preceding dialogue, FRANK *and* MARY *have been talking in dumb-show.*

FRANK. And I—what is to become of me, madam? [*To* MARY.] Will nobody ask me for my company? Upon my credit, there's nothing I'd sooner give away just now.

MARY. Why—come—since you are so modest as not to think it a favor, as most of our fashionable beaux do, I will permit you to remain here and read to me till my father or aunt returns.

FRANK. Ten thousand thanks! I long to begin our studies.

JANE. Well, as all are agreed, let us go, Mr. Tudor.—My sister will be lonely. My lord, I suppose you attend court tonight?

NOLAND. Court, madam?

JANE. Yes, my lord—where kings and queens, to say nothing of knaves, take precedence, and share all the honors.
[*Exeunt all but* NOLAND.

NOLAND [*looking after her*]. I understand you, my lady—and shall have a card to play with you ere long. She certainly begins to affect this Bucktail. Well—birds of a feather, they say. My affairs are drawing to a crisis, and I must either make her love me, or run away with her, and make her a lady against her will. [*Exit.*

END OF THIRD ACT

ACT IV

SCENE I. LORD NOLAND'S *Lodgings*

LORD NOLAND *and* PADDY WHACK

PADDY. Faith, my lord, here's an invitation, I believe. The genius that brought it, insisted upon coming in; but I gave him my honor it should be safely delivered. [*Gives a note.*]

NOLAND [*opening the note*]. An invitation with a vengeance! Go and tell the fellow to call next week. [*Exit* PADDY.]—The rascal threatens extremities unless he's paid. Confound these impudent clowns, that are so unreasonable as to expect their money, when a man has spent it, every sous. Well, if I must, I must. Fate's a spaniel—we can't drive her from us. I must marry Jane Warfield, whether she will or no, and that off hand, too, by a *coup de main.*—Um—carry her off? Faith, 'twill be a piece of gallantry few women can resist—a proof of love of which this shilly-shally age affords no parallel.—'Twill be talked of, too! I'faith, I'll do—um—ay—it shall be so—my old ruined castle in the wood.—Servants are necessary implements of villany and mischief—um—I'll trust him.

Enter WHACK

WHACK. Faith, he says your lordship has been telling him to call next week till he begins to doubt whether that same next week doesn't mean Doomsday. He talks about an execution. I hope he don't mean to hang your lordship.

NOLAND. Well, well, let the fellow go—Mr. Whack!

PADDY. Sir—my lord?

NOLAND. Hast any skill in elopements?

PADDY. Elopements? Sure, that's my forte.—I ran away from three sweethearts extempore, in my own country.

NOLAND. It's not running away from, but with a woman I speak of.

PADDY. Just the same, my lord, if the lady is as willing as I was.

NOLAND. But suppose she is not willing?

PADDY. Why, then—the next thing is to persuade her to be willing.

NOLAND. But suppose, Mr. Whack, she can't be persuaded?

PADDY. Why, then, the next best thing is to persuade the world she was willing. 'Tis a great matter to keep up appearances, for though I don't mind running away *from* a woman against her will, it's rather against my morality to run away *with* her, contrary to her conscience—

NOLAND. You make nice distinctions, Mr. Whack. But wouldn't being well paid make it one and the same thing?

PADDY. Why, I can't tell, my lord, till I'm tried. A bright guinea, like a bright sun, is very apt to throw light upon a case of conscience.

NOLAND. Very well, Mr. Whack, the argument shall not be wanting. In the mean time, by way of quieting that troublesome monitor of yours, I promise you my wife shall have an excellent place at the coronation. Rank for money is a fair exchange, you know.

PADDY. Sure, my lord. Don't we every day see plenty of people who will not only part with their lands, but their consciences too, for this same rank and honor?

NOLAND. Nay, Mr. Whack, no reflections upon Parliament, if you please. But, harkee! You must be as discreet as a prime minister, or a gentleman in the secretary's department.

PADDY. I warrant, your honor, I'll be as secret as a Scotch wizard, who don't let even his shadow be seen. But may I be so bold as to ax your lordship who is the lady for whom you intend this great favor?

NOLAND. Follow me into the next room, where nobody will interrupt us, and we'll settle the preliminaries.

PADDY. Ay, your honor—the protocol, as they say. [*Exeunt.*

SCENE 2. *A Sitting-Room*

JANE WARFIELD, *solus*

JANE. Heigho! surely there's something in the very air of this island that makes one dull. When I was in the sprightly land of liberty, I used to skip about like a lamb, and if I happened to be out of the way for half an hour, nobody was frightened lest I had run away to Gretna Green. But here my feet are tied, and my tongue, too, so that I am fain to talk to myself when alone, to keep it in exercise. I've a great mind to fall in love, if it were only to pass the time—Yes—

Enter SERVANT

SERVANT. Mr. Tudor, madam. [*Exit.*

JANE. Heaven preserve us! there's certainly a great deal of truth in the old proverb.

Enter HENRY TUDOR

HENRY. Good day to you, Miss Warfield.

JANE. O, Mr. Tudor, I'm rejoiced to see you. Do you know I was actually talking to myself for want of better company? My sister has just set off for London, to meet her husband.

HENRY. Suppose *me* a second self, Miss Warfield, and continue the conversation.

JANE. No—no—sir, that would be worse than making you my confessor at once. You're too young to be trusted with a lady's secrets.

HENRY. And too indulgent; I should pardon every sin, but that of falling in love—except with a person of my choosing.

JANE. O—I suppose you mean Mr. Obsolete?

HENRY. No—he's not the man.—You'd be rival'd by the mummy.

JANE. The spruce banker?

HENRY. No—you'd be rival'd by his horse.

JANE. Sir Christopher?

HENRY. No—you'd be rival'd by a unique black-letter folio.

JANE. My lord?

HENRY. No—you'd be forsaken for dice, drinking and debauchery.

JANE. The major?

HENRY. No—you'd be rival'd by the whole sex.

JANE. And yet he's constant to one lady, I'll swear.

HENRY. O, every woman of course makes an exception in her own favor.

JANE. I mean the Lady Fortune, sir.

HENRY. There, indeed, I believe the major may be depended upon.

JANE. You're very hard to be pleased, good father.—What say you to the admiral?

HENRY. Dear Miss Warfield, I can't think of your sailing under an enemy's flag.

JANE. Alas! for me—my list of beaux is exhausted! I can think of no other.

HENRY. And yet there is another, who, if he dared name himself—would offer you his name—who, did he dare to hope, would lay his heart at your feet, and beg you not to trample on it—One who, though almost a stranger to you, would rely upon your virtues, as on the mercy of Heaven—whose faith is equal to that of a martyr—whose devotion exceeds that of a saint—whose love, like—

JANE. O, say no more! Where is this wonder to be seen? I'll go a pilgrimage barefoot to find him, even to the snowy summit of Ætna. Where dwells he—in earth, sea or air?

HENRY. Here—[*Dropping on his knee.*]

JANE. Where? [*Looks wistfully about the room.*]—I don't see him! I thought it must be some invisible spirit, for I never yet saw such a man.

HENRY [*rising, and placing himself before her*]. Nay, look at me. Her sprightliness makes me bold. [*Aside.*]

JANE. I can't see him, not I—Alas! he has flown away! 'Twas a spirit, sure!

HENRY. True flesh and blood, I promise you, Miss Warfield. But pray, now, do be serious for once.

JANE [*looking prim*]. Well, sir—May I ask how long, according to the best of your knowledge and belief, we two have known each other? I believe it is little more than a day for every year that Jacob labored for a helpmate.

HENRY. Where hearts are pure, an hour's acquaintance is equal to an age of hypocritical contest, who shall deceive the other. What if we have not known each other long? A woman's curiosity has the better chance of being gratified in finding out my virtues. Were I a woman, I should begin to hate a man as soon as I knew all about him.

JANE. Why, so we do, generally, and that's the reason I never mean to marry. I intend to live single, and employ the rest of my life in studying the virtues of your sex, only to gratify my curiosity.

HENRY. Nay, charming Miss Warfield, for once be serious. Though it was thy innocent unaffected gayety that first caught my fancy, and soon engaged my heart, yet there is a time when sprightliness is levity, and laughter cruel. Stab me, but do not tickle me to death in sport.

JANE. Well, good sir. Seriously, then, thou art a bold and a rash man in thy love. Strangers as we are, unknowing whether like flint and steel, we may strike out consuming fires by meeting—ignorant whether our tastes or habits mingle in the sweet accord so necessary to the happiness of wedlock. Surely you can't be serious; or if you are, surely, Mr. Tudor, you cannot expect me to be so, in order to prosper your suit. Believe me, sir, my gayety is not levity, nor my frankness, folly. The interchange of sentiments is not that of hearts. Go you to the ball tonight?

HENRY. The ball!—But—I understand you, madam. Beshrew me, but I can take a hint—I–I–I can laugh, too—be gay—and wither in an hour afterwards. I can frisk and giggle, while I stab—Farewell, madam—thou hast wounded a true bosom—[*Going out he sinks into a chair, as though exhausted with his emotions.*]

JANE. What, is it so, dear youth? Then heart speak, and be heard at last. You are ill, sir. [*Takes his hand.*]

HENRY [*with effort*]. 'Tis over, now—a mere faintness, common with me at times. [*Turning from her.*] I'll swallow my feelings, though they were live coals. Were it Prometheus' vulture, I'd hug it, rather than its fluttering should be seen by this unfeeling woman. [*Aside.*] Farewell—madam—It is all over now.—[*Going.*]

JANE. But it is not all over—listen to me, sir. I have a heart as warm as thine; but lately I have been plagued by a swarm of flies, in the shape of lovers, who came to suck my blood, and then be gone. Men without heads or hearts—who have no feelings left but selfish ones; who throng about our sex to sate themselves with their spoils—to stake their miserable remnant of man, against our unsoil'd hearts, our unworn sensibilities, our fortunes, and our happiness. To such I have opposed the bitterness of unfeeling scorn, for they deserved it. But you are not of these, I think.

HENRY. In faith, I am not. It was thy laughing eyes darting a thousand innocent meanings—thy heart that calls down a thousand blessings on the head—thy worth, thy beauty that won me. It is thy scorn, and not the loss of fortune, that wounds my heart to its very core.

JANE. I do believe it. And now [*Sighing.*]—though knowing what I pledge and what I hazard—knowing that when a woman puts her trust in man, she risks all, and places her stock of happiness where full oft the principal and interest both are lost,—knowing too she puts almost beyond her power, not only her present safety but the welfare of her immortal soul,—knowing and feeling all this—here is my hand. He that turns pale and trembles at a woman, must love her.

HENRY [*kneeling*]. And here do I receive that hand, as the best gift of Heaven. [*Kisses her.*] Thus do I seal thee mine forever. I cannot speak my happiness.

Enter SERVANT

SERVANT. Madam, Miss Obsolete to wait on you. [*Exit.*

HENRY. Then pray excuse me. I wish to be alone awhile to realize my bliss. Adieu, my best beloved! [*Exit.*

Enter MISS OBSOLETE

MISS OBSOLETE. O, Miss Warfield, I've the most delightful excursion to propose to you!

JANE. And I am delighted to hear it, madam, for I do long to get into the fields and skip and chirp like a grasshopper. Where is it, and when shall we set out?

MISS OBSOLETE. As soon as you can get ready. See here—read this letter—this charming letter. [*Gives a letter.*]

JANE [*reads*].

Honored madam:

Hearing of your kind dispositions to the poor, I make bold to address you with my sad tale of woe. I lost my husband at the great victory of the Nile, a long time ago. I have five small children, one deaf, another blind, and my situation prevents me from doing anything for their support. Honored madam, if you will honor me with a visit, and bring with you some coffee, tea, and sugar, you will have an opportunity of witnessing the truth of my statement.

Your unfortunate petitioner,
ELIZABETH DUMPS.

P.S.—My son little Billy, who is a cripple, will show the way, if you honor me with a visit. P.S.—Honored madam, you will do me a great favor, if you will let the tea be Souchong, as my nerves will not bear green tea, and the sugar, loaf sugar, for I am a little particular in these matters. If you are afraid to come by yourself, bring Miss Warfield with you. I hear she is very charitable.

MISS OBSOLETE [*eagerly and delighted*]. There—there, Jane—did you ever hear such a delightful tale of woe? A widow with five children, one dumb, deaf and crippled. I must positively go immediately—I wouldn't miss the sight for the whole world. I'd rather see it than the coronation.

JANE. Indeed, madam, to tell you the truth, though I have but little experience in these matters, this seems to be one of those tales expressly got up to impose upon your goodness of heart. They say, indeed, that misfortunes seldom come single, but here are half a dozen pairs, all following at the heels of each other. I can't help doubting the whole story.

MISS OBSOLETE. My dear Jane, you must positively go, or I shall think you hard-hearted—I can't go without you—it will be such a beautiful sight. I've got the tea and the sugar, and the coffee—and little Billy is waiting at the door with them. You never saw such a beautiful cripple.

JANE. Well—How far does he say it is?

MISS OBSOLETE. O, just at the skirts of the town.

JANE. But hadn't we better take a servant, or ask Mr. Obsolete to go with us? I don't like the idea of being escorted by little Billy alone.

MISS OBSOLETE. No—no—my brother won't hear of such things ever since I took his daughter to the Penitentiary to see some bad women that talked of being good—And besides, I forgot to tell you—little Billy says—[*Whispers in her ear.*]—and don't like to be seen by the gentlemen.

JANE. Well—the motive must excuse the act. I would not willingly forego the chance of doing good, but I really dislike this strolling about the skirts of the city alone.

MISS OBSOLETE. Mercy upon us, Miss Jane, do you suppose I would lead you into any impropriety? You'll meet no Bucktails there, I promise you, nor any of those desperate knights that run away with beauteous and rich damsels in romance. Our present race of beaux are not quite so enterprising. I believe they'd rather run away from me than with me at any time.

JANE. Well, madam—go with me to the next room, where I will get ready, for this piece of lady-errantry. But why not order your carriage?

MISS OBSOLETE. O, that would look like an ostentatious display of charity, you know. Lord Noland just now offered to send a hack to the door, which Billy says we shall be obliged to leave at some little distance; so his lordship desired me to take a female companion. [*Exeunt.*

SCENE 3. *A Room in the Hotel*

JONATHAN *and* PADDY WHACK

PADDY. As I was saying, Governor Peabody, I've been looking for you all about town. I want to speak to you.

JONATHAN. I calculate I've not been out this blessed day. I wonder you didn't find me at home before now.

PADDY. Faith, it never came across me that you might be at home till I'd looked for you everywhere else, honeycomb.

JONATHAN. Why, I should guess it was nateral to look for a man first at home, Mr. Whack.

PADDY. Booh! That only shows your ignorance. My master, who is a lord, is always out, or never at home when he isn't; and I his man am just as seldom there as a bishop at his church.

JONATHAN. May be so—but what might your business be with me, Mr. Whack?

PADDY. Why, governor, I came to talk over the affair of the governorship, you as good as promised me.

JONATHAN. Um—I guess I remember you didn't finish your biography. I think you said you came over in the King's suit?

PADDY. Right—I belonged to the court.

JONATHAN. Did you now, by gum—marry?

PADDY. Marry? No, marry I did not—I left my sweetheart in Ireland, and came over a single jontleman, governor.

JONATHAN. Sartin?—Ay, I've heard that neither witches nor women have any power over men when the water is between 'em. But how did you come?

PADDY. Faith, as an attaché, I think they call it. I attached myself to the fat assistant cook of the royal squadron, in which capacity I gain'd the good will of a certain great lord, who had been an old clothesman in his time. He took me into his service when we landed, upon account of my wardrobe.

JONATHAN. Um—I guess he was smitten with your old clothes, Mr. Whack.

PADDY. You say right, bully governor, but it proved the ruin of our friendship.

JONATHAN. How so, Mr. Whack?

PADDY. Why, as bad luck would have it, I caught my lord one day robbing my trunk of a pair of old breeches, and sundry other articles of no value but to the owner.

JONATHAN. I reckon what's bred in the bone, Mister Whack, is apt to stick in the flesh, even of a lord. By the way, you seem to have a *power* of lords here.

PADDY. Plenty, dear—There's but one lord above, and thousands below. Howsomever, finding my lord not to be trusted, I discharged him, and got with another lord, who hired me on account of my skill in elopements.

JONATHAN. Lord Noland, may be?

PADDY. Right, governor—I believe you were born by guess, you're such a great hand at it. We've an elopement on hand just at present. [*Bell rings.*]

JONATHAN. You don't say so? But I hear my pupil's bell ring, and reckon he wants my advice. So good day, Mr. Whack.

PADDY. I hope you are pleased with my biography, governor? My sarvice—good day to you. I'll call again tomorrow, if the elopement will permit me that honor.

JONATHAN. Do so, Mr. Whack—Um—An elopement—I guess I begin to—Um—That Lord Noland, to my sartin knowledge, has been casting sheep's eyes at Mister Henry's sweetheart, Miss Jane. I snore I reckon he wants to be sweet upon her. Um—I'll pump Paddy Whack the next time we meet—I will, by gum. [*Exit.*

SCENE 4. *A Wood*

LORD NOLAND, *and three ill-looking fellows. A carriage seen in the back-ground*

NOLAND. I have made sure that Miss Warfield accompanies the good lady. [*Whistle.*] Hush!—the signal! The game approaches—be quick, silent and steady! Confound that blundering Irishman, to be absent now! I'm afraid he has played the traitor. Faith, perhaps it's all the better; the rascal would be just as likely to mistake, and carry off the old woman instead of the young one. [*Another whistle.*] Whisht! they come. Use no unnecessary violence, and when the prize is safe, away for life to St. Briaval's Castle in the forest. I must not be seen. [*Retires, and the three* RUFFIANS *hide behind the trees.*]

Enter MISS OBSOLETE, JANE *and* BILLY, *an ill-looking imp, lame*

MISS OBSOLETE. Why, Billy! I protest I'll not go a step further. You're a perfect will-o'-the-wisp for leading people astray. I'll not stir a step further, Billy!

BILLY. It's jist nigh hand, now—it's jist t'other side the woods—this path leads to it.

JANE. I begin to distrust this boy;—some mischief is on foot, I fear. The place is so lonely, and there's not a house or a human being in sight, madam. I'm almost sure I heard a whistle just now.

MISS OBSOLETE. A whistle! mercy on us! That's just like a story of robbers! Billy, you look like a good boy, and have the most graceful limp—Billy—I hope you don't mean any harm. A whistle!—Mercy upon me—O dear! Billy.

BILLY. It's ony my brother Sim. Brother Sim's fond of moosick, and blows the whistle all day long. We're nigh hand, now—This way, ladies—here's the path—hem!

[*During this scene the three* RUFFIANS *are seen peeping from behind the trees, and making signs to each other. At the signal of* "Hem" *made by* BILLY, *they rush out and seize* MISS WARFIELD, *who faints.*]

MISS OBSOLETE. Thieves! murder! fire! rape! [*Falls on her knees.*] B–B–Pray, good Mr. Highwayman, don't rav—I mean murder me, for I'm a great friend to all sorts of criminals—Thieves! murder! rape! O! Billy! Billy! I'll never trust to a lame leg again—Thieves! Th—

FIRST RUFFIAN. Silence, you old Tabby—d'ye see this? [*Holds a pistol.*]

MISS OBSOLETE. I'll not breathe a whisper—indeed I won't—Old Tabby!—Th—Ah!—pray, sir, don't shoot me!—I promise to sign a petition for your pardon whenever you are condemned to be hanged. Thieves! Th—

FIRST RUFFIAN. Quiet, you old Tabby—It's not you, nor your money, nor your vartue that's in danger. Be quiet, and no harm shall come to you.

During this scene the two other RUFFIANS *place* JANE, *who still continues insensible, in the carriage, which drives off.*

SECOND RUFFIAN. Come—come away. It's all finished—Leave the old Tabby alone. There's no danger anybody will run away with *her*. [*Exeunt* RUFFIANS *with* BILLY.

MISS OBSOLETE. Old Tabby! marry come up—a set of polite gentlemen! Nobody will run away with *me*, forsooth! I'd have the brute to know I can be run away with whenever I please. [*Fanning herself violently.*] Old Tabby!—the unmannerly wretches, to show such a preference to one lady before another. But—mercy on us!—I forgot—Thieves! Robbers! Rapes! Billy!—Miss

Jane! O Lord, what will become of me! Thieves! Rob—Old Tabby! marry come up, forsooth! Th— [*Runs out.*

END OF ACT FOURTH

ACT V

Scene i. *A Garden*

Mary, *alone*

Mary. I wish I could get that young fellow out of my head, or perhaps I may as well tell the truth, now there is nobody to listen—out of my heart. Heigho—I begin to believe in love at first sight, for I have only known him three weeks, and am already far gone. I fear I've caught the infection from the New World, where they say everything grows up in a hurry—Heigho! [*Sighs and muses.*]

Frank *leaps over the wall*

Frank. Don't be alarmed, I beseech you. I just borrowed your cousin Cupid's wings, and like our little humming bird flew into your garden, to sip the dews of the morning from the bud of the rose.

Mary. Really, Mr. Tudor, you make yourself no stranger. Assist me, my sex's dear ally Hypocrisy. [*Aside.*] And now, sir, permit me to request that you will avail yourself of my cousin Cupid's wings to fly out again as soon as possible.

Frank. What! and leave the honey-dew unsipped? You cannot be so cruel. Since we parted last I have not slept; I cannot sleep or think, but of one thing. My spirit hovers and flutters about you, like a bird around its nest, and can you blame me that my body follows?

Mary. Really, sir, if you had not told me freedom of speech was the birthright of every American, I should be tempted to give your forwardness a very different name. Leave me, sir, and learn to respect the privilege of woman to be alone at pleasure.

Frank. What, in a garden? That's not according to Scripture. Remember Eve had a companion in Eden.

Mary. Yes, two—the man and the serpent, twin brothers and equally dangerous. But enough of this. Do the women of your country permit such freedoms?

Frank. Why—ay—yes—hush—on special occasions.

Mary. And what are these special occasions?

Frank. Why—why—when they can't help it. But don't drive me away, I beseech you. In a few days I shall be obliged to leave you, never perhaps to meet again. The present moment is all I have, and if I am in too great haste, 'tis but the drowning man catching at—

Mary. Straws? Thank you, sir—[*Courtesies.*]

Frank. No—life and happiness. Last night I dared to tell you of my love. You did not spurn me. Nay, I thought I saw you blush; and if my ears did not deceive me, I heard a gentle sigh, answering like whispering leaves, when Zephyrs woo them, with sweet assenting welcome. Do not, ah! do not crush the hopes that cheered me all last night, and made the misty morning bright as my native skies. Don't crush the heart you've won.

Mary. I can't play the hypocrite much longer. [*Aside.*] My winning has been like the gamester's, with a single throw, and your love has grown up like the mushroom, in a single night. Do you think I am a fool to believe such wonders?

Frank. Ah! gentle lady! hast thou yet to learn,
Love is no child of Time, unless it be
The offspring of a moment?
True love requires no blowing of the spark
To light it to a bright consuming flame.
To linger on through years of sighing dolor;
To write, to reason, to persuade, to worry
Some cold heart into something like an ague—
An icy shivering fit—this is not love;
'Tis habit; 'tis like that we often feel
For some old tree, because we've known it long.
'Tis to put out the feeling heart to nurse,
Or send it like a lazy schoolboy forth,
Unwilling to learn his A B C
Under some graybeard flogging pedagogue.
Time's office is to throw cold water on—
Not feed the flame with oil.

So the old poets sing, when wooing Truth
From Love and Inspiration.

MARY. Well, sir, you know, I suppose, that blank verse is neither rhyme nor reason, and cannot hope to convince without one or the other. I'll try him. [*Aside.*] Say, if I could find in my heart to love you, as it were extempore—what then?

FRANK. A wedding, and an age of happiness.

MARY. Would you then forsake your country?

FRANK. Ah!—do not undervalue my true affection if I should pause at this. Long before I saw you, my country was my darling. Her waving woods, her boundless fields, her freedom, and the generous plenty that reigns throughout her vast circumference, have, till now, made her my only mistress. Nay, the very scorn which the proud slaves of kings have cast upon her dear and honored name, has made me love her a thousand times more than if they had overwhelmed her with their hollow praise. O! such a country—if you were but there!

MARY. But there I cannot be—even if I wished it. My dear father has no wife, no kindred, and I might say perhaps no friends, to take care of him when I am gone. What if the world scoffs at his little whims and foibles? 'Tis only reason that I should love him the more, since the world's laugh is food for true affection. I would not leave him though I died for love.

FRANK. By Heaven, I only love you the dearer for that thought. Who would trust a wife that, as a daughter, forgot a duty that a score of years had brought to its full growth? She that forgets her duty to a parent will never learn it for a husband.

MARY. I'm glad you think so. [*Sighs.*]

FRANK. But perhaps he will go with us, and live to see his race prolonged in the land where I trust they will be free till Doomsday; to see each thrifty sprig shoot to an oak deep rooted in the soil, a lord of the creation; or a blooming girl, as lovely as thyself, the mother of the Gracchi.

MARY. What airy dreams are these? My father is too old to seek a new world and new objects.

FRANK. Trees grow most thrifty, and bear the choicest fruit when transplanted, and why not men?

MARY. Ay, but you know that trees transplanted too late, never take root again. So with men.

FRANK. But there will be such novelty for him—Tumuli—old fortifications—ay, and mummies, too.

MARY. You cannot love me, if you jeer at my father.

FRANK. Forgive me—pray, forgive me. But if you consent, the rest is nothing. He'll follow you to the world's end, as the shepherd follows his pet lamb. Trust me, he'll go.

MARY. But I have not yet said I will go.

FRANK. O! but you will, you must, you shall. Say you will go if he will.

MARY. My answer follows his. [*Exit hastily.*

Enter OBSOLETE

OBSOLETE. I don't like this stealing away, not I. Among the ancients it was held a *sequitur*, that when a young woman ran away from her father, the next step would be running away with her lover. I'll sound this juvenile novelty. Pray, Mr. Tudor, what think you of my daughter, marry?

FRANK. Marry? Faith, sir, that was just what I was thinking of. Your daughter is an angel.

OBSOLETE. You admire her, then?

FRANK. Admire? I adore her. She has referred me to you for an answer to a question of a very interesting nature, sir.

OBSOLETE. Indeed! I hope it relates to antiquity.

FRANK. No, sir. Unfortunately it relates to something very young and beautiful, that I wish to beg of you—your daughter, sir.

OBSOLETE. Marry, that's a modern idea, indeed. But harkee, Mr. Tudor, to convince you I'm a reasonable man, and a kind father, I hereby give my full and free consent—

FRANK. O! sir, you overwhelm me with gratitude!

OBSOLETE. Don't be in too great a hurry to be grateful—To your immediately quitting this place, and never seeing my daughter more.

FRANK. But, sir, may I ask what are your objections? To my fortune?

OBSOLETE. Marry, yea. I'm told it is all in new lands, and I hate new lands.

FRANK. To my character?

OBSOLETE. Marry, yea. You've no mystery about you—no hieroglyphical obscurity. One can read you at first sight, like a modern book. Now I hate anything that everybody can understand.

FRANK. My person, sir?

OBSOLETE. Marry, yea. You're not in the least like a mummy, or like one of our fashionable young fellows, who look as old as their family pictures before they come to years of discretion. You've no mark of antiquity about you.

FRANK. But perhaps your daughter may not object to that, sir.

OBSOLETE. But I do, sir, and that's quite as much as to the purpose. I always give a preference to old wine, old fiddles, old friends, and, in short, everything old.

FRANK. Except women, Mr. Obsolete. Miss Warfield, for example. But seriously, sir, if you find any fault in my conduct, I'll turn over a new leaf.

OBSOLETE. A new leaf? That phrase does your business. If you had promised to stick to your old ways, they might in time have become respectable by age. You're not in my book, Mr. Tudor; there's not a new leaf there.

FRANK. Alas! sir, if you don't like me as I am, and won't permit me to change, my case is indeed desperate. But I will live in hope. You may in time become reconciled to my being neither a mummy, a hieroglyphic, or a black-letter volume, and look upon me in a new light. Farewell, sir.

[*Exit.*

OBSOLETE. New light! There it is, again. Everything is new with these natives of the New World. I wonder what has become of Miss Obsolete, who was out all last night? But I suppose she was with her accomplice Mrs. Toogood, plotting as usual the encouragement of idleness, poverty and vice, under cover of charity. Pray Heaven she is not shut up in Bridewell, or the poor-house!

Enter MISS OBSOLETE. *Her clothes draggled, &c.*

MISS OBSOLETE. O, brother, brother—I've had such an escape. I've been—

OBSOLETE. Mistaken for a pauper, I suppose, or some one of those compunctious criminals you're so fond of keeping company with, and carried to the Bridewell?

MISS OBSOLETE. Bridewell, indeed? No such good luck, brother. I've been like to be run away with.

OBSOLETE. The d—l you have! What mortal man undertook that feat?

MISS OBSOLETE. Why, you must know, little Billy—

OBSOLETE. And who in the name of wonder is little Billy?

MISS OBSOLETE. Why, little Billy, whose mother lost her husband, seven brothers, and twelve sons, in the last war—

OBSOLETE. Hum—well, what next?

MISS OBSOLETE. Why, he brought me the most affecting letter! and so I took Miss Warfield with me to see the poor woman—

OBSOLETE. Well—well—

MISS OBSOLETE. Well, little Billy led us over the fields, the Lord knows where, till we came to a wood, where twelve ruffians armed with pistols rushed out, and were going to carry me off. But they made a mistake, and left me alone by myself.

OBSOLETE. Alone by yourself!—Why, what is the woman talking about?

MISS OBSOLETE. Why, little Billy ran away—and they forced Miss Jane into a post-chaise, and drove off with her.—O! that ever I should live to be called an old Tabby!

[*Weeps.*]

OBSOLETE. Good Heavens! You say they forced her away in a post-chaise—Why—

MISS OBSOLETE. Yes—and called me an old Tabby. [*Weeps.*]

OBSOLETE. What can this mean? I begin to suspect some mischief. Did she seem to go willingly?

MISS OBSOLETE. No, they forced her away, I tell you—and called me old Tabby—and swore they'd shoot me if I didn't stop mewing. [*Weeps.*]

OBSOLETE [*apart*]. Forced away!—doubtless

by some admirer of antiquity who has read of the abduction of Helen, and wishes to revive the good old customs of antiquity. Who can it be?

MISS OBSOLETE [*whimpering*]. Old Tabby—old Tabby!

OBSOLETE. D—n old Tabby—I beg pardon, sister. I didn't mean any personal reflection. Who can it be? Hum—ah! I have it—Lord Noland. I know he admires her fortune, and is desperately, not in love, but debt. My life on it, 'tis he. My sprightly Jane!

MISS OBSOLETE. Old Tabby! old Tabby! [*Whimpering.*]

OBSOLETE. Pshaw!—A stranger too, in a strange land, and committed to our protection by her sister in her absence. Love, honor, patriotism all combine to inspire me to follow, and if possible rescue her. Hum—yes—I will immediately to Sir Kit and the admiral. We'll scour the country far and wide; rescue my sprightly Jane, and then trust to her gratitude for rewarding at least one of us. Where's my daughter?

MISS OBSOLETE. In her chamber, crying her eyes out.

OBSOLETE. Ah! there's another pretty affair. I must take her with me, or there'll be another elopement before I get back. Sister, take care of the house—I go in pursuit of my sprightly Jane. [*Exit.*

MISS OBSOLETE. Well, take thy ways for an old gray goose—I'll go and tell Mrs. Toogood all about it—except the old Tabby. [*Exit.*

SCENE 2. *The Street*

Enter PADDY WHACK, *fuddled*

PADDY. So, Mister Whack, you're in a pretty sort of a botheration, I take it. You must be drinking at the tavern instead of minding your master's business—and disgracing your country by neglecting a love affair. Fait, now I should like to meet some ill-looking knave, that I might be revenged for this blunder of mine, by bating him soundly. But I'll have satisfaction of somebody, I'm resolved. Look you, Mr. Whack, you must needs be drinking, must you? There's for that [*Cuffs one cheek.*]—and neglecting your master's business—there's for that, Mr. Whack [*Cuffs the other cheek.*];—and you must be staggering about the street instead of being in the country, tending upon the elopement—you great blundering blockhead—Take that, honey, for your pains—[*Knocks himself down.*]—Fait—I think you've got your bitters now, Mister Whack.

Enter JONATHAN

JONATHAN. Why, tarnation, Mr. Whack, what are you arter now, there! This beats all the assaults and batteries I ever heard on, in my country. Can't you find some better employment than knocking yourself on the head?

PADDY. Honey governor, jist lend me a hand to get up, and mingle your briny tears with mine. Och! I've jist miss'd the prettiest affair of an E–elopement—that's the word. I'm the most disconsolate jontleman. Ill luck follows me like an intermitting faver—a little space of health, and then slap-dash comes the quaver again. I shall fall away into an extemporary skeleton, Governor Hebiddy.

JONATHAN. No, sure! But you say you've had an elopement, Mr. Whack.—How d'ye make that out?

PADDY. Why, as asy as kiss your hand, governor.—My master, Lord Noland, is jist run away from me with a young lady. I don't know what will become of him, not I, without my discretion in this business. I met the old jontleman, Mr. Ob–Obsolete jist now, who ax'd me after my lord, and I told him all about the elopement, in hope he would put me on the track, but he only called me a prepasterous Paddy, and cut me quite unhandsomely.

JONATHAN. Now you don't say as much? But what may the lady's name be, and what is my lord going to do with her? I guess he can't sell her, as they do kidnapp'd negers?

PADDY. Sell!—why her name's—her name's Miss Jane Warfield, the young Bucktail lady—and my lord is going to do with her —[*Laughs.*] By the powers, governor, you must be a green one not to know what they run away with women for now-a-days.

Money—money—what the French call *large-on*, governor.

JONATHAN. And where is my lord going to carry her—maybe?

PADDY. Why, to a great big wood, yonderways.—I think they call it a forest, with an old wreck of a castle in it belonging to his lordship's ancestors, governor.—But hub-a-boo—here am I talking all this time when I ought to be taking care of the young lady.—By St. Patrick, if my master misuses her, I'll be into his mutton—I must be after him straight—[*Staggers.*]

JONATHAN. Crooked, you mean, I guess.—But Mr. Whack, what's your hurry?—Hadn't you better take somebody with you?—Hum—There'll be likely robbers in this wood—or great wild beasts, bears, wolves, catamounts and the like. Suppose we go to Mr. Tudor, and ask him to lend a hand.—He's right good-natur'd, and will start with us, I dare snore.

PADDY. Snore! You'd better be wide awake, governor.—But I dare say my master will be delighted with this new reinforcement—the more the merrier—

JONATHAN. Yes—but the less the better sheer—I guess—

PADDY. That's a niggardly notion, governor—But come along, honey—D'ye understand the use of firearms, governor?

JONATHAN. The rifle a little, I reckon—I've liv'd in the back parts something. I'm half horse, half alligator, and a little of the *Ingen*, I guess.

PADDY. The divil you are! Then you're the very man for my money—Come along, governor. It's growing dark already, and there's no time to be lost.

[*Exeunt hastily.*

SCENE 3. *A Parlor*

OBSOLETE, MARY, SIR KIT *and the* ADMIRAL

OBSOLETE [*ringing*]. My horses are snails, and my people sloths.—[*Rings again.*]

ADMIRAL. This is a wild goose chase, sir knight. Faith, I don't half like it.

SIR KIT. But consider the prize, admiral. If we recapture the lady, what glorious salvage! I wouldn't take twenty thousand for my share.

MARY. I wish to Heaven they would make haste. Poor Jane! I fear we shall never overtake her till too late.

OBSOLETE [*worrying about*]. One would think the fellows were breaking the horses, and building the carriage. Hark! I think I hear it drawing up.—No—it's only a hack passing—confound this delay! [*Rings.*]

Enter SERVANT

SERVANT. Sir, the carriage is ready.

OBSOLETE. Then let's be gone! Harkee, sir—Order the carriage to drive to the small alehouse, on the skirts of the forest hard by, and let the lamps be lighted. Come, Mary—

ADMIRAL. Well, if I miss stays this time, I'll never go to sea again. [*Exeunt.*

SCENE 4. *A Forest at Night*

Enter HENRY, FRANK, PADDY *and* JONATHAN *armed; the latter with a rifle*

PADDY. Och! for a walking fire, or a bit of a Jack a lantern, if it be only to show us the way into another ditch—I've been in fifteen already. A big fiend with saucer eyes would be tolerable in this outer darkness. Now I'd give one of my lord's guineas, he promised me, to know how we lost our way.

JONATHAN. And I'd give another to know how to find it again, Master Whack.

FRANK. Faith, brother, we seem like two great metaphysicians, that after disputing their way through all the snares of argument, end just where they began. I do believe this is the very bramble that disputed my passage some time ago. I think I know the touch.

HENRY. Well, Frank, as you've no mistress in the case, I'll forgive you if you decline advancing a foot further.

FRANK. Say no more, dear Hal, I'd follow you if every step brought me so much nearer the grave. [*Hallooing heard in the wood.*]

HENRY. Hark! I hear the sound of voices at a distance. Be silent, and let us follow the direction. [*Exeunt.*

SCENE 5. *Another Part of the Forest*

Enter OBSOLETE, MARY, SIR KIT *and the* ADMIRAL

OBSOLETE. How unfortunate that we should be benighted, and lose our way. This is a perfect Hercynian forest. It's more intricate than the Hebrew Points.

ADMIRAL. Faith, you may say that. I'd sooner navigate the frozen sea, without compass or chart, than this confounded wood at night. For a man dismasted like myself, it's the very devil.

SIR KIT. Tut, admiral—don't you see the advantages of a wooden leg here? You've only to put that foremost, and these cursed briers that tickle me so delightfully, will give way before you. You ought in conscience to go first and make a path for us.

OBSOLETE. My poor girl, how fares it with you?

MARY. O, never mind me, sir—let us get on as fast as we can.

[*Hallooing heard in the wood.*]

OBSOLETE. Hark! 'tis the keepers going their rounds in the forest. If they catch us at this time of the night, we shall be taken for deer-stealers, caught in actual commission of dog-straw, stable stand, back bear, and bloody hand. Let's away, or we shall be transported at least.

SIR KIT. Yes, in faith—stealing a doe is felony, while stealing a young lady is a mere flea-bite, now-a-days. [*Hallooing again.*]

OBSOLETE. Again! Let's get out of the way; they seem to approach nearer. My arm, Mary. [*Exeunt.*

SCENE 6. *Another Part of the Forest*

Enter JANE, *pale and fatigued*

JANE. Alas! alas! I seem to have escaped from man, only to perish in the wild wood. I dare not call, for fear of being overheard by the ruffian crew I left drinking in the ruined old castle, and yet, if I stay here alone, Heaven knows what will become of me. Alas! whither shall I go? O! Henry, where art thou? Does he know that I am in danger of being lost to him forever?

[*A clock at a distance strikes three.*]

One, two, three. Thank Heaven, 'twill soon be daylight. I'll follow the direction of the sound; it must lead to some inhabited place.

[*Hallooing at a distance.*]

Heavenly Powers, protect me! they come!

[*Runs out.*]

Enter LORD NOLAND *and three* RUFFIANS

NOLAND. Infernal blockheads! knaves and fools combined—how came you to let her escape?

FIRST RUFFIAN. Why, please your honor, we just sat down at the old castle to drink to your lordship's happy marriage, when she somehow contrived to flit by us without being seen—and ran away into the forest. For my part, I believe she is a witch, and made herself invisible—don't you, Tom?

SECOND RUFFIAN. Ay, dammee—She couldn't have got off else, without our seeing her.

NOLAND. You careless scoundrels! Must a man trust his fortune and reputation to such drunken curs?

FIRST RUFFIAN. Drunken curs? If Tom and I had been drunk, as you say, we should have seen double, and then one of us might have kept an eye on each of the ladies—Hey, Tom?

NOLAND. Silence, you ribald rascals!—Pshaw! I cannot do without them now, and must keep well with these wretches. Hark! let's follow—

[*Hallooing at a distance. Exeunt.*

SCENE 7. *A Church with a Graveyard*

Enter JANE

JANE. Behold! A Christian temple!—
Hail, dear asylum, I will rest me here,
Within the peaceful precincts of the dead!
If guilt and crime, hypocrisy and fraud,
In shrines like this from their just punishment
Have oft found refuge, I can't seek in vain,
That flee not from my own, but other's wrongs. [*Seats herself in the porch.*]
How solemn is the night! I, I alone
Here breathe among the dead of ages past!
See! where the stones point to the dust below,
And tell a tale of flattery, that would make
The bloodless corses blush if they could hear it.
Why should I tremble? "Dead men tell no tales,"
And such a scene seems fit for deeds of guilt
That never should be told!

But dead men do no harm, and ev'n the wretch
Whose harden'd soul ne'er shrunk before *His* eye,
Who sees all that is done, or will'd, or thought,
Quails at the glaring of the sightless corse,
And stands corrected by its mute cold lips,
That tell what all must come to.
I'll rest me here till morning.

Lightning and peals of thunder. By the flashes, JONATHAN *and* PADDY *are seen at the back of the stage.*

PADDY. Governor! Governor Hebiddy! By the powers, I think I saw a house or a church, by that flash. Burn the young Bucktail jontlemen, I say, for dividing this pretty party of pleasure. I knew we should lose our way.

JONATHAN. N—Yes—I guess you've a genius for that. If you'd studied ten years for a blunder, you couldn't have beat this, I calculate. [*Lightning and thunder.*]

PADDY. Och! murder—m—murder—Ye—ye—ye—O, b—b—b—

JONATHAN. What's the matter, Mr. Whack? —You seem partly thunderstruck.

PADDY. Thunderstruck!—If I ever saw a ghost in my born days, there's one setting in the church porch now—I saw it as plain as the white of my eye—[*Lightning.*]—There! there! there again—'tis surrounded by a hundred cats with eyes like lanterns—[*Lightning.*]—There! there! I see two dozen spirits capering in the fire—They must be evil spirits, or they wouldn't be there—[*Lightning.*]—There—there—there again—Why, governor, an't you afeard?

JONATHAN. I guess not—I wasn't born in the woods to be scared by an owl—nor brought up in the fear of ghosts. Let's go and see what it is, Mr. Whack.

PADDY. Tank you, master governor—I don't fear anything that's alive above ground, but I'm not in spirits to face a ghost.

JONATHAN. I swow I'll soon see whether it's a *spook* or no. [*Levels his rifle.*]

PADDY. Why, arrah, governor, I thought you knew more of mankind than to shoot at a ghost with a bullet of lead—If you havn't a silver one, you'll only be shooting flying, honey.

JONATHAN. I'll see, I guess—I never saw a *spook* yet that wasn't afraid of a rifle ball. Hollo there, mister, if you don't speak out, I calculate I'll shoot you, as sure as a gun.

JANE. Heavens! Who's that! Still chas'd like the wounded deer! Alas! is there no rest even among the dead?

JONATHAN. Sing out, I say, mister—or I shoot.

JANE. 'Tis some ruffian robber! O, what will become of me!

[*Flies in an opposite direction.* JONATHAN *fires.*]

PADDY. What a Judy you are, governor—I saw the ghost vanish, in a cloud of fire, just like a bird at a flash in the pan.

Enter HENRY *and* FRANK *alarmed*

HENRY. What gun was that?

PADDY. Why, the governor jist let fly at a ghost yonder at the church door.

HENRY. A ghost, you goose.—You've roused all the keepers of the forest by this time.—Let's away, or we shall be taken for poachers. [*Exeunt.*

SCENE 8. *An Old Ruined Castle*

Enter JANE

JANE. Is there no rest except in Heaven?—There seems a storm coming, and this ruin may shelter me the while—I'll venture. [*Looks in at an old dilapidated window.*] Ah! [*Shrieks.*]—now I am lost indeed!

As she starts back, some pieces of the ruin are displaced; part of the wall tumbles down, and discovers to the audience a group of ragged men, women and children, gathered about a fire. One of the men, dressed in tattered finery, advances and speaks.

KING *of the gipsy beggars.* What noise was that, Potluck?

POTLUCK. Nothing but the thunder, taking a few freedoms with your royal palace.

KING. But I'm sure I heard a voice! Run—skip—and see whether it isn't some spy.

[*Some go out and return with* JANE.]

JANE. Oh! for Heaven's sake—for the sake of mercy, don't murder me!

KING. Murder you, damsel!—O, no, we

never kill anything but fleas and other troublesome visitors.—We beg, borrow, and sometimes steal—but we never murder. Quiet thy fears, fair damsel. On my royal word, we'll take nothing from you—except what you are pleased to give.

JANE. In the name of Heaven, who and what are you?

KING. Gentlemen commoners—that belong to the most thriving commonwealth in the world. We are free from Scot and Lot—observe no law, pay no taxes—obey no authority—and fear nothing but the parish officers. In one word, we're stockant, whippant, rampant beggars, and I am their legitimate sovereign, at your service. Only give us what you have about you, and I pledge my royal word, we'll not rob you of the rest; and besides, "will beg a blessing on your head"—[*Whining.*]

[*The rest of the beggars whine out in concert*—"Bless your sweet face—bless your sweet face."]

JANE. O! only beggars—Heaven be praised! I'm safe now. [*Aside.*]—King!—I never heard the beggars had a king. [*Beginning to recover her sprightliness.*]—You don't look much like a king. [*Smiling.*]

KING. King, ay, damsel—though I don't look like one. And yet the difference betwixt a king and a beggar after all is only that between two bricks, one at the top, the other at the bottom of the chimney. But you seem tired—there's a bed of straw fit for a queen in the other room, and one of my maids of honor shall attend you.

JANE. Indeed, I am almost worn down. Shall I be safe?

KING. From man—I won't promise for the beasts, lady.

JANE. Well, I will try. In my proud days, how I should have shrunk from such a lodging—but fatigue makes equal the bed of straw and couch of down.

Exit with one of the women, more decently dressed than the rest. Then enter some beggars with PADDY *and* JONATHAN, *crying out*, "A prisoner! a prisoner!"

JONATHAN. Mister Whack, we're nabb'd, I guess.

PADDY. Faith, and I'm pretty sartin of it, governor.

KING. Two spies! That tall splice looks for all the world like a lean parish officer. I can smell him afar off, as crows do powder. Pray, fellows, what brought you here?

PADDY. A blunder—Mr. Robber.

KING. Robber!—Slave, if you say that again, I'll hang you for high treason. I will—Robber! Know, slave, that in me you behold the representative of royalty—sole monarch of millions of—fleas!

JONATHAN. No, sure?—You don't say so, I guess.—By gum, I've wanted to see the king ever since I came to this country.

KING. Then behold him now! Know, caitiff, that I reign by legitimate hereditary right—for my ancestor was one of King Charles' courtiers, who—

JONATHAN. Ay, King Charles—he who lost his head for slipping his bridle, I calculate.

KING. You do, do you?—and I calculate, if you dare to interrupt majesty again, I will consign you to a dark room, there to be put to the torture—by an Inquisition of fleas. I will—I say, slave—

JONATHAN. I'm no slave—I'm a free man, I guess.

KING. Silence, I say. Know that mine ancestors, one of them was a courtier, who gained a habit of begging, which descended to his posterity—and the other a maid of honor, who kept her virtue so snugly that nobody suspected she had any.

JONATHAN. O—ay—I guess that's being what they call a legitimate king?

KING. To be sure it is, varlet. Half the kings in the world can't show a better pedigree, if the truth were known. And as for begging, they get millions by it, where we get but pennies.

Hallooing, and enter beggars with OBSOLETE, MARY, SIR KIT, *and the* ADMIRAL

KING. Is the whole world abroad in the forest tonight? One would think I was to have a coronation, by the number of my visitors.

OBSOLETE [*looking about*]. What a venerable ruin! Saxon by the arches, fine—very fine!

ADMIRAL. The four winds take the ruin, and everything in it, say I—'Sblood! don't you see we're among a set of land pirates?

KING. Welcome—welcome, gentlemen, to my court—and if you'll only grant me a subsidy, or vote a poll-tax, I'll promise, on the word of a king, to entertain you royally—that is, at other people's expense. [*Aside.*]

OBSOLETE. Pray, sir, who are you? The lord of this castle, I suppose—Hem!—both a little out at the elbows. [*Aside.*]

KING. Yes—slave—the king!—You might kneel and kiss my hand, I think, sirrah!

OBSOLETE. A king!

KING. "Ay—every inch a king!" [*In a lofty style.*]

OBSOLETE. "Of shreds and patches," marry. [*Aside.*]

During this interval, PADDY *has been flirting with a beggar girl, and* JONATHAN *gazing out at a window, looking, as he says, for his master.*

PADDY. Faith, you're as pretty a creature as ever grew at the side of a ditch or a hedge, like a jewel in a pig's ear, mistress—[*Beckons.*] —this way, this way, honey. [*Whispers her—she shakes her head.*] You shall have a looking-glass all to yourself—[*Shakes her head.*] No! By the powers then, you ugly affair, but if I had you at home, I'd turn you over to the road masters, that they might make that rough face of yours passable.

OBSOLETE. And may it please your majesty, who are these worthy persons?

[*Pointing to the beggars in a corner.*]

KING. Courtiers, sir, courtiers.—This, now, is my prime minister. He's the keenest hand at raising the wind—that is to say, smelling out a new tax, in my whole kingdom. There's not a hedge that he don't assess for a shirt or a petticoat, and, like another Titus, he thinks he has lost a day if he hasn't cheated somebody.

SIR KIT. Cheated!

KING. Ay, marry, slave. What makes the great politician but superior skill in cheating? Men are slaves to fools; they to knaves; and knaves to wealth and power. The cheated and the cheats make up the body politic!

OBSOLETE. This fellow must be some satirist fresh from the pillory—[*Aside.*] And pray who is that gentleman yonder, so busy with his pencil and paper?

KING. That? O, that's my poet laureate. He's considered the best beggar in the commonwealth, and finds himself in sack and sugar by writing dedications and birth-day odes. He's now hard at a poem or poetical law-case, in which the devil is chief justice, and the ghost of a king defendant.

OBSOLETE. And this?

KING. That's my attorney-general, a learned limb of the law. 'Tis true the only cause he ever pleaded was when he was brought up for cozening a client. But then he's been up since so often before the justice, that I'll pit him against any Cicero of the Quarter Sessions.

OBSOLETE. And this?

KING. O, he's my first physician. He's had great practice in his day, I assure you, and this I'll be bold to say, not one of his patients ever complained of his skill.

OBSOLETE. Hem! I suppose not.—"Dead men tell no tales"—[*Aside.*] And this?

KING. This? mine oracle of Delphos.—If you wish to know what will happen to you a hundred years hence, she's your man, for a shilling.

OBSOLETE. Not I, marry.—But here's my friend Sir Christopher, a most learned physician, who is curious in these matters.

KING. Well, come forth, old second-sight. [*Waves to one of the crew.*] She knows what will come to pass, as well as any priestess of Apollo, living or dead—But what is worthy of note, she can never foretell the approach of a constable.

FORTUNE TELLER. Hold out your hand, your honor—[*To* SIR KIT.] Bless me, what a bloody palm! The fates ordain you'll be a great man-killer in your time, and at last come to be hung.

OBSOLETE. Ha! ha! ha! good.—The old sybil has hit the nail on the head. The English of all this is, that your practice will increase, and that your picture will one day be hung up in the medical college. Ha! ha! ha!

FORTUNE TELLER. Perhaps the young lady

here would like to have her fortune told—Ah! pretty soul, I warrant it has a dozen sweethearts. Give me your hand, pretty one.

OBSOLETE. Ay, do, Mary. 'Tis an ancient and venerable custom, that of consulting the oracle.

MARY. Excuse me, sir. What is written in the book of fate can neither be altered by the power, nor shunn'd by the prudence of man. Where, then, is the use of heeding it, dear father?

OBSOLETE. You say true, my girl. But here are we trifling away the time, while my sprightly Jane is in the claws of the ravisher. [*Thunder.*] Zounds, what a clap! 'Twere best stay where we are till morning dawns. Your court seems quite complete, may it please your majesty.

KING. Why, yes—except that we lack a lord high admiral. May be, sir [*To the* ADMIRAL.], you'd like the place? Your wooden leg would be a marvelous recommendation to my service.

[ADMIRAL *stumps away in a rage.*]

[HENRY *and* FRANK *appear in the wood, just outside the ruin.*]

KING. Whisht! I smell an officer! We shall have the whole *posse* upon us directly. Fly! skip like fleas, ye flea-bitten knaves. Meet me at the old hollow oak. Away! I'm not the first king that has been oblig'd to flee his dominions of late years. We're surrounded—Run! skip, ye imps!—away!

NOLAND *and his party appear during the foregoing speech on the opposite side to* HENRY *and* FRANK. *The beggars, who before appeared crippled and deformed, in various ways recover the use of their limbs, and disappear, jumping out of the windows, over the walls, &c., with great activity.*

OBSOLETE. Ha! ha! a miracle! What wouldst give, Sir Kit, for the power of working such astonishing cures of wooden legs, humpbacks, and crippled arms, hey!—But by the way, if the officers are coming, we'd better retire into the interior for fear of being confounded with his sacred majesty and his courtiers. Here's a door—follow me.

[*Exeunt omnes.*

HENRY *and* FRANK *without the castle walls on one side, and* LORD NOLAND *with his party on the other. Lightning and thunder at intervals.*

NOLAND. I see a light in the old castle. What can it mean?

FIRST RUFFIAN. Most likely the gipsy beggars—they've been about the forest lately.

NOLAND. Well, well, no matter what it is. We are armed, and I hear the rain beginning to patter.—Let's in awhile. [*Lightning.*] Whisht! I'm sure I saw two figures watching us yonder.

FIRST RUFFIAN. Where, my lord?

NOLAND. Whisht! Yonder.—This way, behind these stones. There's something brewing besides the storm. [*They retire.*]

HENRY *and* FRANK *advance*

FRANK. There seems something like a shelter here. 'Tis useless to wander about in the dark. There is a storm approaching. Let's in, and wait quietly till it is past.

HENRY. Well, well—I despair of finding her now.—O, God! what will become of her and me!

[*They go into the ruin, and* LORD NOLAND *and his party appear again.*]

NOLAND. 'Tis the Bucktail brothers! And doubtless in pursuit of the lady. I'll beard them, by this hand.

FIRST RUFFIAN. To what purpose, my lord? The lady is not in their possession, you see.

NOLAND. I care not, sir. I feel she's lost to me. By this time she's out of my reach—perhaps out of the reach of friend and foe. Living or dead, I'm baffled, disgraced and desperate.—Come on, let what will follow.

They enter. And the scene shifts at the instant to the inside of the castle.

SCENE 9

NOLAND. "'Tis I—Hamlet the Dane!"

HENRY. Rather say Lord Noland the ravisher—the gallant noble who wins a lady as thieves do lambs—by running away with them—But I've found you, thank Heaven!

NOLAND. Found *me*, sir? I sought you—I knew you were here. What then?

HENRY. In three words then, you're a villain.

Tell me where you have hid the innocent girl you stole from her friends in a land of strangers, or—

NOLAND. Or what then, sir?

HENRY. What then! Death to one or both of us; for by the worth of my immortal soul, one of us shall never leave this place alive.—We are both armed, and death or the lady is the word.

NOLAND. Look'ee, Mr. Tudor—we'll settle this matter at once. Miss Warfield is not in my possession—she escaped last night—I swear it, on the honor of a nobleman.

HENRY. The honor of a nobleman! Pish!—Escap'd, did she? Pshaw! But he who is ashamed of his actions, will seldom care about his words. Do not oblige me to believe you're a coward as well as a villain.

NOLAND. Very well—very well, sir! But I have injured you and will be patient as long as I can. To show you I am in earnest, I here offer to accompany you in search of Miss Warfield.

HENRY. Cold-blooded poltroon! Yes! to lead us astray from the place where you've conceal'd your prize! No, no, my lord, I parley no longer. Restore the lady, or take your distance. Our bullets will find their way by the light of this fire, I warrant you.

FRANK. And don't forget, my worthy lord, that if any accident happens to one brother, there's another one to settle the account with, principal and interest.

NOLAND. Say you so, my bully Bucktails? Come on then, and you precious mischiefs go your ways, and be silent, or I'll hang you all—Begone!—[*Exit* RUFFIANS.] I'll trust to your honor, gentlemen, for fair play, though you won't to mine. *Allons*—take your distance and give the word.

[*They take their distance and point their pistols, when* JANE *and the rest rush in and interfere.*]

JANE. Hold! hold! in the name of him who made the first murderer and his posterity wanderers on the face of the earth! Dear Henry, I am safe, and thine! [*Sinks down between them.*]

HENRY [*drops his pistol and supports her*]. Is it a blessed vision? No—it is my own, my sprightly Jane.—Here is thy shelter.—[*Embrace.*]

JANE [*after a pause*]. But you don't bid my kind friends welcome, who came, like you, to rescue me.

HENRY. Thanks to them all and blessings on their heads. But where was my treasure found?

OBSOLETE [*apart to* SIR KIT *and the* ADMIRAL]. It's all over with us now, so we may as well put a good face on the matter.—Why, Mr. Tudor, we found her fast asleep in the lap of a maid of honor.

FRANK [*apart to* NOLAND]. As my brother is better engaged, suppose you and I retire and settle the affair.—The day begins to dawn, and the sooner the better.

NOLAND. I owe you no grudge, sir—you've not robbed me of my mistress. Now do I see no special reason why I shouldn't go and hang myself on the next tree; yet still I cling to life like ivy to an old wall—the more decayed the closer it sticks—[*Aside.*] [*Then turning to* HENRY.] Mr. Tudor, you must have perceived that I dare fight even in a bad cause, and when I beg pardon, as I do now, of you and this injured lady, you will do me the justice to believe that not fear, but compunction and shame, have brought me to this avowal. Farewell—forgive me—and be happy. [*Exit.*

PADDY. Fait, governor, my master cuts such a figure, I'm asham'd to keep company wid him—so I'll stay and make interest for a government, I tink, with one of these Bucktail jontlemen. You see now, governor, what a providential thing is a blunder. If I hadn't lost my way with you all in the forest, you'd never have found the lady, honey.

JONATHAN. Y-e-s—I calculate I've known a heap of people stumble upon good luck, Mister Whack.

During the preceding, FRANK *and* MARY *have been talking in dumb-show.*

FRANK. And so, my lady-errant, you too went forth in pursuit of the stray damsel?

MARY. O, my father wouldn't leave me behind, in his absence.

FRANK. No! why not?

MARY. Why—why—he was afraid I might be run away with in the fashion.

FRANK. No! [*Smiling.*]

OBSOLETE [*observing them*]. Hum! If I don't take care there'll be more running away soon. Hum—Well, I've lost my sprightly Jane, that's clear—and must find my happiness in making others happy. Hum—If I stay at Bath, I shall be laugh'd at a thousand years hence for an amorous old knight-errant—Hum—It shall be so—Mary!

MARY. Sir! [*Confused.*]

OBSOLETE. Come hither, and you too, Mr. Bucktail.—How would you like a trip to the New World—Hey?

MARY. If—if—[*Hesitating.*]—if you'd go with me, sir.

OBSOLETE. Why, I don't know—this lad here has almost persuaded me. He talks of a mummy found in a cave in Kentucky. I should like to see if it resembles that of the Signior Belzoni.

FRANK [*eagerly*]. And then, sir—the ancient fortifications on the Ohio and Muskingum!

OBSOLETE. And the Tumuli—[*Rubbing his hands.*]

FRANK. And the people that talk Welsh!

OBSOLETE. And the unaccountable medal dug out of a well in the western country!—[*Rubbing his hands.*]

FRANK. And the ancient specimens of stone jars!

OBSOLETE. And the nation of pigmy skeletons three feet high! I'll go—I'll go, I'm resolved.—What a noble field for the antiquary! Harkee, young Bucktail—see if you can persuade my daughter.

FRANK [*kneels*]. Wilt thou?

MARY. Will I what?

FRANK. Will you go with me towards the setting sun, and be my mate in weal and woe?

MARY. I've told you I'll go anywhere with—my father.

OBSOLETE [*joining their hands*]. Then thus I pair you two little turtles for the woods. And now hey for the New World—'tis the land of unexplored antiquities.

JANE. And hey for the New World—'tis the land of free maids and happy wives.

PADDY. And hey for the New World—say I, 'tis the land of the exile, the foster-home of the poor Irishman!

HENRY. And hey for the New World—'tis "the land of the free, and the home of the brave!"

[*Exeunt omnes.*

END OF "THE BUCKTAILS"

SUPERSTITION

By James Nelson Barker

JAMES NELSON BARKER

[1784–1858]

James Nelson Barker was born of a family active and prominent in the political and social life of Philadelphia; he inherited some of his father's "fiery traits" of personality and profited by his father's influential political position, though the son, to be sure, possessed qualities of his own that would have secured him advancement in public life.[1] His birth in 1784 meant that he grew up during the period of strenuous political activity attendant upon the two wars with England, and as a consequence he tended to confuse patriotic and aesthetic standards, as did many of his contemporaries.[2] Evidence of this is suggested in Barker's second play, *America* (1805), a patriotic masque, and in his *Embargo; or, What News?* (1808) which contained "patriotic sentiments" in support of the current embargo bills.

Barker's career included service in the army, where he rose to the rank of major; activity in Philadelphia politics, which culminated in his election as mayor; and participation in governmental affairs at Washington, where he became Comptroller of the Treasury in 1838 under Van Buren. He had been active with the Democrats, had supported "Old Hickory," and was a decided anti-Federalist: "The Federalists have damped the powder—as they would damp the spirit of the nation." [3] "The salvation of the people rests with themselves." [4] The observer-playwright in him was not submerged by politics, however, for he regarded the gay social scene of the capital as a "fine field for the study of human character," [5] and managed occasionally to produce a drama. Barker continued his connection with the Treasury Department until his death, March 9, 1858.

According to Barker's own account of his plays given in a letter to William Dunlap,[6] he completed only one act of his first play, *The Spanish Rover* (1804), which concerned "a marquis and a banditti." This play Barker later committed to the flames. The second play, *America*, was a masque modelled in part after *The Tempest*, and his third play, *Attila*, was a tragedy based on Gibbon. Both of these plays have been lost. Barker's next attempt, *Tears and Smiles*, produced in 1807, was a distinct theatrical success. It is a sentimental comedy of manners

[1] A short biographical account of Barker appears in Henry Simpson's *The Lives of Eminent Philadelphians Now Deceased*. Philadelphia: 1859, pp. 26–28. The most extended study of his life and writings is Paul H. Musser's *James Nelson Barker* (Philadelphia: 1929) which contains a reprint of Barker's *Tears and Smiles*.

[2] See Spiller, R. E., review of Musser's *Barker*. *Modern Language Notes*, XLV, 407–409 (June, 1930).

[3] Musser, *op. cit.*, p. 38. Quotes letter of March 1, 1810.

[4] *Ibid.*, p. 41. Letter, undated.

[5] *Ibid.*, p. 32.

[6] Dunlap, *History of the American Theatre*. New York: 1832, pp. 376–380.

representing the contrast between the Frenchified American and one who has not yielded up his native simplicity and honesty; the play includes two widows, personifying "tears" and "smiles" respectively, and a stupid servant, Nathan Yank, obviously suggested by Jonathan in Tyler's *The Contrast* [1] and belonging to that long line of stage Yankees which was to follow. The international contrasts in *Tears and Smiles* are similar to those in Tyler's play and are a part of the contemporary thought which deplored the invasion of foreign influences at the expense of native American culture.

The Embargo; or, What News? already mentioned, was followed in 1808 by *The Indian Princess; or, La Belle Sauvage*, based on the story of Pocahontas as related by Captain John Smith. This latter play is one of the earliest of our Indian dramas.[2] *Marmion; or, the Battle of Flodden Field* (1812) reflects the vogue of Scott in America, though Barker used Holinshed's *Chronicles of England, Scotland and Ireland* in addition to Scott's poem. *The Armourer's Escape; or, Three Years at Nootka Sound* (1817) was a "melo-dramatic sketch" in two acts founded on the adventures of a ship armorer; Barker's comedy, *How to Try a Lover* (1817), suggested by a novel of Le Brun's, was not acted until 1836, when it was produced under the title, *A Court of Love*. This was the only play Barker was entirely satisfied with, though by common acknowledgment his last play, *Superstition*, is his finest.[3]

Like Longfellow's *New England Tragedies*, many years later, *Superstition* deals with the Puritan persecution of witches and nonconforming or opposing sects. Ravensworth embodies clearly the New England "witch-hunting" spirit which Professor G. L. Kittredge has analyzed so interestingly in his *Witchcraft in Old England and New*. According to Ravensworth, "the powers of darkness are at work among us"; Charles grew up "without one gleam of virtue to redeem"; and Isabella is a witch "swelling with earth-born vanity. . . ." In the view of Ravensworth it is Isabella who has brought "the afflictions which this groaning land is vex'd with." Ravensworth reconciles a belief in "the wonders of the invisible world" with the doctrines of his theology:

"Is there in our religion aught forbidding
Belief in sorcery!" [4]

And with the tenacity characteristic of the fanatic he hunts down his innocent victims until "mere suspicion" does "with a hint destroy," bringing unjust death upon them.

[1] Barker acknowledges in his letter to Dunlap that he "had never seen a Yankee at the time."

[2] Quinn, *A History of the American Drama from the Beginning to the Civil War*, p. 270.

[3] Quinn states: "With his last and greatest play Barker returned to his native country for a theme. . . ." (*Op. cit.*, p. 147.) Musser: "*Superstition* is without question the best of his plays." (*Op. cit.*, p. 96.) Contemporary comment was very favorable; the *Democratic Press* for March 17, 1824, says it was "received with the most flattering approbation."

[4] Act IV, sc. 1, p. 140.

But Ravensworth undermines the validity of his own point of view by false interpretation of fact and by his complete willingness to prefer charges without a shred of real evidence; community afflictions and hearsay are for him sufficient proof of witchcraft. His position is hardly strengthened by his entire oversight of Mary during the Indian raid; she is rescued by Charles, whose course of boyhood, according to Ravensworth, has been run

"Without one gleam of virtue to redeem
The darkness of his vices." [1]

Moderation and common sense characterize the point of view of Walford, who tries to mollify Ravensworth by appealing to his intelligence:

"Ah, my friend,
If reason in a mind like yours, so form'd,
So fortified by knowledge, can bow down
Before the popular breath, what shall protect
From the all-with'ring blasts of superstition
The unthinking crowd, in whom credulity,
Is ever the first born of ignorance?" [2]

He warns against the dangers of erroneous belief becoming widespread:

"Abstract points
In science, may be safely tolerated,
Altho' erroneous—But there may be doctrines
So fatal in their influence, that, until
Their truth is manifest, 'twere well not cast them,
With lavish hand, among the multitude." [3]

And Walford offers a rationalistic explanation of the source of superstition:

"The ignorant and envious
May find, in her superior intellect—
E'en in her ample wealth and proud reserve,
Food for their hate, and therefore their suspicion. . . ." [4]

Isabella, also, appeals to reason in defense of herself:

"Sorcery! Gracious Heaven!
Is it necessary, in this age of light,
And before men and Christians, I should deny
A charge so monstrous!" [5]

Even Ravensworth's daughter charges unfairness in the persecution of Isabella: "Her very virtues they distort to crimes"; and according to Charles, "Nothing is too ridiculous for those whom bigotry has brutaliz'd." As the play indicates,

[1] Act I, sc. 1, p. 128.
[2] Act IV, sc. 1, p. 140.
[3] Act IV, sc. 1, p. 141.
[4] Act I, sc. 1, p. 127.
[5] Act V, sc. 2, p. 147.

there was contemporary criticism of witch-persecution, but the arguments advanced and language used are nearer the eighteenth than the seventeenth century. The appeal to reason and knowledge, and such terms as "age of light" and "abstract points in science" suggest that Barker was reflecting the rationalistic thought current shortly before and partly during the period in which he was writing.[1]

True to the seventeenth century, and eighteenth as well, the thought of the play is ultimately theistic: the Unknown acknowledges God and even the "accursed" Isabella, "who scorns religion," prays to a power above.[2] The types of religious belief, however, differ appreciably. The Calvinistic philosophy of Divine wrath and punishment for sins is represented in Ravensworth's brimstone denunciations of Isabella and her son:

"Ye all remember
The terror and despair that fill'd each bosom
When the red comet, signal of Heaven's wrath,
Shook its portentous fires above our heads." [3]

When the thunderstorm crashes above the trial, Ravensworth interprets this as a sign from above:

"The angry Heavens—
Hark, how they chide in thunder!" [4]

On another occasion "death has been here guided by Heaven's vengeance." Chastisement is the inevitable consequence of sin: upon hearing of the Indian attacks, Ravensworth asks: ". . . Will you now believe, our sins bring these afflictions on us?"

Ironically (but perhaps plausibly) enough the opposing view of the Deity as merciful finds expression in the daughter of the Calvinistic minister:

"Sure, ah sure, Religion
Descends not like the vulture in its wrath;
But rather like the mild and gentle dove,
Emblem of peace and harbinger of joy,
Love in its eye and healing on its wing. . . ." [5]

Walford argues in behalf of man's weakness:

". . . surely, the necessity is pass'd
For trampling on our nature." [6]

As one might well expect, considering the scene of action and date of composition, both royalty and the court appear in the play in an unfavorable light.

[1] For an excellent study of eighteenth-century rationalism see Harry Hayden Clark's "An Historical Interpretation of Thomas Paine's Religion," *University of California Chronicle*, XXXV, no. 1 (Jan., 1933).

[2] . . . "God, to thee
The mother turns. Not for myself,
Not for my sinful self—but for my son—
My innocent son I plead. . . ."

[3] Act V, sc. 2, p. 147.

[4] Act V, sc. 2, p. 149.

[5] Act I, sc. 1, p. 125.

[6] Act I, sc. 1, p. 127.

George and his uncle brazenly pursue Mary; George openly avows that he fears "nor law, nor gospel . . . ," and Sir Reginald jestingly warns his nephew:

"You're not in London now, where our gay monarch
Sets such fine example, in these matters.
They'll have no poaching here, that I can tell you,
Among their wives and daughters." [1]

Referring to the regicides, Sir Reginald reports that Charles

". . . finds it decorous
To grow a little angry with the persons
That kill'd his father." [2]

It is Cromwell, naturally, who commands the respect of the Puritans:

"Your saints
Climb'd to high places—Cromwell to the highest—" [3]

Anti-royalist as the Puritans were, still, with their doctrine of the elect, they were not democrats in the Jeffersonian sense of the term; the wise Walford speaks of the "unthinking crowd" and warns against trusting the multitude with controversial and undemonstrated theories.

Socially we see the filial obedience, almost to the point of slavery, which prevailed in the Puritan families. Alice is

". . . content to follow
Where e'er our fathers lead," [4]

and when Ravensworth commands Mary to repent for having defended her lover, Charles, she meekly obeys.

The general concepts of liberality, intelligence, and patriotism underlying *Superstition* are consonant with Barker's expressed hope for the drama "that with a free people and under the liberal care of a government such as ours it might tend to keep alive the spirit of freedom; and to unite conflicting parties in common love of liberty and devotedness to country." [5]

According to Barker the central events of *Superstition* were "said to have actually occurred in New England, in the latter part of the 17th century . . . found recorded in the authentic history of that dark period." [6]

Other treatments of the same or related themes are Cooper's *The Wept of Wish-ton-Wish* (1829), Hawthorne's *The Gray Champion* (1833), Cornelius Mathews' *Witchcraft, or the Martyrs of Salem* (1846), and Longfellow's *Giles Corey* (1868).

The present text of the play follows the original edition published by Lopez and Wemyss in *The Acting American Theatre*, 1826.

[1] Act I, sc. 1, p. 128.
[2] Act I, sc. 1, p. 129.
[3] Act V, sc. 2, p. 148.
[4] Act I, sc. 1, p. 125.
[5] *Democratic Press*, December 18, 1816.
[6] Lopez and Wemyss edition of *Superstition*, 1826; prefatory note. For an able discussion of Barker's use of his sources see Musser, *op. cit.*, pp. 92–94, 215.

AUTHOR'S NOTE

The principal incidents of the following humble attempt at a Domestic Tragedy, are said to have actually occurred in New England, in the latter part of the 17th Century. If objections be made to the catastrophe as improbable, the best answer is, that such an event is found recorded in the authentic history of that dark period. The author would willingly have made his lovers happy, if, as a faithful chronicler, he could have done so; but he thought he was bound to give the story as he found it. Perhaps it may not be so well calculated for scenic representation; but it is still more likely that any failure observable in stage effect, may be owing to the author's want of dramatic skill.

DRAMATIS PERSONÆ

Performed (first time) at the Chestnut Street Theatre, Philadelphia, March 12, 1824

Sir Reginald Egerton .... Mr. Warren
George Egerton .... Mr. Wemyss
Ravensworth .... Mr. Darley
Walford .... Mr. Wheatly
The Unknown .... Mr. Duff
Charles .... Mr. Wood
Judge .... Mr. Greene
First Villager .... Mr. Hathwell
Second Villager .... Mr. Jones
Messenger .... Mr. Bignall
First Officer .... Mr. Johnston
Second Officer .... Mr. Murray
Edward .... Mr. Parker
Boy .... Master H. Mestayer
Second Judge .... Mr. Mestayer
Officer .... Mr. J. Mestayer

Villagers, Indians, Sups.

Isabella .... Mrs. Wood
Mary .... Mrs. Duff
Alice .... Mrs. Durang
Lucy .... Mrs. Greene
Female Villagers .... Mrs. Mestayer, Bignall, Murray, Misses Parker, Hathwells, Mestayers

Scene *in New England, about the year 1675*

Time, *a little more than Twenty-four hours*

SUPERSTITION

ACT I

SCENE I. *A Village at a little distance. In front, on the left of the Stage, the cottage of* RAVENSWORTH; *a handsome rustic building. A large mansion, on an eminence nearer the Village, on the right.*

Enter from the Cottage, MARY *and* ALICE

MARY. Nay, come away, dear Alice, every moment
Of your brief visit must be wholly mine;
Let's leave our fathers to their grave discourse
Of witch and wizard, ere we laugh outright.

ALICE. It is a subject that the country round
Deems a most solemn one.

MARY. True: but to me,
'Tis not the less absurd on that account.

ALICE. This levity's misplac'd: your father claims
Your love and reverence—

MARY. And I do revere him,
And love him dearly, Alice; do I not?
How often have I striven to melt his sternness;
And, when my heart was sick of its own cares,
Lock'd up my selfish sorrows from his view,
And tried, by every filial endearment,
To win his smiles. E'en when his brow was darkest,
I've brav'd its terrors; hung upon his neck,
And spoken of my mother: O how sweet
It were methought, even to weep with him.

ALICE. You're an enthusiast, Mary. Ah, beware,
Lest this impetuous current of your feeling
Urge you, one day, against the perilous rock.

MARY. I'm young, and youth is ardent, and should be
Cheerful, and full of bright and sunny thoughts;
I would be if I dared. You, too, are young,
Yet may be happy; for you have a parent
Who, tho' he guide you safely down the stream,
Does not, like angry pilots, chide, e'en louder
Than the loud storm.

ALICE. His high and holy office
May, haply give to your good father's manner,
A grave solemnity, perhaps, a harshness—

MARY. And why a harshness? Sure, ah sure, Religion
Descends not like the vulture in its wrath;
But rather like the mild and gentle dove,
Emblem of peace and harbinger of joy,
Love in its eye and healing on its wing;
With pure and snowy plumage, downy soft,
To nestle in the bosom of its votaries.

ALICE. I cannot argue; I'm content to follow
Where e'er our fathers lead. For you, I fear
You've learn'd too much from this mysterious stranger.

MARY. O Alice, join not you with the slanderous crowd,
Against a noble lady, whom you know not.
For me, be satisfied I never more
Perhaps, shall see her: I've obeyed my father;
And must, tho' it should break my heart: tho' Charles—[*Pauses.*]

ALICE. And what of Charles?

MARY. Her son—

ALICE. I know: her son,
And what of him?

MARY. This very day, 'tis said,
He will be here—

ALICE. Expell'd, they say, from college.

MARY. Disgraced—'Tis false: Charles cannot be disgraced;
If envy, persecution, drive him thence,
They but disgrace themselves, and not poor Charles.

ALICE. Mary?

MARY. Yes; take my secret; take it quickly,
Or it will burst my heart.

ALICE. Nay, but be calm.

MARY. You shall know all—surely you'll pity, Alice,
And perhaps, pardon me. Three years ago
When Charles's mother first came here to live;
From England, was it not—the village then
Had scarce begun to hate her, for as yet
She had not lavish'd charities abroad,
To purchase up ingratitude and envy.
Being her nearest neighbor, (my dear mother
Was then alive,) there rose at once between us
That intercourse which neighborhood compels
At times, e'en with the most reserved. The lady
I know not why, unless out of her goodness,
Graced me with her regard, and when my mother
Died, she took the desolate child to her bosom.

ALICE. 'Twas kindly done.

MARY. O she was goodness all,
Her words so sweet and soothing; as she spoke,
Alice, methought I saw my sainted mother
Lean o'er the bright edge of a silvery cloud
And smile upon her happy orphan girl,—
And there was Charles, so busy still around me,
Exhausting all his boyish gallantries,
With brotherly affection.—

ALICE. Charles, still Charles?

MARY. Can I forget it!—

ALICE. Nay, go on.

MARY. The winter
Soon pass'd away, and then the spring came on
With all its flowers, and still the earliest blossom
Was cull'd for me. O, we were then so happy—
I always lov'd the spring. Young nature then
Came to me like a play-mate. Ere the snows
Had left the hills, I've often wander'd forth,
And, all impatient for the verdure, clear'd
A patch of infant green; or even turn'd
With mighty effort, some recumbent stone,
To find the fresh grass under it.

ALICE. This is childish.

MARY. I was a child, then,—would I were e'en now,
As then I was—my life, I fear will prove
A wintry waste with no green spot to cheer it—

ALICE. More visionary still.

MARY. Well, to my story:—
My father took me home, I think it was
About the time you came into the village.
Fell superstition now had spread around.
Reports—I scarce know what they meant—arose
Concerning Isabella; and my father
Made gloomier by my mother's death, and yielding
His strong mind to the doctrine of the times,
Grew daily still more stern, until at length,
At peril of his curse, he bade me never
To hold communion with that family.

ALICE. And you obeyed?

MARY. All that I could, I did.
But O the tales they tell—the horrid stories—
Her very virtues they distort to crimes.
And for poor Charles, his manliness and spirit,
The gayety of youth and innocence,
In him are vices. Could I help defending,
Knowing them as I did:—all others hating,
Could I help loving!—

ALICE. Loving, Mary?

MARY. Ay; most deeply, strongly loving
Charles and his mother.

ALICE. But sure you have not seen this Charles?

MARY. Not often.—
Nay, frown not friend, for how could I avoid it,
When chance insisted on an interview?

ALICE. Have ye met lately?

MARY. Yes.

ALICE. What pass'd between you?

MARY. A plight of faith: A vow to live or die,
Each for the other.

ALICE. Lost, lost girl.

MARY. Why, ay,

It may be so; if so, 'tis Heaven's will.
You have my secret, Alice.

Enter from the House, RAVENSWORTH *and* WALFORD

ALICE. Peace; our fathers.
[*They retire into house.*]

RAVENSWORTH. No, Walford, no: I have no charity
For what you term the weakness of our nature.
The soul should rise above it. It was this
That made the fathers of this land prevail,
When man and the elements opposed, and win
Their heritage from the heathen.

WALFORD. True; the times
Impos'd a virtue, almost superhuman.
But surely, the necessity is pass'd
For trampling on our nature.

RAVENSWORTH. We have grown
Luke-warm in zeal, degenerate in spirit;—
I would root out with an unsparing hand,
The weeds that choke the soil;—pride and rank luxury
Spring up around us;—alien sectaries,
Spite of the whip and axe, infest our limits;
Bold infidelity, dark sorcery—

WALFORD. Nay,
Nay, Ravensworth—

RAVENSWORTH. I tell thee, Walford, yea:
The powers of darkness are at work among us.
Not distant we have seen the fagot blaze,
And soon the stake may ask its victim here.

WALFORD. What victim point you at?

RAVENSWORTH. Turn your eye—thither
Upon yon haughty mansion—you have heard?—

WALFORD. Much idle rumor.

RAVENSWORTH. Do you deem it so?
Whence then, and who is this imperious dame,
That holds herself above her fellow creatures,
And scorns our church's discipline: her means—
Her business here?

WALFORD. The ignorant and envious
May find, in her superior intellect—
E'en in her ample wealth and proud reserve
Food for their hate, and therefore their suspicion;
But for us, Ravensworth—

RAVENSWORTH. No more, ere long,
These questions must be answer'd.

WALFORD. Be it so;
I shall be ready in all lawful ways
To seek the truth.

RAVENSWORTH. 'Tis well, we soon may need you.
What public tidings hear you?

WALFORD. That King Philip
Our savage foe, after his late defeat,
Has gained his rocky hold, where he now lies,
With scarce a fragment of his former force.

RAVENSWORTH. Where are our troops?

WALFORD. They watch the enemy.

RAVENSWORTH. They should have followed up their victory,
To the extermination of the heathen.—
Has there aught chanc'd in the village?

WALFORD. There have arrived
Two persons from the court of Charles.

RAVENSWORTH. More vanity!
What do they here?

WALFORD. The elder, it is said,
Brings letters to the government. [*Crosses.*]

RAVENSWORTH. Charles Stuart,
Is growing much concern'd about the people
His family have scourg'd, hunted and driven
From shed and shelter in their native land.
We needs must thank that most paternal care,
That, when the expos'd infant climbs to manhood
Comes for the first time, then, to claim his service.

WALFORD. You broach a startling topic—
But the day wears—
Fare thee well, Ravensworth.

RAVENSWORTH. Farewell, farewell.
[*Exit* WALFORD.
Timid, weak minded man.

Enter MARY, *from House*

Come hither, daughter.

MARY. Father! [*Running to him.*]

RAVENSWORTH. What mean these tears?

MARY. I cannot check them.

RAVENSWORTH. They do displease me, tears can only flow
From frailty or from folly, dry them straight,
And listen to me. I have heard, the son
Of this strange woman is returning home,
And will again pollute our neighborhood;
Remember my command, and shun his presence
As you would shun the adder. If report
Err not, his course of boyhood has been run
Without one gleam of virtue to redeem
The darkness of his vices.

MARY. I'll obey—
To the utmost of my power.—But, my dear father,
May not report err sometimes? You were wont
To instruct me never to withhold the truth;
And fearlessly to speak in their defense,
Whom I could vindicate from calumny;
That to protect the innocent, the absent—

RAVENSWORTH. How's this! the innocent—and calumny?
And whence do you presume to throw discredit
On general report—What can you know?

MARY. Not much perhaps, of late: while I remain'd
At his mother's—he was in his boyhood then;
I knew him well: and there's one incident
Much dwelt on to his prejudice, that I
Was witness to—if you would bid me tell it.

RAVENSWORTH. O, by all means, come, your romance.

MARY. 'Tis truth.
It was a wintry day, the snow was deep,
And the chill rain had fallen and was frozen,
That all the surface was a glittering crust.—
We were all gather'd in the lady's hall,
That overlook'd the lawn; a poor stray fawn
Came limping toward us. It had lost, perhaps,
It's dam, and chas'd by cruel hunters, came
To seek a refuge with us. Every bound
The forlorn creature made, its little feet
Broke through the crust, and we could mark that one
Of its delicate limbs was broken. A rude boy
Follow'd it fast, as it would seem, to kill it;
I could not choose but wish its life were sav'd,
And at the word Charles ran and took it up,
And gave it to me, and I cherish'd it
And bound its broken limb up; and it liv'd,
And seem'd to thank me for my care of it.

RAVENSWORTH. But was this all? Was not the village lad
Assailed and beaten?

MARY. He was rude and churlish,
And would have forc'd the animal from Charles.
And tho' 'twas on his mother's grounds, Charles proffer'd him
The price of the fawn. But nothing would content him,
And he struck Charles; he was a larger boy,
But did not prove the stronger—so he went
And made the village all believe his story,
That Charles had robb'd and beaten him, for Charles
Had none to speak for him.

RAVENSWORTH. No more of this—
And never let me hear the name you've utter'd
Pass from your lips again. It is enough
I know this youth for a lewd libertine;
The woman, for a scoffer at things sacred,
At me, and at my functions—and perhaps,
Given to practices, that yet may need
A dreadful expiation. Get you gone,
And on your knees petition that you may not
Deserve my malediction.

MARY. I obey.

[*Exit* MARY, *into cottage, followed by* RAVENSWORTH.]

Enter GEORGE EGERTON, *followed by* SIR REGINALD, *both in shooting dresses*

GEORGE. By Heaven, a lovely creature!

SIR REGINALD. Softly, George,
Is this the game you point at? Have a care,
You're not in London now, where our gay monarch
Sets such a fine example, in these matters.
They'll have no poaching here, that I can tell you,
Among their wives and daughters. These same roundheads,

That crop their hair so short—a plague upon 'em—
Will cut your ears as close, if you're caught meddling.

GEORGE. Why, what a heathen region have we come to.
What a deuce, uncle, did you bring me here for?
To shoot at bears and panthers; pleasant sport;
No women: zounds; I'll back to court again—
No women!

SIR REGINALD. None: the old they burn for witches,
The young they keep clos'd up, (like flies in amber)
In adamantine ice.—

GEORGE. They should be hang'd
For treason against nature. Let the old ones
Freeze, 'tis their charter; but youth should have fire.

SIR REGINALD. They've good laws here for gallants—t'other day
They put a man i' the stocks because he kiss'd
His wife o' Sunday.

GEORGE. They were in the right.
Kiss his own wife! it is a work-day business;
Play-days and holy-days are made for lovers.

SIR REGINALD. To lay hands on a maid here's present death.

GEORGE. It might be so in London, and no lives lost:
The law were a dead letter there—

SIR REGINALD. And widows
May not be spoken to, under the pain
Of fine and pillory.

GEORGE. Uncle, let's embark,
Tho' for the north pole; this clime is too cold—
Or to some catholic country, where a man
May have flesh sometimes: here 'tis always lent.

SIR REGINALD. No: you must stay, your stomach must endure it.

GEORGE. I' faith, dear uncle, being a cavalier,
A gentleman of honor and of breeding,
I marvel much you could come hither; but
The greater wonder is, you'd have me with you,
Knowing my humor.

SIR REGINALD. Troth, my gentle nephew,
Knowing your humor, I could do no better
Than take you from the sphere of Charles's court;
From Rochester, and his dissolute companions,
To cool your blood here in the wilderness.

GEORGE. Well! there may come a time.

SIR REGINALD. As for my voyage,
Perhaps it was a royal jest: or, haply
My clothes had grown too rusty for the court,
Or Charles was tired of the old cavalier,
Who had fought some battles for him, and consum'd
Some certain paltry acres—all he had—
And having left no vacant place at court,
He sent me here Ambassador.

GEORGE. But uncle,
Is that your character?

SIR REGINALD. Much the same thing,
In Christian countries, nephew; I'm a spy.

GEORGE. The devil!

SIR REGINALD. Yes: we read in ancient history,
Of Kings and Emperors, who have kept the men
Who help'd them to the Throne, (by simply putting
Their fathers out o' the way)—about their persons,
As their prime friends. But Charles, being advis'd
That this was in bad taste, and took place only
In semi-barbarous courts, finds it decorous
To grow a little angry with the persons
That kill'd his father. And being told, besides,
That his most loving and beloved subjects
This side the water—who, by the way, he never
Thought of before—had given food and shelter
To certain of the regicides, he sends me
To—

GEORGE. Well, Sir?

SIR REGINALD. Nothing. Come, 'tis growing late.
We must regain our cottage. In the morning,
We leave the village.

GEORGE. 'Gad, with all my soul—
And so to England?

SIR REGINALD. Not so fast, good Springal,
We must have patience yet. Come, let's begone.

GEORGE. I'll see her in the morning, tho' they hang me.

[*Exeunt*, GEORGE *looking back.*

END OF ACT I

ACT II

SCENE I.—*A Forest. In the background an insulated caverned rock. Night. The* UNKNOWN *enters by a bridge formed of the trunk of a tree, which is let down from the rock.* (*His dress is of Skins: his general appearance, wild—but his air and manner dignified. He is armed.*)

UNKNOWN. Yes: it is near the dawn—the dawn! when man
Again shall greet his fellow man, and nature,
Through all her living kingdom shall rejoice.
I only of the human race, condemn'd
To shun my species, and in caves of night
Shut out the common day. Ye glorious stars,
I gaze on you—I look on you, ye Heavens,
With an unblenching eye. You read the heart,
And you can judge the act. If I was wrong,
If innocent blood rest on me—here I stand
To pay the dreadful forfeiture,—let fall
In drops of fire your red-hot vengeance on me.
Am I a murderer? Is the mark of Cain
Imprinted on my front!—I would not murmur—
But as I am but man, forgive it Heaven.
Torn from the beings that I fondly lov'd.—
For nineteen years an outlaw and a wanderer—
Proscribed and hunted like the ravening wolf;—
A price set on my felon head—A felon!
Am I so, Heaven! Did these wounds, receiv'd
In thy holy cause, stream with a felon's blood,
Was it a felon's courage nerv'd my arm,
A felon's zeal that burn'd within my heart?
Yet this I could endure—but when I think
Of thee my child—my daughter—Ha! a step!
Perhaps a beast of prey! I fear not that,
The panther is my co-mate and my brother;
Man only is mine enemy—He comes.

[*Retires into cave.*

Enter CHARLES, *in a neat hunting dress of green, cap, &c., a short sword, or couteau-de-chasse slung, and a gun in his hand*

CHARLES. Each step I take but plunges me the deeper
In this wild labyrinth.—Here's a pretty scene
For those whose love o' the picturesque could make them
Forget their bed and supper. My poor mother
Will be so disappointed—and, dear Mary,
Will not your hopes, too, rise with the lark: I'll on
But whither? May I not be straying further:
I must needs make my couch e'en here.—What's this?
A bridge; and further on, methinks, a cavern,
'Twill serve—But hold—perhaps I shall disturb
Some wild beast in his lair. Tut! 'tis some hunter
Has made his cabin here—I'll try. [*Going to cavern.*]

UNKNOWN. Pass not.

[*Enters from cave.*]

CHARLES. You speak commandingly.

UNKNOWN. And may, when strangers
Intrude upon my privacy. That cave
Is mine, my castle.

CHARLES. It must be confess'd
You play the Castellain right courteously.

UNKNOWN. No trifling, boy. Are you a spy?
—What are you?

CHARLES. My answer's here. [*Levelling his gun.*]

UNKNOWN. Tut, overweening child,
Level thy weapon at the timid deer

That fears thy puny skill. The wither'd leaf
Stirr'd by the falling nut, or passing breeze,
Startles as much as does thy idle menace.

CHARLES. To prove it is not idle—

UNKNOWN. Hold, rash boy;
If but this tube is rais'd, thou perish'st.
For years, as many as thou tell'st of life,
I've wielded it.

CHARLES. I've had some practice, too.

UNKNOWN. Do you provoke your fate!—
But hold; no, no—
Though 'twere my sole security, no blood.
He spoke of his mother, too; I'll not deprive
The mother of her child—Hear me, bold youth.
'Tis meet that I should know so much of thee,
As to be well assur'd thou com'st not hither,
At this dark hour, for evil purpose—tell me—
I do not now command, but I request thee—
Wherefore this visit?

CHARLES. Now, sir, that your question
Is one a gentleman may give reply to,
I'll frankly tell you. I've a mother lives,
I trust, in the next town. A short time since
I left her, for the second time, for college,
To make a second trial for the honors,
I think, with due humility, I'd merited.
Their worships as before play'd with my patience,
'Till I grew tired of it, and told them so,
In good round terms. Glad of the fit excuse,
They just discover'd then, I was too wild
For their strait limits, and so they expell'd me.

UNKNOWN. You speak but lightly of a circumstance
That an ingenuous and aspiring youth,
And, such you seem, might well think serious.

CHARLES. I cannot be a hypocrite, and deem
The acts of solemn folly serious.
When I shall cease to scorn malevolence
And learn to reverence cant and superstition,
Then, not till then, I'll weep at my expulsion.

UNKNOWN. But to your tale.

CHARLES. 'Tis told: I turn'd my back
On my grave censors; seized my hunter's arms,
And struck into the wilderness for home;
Which by the forest route I hoped to reach
Ere the light closed today. I was deceiv'd.
Night came upon me; yet, I travell'd on,
For by a civil horseman that pass'd by
I had sent letters bidding them expect me.
Briefly, when I had fairly lost myself
I met a hunter, whose bark cabin stands
A few miles hence. He put me in the track,
And pointed out a certain star to steer by;
But passing clouds, and intervening boughs,
And perhaps thoughts of home, and those at home,
Marr'd my astronomy. I lost my star,
And then I lost my path, and then myself.
And so, through swamp and thicket, brake and bramble,
I've scrambled on thus far—and, there's my story.

UNKNOWN. Your way was perilous—Did you meet nothing?

CHARLES. Not much. Sometimes a snake I trod on coil'd
Around my leg, but I soon shook him off;
A howl at times approach'd—and as I pass'd,
The brake stirr'd near me with some living thing
Beside myself—but this was all.

UNKNOWN. 'Twas wrong,
Rashly to tempt these dangers. If your air
Deceive me not, you are of foreign birth.

CHARLES. Not four years since, we left our native England.

UNKNOWN. England!

CHARLES. But why's a mystery. We're not known
Nor understood here; we're of another world.

UNKNOWN. Your name?

CHARLES. 'Tis Charles Fitzroy.

UNKNOWN. Fitzroy! Your mother's?

CHARLES. You're somewhat curious: Isabella.

UNKNOWN. Ha!

CHARLES. What is it moves you?

UNKNOWN. Isabella, say you?

CHARLES. This strong emotion—

UNKNOWN. It is nothing, nothing.—

Or—is it strange that I should feel emotion
At the sad tale you tell?

CHARLES. Sad tale!

UNKNOWN. I wander.—
I've been a solitary man so long
That—'Tis no matter.—What dost think me, youth?

CHARLES. A hunter who loves freedom and the forest;
Who'd rather kill his venison in the wood
Than toil for it in the town. Am I not right?

UNKNOWN. 'Tis true—I am—a hunter—

CHARLES. But a strange one.—
But come, sir, will you put me on my way?

UNKNOWN. Will you not rather enter my poor cave
And take its shelter till the morning breaks?
'Twill not be long.

CHARLES. I cannot lose a moment
In selfish rest, while those who love me suffer.

UNKNOWN. Give me your hand then. I'm your friend.

CHARLES. I thank you.
'Tis the first cordial grasp I've had from man.

UNKNOWN. Poor youth! But hold—Give me your solemn promise
To keep this meeting secret.

CHARLES. I hate secrets;
Lovers alone should have them.

UNKNOWN. There are reasons:—
I cannot now disclose them—solemn reasons.—
I do implore you—

CHARLES. Sir, be satisfied;
I'll not reveal it.

UNKNOWN. Nor allude to it,
However press'd—Nor give the darkest hint
That such a man as I exist!

CHARLES. I promise.

UNKNOWN. I'm satisfied. Your words are from the heart.
Fidelity and truth sit on your brow.
The blush of morn begins to tinge the east;
You are not far from home; you'll soon embrace
Your mother, Charles. Come, this way lies the path.

[*Exeunt.*

SCENE 2. *An open Wood near the cottage of* RAVENSWORTH. *Early dawn.*

Enter GEORGE EGERTON

GEORGE. Poor uncle! little does your wisdom dream,
(Being abed) what ramble I'm upon.
A hopeful enterprize, this of my uncle's—
To tame me in a wild wood. Ay, and then
His bug-bear stories of the laws—confound 'em,
Last night they spoil'd the sweetest vision for me;
Methought I saw this beauteous puritan,
The parson's daughter; well, I woo'd and won—
A thing of course—But going to embrace her,
I hugg'd—my pillow, think you? no; a pillory!
Well: I'm resolved in spite of dream and omen,
To see her, if I can, before we go.
I've three hours, good; and three hours may do much.—
By Vulcan, the intruding and lame God,
My uncle limping this way! Gout confound him.
A royal oak! Bend your umbrageous branches,
And saving me, be twice immortalized.

[*Conceals himself in a tree.*]

Enter SIR REGINALD

SIR REGINALD. S'blood! the young rebel, what a march he's led me!
Tortur'd, too, all the route, like a poor prisoner
By my own natural enemy the gout.
The worst of 't is I cannot find the rascal,
I've been around the house; and I'd ha' sworn
That was his mark. If I but catch him—Hey!

Enter MARY

A pretty girl—I' faith, a pretty girl!
I'll speak to her, I will; there's no one near—
Hem! Save you, lady.—

MARY [*who is anxiously looking another way*].
Would you aught with me, sir!

SIR REGINALD. Aught? Yes, egad: a very pretty girl—
My dear, I—that is—
GEORGE. So, so, my grave uncle.—
SIR REGINALD. I meant to say—'tis somewhat early, child,
For youth like yours—She's beautiful, by gad:—
To leave your downy slumbers—
GEORGE. Poetry!
MARY. It is my custom, sir—But age like yours
May suffer from the chill air of the morning.
GEORGE. A brave girl, faith!
MARY [*aside*]. 'Tis one of those strange persons,
My father spoke of—would that he would go.
SIR REGINALD. Why, as you say, my dear,—that is—in fact—
GEORGE. Nay, charge again, brave cavalier.
SIR REGINALD. In truth then,
My errand here so early, was to seek
A runagate nephew.
GEORGE. Meaning me.—
SIR REGINALD. A rascal!
Pray, lady, have you met him?
MARY. Sir, I know not
The person you enquire for.
SIR REGINALD. I'll describe him.
GEORGE. Now for a flattering portrait.
SIR REGINALD [*aside*]. I'll disgust her
Lest he, perchance, should meet her—He's a fellow
Of an indifferent person, which his tailor
Cannot make handsome; yet he thinks himself
The only true Adonis. He has language
If you can understand it. When he speaks,
'Tis in a lisp or oath. His gait's between
A swagger and a dance. His grin's from France,
His leer from Cyprus. He's a Turk in morals,
And is of that religion no man knows of:
In fine, he's as ridiculous as dangerous—
A mongrel thing; a slip of the coxcomb, madam,
Grafted upon the rake.
MARY. Sir, you describe
A monster.
SIR REGINALD. You have hit it: that is he,
Should he approach you, shun him.
MARY. Sir, I shall.
GEORGE. Here's a kind uncle: but I'll be reveng'd.
[SIR REGINALD *bows and exit.*
MARY. He should have come last night: yet here's the morning,
And yet he comes not. He cannot have pass'd me.
Is it because this is his homeward path
That I am loitering here? I fear it is—
O, I am most imprudent—most forgetful—
I fear most sinful.
GEORGE [*descending*]. Now he's out of sight.
And now for the encounter—Madam, your slave.
Nay, start not; I am not the monster, lady,
That gouty person pictur'd. Did you know him
But half so well as I, you'd not believe him,
Or did you but know me, but half so well
As I would have you, and you would believe him
To be the most transcendant of romancers.
Bunyan's book, madam, is true history,
To that he speaks. He was a soldier once,
But was cashier'd for lying. Mandeville,
The greatest liar of antiquity,
May be hereafter quoted as authentic,
When he's believ'd.—And I'm his nephew, too!
A pleasant jest: he kept the wild beasts, madam,
In London, till they turn'd him off for stealing
The lion's supper—Yet a single moment.
MARY. What would you, sir?
GEORGE. You see, before you, lady,
The most unfortunate young fellow breathing,
Banish'd to this strange country for the crime
Of being susceptible—and sentenc'd
To die a lingering death upon the rack,
Unless your smile reprieve him.
MARY. This is strange:
I do not understand you.
GEORGE. If my words
Lack meaning, lady, look into my eyes,

And thro' them to my heart, and see enshrin'd
Your worshipp'd image there—

MARY. Most wonderful,
What language is't you speak, sir?

GEORGE. Ma'am: what language?
English, I think. The pretty simpleton!
Bred in the woods, to her a metaphor
Is Heathen Greek. Madam, those foolish figures
Are all the mode at court; and mean, my dear,
In simple phrase—

MARY. I pray, sir, let me pass—

GEORGE. Not yet, my child—

MARY. Sure 'tis a madman.

GEORGE. True,
And therefore treat me soothingly and kindly,
For of all madmen, your mad lover's maddest.
Do you not fear me?

MARY. No.

GEORGE. Why, then you love me.
Come; I have seen such clouds before; they tell
Of coming sunshine—nay, you must not go.—
I will be monstrous kind to thee, and love thee
Most constantly—

MARY. Release me.

GEORGE. Ay, and take thee
To England, child, and make thee there, my dear,
The envy of thy sex.

MARY. If you're a gentleman—

GEORGE. The conscious grove would blush its green leaves red,
Should I give back.

MARY. Do you not fear the laws?

GEORGE. Nor law, nor gospel now—Come, come, 'tis folly—

MARY. O Heav'n: help, help!

Enter CHARLES

CHARLES. Ruffian, unhand the lady!

GEORGE. So peremptory, boy?

CHARLES. Do you delay?
[*Throws him off.*]

GEORGE. Curse on my haste: I have forgot my sword.

MARY. O Charles!

CHARLES. My dearest Mary; my belov'd!
[MARY *retires up.*]

GEORGE. Hum: Is it so? But s'death! I mustn't bear it.
Hark ye, Sir.

CHARLES. Well, Sir.

GEORGE. I shall find a time.—

CHARLES. Best make it.

GEORGE. When?

CHARLES. Two hours hence, in the grove
East of the village.

GEORGE. I shall meet you there.
But look ye, Sir, be punctual: I've engagements.

CHARLES. I shall not fail you.

GEORGE. 'Gad, a pretty fellow.
I'll pink him first, and then I'll patronize him. [*Exit.*

MARY. O Charles! what pass'd between you? surely, surely
You will not honor him with further notice.

CHARLES. Speak not of him—he is not worth a thought—
We can employ our time to better purpose.
Tell me, have yet the calumnies against me
Found shelter here?

MARY. You know they have not, Charles.
But I have much to tell you—We must part!
Heav'n! is not that my father? Oh, it is!
He comes this way; but has not yet descried us—
Ah! fly, fly quickly!

CHARLES. Fly!

MARY. Yes, if you wish
That we should ever meet—

CHARLES. But shall we meet?

MARY. That way—behind the trees—O quickly, quickly! [CHARLES *goes up.*]

CHARLES [*from the grove*]. But tell me, Mary, will you walk this way
In the evening?

MARY. It is impossible; my father
Forbids my walks.—

CHARLES. Why, then, one place remains—
One only—I will visit you tonight—
You do not answer—Shall I?

MARY. O, begone!
[*Exit* CHARLES, *behind the trees.*

Did I consent? I fear he'll think I did.
My father comes—should he have seen us part!
Am I the guilty creature that I feel?
He's here—I cannot look him in the face.

Enter RAVENSWORTH, *looks at* MARY *sternly for some time*

RAVENSWORTH. 'Tis well: that air of shame becomes you well,
Is this your duty? Did I not forbid
These lonely walks? But get you home; anon,
I'll talk with you.
MARY [*as she goes out*]. He did not see him!
RAVENSWORTH. Home.
[*Exeunt.*

SCENE 3. *An Apartment at* ISABELLA'S

Enter ISABELLA, *meeting* LUCY

ISABELLA. Speak; is he yet in sight?
LUCY. No, madam.
ISABELLA. Go,
O! go again, good Lucy, and be swift
When he appears. [*Exit* LUCY.
My poor, poor boy! my Charles—
To be thus treated, and thy gentle heart
So full of kindness to all living creatures:
To have thy aspirations after fame,
Thus rudely scorn'd, thy youthful hopes thus blighted!
But he deserves it not; there's comfort yet,
And he may rise above it.—Not yet come.
He promis'd, and he would not break his word,
And to his mother, without serious cause—
The way is full of peril, and I know
His temper shuns not danger. Gracious Heav'n!
If I should lose him—him, the only being—

Enter LUCY, *hastily*

Now Lucy, quick!
LUCY. Madam, he is in sight;
And flying up the avenue.
Thank Heaven!

Enter CHARLES

CHARLES. Mother!
ISABELLA. My son. [*Falls into his arms.*]
CHARLES. My ever dearest mother!
ISABELLA. O Charles, how could you thus delay your coming?
The night was pass'd in watch.
CHARLES. I grieve to know it.
I was benighted in the forest, mother,
And lost my way.
ISABELLA. Alas! thou art spent with toil.
CHARLES. Not much.
ISABELLA. Poor Charles: And so they have expell'd thee—
Expell'd!
CHARLES. Nay, pry'thee let us forget it.
ISABELLA. Wretches!
I could have borne all else—but to disgrace thee—
To spurn thee from them—thee! I could endure
The daily persecutions that assail me
With patience and with firmness—But I have thee.
Come, let us in: you need rest and refreshment.
You shall not leave me soon again, my son—
I am a child without you.
CHARLES [*aside*]. My poor mother.
ISABELLA. But let us in—
CHARLES. I'll follow you, my mother.
I will but give an order. [*Exit* ISABELLA.
Edward.

Enter EDWARD

EDWARD. Sir.
CHARLES. Go, get my rapier ready, wrap it close,
And some hour hence, not later, choose a time,
And speed with it to the wood, east of the village.
There wait my coming.
EDWARD. Yes, sir.
CHARLES. But be sure
That no one see it.
EDWARD. I'll be careful, sir.
[*Exit* EDWARD.

Enter ISABELLA

ISABELLA. Fye, sir; is this your breeding? must I wait?
CHARLES. Forgive me, madam, I am ready now. [*Exeunt.*

END OF ACT II

ACT III

SCENE I. *An open Wood*

Enter CHARLES, *followed by* EDWARD

CHARLES. Give me the sword; remain at the edge of the wood;
If any one approach, haste to inform me.
[*Exit* EDWARD.
I am here first, 'tis well. My mother thinks
It is a softer interview I seek;
And while she cautioned me, her sad smile seem'd
To sanction what she fear'd. My dear, kind mother.
And should I fall—well: it would be my fate.
We are but barques upon the sea of life,
And when the storm is up, we greet the port,
Or meet the rock, as destiny determines,
Spite of our feeble efforts. Mary, too!
These thoughts are not in season. Here's my man.

Enter GEORGE EGERTON, *hastily*

Well met, sir.
GEORGE. Sir, I kiss your hands. I' faith,
I've had a race to get here. My wise uncle
Hung round me like a bride in the first month—
Or rather like a wife in the second year,
When jealousy commences.—Come on, sir.
CHARLES. Best breathe awhile; I have the advantage of you.
GEORGE. You will not keep it long. My greatest skill
Will give me still the odds.
CHARLES. It may be so,
Yet you may be deceived. My masters flatter'd
Or I, too, have some science.
GEORGE. I'm glad of it;
For you're a pretty fellow, and deserve
To fall with credit. Come, sir, to your guard.
We shall be interrupted.
CHARLES. Better so,
Than that we fight unfairly. You pant still, sir.
GEORGE. You are a soul of honor, and, were't possible—
But no; the person of an Egerton
Must never be profan'd. Come, Sir, *en garde*.
CHARLES. If you will have it so.
GEORGE. I will.
CHARLES. Come on, then.
[*They fight*. GEORGE *is wounded*.]
GEORGE. I'm pink'd, egad; who would have thought it? S'death!
I'm out of practice.
CHARLES. Here, Sir, on this bank,
Your head against this tree.—Your wound's not deep
I hope. How feel you now?
GEORGE. I' faith, but faintly.

Enter EDWARD

EDWARD. There is a gentleman approaching, Sir.
GEORGE. It is my uncle, like a keen old sportsman,
In at the death. Pry'thee begone, my friend,
'Twere well you were not known.
CHARLES. This handkerchief—
So, press it close—I'll haste to send you aid—
But for the lady's fame, and your own honor,
The cause of this our meeting is a secret.
GEORGE. It shall be so: I thank you. But away!
[*Exeunt* CHARLES *and* EDWARD.
That's a fine lad. But where i' the devil's name,
Learn'd he to fence? I wonder, now I think on't,
Who'll write my epitaph. My uncle can't,
He has no genius. I would do't myself,
Had I an amanuensis: let me see—
Hic jacet—[*Faints*.]

Enter SIR REGINALD

SIR REGINALD. Gracious Heav'n, what is this!
My nephew bleeding, dead! no, he but faints,
With loss of blood. Soft, he revives; why nephew—
My poor mad George, how fares it?
GEORGE. How d'ye, uncle?
Is't day or night? Faith, my eyes twinkle strangely.
SIR REGINALD. Cheerly, George, cheerly, we'll do well enough,—

What shall I do?—But how came this about?
Was't fairly done?

GEORGE. According to the rules.
Should I die, uncle, and my adversary
E'er be discover'd, testify for him—
He kill'd me like a gentleman and Christian.

SIR REGINALD. A duel! ah, George, George.
But zounds! do the roundheads
Fight duels too! a pretty school I've chosen
To teach you prudence in! will no one come!

Enter TWO MEN, *with a Bier*

Ah, you are welcome, set it down: so, so.

GEORGE. A pretty ominous conveyance, this.

SIR REGINALD. I pry'thee hold thy peace, and get thee in.

GEORGE. A grain of opium now, were worth a jewel,
Uncle, I'll never fight again without it.

SIR REGINALD. Be quiet George—you waste your strength.
So, so.
[*The men take him up and are about moving.*]

GEORGE. Head foremost if you please, my worthy friends;
'Tis but fair play—heels first perhaps, to-morrow.
[*The men carry him a few paces.*]
Halt, if it please ye, gentlemen, one moment.
Two hobbles more and I'm defunct.—Pray, general,
Drill those recruits to the step. In camp, now, uncle,
It were a pleasure to be carried out.

SIR REGINALD. Wilt hold thy peace then?

GEORGE. Yes.—The left foot, uncle—

SIR REGINALD. Now, gentlemen, at the word "march" lift up
The left foot of each of you, and so move on.

GEORGE. Right, uncle.

SIR REGINALD. Hold your tongue. March!

GEORGE. Ay; so, so.
[*Exeunt.*

SCENE 2. *The Village*

Enter CHARLES *and* EDWARD

CHARLES. Can it be true! the savages so near?

EDWARD. It is so said.

CHARLES. Edward, do you return,
And see the unfortunate gentleman I wounded
Placed in security. I'll hasten home.
[*Exit* EDWARD.
My first care is my mother—then for Mary!
[*Exit* CHARLES.

Enter WALFORD, *meeting* ALICE

WALFORD. Whence this alarm?

ALICE. O father, we are lost.
A hunter has come in nigh dead with speed,
With tidings that the savages are coming.

WALFORD. How near?

ALICE. Alas! a few miles from the village.

WALFORD. Is't possible! can they have thus eluded
Our watchful troops! we must prepare—O welcome!

Enter RAVENSWORTH

Heard you the fearful tidings, Ravensworth?

RAVENSWORTH. I have, and will you now believe, our sins
Bring these afflictions on us? We have murderers
Lurking among us.

WALFORD. How!

RAVENSWORTH. This moment pass'd me
The relative of the Knight, Sir Reginald;
Dying, or dead.

WALFORD. Whose was the act?

RAVENSWORTH. Whose was't?
The act of him, whose every act is crime.
The son of this dark woman.

WALFORD. How is it known?

RAVENSWORTH. His sword and handkerchief stain'd both with blood,
And mark'd with his vile name, were found in the wood.
He has not been one day yet in the village,
And lo! these visitations. On the instant
He must be dealt with.

WALFORD. First for our defense—
What do you counsel?

RAVENSWORTH. Prayer and sacrifice.

WALFORD. 'Tis too late now, we must take other means.

The VILLAGERS *enter*, *exhibiting signs of wild affright*

WALFORD. Hark ye, my friend, have messengers been sent
To warn the scatter'd settlers round?

1ST VILLAGER. They have.

WALFORD. Why rings not the alarum bell!

1ST VILLAGER. I know not,
Unless the exposed position of the church—

WALFORD. Go, some of you and do it.—Hasten, friends,
Seize every man his arms.

[*Exeunt* VILLAGERS.

RAVENSWORTH. Behold where comes
In all her pride, one of the moving causes
Of all this horror—mark with what an air,
How tranquil and compos'd she looks around
Upon the growing evil—safe, 'midst the fury
Of her own tempest.

As he speaks, enter ISABELLA; *the women shrink from her in fear.* ALICE *gazes upon her with interest;* RAVENSWORTH *fixes his eyes sternly upon her. She remains unmoved.*

WALFORD. Ravensworth, forbear.
Is this a time —

Enter 2D VILLAGER

Now, friend, what news have you?

2D VILLAGER. They have begun to issue from the wood.—

Enter SIR REGINALD

SIR REGINALD. What is this I hear? the savages approaching!
Now plague upon this gout!—But I've an arm left
That yet can wield a sword.

WALFORD. Your nephew, Sir,
May need your care. You're strange to our wild warfare.

SIR REGINALD. True; I'd forgot poor George. They'll cut thro' me,
Before they get a hair of him. [*Retires.*

Re-enter 1ST VILLAGER

WALFORD. How now?

1ST VILLAGER. We've rallied at the church; but want a leader.

WALFORD. You shall not want one longer.

ALICE. O, my father!

WALFORD. Heav'n bless you, my dear daughter. Follow me.

[*Exit* WALFORD, *followed by* VILLAGERS. *Distant yell. The alarm bell rings, a few distant and straggling shots heard. Houses at a distance beginning to blaze;—a pause of the bell.*]

RAVENSWORTH. Now, where's your son?

ISABELLA. Gone, Sir, to save your daughter.

RAVENSWORTH. My daughter! I'd forgot.—Is she not here?

[*Runs wildly around. Bell rings. The shots are nearer and more frequent. The blaze increases.*]

RAVENSWORTH. My daughter! where, O, where's my daughter!

Enter CHARLES, *bearing* MARY

CHARLES. There, Sir.

[RAVENSWORTH *receives her, and for a moment yields to his paternal feeling. But instantly withdraws from* CHARLES *with a scowl.* CHARLES, *after affectionately recognizing his mother, rushes out.* ALICE *joins* MARY; *who is prevented from addressing* ISABELLA, *by her father's frown.* ISABELLA *maintains her dignity and composure. Alarm continues, shouts, yells, &c.*]

The VILLAGERS *enter in disorder, followed by* CHARLES *and* WALFORD

CHARLES. One effort more.

WALFORD. It is impossible,
Panic has seiz'd them all and we must perish.

[*The bell has ceased. A dreadful yell. The* VILLAGERS *turn and are about to fly in despair, when—*

Enter the UNKNOWN

UNKNOWN. Turn back for shame—as ye are men, turn back!
As ye are husbands, fathers, turn, and save
From death and violation those ye love.—
If this not move you, as ye are Christian men
And do believe in God, tempt not his wrath
By doubting thus his providence. Behold
I am sent to save you.

OMNES. Save us, save us.

WALFORD. Say,
What shall we do; we're ready to obey thee.

UNKNOWN. Front then and bear yourselves like men—'Tis well.
The savage sees us rally; and the pause
His caution grants, secures us the advantage.

[*He passes rapidly along the line, dividing them into three bodies. Then addresses* WALFORD *and* CHARLES.]

This band be yours—this yours—Quick, lead them forth,
And each by a rapid circuit, turn the foe
By either flank. This will I lead myself
Against his front—holding him thus in check
Until I hear the horn sound your arrival—
Then while perplex'd he hesitates between us,
Rush to the onset all—close on the heathen,
And shower destruction on him—haste, away.

[*Exeunt* UNKNOWN, WALFORD *and* CHARLES, *leading their bands.*]

ISABELLA. How awful is this pause, that but precedes
The shock that may o'erwhelm us. God, to thee,
The mother turns. Not for myself,
Not for my sinful self—but for my son—
My innocent son I plead. Cut him not off
In the blossom of his days.

RAVENSWORTH. Mark, if the hag
Mutter not, even now, her incantations.
[*A few scattering shots heard.*]
The fronts have met, and from the forest coverts,
Exchange their cautious fire.

[*A bugle sounds, answered by another from a different quarter. Shouts, yells, a general and continued discharge of musketry. Shouts and bugles.*]

RAVENSWORTH. The crisis has arrived—the fire has ceased,
And now the closer work of death commences.
Ascend yon tree, and say what thou observest.
[*To a boy, who ascends the tree.*]

BOY. I see them now. The Indians stand dismay'd.
We're pouring now upon them from the forest,
From every side.—Now, now the Indians turn—
They meet—they close—they're struggling man to man.
Sword, knife and tomahawk are glancing.

ISABELLA. Heaven!
Protect, protect my Charles!

ALICE. Save my dear father. [*Shout.*]

RAVENSWORTH. What shout is that? Hear ye the savage yell?

BOY. No, no, 'twas ours—we've conquer'd—and they come,
Dragging their prisoners with them. Here's my father.

Enter 1ST VILLAGER *shouting "Victory," meets and caresses the boy*

General shout, bugles. Enter WALFORD, CHARLES, VILLAGERS, *with* INDIAN PRISONERS. *They arrange themselves on each side; the Indians in the background.* CHARLES *flies to his mother who sinks on her knees in his embrace.* ALICE *joins her father, various groups formed.* MARY *manifests much interest for* CHARLES, *who regards her tenderly.* RAVENSWORTH *preserves his suspicious and reserved demeanour.*

Enter the UNKNOWN. *He passes down the centre. All gaze on him with awe, and stretch forth their hands towards him, bending their bodies.*

UNKNOWN. No; not to me this homage—not to man
Is your this day's deliverance owing. There—
To heaven address your gratitude. To God
Stretch forth your hands and raise your swimming eyes.
Before Jehovah bend your bodies down,
And from your humble hearts pour out the flood
Of Thankfulness. It was his care that watch'd,
His eye that saw; his arm that smote the heathen—
His be the praise and glory.

[*All bend in adoration. The* UNKNOWN *casts a glance at* ISABELLA, *and exclaims as he goes out:*]

Yes; 'tis she. [*Exit* UNKNOWN.

[*After a short pause, they raise their heads and look around anxiously for the* UNKNOWN.]

Enter SIR REGINALD

WALFORD. Has this thing been? Where is he? did he pass you?

SIR REGINALD. Who?

WALFORD. Our mysterious leader—
SIR REGINALD. I saw him not.
WALFORD. Was't an earthly being?
ALICE. O my father!
It was not mortal.
CHARLES. In the fight his arm,
Like the fierce lightning wither'd where it fell.
SIR REGINALD. You speak of wonders!
RAVENSWORTH. Woman, what think you—
Was it an angel—or a fiend?
WALFORD. What mean you?
[ISABELLA *turns from him proudly*. CHARLES *represses his anger on exchanging glances with* MARY.]
RAVENSWORTH. You'll know anon. Walford, you bleed.
WALFORD. A trifle.
RAVENSWORTH. *He* does not bleed—
WALFORD. I think not; yet he dar'd
The thickest of the fight.
RAVENSWORTH. Can you not see?
Do you not mark?
WALFORD. Your meaning is most dark.
RAVENSWORTH. The murkiest night must fly before the day;
Illusion, strong as Hell must yield to Truth.
You understand me not—No matter—come—
Let these vile heathens be securely plac'd
To await their certain death—then to the temple—
There, to the Throne of Mercy to present
Our sacrifice of prayer and of thanksgiving.
[*Exeunt* CHARLES, ISABELLA, *and others.*

END OF ACT THREE

ACT IV

SCENE I.[1] *Before the house of* RAVENSWORTH

Enter RAVENSWORTH *from the house, meeting* WALFORD

RAVENSWORTH. You come in happy time; I would have sought you
Walford, my soul is sick, even to death,
To look upon the miseries, our sins
Bring down upon us. But I am resolv'd;—
This day's events at length have steel'd my heart
Against the accursed cause; who must not longer
Pollute, unquestion'd thus, our wholesome air.
WALFORD. You know the cause then?
RAVENSWORTH. Who can know this woman,
This Isabella, and be ignorant!
But she must answer it—the time is come;
She and her son must answer for their deeds.
And since my letters to the government
Have fail'd to bring their aid—ourselves, my friend,
Must call them to the judgment seat.
WALFORD. Not so;
Your efforts have been crown'd with sad success.
Commissioners have even now arriv'd.—
I came to let you know it.
RAVENSWORTH. Thanks, my friend,
You make me happy.
WALFORD. Happy, Ravensworth!
RAVENSWORTH. And should I not rejoice that guilt like theirs
Should cease to spread its poison thro' the land?
WALFORD. Where shall we find the evidence of guilt?
RAVENSWORTH. The trial shall produce it, doubt it not;
Meantime, methinks the general belief
In their dark crimes; the universal horror
Inspir'd e'en by their presence—as if nature
Shudder'd instinctively at what was monstrous,
And hostile to its laws, were, of themselves,
A ground to rest the charge on.
WALFORD. Ah, my friend,
If reason in a mind like yours, so form'd,
So fortified by knowledge, can bow down
Before the popular breath, what shall protect
From the all-with'ring blasts of superstition
The unthinking crowd, in whom credulity,
Is ever the first born of ignorance?
RAVENSWORTH. Walford, what meanest thou by superstition!
Is there in our religion aught forbidding
Belief in sorcery! Look thro' this land,
Or turn thine eyes abroad—are not the men

[1] This scene was omitted in the representation.

Most eminent for piety and knowledge—
The shining lights of a benighted age,
Are they not, too, believers?

WALFORD. There have been,
In every age, among the learn'd, divines,
Statesmen, philosophers, astronomers,
Who have upheld with much ability,
The errors they believ'd in. Abstract points
In science, may be safely tolerated,
Altho' erroneous—But there may be doctrines,
So fatal in their influence, that, until
Their truth is manifest, 'twere well not cast them,
With lavish hand, among the multitude.

RAVENSWORTH. And is not sorcery manifest as day?
Have not our senses testified unto it?

WALFORD. We have heard infant witnesses aver it,
And seen them while they seem'd to suffer it;
We have heard wretches in despair confess it,
And have seen helpless creatures perish for it;
And yet—

RAVENSWORTH. What yet?

WALFORD. O Ravensworth! these things
Have happened: on a day of gloom and terror,
When but to doubt was danger, to deny, death;
When childish petulance, e'en idiocy,
Were gravely listened to, when mere suspicion,
Could, with a hint destroy, and coward malice,
With whispers, reach'd at life; when frenzy's flame,
Like fire in tow, ran thro' the minds of men,
Fann'd by the breath of those in highest places,
E'en from the bench, yea, from the sacred desk.

RAVENSWORTH. Hold, Walford, I have held thee as my friend,
For many years, beware—

WALFORD. I know thy power
Over the multitude, but fear it not.
I have discharged my duty, fare thee well.

RAVENSWORTH. Stay, Walford, thou art honest, but mistaken,
We will dispute no more. But tell me, friend,
Have the commissioners enquired for me?

WALFORD. They have. Before they enter on their duties,
They'd have thy counsel.

RAVENSWORTH. They shall have it straight,
I'll go to them at once. 'Tis almost night—
There is no hour to lose. I pray thee, Walford,
As I may, haply, be detain'd abroad,
Let thy good Alice stay here with my daughter
Till my return.

WALFORD. Most willingly. I'll haste,
And bring her hither.

RAVENSWORTH. Nay, we'll go together.
[*Exeunt.*

SCENE 2. *An Apartment at* ISABELLA'S

Enter ISABELLA *and* CHARLES

ISABELLA. Ungrateful people!

CHARLES. Had they not presum'd
To cloud your clear name with their viperous breath,
I could forgive them. 'Twas not for the herd
I drew my sword.

ISABELLA. Unthankful wretches; what!
Upon the very act that saved their lives,
To found a charge that might endanger thine!

CHARLES. 'Tis even so: I am in league, it seems,
With fiends, so say their worships; and the stranger,
Is no less, than the prince of fiends himself.
Nothing is too ridiculous for those
Whom bigotry has brutaliz'd, I laugh
At their most monstrous folly.

ISABELLA. But such folly,
When it infects the crowd, is dangerous.
Already we've had proof what dreadful acts
Their madness may commit, and each new day
The frenzy spreads. We are suspected, too—
Then your imprudent duel—O my son,
We must remove from hence.

CHARLES. Remove, from hence?

ISABELLA. Yes; ere the monsters catch us in the toils
They are preparing.

CHARLES. Mother, you were wont
To bear a mind whose firmness could resist
Your sex's common weaknesses!

ISABELLA. I know not
How it is, Charles, but dark and sad forebodings
Hang o'er my subdued spirit; and I tremble
E'en for thy life.

CHARLES. Banish those thoughts, my mother.

ISABELLA. I try, but cannot.—Yes; we will hence; my son.
Tho' on the verge, perhaps, of that discovery
The hope of which has held me here so long,
We will begone tomorrow.

CHARLES. So soon, mother?

ISABELLA. You do not wish it. Charles, a mother's eye
Can penetrate the heart. The gentle Mary—
She will be left behind—is it not so?
But this is boyish, you are yet too young
To entertain such fantasies—and then,
You know her father—sadder still, my son;
Well, we'll not cross the ocean—we'll but seek
The nearest spot that is inhabited
By rational beings. And besides, your youth
Will wear a year or two. How say you, Charles,
Are you contented?

CHARLES. You're the best of mothers.
And were my heart strings fasten'd to the spot,
I'd with you, tho' they sunder'd. But you spoke
A moment since, of some discovery
You were near making: what discovery?

ISABELLA. It was an inadvertence—

CHARLES. Must I never
Hope to enjoy your confidence?

ISABELLA. Not now—
Another time, my son.

CHARLES. Another time—
'Tis ever thus you put my questions by.
Rather forbid me e'er again to ask
Of what so much concerns me, and I promise
However hard the task, I will obey you.
I trust you have ne'er found me disobedient!

ISABELLA. You have been all a mother's heart could wish.
You ask but what you have a right to ask,
And I have always purpos'd a fit time—
When that your age were ripe enough—

CHARLES. Well, mother,
Has not that time arrived?

ISABELLA. Your age, dear Charles,
Has scarce reach'd manhood yet. 'Tis true, your courage,
Your conduct amidst danger—manly virtues,—
Are well approv'd. Your judgment, too—so much,
A mother may believe and say—is far
Beyond the years you count. But there's a quality;
A virtue it may be, which is the growth
Only of minds well disciplin'd; which looks
On human actions with a liberal eye.
That knows the weakness of the human heart,
Because it feels it; and will not condemn
In others, what itself is conscious of—
That will not with the tyrant prejudice,
Without allowance or extenuation,
Yea, without hearing, pass its dreadful sentence.

CHARLES. And am I such a one? thanks to my nature,
Which I feel is not quite so vile. My breeding,
Which has been liberal. Nay, thanks to those
Who daily here exhibit its deformity,
I scorn this monster prejudice.

ISABELLA. And yet—
Should you—I could not live if you should hate me.

CHARLES. Hate you, my mother? Had not all your actions
Been, as I've seen them, noble; all your precepts
As I have ever found them, full of goodness,
Could I recall the tenderness you've shewn
Towards me, and cease to love you.—Never, never!
All crimes however great, dwindle to atoms
Near filial ingratitude: the heart

That is that monster's throne, ne'er knew a virtue.

ISABELLA. Ah! how shall I commence!—What would you know?

CHARLES. Why you left England? Why in this wilderness,
Amidst a race that scorn, that shun and loathe us,
You linger out existence? Chiefly, mother;
Who is my father? [*Taking her hand.*]

ISABELLA. Ah! [*Turning away.*]

CHARLES. In our own England,
At school, among my frank and laughing mates,
When they have put this question, it was done
In merry mood, and I could bear it—well—
Although I could not answer it; but here,
O mother—to these cold and selfish beings,
Their smooth tongues dipp'd in bitterness, their eyes
Scowling suspicion—what can I reply?

ISABELLA. Poor boy, poor boy! Well, Charles, the time is come
And if my spirits fail not—you shall know all.
Your father—but I cannot, no, I cannot
Commence my story there.—I was left, Charles,
Without a parent's care, just at that age
That needs it most. I had ne'er known my mother,
And was scarce fifteen when my father's fate
Forc'd him to abandon child and home and country;
For he had been a patriot, as he deemed it,
Or, as his destiny decreed, a traitor.—
He fled to this new world.

CHARLES. Does he yet live?

ISABELLA. Alas! I know not, rumors came to England
That he survived. It was to find my father,
And on my knees implore his benediction;—
Haply, should he forgive, to minister
Unto his age's comfort—I came hither.

CHARLES. 'Tis strange, if living, he should seek concealment,
After the general amnesty.

ISABELLA. O! Charles;
He was excepted in that act of mercy:
He had done that, the king might never pardon.

CHARLES. Unhappy man!

ISABELLA. Most true.—But let me haste
To close my dark recital. I was plac'd
In charge of a kinsman—a perfidious villain
Whose avarice sold, betray'd me.—O my son,
It is not fit thy ears should hear the tale,
And from my lips. I wept, implor'd, resisted—
Riches and pleasure tempted me in vain,
Coupled with shame. But hellish craft at length
Triumph'd o'er credulous vanity—The altar
Was made the scene of sacrilegious mockery,
The holy vestments of the priest, became
A profane masking habit—

CHARLES. Power of Justice!
Could you behold this and forbear to strike!

ISABELLA. The illusion vanish'd, and I fled, I fled
In horror and in madness.

CHARLES. Dreadful, dreadful!

ISABELLA. It was thy birth that sav'd me from destruction—
I had thee to live for, and I liv'd; deep hid
In solitude, under an assum'd name,
Thou wer't rear'd, Charles, amidst thy mother's tears.

CHARLES. An assum'd name—in solitude—Shame, shame!
Why not unmask the villain to the world,
And boldly challenge what was yours?

ISABELLA. His rank—

CHARLES. No rank should shield injustice. Quick, inform me
Who was the wretch? Give me the villain's name.

ISABELLA. He was thy father, Charles.

CHARLES. In the sight of Heaven
I here disclaim and curse—

ISABELLA. Forbear, forbear—
Or curse me too—

CHARLES. His name, his name—

ISABELLA. You will destroy me!
[*She falls into his arms.*]

CHARLES. What have I done? I will be calm—forgive me.

Enter LUCY

LUCY. A person from the village, madam, asks
To be admitted to your presence.

ISABELLA. How!
Does he declare his business?

LUCY. He declines it,
Until he see yourself.

ISABELLA. Admit him, Lucy. [*Exit* LUCY.

CHARLES. Madam, you tremble still, let me support you.

ISABELLA. No; I must learn to overcome this weakness.

Enter MESSENGER

Now, Sir, I'm she you ask for—to your business.

MESSENGER. My business is with both. You, Isabella
And Charles, surnam'd Fitzroy, are cited both,
By a commission of the government,
To attend them at their session on the morrow
At nine in the morning.

CHARLES. And to what purpose?

MESSENGER. That
You'll learn from them, farewell.
[*Exit* MESSENGER.

CHARLES. Why farewell, gravity.

ISABELLA. What can this mean?

CHARLES. They do not know themselves.

ISABELLA. I fear I've been too tardy.

CHARLES. Nay, 'tis nothing.
To question us, perhaps, upon our means,
And pack us from the parish, nothing more.
But, madam, you were interrupted, ere
I learn'd the name—

ISABELLA. Not at this moment, Charles.

CHARLES. Well, then, enough of sorrow for today.—
I will return anon, and laugh with you
At the absurdities of these strange people.
At supper we'll discuss our plans for the future.
We may be happy yet.—

ISABELLA. But whither go you?

CHARLES. I ought to visit him I wounded, madam,
And perhaps I may gather in the village,
Something that may concern us—and perhaps—

ISABELLA. Well, do not be long absent; it is night.

CHARLES. I will not, madam: I shall soon return. [*Exit* CHARLES.

ISABELLA. He does not feel the danger, his frank spirit,
His careless youth, disdains it. We must fly.—

Enter LUCY

Bid Edward, with all speed, prepare the horses,
Then follow to my chamber. We must prepare
In all haste, for a journey—

LUCY. Madam, a journey—
Tonight?

ISABELLA. Tonight: it is most necessary. So, bid Edward
Be secret.

LUCY. He is here.

EDWARD [*within*]. You cannot pass.

Enter EDWARD

ISABELLA. What noise is this?

EDWARD. Madam, in spite of me
They press into your presence.

ISABELLA. We are lost!

Enter several OFFICERS

1ST OFFICER. For that we do we have sufficient warrant.

ISABELLA. What means this rudeness?

1ST OFFICER. Answer; where's your son?

ISABELLA. He is not in the house.

1ST OFFICER [*to attendants who go out*]. Go you, make search.

ISABELLA. Again I ask, what is your business here?

1ST OFFICER. Read. [*Hands her a paper.*]

ISABELLA. Gracious Heav'n! Is this the charge against us!
But why this second visit! we are cited
To answer in the morning.

1ST OFFICER. But the judges
Have chang'd their mind. Your chamber is your prison
Till you are sent for. We'll attend you thither.

ISABELLA. But one word with my servant—
1ST OFFICER. Not one word;
It is forbidden, come—
ISABELLA. My son, my son! [*She exchanges significant looks with* LUCY, *and exit guarded.*]
LUCY. I understand. [*Going.*]
2ND OFFICER. And so do we—our duty.
You are not to stir hence, nor hold discourse
One with another. Lead them in—away.
[*Officers lead off* LUCY *and* EDWARD.]

SCENE 3. *Before the house of* RAVENSWORTH

Enter MARY *from house*

MARY. He does not come. I do not wish it, sure—
At least I ought not. But has he forgotten?—
That is impossible.—Perhaps he fears—
O no! Charles never fears—should he not come—
I ought to hope he could not—ah! a figure,
Stealing between the trees—should it be he:
But may it not be a stranger! ah, let me fly.
[*Exit, into the house.*

Enter CHARLES *cautiously*

CHARLES. 'Twas she, her white robe, emblem of her innocence,
Dispels the darkness of the libertine night,
And all around her's purity and brightness.
She is alone. As I pass'd thro' the village
I learn'd her father was in council there.—
She is alone and unprotected quite—
She loves me and confides in me—be that,
Tho' passion mount to madness, her protection.
The door is fasten'd, right; a common guest
Comes by a common passage—there are posterns
And wickets for the lover. Let me try.
[*Exit behind the house.*

SCENE 4. *A chamber: a window in the flat; a light burning near the window*

MARY *discovered, a book in her hand*

MARY. I cannot read,—my thoughts are all confusion,
If it be he, will he not think the light
Was plac'd designedly. I will remove it.
[*Goes towards the window, starts on* CHARLES *appearing at it.*]
CHARLES. Be not alarm'd, my Mary: it is I.
MARY. O Charles, how could you?—
CHARLES. How could I refrain
When that the beacon light so fairly blaz'd,
From steering to this haven.
MARY. There! I fear'd
You would presume to think—
CHARLES. But I think nothing—
Presume, know nothing, but that thou, my Mary,
Art the divinest creature on the earth
And I the happiest—O my best, my dearest,
That thou might'st live forever near this heart;
And why not there forever! What prevents it,
What can—what shall? My beauteous, my beloved.
MARY. No more; this warmth alarms me—hear me, Charles—
I've given to thee my heart and maiden vow,
O, be content—and—leave me—
CHARLES. Leave thee, Love?
MARY. Before you teach me to despise myself;
Ere you yourself despise me.
CHARLES. Have I, Mary,
Have I deserv'd that from thee? Lo, I'm calm—
And gaze upon thee as the pilgrim looks
Upon the shrine he kneels at; the pure stars
Look not on angels with a holier light.
MARY. I do believe you, Charles—But O this meeting,
So rash, so—
CHARLES. 'Twas presumptuous in me, Mary,
I do confess it.
MARY. Still you mistake me, Charles.
I do not say, I did not wish you here—
Yet I must wish you gone. It is so wrong—
I am so much to blame—
CHARLES. I will not stay,
To give you pain.
MARY. But do not go in anger—
CHARLES. Anger! at you!
MARY. A happier time will come—
Each moment now is full of peril, Charles;

My father may return, and should he find you!—

CHARLES. One word and I will leave you. You will hear,
Tomorrow, that we've left this place for ever.

MARY. How, Charles?

CHARLES. My mother has resolv'd to fly
The persecutions that surround her here
And we depart tomorrow—if we may—
For we're already cited—

MARY. Heav'ns! for what?

CHARLES. It can be nothing, surely. But, dear Mary
Tho' absent, ah remember there is one
Who lives for you alone.

MARY. Charles, can you doubt it?

CHARLES. And should there, Mary, should there come an hour
Propitious to our loves; secure and safe—
Suspicion dead, her eye, nor ear to mark us—
And should the lover that adores you, Mary,
Appear at that blest hour, with certain means
To bear you far from cruelty and slav'ry,
To love and happiness—

MARY. No more, no more—

CHARLES. Would you consent?

MARY. O tempt me not to sin—
'Twould break my father's heart—

CHARLES. Give me your promise.

Enter RAVENSWORTH, WALFORD, ALICE

MARY [*observing her father*]. Unhand me, oh unhand me—Father, father!

[*Faints in* CHARLES' *arms.*]

RAVENSWORTH. Thy father's here to save thee, hapless girl,
And hurl confusion on thy base betrayer.

CHARLES [*attending only to* MARY]. She's dead, she's dead!

RAVENSWORTH. Haste, tear her from his arms
Ere the pollution of his touch destroy her.

[ALICE *and* WALFORD *convey* MARY *out.*]

CHARLES. And have I killed her! [*Gazing after her.*]

RAVENSWORTH. Wretch, and do you mourn
Over the clay, that would have kill'd the soul?

Re-enter WALFORD

WALFORD. She has reviv'd, and calls for thee, my friend.

CHARLES. She lives, she lives! Then I defy my fate.

RAVENSWORTH. Outcast from Heav'n, thy doom is near at hand.
Walford, we'll strait convey him to the church,
Where by this time the judges have assembled,
To try his sinful mother.

CHARLES. How? my mother!
And have ye laid your sacrilegious hands
Upon my mother?

RAVENSWORTH. Silence, wretched youth.
I will but see my daughter—meantime, Walford,
Guard well your prisoner.

CHARLES. Guard me! heartless father,
That feelest not the ties of blood and nature—
Think you, at such an hour, I'd quit my mother?

[*Exeunt* RAVENSWORTH, CHARLES *and* WALFORD.]

END OF ACT IV

ACT V

SCENE I. *A Wood.* [*Stage dark.*]

Enter the UNKNOWN

At length, unseen by human eye, I've gain'd
Her neighborhood. The village lies before me;
And on the right rises the eminence
On which she dwells—She dwells! who dwells? O heart,
Hold till thou art assur'd. Such were the features,
The stately form of her, whose cherish'd image,
Time spares my widow'd heart, fresh and unchang'd.—
I must be satisfied.—The night has fallen
Murky and thick; and in the western Heavens,
The last of day was shrouded in the folds
Of gathering clouds, from whose dark confines come,

At intervals, faint flashes, and the voice
Of muttering thunder: there will be a storm.
How is it that I feel, as never yet
I felt before, the threatening elements;
My courage is bow'd down and cowers, as though
The lowering canopy would fall in streams
Of death and desolation. Dark portents,
Hence! There's a Heaven beyond the tempest's scope,
Above the clouds of death. Wing your flight thither,
Thoughts—hopes, desires; there is your resting place. [*Exit.*

SCENE 2. *The interior of the Church, arranged as a Hall of Justice. Passages lead to doors on each side of the desk.*

The JUDGES *seated at the desk.* CHARLES *stands on the left, near the* JUDGES. ISABELLA *nearer the front; on the same side* RAVENSWORTH, WALFORD, MARY, *and* ALICE; *on the opposite side,* VILLAGERS, OFFICERS, *&c.*

JUDGE. Ye have heard the charge—but ere ye answer to it
Bethink ye well. Confession may do much
To save you from the penalty; or mitigate
Your punishment. Denial must deprive you
Of every hope of mercy.—Answer then—
And first, you, madam.

ISABELLA. Sorcery! Gracious Heaven!
Is it necessary, in this age of light,
And before men and Christians, I should deny
A charge so monstrous!

JUDGE. Answer to the question.

ISABELLA. We are not guilty then; so aid us Heaven!

JUDGE. Speak for yourself alone. Will you disclose
Who—what ye are?

ISABELLA. I am a gentlewoman—
More I cannot disclose.

JUDGE. Say, wherefore, madam,
You came among us?

ISABELLA. Sir, I came to seek
A father.

JUDGE. Who is he?

ISABELLA. I dare not name him.

RAVENSWORTH. Mark you, how she prevaricates?

JUDGE. What evidence
Have you against this woman?

RAVENSWORTH. Ye all remember
The terror and despair that fill'd each bosom
When the red comet, signal of Heaven's wrath,
Shook its portentous fires above our heads.
Ye all have seen, and most of ye have felt
The afflictions which this groaning land is vex'd with—
Our smiling fields wither'd by blight and blast,
The fruitful earth parch'd into eddying dust,—
On our fair coast the strewings of wreck'd commerce;
In town and city, fire and pestilence,
And famine, walking their destroying rounds—
Our peaceful villages, the scene of slaughter,
Echoing the savage yell, and frenzied shriek
Of maid and matron, or the piercing wail
Of widows and of orphans—

JUDGE. We deplore
The evils you recite; but what avails
Their repetition here; and how do they
Affect the cause in question?

RAVENSWORTH. Shall we forget
That worldly pride and irreligious lightness,
Are the provoking sins, which our grave synod
Have urg'd us to root out? Turn then to her,
Swelling with earth-born vanity, to her
Who scorns religion, and its meek professors;
And, to this hour—until compell'd, ne'er stood
Within these holy walls.

JUDGE. Yet this is nothing,
Touching the charge against her—you must be
Less vague and general. Produce your proofs.

RAVENSWORTH. There are two witnesses at hand; her servants—
Who have confess'd she had prepared to fly
This very night—a proof most clear and potent
Of conscious guilt. But why refer to this!

Each one that hears me is a witness of it,
It is the village horror. Call, at random,
One from the crowd, and mark if he will dare
To doubt the thing I speak of.

JUDGE. 'T must not be,
Nor can we listen further.

ISABELLA. I beseech you
Let him proceed; let him endeavor still,
To excite the passions of his auditors;
It will but shew how weak he deems his proof
Who lays such stress on prejudice. I fear not,
But I can answer all his accusations.—
If I intended flight—need I remind you
Of what your fathers—what yourselves have done?
It was not conscious guilt bade them or you
Escape from that, was felt was persecution—
If I have thought the manner of my worship
A matter between Heaven and my conscience,
How can ye blame me, who in caves and rocks
Shunning the church, offer'd your secret prayers?
Or does my state offend? Habit and taste
May make some difference, and humble things
Seem great to those more humble; yet I have used
My little wealth in benefits. Your saints
Climb'd to high places—Cromwell to the highest—
As the sun seeks the eminence from which
He can diffuse his beams most bounteously.

RAVENSWORTH. The subtle power she serves does not withhold
The aid of sophistry.

ISABELLA. I pray my judges
To shield me from the malice of this man,
And bring me to the trial. I will meet it,
As it concerns myself with firm indifference;
But as it touches him whom I exist in,
With hope that my acquittal shall dissolve
The fetters of my son.

RAVENSWORTH [*aside*]. That must not be.

JUDGE. Bring forth your proofs, and let the cause proceed.

RAVENSWORTH. Perhaps it is the weakness of the father
Prompts the suggestion—But I have bethought me,
It were most fit this youth should first be dealt with,
'Gainst whom there are a host of witnesses
Ready to testify—unless his actions,
Obvious and known, are proof enough—his life
Which is a course of crime and profligacy,
Ending, with contemplated rape and murder.

ISABELLA. What do I hear?

JUDGE. How say you? rape and murder!

RAVENSWORTH. The victim of his bloody purpose lingers
Upon the verge of death—Here are the proofs
That point out the assassin! [*Showing the sword and handkerchief, which are held by a* VILLAGER *who is standing near him.*] For the violence—
Myself, my daughter here—

MARY. O father, father!

JUDGE. These things are terrible. But you forget,
They are not now the charge.

RAVENSWORTH. What matters it,
Whether by hellish arts of sorcery
He wrought upon the maiden,—or with force
Attempted violation—Let him answer—
Denying one, he but admits the other.

JUDGE. Bid him stand forth. We wait your answer, youth.

CHARLES. You wait in vain—I shall not plead.

JUDGE. Not plead!

RAVENSWORTH [*aside*]. This is beyond my hopes.

ISABELLA. O Charles, my son!

JUDGE. What do you mean?

CHARLES. Simply, sir, that I will not
Place myself on my trial here.

JUDGE. Your reason?
Do you question then the justice of the court?

RAVENSWORTH. He does, no doubt he does.

CHARLES. However strong
Might be the ground for question—'tis not that
Determines me to silence.

JUDGE. If you hope
To purchase safety by this contumacy;
'Tis fit you be aware that clinging there,
You may pull ruin on your head.

CHARLES. I know
The danger I incur, but dare to meet it.

ISABELLA. O Charles, reflect—

CHARLES. Mother, my soul is fixed;
They shall not call yon maiden to the bar.
Tremble not, weep not, pure and timid soul,
They shall not question thee.

RAVENSWORTH. Hence with thy spells—
Take thine eyes off my child, ere her weak frame
Yield to the charm she shakes with—hence, I say!

[MARY *attempts to speak, but is prevented by her Father.*]

JUDGE. Prisoner, attend: at once inform the court
Of all you know concerning the strange being,
Who, like a supernatural visitant,
Appear'd this day among us. What connexion
Subsists between you?

CHARLES. None. I know him not.

RAVENSWORTH. And yet this morning, ere the dawn had broken,
They were both seen together in the forest,
Holding mysterious converse. Here's a witness
Who will avouch the fact; and that the stranger
With the first day-beam, vanished from his sight.

ISABELLA [*aside*]. He never told me this. Can he have met him?

JUDGE. Look on these things. They are mark'd with your name,
And stain'd with blood. They were found near the spot
Where a poor wretch lay bleeding. Can you explain it?

CHARLES. They are mine—I do confess it. I encounter'd
A person near that spot, and wounded him
In honorable duel. Nothing more
Can I explain.

MARY [*struggling*]. O father, let me speak.

RAVENSWORTH. Silence! Now answer me, and let the powers
Of darkness, that sustain you in your pride
Yield and abandon you unto your fate.
Did you not robber like, this night break in
My unguarded house, and there, with ruffian force
Attempt the honor of this maiden?

ISABELLA. Heaven!

RAVENSWORTH. D'ye hesitate! you dare not answer nay;
For here are witnesses to your confusion,
Who saw you clasp her in your vile embrace,
And heard her shrieks for help. Nay, here's the maiden,
Who will herself aver it.

MARY. Father, father!

RAVENSWORTH. Come forth, my child.

[*Attempting to lead her forward.*]

CHARLES. Forbear! it shall not need.

RAVENSWORTH. Do you confess?

CHARLES. Whate'er you will.

ISABELLA. 'Tis past.

[MARY *faints in the arms of* ALICE.]

RAVENSWORTH. Hear ye this, Judges! People, hear ye this? [*Storm commences.*]
And why do we delay! His doom were death,
Disdaining as he has to make his plea
To the charge of sorcery. Now, his full confession,
Which ye have heard, dooms him a second time.

[*Storm increases; Thunder and Lightning.*]

Then why do ye delay? The angry Heavens—
Hark, how they chide in thunder! Mark their lightnings.

[*The storm rages; the* JUDGES *rise; all is confusion; the* PEOPLE *and two* OFFICERS *gather around* CHARLES; OFFICERS *seize him.*]

ISABELLA. Save him! O Heaven! As ye are men, have mercy!

RAVENSWORTH. No; not beneath this roof: among the tombs,
Under the fury of the madden'd sky;
Fit time and place!

CHARLES [*as they are dragging him out*]. Mary; my mother! Mary!

ISABELLA. My son!
[*Leans nearly fainting in* LUCY'S *arms.*]
MARY [*reviving*]. Who calls me? Ah! What would ye do?
He's innocent—he's my betroth'd—my husband!
He came with my consent—he's innocent!
RAVENSWORTH. Listen not to her; 'tis his hellish magic
Speaks in her voice—away!
MARY. O Charles, my Charles!—
[*She faints.*]
[*They bear* CHARLES *out. The storm continues.*]
RAVENSWORTH. It is accomplish'd.

Enter the UNKNOWN

UNKNOWN. What? what is accomplish'd?
RAVENSWORTH. Who'rt thou that ask'st?
UNKNOWN. Nay, answer me. They tell
Of dreadful deeds ye are performing here.—
How's this! Has death been here among you?
RAVENSWORTH. Yes,
Whatever thou may'st be, death has been here
Guided by Heaven's vengeance.
UNKNOWN. Who is this?
'Tis she, 'tis she! Dost know me, Isabella?
ISABELLA. Is it not—?
UNKNOWN. 'Tis thy father.
ISABELLA. Father, father!
Have I then found thee! But my son! my son!
UNKNOWN. Unhappy child, be calm—I know thy story;
And do forgive and bless thee.
ISABELLA. Thanks, my father,—
[*Struggling to speak.*]
But—
UNKNOWN. What means this?
ISABELLA. O, for a moment's strength—
Haste—haste—they murder him—my son—
UNKNOWN. Thy son,
O, where?
ISABELLA. There—there—O Heaven! it is too late!

They enter with a Bier, carrying CHARLES. *The* UNKNOWN *leads* ISABELLA *slowly towards it.*

Enter SIR REGINALD

SIR REGINALD. O fatal tardiness! and yet I came
The instant that I learned it. Bloody monsters!
How will ye answer this? Behold these papers,
They're from the king! They bid me seek a lady,
Nam'd Isabella, whom he espoused in secret,
And her son Charles Fitzroy—And is it thus—

Enter GEORGE EGERTON, *pale and weak*

O George, look there!
GEORGE. O, brave, unhappy youth!
My generous foe, my honorable conqueror!
MARY [*reviving*]. Nay, ye shall not detain me—I will go,
And tell them all. Before I could not speak—
My father held me here fast by the throat.
Why will you hold me? they will murder him,
Unless I speak for him. He spoke for me—
He sav'd my honor; Ah! what's here? O Heaven!
'Tis he—Is he asleep?—No, it is not he.—
I'd think 'twere he, but that his eyes are swoll'n
Out of their sockets—and his face is black
With settled blood.—It is a murder'd man
You've brought me to—and not my Charles—my Charles!
He was so young and lovely.—Soft, soft, soft!
Now I remember.—They have made you look so,
To fright me from your love. It will not do—
I know you well enough—I know those lips
Tho' I have never touch'd them. There, love, there,
It is our nuptial kiss. They shall not cheat us—
Hark in thine ear, how we will laugh at them.
[*Leans her head down on the body, as if whispering.*]
SIR REGINALD. Alas! poor maniac.
[ISABELLA *who, supported by her father, had been bending over the body in mute despair is now sinking.*]

UNKNOWN. Daughter—Isabella—

ISABELLA. Father— [*Looking up in his face.*]

UNKNOWN. You will not leave me, Isabella?

ISABELLA. I would remain to comfort you, my father,
But there's a tightness here.—For nineteen years
He was my only stay on earth—my good,
My duteous son. Ere I found thee, my father,
The cord was snapp'd—Forgive me—

[ISABELLA *falls, and is received in the arms of* LUCY.]

UNKNOWN. Bless thee, child—
I will not linger long behind thee.

[*Storm subsides.*]

SIR REGINALD. Sir,
If you're that lady's father, I have here
A pardon for you from the king.

UNKNOWN. I thank him;
But it is now too late.—She's gone.—The world
Has nothing left for me—deep in the wilderness,
I'll seek a grave, unknown, unseen by man.—

WALFORD. How fares your hapless friend?

ALICE. Her cold cheek rests
Against his cheek—not colder—

WALFORD. Place your hand
Upon her heart: is there no beating there?

ALICE. There is no beating there—She's dead!

RAVENSWORTH. Dead, dead!—

[RAVENSWORTH, *who thro' this scene, had shewn the signs of stern and settled despair, occasionally casting his eyes upon his daughter, or raising them to Heaven, but withdrawing them again in utter hopelessness, now sinks groaning into the arms of* WALFORD. ISABELLA *is on her knees, on the upper side of the bier, leaning on* LUCY. *The* UNKNOWN, *with his hands clasp'd, bends over his daughter.* ALICE *is kneeling at the side of her friend.* SIR REGINALD *and* GEORGE EGERTON *stand near the head of the bier.* LUCY *and* EDWARD *behind their mistress. The background filled up by the* JUDGES, VILLAGERS, *&c.*]

The CURTAIN *falls amidst a burst of the Storm, accompanied by* THUNDER *and* LIGHTNING.

THE GLADIATOR

By Robert Montgomery Bird

ROBERT MONTGOMERY BIRD

[1806–1854]

Robert Montgomery Bird was born February 5, 1806, of a socially conservative and intellectually alert family. His boyhood was passed in his birthplace, New Castle, Delaware, a town rich in historic associations; he enjoyed nature and solitude, and early gave evidence of the imagination which later revealed itself so abundantly. After an early severe schooling, vividly described in *The Adventures of Robin Day*, Bird was allowed to follow his own interests, which led him to a reading of history, romance, and adventure, sources that he was later to draw upon in his plays. He subsequently re-entered school, benefited from the association with several talented instructors, and finished the academy at Germantown, in 1824, "with a distinguished literary rank among his fellow students."[1] During his course of study at the Medical School of the University of Pennsylvania, from which he was graduated as a doctor in 1827, he read widely and wrote a number of poems and plays.

After a year of practice he gave up medicine, owing to temperamental dislike for the work, and systematically set about a course of historical study to equip himself for the writing of "fifty-five plays besides a number of romances and stories. . . ."[2] These objectives, however, were never realized. In response to a prize offered by Edwin Forrest, the actor, for the best American play submitted, Bird wrote the blank verse tragedy *Pelopidas, or the Fall of the Polemarchs*. Dealing as it does with the successful revolt of Pelopidas against the tyrants of Thebes, its theme was adapted to Forrest's energetic talents and he awarded first place to Bird's manuscript; he never produced *Pelopidas*, however, for Bird soon presented a second prize play, *The Gladiator*, which was even more to Forrest's liking. This play was extremely successful as a stage production, being acted occasionally for three-quarters of a century in this country and abroad.[3]

Bird's third prize play, *Oralloossa, Son of the Incas*, was an outgrowth of his studies in South American history; it takes place during the Spanish colonization of Peru and deals with the uprising of Almagro and the killing of the Viceroy Pizarro. Though praised by contemporary critics, the play, in Forrest's reconsidered view, was neither a dramatic nor an artistic success. After an extensive

[1] Foust, Clement E., *The Life and Dramatic Works of Robert Montgomery Bird*. New York: 1919, p. 23. By the kind permission of Mr. Foust the biographical data for this account have been taken from his work, which gives a definitive account of Bird.

[2] *Ibid.*, p. 33.

[3] For details of its stage history see *ibid.*, pp. 39 ff.

trip through parts of South America Bird wrote his last and one of his best plays, *The Broker of Bogota*, produced in 1834. In contrast to his heroic plays, *The Broker of Bogota* deals with the domestic theme of a money lender's tragic difficulties over his son's marital affairs. Bird also revised a play, *Metamora, or the Last of the Wampanoags*, by John Augustus Stone; the plot of this Bird affirmed had been taken originally from a play of his own.[1]

The dramatist then turned to the writing of novels; these include: *Calavar*, *The Infidel*, *The Hawks of Hawk Hollow*, *Shepherd Lee*, *Nick of the Woods*, and *The Adventures of Robin Day*. Bird devoted his later years to journalism, being editor of the Philadelphia *North American*. His death occurred in 1854.

Most of the contemporary references to *The Gladiator* emphasize the splendid physical energies of Forrest's acting in the role of Spartacus. A few commentators took exception to his "physical" and "melodramatic" reading of the part, but William R. Alger, biographer of Forrest, defends this interpretation on the ground that a gladiator, under the circumstances, would have been physical and melodramatic. There is little doubt that the more obvious aspects of the play do, in some measure, answer to this description; but the concept of the piece as a whole stems from a consistent philosophy. Largely a play of action, courage, and heroic speeches as it is, *The Gladiator* nevertheless reflects, in its picture of Roman slavery, concepts of social freedom and equality current in Bird's own time. The power of the Roman master over his slaves, his abuse of that power in gaming with human life, and the destruction of slave families are graphically portrayed with unmistakable implication. Slavery destroys not only life but also the desire for it:

> "... being slaves,
> We care not much for life. . . ." [2]

Merchandising of slaves is held up to scorn: "The miserable rich man, the patrician monger, that, by traffic in human flesh, has turned a patrimony of an hundred talents into an hundred thousand!" [3]

> "Villains, do you put them up for sale, like beasts?
> Look at them: they are human." [4]

The gladiatorial contests, in which the slaves are forced to "tear each other for their masters' pleasure," take place in

> "... the temple, where they mock the Gods
> With human butchery . . ." [5]

and for their "cold blood" victories the contestants earn a "bulldog's reputation." The reason the masters could treat their slaves so cruelly is that the Romans re-

[1] For a discussion of this involved question see Foust, *op. cit.*, pp. 60–61.

[2] Act II, sc. 2, p. 170.

[3] Act I, sc. 1, p. 161.

[4] Act I, sc. 1, p. 166.

[5] Act II, sc. 3, p. 171.

garded the barbarians (i.e., non-Romans), from whom they recruited their slaves, as inferior to men:

> "Why, yes, a sort of men.
> They had legs and arms, noses and eyes like men,
> They bled like men; but being barbarians,
> Of not much matter of account as men." [1]

Though Bird's primary aim in *The Gladiator* may not have been abolition,[2] yet it is significant that the play appeared at a time when anti-slavery sentiment was beginning to make itself felt in American literature: the play was completed and produced in 1831, the year that Whittier's lines *To William Lloyd Garrison* appeared and the year that Garrison founded *The Liberator*. Bird intended that the anti-slavery sentiment in the play should be strong, for among his notes appears the direction to insert "an impassioned and strong dialogue about slavery";[3] and he later realized the success of his efforts at this point, for he feared that if *The Gladiator* were to be produced in a slave state, "the managers, actors, and author as well would probably be rewarded with the penitentiary." [4] It is to be noted also that the conclusion of *Pelopidas* is anti-slavery in feeling.

The thought of Spartacus with reference to the natural man is consonant with the philosophy that underlay much of the nineteenth-century humanitarianism; although Spartacus is on occasion moved by pure blood-lust,[5] he is normally benevolent, his heart "can melt to pity," [6] and he believes that man in his native state is good: "Man is heaven's work," and

> "Nature
> Makes fewer rogues, than misery." [7]

Spartacus is impressed with the equality and freedom of men in view of their common origin in a superior power: he speaks of himself as

> ". . . a free son of a free sire, and imaged
> After the semblance of the Only Master. . . ." [8]

A corollary of Spartacus' trust in the natural man is his conception of the ideality in rural life; amidst the "beasts of Rome" he pictures to himself, in a passage of fine poetry:

[1] Act II, sc. 1, p. 169.

[2] According to Foust, "his central aim in *The Gladiator* was to fashion a part which should fit and display the individuality of the first American tragedian of the day." (*Op. cit.*, p. 156.)

[3] Quinn, A. H., *A History of the American Drama from the Beginning to the Civil War*, p. 230, n. 2.

[4] Foust, *op. cit.*, p. 51.

[5] When "goaded into fury" he says:

> "There's nothing now but blood
> Can give me joy. . . .
> I'll decimate them."

[6] He twice softens in behalf of Julia, a valuable hostage:

> "Lo you, she weeps, and she is fatherless.
> Thou wouldst not harm an orphan?"

[7] Act V, sc. 4, p. 194. It must be noted, however, that several years later, in *Nick of the Woods*, Bird pictured the American Indian as debased and ignorant.

[8] Act III, sc. 3, p. 180.

"... the glory of those lands,
Where peace was tinkling on the shepherd's bell
And singing with the reapers...." [1]

Spartacus' last words before his death express this thought of country peace—perhaps they are symbolic of the life to be (certainly they are suggestive of Tennyson's *Ulysses*):

"Well—never heed the tempest—
There are green valleys in our mountains yet.—
Set forth the sails.—We'll be in Thrace anon.—" [2]

But a symbolic interpretation of this passage would be problematical at best, for the religious aspects of Spartacus and of the play are minor: only on two or three occasions is the subject approached. Spartacus speaks of himself as being imaged "After the semblance of the Only Master—" and he recalls the time when he carried his brother in his arms

"To mountain-tops, to worship the great God...." [3]

The anguish occasioned by the murder of Spartacus' wife and child, however, drives him to temporary atheism. "There are no gods in heaven ...",[4] and it leaves him with a Macbeth-like disbelief in life:

"Why should we struggle longer, in this dream
Of life, which is a mocking lunacy,
With ever sunshine playing far ahead,
But thunderbolts about us?...
There is no Orcus blacker than the hell
That life breeds in the heart." [5]

Thus "this hell of Rome" has robbed him of his humanity prior to the taking of his life.

Anti-imperialism is evident in the picture of Rome as a cruel and tyrannical mistress, populated with

"... fiends, that make their mirth
Out of the groans of bleeding misery!" [6]

A nation can extend its sovereignty only at the cost of the vanquished people; greatness comes from the "miseries of subjugated nations." "How many myriads of happy people ... were slain like the beasts of the field, that Rome might fatten upon their blood, and become *great?*" [7] Wealth, a product of empire, "is

[1] Act IV, sc. 3, p. 187. Also:
"Ah, would to heaven, Phasarius,
I were with her now and my smiling boy,
In Thrace again, beside our mountain cot,
Or in those vales, where babbling Hebrus tumbles
Along his golden sands. . . ." (Act III, sc. 2, p. 178.)

[2] Act V, sc. 7, p. 198.

[3] Act IV, sc. 1, p. 184.

[4] Act V, sc. 4, p. 195.

[5] Act V, sc. 4, p. 196.

[6] Act II, sc. 3, p. 174.

[7] Act I, sc. 1, p. 165.

the key to office, here in Rome—";[1] it is the basis of favor,[2] honor,[3] even of love.[4]

We see, then, that the play reflects the American environment in the form of political democracy opposing itself to the rule of the few.[5] Alger notes the play's "extreme democratic quality," [6] and when the play was taken to London, the Americans in attendance were apprehensive of the reaction these views would produce on the British. The latter, in the main, were enthusiastic, except that they wanted Forrest to play in Shakespeare; they did not fail to notice, however, the democracy in the play: Forrest "has all the energy, all the indomitable love of freedom that characterizes the transatlantic world. We say this because there were many republican allusions in the play where the man spoke out quite as much as the actor, if not more." [7] That the strong democratic ideas expressed in the play are integrated with Bird's own views is suggested by his profession of political faith: "I am a Whig, a very good one." [8]

It is pertinent to note that contemporary with *The Gladiator* there were several plays containing "revolt" themes, among them Bird's other plays and the following: *Caius Marius*, *Metamora*, *Tortesa the Usurer*, *The Bride of Genoa*, *Sertorius*, and *Jack Cade*.[9]

Though Bird made a careful study to ascertain the historical facts for the background of his tragedy,[10] yet he resorted to changes of time and situation where they seemed dramatically necessary.

The Gladiator was a distinct dramatic success, it has many poetic passages of real merit,[11] and it derives from the American thought contemporary with it.

Through the kind permission of Clement E. Foust the present text is based on his version of the play printed in *The Life and Dramatic Works of Robert Montgomery Bird*. Passages omitted in the stage representation are indicated by enclosure within brackets of this shape < >.

[1] Act II, sc. 1:
"They ask not if their candidate have honor,
Or honesty, or proper qualities;
But, with an eager grin, *What is his wealth?*"

[2] Act II, sc. 1: ". . . men
Consider none, but those can profit them."

[3] Act II, sc. 1: "For what is honor,
With empty pockets, in this thievish world?"

[4] Act II, sc. 1: "I am ashamed
You have so poor a spirit as to love
This base-born Capuan, whose whole wealth you might,
Piled up in coin, base on a puny drachma."

[5] It will be remembered that Andrew Jackson came into office in 1828.

[6] Alger, William R., *Life of Edwin Forrest*. Philadelphia: 1877. I, 298.

[7] *Ibid.*, 300–301. Quoted from the London *Sun*, October 18, 1836.

[8] Foust, *op. cit.*, p. 125.

[9] See Quinn, *op. cit.*, pp. 267–268.

[10] Foust points out that Bird probably used the following sources in conjunction with this play: Plutarch, *Crassus* [8–12]; Livy, *Epit.*, xcv; Florus, iii, 20; Eutropius, vi, 2; Tacitus, *Ann.*, xv, 46; Paterculus, ii, 30; Appian [*De Bellis Civilibus*, i, 116–121]; Sallust [Hist., iii, frag. 90, 93, 96, 100, 101; iv, frag. 41]; Caecilius; A. Ferguson, *History of the Progress and Termination of the Roman Republic;* N. Hooke, *Roman History from the Building of Rome to the Ruin of the Commonwealth.*

[11] "Although written exclusively with a view to the stage, it abounds with poetic passages, and possesses no ordinary share of literary merit." (James Rees, *The Life of Edwin Forrest*, p. 423.)

PERSONS REPRESENTED

Marcus Licinius Crassus, a Roman Prætor

Lucius Gellius, a Consul

Scropha, a Quæstor

Jovius, a Centurion

Mummius, lieutenant to Crassus

Batiatus Lentulus, a Capuan Lanista, or master of gladiators

Bracchius, a Roman Lanista

Florus, son of B. Lentulus

Spartacus, a Thracian,
Phasarius, his brother,
Ænomaiis, a Gaul,
Crixus, a German,
and others
} Gladiators

A boy, son of Spartacus

Julia, niece of Crassus

Senona, wife of Spartacus

Citizens, soldiers, etc.

Scene. *Rome, and parts of Italy.* Time, b.c. 73

THE GLADIATOR

ACT I

SCENE I. *Rome. The Street before* BRACCHIUS'S *house*

Enter PHASARIUS, ÆNOMAIIS, *and other gladiators*

PHASARIUS. There never was a properer moment. I look around me on the Roman flocks, that are deserted by their watch-dogs and shepherds, and my fingers itch to be at their throats. Rome has sent forth her generals to conquer the world, and left nothing but her name for the protection of her citizens. Where now is that warlike, arrogant, and envious coxcomb, Pompey? Quarrelling,—he and that old brawler, Metellus,—in Spain, with the rebel, Sertorius: Lucullus, the Spoiler? Chasing the braggart, Mithridates, over his Pontic mountains: and Marcus, his brother? Killing the rest of my countrymen, the furies speed him! That restless boy, young Cæsar? Among the islands, crucifying the pirates. Marius dead, Sylla rotting.—There is not a man in Rome, that Rome could now look to for service.

ÆNOMAIIS. The prætor, Crassus.

PHASARIUS. The miserable rich man, the patrician monger, that, by traffic in human flesh, has turned a patrimony of an hundred talents into an hundred thousand! If there be any virtue in the love of wealth, then is the prætor a most virtuous man; for he loves it better than he loves the gods. And if he be great and magnanimous, who coins his gold from the sinews of his bondsmen, set me down Crassus as the beloved of all greatness. 'Sblood, brother sworder, what were such a counter of silver in the iron wars? Get me up a rebellion, and you shall see this great man brained by the least of his merchandise.

ÆNOMAIIS. Well, I should like to be at the killing of some dozen such tyrants.

PHASARIUS. Why should you not? Some thousands like ourselves,
Most scurvy fellows, that have been trained, like dogs,
To tear each other for their masters' pleasure,
Shed blood, cut throats, and do such mortal mischiefs
As men love best to work upon their foes,—
Of these there are some thousands in this realm,
Have the same wish with us, to turn their swords
Upon their masters. And, 'tis natural,
That wish, and reasonable, very reasonable.
I am tired of slaying bondmen like myself,
I am sick of it. That day the Roman knight,
To win the smile of the rich quæstor's daughter,
In the arena sprung, and volunteered
To kill a gladiator, and did find
His liver spitted, like a thing of naught,
Upon my weapon,—since that day I tasted
Of Roman blood, I have had no desire
To kill poor slaves—I've longed for naught but Romans!

ÆNOMAIIS. Well, we can die, and kill some, ere we die.

PHASARIUS. Ay, marry, some dozens;
And should those wretches be but moved to join us,
We might, for dozens, count us glorious thousands.

ÆNOMAIIS. Well, we are all agreed to this. We are thirty. But how
Shall we get weapons?

PHASARIUS. Set our dens afire,
And force the armory.

ÆNOMAIIS. Our master, Bracchius,
Has a sharp watch to that.

PHASARIUS. In half an hour,
We are at our morning's practice. Now, thou knowest,

To keep me in good heart, he humors me
Most fulsomely. I have won him some great wagers,
So I am worth his fooling. I will urge him,
For this day's play, instead of laths, to give us
True brands, for keener practice, that we may
Show nobler for him at the prætor's games.

ÆNOMAIIS. <He knows, indeed, 'tis needful we have ready,
For these same games, the best of skill:> I've heard
That Lentulus the Capuan brings a troop
Of excellent swordsmen on that day.

PHASARIUS. What, excellent?
Did I not beat his boaster?—Excellent?

ÆNOMAIIS. 'Tis rumored so.

PHASARIUS. By Jove, we will put off
This thing a day! I have seen no excellence
In weapons for a month.

ÆNOMAIIS. Why need you see it?

PHASARIUS. Nay, if he have a man to meet a man,
I must be in the arena: No desertion,
When there's a peril to be dared and ended!
Faith, I will have a bout, if it but be
To make Rome talk. You shall see, Ænomaiis,
If he be matched with me in the Thracian combat,
How I will use that trick my brother taught me,
When first I flashed a weapon.

ÆNOMAIIS. I doubt not,
You will maintain your reputation.

PHASARIUS. Faith,
I'll hear once more this Roman acclamation,
Ere it be changed to curses.

ÆNOMAIIS. See! Our master—

PHASARIUS. Well, get you gone.

ÆNOMAIIS. Forget not for the weapons.

PHASARIUS. Ay, ay—after the shows.

[*Exit* ÆNOMAIIS *and the Gladiators.*

Enter BRACCHIUS

BRACCHIUS. How now, Phasarius; what did these cutthroats here? Idling, sirrah?

PHASARIUS. No; they were moralizing over their scars, and asking what they had got by 'em.

BRACCHIUS. Do the rogues think themselves soldiers, that their cuts should be worth anything but showing?

PHASARIUS. No. But some of them hope to be made freedmen one day, when they are no longer fit for the arena.

BRACCHIUS. Fellow, thou knowest I love thee, and will enfranchise thee.

PHASARIUS. Yes,—when my eye is dimmed, my arm stiffened, my heart chilled, my head gray: I look for redemption no sooner. I am a lusty, serviceable rogue yet: Why should you free me now?

BRACCHIUS. Sirrah, are you insolent? I will have the centupondium to your heels, and the lash to your shoulders.

PHASARIUS. Which will make me fight the better at the prætor's games, hah! Which of us is the lunatic?

BRACCHIUS. What, you knave!

PHASARIUS. Thou art my master; but I know, thou wouldst as soon set me free, as scourge me. Both would destroy thy subsistence, and one thy life; in either case, I would fight no more. And if thou wert to touch me lawfully with the thong, thou knowest, I would unlawfully murder thee.

BRACCHIUS. You shall be crucified!

PHASARIUS. Then shall the crows pick forty thousand crowns from my bones; for so much are these muscles worth.

BRACCHIUS. Out upon you, villain! It is my favor has made thee so insolent.

PHASARIUS. It is my knowledge of my own price, and not thy favor, which is more perilous than thine anger. Pr'ythee, threaten me no more; or I shall grow peaceable, and spoil thy fortune.

BRACCHIUS. You have sworn never to decline the combat.

PHASARIUS. Ay; so I have. But I have found no one regards a slave's oath; and why now should the slave? It is my humor, and not my oath, makes me a shedder of blood. But the humor may change.

BRACCHIUS. Well, thou art a most impudent talker; it is eternal Saturnalia with thee. But I forgive thee, and will do thee more kindness than I have done already.

PHASARIUS. Which is to say, you have some new jeopardy to put my neck in. You have some gladiator of fame you would have me fight, is it not?

BRACCHIUS. Ay, if rumor be worth the noting. Crassus has hired the gladiators from Capua; and, 'tis said, Lentulus will bring with them a man that will cut the coxcomb from thy pate, and utterly annihilate thee.

PHASARIUS. They say so? Annihilate me!

BRACCHIUS. Faith, 'tis so reckoned, and strong wagers are making against you.

PHASARIUS. Hah? Against me? Annihilate me! If he have a head of adamant and a breast of brass, he may do it; but if his scull be common bone, and his skin no thicker than bullhide—Mehercle! let me see this Cyclops.

BRACCHIUS. Now, by Jupiter, I love thy spirit.

PHASARIUS. Has he no name? No country? No voucher of triumphs? Marry, for a mushroom, a thing that was yesterday unknown, his credit is a jot too arrogant; and, as I am a Thracian, and feel the blood of the warlike god, the father of Thrace, still tingle in my fingers, I will make my iron acquainted with his ribs.—Out upon him,—Annihilate me!

BRACCHIUS. Come, thou art his better; but he is noted enough to make thy triumph the more glorious. Put thyself in the meanwhile to practice. But who comes here? What, Lentulus of Capua?

Enter LENTULUS

By mine honesty, I am glad to see thee. Bringest thou any new cutthroats? What, man, here is my Mars of gladiators, my most unmatched and unmatchable, Phasarius the Thracian. Look how lusty the knave looks! Hast anything fit to be slashed by such a fellow?

LENTULUS. Nay, I know not. 'Tis a most gallant villain. <Slew he not six at the shows given by Gellius the consul?

BRACCHIUS. Yes, by Mars; and would have made eel's meat of the seventh, but that the people grew pitiful and pointed their thumbs.—I could have cuffed 'em, senators and all.—He had him on his hip, his body bent round him thus, his fist to his poll, his dagger to his throat. By Mars, 'twas the noblest sight I had seen for a month: and yet when he looked to them for the doom, the pitiful things cried *Nay*.—I could have cuffed 'em! >

LENTULUS. But is he thy best man?

BRACCHIUS. The best in Rome. I have a Gaul, too; but he is not his equal. I would thou hadst a match for either. Crassus will pay: the best gladiator in the land were no loss, if killed in his service.

LENTULUS. I have brought some indifferent good fellows: and one of them, I think, I would wager against your unmatchable.

BRACCHIUS. Hearest thou that, Phasarius? Get in and practice. [*Exit* PHASARIUS.

LENTULUS. But he will not take the gladiator's oaths.

BRACCHIUS. What, is he slave or felon?

LENTULUS. A slave that I bought of the quæstor just returned from the army of Thrace; a shepherd, I think, they told me, and leader of a horde of his savage countrymen. I bought him on the faith of the fame he brought with him, of being the most desperate, unconquerable, and, indeed, skilful barbarian in the province. <Thou hast not forgot Caius Clypeus, the centurion, that fought in the shows at the funeral of Sylla?

BRACCHIUS. He was accounted on that day the second swordsman in Rome.

LENTULUS. His bones, with those of two of his followers, are rotting on the banks of the Strymon. The three attacked the valiant savage, my bondman; and by Jupiter, without other help than fortune and extraordinary prowess, he slew them all.

BRACCHIUS. Hercules! he has magic weapons! >But how was he taken?

LENTULUS. Betrayed by his follower, while he slept; and yet he had vengeance on his betrayer, for he dashed his brains out upon a rock.

BRACCHIUS. Excellent! Dash his brains out! He is a Titan. I would have given a dozen common slaves to have seen him do that thing!

LENTULUS. But he will not swear.

BRACCHIUS. Come, thou knowest not the nature of these fellows. Didst thou speak him kindly?

LENTULUS. Ay: but I had better have talked softly to a hyena: he did but scowl at me. Faith, he will sit yon by the day, looking at his chains, or the wall; and if one has a word from him, it is commonly a question, How many leagues he is away from Thrace.

BRACCHIUS. Didst thou tell him of the honors of a gladiator?

LENTULUS. Ay; and he asked if cutting throats was the most honorable occupation in Rome?

BRACCHIUS. By Mars, thou shouldst have scourged him.

LENTULUS. I did.

BRACCHIUS. And how wrought it?

LENTULUS. I think the knave had killed me, when I struck him,—ay, even with his manacled fist,—but that he was felled by the staff of my freedman. I should have hanged him, but was loath to lose so bold a varlet. Wherefore I had him scourged again, and, faith, he took it as passively as a stone. But it will not make him swear.

BRACCHIUS. Didst thou vow to the gods to hang him up like a dog, if he were so obstinate?

LENTULUS. I had a halter put to his neck; but then he laughed, and thanked his barbarous gods for such indulgence.

BRACCHIUS. Nay, this is a madman.

LENTULUS. I had the fetters taken from his arm, and sent one to attack him with a weapon. But although I laid a sword by him, he would not use it; yet he struck the assailant with his fist, and felled him as one would a wall with a battering ram. But then he was angry. Another time, he sat still, and let the slave wound him, unresisting.

BRACCHIUS. Moody caitiff! Thou hadst better drown him.—Look thou—Mine eyes are dim—I have bought a troop of women and children—Thracians too—and I think those be they coming yonder.

LENTULUS. Thou art mistaken. Those are mine own cutthroats, and the wild Thracian among them.

BRACCHIUS. Why didst thou bring him to Rome?

LENTULUS. In a last hope to urge him to the oath. Look, is he not a most warlike and promising fellow?

Enter SPARTACUS, *chained, and* FLORUS *with the* CAPUAN *Gladiators*

BRACCHIUS. A Hercules, a Mars! What, thou rogue, why dost thou droop thus? Why art thou so sullen and obstinate? No words? What, canst thou not speak?—Fetch me a scourge hither—I'll find thee a tongue.

LENTULUS. Come, sirrah, look up, speak, show thyself.

SPARTACUS. Is it a thousand leagues away to Thrace?

LENTULUS. What, thou fool, wilt thou always be harping on Thrace? 'Tis so far away, thou wilt never see it more.

SPARTACUS. Never.

LENTULUS. Why, I say, never. Why wilt thou be so mad as to think of it?

SPARTACUS. Have Romans fathers, and wives, and children?

BRACCHIUS. Truly! Thou art a Thracian; what is thy name?

SPARTACUS. Misery.

LENTULUS. Thou seest!

BRACCHIUS. Faith, thou hast scourged him too much; thou hast broke his heart. Come, sirrah, dost thou love thy country?

SPARTACUS. I have none,—I am a slave. I was bought; I say, I was bought. Do you doubt it? That man scourges me; *thou* didst threaten me with stripes; every Roman I look upon, speaks to me of scourging. Nay, they may: I was bought.

LENTULUS. Thou seest, Bracchius! This is the manner of his obstinacy.

BRACCHIUS. Nay, I see more than thou thinkest. I can move him yet.—Observe him.—He mutters to himself.

SPARTACUS. Is not this Rome? The great city?

BRACCHIUS. Ay; and thou shouldst thank the gods they have suffered thee to see it, before thou diest.—

SPARTACUS. I heard of it, when I was a boy among the hills, piping to my father's flocks. They said, that spoke of it, it was the queen of cities, the metropolis of the world. My heart grew big within me, to hear of its greatness. I thought those men who could make it so, were greater than men; they were gods.

LENTULUS. And are they not, sirrah?—

SPARTACUS. How many palaces, that look like the habitations of divinities, are here about me! Here are marble mountains, that have been hewn down and shaped anew, for men to dwell among. Gold, and silver, and purple, and a million of men thronging the pillared hills!

BRACCHIUS. And what thinkest thou, now thou hast seen it?

SPARTACUS. That,—if Romans had not been fiends, Rome had never been great! Whence came this greatness, but from the miseries of subjugated nations? How many myriads of happy people—people that had not wronged Rome, for they knew not Rome—how many myriads of these were slain like the beasts of the field, that Rome might fatten upon their blood, and become *great?* Look ye, Roman,—there is not a palace upon these hills that cost not the lives of a thousand innocent men; there is no deed of greatness ye can boast, but it was achieved upon the ruin of a nation; there is no joy ye can feel, but its ingredients are blood and tears.

LENTULUS. Now marry, villain, thou wert bought not to prate, but to fight.

SPARTACUS. I will not fight. I will contend with mine enemy, when there is strife between us; and if that enemy be one of these same fiends, a Roman, I will give him advantage of weapon and place; he shall take a helmet and buckler; while I, with my head bare, my breast naked, and nothing in my hand but my shepherd's staff, will beat him to my feet and slay him. But I will not slay a man for the diversion of Romans.

BRACCHIUS. Thou canst boast, barbarian! If thou canst do this, what brought thee to Rome, a captive?

SPARTACUS. Treachery! I was friendless, sick, famished. My enemies came in numbers. They were like the rats in Egypt, that will not come near the crocodile while he is awake: they attacked me sleeping. Had they found me with a weapon in my hands, Gods! I had not now been a thing for Romans to scourge.

BRACCHIUS. Fellow, I love thee. What is thy name?

SPARTACUS. What matters it?

BRACCHIUS. Wilt thou be free?

SPARTACUS. Free!

BRACCHIUS. Take the oaths of a gladiator, and kill me a score of lusty fellows—

SPARTACUS. A score! kill a score of men? in cold blood? and for the diversion of Rome's rabble? I will not.

BRACCHIUS. By Mars, then you shall be sent to man young Cæsar's galleys, and be whipped daily.

LENTULUS. Fight me half a score, and, by Jupiter, I will send thee back to thy wife.

SPARTACUS. My wife!—The last thing that mine eyes looked on,
When my steps turned from Thrace, it was my cottage,
A hideous ruin; the Roman fires had scorched it:
No wife sat sobbing by the wreck; no child
Wept on the sward; not even the watchdog howled:
There was no life there.—Well, why should I talk?
'Tis better they are perished.

LENTULUS. This is despair:
The slave is reckless.—

SPARTACUS. O ye heavens! that sight
Withered my heart; I was a man no more.
I had been happy, too!—Had ye spared them,
Then spoke of freedom, you should have had my blood,
For beastly ransome: All integrity
And pride of heart I would have sold for it.

BRACCHIUS. Sirrah, there are more wives in Thrace.

LENTULUS. Lo now!
He'll speak no more.—You, Bracchius, have more skill
To move these obstinates. You shall buy him of me.

BRACCHIUS. And hang him! Marry, not I. He is a madman.
I have some better merchandise here now,
Not warlike, but as gainful.

Enter SENONA, *with a child, and other slaves*

Thou seest these creatures:
Here are some Thracians, too.—The moody villain!
He should be hanged.—The Thracian women are
Most excellent spinners. Buy a brace of them
For your wife. I care not for so many.

LENTULUS. This woman
That weeps so, she with the brat,—is she a Thracian?

BRACCHIUS. Hark ye, mistress, answer—are you of Thrace?
One might swear it by her silence; for these savages
Are always obstinate at the first. You like her?
Well, out of my friendship now, I'll almost give her to you.
Three thousand drachmas—

LENTULUS. Three thousand furies!

BRACCHIUS. Ay, with the boy, too—'Tis a lusty imp.

LENTULUS. Three thousand sesterces; and that's too much.

BRACCHIUS. Jove! talk of sesterces? This cub is worth it!
[BRACCHIUS *handling the child roughly*.]

SENONA. Ah, hurt him not.

SPARTACUS. Hah!

LENTULUS. Three thousand sesterces.—

SPARTACUS. Did my ears mock me?

BRACCHIUS. Well, then, sesterces,
For the woman alone.

SENONA. You will not part us?

SPARTACUS. Hah!
Gods, pity me! does the grave give back the dead?
Senona!

SENONA. Hah! Hah! My husband!

BRACCHIUS. What's the matter?

LENTULUS. A bargain—

BRACCHIUS. What, his wife? Six thousand drachmas.
No more sesterces!—Caitiff, is this thy wife?—[*To* SPARTACUS.]

SPARTACUS. And my miserable boy, too,
Exposed in the street to sell!

BRACCHIUS. By Jove, I have you.
Six thousand drachmas.

SPARTACUS. Why didst thou not die?—
Villains, do you put them up for sale, like beasts?
Look at them: they are human.

LENTULUS. Silence, rogue.—

SPARTACUS. I will not silence. I will ransome them,
What way you will, with life or blood.—

BRACCHIUS. By Jove,
I will not sell her. Into the house, get in.—
Take her along.

SPARTACUS. You shall not—I will brain that man
That lays his hand upon her.

BRACCHIUS. Kill the villain.—

SPARTACUS. Man, master!—See, I am at your feet, and call you,
Of mine own will, *My Master!*—I will serve you
Better than slave e'er served;—grant me this prayer,
And hire my blood out. Buy—yes, that's the word;
It does not choke me—buy her, buy the boy;
Keep us together—

BRACCHIUS. Six thousand drachmas—

SPARTACUS. I will earn them,
Though they were doubled.

LENTULUS. Will you fight?

SPARTACUS. And die.

LENTULUS. Die! Then my gold is lost.

SPARTACUS. I will not die.—
Buy them, buy them.

LENTULUS. And you will swear?

SPARTACUS. I will,—
To be a cutthroat and a murderer,—
Whate'er you will,—so you will buy them.

LENTULUS. Unbind him.

BRACCHIUS. Six thousand—

LENTULUS. Three. Remember, Bracchius,
If you prevent his fighting, your own profit
Suffers as well as mine.

BRACCHIUS. Five thousand then.

LENTULUS. Nay, pr'ythee, four.

BRACCHIUS. Well, out of friendship,
It shall be four.—But, faith, my Gaul shall kill him.

LENTULUS. We shall see. I'll wager even, and no less
Than the purchase money.—

SPARTACUS. Come, dry your tears, Senona:
We are slaves: Why should slaves weep?

SENONA. O, dear my husband,
Though I ne'er thought to have the joy to meet you
Again, in this dark world, I scarce feel joy—
I think, my heart is burst.

SPARTACUS. Come, be of better cheer:—
Art thou not now amid the gorgeous piles
Of the potential and the far-famed Rome?

SENONA. But oh, the hills of our own native land!
The brooks and forests—

SPARTACUS. Ah! no more, no more:
Think of them not.—

SENONA. Where we fed sheep, and laughed
To think there could be sorrow in the world;
The bright, clear rivers, even that washed the walls
Of our burned cottage—

SPARTACUS. No more, no more, no more.
Are there not hills and brooks in Italy,
Fairer than ours? Content you, girl.

SENONA. Alas,
This boy must be a Roman, and a slave.

SPARTACUS. By heaven, he shall not! Free as rock-hatched eagles,
Thy boy was born, and so shall live and die!—
We wear our fetters only for a time—
Romans are not all like these men. We'll see
Our home yet. We are slaves but for a time.—
I need not ask thee for my mother, girl:
I know this thing has slain her. Her heart cracked,
When they bore off my brother.

LENTULUS. With the Gaul then:
And if he beat him, as I think he will,
Then shall he battle with your best.—Now, sirrah.

SPARTACUS. Hah!

SENONA. Husband!

SPARTACUS. Well, it is not chains alone
That make the slave. What will my master have?

LENTULUS. I'll have thee exercise thine arm in practice.
Thou wilt have brave men to contend with.

SPARTACUS. Well,
I will do so: but speak it not before my wife.

LENTULUS. Get thee along. Florus, conduct them to
Their lodgings. See this Thracian exercised.
[*Exeunt.*

END OF ACT I

ACT II

SCENE I. *A room in* CRASSUS'S *house*

Enter CRASSUS, JOVIUS, *an Artificer, and a Slave*

CRASSUS. To the full letter of the law. What, use
My excellent slave in thy most gainful craft,
And groan at the reckoning? By Jupiter,
Thou shalt his hire pay to the utmost sesterce,
Or have a quittance writ upon thy back.
Breed I then servants for the good of knaves?
Find me the money, or I'll have thee whipped.
Begone. [*Exit Artificer.*] I built not up my fortunes thus,
By taking sighs for coin: had I done so,
Foul breath had ruined me. How should I then
Have borne the hard expenses of these games,
The uproarious voters clamor for?

JOVIUS. What! true.
Wealth is the key to office, here in Rome,—
Or is the lock that best secures it.

CRASSUS. Sirrah,
Thou dost not mean, the officers bribe the people?

JOVIUS. I had sooner lug old Cerberus by the ears,
Than do aught to our citizens, but praise 'em.
But, in your gracious ears,—our sovereign Romans
Are something bauble-brained; and, like to children,
Pass qualmish by their needful medicines,
To snatch at sugary playthings. What do they
In their elections? Faith, I have observed,
They ask not if their candidate have honor,

Or honesty, or proper qualities;
But, with an eager grin, *What is his wealth?*
If thus and thus—*Then he can give us shows*
And feasts; and therefore is the proper man.
An excellent mode of judging!

CRASSUS. Ancient comrade,
At me thou point'st now.

JOVIUS. Not irreverently:
I question of the people; and, I think,
They loved great Marius more for his rich feasts,
Than his rich victories. Sooth, when angry Sylla
Swept them, like dogs, out of his bloody path,
And made their hearts sore, they forgot their fury,
When once they had looked upon his fighting lions.

CRASSUS. Hence, thou inferrest, they have chose me prætor,
Being rich enough to purchase them diversions!
But I have done them service in the wars,
And, out of gratitude—But no more of that.—
They shall be pleased: the games go bravely on.
The Capuan hath brought me a new sworder.—
Sirrah, go bid my niece here. [*Exit* SLAVE.
This Capuan hath
A son most insolent and troublesome.

Enter FLORUS

What, Sirrah, again? Hast thou not had thy answer?
<Kill me these flies that being lean themselves,
Swarm after fatness.> Why art thou this fool,
To covet my rich niece?

FLORUS. I seek not riches.

CRASSUS. Pah! Will poor lovers sing eternally
The self-same song? They seek not riches! Jove,
Why pass they then all poverty, where their choice
Might find a wider compass?

FLORUS. Excellent prætor,
Give me the maid, and keep her lands thyself.

CRASSUS. Sirrah, thou know'st, the girl abhors thee. Look,
She has the blood of nobles in her veins,
Distilling purely through a thousand years;
And thine comes grossly from a German slave's,
That was thy grandsire.

FLORUS. Worth and deserving toil can raise me up,
Even from my poverty, to wealth and honors.
And these shall do it.

CRASSUS. Get thee away, then,
To warring Pompey, and, with thy soiled sword,
Carve out clean honors; not forgetting, whilst
Thy right hand grasps the enemy's throat, to thrust
The left into his purse: For what is honor,
With empty pockets, in this thievish world?
Honor is men's consideration: men
Consider none, but those can profit them.
Therefore, if thou'lt be quick
In gaining honor, use thy right hand rather
For gathering gold than killing—or rather use them both:
Make much, and thou shalt be most honorable.

JOVIUS. Thou hearest, Florus? This is the truer wisdom.
I've fought for honor some good thirty years,—
<Courting her with such madman freaks, as leaping,
First man, upon an arm'd wall in the storm;
Saving a comrade's life (some dozen of 'em,)
Out of the jaws of death; contesting singly
With scores, in divers places.> But being foolish,
In my hot haste for slaughter, I forgot
To look for spoil; and lo, the consequence!
I bear the vine-branch,[1] and am only honored
As a gray-haired centurion.

[1] The MS. contains the following note, written in Bird's hand: "This (the vine-branch) was the badge of a centurion's office, and he should carry it—at least in camp and in his embassies." [*Foust's note.*]

CRASSUS. Get thee gone.
When thou art worthy, ask her, and no sooner. [*Exit* FLORUS.
A most mad, insolent boy, and honest son
Of a breeder of cutthroats! Would some knave would hang him.
He has the damsel's heart, too. See, she comes.—
Is the litter ready?

Enter JULIA

JULIA. It cannot be, dear uncle,
You will send me to the country?
CRASSUS. It cannot be!
What, chuff, it cannot be? In faith, it can be,
And, instantly, it shall be:—Into the country,
To weep and meditate. I am ashamed
You have so poor a spirit as to love
This base-born Capuan, whose whole wealth you might,
Piled up in coin, base on a puny drachma.
JULIA. Ah! When did love e'er think of drachmas, uncle?
<You would have me, when a lover moans, demand him,
Could he coin gold, as easily as sighs;
Or when he wept, ask if his pockets had
As many talents as his eyes had tears.
Then should he change his manner, and where he might
Have wooed me with soft words, assault me with
A schedule of his properties; instead
Of flattering, boast me of his lands; his vows
Change into oaths of, lord, how rich he was.
How could I say him nay?>
CRASSUS. A milksop boy,
That has done nothing in the world but breathe,—
Has won no name or fortune. Why should such
A natural expletive, <a sack of breath,>
Aspire to wealth or woman? When he proves him
Worth his existence, then let him aspire.
Till then thou shalt be hid from his presumption,
Even in Campania.
JULIA. Oh, but not today.
Tomorrow, or the next day, when the games are done.
I must see them: 'twould kill me not to look
Once more upon the fighting gladiators.
CRASSUS. Pho!
Thou a green girl, and talk of gladiators!
My youth was pass'd in battles, and I am not
Unused to blood; but my flesh always creeps,
To see these cold-blood slaughters.
JULIA. So does mine.
Ugh! my heart stops with terror, and my eyes
Seem parting from their sockets; my brain reels,
While I look on; and while I look, each time,
I swear I ne'er will look again. But when
They battle boldly, and the people shout,
And the poor creatures look so fearless,—frowning,
Not groaning, when they are hurt:—Indeed 'tis noble!
<And though they fright me, always make me weep,
I love to see them. These are your own shows:>
Oh, I must see them.
JOVIUS. This is a brave maiden.
<You should look on a battle—two great armies,
(Perhaps a hundred thousand men apiece:)
Fighting as staunchly as so many wolves,
Throttling and stabbing, dying in multitudes,—
A chaos of death:—Even such a one as that
(My own first fight) at Aqua Sextia,
Against the Ambrones, where a hundred thousand
Of the barbarians fell.
JULIA. An hundred thousand!
JOVIUS. Was it not glorious?
JULIA. Horrid!
JOVIUS. Horrid! Humph,
Still woman.—But these were barbarians.
JULIA. Were they not men?
JOVIUS. Why, yes, a sort of men.
They had legs and arms, noses and eyes like men,
They bled like men; but, being barbarians,
Of not much matter of account as men.

JULIA. That makes a difference. But an hundred thousand
Was many to kill, even of barbarians.

CRASSUS. Come, you're a goose, you know not what you say.

JULIA. O but these gladiators! My friend, Caloeia,
Told me that famous one, Phasarius,
Would fight today. He is a handsome rogue,
And kills a man the prettiest in the world. >

CRASSUS. You shall not see him.

JULIA. Dear my uncle!

CRASSUS. You came
Into this city, modest and obedient;
Now you have learnt to cog, cajole and cozen;
And, in the teeth of my authority,
Give private hopes to this low Capuan;
And, while mine eyes are tied upon the games,
Would—But I'll balk your hoped for interviews.
The litter waits you at the door. Farewell.
This good old man, who once was my tried client,
Shall have you in charge. Now no more opposition.
Farewell. Be wise, and love none but the worthy. [*Exeunt.*

SCENE 2. *A court before* LENTULUS'S *house*

Enter FLORUS *with* SPARTACUS, CRIXUS, *and other Gladiators*

FLORUS. You have played well, and beaten Crixus fairly.
Carry this skilfulness to the arena,
And you shall win great honor.

SPARTACUS. Great degradation.
No matter: I am sworn to be a caitiff.
Where have you placed my wife? It was conditioned,
You should not part us.

FLORUS. She is lodged hard by:
After the combat, you shall see her.—Come,
Play me a bout here with Soturius.
I'll fetch you foils.

SPARTACUS. I'll play no more: I was not sworn to that.

FLORUS. You cannot go too well prepared.

SPARTACUS. Even as I stand,
Awkward or skilful, doomed to die or kill,
So will I go.—I'll train no more for murder.

FLORUS. Well, as you will.

SPARTACUS. Will it not be enough,
If I disarm or worst my enemy?
May I not spare him?

FLORUS. Not unless the people
Grant you permission. <When you have him at
Your mercy, look to the spectators then.
If they consent, they will their thumbs raise—thus:
Then you shall spare. But if their hands be clenched,
And the thumbs hid, then must you slay. >

SPARTACUS. Well, well;
I understand.

FLORUS. Breathe yourselves here awhile,
Then follow to the armory. [*Exit.*

SPARTACUS. Good brother,
Have you yet fought i' th' Amphitheatre?

CRIXUS. Ay.

SPARTACUS. And killed
Your adversary?

CRIXUS. Ay. Each one of us
Has won some reputation.

SPARTACUS. Reputation!
Call you this reputation?
This is the bulldog's reputation:
He and the gladiator only need
The voice o' the master, to set on to mischief.—
Love you your masters?

CRIXUS. No.

SPARTACUS. Or of your own wishes
Go ye to perish?

CRIXUS. No; but being slaves,
We care not much for life; and think it better
To die upon the arena, than the cross.

SPARTACUS. If ye care not for life, why die ye not
Rather like men, than dogs?

CRIXUS. What mean you?

SPARTACUS. Were it not better
To turn upon your masters, and so die,
Killing them that oppress you, rather than fall,
Killing your brother wretches?

CRIXUS. True, it were.
Put arms into our hands, unlock our dungeons,

And set us out among the citizens;
Then ask this question.
SPARTACUS. Do you say this? By heaven,
This spirit joys me.—Fight ye all today?
CRIXUS. We are so ordered.
SPARTACUS. How many do you number?
CRIXUS. Fifty.
SPARTACUS. Fifty? How many hath this Roman,
This villain Bracchius?
CRIXUS. Some five and thirty.
SPARTACUS. And fight they all?
CRIXUS. Some forty pairs today.
SPARTACUS. O heaven, what, forty?
CRIXUS. And ere the shows are done,
Two hundred pairs.
SPARTACUS. Two hundred pairs!—Four hundred
Arm'd slaves, that hate their masters!
CRIXUS. On the third day,
All that survive, will fight in general battle.
SPARTACUS. In general battle!—If Senona now,
And the young infant were in Thrace.—Alas,
To peril them.—
CRIXUS. What say'st thou, Thracian?
SPARTACUS. Nothing;
At least, not much.—Are there now troops in Rome?
CRIXUS. Four legions of Prætorian Guards; and now
Each legion counts five thousand.
SPARTACUS. 'Twill not do.
CRIXUS. What will not do?
SPARTACUS. I'll tell you by and by:
'Tis worth your ear.—But let us now go arm,
Then to the Arena, to begin the work
Of slavish murder.—We are gladiators.
[*Exeunt.*

SCENE 3. *The Arena of an Amphitheatre, behind which are many citizens.* CRASSUS *seated with his Lictors,* MUMMIUS, LENTULUS, BRACCHIUS, FLORUS, *and many officers,—Ædiles, Conquisitores, etc.*

CRASSUS. Let our good friends, the citizens, be seated.
We purpose to delight their humors with
The bravest gladiators of this realm.—
What say'st thou, Capuan? Why, tell me, thou
Hast brought me some brave cutthroats, to be pitched,
Through the first hours, in single combat, with
The best slaves of our Bracchius.
LENTULUS. Even so,
Most noble prætor; and, with the consent
Of your appointed officers, we first
Will bring a lusty Thracian, who, although
Yet unadventured in the Arena, bears
A name of valor.
CRASSUS. Let him before us.
[*Exit* FLORUS.
Had Thracians, by their firesides, fought as fiercely
As now they fight upon the Roman sand,
The cranes o' the Strymon still had been their sentries.

Reënter FLORUS, *with* SPARTACUS, *as a gladiator*

Is this the man? A very capital knave;
Yet, or I err, of but a little spirit.
Where is the fiery confidence, should flash
From his bold eyes? the keen and tameless spirit,
Should brace his strong limbs to activity?
LENTULUS. Driveller, arouse thee!—Let not his gloom condemn him:
He is most wayward, but, in truth, right valiant.
What, sirrah, shake off these clouds, and do thy homage
To the most noble prætor. Bend thy knee.
SPARTACUS. Did I swear that? Kneel *thou,* whose servile soul
Was given for crouching. I am here to fight!
CRASSUS. This is some madman!
LENTULUS. A barbarian,
Bred in a savage roughness.
SPARTACUS. Well, I am here,
Among these beasts of Rome, a spectacle.
This is the temple, where they mock the Gods
With human butchery,—Most grand and glorious
Of structure and device!—It should have been a cave,

Some foul and midnight pit, or den of bones,
Where murder best might veil himself from sight.—
Women and children, too, to see men die,
And clap their hands at every stab! This is
The boastful excellence of Rome! I thank the Gods
There are Barbarians.

CRASSUS. Now, by Jupiter,
The rogue speaks well—But Romans must be pleased—
Sirrah,—[*Comes down center.*]

SPARTACUS. Roman!

CRASSUS. Most impudently bold.
I did mistake him. Prepare thyself.

SPARTACUS. I am ready,
As ready to die, as thou to see me die.
Where is the opponent? Of what nation comes
The man that I must kill?

CRASSUS. What matters it?

SPARTACUS. Much, very much. Bring me some base ally
Of Roman rapine, or, if ye can, a Roman:—
I will not grieve to slay him.

CRASSUS. Faith, I like
This fearless taunting, and will sound it further.
Thy foe shall be a Spaniard.

SPARTACUS. Alas, I should
Bethink me of his country, as of mine,
Ruined and harried by our common foe;
His kinsmen slain, his wife and children sold,
And nothing left of all his country's greatness,
Save groans and curses on the conquerors.

CRASSUS. A Carthaginian.

SPARTACUS. What, a Carthaginian?
A relic of that noble tribe, that ne'er
Would call Rome friend, and perished rather than
Become Rome's vassal? I could not fight with him:
We should drop swords, and recollect together,
As brothers, how the Punic steel had smote,
Of yore, to Rome's chill'd heart; yea, how Rome quaked,
How shook her proud sons, when the African
Burst from the sea, like to its mightiest surge,
Swept your vain shores, and swallow'd up your armies!
How, when his weapons, gored with consular blood,
Waved o'er your towns, your bucklered boasters fled,
Or shook, like aguish boys, and wept and prayed:—
Yea, feared to die, and wept and prayed.

LENTULUS. <Peace, villain.>

CRASSUS. Strike him not, Lentulus. The prattler knows
There's scarce a man of the Punic stock left living,
To boast of these mishaps.—Thy adversary
Is a brave Gaul.

SPARTACUS. Why, there again! The name
Speaks of Rome's shame. Name but a Gaul, and I
Bethink me of the Tiber running blood,
His tributaries choked with knightly corses;
Of Rome in ashes, and of Brennus laughing
At the starved cravens in the Capitol.

CRASSUS. Sirrah, no more.
Be but thy sword as biting as thy tongue,
And I'll assure thee victory.—Bring in
The Gaul. Use thy best skill, if skill thou hast,
Or I'll not lay an obolus on thy life.—
[*A Gallic Gladiator is brought in.*]
Clear the Arena. [*Ascends chair again.*]

SPARTACUS. I will fight with him;
But give me to spare his life.

CRASSUS. That privilege
Rests with the people. Remember thy oath.—Sound, trumpets. [*A flourish.*]

SPARTACUS. Brother—

CRASSUS. No words; but do thy best. <He'll spit thee.>

[*They fight. The* GAUL *is disarmed, and thrown on his knees.* SPARTACUS *looks to the people.*]

Thine oath! Strike, <villain!> Hah!

[SPARTACUS *kills the* GAUL.]

Why, that was bravely done.

SPARTACUS. Well, I have done it. Let me go hence.

CRASSUS. Not so.—
Most nobly fought!

SPARTACUS. Alas, alas, poor slave!—

CRASSUS. Bring me another.
[*The body is taken away.*]
SPARTACUS. I will fight no more.
CRASSUS. Sirrah!
SPARTACUS. I have heart enough to die, but not to kill.
CRASSUS. Why, 'twas most capitally done! Remember
Thy oath.
SPARTACUS. I care not. I will fight no more.
CRASSUS. Thou shalt have freedom. Nay, I'll ransome for thee,
Thy wife and boy.
SPARTACUS. Wilt thou?
CRASSUS. By Mars, I will.
Fight through these games; and thou and they shall be
Sent back to Thrace.
SPARTACUS. Shall we see Thrace again?—
Let him come on; yes, though it sick my soul,—
Let him come on.
CRASSUS. Bring in the Thracian!
[*Exit* BRACCHIUS.
SPARTACUS. Thracian?
I will not fight a Thracian! 'Tis my countryman.
CRASSUS. Nay, but thou shalt, and kill him too; or thou
And they, are slaves eternally.
SPARTACUS. O heaven!
Bring me a Spaniard, German, Carthaginian,
Another Gaul, a Greek—any but Thracian.
CRASSUS. None
But this same Thracian is thy match; and truly
If thou slay him, there will remain no other
Worthy of thee. Thou shalt be quickly free.
SPARTACUS. I will fight two—three—so they be not Thracians.
CRASSUS. The Thracian, or eternal bondage; bondage
For wife and child, too.
SPARTACUS. Wilt thou swear to free us?
Fight with a Thracian!—Wilt thou *swear* to free us?
CRASSUS. Bring hither the *Vindicta:* With this rod,
If thou escape this man, the prætor frees thee.

Reënter BRACCHIUS, *with* PHASARIUS.

This is thy foe.
PHASARIUS [*aside*]. What, do I dream?
SPARTACUS. Alas,
Thou art a Thracian and my countryman,
And yet we meet as deadly foes. Forgive me.
PHASARIUS [*aside*]. This is no fantasy!
CRASSUS. Observe them, Bracchius:
Thy boaster hesitates.
PHASARIUS. Thou art a Thracian?
SPARTACUS. Would thou wert not.
PHASARIUS. Of the Ciconian tribe—
A son of blue-waved Hebrus?
SPARTACUS. Such I am.
And comest thou too of the same race? and set
Against thy brother?
PHASARIUS. Brother, indeed!
Thy name is Spartacus.
SPARTACUS. Where learnt you that?
Freemen have heard it, but not slaves.
PHASARIUS. How fares thy father?
SPARTACUS. Didst thou know him?—Dead—
I cannot fight thee.
PHASARIUS. Hadst thou not a brother?
CRASSUS. Why prate these cutthroats? Come, prepare, prepare—
SPARTACUS. A young, brave heart, whose steps I taught to dare
The crags and chasms and roaring cataracts
Of his own native hills, till he was freer
Among them than the eagles. What art thou,
That seem'st to know him? I would be angry with thee:
These words make me look on thee as a friend.
PHASARIUS. Seem I not like Phasarius?
SPARTACUS. What, thou?
A mailed warrior like a singing boy?
The Romans slew him.
PHASARIUS. They enslaved him—Brother,
Changed as I am, and from a harmless boy,
Turned to a rough destroyer, still am I
The selfsame fool that once thou called'st brother.
SPARTACUS. Thou mock'st me. Thou!
PHASARIUS. My father, Menalon—
SPARTACUS. Thy father, Menalon?

PHASARIUS. My mother—
SPARTACUS. Ay, thy mother?
PHASARIUS. Laödice.
SPARTACUS. My brother!
CRASSUS. What mean these rogues, that they have dropped their swords,
And faln, like friends, about each other's necks?
What ho, ye slaves, give o'er this timeless juggling:
Take up your swords, and look ye to the signal.
SPARTACUS. I do believe the gods have given me o'er
To some new madness: First, I find in Rome,
Where naught I looked for but despair, my wife
And then my brother!
<CRASSUS. Villains!
SPARTACUS. But I am sorry
To find thee here, Phasarius.>
LENTULUS. <Whining miscreant,>
Why mark'st thou not the prætor?
CRASSUS. <Rogues, prepare.>
Let the trumpet sound.
SPARTACUS. Bring me my adversary.
CRASSUS. Thou hast him there.
SPARTACUS. What, he? This is my brother.
You would not have me fight with him!
CRASSUS. His brother?
PHASARIUS. 'Tis true, most excellent prætor.
CRASSUS. Now, by Hercules,
This is too strange for truth.
LENTULUS. Ye cogging rogues,
Think ye to balk us thus?
<BRACCHIUS. Conspiracy!
Shameful collusion! Out on you, Phasarius,
You're not afeard now? Out, ye cheating villain.>
PHASARIUS. Hear me, good prætor—
CRASSUS. <Rogues>, prepare yourselves.
This is a most evident knavery, to 'scape
From one another.—Brothers indeed!—Prepare;
Take up your arms.
SPARTACUS. Foul Roman—
CRASSUS. Bring me in
The guarding cohort: [*An Officer goes out.*]
I'll have them cut to pieces,
If they refuse the battle.—Brothers indeed!
SPARTACUS. Thou hard, unnatural man—
PHASARIUS. Patience, brother—
SPARTACUS. Let them come in—We are armed.—
CRASSUS. Most strange and insolent contumacy!
PHASARIUS [*aside*]. 'Tis something sudden—and in Rome!—Peace, brother.—
SPARTACUS. We will resist them, armed as we are.
Can we not die?
PHASARIUS. Most worthy prætor, pardon.
Grant us a word together, and we are ready.
CRASSUS. Fine knavery! I did almost suspect
Yon cutthroat for a coward—that 'twas skill alone
Gave him his courage, which he fear'd to try
With that more skilful savage. For the barbarian,
His soul is made of contrariety.
PHASARIUS [*apart to* SPARTACUS]. I know them all—This thing was hatch'd before.—
They wait without,
Circled by cohorts, but all arm'd for combat.
Let me but raise the cry of *Freedom* to them,
And each man strikes his Roman to the earth.
SPARTACUS. The slaves of Lentulus—they will strike, too:
Let us but reach them, and they rise with us.—
PHASARIUS. One moment, princely prætor.
CRASSUS. Not an instant.
What, shall our shows wait on the time and pleasure
Of our base bondmen? Sound the trumpets there—
What, treachery, ho! Call in the soldiers!—
PHASARIUS. Freedom
For gladiators!
SPARTACUS. Death to all their masters!—
CRASSUS. Treachery!—
SPARTACUS. Death to the Roman fiends, that make their mirth
Out of the groans of bleeding misery!
Ho, slaves, arise! it is your hour to kill!
Kill and spare not—For wrath and liberty!—

Freedom for bondmen—freedom and revenge!—

[*Shouts and trumpets—The guards and gladiators rush and engage in combat, as the curtain falls.*]

END OF ACT II

ACT III

SCENE I.[1] *A room in* CRASSUS'S *house*

Enter CRASSUS, JOVIUS, LENTULUS, BRACCHIUS, MUMMIUS

<CRASSUS. Incredible! What, fight a consular army?
Or look one in the face?

JOVIUS. So says the courier.
'Tis sworn, that half the slaves of Italy
Are flocking to his banner.

CRASSUS. Fight a consul!
Fight Cneus Lentulus!

JOVIUS. 'Tis not so much
To one who has already beat a proconsul.
You'll not doubt that? nor that these madman slaves,
Led by this whirlwind slayer—

LENTULUS. My precious Thracian!—

JOVIUS. Have vanquished severally, and in pitched battles,
Three prætors of the provinces.

CRASSUS. Shame upon them!
Sneers for their lives, contempt for epitaphs!
Beaten by slaves!—I warrant me, by mine—
Two thousand costly and ungrateful villains:—
I'll hang them, every man.—Beaten by slaves,
Gross, starving, unarmed slaves!

JOVIUS. Not now unarmed.
Each rogue has got a Roman harness on,
Filched from the carcass of a Roman veteran.
Not starving neither, whilst every day they sack
Some camp or city—pouncing sudden down,
Like vultures, from their hills upon our troops.

CRASSUS. Scandalous, scandalous! Slaves, wretched slaves,
Led by a slave, too!

LENTULUS. Still my precious Thracian!

CRASSUS. A scurvy gladiator, with no brains;
An ignorant savage.—

JOVIUS. Come, give the rogue his due:
He has more brains than all our generals,
For he has beaten them; that's a soldier's proof.
This Spartacus, so late a bondman, has
A soul for master; though a shepherd bred,
He has fought battles, ay, and led men, too,—
Some mountain malcontents in his own land,—
'Gainst Roman conquerors; and, by the faith
Of honesty, for honest I will be,
In courage, stratagem, resource, exploits,
He shows a good commander. He has formed,
Out of this slavish, ragged scum, an army;
Arms it and feeds it at his foeman's cost,
Recruits it in his foeman's territory;
Which foe is renowned Rome, resistless Rome,
Rome the great head and empress of the world!
Is he not then a general?

CRASSUS. I grant you,
The rogue is not a common one; but still
A slave. And much it shames me that the senate
Finds me no worthier enemy; whom to conquer,
Wins neither spoil nor honor.

JOVIUS. No spoil indeed,
Unless you count their arms and bodies such;
But honor enough to him that beats the vanquisher
Of some half score commanders: There's your honor.
Come, stir these centuries: My old bones are aching
For one more battering, ere they fall to dust.
The reprobates must be put down, that's certain,
And by yourself, or Pompey.>

[1] There is a query in Bird's handwriting "whether to restore the beginning of this scene or some part of it?" It seems that Dr. Bird submitted the MS. of *The Gladiator* to Edwin Forrest for revision, who no doubt suggested many of the cuts indicated. [*Foust's note.*]

CRASSUS. Now the gods rest him!
Is there no trouble can befall the state,
But men must cry for Pompey? As if Rome
Had whelped no other fit to do her service.
<Still is it Pompey, great and valiant Pompey,
Must all our state thorns conjure into laurels.—
Well, Crassus is not Pompey, but may serve
For the besom.

JOVIUS. What, a besom?

CRASSUS. Ay, to sweep away
This filthy blush out of Rome's cheek. >—These varlets,
These fooled *lanistæ*, that have trained slaves up
To fight their masters, shall to camp with me,
And of the evils they have caused, partake.

LENTULUS. I am willing.
I'll kill my Thracian, though he be a general.

BRACCHIUS. It matters not how soon I am knock'd o' the head.
I have not now a gladiator left.—
The rogues have ruined me.

CRASSUS. Where is thy son?
This knave shall march, too. Have you brought the woman,
The wife o' the Thracian, here to Rome?

LENTULUS. I have sent for her.
My son has gone into Campania.

CRASSUS. What, to Campania? Now, by Jupiter,
This fool will set me mad.

LENTULUS. I know not that.
He went with the band of youthful volunteers,
To the camp of Gellius, the consul.

JOVIUS. Bravely done.
That was in memory of our counselling.
But now for action. <You remember, prætor,
This consul prays immediate succors, being
But ill provided, should the Gladiator,
In contest with his colleague, prove victorious,
As there is ground to fear; for Lentulus,
At the last word, was at extremities.
Being deprived, too, by the angry senate
Of their authority, their mutinous troops
But scurvily obey them. > Should the rebels
Come near your country-seat—

CRASSUS. No more of that:
The consul shall protect her.—Presently
Bring me six legions; which, being added to
The consular troops and the knights volunteers,
We'll have appointed to this service. Then
There shall be knocks enough, I promise you.
See that these people follow, and all men
Whose slaves have joined the rebels. It is reason,
The rogues should kill no masters but their own. [*Exeunt.*

SCENE 2. *A plain in Campania, after the battle. Some corses lying about. March of trumpets.*

Enter, sumptuously armed, SPARTACUS, PHASARIUS, CRIXUS, ÆNOMAIIS, *and Attendants*

SPARTACUS. So, we are victors, conquerors again.
The hotbrained boasters, that in mockery thought
To ape the angry Scythian, and subdue us
With whips, instead of warlike instruments,
Lie hush'd and gory; and, despite the claim
Of their high honors and nobility,
There is no slave too base to tread upon them.
There he's a Consul.—I have known that word
Fright men more than the name of gorgeous kings.
Say to barbaric States, *A Consul Comes,*
A Roman Consul, and their preparation
Of war or welcome, speaks a demigod.
And yet lies he on the opprobrious earth,
A palmy Consul, by a slave's hand slain,
No nobler than his horse—a thing to glut
The starved hyena's maw.[1]

PHASARIUS. Ay—and there's another
Must lie beside him.

SPARTACUS. Speak you of Gellius?

[1] The original reading, struck out in the MS., was,—
"—a thing to rot
In a hyena's paunch."
The reading I have adopted is written in a hand resembling Forrest's, in pencil, and is probably his suggestion. [*Foust's note.*]

PHASARIUS. Ay, marry. I'll fight now nothing less than consuls.
There is another of them, and I say,
Another battle and another victory.

CRIXUS. 'Tis but to will, and we have won it.

SPARTACUS. Ay;
But not today. Our medly bands have earned
Their armor, and are weary.—'Tis full six leagues
To Gellius' camp.

CRIXUS. My Germans will not fear it.

SPARTACUS. It cannot be, and must not.

CRIXUS. Must not, Spartacus?

SPARTACUS. Ay, man, I say so: this thing must not be.
When ye were few, with one consent, ye chose me
Your leader, with each man an oath to yield
To me sole guidance. This was little honor,
To be the chief of fourscore fugitives,
And none would have it, save myself. I took it,
And ye have prospered. Under my authority,
In a few days your ranks have been swell'd up
To fearful thousands; and from a band of slaves,
Skulking in caves, you have become an army
Can fight a Roman Consul. This is proof,
I have deserved obedience; and therefore,
I still command it.

CRIXUS. And my countrymen
Myself have made their leader; and they bid me
Lead them to Gellius.

SPARTACUS. We are but one army,
With but one object, howsoe'er our ranks
Are filled with various nations. We are slaves,
All of us slaves, contesting for our freedom;
And so far free, that we have arms and kill;
No further. We have yet to cut our way
Out of this tyrant empire; which to do,
We must destroy more armies, that are gathering
To hem us in. We do not fight for conquest,
But conquer for our liberties; and they
Are lost by rashness. Let us rest our troops,
And think of Gellius on the morrow.

CRIXUS. Today, today,
Ere he have rallied this fight's fugitives.

SPARTACUS. The thousands that are crowding to our lines
Will, by the dawn, have trebled all his gain.

CRIXUS. I will beat him with the Germans alone.

SPARTACUS. You shall not;
I am your general, and forbid you.

CRIXUS. Thracian,
I was a slave, but am not now.

PHASARIUS. Brother Crixus,
On second thoughts, 'tis better put this off,
According as the general commands.

CRIXUS. I am sole leader of my countrymen.

PHASARIUS. Sirrah, thou art a mutineer.—

SPARTACUS. Peace, brother.—

PHASARIUS. Defy the general! If one beggar's rogue
Of all his Germans dare to leave the lines,
I'll have him spitted like a cur.

SPARTACUS. Peace, brother.
Contention will harm worse than this partition.
German, thou hast thy wish: depart in peace,
But without hope of succor, if the Roman
Prevail above thee.

PHASARIUS. Pray the gods he do!
<And thwack them till they are skinless, all. Base rascals
And mutineers!>

SPARTACUS. Take all thy countrymen,
Or all that wish to follow thee.

[*Exit* CRIXUS.

PHASARIUS. Rank mutiny!
Why did you let him go?

SPARTACUS. To teach him, brother,
Him and some others of our lieutenants,
(For we are growing mad upon success,)
An humbling lesson. A defeat were now
Better than victory; and, in his Germans,
We best can bear it.

PHASARIUS. Let them go, and hang;
They are all villanous hotheads, and presumptuous
Beyond all tolerance. And, to punish them,

They shall not share with us the fame and spoil
Of the sack'd city.

SPARTACUS. Brother, I think thou art
Almost as madbrained as the rest.

PHASARIUS. I have
A kind of ardor, that, for aught I know,
May be a lunacy. But this is clear:
Rome is a city; cities may be sack'd;
So Rome may be.

SPARTACUS. A city, that the world
Looks frighted at, even in her sleep of peace,
As gazers look at sleeping lions. I told
This German fool, we did not fight for conquest,
But for a passport to our several homes.
What care we then to waste our vigor on
The gates of fortressed cities?

PHASARIUS. But this city—

SPARTACUS. Is as impregnable as the storm-arm'd sea.
Why should we talk of it? Great Mithridates,
Though populous Asia followed at his back,
Should, were his frothy hopes to point at it,
Be laughed at for a kingly maniac.
What should be said of us, the mushroom warriors
Of Roman dunghills, should our arrogance
Mad us so far? I think, we do not fight
To make the world talk?

PHASARIUS. I would have you do so;
Fight now for glory; let ambition raise you
Among the deathless, now while fate invites you.
Rome has no greatness, but is now employed
In foreign climes: You have well tried yourself;
And consuls vanish, when your trumpet sounds.
March on the city, and there swear to die,
Or live its master, and you are its master.
Think, brother, think what glorious fame were ours,
As lasting as the eternal world, should we,
The upturned dregs of servitude, destroy,
As, by the inviting fates! We may destroy,
This lair of lions, this den of conquerors,
This womb of heroes, whose boastings fright the earth,
And whose ambition (—look, Ambition!)—chains it!

<SPARTACUS. This is a wild and most preposterous hope.
Even the fierce Hannibal, with veteran troops,
And all the towns of Italy at his feet,
Save this alone, here paused his hopes.

PHASARIUS. Hope thou
T' excel the vaunted African, and dare
Beyond his daring. Hast thou not a heart
Bigger than his, that, with a herd of slaves,
Hast wrought as much as all his veterans?
Smiles heaven upon thee less, which, in an hour,
Has, from a dungeon, raised thee to an army,
Still growing, still victorious? Do this deed,
And live for ever.>

SPARTACUS. Well, well, I'll think of it.
Perhaps Senona's there:—Ah, would to heaven, Phasarius,
I were with her now and my smiling boy,
In Thrace again, beside our mountain cot,
Or in those vales, where babbling Hebrus tumbles
Along his golden sands; and dreamt no more
Of sacks and battles.

PHASARIUS. Whilst this city stands,
This ne'er can be; for just so long our country
Remains a Roman province. Tear it down,
And you enfranchise Thrace, and half the world.

SPARTACUS. We'll think of this again, when we are stronger,
And when we have Senona sent to us.
Meanwhile we must the final effort make
To ransome her. <Did you secure a guide,
To lead us through the mountains? I have seen
The camp most strongly guarded, and fear not
To trust it with the trusty Ænomaiis.
When the tired troops have slept an hour, I'll order
To bring them after us, to see indeed
How we may end, what Crixus may begin,
Disastrously for him, on Gellius,
In the confusion of the Consul's triumph.>
Pick me an hundred of our swiftest horses,

And have them presently in wait for me.
I shall fight better, when I know each blow
Strikes a protection for my family.
[*Exeunt.*

SCENE 3. *A room in* CRASSUS'S *Villa*
Enter JULIA *and* FLORUS

JULIA. I am glad to see thee. This terrific din
Of the near battle made a sparrow of me.
I was afeard to breathe, <lest I should swallow
Some of your horrid missiles; for I ran
Unto the housetop, to look on the fight.
But the moon was more coward than myself,
And hid her pale face in a cloud: so nothing
I saw. But I could hear the brazen trumps,
The conchs and cornets, the shouts and yells of fury,
The clang of arms, and whistling in the air
Of stones and arrows. But, come tell me now,
My general, have you killed a foe tonight?
FLORUS. And won a civic crown, by saving a friend.
JULIA. That's good; I am glad to hear it.>
FLORUS. But I am sorry
To find you here among these fears and perils.
I would you were in Rome.
JULIA. There is no peril.
Have you not beaten these wild gladiators?
A shepherd flying from his pastures, told me,
That Gellius had the victory, and had taken
Or killed the insurgent, bloody Spartacus.
FLORUS. I know not that. 'Tis true, that we have beaten
A band of mad rogues, that assaulted us;
And 'tis believed, their general, Spartacus,
Is dead upon our trenches; for whose body
Search is now made. But one poor prisoner,
<I think, the only one whose life was spared,>
Declared these troops to be but a small band
Of mutinous runagates, that had left their leader,
Being thereto moved by their late victory
Over the consul Lentulus.
JULIA. What, Florus!
A victory over Lentulus?
FLORUS. 'Tis even so:
His army has been vanquished, himself slain
By the late bondman. And those, who give faith
To the assurance of our prisoner,
Fear for *our* consul, should the Thracian march,
After his mutineers, upon us now;
Our camp being all a confused festival
Of drunken triumph,—half our soldiers scattered
In search of spoil and fugitives.—
SPARTACUS [*within*]. Guard the doors:
Let none go out.
FLORUS. What voice is that? By heaven,
We are betrayed!

Enter SPARTACUS, PHASARIUS, *and others.*
ÆNOMAIIS

SPARTACUS. <Sold, lost, and dead!>—
Look to the maiden.
<What, flourishing fool,> drop thy sword's point, or die.
FLORUS. A thousand times, ere thou, malicious rebel,
Touch this endangered lady.
SPARTACUS. Straw, I say!
[*He disarms* FLORUS.]
Know I not this boy's face? [1]
FLORUS. I think thou should'st.
Spare thou the lady, rich will be her ransome.
And for myself, I know, thy deadly fury
Grants never quarter.
SPARTACUS. By the stripes not yet
Fled from mine outraged limbs, thou art the son
Of Lentulus the scourger!
PHASARIUS. Ay, the same.
Let him atone his rascal father's sins:
Scourge him to death.
FLORUS. Give me a soldier's death:

[1] There are the following notes in Bird's hand, evidently in answer to Forrest's suggested cuts.

"Think you had better keep these expressions particularly the *flourishing fool* and *straw.* They express, in a very lofty and furious style, the contempt which such a man as Spartacus would feel at finding himself resisted by a younker."

"The term *boy's* was meant as a substitute for boyish; not, as if asking the question of others, *the face of this boy.*" [*Foust's note.*]

Let me die by the sword. I never scourged thee.

SPARTACUS. Thou! Miserable boy!

FLORUS. And well thou knowest,
Thou fierce and fiendish man, this tongue of mine
Was oft thy intercessor.

SPARTACUS. I do know,
One of thy blood did give me to the scourge—
Me, a free son of a free sire, and imaged
After the semblance of the Only Master—
Gave me to thongs and whips, as a poor beast,
Till I became one. This I know; know thou,
From that shamed hour, when first my body writhed
Under the merciless lash, I did devote
The scourger and his household to the furies,
To quick and murderous death. And thinkest thou,
Thy whining kindness took away a pang?
Thou art the Roman's son, and thou shalt die.

FLORUS. Let it be so—

SPARTACUS. It shall be so. Thou seest,
Command and dignities have not wiped out
The memory of wrongs; and Roman blood,
Running in rivers ever at my feet,
Sates not the thirst for more!—Take him away;
Scourge him to death.

JULIA [*to* SPARTACUS]. Thou horrible monster, spare him,
And name whate'er thou wilt for ransome.

SPARTACUS. Ransome!
Drachmas for stripes!

FLORUS. Beeseech him not, fair Julia.
Think of thyself, or let me think for thee.

JULIA. He never did thee hurt.

SPARTACUS. Let her be ta'en away.

FLORUS. Let her be ransomed, and for thine own wife.

SPARTACUS. Ay, so I will: 'twas e'en for that I took her.

FLORUS. Then may'st thou instantly exchange them.—

SPARTACUS. How!

FLORUS. Thy wife is in the consul's camp—

SPARTACUS. In the consul's camp?

FLORUS. There driven by the fright of her conductors.
And thou may'st instant ransome her.—

SPARTACUS. Ha, ha!
Now does Jove smile. What, ransome her?
Ay, ransome;
But with the steel.—I can almost forgive thee,
For this good news.—Prætor, I have thee now
In the same trap thou set'dst for me!—
What, sirrah,
Ye have beaten my refractory lieutenant,
The German Crixus?

FLORUS. Ay, I thank the gods.

SPARTACUS. And so do I; it wins me victory,
And puts the second consul in my hands.—
Antistheus, see these captives safely guarded.—
Brother, the troops must now be nigh upon us.—
Take thou the Thracian cohorts, and in secret
Steal to the heights that overhang his rear,
Posting a strong guard on the river. Let none 'scape,
And let none live. Myself will force the camp,
And drive the rioting fools upon your swords.—
I say, spare none.

PHASARIUS. 'Twere much too troublesome
To imitate them, and build crucifixes
For the prisoners.

SPARTACUS. Let not a moment's rashness
Bring us a limping victory. Stand fast
Upon your post, and every rogue is dead.—
Roman, thou shalt see how I'll ransome her!
[*Exeunt.*

SCENE 4. *The Tent of* GELLIUS, *the Consul*
GELLIUS *discovered, with* SCROPHA, SENONA *and her child, and attendants.*

GELLIUS. There is no doubt, this foolish German lies.
'Twas the main body of the rebels surely.
No mere detachment would have impudence
To march upon a consul. Now this victory,
Which, on the morn, I'll follow up, will change

The tone o' the angry Senate, and restore me
To my full rank, and, what is better, send
The scheming Crassus empty-handed back.
This is a man should fight in the Velabrum,
Among the cheating mongers, and not bring
His brains of a broker to a glorious camp.
This woman here, the wife o' the Gladiator,
That cutthroat caitiff—

SENONA. Why dost thou slander him?
Has he not fought a consul?

GELLIUS. Pr'ythee, be silent.
He's a brave rebel, and will be renowned.—
Now, as I said, with this same woman here,
The Greek-brained Crassus did design some trick,
Some scurvy plot upon the Gladiator—
[*Alarums.*]

SCROPHA. Hark!

GELLIUS. A device of the rejoicing drunkards.—
This thing meant Crassus, this—

SCROPHA. The clang increases!
[*A great shout is heard.*]

GELLIUS. The knaves are noisy.—

Enter a CENTURION, *wounded*

CENTURION. Fly for your lives! The camp is forced—

GELLIUS. What camp?

CENTURION. Your own. The Gladiators are upon us:
We are surprised, and all is lost. [*Exit.*

GELLIUS. My armor!
What ho, my armor!
[*Exeunt all but* SENONA *and child.*

Enter SPARTACUS, ÆNOMAIIS, *and Gladiators*

SPARTACUS.[1] Victory! Ha! ha!
Romans are sheep—search every tent—ah! Jove!
I have found ye wife, aye, and have ransomed ye.

[1] I have followed the reading probably suggested by Forrest. The original lines, crossed out in the MS., are:

"Victory! ha, ha.
Romans are sheep.—Search every tent—Ah, Jove!
I have found ye, wife, and in a noble hour.
When we met last, I was a slave; and now,
In a consul's camp, I stand a conqueror!
"(Drop.)"
[*Foust's note.*]

What, did you think I had deserted you?
Look, I have found you in a noble hour:
When last we met I was a slave: and now
In a Consul's camp I stand a conqueror!

Curtain

END OF ACT III

ACT IV

SCENE I.[1] *The Camp of* CRASSUS

Enter CRASSUS, MUMMIUS, JOVIUS, LENTULUS, BRACCHIUS, *and Attendants*

CRASSUS. And Gellius beaten, too? both consuls beaten?
This is some demigod that hath ta'en man's shape,
To whip us for our sins.—Both consuls beaten?
I would I had those Macedonian legions.

JOVIUS. Have them thou shalt; ay, and the Spanish, too:
The senate, in their terror, (for the victories
Of this great savage now add fright to shame,)
Bid Pompey and Lucullus, with their troops,
Instant embark for Rome.

CRASSUS. Why should they send
For Pompey, too?—Perhaps it may be better.—
See that the fugitives from the consular camps
Be decimated, and so punished. The cowards should
Be slain by duplates rather than by tithes:
I'll make example of them.—Jovius,
Lay not this consul near my villa? I would not
My niece should come to harm; and it is horrid
To think her in the hands of the barbarians.

JOVIUS. I am sorry, prætor—

CRASSUS. What, man, is it so?

JOVIUS. A herdsman, fled that night from the estate,
Just on the eve of battle, saw the house
Beset by numerous slaves.—

CRASSUS. The gods be with her:

[1] This scene is struck out in the MS. and, according to a note in Bird's handwriting, was "omitted in the representation." [*Foust's note.*]

I loved her well.—Sirrah, where is that woman,
I bade thee bring me?

LENTULUS. Not yet reached the camp,
But on the road.

CRASSUS. Let her be hastened hither.
I did intend to use her as a check
On the uxorious chief. Now shall she ransome
My Julia from him.—Where lies the enemy?

JOVIUS. He is advancing on us.

CRASSUS. What, advancing?

JOVIUS. With countless multitudes at his heels.—

CRASSUS. What! come,
Intrench, intrench.

JOVIUS. Rather march out to meet him.
Shall it be said, that Crassus, the lieutenant
Of valiant Sylla, hid behind a trench,
When bondmen menaced him?

CRASSUS. Shall it be said,
Crassus, the prætor, like a hair-brained fool,
Helped these same bondmen to a victory?
Spear me these cowards; and intrench, I say.—
What, sirrah?

Enter a Messenger, who speaks with JOVIUS

JOVIUS. Happy tidings! Marcus Lucullus
Hath landed his army at Brundisium;—

CRASSUS. The gods be thank'd.—

JOVIUS. And legion'd Pompey, too,
At Ostia.

CRASSUS. Still thanks. Let messengers
Be sent o' the instant to both generals,
Praying them, as they love the gods and Rome,
Their march to hasten. [*Exit Messenger.*
Good centurion,
I will employ thee in a difficult office,
Wherein thou may'st the state and me do service.

JOVIUS. Let it be honest, then, and soldier-like.

CRASSUS. So it shall be. I'll have thee an ambassador
To this mad Thracian, to propose a ransome
For my unhappy niece, if niece I have;
Or to exchange for her his wife and brat,
Now in our hands. If she be living, have her
At any ransome; stick not at the sum.—
And hark ye, use your eyes and wisdom well.
Look me out, as a soldier, what 'twould profit
A soldier to have known; and if thou find'st
A man among his officers to be bribed
To any treason may advantage us,
Make him what gain thou wilt.—But see thou bring
My Julia with thee.—If thou find'st a man,
That may be bought, at any price, to murder
The Thracian, buy him for that act.

JOVIUS. Not I:
No foul and dastard blows i' the back.

CRASSUS. Ay, none
For honest enemies; but felon foes
E'en crush feloniously.—Away: heaven speed thee.
Kill we the chief, and I will end the war,
Ere Pompey comes to share with me the honor. [*Exeunt.*

(In the acting version of the play, Act IV begins at this point.)

SCENE I. *The Camp of* SPARTACUS

Enter SENONA, JULIA, FLORUS, *and* ÆNOMAIIS

SENONA. Weep not, poor lady.—

JULIA. Why bid'st thou me not weep?
Hadst thou no tears, when thou didst find thyself
The slave of strangers? Yes, thou hadst, although
In bond of the merciful, who were never used
To aught but gentleness with woman. Yet me,
The lily-cradled daughter of great nobles,
Brought to the slavish[1] thrall of slaves, exposed
To all their brutal cruelty, thou bid'st
To weep no more.

SENONA. It is thy fright, that conjures
These shapes of danger. Thou art here as safe
As woman may be in a troubled camp.
Thou art no slave; but, I am sure, art held

[1] There is a query in Bird's hand, — "Shall I substitute vile, odious, degrading, or some other word?" [*Foust's note.*]

To timely ransome. Pray be comforted:—
I know, thou art safe.

JULIA. I have, I know, that safety
That may be found in den of wolves or bears.—
Would I had died or e'er my fate had thrust me
Among these dreadful murderers.

SENONA. They are such
To none my husband favors.

JULIA. Is not he
As fierce and pitiless as the rest, who seeks
To venge his wrongs upon the innocent?
He that has madly doomed that hapless captive
His father's crime in blood to expiate?

SENONA. He has not doomed him; nay, if he said so,
It was in wrath; and he will pardon him.
The heart that throbs beneath his bloody mail,
Can melt to pity quickly as thine own.
I think, he'll free him; for thyself, I know,
Thou art protected.

JULIA. Am I from his brother,
The insolent Phasarius?—Heard I not
What claim that villain made to me? Alas,
Thou art a woman, and can pity me.

SENONA. Thine ears deceived thee; did they not, Ænomaiis?

ÆNOMAIIS. I think so, lady.

SENONA. Did not this argument
Point to some claim of war?

ÆNOMAIIS. A bold proposal
Made by Phasarius, by the chief denied:
This was their argument.

Enter SPARTACUS

JULIA. Alas, behold
How frowns the angry fury on his face!
Bodes this no ill to Florus or to me?

SENONA. What is the matter, husband, that you look
So sad and heavy?

SPARTACUS. Sad and heavy, am I?—
[*Aside.*] And shall I, for this face of snow provoke
A threatening ruin? Out of foolish pity
For one that loves me not, drive from my heart,
The heart that loves me well?

SENONA. What say'st thou, Spartacus?

SPARTACUS [*aside*]. To save her girlish body from the shame,
Her baby bosom from the pang,— to rescue
From a short dream of sorrow, one young fool
Out of the million millions of the mourning,
Kill mine own coming glory and the hopes
Of a wrong'd world?

SENONA. I fear me, thou art angry.

SPARTACUS. Hark ye, my girl—that fool that trembles yonder—

SENONA. I pity her.

SPARTACUS. Dost thou indeed? And art thou
Assured she is worth thy pity? Were the world
A jot the worse, were she removed from it?

SENONA. Alas, you will not harm her? She has indeed
A kind and foolish heart.

SPARTACUS. Has she indeed?
Well, she shall to her father.

SENONA. She has none.

SPARTACUS. What, wife, an orphan? Now the incensed heaven
Smite my hard heart! A poor and feeble child
Left struggling fatherless in the world, and I
Consent to wrong her!

SENONA. What is't you say?

SPARTACUS. Not I,
Though forty thousand unjust brothers storm'd.—
One day mine own child will be fatherless.—
We'll ransome her.

SENONA. I'm glad to hear you say so.

SPARTACUS [*to* JULIA]. What, foolish maid, why dost thou weep? Come, smile,
I'll send thee to the prætor—and the boy too.—
I think 'twould break her heart to kill him.—

Enter PHASARIUS

Brother—
Brother, I hope thou hast forgot this folly.

PHASARIUS. I claim the captive.

SPARTACUS. Thou shalt have a thousand;
But not these twain.

PHASARIUS. I care not for the boy.

The girl is mine,—captured by mine own hands;
Therefore mine own.
FLORUS. Base caitiff!
SPARTACUS. Sirrah, begone.—
PHASARIUS. Deny me her, and, by the fates, thou art
No longer brother of mine. 'Twas I that helped thee
To this high station; and the troops thou rulest,
Are but my lending; for that hour I leave thee,
They leave thee, too.
SPARTACUS. Come,—look me in the face,
And let me see how bad desires have changed thee.
PHASARIUS. I claim the captive.
SPARTACUS. Set thine eye on *her:*
Lo you, she weeps, and she is fatherless.
Thou wouldst not harm an orphan? What, I say,
Art thou, whom I have carried in my arms
To mountain-tops, to worship the great God,
Art thou a man to plot a wrong and sorrow
(And thou a *man!*) against a feeble orphan?
Wilt thou now ask her?
PHASARIUS. Ay.
SPARTACUS. Thou art a changeling!
My father ne'er begot so base a heart.—
Brother, I do conjure thee, for I love thee,
Forget this thing.
PHASARIUS. Farewell.
SPARTACUS. Thou wilt not go?
PHASARIUS. Ay, by great Jove, I will. Play thou the tyrant
On those that follow thee.
SPARTACUS. My younger brother:—
Nay, I'll not call thee such,—but a hot fool
And heartless enemy.—
PHASARIUS. Call what thou wilt:
I am a man not to be mock'd and wrong'd,
Nor flouted in my counsels. I did ask you,
Now that you had the wind of the fooled prætor,
Now when rich Rome is emptied by her levies,
Now when the eager troops cry all, *for Rome,*
To march upon it, ere the joining armies
Of Pompey and Lucullus should prevent you.
This I did ask, and this you did deny,
Though, by a former promise, pledged thereto.
SPARTACUS. I promised not.
PHASARIUS. By heaven, you did—*when stronger.*
This you refuse; and when, forgiving this,
I ask my captive, you deny me her,
With many a sharp and contumelious word,
Such as is fitter for a dog than me.
SPARTACUS. Forgive me, if my anger used such shame;
I knew not what I said.
PHASARIUS. March then to Rome.
SPARTACUS. It cannot be. We should but set us down
Under her walls, where the three generals,
Ere we could force the gates, would hedge us in.
We cannot stand against them all even here;
But, when in Sicily, are invincible.
PHASARIUS. Rome, or the captive: no more Sicily.
SPARTACUS. To Sicily:
There, by the ocean fenced, rouse up and gather
The remnants of those tribes by Rome destroyed,
Invited to their vengeance. Then will come,
Arm'd with retributive and murderous hate,
The sons of fiery Afric,—Carthaginians
Out of their caves, Numidians from their deserts;
The Gaul, the Spaniard, the Sardinian;
The hordes of Thessaly, Thrace, and Macedon,
And swarming Asia;—all at last assembled
In vengeful union 'gainst this hell of Rome.
Then may we crush, but now we crush ourselves.
Let us to Sicily.
PHASARIUS. Those that will. Farewell.
SPARTACUS. Will you desert me?
PHASARIUS. I did think thee meant
For the most godlike enterprise of earth:
Thou fail'st. Farewell; protect thyself.
SPARTACUS. Mad boy,
Remember Crixus.

PHASARIUS. And his thousand Germans!
I go with Gauls and Thracians, and fifty thousand.—
A Roman girl was worth this coil!—Farewell:
Learn to be juster. [*Exit.*

SPARTACUS. Gone! Alas, alas,
Am I unjust? I did not think my brother
Could e'er desert me.

ÆNOMAIIS. Spartacus—

SPARTACUS. Ænomaiis,
Dost thou remain? Why dost thou stay with me?

AENOMAIIS. For that I know thee wiser than thy brother.
I will stand, fight, or die with thee. But look;
If thou speak not, the army to a man,
Will follow this young madman.

SPARTACUS. Mad and ungrateful all! Will none remain?

SENONA. Beseech you, speak with them, my honored husband.

SPARTACUS. And he endanger'd thee, too! By the heavens,
I'll ne'er forgive him.—Nay, go to your couch.
I'll speak with them. They will not all desert me. [*Exeunt.*

SCENE 2. *The Camp of* CRASSUS

Enter CRASSUS *and* LENTULUS

CRASSUS. Thy son was kill'd, then? I am sorry for him.
I heard, he bore him soldier-like, and I,
Upon this promise, did intend him favor.

LENTULUS. I know not that he certainly was killed;
But, I thank Jove, he did not fly his post.

Enter BRACCHIUS

CRASSUS. What of the enemy? does he still approach?

BRACCHIUS. No, he is flying.

LENTULUS. Flying! thou art mad.

BRACCHIUS. That may be, for my slaves have ruined me.
Why should brains stick where gold will not?

CRASSUS. Come, sirrah,
What didst thou mean by saying the foe fled?
<How flies he?

BRACCHIUS. As a hound, that having coursed
A stinking brock, upon a sudden turns,
To chase a noble stag.—Ourselves the badger,
And Rome the worthier quarry.

CRASSUS. Tedious fool,>
What dost thou mean?

BRACCHIUS. That the fierce Gladiators
Instead of dinging us, as seemed designed,
Are now upon the highway to the city.

CRASSUS. To Rome?

BRACCHIUS. Yes, flying to Rome.

CRASSUS. Presumptuous fools!
<Now may we build a forest of crucifixes.
Bid the men cast away their picks, and arm.>
We'll after them.

BRACCHIUS. I think there's some division
Among the leaders; for the herds afoot,
March in disorder.

CRASSUS. Separated! Jove,
I thank thee for this boon.—Another Crixus!
To arms, I say. Send out the cavalry,
<To gain their flanks and front, letting them get
Beyond the leader's camp.>—This is a triumph.—
To arms, I say. [*Exeunt.*

SCENE 3. *The Camp of* SPARTACUS

Enter SPARTACUS *and* ÆNOMAIIS

SPARTACUS. Seven thousand true? A handful, but enough,
Being staunch and prudent, for the enterprise.—
Desert me! Well, well, well.—Among the hills
Are many paths that may be safely trod;
Whereby we'll gain the sea, and so pass o'er
To safer Sicily.—Perhaps I spoke
Too roughly,—but no matter.—Did you send
To hire the shipping of those pirates? Well.—

And all prepared to march at nightfall?—Ænomaiis,
Do you not think they'll beat him?

ÆNOMAIIS. I doubt it not;
Phasarius being a soldier, but no leader.

<SPARTACUS. An excellent leader, but that he is rash.

ÆNOMAIIS. That is the misery. He will fight you hotly
An army of lions; but a troop of foxes
May easily beat him. Now the prætor's brain
Is all o' the fox's color.>

SPARTACUS. Well, I care not:
We will to Rhegium.—Think you, Ænomaiis,
I might not, while the prætor steals upon him,
Steal on the prætor, and so save the army?
What say'st thou?

ÆNOMAIIS. Hang them, no. This brings Lucullus
On our seven thousand. Let the mutineers
Look to themselves.

SPARTACUS. Right, very right, right, Ænomaiis.
Let them look to themselves. He did desert me;
My father's son deserted me, and left me
Circled by foes. I say, 'tis very right.
<He shall no help from me; not though they beat him
An hundred times; no, no, no help from me.>

ÆNOMAIIS. Lo you, a messenger!

SPARTACUS. From Phasarius!—
Perhaps he is sorry.—

Enter JOVIUS

ÆNOMAIIS. Chief, an embassy
From Crassus.

SPARTACUS. And what would Crassus with the Gladiator,
The poor base slave, and fugitive, Spartacus?
Speak, Roman: wherefore does thy master send
Thy gray hairs to the cutthroat's camp?

JOVIUS. Brave rebel,—

SPARTACUS. Why, that's a better name than a rogue or bondman;
But, in this camp, I am call'd general.

JOVIUS. Brave general; for, though a rogue and bondman,
As you have said, I'll still allow you general,
As he that beats a consul surely is,—

SPARTACUS. Say two,—two consuls; and to that e'en add
A proconsul, three prætors, and some generals.

JOVIUS. Why, 'tis no more than true.—Are you a Thracian?

SPARTACUS. Ay.

JOVIUS. There is something in the air of Thrace
Breeds valor up as rank as grass. 'Tis pity
You are a barbarian.

SPARTACUS. Wherefore?

JOVIUS. Had you been born
A Roman, you had won by this a triumph.

SPARTACUS. I thank the gods I am barbarian;
For I can better teach the grace-begot
And heaven-supported masters of the earth,
How a mere dweller of a desert rock
Can bow their crown'd heads to his chariot wheels.
Man is heaven's work, and beggar's brats may 'herit
A soul to mount them up the steeps of fortune,
With regal necks to be their stepping-blocks.—
But come, what is thy message?

JOVIUS. Julia, niece
O' the prætor, is thy captive.

SPARTACUS. Ay.

JOVIUS. For whom
Is offered in exchange thy wife, Senona,
And thy young boy.

SPARTACUS. Tell thou the prætor, Roman,
The Thracian's wife is ransomed.

JOVIUS. How is that?

SPARTACUS. What ho, Senona!
[SENONA *appears with the child at a tent door.*]
Lo, she stands before you,
Ransomed, and by the steel, from out the camp
Of slaughtered Gellius. [*Exit* SENONA.

JOVIUS. This is sorcery!—
But name a ransome for the general's niece.

SPARTACUS. Have I not now the prætor on the hip?
He would, in his extremity, have made

My wife his buckler of defence; perhaps
Have doomed her to the scourge! But this is Roman.
Now the barbarian is instructed. Look,
I hold the prætor by the heart; and he
Shall feel how tightly grip barbarian fingers.

JOVIUS. Men do not war on women. Name her ransome.

SPARTACUS. Men do not war on women! Look you:
One day I clomb upon the ridgy top
Of the cloud-piercing Hæmus, where, among
The eagles and the thunders, from that height,
I look'd upon the world—or, far as where,
Wrestling with storms, the gloomy Euxine chafed
On his recoiling shores; and where dim Adria
In her blue bosom quenched the fiery sphere.
Between those surges lay a land, might once
Have served for paradise, but Rome had made it
A Tartarus.—In my green youth I look'd
From the same frosty peak, where now I stood,
And then beheld the glory of those lands,
Where peace was tinkling on the shepherd's bell
And singing with the reapers; <or beneath
The shade of thatch eaves, smiled with grey old men,
And with their children laughed along the green.>
Since that glad day, Rome's conquerors had past
With withering armies there, and all was changed:
Peace had departed; howling war was there,
Cheered on by Roman hunters: then, methought,
Even as I looked upon the altered scene,
Groans echoed through the valleys, through which ran
Rivers of blood, like smoking Phlegethons;
Fires flashed from burning villages, and famine
Shriek'd in the empty cornfields. Women and children,
Robb'd of their sires and husbands, left to starve—
These were the dwellers of the land!—Say'st thou
Rome wars not then on women?

JOVIUS. This is not to the matter.

SPARTACUS. Now, by Jove,
It is. These things do Romans. But the earth
Is sick of conquerors. There is not a man,
Not Roman, but is Rome's extremest foe;
And such am I, sworn from that hour I saw
These sights of horror, while the gods support me,
To wreak on Rome such havock as Rome wreaks,
Carnage and devastation, wo and ruin.
Why should I ransome, when I swear to slay?—
Begone: this is my answer!

<JOVIUS. With your leave
This prattling scares no Romans; and these threats
Come weakly from a chief of mutineers.

SPARTACUS. Of mutineers?

JOVIUS. Ay, marry, 'tis well known,
Your cutthroats have deserted you. Content you,
Crassus will punish the foul traitors.

SPARTACUS. Crassus!

JOVIUS. Ay, Crassus.—Hercules, how men will talk!
Wreak wo on Rome!—I tell you, your lieutenant
Will hang upon a cross before the morrow.
So name your ransome, while 'tis offered you.

SPARTACUS. Begone, I say. [*Exit* JOVIUS.
Alas, my Ænomaiis,
Should we not strike now? Now while we might fall
Upon their rear, and take them by surprise?

ÆNOMAIIS. Let them be punished, castigated well,
And they'll return to wisdom and obedience.

SPARTACUS. Right, right. Let them be punished, hack'd to the bones:
This will speak better than my words. Prepare
For Rhegium. He'll return to us tomorrow.
[*Exeunt*.>

END OF ACT IV

ACT V

SCENE I. *The Peninsula of* RHEGIUM. *The Camp of the Gladiators*

Enter SPARTACUS *and* ÆNOMAIIS

SPARTACUS. Routed and cut to pieces!—Said I not?
Did I not tell them?—Utterly destroyed!
Scattered like chaff!—Now, by the eternal fates,
They did provoke high heaven, deserting me.—
How many slain?

ÆNOMAIIS. Indeed it is not known.

SPARTACUS. Many, I'm glad; I should be very glad:
Did I not lead them ever on to victory?
And did they not forsake me? Wretched fools,
This was my vengeance, yea, my best of vengeance,
To leave them to themselves, that Roman prætors
Might whip them for me. Art thou not rejoiced?
Art thou not, Ænomaiis, glad of this?
Glad, very glad?

<ÆNOMAIIS. I shall be, when I see
Half of them back again.

SPARTACUS. I'll decimate them:
Even as the Romans punish, so I'll punish.—
Ruin me all these grand and glorious hopes?
Nay, they were certainties.—An excellent army,
That might have fought with Pompey, broke and ruined
By their mad mutiny! An excellent army—

ÆNOMAIIS. Indeed, an excellent.

SPARTACUS. Foolish Ænomaiis,
Why did'st thou stay me, when I would have saved them?

ÆNOMAIIS. Had this been well? Had their ingratitude
Deserved it of thee?

SPARTACUS. Ay, ingratitude.
Did I oppress them? Did I tyrannise?>

ÆNOMAIIS. 'Tis rumored that Phasarius fell.

SPARTACUS. My brother,
My foolish brother—why did he part from me?—
Nay, I'll not mourn him.

ÆNOMAIIS. This evil news must now
Hasten our embarkation. The pirate ships
Already are launching from the shore.

SPARTACUS. Why, now
You are too fast. Bid them be beached again.—
<Alas, that foolish boy! We'll rest awhile,
And see what fugitives may come to us.>
Art sure Phasarius was slain?—the pride
Of his dead mother's heart; and, I do know,
Though prone to anger, of a loving spirit.—
We'll rest awhile here on this promontory.

ÆNOMAIIS. Each moment has a peril. For these pirates
They are most treacherous hounds, and may set sail
Without us; and the prætor, thou know'st well,
Is trenching us in on this peninsula.

SPARTACUS. What care I for the prætor and his trenches?
<This is a boy's trick, and a boy might meet it.>
Trenches to stop a Thracian!—Look you, now,
What drooping slave is that? By all the gods,
It is my brother!—But I'll not be glad.
Lo you, how humbled, spiritless he looks!
Where are his troops?

Enter PHASARIUS

Sirrah, why comest thou here?
Didst thou not part from me, and take mine army?
Did'st thou not teach my followers mutiny,
And lead them to destruction? Thou whipp'd fool,
Why comest thou here?

PHASARIUS. To ask thy pardon, and to die.

SPARTACUS. Couldst thou not die with those thou led'st to death,
That men, who after should have called thee madman,
Might not have called thee craven?

PHASARIUS. I am no craven;
A wretch, I grant you, but no craven.

SPARTACUS. Where are thy troops? that throng'd and valiant army
Thou stol'dst from me?
PHASARIUS. With Pluto. Why demand me?
I am alone of all.
SPARTACUS. Most wretched man,
Thou hast murder'd fifty thousand men, destroyed
Thy brother and thy country, and all hope
Of the earth's disenthralment.
PHASARIUS. I have ruined
My brother, that's enough.
SPARTACUS. Ay, look, behold;
But yestermorn, I was a conqueror,
On the high verge and pinnacle of renown;
Today a skulking, trembling, despised man,
Thrust in a pit. Whose traitorous hand was it,
Pluck'd me from my high seat, and sunk so low?
Who did this thing, this foul, felonious thing?
PHASARIUS. Myself, that was thy brother.
SPARTACUS. Ay, that was!
PHASARIUS. Why shouldst thou stab me with thy words? O brother,
Strike me with thy sharp sword, but speak no more:
Give me to punishment, or drive me forth
To die by Romans; but upbraid no more.
SPARTACUS. Shall I forgive him? Look, he is penitent.
ÆNOMAIIS. But he has lost them all.
SPARTACUS. Ay, so he has.—
Ask'st thou for pardon, when thou hast slain all?
Away! thou didst discard me from thy heart:
I banish thee from mine.
PHASARIUS. It is but just.
Why should I live, when I have ruined thee?
I should have died before. Farewell.
SPARTACUS. Come back:
I will forgive thee: nay, I have.—O brother,
Why didst thou do this wrong? But I'll forget it.—
Let the ships now be launched, now, Ænomaiis;
Now cross to Sicily. [*Exit* ÆNOMAIIS.
With these fifty thousand—
But I've forgot it.—What, were all destroyed?
PHASARIUS. All, all.
SPARTACUS. A disciplined army!—
But no matter.—
All slain upon the field?
PHASARIUS. Six thousand wretches
Yielded them prisoners to the prætor.
SPARTACUS. Well,
He took six thousand prisoners. These will now
Suffer a double wretchedness.
PHASARIUS. Never fear it:
They will not.
SPARTACUS. How is that, Phasarius?
Did not the prætor, in his proclamations,
Threat us with bondmen's deaths by crucifixion?
PHASARIUS. And he will keep his word—nay, he has kept it.
SPARTACUS. What!
PHASARIUS. Are men beasts, that life should count no more
Than a beast's sob?
SPARTACUS. Thou fill'st my soul with terror.
Are they condemned? All?
PHASARIUS. Executed.
SPARTACUS. Horror!
Six thousand men, and crucified!
PHASARIUS. Crucified.
I saw a sight last night, that turned my brain,
And set my comrade mad. The Roman highway
Is, each side, lined with crosses, and on each cross
Is nailed a gladiator.—Well, 'twas night,
When, with a single follower, I did creep
Through the trenched army to that road, and saw
The executed multitude uplifted
Upon the horrid engines. Many lived:
Some moaned and writhed in stupid agony;
Some howled, and prayed for death, and cursed the gods;
Some turned to lunatics, and laughed at horror;
And some with fierce and hellish strength, had torn
Their arms free from the beams, and so had died,

Grasping, headlong, at air. And, oh, the yells,
That rose upon the gusty sighs of night,
And babbled hideously along the skies,
As *they* were fill'd with murder!

SPARTACUS. Say no more:
This is too dreadful for man's ear. I swear
For this to make Rome howl. What, Ænomaiis.

Reënter ÆNOMAIIS

Are the ships all afloat?

ÆNOMAIIS. And gone.

SPARTACUS. What, gone?

ÆNOMAIIS. These same perfidious pirates, with their hire,
Have set their sails, and fled.

SPARTACUS. The ocean god
Meet them with hurricanes, sink their ships, and feed
Sea-monsters with their corses!

ÆNOMAIIS. All is finished:
This is the fruit of mercy for deserters.

SPARTACUS. Be that forgot.

ÆNOMAIIS. What now remains for us,
But to sit down and die?

SPARTACUS. I'll tell thee, what:
To fight the prætor.

ÆNOMAIIS. Though his troops outnumber
Ten times our own!

SPARTACUS. Ay; our despair will make us
Each ten times stronger than his foe. Fill up
This schoolboy ditch with disregarded plunder,
And when the watchdogs sleep, like wolves, steal on them
And take them by the throat. I have no fear,
But we shall find a pathway through their camp.
Then to Tarentum; there we'll find us ships.
Or, if that fail, with a despairing fury,
Turn upon Rome, and perish there.

Enter SENONA, *with the child*

What now?
Com'st thou to mourn o'er our mishaps, Senona?
Be not dismayed: I'll find thee safety yet.

SENONA. Thou wouldst conceal these newer perils from me;
But well I know, that every hour now brings
A menacing cloud about thee.

SPARTACUS. Clouds, ay, clouds:
A cloud is on my path, but my ambition
Sees glory in't: as travellers who stand
On mountains, view upon some neighboring peak,
Among the mists, a figure of themselves,
Traced in sublimer characters; so I
Here see the vapory image of myself,
Distant and dim, but giantlike—I'll make
These perils glories.

SENONA. And the ships have left thee?

SPARTACUS. Thou art a soldier's wife, and wilt not tremble
To share his danger. Look, through yonder camp
Our path lies.

SENONA. I will walk it by thy side.

SPARTACUS. Not so; for though unharmed by steel, the sight
Of the near fray would kill thee. I have discovered
A path almost unguarded; where, whilst I
Assault the Roman in his sleep, thyself
And my war-cradled boy, with my Phasarius
To guard thee, shall in safety pass, and join me
After the battle.

SENONA. Why not lead your army
By that unguarded path?

SPARTACUS. Trust me, dear wife,
I'll make it such for thee, but cannot have it
Safe for an army. The surprised distraction
Of the attack will call the guards away.
This is the safest.

SENONA. Let me go with thee.
I do not fear the horrors of the storm.

SPARTACUS. It cannot be. What, brother—

PHASARIUS. Let some one else
Be made her guard; while I, in fight, find vengeance,
And reparation of my faults.

SPARTACUS. Wilt thou
Refuse me this, Phasarius?

PHASARIUS. Am not I
A rash and witless fool? Trust not to me
What thou so valuest.

SENONA. I beseech you, hear him.
Let me not leave you, Spartacus: my heart

Is full of dismal and of ominous fear,
If I do leave you now, I leave for ever.
If I must die, let me die where thou art.

SPARTACUS. Why talk'st thou now of death? I say, I'll make
This path most safe for thee. How could I fight,
Or play the leader in a bloody storm,
With thy pale visage ever in my eye?

PHASARIUS. I do beseech you, make not me her guard.

SPARTACUS. It must be so. And hear me now, Phasarius;
I put into thy hands more than my soul:
See, my dear wife, and here my innocent boy.—
These are the very jewels of my heart.
Protect them for me. Be not rash; steal softly,
With the small faithful troop I'll send with thee,
Through glens and woods; and when the alarm is sounded,
March fast but wisely. For thy life, and mine,
Avoid all contest, shouldst thou meet a foe;
Nay, though thou know'st thou hast advantage, fight not.
Join me, with these in safety, and assure me
No man has drawn his sword.—And now farewell.
Farewell, Senona: I pray you do not speak.—
Thou art very safe. Farewell.

[*Exeunt* SENONA, *child, and* PHASARIUS.

ÆNOMAIIS. He is too rash.

SPARTACUS. Rash, had I given him a command in battle;
But will not be with them.—Rouse up the troops.
Fill up the ditch with baggage, as I told thee.—
<I'll see that all be schooled for this assault.> [*Exeunt.*

SCENE 2. *Before the tent of* CRASSUS

Enter CRASSUS, MUMMIUS, JOVIUS, LENTULUS *and* BRACCHIUS

CRASSUS. Now I lament me, on this overthrow
Of the chief army of the enemy,
I prayed for Pompey and Lucullus. If
I end not instant, by another blow,
The war I have so maimed, comes me a colleague
To chouse me of my triumphs.

JOVIUS. You must be quick then.
The dawn will show you Pompey by your side;
Or rather, dashing with a Roman scorn,
Amongst the ruffians you have trapp'd.

CRASSUS. I think,
Ourselves may do it.—And this hell-dog holds
The girl to doom?

JOVIUS. He says, he is instructed
By your fore-thought intentions with his spouse.

CRASSUS. But dost thou think he'll slay her?

JOVIUS. Not while he
May purchase mercy with her.

CRASSUS. Shall I take her
Out of his camp by force? or send thee back,
To offer mercy and receive submission?

JOVIUS. Propose him life and liberty, and make him
A Roman citizen.

CRASSUS. What, a rebel slave!

JOVIUS. In these rough, rotten times, we do not scruple
To raise our rogues to honor. Why, then, blush,
To anoint a slave, that's capable and honest?
The genius of this Thracian, had it been
In honorable trust display'd, had quell'd
A score of barbarous nations; and *may* yet,
Make but the man a Roman.

CRASSUS. We will make him
A captive first.—Were my poor Julia free!—

[*Loud Alarums.*]

What is the matter?

JOVIUS. The rats are out! by Jove,
The slaves have pass'd the trenches, and assault us!

CRASSUS. Thou art mad! They dare not—
What, to arms, to arms!
Nay, if they will, let them into the camp,
But let not out.—To arms, to arms!

[*Exeunt.*

SCENE 3. *Another part of the Roman Camp*

Enter CRASSUS, JOVIUS, MUMMIUS, *and* LENTULUS

CRASSUS. Mischiefs and plagues, and slavish stripes disgrace
These shameless cowards? What, ope their ranks, and give
A path to these few madmen! Let them scape us!

JOVIUS. Nay, they are gone, that's certain,—but will drop
Into the jaws of Pompey.

CRASSUS. Bid the legions
Follow them.

JOVIUS. When the day breaks; but not now.

CRASSUS. Shall I let Pompey take them, and have Rome
Laugh at my shame? Have Pompey join the scorners,
And mock me, too? Hie thee away, good Jovius;
Follow the Thracian; offer pardon, freedom,
Whate'er thou wilt. Do but delay his march:
Let him not come near Pompey—Quick, away! [*Exeunt.*

SCENE 4. *The Camp of* SPARTACUS, *among the hills*

Enter SPARTACUS *and* ÆNOMAIIS

SPARTACUS. Was not this well? When desperate men contend,
The brave will fly from them. To fight for life,
Fights surest for a victory. Fought we well?
I would not give these seven thousand poor rogues,
For a whole herd of angry Gauls. We'll win
The highway to Tarentum yet.—Lieutenant,
Should they not now be here?

ÆNOMAIIS. Who?

SPARTACUS. Who! Phasarius
And his care-chosen guard—my brother and my wife.

ÆNOMAIIS. They tread a rough and tangled path.

SPARTACUS. 'Tis true;
And finding there more guards than I had word of,
Their caution journeys them the slower. I
Am almost grieved, I brought them not with me.—
How fare the captives? Bring me to Tarentum,
I'll send that girl unransomed to the prætor.—
Would they were here!—Bring in the prisoner,
And find how march the coming generals.
[BRACCHIUS *is brought in, unguarded.*]

ÆNOMAIIS. This fellow was the master of thy brother.
Question him, and then hang him, for a baser,
More heartless master never yet struck slave.

SPARTACUS. I am sick of blood.—Is not the sun yet up?
If they be seen—but I'll not think of that.—
Be not afeard: hadst thou been worth a blow,
I had not spared thee. Speak, and truly speak,
Or thou shalt fat the kites: When looks the prætor
For Pompey and his Spanish troops?

BRACCHIUS. He looks
Not for, but at him.

SPARTACUS. Wretch!

BRACCHIUS. And so may'st thou,
Yonder among the heights upon thy left.

SPARTACUS. Wretch, if thou mock me, I will strike thee dead.
Know I not well the prætor's craft? These eagles
That spread their golden pinions on the hills,
Were wing'd by Crassus thither, to affright me.
Are they not Crassus's standards? Own me that,
Or look tonight to sup in Acheron.

BRACCHIUS. To sup on earth, then, I'll agree to this;
But I shall lie.

SPARTACUS. Rogue, answer me again:
Are those troops Pompey's?

BRACCHIUS. Ay.

SPARTACUS. The gods forbid!
They are in motion too! Now I begin

To feel my desolation, and despair.
What, Ænomaiis, send me out a scout
To view those hill-perched foes, and quick prepare
The army for the march. And my poor wife!
Why did I trust her with Phasarius?
<Send out a cunning guide to hunt the path.> [*Exit* ÆNOMAIIS.
Roman, if thou speak false, I'll have thee slain.—
Where rests Lucullus?

BRACCHIUS. In no place he rests,
Save nightly on the highroad from Tarentum.

<SPARTACUS. Villain, thou liest! The gods have not so left me.
I say, thou speak'st not true.

BRACCHIUS. Well, I speak false;
But notwithstanding, he is on that road.—
These are the bloodiest cutthroats!—>

SPARTACUS. Now, out on me,
My heart is full of fear. The prætor on my rear,
Lucullus, Pompey on my front and left,
And naught but howling seas upon my right!
Seven thousand men against an hundred thousand!
If Crassus love the girl—He fears disgrace—
'Tis not infeasible—unless, alas,
My wife, perchance, be faln into his hands;
Then can the maiden buy me naught but her.

Reënter ÆNOMAIIS, *with* JOVIUS

ÆNOMAIIS. The Roman prætor
Sends thee again an envoy.

SPARTACUS. Speak, centurion;
What word sends Crassus?

JOVIUS. For the Roman lady,
A princely ransome; for thyself, an offer
Of mercy, pardon, Roman denization,
And martial honor and command; provided—

SPARTACUS. Ay, provided!

JOVIUS. Thou instantly, ere Pompey leave the hills,
Surrender up these malefactious slaves
To whips and crosses. Therefore, most valiant Thracian,
Put by the frenzy, that would fight against
Three circling armies, and accept this boon
Generous and great.

SPARTACUS. I am unfortunate,
Thou know'st that well; but not being Roman yet,
I scorn the foul condition, that makes me
To my true friends a traitor. Give them freedom,
And they lay down their arms; but talk of crosses,
And they have yet the arms that cut a path
Through the proud prætor's camp.

JOVIUS. Why shouldst thou care,
Thou, who hast such a Roman soul, for these
Vile runagate rogues, who, at an opportunity,
Thee would betray as freely as their masters?
Let them be hanged, and be thou made a Roman.
Perhaps thy word may save the least offending;
But let the scum be punished.

SPARTACUS. They shall die,
Like soldiers, on the field, or live in freedom.
But hearken, Roman:
I know the prætor, that he loves his niece,
But honor more; I know, if Pompey strike
At me one blow, the honor all is his,
And nothing left for Crassus, but comparison
Betwixt what Pompey does, and what *he* could not.
He will not then have Pompey strike me, and
He would have back his niece. While I lie here
On this impregnable and forted hill,
Pompey approaches and sits down beside him.
Now he'll consent himself to lose the honor
O' the hunted gladiator's overthrow,
So Pompey wins it not.

JOVIUS. That may be true,
For Crassus loves not Pompey. But on that
What project found you?

SPARTACUS. This: Let him but wink,
While I steal darkly to Tarentum, there
T' embark my army.

JOVIUS. Hah!

SPARTACUS. I'll find a way
To cozen Pompey and pass by Lucullus,
Provided he not follow at my heels.
Gage me but this, and he shall have his niece
Unransomed back; deny me, and by Pluto,
Pompey alone shall gain the laurel.

JOVIUS. Jove!
This is a mad proposal. Help you fly!
Will you surrender, or be cut to pieces?

SPARTACUS. Bring forth the captives.

[JULIA *and* FLORUS *are brought in.*]

Lo, I'll march tonight:
If Crassus follow me, the girl shall die.

JOVIUS. Art thou a savage?

SPARTACUS. Ay; or if you will,
A beast, whose nature not being fierce, the hunters
Have toil'd and goaded into fury. Nature
Makes fewer rogues, than misery. But yesterday,
I had saved that maiden's blood, at cost of mine;
Now, with cool ferocity, I doom her
To perish like a thing abhorred, whene'er
The prætor bids me.

JULIA. Out, alas, alas!
Didst thou not swear thou wouldst not harm my life?
Thou didst, unto thy wife.

SPARTACUS. Well, speak not of it.—
She is surely taken.—Roman, listen to me:
South of thy camp there liest a secret path,
Where, for a certain reason, I did send
A party, to escape the fears of conflict.
Have they been captured?

JOVIUS. I know not, but think so.
Who were they?

SPARTACUS. Well, they are not taken then?

JOVIUS. I'll not say that. A double guard was sent,
Under your one-time master, Lentulus,
Last night, to watch that path.

SPARTACUS. I have some prisoners,
I would exchange for them—Look, all but *her*.

JOVIUS. But who were these?

SPARTACUS. Some women and children. Yes,
Some helpless fools, not fit to look on battle.—
Not that I care for them; but I'll exchange them.

JOVIUS. Some women and children?

SPARTACUS. Sirrah, wilt thou have it?
Why, 'twas my wife then, and my child. If they
Be captured, I'll exchange them for my captives.
Crassus shall have his niece too. Nay, I'll send her,
Without the exchange, provided Crassus swear
To give them freedom, and send back to Thrace.
Let him swear this: let them to Thrace, I say,—
Let them be safe, and I can die.—[*Alarums.*]

ÆNOMAIIS. Look, general!
We are attacked!

SPARTACUS. By heavens, a troop of horse
Rushing against our hill! Why, these are madmen!—
Soft you, they chase some mounted fugitive;
Nay, he has cleared them—Look, man, look! O gods,
Do I not know him?—

JOVIUS. For this proposed exchange—

SPARTACUS. Look, look! 'Tis he! They are lost!

ÆNOMAIIS. His horse has fallen:
He is bloody, too.

SPARTACUS. But where are they?

Enter PHASARIUS, *wounded*

What, brother, brother,
Speak, speak.—Where are they? Ah!

PHASARIUS. My brother!

SPARTACUS. Speak!
Dost thou not know me? By thy soul, I charge thee,
Speak to me; tell me of my love, my boy!
Where hast thou left them?

PHASARIUS. Strike me to the heart:
I have robbed thee, brother, of much more than life;
And all the blood these gaping wounds have left,
Will not repay thee.

SPARTACUS. Art thou mad?
I ask thee of my wife, my boy, my loves!
And thou dost prate to me of wounds and blood!—
Speak!

PHASARIUS. I can better speak than thou canst hear.—
Why madest thou me their escort? Why, O fool!
Thou should'st have known that I would quickly lead them
Through the first perils that invited me;
And where a Roman throat was to be cut,
Would drag them to the hideous spectacle.

SPARTACUS. But thou did'st bear them off! Come, say it, brother;
Thou wert imprudent, but still kind and true.
I'll not be angry—come, I know thou wert worsted,
Thy troops cut off—but thou hast saved them, brother!

PHASARIUS. I would have done it, let my wounds speak for me.

SPARTACUS. They are captives, then? O traitor!—my poor wife,
And my blithe boy!

PHASARIUS. The troops were cut to pieces;
The boy—

SPARTACUS. What of him?

PHASARIUS. Cried for mercy to
A Roman soldier—

SPARTACUS. Who spared him!

PHASARIUS. Struck him to the earth.

SPARTACUS. God!—And his mother?

PHASARIUS. She sprang upon the throat of the black monster—
Ask me no more—I faint.

SPARTACUS. My wife! my wife!
Let furies lash thee into consciousness.
My wife, I say! She sprang upon his throat;
What then?

PHASARIUS. He slew her—but I clove him to the nave.
I could not save, but with my best avenged.

[*Falls*.]

SPARTACUS. There are no gods in heaven;
Pity has fled, and human rage reigns there.—
Wretch, doth the earth still hold thee? Murderer,
Most traitorous, foul, unnatural murderer,
If the warm blood of thy thrice-martyred victims
Reach not thy soul, and strike it dead within thee,
My sword shall sacrifice thee to their fury.—

ÆNOMAIIS. Hold, hold! Thou wilt not strike him? Look, he dies!

[PHASARIUS *dies*.]

SPARTACUS. What, is he dead? All dead? and I alone
Upon the flinty earth? No wife, no child,
[No brother] All slain by Romans? Yes, by Romans.—Look,
I will have vengeance, fierce and bloody vengeance,
Upon the prætor's blood, upon the prætor's.—
Thou grey and hoary wretch,—for being Roman,
A wretch thou art—I'll send back to the prætor
His niece a corse, and thou shalt carry her.—
What ho, my Guards!

Enter Guards

JOVIUS. Savage fiend, forbear;
Shed not the blood o' the innocent.

SPARTACUS. <Foolish man,>
Was not Senona's innocent, and my child's?
Did they e'er harm a Roman?—Blood for blood,
And life for life, and vengeance on the prætor!

FLORUS. Unhappy Spartacus, mar not thy glory
With this unnatural and unjust deed.
Let my head fall for hers.

SPARTACUS. Thy head *and* hers—
<Fools, ye are Romans, and shall die.

JOVIUS. Forbear—>

SPARTACUS. Take them away—

JULIA. Now may the heavens forgive thee.

SPARTACUS. Off, foolish girl; there is no pity left:
My heart now thirsts for blood, and blood will have.

JULIA. I have your promise—

SPARTACUS. Breath, that I revoke.

JULIA. I have Senona's; pity me for her,
For she did love me; pity for your child,
Whom I have nestled in my arms, till it
Did love me, too, and thou, whilst looking on,
Didst swear no harm should ever reach to me.

Yes, for thy babe and wife, thou didst swear this;
And while thou think'st of them, thou canst not kill me.

SPARTACUS. Well, thou art saved.

JOVIUS. Wilt thou, unlucky chief,
Now claim the prætor's mercy? Let thy people
Return to bonds, and have their lives.

SPARTACUS. These twain
Shall go with you; the rest is for my vengeance.
To show thee that the Thracian still defies,—
Even in his hour of misery and despair,—
Still cries for vengeance, still derides the mercy
Of the accursed Roman, thou shalt see
I court his fury.—Hang this Roman cut-throat
Upon a cross, and set it where the Romans
May see him perish.

[BRACCHIUS *is taken out; and the body of* PHASARIUS.]

JOVIUS. This will steel all hearts,
And change all pity into murderous hate.

SPARTACUS. It is for that I hang him to the tree:
There shall no life be spared in fight today.
Look—let the grooms there kill my horse.—'Tis done:
There shall no flight be known; nothing but death.
Begone, centurion and prisoners. Begone or perish.

<FLORUS. I thought thee cruel, but I find thee kind.
Spare that man, and accept the prætor's pardon.

SPARTACUS. Begone, thou foolish boy, while yet thou may'st.

JULIA. Shall I not thank thee, Thracian, for my life?

SPARTACUS. Begone, or die,—and all the hearted griefs,
That rack more bitterly than death, go with you,
And reach your abhorred country: May the gods,
Who have seen Rome fill the earth with wo and death.
Bring worse than wo and death on Rome; light up
The fires of civil war and anarchy,
Curse her with kings, imperial torturers;
And while these rend her bowels, bring the hosts
Of Northern savages, to slay, and feed
Upon her festering fatness; till the earth,
Shall know, as it has known no land so great,
No land so curst as miserable Rome!—
Begone, or perish. >

[*Exeunt* JOVIUS, JULIA, *and* FLORUS.

Let the troops array.
And all that would not die upon the cross,
Slaying their horses, to the plain descend,
And die in battle.

<ÆNOMAIIS. You will not fight today?

SPARTACUS. This day, this hour, this minute, fight and die.
Why should we struggle longer, in this dream
Of life, which is a mocking lunacy,
With ever sunshine playing far ahead,
But thunderbolts about us? Fight, I say.
There is no Orcus blacker than the hell
That life breeds in the heart. >

ÆNOMAIIS. Alas, dear general,
You are not fit for battle.

SPARTACUS. Fit to make
The Roman mothers howl.—Spare not one life;
Shed blood, and laugh; and if ye meet a woman
Hiding her babe in her scared bosom, slay her,
Slay both.—O Ænomaiis, but to think
How lone I stand now on this pitiless earth!—
Had I not parted with them!—O ye heavens,
Could ye look on and see the merciless steel
Struck at their sinless hearts?

<ÆNOMAIIS. Alas, alas,
Give not this way to grief.

SPARTACUS. I will not, brother;
My grief is blackened into scowling vengeance. >

ÆNOMAIIS. Pray you, come to your tent.

SPARTACUS. To tents no more;
I couch no more but on the corse-strown plain,—

Draw out the troops—I say, upon the ground,
Pillow'd on death; thus shall my slumbers be.
Come, battle, battle. [*Exeunt.*

SCENE 5. *The Camp of* CRASSUS

Enter CRASSUS, MUMMIUS, JOVIUS, LENTULUS, FLORUS, *etc. Alarums*

CRASSUS. Thus ends rebellious rage in lunacy;
Despair hath set the gladiator mad.
Look, how with wild and impotent wrath, he rushes
Upon our ready spearmen!—Lentulus,
I am sorry thou didst slay his family.

LENTULUS. Nay, 'twas not I. Perhaps, *I* am not sorry;
They were my slaves, punish'd as fugitives.

CRASSUS. Detach the third rank and the cavalry,
On all sides to surround them. Take them prisoners:
This soldier death befits them not. Ten thousand
Greek drachmæ to the man that brings alive
The leader Spartacus. [*Exit* LENTULUS.

<JOVIUS. That ne'er will be.
He slew his horse, and thus rejecting flight,
His life devoted to the infernal gods.

CRASSUS. A valiant madman!—Had he held my girl—
Nay, but I should have storm'd his mountain camp.
Look, moves not Pompey from the hills? What, friends,
Shall we stand staring at this handful foes,
Till Pompey comes to help us? To the front,
Away, to the front. [*Exeunt.* >

SCENE 6. *Another part of the same*

Enter SPARTACUS, ÆNOMAIIS, *and others*

SPARTACUS. Leave slaying in the ranks, and rush with me
Even to the forum and prætorium,
To strike the officers.

<ÆNOMAIIS. See, the troops of Pompey,
Are following on our rear!

SPARTACUS. What care I for the rear? I see alone
The inviting vengeance beck'ning to the front,
Where flows the blood that Rome may bitterest mourn.
Let me beside the prætor. Mark, no prisoners;
Kill, kill, kill all! There's nothing now but blood
Can give me joy. Now can I tell how gore
Inspires the thirsty tiger, and gives strength
Unto the fainting wolf.—No prisoners!
On to the general! >

Enter LENTULUS, *with others*

LENTULUS. Lo, the bloody chief!
Now yield thee, villain.

SPARTACUS. Murder-spotted fiend,
Thou led'st the band that slew my wife and boy!
Kill, kill, kill all!
[*He kills* LENTULUS, *and exit with the rest fighting.*]

SCENE 7. *The prætorium*

Enter CRASSUS, JOVIUS, JULIA, *etc.*

CRASSUS. Get thee away; thou wilt be slain.

JULIA. I fear not:
Let me look on the battle, and perhaps
Return the gift of life to Spartacus.

CRASSUS. Pr'ythee, retire. This man has won more honor,
Than even the braggart Pompey; for all ages
Shall own there needed two united armies
To quell him, yea, two Roman armies.
What now? Why fliest thou?

Enter FLORUS

FLORUS. He has broken through
The second rank. Give me more troops, and fresh,
To venge my father's death.

CRASSUS. Nay, tarry here,
And mark, how like the timbers of a ship,
Crushed in the mighty seas, the sundered wrecks
Of this rebellion vanish from our eyes.

SPARTACUS [*within*]. On to the general!

CRASSUS. What is that cry?
This is a victory, but Pompey shares it.—

What rout is this here at our tents? By heaven,
My guards are reeling in confusion!—Lo,
What man is this, unbuckler'd and unhelm'd,
Gored with a thousand deaths, that waves so wildly,
A broken weapon?

Enter SPARTACUS, *wounded, etc.*

SPARTACUS. All is lost; but cry
Victory! On: I'll reach the general.

CRASSUS. Smite him! 'tis Spartacus.

[SPARTACUS *is wounded by several.*]

SPARTACUS. Hah! Victory!
Crassus, thou diest! I know thee very well.—
Romans are straws.—No prisoners.—Naught but blood.
Why should there be night now?—

[*He falls.*]

JULIA. O dear uncle, strike not.
Let him be spared.—He gave me life.—Alas,
He dies, he dies!

SPARTACUS. Well—never heed the tempest—
There are green valleys in our mountains yet.—
Set forth the sails.—We'll be in Thrace anon.—

[*Dies.*]

<CRASSUS. Thy bark is wreck'd, but nobly did she buffet
These waves of war, and grandly lies at last,
A stranded ruin on this fatal shore.
Let him have burial; not as a base bondman,
But as a chief enfranchised and ennobled.
If we denied him honor while he lived,
Justice shall carve it on his monument.>

[*Dead March, etc. Curtain.*]

THE END

BIANCA VISCONTI; OR THE HEART OVERTASKED

By Nathaniel Parker Willis

NATHANIEL PARKER WILLIS

[1806–1867]

NATHANIEL PARKER WILLIS was born January 20, 1806, in Portland, Maine; he came from a family of good New England ancestry and grew up under the influence of a Puritan father whose training was to show itself, in varying degrees, all through the son's life. After a preparatory schooling at Andover, where he was "converted" to Calvinism, he was sent to the orthodox Yale where he was to learn "the mysteries of 'election and free grace,' whether or no." [1] His religious zeal cooled somewhat, much to the disappointment of his father, but his literary tastes were nourished by his college contacts, especially by the poet Hillhouse, whose *Hadad* dominated Willis's imagination for a long period of time. During his college career he wrote a comedy which was acted privately with some success; he became known as a "great wit and a great beau," but was in no way dissipated; he graduated valedictorian poet of his class in 1827, having already achieved something of a national reputation as a writer.

Coming from a family of journalists, Willis naturally continued his activities in the literary field. In Boston as editor of the *American Monthly Magazine*, most of which he composed himself, he became an adept in the easy-flowing, conversational style of writing, but he did not win his way to the literary or social prominence he had hoped for. In fact, his Boston residence was to prove a bitter experience, for besides his other disappointments he was eventually asked to leave the church because of his indifference. Willis did not renounce religion, however: "Worldling as I am and hardly as I dare claim any virtue as a Christian, there is that within me which sin and folly never reached or tainted." [2] After the failure of the *American Monthly Magazine* in 1831, Willis went to New York, where he became associated with George P. Morris in editing the *New York Mirror*. It was for this publication that he undertook a trip to Europe, where the wealth of scene and incident proved highly fruitful for him. He was well received in the higher social circles, especially in England; his intense personal enjoyment in the places he visited and the persons he met is clearly portrayed in letters to the *New York Mirror* and also in one of his best-known books, *Pencillings by the Way*. In many of his sketches can be seen his interest in the colorful, the unusual, the striking—an interest which again reveals itself in his plays.

While in England, Willis married a religious young woman, Mary Stace;

[1] This biographical account is based on Henry Augustin Beers' *Nathaniel Parker Willis*. Boston: 1885.

[2] *Ibid.*, p. 96.

bluntly he writes: "I should never have wished to marry you if you had not been religious. . . ." [1] Apparently his marriage marked a departure from his past social activity: "I have lived the past ten years in gay society, and I am sick at heart of it. . . . I feel sincerely that this is the turning point of both mind and heart. . . ." [2]

After Willis's return to this country he wrote his two important dramas, *Bianca Visconti; or the Heart Overtasked*, and *Tortesa the Usurer*. He continued his journalism by editing the *New Mirror* with Morris, and in 1846 these two men brought out their last and most successful periodical, the *Home Journal*, which had as its motto: "We should do our utmost to encourage the beautiful, for the useful encourages itself." Willis continued writing for this periodical until his death in 1867.

Tortesa the Usurer concerns the scheming of a Florentine moneylender to gain the hand of a count's daughter; after a series of disguises, feignings, potions, and so on, the usurer is brought to better ways upon discovering the lady's pure love for a young painter. The play, in its poetry and delineation of character, is held by Professor Quinn to be especially meritorious; [3] it is the subject of extended commentary by Poe who, though asserting that it is "over-clouded—rendered misty—by a world of unnecessary and impertinent intrigue," really does "think highly of the drama as a whole. . . ." [4] The Shakespearean influence is evident in the "love at first sight" scene between Angelo and Isabella, and in the portrait of Isabella "coming to life."

Bianca Visconti is based on the historical Francesco Sforza, who married the daughter of Philip Visconti, but the facts are altered to suit the dramatic purposes; one critic condemns Willis for putting a "wholly wrong face upon history." [5] Though the role of Bianca is derived from history, it was written expressly for Josephine Clifton, a popular actress "of great physical force and beauty of the large, queenly type, who took the part of the heroine," and the role of Pasquali was created for Harry Placide, a well-known actor of the time.[6] Numerous productions of the play marked it as a distinct dramatic success.

From a literary point of view, *Bianca Visconti* is directly related to the writings contemporary with it by reason of the romanticism which permeates its plot, characters, and expression.[7] Just as Irving was fictionizing history in *The Conquest of Granada* (1829) and in *The Alhambra* (1832), Cooper in *The Spy* (1821) and *The Pilot* (1823); just as Longfellow was putting historic materials into poetic

[1] Beers, *op. cit.*, p. 176.

[2] *Ibid.*, p. 117.

[3] Quinn, *A History of the American Drama from the Beginning to the Civil War*, p. 529.

[4] *The Works of Edgar Allan Poe*, edited by Stedman and Woodberry. New York: 1914. VI, 270.

[5] C. C. Felton in *North American Review*, LI, 153 (July, 1840).

[6] Beers, *op. cit.*, p. 231.

[7] The romanticism of Willis is consonant with his critical dictum: "Whatever I accomplish must be gained by ardor, and not by patience." (Beers, *op. cit.*, p. 14.)

form in such poems as *Evangeline* (1847) and *Miles Standish* (1858); and just as Robert Montgomery Bird was dramatizing historical incidents in *The Gladiator* (1831), *Oralloossa* (1832), and *The Broker of Bogota* (1834); so Willis, in his verse tragedy *Bianca Visconti*, was participating in the romantic "revival of the past." In his poetry, too, he evinced this same interest, as may be seen in *Parrhasius*, dealing with an Athenian painter, and in *The Scholar of Thebet Ben Khorat*, an Arabian astrologer. The *Poem Delivered at Brown University* (September 6, 1831) at one point apostrophizes the "rapt sages of old time."[1] With the setting of *Bianca Visconti* at Milan in the fourteenth century, Willis is particularly representative of the romantic interest in the Middle Ages.[2] Romantic sensationalism is evident in the various aspects of the plot, such as concealed identities, conspiracies, betrayals, druggings, substituted victims, deaths, murders; the ascendancy of feeling reveals itself in the passionate love of Bianca which transcends self, fraternity, heaven; in Bianca, too, is lightly suggested the Shelleyan desire to flee the world in search of a remote, idyllic isle:

"Love's a miser,
That plucks his treasure from the prying world . . .
. . . Oh, I'll build
A home upon some green and flowery isle
In the lone lakes, where we will use our empire
Only to keep away the gazing world.
The purple mountains and the glassy waters
Shall make a hushed pavilion with the sky,
And we two in the midst will live alone. . . ." [3]

Human speech is frequently heightened to poetry, even in the sword-loving Sforza, "who never learned the courtly phrase of love":

"The sun of woman's world is love, Rossano!
When that sun sets, if no unpitying cloud
Trouble her sky, there rises oftentimes
A crescent moon of memory, whose light
Makes the dark pathway clear again." [4]

The romantic interest in nature appears in the numerous figures of speech employed by the characters, and a departure from the conventional is suggested in Pasquali's dictum that "there is no hope for her in poetry if she be not a sinner." [5]

A more traditional view of poetry is expressed by Pasquali when he points out that though in specific or literal application poetry may be false, yet basically it should be universally true: "Though poetry be full of lies, it is unworthy to be called poetry if it be not true as prophecy." This same thought is suggested else-

[1] *Poems*. New York: 1882, p. 374.

[2] Cf. also Willis's *Tortesa the Usurer;* Longfellow's *Nuremberg* and *The Golden Legend;* Lowell's *The Vision of Sir Launfal;* Boker's *Francesca da Rimini*, etc.

[3] Act I, sc. 3, p. 212.

[4] Act II, sc. 3, p. 215.

[5] Act I, sc. 1, p. 207.

where in Willis: in *Poem Delivered at Brown University* (1831) he states that "truth is *vitality*. . . ." [1] Pasquali is characteristically aware of the perpetuative power of poetry: ". . . To be the friend of a poet is to be immortal." [2] And he defines the role of the imaginative faculty in enriching life: "There be gems in the earth, qualities in the flowers, creatures in the air, the duke ne'er dreams of. There be treasuries of gold and silver, temples and palaces of glorious work, rapturous music, and feasts the gods sit at—and all seen only by a sun, which, to the duke, is black as Erebus. . . . All these gems, treasuries, palaces, and fairy harmonies I see by the imagination I spoke of." It is by virtue of this pictorial power, which the duke lacks, that the poet is richer than his social superior.

Religiously the play indicates the Catholic background of the Middle Ages: there are phrasal references to the Deity, and Sforza presses the crucifix to his lips as a seal to his prayer for filial worthiness. Conscience chastises Bianca severely for her complicity in her brother's death:

"Ah, who murdered Giulio!
Not I!—not I!—not I!" [3]

She is so distraught by the anguish of remorse that she is driven to the psychological escape of believing reality to be a dream:

"Is it not strange
That we can dream such things?"
. . . .
"Was't not a hellish dream?" [4]

It has been pointed out that the Puritan environment which surrounded Willis in his earlier years left definite traces upon his character; he himself testifies: "I am under one ceaseless and enduring conviction of sin; one wearing anxiety about my soul, without making any visible progress." [5] This suggestion of duality is also found in his poetry, especially in the *Poem Delivered at Brown University*, where he sets against "a heavenward spirit" another which is

". . . a child of clay,
And born of human passions. In its train
Follow all things unholy—Love of Gold,
Ambition, Pleasure, Pride of place or name,
All that we worship for itself alone,
All that we may not carry through the grave." [6]

However, it is Bianca's desire for Sforza's love that finally surmounts all other considerations: she has denied herself in reaching for his love; though she calls him a devil,

[1] *Poems*, p. 375.

[2] Petrarch's Laura and Homer's Priam are instanced as classic illustrations of this point.

[3] Act V, sc. 3, p. 228.

[4] Act V, sc. 3, p. 229.

[5] Beers, *op. cit.*, p. 59.

[6] *Poems*, pp. 368–369.

"... the shape of one
Who upon earth had no heart!" [1]

yet she finally grants him the crown; also, in the name of love she has plotted her brother's death and will forego the reward of heaven:

"... heaven without him
Were but a hell—for I've no soul to go there!
Nothing but love! no memory but that!
No hope! no sense!—Heaven were a madhouse to me!" [2]

This strong personal love stands in contrast to the more general love for man that Willis portrays, for example, in *The Dying Alchymist:*

"And more, much more—for now
The life-seal'd fountains of my nature move—
To nurse and purify this human love—
To clear the godlike brow
Of weakness and mistrust, and bow it down,
Worthy and beautiful, to the much-loved one—" [3]

And in *Poem*, above referred to, love and heaven are not at odds; in fact, "The law of heaven is *love*." But in the main, as we have seen, *Bianca Visconti* emerges naturally from the characteristics of its author and blends directly with the literary features of its age.

The present text of the play is taken from the *Mirror Library*, no. 30 (1844), published by Morris and Willis, New York. It contains *Tortesa the Usurer* and *Bianca Visconti.*

[1] Act V, sc. 3, p. 230.
[2] Act IV, sc. 2, p. 224.
[3] *Poems*, p. 244.

DRAMATIS PERSONÆ

FRANCESCO SFORZA—A Condottiero of the 14th century, afterwards Duke of Milan
BRUNORIO—His Lieutenant
SARPELLIONE—Ambassador at Milan from Alfonso, king of Naples
ROSSANO—A Milanese Captain, formerly companion in arms to Sforza
PASQUALI—A whimsical Poet

* * *

BIANCA VISCONTI—Daughter of Philip Visconti,[1] the bed-ridden Duke of Milan, and heiress-apparent to the crown
GIULIO—Her Page, afterwards discovered to be her brother and heir to the crown
FIAMETTA—Waiting Woman to Bianca, and partial to Pasquali
Lords of Council, Priest, Messengers, Sentinels, &c.

[1] This eccentric duke, the last of the Viscontis, passed the latter part of his life in utter seclusion, seen by no one but his physician. His habits were loathsome, and his character harsh and unnatural. [*Willis's note.*]

BIANCA VISCONTI; OR THE HEART OVERTASKED

ACT I

SCENE I. PASQUALI *the poet's chamber.* FIAMETTA *mending his hose while he writes.*

FIAMETTA. Why dost thou never write verses upon me?

PASQUALI. Didst thou ever hear of a cauliflower struck by lightning?

FIAMETTA. If there were honesty in verses, thou wouldst sooner write of me than of Minerva thou talkst of. Did she ever mend thy hose for thee?

PASQUALI. There is good reason to doubt if Minerva ever had hose on her leg.

FIAMETTA. There now! She can be no honest woman! I thought so when thou saidst she was most willing at night.

PASQUALI. If thy ignorance were not endless, I would instruct thee in the meanings of poetry. But thou'lt call Jupiter a cow driver, till the thunderbolt thou takest for a bunch of twigs, strike thee dead for profanity. This once understand: Minerva is no *woman*, but *wit;* and when the poet speaks of unwilling Minerva, he talks of sluggish wit—that hath nothing to do with chastity.

FIAMETTA. Are there two names for all things, then, Master Pasquali?

PASQUALI. Ay—nearly.

FIAMETTA. What is the learned name for honest wife?

PASQUALI. Spouse.

FIAMETTA. When shall I be thy spouse, then?

PASQUALI. When thou canst make up thy mind to forego all hope of living in poetry.

FIAMETTA. Nay, if I am not to be put in verse, I may as well have a plain man for a husband.

PASQUALI. If thou wouldst be put in verse, thou shalt have no husband at all.

FIAMETTA. Now, wilt thou tell me why—in good common words, Master Pasquali.

PASQUALI. Thus:—dost thou think Petrarch had e'er made Laura so famous if she had been honestly his wife?

FIAMETTA. An she were thrifty, I think he might.

PASQUALI. I tell thee no! His sonnets had then been as dull as the praises of the just. No man would remember them.

FIAMETTA. Can no honest women be famous, then?

PASQUALI. Virtue disqualifies. There is no hope for her in poetry if she be not a sinner. Mention me the most famous woman in history.

FIAMETTA. Helen of Troy, in the ballad, I think.

PASQUALI. Wouldst thou be more virtuous than she?

FIAMETTA. Nay, that were presumption.

PASQUALI. Knowest thou why she is sung in an Iliad? I will tell thee: being the wife to Menelaus, she ran away with the prince of Troy.

FIAMETTA. Then is it a shame to remember her.

PASQUALI. So thou sayest in thy ignorance. Yet for that sin she hath been remembered near three thousand years. Look through all poetry, and thou'lt find it thrives upon making sinners memorable. To be famous, thou must sin. Wilt thou qualify?

[*A rap at the door.*]

PAGE. Master Pasquali! Master Pasquali!

FIAMETTA. Holy Virgin! it is my mistress's page. An I be found here now, I were as qualified as Helen of Troy.

[*She conceals herself. Enter the* PAGE.]

PASQUALI. How now, Master Giulio? Thou'rt impatient.

PAGE. Zounds, Pasquali! If thou hadst been a prince, I had not been kept longer at the door.

PASQUALI. If thou wert of age to relish true philosophy, I could prove to thee that the poet were the better waited for of the two. But what is thy errand?

PAGE. A song—I want a new song!

PASQUALI. To what tune?

PAGE. To a new tune on the old theme. Could I tell thee a secret without danger now! Hast thou ne'er a cat that will mew it out?

PASQUALI. No! not even a wall that has ears. What is thy news?

PAGE. My mistress Bianca hath lost all taste for my singing!

PASQUALI. A pin's head might pay for that news.

PAGE. But, good Pasquali, wilt thou not write me a new song?

PASQUALI. Upon what theme?

PAGE. Sforza—still Sforza! But it must be melancholy.

PASQUALI. Why melancholy?

PAGE. Did I not tell thee once in confidence that she loved him?

PASQUALI. Ay—and I writ a song in his praise.

PAGE. I now tell thee in confidence that she hath lost him; for she is to marry Lionel of Ferrara!

PASQUALI. Here's news indeed!

PAGE. It's the duke's will, and my lady is grieved to the degree I tell thee. She'll have none of my music. Wilt thou write me the song?

PASQUALI. Must it be mournful, say you?

PAGE. Ay—as the jug-jug of her nightingale. She's full of tears. Wilt thou write it now? Shall I hold the ink while thou writest it?

PASQUALI. Bless the boy's wits! Dost thou think songs are made like pancakes, by turning the hand over?

PAGE. Why, is't not in thy head?

PASQUALI. Ay—it is.

PAGE. And how long will it take thee to write eight lines upon parchment?

PASQUALI. Not long—if Minerva were willing.

PAGE. Shall I have it by vespers, then?

PASQUALI. Ay—if thou wilt leave me presently.

PAGE. Farewell, then! Let it be melancholy, good Pasquali. [*Exit.*

[FIAMETTA *comes out.*]

FIAMETTA. Now must I hurry to my mistress, ere that monkey-page gets to the palace.

PASQUALI. Stands he well with her?

FIAMETTA. If he were her born child, she could not love him more. She fancies the puppy-dog has an eye of her color. Good day, Master Pasquali.

PASQUALI. Stay! will she marry this Lionel, think you?

FIAMETTA. Can you know anything by tears?

PASQUALI. Not so much by a woman's—but doth your lady weep?

FIAMETTA. Ay—like an aqueduct!

PASQUALI. Then it's more like she loves than hates him!

FIAMETTA. Now, enlighten me that!

PASQUALI. Thus:—a woman, if she be a lady (for clowns like thee, are of a constitution more dull and reasonable), a lady, I say, hath usually in her composition, two spirits—one angelical, the other diabolical. Now, if you stir me up the devil, he will frown—but if you touch me the angel, he will weep! If your lady weep, therefore, it is more like this match hath waked the angel than stirred the devil—for I never saw woman yet, who, if her heart were crossed, would not play the devil ere she knocked under!

FIAMETTA. How canst thou think such brave thoughts on what does not concern thee!

PASQUALI. Does it concern me if I shall live for ever?

FIAMETTA. Surely it doth!

PASQUALI. By what shall I live, then?

FIAMETTA. By faith in the catechism, I think!

PASQUALI. By poetry, I tell thee! And now digest this paradox! Though poetry be full of lies, it is unworthy to be called poetry if it be not true as prophecy.

FIAMETTA. But how can that be true which is false?

PASQUALI. I will show thee! Thy lady's page would have a song, now, full of lamentation for Sforza. In it, I should say, the heavens wept—(which would be a lie)—that the winds whispered mournfully his name (which would be a lie), and that life without him were but music out of tune (which would be a consumed lie)! Yet if she loved Sforza, see you not that my verses, which are nothing but lies, have a poetic truth? When if she love him not—they are poetically false!

FIAMETTA. 'Tis like thy flatteries, then! When thou sayest my cheek is like a peach, it is true, because it hath down upon it, and so hath a peach—yet it is false—because my cheek hath no stone in it!

PASQUALI. Let me taste the savor of that peach. Thou art wiser than I thought thee.

FIAMETTA. I must go now.

PASQUALI. Find me out if she love him! I would fain write no more verses on Sforza—whom I hate that he hath only a brute courage, and no taste for poesy. Now, Lionel's father was Petrarch's friend, and thy lady loving my verses, it were more convenient if she loved Lionel, who would love them, too. Go thy ways now.

FIAMETTA. Farewell, Master Pasquali!

PASQUALI. Stay—there be rude men in this poor quarter, I will come with thee to the piazza. Come along, mistress!

SCENE 2. *The Camp before Milan. The tent of* SFORZA *at the side and watch-fires in the distance.*

Enter SFORZA *and* BRUNORIO

SFORZA. Is the guard set?
BRUNORIO. All set, my lord!
SFORZA. And blaze
The watch-fires where I ordered?
BRUNORIO. Every one.
Hold you your purpose, sir?
SFORZA. Tonight, at twelve,
I will set on! This fickle Duke of Milan
Has changed for the last time. Brunorio!
BRUNORIO. You seem disturbed, sir.
SFORZA. I would have tonight
The best blood up that ever rose for Sforza.
Are your spears resolute?
BRUNORIO. As yourself, my lord!
SFORZA. We'll sleep in Milan, then. By Heaven! I know not
Why I have waited on the changing pleasure
Of this old duke so long.
BRUNORIO. Twelve years ago
He promised you his daughter.
SFORZA. Did he not?
And every year he has renewed and broken
This promise of alliance.
BRUNORIO. Can you hold
Milan against the Florentine, my lord?
'Tis said the fair Bianca is betrothed
To their ally Ferrara! They will join
Naples against you, and cry out "usurper!"
SFORZA. Ay—I have thought on't. I'm the *second* Sforza!
The *first* hewed wood! *There* lies enough to bar me,
Were I another Cæsar, from authority!
'Tis by this whip I have been driven so long—
'Tis by the bait of this old man's alliance
I have for ten years fought the wars of Milan.
They've fooled me year by year, and still found means
With their cursed policy, to put me off—
And, by the saints, they've reason. Could I point
The world to such a thread 'twixt me and Milan
As weaves a spider through the summer air,
I'd hang a crown upon it. Once possessed
Of a fair seat in Lombardy, my spears
Would glisten in St. Mark's!
BRUNORIO. And thence to Naples!
SFORZA. Ay—with what speed we might! My brave lieutenant,
You echo my own thought!

Enter a SENTINEL

SENTINEL. A flag of truce
By torch-light comes from Milan.

Enter SARPELLIONE, *in haste*

SARPELLIONE. Noble Sforza!
I've rudely used my privilege to seek you!
SFORZA. By right of office you are ever welcome.
SARPELLIONE. If I might speak to you a timely word
In haste and privacy?
SFORZA. Brunorio, leave us!
SARPELLIONE. A flag of truce comes presently from Milan
With terms of peace. The duke would give his daughter
To save his capital.
SFORZA. The duke does well!
SARPELLIONE. You'll wed her then!
SFORZA. If fairly offered me,

Free of all other terms save peace between us,
I'll wed her freely.

SARPELLIONE. Then I pray you pardon!
You're not the Sforza that should be the son
Of him who made the name!

SFORZA. Bold words, ambassador!
But you are politic, and speak advisedly.
What bars my marriage with Duke Philip's daughter?

SARPELLIONE. Brief—for this herald treads upon my heels—
Bianca was not born in wedlock!

SFORZA. Well!

SARPELLIONE. She's been betrothed to other suitors—

SFORZA. Well!

SARPELLIONE. Is't well that you can ne'er through her inherit
The ducal crown? Is't well to have a wife
Who has made up her mind to other husbands—
Who has been sold to every paltry prince
Twixt Sicily and Venice?

SFORZA. Is that all?

SARPELLIONE. No—nor the best of it. *There lives a son,*
By the same mother, to the Duke of Milan.

SFORZA [*seizing him by the arm*]. Said you a son?

SARPELLIONE. A son!—and—had I time—

SFORZA. Without there! Pray the embassy from Milan
To grant me but a moment.
[*Turning to* SARPELLIONE.]
Is it sure?

SARPELLIONE. Upon the honor of my royal master,
Who'll make it good.

SFORZA. Have you authority
For what you say?

SARPELLIONE. In court or camp, Alfonso
Will prove this story true. His mother fled,
As the world knows—in peril of her life—
To Naples.

SFORZA. From the jealousy of the duke—
I well remember.

SARPELLIONE. Ere he could demand her
From young Alfonso, newly king, she died;
But in her throes brought prematurely forth
A son; whom, fearing for his life, she hid,
And reared him, ever like a prince, till now.

SFORZA. Some fourteen years.

SARPELLIONE. Scarce that—but he is forward,
And feels his blood already.

SFORZA. Say he does—
What make you out of it to change my purpose?

SARPELLIONE. Seeing you cannot thrive by conquering Milan,
Which Milan's allies will pluck back from you
To put the prince upon his father's seat—
My royal master wishes you forewarned.

SFORZA. He's kind—if that is all!

SARPELLIONE. He'd make a friend
Of the best sword in Italy.

SFORZA. What scheme
Lies under this?

SARPELLIONE. No scheme—but your own glory!
Your star stoops to the south. Alfonso's army
Gathers at Capua to war on Florence!
[*More earnestly.*] He'll add Ravenna to your marquisate
For but a thousand spears!

SFORZA. I'll take Ravenna
Without his leave! Admit the herald there!
No, Count! your policy has overshot!
The King Alfonso needs no spears of mine—
But he would have them farther off from Milan—
A blind mole would see that!

SARPELLIONE. My lord! My lord!

SFORZA. Hear me, Sarpellione! I have been
Too long the sport of your fine policy,
With promises of power and fair alliance
I've fought for every prince in Italy—
And *against* all, in turn; now leagued with Venice
To beat back Florence from the Brenta; now
With Florence against Milan; then with Milan
To drive the Tuscan home again, and all
For my *own glory*, by some politic reason.
I'll have a place, or I'll be in the track on't—
Where the poor honor that my hand may pluck

Shall be well garnered. By Visconti's daughter
I set my foot in Milan. My poor laurels,
Such as they are, shall root there!—and, by Heaven,
I'll find a way to make their branches flourish!
Call in the herald, there!

SARPELLIONE. But Lionel,
Prince of Ferrara, whom Bianca loves—

SFORZA. Glory has been my mistress many years
And will suffice me still. If it should chance
Bianca loves another, 'tis an evil
To wed with *me*, which I will recompense
With chainless freedom after. In my glory
She'll find a bright veil that will hide all errors,
Save from the heart that pardons her.

SARPELLIONE. Farewell!
You'll hear o' the young prince soon!

SFORZA. I'll never wrong him—
If there be one!—Our stars will rise together!
There's room enough!

[*Exit* SARPELLIONE *and enter* ROSSANO.
Fair welcome, brave Rossano!
I know your news.

ROSSANO. The duke sends greeting to you—

SFORZA. And offers me his daughter—is't not so?

ROSSANO. Seeing your preparations as I came
I marvel you anticipate so well!

SFORZA. A bird i' the air brings news, they say—but this
Came by a serpent. How's the spear-wound now,
You took for me at Pisa? Brave Rossano!
We'll break a lance once more in company.
It warms my blood to find myself again
Of the same side. Come out in the open air!
We'll talk more freely, as we used to do,
Over a watch-fire. Come out, old comrade!

[*Exeunt* SFORZA *and* ROSSANO.

SCENE 3. *The apartment of* BIANCA. FIAMETTA *embroidering, and the* PAGE *thrumming his guitar.*

PAGE. I'd give my greyhound now—gold collar and silken leash—to know why the duke sent for my lady.

FIAMETTA. *Would* you, Master Curiosity?

PAGE. Mistress Pert, I would—and thy acquaintance into the bargain.

FIAMETTA. Better keep the goods you come honestly by. I would you knew as well how your mistress came by *you.*

PAGE. I came to her from heaven—like her taste for my music. [*Hums a tune.*]

FIAMETTA. *Did* you! do they make sacks in heaven?

PAGE. There's a waiting woman's question for you! Why sacks?

FIAMETTA. Because I think you came in one, like a present of a puppy-dog.

PAGE. Silence, dull pin-woman! here comes my mistress!

[*Takes off his cap as* BIANCA *enters. She walks across the stage without heeding her attendants.*]

BIANCA. To marry Sforza!
My dream come true! my long, long cherished dream!
The star come out of heaven that I had worshipped!
The paradise I built with soaring fancy
And filled with rapture like a honey-bee
Dropped from the clouds at last! Am I awake?—
Am I awake, dear Giulio?

PAGE [*half advancing to her*]. Noble mistress!

BIANCA. Thank God, they speak to me! It is no dream!
It was *this* hand my father took to tell me—
It was with *these* lips that I tried to speak—
It was *this* heart that beat its giddy prison
As if the exulting joy new-sprung within it
Would out and fill the world! . . . . . .
. . . . Wed him tomorrow!
So suddenly a wife! Will it seem modest,
With but twelve hours of giddy preparation
To come a bride to church! Will he remember
I was ten years ago affianced to him?
I have had time to think on't! Oh, I'll tell him—
When I dare speak, I'll tell him—how I've loved him!
And day and night dreamed of him, and through all
The changing wars treasured the solemn troth

Broke by my father! If he listens kindly,
I'll tell him how I fed my eyes upon him
In Venice at his triumph—when he walked
Like a descended god beside the Doge,
Who thanked him for his victories, and the people,
From every roof and balcony, by thousands
Shouted out "Sforza! Live the gallant Sforza!"
I was a child then—but I felt my heart
Grow, in one hour, to woman!

PAGE. Would it please you
To hear my new song, lady?

BIANCA. No, good Giulio!
My spirits are too troubled now for music.
Get thee to bed! Yet stay! hast heard the news?

PAGE. Is't from the camp?

BIANCA. Ay—Sforza's taken prisoner!

PAGE. I'm vexed for that.

BIANCA. Why vexed?

PAGE. In four years more
I shall bear sword and lance. There'll be no Sforza
To kill when I'm a man! Who took him, lady?

BIANCA. A blind boy, scarcely bigger than yourself;
And gave him, bound, to me! In brief, dear Giulio!
Not to perplex those winking eyelids more,
The wars are done, and Sforza weds to-morrow
Your happy mistress!

PAGE. Sforza! We shall have
A bonfire, then!

BIANCA. Ay—twenty!

PAGE. And you'll live
Here in the palace, and have masks and gambols
The year round, will you not?

BIANCA. My pretty minion,
You know not yet what love is! Love's a miser,
That plucks his treasure from the prying world
And grudges e'en the eye of daylight on it!
Another's look is theft—another's touch
Robs it of all its value. Love conceives
No paradise but such as Eden was
With *two* hearts beating in it.

[*Leaves the* PAGE *and walks thoughtfully away.*]

Oh, I'll build
A home upon some green and flowery isle
In the lone lakes, where we will use our empire
Only to keep away the gazing world.
The purple mountains and the glassy waters
Shall make a hushed pavilion with the sky,
And we two in the midst will live alone,
Counting the hours by stars and waking birds,
And jealous but of sleep! To bed, dear Giulio!
And wake betimes.

PAGE. Good night, my dearest lady!

BIANCA. To bed, Fiametta! I have busy thoughts,
That needs will keep me waking.

FIAMETTA. Good night, lady.

BIANCA. Good night, good night! The moon has fellowship
For moods like mine. I'll forth upon the terrace,
And watch her while my heart beats warm and fast.

ACT II

SCENE I. *The square of Milan. The front of the cathedral on the right. People kneeling round the steps, and the organ heard within.*

Enter PASQUALI *and* FIAMETTA *in haste*

FIAMETTA. Now, Master Pasquali! said I not we should be too late?

PASQUALI. Truly, there seems no room!

FIAMETTA. And I her first serving-woman! If it were my own wedding I should not grieve more to have missed it. You would keep scribbling, scribbling, and I knew it was past twelve.

PASQUALI. Consider, Mistress Fiametta! I had no news of this marriage till the chimes began; and the epithalamium must be writ! I were shamed else, being the bard of Milan.

FIAMETTA. The what, of Milan?

PASQUALI. The bard, I say! Come aside, and thou shalt be consoled. I'll read thee my epithalamium.

FIAMETTA. Is it something to ask money of the bridegroom?

PASQUALI. Dost thou think I would beg?

FIAMETTA. Nay, thou'rt very poor!

PASQUALI. Look thee, Mistress Fiametta! that's a vulgar error, thou hadst best be rid of. I, whom thou callest poor, am richer than the duke.

FIAMETTA. Now if thou'rt not out of thy ten senses, the Virgin bless us.

PASQUALI. I'll prove it even to thy dull apprehension. Answer me truly. How many meals eats the duke in a day?

FIAMETTA. Three, I think, if he be well.

PASQUALI. So does Pasquali! How much covering has he?

FIAMETTA. Nay—what keeps him warm.

PASQUALI. So has Pasquali! How much money carries he on his person?

FIAMETTA. None, I think. He is a duke, and needs none.

PASQUALI. Even so Pasquali! He is a poet, and needs none. What good does him the gold in his treasury?

FIAMETTA. He thinks of it.

PASQUALI. So can Pasquali! What pleasure hath he in his soldiers?

FIAMETTA. They keep him safe in his palace.

PASQUALI. So they do Pasquali in his chamber. Thus far, thou'lt allow, my state is as good as his—and better—for I can think of his gold, and sleep safe by his soldiers, yet have no care of them.

FIAMETTA. I warrant he has troubled thoughts.

PASQUALI. Thou sayest well. Answer me once more, and I'll prove to thee in what I am richer. Thou'st ne'er heard, I dare swear, of imagination.

FIAMETTA. Is't a pagan nation or a Christian?

PASQUALI. Stay—I'll convey it to thee by a figure. What were the value of thy red stockings over black, if it were always night?

FIAMETTA. None.

PASQUALI. What were beauty if it were always dark?

FIAMETTA. The same as none.

PASQUALI. What were green leaves better than brown—diamonds better than pebbles—gold better than brass—if it were always dark?

FIAMETTA. No better, truly.

PASQUALI. Then the shining of the sun, in a manner, dyes your stockings, creates beauty, makes gold and diamonds, and paints the leaves green?

FIAMETTA. I think it doth.

PASQUALI. Now mark! There be gems in the earth, qualities in the flowers, creatures in the air, the duke ne'er dreams of. There be treasuries of gold and silver, temples and palaces of glorious work, rapturous music, and feasts the gods sit at—and all seen only by a sun, which, to the duke, is black as Erebus.

FIAMETTA. Lord! Lord! Where is it, Master Pasquali!

PASQUALI. In my head. [FIAMETTA *discovers signs of fear.*] All these gems, treasuries, palaces, and fairy harmonies I see by the imagination I spoke of. Am I not richer now?

FIAMETTA [*retreating from him*]. The Virgin help us! He thinks there's a sun in his head! I thought to have married him, but he's mad! [*She falls to weeping.*]

[*The cathedral is flung open, and the organ plays louder. The bridal procession comes out of church and passes across the stage. As they pass* PASQUALI, *he offers his epithalamium to* SFORZA.]

SFORZA. What have we here—petitions?

BIANCA. Nay, my lord!
Pasquali's not a beggar. You shall read
Something inventive here! He's a clear fancy,
And sings your praises well. Good chamberlain!
Bring him with honor to the palace! Please you,
My lord, wilt on!

PAGE [*to* PASQUALI]. You'll come to the feast now, won't you?
We'll sit together, and have songs and stories,
And keep the merriest end on't!

[*As the procession passes off*, SARPELLIONE *plucks* PASQUALI *by the sleeve, and retains him.*]

SARPELLIONE. A fair bride, sir!

PASQUALI. What would you, noble Count?

SARPELLIONE. The bridegroom, now,

Should be a poet, like yourself, to know
The worth of such a jewel!

PASQUALI. Haply so—
But we are staying from the marriage feast—

SARPELLIONE. One word! [*Pulls him aside.*]
Have you ambition?

PASQUALI. Like the wings
Upon a marble cherub—always spread,
But fastened to a body of such weight
'Twill never rise till doomsday. I would drink
Sooner than talk of it!—Come on! my lord!

SARPELLIONE. Signor Pasquali—I have marked you oft
For a shrewd, rapid wit. As one who looks
Oft on the sun, there needs no tedious care
Lest the light break too suddenly upon you.
Is it not so?

PASQUALI. Say on!

SARPELLIONE. You know how Naples
Has over it a sky all poetry.

PASQUALI. I know it well.

SARPELLIONE. The radiant Giovanna
Cherished Boccaccio and Petrarch there,
And 'tis the quality of the air they breathed—
Alfonso feels it! Brief and to the point!
My royal master sends for you. He'd have
A galaxy around him!

PASQUALI. Noble Count!

Enter PAGE

PAGE. I'm sent to bid you to the feast, sirs!

SARPELLIONE. Go!
We'll follow straight. [*Exit* PAGE.
This leaden-headed soldier
Slights you, I see—He took you for a beggar!

PASQUALI. Humph! 'tis his wedding day, and I forgive him!

SARPELLIONE. You're used to wrong, I knew.

PASQUALI. Today, my lord,
I'm bent upon a feast—wake not a devil
To mar my appetite!

SARPELLIONE. One single word!
This brainless spear-head would be Duke of Milan.

PASQUALI. What! while the duke lives!

SARPELLIONE. While the duke's *son* lives,
For there *is* one—I'll prove it when you will—
And he will murder him to take his crown.

PASQUALI. How know you that?

SARPELLIONE. Alfonso, king of Naples,
Would have this usurpation and this murder
In time prevented.

PASQUALI. How!

SARPELLIONE. By Sforza's death.
There's no way else—but 'tis a dangerous theme
To talk on here—come out o' the way a little,
And you shall have such reasons for the deed—

PASQUALI [*flings him from him with contempt*].
What "deed"? Dost take me for a murderer?
My lord! I'm poor. I have a thirst for honors
Such as you offered me but now, that burns
Like fire upon my lips—I could be tortured
Through twenty deaths to leave a name behind me.
But nay, I prate—I'll turn not out to *thee*
The golden inside of a soul of honor—
[*Leaving him.*] When next you want a hand for a bad deed,
Look to your *equals*—there are those *beneath* you
Who, from their darkling wells, see guiding-stars
Far o'er *your* head, my lord! [*Exit.*

SARPELLIONE. Such men as this
Do not betray e'en villains! I shall find
Another and a fitter. To the feast now!
And watch my time and means. [*Exit.*

SCENE 2. *An ante-room, with a feast seen beyond*

Enter SFORZA *and* ROSSANO

ROSSANO. I've a new culverin
Invented here by the duke's armorer;
Will you walk forth?

SFORZA. Most willingly. Within there!
My helmet!

Enter BIANCA

BIANCA. Is there fresh alarm, my lord?
You would not go abroad?
[*She takes the helmet from the* PAGE *as he brings it in.*]

SFORZA. A little way, sweet,
To look at some new arms.

BIANCA. Tomorrow, surely,
Will do as well. Here are some loving verses
Writ on your marriage!

ROSSANO. I've the gonfalon
Your father gave me at the siege of Parma.
The rags wave yet!

SFORZA. I'd rather see a thread on't
Than feast a hundred years!

BIANCA. My lord, will't please you
Come in, and hear the verses? There's a wine
You did not taste, grown on Vesuvius;
Pray you, come in!

ROSSANO. I've, in my tent, the sword
Your father plucked from a retreating soldier
To head the fight at Pisa. 'Tis well hacked!

SFORZA. I'll come, Rossano! [*To* BIANCA.]
Nay, sweet! by your leave
[*Takes his helmet.*]
We'll go abroad a little! You shall see us
Betimes at supper. Keep the revels toward!
We'll taste your wine anon. Come, brave Rossano!

[*They go out.* BIANCA *looks after them thoughtfully a few moments, and then walks back slowly to the banqueting room.*]

SCENE 3. *The ramparts at night*

Enter SFORZA *and* ROSSANO

ROSSANO. She's loving in her nature, and methought
Seemed grieved when you came forth!

SFORZA. I should have thought so,
But that I had some private information
She loved another!

ROSSANO. You're perhaps abused!

SFORZA. Nay—nay—how should she love me? I'm well on
To my meridian, see you!—a rough soldier—
Who never learned the courtly phrase of love.
And she—the simplest maiden in a cot,
Is not more tender-eyed, nor has a heart
Apter to know love's lesson ere 'tis time.
She's loved ere now, Rossano!

ROSSANO. Haply so—
Yet be not rude too rashly.

SFORZA. Rude! I'll make
This forced link that policy puts on her
Loose as a smoke-curl! She shall know no master,
And be no slave for me!

ROSSANO. You'll not neglect her!

SFORZA. The sun of woman's world is love, Rossano!
When that sun sets, if no unpitying cloud
Trouble her sky, there rises oftentimes
A crescent moon of memory, whose light
Makes the dark pathway clear again. Bianca's
May have gone down for me! I'll be no cloud
To mar the moon as well.

ROSSANO. Stand by—there comes
A footfall this way. [*They stand aside.*]

Enter PASQUALI, *hiccupping, and talking to himself*

PASQUALI. That wine was grown on Vesuvius. That's the reason it makes such an eruption. If it breaks out o' the top o' my head now—as I think it will—for it gets hotter and hotter—I shall know if wit be in the brains or the belly.

ROSSANO [*aside*]. (Stay—my lord! This is Pasquali, whose verses Bianca sometimes sings to her lute. Ten to one now but you may gather from his drunkenness if Bianca loves another.) [ROSSANO *comes forward.*] Good even, Master Pasquali.

PASQUALI. That's an everyday phrase—this is holyday!

ROSSANO. A *merry* good even, then!

PASQUALI. Ay, that's better! For we're all merry—except the bride. And that's the way of it.

ROSSANO. What's the way of it?

PASQUALI. See here! Who is it that never weeps at a funeral?

ROSSANO. You shall tell me.

PASQUALI. The dead man, that hath most cause.

ROSSANO. And what hath that to do with a bridal?

PASQUALI. A great deal. Of all people at a bridal, who should be most merry? Why, the bride! now I have just left a bride that is sad enough for a funeral.

ROSSANO. For what cause, think you?

PASQUALI. There are some things which can have but one cause. There's but one cause for drunkenness, and there's but one for grief on a wedding-day.

ROSSANO. And what's that?

PASQUALI. Wine—causes drunkenness!

ROSSANO. And what causes grief in a bride?

PASQUALI. Want of love for the bridegroom.

ROSSANO. How know you that, sir?

PASQUALI. Listen to in-spi-ra-tion!

"When first young Lionel did catch mine eye,
Sforza, the valiant, passed unheeded by!"

ROSSANO. Villain! these are thine own lying verses!

PASQUALI [*pulling out his sword*]. The figures of speech are lies of verse. But if thou sayest that it is a lie that Bianca loves Lionel best, *thou* liest in prose, and so, come on! [*Attacks* ROSSANO, *and* SFORZA *comes forward, and strikes up their swords.*]

SFORZA. Get home, thou drunkard! Come, away, Rossano.
He writes what's palatable, and but echoes
That which is rung at court. She loved this prince—
Sarpellione told me so before.
We'll to the field and our old mistress, glory.
Come on—we'll talk of battles and forget her. [*Exeunt.*

PASQUALI. Fighting's not my vocation; but I have an itching that way, and I'll after him. Halloo! Were there two men? I think there were two. The last man called me a drunkard! That's no offence! a poet may be a drunkard! But "villain!" that's incompatible, and must be pricked back. Halloo! [*Exit.*

SCENE 4. BIANCA'S *chamber at midnight. She sits on a couch in a white undress, and* SFORZA *beside her in his armor.*

BIANCA. Dost think this ring a pretty one, my lord?

SFORZA. Ay, 'tis a pretty ring! I have one here
Marancio gave me—Giacomo Marancio.
The ring his wife sent—but you've heard the story?

BIANCA. I think I never heard it.

SFORZA. She's a woman
The heart grows but to speak of. She was held
A hostage by the Milanese (I pray you
Pardon the mention), when, 'twixt them and me
Marancio held a pass. Her life was threatened
If by his means I crossed the Adige. She—
(Brave heart! I warm to speak of her!) found means
To send to him this ring; wherein is writ
"He who loves most, loves honor best." You'll see it
Here o' the inside.

BIANCA. Did you see this lady?

SFORZA. I hazarded a battle three days after
With perilous odds, only to bring her off—
And would have sold my life for't.

BIANCA. Did you *see* her?

SFORZA. I gave her to Marancio when I took
The ring of him.

BIANCA. My lord! speak you so warmly
Of any other woman?

SFORZA [*rising and taking his helmet*]. Nay, I know not.
There are some qualities that women have
Which are less worthy, but which warm us more
Than speaking of their virtues. I remember
The fair Giovanna in her pride at Naples.
Gods! what a light enveloped her! She left
Little to shine in history—but her beauty
Was of that order that the universe
Seemed governed by her motion. Men looked on her
As if her next step would arrest the world;
And as the sea-bird seems to rule the wave
He rides so buoyantly, all things around her—
The glittering army, the spread gonfalon,
The pomp, the music, the bright sun in heaven—
Seemed glorious by her leave.

BIANCA [*rising and going to the window*]. There's emulation
Of such sweet praise, my lord! Did you not hear
The faint note of a nightingale?

SFORZA. More like
A far-heard clarion, methought! They change

The sentinels, perchance. 'Tis time Rossano
Awaits me on the ramparts.

BIANCA. Not tonight!
Go not abroad again tonight, my lord!

SFORZA. For a brief hour, sweet! the old soldier loves
To gossip of the fields he's lost and won,
And I, no less, to listen. Get to bed!
I'll follow you anon. [*Exit* SFORZA.

BIANCA. He does not love me!
I never dreamed of this! To be his bride
Was all the heaven I looked for! Not to love me
When I have been ten years affianced to him!—
When I have lived for him—shut up my heart,
With every pulse and hope, for his use only—
Worshipped—oh God! idolatrously loved him!
. . . .
Why has he sought to marry me? Why still
Renew the broken pledge my father made him?
Why, for ten years, with war and policy,
Strive for my poor alliance? . . . . . .
. . . . He *must* love me,
Or I shall break my heart! I never had
One other hope in life! I never linked
One thought, but to this chain! I have no blood—
No breath—no being—separate from Sforza!
Nothing has any other name! The sun
Shined like his smile—the lightning was his glory—
The night his sleep, and the hushed moon watched o'er him;—
Stars writ his name—his breath hung on the flowers—
Music had no voice but to say *I love him*,
And life no future, but his love for me!
Whom does he love? Marancio's wife? He praised
Only her courage! Queen Giovanna's beauty?
'Tis dust these many years! There is no sign
He loves another; and report said ever
His *glory* was his mistress. *Can* he love?
Shame on the doubt! 'Twas written in the ring
"He who loves *most*, loves honor best"—and Sforza
Is made too like a god to lack a heart.
And so, I breathe again! To make him love me
Is all my life now! to pry through his nature,
And find his heart out. *That's* wrapt in his glory!
I'll feed his glory, then! He praised Giovanna
That she was royal and magnificent—
Ay—that's well thought on, too! How should an eye,
Dazzled with war and warlike pomp, like Sforza's,
Find pleasure in simplicity like mine!
[*Looks at her dress.*]
I'm a duke's daughter, and I'll wear the look on't!
Unlock my jewels and my costly robes,
And while I keep his show-struck eye upon me,
Watch for a golden opportunity
To build up his renown! . . . .
. . . . And so farewell
The gentle world I've lived in! Farewell all
My visions of a world for two hearts only—
Sforza's and mine! If I outlive this change,
So brief and yet so violent within me,
I'll come back in my dreams, oh, childish world!
If not—a broken heart blots out remembrance.
[*Exit into her bridal chamber, which is seen beyond on opening the door.*]

ACT III

SCENE I. *An ante-chamber of the palace.* BRUNORIO *leaning sullenly on his sword by the door.*

Enter SARPELLIONE

SARPELLIONE. What's this?—the brave Brunorio turned lackey?

BRUNORIO. Nay, Count! I wait my turn.

SARPELLIONE. If a civilian
May have a judgment of a soldier's duty,
You're out of place, sir! This is not the camp!

You're not on guard here! There's a difference
'Twixt patience at your post, and kicking heels
In my lord's ante-chamber!

BRUNORIO. By the saints
My own thought, noble Count! As you came in
I brooded on't.

SARPELLIONE [*aside*]. (This blockhead may be turned
To a shrewd use now! I have marked his brows
Blackening upon Rossano, who usurps
His confidence with Sforza. Could I seize
The lightning in this jealous thunder-cloud—
I'll see the depth on't.) Sforza *knows* you're *here?*

BRUNORIO. I had a message by a varlet page,
Who bid me wait here.

SARPELLIONE. By a page? Sacristie!
Fair treatment for a soldier! Say, Brunorio!
What was't I heard of the Pope's standard-bearer
Clove to the wrist?

BRUNORIO. Heard you of *that*, my lord?
You see the weapon here!

SARPELLIONE. Was't thine, i'faith?
I thought *promotion* had been won with service!
Was't thou, indeed? I heard the King Alfonso
Say 'twas the best blow and the bravest followed
He'd known in his time. How it came to his ears
I know not—but he made the court ring with it!

BRUNORIO. The king?

SARPELLIONE. How long since thou wast made lieutenant?

BRUNORIO. Five years come March!

SARPELLIONE. Zounds! how this peasant's son
Treads merit in the dust! Sforza keeps back
His betters, brave Brunorio!

[ROSSANO *passes out.*]

Ay—there!
That man cuts off your sunshine, or I know
Nothing of courts! I, that have no part in it,
Have marked how you are slighted for Rossano!
Forgive my touching on't! 'Tis my respect
For a brave soldier makes me speak so freely.
But were I of your counsel—

BRUNORIO. Noble Count,
My heart speaks through your lips. Since this Rossano
Has had my lord's ear, I've been thrust aside
Like a disgraced hound.

SARPELLIONE. Frankly, brave Brunorio!
And between us,—I've heard you lightly mentioned
By this ungrateful Sforza!

BRUNORIO. How, my lord?

SARPELLIONE. I would not tell you but to serve you in it—
He told Rossano, there, that you had strength,
And struck a sharp blow—and so did an axe!
But for your brains—and then he tossed his head—
You've seen the scorn upon his lip?

BRUNORIO. Curse on him!
I've a sharp blow left yet—and brains enough
To find a time to strike it! Did you say
Alfonso had spoke well of me, my lord?

SARPELLIONE. So well, that, on my own authority—
If you'd take service with a better master—
You're captain from this hour.

BRUNORIO. My lord! So promptly
I take your offer, that your commendations
Will find no swifter bearer than myself
To King Alfonso.

SARPELLIONE. Stay—I'm not just now
On the best terms with Sforza, and you'll see
With half a glance, that while he's here in Milan
His best sword could not leave him for Alfonso,
But it would throw suspicion upon me,
And touch my credit here. I'll write your warrant,
Which you shall keep, and use it when you please.
But for the present shut your bosom up,

And bear your wrongs. Sforza awaits you now—
Go in. I'll see you as you pass again!
[*Exit* BRUNORIO.
He's a fit tool! This o'er-ambitious Sforza
Must not be duke—and if I fret this cur
Till he will tear his master, why, 'twill save
A worthier hand the trouble on't.
[*Exit* SARPELLIONE.

SCENE 2. SFORZA *discovered sitting thoughtfully in his apartment. The* PAGE *curiously examining his sword.*

SFORZA [*yawning*]. This is dull work!
PAGE. My lord, will't please you, teach me
A trick of fence?
SFORZA. Ay—willingly! Hast thou
A weapon in that needle-case of thine?
PAGE [*drawing*]. A weapon! If I had your legs to stand on
I'd give you all the odds 'twixt it and yours!
Look at that blade! [*Bends it.*] Damascus!
[SFORZA *smiles, and unbuckles his scabbard.*]
By the gods,
You shall not laugh at me! I'll give you odds,—
With anything to stand on!
SFORZA. Nay—I'll sit—
And you shall touch me if you can! Come on!
And see I do not rap you o'er the coxcomb!
PAGE. Have at you fairly! Mind! for I'm in earnest!
[*They fence.*]
SFORZA. One—two—well thrust, by Jupiter! Again!
One—two!
PAGE [*makes a lunge*]. *Three!* there you have it!
SFORZA [*starting up*]. Zounds!
This is no play.
PAGE. What! does the needle prick?
[*Wipes it with his handkerchief.*]
SFORZA. 'Tis a Damascus if thou wilt! I'll laugh
No more at it or thee. Come here, thou varlet!
Where got thy mistress such a ready hand
As thou art?
PAGE [*fencing with the chair*]. From an eagle's nest, my lord!
SFORZA. I'll swear to it! Thou hast the eagle's eye!
But tell me—what brave gentleman of Milan
Has thy blood in his veins?
PAGE. I'm not of Milan.
Sarpellione brought me here from Naples.
SFORZA. Thou'rt not his child. I'll answer for't.
PAGE. Not I!
I hate him! Come! Wilt try another pass?
SFORZA. Stay! is the count thy master, then?
PAGE. *My* master?
He's an old snake! But I'll say this for him,
Were I a royal prince—(as I may be—
Who knows!)—Sarpellione could not treat me
With more becoming honor.
SFORZA [*starting up suddenly*]. What if this
Should be the duke's son that he told me of?
Come hither, sir! What know you of your father?
[*Aside.*] ('Tis the Visconti's lip!)
PAGE. I'll tell you all
I know, my lord. Alfonso sent me here,
Five years ago, in quality of page.
I was to serve my lady and no other,
And to be gently nurtured. The king gave me
A smart new feather—bade me bear myself
Like a young prince at Milan—
SFORZA [*starting away from him*]. It is he!—
Princely in spirit, and Visconti's impress
On every feature! He'll be duke of Milan!
PAGE. Heard you the duke was worse today, my lord?
SFORZA. What duke?
PAGE. Nay, sir! you ought to know what duke!
I heard the doctor say you'd wear his crown
In three days. Never say I told you of it!
He whispered it to old Sarpellione,
Who—
SFORZA. What?
PAGE. Looked daggers at him!
SFORZA [*aside*]. (Now the devil
Plucks at my soul indeed! If the duke die,
The crown lies in the gift of my new wife,

And I were duke as sure as he were dead—
But for this boy!
[*Walks rapidly up and down.*]
I'd set my foot in Venice
In half a year!—Ferrara—then Bologna—
Florence—and thence to Naples! I'd be king
Of Italy before their mourning's threadbare—
But for this boy! . . . .
[*The page still fences with the chair.*]
. . . . I'd found a dynasty!—
Be second of the name—but the first king—
And there should go, e'en with the news, to France,
A bold ambassador from one Francesco,—
Sforza by birth and king of Italy—
But for this boy! . . . .
. . . . I would he were a man!
I would an army barred me from the crown,
Sooner than this boy's right! But he might die!
He might have run upon my sword just now!
'Twere natural,—and so it were to fall
In playing with't, and bleed to death unheard,
From a ripped vein. That would be natural!
He might have died in *many ways* and *I*
Have no part in't.)

PAGE. Will you fence, my lord?

SFORZA [*clutches his sword, and suddenly sheaths it, and walks from him. Aside*].
(Get thee gone, devil! After all his glory
Shall Sforza be the murderer of a child?)
No—No! I'll not fence with thee! Go and play!
I—I—I—[*Turns from him*]. Stay! shall such a grain of sand
As a boy's life, check Sforza's bold ambition?
I, who have hewn down thousands in a day
For but the play on't—I, upon whose hand
Sat slaughter, like a falcon, to let loose
At all that flew above me! I—whose conscience
Carries the reckoning of unnumbered souls
Sped unto hell or heaven, for this ambition!—
Shall I mar all now with a woman's pity
For a fair stripling!

[*Draws his sword, and the* PAGE, *who has been regarding him attentively, comes up and pulls him by his sleeve.*]

PAGE. Look you here, my lord!
If I have harmed you—for you seem so angry
I *think* I have—more than I meant to do—
Take my own sword, and wound me back again!
I'll not cry out—and when you see me bleed,
You'll pardon me that I was so unhappy
As to have chanced to wound you!

[*Kneels, opens his bosom, and offers his sword-hilt to* SFORZA.]

SFORZA. Angels keep me!
Give me thy hand, boy!
[*Looks at him a moment, and passes his hand across his eyes.*]

PAGE. You'll forgive me, sir?
Letting of blood—*when done in fair play, mind you!*—
Has no offence in't.

SFORZA. Leave me now, sweet boy!
I'll see thee at the feast tonight! Farewell!
[PAGE *kisses his hand, and exit.*
Shade of my father! If from Heaven thou lookest
Upon the bright inheritance of glory
I took from thee—pluck from my tortured soul
These thoughts of hell—and keep me worthy of thee!
[*Walks up and down thoughtfully, and then presses the crucifix to his lips.*]
As I am true to honor and that child,
Help me, just Heaven!

SCENE 3. *A bridal feast seen through a glass door in the rear of the stage.*

Enter from the banqueting room, BIANCA, *dressed with great magnificence, followed by* SFORZA, ROSSANO, BRUNORIO, *and* SARPELLIONE. *A raised throne at the side. Music heard till the door is closed.*

BIANCA. They who love stillness follow us! The brain
Grown giddy with the never-wearying dance,
And music's pause is sweet as its beginning.

Shut the doors, Giulio! Sarpellione! enter!
You're welcome to Trophonius' cave! We'll hold
The Court of Silence, and I'll play the Queen.
My brave lord, you shall doff that serious air,
And be court favorite—sit you at our feet!

SFORZA. Too envious a place and office both!
I'll sit here with Rossano. Honor's flower—
That lifts a bold head in the world—at court,
Looks for the lily's hiding-place.

SARPELLIONE [*aside*]. (What trick
Lies in this new humility?) The lily
Is lowly born, and knows its place, my lord!

BIANCA. Yet is it sought with pains while the rose withers!

SARPELLIONE. The rose lifts to the sun its flowering tree,
And all its parts are honored—while the lily
Upon one fragile stem rears all its beauty—
And its coarse family of leaves are left
To lie on the earth they cling to.

SFORZA [*to* ROSSANO, *with whom he has been conversing apart*]. (I've sure news
He was worse yesterday.)

BIANCA [*rising with dignity, and descending from the ducal chair*]. Now, since the serpent
Misled our mother, never was fair truth
So subtly turned to error. If the rose
Were born a lily, and, by force of heart
And eagerness for light, grew tall and fair,
'Twere a true type of the first fiery soul
That makes a low name honorable. They
Who take it by inheritance alone—
Adding no brightness to it—are like stars
Seen in the ocean, that were never there
But for the bright originals in heaven!

SARPELLIONE [*sneeringly*]. Rest to the gallant soul of the *first* Sforza!

BIANCA. Amen! but triple glory to the second!
I have a brief tale for thine ear, ambassador!

SARPELLIONE. I listen, lady!

BIANCA. Mark the moral, sir!
An eagle once from the Euganean hills
Soared bravely to the sky. [*To* SFORZA.] (Wilt please my lord
List to my story?) In his giddy track
Scarce marked by them who gazed upon the first,
Followed a new-fledged eaglet, fast and well.
Upward they sped, and all eyes on their flight
Gazed with admiring awe, when suddenly,
The parent bird, struck by a thunderbolt,
Dropped lifeless through the air. The eaglet paused,
And hung upon his wings; and as his sire
Plashed in the far-down wave, men looked to see him
Flee to his nest affrighted!

SFORZA [*with great interest*]. Did he so?

BIANCA. My noble lord—he had a monarch's heart!
He wheeled a moment in mid air, and shook
Proudly his royal wings, and then right on,
With crest uplifted and unwavering flight,
Sped to the sun's eye, straight and gloriously.

PAGE. Lady—is that true?

BIANCA. Ay—men call those eagles
Sforza the First and Second!

[*The bell tolls, and enter a* MESSENGER.]

MESSENGER. Pardon, madam!
For my sad news! your royal father's dead!

BIANCA [*aside, with great energy*]. (Sforza'll be duke!)

[*Turning to the* MESSENGER.]

Died he in much pain, know you?

MESSENGER. Madam—

BIANCA [*aside*]. (The crown is mine! He will remember
The crown was *mine*.)

[*Turns to the* MESSENGER.]

Sent he for any one
In his extremity?

MESSENGER. Most honored madam—

BIANCA [*aside*]. (Ingratitude is not the lion's fault—
He cannot hate me when I make him royal!
It would be monstrous if he did not love me!)

[*To the* MESSENGER.]

Said you my father sent for me?

MESSENGER. No! Madam,
He died as he had lived, unseen of any
Save his physician!

BIANCA [*aside*]. (Sforza must be crowned

And then our mourning will shut out the world!
He'll be alone with me and his new glory—
All royal, and all *mine!*) [*To* SFORZA.] Please you, my lord,
Dismiss the revellers! My father's dead!
[*Aside.*] (There are no more Viscontis—Sforza's children
Shall now be dukes of Milan! Think on that!
He'll think on't, and his heart will come down to me,
Or there's no truth in nature!) [*To* SFORZA.] My brave lord!
Shall we go in?

SFORZA. Go you in first! [*Hands her in.*] Rossano
Will forth with me, to see the funeral
Fitly arranged.

BIANCA. You'll come back soon, my lord!

SFORZA. Ay—presently! [*Exit* BIANCA.

ROSSANO. With what a majesty
She walks!

SFORZA. She knows not that she has a brother,
And in her port already mocks the duchess.

ROSSANO. She would have made a glorious queen, my lord!

SFORZA. She *should* have made one—but I cannot talk on't!
Let's forth upon our errand, and forget
There was a crown in Milan. [*Exeunt.*

ACT IV

SCENE I. PASQUALI'S *chamber.* FIAMETTA *sitting with his cap in her hand.*

FIAMETTA. What wilt thou do for a black feather, Pasquali?

PASQUALI. Hast thou no money?

FIAMETTA. No—save my dowry of six pieces.

PASQUALI. Give the pieces to me, and thy dowry will be ten times greater.

FIAMETTA. An it be not six times less, I will never trust counting upon fingers.

PASQUALI. Hast thou no dread of dying uncelebrated?

FIAMETTA. If it be sin, I have a dread of it by baptism.

PASQUALI. Is it a sin to neglect thy immortality?

FIAMETTA. Ay—it is.

PASQUALI. Then take heed how thou fallest into sin—for to be the friend of a poet is to be immortal, and thou art no friend of mine if I have not thy six pieces.

FIAMETTA. But how shall I have six times more, Master Pasquali?

PASQUALI. In reputation! Wouldst thou marry a fool?

FIAMETTA. No, truly.

PASQUALI. Then if thy husband be wise, he will be more proud that thou art famous, than covetous of thy six pieces.

FIAMETTA. And shall I be famous? [*Gives him the money.*]

PASQUALI. Thou wilt live when Sforza is dead!

FIAMETTA. Is not Sforza famous, then?

PASQUALI. He hath fame while he lives, and so had King Priam of Troy. But if Homer had not written, Priam would have been forgot and Troy too; and if Sforza live not in poetry, he is as dead in a century—as thou and Laura were, but for thy favors to Petrarch and Pasquali.

FIAMETTA. Why does not Sforza give thee six pieces and be immortal?

PASQUALI. Truly—he pays more for a less matter. It is the blindness of great men that they slight the poets. Look here, now—hath not Sforza shed blood, and wasted treasure, and taken a thousand murders on his soul, to leave a name after him?

FIAMETTA. I misdoubt he hath.

PASQUALI. Now will I, whom he thinks less worthy than a trumpeter, sit down, and with a scrape of my pen, make a dog's name more known to posterity.

FIAMETTA. When thou speakest of a dog, I think of my lady's page. Canst thou tell me why she should love him so out of reason?

PASQUALI. Canst thou tell me why the moon riseth not every night, as the sun every day?

FIAMETTA. No—truly.

PASQUALI. Neither can I give thee reason for a woman's fancy—which is as unaccountable in its caprice as the moon in its changes. Hence the sun is called "*he*," the moon "*she*."

FIAMETTA. Holy Virgin—what it is to be learned!

PASQUALI. Come, Fiametta! spend thy dowry while thy mind is enlightened!

FIAMETTA. If I should repent now!

PASQUALI. Think not of it. If thou shouldst repent tomorrow, I shall still go beseemingly to the funeral, and thou wilt be famous past praying for. Come away!

SCENE 2. *The garden of the palace of Milan*

Enter BIANCA *in mourning, followed by* SARPELLIONE

BIANCA. Liar—'tis not true!

SARPELLIONE. Will't please you read this letter from the king,
Writ when he sent him to you—

BIANCA [*plucks it from him, and tears it to pieces*]. 'Tis a lie
Writ by thyself—

SARPELLIONE [*taking up the pieces*]. The king has written here
The story of his birth, and that he is
Your brother, pledges his most royal honor—

BIANCA. Lie upon lie—

SARPELLIONE. And will maintain the same
With sword and battle!

BIANCA. Let him! There's a Sforza
Will whip him back to Naples! Tell him so!
There'll be a duke upon the throne of Milan
In three days more, whose children will be kings!

SARPELLIONE. Your brother, madam!

BIANCA. Liar, no! my husband!
The crown is mine, and *I* will give it him!

SARPELLIONE. Pardon me, lady, 'tis not yours to give!
While a Visconti lives—and one *does* live—
Princely and like his father—'tis not yours—
And Sforza dare not take it.

BIANCA. He *has* taken it,
In taking me. Sforza is duke, I say!

SARPELLIONE. Am I dismissed to Naples with this news?

BIANCA. Ay—on the instant!

SARPELLIONE. Will you give me leave
To bid the prince make ready for his journey?

BIANCA. What prince?

SARPELLIONE. Your brother, madam, who'll come back
With the whole league of armed Italy
To take the crown he's born to.

BIANCA. I've a page
I love, called Giulio! If you mean to ask me
If he goes with you—lying traitor! no!
I love him, and will keep him!

SARPELLIONE. Ay—till Milan
Knows him for prince, and then farewell to Sforza!
He's flown too near the sun!

BIANCA. Foul raven, silence!
What dost *thou* know of eagles who wert born
To mumble over carrion! Hast thou looked
On the high front of Sforza? Hast thou heard
The thunder of his voice? Hast met his eye?
'Tis writ upon his forehead: *Born a king!*
Read it, blind liar!

SARPELLIONE. Upon your brother's, lady,
The world shall read it.

BIANCA. Wilt thou drive me mad?
They say all breathing nature has an instinct
Of that which would destroy it. I of thee
Feel that abhorrence! If a glistering serpent
Hissed in my path, I could not shudder more,
Nor would I kill it sooner—so begone!
I'll strike thee dead else!

SARPELLIONE. Madam!

[*Exit* SARPELLIONE.

BIANCA. 'Tis my brother!
At the first word with which he broke it to me
My heart gave nature's echo! 'Tis my brother!
I would that he were dead—and yet I love him—
Love him so well, that I could die for him—
Yet hate him that he bars the crown from Sforza.
He's betwixt me and heaven! were *he* but dead!
Sforza and I would, like the sun and moon,
Have all the light the world has! He must die!
Milan will rise for him—his boyish spirit

Is known and loved in every quarter of it.
Naples is powerful, and Venice holds
Direct succession holy, and the lords
Of all the Marches will cry "down usurper!"
For Sforza's glory has o'ershadowed theirs.
Both cannot live or I must live unloved—
And that were hell—or die, and heaven without him
Were but a hell—for I've no soul to go there!
Nothing but love! no memory but that!
No hope! no sense!—Heaven were a madhouse to me!
Hark! who comes here?

Enter SARPELLIONE *and* BRUNORIO. BIANCA *conceals herself*

SARPELLIONE. Strike but this blow, Brunorio—
And thou'rt a made man!
BRUNORIO. Sforza sleeps not well.
SARPELLIONE. Art thou less strong of arm than he who called thee
A brainless ass?
BRUNORIO. 'Sdeath, he did call me so!
SARPELLIONE. And more I never told thee. Pay him for it—
And thou wilt save a prince who'll cherish thee,
And Sforza's soul a murder—for he'll kill him
Ere one might ride to Naples.
BRUNORIO. Think'st thou so?
SARPELLIONE. Is it not certain? If this boy were dead
Sforza were duke. With Milan at his back
He were the devil. Rather than see this,
Alfonso would share half his kingdom with thee.
BRUNORIO. I'll do it!
SARPELLIONE. Thou wilt save a prince's life
Whom he would murder. Now collect thy senses,
And look around thee! On that rustic bank,
Close by the fountain, with his armor off,
He sleeps away the noon.
BRUNORIO. With face uncovered?
SARPELLIONE. Sometimes—but oftener with his mantle drawn
Quite over him! But thou must strike so well,
That, should he see thee, he will never tell on't.
BRUNORIO. I'd rather he were covered.
SARPELLIONE. 'Tis most likely—
But mark the ground well. By this alley here,
You'll creep on unperceived. If he's awake—
You're his lieutenant, and may have good reason
To seek him any hour? Are you resolved?
BRUNORIO. I am!
SARPELLIONE. Once more look round you!
BRUNORIO. If he sleep
Tomorrow, he'll ne'er wake!
SARPELLIONE. Why, that's well said—
Come now and try the horse I've chosen for you.
We'll fly like birds with welcome news to Naples!
[*Exeunt* SARPELLIONE *and* BRUNORIO.
BIANCA. Thank God that I was here! Can there be souls
So black as these—to plot so foul a murder!
Oh, unretributive and silent Heavens!
Heard you these men? Thank God that I can save him!
The sun shone on them—*on these murderers*—
As it shines now on *me!*—Would it were Giulio
They thought to murder!—Ha! what ready fiend
Whispered me that? Giulio *instead* of Sforza!
Why, that were murder—*too!*—Brunorio's murder!—
Not mine! my hands would show no blood for it!
If Giulio were asleep beneath the mantle
Tomorrow noon, and Sforza in his chamber—
What murder lies upon my soul for that?
. . . .
I'll come again tonight, and see the place,
And think on't in the dark!
[*Exit* BIANCA.

ACT V

SCENE I. *Same scene in the garden*

Enter BIANCA

BIANCA. No! no! come hate—come worse indifference!

Come anything—I will not! He is gone
To bring me flowers now, for he sees I'm sad;
Yet, with his delicate thought, asks not the reason,
But tries to steal it from me! *could* I kill him!
His eyes grew moist this morn, for I was pale—
With thinking of his murder! could I kill him!
Oh, Sforza! I could walk on burning ploughshares,
But not kill pitying Giulio! I could starve—
Or freeze with wintry cold—or swallow fire—
Or die a death for every drop of blood
Kneeling at my sad heart, but not kill Giulio!
No—no—no! no!

SFORZA *comes in dejectedly*

My lord! My noble lord!

SFORZA. Give you good day, Bianca!

BIANCA. Are you ill,
That you should drop your words so sorrowfully?

SFORZA. I am not ill, nor well!

BIANCA. Not well?

SFORZA. The pulse
Beats on sometimes, when the heart quite runs down.
I'm very well!

BIANCA. My lord, you married me—
The priest said so—to share both joy and sorrow.
For the last privilege I've shed sweet tears!—
If I'm not worthy—

SFORZA. Nay—you are!—I thank you
For many proofs of gentle disposition,
Which, to say truth, I scarcely looked for in you—
Knowing that policy, and not your choice,
United us!

BIANCA. My lord!

SFORZA. I say you're worthy,
For this, to see my heart—if you could do so,
But there's a grief in't now which brings you joy,
And so you'll pardon me!

GIULIO *comes in with a heap of flowers, which he throws down and listens*

BIANCA. That cannot be!

SFORZA. Listen to this. I had a falcon lately,
That I had trained, till, in the sky above him,
He was the monarch of all birds that flew.
I loved him next my heart, and had no joy,
But to unloose his feet, and see the eagle
Quail at his fiery swoop! I brought him here!
Sitting one day upon my wrist, he heard
The nightingale you love, sing in the tree,
While I applauded him. With jealous heart
My falcon sprang to kill him; and with fear
For your sweet bird, I struck him to my feet;
And since that hour, he droops. His heart is broke,
And he'll ne'er soar again!

PAGE. Why, one such bird
Were worth a thousand nightingales.

BIANCA [*aside*]. (Poor boy!
He utters his own doom!) [*To* SFORZA.] My Lord, I have
A slight request, which you will not refuse me.
Please you, today sleep in your chamber. I
Will give you reason for't.

SFORZA. Be't as you will!
The noon creeps on apace, and in my dreams
I may forget this heaviness. [*Goes in.*]

BIANCA. Be stern,
Strong heart! and think on Sforza! Giulio!

PAGE. Madam!

BIANCA [*aside*]. (He's hot and weary now, and will drink freely
This opiate in his cup, and from his sound
And sudden sleep he'll wake in Paradise.)
Giulio, I say! [*She mixes an opiate.*]

PAGE. Sweet lady, pardon me!
I dreamed I was in heaven, and feared to stir
Lest I should jar some music. Was't your voice
I heard sing, "Giulio"?

BIANCA [*aside*]. (Oh, ye pitying angels,
Let him not love me most, when I would kill him.)
Drink! Giulio!

PAGE. Is it sweet?

BIANCA. The sweetest cup
You'll drink in this world!

PAGE. I can make it sweeter—

BIANCA. And how?

PAGE. With your health in it!

BIANCA. Drink it not!
Not my health! Drink what other health thou wilt!
Not mine—not mine!

PAGE. Then here's the noble falcon
That Sforza told us of! Would you not kill
The nightingale that broke his spirit, madam?

BIANCA. Oh, Giulio! Giulio! [*Weeps.*]

PAGE. Nay—I did not think
You loved your singing bird so well, dear lady!

BIANCA. (He'll break my heart!)

PAGE. Say truly! if the falcon
Must pine unless the nightingale were dead,
Would you not kill it?

BIANCA. Though my life went with it—
I must do so!

PAGE. Why—so I think! And yet
If I had fed the nightingale, and loved him;
And he were innocent, as, after all
He is, you know—I should not like to kill him—
Not with my own hands!

BIANCA. Now, relentless heavens,
Must I be struck with daggers through and through!
Speaks not a mocking demon with his lips?
I will not kill him!

PAGE. Sforza has gone in—
May I sleep there, sweet lady, in his place?

BIANCA. No, boy! thou shalt not!

PAGE. Then will you?

BIANCA. Oh, God!
I would I could! and have no waking after!
Come hither, Giulio! nay—nay—stop not there!
Come on a little, and I'll make thy pillow
Softer than ever mine will be again.
Tell me you love me ere you go to sleep!

PAGE. With all my soul, dear mistress! [*Drops asleep.*]

BIANCA. Now he sleeps!
This mantle for his pall—but stay—his shape
Looks not like Sforza under it. Fair flowers,
[*Heaps them at his feet, and spreads the mantle over all.*]
Your innocence to his! Exhale together,
Pure spirit and sweet fragrance! So—one kiss!
Giulio! my brother! Who comes there? Wake, Giulio!
Or thou'lt be murdered! Nay—'twas but the wind!
[*Withdraws on tiptoe, and crouches behind a tree.*]
I will kneel here and pray!

BRUNORIO *creeps in, followed by* SARPELLIONE *at a distance*

Hark!

SARPELLIONE. See—he sleeps.
Strike well, and fear not!

BIANCA [*springing forward as he strikes*].
Giulio! Giulio! wake!
Ah, God!

[*She drops on the body, the murderer escapes and* SFORZA *rushes in. As he bends over her the scene closes.*]

SCENE 2. *A road outside the walls of Milan*

Enter SARPELLIONE *and* BRUNORIO, *flying from the city, and met by* PASQUALI

PASQUALI. What news, sirs?
[*As they attempt to pass him without answer, he steps before* SARPELLIONE.]
Stay, Count, I've a word with you!

SARPELLIONE. Stand off, and let me pass!

PASQUALI. Nay, with your leave
One single word!

SARPELLIONE. Brunorio! hasten forward,
And loose my bridle! I'll be there o' the instant! [BRUNORIO *hastens on.*]
What would you say?

PASQUALI. My lord! I hear the bell
Tolling in Milan, that is never heard
But at some dread alarm.

SARPELLIONE [*pressing to go on*]. Is that all?

PASQUALI. Stay!
I met a flying peasant here just now,
Who muttered of some *murder*, and flew on!

SARPELLIONE. Slave! let me pass!
[*Draws, and* PASQUALI *confronts him with his sword.*]

PASQUALI. My lord! you once essayed
To tempt me to a murder. Something tells me
That this hot haste has guilt upon its heels,
And you shall stay till I know more of it.
Down with your point!

SARPELLIONE. Villain! respect my office!

PASQUALI. No "villain," and no murderer! In Milan
They've soldiers' law, and if your skirts are bloody,
You'll get small honor for your coat, ambassador!
Bear back, I say!

[*They fight, and* SARPELLIONE *falls, disarmed, on his knee.*]

SARPELLIONE. In mercy, spare my life!

PASQUALI. Up, coward! You shall go before to Milan,
And meet the news! If you are innocent,
I'll ne'er believe a secret prompting more.
If not, I've done the state a worthy service.
On, on, I say!

[*Drives* SARPELLIONE *out before him at the point of his sword.*]

SCENE 3. *A room of state in the palace*

Enter ROSSANO *and a* PRIEST

ROSSANO. Will she not eat?

PRIEST. She hath not taken food
Since the boy died!

ROSSANO. Nor slept?

PRIEST. Nor closed an eyelid!

ROSSANO. What does she?

PRIEST. Still, with breathless repetition,
Goes through the page's murder—makes his couch
As he lay down i' the garden—heaps again
The flowers upon him to eke out his length;
Then kisses him, and hides to see him killed!
'Twould break your heart to look on't.

ROSSANO. Is't the law
That she must crown him?

PRIEST. If, upon the death
Of any Duke of Milan, the succession
Fall to a daughter, she may rule alone,
Giving her husband neither voice nor power
If she so please. But if she delegate
The crown to him, or in extremity
Impose it, it is not legitimate,
Save he is crowned by her own living hands
In presence of the council.

Enter SFORZA, *hastily, in full armor, except the helmet*

SFORZA. Ho! Rossano!

ROSSANO. My lord!

SFORZA. Send quick, and summon in the council
To see the crown imposed! Bianca dies!
My throne hangs on your speed! Fly!

[*Exit* ROSSANO.

Sentry, ho!
Despatch a hundred of my swiftest horse
Toward Naples! Bring me back Sarpellione!
Alive or dead, a thousand ducats for him!
Quick!

[*Exit sentinel, re-enter* ROSSANO.]

ROSSANO. I have sped your orders!

Enter a MESSENGER

MESSENGER. Please, my lord,
Lady Bianca prays your presence with her!

SFORZA. Away! I'll come! [*To* ROSSANO.]
Go, man the citadel
With my choice troops! Post them at every gate!
Send for the Milanese to scout or forage,
I care not what, so they're without the wall!
And hark, Rossano! if you hear a knell
Wail out before the coronation peal,—
Telling to Milan that Bianca's dead,
And there's no duke—down with the ducal banner,
And, like an eagle, to the topmost tower
Up with my gonfalon! Away!

Re-enter the MESSENGER *from* BIANCA

MESSENGER. My lord—

SFORZA. I come! I come!

PASQUALI [*without*]. In, in!

Enter SARPELLIONE, *followed by* PASQUALI

SARPELLIONE [*aghast at the sight of* SFORZA].
Alive!

SFORZA. Ha, devil!
Have you come back to get some fresher news?
Alfonso'd know who's duke! While you are hanging,
I'll ride to Naples with the news myself!
Ha! ha! my star smiles on me!

BIANCA *rushes in and crouches at the side of* SFORZA, *as if hiding from something beyond him.*

BIANCA. Hark! I hear them!
Come! come! Brunorio!—If you come not quick,
My heart will break and wake him!
[*Presses her hand painfully to her side.*]
Crack not yet!
Nay, think on Sforza! Think 'tis for his love!
Giulio will be an angel up in Heaven,
And Sforza will drink glory from *my* hand!
Come! come! Brunorio! [*Screams piercingly.*]
Ah, who murdered Giulio!
Not I!—not I!—not I!

SFORZA [*watching her with emotion*].
Oh, God! how dearly
Are bought the proudest triumphs of this world!

BIANCA. Will the bell never peal!

PRIEST [*to an* ATTENDANT]. On that string only
Her mind plays truly now. Her life hangs on it!
The waiting for the bell of coronation
Is the last link that holds!

SFORZA [*raising her*]. My much-loved wife!

BIANCA. Is it thee, Sforza? Has the bell pealed yet?

SFORZA. Think not of that, but take some drink, Bianca!
You'll kill me this way!

BIANCA [*dashing down the cup*]. Think you I'll drink fire!

SFORZA. Then taste of this! [*Offers her a pomegranate.*]

BIANCA [*laughing bitterly*]. I'm not a fool! I know
The fruit of hell has ashes at the core!
Mock me some other way!

SFORZA. My poor Bianca!

BIANCA. Ha! ha! that's well done! You've the shape of Sforza,
And you're a devil, and can mock his voice,
But Sforza never spoke so tenderly!
You *overdo* it! Ha! ha! ha!

SFORZA. God help me,
I would her brother had been duke in Milan
And I his slave—so she had lived and loved me!

BIANCA. Can you see Heaven from hence! I thought 'twas part
Of a soul's agony in hell to see
The blest afar off? Can I not see Giulio?
[*Struggles, as if to escape something before her eyes.*]
Sforza's between!

SFORZA. Bianca! sayst thou that?
[*Struggles with himself a moment.*]
Nay, then, 'tis time to say farewell Ambition!
[*Turns to the* PRIEST.]
Look, father! I'm unskilled in holy things,
But I have heard, the sacrifice of that
Which the repenting soul loved more than Heaven,
Will work a miracle!
[*Takes his sword from his scabbard, and proceeds in a deeper voice.*]
I love my sword
As never mother loved her rosy child!
My heart is in its hilt—my life, my soul,
Follow it like the light! Say thou dost think
If I give that up for a life of peace,
Heaven will give back her reason—

PRIEST [*eagerly*]. Doubt it not!

SFORZA. Then—take it!
[*Drops the hilt into his hand, and holds it a moment.*]

SARPELLIONE [*in a hoarse whisper*]. Welcome news for King Alfonso!

SFORZA [*starting*]. Fiend! sayest thou so!
Nay, then, come back, my sword.
I'll follow in its gleaming track to Naples
If the world perish!

Enter ROSSANO

Now, what news, Rossano?

ROSSANO. In answer to your wish, the noble council
Consent to see the crown imposed in private,
Three delegated lords will presently
Attend you here!

SFORZA [*energetically*]. Tell him who strikes the bell,
To look forth from his tower and watch this window!
When he shall see a handkerchief wave hence
Let him peal out. [ATTENDANT *goes out.*]

My gonfalon shall float
Over St. Mark's before Foscari dreams
There's a new duke in Milan! Let Alfonso
Look to the north!

Enter ATTENDANT

ATTENDANT. My lord! the noble council
Wait to come in!
[SFORZA *waves his hand, and they enter.*]

1ST LORD. Health to the noble Sforza!

SFORZA. My lords, the deep calamity we suffer
Must cut off ceremony. Milan's heiress
Lies there before you, failing momently,
But holds in life to give away the crown.
If you're content to see her put it on me
Let it be so as quickly as it may!
Give signal for the bell!
[*The handkerchief is waved and the bell peals.* BIANCA *rises to her feet.*]

BIANCA. It peals at last!
Where am I? Bring some wine, dear Giulio!
[*Looks round fearfully.*]
Am I awake now! I've been dreaming here
That he was dead! Oh, God! a horrid dream!
Come hither, Sforza! I have dreamt a dream,
If I can tell it you—will make your hair
Stand up with horror!

SFORZA. Tell it not!

BIANCA. This Giulio
Was, in my dream, my brother! how I knew it
I do not now remember—but I *did!*
And loved him—(that you *know* must be a dream)
Better than you!

SFORZA. What—better?

BIANCA. Was't not strange?
Being my brother, he must have the crown!
Stay?—is my father dead—or was't i' the dream too?

SFORZA. He's dead, Bianca!

BIANCA. Well, you loved me not,
And Giulio *did*—and somehow you should hate me
If he were duke; and so I killed him, *loving me,*
For you that *loved me not!* Is it not strange
That we can dream such things? The manner of it—
To see it in a play would break your heart—
It was so pitiless! Look here! this boy
Brings me a heap of flowers!—I'll show it you
As it was done before me in the dream!
Don't weep! 'twas but a dream—but I'll not sleep
Again till I've seen Giulio—the blood seemed
So ghastly natural! I shall see it, Sforza,
Till I have passed my hand across his side!
[*Turning to the attendants.*]
Will some one call my page?

SFORZA. My own Bianca,
Will you not drink?
[*She drops the cup in horror.*]

BIANCA. Just such a cup as that
Had liquid fire in't when the deed was done—
A devil mocked me with it!
[*Another cup is brought, and she drinks.*]
This is wine!
Thank God, I wake now!
[*She turns to an attendant.*]
Will you see if Giulio
Is in the garden?

SFORZA. Strike the bell once more!

BIANCA. He kissed me ere he slept—wilt listen, Sforza?

SFORZA. Tell me no more, sweet one!

BIANCA. And then I heaped
The very flowers he brought me, at his feet,
To eke his body out as long as yours—
Was't not a hellish dream?
[*The bell strikes again, and she covers her ears in horror.*]
That bell! Oh, God,
'Tis no dream—now I know—yes—yes—I know
These be the councillors—and you are Sforza,
And that's Rossano—and I killed my brother
To make you duke! Yes, yes! I see it all!
Oh, God! Oh, God!
[*She covers her face, and weeps.*]

SFORZA. My lords! her reason rallies
Little by little. With this flood of tears,
Her brain's relieved, and she'll give over raving.
My wife! Bianca! If thou ever loved'st me,
Look on my face!

BIANCA. Oh, Sforza, I have given
For thy dear love, the eyes I had to see it,
The ears to hear it. I have broke my heart
In reaching for't.

SFORZA. Ay—but 'tis thine *now*, sweet one!
The life-drops in my heart are less dear to me!

BIANCA. Too late! you've crushed the light out of a gem
You did not know the price of! Had you spoken
But *one* kind word upon my bridal night!

SFORZA. Forgive me, my Bianca!

BIANCA. I am parched
With thirst now, and my eyes grow faint and dim.
Are you here, Sforza? Mourn not for me long!
But bury me with Giulio! [*Starts from him.*] Hark! I hear
His voice now! Do the walls of Paradise
Jut over hell? I heard his voice, I say!
[*Strikes off* SFORZA, *who approaches her.*]
Unhand me, devil! You've the shape of one
Who upon earth had no heart! Can you take
No shape but that? Can you not look like Giulio?
[SFORZA *falls back, struck with remorse.*]
Hark! 'tis his low, imploring voice again—
He prays for poor Bianca! And look, see you!
The portals stir! Slow, slow—and difficult—
[*Creeps forward with her eyes upward.*]
Pray on, my brother! Pray on, Giulio!
I come! [*Falls on her face.*]

[SFORZA *drops on his knee, pale and trembling.*]

SFORZA. My soul shrinks with unnatural fear!
What heard I then? "Sforza, give up thy sword!"
Was it from heaven or hell?
[*Shrinks, as if from some spectre in the air.*]
I will! I will!

[*Holds out his sword as if to the monk, and* SARPELLIONE, *who has been straining forward to watch* BIANCA, *springs suddenly to her side.*]

SARPELLIONE. She's dead! Ha! ha! who's duke in Milan now?

[SFORZA *rises with a bound.*]

SFORZA. Sforza!

[*He flies to the window, and waves the handkerchief. The bell peals out, and as he rushes to* BIANCA, *she moves, lifts her head, looks wildly around, and struggles to her feet.* ROSSANO *gives her the crown—she looks an instant smilingly on* SFORZA, *and with a difficult but calm effort places it on his head. All drop on one knee to do allegiance, and as* SFORZA *lifts himself to his loftiest height, with a look of triumph at* SARPELLIONE, BIANCA *sinks dead at his feet.*]

[*Curtain falls.*]

THE END OF "BIANCA VISCONTI"

FASHION

By Mrs. Anna Cora Mowatt

MRS. ANNA CORA MOWATT

[1819–1870]

Anna Cora Ogden was born in the country whose manners later came to provide an important theme in her distinguished play, *Fashion.* Born in 1819 of American parents temporarily residing in Bordeaux, France, she learned French as her native language, acted the part of a judge in a French *Othello* at the age of four, and at the age of ten had read all of Shakespeare. After seven years of residence on a French estate, where she frequently took part in private theatricals, she was brought to New York with her family and subsequently enjoyed the privileges of social life in the American metropolis.[1] At the age of fifteen she married a lawyer, James Mowatt, and upon his financial reverses several years later, she turned to elocutionary readings in Boston and New York, a vocation much frowned upon by her intimate associates.[2] It was during this period also that she was induced to write *Fashion*, as well as another play, and to become a professional actress, in which capacity she gained a wide fame. A few years after her husband's death in 1851, she married William F. Ritchie, a journalist of Richmond, Virginia. She lived abroad during the latter years of her life and died in England, July 28, 1870.

Mrs. Mowatt wrote her first play in 1840, *Gulzara; or, the Persian Slave*, which was acted in her own home.[3] This was followed in 1842 by a long novel, *The Fortune Hunter*, and in 1845 by *Fashion.* A five-act, semi-historical play, *Armand; or, the Peer and the Peasant*, was produced with success in 1847. Her *Autobiography of an Actress* appeared in 1854 and *Mimic Life, or Before and Behind the Curtain* in 1855; the latter is a series of stage stories and experiences.

It has been said that *Fashion* was an "accident," [4] and, to be sure, Mrs. Mowatt gives the following account of it in her *Autobiography:*

> "Why do you not write a play?" said E. S——[Epes Sargent] to me one morning. "You have more decided talent for the stage than for any thing else. . . ."
>
> "What shall I attempt, comedy or tragedy?"
>
> "Comedy, decidedly; because you can only write what you feel, and you are 'nothing if not critical'—besides, you will have a fresh channel for the sarcastic ebullitions with which you so constantly indulge us." [5]

[1] Most of the biographical data here given are taken from Mrs. Mowatt's *Autobiography of an Actress; or, Eight Years on the Stage.* Boston: 1854.

[2] It was this disapproval, so sharply felt by Mrs. Mowatt, that no doubt motivated her elaborate defense of public acting at the conclusion of her *Autobiography.*

[3] Published in *The New World*, 1840. For an account of the play see the *Autobiography*, pp. 132–137.

[4] Moses, Montrose J., *Representative Plays by American Dramatists, 1815–1858.* New York: 1925, p. 524.

[5] *Autobiography*, p. 202.

Also, Mr. Mowatt's failure in business was a further incentive. But to say that *Fashion* was therefore an accident is hardly tenable in view of the fact that the author had been actively interested in the drama since she was four and had already published one play. It is likewise pertinent, as well as illuminating, to note that *Fashion* grew directly from her own experience and previous observation. That some of the ideas had taken root in her mind long before she wrote the play we can see from one of the letters written during her first trip abroad (seven or eight years prior to the composition of *Fashion*):

> "The customs and fashions which we imitate as *Parisian* are not unfrequently mere caricatures of those that exist in Paris. For instance, it is the present *mode* not to introduce persons who meet at parties or in visiting, but the custom is intended to obviate the ceremoniousness of formal introductions. . . . As yet, we only *follow* the fashions; we do not conceive the spirit which dictated them." [1]

It is evident, then, that the ideas expressed in *Fashion* derive from Mrs. Mowatt's own thinking on the subject.

The point of view underlying *Fashion* is that of a sober and clear-eyed observer looking upon the American social scene and humorously pointing out some of its pretenses, stupidities, and gullibilities. If those who have become socially prominent are of obscure or humble origin (Mrs. Tiffany), they frequently conceal the fact or deny it indignantly when brought to light. One must be aware of the "necessity of *keeping up appearances*," especially on the eve of bankruptcy, for the illusion of wealth must be maintained though its reality be withdrawn. Money, thinks Mrs. Tiffany, determines taste as well as position: "My conservatory is well worthy a visit. It cost an immense sum of money." [2] Millinette understands the power of wealth: ". . . De money is all dat is *necessaire* in dis country to make one lady of fashion." [3]

Mrs. Tiffany's unwitting perversions of social concepts make irretrievably ridiculous the spectacle of an incompetent woman attempting to be a connoisseur of life and fashion. "A woman of fashion *never* grows old. Age is always out of fashion." [4] "I hear the *ee-light* never condescend to do anything of the kind [i.e., pay their bills]." [5] No less provocative is her monstrous use of French and her distorted aping of French customs. "You are quite sure that it is strictly a Parisian mode, Millinette?" "It is not the fashion in Paris to introduce—Millinette told me so." So slavish is Mrs. Tiffany to Millinette's French dictates that the latter regards herself as the arbiter of American society (and in a measure she is): ". . . It is me, *moi-même*, dat do lead de fashion for all de American *beau monde*." The *pièce de résistance* of Mrs. Tiffany's gullibility is the alliance she arranges for her daughter with a sham count.

[1] *Autobiography*, p. 125.
[2] Act I, sc. 1, p. 246.
[3] Act I, sc. 1, p. 241.
[4] Act I, sc. 1, p. 244.
[5] Act V, sc. 1, p. 266.

This exposé of American society has its direct as well as its satiric expression. In the character of Adam Trueman pertinent commentary is made upon the action of the play. Shallowness and hypocrisy in society are censured: "This *fashion*-worship has made heathens and hypocrites of you all! *Deception* is your household God! A man laughs as if he were crying, and cries as if he were laughing in his sleeve. Everything is something else from what it seems to be. I have lived in your house only three days, and I've heard more lies than were ever invented during a presidential election!" [1] Wealth is inimical to spirit: "You look as if you'd melted down your flesh into dollars, and mortgaged your soul in the bargain! Your warm heart has grown cold over your ledger—your light spirits heavy with calculation! You have traded away your youth—your hopes—your tastes for wealth! and now you *have* the wealth you coveted, what does it profit you?" [2] Social freedom is an end to be sought after; complaining about the servant's livery, Trueman decries domestic slavery: "To make men wear the *badge of servitude* in a free land,—that's the fashion, is it? Hurrah, for republican simplicity!" [3] Fashion, according to Trueman, is essentially "an agreement between certain persons to live without using their souls." Intrinsic worth of character is honored in contrast to exterior decoration and position: "But we *have* kings, princes, and nobles in abundance—of *Nature's stamp*, if not of *Fashion's*,—we have honest men, warm hearted and brave, and we have women—gentle, fair, and true, to whom no *title* could add *nobility*." [4]

The question may here be raised, as in the case of Manly in *The Contrast*, as to whether Trueman is to be taken seriously.[5] If not, the foregoing interpretation is without basis; but there is fairly conclusive evidence that Mrs. Mowatt intended Trueman's character to be taken literally and not satirically. In her *Autobiography* she refers to the play as a "satire on American *parvenuism*" [6] (she says nothing about satire on American provincialism), and she particularly comments on Trueman as follows:

"The only character in the play which was sketched from life was that of the blunt, warm hearted old farmer. I was told that the original was seen in the pit vociferously applauding Adam Trueman's strictures on fashionable society. It was not very wonderful that his sentiments found an echo in my friend's bosom. I longed to ask the latter whether he recognized his own portrait; but we have never met since the likeness was taken." [7]

[1] Act II, sc. 1, p. 249.

[2] Act II, sc. 1, p. 249.

[3] Act I, sc. 1, p. 247.

[4] Act V, sc. 1, p. 271.

[5] Moses speaks of Trueman as a "cartoon of American character." A recent production of *Fashion* at the University of Wisconsin interpreted both Trueman and Gertrude satirically as comic characters. Margaret G. Mayorga, in *A Short History of the American Drama*, states, without qualification: "The play is written very much in the spirit of burlesque. . . ." (P. 145.) Her failure to make the necessary distinction here is explained by the fact that her impression of the intent of the play was derived from recent productions of it in New York; it would seem that it is safer to consult the author on the subject rather than producers seventy-five years later.

[6] P. 203.

[7] *Ibid.*

Upon witnessing one of Blake's performances of Trueman, Mrs. Mowatt spoke of it as "more truthful and touching than ever." [1] Satire is seldom "touching." Even more tempting for satirical interpretation is the part of Gertrude, which is laden with sentimentalism; but that Mrs. Mowatt herself was capable of Gertrude's type of sentimentalism can be seen from her introduction to the *Autobiography*.[2] Incredible as Trueman's actions are in solving plot difficulties, yet his reflections are to be taken seriously.

It is probable that this whole commentary on foreign manners and conduct invading American life derives from that movement toward independence and nationalism which reached its climax in the Revolution and found its first dramatic expression in *The Contrast*. Thus *Fashion* may be considered—in a light vein, to be sure—a part of that feeling for cultural independence which is so trenchantly set forth in Emerson's *The American Scholar*. Several other plays express this nationalism, especially James Kirke Paulding's *The Bucktails; or, Americans in England*.

Allied to the foregoing sense of independence and nationalism [3] is the political aversion to aristocracy implied in Mrs. Tiffany's ludicrous dotage on all things aristocratic and her childish awe at the mention of titles. "I do dote on all aristocracy!" she says, and adds the garbled idea that "nothing is more positively vulgarian—more *unaristocratic* than any allusion to the past!" [4] It may be reasonable to assume that from the spurious count we get spurious philosophy: ". . . You would find America—where you have no kings, queens, lords, nor ladies—insupportable." [5] But the itinerant aristocrat does find something of value in America: "I find but one redeeming charm in America—the superlative loveliness of the feminine portion of creation,—and the wealth of their obliging papas." [6]

The play acknowledges the reality of evil and the punitive powers of an offended conscience. Upon learning of Mr. Tiffany's forgery, Trueman says, "Your face speaks for itself,—the crime has brought its punishment along with it." Tiffany admits the truth of this: "In *one year* I have lived a *century* of misery." [7]

[1] *Autobiography*, p. 232.

[2] "If one struggling sister in the great human family, while listening to the history of my life, gain courage to meet and brave severest trials; if she learn to look upon them as blessings in disguise: if she be strengthened in the performance of 'daily duties,' however 'hardly paid;' if she be inspired with faith in the power imparted to a strong *will*, whose end is *good*,—then I am amply rewarded for my labor." (Introduction, pp. 3–4.)

Relative to the above discussion, it may be further noted that the satire of the play is directed at the same objects as Trueman's moralizings. Also, there is little evidence in the lines that Trueman was intended as a comic character: had Mrs. Mowatt meant this to be the case, her failure in this instance is difficult to understand in view of her abundant success with the other comic characters. Trueman's speeches are sensible, not bucolically senile; his language is almost entirely that of an intelligent urbanite, not that of a country bumpkin. Had Mrs. Mowatt intended to make a Jonathan Yank out of Trueman, her dialectical inventiveness would hardly have failed her in this particular.

[3] When Count Jolimaitre proposes a French amour to Gertrude, she replies: "But I am an *American!* Your conduct proves that you are not one!" (Act II, sc. 2, p. 251.)

[4] Act III, sc. 1, p. 254.

[5] Act I, sc. 1, p. 246.

[6] Act I, sc. 1, p. 245.

[7] Act V, sc. 1, p. 270.

The thought has evidently penetrated deeply, for it is still with Tiffany in the epilogue:

> "Ah! there's punishment within!
> Guilt ever carries his own scourge along."

Moderation is the corrective for the excesses which lead one into evil: ". . . Let moderation, in future, be your counsellor, and let *honesty* be your confidential clerk." According to Gertrude, the virtuous do not look for evil: ". . . The truly pure see no imaginary evil in others! It is only vice, that reflecting its own image, suspects even the innocent." [1] Spirit and soul are affirmed as against wealth and fashion, virtue as against folly; Trueman says, ". . . let them learn economy, true independence, and home virtues, instead of foreign follies." [2]

On the basis of the foregoing it appears that Mrs. Mowatt has in a measure put into practice one of her theories with respect to drama in general: "If the acting of a play has been instrumental in causing 'joy among the angels of heaven over one sinner that repenteth,' what stronger proof can there be that the theatre is a useful institution?" [3] She states the didactic aspect of the play in another way: "The drama merely represents in action what the parable and similar fictions inculcate by written or oral teaching." [4] Her theory, however, of the play as a purging agent through the presentation of "sterner battles" is hardly worked out in the case of *Fashion*.

Foppish and superficial poets are satirized in T. Tennyson Twinkle, who explains with respect to his poems that "you must take into consideration, ladies, the rapidity with which they were written. Four minutes and a half by the stop watch! The true test of a poet is the *velocity* with which he composes." [5] We see in Mrs. Tiffany the mock admirer who does not read poetry but is only *seen* with it on advantageous occasions; and we find also in her the sham linguist for whom "a week's study of that invaluable work—'*French without a Master*,' has made me quite at home in the court language of Europe!" The creator of Mrs. Tiffany has a right to bestow the ridicule as she does; that Mrs. Mowatt herself is a woman of culture is evidenced by the learning she brings forth at the conclusion of her *Autobiography*.[6]

Particularly interesting from the standpoint of criticism is Poe's commentary on the play; his first reactions were distinctly unfavorable, but repeated attendance at the play induced him to modify his views appreciably. His censure of the play is at first strong:

"Had it, indeed, been designed as a burlesque upon the arrant conventionality of stage incidents in general, it might have been received as a palpable hit. There is not an event, a

[1] Act V, sc. 1, p. 264

[2] Act V, sc. 1, p. 271.

[3] *Autobiography*, pp. 444–445.

[4] *Ibid.*, p. 432.

[5] Act I, sc. 1, p. 244.

[6] Among others Mrs. Mowatt quotes the following: Bacon, Joshua Reynolds, D'Israeli (the elder), St. Paul, Marcus Aurelius, Martin Luther, The Rev. Dr. Knox, Dr. Blair, Sir Philip Sidney, Sir Walter Scott.

character, a jest, which is not a well-understood thing, a matter of course, a stage property time out of mind. The general tone is adapted from 'The School for Scandal,' to which, indeed, the whole composition bears just such an affinity as the shell of a locust to the locust that tenants it. . . ." [1]

Mrs. Mowatt's answer to this criticism is pointed: "If his severity were but justice, it must be that the spirits of the performers infused themselves into the empty shell, and produced a very effective counterfeit of *life*." [2] In the *Broadway Journal* for April 5, 1845, after witnessing the play every night for a week, Poe revises his earlier strictures on its conventionality: "We are not quite sure, upon reflection, that her entire thesis is not an original one"; [3] he also applauds the "effective manner in which *Fashion* has been brought forward at the Park" [4] and speaks of his "enthusiastic admiration" for Mrs. Mowatt's acting. If a week of continued attendance at a play has the effect of changing a person's impression of it for the better (especially a person whose attention-span is professedly short), then it is likely that the drama has underlying qualities either subtle enough to escape the first hearing or provocative enough to warrant repetition.

The text follows the Boston edition of 1855, virtually the same as the London edition of 1850.

[1] Poe, Edgar Allan, *Works*. New York: 1914. VIII, 37.

[2] *Autobiography*, p. 213.

[3] Poe, Edgar Allan, *Works*. Virginia edition, XII, 124.

[4] *Ibid.*, p. 128.

DRAMATIS PERSONÆ

ADAM TRUEMAN, a Farmer from Catteraugus
COUNT JOLIMAITRE, a fashionable European Importation
COLONEL HOWARD, an Officer in the U. S. Army
MR. TIFFANY, a New York Merchant
T. TENNYSON TWINKLE, a Modern Poet
AUGUSTUS FOGG, a Drawing Room Appendage
SNOBSON, a rare species of Confidential Clerk
ZEKE, a colored Servant

MRS. TIFFANY, a Lady who imagines herself fashionable
PRUDENCE, a Maiden Lady of a certain age
MILLINETTE, a French Lady's Maid
GERTRUDE, a Governess
SERAPHINA TIFFANY, a Belle

Ladies and Gentlemen of the Ball Room

FASHION

ACT I

SCENE I. *A splendid Drawing Room in the House of* MRS. TIFFANY. *Open folding doors discovering a Conservatory. On either side glass windows down to the ground. Doors on right and left. Mirror, couches, ottomans, a table with albums, &c., beside it an arm-chair.* MILLINETTE *dusting furniture, &c.* ZEKE *in a dashing livery, scarlet coat, &c.*

ZEKE. Dere's a coat to take de eyes ob all Broadway! Ah! Missy, it am de fixins dat make de natural *born* gemman. A libery for ever! Dere's a pair ob insuppressibles to 'stonish de colored population.

MILLINETTE. Oh, *oui*, Monsieur Zeke [*Very politely.*] I not *comprend* one word he say! [*Aside.*]

ZEKE. I tell 'ee what, Missy, I'm 'stordinary glad to find dis a bery spectabul like situation! Now as you've made de acquaintance ob dis here family, and dere you've had a supernumerary advantage ob me—seeing dat I only receibed my appointment dis morning. What I wants to know is your publicated opinion, privately expressed, ob de domestic circle.

MILLINETTE. You mean vat *espèce*, vat kind of personnes are Monsieur and Madame Tiffany? Ah! Monsieur is not de same ting as Madame,—not at all.

ZEKE. Well, I s'pose he ain't altogether.

MILLINETTE. Monsieur is man of business,—Madame is lady of fashion. Monsieur make de money,—Madame spend it. Monsieur nobody at all,—Madame everybody altogether. Ah! Monsieur Zeke, de money is all dat is *necessaire* in dis country to make one lady of fashion. Oh! it is quite anoder ting in *la belle France!*

ZEKE. A bery lucifer explanation. Well, now we've disposed ob de heads ob de family, who come next?

MILLINETTE. First, dere is Mademoiselle Seraphina Tiffany. Mademoiselle is not at all one proper *personne*. Mademoiselle Seraphina is one coquette. Dat is not de mode in *la belle France;* de ladies, dere, never learn *la coquetrie* until dey do get one husband.

ZEKE. I tell 'ee what, Missy, I disreprobate dat proceeding altogeder!

MILLINETTE. Vait! I have not tell you all *la famille* yet. Dere is Ma'mselle Prudence—Madame's sister, one very *bizarre* personne. Den dere is Ma'mselle Gertrude, but she not anybody at all; she only teach Mademoiselle Seraphina *la musique*.

ZEKE. Well, now, Missy, what's your own special defunctions?

MILLINETTE. I not understand, Monsieur Zeke.

ZEKE. Den I'll amplify. What's de nature ob your exclusive services?

MILLINETTE. *Ah, oui! je comprend.* I am Madame's *femme de chambre*—her lady's maid, Monsieur Zeke. I teach Madame *les modes de Paris*, and Madame set de fashion for all New York. You see, Monsieur Zeke, dat it is me, *moi-même*, dat do lead de fashion for all de American *beau monde!*

ZEKE. Yah! yah! yah! I hab de idea by de heel. Well, now, p'raps you can 'lustrify my officials?

MILLINETTE. Vat you will have to do? Oh! much tings, much tings. You vait on de table,—you tend de door,—you clean de boots,—you run de errands,—you drive de carriage,—you rub de horses,—you take care of de flowers,—you carry de water,—you help cook de dinner,—you wash de dishes,—and den you always remember to do everyting I tell you to!

ZEKE. Wheugh, am dat *all?*

MILLINETTE. All I can tink of now. Today is Madame's day of reception, and all her grand friends do make her one *petite* visit. You mind run fast ven de bell do ring.

ZEKE. Run? If it wasn't for dese superfluminous trimmings, I tell 'ee what, Missy, I'd run—

MRS. TIFFANY [*outside*]. Millinette!

MILLINETTE. Here comes Madame! You better go, Monsieur Zeke.

ZEKE. Look ahea, Massa Zeke, doesn't dis open rich! [*Aside.*] [*Exit* ZEKE.

Enter MRS. TIFFANY *dressed in the most extravagant height of fashion*

MRS. TIFFANY. Is everything in order, Millinette? Ah! very elegant, very elegant indeed! There is a *jenny-says-quoi* look about this furniture,—an air of fashion and gentility perfectly bewitching. Is there not, Millinette?

MILLINETTE. Oh, *oui,* Madame!

MRS. TIFFANY. But where is Miss Seraphina? It is twelve o'clock; our visitors will be pouring in, and she has not made her appearance. But I hear that nothing is more fashionable than to keep people waiting.—None but vulgar persons pay any attention to punctuality. Is it not so, Millinette?

MILLINETTE. Quite *comme il faut.*—Great personnes always do make little personnes wait, Madame.

MRS. TIFFANY. This mode of receiving visitors only upon one specified day of the week is a most convenient custom! It saves the trouble of keeping the house continually in order and of being always dressed. I flatter myself that *I* was the first to introduce it amongst the New York *ee-light*. You are quite sure that it is strictly a Parisian mode, Millinette?

MILLINETTE. Oh, *oui*, Madame; entirely *mode de Paris*.

MRS. TIFFANY. This girl is worth her weight in gold. [*Aside.*] Millinette, how do you say *arm-chair* in French?

MILLINETTE. *Fauteuil*, Madame.

MRS. TIFFANY. *Fo-tool!* That has a foreign—an out-of-the-wayish sound that is perfectly charming—and so genteel! There is something about our American words decidedly vulgar. *Fowtool!* how refined. *Fowtool! Arm-chair!* what a difference!

MILLINETTE. Madame have one charmante pronunciation. *Fowtool!* [*Mimicking aside.*] Charmante, Madame!

MRS. TIFFANY. Do you think so, Millinette? Well, I believe I have. But a woman of refinement and of fashion can always accommodate herself to everything foreign! And a week's study of that invaluable work—"*French without a Master*," has made me quite at home in the court language of Europe! But where is the new valet? I'm rather sorry that he is black, but to obtain a white American for a domestic is almost impossible; and they call this a free country! What did you say was the name of this new servant, Millinette?

MILLINETTE. He do say his name is Monsieur Zeke.

MRS. TIFFANY. Ezekiel, I suppose. Zeke! Dear me, such a vulgar name will compromise the dignity of the whole family. Can you not suggest something more aristocratic, Millinette? Something *French!*

MILLINETTE. Oh, *oui*, Madame; *Adolph* is one very fine name.

MRS. TIFFANY. A-dolph! Charming! Ring the bell, Millinette! [MILLINETTE *rings the bell.*] I will change his name immediately, besides giving him a few directions.

Enter ZEKE. MRS. TIFFANY *addresses him with great dignity*

Your name, I hear, is *Ezekiel.*—I consider it too plebeian an appellation to be uttered in my presence. In future you are called A-dolph. Don't reply,—never interrupt me when I am speaking. A-dolph, as my guests arrive, I desire that you will inquire the name of every person, and then announce it in a loud, clear tone. *That* is the fashion in Paris.

[MILLINETTE *retires up the stage.*]

ZEKE. Consider de office discharged, Missus. [*Speaking very loudly.*]

MRS. TIFFANY. Silence! Your business is to obey and not to talk.

ZEKE. I'm dumb, Missus!

MRS. TIFFANY [*pointing up stage*]. A-dolph, place that *fow-tool* behind me.

ZEKE [*looking about him*]. I habn't got dat far in de dictionary yet. No matter, a genus gets his learning by nature. [*Takes up the table and places it behind* MRS. TIFFANY, *then expresses in dumb show great satisfac-*

tion. MRS. TIFFANY, *as she goes to sit, discovers the mistake.*]

MRS. TIFFANY. You dolt! Where have you lived not to know that *fow-tool* is the French for *arm-chair?* What ignorance! Leave the room this instant.

[MRS. TIFFANY *draws forward an arm-chair and sits.* MILLINETTE *comes forward suppressing her merriment at* ZEKE'S *mistake and removes the table.*]

ZEKE. Dem's de defects ob not having a libery education. [*Exit.*

[PRUDENCE *peeps in.*]

PRUDENCE. I wonder if any of the fine folks have come yet. Not a soul,—I knew they hadn't. There's Betsy all alone. [*Walks in.*] Sister Betsy!

MRS. TIFFANY. Prudence! how many times have I desired you to call me *Elizabeth? Betsy* is the height of vulgarity.

PRUDENCE. Oh! I forgot. Dear me, how spruce we do look here, to be sure,—everything in first rate style now, Betsy.

[MRS. TIFFANY *looks at her angrily.*]

Elizabeth, I mean. Who would have thought, when you and I were sitting behind that little mahogany-colored counter, in Canal Street, making up flashy hats and caps—

MRS. TIFFANY. Prudence, what *do* you mean? Millinette, leave the room.

MILLINETTE. *Oui*, Madame.

[MILLINETTE *pretends to arrange the books upon a side table, but lingers to listen.*]

PRUDENCE. But I always predicted it,—I always told you so, Betsy,—I always said you were destined to rise above your station!

MRS. TIFFANY. Prudence! Prudence! have I not told you that—

PRUDENCE. No, Betsy, it was *I* that told *you*, when we used to buy our silks and ribbons of Mr. Antony Tiffany—"*talking Tony*," you know we used to call him, and when you always put on the finest bonnet in our shop to go to his,—and when you staid so long smiling and chattering with him, I always told you that *something* would grow out of it—and didn't it?

MRS. TIFFANY. Millinette, send Seraphina here instantly. Leave the room.

MILLINETTE. *Oui*, Madame. So dis Americaine ladi of fashion vas one *milliner?* Oh, vat a fine country for *les marchandes des modes!* I shall send for all my relation by de next packet! [*Aside.*] [*Exit* MILLINETTE.

MRS. TIFFANY. Prudence! never let me hear you mention this subject again. Forget what we *have* been, it is enough to remember that we *are* of the *upper ten thousand!*

[PRUDENCE *goes up and sits down.*]

Enter SERAPHINA, *very extravagantly dressed*

MRS. TIFFANY. How bewitchingly you look, my dear! Does Millinette say that that head dress is strictly Parisian?

SERAPHINA. Oh yes, Mamma, all the rage! They call it a *lady's tarpaulin*, and it is the exact pattern of one worn by the Princess Clementina at the last court ball.

MRS. TIFFANY. Now, Seraphina, my dear, don't be too particular in your attentions to gentlemen not eligible. There is Count Jolimaitre, decidedly the most fashionable foreigner in town,—and so refined,—so much accustomed to associate with the first nobility in his own country that he can hardly tolerate the vulgarity of Americans in general. You may devote yourself to him. Mrs. Proudacre is dying to become acquainted with him. By the by, if she or her daughters should happen to drop in, be sure you don't introduce them to the Count. It is not the fashion in Paris to introduce—Millinette told me so.

Enter ZEKE

ZEKE [*in a very loud voice*]. Mister T. Tennyson Twinkle!

MRS. TIFFANY. Show him up. [*Exit* ZEKE.

PRUDENCE. I must be running away! [*Going.*]

MRS. TIFFANY. Mr. T. Tennyson Twinkle—a very literary young man and a sweet poet! It is all the rage to patronize poets! Quick, Seraphina, hand me that magazine.—Mr. Twinkle writes for it.

[SERAPHINA *hands the magazine*, MRS. TIFFANY *seats herself in an arm-chair and opens the book.*]

PRUDENCE [*returning*]. There's Betsy trying to make out that reading without her spectacles. [*Takes a pair of spectacles out of her pocket and hands them to* MRS. TIFFANY.]

There, Betsy, I knew you were going to ask for them. Ah! they're a blessing when one is growing old!

MRS. TIFFANY. What do you mean, Prudence? a woman of fashion *never* grows old! Age is always out of fashion.

PRUDENCE. Oh, dear! what a delightful thing it is to be fashionable. [*Exit* PRUDENCE.

[MRS. TIFFANY *resumes her seat.*]

Enter TWINKLE. *He salutes* SERAPHINA

TWINKLE. Fair Seraphina! the sun itself grows dim,
Unless you aid his light and shine on him!

SERAPHINA. Ah! Mr. Twinkle, there is no such thing as answering you.

TWINKLE [*looks around and perceives* MRS. TIFFANY]. The "New Monthly Vernal Galaxy." Reading my verses, by all that's charming! Sensible woman! I won't interrupt her. [*Aside.*]

MRS. TIFFANY [*rising and coming forward*]. Ah! Mr. Twinkle, is that you? I was perfectly *abimé* at the perusal of your very *distingué* verses.

TWINKLE. I am overwhelmed, Madam. Permit me. [*Taking the magazine.*] Yes, they do read tolerably. And you must take into consideration, ladies, the rapidity with which they were written. Four minutes and a half by the stop watch! The true test of a poet is the *velocity* with which he composes. Really they do look very prettily, and they read tolerably—*quite* tolerably—*very* tolerably,—especially the first verse. [*Reads.*] "To Seraphina T——."

SERAPHINA. Oh! Mr. Twinkle!

TWINKLE [*reads*]. "Around my heart"—

MRS. TIFFANY. How touching! Really, Mr. Twinkle, quite tender!

TWINKLE [*recommencing*]. "Around my heart"—

MRS. TIFFANY. Oh, I must tell you. Mr. Twinkle! I heard the other day that poets were the aristocrats of literature. That's one reason I like them, for I do dote on all aristocracy!

TWINKLE. Oh, Madam, how flattering! Now pray lend me your ears! [*Reads.*]
"Around my heart thou weavest"—

SERAPHINA. That is such a *sweet* commencement, Mr. Twinkle!

TWINKLE [*aside*]. I wish she wouldn't interrupt me!
[*Reads.*] "Around my heart thou weavest a spell"—

MRS. TIFFANY. Beautiful! But excuse me one moment, while I say a word to Seraphina! Don't be too affable, my dear! Poets are very ornamental appendages to the drawing room, but they are always as poor as their own verses. They don't make eligible husbands! [*Aside to* SERAPHINA.]

TWINKLE. Confound their interruptions! [*Aside.*] My dear Madam, unless you pay the utmost attention you cannot catch the ideas. Are you ready? Well, now you shall hear it to the end! [*Reads.*]
"Around my heart thou weavest a spell
"Whose"—

Enter ZEKE

ZEKE. Mister Augustus Fogg! A bery misty lookin young gemman! [*Aside.*]

MRS. TIFFANY. Show him up, Adolph! [*Exit* ZEKE.

TWINKLE. This is too much!

SERAPHINA. Exquisite verses, Mr. Twinkle, —exquisite!

TWINKLE. Ah, lovely Seraphina! your smile of approval transports me to the summit of Olympus.

SERAPHINA. Then I must frown, for I would not send you so far away.

TWINKLE. Enchantress! It's all over with her. [*Aside.*] [*Retire up and converse.*]

MRS. TIFFANY. Mr. Fogg belongs to one of our oldest families,—to be sure he is the most difficult person in the world to entertain, for he never takes the trouble to talk, and never notices anything or anybody,—but then I hear that nothing is considered so vulgar as to betray any emotion, or to attempt to render oneself agreeable!

Enter MR. FOGG, *fashionably attired but in very dark clothes*

FOGG [*bowing stiffly*]. Mrs. Tiffany, your most obedient. Miss Seraphina, yours. How d'ye do, Twinkle?

MRS. TIFFANY. Mr. Fogg, how do you do? Fine weather,—delightful, isn't it?

FOGG. I am indifferent to weather, Madam.

MRS. TIFFANY. Been to the opera, Mr. Fogg? I hear that the *bow monde* make their *debutt* there every evening.

FOGG. I consider operas a bore, Madam.

SERAPHINA [*advancing*]. You must hear Mr. Twinkle's verses, Mr. Fogg!

FOGG. I am indifferent to verses, Miss Seraphina.

SERAPHINA. But Mr. Twinkle's verses are addressed to me!

TWINKLE. Now pay attention, Fogg! [*Reads.*]
"Around my heart thou weavest a spell
"Whose magic I"—

Enter ZEKE

ZEKE. Mister—No, he say he ain't no Mister—

TWINKLE. "Around my heart thou weavest a spell
"Whose magic I can never tell!"

MRS. TIFFANY. Speak in a loud, clear tone, A-dolph!

TWINKLE. This is terrible!

ZEKE. Mister Count Jolly-made-her!

MRS. TIFFANY. Count Jolimaitre! Good gracious! Zeke, Zeke—A-dolph I mean.—Dear me, what a mistake! [*Aside.*] Set that chair out of the way,—put that table back. Seraphina, my dear, are you all in order? Dear me! dear me! Your dress is so tumbled! [*Arranges her dress.*] What are you grinning at? [*To* ZEKE.] Beg the Count to *honor* us by walking up! [*Exit* ZEKE. Seraphina, my dear [*Aside to her.*], remember now what I told you about the Count. He is a man of the highest,—good gracious! I am so flurried; and nothing is so ungenteel as agitation! what will the Count think! Mr. Twinkle, pray stand out of the way! Seraphina, my dear, place yourself on my right! Mr. Fogg, the conservatory—beautiful flowers,—pray amuse yourself in the conservatory.

FOGG. I am indifferent to flowers, Madam.

MRS. TIFFANY. Dear me! the man stands right in the way,—just where the Count must make his *entray!* [*Aside.*] Mr. Fogg,—pray—

Enter COUNT JOLIMAITRE, *very dashingly dressed, wears a moustache*

MRS. TIFFANY. Oh, Count, this unexpected honor—

SERAPHINA. Count, this inexpressible pleasure—

COUNT. Beg you won't mention it, Madam! Miss Seraphina, your most devoted! [*Crosses.*]

MRS. TIFFANY. What condescension! [*Aside.*] Count, may I take the liberty to introduce—Good gracious! I forgot. [*Aside.*] Count, I was about to remark that we never introduce in America. All our fashions are foreign, Count.

[TWINKLE, *who has stepped forward to be introduced, shows great indignation.*]

COUNT. Excuse me, Madam, our fashions have grown antediluvian before you Americans discover their existence. You are lamentably behind the age—lamentably! 'Pon my honor, a foreigner of refinement finds great difficulty in existing in this provincial atmosphere.

MRS. TIFFANY. How dreadful, Count! I am very much concerned. If there is anything which I can do, Count—

SERAPHINA. Or I, Count, to render your situation less deplorable—

COUNT. Ah! I find but one redeeming charm in America—the superlative loveliness of the feminine portion of creation,—and the wealth of their obliging papas. [*Aside.*]

MRS. TIFFANY. How flattering! Ah! Count, I am afraid you will turn the head of my simple girl here. She is a perfect child of nature, Count.

COUNT. Very possibly, for though you American women are quite charming, yet, demme, there's a deal of native rust to rub off!

MRS. TIFFANY. *Rust?* Good gracious, Count! where do you find any rust? [*Looking about the room.*]

COUNT. How very unsophisticated!

MRS. TIFFANY. Count, I am so much ashamed, —pray excuse me! Although a lady of large fortune, and one, Count, who can boast of the highest connections, I blush to confess that I have never travelled,—while you,

Count, I presume are at home in all the courts of Europe.

COUNT. *Courts?* Eh? Oh, yes, Madam, very true. I believe I am pretty well known in some of the courts of Europe—*police courts.* [*Aside, crossing.*] In a word, Madam, I had seen enough of civilized life—wanted to refresh myself by a sight of barbarous countries and customs—had my choice between the Sandwich Islands and New York—chose New York!

MRS. TIFFANY. How complimentary to our country! And, Count, I have no doubt you speak every conceivable language? You talk English like a native.

COUNT. Eh, what? Like a native? Oh, ah, demme, yes, I am something of an Englishman. Passed one year and eight months with the Duke of Wellington, six months with Lord Brougham, two and a half with Count d'Orsay—knew them all more intimately than their best friends—no heroes to me—hadn't a secret from me, I assure you,—*especially of the toilet.* [*Aside.*]

MRS. TIFFANY. Think of that, my dear! Lord Wellington and Duke Broom! [*Aside to* SERAPHINA.]

SERAPHINA. And only think of Count d'Orsay, Mamma! [*Aside to* MRS. TIFFANY.] I am so wild to see Count d'Orsay!

COUNT. Oh! a mere man milliner. Very little refinement out of Paris! Why, at the very last dinner given at Lord—Lord Knows-who, would you believe it, Madam, there was an individual present who wore a *black* cravat and took *soup twice!*

MRS. TIFFANY. How shocking! the sight of him would have spoilt my appetite! Think what a great man he must be, my dear, to despise lords and counts in that way. [*Aside to* SERAPHINA.] I must leave them together. [*Aside.*] Mr. Twinkle, your arm. I have some really very *foreign exotics* to show you.

TWINKLE. I fly at your command. I wish all her exotics were blooming in their native soil! [*Aside, and glancing at the* COUNT.]

MRS. TIFFANY. Mr. Fogg, will you accompany us? My conservatory is well worthy a visit. It cost an immense sum of money.

FOGG. I am indifferent to conservatories, Madam; flowers are such a bore!

MRS. TIFFANY. I shall take no refusal. Conservatories are all the rage,—I could not exist without mine! Let me show you,—let me show you.

[*Places her arm through* MR. FOGG'S, *without his consent. Exeunt* MRS. TIFFANY, FOGG, *and* TWINKLE *into the conservatory, where they are seen walking about.*]

SERAPHINA. America, then, has no charms for you, Count?

COUNT. Excuse me,—some exceptions. I find you, for instance, particularly charming! Can't say I admire your country. Ah! if you had ever breathed the exhilarating air of Paris, ate creams at Tortoni's, dined at the Café Royale, or if you had lived in London—felt at home at St. James's, and every afternoon driven a couple of Lords and a Duchess through Hyde Park, you would find America—where you have no kings, queens, lords, nor ladies—insupportable!

SERAPHINA. Not while there was a Count in it?

Enter ZEKE, *very indignant*

ZEKE. Where's de Missus?

Enter MRS. TIFFANY, FOGG, *and* TWINKLE, *from the conservatory*

MRS. TIFFANY. Whom do you come to announce, A-dolph?

ZEKE. He said he wouldn't trust me—no, not eben wid so much as his name; so I wouldn't trust him up stairs, den he ups wid *his stick* and I *cuts mine.*

MRS. TIFFANY. Some of Mr. Tiffany's vulgar acquaintances. I shall die with shame. [*Aside.*] A-dolph, inform him that I am *not at home.* [*Exit* ZEKE.

My nerves are so shattered, I am ready to sink. Mr. Twinkle, that *fow tool*, if you please!

TWINKLE. What? What do you wish, Madam?

MRS. TIFFANY. The ignorance of these Americans! [*Aside.*] Count, may I trouble you? That *fow tool*, if you please!

COUNT. She's not talking English, nor French, but I suppose it's American. [*Aside.*]

TRUEMAN [*outside*]. Not at home!

ZEKE. No, Sar—Missus say she's not at home.

TRUEMAN. Out of the way, you grinning nigger!

Enter ADAM TRUEMAN, *dressed as a farmer, a stout cane in his hand, his boots covered with dust.* ZEKE *jumps out of his way as he enters.* [*Exit* ZEKE.

TRUEMAN. Where's this woman that's not *at home* in her own house? May I be shot! if I wonder at it! I shouldn't think she'd ever feel *at home* in such a show-box as this! [*Looking round.*]

MRS. TIFFANY. What a plebeian looking old farmer! I wonder who he is? [*Aside.*] Sir—[*Advancing very agitatedly.*] what do you mean, Sir, by this *ow*dacious conduct? How dare you intrude yourself into my parlor? Do you know who I am, Sir? [*With great dignity.*] You are in the presence of Mrs. Tiffany, Sir!

TRUEMAN. Antony's wife, eh. Well now, I might have guessed that—ha! ha! ha! for I see you make it a point to carry half your husband's shop upon your back! No matter; that's being a good helpmate—for he carried the whole of it once in a pack on his own shoulders—now you bear a share!

MRS. TIFFANY. How dare you, you impertinent, *ow*dacious, ignorant old man! It's all an invention. You're talking of somebody else. What will the Count think! [*Aside.*]

TRUEMAN. Why, I thought folks had better manners in the city! This is a civil welcome for your husband's old friend, and after my coming all the way from Catteraugus to see you and yours! First a grinning nigger tricked out in scarlet regimentals—

MRS. TIFFANY. Let me tell you, Sir, that liveries are all the fashion!

TRUEMAN. The fashion, are they? To make men wear the *badge of servitude* in a free land,—that's the fashion, is it? Hurrah, for republican simplicity! I will venture to say, now, that you have your coat of arms too!

MRS. TIFFANY. Certainly, Sir; you can see it on the panels of my *voyture.*

TRUEMAN. Oh! no need of that. I know what your escutcheon must be! A bandbox *rampant* with a bonnet *couchant*, and a pedlar's pack *passant!* Ha, ha, ha! that shows both houses united!

MRS. TIFFANY. Sir! you are most profoundly ignorant,—what do you mean by this insolence, Sir? How shall I get rid of him? [*Aside.*]

TRUEMAN [*looking at* SERAPHINA]. I hope that is not Gertrude! [*Aside.*]

MRS. TIFFANY. Sir, I'd have you know that —Seraphina, my child, walk with the gentlemen into the conservatory.

[*Exeunt* SERAPHINA, TWINKLE, FOGG *into conservatory.*]

Count Jolimaitre, pray make due allowances for the errors of this rustic! I do assure you, Count—[*Whispers to him.*]

TRUEMAN. Count! She calls that critter with a shoe brush over his mouth, Count! To look at him, I should have thought he was a tailor's walking advertisement! [*Aside.*]

COUNT [*addressing* TRUEMAN *whom he has been inspecting through his eye-glass*]. Where did you say you belonged, my friend? Dug out of the ruins of Pompeii, eh?

TRUEMAN. I belong to a land in which I rejoice to find that you are a foreigner.

COUNT. What a barbarian! He doesn't see the honor I'm doing his country! Pray, Madam, is it one of the aboriginal inhabitants of the soil? To what tribe of Indians does he belong—the Pawnee or Choctaw? Does he carry a tomahawk?

TRUEMAN. Something quite as useful,—do you see that?

[*Shaking his stick.* COUNT *runs behind* MRS. TIFFANY.]

MRS. TIFFANY. Oh, dear! I shall faint! Millinette! [*Approaching.*] Millinette!

Enter MILLINETTE, *without advancing into the room*

MILLINETTE. *Oui*, Madame.

MRS. TIFFANY. A glass of water! [*Exit* MILLINETTE.] Sir, [*Crossing to* TRUEMAN.] I am shocked at your plebeian conduct! This is a gentleman of the highest standing, Sir! He is a *Count*, Sir!

Enter MILLINETTE, *bearing a salver with a glass of water. In advancing towards* MRS. TIFFANY, *she passes in front of the* COUNT, *starts and screams. The* COUNT, *after a start of surprise, regains his composure, plays with his eye-glass, and looks perfectly unconcerned.*

MRS. TIFFANY. What is the matter? What *is* the matter?

MILLINETTE. Noting, noting,—only—[*Looks at* COUNT *and turns away her eyes again.*] only—noting at all!

TRUEMAN. Don't be afraid, girl! Why, did you never see a live Count before? He's tame,—I dare say your mistress there leads him about by the ears.

MRS. TIFFANY. This is too much! Millinette, send for Mr. Tiffany instantly!

[*Crosses to* MILLINETTE, *who is going.*]

MILLINETTE. He just come in, Madame!

TRUEMAN. My old friend! Where is he? Take me to him,—I long to have one more hearty shake of the hand!

MRS. TIFFANY [*crosses to him*]. Count, honor me by joining my daughter in the conservatory, I will return immediately.

[COUNT *bows and walks towards conservatory.* MRS. TIFFANY *following part of the way and then returning to* TRUEMAN.]

TRUEMAN. What a Jezebel! These women always play the very devil with a man, and yet I don't believe such a damaged bale of goods as *that* [*Looking at* MRS. TIFFANY.] has smothered the heart of little Antony!

MRS. TIFFANY. This way, Sir, sal vous plait.

[*Exit with great dignity.*

TRUEMAN. *Sal vous plait.* Ha, ha, ha! We'll see what Fashion has done for him. [*Exit.*

END OF ACT I

ACT II

SCENE I. *Inner apartment of* MR. TIFFANY'S *Counting House.* MR. TIFFANY, *seated at a desk looking over papers.* MR. SNOBSON, *on a high stool at another desk, with a pen behind his ear.*

SNOBSON [*rising, advances to the front of the stage, regards* TIFFANY *and shrugs his shoulders*]. How the old boy frets and fumes over those papers, to be sure! He's working himself into a perfect fever—ex-actly,—therefore *bleeding's* the prescription! So here goes! [*Aside.*] Mr. Tiffany, a word with you, if you please, Sir?

TIFFANY [*sitting still*]. Speak on, Mr. Snobson, I attend.

SNOBSON. What I have to say, Sir, is a matter of the first importance to the credit of the concern—the *credit* of the concern, Mr. Tiffany!

TIFFANY. Proceed, Mr. Snobson.

SNOBSON. Sir, you've a handsome house—fine carriage—nigger in livery—feed on the fat of the land—everything first rate—

TIFFANY. Well, Sir?

SNOBSON. My salary, Mr. Tiffany!

TIFFANY. It has been raised three times within the last year.

SNOBSON. Still it is insufficient for the necessities of an honest man,—mark me, an *honest* man, Mr. Tiffany.

TIFFANY [*crossing*]. What a weapon he has made of that word! [*Aside.*] Enough—another hundred shall be added. Does that content you?

SNOBSON. There is one other subject which I have before mentioned, Mr. Tiffany,—your daughter,—what's the reason you can't let the folks at home know at once that I'm to be *the man?*

TIFFANY. Villain! And must the only seal upon this scoundrel's lips be placed there by the hand of my daughter? [*Aside.*] Well, Sir, it shall be as you desire.

SNOBSON. And Mrs. Tiffany shall be informed of your resolution?

TIFFANY. Yes.

SNOBSON. Enough said! That's the ticket! The CREDIT *of the concern's safe*, Sir!

[*Returns to his seat.*]

TIFFANY. How low have I bowed to this insolent rascal! To rise himself he mounts upon my shoulders, and unless I can shake him off he must crush me! [*Aside.*]

Enter TRUEMAN

TRUEMAN. Here I am, Antony, man! I told you I'd pay you a visit in your money-making quarters. [*Looks around.*] But it looks as dismal here as a cell in the States' prison!

TIFFANY [*forcing a laugh*]. Ha, ha, ha! States' prison! You are so facetious! Ha, ha, ha!

TRUEMAN. Well, for the life of me I can't see anything so amusing in that! I should think the States' prison plaguy uncomfortable lodgings. And you laugh, man, as though you fancied yourself there already.

TIFFANY. Ha, ha, ha!

TRUEMAN [*imitating him*]. Ha, ha, ha! What on earth do you mean by that ill-sounding laugh, that has nothing of a laugh about it! This *fashion*-worship has made heathens and hypocrites of you all! *Deception* is your household God! A man laughs as if he were crying, and cries as if he were laughing in his sleeve. Everything is something else from what it seems to be. I have lived in your house only three days, and I've heard more lies than were ever invented during a Presidential election! First your fine lady of a wife sends me word that she's not at home—I walk up stairs, and she takes good care that *I* shall not be *at home*—wants to turn me out of doors. Then *you* come in—take your old friend by the hand—whisper, the deuce knows what, in your wife's ear, and the tables are turned in a tangent! Madam curtsies—says she's enchanted to see me—and orders her grinning nigger to show me a room.

TIFFANY. We were exceedingly happy to welcome you as our guest!

TRUEMAN. Happy? *You* happy? Ah! Antony! Antony! that hatchet face of yours, and those criss-cross furrows tell quite another story! It's many a long day since you were *happy* at anything! You look as if you'd melted down your flesh into dollars, and mortgaged your soul in the bargain! Your warm heart has grown cold over your ledger—your light spirits heavy with calculation! You have traded away your youth—your hopes—your tastes for wealth! and now you *have* the wealth you coveted, what does it profit you? Pleasure it cannot buy; for you have lost your *capacity* for enjoyment—Ease it will not bring; for the love of gain is never satisfied! It has made your counting-house a penitentiary, and your home a fashionable *museum* where there is no niche for you! You have spent so much time *ciphering* in the one, that you find yourself at last a very *cipher* in the other! See me, man! seventy-two last August!—strong as a hickory and every whit as sound!

TIFFANY. I take the greatest pleasure in remarking your superiority, Sir.

TRUEMAN. Bah! no man takes pleasure in remarking the superiority of another! Why the deuce, can't you speak the truth, man? But it's not the *fashion*, I suppose! I have not seen one frank, open face since—no, no, I can't say that either, though lying *is* catching! There's that girl, Gertrude, who is trying to teach your daughter music—but Gertrude was bred in the country!

TIFFANY. A good girl; my wife and daughter find her very useful.

TRUEMAN. Useful? Well, I must say you have queer notions of *use!*—But come, cheer up, man! I'd rather see one of your old smiles, than know you'd realized another thousand! I hear you are making money on the true, American, high pressure system—better go slow and sure—the more steam, the greater danger of the boiler's bursting! All sound, I hope? Nothing rotten at the core?

TIFFANY. Oh, sound—quite sound!

TRUEMAN. Well, that's pleasant—though I must say you don't look very pleasant about it!

TIFFANY. My good friend, although I am solvent, I may say, perfectly solvent—yet you—the fact is, you can be of some assistance to me!

TRUEMAN. That's the *fact*, is it? I'm glad we've hit upon one *fact* at last! Well—

[SNOBSON, *who during this conversation has been employed in writing, but stops occasionally to listen, now gives vent to a dry, chuckling laugh.*]

TRUEMAN. Hey? What's that? Another of those deuced ill-sounding, city laughs! [*Sees* SNOBSON.] Who's that perched up on the stool of repentance—eh, Antony?

SNOBSON. The old boy has missed his text there—*that's* the stool of repentance!

[*Aside and looking at* TIFFANY'S *seat.*]

TIFFANY. One of my clerks—my confidential clerk!

TRUEMAN. Confidential? Why, he looks for all the world like a spy—the most inquisitorial, hang-dog face—ugh! the sight of it makes my blood run cold! Come, [*Crosses.*]

let us talk over matters where this critter can't give us the benefit of his opinion! Antony, the next time you choose a confidential clerk, take one that carries his credentials in his face—those in his pocket are not worth much without!

[*Exeunt* TRUEMAN *and* TIFFANY.

SNOBSON [*jumping from his stool and advancing*]. The old prig has got the tin, or Tiff would never be so civil! All right—Tiff will work every shiner into the concern—all the better for me! Now I'll go and make love to Seraphina. The old woman needn't try to knock me down with any of her French lingo! Six months from today if I ain't driving my two footmen tandem, down Broadway—and as fashionable as Mrs. Tiffany herself, then I ain't the trump I thought I was! that's all. [*Looks at his watch.*] Bless me! eleven o'clock and I haven't had my julep yet! Snobson, I'm ashamed of you!

[*Exit.*

SCENE 2. *The interior of a beautiful conservatory; walk through the centre; stands of flower pots in bloom; a couple of rustic seats.* GERTRUDE, *attired in white, with a white rose in her hair; watering the flowers.* COLONEL HOWARD, *regarding her.*

HOWARD. I am afraid you lead a sad life here, Miss Gertrude?

GERTRUDE [*turning round gaily*]. What! amongst the flowers?

[*Continues her occupation.*]

HOWARD. No, amongst the thistles, with which Mrs. Tiffany surrounds you; the tempests, which her temper raises!

GERTRUDE. They never harm me. Flowers and herbs are excellent tutors. I learn prudence from the reed, and bend until the storm has swept over me!

HOWARD. Admirable philosophy! But still this frigid atmosphere of fashion must be uncongenial to you? Accustomed to the pleasant companionship of your kind friends in Geneva, surely you must regret this cold exchange?

GERTRUDE. Do you think so? Can you suppose that I could possibly prefer a ramble in the woods to a promenade in Broadway? A wreath of scented wild flowers to a bouquet of these sickly exotics? The odor of new-mown hay to the heated air of this crowded conservatory? Or can you imagine that I could enjoy the quiet conversation of my Geneva friends, more than the edifying chit-chat of a fashionable drawing room? But I see you think me totally destitute of taste?

HOWARD. You have a merry spirit to jest thus at your grievances!

GERTRUDE. I have my *mania*,—as some wise person declares that all mankind have,—and mine is a love of independence! In Geneva, my wants were supplied by two kind old maiden ladies, upon whom I know not that I have any claim. I had abilities, and desired to use them. I came here at my own request; for here I am no longer *dependent! Voilà tout*, as Mrs. Tiffany would say.

HOWARD. Believe me, I appreciate the confidence you repose in me!

GERTRUDE. Confidence! Truly, Colonel Howard, the *confidence* is entirely on your part, in supposing that I confide that which I have no reason to conceal! I think I informed you that Mrs. Tiffany only received visitors on her reception day—she is therefore not prepared to see you. Zeke—Oh! I beg his pardon—Adolph, made some mistake in admitting you.

HOWARD. Nay, Gertrude, it was not Mrs. Tiffany, nor Miss Tiffany, whom I came to see; it—it was—

GERTRUDE. The conservatory perhaps? I will leave you to examine the flowers at leisure!

[*Crosses.*]

HOWARD. Gertrude—listen to me. If I only dared to give utterance to what is hovering upon my lips! [*Aside.*] Gertrude!

GERTRUDE. Colonel Howard!

HOWARD. Gertrude, I must—must—

GERTRUDE. Yes, indeed you *must*, must leave me! I think I hear somebody coming—Mrs. Tiffany would not be well pleased to find you here—pray, pray leave me—that door will lead you into the street.

[*Hurries him out through door; takes up her watering pot, and commences watering flowers, tying up branches, &c.*]

What a strange being is man! Why should

he hesitate to say—nay, why should I prevent his saying, what I would most delight to hear? Truly man *is* strange—but woman is quite as incomprehensible!

[*Walks about gathering flowers.*]

Enter Count JOLIMAITRE

COUNT. There she is—the bewitching little creature! Mrs. Tiffany and her daughter are out of ear-shot. I caught a glimpse of their feathers floating down Broadway, not ten minutes ago. Just the opportunity I have been looking for! Now for an engagement with this captivating little piece of prudery! 'Pon honor, I am almost afraid she will not resist a *Count* long enough to give value to the conquest. [*Approaches her.*] *Ma belle petite*, were you gathering roses for me?

GERTRUDE [*starts on first perceiving him, but instantly regains her self-possession*]. The roses here, Sir, are carefully guarded with thorns—if you have the right to gather, pluck for yourself!

COUNT. Sharp as ever, little Gertrude! But now that we are alone, throw off this frigidity, and be at your ease.

GERTRUDE. Permit me to *be alone*, Sir, that I *may* be at my ease!

COUNT. Very good, *ma belle*, well said! [*Applauding her with his hands.*] Never yield too soon, even to a *title!* But, as the old girl may find her way back before long, we may as well come to particulars at once. I love you; but that you know already. [*Rubbing his eye-glass unconcernedly with his handkerchief.*] Before long I shall make Mademoiselle Seraphina my wife, and, of course, you shall remain in the family!

GERTRUDE [*indignantly*]. Sir—

COUNT. 'Pon my honor you shall! In France we arrange these little matters without difficulty!

GERTRUDE. But I am an *American!* Your conduct proves that you are not one!

[*Going, crosses.*]

COUNT [*preventing her*]. Don't run away, my immaculate *petite Américaine!* Demme, you've quite overlooked my condescension—the difference of our stations—you a species of upper servant—an orphan—no friends.

Enter TRUEMAN *unperceived*

GERTRUDE. And therefore more entitled to the respect and protection of every *true gentleman!* Had you been one, you would not have insulted me!

COUNT. My charming little orator, patriotism and declamation become you particularly! [*Approaches her.*] I feel quite tempted to taste—

TRUEMAN [*thrusting him aside*]. An American hickory switch! [*Strikes him.*] Well, how do you like it?

COUNT. Old matter-of-fact! [*Aside.*] Sir, how dare you?

TRUEMAN. My stick has answered that question!

GERTRUDE. Oh! now I am quite safe!

TRUEMAN. Safe! not a bit safer than before! All women would be safe, if they knew how virtue became them! As for you, Mr. Count, what have you to say for yourself? Come, speak out!

COUNT. Sir,—aw—aw—you don't understand these matters!

TRUEMAN. That's a fact! Not having had *your* experience, I don't believe I *do* understand them!

COUNT. A piece of pleasantry—a mere joke—

TRUEMAN. A joke was it? I'll show you a joke worth two of that! I'll teach you the way we natives joke with a puppy who don't respect an honest woman! [*Seizing him.*]

COUNT. Oh! oh! demme—you old ruffian! let me go. What do you mean?

TRUEMAN. Oh! a piece of pleasantry—a mere joke—very pleasant, isn't it?

[*Attempts to strike him again;* COUNT *struggles with him. Enter* MRS. TIFFANY *hastily, in her bonnet and shawl.*]

MRS. TIFFANY. What IS the matter? I am perfectly *abimé* with terror. Mr. Trueman, what has happened?

TRUEMAN. Oh! we have been *joking!*

MRS. TIFFANY [*to* COUNT, *who is re-arranging his dress*]. My *dear* Count, I did not expect to find you here—how kind of you!

TRUEMAN. Your *dear* Count has been showing his *kindness* in a very *foreign* manner.

Too *foreign*, I think he found it to be relished by an *unfashionable native!* What do you think of a puppy, who insults an innocent girl all in the way of *kindness?* This Count of yours—this importation of—

COUNT. My dear Madam, demme, permit me to explain. It would be unbecoming—demme—particularly unbecoming of you—aw—aw—to pay any attention to this ignorant person. [*Crosses to* TRUEMAN.] Anything that he says concerning a man of my standing—aw—the truth is, Madam—

TRUEMAN. Let us have the truth by all means,—if it is only for the novelty's sake!

COUNT [*turning his back to* TRUEMAN]. You see, madam, hoping to obtain a few moments' private conversation with Miss Seraphina—with *Miss Seraphina* I say—and—aw—and knowing her passion for flowers, I found my way to your very tasteful and *recherché* conservatory. [*Looks about him approvingly*.] *Very* beautifully arranged—does you great credit, madam! Here I encountered this young person. She was inclined to be talkative; and I indulged her with—with a—aw—demme—a few *common places!* What passed between us was mere *harmless badinage*—on *my* part. You, madam, you—so conversant with our European manners—you are aware that when a man of fashion—that is, when a woman—a man is bound—amongst noblemen, you know—

MRS. TIFFANY. I comprehend you perfectly—*parfittement*, my dear Count.

COUNT. 'Pon my honor, that's very obliging of her. [*Aside*.]

MRS. TIFFANY. I am shocked at the plebeian forwardness of this conceited girl!

TRUEMAN [*walking up to* COUNT]. Did you ever keep a reckoning of the lies you tell in an hour?

MRS. TIFFANY. Mr. Trueman, I blush for you! [*Crosses to* TRUEMAN.]

TRUEMAN. Don't do that—you have no blushes to spare!

MRS. TIFFANY. It is a man of rank whom you are addressing, Sir!

TRUEMAN. A rank villain, Mrs. Antony Tiffany! A *rich one* he would be, had he as much *gold* as *brass!*

MRS. TIFFANY. Pray pardon him, Count; he knows nothing of *how ton!*

COUNT. Demme, he's beneath my notice. I tell you what, old fellow—[TRUEMAN *raises his stick as* COUNT *approaches, the latter starts back*.] the sight of him discomposes me—aw—I feel quite uncomfortable—aw—let us join your charming daughter? I can't do you the honor to shoot you, Sir—[*To* TRUEMAN.] you are beneath me—a nobleman can't fight a commoner! Good bye, old Truepenny! I—aw—I'm insensible to your insolence!

[*Exeunt* COUNT *and* MRS. TIFFANY.

TRUEMAN. You won't be insensible to a cow hide in spite of your nobility! The next time he practises any of his foreign fashions on you, Gertrude, you'll see how I'll wake up his sensibilities!

GERTRUDE. I do not know what I should have done without you, sir.

TRUEMAN. Yes, you do—you know that you would have done well enough! Never tell a lie, girl! not even for the sake of pleasing an old man! When you open your lips let your heart speak. Never tell a lie! Let your face be the looking-glass of your soul—your heart its clock—while your tongue rings the hours! But the glass must be clear, the clock true, and then there's no fear but the tongue will do its duty in a woman's head!

GERTRUDE. You are very good, Sir!

TRUEMAN. That's as it may be!—How my heart warms towards her! [*Aside*.] Gertrude, I hear that you have no mother?

GERTRUDE. Ah! no, Sir; I wish I had.

TRUEMAN. So do I! Heaven knows, so do I! [*Aside, and with emotion*.] And you have no father, Gertrude?

GERTRUDE. No, Sir—I often wish I had!

TRUEMAN [*hurriedly*]. Don't do that, girl! don't do that! Wish you had a mother—but never wish that you had a father again! Perhaps the one you had did not deserve such a child!

Enter PRUDENCE

PRUDENCE. Seraphina is looking for you, Gertrude.

GERTRUDE. I will go to her. Mr. Trueman,

you will not permit me to thank you, but you cannot prevent my gratitude! [*Exit.*

TRUEMAN [*looking after her*]. If falsehood harbors there, I'll give up searching after truth!

[*Crosses, retires up the stage musingly, and commences examining the flowers.*]

PRUDENCE. What a nice old man he is, to be sure! I wish he would say something! [*Aside.*]

[*Crosses, walks after him, turning when he turns—after a pause.*]

Don't mind *me*, Mr. Trueman!

TRUEMAN. Mind you? Oh, no, don't be afraid—I wasn't minding you. Nobody seems to mind you much!

[*Continues walking and examining the flowers*—PRUDENCE *follows.*]

PRUDENCE. Very pretty flowers, ain't they? Gertrude takes care of them.

TRUEMAN. Gertrude? So I hear—I suppose you can tell me now who this Gertrude—

PRUDENCE. Who she's in love with? I *knew* you were going to say that! I'll tell you all about it! Gertrude, she's in love with—Mr. Twinkle! and he's in love with her. And Seraphina she's in love with Count Jolly—what-d'ye-call-it: but Count Jolly don't take to her at all—but Colonel Howard—he's the man—he's desperate about her!

TRUEMAN. Why, you feminine newspaper! Howard in love with that quintessence of affectation! Howard—the only, frank, straightforward fellow that I've met since—I'll tell him my mind on the subject! And Gertrude hunting for happiness in a rhyming dictionary! The girl's a greater fool than I took her for!

PRUDENCE. So she is—you see I know all about them!

TRUEMAN. I see you do! You've a wonderful knowledge—wonderful—of *other people's concerns!* It may do here, but take my word for it, in the county of Catteraugus you'd get the name of a great *busy-body*. But perhaps you know that, too?

PRUDENCE. Oh! I always know what's coming. I feel it beforehand all over me. I knew something was going to happen the day you came here—and what's more I can always tell a married man from a single—I felt right off that you were a bachelor!

TRUEMAN. Felt right off I was a bachelor, did you? you were sure of it—sure?—quite sure? [PRUDENCE *assents delightedly.*] Then you felt wrong!—a bachelor and a widower are not the same thing!

PRUDENCE. Oh! but it all comes to the same thing—a widower's as good as a bachelor any day! And besides I knew that you were a farmer *right off.*

TRUEMAN. On the spot, eh? I suppose you saw cabbages and green peas growing out of my hat?

PRUDENCE. No, I didn't—but I knew all about you. And I knew—[*Looking down and fidgeting with her apron.*] I knew you were for getting married soon! For last night I dream't I saw your funeral going along the streets, and the mourners all dressed in white. And a funeral is a sure sign of a wedding, you know! [*Nudging him with her elbow.*]

TRUEMAN [*imitating her voice*]. Well, I can't say that I *know* any such thing! you know! [*Nudging her back.*]

PRUDENCE. Oh! it does, and there's no getting over it! For my part, I like farmers—and I know all about setting hens and turkeys, and feeding chickens, and laying eggs, and all that sort of thing!

TRUEMAN. May I be shot! if mistress newspaper is not putting in an advertisement for herself! This is your city mode of courting, I suppose, ha, ha, ha! [*Aside.*]

PRUDENCE. I've been west, a little; but I never was in the county of Catteraugus, myself.

TRUEMAN. Oh! you were not? And you have taken a particular fancy to go there, eh?

PRUDENCE. Perhaps I shouldn't object—

TRUEMAN. Oh!—ah!—so I suppose. Now pay attention to what I am going to say, for it is a matter of great importance to yourself.

PRUDENCE. Now it's coming—I know what he's going to say! [*Aside.*]

TRUEMAN. The next time you want to tie a man for life to your apron-strings, pick out one that don't come from the county of Catteraugus—for green horns are scarce in those parts, and modest women plenty!

[*Exit.*

PRUDENCE. Now who'd have thought he was going to say that! But I won't give him up yet—I won't give him up. [*Exit.*

END OF ACT II

ACT III

SCENE I. MRS. TIFFANY'S *Parlor*

Enter MRS. TIFFANY, *followed by* MR. TIFFANY

TIFFANY. Your extravagance will ruin me, Mrs. Tiffany!

MRS. TIFFANY. And your stinginess will ruin me, Mr. Tiffany! It is totally and *toot a fate* impossible to convince you of the necessity of *keeping up appearances*. There is a certain display which every woman of fashion is forced to make!

TIFFANY. And pray who made *you* a woman of fashion?

MRS. TIFFANY. What a vulgar question! All women of fashion, Mr. Tiffany—

TIFFANY. In this land are *self-constituted*, like you, Madam—and *fashion* is the cloak for more sins than charity ever covered! It was for *fashion's* sake that you insisted upon my purchasing this expensive house—it was for *fashion's* sake that you ran me in debt at every exorbitant upholsterer's and extravagant furniture warehouse in the city—it was for *fashion's* sake that you built that ruinous conservatory—hired more servants than they have persons to wait upon—and dressed your footman like a harlequin!

MRS. TIFFANY. Mr. Tiffany, you are thoroughly plebeian, and insufferably *American*, in your grovelling ideas! And, pray, what was the occasion of these very *mal-ap-propos* remarks? Merely because I requested a paltry fifty dollars to purchase a new style of headdress—a *bijou* of an article just introduced in France.

TIFFANY. Time was, Mrs. Tiffany, when you manufactured your own French headdresses—took off their first gloss at the public balls, and then sold them to your shortest-sighted customers. And all you knew about France, or French either, was what you spelt out at the bottom of your fashion plates—but now you have grown so fashionable, forsooth, that you have forgotten how to speak your mother tongue!

MRS. TIFFANY. Mr. Tiffany, Mr. Tiffany! Nothing is more positively vulgarian—more *unaristocratic* than any allusion to the past!

TIFFANY. Why, I thought, my dear, that *aristocrats* lived principally upon the past—and traded in the market of fashion with the bones of their ancestors for capital?

MRS. TIFFANY. Mr. Tiffany, such vulgar remarks are only suitable to the counting house, in my drawing room you should—

TIFFANY. Vary my sentiments with my locality, as you change your *manners* with your *dress!*

MRS. TIFFANY. Mr. Tiffany, I desire that you will purchase Count d'Orsay's "Science of Etiquette," and learn how to conduct yourself—especially before you appear at the grand ball, which I shall give on Friday!

TIFFANY. Confound your balls, Madam; they make *footballs* of my money, while you dance away all that I am worth! A pretty time to give a ball when you know that I am on the very brink of bankruptcy!

MRS. TIFFANY. So much the greater reason that nobody should suspect your circumstances, or you would lose your credit at once. Just at this crisis a ball is absolutely *necessary* to save your reputation! There is Mrs. Adolphus Dashaway—she gave the most splendid fête of the season—and I hear on very good authority that her husband has not paid his baker's bill in three months. Then there was Mrs. Honeywood—

TIFFANY. Gave a ball the night before her husband shot himself—perhaps you wish to drive me to follow his example?

MRS. TIFFANY. Good gracious! Mr. Tiffany, how you talk! I beg you won't mention anything of the kind. I consider black the most unbecoming color. I'm sure I've done all that I could to gratify you. There is that vulgar old torment, Trueman, who gives one the lie fifty times a day—haven't I been very civil to him?

TIFFANY. Civil to his *wealth*, Mrs. Tiffany! I told you that he was a rich, old farmer—the early friend of my father—my own benefactor—and that I had reason to think he might assist me in my present embarrassments. Your civility was *bought*—and like most of your *own* purchases has yet to be *paid* for. [*Crosses.*]

MRS. TIFFANY. And will be, no doubt! The condescension of a woman of fashion should command any price. Mr. Trueman is insupportably indecorous—he has insulted Count Jolimaitre in the most outrageous manner. If the Count was not so deeply interested—so *abimé* with Seraphina, I am sure he would never honor us by his visits again!

TIFFANY. So much the better—he shall never marry my daughter!—I am resolved on that. Why, Madam, I am told there is in Paris a regular matrimonial stock company, who fit out indigent dandies for this market. How do I know but this fellow is one of its creatures, and that he has come here to increase its dividends by marrying a fortune?

MRS. TIFFANY. Nonsense, Mr. Tiffany. The Count, the most fashionable young man in all New York—the intimate friend of all the dukes and lords in Europe—not marry my daughter? Not permit Seraphina to become a Countess? Mr. Tiffany, you are out of your senses!

TIFFANY. That would not be very wonderful, considering how many years I have been united to you, my dear. Modern physicians pronounce lunacy infectious!

MRS. TIFFANY. Mr. Tiffany, he is a man of fashion—

TIFFANY. Fashion makes fools, but cannot *feed* them. By the bye, I have a request,—since you are bent upon ruining me by this ball, and there is no help for it,—I desire that you will send an invitation to my confidential clerk, Mr. Snobson.

MRS. TIFFANY. Mr. Snobson! Was there ever such an *you-nick* demand! Mr. Snobson would cut a pretty figure amongst my fashionable friends! I shall do no such thing, Mr. Tiffany.

TIFFANY. Then, Madam, the ball shall not take place. Have I not told you that I am in the power of this man? That there are circumstances which it is happy for you that you do not know—which you cannot comprehend,—but which render it essential that you should be civil to Mr. Snobson? Not you merely, but Seraphina also? He is a more appropriate match for her than your foreign favorite.

MRS. TIFFANY. A match for Seraphina, indeed! [*Crosses.*] Mr. Tiffany, you are determined to make a *fow pas.*

TIFFANY. Mr. Snobson intends calling this morning.

MRS. TIFFANY. But, Mr. Tiffany, this is not reception day—my drawing rooms are in the most terrible disorder—

TIFFANY. Mr. Snobson is not particular—he must be admitted.

Enter ZEKE

ZEKE. Mr. Snobson.

Enter SNOBSON; *exit* ZEKE

SNOBSON. How d'ye do, Marm? [*Crosses.*] How are you? Mr. Tiffany, your most!—

MRS. TIFFANY [*formally*]. *Bung jure. Comment vow portè vow, Monsur Snobson?*

SNOBSON. Oh, to be sure—very good of you—fine day.

MRS. TIFFANY [*pointing to a chair with great dignity*]. *Sassoyez vow*, Monsur Snobson.

SNOBSON. I wonder what she's driving at? I ain't up to the fashionable lingo yet! [*Aside.*] Eh? what? Speak a little louder, Marm?

MRS. TIFFANY. What ignorance! [*Aside.*]

TIFFANY. I presume Mrs. Tiffany means that you are to take a seat.

SNOBSON. Ex-actly—very obliging of her—so I will. [*Sits.*] No ceremony amongst friends, you know—and likely to be nearer—you understand? *O.K.*, all correct. How *is* Seraphina?

MRS. TIFFANY. Miss Tiffany is not visible this morning. [*Retires up.*]

SNOBSON. Not visible? [*Jumping up, crosses.*] I suppose that's the English for can't see her? Mr. Tiffany, Sir—[*Walking up to him.*] what am I to understand by this *de-fal-ca-tion*, Sir? I expected your word to be as good as your bond—beg pardon, Sir—I mean *better*—considerably better—no humbug about it, Sir.

TIFFANY. Have patience, Mr. Snobson. [*Rings bell.*]

Enter ZEKE

Zeke, desire my daughter to come here.

MRS. TIFFANY [*coming down*]. Adolph—I say, Adolph—

[ZEKE *straightens himself and assumes foppish airs, as he turns to* MRS. TIFFANY.]

TIFFANY. Zeke.

ZEKE. Don't know any such nigga, Boss.

TIFFANY. Do as I bid you instantly, or off with your livery and quit the house!

ZEKE. Wheugh! I'se all dismission! [*Exit.*

MRS. TIFFANY. A-dolph, A-dolph! [*Calling after him.*]

SNOBSON. I brought the old boy to his bearings, didn't I though! Pull that string, and he is sure to work right. [*Aside.*] Don't make any stranger of me, Marm—I'm quite at home. If you've got any odd jobs about the house to do up, I sha'n't miss you. I'll amuse myself with Seraphina when she comes—we'll get along very cosily by ourselves.

MRS. TIFFANY. Permit me to inform you, Mr. Snobson, that a French mother never leaves her daughter alone with a young man—she knows your sex too well for that!

SNOBSON. Very *dis*-obliging of her—but as we're none French—

MRS. TIFFANY. You have yet to learn, Mr. Snobson, that the American *ee-light*—the aristocracy—the *how-ton*—as a matter of conscience, scrupulously follow the foreign fashions.

SNOBSON. Not when they are foreign to their interests, Marm—for instance—[*Enter* SERAPHINA.] There you are at last, eh, Miss? How d'ye do? Ma said you weren't visible. Managed to get a peep at her, eh, Mr. Tiffany?

SERAPHINA. I heard you were here, Mr. Snobson, and came without even arranging my toilette; you will excuse my negligence?

SNOBSON. Of everything but *me*, Miss.

SERAPHINA. I shall never have to ask your pardon for *that*, Mr. Snobson.

MRS. TIFFANY. Seraphina—child—really—

[*As she is approaching* SERAPHINA, MR. TIFFANY *plants himself in front of his wife.*]

TIFFANY. Walk this way, Madam, if you please. To see that she fancies the surly fellow takes a weight from my heart. [*Aside.*]

MRS. TIFFANY. Mr. Tiffany, it is highly improper and not at all *distingué* to leave a young girl—

Enter ZEKE

ZEKE. Mr. Count Jolly-made-her!

MRS. TIFFANY. Good gracious! The Count—Oh, dear!—Seraphina, run and change your dress,—no, there's no time! A-dolph, admit him. [*Exit* ZEKE. Mr. Snobson, get out of the way, will you? Mr. Tiffany, what are you doing at home at this hour?

Enter COUNT JOLIMAITRE, *ushered by* ZEKE

ZEKE. Dat's de genuine article ob a gemman. [*Aside.*]

MRS. TIFFANY. My dear Count, I am overjoyed at the very sight of you.

COUNT. Flattered myself you'd be glad to see me, Madam—knew it was not your *jour de reception.*

MRS. TIFFANY. But for you, Count, all days—

COUNT. I thought so. Ah, Miss Tiffany, on my honor, you're looking beautiful.

SERAPHINA. Count, flattery from you—

SNOBSON. What? Eh? What's that you say?

SERAPHINA. Nothing but what etiquette requires. [*Aside to him.*]

COUNT [*regarding* MR. TIFFANY *through his eye-glass*]. Your worthy Papa, I believe? Sir, your most obedient.

[MR. TIFFANY *bows coldly;* COUNT *regards* SNOBSON *through his glass, shrugs his shoulders and turns away.*]

SNOBSON [*to* MRS. TIFFANY]. Introduce me, will you? I never knew a Count in all my life—what a strange-looking animal!

MRS. TIFFANY. Mr. Snobson, it is not the fashion to introduce in France!

SNOBSON. But, Marm, we're in America. The woman thinks she's somewhere else than where she is—she wants to make an *alibi?* [*Aside.*]

MRS. TIFFANY. I hope that we shall have the pleasure of seeing you on Friday evening, Count?

COUNT. Really, madam, my invitations—my engagements—so numerous—I can hardly answer for myself: and you Americans take offence so easily—

MRS. TIFFANY. But, Count, everybody expects you at our ball—you are the principal attraction—

SERAPHINA. Count, you *must* come!

COUNT. Since you insist—aw—aw—there's no resisting you, Miss Tiffany.

MRS. TIFFANY. I am so thankful. How can I repay your condescension! [COUNT *and* SERAPHINA *converse.*] Mr. Snobson, will you walk this way?—I have *such* a cactus in full bloom—remarkable flower! Mr. Tiffany, pray come here—I have something particular to say.

TIFFANY. Then speak out, my dear—I thought it was highly improper just now to leave a girl with a young man? [*Aside to her.*]

MRS. TIFFANY. Oh, but the Count—that is different!

TIFFANY. I suppose you mean to say there's nothing of *the man* about him?

Enter MILLINETTE, *with a scarf in her hand*

MILLINETTE. Adolph tell me he vas here. [*Aside.*] Pardon, Madame, I bring dis scarf for Mademoiselle.

MRS. TIFFANY. Very well, Millinette; you know best what is proper for her to wear.

[MR. *and* MRS. TIFFANY *and* SNOBSON *retire up; she engages the attention of both gentlemen.*]

[MILLINETTE *crosses towards* SERAPHINA, *gives the* COUNT *a threatening look, and commences arranging the scarf over* SERAPHINA'S *shoulders.*]

MILLINETTE. Mademoiselle, *permettez-moi.* Perfide! [*Aside to* COUNT.] If Mademoiselle vil stand *tranquille* one *petit moment.* [*Turns* SERAPHINA'S *back to the* COUNT, *and pretends to arrange the scarf.*] I must speak vid you today, or I tell all—you find me at de foot of de stair ven you go. *Prends garde!* [*Aside to* COUNT.]

SERAPHINA. What is that you say, Millinette?

MILLINETTE. Dis scarf make you so very beautiful, Mademoiselle—*Je vous salue, mes dames.* [*Curtsies.*] [*Exit.*

COUNT. Not a moment to lose! [*Aside.*] Miss Tiffany, I have an unpleasant—a particularly unpleasant piece of intelligence—you see, I have just received a letter from my friend—the—aw—the Earl of Airshire; the truth is, the Earl's daughter—beg you won't mention it—has distinguished me by a tender *penchant.*

SERAPHINA. I understand—and they wish you to return and marry the young lady; but surely you will not leave us, Count?

COUNT. If *you* bid me stay—I shouldn't have the conscience—I couldn't *afford* to tear myself away. I'm sure that's honest. [*Aside.*]

SERAPHINA. Oh, Count!

COUNT. Say but one word—say that you shouldn't mind being made a Countess—and I'll break with the Earl tomorrow.

SERAPHINA. Count, this surprise—but don't think of leaving the country, Count—we could not pass the time without you! I—yes—yes, Count—I do consent!

COUNT. I thought she would! [*Aside, while he embraces her.*] Enchanted, rapture, bliss, ecstacy, and all that sort of thing—words can't express it, but you understand. But it must be kept a secret—positively it *must!* If the rumor of our engagement were whispered abroad—the Earl's daughter—the delicacy of my situation, aw—you comprehend? It is even possible that our nuptials, my charming Miss Tiffany, *our nuptials* must take place in private!

SERAPHINA. Oh, that is quite impossible!

COUNT. It's the latest fashion abroad—the very latest! Ah, I knew that would determine you. Can I depend on your secrecy?

SERAPHINA. Oh, yes! Believe me.

SNOBSON [*coming forward in spite of* MRS. TIFFANY'S *efforts to detain him*]. Why, Seraphina, haven't you a word to throw to a dog?

TIFFANY. I shouldn't think she had after wasting so many upon a puppy. [*Aside.*]

Enter ZEKE, *wearing a three-cornered hat*

ZEKE. Missus, de bran new carriage am below.

MRS. TIFFANY. Show it up,—I mean, very well, A-dolph. [*Exit* ZEKE.
Count, my daughter and I are about to take an airing in our new *voyture,*—will you honor us with your company?

COUNT. Madam, I—I have a most *pressing*

engagement. A letter to write to the *Earl of Airshire*—who is at present residing in the *Isle of Skye*. I must bid you good morning.

MRS. TIFFANY. Good morning, Count.

[*Exit* COUNT.

SNOBSON. *I'm* quite at leisure, [*Crosses to* MRS. TIFFANY.] Marm. Books balanced—ledger closed—nothing to do all the afternoon,—I'm for you.

MRS. TIFFANY [*without noticing him*]. Come, Seraphina, come! [*As they are going* SNOBSON *follows them.*]

SNOBSON. But Marm—I was saying, Marm, I am quite at leisure—not a thing to do; have I, Mr. Tiffany?

MRS. TIFFANY. Seraphina, child—your red shawl—remember—Mr. Snobson, *bon swear!*

[*Exit, leading* SERAPHINA.

SNOBSON. Swear! Mr. Tiffany, Sir, am I to be fobbed off with a *bon swear?* D—n it, I will swear!

TIFFANY. Have patience, Mr. Snobson, if you will accompany me to the counting house—

SNOBSON. Don't count too much on me, Sir. I'll make up no more accounts until these are settled! I'll run down and jump into the carriage in spite of her *bon swear*. [*Exit.*

TIFFANY. You'll jump into a hornet's nest, if you do! Mr. Snobson, Mr. Snobson!

[*Exit after him.*

SCENE 2. *Housekeeper's Room*

Enter MILLINETTE

MILLINETTE. I have set dat bête, Adolph, to vatch for him. He say he would come back so soon as Madame's voiture drive from de door. If he not come—but he vill—he vill—he *bien étourdi*, but he have *bon cœur*.

Enter COUNT

COUNT. Ah! Millinette, my dear, you see what a good-natured dog I am to fly at your bidding—

MILLINETTE. Fly? Ah! *trompeur!* Vat for you fly from Paris? Vat for you leave me—and I love you so much? Ven you sick—you almost die—did I not stay by you—take care of you—and you have no else friend? Vat for you leave Paris?

COUNT. Never allude to disagreeable subjects, *mon enfant!* I was forced by uncontrollable circumstances to fly to the land of liberty—

MILLINETTE. Vat you do vid all de money I give you? The last sou I had—did I not give you?

COUNT. I dare say you did, *ma petite*—wish you'd been better supplied! [*Aside.*] Don't ask any questions here—can't explain now—the next time we meet—

MILLINETTE. But, ah! ven shall ve meet—ven? You not deceive me, not any more.

COUNT. Deceive you! I'd rather deceive myself—I wish I could! I'd persuade myself you were once more washing linen in the Seine! [*Aside.*]

MILLINETTE. I vil tell you ven ve shall meet—On Friday night Madame give one grand ball—you come *sans doute*—den ven de supper is served—de Americans tink of noting else ven de supper come—den you steal out of de room, and you find me here—and you give me one grand *explanation!*

Enter GERTRUDE, *unperceived*

COUNT. Friday night—while supper is serving—*parole d'honneur* I will be here—I will explain every thing—my sudden departure from Paris—my—demme, my countship—every thing! Now let me go—if any of the family should discover us—

GERTRUDE [*who during the last speech has gradually advanced*]. They might discover more than you think it advisable for them to know!

COUNT. The devil!

MILLINETTE. *Mon Dieu!* Mademoiselle Gertrude!

COUNT [*recovering himself*]. My dear Miss Gertrude, let me explain—aw—aw—nothing is more natural than the situation in which you find me—

GERTRUDE. I am inclined to believe that, Sir.

COUNT. Now—'pon my honor, that's not fair. Here is Millinette will bear witness to what I am about to say—

GERTRUDE. Oh, I have not the slightest doubt of that, Sir.

COUNT. You see, Millinette happened to be lady's-maid in the family of—of—

the Duchess Chateau D'Espagne—and I chanced to be a particular friend of the Duchess—*very particular*, I assure you! Of course I saw Millinette, and she, demme, she saw me! Didn't you, Millinette?

MILLINETTE. Oh! *oui*—Mademoiselle, I knew him ver vell.

COUNT. Well, it is a remarkable fact that—being in correspondence with this very Duchess—at this very time—

GERTRUDE. That is sufficient, Sir—I am already so well acquainted with your extraordinary talents for improvisation, that I will not further tax your invention—

MILLINETTE. Ah! Mademoiselle Gertrude, do not betray us—have pity!

COUNT [*assuming an air of dignity*]. Silence, Millinette! My word has been doubted—the word of a nobleman! I will inform my friend, Mrs. Tiffany, of this young person's audacity. [*Going*.]

GERTRUDE. His own weapons alone can foil this villain! [*Aside*.] Sir—Sir—Count! [*At the last word the* COUNT *turns*.] Perhaps, Sir, the least said about this matter the better!

COUNT [*delightedly*]. The least said? We won't say anything at all. She's coming round—couldn't resist me! [*Aside*.] Charming Gertrude—

MILLINETTE. *Quoi?* Vat that you say?

COUNT. My sweet, adorable Millinette, hold your tongue, will you? [*Aside to her*.]

MILLINETTE [*aloud*]. No, I vill not! If you do look so from out your eyes at her again, I vill tell all!

COUNT. Oh, I never could manage two women at once,—jealousy makes the dear creatures so spiteful. The only valor is in flight! [*Aside*.] Miss Gertrude, I wish you good morning. Millinette, *mon enfant*, adieu. [*Exit*.

MILLINETTE. But I have one word more to say. Stop, stop! [*Exit after him*.

GERTRUDE [*musingly*]. Friday night, while supper is serving, he is to meet Millinette here and explain—what? This man is an impostor! His insulting me—his familiarity with Millinette—his whole conduct—prove it. If I tell Mrs. Tiffany this she will disbelieve me, and one word may place this so-called Count on his guard. To convince Seraphina would be equally difficult, and her rashness and infatuation may render her miserable for life. No—she shall be saved! I must devise some plan for opening their eyes. Truly, if I *cannot* invent one, I shall be the first woman who was ever at a loss for a stratagem—especially to punish a villain or to shield a friend. [*Exit*.

END OF ACT III

ACT IV

SCENE I. *Ball Room splendidly illuminated. A curtain hung at the further end.* MR. *and* MRS. TIFFANY, SERAPHINA, GERTRUDE, FOGG, TWINKLE, COUNT, SNOBSON, COLONEL HOWARD, *a number of guests—some seated, some standing. As the curtain rises, a cotillion is danced;* GERTRUDE *dancing with* HOWARD, SERAPHINA *with* COUNT.

COUNT [*advancing with* SERAPHINA *to the front of the stage*]. Tomorrow then—tomorrow—I may salute you as my bride—demme, my Countess!

Enter ZEKE, *with refreshments*

SERAPHINA. Yes, tomorrow.

[*As the* COUNT *is about to reply*, SNOBSON *thrusts himself in front of* SERAPHINA.]

SNOBSON. You said you'd dance with me, Miss—now take my fin, and we'll walk about and see what's going on.

[COUNT *raises his eye-glass, regards* SNOBSON, *and leads* SERAPHINA *away;* SNOBSON *follows, endeavoring to attract her attention, but encounters* ZEKE, *bearing a waiter of refreshments; stops, helps himself, and puts some in his pockets*.]

Here's the treat! get my tomorrow's luncheon out of Tiff.

Enter TRUEMAN, *yawning and rubbing his eyes*

TRUEMAN. What a nap I've had, to be sure! [*Looks at his watch*.] Eleven o'clock, as I'm alive! Just the time when country folks are comfortably *turned in*, and here your grand *turn-out* has hardly begun yet! [*To* TIFFANY, *who approaches*.]

GERTRUDE [*advancing*]. I was just coming to look for you, Mr. Trueman. I began to fancy that you were paying a visit to dreamland.

TRUEMAN. So I was, child—so I was—and I saw a face—like yours—but brighter!—even brighter. [*To* TIFFANY.] There's a smile for you, man! It makes one feel that the world has something worth living for in it yet! Do you remember a smile like that, Antony? Ah! I see you don't—but I do—I do! [*Much moved.*]

HOWARD [*advancing*]. Good evening, Mr. Trueman. [*Offers his hand.*]

TRUEMAN. That's right, man; give me your whole hand! When a man offers me the tips of his fingers, I know at once there's nothing in him worth seeking beyond his fingers ends.

[TRUEMAN *and* HOWARD, GERTRUDE *and* TIFFANY *converse.*]

MRS. TIFFANY [*advancing*]. I'm in such a fidget lest that vulgar old fellow should disgrace us by some of his plebeian remarks! What it is to give a ball, when one is forced to invite vulgar people!

[MRS. TIFFANY *advances towards* TRUEMAN; SERAPHINA *stands conversing flippantly with the gentlemen who surround her; amongst them is* TWINKLE, *who having taken a magazine from his pocket, is reading to her, much to the undisguised annoyance of* SNOBSON.]

Dear me, Mr. Trueman, you are very late—quite in the fashion, I declare!

TRUEMAN. Fashion! And pray what is *fashion*, madam? An agreement between certain persons to live without using their souls! to substitute etiquette for virtue—decorum for purity—manners for morals! to affect a shame for the works of their Creator! and expend all their rapture upon the works of their tailors and dressmakers!

MRS. TIFFANY. You have the most *ow-tray* ideas, Mr. Trueman—quite rustic, and deplorably *American!* But pray walk this way.

[MRS. TIFFANY *and* TRUEMAN *go up.*]

COUNT [*advancing to* GERTRUDE, HOWARD *a short distance behind her*]. Miss Gertrude—no opportunity of speaking to you before—in demand, you know!

GERTRUDE. I have no choice, I must be civil to him. [*Aside.*] What were you remarking, Sir?

COUNT. Miss Gertrude—charming Ger—aw—aw—I never found it so difficult to speak to a woman before. [*Aside.*]

GERTRUDE. Yes, a very charming ball—many beautiful faces here.

COUNT. Only one!—aw—aw—one—the fact is—

[*Talks to her in dumb show.*]

HOWARD. What could old Trueman have meant by saying she fancied that puppy of a Count—that paste jewel thrust upon the little finger of society.

COUNT. Miss Gertrude—aw—'pon my honor—you don't understand—really—aw—aw—will you dance the polka with me?

[GERTRUDE *bows and gives him her hand; he leads her to the set forming;* HOWARD *remains looking after them.*]

HOWARD. Going to dance with him, too! A few days ago she would hardly bow to him civilly—could old Trueman have had reasons for what he said? [*Retires up.*]

[*Dance, the polka;* SERAPHINA, *after having distributed her bouquet, vinaigrette and fan amongst the gentlemen, dances with* SNOBSON.]

PRUDENCE [*peeping in as dance concludes*]. I don't like dancing on Friday; something strange is always sure to happen! I'll be on the look out.

[*Remains peeping and concealing herself when any of the company approach.*]

GERTRUDE [*advancing hastily*]. They are preparing the supper—now if I can only dispose of Millinette while I unmask this insolent pretender! [*Exit.*

PRUDENCE [*peeping*]. What's that she said? It's coming!

Re-enter GERTRUDE, *bearing a small basket filled with bouquets; approaches* MRS. TIFFANY; *they walk to the front of the stage.*

GERTRUDE. Excuse me, Madam—I believe this is just the hour at which you ordered supper?

MRS. TIFFANY. Well, what's that to you! So you've been dancing with the Count—how dare you dance with a nobleman—*you?*

GERTRUDE. I will answer that question half an hour hence. At present I have something to propose, which I think will gratify you and please your guests. I have heard that at the most elegant balls in Paris, it is customary—

MRS. TIFFANY. What? what?

GERTRUDE. To station a servant at the door with a basket of flowers. A bouquet is then presented to every lady as she passes in—I prepared this basket a short time ago. As the company walk in to supper, might not the flowers be distributed to advantage?

MRS. TIFFANY. How *distingué!* You are a good creature, Gertrude—there, run and hand the *bokettes* to them yourself! You shall have the whole credit of the thing.

GERTRUDE. Caught in my own net! [*Aside.*] But, madam, *I* know so little of fashions—Millinette, being French herself, will do it with so much more grace. I am sure Millinette—

MRS. TIFFANY. So am I. She will do it a thousand times better than you—there, go call her.

GERTRUDE [*giving basket*]. But madam, pray order Millinette not to leave her station till supper is ended—as the company pass out of the supper room she may find that some of the ladies have been overlooked.

MRS. TIFFANY. That is true—very thoughtful of you, Gertrude. [*Exit* GERTRUDE. What a *recherché* idea!

Enter MILLINETTE

Here, Millinette, take this basket. Place yourself there, and distribute these *bokettes* as the company pass in to supper; but remember not to stir from the spot until supper is over. It is a French fashion, you know, Millinette. I am so delighted to be the first to introduce it—it will be all the rage in the *bow-monde!*

MILLINETTE. Mon Dieu! dis vill ruin all! [*Aside.*] Madame, Madame, let me tell you, Madame, dat in France, in Paris, it is de custom to present *les* bouquets ven every body first come—long before de supper. Dis vould be *outré! barbare!* not at all *la mode!* Ven dey do come in—dat is de fashion in Paris!

MRS. TIFFANY. Dear me! Millinette, what is the difference? besides I'd have you to know that Americans always improve upon French fashions! here, take the basket, and let me see that you do it in the most *you-nick* and genteel manner.

[MILLINETTE *poutingly takes the basket and retires up stage. A March. Curtain hung at the further end of the room is drawn back, and discloses a room, in the centre of which stands a supper table, beautifully decorated and illuminated; the company promenade two by two into the supper room;* MILLINETTE *presents bouquets as they pass;* COUNT *leads* MRS. TIFFANY.]

TRUEMAN [*encountering* FOGG, *who is hurrying alone to the supper room*]. Mr. Fogg, never mind the supper, man! Ha, ha, ha! Of course you are indifferent to suppers!

FOGG. Indifferent! suppers—oh, ah—no, Sir—suppers? no—no—I'm not indifferent to suppers! [*Hurries away towards table.*]

TRUEMAN. Ha, ha, ha! Here's a new discovery I've made in the fashionable world! Fashion don't permit the critters to have *heads* or *hearts*, but it allows them stomachs! [*To* TIFFANY, *who advances.*] So it's not fashionable to *feel*, but it's fashionable to *feed*, eh, Antony? ha, ha, ha!

[TRUEMAN *and* TIFFANY *retire towards supper room. Enter* GERTRUDE, *followed by* ZEKE.]

GERTRUDE. Zeke, go to the supper room instantly,—whisper to Count Jolimaitre that all is ready, and that he must keep his appointment without delay,—then watch him, and as he passes out of the room, place yourself in front of Millinette in such a manner, that the Count cannot see her nor she him. Be sure that they do not see each other—every thing depends upon that.

ZEKE. Missey, consider dat business brought to a scientific conclusion.

[*Exit into supper room. Exit* GERTRUDE.

PRUDENCE [*who has been listening*]. What can she want of the Count? I always suspected that Gertrude, because she is so merry and busy! Mr. Trueman thinks so much of her, too—I'll tell him this! There's something wrong—but it all comes of giving a ball on a Friday! How astonished the dear old man will be when he finds out how much I know! [*Advances timidly towards the supper room.*]

SCENE 2. *Housekeeper's room; dark stage; table, two chairs*

Enter GERTRUDE, *with a lighted candle in her hand*

GERTRUDE. So far the scheme prospers! and yet this imprudence—if I fail? Fail! to lack courage in a difficulty, or ingenuity in a dilemma, are not woman's failings!

Enter ZEKE, *with a napkin over his arm, and a bottle of champagne in his hand*

Well, Zeke—Adolph!

ZEKE. Dat's right, Missey; I feels just now as if dat was my legitimate title; dis here's de stuff to make a nigger feel like a gemman!

GERTRUDE. But is he coming?

ZEKE. He's coming! [*Sound of a champagne cork heard.*] Do you hear dat, Missey? Don't it put you all in a froth, and make you feel as light as a cork? Dere's nothing like the *union brand*, to wake up de harmonies ob de heart. [*Drinks from bottle.*]

GERTRUDE. Remember to keep watch upon the outside—do not stir from the spot; when I call you, come in quickly with a light—now, will you be gone!

ZEKE. I'm off, Missey, like a champagne cork wid de strings cut. [*Exit.*

GERTRUDE. I think I hear the Count's step. [*Crosses, stage dark; she blows out candle.*] Now if I can but disguise my voice, and make the best of my French.

Enter COUNT

COUNT. Millinette, where are you? How am I to see you in the dark?

GERTRUDE [*imitating* MILLINETTE'S *voice in a whisper*]. Hush! *parle bas.*

COUNT. Come here and give me a kiss.

GERTRUDE. *Non—non—*[*Retreating alarmed,* COUNT *follows.*] make haste, I must know all.

COUNT. You did not use to be so deuced particular.

ZEKE [*without*]. No admission, gemman! Box office closed, tickets stopped!

TRUEMAN [*without*]. Out of my way; do you want me to try if your head is as hard as my stick?

GERTRUDE. What shall I do? Ruined, ruined! [*She stands with her hand clasped in speechless despair.*]

COUNT. Halloa! they are coming here, Millinette! Millinette, why don't you speak? Where can I hide myself? [*Running about stage, feeling for a door.*] Where are all your closets? If I could only get out—or get in somewhere; may I be smothered in a clothes' basket, if you ever catch me in such a scrape again! [*His hand accidentally touches the knob of a door opening into a closet.*] Fortune's favorite yet! I'm safe!

[*Gets into closet and closes door. Enter* PRUDENCE, TRUEMAN, MRS. TIFFANY, *and* COLONEL HOWARD, *followed by* ZEKE, *bearing a light; lights up.*]

PRUDENCE. Here they are, the Count and Gertrude! I told you so!

[*Stops in surprise on seeing only* GERTRUDE.]

TRUEMAN. And you see what a lie you told!

MRS. TIFFANY. Prudence, how dare you create this disturbance in my house? to suspect the Count, too—a nobleman!

HOWARD. My sweet Gertrude, this foolish old woman would—

PRUDENCE. Oh! you needn't talk—I heard her make the appointment—I know he's here—or he's been here. I wonder if she hasn't hid him away!

[*Runs peeping about the room.*]

TRUEMAN [*following her angrily*]. You're what I call a confounded—troublesome—meddling—old—prying—[*As he says the last word,* PRUDENCE *opens closet where the* COUNT *is concealed.*] Thunder and lightning!

PRUDENCE. I told you so!

[*They all stand aghast;* MRS. TIFFANY, *with her hands lifted in surprise and anger;* TRUEMAN, *clutching his stick;* HOWARD, *looking with an expression of bewildered horror from the* COUNT *to* GERTRUDE.]

MRS. TIFFANY [*shaking her fist at* GERTRUDE]. You depraved little minx! this is the meaning of your dancing with the Count!

COUNT [*stepping from the closet and advancing*]. I don't know what to make of it! Millinette not here! Miss Gertrude—oh! I see—a disguise—the girl's desperate about me—the way with them all. [*Aside.*]

TRUEMAN. I'm choking—I can't speak—

Gertrude—no—no—it is some horrid mistake! [*Partly aside, changes his tone suddenly.*] The villain! I'll hunt the truth out of him, if there's any in—[*Crosses, approaches* COUNT *threateningly.*] do you see this stick? You made its first acquaintance a few days ago; it is time you were better known to each other.

[*As* TRUEMAN *attempts to seize him,* COUNT *escapes, crosses, and shields himself behind* MRS. TIFFANY, TRUEMAN *following.*]

COUNT. You ruffian! would you strike a woman?—Madam—my dear Madam—keep off that barbarous old man, and I will explain! Madam, with—aw—your natural *bon gout*—aw—your fashionable refinement—aw—your—aw—your knowledge of *foreign customs*—

MRS. TIFFANY. Oh! Count, I hope it ain't a *foreign custom* for the nobility to shut themselves up in the dark with young women? We think such things *dreadful* in *America.*

COUNT. Demme—aw—hear what I have to say, Madam—I'll satisfy all sides—I am perfectly innocent in this affair—'pon my honor I am! That young lady shall inform you that I am so herself!—can't help it, sorry for her. Old matter-of-fact won't be convinced any other way,—that club of his is so particularly unpleasant! [*Aside.*] Madam, I was summoned here *malgré moi*, and not knowing whom I was to meet—Miss Gertrude, favor this company by saying whether or not you directed—that—aw—aw—that colored individual to conduct me here?

GERTRUDE. Sir, you well know—

COUNT. A simple yes or no will suffice.

MRS. TIFFANY. Answer the Count's question instantly, Miss.

GERTRUDE. I did—but—

TRUEMAN. I won't believe it—I can't! Here, you nigger, stop rolling up your eyes, and let us know whether she told you to bring that critter here?

ZEKE. I'se refuse to gib ebidence; dat's de device ob de skilfullest counsels ob de day! Can't answer, Boss—neber git a word out ob dis child—Yah! yah! [*Exit.*

GERTRUDE. Mrs. Tiffany,—Mr. Trueman, if you will but have patience—

TRUEMAN. Patience! Oh, Gertrude, you've taken from an old man something better and dearer than his patience—the one bright hope of nineteen years of self-denial—of nineteen years of—

[*Throws himself upon a chair, his head leaning on table.*]

MRS. TIFFANY. Get out of my house, you *ow*dacious—you ruined—you *abimé* young woman! You will corrupt all my family. Good gracious! don't touch me,—don't come near me. Never let me see your face after tomorrow. Pack. [*Goes up.*]

HOWARD. Gertrude, I have striven to find some excuse for you—to doubt—to disbelieve—but this is beyond all endurance! [*Exit.*

Enter MILLINETTE *in haste*

MILLINETTE. I could not come before—[*Stops in surprise at seeing the persons assembled.*] *Mon Dieu!* vat does dis mean?

COUNT. Hold your tongue, fool! You will ruin everything, I will explain tomorrow. [*Aside to her.*] Mrs. Tiffany—Madam—my dear Madam, let me conduct you back to the ball-room. [*She takes his arm.*] You see I am quite innocent in this matter; a man of my standing, you know,—aw, aw—you comprehend the whole affair.

[*Exit* COUNT *leading* MRS. TIFFANY.

MILLINETTE. I vill say to him von vord, I will! [*Exit.*

GERTRUDE. Mr. Trueman, I beseech you—I insist upon being heard,—I claim it as a right!

TRUEMAN. Right? How dare you have the face, girl, to talk of rights? You had more rights than you thought for, but you have forfeited them all! All right to love, respect, protection, and to not a little else that you don't dream of. Go, go! I'll start for Catteraugus tomorrow,—I've seen enough of what fashion can do! [*Exit.*

PRUDENCE [*wiping her eyes*]. Dear old man, how he takes on! I'll go and console him! [*Exit.*

GERTRUDE. This is too much! How heavy a penalty has my imprudence cost me!—his esteem, and that of one dearer—my home—my—[*Burst of lively music from ball-

room.] They are dancing, and I—I should be weeping, if pride had not sealed up my tears.

[*She sinks into a chair. Band plays the polka behind till Curtain falls.*]

END OF ACT IV

ACT V

SCENE I. MRS. TIFFANY'S *Drawing Room—same Scene as Act First.* GERTRUDE *seated at a table, with her head leaning on her hand; in the other she holds a pen. A sheet of paper and an inkstand before her.*

GERTRUDE. How shall I write to them? What shall I say? Prevaricate I cannot—[*Rises and comes forward.*] and yet if I write the truth—simple souls! how can they comprehend the motives for my conduct? Nay—the truly pure see no imaginary evil in others! It is only vice, that reflecting its own image, suspects even the innocent. I have no time to lose—I must prepare them for my return. [*Resumes her seat and writes.*] What a true pleasure there is in daring to be frank! [*After writing a few lines more pauses.*] Not so frank either,—there is one name that I cannot mention. Ah! that he should suspect—should despise me. [*Writes.*]

Enter TRUEMAN

TRUEMAN. There she is! If this girl's soul had only been as fair as her face,—yet she dared to speak the truth,—I'll not forget that! A woman who refuses to tell a lie has one spark of heaven in her still. [*Approaches her.*] Gertrude, [GERTRUDE *starts and looks up.*] what are you writing there? Plotting more mischief, eh, girl?

GERTRUDE. I was writing a few lines to some friends in Geneva.

TRUEMAN. The Wilsons, eh?

GERTRUDE [*surprised, rising*]. Are you acquainted with them, Sir?

TRUEMAN. I shouldn't wonder if I was. I suppose you have taken good care not to mention the dark room—that foreign puppy in the closet—the pleasant surprise—and all that sort of thing, eh?

GERTRUDE. I have no reason for concealment, Sir! for I have done nothing of which I am shamed!

TRUEMAN. Then I can't say much for your modesty.

GERTRUDE. I should not wish you to say more than I deserve.

TRUEMAN. There's a bold minx! [*Aside.*]

GERTRUDE. Since my affairs seem to have excited your interest—I will not say *curiosity*, perhaps you even feel a desire to inspect my correspondence? There, [*Handing the letter.*] I pride myself upon my good nature,—you may like to take advantage of it?

TRUEMAN. With what an air she carries it off! [*Aside.*] Take advantage of it? So I will. [*Reads.*] What's this? "French chambermaid— Count— impostor—infatuation—Seraphina—Millinette—disguised myself—expose him." Thunder and lightning! I see it all! Come and kiss me, girl! [GERTRUDE *evinces surprise.*] No, no—I forgot—it won't do to come to that yet! She's a rare girl! I'm out of my senses with joy! I don't know what to do with myself! Tol, de rol, de rol, de ra! [*Capers and sings.*]

GERTRUDE. What a remarkable old man! [*Aside.*] Then you do me justice, Mr. Trueman?

TRUEMAN. I say I don't! Justice! You're above all dependence upon justice! Hurrah! I've found one true woman at last! *True?* [*Pauses thoughtfully.*] Humph! I didn't think of that flaw! Plotting and manœuvering—not much truth in that? An honest girl should be above stratagems!

GERTRUDE. But my *motive*, Sir, was good.

TRUEMAN. That's not enough—your *actions* must be *good* as well as your *motives!* Why could you not tell the silly girl that the man was an impostor?

GERTRUDE. I did inform her of my suspicions—she ridiculed them; the plan I chose was an imprudent one, but I could not devise—

TRUEMAN. I hate devising! Give me a woman with the *firmness* to be *frank!* But no matter—I had no right to look for an angel out of Paradise; and I am as happy—as happy as a Lord! that is, ten times happier than any Lord ever was! Tol, de rol, de rol! Oh! you—you—I'll thrash every fellow that says a word against you!

GERTRUDE. You will have plenty of employment then, Sir, for I do not know of one just now who would speak in my favor!

TRUEMAN. Not *one*, eh? Why, where's your dear Mr. Twinkle? I know all about it—can't say that I admire your choice of a husband! But there's no accounting for a girl's taste.

GERTRUDE. Mr. Twinkle! Indeed you are quite mistaken!

TRUEMAN. No—really? Then you're not taken with him, eh?

GERTRUDE. Not even with his rhymes.

TRUEMAN. Hang that old mother meddlemuch! What a fool she has made of me. And so you're quite free, and I may choose a husband for you myself? Heart-whole, eh?

GERTRUDE. I—I—I trust there is nothing *unsound* about my heart.

TRUEMAN. There it is again. Don't prevaricate, girl! I tell you an *evasion* is a *lie in contemplation*, and I hate lying! Out with the truth! Is your heart *free* or not?

GERTRUDE. Nay, Sir, since you *demand* an answer, permit *me* to demand by what right you ask the question?

Enter HOWARD

Colonel Howard here!

TRUEMAN. I'm out again! What's the Colonel to her? [*Retires up.*]

HOWARD [*crosses to her*]. I have come, Gertrude, to bid you farewell. Tomorrow I resign my commission and leave this city, perhaps for ever. You, Gertrude, it is you who have exiled me! After last evening—

TRUEMAN [*coming forward to* HOWARD]. What the plague have you got to say about last evening?

HOWARD. Mr. Trueman!

TRUEMAN. What have you got to say about last evening? and what have you to say to that little girl at all? It's Tiffany's precious daughter you're in love with.

HOWARD. Miss Tiffany? Never! I never had the slightest pretension—

TRUEMAN. That lying old woman! But I'm glad of it! Oh! Ah! Um! [*Looking significantly at* GERTRUDE *and then at* HOWARD.] I see how it is. So you don't choose to marry Seraphina, eh? Well, now, whom do you choose to marry? [*Glancing at* GERTRUDE.]

HOWARD. I shall not marry at all!

TRUEMAN. You won't? [*Looking at them both again.*] Why, you don't mean to say that you don't like—

[*Points with his thumb to* GERTRUDE.]

GERTRUDE. Mr. Trueman, I may have been wrong to boast of my good nature, but do not presume too far upon it.

HOWARD. You like frankness, Mr. Trueman, therefore I will speak plainly. I have long cherished a dream from which I was last night rudely awakened.

TRUEMAN. And that's what you call speaking plainly? Well, I differ with you! But I can guess what you mean. Last night you suspected Gertrude there of—[*Angrily.*] of what no man shall ever suspect her again while I'm above ground! You did her injustice,—it was a mistake! There, now that matter's settled. Go, and ask her to forgive you,—she's woman enough to do it! Go, go!

HOWARD. Mr. Trueman, you have forgotten to whom you dictate.

TRUEMAN. Then you won't do it? you won't ask her pardon?

HOWARD. Most undoubtedly I will not—not at any man's bidding. I must first know—

TRUEMAN. You won't do it? Then if I don't give you a lesson in politeness—

HOWARD. It will be because you find me your *tutor* in the same science. I am not a man to brook an insult, Mr. Trueman! but we'll not quarrel in presence of the lady.

TRUEMAN. Won't we? I don't know that—

[*Crosses.*]

GERTRUDE. Pray, Mr. Trueman—Colonel Howard, pray desist, Mr. Trueman, for my sake! [*Taking hold of his arm to hold him back.*] Colonel Howard, if you will read this letter it will explain everything.

[*Hands letter to* HOWARD, *who reads.*]

TRUEMAN. He don't deserve an explanation! Didn't I tell him that it was a mistake? Refuse to beg your pardon! I'll teach him, I'll teach him!

HOWARD [*after reading*]. Gertrude, how have I wronged you!

TRUEMAN. Oh, you'll beg her pardon now? [*Between them.*]

HOWARD. Hers, Sir, and yours! Gertrude, I fear—

TRUEMAN. You needn't,—she'll forgive you. You don't know these women as well as I do,—they're always ready to pardon; it's their nature, and they can't help it. Come along, I left Antony and his wife in the dining room; we'll go and find them. I've a story of my own to tell! As for you, Colonel, you may follow. Come along, come along!

[*Leads out* GERTRUDE, *followed by* HOWARD.]

Enter MR. *and* MRS. TIFFANY, MR. TIFFANY *with a bundle of bills in his hand*

MRS. TIFFANY. I beg you won't mention the subject again, Mr. Tiffany. Nothing is more plebeian than a discussion upon economy—nothing more *ungenteel* than looking over and fretting over one's bills!

TIFFANY. Then I suppose, my dear, it is quite as ungenteel to *pay* one's bills?

MRS. TIFFANY. Certainly! I hear the *ee-light* never condescend to do anything of the kind. The honor of their invaluable patronage is sufficient for the persons they employ!

TIFFANY. *Patronage* then is a newly invented food upon which the working classes fatten? What convenient appetites poor people must have! Now listen to what I am going to say. As soon as my daughter marries Mr. Snobson—

Enter PRUDENCE, *a three-cornered note in her hand*

PRUDENCE. Oh, dear! oh, dear! what shall we do! Such a misfortune! Such a disaster! Oh, dear! oh, dear!

MRS. TIFFANY. Prudence, you are the most tiresome creature! What *is* the matter?

PRUDENCE [*pacing up and down the stage*]. Such a disgrace to the whole family! But I always expected it. Oh, dear! oh, dear!

MRS. TIFFANY [*following her up and down the stage*]. What are you talking about, Prudence? Will you tell me what has happened?

PRUDENCE [*still pacing*, MRS. TIFFANY *following*]. Oh! I can't, I can't! You'll feel so dreadfully! How could she do such a thing! But I expected nothing else! I never did, I never did!

MRS. TIFFANY [*still following*]. Good gracious! what do you mean, Prudence? Tell me, will you tell me? I shall get into such a passion! What *is* the matter?

PRUDENCE [*still pacing*]. Oh, Betsy, Betsy! That your daughter should have come to that! Dear me, dear me!

TIFFANY. Seraphina? Did you say Seraphina? What has happened to her? what has she done?

[*Following* PRUDENCE *up and down the stage on the opposite side from* MRS. TIFFANY.]

MRS. TIFFANY [*still following*]. What *has* she done? what *has* she done?

PRUDENCE Oh! something dreadful—dreadful—shocking!

TIFFANY [*still following*]. Speak quickly and plainly—you torture me by this delay,—Prudence, be calm, and speak! What is it?

PRUDENCE [*stopping*]. Zeke just told me—he carried her travelling trunk himself—she gave him a whole dollar! Oh, my!

TIFFANY. Her trunk? where? where?

PRUDENCE. Round the corner!

MRS. TIFFANY. What did she want with her trunk? You are the most vexatious creature, Prudence! There is no bearing your ridiculous conduct!

PRUDENCE. Oh, you will have worse to bear—worse! Seraphina's gone!

TIFFANY. Gone! where?

PRUDENCE. Off!—eloped—eloped with the Count! Dear me, dear me! I always told you she would!

TIFFANY. Then I am ruined!

[*Stands with his face buried in his hands.*]

MRS. TIFFANY. Oh, what a ridiculous girl! And she might have had such a splendid wedding! What could have possessed her?

TIFFANY. The devil himself possessed her, for she has ruined me past all redemption! Gone, Prudence, did you say gone? Are you *sure* they are gone?

PRUDENCE. Didn't I tell you so! Just look at this note—one might know by the very fold of it—

TIFFANY [*snatching the note*]. Let me see it! [*Opens the note and reads.*] "My dear Ma,—When you receive this I shall be a *countess!*

Isn't it a sweet title? The Count and I were forced to be married privately, for reasons which I will explain in my next. You must pacify Pa, and put him in a good humor before I come back, though now I'm to be a countess I suppose I shouldn't care!" Undutiful huzzy! "We are going to make a little excursion and will be back in a week.

"Your dutiful daughter—Seraphina."

A man's curse is sure to spring up at his own hearth,—here is mine! The sole curb upon that villain gone, I am wholly in his power! Oh! the first downward step from honor—he who takes it cannot pause in his mad descent and is sure to be hurried on to ruin!

MRS. TIFFANY. Why, Mr. Tiffany, how you do take on! And I dare say to elope was the most fashionable way after all!

Enter TRUEMAN, *leading* GERTRUDE, *and followed by* HOWARD

TRUEMAN. Where are all the folks? Here, Antony, you are the man I want. We've been hunting for you all over the house. Why—what's the matter? There's a face for a thriving city merchant! Ah! Antony, you never wore such a hang-dog look as that when you trotted about the country with your pack upon your back! Your shoulders are no broader now—but they've a heavier load to carry—that's plain!

MRS. TIFFANY. Mr. Trueman, such allusions are highly improper! What would my daughter, *the Countess*, say!

GERTRUDE. The Countess? Oh! Madam!

MRS. TIFFANY. Yes, the Countess! My daughter Seraphina, the Countess *dee* Jolimaitre! What have you to say to that? No wonder you are surprised after your *recherché*, *abimé* conduct! I have told you already, Miss Gertrude, that you were not a proper person to enjoy the inestimable advantages of my patronage. You are dismissed—do you understand? Discharged!

TRUEMAN. Have you done? Very well, it's my turn now. Antony, perhaps what I have to say don't concern you as much as some others—but I want you to listen to me. You remember, Antony, [*His tone becomes serious.*] a blue-eyed, smiling girl—

TIFFANY. Your daughter, Sir? I remember her well.

TRUEMAN. None ever saw her to forget her! Give me your hand, man. There—that will do! Now let me go on. I never coveted wealth—yet twenty years ago I found myself the richest farmer in Catteraugus. This cursed money made my girl an object of speculation. Every idle fellow that wanted to feather his nest was sure to come courting Ruth. There was one—my heart misgave me the instant I laid eyes upon him—for he was a city chap, and not over fond of the truth. But Ruth—ah! she was too pure herself to look for guile! His fine words and his fair looks—the old story—she was taken with him—I said, "no"—but the girl liked her own way better than her old father's—girls always do! and one morning—the rascal robbed me—not of my money, he would have been welcome to that—but of the only treasure I cherished—my daughter!

TIFFANY. But you forgave her!

TRUEMAN. I did! I knew she would never forgive herself—that was punishment enough! The scoundrel thought he was marrying my gold with my daughter—he was mistaken! I took care that they should never want; but that was all. She loved him—what will not woman love? The villain broke her heart—mine was tougher, or it wouldn't have stood what it did. A year after they were married, he forsook her! She came back to her old home—her old father! It couldn't last long—she pined—and pined—and—then—she died! Don't think me an old fool—though I am one—for grieving won't bring her back. [*Bursts into tears.*]

TIFFANY. It was a heavy loss!

TRUEMAN. So heavy, that I should not have cared how soon I followed her, but for the child she left! As I pressed that child in my arms, I swore that my unlucky wealth should never curse it, as it had cursed its mother! It was all I had to love—but I sent it away—and the neighbors thought it was dead. The girl was brought up tenderly but humbly by my wife's relatives in Geneva. I had her taught true independence—she had hands—capacities—and should use them! Money should never buy her a husband! for I resolved not to claim her until she had made her choice, and found the man who was willing to take her for herself alone. She turned out a rare girl! and it's time her old grandfather claimed her. Here he is to do it! And there stands Ruth's child! Old Adam's heiress! Gertrude, Gertrude!—my child!

[GERTRUDE *rushes into his arms.*]

PRUDENCE [*after a pause*]. Do tell; I want to know! But I knew it! I always said Gertrude would turn out somebody, after all!

MRS. TIFFANY. Dear me! Gertrude an heiress! My dear Gertrude, I always thought you a very charming girl—quite YOUNICK—an heiress! I must give her a ball! I'll introduce her into society myself—of course an heiress must make a sensation! [*Aside.*]

HOWARD. I am too bewildered even to wish her joy. Ah! there will be plenty to do that now—but the gulf between us is wider than ever. [*Aside.*]

TRUEMAN. Step forward, young man, and let us know what you are muttering about. I said I would never claim her until she had found the man who loved her for herself. I *have* claimed her—yet I never break my word—I think I *have* found that man! and here he is. [*Strikes* HOWARD *on the shoulder.*] Gertrude's yours! There—never say a word, man—don't bore me with your thanks—you can cancel all obligations by making that child happy! There—take her!—Well, girl, and what do you say?

GERTRUDE. That I rejoice too much at having found a parent for my first act to be one of disobedience!

[*Gives her hand to* HOWARD.]

TRUEMAN. How very dutiful! and how disinterested!

[TIFFANY *retires up—and paces the stage, exhibiting great agitation.*]

PRUDENCE [*to* TRUEMAN]. All the *single folks* are getting married!

TRUEMAN. No, they are not. You and I are single folks, and we're not likely to get married.

MRS. TIFFANY. My dear Mr. Trueman—my sweet Gertrude, when my daughter, the Countess, returns, she will be delighted to hear of this *deenooment!* I assure you that the Countess will be quite charmed!

GERTRUDE. The Countess? Pray, Madam, where *is* Seraphina?

MRS. TIFFANY. The Countess *dee* Jolimaitre, my dear, is at this moment on her way to—to Washington! Where after visiting all the fashionable curiosities of the day—including the President—she will return to grace her native city!

GERTRUDE. I hope you are only jesting, Madam? Seraphina is not married?

MRS. TIFFANY. Excuse me, my dear, my daughter had this morning the honor of being united to the Count *dee* Jolimaitre!

GERTRUDE. Madam! He is an impostor!

MRS. TIFFANY. Good gracious! Gertrude, how can you talk in that disrespectful way of a man of rank? An heiress, my dear, should have better manners! The Count—

Enter MILLINETTE, *crying*

MILLINETTE. Oh! Madame! I will tell everyting—oh! dat *monstre!* He break my heart!

MRS. TIFFANY. Millinette, what is the matter?

MILLINETTE. Oh! he promise to marry me—I love him much—and now Zeke say he run away vid Mademoiselle Seraphina!

MRS. TIFFANY. What insolence! The girl is mad! Count Jolimaitre marry my *femmy de chamber!*

MILLINETTE. Oh! Madam, he is not one Count, not at all! Dat is only de title he go by in dis country. De foreigners always take de large title ven dey do come here. His name *à Paris* vas Gustave Tread-mill. But he not one Frenchman at all, but he do live one long time *à Paris*. First he live vid Monsieur Vermicelle—dere he vas de head cook! Den he live vid Monsieur Tire-nez, de barber! After dat he live vid Monsieur le Comte Frippon-fin—and dere he vas le Comte's valet! Dere, now I tell everyting I feel one great deal better!

MRS. TIFFANY. Oh! good gracious! I shall faint! Not a Count! What will every body say? It's no such thing! I say he *is* a Count! One can see the foreign *jenny says quoi* in his face! Don't you think I can tell a Count when I see one? I say he *is* a Count!

Enter SNOBSON, *his hat on—his hands thrust in his pocket—evidently a little intoxicated*

SNOBSON. I won't stand it! I say I won't!

TIFFANY [*rushing up to him*]. Mr. Snobson, for heaven's sake—[*Aside.*]

SNOBSON. Keep off! I'm a hard customer to get the better of! You'll see if I don't come out strong!

TRUEMAN [*quietly knocking off* SNOBSON'S *hat with his stick*]. Where are your manners, man?

SNOBSON. My business ain't with you, Catteraugus; you've waked up the wrong passenger!—Now the way I'll put it into Tiff will be a caution. I'll make him wince! That extra mint julep has put the true pluck in me. Now for it! [*Aside.*] Mr. Tiffany, Sir—you needn't think to come over me, Sir—you'll have to get up a little earlier in the morning before you do *that*, Sir! I'd like to know, Sir, how you came to assist your daughter in running away with that foreign loafer? It was a downright swindle, Sir. After the conversation I and you had on that subject she wasn't your property, Sir.

TRUEMAN. What, Antony, is that the way your city clerk bullies his boss?

SNOBSON. You're drunk, Catteraugus—don't expose yourself—you're drunk! Taken a little too much toddy, my old boy! Be quiet! I'll look after you, and they won't find it out. If you want to be busy, you may take care of my *hat*—I feel so deuced weak in the chest, I don't think I *could* pick it up myself.—Now to put the screws to Tiff. [*Aside.*] Mr. Tiffany, Sir—you have broken your word, as no virtuous individual—no honorable member—of—the—com—mu—ni—ty—

TIFFANY. Have some pity, Mr. Snobson, I beseech you! I had nothing to do with my daughter's elopement! I will agree to anything you desire—your salary shall be doubled—trebled—[*Aside to him.*]

SNOBSON [*aloud*]. No, you don't. No bribery and corruption.

TIFFANY. I implore you to be silent. You shall become partner of the concern, if you please—only do not speak. You are not yourself at this moment. [*Aside to him.*]

SNOBSON. Ain't I, though? I feel *twice* myself. I feel like two Snobsons rolled into one, and I'm chock full of the spunk of a dozen! Now, Mr. Tiffany, Sir—

TIFFANY. I shall go distracted! Mr. Snobson, if you have one spark of manly feeling— [*Aside to him.*]

TRUEMAN. Antony, why do you stand disputing with that drunken jackass? Where's your nigger? Let him kick the critter out, and be of use for once in his life.

SNOBSON. Better be quiet, Catteraugus. This ain't your hash, so keep your spoon out of the dish. Don't expose yourself, old boy.

TRUEMAN. Turn him out, Antony!

SNOBSON. He daren't do it! Ain't I up to him? Ain't he in my power? Can't I knock him into a cocked hat with a word? And now he's got my steam up—I *will* do it!

TIFFANY [*beseechingly*]. Mr. Snobson—my friend—

SNOBSON. It's no go—steam's up—and I don't stand at anything!

TRUEMAN. You won't *stand* here long unless you mend your manners—you're not the first man I've *upset* because he didn't know his place.

SNOBSON. I know where Tiff's place is, and that's in the *States' Prison!* It's bespoke already. He would have it! He wouldn't take pattern of me, and behave like a gentleman! He's a *forger*, Sir! [TIFFANY *throws himself into a chair in an attitude of despair; the others stand transfixed with astonishment.*] He's been forging Dick Anderson's endorsements of his notes these ten months. He's got a couple in the bank that will send him to the wall any how—if he can't make a raise. I took them there myself! Now you know what he's worth. I said I'd expose him, and I have done it!

MRS. TIFFANY. Get out of the house! You ugly, little, drunken brute, get out! It's not true. Mr. Trueman, put him out; you have got a stick—put him out!

Enter SERAPHINA, *in her bonnet and shawl—a parasol in her hand*

SERAPHINA. I hope Zeke hasn't delivered my note.

[*Stops in surprise at seeing the persons assembled.*]

MRS. TIFFANY. Oh, here is the Countess! [*Advances to embrace her.*]

TIFFANY [*starting from his seat, and seizing* SERAPHINA *violently by the arm*]. Are—you—married?

SERAPHINA. Goodness, Pa, how you frighten me! No, I'm not married, *quite.*

TIFFANY. Thank heaven.

MRS. TIFFANY [*drawing* SERAPHINA *aside*]. What's the matter? Why did you come back?

SERAPHINA. The clergyman wasn't at home—I came back for my jewels—the Count said nobility couldn't get on without them.

TIFFANY. I may be saved yet! Seraphina, my child, you will not see me disgraced—ruined! I have been a kind father to you—at least I have tried to be one—although your mother's extravagance made a *madman* of me! The Count is an impostor—you seemed to like him—[*Pointing to* SNOBSON.] Heaven forgive me! [*Aside.*] Marry *him* and save *me.* You, Mr. Trueman, you will be my friend in this hour of extreme need—you will advance the sum which I require—I pledge myself to return it. My wife—my child—who will support them were I—the thought makes me frantic! You will aid me? You had a child yourself.

TRUEMAN. But I did not *sell* her—it was her own doings. Shame on you, Antony! Put a price on your own flesh and blood! Shame on such foul traffic!

TIFFANY. Save me—I conjure you—for my father's sake.

TRUEMAN. For your *father's* SON's sake I will *not* aid you in becoming a greater villain than you are!

GERTRUDE. Mr. Trueman—Father, I should say—save him—do not embitter our happiness by permitting this calamity to fall upon another—

TRUEMAN. Enough—I did not need your voice, child. I am going to settle this matter my own way.

[*Goes up to* SNOBSON—*who has seated himself and fallen asleep—tilts him out of the chair.*]

SNOBSON [*waking up*]. Eh? Where's the fire? Oh! it's you, Catteraugus.

TRUEMAN. If I comprehend aright, you have been for some time aware of your principal's forgeries?

[*As he says this, he beckons to* HOWARD, *who advances as witness.*]

SNOBSON. You've hit the nail, Catteraugus! Old chap saw that I was up to him six months ago; left off throwing dust into my eyes—

TRUEMAN. Oh, he did!

SNOBSON. Made no bones of forging Anderson's name at my elbow.

TRUEMAN. Forged at your elbow? You saw him do it?

SNOBSON. I did.

TRUEMAN. Repeatedly?

SNOBSON. Re—pea—ted—ly.

TRUEMAN. Then you, Rattlesnake, if he goes to the States' Prison, you'll take up your quarters there too. You are an accomplice, an *accessory!*

[TRUEMAN *walks away and seats himself,* HOWARD *rejoins* GERTRUDE. SNOBSON *stands for some time bewildered.*]

SNOBSON. The deuce, so I am! I never thought of that! I must make myself scarce. I'll be off! Tif, I say, Tif! [*Going up to him and speaking confidentially.*] that drunken old rip has got us in his power. Let's give him the slip and be off. They want men of genius at the West,—we're sure to get on! You—you can set up for a writing master, and teach copying *signatures;* and I—I'll give lectures on *temperance!* You won't come, eh? Then I'm off without you. Good bye, Catteraugus! Which is the way to California? [*Steals off.*]

TRUEMAN. There's one debt your city owes me. And now let us see what other nuisances we can abate. Antony, I'm not given to preaching, therefore I shall not say much about what you have done. Your face speaks for itself,—the crime has brought its punishment along with it.

TIFFANY. Indeed it has, Sir! In *one year* I have lived a *century* of misery.

TRUEMAN. I believe you, and upon one condition I will assist you—

TIFFANY. My friend—my first, ever kind friend,—only name it!

TRUEMAN. You must sell your house and all

these gew gaws, and bundle your wife and daughter off to the country. There let them learn economy, true independence, and home virtues, instead of foreign follies. As for yourself, continue your business—but let moderation, in future, be your counsellor, and let *honesty* be your confidential clerk.

TIFFANY. Mr. Trueman, you have made existence once more precious to me! My wife and daughter shall quit the city tomorrow, and—

PRUDENCE. It's all coming right! It's all coming right! We'll go to the county of Catteraugus. [*Walking up to* TRUEMAN.]

TRUEMAN. No, you won't,—I make that a stipulation, Antony; keep clear of Catteraugus. None of your fashionable examples there!

JOLIMAITRE *appears in the Conservatory and peeps into the room unperceived*

COUNT. What can detain Seraphina? We ought to be off!

MILLINETTE [*turns round, perceives him, runs and forces him into the room*]. Here he is! Ah, Gustave, *mon cher* Gustave! I have you now and we never part no more. Don't frown, Gustave, don't frown—

TRUEMAN. Come forward, Mr. Count! and for the edification of fashionable society confess that you're an impostor.

COUNT. An impostor? Why, you abominable old—

TRUEMAN. Oh, your feminine friend has told us all about it, the cook—the valet—barber and all that sort of thing. Come, confess, and something may be done for you.

COUNT. Well, then, I do confess I am no count; but really, ladies and gentlemen, I may recommend myself as the most capital cook.

MRS. TIFFANY. Oh, Seraphina!

SERAPHINA. Oh, Ma! [*They embrace and retire up.*]

TRUEMAN. Promise me to call upon the whole circle of your fashionable acquaintances with your own advertisements and in your cook's attire, and I will set you up in business tomorrow. Better turn stomachs than turn heads!

MILLINETTE. But you will marry me?

COUNT. Give us your hand, Millinette! Sir, command me for the most delicate *paté*—the daintiest *croquette à la royale*—the most transcendent *omelette soufflée* that ever issued from a French pastry-cook's oven. I hope you will pardon my conduct, but I heard that in America, where you pay homage to titles while you profess to scorn them—where *Fashion* makes the basest coin current—where you have no kings, no princes, no *nobility*—

TRUEMAN. Stop there! I object to your use of that word. When justice is found only among lawyers—health among physicians—and patriotism among politicians, *then* may you say that there is no *nobility* where there are no titles! But we *have* kings, princes, and nobles in abundance—of *Nature's stamp*, if not of *Fashion's*,—we have honest men, warm hearted and brave, and we have women—gentle, fair, and true, to whom no *title* could add *nobility*.

EPILOGUE

PRUDENCE. I told you so! And now you hear and see.
I told you *Fashion* would the fashion be!
TRUEMAN. Then both its point and moral I distrust.
COUNT. Sir, is that liberal?
HOWARD. Or is it just?
TRUEMAN. The guilty have escaped!
TIFFANY. Is, therefore, sin
Made charming? Ah! there's punishment within!
Guilt ever carries his own scourge along.
GERTRUDE. Virtue her own reward!
TRUEMAN. You're right, I'm wrong.
MRS. TIFFANY. How we have been deceived!
PRUDENCE. I told you so.
SERAPHINA. To lose at once a title and a beau!
COUNT. A count no more, I'm no more of *account*.
TRUEMAN. But to a nobler title you may mount,
And be in time—who knows?—an honest man!
COUNT. Eh, Millinette?

MILLINETTE. Oh, *oui,*—I know you can!

GERTRUDE [*to audience*]. But, ere we close the scene, a word with you,—

We charge you answer,—Is this picture true?

Some little mercy to our efforts show,

Then let the world your honest verdict know.

Here let it see portrayed its ruling passion,

And learn to prize at its just value—*Fashion.*

THE END

FRANCESCA DA RIMINI

By George Henry Boker

GEORGE HENRY BOKER

[1823–1890]

George Henry Boker was born in Philadelphia on October 6, 1823;[1] he was brought up in a home of comfortable means, gracious living, and conservative atmosphere. In his boyhood and youth he was educated by a tutor and attended a private school; much of his reading was in romantic literature, including such names as Cooper, Bulwer-Lytton, Irving, Scott, and Byron. Boker's father was not influenced by the Quakerism of Philadelphia and he frequently took his son to the theatre, where the impressionable youth soon developed a taste for the plays and an acquaintance with the players.

At the age of fifteen Boker entered the College of New Jersey (now Princeton) where he read widely in English, French, and Italian literature, partly at the invitation of the school and partly on his own initiative; he especially admired the Elizabethans, Shakespeare most of all. During his residence at college, the *Nassau Literary Monthly* was begun; to this Boker contributed several poems, including three sonnets, a form which he later mastered to a high degree.

Upon his graduation in 1842 he was offered a diplomatic post at Vienna and also had the opportunity of going into his father's successful banking business; he declined both for fear that they might interfere with his chosen career as an author, but he later agreed to read law as a compromise. This apprenticeship lasted only two years, however, until his marriage to Julia Riggs in 1844. From this time on he devoted much of his energy to writing, though he was active in the "civilian army" of the North during the Civil War. He later served during the years from 1871 to 1878 as American Minister first to Turkey and then to Russia, thus joining the ranks of the numerous distinguished men of letters who have served as ambassadors to foreign countries. His death occurred January 2, 1890.

His first book of poetry, *A Lesson of Life*, appeared in 1848 and included five sonnets as well as some poems in blank verse. His first play, *Calaynos*, produced in 1849, is a romantic tragedy of medieval Spain; it is concerned with a noble, studious Spanish lord, of Moorish extraction, who finds his peaceful country estate invaded by tragedy in the person of an unscrupulous gambler whom Calaynos has befriended. The Spanish hatred of Moorish blood forms part of the motivation in the play. Conflict between vice and virtue, and the problem of

[1] Edward Sculley Bradley's *George Henry Boker: Poet and Patriot* (Philadelphia: 1927) is the definitive life of the dramatist; it is used as the authority for the biographical facts here presented.

evil in a world of Divine origin, are effectively dealt with in this moving drama. Parts of the play are reminiscent of *The Merchant of Venice*, and Boker's blank verse frequently attains that Shakespearean quality of organic relevancy. *Calaynos* was successful on the stage both in England and America.

Anne Boleyn, written in 1849 but not produced, is an historic romance in blank verse recounting the decline of Anne, her questionable trial, and her consequent execution. Conspicuous among the characters of the play, and among the lovers of Anne, is Sir Thomas Wyatt, whom Boker pictures sympathetically and, as one would expect, poetically. *The Betrothal*, Boker's most successful comedy, was produced in 1850, and *All the World a Mask*, a social satire, appeared on the stage the following year. Two inferior plays, *The Bankrupt* and *The Sycophant*, were written during this period. *The Widow's Marriage*, a social comedy of the time of George II, was written in 1852 but not published until four years later. *Leonor de Guzman* (1853) is a tragedy based on the "Spanish Chronicles relating to the reign of Alfonso XII and his son, Pedro of Castile."[1] It portrays the conflict, after the death of Alfonso, between his wife, Maria, and his mistress, Leonor; directing the interplay of plot on plot are the subtle maneuverings of an ambitious prime minister and also the outraged feelings of a displaced wife. Strong as *Leonor de Guzman* is in its dramatic and poetic power, it did not enjoy the stage success of some of Boker's other plays.

Francesca da Rimini, the best as well as the most successful of Boker's plays, was written in 1853 and put on the stage in 1855. The revival of *Francesca da Rimini* in 1882 led Boker to write two other plays on the same subject, *Nydia* and *Glaucus*, written in 1885–1886.

Francesca da Rimini belongs to romantic literature because of its emphasis on feeling, as in the central Paolo and Francesca theme and in Lanciotto's pathetic bid for beauty; because of its recovery of the past (medieval Italy); because of its representation of the mysterious (the sword leaping from its scabbard to the oaken floor); and because of its colorful, striking language. The play belongs to its age, one of romantic literature. In the field of the drama Charles James Cannon was dealing with Irish history in *The Oath of Office* (1850), as was James Pilgrim in *Robert Emmet* (1853); *The Italian Bride* was published anonymously in 1856 and in the next year appeared *Leonora, or the World's Own*, by Julia Ward Howe, set in Italy during the early eighteenth century; *Fate, or the Prophecy*, by Oliver Bell Bunce, appeared in 1856 and its scene was "Altenburg in the Early Feudal Times."[2] Prominent among the writers of romantic verse were Bryant, Taylor (a close friend of Boker's), Whittier, Lowell (lover of Italy and Dante), Longfellow (devoted to the New England past and translator of

[1] Letter from Boker to Bayard Taylor, Nov. 25, 1852.

[2] See Quinn, *A History of the American Drama from the Beginning to the Civil War*, p. 364. Cf. ch. XII for treatment of romantic tragedies.

Dante); in the field of the romantic novel were Hawthorne, Simms, and Melville.

Sharing a quality with Shakespearean drama, *Francesca da Rimini* is not all of a color; though dominantly romantic, it contains numerous passages which could proceed only from realistic thinking. The character of Lanciotto (which will be discussed more fully later) is conspicuous in this respect: to be noted especially is his scalpel-like treatment of Seneca's consolation for cripples:

"Doubtless he can tell,
As he skips nimbly through his dancing-girls,
How sad it is to limp about the world
A sightless cripple! Let him feel the crutch
Wearing against his heart, and then I'd hear
This sage talk glibly; or provide a pad,
Stuffed with his soft philosophy, to ease
His aching shoulder." [1]

It was in the midst of consuming romance that Romeo said:

"He jests at scars, that never felt a wound."

With skillful blending, Boker introduces into the atmosphere of medievalism a philosophic concept ordinarily beyond the range of romantic speculation and evidencing Boker's insight into social forces whose meaning and significance had engaged the attention of penetrating thinkers. Fontenelle, in his *Dialogues of the Dead* (1683), had said:

"The heart always the same, the intellect perfecting itself; passions, virtues, vices unaltered; knowledge increasing." [2]

Lanciotto remarks to Pepe, the jester:

"Mechanic means advance;
Nature bows down to science' haughty tread,
And turns the wheel of smutty artifice;
New governments arise, dilate, decay,
And foster creeds and churches to their tastes;
At each advance, we cry, 'Behold, the end!'
Till some fresh wonder breaks upon the age.
But man, the moral creature, midst it all
Stands still unchanged; nor moves towards virtue more,
Nor comprehends the mysteries in himself,
More than when Plato taught academies,
Or Zeno thundered from his Attic porch." [3]

No evidence appears that Boker read Fontenelle, but "Condorcet, Voltaire and the satires of Juvenal opened up new realms of thought. . . ." [4] It is not in a

[1] Act III, sc. 1, p. 305.

[2] Fontenelle, Bernard le Bovier de. *Œuvres Choisies.* Londres, J. M. Dent & Sons, p. 145.

[3] Act III, sc. 1, p. 306.

[4] Bradley, *op. cit.*, p. 17. See J. B. Bury, *The Idea of Progress*, New York, 1932.

proselytizing temper that this idea is advanced, however, for a few moments later Pepe's mock-zeal for reform, "I have an itching to reform the world," elicits from Lanciotto the admonition: "Begin at home, then."

The concept of duality in man's nature appears:

"These mystic shades
Are of the earth; the light that causes them,
And teaches us the quick comparison,
Is all from heaven. Ah! restless man might crawl
With patience through his shadowy destiny,
If he were senseless to the higher light
Towards which his soul aspires." [1]

When Lanciotto is at last convinced that Paolo and Francesca may be in love, he wishes to be reassured that he is calm before seeking them out:

"You see
No trace of passion on my face?—No sign
Of ugly humors, doubts, or fears, or aught
That may disfigure God's intelligence?" [2]

It appears that man is not necessarily good in a state of nature, for nature will

"make fifty kings—
Good, hearty tyrants, sound, cruel governors—
For one fine fool." [3]

A parallel thought is reflected in a sonnet belonging to the series recently discovered by E. S. Bradley:

"Oh! surely this is cause for honest pride,
And long thanksgiving to the hand above;
That through coarse clay and coarser lusts can move
His chosen one to ends so pure and wide." [4]

But still, physical nature seems to be related to Divinity:

"Magnificent,
O God, art thou amid the sunsets!" [5]

Political rivalry and bargaining, especially when human beings are employed as counters, can lead directly to tragedy; at the deaths of Paolo and Francesca, Lanciotto says to Malatesta and Guido, the rival lords:

"You two
Began this tragedy." [6]

[1] Act V, sc. 2, p. 324.

[2] Act V, sc. 2, p. 328. In his biography, Bradley speaks of Boker's "patrician self-control" which he exhibited through life. (*Op. cit.*, p. 40.)

[3] Act V, sc. 1, p. 320.

[4] *Sonnets: a Sequence on Profane Love.* Philadelphia: 1929. Ed. by Edward Sculley Bradley. Sonnet LXIII, p. 48. This series of Boker's sonnets, recently brought to light by Bradley, places Boker second only to Longellow as an American sonnet writer. See also L. G. Sterner, *The Sonnet in American Literature*, Philadelphia, 1930.

[5] Act V, sc. 2, p. 324.

[6] Act V, sc. 3, p. 331.

In the character of Pepe, Boker toys with an idea of commonwealth that has well-nigh become a political theory in some quarters:

"I'd have no families, no Malatesti,
Strutting about the land, with pedigrees
And claims bequeathed them by their ancestors;
No fellows vaporing of their royal blood;
No one to seize a whole inheritance,
And rob the other children of the earth.
By Jove! you should not know your fathers, even!
I'd have you spring, like toadstools, from the soil—
Mere sons of women—nothing more nor less—
All base-born, and all equal. There, my lord,
There is a simple commonwealth for you!" [1]

Francesca da Rimini, as well as other plays of Boker, bears a direct relationship to his life and it is probable that the Paolo story adumbrates a situation in Boker's own experience. In *Francesca da Rimini*, composed between March 1 and March 21, 1853, we have the situation of Paolo's love for Francesca rendered illegal by her betrothal and marriage to Lanciotto; in this social barrier resides the Nemesis which controls the course of their loves. Judging by a sonnet series begun in 1851 and completed in all probability by 1854, Boker was enamored of a "dear maid," "the sun whence all my light doth flow," "the fount of every feeling, slow or fleet," [2] and it is evident from the sonnets themselves that "the harsh world's command" stands between the poet and the one whom he had loved "beyond the prudent line."

So if we are to accept these sonnets at their face value, it appears that the inner conflict of Paolo has its poignant counterpart in Boker's own experience. That the whole series is a piece of Renaissance imagination is a possibility suggested by Bradley in his biography of Boker,[3] but two years later when he published the newly-discovered sonnet sequence, he accepted their validity and went so far as to identify the woman addressed. The psychology of the writer as revealed in the sonnets points to the reality of the experience:

"No lyric song, no stately tragedy,
  No cry of joy nor pain, but shall be rife
  With thy sweet self. More close than man to wife
Shall we be joined through all futurity.
Doubt not the issue. While my melody
  Shall move the world, in each applauded lay
  Men shall behold my love's undimmed display . . ." [4]

In this sonnet series and in its probable continuation, the series unearthed by Bradley, we find a close parallel of emotional reaction with that delineated in

[1] Act III, sc. 1, p. 306.

[2] Boker, George H. *Plays and Poems*, Boston: 1856, II, 398.

[3] *George Henry Boker*, pp. 317 ff.

[4] Boker, *Plays and Poems*, II, 441.

Francesca da Rimini: there is an alternation between self-condemnation for "our sin" and self-justification for having touched "the height of human bliss"; there is also that "dark prophetic soul," that sense of "coming fears," together with a headlong defiance of the "sharp rebound" from the "spite of fate"; and we find too the feeling that their love has been a reality which will survive all vicissitudes:

> "If they cast us, now,
> Amid the furies, shall we not go down
> With rich ambrosia clinging to our lips,
> And richer memories settled in our hearts?" [1]

Or, this passage from the sonnets:

> "I, like a victor, hold these glories fast;
> . . . .
> For, with this myrtle symbol of my love,
> I reign exultant, and am fixed above
> The petty fates that other joys consume." [2]

The lovers welcome death in the midst of ecstasy:

> " 'Come, strike me now!—
> Now, while I hold my kingdom, while my crown
> Of amaranth and myrtle is yet green
> Undimmed, unwithered. . . .' " [3]

With this close interlocking of emotional psychology, there can be little doubt that the Paolo-Francesca theme is in a large measure the dramatic form of the sonnet material, and since the sonnets themselves embody relationships "actual rather than imaginary," as Bradley affirms, it is with factual and, it may be added, aesthetic justification that one can speak of *Francesca da Rimini* as the "life blood of a master spirit."

Especially striking among the characters in Boker's play is Lanciotto. In Boccaccio's account,[4] which Boker drew upon, Lanciotto was a "man of great spirit," "rude in appearance and a cripple." Though some of the versions of the story do not retain the deformity of Lanciotto (as in Hunt's *Story of Rimini*), it becomes a controlling concept in Boker's character. The galling consciousness of his "gnarled, blighted trunk," his "broken hip," and "huge swart arms" besets Lanciotto at almost every turn, even from the first proposal of the match:

> "I, the great twisted monster of the wars,
> The brawny cripple, the herculean dwarf,
> . . . .
> I be a bridegroom!"

[1] Act V, sc. 1, p. 323.

[2] *Plays and Poems*, II, 450.

[3] Act V, sc. 1, p. 323.

[4] Boccaccio, Giovanni. *Il Comento Alla Divina Commedia*. Bari: 1918. Volume secondo, pp. 137–146. Appears in translation in Longfellow's *The Divine Comedy*. Boston: 1913, p. 127.

to the point when he at length comes to hope for Francesca's love:

"What heart in Rimini is softened now,
Towards my defects?"

This continual affliction, played upon by a probing intellect, lies back of Lanciotto's vivid sense of reality, his exposure of sham or artificiality. His rejection of Seneca's philosophy has already been referred to; in Lanciotto's attempt at suicide Paolo stays his hand and admonishes him for his act, reminding him that "we're bound Life into life, a chain of loving hearts," but Lanciotto, in a passage uncannily Shakespearean, is of another mind about the "loving hearts":

"I know the seasons of our human grief,
And can predict them without almanac.
A few sobs o'er the body, and a few
Over the coffin; then a sigh or two,
Whose windy passage dries the hanging tear;
Perchance, some wandering memories, some regrets;
Then a vast influx of consoling thoughts—
Based on the trials of the sadder days
Which the dead missed; and then a smiling face
Turned on tomorrow. Such is mortal grief." [1]

Lanciotto strips the "vestal whiteness" from the judge, from the priest, from the doctor, from the soldier, from himself; in his relationship with Francesca he tries repeatedly to be honest with himself:

"Dreams, dreams! Poor fools, we squander love away
On thankless borrowers. . . ."

But this visitation of loveliness gives him a glimpse of something he has never known, and though he is one who exalts self-control, yet

". . . 'tis sweet,
Sweeter than slumber to the lids of pain,
To fancy that a shadow of true love
May fall on this God-stricken mould of woe,
From so serene a nature."

When he surprises Paolo and Francesca in a kiss, he desperately pleads, well knowing the futility of his hope, that they deny their love for one another:

"Deny it—but a word—say no. Lie, lie!
And I'll believe."

It is a sense of duty to the "laws of Italy" and to the honor of the family that ultimately compels Lanciotto to evoke eternity for the woman who could have slaked his "thirsting soul" and for the brother whom he loved "more than honor."

In regard to Lanciotto, Bradley says: "His real nature is infinitely tender." [2]

[1] Act I, sc. 3, p. 290.

[2] *Op. cit.*, p. 133.

As illustrative of this trait he cites the moderately long speech of Lanciotto's beginning:

"I pity those who fought, and bled, and died,
Before the armies of this Ghibelin."

To be sure, this shows a real capacity for pity, but it would seem as if this tenderness is circumscribed by nationality; it is to be observed that Lanciotto pities those who suffered "*Before* the armies of this Ghibelin," and in his very next speech his tenderness is open to question:

"I'd see Ravenna burn,
Flame into heaven, and scorch the flying clouds;
I'd choke her streets with ruined palaces;
I'd hear her women scream with fear and grief,
As I have heard the maids of Rimini." [1]

It must be admitted, of course, that a Guelph loving a Ghibelline would be something of an anomaly. Lanciotto *is* sensitive, not only to the sufferings of fellow-countrymen, but also to the beauties of nature, and his speech is often flavored with poetry. This feeling for nature has in a measure induced visions of a higher reality on the part of Lanciotto and has led to a concept of duality, already pointed out, in which man's earthly nature lies beneath the divinity above:

"These mystic shades
Are of the earth; the light that causes them,
And teaches us the quick comparison,
Is all from heaven."

Although the Francesca story existed in several versions before Boker wrote his, it is probable that he consulted only the original in Dante, who took the story from life, and the account given by Boccaccio in his Commentary. In the "grim Florentine's" [2] version is a suggestive picture of the lovers in "all the woes of his material hell," and a relation of how they were drawn together in reading of Lancelot's love, an incident which Boker takes over in his play. From Boccaccio it appears that Boker adopted the main outlines of his plot. The names of the principal characters are the same, with a few variations in spelling, such as Lanciotto for Gianciotto, and Paolo for Polo. In both versions appear the following: Francesca is given in marriage to the crippled son of Malatesta as a pledge of peace; the handsome Paolo is sent as a messenger of love to bring Francesca from Ravenna to Rimini; Francesca mistakes Paolo for Lanciotto and falls in love with him at sight; the love is reciprocated and continues after Francesca's marriage to Lanciotto; a servant discovers the lovers and informs Lanciotto; Lanciotto seeks them out and puts them to death. In Boccaccio, however, Gianciotto surprises the lovers behind a locked door and catches Polo as he

[1] Act I, sc. 2, p. 287.

[2] Boker, *Sonnets*, p. 50.

is trying to escape from the room; Gianciotto rushes upon Polo with intent to kill, but Francesca intercepts the dagger with her own bosom and Gianciotto is compelled to strike again to kill Polo; thereupon Gianciotto goes off to his "wonted affairs." In Boker, Lanciotto first pleads with the lovers to deny their guilt and deals the death blow only when they refuse to do so. Another variation is that in Boccaccio, Francesca does not learn of her mistake in identity until she wakes up after the wedding night to find her husband Gianciotto at her side; in Boker she learns of it even before leaving Ravenna, but she goes through with the marriage in order to protect her father.

Boccaccio's account is comparatively short, and one must realize that the emotional, artistic, and philosophical development of the story, together with the addition of the jester Pepe, is entirely Boker's own creation.[1]

The present text of *Francesca da Rimini* is from the version printed in *Plays and Poems*, 1856.

[1] The other versions of the Francesca story include: Uhland, Johann Ludwig, *Franceska da Rimino*, a play, 1807; Hunt, Leigh, *The Story of Rimini*, a poem, 1816; Pellico, Silvio, *Francesca da Rimini*, a tragedy, 1818; Greif, Martin, *Francesca da Rimini*, a tragedy, 1892; Phillips, Stephen, *Paolo and Francesca*, a tragedy, 1899; D'Annunzio, Gabriele, *Francesca da Rimini*, a tragedy, 1901; Crawford, F. Marion, *Francesca da Rimini*, a play, 1902; Birrini, Nino, *Francesca da Rimini*, a play, 1924. (For a discussion of these versions see Bradley's life of Boker, pp. 152 ff.)

DRAMATIS PERSONÆ

MALATESTA	Lord of Rimini
GUIDO DA POLENTA	Lord of Ravenna
LANCIOTTO	Malatesta's son
PAOLO	His brother
PEPE	Malatesta's jester
CARDINAL	Friend to Guido
RENE	A troubadour
FRANCESCA DA RIMINI	Guido's daughter
RITTA	Her maid

Lords, Ladies, Knights, Priests, Soldiers, Pages, Attendants, etc.

SCENE: *Rimini, Ravenna, and the neighborhood.*

TIME: *About 1300 A.D.*

FRANCESCA DA RIMINI

ACT I

SCENE I. *Rimini. The Garden of the Palace.* PAOLO *and a number of Noblemen are discovered, seated under an arbor, surrounded by* RENE, *and other Troubadours, attendants, &c.*

PAOLO. I prithee, Rene, charm our ears again
With the same song you sang me yesterday.
Here are fresh listeners.

RENE. Really, my good lord,
My voice is out of joint. A grievous cold— [*Coughs.*]

PAOLO. A very grievous, but convenient cold,
Which always racks you when you would not sing.

RENE. O, no, my lord! Besides, I hoped to hear
My ditty warbled into fairer ears,
By your own lips; to better purpose, too. [*The Noblemen all laugh.*]

FIRST NOBLEMAN. Rene has hit it. Music runs to waste
In ears like ours.

SECOND NOBLEMAN. Nay, nay; chaunt on, sweet Count.

PAOLO [*coughing*]. Alack! you hear, I've caught poor Rene's cough.

FIRST NOBLEMAN. That would not be, if we wore petticoats. [*The others laugh.*]

PAOLO. O, fie!

FIRST NOBLEMAN. So runs the scandal to our ears.

SECOND NOBLEMAN. Confirmed by all our other senses, Count.

FIRST NOBLEMAN. Witnessed by many a doleful sigh, poured out
By many a breaking heart in Rimini.

SECOND NOBLEMAN. Poor girls!

FIRST NOBLEMAN [*mimicking a lady*]. Sweet Count! sweet Count Paolo! O!
Plant early violets upon my grave!
Thus go a thousand voices to one tune. [*The others laugh.*]

PAOLO. 'Ods mercy! gentlemen, you do me wrong.

FIRST NOBLEMAN. And by how many hundred, more or less?

PAOLO. Ah! rogues, you'd shift your sins upon my shoulders.

SECOND NOBLEMAN. You'd bear them stoutly.

FIRST NOBLEMAN. It were vain to give
Drops to god Neptune. You're the sea of love
That swallows all things.

SECOND NOBLEMAN. We the little fish
That meanly scull about within your depths.

PAOLO. Go on, go on! Talk yourselves fairly out. [PEPE *laughs without.*]
But, hark! here comes the fool! Fit company
For this most noble company of wits!

Enter PEPE, *laughing violently*

Why do you laugh?

PEPE. I'm laughing at the world.
It has laughed long enough at me; and so
I'll turn the tables. Ho! ho! ho! I've heard
A better joke of Uncle Malatesta's
Than any I e'er uttered. [*Laughing.*]

ALL. Tell it, fool.

PEPE. Why, do you know—upon my life, the best
And most original idea on earth:
A joke to put in practice, too. By Jove!
I'll bet my wit 'gainst the stupidity
Of the best gentlemen among you all,
You cannot guess it.

ALL. Tell us, tell us, fool.

PEPE. Guess it, guess it, fools.

PAOLO. Come, disclose, disclose!

PEPE. He has a match afoot.—

ALL. A match!

PEPE. A marriage.

ALL. Who?—who?

PEPE. A marriage in his family.

ALL. But, who?

PEPE. Ah! there's the point.

ALL. Paolo?

PEPE. No.

FIRST NOBLEMAN. The others are well wived. Shall we turn Turks?

PEPE. Why, there's the summit of his joke, good sirs.
By all the sacred symbols of my art—
By cap and bauble, by my tinkling bell—
He means to marry Lanciotto!
[*Laughs violently.*]

ALL [*laughing*]. Ho!—

PAOLO. Peace! peace! What tongue dare echo yon fool's laugh?
Nay, never raise your hands in wonderment;
I'll strike the dearest friend among ye all
Beneath my feet, as if he were a slave,
Who dares insult my brother with a laugh!

PEPE. By Jove! ye're sad enough. Here's mirth's quick cure!
Pretty Paolo has a heavy fist,
I warn you, sirs. Ho! ho! I trapped them all; [*Laughing.*]
Now I'll go mar old Malatesta's message.
[*Aside.*] [*Exit.*

PAOLO. Shame on ye, sirs! I have mistaken you.
I thought I harbored better friends. Poor fops,
Who've slept in down and satin all your years,
Within the circle Lanciotto charmed
Round Rimini with his most potent sword!—
Fellows whose brows would melt beneath a casque,
Whose hands would fray to grasp a brand's rough hilt,
Who ne'er launched more than braggart threats at foes!—
Girlish companions of luxurious girls!—
Danglers round troubadours and wine-cups!—Men
Whose best parts are their clothes! bundles of silk,
Scented like summer! rag-men, nothing more!—
Creatures as generous as monkeys—brave
As hunted hares—courteous as grinning apes—
Grateful as serpents—useful as lap-dogs—
[*During this, the Noblemen, &c., steal off.*]
Ha!
I am alone at last! So let me be,
Till Lanciotto fill the vacant room
Of these mean knaves, whose friendship is but breath. [*Exit.*

SCENE 2. *The Same. A Hall in the Castle*

Enter MALATESTA *and* LANCIOTTO

MALATESTA. Guido, ay, Guido of Ravenna, son—
Down on his knees, as full of abject prayers
For peace and mercy as a penitent.

LANCIOTTO. His old trick, father. While his wearied arm
Is raised in seeming prayer, it only rests.
Anon, he'll deal you such a staggering blow,
With its recovered strength, as shall convert
You, and not him, into a penitent.

MALATESTA. No, no; your last bout levelled him. He reeled,
Into Ravenna, from the battle-field,
Like a stripped drunkard, and there headlong fell—
A mass of squalid misery, a thing
To draw the jeering urchins. I have this
From faithful spies. There's not a hope remains
To break the shock of his great overthrow.
I pity Guido.

LANCIOTTO. 'Sdeath! go comfort him!
I pity those who fought, and bled, and died,
Before the armies of this Ghibelin.
I pity those who halted home with wounds
Dealt by his hand. I pity widowed eyes
That he set running; maiden hearts that turn,
Sick with despair, from ranks thinned down by him;
Mothers that shriek, as the last stragglers fling
Their feverish bodies by the fountain-side,
Dumb with mere thirst, and faintly point to him,
Answering the dame's quick questions. I have seen
Unburied bones, and skulls—that seemed to ask,
From their blank eye-holes, vengeance at my hand—

Shine in the moonlight on old battle-fields;
And even these—the happy dead, my lord—
I pity more than Guido of Ravenna!

MALATESTA. What would you have?

LANCIOTTO. I'd see Ravenna burn,
Flame into heaven, and scorch the flying clouds;
I'd choke her streets with ruined palaces;
I'd hear her women scream with fear and grief,
As I have heard the maids of Rimini.
All this I'd sprinkle with old Guido's blood,
And bless the baptism.

MALATESTA. You are cruel.

LANCIOTTO. Not I;
But these things ache within my fretting brain.
The sight I first beheld was from the arms
Of my wild nurse, her husband hacked to death
By the fierce edges of these Ghibelins.
One cut across the neck—I see it now,
Ay, and have mimicked it a thousand times,
Just as I saw it, on our enemies.—
Why, that cut seemed as if it meant to bleed
On till the judgment. My distracted nurse
Stooped down, and paddled in the running gore
With her poor fingers; then a prophetess,
Pale with the inspiration of the god,
She towered aloft, and with her dripping hand
Three times she signed me with the holy cross.
'Tis all as plain as noon-day. Thus she spake,—
"May this spot stand till Guido's dearest blood
Be mingled with thy own!" The soldiers say,
In the close battle, when my wrath is up,
The dead man's blood flames on my vengeful brow
Like a red planet; and when war is o'er,
It shrinks into my brain, defiling all
My better nature with its slaughterous lusts.
Howe'er it be, it shaped my earliest thought,
And it will shape my last.

MALATESTA. You moody churl!
You dismal knot of superstitious dreams!
Do you not blush to empty such a head
Before a sober man? Why, son, the world
Has not given o'er its laughing humor yet,
That you should try it with such vagaries.—
Poh!
I'll get a wife to teach you common sense.

LANCIOTTO. A wife for me! [*Laughing.*]

MALATESTA. Ay, sir, a wife for you.
You shall be married, to insure your wits.

LANCIOTTO. 'Tis not your wont to mock me.

MALATESTA. How now, son!
I am not given to jesting. I have chosen
The fairest wife in Italy for you.
You won her bravely, as a soldier should:
And when you'd woo her, stretch your gauntlet out
And crush her fingers in its steely grip.
If you will plead, I ween, she dare not say—
No, by your leave. Should she refuse, howe'er,
With that same iron hand you shall go knock
Upon Ravenna's gates, till all the town
Ring with your courtship. I have made her hand
The price and pledge of Guido's future peace.

LANCIOTTO. All this is done!

MALATESTA. Done, out of hand; and now
I wait a formal answer, nothing more.
Guido dare not decline. No, by the saints,
He'd send Ravenna's virgins here in droves,
To buy a ten days' truce.

LANCIOTTO. Sir, let me say,
You stretch paternal privilege too far,
To pledge my hand without my own consent.
Am I a portion of your household stuff,
That you should trade me off to Guido thus?
Who is the lady I am bartered for?

MALATESTA. Francesca, Guido's daughter.—
Never frown;
It shall be so!

LANCIOTTO. By heaven, it shall not be!
My blood shall never mingle with his race.

MALATESTA. According to your nurse's prophecy,
Fate orders it.

LANCIOTTO. Ha!

MALATESTA. Now, then, I have struck
The chord that answers to your gloomy thoughts.

Bah! on your sibyl and her prophecy!
Put Guido's blood aside, and yet, I say,
Marry you shall.

LANCIOTTO. 'Tis most distasteful, sir.

MALATESTA. Lanciotto, look ye! You brave gentlemen,
So fond of knocking out poor people's brains,
In time must come to have your own knocked out:
What, then, if you bequeath us no new hands,
To carry on your business, and our house
Die out for lack of princes?

LANCIOTTO. Wed my brothers:
They'll rear you sons, I'll slay you enemies.
Paolo and Francesca! Note their names;
They chime together like sweet marriage-bells.
A proper match. 'Tis said she's beautiful;
And he is the delight of Rimini,—
The pride and conscious centre of all eyes,
The theme of poets, the ideal of art,
The earthly treasury of Heaven's best gifts!
I am a soldier; from my very birth,
Heaven cut me out for terror, not for love.
I had such fancies once, but now—

MALATESTA. Pshaw! son,
My faith is bound to Guido; and if you
Do not throw off your duty, and defy,
Through sickly scruples, my express commands,
You'll yield at once. No more: I'll have it so! [*Exit.*

LANCIOTTO. Curses upon my destiny! What, I—
Ho! I have found my use at last—What, I,
I, the great twisted monster of the wars,
The brawny cripple, the herculean dwarf,
The spur of panic, and the butt of scorn—
I be a bridegroom! Heaven, was I not cursed
More than enough, when thou didst fashion me
To be a type of ugliness,—a thing
By whose comparison all Rimini
Holds itself beautiful? Lo! here I stand,
A gnarléd, blighted trunk! There's not a knave
So spindle-shanked, so wry-faced, so infirm,
Who looks at me, and smiles not on himself.
And I have friends to pity me—great Heaven!
One has a favorite leg that he bewails,—
Another sees my hip with doleful plaints,—
A third is sorry o'er my huge swart arms,—
A fourth aspires to mount my very hump,
And thence harangue his weeping brotherhood!
Pah! it is nauseous! Must I further bear
The sidelong shuddering glances of a wife?
The degradation of a showy love,
That over-acts, and proves the mummer's craft
Untouched by nature? And a fair wife, too!—
Francesca, whom the minstrels sing about!
Though, by my side, what woman were not fair?
Circe looked well among her swine, no doubt;
Next me, she'd pass for Venus. Ho! ho! ho! [*Laughing.*]
Would there were something merry in my laugh!
Now, in the battle, if a Ghibelin
Cry, "Wry-hip! hunchback!" I can trample him
Under my stallion's hoofs; or haggle him
Into a monstrous likeness of myself:
But to be pitied,—to endure a sting
Thrust in by kindness, with a sort of smile!—
'Sdeath! it is miserable!

Enter PEPE

PEPE. My lord—

LANCIOTTO. My fool!

PEPE. We'll change our titles when your bride's bells ring—
Ha, cousin?

LANCIOTTO. Even this poor fool has eyes,
To see the wretched plight in which I stand. [*Aside.*]
How, gossip, how?

PEPE. I, being the court-fool,
Am lord of fools by my prerogative.

LANCIOTTO. Who told you of my marriage?

PEPE. Rimini!
A frightful liar; but true for once, I fear.
The messenger from Guido has returned,
And the whole town is wailing over him.

Some pity you, and some the bride; but I,
Being more catholic, I pity both.

LANCIOTTO. Still, pity, pity! [*Aside. Bells toll.*] Ha! whose knell is that?

PEPE. Lord Malatesta sent me to the tower.
To have the bells rung for your marriage-news.
How, he said not; so I, as I thought fit,
Told the deaf sexton to ring out a knell.
[*Bells toll.*]
How do you like it?

LANCIOTTO. Varlet, have you bones,
To risk their breaking? I have half a mind
To thrash you from your motley coat!
[*Seizes him.*]

PEPE. Pardee!
Respect my coxcomb, cousin. Hark! ha, ha!
[*Laughing.*]
[*Bells ring a joyful peal.*]
Some one has changed my music. Heaven defend!
How the bells jangle! Yonder graybeard, now,
Rings a peal vilely. He's more used to knells,
And sounds them grandly. Only give him time,
And, I'll be sworn, he'll ring your knell out yet.

LANCIOTTO. Pepe, you are but half a fool.

PEPE. My lord,
I can return the compliment in full.

LANCIOTTO. So, you are ready.

PEPE. Truth is always so.

LANCIOTTO. I shook you rudely; here's a florin. [*Offers money.*]

PEPE. No:
My wit is merchandise, but not my honor.

LANCIOTTO. Your honor, sirrah!

PEPE. Why not? You great lords
Have something you call lordly honor; pray,
May not a fool have foolish honor too?
Cousin, you laid your hand upon my coat—
'Twas the first sacrilege it ever knew—
And you shall pay it. Mark! I promise you.

LANCIOTTO [*laughing*]. Ha, ha! you bluster well. Upon my life,
You have the tilt-yard jargon to a breath.
Pepe, if I should smite you on the cheek—
Thus, gossip, thus—[*Strikes him.*] what would you then demand?

PEPE. Your life!

LANCIOTTO [*laughing*]. Ha, ha! there is the camp-style, too—
A very cut-throat air! How this shrewd fool
Makes the punctilio of honor show!
Change helmets into coxcombs, swords to baubles,
And what a figure is poor chivalry!
Thanks for your lesson, Pepe. [*Exit.*

PEPE. Ere I'm done,
You'll curse as heartily, you limping beast!
Ha! so we go—Lord Lanciotto, look!
[*Walks about, mimicking him.*]
Here is a leg and camel-back, forsooth,
To match your honor and nobility!
You miscreated scarecrow, dare you shake,
Or strike in jest, a natural man like me?—
You cursèd lump, you chaos of a man,
To buffet one whom Heaven pronounces good! [*Bells ring.*]
There go the bells rejoicing over you:
I'll change them back to the old knell again.
You marry, faugh! Beget a race of elves;
Wed a she-crocodile, and keep within
The limits of your nature! Here we go,
Tripping along to meet our promised bride,
Like a rheumatic elephant!—ha, ha!
[*Laughing.*]
[*Exit, mimicking* LANCIOTTO.

SCENE 3. *The Same. A Room in the Same*

Enter LANCIOTTO, *hastily*

LANCIOTTO. Why do these prodigies environ me?
In ancient Rome, the words a fool might drop,
From the confusion of his vagrant thoughts,
Were held as omens, prophecies; and men
Who made earth tremble with majestic deeds,
Trembled themselves at fortune's lightest threat.
I like it not. My father named this match
While I boiled over with vindictive wrath
Towards Guido and Ravenna. Straight my heart
Sank down like lead; a weakness seized on me,
A dismal gloom that I could not resist;
I lacked the power to take my stand, and say—

Bluntly, I will not! Am I in the toils?
Has fate so weakened me, to work its end?
There seems a fascination in it, too,—
A morbid craving to pursue a thing
Whose issue may be fatal. Would that I
Were in the wars again! These mental weeds
Grow on the surface of inactive peace.
I'm haunted by myself. Thought preys on thought.
My mind seems crowded in the hideous mould
That shaped my body. What a fool am I
To bear the burden of my wretched life,
To sweat and toil under the world's broad eye,
Climb into fame, and find myself—O, what?—
A most conspicuous monster! Crown my head,
Pile Cæsar's purple on me—and what then?
My hump shall shorten the imperial robe,
My leg peep out beneath the scanty hem,
My broken hip shall twist the gown awry;
And pomp, instead of dignifying me,
Shall be by me made quite ridiculous.
The faintest coward would not bear all this:
Prodigious courage must be mine, to live;
To die asks nothing but weak will, and I
Feel like a craven. Let me skulk away
Ere life o'ertask me.

[*Offers to stab himself.*]

Enter PAOLO

PAOLO [*seizing his hand*]. Brother! what is this?
Lanciotto, are you mad? Kind Heaven! look here—
Straight in my eyes. Now answer, do you know
How near you were to murder? Dare you bend
Your wicked hand against a heart I love?
Were it for you to mourn your wilful death,
With such a bitterness as would be ours,
The wish would ne'er have crossed you. While we're bound
Life into life, a chain of loving hearts,
Were it not base in you, the middle link,
To snap, and scatter all? Shame, brother, shame!
I thought you better metal.

LANCIOTTO. Spare your words.
I know the seasons of our human grief,
And can predict them without almanac.
A few sobs o'er the body, and a few
Over the coffin; then a sigh or two,
Whose windy passage dries the hanging tear;
Perchance, some wandering memories, some regrets;
Then a vast influx of consoling thoughts—
Based on the trials of the sadder days
Which the dead missed; and then a smiling face
Turned on tomorrow. Such is mortal grief.
It writes its histories within a span,
And never lives to read them.

PAOLO. Lanciotto,
I heard the bells of Rimini, just now,
Exulting o'er your coming marriage-day,
While you conspire to teach them gloomier sounds.
Why are you sad?

LANCIOTTO. Paolo, I am wretched;
Sad's a faint word. But of my marriage-bells—
Heard you the knell that Pepe rang?

PAOLO. 'Twas strange:
A sullen antic of his crabbed wit.

LANCIOTTO. It was portentous. All dumb things find tongues
Against this marriage. As I passed the hall,
My armor glittered on the wall, and I
Paused by the harness, as before a friend
Whose well-known features slack our hurried gait;
Francesca's name was fresh upon my mind,
So I half-uttered it. Instant, my sword
Leaped from its scabbard, as with sudden life,
Plunged down and pierced into the oaken floor,
Shivering with fear! Lo! while I gazed upon it—
Doubting the nature of the accident—
Around the point appeared a spot of blood,
Oozing upon the floor, that spread and spread—
As I stood gasping by in speechless horror—
Ring beyond ring, until the odious tide
Crawled to my feet, and lapped them, like the tongues

Of angry serpents! O, my God! I fled
At the first touch of the infernal stain!
Go—you may see—go to the hall!

PAOLO. Fie! man,
You have been ever played on in this sort
By your wild fancies. When your heart is high,
You make them playthings; but in lower moods,
They seem to sap the essence of your soul,
And drain your manhood to its poorest dregs.

LANCIOTTO. Go look, go look!

PAOLO [*goes to the door, and returns*]. There sticks the sword, indeed,
Just as your tread detached it from its sheath;
Looking more like a blessed cross, I think,
Than a bad omen. As for blood—Ha, ha! [*Laughing.*]
It sets mine dancing. Pshaw! away with this!
Deck up your face with smiles. Go trim yourself
For the young bride. New velvet, gold, and gems,
Do wonders for us. Brother, come; I'll be
Your tiring-man, for once.

LANCIOTTO. Array this lump—
Paolo, hark! There are some human thoughts
Best left imprisoned in the aching heart,
Lest the freed malefactors should dispread
Infamous ruin with their liberty.
There's not a man—the fairest of ye all—
Who is not fouler than he seems. This life
Is one unending struggle to conceal
Our baseness from our fellows. Here stands one
In vestal whiteness with a lecher's lust;—
There sits a judge, holding law's scales in hands
That itch to take the bribe he dare not touch;—
Here goes a priest with heavenward eyes, whose soul
Is Satan's council-chamber;—there a doctor,
With nature's secrets wrinkled round a brow
Guilty with conscious ignorance;—and here
A soldier rivals Hector's bloody deeds—
Out-does the devil in audacity—
With craven longings fluttering in a heart
That dares do aught but fly! Thus are we all
Mere slaves and alms-men to a scornful world,
That takes us at our seeming.

PAOLO. Say 'tis true;
What do you drive at?

LANCIOTTO. At myself, full tilt.
I, like the others, am not what I seem.
Men call me gentle, courteous, brave.—They lie!
I'm harsh, rude, and a coward. Had I nerve
To cast my devils out upon the earth,
I'd show this laughing planet what a hell
Of envy, malice, cruelty, and scorn,
It has forced back to canker in the heart
Of one poor cripple!

PAOLO. Ha!

LANCIOTTO. Ay, now 'tis out!
A word I never breathed to man before.
Can you, who are a miracle of grace,
Feel what it is to be a wreck like me?
Paolo, look at me. Is there a line,
In my whole bulk of wretched contraries,
That nature in a nightmare ever used
Upon her shapes till now? Find me the man,
Or beast, or tree, or rock, or nameless thing,
So out of harmony with all things else,
And I'll go raving with bare happiness,—
Ay, and I'll marry Helena of Greece,
And swear I do her honor!

PAOLO. Lanciotto,
I, who have known you from a stripling up,
Never observed, or, if I did, ne'er weighed
Your special difference from the rest of men.
You're not Apollo—

LANCIOTTO. No!

PAOLO. Nor yet are you
A second Pluto. Could I change with you—
My graces for your nobler qualities—
Your strength, your courage, your renown—by heaven,
We'd e'en change persons, to the finest hair.

LANCIOTTO. You should be flatterer to an emperor.

PAOLO. I am but just. Let me beseech you, brother,
To look with greater favor on yourself;
Nor suffer misty phantoms of your brain

To take the place of sound realities.
Go to Ravenna, wed your bride, and lull
Your cruel delusions in domestic peace.
Ghosts fly a fireside: 'tis their wont to stalk
Through empty houses, and through empty hearts.
I know Francesca will be proud of you.
Women admire you heroes. Rusty sages,
Pale poets, and scarred warriors, have been
Their idols ever; while we fair plump fools
Are elbowed to the wall, or only used
For vacant pastime.

LANCIOTTO. To Ravenna?—no!
In Rimini they know me; at Ravenna
I'd be a new-come monster, and exposed
To curious wonder. There will be parade
Of all the usual follies of the state;
Fellows with trumpets, tinselled coats, and wands,
Would strut before me, like vain mountebanks
Before their monkeys. Then, I should be stared
Out of my modesty; and when they look,
How can I tell if 'tis the bridegroom's face
Or hump that draws their eyes? I will not go.
To please you all, I'll marry; but to please
The wonder-mongers of Ravenna—Ha!
Paolo, now I have it. You shall go,
To bring Francesca; and you'll speak of me,
Not as I ought to be, but as I am.
If she draw backward, give her rein; and say
That neither Guido nor herself shall feel
The weight of my displeasure. You may say,
I pity her—

PAOLO. For what?

LANCIOTTO. For wedding me.
In sooth, she'll need it. Say—

PAOLO. Nay, Lanciotto,
I'll be a better orator in your behalf,
Without your promptings.

LANCIOTTO. She is fair, 'tis said;
And, dear Paolo, if she please your eye,
And move your heart to anything like love,
Wed her yourself. The peace would stand as firm
By such a match.

PAOLO [*laughing*]. Ha! that is right: be gay!
Ply me with jokes! I'd rather see you smile
Than see the sun shine.

LANCIOTTO. I am serious.
I'll find another wife, less beautiful,
More on my level, and—

PAOLO. An empress, brother,
Were honored by your hand. You are by much
Too humble in your reckoning of yourself.
I can count virtues in you, to supply
Half Italy, if they were parcelled out.
Look up!

LANCIOTTO. I cannot: Heaven has bent me down.
To you, Paolo, I could look, however,
Were my hump made a mountain. Bless him, God!
Pour everlasting bounties on his head!
Make Crœsus jealous of his treasury,
Achilles of his arms, Endymion
Of his fresh beauties,—though the coy one lay
Blushing beneath Diana's earliest kiss,
On grassy Latmos; and may every good,
Beyond man's sight, though in the ken of Heaven,
Round his fair fortune to a perfect end!
O, you have dried the sorrow of my eyes;
My heart is beating with a lighter pulse;
The air is musical; the total earth
Puts on new beauty, and within the arms
Of girdling ocean dreams her time away,
And visions bright tomorrows!

Enter MALATESTA *and* PEPE

MALATESTA. Mount, to horse!

PEPE [*aside*]. Good Lord! he's smiling! What's the matter now?
Has anybody broken a leg or back?
Has a more monstrous monster come to life?
Is hell burst open?—heaven burnt up? What, what
Can make yon eyesore grin?—I say, my lord,
What cow has calved?

PAOLO. Your mother, by the bleat.

PEPE. Right fairly answered—for a gentleman!
When did you take my trade up?

PAOLO. When your wit
Went begging, sirrah.

PEPE. Well again! My lord,
I think he'll do.

MALATESTA. For what?
PEPE. To take my place.
Once fools were rare, and then my office sped;
But now the world is overrun with them:
One gets one's fool in one's own family,
Without much searching.
MALATESTA. Pepe, gently now.
Lanciotto, you are waited for. The train
Has passed the gate, and halted there for you.
LANCIOTTO. I go not to Ravenna.
MALATESTA. Hey! why not?
PAOLO. For weighty reasons, father. Will you trust
Your greatest captain, hope of all the Guelfs,
With crafty Guido? Should the Ghibelins
Break faith, and shut Lanciotto in their walls—
Sure the temptation would be great enough—
What would you do?
MALATESTA. I'd eat Ravenna up!
PEPE. Lord! what an appetite!
PAOLO. But Lanciotto
Would be a precious hostage.
MALATESTA. True; you're wise;
Guido's a fox. Well, have it your own way.
What is your plan?
PAOLO. I go there in his place.
MALATESTA. Good! I will send a letter with the news.
LANCIOTTO. I thank you, brother. [*Apart to* PAOLO.]
PEPE. Ha! ha! ha!—O! O! [*Laughing.*]
MALATESTA. Pepe, what now?
PEPE. O! lord, O!—ho! ho! ho! [*Laughing.*]
PAOLO. Well, giggler?
PEPE. Hear my fable, uncle.
MALATESTA. Ay.
PEPE. Once on a time, Vulcan sent Mercury
To fetch dame Venus from a romp in heaven.
Well, they were long in coming, as he thought;
And so the god of spits and gridirons
Railed like himself—the devil. But—now mark—
Here comes the moral. In a little while,
Vulcan grew proud, because he saw plain signs
That he should be a father; and so he
Strutted through hell, and pushed the devils by,
Like a magnifico of Venice. Ere long,
His heir was born; but then—ho! ho!—the brat
Had wings upon his heels, and thievish ways,
And a vile squint, like errant Mercury's,
Which honest Vulcan could not understand;—
Can you?
PAOLO. 'Sdeath! fool, I'll have you in the stocks.
Father, your fool exceeds his privilege.
PEPE [*apart to* PAOLO]. Keep your own bounds, Paolo. In the stocks
I'd tell more fables than you'd wish to hear.
And so ride forth. But, cousin, don't forget
To take Lanciotto's picture to the bride.
Ask her to choose between it and yourself.
I'll count the moments, while she hesitates,
And not grow gray at it.
PAOLO. Peace, varlet, peace!
PEPE [*apart to him*]. Ah, now I have it. There's an elephant
Upon the scutcheon; show her that, and say—
Here's Lanciotto in our heraldry!
PAOLO. Here's for your counsel!
[*Strikes* PEPE, *who runs behind* MALATESTA.]
MALATESTA. Son, son, have a care!
We who keep pets must bear their pecks sometimes.
Poor knave! Ha! ha! thou'rt growing villainous! [*Laughs and pats* PEPE.]
PEPE. Another blow! another life for that! [*Aside.*]
PAOLO. Farewell, Lanciotto. You are dull again.
LANCIOTTO. Nature will rule.
MALATESTA. Come, come!
LANCIOTTO. God speed you, brother!
I am too sad; my smiles all turn to sighs.
PAOLO. More cause to haste me on my happy work. [*Exit with* MALATESTA.
PEPE. I'm going, cousin.
LANCIOTTO. Go.
PEPE. Pray, ask me where.
LANCIOTTO. Where, then?
PEPE. To have my jewel carried home:

And, as I'm wise, the carrier shall be
A thief, a thief, by Jove! The fashion's new.
[*Exit.*

LANCIOTTO. In truth, I am too gloomy and irrational.
Paolo must be right. I always had
These moody hours and dark presentiments,
Without mischances following after them.
The camp is my abode. A neighing steed,
A fiery onset, and a stubborn fight,
Rouse my dull blood, and tire my body down
To quiet slumbers when the day is o'er,
And night above me spreads her spangled tent,
Lit by the dying cresset of the moon.
Ay, that is it; I'm homesick for the camp.
[*Exit.*

ACT II

SCENE I. *Ravenna. A Room in Guido's Palace*

Enter GUIDO *and a* CARDINAL

CARDINAL. I warn thee, Count.
GUIDO. I'll take the warning, father,
On one condition: show me but a way
For safe escape.
CARDINAL. I cannot.
GUIDO. There's the point.
We Ghibelins are fettered hand and foot.
There's not a florin in my treasury;
Not a lame soldier, I can lead to war;
Not one to man the walls. A present siege,
Pushed with the wonted heat of Lanciotto,
Would deal Ravenna such a mortal blow
As ages could not mend. Give me but time
To fill the drainéd arteries of the land.
The Guelfs are masters, we their slaves; and we
Were wiser to confess it, ere the lash
Teach it too sternly. It is well for you
To say you love Francesca. So do I;
But neither you nor I have any voice
For or against this marriage.
CARDINAL. 'Tis too true.
GUIDO. Say we refuse: Why, then, before a week,
We'll hear Lanciotto rapping at our door,
With twenty hundred ruffians at his back.
What's to say then? My lord, we waste our breath.
Let us look fortune in the face, and draw
Such comfort from the wanton as we may.
CARDINAL. And yet I fear—
GUIDO. You fear! and so do I.
I fear Lanciotto as a soldier, though,
More than a son-in-law.
CARDINAL. But have you seen him?
GUIDO. Ay, ay, and felt him, too. I've seen him ride
The best battalions of my horse and foot
Down like mere stubble: I have seen his sword
Hollow a square of pikemen, with the ease
You'd scoop a melon out.
CARDINAL. Report declares him
A prodigy of strength and ugliness.
GUIDO. Were he the devil—But why talk of this?—
Here comes Francesca.
CARDINAL. Ah, unhappy child!
GUIDO. Look you, my lord! you'll make the best of it;
You will not whimper. Add your voice to mine,
Or woe to poor Ravenna!

Enter FRANCESCA *and* RITTA

FRANCESCA. Ha! my lord—
And you, my father!—But do I intrude
Upon your counsels? How severe you look!
Shall I retire?
GUIDO. No, no.
FRANCESCA. You moody men
Seem leagued against me. As I passed the hall,
I met your solemn Dante, with huge strides
Pacing in measure to his stately verse.
The sweeping sleeves of his broad scarlet robe
Blew out behind, like wide-expanded wings,
And seemed to buoy him in his level flight.
Thinking to pass, without disturbing him,
I stole on tip-toe; but the poet paused,
Subsiding into man, and steadily
Bent on my face the lustre of his eyes.
Then, taking both my trembling hands in his—
You know how his God-troubled forehead awes—
He looked into my eyes, and shook his head,

As if he dared not speak of what he saw;
Then muttered, sighed, and slowly turned away
The weight of his intolerable brow.
When I glanced back, I saw him, as before,
Sailing adown the hall on out-spread wings.
Indeed, my lord, he should not do these things:
They strain the weakness of mortality
A jot too far. As for poor Ritta, she
Fled like a doe, the truant.

RITTA. Yes, forsooth:
There's something terrible about the man.
Ugh! if he touched me, I should turn to ice.
I wonder if Count Lanciotto looks—

GUIDO. Ritta, come here. [*Takes her apart.*]

RITTA. My lord.

GUIDO. 'Twas my command,
You should say nothing of Count Lanciotto.

RITTA. Nothing, my lord.

GUIDO. You have said nothing, then?

RITTA. Indeed, my lord.

GUIDO. 'Tis well. Some years ago,
My daughter had a very silly maid,
Who told her sillier stories. So, one day,
This maiden whispered something I forbade—
In strictest confidence, for she was sly:
What happened, think you?

RITTA. I know not, my lord.

GUIDO. I boiled her in a pot.

RITTA. Good heaven! my lord.

GUIDO. She did not like it. I shall keep that pot
Ready for the next boiling.
[*Walks back to the others.*]

RITTA. Saints above!
I wonder if he ate her! Boil me—me!
I'll roast or stew with pleasure; but to boil
Implies a want of tenderness,—or rather
A downright toughness—in the matter boiled,
That's slanderous to a maiden. What, boil me—
Boil me! O! mercy, how ridiculous!
[*Retires, laughing.*]

Enter a MESSENGER

MESSENGER. Letters, my lord, from great Prince Malatesta.
[*Presents them, and exit.*

GUIDO [*aside*]. Hear him, ye gods!—"from great Prince Malatesta!"
Greeting, no doubt, his little cousin Guido.
Well, well, just so we see-saw up and down.
[*Reads.*]
"*Fearing our treachery*,"—by heaven, that's blunt,
And Malatesta-like!—"*he will not send*
His son, Lanciotto, to Ravenna, but"—
But what?—a groom, a porter? or will he
Have his prey sent him in an iron cage?
By Jove, he shall not have her! O! no, no;
"*He sends his younger son, the Count Paolo,*
To fetch Francesca back to Rimini."
That's well, if he had left his reasons out.
And, in a postscript—by the saints, 'tis droll!—
"'*Twould not be worth your lordship's while, to shut*
Paolo in a prison; for, my lord,
I'll only pay his ransom in plain steel:
Besides, he's not worth having." Is there one,
Save this ignoble offshoot of the Goths,
Who'd write such garbage to a gentleman?
Take that, and read it. [*Gives letter to* CARDINAL.]

CARDINAL. I have done the most.
She seems suspicious.

GUIDO. Ritta's work.

CARDINAL. Farewell! [*Exit.*

FRANCESCA. Father, you seem distempered.

GUIDO. No, my child,
I am but vexed. Your husband's on the road,
Close to Ravenna. What's the time of day?

FRANCESCA. Past noon, my lord.

GUIDO. We must be stirring, then.

FRANCESCA. I do not like this marriage.

GUIDO. But I do.

FRANCESCA. But I do not. Poh! to be given away,
Like a fine horse or falcon, to a man
Whose face I never saw!

RITTA. That's it, my lady.

GUIDO. Ritta, run down, and see if my great pot
Boils to your liking.

RITTA [*aside*]. O! that pot again!
My lord, my heart betrays me; but you know
How true 'tis to my lady. [*Exit.*

FRANCESCA. What ails Ritta?

GUIDO. The ailing of your sex, a running tongue.
Francesca, 'tis too late to beat retreat:
Old Malatesta has me—you, too, child—
Safe in his clutch. If you are not content,
I must unclose Ravenna, and allow
His son to take you. Poh, poh! have a soul
Equal with your estate. A prince's child
Cannot choose husbands. Her desires must aim,
Not at herself, but at the public good.
Both as your prince and father, I command;
As subject and good daughter, you'll obey.

FRANCESCA. I knew that it must be my destiny,
Some day, to give my hand without my heart;
But—

GUIDO. But, and I will but you back again!
When Guido da Polenta says to you,
Daughter, you must be married,—what were best?

FRANCESCA. 'Twere best Francesca, of the self-same name,
Made herself bridal-garments. [*Laughing.*]

GUIDO. Right!

FRANCESCA. My lord,
Is Lanciotto handsome—ugly—fair—
Black—sallow—crabbed—kind—or what is he?

GUIDO. You'll know ere long. I could not alter him,
To please your taste.

FRANCESCA. You always put me off;
You never have a whisper in his praise.

GUIDO. The world reports it.—Count my soldiers' scars,
And you may sum Lanciotto's glories up.

FRANCESCA. I shall be dutiful, to please you, father.
If aught befall me through my blind submission,
Though I may suffer, you must bear the sin.
Beware, my lord, for your own peace of mind!
My part has been obedience; and now
I play it over to complete my task;
And it shall be with smiles upon my lips,—
Heaven only knows with what a sinking heart! [*Exeunt.*

SCENE 2. *The Same. Before the Gates of the City. The walls hung with banners, flowers, &c., and crowded with citizens. At the side of the scene is a canopied dais, with chairs of state upon it. Music, bells, shouts, and other sounds of rejoicing, are occasionally heard.*

Enter GUIDO, *the* CARDINAL, *Noblemen, Knights, Guards, &c., with banners, arms, &c.*

GUIDO. My lord, I'll have it so. You talk in vain.
Paolo is a marvel in his way:
I've seen him often. If Francesca take
A fancy to his beauty, all the better;
For she may think that he and Lanciotto
Are like as blossoms of one parent branch.
In truth, they are, so far as features go—
Heaven help the rest! Get her to Rimini,
By any means, and I shall be content.
The fraud cannot last long; but long enough
To win her favor to the family.

CARDINAL. 'Tis a dull trick. Thou hast not dealt with her
Wisely nor kindly, and I dread the end.
If, when this marriage was enjoined on thee,
Thou hadst informed Francesca of the truth,
And said, Now, daughter, choose between
Thy peace and all Ravenna's; who that knows
The constant nature of her noble heart
Could doubt the issue? There'd have been some tears,
Some frightful fancies of her husband's looks;
And then she'd calmly walk up to her fate,
And bear it bravely. Afterwards, perchance,
Lanciotto might prove better than her fears,—
No one denies him many an excellence,—
And all go happily. But, as thou wouldst plot,
She'll be prepared to see a paragon,
And find a satyr. It is dangerous.
Treachery with enemies is bad enough,
With friends 'tis fatal.

GUIDO. Has your lordship done?

CARDINAL. Never, Count Guido, with so good a text.
Do not stand looking sideways at the truth;
Craft has become thy nature. Go to her.

GUIDO. I have not heart.
CARDINAL. I have. [*Going.*]
GUIDO. Hold, Cardinal!
My plan is better. Get her off my hands,
And I care not.
CARDINAL. What will she say of thee,
In Rimini, when she detects the cheat?
GUIDO. I'll stop my ears up.
CARDINAL. Guido, thou art weak,
And lack the common fortitude of man.
GUIDO. And you abuse the license of your garb,
To lessen me. My lord, I do not dare
To move a finger in these marriage-rites.
Francesca is a sacrifice, I know,—
A limb delivered to the surgeon's knife,
To save our general health. A truce to this.
Paolo has the business in his hands:
Let him arrange it as he will; for I
Will give Count Malatesta no pretext
To recommence the war.
CARDINAL. Farewell, my lord.
I'll neither help nor countenance a fraud.
You crafty men take comfort to yourselves,
Saying, deceit dies with discovery.
'Tis false; each wicked action spawns a brood,
And lives in its succession. You, who shake
Man's moral nature into storm, should know
That the last wave which passes from your sight
Rolls in and breaks upon eternity! [*Exit.*
GUIDO. Why, that's a very grand and solemn thought:
I'll mention it to Dante. Gentlemen,
What see they from the wall?
NOBLEMAN. The train, my lord.
GUIDO. Inform my daughter.
NOBLEMAN. She is here, my lord.

Enter FRANCESCA, RITTA, *Ladies, Attendants, &c.*

FRANCESCA. See, father, what a merry face I have,
And how my ladies glisten! I will try
To do my utmost, in my love for you
And the good people of Ravenna. Now,
As the first shock is over, I expect
To feel quite happy. I will wed the Count,
Be he whate'er he may. I do not speak
In giddy recklessness. I've weighed it all,—
'Twixt hope and fear, knowledge and ignorance,—
And reasoned out my duty to your wish.
I have no yearnings towards another love:
So, if I show my husband a desire
To fill the place with which he honors me,
According to its duties, even he—
Were he less noble than Count Lanciotto—
Must smile upon my efforts, and reward
Good will with willing grace. One pang remains.
Parting from home and kindred is a thing
None but the heartless, or the miserable,
Can do without a tear. This home of mine
Has filled my heart with two-fold happiness,
Taking and giving love abundantly.
Farewell, Ravenna! If I bless thee not,
'Tis that thou seem'st too blessed; and 'twere strange
In me to offer what thou'st always given.
GUIDO [*aside*]. This is too much! If she would rail a while
At me and fortune, it could be endured.
[*Shouts, music, &c., within.*]
FRANCESCA. Ha! there's the van just breaking through the wood!
Music! that's well; a welcome forerunner.
Now, Ritta—here—come talk to me. Alas!
How my heart trembles! What a world to me
Lies 'neath the glitter of yon cavalcade!
Is that the Count?
RITTA. Upon the dapple-gray?
FRANCESCA. Yes, yes.
RITTA. No; that's his—
GUIDO [*apart to her*]. Ritta!
RITTA. Ay; that's—that's—
GUIDO. Ritta, the pot! [*Apart to her.*]
RITTA. O! but this lying chokes! [*Aside.*]
Ay, that's Count Somebody, from Rimini.
FRANCESCA. I knew it was. Is that not glorious?
RITTA. My lady, what?
FRANCESCA. To see a cavalier
Sit on his steed with such familiar grace.
RITTA. To see a man astraddle on a horse!
It don't seem much to me.
FRANCESCA. Fie! stupid girl!
But mark! the minstrels thronging round the Count!

Ah! that is more than gallant horsemanship.
The soul that feeds itself on poesy,
Is of a quality more fine and rare
Than Heaven allows the ruder multitude.
I tell you, Ritta, when you see a man
Beloved by poets, made the theme of song,
And chaunted down to ages, as a gift
Fit for the rich embalmment of their verse,
There's more about him than the patron's gold.
If that's the gentleman my father chose,
He must have picked him out from all the world.
The Count alights. Why, what a noble grace
Runs through his slightest action! Are you sad?
You, too, my father? Have I given you cause?
I am content. If Lanciotto's mind
Bear any impress of his fair outside,
We shall not quarrel ere our marriage-day.
Can I say more? My blushes speak for me:
Interpret them as modesty's excuse
For the short-comings of a maiden's speech.

RITTA. Alas! dear lady! [*Aside.*]

GUIDO [*aside*]. 'Sdeath! my plot has failed,
By overworking its design. Come, come;
Get to your places. See, the Count draws nigh.

[GUIDO *and* FRANCESCA *seat themselves upon the dais, surrounded by* RITTA, *Ladies, Attendants, Guards, &c. Music, shouts, ringing of bells, &c. Enter Men-at-arms, with banners, &c.; Pages bearing costly presents on cushions; then* PAOLO, *surrounded by Noblemen, Knights, Minstrels, &c., and followed by other Men-at-arms. They range themselves opposite the dais.*]

GUIDO. Ravenna welcomes you, my lord, and I
Add my best greeting to the general voice.
This peaceful show of arms from Rimini
Is a new pleasure, stranger to our sense
Than if the East blew zephyrs, or the balm
Of Summer loaded rough December's gales,
And turned his snows to roses.

PAOLO. Noble sir,
We looked for welcome from your courtesy,
Not from your love; but this unhoped for sight
Of smiling faces, and the gentle tone
In which you greet us, leave us naught to win
Within your hearts. I need not ask, my lord,
Where bides the precious object of my search;
For I was sent to find the fairest maid
Ravenna boasts, among her many fair.
I might extend my travel many a league,
And yet return, to take her from your side.
I blush to bear so rich a treasure home,
As pledge and hostage of a sluggish peace;
For beauty such as hers was meant by Heaven
To spur our race to gallant enterprise,
And draw contending deities around
The dubious battles of a second Troy.

GUIDO. Sir Count, you please to lavish on my child
The high-strained courtesy of chivalry;
Yet she has homely virtues that, I hope,
May take a deeper hold in Rimini,
After the fleeting beauty of her face
Is spoiled by time, or faded to the eye
By its familiar usage.

PAOLO. As a man
Who ever sees Heaven's purpose in its works,
I must suppose so rare a tabernacle
Was framed for rarest virtues. Pardon me
My public admiration. If my praise
Clash with propriety, and bare my words
To cooler judgment, 'tis not that I wish
To win a flatterer's grudged recompense,
And gain by falsehood what I'd win through love.
When I have brushed my travel from my garb,
I'll pay my court in more befitting style.
[*Music. Exit with his train.*

GUIDO [*advancing*]. Now, by the saints, Lanciotto's deputy
Stands in this business with a proper grace,
Stretching his lord's instructions till they crack.
A zealous envoy! Not a word said he
Of Lanciotto—not a single word;
But stood there, staring in Francesca's face
With his devouring eyes.—By Jupiter,
I but half like it!

FRANCESCA [*advancing*]. Father?

GUIDO. Well, my child.
FRANCESCA. How do you like—
GUIDO. The coxcomb! I've done well!
FRANCESCA. No, no; Count Lanciotto?
GUIDO. Well enough.
But hang this fellow—hang your deputies!
I'll never woo by proxy.
FRANCESCA. Deputies!
And woo by proxy!
GUIDO. Come to me anon.
I'll strip this cuckoo of his gallantry!
[*Exit with Guards*, *&c.*
FRANCESCA. Ritta, my father has strange ways of late.
RITTA. I wonder not.
FRANCESCA. You wonder not?
RITTA. No, lady:
He is so used to playing double games,
That even you must come in for your share.
Plague on his boiling! I will out with it.
[*Aside.*]
Lady, the gentleman who passed the gates—
FRANCESCA. Count Lanciotto? As I hope for grace,
A gallant gentleman! How well he spoke!
With what sincere and earnest courtesy
The rounded phrases glided from his lips!
He spoke in compliments that seemed like truth.
Methinks I'd listen through a summer's day,
To hear him woo.—And he must woo to me—
I'll have our privilege—he must woo a space,
Ere I'll be won, I promise.
RITTA. But, my lady,
He'll woo you for another.
FRANCESCA. He?—ha! ha! [*Laughing.*]
I should not think it from the prologue, Ritta.
RITTA. Nor I.
FRANCESCA. Nor any one.
RITTA. 'Tis not the Count—
'Tis not Count Lanciotto.
FRANCESCA. Gracious saints!
Have you gone crazy? Ritta, speak again,
Before I chide you.
RITTA. 'Tis the solemn truth.
That gentleman is Count Paolo, lady,
Brother to Lanciotto, and no more
Like him than—than—
FRANCESCA. Than what?
RITTA. Count Guido's pot,
For boiling waiting-maids, is like the bath
Of Venus on the arras.
FRANCESCA. Are you mad,—
Quite mad, poor Ritta?
RITTA. Yes; perhaps I am,
Perhaps Lanciotto is a proper man—
Perhaps I lie—perhaps I speak the truth—
Perhaps I gabble like a fool. O! heavens,
That dreadful pot!
FRANCESCA. Dear Ritta!—
RITTA. By the mass,
They shall not cozen you, my gentle mistress!
If my lord Guido boiled me, do you think
I should be served up to the garrison,
By way of pottage? Surely they would not waste me.
FRANCESCA. You are an idle talker. Pranks like these
Fit your companions. You forget yourself.
RITTA. Not you, though, lady. Boldly I repeat,
That he who looked so fair, and talked so sweet,
Who rode from Rimini upon a horse
Of dapple-gray, and walked through yonder gate,
Is not Count Lanciotto.
FRANCESCA. This you mean?
RITTA. I do, indeed!
FRANCESCA. Then I am more abused—
More tricked, more trifled with, more played upon—
By him, my father, and by all of you,
Than anything, suspected of a heart,
Was ever yet!
RITTA. In Count Paolo, lady,
Perchance there was no meditated fraud.
FRANCESCA. How, dare you plead for him?
RITTA. I but suppose:
Though in your father—O! I dare not say.
FRANCESCA. I dare. It was ill usage, gross abuse,
Treason to duty, meanness, craft—dishonor!
What if I'd thrown my heart before the feet
Of this sham husband! cast my love away
Upon a counterfeit! I was prepared
To force affection upon any man

Called Lanciotto. Anything of silk,
Tinsel, and gewgaws, if he bore that name,
Might have received me for the asking. Yes,
I was inclined to venture more than half
In this base business—shame upon my thoughts!—
All for my father's peace and poor Ravenna's.
And this Paolo, with his cavalcade,
His minstrels, music, and his pretty airs,
His showy person, and his fulsome talk,
Almost made me contented with my lot.
O! what a fool—in faith, I merit it—
Trapped by mere glitter! What an easy fool!
Ha! ha! I'm glad it went no further, girl; [*Laughing.*]
I'm glad I kept my heart safe, after all.
There was my cunning. I have paid them back,
I warrant you! I'll marry Lanciotto;
I'll seem to shuffle by this treachery. No!
I'll seek my father, put him face to face
With his own falsehood; and I'll stand between,
Awful as justice, meting out to him
Heaven's dreadful canons 'gainst his conscious guilt.
I'll marry Lanciotto. On my faith,
I would not live another wicked day
Here, in Ravenna, only for the fear
That I should take to lying, with the rest.
Ha! ha! it makes me merry, when I think
How safe I kept this little heart of mine! [*Laughing.*]
[*Exit, with Attendants, &c.*

RITTA. So, 'tis all ended—all except my boiling,
And that will make a holiday for some.
Perhaps I'm selfish. Fagot, axe, and gallows,
They have their uses, after all. They give
The lookers-on a deal of harmless sport.
Though one may suffer, twenty hundred laugh;
And that's a point gained. I have seen a man—
Poor Dora's uncle—shake himself with glee,
At the bare thought of the ridiculous style
In which some villain died. "Dancing," quoth he,
"To the poor music of a single string!
Biting," quoth he, "after his head was off!
What use of that?" Or, "Shivering," quoth he,
"As from an ague, with his beard afire!"
And then he'd roar until his ugly mouth
Split at the corners. But to see me boil—
O! that will be the queerest thing of all!
I wonder if they'll put me in a bag,
Like a great suet-ball? I'll go, and tell
Count Guido, on the instant. How he'll laugh
To think his pot has got an occupant!
I wonder if he really takes delight
In such amusements? Nay, I have kept faith:
I only said the man was not Lanciotto;
No word of Lanciotto's ugliness.
I may escape the pot, for all. Pardee!
I wonder if they'll put me in a bag!
[*Exit, laughing.*

SCENE 3. *The Same. A Room in Guido's Palace*

Enter GUIDO *and* RITTA

RITTA. There now, my lord, that is the whole of it:
I love my mistress more than I fear you.
If I could save her finger from the axe,
I'd give my head to do it. So, my lord,
I am prepared to stew.

GUIDO. Boil, Ritta, boil.

RITTA. No; I prefer to stew.

GUIDO. And I to boil.

RITTA. 'Tis very hard, my lord, I cannot choose
My way of cooking. I shall laugh, I vow,
In the grim headsman's face, when I remember
That I am dying for my lady's love.
I leave no one to shed a tear for me;
Father nor mother, kith nor kin, have I,
To say, "Poor Ritta!" o'er my lifeless clay.
They all have gone before me, and 'twere well
If I could hurry after them.

GUIDO. Poor child! [*Aside.*]
But, baggage, said you aught of Lanciotto?

RITTA. No, not a word; and he's so ugly, too!

GUIDO. Is he so ugly?

RITTA. Ugly! he is worse
Than Pilate on the hangings.

GUIDO. Hold your tongue
Here, and at Rimini, about the Count,
And you shall prosper.
RITTA. Am I not to boil?
GUIDO. No, child. But be discreet at Rimini.
Old Malatesta is a dreadful man—
Far worse than I—he bakes his people, Ritta;
Lards them, like geese, and bakes them in an oven.
RITTA. Fire is my fate, I see that.
GUIDO. Have a care
It do not follow you beyond this world.
Where is your mistress?
RITTA. In her room, my lord.
After I told her of the Count Paolo,
She flew to have an interview with you;
But on the way—I know not why it was—
She darted to her chamber, and there stays
Weeping in silence. It would do you good—
More than a hundred sermons—just to see
A single tear, indeed it would, my lord.
GUIDO. Ha! you are saucy. I have humored you
Past prudence, malpert! Get you to your room! [*Exit* RITTA.
More of my blood runs in yon damsel's veins
Than the world knows. Her mother to a shade;
The same high spirit, and strange martyrwish
To sacrifice herself, body and soul,
For some loved end. All that she did for me;
And yet I loved her not. O! memory!
The darkest future has a ray of hope,
But thou art blacker than the sepulchre!
Thy horrid shapes lie round, like scattered bones,
Hopeless forever! I am sick at heart.
The past crowds on the present: as I sowed,
So am I reaping. Shadows from myself
Fall on the picture, as I trace anew
These rising spectres of my early life,
And add their gloom to what was dark before.
O! memory, memory! How my temples throb! [*Sits.*]

Enter FRANCESCA, *hastily*

FRANCESCA. My lord, this outrage—[*He looks up.*] Father, are you ill?
You seem unhappy. Have I troubled you?
You heard how passionate and bad I was,
When Ritta told me of the Count Paolo.
Dear father, calm yourself; and let me ask
A child's forgiveness. 'Twas undutiful
To doubt your wisdom. It is over now.
I only thought you might have trusted me
With any counsel.
GUIDO [*aside*]. Would I had!
FRANCESCA. Ah! well,
I understand it all, and you were right.
Only the danger of it. Think, my lord,
If I had loved this man at the first sight:
We all have heard of such things. Think, again,
If I had loved him—as I then supposed
You wished me to—'twould have been very sad.
But no, dear sir, I kept my heart secure,
Nor will I loose it till you give the word.
I'm wiser than you thought me, you perceive.
But when we saw him, face to face, together,
Surely you might have told me then.
GUIDO. Francesca,
My eyes are old—I did not clearly see—
Faith, it escaped my thoughts. Some other things
Came in my head. I was as ignorant
Of Count Paolo's coming as yourself.
The brothers are so like.
FRANCESCA. Indeed?
GUIDO. Yes, yes.
One is the other's counterpart, in fact;
And even now it may not be—O! shame!
I lie by habit. [*Aside.*]
FRANCESCA. Then there is a hope?
He may be Lanciotto, after all?
O! joy—

Enter a SERVANT

SERVANT. The Count Paolo. [*Exit.*
FRANCESCA. Misery!
That name was not Lanciotto!
GUIDO. Farewell, child.
I'll leave you with the Count: he'll make it plain.
It seems 'twas Count Paolo. [*Going.*]
FRANCESCA. Father!
GUIDO. Well.

FRANCESCA. You knew it from the first!
[*Exit* GUIDO.] Let me begone:
I could not look him in the face again
With the old faith. Besides, 'twould anger him
To have a living witness of his fraud
Ever before him; and I could not trust—
Strive as I might—my happiness to him,
As once I did. I could not lay my hand
Upon his shoulder, and look up to him,
Saying, Dear father, pilot me along
Past this dread rock, through yonder narrow strait.
Saints, no! The gold that gave my life away
Might, even then, be rattling in his purse,
Warm from the buyer's hand. Look on me, Heaven!
Him thou didst sanctify before my eyes,
Him thou didst charge, as thy great deputy,
With guardianship of a weak orphan girl,
Has fallen from grace, has paltered with his trust;
I have no mother to receive thy charge,—
O! take it on thyself; and when I err,
Through mortal blindness, Heaven, be thou my guide!
Worse cannot fall me. Though my husband lack
A parent's tenderness, he yet may have
Faith, truth, and honor—the immortal bonds
That knit together honest hearts as one.
Let me away to Rimini. Alas!
It wrings my heart to have outlived the day
That I can leave my home with no regret!
[*Weeps.*]

Enter PAOLO

PAOLO. Pray, pardon me. [*Going.*]
FRANCESCA. You are quite welcome, Count.
A foolish tear, a weakness, nothing more:
But present weeping clears our future sight.
They tell me you are love's commissioner,
A kind of broker in the trade of hearts:
Is it your usual business? or may I
Flatter myself, by claiming this essay
As your first effort?
PAOLO. Lady, I believed
My post, at starting, one of weight and trust;
When I beheld you, I concluded it
A charge of honor and high dignity.
I did not think to hear you underrate
Your own importance, by dishonoring me.
FRANCESCA. You are severe, my lord.
PAOLO. No, not severe;
Say candid, rather. I am somewhat hurt
By my reception. If I feel the wound,
'Tis not because I suffer from the jest,
But that your lips should deal it.
FRANCESCA. Compliments
Appear to be the staple of your speech.
You ravish one with courtesy, you pour
Fine words upon one, till the listening head
Is bowed with sweetness. Sir, your talk is drugged;
There's secret poppy in your sugared phrase:
I'll taste before I take it.
PAOLO. Gentle lady—
FRANCESCA. I am not gentle, or I missed my aim.
I am no hawk to fly at every lure.
You courtly gentlemen draw one broad rule—
All girls are fools. It may be so, in truth,
Yet so I'll not be treated.
PAOLO. Have you been?
If I implied such slander by my words,
They wrong my purpose. If I compliment,
'Tis not from habit, but because I thought
Your face deserved my homage as its due.
When I have clearer insight, and you spread
Your inner nature o'er your lineaments,
Even that face may darken in the shades
Of my opinion. For mere loveliness
Needs inward light to keep it always bright.
All things look badly to unfriendly eyes.
I spoke my first impression; cooler thought
May work strange changes.
FRANCESCA. Ah, Sir Count, at length
There's matter in your words.
PAOLO. Unpleasant stuff,
To judge by your dark brows. I have essayed
Kindness and coldness, yet you are not pleased.
FRANCESCA. How can I be?
PAOLO. How, lady?
FRANCESCA. Ay, sir, how?
Your brother—my good lord that is to be—
Stings me with his neglect; and in the place

He should have filled, he sends a go-between,
A common carrier of others' love;
How can the sender, or the person sent,
Please overmuch? Now, were I such as you,
I'd be too proud to travel round the land
With other people's feelings in my heart;
Even to fill the void which you confess
By such employment.

PAOLO. Lady, 'tis your wish
To nettle me, to break my breeding down,
And see what natural passions I have hidden
Behind the outworks of my etiquette.
I neither own nor feel the want of heart
With which you charge me. You are more than cruel;
You rouse my nerves until they ache with life,
And then pour fire upon them. For myself
I would not speak, unless you had compelled.
My task is odious to me. Since I came,
Heaven bear me witness how my traitor heart
Has fought against my duty; and how oft
I wished myself in Lanciotto's place,
Or him in mine.

FRANCESCA. You riddle.

PAOLO. Do I? Well,
Let it remain unguessed.

FRANCESCA. You wished yourself
At Rimini, or Lanciotto here?
You may have reasons.

PAOLO. Well interpreted!
The Sphinx were simple in your skilful hands!

FRANCESCA. It has become your turn to sneer.

PAOLO. But I
Have gall to feed my bitterness, while you
Jest in the wanton ease of happiness.
Stop! there is peril in our talk.

FRANCESCA. As how?

PAOLO. 'Tis dangerous to talk about one's self;
It panders selfishness. My duty waits.

FRANCESCA. My future lord's affairs? I quite forgot
Count Lanciotto.

PAOLO. I, too, shame upon me. [*Aside.*]

FRANCESCA. Does he resemble you?

PAOLO. Pray, drop me, lady.

FRANCESCA. Nay, answer me.

PAOLO. Somewhat—in feature.

FRANCESCA. Ha!
Is he so fair?

PAOLO. No, darker. He was tanned
In long campaigns, and battles hotly fought,
While I lounged idly with the troubadours,
Under the shadow of his watchful sword.

FRANCESCA. In person?

PAOLO. He is shorter, I believe,
But broader, stronger, more compactly knit.

FRANCESCA. What of his mind?

PAOLO. Ah, now you strike the key!
A mind just fitted to his history,
An equal balance 'twixt desert and fame.
No future chronicler shall say of him,
His fame outran his merit; or his merit
Halted behind some adverse circumstance,
And never won the glory it deserved.
My love might weary you, if I rehearsed
The simple beauty of his character;
His grandeur and his gentleness of heart,
His warlike fire and peaceful love, his faith,
His courtesy, his truth. I'll not deny
Some human weakness, to attract our love,
Harbors in him, as in the rest of us.
Sometimes against our city's enemies
He thunders in the distance, and devotes
Their homes to ruin. When the brand has fallen,
He ever follows with a healing rain,
And in his pity shoulders by revenge.
A thorough soldier, lady. He grasps crowns,
While I pick at the laurel.

FRANCESCA. Stay, my lord!
I asked your brother's value, with no wish
To hear you underrate yourself. Your worth
May rise in passing through another's lips.
Lanciotto is perfection, then?

PAOLO. To me:
Others may think my brother over-nice
Upon the point of honor; over-keen
To take offence where no offence is meant;
A thought too prodigal of human life,
Holding it naught when weighed against a wrong;
Suspicious of the motives of his friends;
Distrustful of his own high excellence;
And with a certain gloom of temperament,
When thus disturbed, that makes him terrible

And rash in action. I have heard of this.
I never felt it. I distress you, lady?
Perhaps I throw these points too much in shade,
By catching at an enemy's report.
But, then, Lanciotto said, "You'll speak of me,
Not as I ought to be, but as I am."
He loathes deceit.

FRANCESCA. That's noble! Have you done?
I have observed a strange reserve, at times,
An over-carefulness in choosing words,
Both in my father and his nearest friends,
When speaking of your brother; as if they
Picked their way slowly o'er rocky ground,
Fearing to stumble. Ritta, too, my maid,
When her tongue rattles on in full career,
Stops at your brother's name, and with a sigh
Settles herself to dismal silence. Count,
These things have troubled me. From you I look
For perfect frankness. Is there naught withheld?

PAOLO [*aside*]. O, base temptation! What if I betray
His crippled person—imitate his limp—
Laugh at his hip, his back, his sullen moods
Of childish superstition?—tread his heart
Under my feet, to climb into his place?—
Use his own warrant 'gainst himself; and say,
Because I loved her, and misjudged your jest,
Therefore I stole her? Why, a common thief
Would hang for just such thinking! Ha! ha! ha! [*Laughing.*]
I reckon on her love, as if I held
The counsels of her bosom. No, I swear
Francesca would despise so mean a deed.
Have I no honor either? Are my thoughts
All bound by her opinion?

FRANCESCA. This is strange!
Is Lanciotto's name a spell to all?
I ask a simple question, and straight you
Start to one side, and mutter to yourself,
And laugh, and groan, and play the lunatic,
In such a style that you astound me more
Than all the others. It appears to me
I have been singled as a common dupe
By every one. What mystery is this
Surrounds Count Lanciotto? If there be
A single creature in the universe
Who has a right to know him as he is,
I am that one.

PAOLO. I grant it. You shall see,
And shade your judgment by your own remark.
All that my honor calls for I have said.

FRANCESCA. I am content. Unless I greatly err,
Heaven made your breast the seat of honest thoughts.
You know, my lord, that, once at Rimini,
There can be no retreat for me. By you,
Here at Ravenna, in your brother's name,
I shall be solemnly betrothed. And now
I thus extend my maiden hand to you;
If you are conscious of no secret guilt,
Take it.

PAOLO. I do. [*Takes her hand.*]

FRANCESCA. You tremble!

PAOLO. With the hand,
Not with the obligation.

FRANCESCA. Farewell, Count!
'Twere cruel to tax your stock of compliments,
That waste their sweets upon a trammeled heart;
Go fly your fancies at some freer game. [*Exit.*

PAOLO. O, heaven, if I have faltered and am weak,
'Tis from my nature! Fancies, more accursed
Than haunt a murderer's bedside, throng my brain—
Temptations, such as mortal never bore
Since Satan whispered in the ear of Eve,
Sing in my ear—and all, all are accursed!
At heart I have betrayed my brother's trust,
Francesca's openly. Turn where I will,
As if enclosed within a mirrored hall,
I see a traitor. Now to stand erect,
Firm on my base of manly constancy;
Or, if I stagger, let me never quit
The homely path of duty, for the ways
That bloom and glitter with seductive sin! [*Exit.*

ACT III

SCENE I. *Rimini. A Room in the Castle.*
LANCIOTTO *discovered reading*

LANCIOTTO. O! fie, philosophy! This Seneca
Revels in wealth, and whines about the poor!
Talks of starvation while his banquet waits,
And fancies that a two hours' appetite
Throws light on famine! Doubtless he can tell,
As he skips nimbly through his dancing-girls,
How sad it is to limp about the world
A sightless cripple! Let him feel the crutch
Wearing against his heart, and then I'd hear
This sage talk glibly; or provide a pad,
Stuffed with his soft philosophy, to ease
His aching shoulder. Pshaw; he never felt,
Or pain would choke his frothy utterance.
'Tis easy for the doctor to compound
His nauseous simples for a sick man's health;
But let him swallow them, for his disease,
Without wry faces. Ah! the tug is there.
Show me philosophy in rags, in want,
Sick of a fever, with a back like mine,
Creeping to wisdom on these legs, and I
Will drink its comforts. Out! away with you!
There's no such thing as real philosophy!
[*Throws down the book.*]

Enter PEPE

Here is a sage who'll teach a courtier
The laws of etiquette, a statesman rule,
A soldier discipline, a poet verse,
And each mechanic his distinctive trade;
Yet bring him to his motley, and how wide
He shoots from reason! We can understand
All business but our own, and thrust advice
In every gaping cranny of the world;
While habit shapes us to our own dull work,
And reason nods above his proper task.
Just so philosophy would rectify
All things abroad, and be a jade at home.
Pepe, what think you of the Emperor's aim
Towards Hungary?
PEPE. A most unwise design;
For mark, my lord—
LANCIOTTO. Why, there! the fact cries out.
Here's motley thinking for a diadem!—
Ay, and more wisely in his own regard.
PEPE. You flout me, cousin.
LANCIOTTO. Have you aught that's new?—
Some witty trifle, some absurd conceit?
PEPE. Troth, no.
LANCIOTTO. Why not give up the Emperor,
And bend your wisdom on your duties, Pepe?
PEPE. Because the Emperor has more need of wisdom
Than the most barren fool of wit.
LANCIOTTO. Well said!
Mere habit brings the fool back to his art.
This jester is a rare philosopher.
Teach me philosophy, good fool.
PEPE. No need.
You'll get a teacher when you take a wife.
If she do not instruct you in more arts
Than Aristotle ever thought upon,
The good old race of woman has declined
Into a sort of male stupidity.
I had a sweetheart once, she lectured grandly;
No matter on what subject she might hit,
'Twas all the same, she could talk and she would,
She had no silly modesty; she dashed
Straight in the teeth of any argument,
And talked you deaf, dumb, blind. Whatever struck
Upon her ear, by some machinery,
Set her tongue wagging. Thank the Lord, she died!—
Dropped in the middle of a fierce harangue,
Like a spent horse. It was an even thing,
Whether she talked herself or me to death.
The latest sign of life was in her tongue;
It wagged till sundown, like a serpent's tail,
Long after all the rest of her was cold.
Alas! poor Zippa!
LANCIOTTO. Were you married, fool?
PEPE. Married! Have I the scars upon me? No;
I fell in love; and that was bad enough,
And far enough for a mere fool to go.
Married! why, marriage is love's purgatory,
Without a heaven beyond.
LANCIOTTO. Fie, atheist!
Would you abolish marriage?
PEPE. Yes.

LANCIOTTO. What?
PEPE. Yes.
LANCIOTTO. Depopulate the world?
PEPE. No fear of that.
I'd have no families, no Malatesti,
Strutting about the land, with pedigrees
And claims bequeathed them by their ancestors;
No fellows vaporing of their royal blood;
No one to seize a whole inheritance,
And rob the other children of the earth.
By Jove! you should not know your fathers, even!
I'd have you spring, like toadstools, from the soil—
Mere sons of women—nothing more nor less—
All base-born, and all equal. There, my lord,
There is a simple commonwealth for you!
In which aspiring merit takes the lead,
And birth goes begging.
LANCIOTTO. It is so, in truth;
And by the simplest means I ever heard.
PEPE. Think of it, cousin. Tell it to your friends,
The statesmen, soldiers, and philosophers;
Noise it about the earth, and let it stir
The sluggish spirits of the multitudes.
Pursue the thought, scan it, from end to end,
Through all its latent possibilities.
It is a great seed dropped, I promise you,
And it must sprout. Thought never wholly dies;
It only wants a name—a hard Greek name—
Some few apostles, who may live on it—
A crowd of listeners, with the average dulness
That man possesses—and we organize;
Spread our new doctrine, like a general plague;
Talk of man's progress and development,
Wrongs of society, the march of mind,
The Devil, Doctor Faustus, and what not,
And, lo! this pretty world turns upside down,
All with a fool's idea!
LANCIOTTO. By Jupiter,
You hit our modern teachers to a hair!
I knew this fool was a philosopher.
Pepe is right. Mechanic means advance;
Nature bows down to science' haughty tread,
And turns the wheel of smutty artifice;
New governments arise, dilate, decay,
And foster creeds and churches to their tastes;
At each advance, we cry, "Behold, the end!"
Till some fresh wonder breaks upon the age.
But man, the moral creature, midst it all
Stands still unchanged; nor moves towards virtue more,
Nor comprehends the mysteries in himself,
More than when Plato taught academies,
Or Zeno thundered from his Attic porch.
PEPE. I know not that; I only want my scheme
Tried for a while. I am a politician,
A wrongs-of-man man. Hang philosophy!
Let metaphysics swallow, at a gulp,
Its last two syllables, and purge itself
Clean of its filthy humors! I am one
Ready for martyrdom, for stake and fire,
If I can make my great idea take root!
Zounds! cousin, if I had an audience,
I'd make you shudder at my eloquence!
I have an itching to reform the world.
LANCIOTTO. Begin at home, then.
PEPE. Home is not my sphere;
Heaven picked me out to teach my fellow-men.
I am a very firebrand of truth—
A self-consuming, doomed, devoted brand—
That burns to ashes while I light the world!
I feel it in me. I am moved, inspired,
Stirred into utterance, by some mystic power
Of which I am the humble instrument.
LANCIOTTO. A bad digestion, sage, a bilious turn,
A gnawing stomach, or a pinching shoe.
PEPE. O! hear, but spare the scoffer! Spare the wretch
Who sneers at the anointed man of truth!
When we reached that, I and my followers
Would rend you limb from limb. There!—ha! ha! ha! [*Laughing.*]
Have I not caught the slang these fellows preach;

A grand, original idea, to back it;
And all the stock in trade of a reformer?

LANCIOTTO. You have indeed; nor do I wonder, Pepe.
Fool as you are, I promise you success
In your new calling, if you'll set it up.
The thing is far too simple.

[*Trumpet sounds within.*]

PEPE. Hist! my lord.

LANCIOTTO. That calls me to myself.

PEPE. At that alarm,
All Rimini leaped up upon its feet.
Cousin, your bridal-train. You groan! 'Ods wounds!
Here is the bridegroom sorely malcontent—
The sole sad face in Rimini. Since morn,
A quiet man could hardly walk the streets,
For flowers and streamers. All the town is gay.
Perhaps 'tis merry o'er your misery.

LANCIOTTO. Perhaps; but that it knows not.

PEPE. Yes, it does:
It knows that when a man's about to wed,
He's ripe to laugh at. Cousin, tell me, now,
Why is Paolo on the way so long?
Ravenna's but eight leagues from Rimini—

LANCIOTTO. That's just the measure of your tongue, good fool.
You trouble me. I've had enough of you—
Begone!

PEPE. I'm going; but you see I limp.
Have pity on a cripple, gentle Count.

[*Limps.*]

LANCIOTTO. Pepe!

PEPE. A miracle, a miracle!
See, see, my lord, at Pepe's saintly name
The lame jog on.

MALATESTA [*without*]. Come, Lanciotto!

LANCIOTTO. Hark!
My father calls.

PEPE. If he were mine, I'd go—
That's a good boy!

[*Pats* LANCIOTTO'S *back.*]

LANCIOTTO [*starting*]. Hands off! you'll rue it else! [*Exit.*

PEPE [*laughing*]. Ha! ha! I laid my hand upon his hump!
Heavens, how he squirmed! And what a wish I had
To cry, Ho! camel! leap upon his back,
And ride him to the devil! So, we've had
A pleasant flitting round philosophy!
The Count and Fool bumped heads, and struck ideas
Out by the contact! Quite a pleasant talk—
A friendly conversation, nothing more—
'Twixt nobleman and jester. Ho! my bird,
I can toss lures as high as any man.
So, I amuse you with my harmless wit?
Pepe's your friend now—you can trust in him—
An honest, simple fool! Just try it once,
You ugly, misbegotten clod of dirt!
Ay, but the hump—the touch upon the hump—
The start and wriggle—that was rare! Ha! ha! [*Exit, laughing.*

SCENE 2. *The Same. The Grand Square before the Castle. Soldiers on guard, with banners, &c. Citizens, in holiday dresses, cross the scene. The houses are hung with trophies, banners, garlands, &c.*

Enter MALATESTA, *with guards, attendants, &c.*

MALATESTA. Captain, take care the streets be not choked up
By the rude rabble. Send to Cæsar's bridge
A strong detachment of your men, and clear
The way before them. See that nothing check
The bride's first entrance into Rimini.
Station your veterans in the front. Count Guido
Comes with his daughter, and his eyes are sharp.
Keep up a show of strength before him, sir;
And set some laborers to work upon
The broken bastion. Make all things look bright;
As if we stood in eager readiness,
And high condition, to begin a war.

CAPTAIN. I will, my lord.

MALATESTA. Keep Guido in your eye;
And if you see him looking over-long
On any weakness of our walls, just file
Your bulkiest fellows round him; or get up
A scuffle with the people; anything—
Even if you break a head or two—to draw
His vision off. But where our strength is great,

Take heed to make him see it. You conceive?

CAPTAIN. Trust me, my lord.
[*Exit with guards.*

Enter PEPE

PEPE. Room, room! A hall; a hall!
I pray you, good man, has the funeral passed?

MALATESTA. Who is it asks?

PEPE. Pepe of Padua,
A learned doctor of uncivil law.

MALATESTA. But how a funeral?

PEPE. You are weak of wit.
Francesca of Ravenna's borne to church,
And never issues thence.

MALATESTA. How, doctor, pray?

PEPE. Now, for a citizen of Rimini,
You're sadly dull. Does she not issue thence
Fanny of Rimini? A glorious change,—
A kind of resurrection in the flesh!

MALATESTA [*laughing*]. Ha! ha! thou cunning villain! I was caught.
I own it, doctor.

PEPE [*aside*]. This old fool would laugh
To see me break a straw, because the bits
Were of unequal lengths. My character
Carries more dulness, in the guise of wit,
Than would suffice to break an ass's back.
[*Distant shouts, music, &c.*]
Hark! here comes Jeptha's daughter, jogging on
With timbrels and with dances.

MALATESTA. Jeptha's daughter!
How so?

PEPE. Her father's sacrifice.

MALATESTA [*laughing*]. Ho! ho!
You'll burst my belt! O! you outrageous wretch,
To jest at Scripture!

PEPE. You outlandish heathen,
'Tis not in Scripture!

MALATESTA. Is it not?

PEPE. No more
Than you are in heaven. Mere Hebrew history.
She went up to the mountains, to bewail
The too-long keeping of her honesty.
There's woman for you! there's a character!
What man would ever think of such a thing?
Ah! we of Rimini have little cause
For such a sorrow. Would she'd been my wife!
I'll marry any woman in her case.

MALATESTA. Why, Pepe?

PEPE. Why? because, in two months' time,
Along comes father Jeptha with his knife,
And there's an end. Where is your sacrifice?
Where's Isaac, Abraham? Build your altar up:
One pile will do for both.

MALATESTA. That's Scripture, sure.

PEPE. Then I'm a ram, and you may slaughter me
In Isaac's stead.

MALATESTA. Here comes the vanguard. Where,
Where is that laggard?

PEPE. At the mirror, uncle,
Making himself look beautiful. He comes,
[*Looking out.*]
Fresh as a bridegroom! Mark his doublet's fit
Across the shoulders, and his hose!—
By Jove, he nearly looks like any other man!

MALATESTA. You'd best not let him hear you. Sirrah, knave,
I have a mind to swinge you!
[*Seizes his ear.*]

PEPE. Loose my ear!
You've got the wrong sow, swineherd! You're unjust.
Being his father, I was fool sufficient
To think you fashioned him to suit yourself,
By way of a variety. The thought
Was good enough, the practice damnable.

MALATESTA. Hush! or I'll clap you in the pillory.

Enter LANCIOTTO

PEPE [*sings*]. Ho, ho, ho, ho!—old Time has wings—

We're born, we mourn, we wed, we bed,
We have a devilish aching head;
So down we lie,
And die, and fry;
And there's a merry end of things!

[*Music, &c., within.*]

Here come Ravenna's eagles for a roost
In Rimini! The air is black with them.
When go they hence? Wherever yon bird builds,

The nest remains for ages. Have an eye,
Or Malatesta's elephant may feel
The eagle's talons.

LANCIOTTO. You're a raven, croaker.

PEPE. And you no white crow, to insure us luck.

MALATESTA. There's matter in his croak.

PEPE. There always is;
But men lack ears.

MALATESTA. Then eyes must do our work.
Old Guido shall be looked to. If his force
Appear too great, I'll camp him out of town.

LANCIOTTO. Father, you are a sorry host.

MALATESTA. Well, well,
I'm a good landlord, though. I do not like
This flight of eagles more than Pepe. 'Sdeath!
Guido was ever treacherous.

LANCIOTTO. My lord,
You mar my holiday by such a thought.
My holiday! Dear saints! it seems to me
That all of you are mocking me.

PEPE. So—so—
Guido was ever treacherous?—so—so!

MALATESTA. So—so! How so?

PEPE. What if this treachery
Run in the blood? We'll tap a vein then—so!

MALATESTA. Sew up your mouth, and mind your fooling, fool!

PEPE. Am I not fooling? Why, my lord, I thought
The fooling exquisite.

LANCIOTTO [*aside*]. This thoughtless knave
Hits near us sometimes with his random shafts.
Marriage for me! I cannot comprehend,
I cannot take it to my heart; the thing
Seems gross, absurd, ridiculous. Ah! well,
My father bears the folly of it all;
I'm but an actor in his comedy.
My part is bad, but I must through with it.
[*Retires.*]

[*Shouts, music, &c., within.*]

PEPE. Look! here's the whole parade! Mark yonder knave—
The head one with the standard. Nature, nature!
Hadst thou a hand in such a botch-work? Why,
A forest of his legs would scarcely make
A bunch of fagots. Mark old Guido, too!
He looks like Judas with his silver. Ho!
Here's news from sweet Ravenna!

MALATESTA [*laughing*]. Ha! ha! ha!

PEPE. Ah! now the bride!—that's something—she is toothsome.
Look you, my lord—now, while the progress halts—
Cousin Paolo, has he got the dumps?
Mercy! to see him, one might almost think
'Twas his own marriage. What a doleful face!
The boy is ill. He caught a fever, uncle,
Travelling across the marshes. Physic! physic!
If he be really dying, get a doctor,
And cut the matter short. 'Twere merciful.

MALATESTA. For heaven's sake, cease your clamor! I shall have
No face to meet them else. 'Tis strange, for all:
What ails Paolo?

PEPE. Dying, by this hand!

MALATESTA. Then I will hang you.

PEPE. Don't take up my craft.
Wit's such a stranger in your brain that I
Scarce knew my lodger venturing from your mouth.
Now they come on again.

MALATESTA. Stand back!

PEPE [*looking round*]. The bridegroom?
He flies betimes, before the bride shows fight.
[*Walks back, looking for* LANCIOTTO.]

[*Music, shouts, ringing of bells, &c. Enter Men-at-arms, with banners, &c.,* GUIDO, CARDINAL, *Knights, Attendants, &c.; then* PAOLO, *conducting* FRANCESCA, *followed by* RITTA, *Ladies, Pages, &c., and other Men-at-arms. They file around the stage, and halt.*]

MALATESTA. Welcome to Rimini, Count Guido! Welcome.
And fair impressions of our poor abode,
To you, my daughter! You are well returned,
My son, Paolo! Let me bless you, son.
[PAOLO *approaches.*]
How many spears are in old Guido's train?
[*Apart to* PAOLO.]

PAOLO. Some ten-score.

MALATESTA. Footmen?
PAOLO. Double that.
MALATESTA. 'Tis well.
Again I bid you welcome! Make no show
Of useless ceremony with us. Friends
Have closer titles than the empty name.
We have provided entertainment, Count,
For all your followers, in the midst of us.
We trust the veterans of Rimini
May prove your soldiers that our courtesy
Does not lag far behind their warlike zeal.
Let us drop Guelf and Ghibelin henceforth,
Coupling the names of Rimini and Ravenna
As bridegroom's to his bride's.

GUIDO. Count Malatesta,
I am no rhetorician, or my words
Might keep more even with the love I feel:
Simply, I thank you. With an honest hand
I take the hand which you extend to me,
And hope our grasp may never lose its warmth.—
You marked the bastion by the water-side?
Weak as a bulrush. [*Apart to a Knight.*]

KNIGHT. Tottering weak, my lord.

GUIDO. Remember it; and when you're private, sir,
Draw me a plan.

KNIGHT. I will, my lord.

GUIDO. How's this?
I do not see my future son-in-law.

MALATESTA. Lanciotto!

LANCIOTTO [*advancing*]. I am here, my lord.

FRANCESCA [*starting*]. O! heaven!
Is that my husband, Count Paolo? You,
You then, among the rest, have played me false!
He is—[*Apart to* PAOLO.]

PAOLO. My brother.

LANCIOTTO [*aside*]. Ha! she turns from me.

PEPE [*approaching* LANCIOTTO, *sings*].

Around, around the lady turned,
She turned not to her lord;
She turned around to a gallant, gallant knight,
Who ate at his father's board.

A pretty ballad! all on one string though.

LANCIOTTO. Pepe, go hence! [PEPE *retires.*]
[*Aside.*] I saw her start and pale,
Turn off with horror; as if she had seen—
What?—simply me. For, am I not enough,
And something over, to make ladies quail,
Start, hide their faces, whisper to their friends,
Point at me—dare she?—and perform such tricks
As women will when monsters blast their sight?
O! saints above me, have I come so low?
Yon damsel of Ravenna shall bewail
That start and shudder. I am mad, mad, mad!
I must be patient. They have trifled with her:
Lied to her, lied! There's half the misery
Of this broad earth, all crowded in one word.
Lied, lied!—Who has not suffered from a lie?
They're all aghast—all looking at me too.
Francesca's whiter than the brow of fear:
Paolo talks.—Brother, is that well meant?
What if I draw my sword, and fight my way
Out of this cursed town? 'Twould be relief.
Has shame no hiding-place? I've touched the depth
Of human infamy, and there I rest.
By heaven, I'll brave this business out! Shall they
Say at Ravenna that Count Lanciotto,
Who's driven their shivering squadrons to their homes,
Haggard with terror, turned before their eyes
And slunk away? They'll look me from the field,
When we encounter next. Why should not I
Strut with my shapeless body, as old Guido
Struts with his shapeless heart? I'll do it!
[*Offers, but shrinks back.*] 'Sdeath!
Am I so false as to forswear myself?
Lady Francesca! [*Approaches* FRANCESCA.]

FRANCESCA. Sir—my lord—

LANCIOTTO. Dear lady,
I have a share in your embarrassment,
And know the feelings that possess you now.

FRANCESCA. O! you do not.

PAOLO [*advancing*]. My lady—

LANCIOTTO. Gentle brother,
Leave this to me. [PAOLO *retires.*]

FRANCESCA. Pray do not send him off.

LANCIOTTO. 'Tis fitter so.
FRANCESCA. He comforts me.
LANCIOTTO. Indeed?
Do you need comfort?
FRANCESCA. No, no—pardon me!
But then—he is—you are—
LANCIOTTO. Take breath, and speak.
FRANCESCA. I am confused, 'tis true. But, then, my lord;
You are a stranger to me; and Paolo
I've known so long!
LANCIOTTO. Since yesterday.
FRANCESCA. Ah! well:
But the relationship between us two
Is of so close a nature, while the knowledge,
That each may have of each, so slender is
That the two jar. Besides, Paolo is
Nothing to me, while you are everything.
Can I not act? [*Aside.*]
LANCIOTTO. I scarcely understand.
You say your knowledge of me, till today,
Was incomplete. Has naught been said of me
By Count Paolo or your father?
FRANCESCA. Yes;
But nothing definite.
LANCIOTTO. Perchance, no hint
As to my ways, my feelings, manners, or—
Or—or—as I was saying—ha! ha!—or— [*Laughing.*]
As to my person?
FRANCESCA. Nothing, as to that.
LANCIOTTO. To what?
FRANCESCA. Your—person.
LANCIOTTO. That's the least of all. [*Turns aside.*]
Now, had I Guido of Ravenna's head
Under this heel, I'd grind it into dust!
False villain, to betray his simple child!
And thou, Paolo—not a whit behind—
Helping his craft with inconsiderate love!—
Lady Francesca, when my brother left,
I charged him, as he loved me, to conceal
Nothing from you that bore on me: and now
That you have seen me, and conversed with me,
If you object to anything in me,—
Go, I release you.
FRANCESCA. But Ravenna's peace?
LANCIOTTO. Shall not be perilled.
GUIDO [*coming behind, whispers her*]. Trust him not, my child;
I know his ways; he'd rather fight than wed.
'Tis but a wish to have the war afoot.
Stand firm for poor Ravenna!
LANCIOTTO. Well, my lady,
Shall we conclude a lasting peace between us
By truce or marriage rites?
GUIDO [*whispers her*]. The devil tempts thee:
Think of Ravenna, think of me!
LANCIOTTO. My lord,
I see my father waits you. [GUIDO *retires.*]
FRANCESCA. Gentle sir,
You do me little honor in the choice.
LANCIOTTO. My aim is justice.
FRANCESCA. Would you cast me off?
LANCIOTTO. Not for the world, if honestly obtained;
Not for the world would I obtain you falsely.
FRANCESCA. The rites were half concluded ere we met.
LANCIOTTO. Meeting, would you withdraw?
FRANCESCA. No. Bitter word! [*Aside.*]
LANCIOTTO. No! Are you dealing fairly?
FRANCESCA. I have said.
LANCIOTTO. O! rapture, rapture! Can it be that I—
Now I'll speak plainly; for a choice like thine
Implies such love as woman never felt.
Love me! Then monsters beget miracles,
And Heaven provides where human means fall short.
Lady, I'll worship thee! I'll line thy path
With suppliant kings! Thy waiting-maids shall be
Unransomed princesses! Mankind shall bow
One neck to thee, as Persia's multitudes
Before the rising sun! From this small town,
This centre of my conquests, I will spread
An empire touching the extremes of earth!
I'll raise once more the name of ancient Rome;
And what she swayed she shall reclaim again!
If I grow mad because you smile on me,
Think of the glory of thy love; and know
How hard it is, for such an one as I,
To gaze unshaken on divinity!
There's no such love as mine alive in man.
From every corner of the frowning earth,
It has been crowded back into my heart.

Now, take it all! If that be not enough,
Ask, and thy wish shall be omnipotent!
Your hand. [*Takes her hand.*] It wavers.

FRANCESCA. So does not my heart.

LANCIOTTO. Bravo! Thou art every way a soldier's wife;
Thou shouldst have been a Cæsar's! Father, hark!
I blamed your judgment, only to perceive
The weakness of my own.

MALATESTA. What means all this?

LANCIOTTO. It means that this fair lady—though I gave
Release to her, and to Ravenna—placed
The liberal hand, which I restored to her,
Back in my own, of her own free good-will.
Is it not wonderful?

MALATESTA. How so?

LANCIOTTO. How so!

PAOLO. Alas! 'tis as I feared! [*Aside.*]

MALATESTA. You're humble?—How?

LANCIOTTO. Now shall I cry aloud to all the world,
Make my deformity my pride, and say,
Because she loves me, I may boast of it?
[*Aside.*]
No matter, father, I am happy; you,
As the blessed cause, shall share my happiness.
Let us be moving. Revels, dashed with wine,
Shall multiply the joys of this sweet day!
There's not a blessing in the cup of life
I have not tasted of within an hour!

FRANCESCA [*aside*]. Thus I begin the practice of deceit,
Taught by deceivers, at a fearful cost.
The bankrupt gambler has become the cheat,
And lives by arts that erewhile ruined me.
Where it will end, Heaven knows; but I—
I have betrayed the noblest heart of all!

LANCIOTTO. Draw down thy dusky vapors, sullen night—
Refuse, ye stars, to shine upon the world—
Let everlasting blackness wrap the sun,
And whisper terror to the universe!
We need ye not! we'll blind ye, if ye dare
Peer with lack-lustre on our revelry!
I have at heart a passion, that would make
All nature blaze with recreated light!
[*Exeunt.*

ACT IV

SCENE I. *The Same. An Apartment in the Castle*

Enter LANCIOTTO

LANCIOTTO. It cannot be that I have duped myself,
That my desire has played into the hand
Of my belief; yet such a thing might be.
We palm more frauds upon our simple selves
Than knavery puts upon us. Could I trust
The open candor of an angel's brow,
I must believe Francesca's. But the tongue
Should consummate the proof upon the brow,
And give the truth its word. The fault lies there.
I've tried her. Press her as I may to it,
She will not utter those three little words—
"I love thee." She will say, "I'll marry you;—
I'll be your duteous wife;—I'll cheer your days;—
I'll do whate'er I can." But at the point
Of present love, she ever shifts the ground,
Winds round the word, laughs, calls me "Infidel!—
How can I doubt?" So, on and on. But yet,
For all her dainty ways, she never says,
Frankly, I love thee. I am jealous—true!
Suspicious—true! distrustful of myself;—
She knows all that. Ay, and she likewise knows,
A single waking of her morning breath
Would blow these vapors off. I would not take
The barren offer of a heartless hand,
If all the Indies cowered under it.
Perhaps she loves another? No; she said,
"I love you, Count, as well as any man";
And laughed, as if she thought that precious wit.
I turn her nonsense into argument,
And think I reason. Shall I give her up?
Rail at her heartlessness, and bid her go
Back to Ravenna? But she clings to me,
At the least hint of parting. Ah! 'tis sweet,
Sweeter than slumber to the lids of pain,
To fancy that a shadow of true love

May fall on this God-stricken mould of woe,
From so serene a nature. Beautiful
Is the first vision of a desert brook,
Shining beneath its palmy garniture,
To one who travels on his easy way;
What is it to the blood-shot, aching eye
Of some poor wight who crawls with gory feet,
In famished madness, to its very brink;
And throws his sun-scorched limbs upon the cool
And humid margin of its shady strand,
To suck up life at every eager gasp?
Such seems Francesca to my thirsting soul;
Shall I turn off and die?

Enter PEPE

PEPE. Good-morning, cousin!
LANCIOTTO. Good-morning to your foolish majesty!
PEPE. The same to your majestic foolery!
LANCIOTTO. You compliment!
PEPE. I am a troubadour,
A ballad-monger of fine mongrel ballads,
And therefore running o'er with elegance.
Wilt hear my verse?
LANCIOTTO. With patience?
PEPE. No, with rapture.
You must go mad—weep, rend your clothes, and roll
Over and over, like the ancient Greeks,
When listening to the Iliad.
LANCIOTTO. Sing, then, sing!
And if you equal Homer in your song,
Why, roll I must, by sheer compulsion.
PEPE. Nay,
You lack the temper of the fine-eared Greek.
You will not roll; but that shall not disgrace
My gallant ballad, fallen on evil times.
[*Sings.*]

My father had a blue-black head,
My uncle's head was reddish—maybe,
My mother's hair was noways red,
Sing high ho! the pretty baby!

Mark the simplicity of that! 'Tis called
"The Babe's Confession," spoken just before
His father strangled him.
LANCIOTTO. Most marvellous!
You struggle with a legend worth your art.
PEPE. Now to the second stanza. Note the hint
I drop about the baby's parentage:
So delicately too! A maid might sing,
And never blush at it. Girls love these songs
Of sugared wickedness. They'll go miles about,
To say a foul thing in a cleanly way.
A decent immorality, my lord,
Is art's specific. Get the passions up,
But never wring the stomach.
LANCIOTTO. Triumphant art!
[PEPE *sings.*]

My father combed his blue-black head,
My uncle combed his red head—maybe,
My mother combed my head, and said,
Sing high ho! my red-haired baby.

LANCIOTTO. Fie, fie! go comb your hair in private.
PEPE. What!
Will you not hear? Now comes the tragedy
[*Sings.*]

My father tore my red, red head,
My uncle tore my father's—maybe,
My mother tore both till they bled—
Sing high ho! your brother's baby!

LANCIOTTO. Why, what a hair-rending!
PEPE. Thence wigs arose;
A striking epoch in man's history.
But did you notice the concluding line,
Sung by the victim's mother? There's a hit!
"Sing high ho! your brother's baby!"
Which brother's, pray you? That's the mystery,
The adumbration of poetic art,
And there I leave it to perplex mankind.
It has a moral, fathers should regard,—
A black-haired dog breeds not a red-haired cur.
Treasure this knowledge: you're about to wive;
And no one knows what accident—
LANCIOTTO. Peace, fool!
So all this cunning thing was wound about,
To cast a jibe at my deformity? [*Tears off* PEPE'*s cap.*]
There lies your cap, the emblem that protects
Your head from chastisement. Now, Pepe, hark!

Of late you've taken to reviling me;
Under your motley, you have dared to jest
At God's inflictions. Let me tell you, fool,
No man e'er lived, to make a second jest
At me, before your time!

PEPE. Boo! Bloody-bones!
If you're a coward—which I hardly think—
You'll have me flogged, or put into a cell,
Or fed to wolves. If you are bold of heart,
You'll let me run. Do not; I'll work you harm!
I, Beppo Pepe, standing as a man,
Without my motley, tell you, in plain terms,
I'll work you harm—I'll do you mischief, man!

LANCIOTTO. I, Lanciotto, Count of Rimini,
Will hang you, then. Put on your jingling cap;
You please my father. But remember, fool,
No jests at me!

PEPE. I will try earnest next.

LANCIOTTO. And I the gallows.

PEPE. Well, cry quits, cry quits!
I'll stretch your heart, and you my neck—quits, quits!

LANCIOTTO. Go, fool! Your weakness bounds your malice.

PEPE. Yes.
So you all think, you savage gentlemen,
Until you feel my sting. Hang, hang away!
It is an airy, wholesome sort of death,
Much to my liking. When I hang, my friend,
You'll be chief mourner, I can promise you.
Hang me! I've quite a notion to be hung:
I'll do my utmost to deserve it. Hang!
[*Exit*.

LANCIOTTO. I am bemocked on all sides. My sad state
Has given the licensed and unlicensed fool
Charter to challenge me at every turn.
The jester's laughing bauble blunts my sword,
His gibes cut deeper than its fearful edge;
And I, a man, a soldier, and a prince,
Before this motley patchwork of a man,
Stand all appalled, as if he were a glass
Wherein I saw my own deformity.
O Heaven! a tear—one little tear—to wash
This aching dryness of the heart away!

Enter PAOLO

PAOLO. What ails the fool? He passed me, muttering
The strangest garbage in the fiercest tone.
"Ha! ha!" cried he, "they made a fool of me—
A motley man, a slave; as if I felt
No stir in me of manly dignity!
Ha! ha! a fool—a painted plaything, toy—
For men to kick about this dirty world!—
My world as well as theirs.—God's world, I trow!
I will get even with them yet—ha! ha!
In the democracy of death we'll square.
I'll crawl and lie beside a king's own son;
Kiss a young princess, dead lip to dead lip;
Pull the Pope's nose; and kick down Charlemagne,
Throne, crown, and all, where the old idiot sprawls,
Safe as he thinks, rotting in royal state!"
And then he laughed and gibbered, as if drunk
With some infernal ecstasy.

LANCIOTTO. Poor fool!
That is the groundwork of his malice, then,—
His conscious difference from the rest of men?
I, of all men, should pity him the most.
Poor Pepe! I'll be kinder. I have wronged
A feeling heart. Poor Pepe!

PAOLO. Sad again!
Where has the rapture gone of yesterday?

LANCIOTTO. Where are the leaves of Summer? Where the snows
Of last year's Winter? Where the joys and griefs
That shut our eyes to yesternight's repose,
And woke not on the morrow? Joys and griefs,
Huntsmen and hounds, ye follow us as game,
Poor panting outcasts of your forest-law!
Each cheers the others,—one with wild halloos,
And one with whines and howls.—A dreadful chase,
That only closes when horns sound *a mort!*

PAOLO. Thus ever up and down! Arouse yourself,
Balance your mind more evenly, and hunt
For honey in the wormwood.

LANCIOTTO. Or find gall
Hid in the hanging chalice of the rose:
Which think you better? If my mood offend,
We'll turn to business,—to the empty cares
That make such pother in our feverish life.
When at Ravenna, did you ever hear
Of any romance in Francesca's life?
A love-tilt, gallantry, or anything
That might have touched her heart?

PAOLO. Not lightly even.
I think her heart as virgin as her hand.

LANCIOTTO. Then there is hope.

PAOLO. Of what?

LANCIOTTO. Of winning her.

PAOLO. Grammercy! Lanciotto, are you sane?
You boasted yesterday—

LANCIOTTO. And changed today.
Is that so strange? I always mend the fault
Of yesterday with wisdom of today.
She does not love me.

PAOLO. Pshaw! she marries you:
'Twere proof enough for me.

LANCIOTTO. Perhaps, she loves you.

PAOLO. Me, Lanciotto, me! For mercy's sake,
Blot out such thoughts—they madden me! What, love—
She love—yet marry you!

LANCIOTTO. It moves you much.
'Twas but a fleeting fancy, nothing more.

PAOLO. You have such wild conjectures!

LANCIOTTO. Well, to me
They seem quite tame; they are my bedfellows.
Think, to a modest woman, what must be
The loathsome kisses of an unloved man—
A gross, coarse ruffian!

PAOLO. O, good heavens, forbear!

LANCIOTTO. What shocks you so?

PAOLO. The picture which you draw,
Wronging yourself by horrid images.

LANCIOTTO. Until she love me, till I know, beyond
The cavil of a doubt, that she is mine—
Wholly, past question—do you think that I
Could so afflict the woman whom I love?

PAOLO. You love her, Lanciotto!

LANCIOTTO. Next to you,
Dearer than anything in nature's scope.

PAOLO [*aside*]. O! Heaven, that I must bear this! Yes, and more,—
More torture than I dare to think upon,
Spreads out before me with the coming years,
And holds a record blotted with my tears,
As that which I must suffer!

LANCIOTTO. Come, Paolo,
Come help me woo. I need your guiding eye,
To signal me, if I should sail astray.

PAOLO. O! torture, torture! [*Aside.*]

LANCIOTTO. You and I, perchance,
Joining our forces, may prevail at last.
They call love like a battle. As for me,
I'm not a soldier equal to such wars,
Despite my arduous schooling. Tutor me
In the best arts of amorous strategy.
I am quite raw, Paolo. Glances, sighs,
Sweets of the lip, and arrows of the eye,
Shrugs, cringes, compliments, are new to me;
And I shall handle them with little art.
Will you instruct me?

PAOLO. Conquer for yourself.
Two captains share one honor: keep it all.
What if I ask to share the spoils?

LANCIOTTO [*laughing*]. Ha! ha!
I'll trust you, brother. Let us go to her:
Francesca is neglected while we jest.
I know not how it is, but your fair face,
And noble figure, always cheer me up,
More than your words; there's healing in them, too,
For my worst griefs. Dear brother, let us in.
[*Exeunt.*

SCENE 2. *The Same. A Chamber in the Same*

FRANCESCA *and* RITTA *discovered at the bridal toilet*

RITTA [*sings*].

Ring high, ring high! to earth and sky;
  A lady goes a-wedding;
The people shout, the show draws out,
  And smiles the bride is shedding.

No bell for you, ye ragged few;
  A beggar goes a-wedding;
The people sneer, the thing's so queer,
  And tears the bride is shedding.

Ring low, ring low! dull bell of woe,
  One tone will do for either;
The lady glad, and beggar sad,
  Have both lain down together.

FRANCESCA. A mournful ballad!
RITTA. I scarce knew I sang.
I'm weary of this wreath. These orange-flowers
Will never be adjusted to my taste:
Strive as I will, they ever look awry.
My fingers ache!
FRANCESCA. Not more than my poor head.
There, leave them so.
RITTA. That's better, yet not well.
FRANCESCA. They are but fading things, not worth your pains:
They'll scarce outlive the marriage merriment.
Ritta, these flowers are hypocrites; they show
An outside gayety, yet die within,
Minute by minute. You shall see them fall,
Black with decay, before the rites are o'er.
RITTA. How beautiful you are!
FRANCESCA. Fie, flatterer!
White silk and laces, pearls and orange-flowers,
Would do as much for any one.
RITTA. No, no!
You give them grace, they nothing give to you.
Why, after all, you make the wreath look well;
But somewhat dingy, where it lies against
Your pulsing temple, sullen with disgrace.
Ah! well, your Count should be the proudest man
That ever led a lady into church,
Were he a modern Alexander. Poh!
What are his trophies to a face like that?
FRANCESCA. I seem to please you, Ritta.
RITTA. Please yourself,
And you will please me better. You are sad:
I marked it ever since you saw the Count.
I fear the splendor of his victories,
And his sweet grace of manner—for, in faith,
His is the gentlest, grandest character,
Despite his—
FRANCESCA. Well?
RITTA. Despite his—
FRANCESCA. Ritta, what?
RITTA. Despite his difference from Count Paolo.— [FRANCESCA *staggers.*]
What is the matter? [*Supporting her.*]
FRANCESCA. Nothing; mere fatigue.
Hand me my kerchief. I am better now.
What were you saying?
RITTA. That I fear the Count
Has won your love.
FRANCESCA. Would that be cause for fear? [*Laughing.*]
RITTA. O! yes, indeed! Once—long ago—I was
Just fool enough to tangle up my heart
With one of these same men. 'Twas terrible!
Morning or evening, waking or asleep,
I had no peace. Sighs, groans, and standing tears,
Counted my moments through the blessed day.
And then to this there was a dull, strange ache
Forever sleeping in my breast,—a numbing pain,
That would not for an instant be forgot.
O! but I loved him so, that very feeling
Became intolerable. And I believed
This false Giuseppe, too, for all the sneers,
The shrugs and glances, of my intimates.
They slandered me and him, yet I believed.
He was a noble, and his love to me
Was a reproach, a shame, yet I believed.
He wearied of me, tried to shake me off,
Grew cold and formal, yet I would not doubt.
O! lady, I was true! Nor till I saw
Giuseppe walk through the cathedral door
With Dora, the rich usurer's niece, upon
The very arm to which I clung so oft,
Did I so much as doubt him. Even then—
More is my shame—I made excuses for him.
"Just this or that had forced him to the course:
Perhaps, he loved me yet—a little yet.
His fortune, or his family, had driven
My poor Giuseppe thus against his heart.
The low are sorry judges for the great.

Yes, yes, Giuseppe loved me!" But at last
I did awake. It might have been with less:
There was no need of crushing me, to break
My silly dream up. In the street, it chanced,
Dora and he went by me, and he laughed—
A bold, bad laugh—right in my poor pale face,
And turned and whispered Dora, and she laughed.
Ah! then I saw it all. I've been awake,
Ever since then, I warrant you. And now
I only pray for him sometimes, when friends
Tell his base actions towards his hapless wife.
O! I am lying—I pray every night!
[*Weeps.*]

FRANCESCA. Poor Ritta. [*Weeping.*]

RITTA. No! blest Ritta! Thank kind Heaven,
That kept me spotless when he tempted me,
And my weak heart was pleading with his tongue,
Pray, do not weep. You spoil your eyes for me.
But never love; O! it is terrible!

FRANCESCA. I'll strive against it.

RITTA. Do: because, my lady,
Even a husband may be false, you know;
Ay, even to so sweet a wife as you.
Men have odd tastes. They'll surfeit on the charms
Of Cleopatra, and then turn aside
To woo her blackamoor. 'Tis so, in faith;
Or Dora's uncle's gold had ne'er outbid
The boundless measure of a love like mine.
Think of it, lady, to weigh love with gold!
What could be meaner?

FRANCESCA. Nothing, nothing, Ritta.
Though gold's the standard measure of the world,
And seems to lighten everything beside.
Yet heap the other passions in the scale,
And balance them 'gainst that which gold outweighs—
Against this love—and you shall see how light
The most supreme of them are in the poise!
I speak by book and history; for love
Slights my high fortunes. Under cloth of state
The urchin cowers from pompous etiquette,
Waiving his function at the scowl of power,
And seeks the rustic cot to stretch his limbs
In homely freedom. I fulfill a doom.
We who are topmost on this heap of life
Are nearer to Heaven's hand than you below;
And so are used, as ready instruments,
To work its purposes. Let envy hide
Her witless forehead at a prince's name,
And fix her hopes upon a clown's content.
You, happy lowly, know not what it is
To groan beneath the crowned yoke of state,
And bear the goadings of the sceptre. Ah!
Fate drives us onward in a narrow way,
Despite our boasted freedom.

Enter PAOLO, *with Pages bearing torches*

Gracious saints!
What brought you here?

PAOLO. The bridegroom waits.

FRANCESCA. He does?
Let him wait on forever! I'll not go!
O! dear Paolo—

PAOLO. Sister!

FRANCESCA. It is well.
I have been troubled with a sleepless night.
My brain is wild. I know not what I say.
Pray, do not call me sister; it is cold.
I never had a brother, and the name
Sounds harshly to me. When you speak to me,
Call me Francesca.

PAOLO. You shall be obeyed.

FRANCESCA. I would not be obeyed. I'd have you do it
Because—because you love me—as a sister—
And of your own good-will, not my command,
Would please me.—Do you understand?

PAOLO. Too well! [*Aside.*]
'Tis a nice difference.

FRANCESCA. Yet you understand?
Say that you do.

PAOLO. I do.

FRANCESCA. That pleases me.
'Tis flattering if our—friends appreciate
Our nicer feelings.

PAOLO. I await you, lady.

FRANCESCA. Ritta, my gloves.—Ah, yes, I have them on;
Though I'm not quite prepared. Arrange my veil;

It folds too closely. That will do; retire.
[Ritta *retires.*]
So, Count Paolo, you have come, hot haste,
To lead me to the church,—to have your share
In my undoing? And you came, in sooth,
Because they sent you? You are very tame!
And if they sent, was it for you to come?

Paolo. Lady, I do not understand this scorn.
I came, as is my duty, to escort
My brother's bride to him. When next you're called,
I'll send a lackey.

Francesca. I have angered you.

Paolo. With reason: I would not appear to you
Low or contemptible.

Francesca. Why not to me?

Paolo. Lady, I'll not be catechized.

Francesca. Ha! Count!

Paolo. No! if you press me further, I will say
A word to madden you.—Stand still! You stray
Around the margin of a precipice.
I know what pleasure 'tis to pluck the flowers
That hang above destruction, and to gaze
Into the dread abyss, to see such things
As may be safely seen. 'Tis perilous:
The eye grows dizzy as we gaze below,
And a wild wish possesses us to spring
Into the vacant air. Beware, beware!
Lest this unholy fascination grow
Too strong to conquer!

Francesca. You talk wildly, Count;
There's not a gleam of sense in what you say;
I cannot hit your meaning.

Paolo. Lady, come!

Francesca. Count, you are cruel! [*Weeps.*]

Paolo. O! no; I would be kind.
But now, while reason over-rides my heart,
And seeming anger plays its braggart part—
In heaven's name, come!

Francesca. One word—one question more:
Is it your wish this marriage should proceed?

Paolo. It is.

Francesca. Come on! You shall not take my hand:
I'll walk alone—now, and forever!

Paolo [*taking her hand*]. Sister!
[*Exeunt* Paolo *and* Francesca, *with Pages.*

Ritta. O! misery, misery!—it is plain as day—
She loves Paolo! Why will those I love
Forever get themselves ensnared, and Heaven
Forever call on me to succor them?
Here was the mystery, then—the sighs and tears,
The troubled slumbers, and the waking dreams!
And now she's walking through the chapel-door,
Her bridal robe above an aching heart,
Dressed up for sacrifice. 'Tis terrible!
And yet she'll smile and do it. Smile, for years,
Until her heart breaks; and the nurses ask
The doctor of the cause. He'll answer too,
In hard thick Latin, and believe himself.
O! my dear mistress! Heaven, pray torture me!
Send back Giuseppe, let him ruin me,
And scorn me after; but, sweet Heaven, spare her!
I'll follow her. O! what a world is this!
[*Exit.*

Scene 3. *The Same. Interior of the Cathedral.* Lanciotto, Francesca, Paolo, Malatesta, Guido, Ritta, Pepe, *Lords, Knights, Priests, Pages, a bridal-train of Ladies, Soldiers, Citizens, Attendants, &c., discovered before the High Altar. Organ music. The rites being over, they advance.*

Malatesta. By heaven—

Pepe. O! uncle, uncle, you're in church!

Malatesta. I'll break your head, knave!

Pepe. I claim sanctuary.

Malatesta. Why, bridegroom, will you never kiss the bride?
We all are mad to follow you.

Pepe. Yes, yes;
Here was Paolo wetting his red lips
For the last minute. Kiss, and give him room.

Malatesta. You heaven-forsaken imp, be quiet now!

Pepe. Then there'd be naught worth hearing.

Malatesta. Bridegroom, come!

PEPE. Lord! he don't like it! Hey!—I told you so—
He backs at the first step. Does he not know
His trouble's just begun?

LANCIOTTO. Gentle Francesca,
Custom imposes somewhat on thy lips:
I'll make my levy. [*Kisses her. The others follow. Aside.*] Ha! she shrank! I felt
Her body tremble, and her quivering lips
Seemed dying under mine! I heard a sigh,
Such as breaks hearts—O! no, a very groan;
And then she turned a sickly, miserable look
On pale Paolo, and he shivered, too!
There is a mystery hangs around her,—ay,
Paolo knows it, too.—By all the saints,
I'll make him tell it, at the dagger's point!
Paolo!—here! I do adjure you, brother,
By the great love I bear you, to reveal
The secret of Francesca's grief.

PAOLO. I cannot.

LANCIOTTO. She told you nothing?

PAOLO. Nothing.

LANCIOTTO. Not a word?

PAOLO. Not one.

LANCIOTTO. What heard you at Ravenna, then?

PAOLO. Nothing.

LANCIOTTO. Here?

PAOLO. Nothing.

LANCIOTTO. Not the slightest hint?—
Don't stammer, man! Speak quick! I am in haste.

PAOLO. Never.

LANCIOTTO. What know you?

PAOLO. Nothing that concerns
Your happiness, Lanciotto. If I did,
Would I not tell unquestioned?

LANCIOTTO. Would you not?
You ask a question for me: answer it.

PAOLO. I have.

LANCIOTTO. You juggle, you turn deadly pale,
Fumble your dagger, stand with head half round,
Tapping your feet.—You dare not look at me!
By Satan! Count Paolo, let me say,
You look much like a full-convicted thief!

PAOLO. Brother!—

LANCIOTTO. Pshaw! brother! You deceive me, sir:
You and that lady have a devil's league,
To keep a devil's secret. Is it thus
You deal with me? Now, by the light above,
I'd give a dukedom for some fair pretext
To fly you all! She does not love me? Well,
I could bear that, and live away from her.
Love would be sweet, but want of it becomes
An early habit to such men as I.
But you—ah! there's the sorrow—whom I loved
An infant in your cradle; you who grew
Up in my heart, with every inch you gained;
You whom I loved for every quality,
Good, bad, and common, in your natural stock;
Ay, for your very beauty! It is strange, you'll say,
For such a crippled horror to do that,
Against the custom of his kind! O! yes,
I love, and you betray me!

PAOLO. Lanciotto,
This is sheer frenzy. Join your bride.

LANCIOTTO. I'll not!
What, go to her, to feel her very flesh
Crawl from my touch? to hear her sigh and moan,
As if God plagued her? Must I come to that?
Must I endure your hellish mystery
With my own wife, and roll my eyes away
In sentimental bliss? No, no! until
I go to her, with confident belief
In her integrity and candid love,
I'll shun her as a leper! [*Alarm-bells toll.*]

MALATESTA. What is that?

Enter, hastily, a MESSENGER *in disorder*

MESSENGER. My lord, the Ghibelins are up—

LANCIOTTO. And I
Will put them down again! I thank thee, Heaven,
For this unlooked-for aid! [*Aside.*]

MALATESTA. What force have they?

LANCIOTTO. It matters not,—nor yet the time, place, cause,
Of their rebellion. I would throttle it,
Were it a riot, or a drunken brawl!

MALATESTA. Nay, son, your bride—

LANCIOTTO. My bride will pardon me;
Bless me, perhaps, as I am going forth;—

Thank me, perhaps, if I should ne'er return.
[*Aside.*]
A soldier's duty has no bridals in it.

PAOLO. Lanciotto, this is folly. Let me take
Your usual place of honor.

LANCIOTTO [*laughing*]. Ha! ha! ha!
What! thou, a tilt-yard soldier, lead my troops!
My wife will ask it shortly. Not a word
Of opposition from the new-made bride?
Nay, she looks happier. O! accursed day,
That I was mated to an empty heart!
[*Aside.*]

MALATESTA. But, son—

LANCIOTTO. Well, father?

PEPE. Uncle, let him go.
He'll find it cooler on a battle-field
Than in his—

LANCIOTTO. Hark! the fool speaks oracles.
You, soldiers, who are used to follow me,
And front our charges, emulous to bear
The shock of battle on your forward arms,—
Why stand ye in amazement? Do your swords
Stick to their scabbards with inglorious rust?
Or has repose so weakened your big hearts,
That you can dream with trumpets at your ears?
Out with your steel! It shames me to behold
Such tardy welcome to my war-worn blade!
[*Draws.*]
[*The Knights and Soldiers draw.*]
Ho! draw our forces out! Strike camp, sound drums,
And set us on our marches! As I live,
I pity the next foeman who relies
On me for mercy! Farewell! to you all—
To all alike—a soldier's short farewell!
[*Going.*]
[PAOLO *stands before him.*]
Out of my way, thou juggler! [*Exit.*

PAOLO. He is gone!

ACT V

SCENE I. *The Same. The Garden of the Castle*

Enter PEPE, *singing*

'Tis jolly to walk in the shady greenwood
With a damsel by your side;
'Tis jolly to walk from the chapel-door,
With the hand of your pretty bride;
'Tis jolly to rest your weary head,
When life runs low and hope is fled,
On the heart where you confide:
'Tis jolly, jolly, jolly, they say,
They say—but I never tried.

Nor shall I ever till they dress their girls
In motley suits, and pair us, to increase
The race of fools. 'Twould be a noble thing,
A motley woman, had she wit enough
To bear the bell. But there's the misery:
You may make princes out of any stuff;
Fools come by nature. She'll make fifty kings—
Good, hearty tyrants, sound, cruel governors—
For one fine fool. There is Paolo, now,
A sweet-faced fellow with a wicked heart—
Talk of a flea, and you begin to scratch.
Lo! here he comes. And there's fierce crook-back's bride
Walking beside him—O, how gingerly!
Take care, my love! that is the very pace
We trip to hell with. Hunchback is away—
That was a fair escape for you; but, then,
The devil's ever with us, and that's worse.
See, the Ravenna giglet, Mistress Ritta,
And melancholy as a cow.—How's this?
I'll step aside, and watch you, pretty folks.
[*Hides behind the bushes.*]

Enter PAOLO *and* FRANCESCA, *followed by* RITTA. *He seats himself in an arbor, and reads.* RITTA *and* FRANCESCA *advance.*

FRANCESCA. Ritta.

RITTA. My lady.

FRANCESCA. You look tired.

RITTA. I'm not.

FRANCESCA. Go to your chamber.

RITTA. I would rather stay,
If it may please you. I require a walk
And the fresh atmosphere of breathing flowers,
To stir my blood. I am not very well.

FRANCESCA. I knew it, child. Go to your chamber, dear.
Paolo has a book to read to me.

RITTA. What, the romance? I should so love to hear!
I dote on poetry; and Count Paolo
Sweetens the Tuscan with his mellow voice.

I'm weary now, quite weary, and would rest.
FRANCESCA. Just now you wished to walk.
RITTA. Ah! did I so?
Walking, or resting, I would stay with you.
FRANCESCA. The Count objects. He told me, yesterday,
That you were restless while he read to me;
And stirred your feet amid the grass, and sighed,
And yawned, until he almost paused.
RITTA. Indeed
I will be quiet.
FRANCESCA. But he will not read.
RITTA. Let me go ask him. [*Runs toward* PAOLO.]
FRANCESCA. Stop! Come hither, Ritta.
[*She returns.*]
I saw your new embroidery in the hall,—
The needle in the midst of Argus' eyes;
It should be finished.
RITTA. I will bring it here.—
O no! my finger's sore; I cannot work.
FRANCESCA. Go to your room.
RITTA. Let me remain, I pray.
'Tis better, lady; you may wish for me:
I know you will be sorry if I go.
FRANCESCA. I shall not, girl. Do as I order you.
Will you be headstrong?
RITTA. Do you wish it, then?
FRANCESCA. Yes, Ritta.
RITTA. Yet you made pretexts enough,
Before you ordered.
FRANCESCA. You are insolent.
Will you remain against my will?
RITTA. Yes, lady;
Rather than not remain.
FRANCESCA. Ha! impudent!
RITTA. You wrong me, gentle mistress. Love like mine
Does not ask questions of propriety,
Nor stand on manners. I would do you good,
Even while you smote me; I would push you back,
With my last effort, from the crumbling edge
Of some high rock o'er which you toppled me.
FRANCESCA. What do you mean?
RITTA. I know.
FRANCESCA. Know what?
RITTA. Too much.
Pray, do not ask me.
FRANCESCA. Speak!
RITTA. I know—dear lady,
Be not offended—
FRANCESCA. Tell me, simpleton!
RITTA. You know I worship you; you know I'd walk
Straight into ruin for a whim of yours;
You know—
FRANCESCA. I know you act the fool. Talk sense!
RITTA. I know Paolo loves you.
FRANCESCA. Should he not?
He is my brother.
RITTA. More than brother should.
FRANCESCA. Ha! are you certain?
RITTA. Yes, of more than that.
FRANCESCA. Of more?
RITTA. Yes, lady; for you love him, too.
I've said it! Fling me to the carrion crows,
Kill me by inches, boil me in the pot
Count Guido promised me,—but, O, beware!
Back, while you may! Make me the sufferer,
But save yourself!
FRANCESCA. Now, are you not ashamed
To look me in the face with that bold brow?
I am amazed!
RITTA. I am a woman, lady;
I too have been in love; I know its ways,
Its arts, and its deceits. Your frowning face,
And seeming indignation, do not cheat.
Your heart is in my hand.
PAOLO [*calls*]. Francesca!
FRANCESCA. Hence,
Thou wanton-hearted minion! hence, I say!—
And never look me in the face again!—
Hence, thou insulting slave!
RITTA [*clinging to her*]. O lady, lady—
FRANCESCA. Begone! [*Throws her off.*]
RITTA. I have no friends—no one to love—
O, spare me!
FRANCESCA. Hence!
RITTA. Was it for this I loved—
Cared for you more than my own happiness—
Ever at heart your slave—without a wish

For greater recompense than your stray smiles?

PAOLO [*calls*]. Francesca!

FRANCESCA. Hurry!

RITTA. I am gone. Alas!
God bless you, lady! God take care of you,
When I am far away! Alas, alas!
[*Exit weeping.*

FRANCESCA. Poor girl!—but were she all the world to me,
And held my future in her tender grasp,
I'd cast her off, without a second thought,
To savage death, for dear Paolo's sake!
Paolo, hither! Now he comes to me;
I feel his presence, though I see him not,
Stealing upon me like the fervid glow
Of morning sunshine. Now he comes too near—
He touches me—O Heaven!

PAOLO. Our poem waits.
I have been reading while you talked with Ritta.
How did you get her off?

FRANCESCA. By some device.
She will not come again.

PAOLO. I hate the girl:
She seems to stand between me and the light.
And now for the romance. Where left we off?

FRANCESCA. Where Lancelot and Queen Guenevra strayed
Along the forest, in the youth of May.
You marked the figure of the birds that sang
Their melancholy farewell to the sun—
Rich in his loss, their sorrow glorified—
Like gentle mourners o'er a great man's grave.
Was it not there? No, no; 'twas where they sat
Down on the bank, by one impulsive wish
That neither uttered.

PAOLO [*turning over the book*]. Here it is.
[*Reads.*]
"So sat
Guenevra and Sir Lancelot"—'Twere well
To follow them in that. [*They sit upon a bank.*]

FRANCESCA. I listen: read.
Nay, do not; I can wait, if you desire.

PAOLO. My dagger frets me; let me take it off.
[*Rises.*]
In thoughts of love, we'll lay our weapons by.
[*Lays aside his dagger, and sits again.*]
Draw closer: I am weak in voice today.
[*Reads.*]

"So sat Guenevra and Sir Lancelot,
Under the blaze of the descending sun,
But all his cloudy spendors were forgot.
Each bore a thought, the only secret one,
Which each had hidden from the other's heart,
That with sweet mystery well-nigh overrun.
Anon, Sir Lancelot, with gentle start,
Put by the ripples of her golden hair,
Gazing upon her with his lips apart.
He marvelled human thing could be so fair;
Essayed to speak; but, in the very deed,
His words expired of self-betrayed despair.
Little she helped him, at his direst need,
Roving her eyes o'er hill, and wood, and sky,
Peering intently at the meanest weed;
Ay, doing aught but look in Lancelot's eye.
Then, with the small pique of her velvet shoe,
Uprooted she each herb that blossomed nigh;
Or strange wild figures in the dust she drew;
Until she felt Sir Lancelot's arm around
Her waist, upon her cheek his breath like dew.
While through his fingers timidly he wound
Her shining locks; and, haply, when he brushed
Her ivory skin, Guenevra nearly swound:
For where he touched, the quivering surface blushed,
Firing her blood with most contagious heat,
Till brow, cheek, neck, and bosom, all were flushed.
Each heart was listening to the other beat.
As twin-born lilies on one golden stalk,
Drooping with Summer, in warm languor meet,
So met their faces. Down the forest walk
Sir Lancelot looked—he looked east, west, north, south—
No soul was nigh, his dearest wish to balk:
She smiled; he kissed her full upon the mouth."
[*Kisses* FRANCESCA.]

I'll read no more!
[*Starts up, dashing down the book.*]

FRANCESCA. Paolo!

PAOLO. I am mad!
The torture of unnumbered hours is o'er,
The straining cord has broken, and my heart
Riots in free delirium! O, Heaven!
I struggled with it, but it mastered me!
I fought against it, but it beat me down!
I prayed, I wept, but Heaven was deaf to me;

And every tear rolled backward on my heart,
To blight and poison!

FRANCESCA. And dost thou regret?

PAOLO. The love? No, no! I'd dare it all again,
Its direst agonies and meanest fears,
For that one kiss. Away with fond remorse!
Here, on the brink of ruin, we two stand;
Lock hands with me, and brave the fearful plunge!
Thou canst not name a terror so profound
That I will look or falter from. Be bold!
I know thy love—I knew it long ago—
Trembled and fled from it. But now I clasp
The peril to my breast, and ask of thee
A kindred desperation.

FRANCESCA [*throwing herself into his arms*]. Take me all,—
Body and soul! The women of our clime
Do never give away but half a heart:
I have not part to give, part to withhold,
In selfish safety. When I saw thee first,
Riding alone amid a thousand men,
Sole in the lustre of thy majesty,
And Guido da Polenta said to me,
"Daughter, behold thy husband!" with a bound
My heart went forth to meet thee. He deceived,
He lied to me—ah! that's the aptest word—
And I believed. Shall I not turn again,
And meet him, craft with craft? Paolo, love,
Thou'rt dull—thou'rt dying like a feeble fire
Before the sunshine. Was it but a blaze,
A flash of glory, and a long, long night?

PAOLO. No, darling, no! You could not bend me back;
My course is onward; but my heart is sick
With coming fears.

FRANCESCA. Away with them! Must I
Teach thee to love? and reinform the ear
Of thy spent passion with some sorcery
To raise the chilly dead?

PAOLO. Thy lips have not
A sorcery to rouse me as this spell.
[*Kisses her.*]

FRANCESCA. I give thy kisses back to thee again:
And, like a spendthrift, only ask of thee
To take while I can give.

PAOLO. Give, give forever!
Have we not touched the height of human bliss?
And if the sharp rebound may hurl us back
Among the prostrate, did we not soar once?—
Taste heavenly nectar, banquet with the gods
On high Olympus? If they cast us, now,
Amid the furies, shall we not go down
With rich ambrosia clinging to our lips,
And richer memories settled in our hearts?
Francesca.

FRANCESCA. Love?

PAOLO. The sun is sinking low
Upon the ashes of his fading pyre,
And gray possesses the eternal blue;
The evening star is stealing after him,
Fixed, like a beacon, on the prow of night;
The world is shutting up its heavy eye
Upon the stir and bustle of today;—
On what shall it awake?

FRANCESCA. On love that gives
Joy at all seasons, changes night to day,
Makes sorrow smile, plucks out the barbéd dart
Of moaning anguish, pours celestial balm
In all the gaping wounds of earth, and lulls
The nervous fancies of unsheltered fear
Into a slumber sweet as infancy's!
On love that laughs at the impending sword,
And puts aside the shield of caution: cries,
To all its enemies, "Come, strike me now!—
Now, while I hold my kingdom, while my crown
Of amaranth and myrtle is yet green,
Undimmed, unwithered; for I cannot tell
That I shall e'er be happier!" Dear Paolo,
Would you lapse down from misery to death,
Tottering through sorrow and infirmity?
Or would you perish at a single blow,
Cut off amid your wildest revelry,
Falling among the wine-cups and the flowers,
And tasting Bacchus when your drowsy sense
First gazed around eternity? Come, love!

The present whispers joy to us; we'll hear
The voiceless future when its turn arrives.

PAOLO. Thou art a siren. Sing, forever sing;
Hearing thy voice, I cannot tell what fate
Thou hast provided when the song is o'er;—
But I will venture it.

FRANCESCA. In, in, my love! [*Exeunt.*

[PEPE *steals from behind the bushes.*]

PEPE. O, brother Lanciotto!—O, my stars!—
If this thing lasts, I simply shall go mad!
[*Laughs, and rolls on the ground.*]
O Lord! to think my pretty lady puss
Had tricks like this, and we ne'er know of it!
I tell you, Lanciotto, you and I
Must have a patent for our foolery!
"She smiled; he kissed her full upon the mouth!"—
There's the beginning; where's the end of it?
O poesy! debauch thee only once,
And thou'rt the greatest wanton in the world!
O cousin Lanciotto—ho, ho, ho!
[*Laughing.*]
Can a man die of laughter? Here we sat;
Mistress Francesca so demure and calm;
Paolo grand, poetical, sublime!—
Eh! what is this? Paolo's dagger? Good!
Here is more proof, sweet cousin Broken-back.
"In thoughts of love, we'll lay our weapons by!" [*Mimicking* PAOLO.]
That's very pretty! Here's its counterpart:
In thoughts of hate, we'll pick them up again! [*Takes the dagger.*]
Now for my soldier, now for crook-backed Mars!
Ere long all Rimini will be ablaze.
He'll kill me? Yes: what then? That's nothing new,
Except to me: I'll bear for custom's sake.
More blood will follow; like the royal sun,
I shall go down in purple. Fools for luck;
The proverb holds like iron. I must run,
Ere laughter smother me.—O, ho, ho, ho!
[*Exit, laughing.*

SCENE 2. *A camp among the Hills. Before* LANCIOTTO'S *tent*

Enter, from the tent, LANCIOTTO

LANCIOTTO. The camp is strangely quiet. Not a sound
Breaks nature's high solemnity. The sun
Repeats again his every-day decline;
Yet all the world looks sadly after him,
As if the customary sight were new.
Yon moody sentinel goes slowly by,
Through the thick mists of evening, with his spear
Trailed at a funeral hold. Long shadows creep
From things beyond the furthest range of sight,
Up to my very feet. These mystic shades
Are of the earth; the light that causes them,
And teaches us the quick comparison,
Is all from heaven. Ah! restless man might crawl
With patience through his shadowy destiny,
If he were senseless to the higher light
Towards which his soul aspires. How grand and vast
Is yonder show of heavenly pageantry!
How mean and narrow is the earthly stand
From which we gaze on it! Magnificent,
O God, art thou amid the sunsets! Ah,
What heart in Rimini is softened now,
Towards my defects, by this grand spectacle?
Perchance, Paolo now forgives the wrong
Of my hot spleen. Perchance, Francesca now
Wishes me back, and turns a tenderer eye
On my poor person and ill-mannered ways;
Fashions excuses for me, schools her heart
Through duty into love, and ponders o'er
The sacred meaning in the name of wife.
Dreams, dreams! Poor fools, we squander love away
On thankless borrowers; when bankrupt quite,
We sit and wonder of their honesty.
Love, take a lesson from the usurer,
And never lend but on security.
Captain!

Enter a CAPTAIN

CAPTAIN. My lord.

LANCIOTTO. They worsted us today.

CAPTAIN. Not much, my lord.

LANCIOTTO. With little loss, indeed.
Their strength is in position. Mark you, sir.
[*Draws on the ground with his sword.*]

Here is the pass; it opens towards the plain,
With gradual widening, like a lady's fan.
The hills protect their flanks on either hand;
And, as you see, we cannot show more front
Than their advance may give us. Then, the rocks
Are sorry footing for our horse. Just here,
Close in against the left-hand hills, I marked
A strip of wood, extending down the gorge:
Behind that wood dispose your force ere dawn.
I shall begin the onset, then give ground,
And draw them out; while you, behind the wood,
Must steal along, until their flank and rear
Oppose your column. Then set up a shout,
Burst from the wood, and drive them on our spears.
They have no outpost in the wood, I know;
'Tis too far from their centre. On the morrow,
When they are flushed with seeming victory,
And think my whole division in full rout,
They will not pause to scrutinize the wood;
So you may enter boldly. We will use
The heart today's repulse has given to them,
For our advantage. Do you understand?

CAPTAIN. Clearly, my lord.

LANCIOTTO. If they discover you,
Before you gain your point, wheel, and retreat
Upon my rear. If your attack should fail
To strike them with a panic, and they turn
In too great numbers on your small command,
Scatter your soldiers through the wood:
Let each seek safety for himself.

CAPTAIN. I see.

LANCIOTTO. Have Pluto shod; he cast a shoe today:
Let it be done at once. My helmet, too,
Is worn about the lacing; look to that.
Where is my armorer?

CAPTAIN. At his forge.

LANCIOTTO. Your charge
Must be at sunrise—just at sunrise, sir—
Neither before nor after. You must march
At moonset, then, to gain the point ere dawn.
That is enough.

CAPTAIN. Good-even! [*Going.*]

LANCIOTTO. Stay, stay, stay!
My sword-hilt feels uneasy in my grasp;
[*Gives his sword.*]
Have it repaired; and grind the point. Strike hard!
I'll teach these Ghibelins a lesson.
[*Loud laughter within.*]
What is that clamor? Ha!

Enter hastily PEPE, *tattered and travel-stained*

PEPE. News from Rimini! [*Falls exhausted.*]

LANCIOTTO. Is that you, Pepe? Captain, a good-night! [*Exit* CAPTAIN.
I never saw you in such straits before.
Wit without words!

PEPE. That's better than—O!—O!—[*Panting.*]
Words without wit.

LANCIOTTO [*laughing*]. You'll die a jester, Pepe.

PEPE. If so, I'll leave the needy all my wit.
You, you shall have it, cousin.—O! O! O!
[*Panting.*]
Those devils in the hills, the Ghibelins,
Ran me almost to death. My lord—ha! ha!
[*Laughing.*]
It all comes back to me—O! Lord 'a mercy—
The garden, and the lady, and the Count!
Not to forget the poetry—ho! ho!
[*Laughing.*]
O! cousin Lanciotto, such a wife,
And such a brother! Hear me, ere I burst!

LANCIOTTO. You're pleasant, Pepe!

PEPE. Am I?—Ho! ho! ho! [*Laughing.*]
You ought to be; your wife's a—

LANCIOTTO. What?

PEPE. A lady—
A lady, I suppose, like all the rest.
I am not in their secrets. Such a fellow
As Count Paolo is your man for that.
I'll tell you something, if you'll swear a bit.

LANCIOTTO. Swear what?

PEPE. First, swear to listen till the end.—
O! you may rave, curse, howl, and tear your hair;
But you must listen.

LANCIOTTO. For your jest's sake? Well.
PEPE. You swear?
LANCIOTTO. I do.
PEPE. Next, swear to know the truth.
LANCIOTTO. The truth of a fool's story!
PEPE. You mistake.
Now, look you, cousin! You have often marked—
I know, for I have seen—strange glances pass
Between Paolo and your lady wife.—
LANCIOTTO. Ha! Pepe!
PEPE. Now I touch you to the quick.
I know the reason of those glances.
LANCIOTTO. Ha!
Speak! or I'll throttle you! [*Seizes him.*]
PEPE. Your way is odd.
Let go my gullet, and I'll talk you deaf.
Swear my last oath: only to know the truth.
LANCIOTTO. But that may trouble me.
PEPE. Your honor lies—
Your precious honor, cousin Chivalry—
Lies bleeding with a terrible great gash,
Without its knowledge. Swear!
LANCIOTTO. My honor? Speak!
PEPE. You swear?
LANCIOTTO. I swear. Your news is ill, perchance?
PEPE. Ill! would I bring it else? Am I inclined
To run ten leagues with happy news for you?
O, Lord, that's jolly!
LANCIOTTO. You infernal imp,
Out with your story, ere I strangle you!
PEPE. Then take a fast hold on your two great oaths,
To steady tottering manhood, and attend.
Last eve, about this hour, I took a stroll
Into the garden.—Are you listening, cousin?
LANCIOTTO. I am all ears.
PEPE. Why, so an ass might say.
LANCIOTTO. Will you be serious?
PEPE. Wait a while, and we
Will both be graver than a church-yard. Well,
Down the long walk, towards me, came your wife,
With Count Paolo walking at her side.
It was a pretty sight, and so I stepped
Into the bushes. Ritta came with them;
And Lady Fanny had a grievous time
To get her off. That made me curious.
Anon, the pair sat down upon a bank,
To read a poem;—the tenderest romance,
All about Lancelot and Queen Guenevra.
The Count read well—I'll say that much for him—
Only he stuck too closely to the text,
Got too much wrapped up in the poesy,
And played Sir Lancelot's actions, out and out,
On Queen Francesca. Nor in royal parts
Was she so backward. When he struck the line—
"She smiled; he kissed her full upon the mouth;"
Your lady smiled, and, by the saints above,
Paolo carried out the sentiment!
Can I not move you?
LANCIOTTO. With such trash as this?
And so you ran ten leagues to tell a lie?—
Run home again.
PEPE. I am not ready yet.
After the kiss, up springs our amorous Count,
Flings Queen Guenevra and Sir Lancelot
Straight to the devil; growls and snaps his teeth,
Laughs, weeps, howls, dances; talks about his love,
His madness, suffering, and the Lord knows what,
Bullying the lady like a thief. But she,
All this hot time, looked cool and mischievous;
Gave him his halter to the very end;
And when he calmed a little, up she steps
And takes him by the hand. You should have seen
How tame the furious fellow was at once!
How he came down, snivelled, and cowed to her,
And fell to kissing her again! It was
A perfect female triumph! Such a scene
A man might pass through life and never see.
More sentiment then followed,—buckets full
Of washy words, not worth my memory.
But all the while she wound his Countship up,

Closer and closer; till at last—tu!—wit!—
She scoops him up, and off she carries him,
Fish for her table! Follow, if you can;
My fancy fails me. All this time you smile!

LANCIOTTO. You should have been a poet, not a fool.

PEPE. I might be both.

LANCIOTTO. You made no record, then?
Must this fine story die for want of ink?
Left you no trace in writing?

PEPE. None.

LANCIOTTO. Alas!
Then you have told it? 'Tis but stale, my boy;
I'm second hearer.

PEPE. You are first, in faith.

LANCIOTTO. In truth?

PEPE. In sadness. You have got it fresh.
I had no time; I itched to reach your ear.
Now go to Rimini, and see yourself.
You'll find them in the garden. Lovers are
Like walking ghosts, they always haunt the spot
Of their misdeeds.

LANCIOTTO. But have I heard you out?
You told me all?

PEPE. All; I have nothing left.

LANCIOTTO. Why, you brain-stricken idiot, to trust
Your story and your body in my grasp!
[*Seizes him.*]

PEPE. Unhand me, cousin!

LANCIOTTO. When I drop you, Pepe,
You'll be at rest.

PEPE. I will betray you—O!

LANCIOTTO. Not till the judgment day.
[*They struggle.*]

PEPE [*drawing* PAOLO'S *dagger*]. Take that!

LANCIOTTO [*wresting the dagger from him*]. Well meant,
But poorly done! Here's my return.
[*Stabs him.*]

PEPE. O! beast! [*Falls.*]
This I expected; it is naught—Ha! ha!
[*Laughing.*]
I'll go to sleep; but you—what you will bear!
Hunchback, come here!

LANCIOTTO. Fie! say your prayers.

PEPE. Hark, hark!
Paolo hired me, swine, to murder you.

LANCIOTTO. That is a lie; you never cared for gold.

PEPE. He did, I say! I'll swear to it, by heaven!
Do you believe me?

LANCIOTTO. No!

PEPE. You lie! you lie!
Look at the dagger, cousin—Ugh!—good-night!
[*Dies.*]

LANCIOTTO. O! horrible! It was a gift of mine—
He never laid it by. Speak, speak, fool, speak!
[*Shakes the body.*]
How didst thou get it?—speak! Thou'rt warm—not dead—
Thou hast a tongue—O! speak! Come, come, a jest—
Another jest from those thin mocking lips!
Call me a cripple—hunchback—what thou wilt;
But speak to me! He cannot. Now, by heaven,
I'll stir this business till I find the truth!
Am I a fool? It is a silly lie,
Coined by yon villain with his last base breath.
What ho! without there!

Enter CAPTAIN *and Soldiers*

CAPTAIN. Did you call, my lord?

LANCIOTTO. Did Heaven thunder? Are you deaf, you louts?
Saddle my horse! What are you staring at?
Is it your first look at a dead man? Well,
Then look your fill. Saddle my horse, I say!
Black Pluto—stir! Bear that assassin hence.
Chop him to pieces, if he move. My horse!

CAPTAIN. My lord, he's shoeing.

LANCIOTTO. Did I ask for shoes?
I want my horse. Run, fellow, run! Unbarbed—
My lightest harness on his back. Fly, fly!
[*Exit a Soldier.*
[*The others pick up the body.*]
Ask him, I pray you, if he did not lie!

CAPTAIN. The man is dead, my lord.

LANCIOTTO [*laughing*]. Then do not ask him!
[*Exeunt Soldiers with the body.*
By Jupiter, I shall go mad, I think!
[*Walks about.*]

CAPTAIN. Something disturbs him. Do you mark the spot
Of purple on his brow?

[*Apart to a* SOLDIER.]

SOLDIER. Then blood must flow.

LANCIOTTO. Boy, boy! [*Enter a Page.*] My cloak and riding-staff. Quick, quick!
How you all lag! [*Exit Page.*] I ride to Rimini.
Skirmish tomorrow. Wait till my return—
I shall be back at sundown. You shall see
What slaughter is then!

CAPTAIN. Ho! turn out a guard!—

LANCIOTTO. I wish no guard; I ride alone.

Re-enter Page, with a cloak and staff

[*Taking them.*] Well done!
Thou art a pretty boy.—And now my horse!

Enter a SOLDIER

SOLDIER. Pluto is saddled—

LANCIOTTO. 'Tis a damned black lie!

SOLDIER. Indeed, my lord—

LANCIOTTO. O! comrade, pardon me:
I talk at random. What, Paolo too,—
A boy whom I have trotted on my knee!
Poh! I abuse myself by such a thought.
Francesca may not love me, may love him—
Indeed she ought; but when an angel comes
To play the wanton on this filthy earth,
Then I'll believe her guilty. Look you, sir!
Am I quite calm?

CAPTAIN. Quite calm, my lord.

LANCIOTTO. You see
No trace of passion on my face?—No sign
Of ugly humors, doubts, or fears, or aught
That may disfigure God's intelligence?
I have a grievous charge against you, sir,
That may involve your life; and if you doubt
The candor of my judgment, choose your time:
Shall I arraign you now?

CAPTAIN. Now, if you please.
I'll trust my cause to you and innocence
At any time. I am not conscious—

LANCIOTTO. Pshaw!
I try myself, not you. And I am calm—
That is your verdict—and dispassionate?

CAPTAIN. So far as I can judge.

LANCIOTTO. 'Tis well, 'tis well!
Then I will ride to Rimini. Good-night!

[*Exit.*

[*The others look after him, amazedly, and exeunt.*]

SCENE 3. *Rimini. The Garden of the Castle*

Enter PAOLO *and* FRANCESCA

FRANCESCA. Thou hast resolved?

PAOLO. I've sworn it.

FRANCESCA. Ah, you men
Can talk of love and duty in a breath;
Love while you like, forget when you are tired,
And salve your falsehood with some wholesome saw;
But we, poor women, when we give our hearts,
Give all, lose all, and never ask it back.

PAOLO. What couldst thou ask for that I have not given?
With love I gave thee manly probity,
Innocence, honor, self-respect, and peace.
Lanciotto will return, and how shall I—
O! shame, to think of it!—how shall I look
My brother in the face? take his frank hand?
Return his tender glances? I should blaze
With guilty blushes.

FRANCESCA. Thou canst forsake me, then,
To spare thyself a little bashful pain?
Paolo, dost thou know what 'tis for me,
A woman—nay, a dame of highest rank—
To lose my purity? to walk a path
Whose slightest slip may fill my ear with sounds
That hiss me out to infamy and death?
Have I no secret pangs, no self-respect,
No husband's look to bear? O! worse than these,
I must endure his loathsome touch; be kind
When he would dally with his wife, and smile
To see him play thy part. Pah! sickening thought!
From that thou art exempt. Thou shalt not go!
Thou dost not love me!

PAOLO. Love thee! Standing here,
With countless miseries upon my head,
I say, my love for thee grows day by day.

It palters with my conscience, blurs my thoughts
Of duty, and confuses my ideas
Of right and wrong. Ere long, it will persuade
My shaking manhood that all this is just.

FRANCESCA. Let it! I'll blazon it to all the world,
Ere I will lose thee. Nay, if I had choice,
Between our love and my lost innocence,
I tell thee calmly, I would dare again
The deed which we have done. O! thou art cruel
To fly me, like a coward, for thine ease.
When thou art gone, thou'lt flatter thy weak heart
With hopes and speculations; and thou'lt swear
I suffer naught, because thou dost not see.
I will not live to bear it!

PAOLO. Die,—'twere best;
'Tis the last desperate comfort of our sin.

FRANCESCA. I'll kill myself!

PAOLO. And so would I, with joy;
But crime has made a craven of me. O!
For some good cause to perish in! Something
A man might die for, looking in God's face;
Not slinking out of life with guilt like mine
Piled on the shoulders of a suicide!

FRANCESCA. Where wilt thou go?

PAOLO. I care not; anywhere
Out of this Rimini. The very things
That made the pleasures of my innocence
Have turned against me. There is not a tree,
Nor house, nor church, nor monument, whose face
Took hold upon my thoughts, that does not frown
Balefully on me. From their marble tombs
My ancestors scowl at me; and the night
Thickens to hear their hisses. I would pray,
But heaven jeers at it. Turn where'er I will,
A curse pursues me.

FRANCESCA. Heavens! O, say not so!
I never cursed thee, love; I never moved
My little finger, ere I looked to thee
For my instruction.

PAOLO. But thy gentleness
Seems to reproach me; and, instead of joy,
It whispers horror!

FRANCESCA. Cease! cease!

PAOLO. I must go.

FRANCESCA. And I must follow. All that I call life
Is bound in thee. I could endure for thee
More agonies than thou canst catalogue—
For thy sake, love—bearing the ill for thee!
With thee, the devils could not so contrive
That I would blench or falter from my love!
Without thee, heaven were torture!

PAOLO. I must go. [*Going.*]

FRANCESCA. O! no—Paolo—dearest!—
[*Clinging to him.*]

PAOLO. Loose thy hold!
'Tis for thy sake, and Lanciotto's; I
Am as a cipher in the reckoning.
I have resolved. Thou canst but stretch the time.
Keep me today, and I will fly tomorrow—
Steal from thee like a thief.
[*Struggles with her.*]

FRANCESCA. Paolo—love—
Indeed, you hurt me!—Do not use me thus!
Kill me, but do not leave me. I will laugh—
A long, gay, ringing laugh—if thou wilt draw
Thy pitying sword, and stab me to the heart!

Enter LANCIOTTO *behind*

Nay, then, one kiss!

LANCIOTTO [*advancing between them*]. Take it: 'twill be the last.

PAOLO. Lo! Heaven is just!

FRANCESCA. The last! so be it.
[*Kisses* PAOLO.]

LANCIOTTO. Ha!
Dare you these tricks before my very face?

FRANCESCA. Why not? I've kissed him in the sight of heaven;
Are you above it?

PAOLO. Peace, Francesca, peace!

LANCIOTTO. Paolo—why, thou sad and downcast man,
Look up! I have some words to speak with thee.
Thou art not guilty?

PAOLO. Yes, I am. But she
Has been betrayed; so she is innocent.
Her father tampered with her. I—

FRANCESCA. 'Tis false!

The guilt is mine. Paolo was entrapped
By love and cunning. I am shrewder far
Than you suspect.

PAOLO. Lanciotto, shut thy ears;
She would deceive thee.

LANCIOTTO. Silence, both of you!
Is guilt so talkative in its defence?
Then, let me make you judge and advocate
In your own cause. You are not guilty?

PAOLO. Yes.

LANCIOTTO. Deny it—but a word—say no. Lie, lie!
And I'll believe.

PAOLO. I dare not.

LANCIOTTO. Lady, you?

FRANCESCA. If I might speak for him—

LANCIOTTO. It cannot be:
Speak for yourself. Do you deny your guilt?

FRANCESCA. No! I assert it; but—

LANCIOTTO. In heaven's name, hold!
Will neither of you answer no to me?
A nod, a hint, a sign, for your escape.
Bethink you, life is centered in this thing.
Speak! I will credit either. No reply?
What does your crime deserve?

PAOLO. Death.

FRANCESCA. Death to both.

LANCIOTTO. Well said! You speak the law of Italy;
And by the dagger you designed for me,
In Pepe's hand,—your bravo?

PAOLO. It is false!
If you received my dagger from his hand,
He stole it.

LANCIOTTO. There, sweet heaven, I knew! And now
You will deny the rest? You see, my friends,
How easy of belief I have become!—
How easy 'twere to cheat me!

PAOLO. No; enough!
I will not load my groaning spirit more;
A lie would crush it.

LANCIOTTO. Brother, once you gave
Life to this wretched piece of workmanship,
When my own hand resolved its overthrow.
Revoke the gift. [*Offers to stab himself.*]

PAOLO [*preventing him*]. Hold, homicide!

LANCIOTTO. But think,
You and Francesca may live happily,
After my death, as only lovers can.

PAOLO. Live happily, after a deed like this!

LANCIOTTO. Now, look ye! there is not one hour of life
Among us three. Paolo, you are armed—
You have a sword, I but a dagger: see!
I mean to kill you.

FRANCESCA [*whispers* PAOLO]. Give thy sword to me.

PAOLO. Away! thou'rt frantic! I will never lift
This wicked hand against thee.

LANCIOTTO. Coward, slave!
Art thou so faint? Does Malatesta's blood
Run in thy puny veins? Take that!
[*Strikes him.*]

PAOLO. And more:
Thou canst not offer more than I will bear.

LANCIOTTO. Paolo, what a craven has thy guilt
Transformed thee to! Why, I have seen the time
When thou'dst have struck at heaven for such a thing!
Art thou afraid?

PAOLO. I am.

LANCIOTTO. O! infamy!
Can man sink lower? I will wake thee, though:—
Thou shalt not die a coward. See! look here!
[*Stabs* FRANCESCA.]

FRANCESCA. O!—O!— [*Falls.*]

PAOLO. Remorseless man, dare you do this,
And hope to live? Die, murderer!
[*Draws, rushes at him, but pauses.*]

LANCIOTTO. Strike, strike!
Ere thy heart fail.

PAOLO. I cannot. [*Throws away his sword.*]

LANCIOTTO. Dost thou see
Yon bloated spider—hideous as myself—
Climbing aloft, to reach that wavering twig?
When he has touched it, one of us must die.
Here is the dagger.—Look at me, I say!
Keep your eyes from that woman! Look, think, choose!—
Turn here to me: thou shalt not look at her!

PAOLO. O, heaven!

LANCIOTTO. 'Tis done!

PAOLO [*struggling with him*]. O! Lanciotto, hold!
Hold, for thy sake! Thou wilt repent this deed.

LANCIOTTO. I know it.
FRANCESCA [*rising*]. Help!—O! murder!—help, help, help!
[*She totters towards them, and falls.*]
LANCIOTTO. Our honor, boy!
[*Stabs* PAOLO, *he falls.*]
FRANCESCA. Paolo!
PAOLO. Hark! she calls.
I pray thee, brother, help me to her side.
[LANCIOTTO *helps him to* FRANCESCA.]
LANCIOTTO. Why, there!
PAOLO. God bless thee!
LANCIOTTO. Have I not done well?
What were the honor of the Malatesti,
With such a living slander fixed to it?
Cripple! that's something—cuckold! that is damned!
You blame me?
PAOLO. No.
LANCIOTTO. You, lady?
FRANCESCA. No, my lord.
LANCIOTTO. May God forgive you! We are even now:
Your blood has cleared my honor, and our name
Shines to the world as ever.
PAOLO. O!—O!—
FRANCESCA. Love,
Art suffering?
PAOLO. But for thee.
FRANCESCA. Here, rest thy head
Upon my bosom. Fie upon my blood!
It stains thy ringlets. Ha! he dies! Kind saints,
I was first struck, why cannot I die first?
Paolo, wake!—God's mercy! wilt thou go
Alone—without me? Prithee, strike again!
Nay, I am better—love—now—O!
[*Dies.*]
LANCIOTTO [*sinks upon his knees*]. Great heaven!
MALATESTA [*without*]. This way, I heard the cries.
Enter with GUIDO, *Attendants, etc.*
GUIDO. O! horrible!
MALATESTA. O! bloody spectacle! Where is thy brother?
LANCIOTTO. So Cain was asked. Come here, old men! You shrink
From two dead bodies and a pool of blood—
You soldiers, too! Come here!
[*Drags* MALATESTA *and* GUIDO *forward.*]
MALATESTA. O!—O!—
LANCIOTTO. You groan!
What must I do, then? Father, here it is,—
The blood of Guido mingled with our own,
As my old nurse predicted. And the spot
Of her infernal baptism burns my brain
Till reason shudders! Down, upon your knees!
Ay, shake them harder, and perchance they'll wake.
Keep still! Kneel, kneel! You fear them? I shall prowl
About these bodies till the day of doom.
MALATESTA. What hast thou done?
GUIDO. Francesca!—O! my child!
LANCIOTTO. Can howling make this sight more terrible?
Peace! You disturb the angels up in heaven,
While they are hiding from this ugly earth.
Be satisfied with what you see. You two
Began this tragedy, I finished it.
Here, by these bodies, let us reckon up
Our crimes together. Why, how still they lie!
A moment since, they walked, and talked, and kissed!
Defied me to my face, dishonored me!
They had the power to do it then; but now,
Poor souls, who'll shield them in eternity?
Father, the honor of our house is safe:
I have the secret. I will to the wars,
And do more murders, to eclipse this one.
Back to the battles; there I breathe in peace;
And I will take a soldier's honor back.—
Honor! what's that to me now? Ha! ha! ha!
[*Laughing.*]
A great thing, father! I am very ill.
I killed thy son for honor: thou mayst chide.
O God! I cannot cheat myself with words!
I loved him more than honor—more than life—
This man, Paolo—this stark, bleeding corpse!
Here let me rest, till God awake us all!
[*Falls on* PAOLO's *body.*]

HORIZON

By Augustin Daly

AUGUSTIN DALY

[1838–1899]

Augustin Daly was a noteworthy man of the theatre who achieved distinction both as a playwright and a producer, his activities as the latter sometimes overshadowing his abilities as the former. Born in North Carolina (July 20, 1838), Augustin Daly early came to New York with his mother, where he frequented the theatres and various dramatic associations that were forerunners of the present-day Little Theatre groups. He became ardently interested in playwriting and production and his persistent efforts to establish an artistic theatre finally resulted in the organization of an acting company that was preëminent for a quarter of a century. Daly's Theatre was long synonymous with the best in drama. The playwright and producer was still very active in his work at the time of his death in 1899.[1]

His first writing for the stage was *Leah the Forsaken* (1862), an adaptation of a translated German play which had to do with the tragic fate of a Jewess rejected by her Christian lover. After several other adaptations from French, German, English, and American sources, Daly wrote his first original play, *Under the Gaslight*, produced in 1867 by his own newly-organized company. This is a significant play in the history of American literature because of the strong flavor of realism found in the manner of presentation. The plot itself, to be sure, is drenched with melodrama: extremes in wealth and poverty, kidnaping, child-abuse, fights, mysterious strangers, chloroform incidents, attempts at drowning. But the approach to these materials is realistic: the characters are individualized and their speech is natural, with a decided attempt to represent dialectal differences. The strongly-localized settings include the "Tombs," a checkroom at Delmonico's, a river pier, and a railroad crossing. Daly was not the first to place actual New York scenes on the stage: earlier distinctly local-color plays were Baker's *A Glance at New York* (1848), and Boucicault's *The Poor of New York* (1857); but he was influential in advancing realism, and his work is of especial interest when one considers that Howells, the early exponent of American realism, was just beginning to write at this time (*Italian Journeys*, 1867; *A Modern Instance*, 1882; *The Rise of Silas Lapham*, 1885).

The other original plays of Daly include *Judith*, 1864; *A Flash of Lightning*, 1868; *The Red Scarf*, 1869; *Horizon*, 1871; *Divorce*, 1871; *Roughing It*, 1873;

[1] The important biography is Joseph Francis Daly's *Life of Augustin Daly*. New York: 1917.

Pique, 1875; *The Dark City*, 1877.[1] In addition to these, Daly wrote about ninety adaptations from foreign sources; among the latter are *Frou-Frou*, *The Big Bonanza*, *Delmonico's, or Larks up the Hudson*, and *The Princess Royal.*

Daly's *Horizon* is perhaps his most important play, not only because of its dramatic qualities, but also by reason of its literary recognition of the frontier. Not until the publication in 1893 of Turner's account of frontier influences did the full significance of the frontier in American life become recognized.[2] Since that time various studies have demonstrated the effect our expansion westward has had upon our literature,[3] and our dramatic history shows how many plays were directly concerned with the frontier. Some of our earliest plays, like *Ponteach* (1766), dealt with the contact of the white man and the Indian; in 1838 Louisa Medina made a play from Bird's novel, *Nick of the Woods;* and in 1870 T. C. De Walden pictured the pioneer in *Kit the Arkansas Traveller*. An important frontier play, *Davy Crockett* (1872), by Frank Hitchcock Murdoch, portrayed the life of the famous Tennessee hunter and pioneer.

Although Daly's *Horizon* cannot be considered a careful, firsthand study of frontier life, and although much of the action is melodramatic, as in *Under the Gaslight*, yet one finds local color in the settings, accuracy and vividness in characterization, and a sense of the contrast between Western coarseness and Eastern civilization (the contrast so graphically portrayed years later in Moody's *The Great Divide*, 1906). In the opinion of Montrose J. Moses, *Horizon* cannot be considered a "native" play, but unconvincing as parts of it may be, one cannot deny that Daly was serious in his attempt to represent the American scene: "Possibly our national drama, from a literary point of view, will reach its best period when its native writers vie with each other in illustrating native character and contemporaneous fashions and follies." [4]

We see in Daly's play the frontier's independence of traditional legal authority and its tendency to rely on expediency for law; congressional law is scoffed at and local decree is disregarded. The mayor complains, "You've tilted me out of my lawful authority as Mayor of this settlement, and you've taken the law into your own hands." [5] On the frontier "the worst insolvent is elected Sheriff."

[1] This is the grouping made by Arthur Hobson Quinn, who has had the opportunity of examining the Daly manuscripts (comparatively few of his plays have been printed). For further discussion of these plays and an excellent account of the adaptations, see Quinn's *A History of the American Drama from the Civil War to the Present Day*, I, 1–38. For a list of Daly's plays see *ibid.*, II, 278–283.

[2] Reprinted in Turner, Frederick Jackson, *The Frontier in American History*. New York: 1921.

[3] Dondore, Dorothy A., *The Prairie and the Making of Middle America: four centuries of description*, Cedar Rapids, Iowa, 1926; Foerster, Norman, "New Viewpoints in American Literature," *The Saturday Review of Literature*, April 3, 1926; Hazard, Lucy L., *The Frontier in American Literature*, New York, 1927; Hubbell, Jay B., "The Frontier," Ch. III in Foerster's *The Reinterpretation of American Literature*, New York, 1928; Marchand, Ernest, "Emerson and the Frontier," *American Literature*, III, 149–174 (May, 1931); Paine, Gregory, "The Frontier in American Literature," *Sewanee Review*, April, 1928; Rusk, R. L., *The Literature of the Middle Western Frontier*, 2 vols., New York, 1925.

[4] "The American Dramatist," *North American Review*, CXLII, 485–492 (May, 1886).

[5] Act II, p. 348.

Daly's knowledge of the Indian is close enough to keep him from the Rousseauistic delusion of the Indian as the noble savage; to be sure, Daly may be skeptical of certain phases of civilization,[1] but he hardly accepts the idea of innate goodness in the Red Man: "That's civilization, my friend! When the noble savage was in his native state, he went for the hair of your head. Now he's in the midst of civilization, he carries the weapons of enlightenment, and goes for the money in your pocket." [2] The Indian is further represented as one not entirely devoted to scalping, but one who will, upon occasion, play poker for a prize.[3] We have here, and also in the question of property rights raised by the advent of the white man, an indication of Daly's realistic thinking on the subject.[4]

The attitude toward the frontier had up to this time generally been romantic or optimistic, as in the romanticized fiction of Cooper, Emerson's *The Young American*, and (later) Twain's *Life on the Mississippi*. During the latter part of the century, however, a closer observation and a critical temper began to appear. It is significant that Daly's realistic approach to the frontier in *Horizon* corresponds in date with Edward Eggleston's *The Hoosier Schoolmaster* (1871), often considered the earliest treatment of Western life in the light of modern realism.[5] Although Daly's interest in the frontier may be chiefly the utilization of materials rather than the portrayal of a life, it still remains that the drama here exhibits a responsiveness to the new currents of thought beginning to find expression in other forms of literature.[6] Among the later instances of this realistic thought are Edgar Watson Howe's grim novel of Kansas life, *The Story of a Country Town* (1883), Joseph Kirkland's *Zury, The Meanest Man in Spring County* (1887), Garland's *Main-Travelled Roads* (1887–1892) and *A Son of the Middle Border* (1917), Rölvaag's *Giants in the Earth* (1927).[7] In their portrayal of the dull and weary aspects of Western life, in their realization of the harshness, strife, and despair that frequently dwells on the frontier, these men represent the shift from an earlier illusion to a disillusion that becomes almost complete in a *Spoon River Anthology*.[8]

[1] For example, in reference to the commercial settler who gives worthless trinkets in trade for furs, the remark is made: "There's nothing like carrying civilization into the Far West."

[2] Act II, p. 352.

[3] Then, too, Alleyn does not share Columbia's admiration of Cooper's Indians, and points out that in reality they are simply dirty and common.

[4] For a recent discussion of the Indian see Albert Keiser's *The Indian in American Literature*, New York: 1933. Contemporary Indian plays of literary value are William Ellery Leonard's *Red Bird* and *Glory of the Morning*.

[5] Eggleston's other novels of Western life include *The End of the World, The Circuit Rider*, and *The Graysons*.

[6] Later realistic plays of frontier and sectional life include: Herne's *Hearts of Oak* (1879), *Margaret Fleming* (1880), *Shore Acres* (1892); Augustus Thomas's *Alabama* (1891), *In Mizzoura* (1893), *Arizona* (1899); William Vaughn Moody's *The Great Divide* (1906).

[7] The realistic attitude finds discussion in Howells's *Criticism and Fiction*, Garland's *Crumbling Idols*, Norris's *The Responsibilities of the Novelist*.

[8] Important treatments of the development of realism may be found in: Clark, H. H., "Nationalism in American Literature," *University of Toronto Quarterly*, II, 499 ff., (July, 1933); Parrington, V. L., "The Development of Realism," Ch. VII in *The Reinterpretation of American Literature*, ed. by Norman Foerster, New York, 1928; Parrington, V. L., Introduction to Rölvaag's *Giants in the Earth*, New York, 1927; Pattee, F. L., *A History of American Literature Since 1870*, New York, 1915.

Additional social commentary appearing in *Horizon* is the satire on Columbia, who thinks Irving's *Knickerbocker's History* is a social register; in the ridicule of Britisher Smith who is "protected by the British flag"; and in the anti-Chinese feeling caused by the Oriental's willingness to work for half pay. Skepticism of politics is voiced by Alleyn who complains that the politicians "take care of the public's interests. You know the public interest must be cared for. The old adage is: 'What's everybody's business is nobody's business.' Now the politicians do everybody's business, and account to nobody for the way they do it." [1] Rowse seems to be preaching a bit of Jeffersonianism: "Gentlemen, we are here proceeding according to law. Not the musty statutes of effete systems and oligarchies of the Old World, but the natural law implanted in the bosoms of man since our common ancestors were washed, wrung out and hung up to dry by the universal flood." But neither his Jeffersonianism nor his apparent trust in the natural man can be taken too seriously, for Rowse is a satirized character.

The influence of Bret Harte's Oakhurst is clearly seen in Loder, the cool, superior commentator, always equal to the occasion; and the rough villain who can sacrifice his love because he feels unworthy is to be found in Harte's stories. References are made to Cooper's "Leatherstocking Tales"; Irving's *Knickerbocker's History* appears as above indicated.

Heavily laden with physical conflict as the latter part of the play is, such ripened observers as Brander Matthews and Laurence Hutton testify to the drama's merit, and it cannot be denied that had Daly kept up the standard of original observation and accurate characterization found in the first part of the play, he would have written an especially distinguished American drama.

The present text is from the privately printed edition of 1885.

[1] Act I, p. 343.

DRAMATIS PERSONÆ AND ORIGINAL CAST

[An original drama of contemporaneous society and of American frontier perils in five acts and seven tableaux, as acted at the Olympic Theatre, New York City, for the first time, March 21st, 1871.]

ALLEYN VAN DORP, just from West Point with his first commission. Dispatched to the Far West .... Mr. Hart Conway
COKE BALLOU, ESQ., A gentleman, who professes what he practices; *i.e.*, The law; crusty as coke and dry as a whip .... Mr. C. Warwick
SUNDOWN ROWSE, ESQ., A distinguished member of the *Third House* at Washington. Owning a slice of every Territory, and bound for the Far West to survey his new Congressional Land Grant, which lies just this side of the Horizon .... Mr. G. L. Fox
THE UNATTACHED MR. SMITH, not a member of the Joint High Commission, and unattached to the British Legation at Washington .... Mr. H. R. Teesdale
JOHN LODER, alias Panther Loder, alias White Panther—One of the reasons for the establishment of "Vigilance Committees" in the peaceful hamlets of the Plains .... Mr. J. K. Mortimer
WOLF VAN DORP, One of the sort the West opens its arms to receive..... Mr. J. B. Studley
ROCKS OF TENNESSEE, The Mayor of Rogue's Rest, one of the magic cities of the West .... Mr. O. B. Collins
"UNCLE BILLY" BLAKELY, An enfranchised citizen of that enterprising town Mr. G. A. Beane
MR. MACKENZIE, otherwise known as "Sandy Mac,"—another .... Mr. J. L. Debonay
JUDGE SCOTT, the chairman of that Bulwark of Western Liberty:—the Vigilance Committee .... Mr. E. T. Sinclair
SALERATUS BILL, } More of 'em! .... { Mr. F. S. Wilbur
GOPHER JOE, } { Mr. Tyson
CEPHAS, A Fifteenth Amendment .... Mr. I. Pendy
THE HEATHEN CHINEE, who does not understand .... Mr. H. H. Pratt
SERGEANT CROCKETT, One of Uncle Sam's Police of the Prairies .... Mr. Frank Chapman
WANNEMUCKA, The civilized Indian and "Untutored Savage" who dwells with the white settlers in their villages .... Mr. Charles Wheatleigh
WAHCOTAH, The friendly Indian who stops among the white soldiers at their Fort .... Mr. W. H. Pope
GUIDE .... Mr. Atkins
MED, White Flower of the Plains .... Miss Agnes Ethel
MISS COLUMBIA ROWSE, The Belle of *Both Houses* and fascinator of the Lawmakers .... Miss Ada Harland
MRS. VAN DORP, The Abandoned Wife .... Mrs. J. J. Prior
THE WIDOW MULLINS, Emigrant parent, of undoubted extraction .... Mrs. Yeamans
RHODA, her daughter .... Miss Fanny Beane
ONATA, a prairie princess .... Miss Lulu Prior
NOTAH, The little papoose, who'd become the spoil of the stranger .... Jennie Yeamans
ALICE, of the Van Dorp Household .... Flora Lee

Citizens of Rogue's Rest, Indians, Indian Maidens, Soldiers

HORIZON

ACT I

SCENE.—*Parlors in the Van Dorp city house, Waverly Place, New York. Elegant saloon divided by arches. Windows at back, looking upon Washington Park. An apartment seen off, through another arch. Hallway and main entrance at right. Mantel, with framed picture above it, the face turned to the wall. Table, with lamp, books, etc., inkstand and pens, blotting paper, legal paper. Elegant furniture of various patterns about, in each apartment.*

MR. BALLOU *is discovered sitting at table, pen in mouth, pressing blotter on paper. He takes up paper and reads.*

BALLOU. Hum! I think that's about what she wants. A full and particular exhibit of the property, real, personal and mixed, belonging to Margaret Van Dorp. Now, whosoever gets it at her death, gets a very snug fortune. [*Folds paper up, puts it in his pocket with a number of others, which he takes from table, then looks at his watch. Bell, as if of street door—heard.*] Hallo! Some other visitor! We shan't have an opportunity for a private conference after all. [*Rises and crosses to mantel.*]

ALICE *shows in* CAPT. ALLEYN, *who enters with hat, travelling-bag and light overcoat*

ALLEYN. Glad to be home again. That I am. All night on train. Just stopped at the hotel to fix up—ran over after breakfast. [*Gives hat and bag to* ALICE.] No one here? [*Sees* BALLOU.] No! Why, Mr. Ballou! [*They meet and shake hands.*]

BALLOU. This is an unexpected pleasure.

ALLEYN. So it is. I've just come from Washington, by the Owl Train. Where's mother?

BALLOU. Mrs. Van Dorp—I've not seen her yet.

ALLEYN [*to* ALICE]. Will you announce me to mother, and ask if I shall attend her in her own room, or here?

ALICE. Yes, sir! [*To* BALLOU.] I have already told her you were waiting, Mr. Ballou. [*Exit.*

BALLOU. Oh, it don't matter about me. Lawyers can wait. We always charge for that, eh?

ALLEYN. I hope so.

BALLOU. Especially when we are sent for on particular business. [*Sits.*]

ALLEYN [*crossing and standing*]. You lawyers have easy lives. You jog about from house to house, from court to court. Now as to us soldiers—

BALLOU [*yawning and laughing*]. As to you soldiers!

ALLEYN. You may laugh. You think there's no duty for us now.

BALLOU. No! Thank the Lord!

ALLEYN [*quizzically*]. What do you think of the prospect of a war with England?

BALLOU. Bosh!

ALLEYN. Well, then, nearer home; how about the Indian troubles?

BALLOU. They don't hurt us, they're a thousand or two miles off towards sundown.

ALLEYN. That's the very spot.

BALLOU [*interested*]. What spot?

ALLEYN. Where I'm going!

BALLOU [*jumping up, going left*]. You?

ALLEYN [*taking* BALLOU'S *vacated seat*]. Ye-e-es! [*Yawning.*]

BALLOU. And you are to fight the Indians?

ALLEYN. Unless the Indians run away.

BALLOU. What will your mother, I mean Mrs. Van Dorp—pardon me, she regards you as a son; what will she say to this?

ALLEYN. I wrote and told her the whole news. I start tomorrow to join my company.

BALLOU [*slapping his forehead*]. An idea strikes me! She sent for me because you are going away. I see it all!

ALLEYN. Oh, you consider yourself a good substitute for me, eh? [*Sits on ottoman.*]

BALLOU. Badinage aside. Mrs. Van Dorp, ever since she adopted you as a son—.

ALLEYN. Twelve years ago—

BALLOU. And two years after her husband disappeared, so cruelly taking with him their infant daughter, Mrs. Van Dorp, I repeat, has spoken to me about making her will—

ALLEYN. Then I don't want to hear anything more about it—[*Crosses to table, and sits.*]

BALLOU [*takes* ALLEYN'S *seat*]. Don't be afraid. I'm not going to reveal her affairs, for she never told me how she meant to leave her property.

ALLEYN. All right then. Fire away! [*Sits by table.*]

BALLOU. She has sent for me a dozen times, and a dozen times has put off the deed. I remonstrated, but her only excuse was: "We will wait yet a little longer."

ALLEYN. Poor mother! She referred to the expectation she had, that her husband would return and bring back her little girl.

BALLOU. Her husband took his precautions well. If he meant to leave his wife forever, and to punish her, he succeeded.

ALLEYN. To punish her? For what?

BALLOU. Family history! Family history! He was poor and proud, she was rich and proud. They were both aristocrats, but his family, I think, was a little the older, just a little; that is to say, he could count more Knickerbockers for ancestors than she could.

ALLEYN. You are severe!

BALLOU. As I have had the genealogy searched up, I know. Well, they belonged to the first families, she, the richer. They were married. Marriage, my dear boy, is called a union of souls; when it is, it is doubtless a good thing; but when it is a union of pride, passion and violence, it—well—well! They lived a wretched life for five years. They had one daughter. The husband would not bow down to his wife, so she kept him on short allowance of money; he tried to go into business, failed, got dissipated, reformed, broke down again—and was locked out of his wife's house, [*Rises.*] by the way, this very house.

ALLEYN [*rises, sadly*]. Yes, I have heard.

BALLOU [*crosses and sits*]. He watched it; tried to get in to see his child, little Margaret. Was prevented. Laid his plans accordingly, and one night gained admittance by force, and seizing the child, carried it off.

ALLEYN. Yes, so I've heard. And the next day a letter was delivered which told her—

BALLOU. Her child was lost to her forever. His vengeance was complete. At one blow he deprived her of her only pleasure, and closed her doors forever to the gaiety and revelry she loved so much.

ALLEYN. The spiritless, cowardly villain, who lived on her bounty and abused her goodness! [*Sits.*]

BALLOU. Oh, of course. But the world says, she was to blame.

ALLEYN. She, the kindest, most generous of women?

BALLOU. Yes, to all but a husband. There are some girls who never ought to marry. She was one, she had no patience to bear the failings of a husband.

ALICE *enters*

ALICE. My mistress is coming, Mr. Alleyn. [*Speaking outside.*] Come in, John!

SERVANT *enters with a step-ladder, which he places against mantel*

ALICE. Now, then, get up right away and turn the picture.

SERVANT *mounts the steps, but before he can turn the picture*, MRS. VAN DORP *enters*

ALICE. Too late! Stop! [JOHN *descends ladder, as* MRS. VAN DORP *goes to* ALLEYN, *who runs to meet her. She kisses his forehead.*]

MRS. VAN DORP. My boy! [*To* ALICE.] Never mind at present, Alice. Leave the ladder. You can go now.

ALICE. Yes, ma'am! [*Exits, with* JOHN.]

MRS. VAN DORP. My dearest Alleyn! I have looked for you so anxiously. [*Crosses.*] Mr. Ballou, I beg a thousand pardons for keeping you so long. But you know how whimsical I am.

BALLOU. Oh, yes, I know. You have made me run many a wild goose chase before.

MRS. VAN DORP [*to* ALLEYN]. You see how he scolds me.

BALLOU. It's my privilege as your legal adviser.

MRS. VAN DORP [*sits in chair, which* ALLEYN *places for her*]. And you always advise me well.

BALLOU. You are at last resolved to make—

MRS. VAN DORP [*stops him by raising her hand*]. No!

BALLOU. No? Then why am I here?

MRS. VAN DORP. Perhaps to have one more proof of a woman's inconsistency. I sent for you determined to do—[*Stops, then to* ALLEYN.] Alleyn, my dear, will you see if the windows are closed in the reception room yonder?

ALLEYN. Certainly, mother! [*Goes up and off.*]

MRS. VAN DORP [*quickly to* BALLOU]. Say nothing more about this matter. I have changed my mind.

BALLOU. Again, and why?

MRS. VAN DORP. I am ashamed to confess it. You know my old reason.

BALLOU. You used to say, it was because you cherished a very vain hope—

MRS. VAN DORP. What if I tell you, that hope revives again?

BALLOU. It is insanity to encourage such fancies.

MRS. VAN DORP. Enough then! Being in unsound mind, I cannot make my will.

BALLOU. But, madam—

MRS. VAN DORP. Be satisfied with this. By the time Winter comes, I may send for you again. Till then, say nothing.

BALLOU. But your hope—

MRS. VAN DORP [*rising*]. Of that I will never speak to you again.

BALLOU [*crossing*]. Then for the twentieth time, I put my memoranda in my pocket, and take my leave.

MRS. VAN DORP. Stay! You will arrange with the bankers to have Alleyn's allowances sent to him in the West, wherever he may be stationed.

ALLEYN *enters*

BALLOU. Oh, that's easily arranged. Nothing more?

MRS. VAN DORP. Nothing more!

BALLOU. Good morning, then. [*Bows, goes up and meets* ALLEYN.] Well, my dear boy, take care of yourself.

ALLEYN. Going? Good-bye! If I'm scalped, I'll beg the ferocious Indians to send you a lock of my hair. [*Both laugh,* BALLOU *exits.* ALLEYN *comes down quickly.*] My dearest mother!

MRS. VAN DORP. My son! [*She sits, and* ALLEYN *brings an ottoman and sits by her side.*] I have wished so much to see you. Your letter told me all, but not all the little things I wished to know. And so you are a Captain, and you have made influential friends in Washington?

ALLEYN. Yes! I wrote you about the best of them, didn't I? The eccentric Mr. Rowse?

MRS. VAN DORP. Rowse! An odd name, not very distinguished.

ALLEYN. Oh, he's better than his name. A bluff, unpolished, generous heart. A shrewd fellow, but an honest politician, I'll be bound.

MRS. VAN DORP. What is his profession?

ALLEYN. Why, a politician!

MRS. VAN DORP. Is that a profession? What do they do, these politicians?

ALLEYN. Why, they, let me see—they take care of the public's interests. You know the public interest must be cared for. The old adage is: "What's everybody's business is nobody's business." Now the politicians do everybody's business, and account to nobody for the way they do it. That's Rowse's way. He got me my commission.

MRS. VAN DORP. He must be a very influential man.

ALLEYN. Very. He is interested in several railroads—not yet built, and he owns immense tracts of public lands, granted him by Congress to build the railroads on. His daughter, Miss Columbia Rowse, says, he owns a slice of every Territory in the West.

MRS. VAN DORP [*coldly*]. His daughter?

ALLEYN. Why, yes. Didn't I speak of her in my letter? How ungallant of me. She is the belle of the western country; sets the hearts of all the Territory beaux in flames, and is adored by the House of Representatives.

MRS. VAN DORP [*stiffly*]. A very charming person.

ALLEYN. And remember, her father made

me a Captain, and—oh! I quite forgot another.

MRS. VAN DORP. Another daughter?

ALLEYN. No. Another friend, whom I have also invited—Mr. Smith.

MRS. VAN DORP. Mr. Smith! What a name!

ALLEYN. The Honorable Arthur Wellesby Vere de Vere Smith.

MRS. VAN DORP [*interested*]. From England?

ALLEYN. An English nobleman, mother. Sixth son of an Earl, poor, but a good fellow, and no snob. He's not attached to the British Legation at Washington, and he goes with us out West to see life.

MRS. VAN DORP. They must stay with us to dinner.

ALLEYN. Thanks, my dear mother, I now—

MRS. VAN DORP. And now, my dear Alleyn, give me but a moment of your time, while I tell you—you, to whom alone I can confide it, a foolish old woman's troubles. Alas, my boy, I had thought never to see you again.

ALLEYN. How? You alarm me!

MRS. VAN DORP. I have been ill, I thought dying.

ALLEYN. And you never wrote, that I might fly to your side.

MRS. VAN DORP. It was a sudden shock, too sudden, too sudden to call on any human being for aid. Last night—

ALLEYN. So lately—

MRS. VAN DORP. You remember that this is the anniversary of a terrible day to me. I had not the courage to suffer the servants to do, what on this day I have for thirteen years permitted: that picture to be turned from the wall. Go, Alleyn, let me look once more—[ALLEYN *ascends ladder, and turns the picture.*] The picture of the man, who was once my husband, and the father of my child.

ALLEYN [*at foot of ladder*]. I know it well!

MRS. VAN DORP. Little Margaret loved him! loved him more than me. God forgive us all.

ALLEYN [*going to her and kneeling*]. Poor mother!

MRS. VAN DORP. Alleyn, I saw his face last night.

ALLEYN. Last night? In a dream?

MRS. VAN DORP. It must have been, but it seemed real. Listen to me. It seemed that you were in some wild Western place—huts scattered here and there—a sparse and ruffianly crew about you. Among them was that man.

ALLEYN. Your husband.

MRS. VAN DORP. He was unchanged—he looked the same. A man of deadly purpose and cruel eyes. I was by your side. He said to me: "Madam, you have come here to seek me. You have found me. But your child you will never see again." He turned to disappear into a hut. I could not move. I heard a voice, my little Margaret's voice, crying out: "Mother, save me!" She was struggling to be free. Her cries grew fainter, then ceased. I fell in a swoon to the earth. When I awoke, I was upon the floor of my own room, alone, and cold as death.

ALLEYN [*sits*]. It was but a dream.

MRS. VAN DORP. Was it not rather a divine light cast upon the mystery that fate has wrapped around my child's destiny? I feel it to be so. And I say to you now, that I am certain your mission to the Far West is to be the means of restoring her to me.

ALLEYN. I pray it may be so, with all my soul. [*Ring at door.*]

MRS. VAN DORP. Your friends! [*Crossing to door.*]

ALLEYN. Will you see them now?

MRS. VAN DORP. Certainly! One finds good friends so seldom, that yours shall be heartily welcomed at all times.

ALICE *enters with two cards on a salver, which she hands to* MRS. VAN DORP

MRS. VAN DORP [*reading*]. Mr. Smith—Miss Rowse.

ALLEYN. I wonder where papa can be? This is the daughter, and accompanied by the unattached scion of nobility.

MRS. VAN DORP [*to* ALICE]. Ask them in here. [ALICE *exits.*] Is the Honorable Mr. Smith likely to become attached to Miss Columbia?

ALLEYN. Stranger things have happened.

ALICE *ushers in* MR. SMITH *and* MISS COLUMBIA

ALLEYN [*advancing*]. Very happy indeed to see you.

COLUMBIA. We came, you see!

MR. SMITH [*shaking hands with* ALLEYN]. Thanks—very much.

ALLEYN. Allow me to present you. Mrs. Van Dorp, Miss Rowse. [*Crosses to* ALLEYN.] Mr. Smith. [*Salutations.*]

COLUMBIA. I'm sure, delighted. What an elegant house. Quite an old family mansion. Just like the old Knickerbockers. Delightful people.

MR. SMITH. Charmed to have the opportunity. Yes. Van Dorp has spoken of you so much. Yes.

MRS. VAN DORP. You have just arrived in the city, I believe.

MR. SMITH. This morning. Yes. We came—

COLUMBIA. We came by the Owl Train. All of us. Pa, and the Honorable Mr. Smith, and I. We look like owls ourselves, I dare say,—railroad travelling is so scary.

MRS. VAN DORP. I suppose we shall have the pleasure of seeing your father. Pray be seated. [ALLEYN *moves stool.*]

MR. SMITH. [*All sit.*] Yes. Thank you. Mr. Rowse said he would—

COLUMBIA. Said he'd come on after us. Pa is always so full of business. He's got to see at least a dozen prominent men here this morning. Most of the prominent men are in New York now.

MRS. VAN DORP. Indeed.

COLUMBIA. You know pa never has any business with any but prominent men. Pa knows all the prominent men. All the prominent men know pa. I know as many prominent men as pa does.

MRS. VAN DORP. It must be very pleasant.

COLUMBIA. Oh, no! Prominent men are not at all pleasant. You think they are great things till you know them. When you find them out, there's nothing particular about them, except that they are prominent.

MRS. VAN DORP. Your opportunities of judging are very great, no doubt.

COLUMBIA. Oh, very! Pa and I have been in Washington every session for five years. All the prominent characters come to Washington. I know them all, from Maine to Texas.

ALLEYN. Ha! ha! Have you any preferences as to States, Miss Columbia?

COLUMBIA. Not as to States. But the Territories are not nice.

MRS. VAN DORP [*surprise and inquiry*]. The Territories?

COLUMBIA. The prominent men of the Territories. They come to Washington, but they lack polish,—no refinement. I have no sympathy with them. I know all the prominent characters of the Territories; they don't compare with the States. But what I do admire, is the old families.

MRS. VAN DORP. Your acquaintance there is also quite large?

COLUMBIA. Oh, yes! The old families come to Washington, too. Many Knickerbockers. As soon as I heard your son's name, I told pa he was a Knickerbocker. You have a real Knickerbocker name. I've read Washington Irving all through, and I know all the names.

MR. SMITH. It must be awfully fatiguing to remember them all.

COLUMBIA. Oh, dear, no! I've practiced on names. Pa and I never forget a name. We have to remember them. A prominent man never forgives you if you forget his name. I tell the Honorable Mr. Smith he will never rise in America, because he forgets names. Don't I, Honorable?

MR. SMITH. Eh? Yes! Oh, yes! Miss Rowse very often says so. I can't always recollect. I get them mixed, particularly the colonels, and the generals, and the judges.

COLUMBIA. Yes, it was so funny. One day he called the Governor of Montana Colonel, and the Governor's Secretary he called Judge, and Judge Jones he called Governor, and he nearly defeated one of pa's bills. Didn't he? [*To* ALLEYN.]

ALLEYN. I believe something happened.

MR. SMITH. It was distressing. I was very sorry. Yes. But I apologized to the Judge, and the Secretary, and the Governor, and it came out all right.

MRS. VAN DORP. That was fortunate.

ALLEYN. I believe Miss Rowse's powers of fascination had to be exercised.

COLUMBIA. Oh, you bad fellow! [*To* MRS. VAN DORP.] But it's a fact. Pa had to give a dinner, and I had to do the agreeable, and play euchre with the Governor. It's a dreadful thing to be the daughter of a public man, Mrs. Van Dorp. [ALLEYN *moves stool down to left.*]

MRS. VAN DORP. It must be indeed. [*Door bell.*]

COLUMBIA. Oh, that must be pa now. Pa can't be very punctual, but he never breaks his word. In Washington the members say: "Sundown Rowse has given his word he'll square things; we'll go for his bill." If pa broke his word once, he'd never get another bill through.

ALICE *enters*

ALICE. Mr. Rowse.

MRS. VAN DORP. Show Mr. Rowse in, Alice. [ALICE *exits.*

COLUMBIA. It's a real holiday for pa to get away from Washington, he enjoys it so much.

ROWSE [*outside*]. All right, never mind me, I'll find the way.

ROWSE *enters*

ROWSE. Ah, here I am, you see. I knew Columby'd be here before me! Ah, Captain! [*To* MR. SMITH.] How de do again, Honorable.

ALLEYN. Allow me. [*Presents* ROWSE *to* MRS. VAN DORP.] My mother, Mr. Rowse.

ROWSE. Glad to see you, ma'am. Warmish day for the season. Run almost to death. Came straight here from the Fifth Avenue Hotel.

[ALLEYN, COLUMBIA *and* MR. SMITH *withdraw to right, looking over portfolio of pictures.*]

MRS. VAN DORP. Allow me to thank you, Mr. Rowse, most warmly, for the kind interest you have taken in my son, and the great service you have done him.

ROWSE. Don't mention it, ma'am. It wasn't much. I had a cousin wanted the commission, but he didn't like to go and fight the Indians. Your son jumped at the offer. My cousin backed down, asked me if I thought he was a chicken to go for the Chickasaws, and told me, I might go myself and keno the Kiutes.

MRS. VAN DORP. Alleyn is very courageous, and believes a soldier ought to fight.

ROWSE. He's a trump. I appreciate pluck. I come of a fighting family. They were the first settlers of Kansas. Perhaps you have heard of Hefty Bill Rowse of the Prairies?

MRS. VAN DORP. I never had the pleasure.

ROWSE. He was my father; one of the original border ruffians; as honest a man as ever lived. He cleared the settlements, and was elected Mayor twice by thirteen majority. Your son will get some notion of Western life, when he goes out.

MRS. VAN DORP [*going to* ALLEYN *and putting her arm about his neck*]. My hope and belief are, that Alleyn will never forget he is a Christian, even among the lawless settlers of the West.

ROWSE. Oh, I know him. He's a little soft here, perhaps, but he'll get hardened. Men must be hard out West, ma'am. I was too mild myself for it, and father sent me to Washington to dicker. I had a brother, who loved glory and stayed home. He was killed in a fight the very day I got my first bill through Congress. We buried him on my first land grant: two thousand acres near Silver Creek.

MRS. VAN DORP [*returning to center*]. There are many persons from the Eastern States, who settle in the West, are there not?

ROWSE. Thousands! Whole families! Single men—single women—double men—and double women, husbands and wives, you know,—everybody.

MRS. VAN DORP. Do they ever change their names, when they settle there?

ROWSE. If they are absconders, they mostly do. If there ain't no debts, nor no trouble about the law, they don't. I know one town where every inhabitant's got another name. They take ranks there according to the amount of debts they ran away from. The worst insolvent is elected Sheriff.

MRS. VAN DORP. There are many, too, no doubt, who go West to escape domestic troubles.

ROWSE. Oh, yes. The most part of the single people out there are divorced. It's a healthy country for domestic troubles.

MRS. VAN DORP. And the place Alleyn is detailed for, what is it called? Is it much settled?

ROWSE. Fort Jackson! Well, it's pretty well out towards the Horizon.

MRS. VAN DORP. You are familiar with the locality?

ROWSE [*pulling out map*]. [MRS. VAN DORP *and* ROWSE *sit.*] Here's the map. I know it, because my grant takes it in. I run from here on the west bank of the Big Run River down to Dogs' Ears, that's the name of another settlement, then out to All Gone, that's an Indian camp, and then to Hollo Bill, that's a traders' settlement. Queer names, ain't they?

MRS. VAN DORP [*sitting*]. And the inhabitants of these places?

ROWSE [*folding map*]. Queer lot! Native Americans with a sprinkling of the Injun and the least speck of the Chinee. I expect to locate several more towns, when I get out there.

MRS. VAN DORP. You are going, too?

ROWSE. Oh, yes! I'm off with the Captain. C'lumby's going, too, and the Honorable Smith. I'm going to prospect for the first hundred miles of the Fort Jackson and Big Run branch of the Union Pacific Railroad, chartered by Act of Congress and subsidized with twenty thousand acres, well adapted for farms and settlements.

COLUMBIA [*coming down*]. What on earth are you doing, pa? Boring Mrs. Van Dorp with your everlasting railroads and maps. Put 'em up.

ROWSE. Well, C'lumby, I—

COLUMBIA. Put 'em up, I say. This ain't a committee room.

MRS. VAN DORP. Your father has been giving me most valuable information.

COLUMBIA. All about his land grants, I suppose?

MRS. VAN DORP [*significantly to* ALLEYN, *who comes down with* MR. SMITH]. About the people of the West.

MR. SMITH. I'm really anxious to see the great West. Yes. The aboriginal red men and the real original white settlers.

ALLEYN. And I to see that noble territory, destined to be the cradle of a greater republic.

COLUMBIA. And I'm dying to see whether the place has grown any since I was a girl. The Honorable Smith is going to hunt buffaloes and bison, and I'm going with him. Ain't I?

ROWSE. Well, after I've located my railroad—

COLUMBIA. Bother your railroad. It's like a grand picnic. We'll go over the prairies on wild horses and camp out in the woods.

MR. SMITH. And eat buffalo steak cooked by the camp fire. Just as they do in the romances.

MRS. VAN DORP. And the danger—

ALLEYN. Danger, mother! What danger?

MR. SMITH. Danger! Is there danger, truly?

MRS. VAN DORP. The lawless inhabitants of the settlements. I have heard such stories of violence.

MR. SMITH. We'll call in the police. Besides, I'm protected by the British flag.

ALLEYN. They can offer no insult to a soldier of their own land.

COLUMBIA. At least they will respect the softer sex, won't they, Honorable?

ROWSE. Well, if the worst comes to the worst, I'll stand by my Act of Congress and retire behind my land grant.

MRS. VAN DORP. But the Indians—

MR. SMITH. Aw—yes—the noble savage. I'll speak to him as his paleface brother. I've read the Leatherstocking stories, and I think I can manage 'em.

ALLEYN. No quarter to the savages, who murder women and children. But to the weak and oppressed, I may be a friend. Duty commands no more.

ROWSE. Well, I'm going to take a case of dollar store jewelry out with me, and trade it for furs with the simple-minded red man. There's nothing like carrying civilization into the Far West.

ALICE *enters*

ALICE. Dinner is served, ma'am.

MRS. VAN DORP. Come, gentlemen. Come, Miss Rowse.

ROWSE. Dinner—really—bless me—I've half a dozen appointments.

ALLEYN. Oh, you must!

ROWSE. But I've so many engagements.

COLUMBIA. Let them wait for once.

ROWSE. But we start at eight.

Mrs. Van Dorp. And so, at least, we can spare one hour in saying farewell to friends we may never see again.

[*All surround* Rowse, *and preceded by* Mrs. Van Dorp, *they go up.*]

CURTAIN

ACT II

Scene.—*The town of Rogue's Rest—sixty miles from Fort Jackson—one of the wooden cities of the West. Hotel of primitive order at left, with portico, etc. Sign: "Occidental Hotel, on the European plan." Opposite, on right, a building of two stories, upper windows practicable, and reached by door and steps facing audience, over which hangs a lamp and painted thereon "The Clarion of the West." Lower floor with signs, etc., denoting Pacific Express office. At back is a low fence, partly concealing a house and low shed. Gate in fence near left.*

At the rise of the curtain Rocks of Tennessee, *the landlord of the hotel, and late Mayor of the town, is seated on piazza in a wooden arm-chair, smoking, in a loose linen duster.* Wannemucka, *the Indian, is lying, left, in front of hotel, pretending sleep. In center of stage is a group of rough settlers, some sitting, others standing, engaged in loud discussion. Among them are* Blakely, Gopher Joe *and* Mackenzie.

Blakely. Why won't they hang 'em?
Gopher. Quick work, I say!
Mackenzie. No gal's work for us.
Crowd. No nonsense! Clear the settlement! Give us a chaw of terbacker!
Together.

Rocks. Give us a rest, boys, do! What's the use of a row! If the job's to be done, it will be, and there's an end.

Blakely. It oughter been did afore.

Mackenzie. Two months ago.

Rocks. Well, ain't you satisfied now? You've tilted me out of my lawful authority as Mayor of this settlement, and you've taken the law into your own hands.

Blakely. No disrespect to you, boss, you know.

All. Oh, no!

Rocks. I know it, boys, and I'm much obliged. The civil power wasn't able to control. The settlement got overrun with blacklegs, horse-thieves and other alibis and aliases, as we say in the law-books, and so the citizens unite to clean the town themselves.

Blakely [*to others*]. That's it, like a book.

Rocks. You've formed a Vigilance Committee, and the Vigilance Committee cleared the streets effectually.

Blakely. Not quite, governor. After the clearing two weeks ago, a few specks of dirt still stuck to us.

Rocks. You mean Loder, the gambler?

Blakely. Yes, and Wolf!

Rocks. Old Wolf? Why, he's only a nameless old sot. He sleeps his day in that shanty yonder, more like a pigsty than a house. [*All look back at house.*] I'm agin turnin' him off, for the sake of his gal.

Blakely. Let 'em go somewhere else. We're hard-fisted, hard-working men. Mac, pint yer pistol. [*Takes dram from bottle produced by* Mackenzie.] Empty again. That's the fourth time today. Reform is powerful dry work. I say, Mr. Mayor, have her filled up. [Rocks *catches bottle and throws it inside.*] Clear 'em all out, I say, and begin with the Injun.

Mackenzie. Oh, the Injun will go, if we kick him out.

Rocks. Boys, it seems to me there's an almighty powerful talk here by the jury, right afore one of the condemned. [*Points to Indian.*]

Blakely. Oh, he's drunk, as usual.

Mackenzie. Not so early.

Rocks. Listening, I'll swear! [*Significant nod to boys, as he rises and draws pistol.*] Boys, the Injun might as well go at once. I've got my blotter handy, and we might as well wipe him off the records now. I'll just pint his ear and blaze. [*Goes to* Wannemucka, *cocks his pistol audibly, then points the muzzle first at his head, then over it, and fires. The Indian doesn't stir.*] Dead drunk!

All. Oh, he's all right!

Rowse *appears at window of hotel and looks out*

Rowse. Hallo! you there! [*Crowd look up.*]

Blakely. Hallo yourself! Who are you, stranger?

ROCKS. It's all right, gentlemen. There's a party come in last night on their way to Fort Jackson. This is one of them. Mr. Rowse is all right. Let me introduce you to some of our citizens, leading citizens. Leading citizens, Mr. Rowse! Mr. Rowse, leading citizens!

ROWSE. How are you, leading citizens! What are you holding a town meeting for?

BLAKELY. Stranger! The free and independent residents of this place don't usually explain their business to folks from other settlements; but if you want particularly to know, why, we've formed a Vigilance Committee, to reform the character of our population.

ROWSE. A what? A Vigilance Committee? [*Calling inside.*] I say—Smith—here!

MR. SMITH *appears at window*

MR. SMITH. Good gracious! What is it?

ROWSE. Did you ever hear of that peculiar institution of the Far West, called a Vigilance Committee? Here's one, you ignorant Britisher; take a look.

MR. SMITH. Vigilance Committee! Good gracious, yes! Some kind of animal. Where is it?

ROCKS. The Committee is meeting in the newspaper office. [*Points.*]

ROWSE. Ah! The head of the animal is across the street. This is only the tail.

MR. SMITH. Yes! Good gracious!

BLAKELY. Strangers! The Committee is a scary animile, and mustn't be riled. If you ain't got proper respect for it—

ROWSE [*loudly*]. Respect for it! [*Blandly.*] Will you kindly excuse me for a brace of shakes, until I can come down stairs?

ALL. Oh, come down out of that!

ROWSE. Thanks! Honorable, let's descend. [*They disappear.*]

BLAKELY [*to* ROCKS]. Who are these suckers?

ROCKS. Very influential man, Mr. Rowse, from—Washington. Eh, here he is!

ROWSE *and* MR. SMITH *enter from hotel. Crowd observes them sulkily*

ROWSE. Happy to make your acquaintance. May I ask what this Committee is met for?

BLAKELY. To sit on the live bodies of four parties that must get out or be put out.

ROWSE. You propose to expel four of your fellow-citizens?

MACKENZIE [*savagely*]. Yes, we do!

ROWSE. I beg your pardon! How are you? [*Shakes hands with him.*] And may I ask whom you propose to put out?

BLAKELY. First—an old drunken sot, Whiskey Wolf they call him, he hangs out over there.

ROWSE. And what's he done?

MACKENZIE. He's drunk and disorderly. [*Passes bottle around 'mongst crowd.*]

BLAKELY. Secondarily—A scoundrel that calls himself Loder—a gambler and worse, if there can be! [*Takes off hat to wipe face, pack of cards falls out.*]

ROWSE. He's very offensive to the community, I suppose? More so than Whiskey Wolf, eh?

MACKENZIE. Oh, Wolf's only a boozer.

MR. SMITH. A what?

ROWSE. A boozer! From the verb to booze, one who boozes. [*To* MACKENZIE.] When does he booze particularly?

MACKENZIE. All day. Loafs all the time. Never does a day's work. Then there's the Chinee.

ROWSE. You haven't got a Chinee here? Not a regular Heathen Chinee?

BLAKELY. Yes, we have. The varmin!

ROWSE. And what does he do?

BLAKELY. Why, he works for half-pay. Steals the bread out of honest men's mouths.

MR. SMITH. You condemn one fellow because he don't work, and another because he does.

BLAKELY. Stranger! We clear out every feller as don't do as we want him to.

MR. SMITH. Yes, I see!

BLAKELY. Lastly—That Indian yonder—lying over there drunk.

ROWSE. Oh, that's one of the criminals! Where are the others?

BLAKELY. I reckon you'll find Whiskey Wolf drunk in thar. [*Points to fence.*] The Chinee is sent for. He's down in the hollow, making chairs out of swamp rushes, and the boys are laying for Loder down by the Tree Tavern.

ROWSE. Very good! Now, my fellow-citizens, you can leave this job as fast as you please.

ALL [*starting*]. What!

ROWSE. I say you can get an extension of time to perform this contract, and go home with your minds easy.

BLAKELY. What do you mean?

ROWSE. I mean this. From what I see, the people you mean to turn adrift on the plains are no worse than the average crowd that's necessary in pretty nearly every well regulated city. And they may as well stay here, as go to other settlements to steal.

[*Murmurs by the crowd.*]

BLAKELY. Stranger, was your parents particularly long lived?

ROWSE. They stood the chills pretty well for their time of life.

BLAKELY. Well, they never had sich powerful shakes as you'll have, if you don't get into your shafts and travel pretty quickly.

MR. SMITH. Good gracious! What does he mean? Get into your shafts! He takes you for a horse!

ROWSE. All right, gentlemen! I see you want things done regularly, and the papers produced. [*Takes out map.*] Do you see this map? Here's Fort Jackson, there's All Gone, and there's Rogue's Rest—the flourishing city, where we now stand to inhale the breath of freedom.

ALL [*looking over his shoulder*]. Correct!

ROWSE. You observe a red line, which takes in the various localities aforesaid and stretches out to the top of Coyote Hill.

ALL [*as before*]. Correct!

ROWSE. Then, here's a copy of the grant by which the Government of the United States has conveyed to me the whole of this purchase, including your populous city. In other words, I'm the owner of this here settlement, the landlord of the premises, and proprietor generally. In a few words more, I won't have any mob law, and no Vigilance Committees, and no riots, and no games of that sort on my land. How's that for turning up a bower? Do you pass?

BLAKELY [*drawing pistol*]. No, stranger, I order it up.

MR. SMITH. Good gracious! Where's the police?

BLAKELY. Boys, shall we give them a taste of our productions?

ALL. Clear 'em out. [*They draw knives, pistols.*]

BLAKELY. Take up them papers! Put them up, I say! [ROWSE *gathers map nervously.*] Now git!

ROWSE. But I say—

MR. SMITH. Don't touch me—I'm a British subject. I'm under the protection of the British flag.

MACKENZIE [*knocks* MR. SMITH'S *hat off*]. Oh, scissors! [*Hat kicked about.*]

ROWSE. You'll hear from me. I'll—[*The two are hustled towards the hotel, etc.*]

ROCKS. Now, gentlemen,—[*Interposing.*]

SALERATUS BILL *enters running*

BILL. I say, boys, Loder and the Chinee have gone down by the Gulch. Slater thinks they are skedaddling.

BLAKELY. The devil they are! After 'em, lads. Don't let 'em slope till we get through with 'em!

[*The mob run off, headed by* BLAKELY *and* BILL, *crying: "This way," "All right," "Go it," etc.*]

MR. SMITH [*picking up hat, which the mob have given a final kick*]. It's an outrage. It's a blarsted country, altogether.

ROWSE. I'd like to know the good of an Act of Congress, if it ain't respected out here.

ALLEYN *enters gaily*

ALLEYN. Hallo! What's up? You look flushed.

MR. SMITH. Flushed? Yes! By Jove! Just look at my hat, that's flushed.

ROWSE. Cap, you're just the man I want. How long will it take you to bring a company of soldiers from Fort Jackson and put out my tenants?

ALLEYN. Why, I haven't got as far as Fort Jackson yet. We were not to start till this evening.

ROWSE. Well, just start at once, and bring your troops over, won't you? I want this town blown to the devil.

ALLEYN. Why, I thought this place was your property.

ROWSE. And can't I do what I like with my

property? Blow it to the devil. I'll stand the loss.

ALLEYN. What's the trouble? I like the place. I've just seen the prettiest girl you can imagine. A backwoods Venus, lovely, young, delicate. Miss Columbia and I met her down by the post office. A perfect Venus.

ROWSE. Don't talk to me of Venuses. I want Marseses, the gods of war. Alleyn, there's a Vigilance Committee here and they're going to—

ALLEYN. Not harm you or Smith?

ROWSE. No. To turn some poor devils out.

ALLEYN. Oh, that's nothing; they're always doing that.

ROWSE. But I won't have it on my property. Won't you stand up with me and stop it?

ALLEYN. We two against a hundred—nonsense.

ROWSE. Then you won't—

ALLEYN [*looking off*]. Sh! Yonder comes the girl I spoke of.

ROWSE [*down stage, angry*]. Hang the girls. A man is no use to the community till he's married.

ALLEYN. There she goes with Miss Columbia. What a charming step! Smith, just look.

MR. SMITH. Ah, yes! Miss Rowse, monstrous fine girl.

ALLEYN. No, the other!

MR. SMITH. Ah, yes, so she is! Introduce me!

ALLEYN [*taking his arm, impetuously*]. Come along, we'll meet them; hurry up; she may turn off into some of the houses.

[*Exit, dragging* MR. SMITH.

ROWSE. Here, don't go off! What the deuce were girls ever made for? Who'd have thought there'd be a girl out here to turn a chap's head? [*Sees Indian asleep.*] There's one of the poor devils the committee's after. He'll be shot while he's drunk and never know it. [*Touches Indian with his foot.*] Hi! you! Indian! Wake up and let me scare you to death! [WANNEMUCKA *jumps up and confronts* ROWSE, *who jumps back.*] Hello! that's early rising. What kind of whiskey do you drink to freshen up so quick after it?

WANNEMUCKA. Injun no drink whiskey. Stranger think Wannemucka drunk?

ROWSE. It looked like it. What did you say your name was?

WANNEMUCKA. Wannemucka! Wannemucka chief! Big chief! Tribe far away! Down there—sunset!

ROWSE. If your tribe's down by the sunset, they're luckier than you are.

WANNEMUCKA. Wannemucka safe. Ugh! White man think injun sleep. White man talk—injun's nose [*Imitates snore.*] asleep, injun's eyes [*Closing them.*] asleep, but injun's ears awake.

ROWSE. Oh, you've been playing possum and listening. Then you've overheard them. Why don't you run for your life?

WANNEMUCKA. Wannemucka, no fear. [*Shows dirk.*] Wannemucka got this.

ROWSE. Oh, you mean to fight for it, eh? But they'll kill you if you resist.

WANNEMUCKA [*goes to bush behind express office, shows rifle, which he replaces*]. Wannemucka not go alone.

ROWSE. You want to go with the sots and blacklegs, eh? Don't, injun; go back to your tribe in decent company.

WANNEMUCKA [*stealthily approaching*]. White stranger ever love?

ROWSE. Did I ever love? Not much, or if I ever did, it's gone clear out of my head. What of it?

WANNEMUCKA. Wannemucka love! She here! Wannemucka take her, or never go back to his tribe again.

ROWSE. The deuce! Some squaw of yours here, eh? More girls! Even the injun won't save his own bacon, but risks it for a girl. Well, you're a plucky bird anyway. I wish you joy and well out. There's my hand.

[WANNEMUCKA *takes it reluctantly, and then, drawing near, fingers* ROWSE'S *chain.*]

WANNEMUCKA. Ugh! nice!

ROWSE. You like it, eh?

WANNEMUCKA. Heap o' skins to buy that?

ROWSE. Yes, injun, it would take considerable coon skins to reach.

WANNEMUCKA. Injun like it! Injun want it!

ROWSE [*draws back, takes revolver from pocket*]. Stand back! Do you want to rob me, you unsophisticated redman?

WANNEMUCKA. No. Injun play for it.

ROWSE. Play for it?

WANNEMUCKA. Poker! [*Takes greasy pack of cards from his pocket and shuffles them.*]

ROWSE. Moses in the bulrushes! Who'd have thought of this romantic injun sporting a deck and offering to play poker? My feelings are hurt. If you had offered to scalp me, you red rascal, I might have forgiven you. But Poker! That knocks the romance, and I despise you!

LODER, *who has entered at "My feelings are hurt," and carelessly looked on, now comes down.*

LODER [*to* ROWSE]. You won't take a hand then, stranger? [*Laughs and sits on back of chair, pulls out a pencil, commences to whittle it.*]

WANNEMUCKA. Ugh! White panther here! [*Puts up cards.*]

ROWSE. Take a hand? I'm sorry I shook hands with him. I'd rather have seen him carry a tomahawk than a pack of cards.

LODER. That's civilization, my friend! When the noble savage was in his native state, he went for the hair of your head. Now he's in the midst of civilization, he carries the weapons of enlightenment, and goes for the money in your pocket.

ROWSE. I'm sorry for it. I don't want things so progressive on my lands.

LODER. P'raps not. But it's just as well you didn't play with him. Injun is a prime hand at poker. You can't beat him. Why, he almost comes up to me. [*Rises, crosses to* WANNEMUCKA.] Don't you, injun? [WANNEMUCKA *grunts.*]

ROWSE. And who may you be?

LODER. Me? Oh, I'm no account. I travel.

ROWSE. Oh, a traveller!

LODER. You've put it right. My business is to leave. I'm an outpost of progress! I open up the great West to the march of mind. When things get settled about me, I go on! [WANNEMUCKA *plucks his sleeve.*] Eh? What's up?

WANNEMUCKA. Something to tell.

ROWSE [*curious*]. Eh?

LODER [*to* ROWSE]. I reckon your friends are looking for you.

ROWSE. Eh?

LODER [*coolly*]. I reckon your train's about to start.

ROWSE. My train?

LODER [*sternly*]. I reckon you are staying here to mix up in domestic secrets, and worry my mind. Your train's waiting. Get aboard!

ROWSE. Oh, you want me to go! Why didn't you say so? Well, for a new country which belongs to me, and inhabited by people who don't pay me any rent, this is the most impudent—[LODER *points for him to go.*] Oh! This town will certainly have to be blown to the devil. [*Off into hotel.*]

LODER [*whittling*]. Now, Injun, what is it?

WANNEMUCKA. 'Sh! [*Points to Vigilance Committee room.*]

LODER. Well!

WANNEMUCKA. Committee!

LODER. Vigilance? [WANNEMUCKA *nods.*] How do you know?

WANNEMUCKA. Injun sleep there! Crowd! Talk much! Must go, or—[*Imitates hanging.*]

LODER. So soon, and only here four months. [*Puts up knife, puts pencil away calmly.*] And no money to speak of. Just getting into luck, too. Well, if I must, I must. So I'm the marked man?

WANNEMUCKA. Injun, too!

LODER. You? You poor, pitiful sneak! Turn you out! It's a damned disgrace to John Loder to be walked out of a town with a greasy injun!

WANNEMUCKA. More! Old man! [*Points to wall at back.*]

LODER [*excited*]. What! Wolf and his daughter?

WANNEMUCKA. All go!

LODER [*deeply moved*]. She! By the—it will kill her! What has she done? But what the devil am I standing here for? Come! [*Excitedly.*] In with me. We must wake him. We must agree upon some plan. Come! [*Rushes to the door in wall.*] Oh, the cursed wretches! [*Looking back at Vigilance Committee's house.*] If I—!—Oh, get in, and don't waste time. [*Pushes* WANNEMUCKA *and exits after him.*]

ALLEYN *and* MED *enter; he carries her little basket*

MED. This is as far as I go.

ALLEYN. I wish—I wish it were a mile further.

MED. A mile further, and I so tired!

ALLEYN. Pardon me, I didn't think of that. I was only thinking of the pleasure to myself.

MED. And why would you be so pleased? Though I used to love to walk, to run, to play all day in the woods.

ALLEYN. Won't you sit down? Just for a moment! Right here. I love to hear you talk. [*He gently presses her to sit on seat.*] You are a real backwoods girl, ain't you?

MED. And you are from the city?

ALLEYN. Yes! Ever so far away.

MED. It is beautiful in the cities where you come from—is it not?

ALLEYN. Very. Wouldn't you like to leave such life as this, and go to the splendid city?

MED. Yes, and I will too, if I live.

ALLEYN. If you live?

MED. Yes! Didn't I tell you? No, I told her. They say I'm very sick.

ALLEYN. You look delicate and pale—but a little rest, a little care—why don't you see the doctor?

MED. We never have doctors come out here. But there are agents always travelling about with patent medicines. [*Laughs.*] Oh, it was so funny to see the settlers, big fellows, six feet high, who never knew what it was to be sick, coming into father's cabin with big bottles and little bottles, that cured everything—so the agent said—and making me try them all. I think they made me worse, don't you?

ALLEYN [*sits beside* MED]. But, now—surely you are not ill now?

MED. No, I do not suffer now; but the feeling is like—as if the struggle were over.

ALLEYN. Oh, if I could only do something for you!

MED. Yes, that's what they all say.

ALLEYN. Who are all?

MED. Oh, everybody! That is, some particular ones.

ALLEYN. Who are they? Not lovers! [MED *nods, and plays with his buttonhole.*] Lovers! You! Why, you are only a little girl!

MED. Ain't I big enough to love?

ALLEYN. Yes, now.

MED. And I suppose yesterday I wasn't? Oh, that's not true. I've had so many. Everywhere we went, father and I, somebody was sure to say: "I love you."

ALLEYN. And you—what did you say?

MED. Oh, your necktie is all loose.

ALLEYN. No, no! Tell me what you said?

MED. Let me fix the necktie first.

ALLEYN. Yes, on condition that you tell me. [MED *ties it while he speaks.*] What did you say when they told you they loved you?

MED. I said—I said: "I love you, too."

ALLEYN [*vexed*]. You did? [*About to rise.*] Well, you shan't fix my necktie any more.

MED [*pulling him down again*]. Nonsense! Let me fix the necktie.

ALLEYN [*pause, then looking up into her eyes*]. Do you know, you're a little witch?

MED [*rises and goes down stage*]. No! Witches never get sick.

ALLEYN. When I get to Fort Jackson, I'll send the surgeon over to see you.

MED [*archly*]. I don't want to see the surgeon.

ALLEYN [*quickly*]. I'll come with him.

MED. No, indeed, Mr. Assurance, I didn't mean that. But will you come to see Meddie, truly?

ALLEYN. Meddie? What an odd name! What does it mean?

MED. Why, it means me.

ALLEYN. Then it's just the name you ought to have.

MED. But will you come—truly—ever so truly?

ALLEYN. Yes, indeed, I will.

MED. And when are you going away?

ALLEYN. This very day. [*Looking at watch.*] By George, within half an hour! [*Starts up.*] The guides and horses are waiting for me.

MED [*rises*]. And the pretty lady who is coming yonder—is she going with you?

ALLEYN. Oh, no! She and her father, and the tall gentleman are going to take the boat down the Big Run River, to explore his grant.

MED. I know the river. Wannemucka's tribe belongs there. Only think, an Indian loved me, wanted me to be a princess. [*Laughs.*] I didn't tell *him* I loved him. I told Loder, and Loder knocked him down.

ALLEYN. What perils surround you, poor little thing!

MED. I'm so glad the pretty lady is not going with you.

ALLEYN. Why?

MED. Because!

ALLEYN. Nothing could make me ever forget Meddie.

MED. You are sure.

ALLEYN. I know it as I know—

Puts his arm about her waist, when COLUMBIA *and* MR. SMITH *enter*

MED. Oh! [*Runs up and disappears through gate in wall.* ALLEYN *does not see where she goes to in his confusion.*]

COLUMBIA. Oh, Captain! Caught you in the very act.

MR. SMITH. Yes! Very act of besieging the fortress of Beauty.

COLUMBIA. Yes! The very act of throwing the lines of circumvallation around her waist.

MR. SMITH. Where did she go to?

COLUMBIA. Must have run down the street.

ALLEYN [*aside*]. Gone! But I can run over from the Fort and see her, and I will, if I have to—

COLUMBIA. Oh, Captain, don't be so silent. I knew you were struck by her, as soon as we met her. And that was the reason I took the Honorable Mr. Smith around the settlement, while you had a chance to chat with her.

ALLEYN. You were really so good and amiable to—

COLUMBIA. To get out of the way and leave you two alone?

ALLEYN. Oh, I don't mean that! But she really is a charming, original, little thing, just the little angel to—

COLUMBIA. To chat with once, and then forget. Nonsense! A puny, sickly, ignorant little backwoods girl! I'm astonished at you! Come! To Fort Jackson! There's your guide, now.

Enter GUIDE

GUIDE. The horses are saddled, Captain. We only wait for you.

ALLEYN. Baggage all right?

GUIDE. Yes, sir! Mr. Rowse is down by the Tree Tavern, waiting for you. We'll have to start soon, to get over the ford before dark.

ALLEYN [*crosses*]. Then I'm off.

MR. SMITH [*to* COLUMBIA]. We'll see him off, eh?

COLUMBIA. Certainly. We'll see you safe out of here, for fear any other original and charming little girls should detain you.

ALLEYN. Ah! Spare me this time. It's my first and only flirtation. Perhaps I shall never see her again.

COLUMBIA. Oh, how solemn!

MR. SMITH. By Jove, it's heartrending! [*Laugh, and take him off between them.*]

LODER *enters from the gate, pulling* WOLF. *His daughter,* MEDDIE, *follows, clinging to him in fear. After a while* WANNEMUCKA *follows them out moodily.*

LODER [*as he enters*]. I tell you, governor, it's neck or nothing. The town's up, and we've got to go!

WOLF [*staring about him*]. Go! [*Vacantly.*] Where?

MED. Oh, anywhere from this dreadful danger. Father, father, do try and think. Rouse yourself! Do try and understand our peril.

WOLF. Ps'h! My throat's as hot!—Have you got a drop in your flask, Loder?

LODER. Don't think of liquor now, governor. Brace up! Be a man!

WOLF. I'm past it. I'm a gone body, Loder. I feel it here [*Head.*] and here. [*Heart.*] Nothing in me. Let 'em kill, curse 'em. I've travelled thousands of miles, like a madman, for years. Perhaps I'll get a madman's rest now. [*Points to ground.*] The grave!

LODER. If you can't take care of yourself, think of your daughter! If you stop here, they'll shoot you, maybe. I've tried the obstinate dodge, and nearly squalled for it. If you're dead, what becomes of her?

WOLF. Margaret! Meddie! Dear little Med! You won't leave me?

MED. Never, father, while I live. You will go with us. It may not be far. We may find another and kinder settlement; if not, we can go to the Fort.

WOLF. I'll not budge a foot. I'm a desperate man, and I'll dare 'em to do their worst.

LODER. And your daughter? You told me

often that you loved her. You won't trust her to strangers?

WOLF. You coward! You'll desert us, will you?

LODER. Look here, governor, I'm not a coward when I have a show. But I don't fight mobs. Besides, I'm tired of this place. It's getting too civilized for me. When civilization steps in, it's time for John Loder to make a move higher up. I mean to put for some infant settlement a little nearer the Horizon, and give it a lift. [*Goes up.*]

WOLF. Go then! Back out! Leave us!

WANNEMUCKA [*coming forward*]. Wannemucka friend! No leave old Wolf to die by the dogs. Injun honest! Take care of young white girl. [LODER *starts, looks around.*]

WOLF. You! Trust my child to you!

WANNEMUCKA. Indian honest! [LODER *regards him coolly.*] Wannemucka chief of tribes. Take white maiden there. Be a princess.

MED [*terrified*]. Oh, father! [*Clinging to* WOLF.]

WOLF. You copper-colored scoundrel! You dare to think of my daughter—a lady—[*Strikes him.*]

MED. Oh, father, don't! Let us fly together! Oh, Heaven, what will become of me?

LODER [*approaching*]. Whatever happens, little girl, no harm shall come to you, while I have breath and blood to spend. [*Noise of voices and mob heard.*] Come, old man, will you start?

WOLF. No!

LODER. Then put your girl in the house before the pack is on us.

WOLF. Take her!

MED. Oh, bring him with us! [*To* LODER.] Do not leave him!

LODER. Don't fear, I'll do what I can.

Stage growing darker. Voices heard nearer. LODER *leads* MED *to gate, she exits, he closes it. Voices louder. Windows of the newspaper office open, and the heads of* SCOTT, *of Scott Cañon, and others of the Committee, appear. Mob enters, headed by* BLAKELY, MACKENZIE, *etc.*

BLAKELY [*as he enters*]. Here they are, all together! Bring along the other scamp!

[*The other,* CHINEE, *is thrust forward among exiles.*]

SCOTT [*as crowd yell*]. Gentlemen, order! Order!

BLAKELY. Silence, boys—for the Committee.

SCOTT. Gentlemen, the Committee has decided.

MACKENZIE. Three cheers for the Committee!

SCOTT [*puts on glasses, reads from paper*]. The Committee having proceeded according to law and the traditions of the Border, have found the following persons guilty of the following crimes: [*Turning to another leaning over him.*] Colonel, will you jest oblige me by moving your everlasting elbow out of my back! [*Resumes reading.*] John Loder, gambler and fighter!

BLAKELY. Stand out, Loder!

LODER. Anything to oblige, Judge! I say, Scotty!

SCOTT. Well! [*Looks down.*]

LODER. You couldn't give me a reference to the next place, could you? [*Mob laugh and shout: "Good boy!" "Game!"*]

BLAKELY. Order! Order!

SCOTT. Wolf Van Dorp, drunkard, gambler, and nuisance generally!

WOLF [*rousing up*]. Stop! What name was that?

SCOTT. Your own name, I reckon.

WOLF. It's a lie! Strike it out!

SCOTT. Not while the evidence is before the Court. [*Packet is handed him from inside.*] A bundle of old letters, newspaper cuttings, etc., found in your house.

WOLF. You've robbed my house, you thieves!

SCOTT. I reckon we took an everlasting squint about your premises, while you were drunk last night, and found it. But the Court's done with it. You may take it. [*Flings it out.* WOLF *grasps it eagerly, looks over it, then puts it in* LODER'S *hand, and whispers to him.*]

SCOTT. Wannemucka, Indian, gambler and horse-thief, as the Committee suspects! [WANNEMUCKA *folds his blanket and grunts.*] Chinee, heathen and mean-spirited furriner!

CHINEE. Me? No, Melican, me no bad! Love Melican! Work—no play—no gamble—no drunk—poor Chinee man!

SCOTT. Judge, will you give that critter

an all-fired squelcher! [BLAKELY *attends to* CHINEE.] The sentence of the Committee is, that the aforesaid persons, all and singular, git up and git out of this settlement within thirty calendar minutes from the reading of this verdict. [*The mob cry out and menace the group.* SCOTT *folds up paper.*] What do the prisoners at the bar say?

LODER. Gentlemen, for my part, I always bow to the will of the people. The population having unanimously elected me to represent them in some other settlement, I beg leave to thank them, and gracefully retire.

WOLF [*whispers to him*]. Don't fail me, lad! That packet to Med. In your charge I leave her, remember!

LODER. Trust me! [*Bows to mob.*] Gentlemen, good evening! [*Exit.*

WANNEMUCKA [*who had listened*]. Injun remember, too. [*Aloud.*] Palefaces! Wannemucka glad to go to his tribe! [*Stalks off, and during the ensuing scene creeps back stealthily and takes his rifle, then goes off behind houses.*]

SCOTT. Clean out the rest. [*The* CHINEE *is hustled out, and the crowd return to seize* WOLF.]

WOLF. One moment! [*All stop.*] You may kill me, but I don't go!

CROWD. Hang him! Hang him!

WOLF. Well, you can't hang me but once!

The mob rush at him with a yell. One of them, MACKENZIE, *makes a noose, when* ROWSE *enters, and interferes.*

ROWSE. Stop, you fellows! Am I in time? No one hung up yet, I hope?

SCOTT. Who's this?

ROWSE. I'm the landlord here, and I want to know, who gives notice to quit, while I'm about?

BLAKELY [*to* SCOTT]. He's crazy!

SCOTT. Then clean him out! [*Mob advances.*]

ROWSE [*draws a pair of revolvers, crowd halts*]. I thought not. Now, fellow-citizens, listen to me. What are you going to do with this old man?

SCOTT. He's been ordered to leave and he won't.

ROWSE. Well, what then?

MACKENZIE. Then he must be strung up.

ROWSE [*shaking hands*]. Oh, how are you again, neighbor? [*Crowd murmur.*] You won't hang him till he's tried, will you? The committee, as far as I can get at it, only agreed to turn him out. He must be tried before he's sentenced to be hung, mustn't he? [*Mob murmur.*]

SCOTT. That's so, gentlemen. The stranger's correct; we must try him for refusing to go.

ROWSE [*takes off his hat, puts it on ground, and mounts chair on stand*]. Fellow-citizens: Let us not be irregular, let us not proceed to mob law, let us give the prisoner at the bar a fair shake before he steps out on the rope-walk and misses his footing in the circumambient air; is that law? [*Mob assent among themselves.*]

SCOTT [*blandly*]. I beg pardon. What is the gentleman's name?

ROWSE [*blandly*]. Rowse! Sundown Rowse, of Washington, District of Columbia!

SCOTT [*to mob*]. Gentlemen, allow me to introduce Mr. Rowse, of Washington. Mr. Mayor, a glass of water for the speaker. [*Canteens, bottles and flasks passed to* ROWSE.]

ROWSE. Thanks! Gentlemen, we are here proceeding according to law. Not the musty statutes of effete systems and oligarchies of the Old World, but the natural law implanted in the bosoms of man since our common ancestors were washed, wrung out and hung up to dry by the universal flood.

MOB. Hear! hear! Go on! [SCOTT *and committee clap their hands.*]

ROWSE. What do I find? I find the public characters of the town are called upon to do justice to their fellow-man. In such cases, in my experience, it is not uncommon to ask any prominent citizen from another, and friendly settlement, Washington or New York, for instance, to meet with the committee and form a general High Commission to settle all disputed points. Am I right, or am I not?

SCOTT [*who during the proceeding has consulted with the committee*]. Mr. Rowse is correct. Such has been generally the practice. The committee respectfully invite Mr. Rowse to step up and jine the deliberations. [*All applaud,* Rowse *is handed down, his hat is given him and he is escorted to door.*]

Rowse. Thanks! fellow-citizens! Thanks!

Scott. The committee also invite all citizens to keep their feelins suppressed for ten calendar minutes longer, while the deliberations is going on. [*Disappears.*]

Blakely. All right, governor! Boys, come in and see what old Tennessee Rocks has got. [*Shout from crowd, who press forward and exit into hotel.*]

Wolf [*alone and eagerly*]. They mean to do their worst. Life is precious after all. [*Picks up a flask which one of the crowd has dropped and drinks.*] It gives me new courage. I am not too late. I can yet fly with my child.

Runs eagerly up to gate. Shot heard from behind. Wolf *falls.* Wannemucka *appears, throws gun down near body, jumps up on shed.*

Wannemucka. Now injun have white princess!

Loder *and* Med *appear at gateway*

Loder. You red devil! Come and take her!

The mob rush from hotel. The committee and Rowse *appear at windows.*

CURTAIN

ACT III

Scene i.—*The stage represents the head of flatboat navigation on Big Run. Fort Jackson is supposed to be situated here, and on the right, up stage, a low, one story store shed projects, surmounted by a flagstaff and colors flying. The bank of the river extends from right to left. At back is a view of wild country, through which the Big Run winds its course. A flatboat is moored in the stream, a little to the right, and is approached by a sort of gangplank from the bank. The time is afternoon. The curtain rises upon a scene of bustle.*

Sergeant Crockett *is directing soldiers, who are loading the boat with bags, barrels and bundles from shed, right, and* Cephas *and other darkies are loading it with wood from left.* Cephas *carries a single, very small log for each load, singing or whistling with each trip. The* Heathen Chinee, Blakely *and* Wahcotah *are playing cards on the ground by left lower entrance. A sentry is on duty at back on bank. The curtain rises to a chorus of the darkies loading up.*

Cephas and Darkies:—

"I'm proud to be in the service of the Lord,
And I'm bound to die in his army."

[*As darkies go off for another load,* Cephas *comes down and leans on his stick of wood, looking over the group of card players.*]

Cephas. Hi! dars de way dem trash has of musin' dereselves. [*To* Chinee.] Hi! you, play de ace, you cussed fool.

Blakely. Play the ace? Why, not him! He's tried five aces on us already.

Chinee. Me no understand!

Blakely. Don't understand, eh? Well, what you *don't* understand would furnish brains for a mosquito.

Cephas. Hi! golly! Chinee wipe nigger out, eh?

Blakely. Well, for "Ways that are dark and for tricks that are vain." Why, he's won all my terbacker already! Ain't you, Chinee?

Chinee. Me poor chap! No understand Melican. [*Sudden grab at trick* Blakely *is about to take.*] Mine, Melican!

Wahcotah [*throwing down his cards*]. Ugh! Cheatee!

Blakely [*drawing a dirk*]. That's the sixth ace in this hand; let me go for that heathen.

[Chinee *starts up, runs towards shed.* Blakely *after him, stopped by* Sergeant.]

Sergeant. Come! none of that! Let this poor devil alone. Get aboard with you! [Blakely *goes off muttering into boat.*] Come, African, lively with that wood there.

Cephas. All right, massa serjiant. [*Sings as he goes off into boat.*]

"I'm proud to live in the service of the Lord,
And I'm bound to die in his army."

Mr. Smith *enters from left, looking back. He is dressed in Western prairie fashion, but with silk hat, gun and bag.*

Mr. Smith. Yes! This way! come along.

Widow Mullins [*outside*]. Heaven bless your honor, that's what I say.

WIDOW MULLINS *enters, followed by a young girl, her daughter, and a little girl*

SERGEANT. Well, Honorable, what sort of game is that you've got?

COLUMBIA *appears on boat*

MR. SMITH. Game! Yes! you know—oh! there, Miss Columbia! By Jove—good morning!

COLUMBIA. Good morning! Here, you boys, give me a hand.

SOLDIERS. That we will, Miss!

[CEPHAS *again comes. Two men run forward and help her across gang-plank.*]

COLUMBIA. Thanks! [*Comes down and confronts* WIDOW *and others all laden with packs on their backs.*] Mercy, who are these?

SERGEANT. You must ask the Honorable, miss, he brought 'em in.

WIDOW. Faith, an' he did—long life to him and more whiskers if he wants 'em.

COLUMBIA. Irish! Irish out here?

WIDOW. Irish! out here; faix, ma'am, an' did iver ye go anywhere you didn't see the Irish?

MR. SMITH. Yas! I was surprised myself. You see I was out trying to start some game, and all in a minute I came out on the place, about three miles yonder, where these poor people live.

SERGEANT. Oh, you are the Mullinses?

WIDOW. Yis! We are the Mullinses! This is my daughter Rhody, ma'am, an' this is Molly, sir! and we were sitting by our house—more by token, it was no house at all, seein' it had been knocked over by the Indians—crying our eyes out, whin this gentleman come up—

RHODA. Thrue for ye, mother.

COLUMBIA. Your house knocked over?

SERGEANT. By the Indians? When?

MR. SMITH. Last night, they told me.

RHODA. Thrue for ye, sir!

COLUMBIA. Must be the same party Capt. Alleyn has gone after with pa! I hope they'll catch 'em, the red ugly things.

MR. SMITH. When did they go?

COLUMBIA. Just after you left this morning. A scout ran in and told the captain about a party of Indians who had been seen in force along the river.

MR. SMITH. Then, by Jove, I've had a narrow escape. It's well I came back so early with these poor people.

WIDOW. It's well ye did, sir, for if the Indians got ye, they'd make elegant work of that fine head of hair of yours.

MR. SMITH. By Jove, they might have scalped my whiskers.

RHODA. Thrue for ye, sir!

COLUMBIA. But why did the Indians attack you?

WIDOW [WAHCOTAH *listens quietly*]. Faith, they were looking for fire arms and 'munition, they said. An' whin I tould 'em I was only a poor widdy and my husband was dead wid the chills and fever, and divil a gun we had, dey just knocked over the shanty and left us cryin'.

SERGEANT. How many were there?

WIDOW. Faith, I was so worried I couldn't see; a thousand, I'm thinking.

RHODA. Sure, mother, there was only three.

WIDOW. Now, Rhody, how can ye say dat?

RHODA. I observed 'em and heard them speak of a larger party they were going to join.

SERGEANT. Ah! They were scouts then. We'll soon find out when the captain comes back.

RHODA [*to* COLUMBIA]. Please, ma'am, can you tell us what we're to do? We've got no home now, an' sure we're afraid to go back.

COLUMBIA. What do you want to do?

WIDOW. Sure, ma'am, we want to get near some settlement where we'll be snug and safe.

COLUMBIA. We're all going down the river this evening, about thirty miles to a settlement. We go in the boat there; would you like to come?

WIDOW. Sure and that we would, ma'am. [*Distant gun heard.*]

SERGEANT [*going up to boat*]. That must be the captain now.

COLUMBIA. Oh, there comes my pa, then; I'll get him to find room for you, and you shall go with us.

WIDOW. Heaven bless ye, ma'am!
RHODA. Bless ye, ma'am! Thank the lady, Molly. } [*Together.*]

SERGEANT [*on boat, looking off*]. Yes, there's the party.

MR. SMITH. Any captive Indians?

SERGEANT. No! eh? [*Looking off.*] Something very odd. Mr. Rowse has got something. [WAHCOTAH *interested.*] A dog, I think, is following at his heels.

MR. SMITH [*to* COLUMBIA]. By Jove, how odd! I go to hunt buffaloes and bag an Irish family. And your father goes to capture Indians and brings back a bow-wow!

COLUMBIA. Oh, you amusing creature! But don't you like this exciting life? Isn't it romantic? Nothing but alarums, Indians, scouting and scalping—charming!

MR. SMITH. Very!

COLUMBIA. So delicious. You go to bed at night and never know if you'll ever get up to breakfast again.

MR. SMITH. Yes.

COLUMBIA. To go and take a romantic walk by the side of a placid stream, expecting every moment to have your bonnet strings cut by a bullet—

MR. SMITH. Delightful!

COLUMBIA. Let's go and take a walk. We have still time enough, before the boat will be ready to start.

MR. SMITH [*nervously*]. Certainly! with pleasure! and if the Indians surprise us—

COLUMBIA. You will divert their attention—while I run back for help.

MR. SMITH. Oh, ye-es! [*Both exit.*

ALLEYN *and soldiers and darkey enter. Soldiers enter shed*

SERGEANT [*salutes*]. Captain!

ALLEYN. No luck so far, sergeant. We must have a party to scour the river bank tonight. It's not safe to send the boat down unprotected.

SERGEANT. Indians really about, sir; this poor family were surprised last night by three scouts, and they spoke of a larger party.

ALLEYN. We came on the trail of an Indian family, and found an old squaw with her child. The woman fled, leaving the infant.

SERGEANT. That's what we saw with Mr. Rowse then, sir!

ALLEYN [*laughing*]. Yes, he seized the infant, not knowing what he was doing. She has clung to him ever since, and he's rather annoyed at it. Where is the friendly Indian you spoke of this morning, who hangs about the fort?

SERGEANT [*calls*]. Wahcotah!

WAHCOTAH [*advancing*]. Injun here!

ALLEYN. What tribe is it that surprised this poor family?

WAHCOTAH. No tribe. No warriors, only boys. Indian boys love fun.

ALLEYN. Are you sure? But the squaw and child were found today—

WAHCOTAH. Wahcotah not know. Many squaws. Many papoose. [*Waves his hand to take in the whole country.*]

ALLEYN. You are friendly to us, I understand?

WAHCOTAH. Yes! Injun friendly!

ALLEYN. Are there any warriors in this neighborhood?

WAHCOTAH. No!

ALLEYN. It is safe for the boat to go down the stream tonight?

WAHCOTAH. Safe!

ALLEYN. All right then. [*To* SERGEANT.] We'll send a double force out since this friendly Indian is so sure there is no danger. Is every one in? [WAHCOTAH *retires.*]

SERGEANT. All in but two, Captain. The young girl and that gambler chap from Rogue's Rest.

ALLEYN. The young girl. Where is she?

SERGEANT. Miss Rowse said they'd be back before night.

ALLEYN. If they don't, the boat must wait for them.

SERGEANT. Wait for them? They can easily overtake the boat.

ALLEYN. A weak, delicate, little thing like that?

SERGEANT. No better than the rest of the lot, I'm afraid, sir!

ALLEYN. What do you mean?

SERGEANT. Why, she belongs to the worst crowd in the place. I've seen her often at Rogue's Rest. You don't know Western people, sir, like us old hands.

ALLEYN. Perhaps not. But as for her I'd stake my life—! Hem! no matter. Look after the boat. [SERGEANT *goes up*.] These fellows will laugh at me. [*Exits into shed.*

SERGEANT. The captain's struck with her, sure. Well, he ain't the first. I was that way myself when I saw her last, but hallo! [*Looking off.*] Here's Rowse and his little injun sure enough.

MUSIC, "*Little Indians.*" ROWSE *enters in great confusion, followed by* NOTAH *clinging to his coat.* WAHCOTAH *watches.*

ROWSE. Oh, bother, you young sarpint! get out.

NOTAH. No—no—no—no!

ROWSE. You confounded little imp! What do you mean by hanging to me for? I don't want you.

NOTAH. Oona gow ga tcheka!

ROWSE. What?

NOTAH. Oona gow ga tcheka—poo!

ROWSE. Stop swearing! I wonder what she means by that? If she could only speak English, I might reason with her. I don't know any Indian. What's your name?

NOTAH. Oona gow ga tcheka! Chun ge gah! Bees ma!

ROWSE. Bismarck! It can't be possible! I say, why don't you go home?

NOTAH [*impatiently*]. Ugh!

ROWSE. Won't you please go home to your family? I never was a mother, and I don't know what to do for you.

NOTAH [*same*]. Ugh!

SERGEANT. You've got a nice captive there, sir!

ROWSE [*child following*]. I wish I hadn't. I took hold of the little devil when her mother run away, just to look at her, when she caught hold of my coat-tail, and hasn't let go since.

SERGEANT [*to* NOTAH]. Wont-ee come-ee to me-ee?

NOTAH. No—no—no—no!

ROWSE. Oh, no! All of 'em have tried that.

SERGEANT. Here's an Indian, sir, maybe he can tell you what she wants.

ROWSE. Eh? Where is he? Here, you!

WAHCOTAH. Injun here.

ROWSE. What's this little red imp mean by hanging on to me in this way?

WAHCOTAH. Little papoose belong to Wannemucka's tribe.

ROWSE. I don't know Wannemucka's tribe, and I'm not an orphan asylum. Speak to her. [WAHCOTAH *touches* NOTAH *on shoulder. She starts and clings to* ROWSE.]

NOTAH. Oona gow ga tcheka! Chun ge gah!

WAHCOTAH. She say—white father got her —white father keep her always.

ROWSE. The deuce she does!

NOTAH. Looka nah ta poocha. No!

WAHCOTAH. She say her father big chief!

ROWSE. Then why don't she go back to him?

WAHCOTAH. Injun papoose cunning. You capture papoose. Big chief father come after you.

ROWSE. Eh!

WAHCOTAH. She keep close to you—big chief know you took papoose.

ROWSE. And what then?

WAHCOTAH. Big chief kill man steal his papoose.

ROWSE. Then she's hanging on to my coat-tail so as to identify me as the right man for big chief to kill. [*Shakes* NOTAH *off*.] Here, you, get off! Thunder and lightning, what a prospect! [*Walks about followed by* NOTAH.] I might as well have a death-warrant pinned to my back at once. I shall have to dye my hair and black my eyes—I mean my face —to avoid recognition. Let go, you little imp. [*Throws her to* SERGEANT, *who holds her*.]

NOTAH. Ah chee mah poo da! Ah chee! Poo da!

ROWSE. Just hear her swear! I haven't the slightest doubt that's very profane in the Cherokee language.

WAHCOTAH. Me take all trouble. Me take papoose, carry her back to tribe. White man safe den!

ROWSE. Will you? That's a good fellow!

WAHCOTAH. Come! [*About to take* NOTAH.]

SERGEANT. Not so fast. We can't let her go!

WAHCOTAH. No!

ROWSE. Why not?

SERGEANT. Not while the Indians are up and likely to give us trouble. You've made a lucky capture, Mr. Rowse. I think this is the child of some important chief. If so, we can hold her as a hostage, and it may save somebody's life in the event of trouble.

ROWSE. So she may. I recollect that rascally

Wannemucka tried to steal old Wolf's daughter, and when Loder was too sharp for him, he slunk off, swearing he'd have her yet. We'll block his domino with this little hostage.

WAHCOTAH. Me no have papoose?

ROWSE [*crosses to* NOTAH]. Not till I get safe to Big Run settlement, and leave old Wolf's daughter in safety. Then you can tell Big Chief to send me a receipt in full, and I'll give him the chick.

WAHCOTAH. But papoose want to go home.

ROWSE. Does she? We'll see. [*To* NOTAH.] Hanky—panky—hickory—dickory?

NOTAH. Me—ho—na—watee!

ROWSE. She says she won't go home till morning, and don't want to be put in her little bed. Come along. [ROWSE *exits into boat and down hatches.* SERGEANT *laughs and goes up.* WAHCOTAH *slinks off and presently re-appears in the water, climbs into boat and goes below by opening.*]

Gentle music. MED *enters with little bundle, her hand on* LODER'S *shoulder*

MED. See, we are here at last!

LODER. After a very hard day's tramp for you, little girl.

MED. For me? Why, you carried me across all the fords and almost over all the hills. I'm not tired. Tonight we will be floating down the river with our friends, and by tomorrow we will be safe in another settlement.

LODER. But your father's last wishes—

MED [*sinking on mound*]. Poor father! Not even a last word for me.

LODER. You weep for him. Well, well, perhaps it was only because he *was* your father.

MED. Why, what do you mean?

LODER. I mean he didn't do a father's part to drag you—you, a lady—through the world like the child of a thief.

MED. But he loved me, and so I cry for him.

LODER. I won't say another word agin him, princess! I don't know what fine feelings are, and so I'll keep quiet.

MED. Yes, you do! You're kinder to me than anybody—ain't you?

LODER. That's why I want to take you home.

MED. Home? Where?

LODER. To New York.

MED. Oh, yes, so you told me. All about that rich lady who is my mother, and who turned my poor dead father out of her house.

LODER [*taking packet of letters from his pocket*]. So these letters say. And a strange story it is.

MED. Do you think my father's daughter would ever enter that lady's house, sit by her side, live in luxury and comfort, and yet dream every night of the far-off town where *he* was treated like a wild animal, shot down like a dog—and all her fault?

LODER. But you are her daughter!

MED. And he was her husband. If I were married, and the man I promised to love were the greatest villain—[*Crosses to right.*]

LODER [*eagerly*]. You could love him?

MED. Pshaw! I don't know what I'm saying. [*Turning to him.*] Promise me, you won't speak of my mother again nor of taking me back to New York.

LODER. Where will you go, then?

MED. With you. Where you go.

LODER [*recoiling*]. With me?

MED. Can't I go with you?

LODER [*laughs*]. Why, I'm Panther. That's what I'm called out here in this red wilderness. I can't read nor write. I'm always up at knives' point with some one or other! I've been shot at fifty times and turned out of three Territories by Vigilance Committees.

MED. I don't mind that. You are the only friend I have in all the world.

LODER. I tell you, girl, it can't be done!

MED. Why not?

LODER. Your father left you to my care.

MED. Then you must take care of me.

LODER. Yes. I can watch over you day and night. If anything happened to you, I should see ghosts.

MED. And so, if you take care of me, you can't fight, nor drink, nor go off with horrible men to gamble. Do you love these things better than me?

LODER. Well, no! But I know something of the world. People would say I persuaded you to stay with me. I tell you, it's no use talking. I'm a scoundrel, and I must take you to your mother.

MED. If you were as bad as you say, you would not. I don't believe you. You were always good to me. I know you used often to give father money, just when you saw my dress was ragged and my feet were almost on the ground, so that he could buy things for me. Oh, I'm wiser than you think, and I loved you for it.

LODER. You loved! [*Aside.*] Oh, if I were only an honest man. But it's getting too hot for you, Loder. You must think of some damned rascally trick to stop this. If she would only fall in love with somebody who would marry her and take her home!

MED. What are you thinking of? Me? [*She leans against his shoulder, clasps his arm.*]

LODER. Oh, ah, yes! [*Aside.*] I'll pick out some decent chap. Some young fellow who don't play cards. I'll put her in his way; he's sure to love her; who could help it?

MED. I never saw such a stupid, dull fellow as you are.

LODER [*crossing*]. Me? Yes! [*Aside.*] I'll keep out of her sight.

MED. I do believe you hate me!

LODER. Hate you?

MED. Then why don't you love me? I want somebody to love me—now—poor papa is gone. [*Sinks on mound.*]

LODER [*aside*]. Yes, that's how I'll fix it, and if all turns out well! if she falls in love with him [*Moved.*] and marries him! and goes back to New York with him! I'll see them safe off and blow my own worthless brains out comfortably.

ALLEYN *entering*

ALLEYN. Almost time to start. [*Sees* MED.] Why, my little prairie flower!

MED [*coquettishly nestling up to* LODER]. Is that you?

ALLEYN. I have been so anxious about you.

LODER. Who is this?

MED. The young captain from New York.

LODER. From New York? [*Goes up.*]

ALLEYN. Who's your suspicious looking friend?

MED. He is my *best*—my only friend.

ALLEYN. Oh! [*To* LODER.] I say, are you going down in the boat?

LODER. Well, if she goes down, I reckon I'll go down with her.

ALLEYN. Then you'd better jump aboard and be lively. [CEPHAS *and* BLAKELY *appear on boat, getting out poles.* LODER *up,* MED *about to go.*] Med! [*She draws back and looks towards* LODER, *he insists on her remaining.*] Just one word, Med. I'm so happy to see you again. I've never stopped thinking of you since that day. [*Takes her up.*]

LODER [*coming down*]. Curse his soft tongue! He'll capture her heart! Hallo! But that's what I've been wanting! After all, it's a hard thing to stand. She said she loved me—and—! Damn it, I'll take my medicine like a man anyway. [*Goes up and on board and assists the boatmen.*]

ALLEYN [*coming down with* MED]. I'm not going on the boat with you, but I take a party of soldiers with me to guard its course for a few miles down the stream.

MED. Oh! I'm safe now. Panther will take care of me.

ALLEYN. Panther?

MED. Yes! You saw him just now. You don't like him, but I do, and so good-bye!

ALLEYN. But Med—

MED [*running to boat*]. Good-bye! Good-bye! [*Runs to* LODER.]

COLUMBIA *and* MR. SMITH *enter*

COLUMBIA. Now, Honorable! [*To* ALLEYN.] Is papa on board?

ALLEYN. Yes! and everybody else except you and Smith.

COLUMBIA. Come, Honorable! Take care of yourself, Captain.

ALLEYN. I'll try to!

[*As she is going up the gang-plank, noise heard of* ROWSE'S *voice.*]

COLUMBIA. What's that?

WAHCOTAH *appears with* NOTAH *at bow of boat, followed by* ROWSE, *who snatches at* NOTAH

ROWSE. No, you don't, you red devil! [*Seizes* NOTAH *and kicks the Indian over upon bank.*]

WAHCOTAH. Big chief on the trail! Wahcotah warn him!

[*Exit with a run off left.*

COLUMBIA. Why, pa! What have you got there?

ALLEYN. What's all this?

ROWSE. No interference, Cap. I've got this young papoose in safe-keeping. She's a policy of insurance on all our lives. All aboard! [COLUMBIA *is handed up by* MR. SMITH.] Cast off! [SERGEANT *and soldiers draw in gang-plank and draw it off.*] Good-bye, Cap.

[BLAKELY *and* CHINEE *and* CEPHAS *commence to pole the boat off and the scene begins to change. Panorama of river. Scene begins to grow darker.*]

ROWSE. Be hearty now, boys. I guess I'll go below and secure my captive. A piece of bread and butter will do the business. [*Exits below.*

ALLEYN. Sergeant, get the men in line. Good night! [*Goes off.*

[*Group on boat:* MED, *who had taken* COLUMBIA'S *hand, sits in prow, with* MR. SMITH. *The top deck is occupied by boatmen.* LODER *sits in stern. The group of Irish are central figures.*]

MR. SMITH. It's very romantic, 'pon honor!

COLUMBIA [*to* MED]. Are you comfortable, dear?

WIDOW. Faix, can any of ye's give me a light?

CEPHAS. Here you is, old lady.

ROWSE *reappearing*

ROWSE. Come, boys, push her lively.

BLAKELY. All right, Cap.

SONG BY BOATMEN

The boatmen dance, the boatmen sing,
The boatmen are up to everything.
When the boatman goes ashore,
He spends his money and works for more.

DANCE.—The boatman, etc.

I never saw a pretty girl in all my life,
But she was a boatman's wife, etc.

DANCE.—The boatmen, etc.

[*The* WIDOW *dances to this music and the song grows fainter as the panorama closes the scene and forms*—]

SCENE 2.—*A dense wood and dark night.* WAHCOTAH *moves in noiselessly from right and through it as if through shrubbery, and looks about him. Two other Indians emerge from scene, left. The other song merges into music of a march, at first very faint.*

WAHCOTAH. Where is Wannemucka?

INDIAN. Coming, river side! [*Music of march more forte.*]

WAHCOTAH. Sh, soldiers!

The Indians glide back towards right as the music grows louder and ALLEYN, SERGEANT *and file of soldiers with rifles enter.*

ALLEYN. How far can we keep the boat in sight from this path?

SERGEANT. We can keep within three hundred feet of the river bank for at least twelve miles.

ALLEYN. Can we keep up with the boat on foot? At what rate do they pole her down?

SERGEANT. They don't pole the boat after they get into the open stream. The current takes them down about a mile, or a mile and a half an hour.

ALLEYN. Oh, then it will be easy to keep up with it.

SERGEANT. We're half a mile ahead of it now, besides there'll be no fear of any attack tonight, Captain!

ALLEYN. I'm not an old Western campaigner, Sergeant, but it seems to me that your confidence upon that point doesn't justify our neglecting any precautions.

SERGEANT. Of course not, Captain; but it does argufy that we needn't creep through the woods all night at a snail's pace when we might push on, and keep the road clear by driving the Indians before us.

ALLEYN. That's sense. I suppose there's no danger of their closing in our rear and attacking the boat.

SERGEANT. All the Injuns in the wackcinity are ahead of us, I'll swear.

ALLEYN. Well, we can push on, then. [*The chorus again heard faintly.*] Where did you sight the boat last?

SERGEANT. Drifting down behind us safe enough. There! don't you hear 'em?

ALLEYN. Sure enough! Well, come, my boys! On! March!

Music, march. All off. Music fainter. WANNEMUCKA *enters, after them. A pause. He throws himself on the ground.* WAHCOTAH'S *head appears through bushes; they meet.*

WANNEMUCKA. Little snake heard the white braves?

WAHCOTAH. Much talk! White braves talk like Indian squaws!

WANNEMUCKA. Ugh! Boat?

WAHCOTAH. Boat full. Come slow!

WANNEMUCKA. Who?

WAHCOTAH. Papoose! Notah!

WANNEMUCKA. Ugh! Prairie Dog's papoose! [*Other Indians creep through branches.*] What white squaws on boat?

WAHCOTAH. Ugh! Wannemucka's squaw!

WANNEMUCKA. Mine! All mine!

WAHCOTAH. Panther with her!

WANNEMUCKA [*shows knife*]. Wannemucka knows where to strike White Panther!

[*Distant and faint sound of song heard, as if from boat.*]

WAHCOTAH. Boat come. Big chief strike now?

WANNEMUCKA. Now! hist! Braves follow Wannemucka! Close! hist! close! [*Exeunt.*

[*Singing still faint, but nearer. All the Indians off. The scene gradually begins to open and the dense forest to clear, disclosing the moon, and then a large clearing through which is shown*—]

SCENE 3.—*A narrow bend in the Big Run River. From the bank on extreme left, a blasted and fallen tree trunk stretches over to right, dipping the water near the fourth groove.* WANNEMUCKA *and three Indians are concealed on this tree.* WAHCOTAH *and another are in the water near left center. Other Indians concealed behind logs and trees.*

The song is heard more plainly. It is MED *and* COLUMBIA *singing, seated in the extreme bow of boat, a low and plaintive ballad. The boat gradually moves on from right to left, passing beneath the fallen tree. Groups on boat same as before. All asleep.* ROWSE *not in sight.* MR. SMITH *not in sight. As it approaches where* WAHCOTAH *lies concealed, he rises from the water and stops it, raising his body out of the water and grinning at the two girls.*

MED. Why, the boat has stopped. Wake, Loder! [*Turns and sees the Indian.*] Ah! [*Piercing scream and starts back.*]

WANNEMUCKA *drops from branch of tree on deck and seizes* MED *and half raises her.* COLUMBIA *rises in alarm on deck.* WAHCOTAH *threatens her with hatchet.* ROWSE *runs out of cabin to her aid.* LODER *springs up in alarm, as two more Indians drop down upon deck. They fall upon* CEPHAS *and* BLAKELY, *who roll over with them at back.*

MED. Help! help!

WANNEMUCKA. Come!

LODER. Indian, drop that girl!

Indian yell from all sides. WANNEMUCKA *draws dirk and runs at* LODER. WIDOW *seizes* MED *and holds her.* LODER *seizes* WANNEMUCKA, *who bends him over the boat with the dirk at his throat.* ROWSE *engages the Indians, who clamber up sides of boat, and fights them with a bag of meal.* LODER *finally releases one hand, draws a Derringer and fires at* WANNEMUCKA, *who leaps up, staggers front and falls. The drum and sound of approaching soldiers heard as the*—

CURTAIN FALLS

ACT IV

SCENE I.—*A stockade or primitive fort in the prairie. Time—second day from the incidents of last act. The stage represents the interior of the stockade, or two sides of it, with the angle in center. All around it is the horizon. A closed shed, within the stockade, beside the walls. Stakes of stockade about ten feet high. Gate left. A clump of trees, right upper stage outside. Rocks and bush growths, left of stage outside.*

As curtain rises, several groups are formed inside stockade. WIDOW *is cooking with pot swung on sticks over faggot fire and ladle in hand.* CEPHAS *watching and blowing the fire.* RHODA *and* MOLLY *looking on. Soldiers here and there in groups, outside stockade and inside, cleaning rifles.* COLUMBIA *is walking up and down from right to left with* ALLEYN, *his hat on her head coquettishly and carrying his sword.* BLAKELY *and* CHINEE *looking over stockade at back. They come down presently and join* CEPHAS.

COLUMBIA. Oh, you should have seen us!

ALLEYN. Terrific, no doubt!

COLUMBIA. I don't know how many Indians we killed.

ALLEYN. Yes, the enemy was so ashamed of the defeat that even the dead men disappeared.

COLUMBIA. But it's no laughing matter. Indians right up to you in the dead of night!

WIDOW. Faix, you may say that. An' the diviltry of 'em wantin' to run off wid de young creature. [BLAKELY, CEPHAS *and* CHINEE *make a dive at soup and are caught.*]

ALLEYN. If I once lay my sword on Wannemucka I'll make an example of him to every amalgamationist in the territory.

COLUMBIA. So singular that he should be in love with Med.

ALLEYN. Hem, very!

COLUMBIA. You'd suppose, now, that he'd like a bold, brave woman, something like a princess. Med is so timid. I used to think I'd like to have an Indian brave fall in love with me—so romantic.

ALLEYN. Set your cap for Wannemucka.

COLUMBIA. I mean a real noble savage, not a dirty, common Indian.

ALLEYN. They're all the same.

COLUMBIA. Somebody like Fennimore Cooper's braves.

WIDOW. Coopers, is it? Faix, all trades is alike, they're all a dirty pack, and coopers is no better nor any of 'em.

ROWSE *enters, followed by* NOTAH *from gate.* NOTAH *has a newspaper cocked hat and rides a stick, but still holds on to* ROWSE'S *coat, as usual.*

ROWSE. Time to be stirring! All's safe! I've prospected for a quarter of a mile in every direction, and I've come to the conclusion that this is the most desirable spot in the whole country for me to get up and clear out from, as fast as possible. I shan't lay the foundation of Rowseville, the future metropolis of the West, in this spot, I can tell you.

ALLEYN. Then what direction shall we take?

ROWSE. Further in towards that little cluster of woods yonder, just on the stream. That's the spot for Rowseville.

ALLEYN. Then we must be getting ready. Sergeant! [SERGEANT *advances.*] Have the men ready. We must push back to the bend and bring the teams up to carry the ladies and stores. [SERGEANT *retires up to soldiers, who rise and file out of gate.*] Mr. Rowse, will you stay here with the ladies, and act as guard till we return?

ROWSE. Certainly! So will Loder.

ALLEYN. No! Loder, or whatever his name is, must go with us.

ROWSE. Why? Confound you, you young mosquito, do you want to strip me? [*To* NOTAH.]

ALLEYN. I have my suspicions about that Loder. Here he is.

LODER *enters at gate and looks around, then goes to shed, and sits. He carries a rifle, and is followed by* MR. SMITH *with another.*

Watch his eye. [COLUMBIA *goes to meet* MR. SMITH.]

ROWSE. Looks shot. Guess he's been up all night playing poker with your men.

ALLEYN. I tell you he's a rascal. I've watched him when he's been talking to—

ROWSE. To whom?

ALLEYN. Well, never mind. But he's not to be trusted. [*Goes up and off among his men, looking suspiciously towards* LODER.]

ROWSE [*to* COLUMBIA]. And how's our little patient?

COLUMBIA. She's been sleeping in the hut there, all the morning. We made her as comfortable as we could with some of the Captain's army blankets. [*Goes into shed.*

ROWSE. Ah, that's how Uncle Sam's property is diverted from its proper use, is it?

MR. SMITH [*to* LODER]. I say, old fellow, you've been as dull as the deuce all day.

LODER. Well, stranger, I'm sorry for that, it's not my way always.

COLUMBIA *reappears, leading* MED, *very pale and languid.* LODER *draws back*

COLUMBIA. Try a little walk. There's no danger now.

MED. I'm not afraid of the danger.

ROWSE. You'd face a dozen Injuns, if they dropped in now, wouldn't you?

COLUMBIA. Here, some of you men. Give her your arm, and let her take a little walk.

[LODER *and* ALLEYN *both start forward.* LODER *catches* ALLEYN'S *eye, and draws back.*]

ALLEYN. Come with me.

MED. It's so good of you to mind me. But I don't care to walk.

ROWSE [*to* COLUMBIA]. C'lumby, I'm afraid those horrid red wretches have scared what little life there was in her out of her.

MED [*walking to bench by shed*]. You are going to leave us?

ALLEYN. Only to send teams up to bring you down to the bend. [*They sit.*]

ROWSE [*to* COLUMBIA]. Smitten, hey?

COLUMBIA. Yes, and it's so romantic.

ROWSE. Well, just you fight as shy of that sort of nonsense as long as you can and not inconvenience yourself, and I'll be just as glad as you can reckon. [*Off right, followed by* COLUMBIA *and* MR. SMITH. ROWSE *looks back just in time to catch them flirting; they all go off with a laugh.*]

ALLEYN. You don't think I'd leave you in any danger.

MED. I thought I should never see you again, when the Indians attacked our boat.

[LODER *crosses quietly at back and leans against upper end of shed, listening to conversation.*]

ALLEYN. The danger is all over now. Try and brighten a little.

MED. For what?

ALLEYN. Don't say for what? Say for whom?

MED. For whom, then?

ALLEYN. For—[*She looks at him.*] For those who love you.

MED. Everyone who loves me, leaves me. All, except one—

ALLEYN. And he?

MED. Poor Loder! See, how faithful he is.

ALLEYN. You love him, then! [*He rises. She rises, as if to re-assure him.* LODER *makes a step forward.* ALLEYN *turns suddenly on* MED *and steals a kiss, she leans on his shoulder, and they turn to go up, when they confront* LODER.] Well, sir! [*Sternly.*] Are you preparing for the march? [MED *reproves him with a glance, and holds out her hand to* LODER, *who kisses it.*]

ROWSE *re-enters, followed by* NOTAH. *As he comes on* ROWSE *turns around savagely to* NOTAH.

ROWSE. See here, I've had almost enough of this!

MR. SMITH *and* COLUMBIA *in doorway*

MED. Oh, the little Indian. I'm afraid you've captured her heart, Mr. Rowse, and she'll cling to you, for better or for worse.

ROWSE. Cling to me! I should think so! I'm afraid I'll have to adopt her, unless some of you take her off my hands. Don't you want her, Alleyn?

ALLEYN. I—for what?

[MED *disengages herself, and goes quietly to* LODER, *whose downcast look she has been watching. He leans against his gun.*]

ROWSE. To bring her up as an Indian interpreter.

ALLEYN. No, thank you. I'm afraid of the Big Chief.

ROWSE. Here, Smith, suppose you take her.

MR. SMITH. Aw! Where to?

ROWSE. Back to England. She'll be Pocahontas, and you'll be Smith, just the very thing.

MR. SMITH. I'd like to oblige, but I'm afraid she don't deserve it. Pocahontas saved Smith's life, but this little creature is likely to get us all killed.

WIDOW [*coming from right*]. Sure, the dinner's ready.

ROWSE. Dinner! That's handy! Come, lads!

[CEPHAS *and* CHINEE *take pot from fire, as directed by* ROWSE, *and all exit into hut except* MED *and* LODER.]

MED. You look so cross.

LODER. I'm not cross, girl. I'm sorry.

MED. Sorry for what?

LODER. It's a mean thing to confess, but I overheard you talking with the young Captain.

MED. You heard us? Where were you?

LODER. It was wrong, wasn't it?

MED. Yes! It was not like you.

LODER. Yet I wouldn't give away the

memory of what I heard for my life itself. Only tell me, is it so?

MED. Is what so?

LODER. Don't trifle, Med! For God's sake, don't. I heard you speaking.

MED [*bashfully*]. Well!

LODER. You spoke of those who loved you —and of one—

MED. That was you.

LODER. Oh, if it should be so! I would die for you any day—or better than that, I would fight for you and work for you. You could make me an honest man.

MED. I want to do that. You know I do.

LODER. And he asked you if you loved me?

MED [*gladly looking at him, and putting her hand on his shoulder*]. And you heard—

LODER. No, I heard no more.

MED. I told him "yes!" I loved you as if you were a dear brother! [LODER *looks at her stolidly.*] And he seemed so pleased. And you are my brother, ain't you? And you shall always be. And that made him so happy, and then he told me that he loved me, not like a brother, you know—oh, far from that—

ALLEYN [*coming from right*]. Well, Mr. Loder, time's about up. We must leave the ladies here, until we return.

MED. Oh, that will be soon?

ALLEYN. This evening, perhaps.

COLUMBIA [*in door*]. Come, Med, have something to eat.

MED. I'm coming. [*To* ALLEYN.] And you will be ever so careful of yourself, and not fight with the Indians, if you meet them?

ALLEYN. No, I'll stand up, and be shot. [MED *laughs and runs off with* COLUMBIA. ALLEYN *is about to go.*]

LODER. Captain!

ALLEYN. Well, sir!

LODER. May I have a word with you?

ALLEYN. Many as you please, if you're quick about it.

LODER. I'm not one of the drawling sort, stranger, and I say my mind in a few words. You love that girl!

ALLEYN [*angrily*]. What is that to you?

LODER [*smothering his anger*]. I beg pardon. Perhaps I was too plain—she tells me—

ALLEYN. Then keep what you're told to yourself. [*About to go.*]

LODER. Captain!

ALLEYN. Hark ye, my friend, if you address me on that or any other subject again, I'll have you left out on the prairie to look after the redskins alone, without any soldiers to protect you.

LODER. Well, Captain, I've fought the redskins—and alone against odds—before now. I'm not a coward, if I am a—pshaw! I only want to say that the young girl yonder was left by her father to me—

ALLEYN. Just what a drunken brute might do! And I suppose you consider you've a claim on her?

LODER. Yes! [ALLEYN *laughs.*] But not what you supposed. I loved her!

ALLEYN. Oh, I've no objection. I shan't interfere!

LODER. You mean to tell me you don't love her yourself, then! Why, you've just confessed it to her.

ALLEYN [*annoyed*]. She told you—

LODER. Yes, and you're ashamed of it. You think it good sport to fool a friendless creature like her. You're deceiving her, and you know it!

ALLEYN. Whatever you please.

LODER. Captain! I beg pardon again if I'm insulting. But if you only knew all! If I thought you really loved her, I'd be content.

ALLEYN. I'm much obliged, I'm sure.

LODER. Another man who spoke to me as you speak, should fight me until one of us was stretched dead at the other's feet. But she loves you, and I dare not harm you. If you will only say to me that you love her! I have one duty to perform, and then you will see me no more. A secret—

ALLEYN. A secret! About Med?

LODER. To the man who truly loves her, a secret worth the world full of gold. For it tells him she is worthy to be his wife. [ALLEYN *approaches* LODER.] Remember, it is to be told to one only—the man who is to be her husband.

ALLEYN. Whatever your secret is, it is safe with me.

LODER. But you will not answer me!

ALLEYN. Answer what?

LODER. That you love Med!

ALLEYN. Well, then, be answered, I do!

LODER. Come, then; on the road ask me what you will, and every information which this packet does not contain you shall have. [*Shows* WOLF'S *packet.*]

ALLEYN [*kindly*]. My good fellow, I was hasty just now. I do love her; there's my hand upon it.

LODER. No, stranger, I can't take your hand. If she had been poor like me, I'd have taken her far away to the wild West, to be mine, and mine only. I give her up now, as the fretful child must give up the star he sees so far above him.

ALLEYN. I was going to take you with me, but now, that I can trust you, you shall stay here and watch over her till we return.

LODER. No. I won't be tempted. From this time I speak to her no more. She is to be the wife of an honest man and is to become a lady. I know what I am, and that she is too good for me. I'll go with *you.* They are safe here.

ALLEYN. As you will. On the road I will speak with you.

LODER [*going*]. On the road.

MED *reappearing*

MED. Are you going?

ROWSE, COLUMBIA *and* MR. SMITH *enter*

LODER. Only a little way.

MED [*gaily*]. Good-bye, then.

LODER [*struggling with emotion*]. Good-bye! Good-bye! [*Off.*

ROWSE. That fellow's got the worst face I ever saw.

MED. And the best heart that ever beat. [*Goes to* ALLEYN.]

MR. SMITH. I understand he's quite a scoundrel.

COLUMBIA. He looks like some member of Congress, whose name I forget. You know, pa!

ROWSE. Yes! That chap from Maine, that voted against my railroad bill.

ALLEYN. Now we must be off.

ROWSE. So I'm to stay and protect the ladies?

MR. SMITH. Yes! take my gun, it's double barrelled, both barrels loaded. [*Gives it.*]

ROWSE. I never fired one of these things in all my life.

CEPHAS *and* CHINEE *come out from hut*

ALLEYN. Now, then, Sergeant—

SERGEANT [*outside*]. Aye, aye, sir!

ALLEYN [*to* COLUMBIA]. Good-bye! [*To* MED.] Until tomorrow, darling! Now for the road.

[*All off to music.* COLUMBIA *climbs the stockade, waves her handkerchief.* ROWSE *in gateway.* MED *near* COLUMBIA. *The soldiers and all men except* ROWSE *file off.* WIDOW *and others waving them "Good-bye."*]

ROWSE [*coming down*]. Hello! Where's that little Indian of mine? [WIDOW *goes up to gate.*]

COLUMBIA. I don't know, perhaps she's got into your pocket, pa! She's been near it so long.

ROWSE. That's funny. I've taken such a fancy to her that—

WIDOW. Shure, I saw the little crethur yonder running off towards the woods chasing the butterflies.

ROWSE [*laying down gun*]. Chasing fiddlesticks. We mustn't let her get away or she'll be bringing some stray Indians here on us. Which way did you see her go?

WIDOW. Straight down to the gully forninst the wood.

ROWSE. I'll fetch her. [*Goes off running.*]

MED. It's not safe for him to go!

COLUMBIA. Oh, he's got his gun.

WIDOW. Faix, that he hasn't. Shure, here it is. Rhody, dear, run—

MED. Oh, yes, run—call him—take it to him.

[RHODA *takes the gun and afterwards, when the door is barred, she rests it against the barred door.*]

COLUMBIA [*up to gate*]. Pa! pa! Oh, pshaw! he's running so fast and he doesn't hear. [RHODA *stops.*]

MED [*looking over the stockade*]. He's running down to the ravine. He should keep by the open.

COLUMBIA. Oh, pa's wise. He knows what he's about.

WIDOW. Shure, his wisdom wouldn't amount to much if the red divils was about.

COLUMBIA. Pa's a great boxer! Let him alone. [*Coming in.*] Come down, you little canary. [*To* MED.]

MED [*looking off still*]. Yes, in a moment! [*Sunset begins.*]

COLUMBIA. You don't expect to see pa *there*, do you?

MED. No, I was only—

COLUMBIA. You were only looking after somebody else. [*Below, looks up at her.*]

MED [*above, looks down at her*]. No, indeed, I—

COLUMBIA. No fibs! Come down, I want to talk to you.

MED. What about?

COLUMBIA. About yourself and the other one!

MED. Which other one?

COLUMBIA. Oh, you needn't pretend. I saw you flirting.

MED [*coming down*]. Flirting! What's that? [WIDOW *and others sitting back.*]

COLUMBIA. I know your secret. [*They come down.*] You love him! Isn't it so?

MED. Yes!

COLUMBIA. Then why didn't you tell me so that night on the boat?

MED. Because I did not think then he would look at poor little me in such a way as that.

COLUMBIA. Why, you ain't serious, are you? You don't think of marrying him?

MED. I haven't thought of anything but his love.

COLUMBIA. Why, he's ever so rich. He's got an aristocratic mother in New York who wouldn't listen to it. Besides, he's an awful flirt. He'll forget you for the next pretty face he sees. Oh, I know 'em.

MED. Oh, you don't think him like that.

COLUMBIA. They're all alike, my dear. But don't cry over it. There, there. I've been in love myself, often; been deceived, too, my dear, and all that; oh, it's terrible. There was a member of Congress from Indiana, then there was the assistant clerk of the Under Secretary of the German Minister, he made love to me. He was a Baron. I gave him my young heart's affections, and his wife and seven children, all barons, came out in one of the Bremen steamers, and took him home.

MED. I don't know what will come of it, but I love him too much to doubt. Let us talk of something else. Are you not in love now?

COLUMBIA. My affections are hardened.

MED. Even to the tall gentleman?

COLUMBIA. Sh! have you observed him? He's a nobleman.

MED. He's very tall!

COLUMBIA. All English noblemen are!

MED. And does he love you?

COLUMBIA. If any one could restore peace to my solitary heart—[*Darkness deepens.*]

MED. He could—

COLUMBIA. He could—if he would. But I'm afraid it don't enter his mind. His head is a little thick. He doesn't seem to know what's good for him.

[*Distant cry like an owl's heard, as if a signal. All listen, cry repeated.*]

MED. Did you hear that?

COLUMBIA. It must be pa! [*Cry repeated.*]

MED. No! [*Breathlessly putting her ear towards the ground, as though to listen.*]

WIDOW [*looking over wall*]. I don't see anybody at all—at all!

MED. Quick! Close the gate! [*All run to it.*] Bar it!

COLUMBIA. But if pa comes?

MED. We can let him in.

COLUMBIA. Why, what are you afraid of?

MED. We are alone and near the woods. If the Indians should have been concealed there!

COLUMBIA [*laughs*]. Ha! ha! ha! You little scared thing. Why, the soldiers were out all the morning. Come! You must be braver!

MED. I was so once. But when I was a little girl father took me far up the Colorado; we were surprised there by the Indians in our hut.

WIDOW [*others gather*]. Howly Saints!

COLUMBIA. Oh, a story! How delightful! Do tell it!

MED. Alone at night. The darkness gathering, just like now. We had barred the door—there were no windows. I was roused from my sleep by a noise, like the stealthy tread of some animal on the roof.

COLUMBIA. But we have no roof here, and we would see them if they came, and shoot them.

MED. I looked towards the door, the bar seemed to move as if some one pressed against it. [*The gun which* RHODA *has placed against the door, falls.*]

COLUMBIA [*frightened*]. What's that?

WIDOW. Only the gun! [*Runs and places it upright against hut, and runs to center again.*]

MED. My father started up, but too late. With a wild shout the door was broken down, and the savages were upon us.

WAHCOTAH'S *head appears above the stockade.* COLUMBIA *sees him and screams, and points breathlessly while sinking to the ground.* WAHCOTAH *disappears.*

MED. What was it? Speak!

COLUMBIA. Indians! [*Knock heard at gate.*]

WIDOW. We are all murdered!

MED. We can fight for our lives. [*Runs and grasps gun.*]

COLUMBIA. Oh, don't! don't! You'll make them so angry. [*Knock repeated.*] Oh, suppose that is pa! Open the door, quick. [*Going up.*]

MED. Stop! [*Holds her back.*] Who is there? [*Knock repeated.*] It is the Indians! Heaven preserve us!

WANNEMUCKA [*outside*]. Open the gate!

MED. 'Sh!

Several blows are heard, as though stones were hurled against the door. Some of the stakes of the upper part are broken. An Indian puts in his head. MED *fires; he falls. The gate gives way, and the other savages pour in,* WANNEMUCKA *coming last and passing to the front of them. They start back before the gun, which* MED *presents, with the crowd of women clustering around her, all kneeling, but* MED.

WANNEMUCKA. White maiden, put up your gun. Indian too many!

MED. Wannemucka! Coward! to attack women!

WANNEMUCKA. Let the white maiden come with Wannemucka, and her sisters shall be free to go.

COLUMBIA. Never.

WANNEMUCKA. Indian too many. White maiden's gun can kill but one.

MED. Let the *one* who wishes to be killed come forward, then!

WANNEMUCKA [*after a pause*]. Braves no wish to hurt white maiden.

MED. Then go!

WANNEMUCKA [*turns to speak to Indians*]. Yes! Indians go! Indians fight not women. They seek warriors. [*Parleys with tribe.*]

COLUMBIA. Oh, if they will go!

RHODY. See, they seem to be quarrelling.

MED. Oh, if they should! There might be a hope!

[WANNEMUCKA *and tribe seem to disagree. He turns to* MED *softly.*]

WANNEMUCKA. White maiden, Wannemucka is no enemy. His wigwam was cold and his fires unlighted. The eyes of white maiden have warmed his heart, and he would take her to his tribe, their princess! [*Indians murmur.*] Wannemucka would save the white maiden that he loves, and his tribe are angry with him.

MED. I cannot trust you.

WANNEMUCKA. White maiden shall see. [*To Indians, takes a step in advance.*] Warriors! Indian braves fight white braves, not women. Let the warriors of the Caiute follow their chief, and leave the white women in peace.

WAHCOTAH. Ugh! The Caiute knows no difference. Their lodges are hung with the scalps of women. Wannemucka, coward! traitor!

WANNEMUCKA. Wahcotah drunk! Go! Caiute braves know Wannemucka! Go! No harm shall come to white women.

WAHCOTAH. Wannemucka traitor! Stand by—

[*Draws knife and attempts to press by* WANNEMUCKA. *He is stopped. Short struggle, and all the other Indians press forward and strike* WANNEMUCKA; *he falls.* WAHCOTAH *kneels over him, as if to strike again. Women scream.*]

MED. Stop! Another blow, and this bullet strikes you dead! [WAHCOTAH *jumps back.*]

WANNEMUCKA [*faintly*]. White maiden, Indian loved you to his death. [*He stretches out his arms.*]

MED. Chief, I forgive you. Creep to me—they shall not kill you! [*He crawls to her. Indians try to press foward, as he falls. She keeps them at bay with the gun.*] Nearer—nearer! This bullet is for him that touches you. Now—now—you are safe!

WANNEMUCKA. Yes, safe!

[*He crawls to her feet, then suddenly springs up, wrenches the gun from her, throws it to his men, who receive it with a yell, and he grasps her. Indians overpower the rest.*]

WANNEMUCKA. Mine! All mine!

CURTAIN

ACT V

SCENE.—*A ravine, in which the Indians have camped for the night. High ground at sides and at back, surmounted by bushes and thick shrubbery. A path, quite high at the back, across from right to left. Paths down from right and left to center, at back. Mountainous perspective. Time—the dark hour before daylight. A tent of skins in center, midway up stage. Smouldering embers of a camp fire at left. A clump of bushes at a half eminence on right, behind the tent.*

ONATA *and five Indian girls are grouped around the tent, which is closed.* WANNEMUCKA *stands leaning on his rifle, watching his tent. Irish family,* WIDOW, RHODA *and* COLUMBIA, *guarded by a group of Indians. They are seated on the ground, their heads covered with shawls, handkerchiefs, etc. At the eminence on the right is seated an Indian on guard.* WAHCOTAH *seated in buffalo dress.*

WANNEMUCKA. The day is almost here, but the Caiute warriors may rest until it comes. The flight was long, and the way hard. What says Onata?

ONATA. The maidens rejoice that their warriors have returned, but not that they bring white women to the tribe.

WANNEMUCKA. The beloved of Wannemucka need not fear. The white maiden shall be the slave of Onata.

ONATA. Onata needs no slave whose face is like the white moon, and shines through all the lodge.

WANNEMUCKA. She is the prize of Wannemucka, and marks his triumph. Go, look upon her. She is weak and frightened. She is ill.

ONATA. If she die, the Indian women will be glad. [*Exits into the tent.*

WANNEMUCKA. Let the will of the Great Spirit be done.

WAHCOTAH [*rises and goes to* WANNEMUCKA]. The Great Spirit marks out the time of all things. He scatters the flowers and the buds together. [*Aside to* WANNEMUCKA.] The herbs have done their work.

WANNEMUCKA. When will she sink to sleep?

WAHCOTAH. Her eyes close even now.

WANNEMUCKA. Go then! Tell Onata that the white maiden will not see the sun rise.

WAHCOTAH *nods, goes to tent, looks in, then goes off.* ONATA *comes out cautiously, looks at* WANNEMUCKA, *who stands stolidly, and glides out after* WAHCOTAH.

WANNEMUCKA. Ugh! [*When she is off.*] The white woman makes her dark sister angry. [*Calls to Indian scout on eminence.*] Go!

INDIAN [*coming down*]. All is silent!

WANNEMUCKA. The white men will not find us. They have sought us in our ancient hunting grounds. [*The other Indians rise up and come to center, surrounding* WANNEMUCKA. ONATA *steals in behind them and enters tent.*] My brothers ask for council, the braves shall have their wish. Bring in the paleface. [*The Indian scout goes out.*] The warriors have taken no scalps, and their hatchets are unstained.

ROWSE *enters, guarded by the Indian*

Loosen the gag. Let the white warrior speak.

ROWSE. I'm much obliged. I haven't had so much in my mouth for several years.

COLUMBIA [*springs up*]. Oh, pa! is it you? [*Runs towards him, Indians stop her.*] Oh, let me go!

WANNEMUCKA. Let the white maiden go to him. She loves him.

COLUMBIA. Oh, pa, dear! I was afraid I'd

never see you again. Oh, can't we get away? What will they do to us?

ROWSE. I don't know, my child! But if ever I get back to Washington alive, I mean to turn my attention to Indian affairs. I'll bring in a bill to settle this.

WANNEMUCKA. The white maiden loves you!

ROWSE. I guess she does. She's my daughter.

WANNEMUCKA. She is fair, she will make a bride for one of our braves.

COLUMBIA [*screams*]. Oh! the wretches! I won't have any braves! I don't want to be a bride.

WANNEMUCKA. The white woman will learn to love the young warriors. She will bake their bread and dig their corn.

COLUMBIA. Will I? I'll break their heads and scratch their faces.

WANNEMUCKA. Take her away! [*She and* ROWSE *are separated.*] Now, paleface!

ROWSE. Don't call me paleface! My name is Rowse! Sundown Rowse, Washington, D. C.

WANNEMUCKA. The paleface has a double name! What does his name signify? What rank is Rowse? Is he a chief, is he a warrior among the palefaces?

ROWSE [*aside*]. I suppose the greater I am, the more consideration they'll show me. [*Aloud.*] Yes. Rowse big chief! Big warrior!

WANNEMUCKA. Where are the big warrior's hunting grounds? Where does he battle?

ROWSE. Where do I fight? My principal battle ground is the lobby.

INDIANS [*to each other*]. Lobby! [*Seem puzzled.*]

WANNEMUCKA. Rowse take many scalps?

ROWSE. Oh, we don't take scalps any more. We don't want any hair—we sleep on *spring* mattresses now.

WANNEMUCKA. Big chief must have killed many.

ROWSE. Oh, yes. I've killed a great many —bills.

WANNEMUCKA. How he kill them?

ROWSE. Squelched 'em in the Committee of the Whole, or beat 'em on the Third Reading.

WANNEMUCKA. Rowse great warrior then?

ROWSE. Oh, I believe you!

WANNEMUCKA. Rowse lie!

ROWSE. Eh? What's that you say?

WANNEMUCKA. White man lie! Rowse no warrior! Wear no war paint! [*Points to clothes.*] No blue! no gold buttons, no belt for long knife!

ROWSE. The rascals know a soldier when they see one!

COLUMBIA. You horrid savages. My father *is* a great chief. He's one of the prominent men of Washington!

WANNEMUCKA. Prominent man! Ugh! Medicine man!

ROWSE. They're laughing at us, C'lumby. We can't stuff 'em. We'll have to beg off.

COLUMBIA. It's shameful! and to think you own the whole country, too!

ROWSE. Yes. I'm in the hands of some more of my tenants. They couldn't treat me worse if I'd come to collect the rent.

WANNEMUCKA [*consults with Indians, then*]. What says the daughter of the paleface? Does the white man claim the whole country?

COLUMBIA. Yes, he does! All this land belongs to him!

ROWSE. Yes, and I've got the grant in my pocket, much good it's done me.

WANNEMUCKA. Who gave our white brother this land?

ROWSE. Congress, you red rascal!

WANNEMUCKA. Congress give you land and water and trees and all?

ROWSE. Here, C'lumby, take out the grant and show 'em!

COLUMBIA [*takes paper out of his pocket*]. Here it is! [*Opens it.*] And here's the map! [*Spreads the map.*]

ROWSE. Look at that! Every acre of it mine!

WANNEMUCKA. Congress gives it to you. Congress bad spirit! Bad spirit made the lying paper that takes the land and the water from the red man and gives it to the paleface. [*Snatches papers from* COLUMBIA.] Burn the bad spirit. [*Gives them to Indians who carry them to fire.*]

ROWSE. Here, I say! What are you about?

WANNEMUCKA. Ugh! White man prays for bad spirit. [*The paper is in flames, and the Indians shout around it.*]

ROWSE. Well, curse my luck. My grant gone! my map gone! my hands tied, and three thousand miles from Congress! Oh, you infernal rascals.

WANNEMUCKA. Seize the paleface and prepare the stake.

ROWSE. What!

COLUMBIA. Oh, my poor papa! Oh, pa, what do they mean?

ROWSE. I don't know! I'm very sick. [*At a sign from* WANNEMUCKA *Indians seize* ROWSE.]

WANNEMUCKA. Let the paleface pray. When the dawn breaks he dies!

ROWSE *is carried off, struggling.* COLUMBIA *is kept from him at a sign from* WANNEMUCKA, *who also darts an angry glance at him and silences him until he is quite off.* WANNEMUCKA *advances towards the tent, which suddenly opens and* MED *appears, followed by* ONATA. *The Indians draw back in a cluster, up stage about* WAHCOTAH, *and all look on curiously.*

MED. Let us go on! See, the sun is up! the daylight has come! the birds are singing.

WANNEMUCKA. Beautiful maiden! all is dark about you. The night is cold. The earth is wet with dew. Go back to the couch of skins, which your dark sisters have made for you.

MED. No! no! see how bright everything is!

WANNEMUCKA [*aside to* WAHCOTAH]. The herb is making her mad. The Indian women will not hate her now!

COLUMBIA [*running to her*]. Oh, Med! Med!

MED. Who is this?—Alleyn?

COLUMBIA. Don't you know me, Med?

MED. You said you loved me! Come, let us go! [*Sinks on ground.* COLUMBIA *bends over her.*]

COLUMBIA. She is dying!

ONATA. She is favored by the great Manitou! He has taken away her mind.

WAHCOTAH [*approaches, throwing back his buffalo head*]. Fear not! I will speak to the pale sister! [*He kneels and takes her hand.*]

WANNEMUCKA. Will the maiden grow better?

WAHCOTAH. She is near the spirit land! Already she beholds it! [*Rises.*]

MED. Alleyn! Dear Alleyn! [*Takes* COLUMBIA'S *hand.*] I told you, you remember, that I was doomed to die. I did not think so soon! Look! my father! [WANNEMUCKA *turns aside.*] No, father, I will come to *you.* She is not *my* mother, and I will not go to her. Dear father, don't turn from me. I am with you! [*Her eyes grow fixed. She is gently laid back by* COLUMBIA, *who sobs and the Indian maiden takes her.*]

WAHCOTAH. The white maiden is as the leaf upon the ground—as the fallen rosebud.

COLUMBIA. Oh, my poor darling!

The women tenderly raise her, and take her into the tent, followed by ONATA *and* COLUMBIA. *The tent is closed.* WIDOW, RHODA *and* MOLLY *enter.*

WANNEMUCKA. When will she wake?

WAHCOTAH. If she sleeps till the dawn, it will be sunset before she opens her eye to the light. But a little now might rouse her again.

WANNEMUCKA. And Onata?

WAHCOTAH. I gave Onata the drink. She thinks it poison.

WANNEMUCKA. When the sun rises, our march will be resumed, and Onata will seek the land beyond the hills of the south with the tribe. Wannemucka will then return and enjoy the prize which many moons have still found him pursuing, still hopeless, but undespairing.

WAHCOTAH. See, the women begin their lamentations.

[WAHCOTAH *re-covers his head. The tent is opened.* ONATA *and the women crouch on the ground near a couch, on which* MED *lies,* COLUMBIA *kneeling near the head.*]

WANNEMUCKA [*goes to foot of couch, bends over it*]. As the roses on the stalk droop, when one of their number is plucked away, let the fair sisters of our tribe bewail her. She shall be laid under the prairie grass, where the wolf shall not find her, for her grave shall be deep as the red man's love!

ONATA *and the Indian girls break into the following low chant:*

Let us speak of her:
  She was white as the white snow,
And her spirit went away
  Under the breath of Manitou,
As snow flees before the sun.

As the chant is dying away, the distant sound of a drum mingles with it, at first unperceived by the Indians. The music dies away, and the drum continues. The Indians listen.

WANNEMUCKA. The white warriors! [*All start up.*] Quick, cover the fires!

The tent is covered again, concealing all the women. Indians enter, bringing ROWSE. *The fire is scattered. All bend low to the earth.*

ROWSE. Oh, you murdering rascals, you are caught at last!

COLUMBIA [*bursting from tent, with* WIDOW, *etc.*]. It is Alleyn!

WIDOW. Woroo! We are saved!

WANNEMUCKA. Seize them! [*All are seized and held by the Indians with drawn knives.*] If you breathe a cry, you die!

A party of soldiers are seen crossing the high path at back. Drum outside still

ALLEYN [*outside*]. Halt!

SERGEANT [*same*]. Halt! [*The soldiers pause.*]

ALLEYN, SERGEANT *and* MR. SMITH *appear on bridge and look down*

ALLEYN. Is there a path down this ravine?

ROWSE. Oh, if this infernal knife wasn't at my throat!

MR. SMITH [*looking down*]. By Jove, I don't see anything here!

ROWSE. Oh, *you* never could see anything anywhere!

SERGEANT. Black as pitch.

ALLEYN. Listen! don't you hear the branches crack?

ROWSE. I wish some one would sneeze!

MR. SMITH. I can't hear anything!

ROWSE. Of course you can't, you fool!

ALLEYN. Where is Loder?

SERGEANT. He took another cut through the woods, more to the south. He thought he found traces of the scoundrels.

ALLEYN. Then we had better follow his lead. Come, let us hasten.

MR. SMITH. Ya'as, that's what I say. I'll go on through the gully in this direction.

ALLEYN. We'll keep on through the wood. Keep the drum beating, Sergeant, so that if our poor friends hear it, they may know we are near. [*Drum again, soldiers and all off.* MR. SMITH *on left.*]

ROWSE. Well, 'pon my soul! They're precious asses to be sent out here to hunt Indians! [*He kicks over the Indian near him.*]

WANNEMUCKA [*as the drum dies away in the distance*]. The captives may be freed, but let no one speak.

ROWSE. Now, will anybody tell me the use of having friends, when they walk right over you like—

LODER *appears on eminence, pushes aside the branches cautiously and says: "Ah!"* WANNEMUCKA, ROWSE *and* WAHCOTAH *repeat the exclamation and turn and see him. A pause. He dashes away,* ROWSE *following him with his eye, but not moving.* WANNEMUCKA *directs* WAHCOTAH *to follow* LODER, WAHCOTAH *draws his knife and glides out. All breathless attention.*

WANNEMUCKA [*to Indian*]. Quick! Glide by the water course, and stop the flight of White Panther on the north.

ROWSE. Two to one! Loder can't stand that!

WANNEMUCKA. Silence!

All quiet. A pause. LODER *enters, dressed in the disguise of* WAHCOTAH, *and personating him. As he enters, looks backward off left, wiping his knife, as if of blood.*

WANNEMUCKA. Ha! You have slain White Panther. [LODER *shakes head.*] No! Then Cayote will find him there upon the ravine path. Hist!

The Indian enters with MR. SMITH, *who is impelled forward at point of knife*

MR. SMITH. Aw, by Jove, this is what I get for going off on my own account.

ROWSE. The Honorable, by all that's unlucky! Then it wasn't Loder I saw!

MR. SMITH. Here, I say! Use me gently! I'm a British subject, and the British flag—[*He is bound and cast beside* ROWSE.]

WANNEMUCKA [*to Indian*]. White Panther fled?

INDIAN. Yes! Fled!

WANNEMUCKA. Then we must break camp! He will bring them all upon us. [*To* LODER.] Quick, rouse the white lily! She must be carried with us. [LODER *nods and takes rifle.*] No fire! Alarm white warriors!

LODER [*shakes his head*]. No! Gone! [*He approaches* MED *and bends gently over her. Daylight begins to break.*]

ROWSE. Smith, we're lost! We'll be taken to the other end of creation!

MR. SMITH. Oh, Lord!

WANNEMUCKA. No! Indians fly! White women fly! White men remain! [*To Indians.*] Bind the white captives to yonder trees and pin them with your knives. [*Bugle.*]

MR. SMITH *and* ROWSE. Oh, Lord! [*Indians seize them and yell.*]

The drum is heard faintly again. All silent in a moment. MED *starts up at the sound.*

MR. SMITH. They've missed me and are returning.

WANNEMUCKA [*to* LODER *and approaching* MED]. Quick! To the woods! [*Drum nearer.*]

LODER [*casting off his disguise*]. Indian! Stand back!

WANNEMUCKA. White Panther!

LODER. Aye, Loder, White Panther!

WANNEMUCKA. Spy! [*Springs towards him with uplifted knife. All the savages with a yell spring upon their captives.* LODER *seizes* MED *and fires his rifle at* WANNEMUCKA, *who falls.*]

In an instant the ravine is filled with soldiers. ALLEYN *darts forward and* LODER *passes* MED *to him just in time to ward her from a blow aimed by* ONATA, *who darts out of the tent.* ROWSE *and* MR. SMITH *floor their guards.* COLUMBIA *runs to* MR. SMITH, *and, on this picture of triumph, the—*

CURTAIN

THE DANITES IN THE SIERRAS

BY JOAQUIN MILLER

JOAQUIN MILLER

[1841–1913]

According to his own statement Cincinnatus Hiner Miller (later called Joaquin) "was born in a covered wagon pointed west." [1] Thus one of America's significant writers of the frontier found in the circumstances of his birth a symbol for the path his talents were later to follow with such enthusiasm. For thirteen years Miller migrated westward with his family, finally arriving in Oregon where the youth subsequently attended Columbia College, at Eugene.[2] He journeyed far in California, Mexico, and Central America; he became in turn a schoolteacher, pony express rider, newspaper editor, lawyer, judge, and Indian fighter. He went to New York and Europe in 1869 and brought out in London his *Pacific Poems*, *Songs of the Sierras*, and *Songs of the Sun-lands*. His thirst for adventure never satisfied, he voyaged to Europe a second time, joined the gold rush to the Klondike in 1897, and two years later was in China at the time of the Boxer Rebellion. His death occurred in 1913.

The frontier plays that preceded Daly's *Horizon* have already been indicated, and among those that followed were Bret Harte's *The Two Men of Sandy Bar* in 1876 and *Ah Sin* (produced May 7, 1877), written by Bret Harte and Mark Twain in collaboration.[3] Miller's *The Danites in the Sierras*, produced August 22, 1877, was one of the most successful of the frontier plays, achieving the distinction of a favorable reception in England. Miller wrote three other frontier plays, though none of them equalled *The Danites* in quality or popularity; they were *Forty-nine* (1881), *Tally Ho!* and *An Oregon Idyll.*

One aspect of the frontier's influence on American literature was an extended and often deepened attention to the nature which formed such an important part of the pioneer's life. Differing reactions there were, but to a temperament like Miller's it was inevitable that the poetry of nature should make an impressive appeal. In *The Danites* we find Billy apostrophizing nature: "O, what a miracle; the moon and golden stars; and all the majesty and mystery of this calm, still world to love. O, life is not so hard now." [4]

Another phase of frontier life reflected in Miller's play is the informal and impromptu manner in which law is administered. In the absence of properly

[1] The standard biography of Joaquin Miller is Harr Wagner's *Joaquin Miller and His Other Self.* San Francisco: 1929. Much of this is based on Miller's accounts of himself.

[2] See Royal A. Gettman's "A Note on Columbia College," *American Literature*, III, 480–482 (Jan., 1932).

[3] See Quinn, *A History of the American Drama from the Civil War to the Present Day*, I, 105–124.

[4] Act II, p. 389.

organized legal authority, a deputized individual, or the crowd itself, assumes the right to try without jury and to convict without evidence. Exaggerated as certain of the portrayals may be, they nevertheless indicate a reality well known in frontier life. Before seeing the victim, the Judge opines that "we'd best find him guilty on the spot, and execute him when he arrives." [1] The Judge will also hang the Chinaman, without trial, for drawing a pistol in his own defense; and in another instance, referring to a suspect, he counsels that they "hang him first and try him afterwards." [2]

Perhaps there is more of Miller than the frontier in the exaltation of family life as the "edge of God-land," and no doubt there is more of Bret Harte than either in the depiction of the regenerative power that a good woman exerts upon those about her. Just as the youthful innocence of Piney in *The Outcasts of Poker Flat* inspires the dissolute to acts of self-sacrifice, so the Widow in *The Danites* exerts an influence over the coarse men of the West: "You have been the seasons of the year. The spring and summer, and the fruit and flower of the year, to every one of us." [3] The Widow offers hope to the two women: ". . . take my hand," she says, "hold strong and come up and stand by my side." It is she who moves the Judge to say: "I feel as if I'd been to meetin' in Missouri and, and, got religion." [4] Appropriately enough, the Widow evokes the pedestal-veneration of womanhood: "It's a man's place to brighten a woman's name, not to tarnish it." [5]

Conspicuous in the play is the strong current of anti-Mormon feeling personified in the strife between the frontiersmen and the revengeful, atrocity-minded Danites, who hold their commission for murder from Brigham Young—for them the refusal to kill is apostasy. This picture of the Mormons is overdrawn, as Miller subsequently acknowledged: "I have always been sorry I printed it [the play], as it is unfair to the Mormons and the Chinese." [6] Likewise unpopular with the frontiersmen is the proselytizing religion of the East: ". . . of all things under the heavens, or on the earth, what use have we for a missionary here?" [7] The professional religionists are "the white choker gentry" who "will have the best in the land and pay nothing. They never miss a meal and never pay a cent." [8]

In place of these religions is the naturalism above referred to: ". . . the highest, the holiest religion that we can have, is to love this world, and the beauty, the mystery, the majesty that environ us." [9] Then, too, the Widow as missionary came to teach, but she, herself, learned that beneath rough externals the capacity for honor, trust, and self-sacrifice may indeed exist.

[1] Act I, p. 386.

[2] Act IV, p. 401.

[3] Other direct evidence of Bret Harte's influence is of course the character of Sandy, taken over almost entirely.

[4] Act II, p. 391.

[5] Act II, p. 392.

[6] Quoted in Stuart P. Sherman's Introduction to *The Poetical Works of Joaquin Miller*. New York: 1923.

[7] Act I, p. 386.

[8] Act I, p. 386.

[9] Act II, p. 389.

The naturalism and emphasis on feeling in the play link Miller, a reader of Rousseau, firmly with the romantic period during which he wrote. A study of his literary theory reveals not only his association with romantic thought but also how consistently he carried into practice, as in *The Danites*, his general literary reflections. These are, in the main, as follows: (1) "there cannot be a great literature without first a deep, broad, devout, and loving religion"; (2) use new materials; (3) ". . . exalt your theme"; (4) "put your heart in your work"; (5) "a true seer will see that which is before him, and about him, in and of his own land and life"; (6) "use the briefest little bits of baby words at hand": the Messiah will sing in words of one syllable; (7) cultivate peace.[1]

The differences between Daly's *Horizon* and *The Danites*, in content and mood, are numerous and show how unlike may be two works of art having a common source of inspiration. Neither play, in a sense, is a faithful, accurate portrayal of frontier life: but whereas Daly viewed it from a distance with the eye of a realist, Miller viewed it close at hand in the spirit of a romanticist. Despite his portrayal of impromptu justice and vengeful Danites (who were, in fact, motivated by a faith rather than the frontier), Miller's concept of Western life reflected the frontier optimism current during much of the nineteenth century. As we have seen (cf. the Introduction to Daly's *Horizon*), this attitude of hopefulness toward the frontier was later supplanted by the skepticism of Garland in *Main-Travelled Roads* and *A Son of the Middle Border*, of Rölvaag in *Giants in the Earth*, of Masters in the *Spoon River Anthology*. Although preceded by Eggleston and Daly, Miller was among those who felt that the vigorous independence and inspiring magnitude of Western life would regenerate, broaden, quicken men's thoughts and abilities.[2]

The present text of the play is the first edition printed in San Francisco in 1882.

[1] See the preface to *The Complete Poetical Works of Joaquin Miller*. San Francisco: 1904.

[2] For important material on the frontier see authorities listed in n. 3, p. 336. See also Sherman, Stuart P., *Americans*, New York, 1922.

CAST OF CHARACTERS

SANDY.—"A king, this man Sandy; a poet, a painter, a mighty moralist; a man who could not write his own name."

THE PARSON.—So-called because he could "outswear any man in the Camp."

THE JUDGE.—Chosen, because he was fit for nothing else in this "Glorious climate of California."

BILL HICKMAN.—A Danite Chief.

CARTER.—Companion to Hickman.

LIMBER TIM.—Sandy's "Limber Pardner."

WASHEE WASHEE.—"A Helpless little Heathen."

BILLY PIPER.—"That Cussed Boy."

THE WIDOW.—A Missionary to the Mines.

CAPT. TOMMY.—A woman with a bad name but a good heart.

BUNKERHILL.—Companion to Capt. Tommy.

DEDICATED TO MY FELLOW PIONEERS OF THE SIERRAS

Yea, I, the rhymer of wild rhymes,
  Indifferent to blame or praise,
  Still sing of ye as one who plays
The same old air in all strange climes;
  The same wild, piercing Highland air,
  Because, because his heart is there.

JOAQUIN MILLER

"Dan shall be a serpent by the way, an adder in the path, that biteth the horse's heels, so that his rider shall fall backward."—Genesis xlix : 17.

THE DANITES IN THE SIERRAS

ACT I

SCENE. *"The Howlin' Wilderness." Saloon. Bar. Water bucket on table. Mining tools, rocker, etc. Miners discovered lounging about. The* JUDGE *and* LIMBER TIM *at bar, drinking.*

JUDGE. Well, well, well. And so that boy, Billy Piper, is livin' in that old cabin up the Middle Fork where them three miners handed in their checks to the Danites?

LIMBER TIM. Livin' there all alone by hisself, Judge!

JUDGE. Why, I wouldn't live in that 'ere cabin all alone by myself, Tim, for that cradle full of gold.

TIM. It's been empty, that cabin, 'bout a year, Judge.

JUDGE. Empty as a bran new coffin, Tim.

TIM. And folks just about as willin' to get into it, as into a bran new coffin, I guess.

JUDGE. Tim, me and Sandy had gone out to help the emigrants, where we seed that poor gal, Nancy Williams, killed, and we warn't here. But you was. Tell me how it was the Danites killed 'em all three in that cabin, and you fellows didn't smell a mouse till it was all over. [*Miners gather around.*]

TIM. Well, them three miners was kind o' exclusive like, just as if they war a bit afraid of suthin'. They come from Hannibal, Missouri. But they was good miners and good neighbors, too, and was a makin' money like mud.

JUDGE. Yes, hard workers. Struck it, too, in the channel afore Sandy and me went out to meet the emigrants that time.

TIM. Yes, you remember 'em, Judge. All strong, healthy, handsome fellows. But you see—shoo! Be careful, boys, when you speak of it—but they was of that hundred masked men that killed the Mormon Prophet, Joe Smith.

JUDGE. And the Danites hunted 'em down, every one, even away out here in the heart of the Sierras.

TIM. Yes. Three as fine, hearty fellows as ever you see, and a makin' money like dirt, when along comes a chap, gets in with 'em, and the first thing you know, a rope breaks in the shaft, and one of 'em is killed. Then the water breaks in one night, and one is drowned. And then the last one of the three is found dead at the foot of the crag yonder.

JUDGE. And nobody suspectin' nothin' all this time?

TIM. No. But they did, at last, and when me and the boys went there and found that long-haired stranger chap gone, and all their clothes, and all the gold scattered over the floor, why we knew it was—Shoo! Danites!

JUDGE. Left all their clothes, and just lots of gold scattered all over the cabin floor! When I got back, and heard about the gold, I went right up—

TIM. But too late, Judge. The old clothes was there, but the gold—well, that had evaporated.

JUDGE. Yes, you had been there, Tim. I don't want any more old clothes, and come to think, I don't want any gold that comes to fellow's hand like that. Why, boys, that little old cabin is haunted, and that boy a livin' in it.

TIM. And all alone, boys.

JUDGE. Well, if that boy don't see ghosts in that cabin, livin' all alone by hisself like that—there ain't any, that's all. How long's he been there, Tim?

TIM. I don't know. Month or two, maybe. You see, after the men was all dead, and that stranger chap skipped out, nobody liked to go near the cabin; kinder fraid of the Danites.

Enter BILL HICKMAN *and* CARTER

JUDGE. Shoo, Tim! See! [*Miners fall back.*]

HICKMAN [*making sign to Barkeeper*]. Dan

shall be a serpent by the way, an adder in the path, that biteth the horse's heels so that his rider shall fall backward. [*They grasp hands, drink and exit.*]

TIM. Them's Danites.

JUDGE [*grasping pickhandle*]. Well, as Judge of this ar camp, I'd just like to purify this glorious climate of California with—

TIM. Judge! Judge! The Bar keep too? a Danite; didn't you see the grip he gave? You don't know who is and who ain't. Now just you remember them three poor fellows up the Canyon and keep still. Hello! My Pard. [*Enter* SANDY *and the* PARSON *and cross to bar.*]

SANDY. Come, boys. [*All make rush to bar.*] Well, you are all alive here, I see.

PARSON. None of these 'uns dead, Sandy, eh? [*All laugh.*] But poor Dolores. Just been a helpin' Capt. Tommy and Bunkerhill put her in the coffin.

SANDY. Was starved to death. Yes, she was, boys, and right here. Yes, and Tim, when you went to get a subscription for the Dutchman that broke his leg—

TIM. Why, she sot up in bed and took off a ring, and—

SANDY. Took off a ring—her marriage ring—the last one she had, and you didn't have sense enough to see it. Oh, I don't blame you, Tim, that was her way, you know. She was starvin' then. But, boys, look here; the Parson he wrote "Small Pox," on that butcher's door, that refused her meat, and now—well, he'll go into bankruptcy.

ALL. Good! Good! Served him right!

JUDGE. But, I say, Sandy, did you see them strangers?

SANDY. The tall, religious sort of chaps?

JUDGE. Talkin' about Dan bein' a serpent in the path.

SANDY. Yes. Seed 'em lookin' at the dead body of Dolores, down there. What of it? You seem skeered.

JUDGE. Danites!

TIM. Danites in the Sierras!

SANDY. What!

JUDGE. Yes, Danites. And the very fellows too, I think, that you and me run across when we went out to meet the emigrants, after we found this 'ere minin' camp.

SANDY. That shot—that hunted down the last of the Williams and shot, shot her—that pretty, that sweetly pretty girl that, that we found, Judge, and tried to save and bring back to camp to the boys?

JUDGE. The same hungry, Bible-howlin' varmints, I do believe.

SANDY. Judge, I'll be revenged for that poor girl's death if it takes me ten years. Why, there she came to us just at the gray of dawn, just as we seed the gold of the mornin' star croppin' out of the heavens; came to us, weary, torn, half-dead with hunger and fright, flyin' into camp like a wounded dove, there on the bank of the deep, foamin' Truckee river. "Why, poor little bird," I said, and I put my arms about her and took her up when she fell at our feet, boys, and laid her away to rest under the tree, by the bank, Judge, you know, and watched over her, we two did, Judge, as if she'd been our own kid. And then, Judge, when she waked up, you remember, and we fed her, and she talked and told us all. And how we promised and swore to save her, Judge. And then, just as we got all packed up and ready to come back, the Danites came burstin' in upon us, leadin' the Ingins, and all of 'em a shootin' at that poor, helpless baby, that never did anybody any harm.

JUDGE [*crying and wiping eyes*]. That alkali dust out there hurts my eyes yet. [*Rushes to bar and drinks.*] That strengthens the eyes.

SANDY. And then, boys, after the battle was over and I turned to look for her—Gone! Gone! Only the deep, dark river rollin' between its willow walls. Gone! Gone! Only the dark and ugly river gurglin', sweepin' and rollin' by, and the willows leanin' over it and drippin' and drippin' and bendin' to the ugly waters. Leanin' and weepin' as if in tears for her. Only the dark river rollin' there under the bendin' willows and—and—and my heart as cold and empty as a dead man's hand.

TIM. Why, Sandy, my poor old pard, we'll all stand by you and help you git even on 'em.

PARSON. Stand by you agin the Danites, Sandy, till the cows come home; and thar's my hand.

SANDY [*wiping his eyes and going*]. If them's them, Judge, I'll find 'em and raise 'em out of their boots. No, you needn't come, boys. If I can find 'em, that's all I ask. Let me have 'em all to myself, boys. [*Exit.*

JUDGE. Poor Sandy. He loved her, boys. And she was pretty, *so* sweetly pretty. And to go and get shot and drowned like that, when we was fightin' for her.

TIM. Why, he talks about her yet in his sleep, Parson. But he wouldn't know her if he seed her.

JUDGE. Only seed her by the camp-fire, boys. But he hain't been the same man since.

PARSON. Always was a little soft here. [*Taps heart.*] But he's good, Tim. I ain't sayin' nothin' agin' your pard. Only he's tender hearted.

Enter WASHEE WASHEE

WASHEE WASHEE [*down stage*]. I say, Plosson, plack tlain comee.

JUDGE [*aside*]. The pack train! Then there will be some news. And maybe some strangers; and maybe some business. Must brush up a bit.

WASHEE. Yes, plack tlain comee down way uppee mountain, an' a somebodee alle samee a Captin' Tommy; Blunkel hillee.

TIM. All the same Capt. Tommy?

PARSON. All the same Bunkerhill? Now you git out of here. You've been lyin' enough. Git, I tell you. [*Kicks at him and* WASHEE *exits.*] Lie! Why, that Chinaman can lie the bark off of a tree. [*All laugh.*]

JUDGE. Guess he can steal some, too, Parson.

PARSON. Steal? He even steals from himself, just to keep his hand in.

Enter SANDY

SANDY. Couldn't find 'em. And that's what makes me think it *was* Danites. Judge, they come and go as if they came up out of, or sink into the ground, like that.

TIM. Maybe they're gone up to the haunted cabin to see Billy Piper?

JUDGE. Oh, do you know, Parson, Stubbs here, says he's a wearin' of them dead men's old clothes?

PARSON. Hold on, I've got an idea! That boy Billy Piper's a Danite!

SANDY. Now look here, Parson, you don't like that boy, I know.

PARSON. No. I don't like nobody that lives all alone by hisself and in a place like that. Why, the blood ain't hardly dry yet, where them three men died, and he a livin' there.

SANDY. Well, now, maybe he ain't got no other place to stay. And he ain't strong, you know. Why, the first time I ever seed him, I met him in the trail, and he got out of it as I come by, and held down his head, all for the world like a timid bit of a girl, Judge. And when I said, "Boy, what's your name?" he stammered, and as if he wanted to get away, Judge, and at last, with his head still held down, he told me his name—Billy Piper—then smiled so sadly, like *her*, Judge, and went on.

JUDGE. Well, Sandy, ain't nothin' wonderful 'bout it, is there?

SANDY. No, Judge, not that. It's only Billy Piper, that's all. That's his name, boys. And don't you go for to nick-name him. But, Judge, that smile was like her—like her smile, *hers*.

TIM. Oh, now, Sandy, don't; that's a good fellow. Forget all about that.

JUDGE. Yes. Talk about—'bout suthin' new. Talk about the weather—this glorious climate of California, and—and—and—take a drink?

SANDY. Why, of course, boys. That's all right. But you, Parson, don't be too hard on little Billy Piper. I know it does make one feel kind o' skeery to think where he lives, and how he lives. But he's squar', squar', Parson.

TIM. And a poet. Yes. Says pretty things as he stands lookin' up at the moon, a wheelin' through the pine tops; prettier things than you can find in a book.

SANDY. And says things as sets you a thinkin', too. Why, he says to hisself today, kind o' quiet like, when some of the boys was tauntin' Bunker about the hump on her back, says he, takin' Bunkerhill's hand, says he, "God has made some women a little bit plain, in order that He might have some women that is perfectly good."

TIM. Just like a book, ain't it?

JUDGE. A little shaky here. [*Taps head.*] Maybe he's had trouble.

SANDY. Jest so, Judge, jest so. O, but I say, boys. Forgot to tell you. Seed Soapy Dan the storekeeper just now, when I went out to look for them fellows and what do you think? Why, his pack train is comin' in, and a missionary is a comin' in on it, too.

ALL. A missionary!

PARSON. A—a—now look here! Not a missionary? Of all things under the heavens, or on the earth, what use have we for a missionary here?

ALL. No use, no use at all.

JUDGE. No! We're too good *now*.

PARSON. A derned sight too good!

JUDGE. Why, it's insinervatious, that's what it is.

TIM. Better send him to the Cannibal Islands, eh, Parson?

PARSON. Do they take us for Cannibals out here, in this 'ere camp?

JUDGE. He'll want to be Judge and everything else.

PARSON. It is an insult. A roarin', howlin' insult, for that 'ere storekeeper to let 'em come in here on his mules. And if he sets foot in here, boys, and he will set foot in here, he'll come in here to take up a collection right off—O, yes, I know 'em. I seed 'em in Missouri and on the Mississippi, and seed 'em when I went down the river and took ship. Oh, I know the white choker gentry. They will have the best in the land and pay nothing. They never miss a meal and never pay a cent. A Boston missionary, bah!

JUDGE [*shakes pickhandle*]. Well, then, gentlemen, it's my official opinion, as judge of this 'ere camp, that we'd best find him guilty on the spot, and execute him when he arrives.

PARSON. Tried, and found guilty.

ALL. Yes; let's all go for him.

TIM. O, but he won't come in here.

PARSON. Won't he, though? This is the sittin' room of the hotel. He'll come to the hotel to get his fodder, won't he? O, they always have the best in the land, the broad-brimmed, long-legged, lean, lantern-jawed, hymn-howlin', white-chokered sons of guns. I'm down on 'em, I am.

SANDY. Well, guess we'd better all go for him, eh, boys?

PARSON. O, no. Don't let's go for him. Let's pass around the hat for brother Tomkinsonsonson; let's take up a collection; do suthin' religious.

TIM [*taking drink from bucket*]. Let's all be baptized. [*All laugh.*]

PARSON. Bully for Tim! Let's baptize the missionary!

SANDY. That's the idea, boys. Say, boys. Look here. When he comes in at that door—

PARSON. Baptize him, then and thar. Yes! Let's baptize him and give him his new name, like all the rest of us.

SANDY [*all sitting; pans; water*]. We'll do it, and I'll be chief mourner.

TIM. Wonder if he's a sprinkler or a dipper?

SANDY. Well, we'll make him think he's a dipper.

PARSON. Won't he look funny though, with his broad-brimmed Quaker hat all wilted down like a cabbage leaf?

TIM. An' his long-tailed coat all a streamin'.

SANDY. And his umbrella won't do him no good, for the water will rain from below. [*All roar.*]

Enter WASHEE WASHEE

WASHEE. Missonalie—longee cloatee—comee.

PARSON. He's a comin' right in. Told you so, boys. Washee, take that, and give him one for his mother. [*Hands water.*] Comin' in. Told you so.

SANDY. There, boys! Pullin' at the latch-string. Give it to him.

Enter WIDOW, *bag in hand; scar on cheek. Miners fall back*

ALL. Calico!

WIDOW. I am the missionary.

PARSON. The missionary!

SANDY [*to miners; down water*]. Yes, and the very kind of missionary the camp wanted.

WIDOW [*aside*]. Why, they all had gold-pans in their hands. How industrious these honest miners are.

PARSON. Say, Sandy, let's send to the Board of Missions for a thousand missionaries.

WIDOW. I sent word by the storekeeper that I was coming. I hope you were ready to receive the missionary?

JUDGE. Hem! We—we was ready to receive the missionary, mum, but—but not that kind of a missionary, mum.

SANDY. But we're glad, we're glad it *is* this kind of one, all the same.

PARSON [*brushing up and coming close to the* WIDOW]. Yes, we are, mum, by the—[*Hand over mouth.*]

SANDY. The biggest strike, Judge, since we found the Forks. Now go in. Make a speech. Speak for me. Don't let the Parson have it all to say.

JUDGE. This glorious climate, California, mum. Mum, mum, welcome. Welcome, mum, to the—the—to—Married, mum? [WIDOW *shakes head. Miners wild with delight.*] California widow, perhaps? [*She modestly turns away.*] A widder, boys. A real, squar', modest mite of a widder.

PARSON. Yes, she's a widder. And pretty. God bless the pretty widder.

SANDY. A widder! A California widder?

JUDGE. Yes, yes, Sandy. That's all right. You see, the other kind never gets this far. They seem to spile first.

PARSON. Have suthin' to drink, widder?

WIDOW. O, no, thank you. But if you could show me a room—

PARSON. The best room in the Forks is yourn till you can get a cabin of your own. This way. [*Showing her off.*]

SANDY. Yes; but we all must be allowed to pay for it together, Parson.

WIDOW. Parson?

SANDY. This is the Parson, mum.

WIDOW. O, I'm so glad. I shall have you preach at every service. [*Exit.*

ALL. Have you preach? [*All laugh.*]

PARSON. Have me preach?

SANDY. Why, she don't know we call you the Parson because you can out cuss any man in the camp. Come! My treat! [*All rush to bar.*]

JUDGE. Who's goin' to be baptized now, Parson?

PARSON. I am. Yes, I am, boys. I'm converted; and I'm willin' to be baptized.

SANDY. Leastwise, we don't baptize the widder, no way. [*Sadly.*] But what strange wind or storm blew her away in here among the crags and pines, boys? And so pretty, too; pretty as poor little Nancy Williams. And the scar? But pshaw, no. This cannot be her.

PARSON. Pretty, pretty, and good as gold. But she's had trouble, old pard. That's been a bullet made that scar.

SANDY. That's just what set me to thinkin' just now. And I want to look at her pretty face agin, boys. For you see them Danites came just as she came. Now we couldn't find the body of Nancy Williams, Judge, you know, and with that scar and them Danites, I tell you this might be Nancy Williams, and if—

JUDGE. Sandy! Sandy! You—That's not possible. You're always thinkin' of poor Nancy Williams. Why, that river rolls over her, Sandy. Forget her, do. Now, here's this 'ar widder—

TIM. O, that pretty widder. [*Straightening up collar.*] I'm goin' to fix myself up.

PARSON. And me, too. [*Miners repeat this and all exit, leaving* SANDY.]

WIDOW [*entering*]. All alone? And so thoughtful and still.

SANDY [*starts*]. Why, I—I was a thinkin' a bit, widder. I—the boys have gone to fix up, I guess. You see you're the first woman in the Forks, mum.

WIDOW. And are there no ladies here, then?

SANDY. Ladies? No, no ladies, mum. No children. No young folks at all. Only one. Billy Piper. A pale-faced, lonesome little fellow that lives all alone by hisself.

WIDOW. Why, how sad for him. I shall seek him out and console him.

SANDY. You mind me, mum, of a face that I saw once in the dusk and in trouble; a sweet, sad face, that vanished away like a dear, tender dream. But no, no, you are taller than she.

WIDOW. Why, how strange. I must have you tell me all about it. But here are your friends.

Miners entering dressed loudly, drink, and edge up to WIDOW

PARSON. Now Sandy's had her five minutes all by hisself. She's talked to him five whole minutes. I'd a been converted and baptized by this time.

Enter BILLY PIPER; *pick and pan*

SANDY. This is the boy Billy Piper, mum, that lives all alone by hisself.

WIDOW. I'm very glad to know you. We shall be the best of friends.

BILLY. O, I thank you so much. [*Aside.*] A woman. And a kind, true woman too. Life will not be so hard now. No, not so utterly desolate. But Sandy! How he looks at her. Looks at her tenderly as he once looked at me.

WIDOW. And you are a little miner. I should so like to dig the pure gold from the earth, too.

BILLY. Then come, and I will show you how it is done. [*Exit.*

PARSON. Curse that Danite boy! His smooth tongue and face will win that widder's heart in five minutes. Well, if she don't baptize him, I will, and in deeper water than he thinks. [*Goes to door. Shouts outside.*] Hello! Boys after that Chinaman again. Come. Let's go to work. It's dull here now, with the widder gone. [*All exit.*

Enter WASHEE WASHEE, *blouse stuffed with clothes. Takes bottle, drinks*

WASHEE. Blandee! Blandee! Me likee blandee. [*Drinks again.*] Blandee makee Chinaman feel allee same likee flighten clock. [*Going to door.*] Melican man no comee. No catchee Chinaman. [*Drinks.*] Melican man he no comee. Chinaman he no go. [*Shouts outside.*]

Enter miners, excited

SANDY. There he is, boys. [*Rush at* WASHEE.]

TIM. Well, he's got 'em. You bet he has. Let's search him for the shirts.

JUDGE. Yes, search him. And if you find your shirts, I'll find him guilty.

PARSON. Yes, and if you find him guilty, Judge, he's got to swing. Look here. [*Miners seize Chinaman and pull shirts from blouse.*] And here, and here, and there! A hull cargo! You heathen! Got anything more?

JUDGE. Got anything more, Washee? If you got anything more the law will make you give it up. You can't go on breakin' the seventh commandment like that, in this glorious climate of California, I can tell you. No, not while I'm Judge, you can't. Got anything else about you? [*Seizes queue, and pulls about.*] Got anything else about you, I say?

WASHEE. Yesee. My gotee that! [*Draws pistol,* JUDGE *back.*]

PARSON. He's drawed a pistol! A Chinaman dares to draw a pistol! Has it come to this in California? A Chinaman draws a pistol on a white man in California! Bring that rope. [*Miners hand rope.*]

JUDGE [*hiding behind* SANDY]. Hang him! Hang him! And I'll pronounce sentence of death on him afterwards.

SANDY [*takes pistol*]. Hand in your checks, Washee Washee.

PARSON. Here, boys! Out to the nearest tree. [*Throws noose over* WASHEE'S *head; other end to miners. Dragging to door. Shouting wildly:* "Hang him!" *Enter* WIDOW, *with* BILLY. *She lifts hand; all let go.* WASHEE *at her feet. She throws off rope. Miners down stage in shame.*]

CURTAIN

ACT II

SCENE. *Moonlight on the Sierras. Rocky Run crossing stage; ledge overhanging; set cabin, practical door, foot of run; background of distant snow-capped peaks.*

Enter HICKMAN *and* CARTER

HICKMAN. That's her cabin. The missionary. Humph! As if we could not find her out, though she professed herself a saint. Her time has come.

CARTER. Yes. But it seems to me, after she has escaped the bullet and the flood, and hid away here, toiling too as she does, it is hard to kill her. Maybe the Lord has willed to spare her.

HICKMAN [*close and solemn*]. And Dan shall be a serpent in the path, that biteth the horse's heel till his rider falleth backward. Have we not our orders from the Church? Is she not sentenced to death? Do we not hold our commission from Brigham Young for her execution?

CARTER. But I—I'm tired of this hunting down helpless women. As long as it was men I did my part, but now—well, she had no hand in the Prophet's death.

HICKMAN. But her father had. And are *you* to sit in judgment now on this? You are not the judge. You are only the executioner. No! She and all her kindred shall perish from the earth. For I will be revenged, saith the Lord, unto the third and fourth generation.

CARTER. And I am to kill her? Enter that cabin like a thief and kill her with this knife? This hand? I will not! I—

HICKMAN. And be an apostate? And die by *this* knife? And *this* hand?

CARTER. I will defend myself.

HICKMAN. Fool! Defend yourself against the destroying angels? Whistle against the winds of the Sierras, but defy not the Danites of the Church. Hush! [*Exit.*

Enter WIDOW *and* BILLY *from cabin*

BILLY. How beautiful! The whole moon's heart is poured out into the mighty Sierras. O, what a miracle; the moon and golden stars; and all the majesty and mystery of this calm, still world to love. O, life is not so hard now.

WIDOW. And you love the world, with all your sad, hard life?

BILLY. And why not? Is it less beautiful because *I* have had troubles? My sweet friend, it seems to me the highest, the holiest religion that we can have, is to love this world, and the beauty, the mystery, the majesty that environ us.

WIDOW. How strange all this from one so young. I came here, a missionary, to teach; I am being taught. But stay awhile yet. You see by the moonlight on the mountain, it is not so late as you thought. We may still read another chapter of your little Testament.

BILLY. No, I must go now. Besides, I know Sandy is coming this evening. Oh, I know you expect him. And he, he would not like to see me here.

WIDOW. And why not? His is a high, loyal nature, above the petty quarrels and jealousies of the camp. Come, come in and wait till he calls. Then, you see, you will not leave me alone.

BILLY. Alone? And do you fear to be alone? Oh! do you, too, shudder and start at strange sounds and signs as I do? Last night, up yonder on the banks of the stream, in my cabin in the thick wood, as I lay there I heard footsteps about my cabin. I heard the chapparal and the manzanitti crackle, as if monsters prowled about; wild beasts, waiting to devour me.

WIDOW. Then come in. You shall not go till you are at least in better heart. [*Into cabin.*]

Enter PARSON *up canyon at back, breathless, pick on shoulder*

PARSON. Well! That is a climb for you. If I'd a lost my footin' comin' up that precipice, good-bye Parson. But it was a mile around by the trail, and I wanted to get to the widder's cabin afore Sandy. She's in thar'. Lord love her! The sweetest thing in these 'ere Sierras. These 'ere Sierras? The sweetest and the prettiest in this universal world. Yes, and the boys all know it. They all knowed it when she came. But when she took this 'ere cabin, and took in that cussed, thievin' little heathen, kind o' absorbed him like, and set up to washin' the boys' clothes; workin' like the rest of us—when I seed that 'ere little widder a bendin' over a wash-tub, earnin' her bread by the sweat of her brow; wearin' a diadem of diamonds on her forehead; well, I thought of my mother and my sister, an' it made me better—better—and I loved her so, I loved her so. [*Has been coming down Run; is at door. Stops and listens.*] The widder readin'? And—and to him—that boy Piper. That brat that's either Danite, Devil or imp? I'll—I'll strangle him. I'll take him by the throat and choke the life out of him with these two hands and chuckle with delight while doin' it. He's comin' out. I'll wait till I catch him alone and then I'll throttle him. [*Exit.*

Enter BILLY *and* WIDOW

BILLY. O, yes. I am quite strong now. It was only a passing shadow; as the clouds will sometimes shut out the light of the sun or the beauty of yon moon. I suppose such moments come to us all. Good-night. My cabin is not far.

Widow. And if anything happens, or you feel at all sad or lonely, come back, and Sandy, if he comes, I am sure will be glad to take you to his own cabin and cheer you up.

Billy. Sandy! You know not what you say. But no. It is *I* rather, that know not what *I* say. Good-night.

Widow. Good-night. And come again soon to read the other chapters.

Billy. I will come. Good-night. [Widow *closes door*. Billy *looks off*.] How full of rest and peace the whole world seems. But I? I am as the dove that was sent forth from out the ark and found not where to set its foot. The olive branch? It is not for me.

Enter Judge *and* Tim

Tim. Yes, Judge, my pard's cut the sand clean from under the Parson's feet, I guess. He's goin' to pop tonight, he tells me, if he can only pump up the spunk to do it. [*Takes bottle from boot leg; they drink; he returns it.*]

Judge. Goin' to get married? Well, Tim, in this glorious climate of California, I tell you one feels like—like—well, as if he must do suthin', Tim.

Tim. If there was only more women, Judge.

Judge. That's it, Tim. I tell you, it makes me feel sort of, of warlike to think about what Sandy's goin' to do. I tell you, in this glorious climate of California—[Billy *down stage and they meet.*]

Tim. Billy Piper at the widder's agin? Judge, you're the Judge of this 'ere camp. Set him up.

Judge. Billy, as Judge of this 'ere camp I must say that you ain't doin' the squar'. The boys talk powerful rough about you and her. You're a cryin' shame to the—the—the—this glorious climate of California. And Billy, for the reputation of this 'ere camp, I think I'll punch your head. [*About to strike.*]

Enter Capt. Tommy *and* Bunkerhill

Capt. Tommy [*fist in* Judge's *face*]. Touch that boy and I'll knock the corn juice out of you. Yes, I will, and you, too. Light out, Billy. [*Exit* Billy.] You bald-headed, gum suckin' old idiot.

Bunkerhill. Tackle a boy, eh? 'Bout the only thing in the camp you could lick anyhow; both of you.

Judge. Well, Capt. Tommy, I'm a magistrate and must not fight. But Tim—speak to her, Tim.

Tim. Yes, he's a magistrate; and you've got to keep the peace, too, or he'll—

Capt. Tommy. Well, do *you* want to take it up? You long-legged, jackass rabbit you. Come on, both of you. I'm your match.

Bunkerhill. Take both of 'em to make one man.

Enter Widow *from cabin*

Judge. Ahem! The widder! Good evenin', marm. I'll put 'em under arrest for bein' drunk and disorderly, if they disturb you, marm.

Capt. Tommy. Widder, sorry to disturb you. Bunker and me is allers in trouble. Allers, allers. And not allers for faults of our own, mum; it's the bad name, mum.

Bunkerhill. It's the bad name, mum. And we must bear it. Good-night, Widder, good-night. [*Going.*]

Capt. Tommy. Don't think too hard of us. We hain't had no bringin' up, like better women has. But we won't never make no rows any more, mum, if you'll forgive us.

Widow. Forgive you? You have done me no harm, and if you have trouble, young ladies, remember it is yourselves you harm. You do yourselves harm, young ladies.

Capt. Tommy [*to* Bunkerhill]. Young ladies! She called us young ladies.

Bunkerhill. She's a good 'un, Tommy. A good, squar' woman. [*Both returning.*]

Capt. Tommy [*weeping*]. Widder, between us rolls a wide river that has borne Bunker and me from the high, sunny shore where you stand to the dark, muddy t'other side: and I'll not try to cross it, Widder. But God bless you for callin' us young ladies. We was good once, and we had mothers once. Yes, we had, mothers, and fathers, and little baby brothers and sisters, and—[Tim *affected*. Judge *takes out handkerchief.*]

Bunkerhill. Yes, fathers and mothers and little brothers and sisters that loved us, before we fell into the dark river that bore us far from the high, white shore where you stand, Widder.

WIDOW [*offering hands*]. The river is not so wide that my hands will not reach across it. If my feet are on the solid bank, take my hand, hold strong and come up and stand by my side. [*They hesitate, grasp her hands and kiss them.*]

JUDGE. Tim, I feel as if I'd been to meetin' in Missouri and, and, got religion.

TIM. You old fool, you're a cryin'; Capt. Tommy, she's a cryin'; and Bunker—she's a—[*Breaks down.*]

JUDGE. Capt. Tommy, I'm an old, busted, bald-headed old—well, I guess I am an old fool. But you've made me better. And if you'll take me for better or for worse—

TIM. And me, too, Bunker. I'm hot lead in a bullet-ladle. All melted up. Take me? [*Both greatly amazed. Confer aside, then frankly forward.*]

BUNKERHILL. Well, if you'll be good to Billy, and to everybody.

TIM. Good to Billy? You will make us good to all. Good! But come. Now let us go tell Sandy. [*Both embrace; ladies take arms and going.*]

JUDGE. O, this glorious climate of California!

WIDOW. You will all come to see me?

JUDGE. We will come. Good-night.

[*Exit;* WIDOW *looking after.*

Enter SANDY

SANDY. Why, Widder, you—you out here? You—you waitin' here for me, Widder? Say yes, Widder. Say you were waitin' for me, and it will be as if the sun, and the moon, and the stars all together shone out over the Sierras, and made this another Eden, with its one sweet woman in the centre of God's own garden of fruit and flowers, and—and—

WIDOW. Why, Sandy! You used to sit for hours in my cabin and not say one word, and now, you talk like a running brook.

SANDY. No, no, Widder. I can't talk. I never could. I never can, Widder. But Widder, it's not them that can talk that feel. You hear the waters thunderin' down that ar canyon over thar'? They are shallow, and foamy, and wild. But where they meet the river away down below, they are calm and still. But, they are deep and strong, and clear. So, widder, it seems to me with the hearts of men and women. And Widder, when I stood thinkin' of you, today—

WIDOW. You thought of me today?

SANDY. Today? Yesterday! Tomorrow! Forever! O, Widder, as I bent to my work in the runnin' water, the white clouds far up above me tangled in the high, dark tops of the pines, the gold shinin' there in the dark loam and muck, as the pure waters poured over it; the gold as pure and true, and as beautiful as your noble life, my lady, I thought of you, how that you was like that gold in the loam and in the muck, among us all. And—and—

WIDOW. Us all? [*Aside.*] Why can't he speak up for himself, now that he has learned to speak? [*Aloud.*] And you think I have done good here—for *us* all?

SANDY. Good! You have been the seasons of the year. The spring and summer, and the fruit and flower of the year, to every one of us. Why, we'd a hung that cussed Chinaman. We would. Yes, and never a thought about it after he was buried. And, why, we hain't hardly had a funeral since you came, and we used to have 'em every Sunday, when only Bunker and Capt. Tommy and poor dead Dolores was here. O, yes, you've helped us, Widder.

WIDOW. Helped *us*. Has the little missionary done *you* no good, Sandy?

SANDY. O, yes, you—yes, you—you—you—washed my shirt.

WIDOW. Oh, Sandy!

SANDY. Yes, that was good in you, widder. But you see that's considerable trouble to a feller, too, as well as help. For when a feller has to send his pard with his shirt and go to bed till it gets back—

WIDOW. Why, Sandy, haven't you but one shirt?

SANDY. But one shirt? Do you think a man wants a thousand shirts in the Sierras?

WIDOW. O, Sandy, you do need a missionary, indeed you do, Sandy. You want a missionary badly. [SANDY *starts, and for the first time seems to understand.*]

SANDY. I—I—yes, Widder, I do want a missionary; I need a missionary. *I—I*—the great, rough heathen of this 'ere camp. Never did a cannibal hunger for a missionary as my heart hungers for—for—Widder, will you—can you—can you—will you be my missionary?—my wife?

WIDOW. Sandy, here is my hand; my heart, you ought to have known, has long been yours. [*Offering hand.*]

SANDY. You—you—you don't mean it? Is it me that's to have you? Rough, bluff, bearded old Sandy. Not the Parson; not slim Limber Tim, not that gentle, sweet boy, Billy Piper, but Sandy? Sandy, strong as a pine in Winter, and rough as the bark of a tree. And this—this soft, lily-like hand to be laid in his! O, Widder, you don't mean to give me this dear, tremblin' little hand, do you? Soft and white, and flutterin' like a dove that has just been caught. Is this little hand to be mine for storms or sunny weather, Widder?

WIDOW. Yes, Sandy.

SANDY [*taking her in his arms*]. Jerusalem! Mine! Mine! My wife! Mine, to work for, to plan for, to love and to live for! Mine! Mine! Mine! My beauty! Mine! Mine, at last! [*Reflecting.*] But, Widder, my cabin is a rough place. Only a little log hut.

WIDOW. Sandy, true love is content to live in a very small house.

SANDY. True, Widder, true. Love, real unselfish love, it seems to me, could be content under the trees; in the boughs of the trees, like the birds; in the mountains; everywhere that love—that love—finds love—to—love, love.

WIDOW. Yes, Sandy. Anywhere that love finds love.

SANDY. Yes, yes. You see, I know about what it is I want to say, but I can't say it as well as you can.

WIDOW. Nonsense, Sandy. But the moon is low, and—

SANDY. And I must go. Well, you're right. But before I go, Widder, if you love me—[*Embraces and kisses her.*] Moses in the bulrushes! The world is a bigger world now. I seem to stand on the summit of the Sierras, six feet two inches taller than the tallest mountain. Oh, Widder, this is Paradise with its one little woman, and now you're goin' to drive me out of it.

WIDOW. Yes, you must go now. You see we are here in the open trail, and the miners on the night-watch, passing to and from their tunnels, will think it strange on seeing us together so late.

SANDY. Right, Widder. It's a man's place to brighten a woman's name, not to tarnish it. Good-night.

WIDOW. Tomorrow, Sandy. Good-night.

[*Exits into cabin.*

SANDY. Tomorrow! O, moon, go down! And sun rise up and set, for I can never wait. Tomorrow! And I kissed her! And her soul overflowed and filled mine full as a river flooding its willow banks. I must tell Tim, and Tim will tell the Judge, and the Judge will tell the boys, and the boys will bust. For it's too much happiness for one little camp to hold. Tomorrow! Mine! My wife! [*Starting to go.*] And I kissed her, and kissed her, and—[*Turns to go up stage, and meets* PARSON *face to face.*]

PARSON. Talkin' in your sleep, Sandy? 'Pears to me you're actin' mighty queer, eh? Been seein' the widder agin? Mustn't get excited where woman is concerned. Sort of like buck ager. Miss your game, sure, if you get excited, Sandy.

SANDY. O, yes, I know all about that, you know. Oh, I'm not—not afraid of a little woman like that.

PARSON. Well, say, old pard, Sandy, you—you didn't really have a serious talk with her? Squar', now, Sandy. Squar' as a coffin lid, Sandy. We were old pards once, you and me, Sandy. We don't want to send each other up on the hill thar, Sandy. So you'll be squar' with me, an' I'll be squar' with you. I love that 'ere woman thar, and—

SANDY. Well—well. The fact is, Parson—you can't help it, I guess. Now, I'll tell you. That 'ere little woman, she's—come and take a drink.

PARSON. No, thank you, Sandy. Got to set my night-watch in the tunnel, and change my drifters. But it's to be a squar' fight, Sandy, and there's my hand. And if you git her, Sandy—git her squar'!

SANDY. Squar', Parson. Squar'! [*Exit.*

PARSON. Good-night. Got him out of the way, and I'll see her right off, and tell her—tell her like a man I love her. [*About to enter cabin.* LIMBER TIM *and* BILLY *enter.*] Pshaw! Here comes Tim and that cussed boy. [*Exit, behind cabin.*

BILLY. There is somebody prowling about my cabin, Tim. I can't; I won't stay there tonight.

TIM. Well, you do look skeered. [*Aside.*] Ghosts, I'll bet a gold mine! [*Aloud.*] Three men, wasn't there? Your face is white as snow, Billy.

BILLY. And my hair will be as white. O, Tim, I tell you there are two men, and—

TIM. Three! [*Aside.*] There was three of 'em killed, and they've come back. [*To* BILLY.] Pull up, Billy. I'll tell my pard, Sandy. But you see his mind is awful full now. O, he's got a powerful mind. But it takes it all, and more too, to tend to her. [*Pointing to cabin.*]

BILLY. And he really loves, and will marry her?

TIM. That's the little game he's tryin' to play, Billy. Guess he's got the keerds to do it, too. I tell you the moon shines mighty bright for my pard tonight, Billy. Oh, he's a happy man, I can tell you.

BILLY. Tim, tell me this. Why is it that the grave yards are always on a hill? Is it because it is a little nearer heaven?

TIM [*turning away*]. Well, I—I—well, Billy, I don't take to grave yards and sich like. May be it's a prettier view up thar. But then they can't see, with thar eyes full of dust.

BILLY. No. Nor feel, nor understand, nor suffer. Love and be unloved, know and be unknown through all the weary years of this weary, loveless life. Oh, Tim, Tim! [TIM *knocks at door.*]

Enter WIDOW

TIM. Widder! Billy's took sick. Poetry; pretty; stars; grave yards and sich. Mustard plaster, physic and peppermint tea. Take care of him, Widder, till I tell Sandy. [*Exit.*

WIDOW. What is the matter, Billy?

BILLY. Sandy. Has he been here, as you expected, and told you all?

WIDOW. All, all. And I am so happy.

BILLY. And *I* am so miserable.

WIDOW. O, Billy, why is this? Why are you so miserable when your friends are to be so happy? Can you not tell me? Can you not trust me? And can you not trust Sandy, too?

BILLY. No, no, no. Down to the door of the tomb, even over the dark river, alone I must bear my secret, my sufferings and my cross. O, you cannot guess. You will never know the dark and dreadful truth, the mystery, the awful crimes—

WIDOW. Crimes! Crimes! Then you are—you are a Danite?

BILLY. I, a Danite? I?

WIDOW. Yes, I see it all now. Men have been seen prowling about your cabin at night. They have been seen to enter it in your absence.

BILLY. Merciful heavens, what do you say? Then I am doomed. Oh, if it would come. If it would come now! Now! Sudden, and swift, and certain. Now! Oh, this suspense is more than death. This waiting day and night, night and day, for the executioner to strike. Come! Come! O, I cannot bear this any longer. Come, death! Father in heaven take—take me! Pity and take me now. Oh! Oh! This is death! [*Falls.*]

WIDOW. What terrible thing is this? Will no one come? He is dying, and no one to help. Dying, choking to death. [*Opens collar.*] A woman!

BILLY. Hush. A whisper would be my death warrant. [*Danites appear on cliff watching.*] You hold the secret of my life. You hold my *life* itself.

WIDOW. You are—

BILLY. Nancy Williams. [*Danites disappear.*] But you will keep my secret?

WIDOW. As these Sierras keep the secrets of their Creator.

BILLY. Thank you! thank you! My sister, my friend. And when all is over; when dying from this constant strain and terror; when dead in my cabin yonder; then bring him, with some wild flowers, and once let him, whom you so love, stoop and kiss the cold, cold face of her who loved him, oh, so tenderly.

WIDOW. And you love him as he loved you?

BILLY. As *you* love him, and as I shall love him while life lasts, my sister and my friend. But from him, even until death, this secret is sacred as the secrets of the grave.

WIDOW. As you will; sacred as the grave.

BILLY. And now good-night. Tim will be back soon. No, I dare not enter your cabin now. Let them still believe me of the Danites. I hear footsteps, go! Good-night. [*Exit* WIDOW *into cabin.*

Enter Danites

BILLY. The Danites! [*Exits.*

HICKMAN. Keep watch down the trail. Men will be passing soon to and from the tunnels on the night-watch. We must not be seen. Look sharp. This is the woman. I heard the boy call her name—Nancy Williams—as I leaned from the cliff there. The work must be done, and done now. [*Tests knife, and cautiously opens door.*]

CARTER. Shoo! Some one is coming down the trail. Out! Back!

Enter WIDOW

WIDOW. Some one opening my door. Well, what is it you want, sir?

HICKMAN. You. Your time has come. [*Throws light of lantern in her face, and grasping knife.*]

Enter PARSON

PARSON. Hello! Hello! Now what are you doin' around the widder's cabin, eh? 'Pears to me everybody in camp, night and day's a hoverin' round this 'ere cabin of yourn, Widder. Who are they? Say, who are you fellows, anyhow? [HICKMAN *and* CARTER *retreat.* PARSON *following them, seizes* HICKMAN, *holds him, and looks long and hard in his face.*]

HICKMAN. Well, friend, you'll know me when you see me again, won't you?

PARSON. Yes, I will. Yes, I will know you, and know you in a way that you will remember, if ever I see you hangin' 'round this little woman's cabin agin. Know you when I see you? Now, you just set a peg thar, and remember that the longest day you live I'll know you, you bet.

HICKMAN. Be patient, my friend, I meant no offence.

PARSON. Didn't you, though? Well, I'll remember you, and know you all the same when I see you. Who are you, anyhow?

HICKMAN. Only prospectors. Good-night, Sir. [*Exit both.*

PARSON. Prospectors, eh? Well, prospectors don't prospect at midnight. They're ground-sluice robbers, I'll bet. You look out for them fellers, Widder, they're on the steal. [*Aside.*] All by herself; and Sandy sound asleep. Bet I'll never get another such a chance. [*To* WIDOW.] Pretty late, ain't it, Widder? Pretty fine night, but pretty late.

WIDOW. Yes! late. But it seems to me nights like this were not made for sleep.

PARSON [*aside*]. Not made for sleep; but made for love. O, what a hint. That's what she means. Oh, was there ever anything so smart as a smart woman in such things? [*Aloud.*] Ahem! No, not made for sleep. You're right there, Widder. [*Aside.*] Ain't she pretty and smart? Ain't she smart? I'll just press her here on that point. [*Aloud.*] No, these moonlight nights were not made for sleep, but for—for—Now what were these moonlight nights in the Sierras made for, Widder?

WIDOW. For meditation and prayer.

PARSON [*aside*]. Won't somebody please set down on my head? This is the end of the Parson. [*To* WIDOW.] Why, Widder, you—you—I understand now. And it's Billy—but to have you love a thing like Billy, Widder, that there's been so much talk and secrets about. I tell you to beware of Billy. Beware of Billy. He's a sneak; a sneak. A Danite! And I'll throttle him yet. Yes, he is a Danite; and I will kill him.

WIDOW. Parson, for shame! You asked me if you could do me a favor just now; you can.

PARSON. Name it! And if it's to throw him over that cliff, I'll do it. I'll do it.

WIDOW. No. You will befriend and defend poor little Billy Piper. Do it with your life!

PARSON. Oh, Widder, anything but that. Why, he's a snake. A snake in the grass. He has put you to shame before all the camp. All the camp is talkin' about his sneakin' in and out of your cabin, day and night, and—

WIDOW. You insult me! [*Going.*] And now show me that you are the man Sandy is, by befriending that boy, or never speak to me again. [*Exit into cabin.*

PARSON. By defending that boy! that boy who seeks to ruin her! And to have her slam the door in my face. O, I could twist his neck as if it were a wisp of straw. Slam your door in my face like that? I'll be revenged on you and on him if ever I—

Enter BILLY, *running and looking back*

BILLY. By my cabin! I dare not go home!

PARSON [*suddenly confronts* BILLY]. So, youngster! [*Seizing him.*] Come here! [*Pulls him down.*] Come here with me! Now, look here! What have you been doin' at the widder's? Do you hear? Answer! Say—I'll just pitch you over them rocks there, and break your infernal slim neck—[*Pulls him up, run.*] Come here! Now you tell me the truth! What a' you been doin' at the widder's? Say! [*Shakes him.*] Don't you know that if you go on in this way, you will fall over this bluff some night, and break your infernal little neck? Don't you know that? Speak! you boy—you brat. [*Shaking him.*] Well, I'll save you the trouble of slippin' off of here; yes, the boys will like it. They'll all say, they knew you'd break your neck some night. Now look here, sir! You've got just one minute to live; to say what you want to say, quick. When that flyin' cloud covers that 'ere star yonder, you die, and may God help you and me. Speak now! Come! come! speak but once before I—murder you.

BILLY [*falling on knees, hands clasped*]. Please, Parson, may I pray? [PARSON *lets go; staggers back;* WIDOW *appears at door of cabin with candle, shading eyes.*]

CURTAIN

ACT III

SCENE. SANDY'S *cabin. Flowers on table, curtains on walls and at window; practical door; fire; gun; door; cradle;* WIDOW *discovered rocking cradle;* CAPT. TOMMY *and* BUNKERHILL *sewing; both greatly improved.*

BUNKERHILL. Well, if I was Billy, I'd take the hint, I would, and leave camp. He won't fight; he can't work. He's got no spirit for nothin'.

CAPT. TOMMY. Guess we'd better 'ave let Limber and Judge shake him out of his boots, that night, eh? He's no good, I guess, eh?

BUNKERHILL. Yes, but it ain't in me, and it ain't in you, Tommy, for to see two on one. The bottom dog in the fight, that captures me. But guess Limber and Judge were right when they wanted him to git.

CAPT. TOMMY. Well, what is he, anyhow? Danite or devil?

BUNKERHILL. Can't say, Capt. Tommy. Mrs. Judge. Beg pardon, Mrs. Judge.

CAPT. TOMMY. All right, Mrs. Tim, 'pology is accepted.

BUNKERHILL. Well, as I was sayin', I don't know whether he's Danite or devil. But I do know he's no man. [WIDOW *starts.*] Why, yes, Widder. And the sooner you know it the better. Why, don't the whole camp hate and despise him? You're the only friend he's got. You and Sandy. And you're the very ones he hurts the most.

CAPT. TOMMY. Why, he's just a ruinin' of your character in this 'ere camp, Widder. Society must be respected.

BUNKERHILL. Yes, Widder; we ladies can't afford to fly into the face of society.

CAPT. TOMMY. Yes, Widder; only last night, the Judge he says to me, he says, says he, "Now that I'm a family man," says he, "I must have respect for society."

BUNKERHILL. O, I tell you, I wouldn't fly into the face of society for nothin' in this world. [*To* CAPT. TOMMY.] It would be the saddest day of my life when I'd have to cut the widder for the sake of society, but she must be keerful.

WIDOW. And why should all men hate poor little Billy Piper so?

BUNKERHILL [*to* CAPT. TOMMY]. Shall I tell her, Tommy?

CAPT. TOMMY. Yes, tell her. Hit's for her own good.

BUNKERHILL. Well, then, they hates him so because you loves him so.

WIDOW. Love him? Well, yes, I do, and pity him from the bottom of my heart. Oh, if we but had money, gold, plenty of gold,

Sandy and me, we would leave here. We would go away silently and secretly some night, to another land, and take him away out of it all. Yes, I do love him.

CAPT. TOMMY [*to* BUNKERHILL]. Well, that just fetches me. What will society say to that?

BUNKERHILL. The butcher's wife will cut her.

CAPT. TOMMY. The baker's wife turned all streaked and striped last night as she told me about Billy comin' here so much. I never!

BUNKERHILL. Well, *I* never.

CAPT. TOMMY. Why, the new Parson's wife won't even look this way.

BUNKERHILL. Hexcept when she goes out to take up a collection. Capt. Tommy, Mrs. Judge; beggin' pardon, Mrs. Judge.

CAPT. TOMMY. Well, if she'd a married the Parson, I tell you, ther'd been [no] hangin' round of Billy Piper at the parsonage. Why, he'd a kicked him out, and respected society, he would.

BUNKERHILL. Poor Parson. Wish he had a got her. Why, he's all broke up. He's a perfect walkin' corpse. Asks always 'bout the widder when I meets him on the trail; tender like; so tender like, Capt. Tommy, with his eyes all wet, and a lookin' to the ground.

CAPT. TOMMY. Well, now, the Parson's not a corpse, I guess. Look here, I seed him at the store, a fixin' of his irons; heelin' himself like a fightin' cock. Yes, he did look powerful pale. But the Judge says to me, last night, says he, "Mrs. Judge, I hearn the Parson's bull pup bark;" that's his pistol, you know, Bunker. And the Judge, he says to me, says he, "There's goin' to be a row." And the Judge, he says to me, says he, "I know there's goin' to be a row, because, as I came home, I heard the Dutch undertaker hammerin' away like mad." And the Judge, he says to me, says he, "Mrs. Judge, that undertaker is a good business man, and a very obligin' man; he allers looks ahead, and when he's sure there's goin' to be a row at the Forks, he takes the size of his man and makes his coffin in adwance."

Enter JUDGE *and* TIM; *dressed; polite*

JUDGE. Good mornin', madam; Mrs. Sandy, good mornin'. A very infusin' sermon last Sunday, Mrs. Sandy. Sorry you was not out. Mustn't neglect the church, Mrs. Sandy. Splendid sermon 'bout—'bout—And splendid collection. Took up a damned splendid collection. Got my handkerchief hemmed, Capt. Tommy? [*Glasses; to table, takes up baby garment;* CAPT. TOMMY *hides face.*] You don't mean to say that—that—that—God bless you, Tommy, God bless you. Oh, this glorious climate of California. Tim, let's take our wives home and go on a tear. [*Arms to ladies.*] Good-bye, Widder.

CAPT. TOMMY. Good-bye, Widder. And, say, Widder, we love you, but be careful about Billy Piper, won't you?

BUNKERHILL. Widder, that's so; we loves you. You made suthin' of us, and we'll try to don't forgit it. But there's trouble comin', Widder. Cut Billy, and tell Sandy to look out for the Parson.

JUDGE. Come, my family. Oh, this glorious climate of California. [*Exit* JUDGE, TIM, CAPT. TOMMY *and* BUNKERHILL.]

WIDOW. They are so happy. And the great bald-headed boy, the Judge, is the happiest of all. O, they have so improved the poor girls. 'Tis love that makes the world go round, my baby. And you, my little pet, smiling there, I wonder what these Sierras hold in their hearts for you? And I wonder, as I look in your rosebud face, what manner of men and women will grow here in this strong, strange land, so new from the Creator's hand? Shall there be born under the burning sun of the Sierras a race of poets? Of good and eloquent men? Or men, mighty for ill? These are your mother's thoughts, my darling, as she tries to fill her little place in life and do her duty to her baby and to her husband. [*Enter* SANDY; *gold pan, pick, shovel; pan on table; pick and shovel by door.*] Oh, Sandy, I was just thinking of you, just saying, *my husband.*

SANDY. My wife! And the baby is well?

WIDOW. Smiling, Sandy.

SANDY. So it is; smilin' like a new Spring mornin', when the sun leaps up a laughin' from its bed. Now this is happiness. This 'ere is the edge of God-land, my pretty. I think if I should go on and on a thousand years, a hundred thousand miles, my darlin',

I wouldn't get nearer to the Garden of Eden, that the preacher tells about, than I am now.

WIDOW. And this little home is Paradise to you, as it is to me, Sandy?

SANDY. Paradise! It is the best part of Paradise. It is the warm south side of Paradise, my darlin'. But there, I must put up the gold in the bag, and put it under the hearthstone for baby. [*Cleaning gold.*]

WIDOW. If we only had plenty of it, Sandy.

SANDY. My pretty, is there anything you want?

WIDOW. No, Sandy. Not that I really want.

SANDY. But what is it, my pretty? Now, come, there's a cloud over your face. Don't, my darlin', don't. This is Paradise; and the new preacher tells us that never a cloud or a rude wind crossed the Garden of Eden. Yonder are our walls; the white watch towers of the Sierras, keeping eternal guard over *our* Garden of Eden here in the heart of the Sierras. Now, what is it?

WIDOW. Why, nothing at all, Sandy. Only I was thinking this morning that if we had plenty of gold, a great, great plenty, Sandy; so that you had so much, you might never have to work so hard any more, that,—that—

SANDY. Well, my pretty? O, I see. You would give it to my old pard, the Parson. That's right; that's good. He's goin' away and will need it. I'll make him take this—

WIDOW. No, no, Sandy. He is not going. He is mad, desperate; and will do you harm if you go near him. Do not speak to him. Do not go near him.

SANDY. Well, I won't then, if he's mad with me, my pretty. No sir'ee. And I'll buckle on a bull-dog, too. [*Buckles on and tapping pistol.*] Bark at him, boy. Bark at him. Bite him if he bothers us. But I say, what is this you want with gold? Take all there is. Take it, my pretty, and do as you please with it. Is it Washee Washee that wants to bring out some more of his seventy cousins? Or is it the old man that got washed through the ground sluice? No; I won't ask you; take it. For what do I want with it but to please you? What good is all the gold in the Sierras if you are not satisfied and happy?

WIDOW. No! Take it back, Sandy; you have worked too hard for this, for me to give it away to poor little—[*Shouts*, WIDOW *to window.*] Why, what can that be, Sandy?

SANDY. Is it the Parson, my pretty?

WIDOW. Why, no, it's Billy Piper! And the boys howling and running after him! Oh, Sandy!

Enter BILLY, *breathless*

BILLY [*behind* SANDY; *enter mob*]. Sandy! Sandy! They have run me out of my cabin. They threaten to kill me.

SANDY. Run him out of his cabin?

TIM. Yes, and we'll hang him to the nearest tree!

SANDY. Now hold up, Tim! And tell me what's he done? And what all you men are runnin' after a boy like that for?

ALL. Bah!

JUDGE. A boy like that! And you a family man?

TIM. Them Danites was seen a sneakin' about his cabin only ten minutes ago. And that's why I say run him out.

JUDGE. Yes, I say git.

ALL. Yes, run him out!

CAPT. TOMMY. Too many on one, Bunker. I'm goin' in for the bottom dog, and society can just go to the devil. [*Throws off bonnet and rolls up sleeves.*]

JUDGE. Now, my Capt. Tommy, just think what society—

CAPT. TOMMY. Shut up! You bald-headed old jackass! I'm just goin' in on this fight, bet your life.

BUNKERHILL. Yes; we're all gettin' too dern'd respectable, anyhow. [*Throws hat.*]

WIDOW. Sandy, Sandy, stand by Billy.

ALL. He's a Danite!

SANDY. Stand back! I don't care what he is, or what he has done. He has come to me for protection. Why, if the meanest Digger Injin runs to another Injin for protection, won't he protect him? Well, now, this boy is as safe here as if he were my own kid.

BILLY. O, thank you, Sandy! Thank you with all my poor broken heart. But it won't be for long, Sandy. It won't be for long, and then you shall know all. She will tell you all. [*Exit.*

SANDY. She! She will tell me all? Why this mystery? Why this—

WIDOW. Sandy, what do you mean? Can you not trust your wife?

SANDY. I *can* trust you. I *do* and I *will* to the end of my life and of yours.

JUDGE. That's right. Family man myself; trust your wife. Now you see, Sandy, the boys been askin' me to make a sort of explanation of this 'ere intrudin' into your house like this 'ere. You see, Sandy, we was makin' up a purse for—for your family. And as the boys had never seed a baby, and—and as I—as we wanted to see how they look, we had concluded to call *en masse*. But just as we was a comin' down the trail we seed two Danites skulkin' about Billy Piper's cabin. And on the spur the boys went for him. But we brought the purse all the same, and here it is. [*Purse to* TIM.]

TIM. As the pardner of—of my pardner. I—I have been appointed a committee of this 'ere delegation to deliver this 'ere dust and make the speech for the occasion. Widder—[*Breaks down.*]

JUDGE [*pushing himself forward*]. Widder, in—in this—glorious climate of California—[*Breaks down.*]

TIM. Widder, this 'ere bag of gold what you now behold; this purse of pure bright gold, dug from out the—the Sierras. This purse of gold, Widder, is—is—is—yourn.

WIDOW. Mine, mine? All mine to do what I will with it?

TIM. Yourn, Widder, all yourn. Yourn to git up and git, out of this hole in the ground, to go back to the States and live like a Christian, as you are, and git away from all that's bad here in this hole in the ground, like a wild beast in a carawan.

ALL. Bully for Tim!

JUDGE. And now let the boys see your family, Sandy.

SANDY. Here, Washee Washee, give *it* to Mrs. Sandy and set up the bottles for the boys. [WASHEE, *who has been feeding baby by fire, with bottle and spoon, gives baby, bottles, etc.* WIDOW *sits.*]

ALL. Oh! Oh! what is that? The little cuss!

TIM. Little thing to make sich a big row, eh, Sandy?

WASHEE. He judgee babee, baldee headee. He no Sandee.

TIM. You speak to the boys, Judge; that effort of mine exhausted me.

[JUDGE, *attitude for speech; to table, drinks, and again striking attitude; drinks again.*]

JUDGE. Gentlemen of—of the committee! Fellow citizens, this, what you now behold is—is—[*Stops and* WIDOW *whispers in ear.*] This which you now behold before you is—is an—an infant. The first white born baby citizen ever born in these Sierras. The first, but not the—the—[CAPT. TOMMY *stops him.*] Feller citizens, this little infant sleeping here in its mother's arms, with the mighty snow-peaks of the Sierras about us; this innocent little sleepin' infant, which has been born to us here, gentlemen, shows us that—well, in fact, shows us—shows us what can be done in this glorious climate of California. [*All shout and file past, and look at baby.*]

TIM [*going*]. Well, come, boys, I've got a family myself and must be lookin' after my mine. [*Exit. Re-enter.*] Sandy! Sandy! Heel yourself! The Parson! The Parson with his bull pups—shootin' irons.

WIDOW. Oh, Sandy! Sandy!

SANDY [*hand on pistol*]. Stand back, boys, and let him come. Quiet, quiet, my girl.

PARSON *enters, hand behind; down, and walks quickly towards* SANDY; SANDY *raises pistol;* PARSON, *after emotion*

PARSON. I've been a waitin' to see you, Sandy, a waitin' a long time.

SANDY. Stop!

PARSON. Sandy, I'm goin' away from here. I can't stand it any longer. Your cabin here will be too small now, so I want you to promise me to take care of the parsonage till I come back.

SANDY. The parsonage?

PARSON. Yes, that's what the boys call my cabin. The parsonage. You'll move in there, at once. It's full of good things for winter. You'll take my cabin, and all that's there in it, I say you'll take it at once. Promise me that. [*Handing key.*] There's the key. Now say you will.

SANDY. Yes, I will.

PARSON. It was your luck, Sandy, to git her. Good-bye, old pard. Widder—I—what! You shake hands with me, the poor, old, played out Parson, after I broke my word with you! Widder! God bless you! Yes, Yes! God bless you both! [*Exit.*

SANDY. Poor, honest old Parson. Thar's many a worse man than he in mighty high places, boys.

TIM [*at door looking up*]. Yes, Sandy, and he is climbing for a high place now.

SANDY. What! Gone already! And it's dark and snowin'.

TIM. Started up the steep mountain right here. A climbin' and climbin' right straight up the mountain; as if he was a climbin' for the mornin' star.

SANDY. And may he reach it, and find rest at last, Tim.

ALL. And find rest at last.

TIM. But Sandy, you must move into the parsonage. Yes, you must. You see, you promised it. And then it takes a pretty big cabin to hold a pretty small baby. [*All laugh and gather around table and drink.*]

JUDGE. Well, one more boys, to—to—

TIM. To *it*. But come, boys, it's gettin' dark. [*All drink and exit.*

WIDOW. My baby! What a name, Sandy. IT!

SANDY. Poor, poor old Parson. It's a hard world on some of us, Widder.

WIDOW. It *is* hard on some, those who cannot work and are all the time persecuted and misunderstood. Now, Sandy, dear, do you know who I am going to give that gold to which the miners gave me just now? Come, guess. Can't you guess, Sandy, dear?

SANDY. Why, no, Widder. I can't guess. To who?

WIDOW. Why, to Billy Piper.

SANDY [*starting*]. To Billy Piper! No, no, not to him. You know not what you say. You know not what you ask of me to bear. You know not what you are asking me to bear, my wife. That boy? Why, now that he is once out of my cabin I will kill him as I would a rattlesnake wherever I can find him.

Enter TIM, *running and breathless*

TIM. Sandy! Sandy! The Danites! Your gun, Sandy! The two Danites have just left Billy Piper's cabin, their dark lanterns in their hands and are coming this way through the chapparal. Quick, your gun! Billy's in with them.

SANDY [*reaching gun*]. Billy Piper in with them! Danite or devil, this shall be the end of him.

WIDOW. Sandy, you will not, you *shall* not harm him. You shall not leave this cabin till you promise you will not harm him. See, Sandy, see, on my knees I beg of you. Never before on my knees to aught but my maker, Sandy, yet you see me here now on my knees to you.

SANDY. You take from me my life and my honor.

WIDOW. Sandy, Sandy! Do not be so blind. It is to save your soul.

SANDY. What!

WIDOW. It is to save your soul from the stain of innocent blood. Will you not believe her whom you promised to trust to the end of your life, and of hers?

SANDY. Yes, yes! I *can*, and I *do* trust you. I will not harm him.

WIDOW. O brave, generous Sandy. But I ask more still. Promise me that you will protect him. Yes, protect him as you would protect me with this strong right arm, Sandy.

SANDY. Why, Widder, I—

WIDOW. O Sandy, promise me, promise me. I feel that something dark and dreadful is about to happen. I see him lying dead in his innocent blood with no one to pity, to pray for, or to understand. Oh, promise me, Sandy, that whatever happens, you will be his friend and defender to the end.

SANDY. I promise.

WIDOW. Swear it.

SANDY. I swear it. [*Exit with* TIM.

WIDOW. The Danites here, and on his track! Oh, this is too dreadful to believe. [*Noises.*] What is that? It may be poor Billy now trying to find his way to my door, in the dark and cold. I will go find him, help him, save him. [*Snatches up candle.*] Lie still, my baby. [*Exit hastily.*

Enter BILLY, *cold and snow*

BILLY. It is a fit night for the bloody deeds of the Danites. But I must not stay here.

Where can she be! I must see her, and then fly, fly, fly! [*Sees cradle.*] Oh she's not far off. [*Kneels by cradle.*]

Enter WIDOW. *Very dark stage*

WIDOW. Why, how dark it has grown! The wind has blown out my candle, too. I left some matches here somewhere. [*Feels about, comes to cradle and finds* BILLY.] Billy! You here! But Sandy must not see you here now. Quick! hide here; I hear some one. [*Hides* BILLY *behind curtain, and down stage. Door opens softly.*]

Danites enter and come stealthily down stage

HICKMAN. I saw her enter at that door, not a minute since. She *must* be here. [*Sees* WIDOW.] Ah, there! [HICKMAN *conceals lantern; advances on* WIDOW *from behind with knife and strikes her; then child.* WIDOW *screams and dies as crowd rushes in. Danites exit unseen.* SANDY *and* CAPT. TOMMY *bend over* WIDOW.]

CAPT. TOMMY. She is dead! Murdered in cold blood!

SANDY. Dead! My wife dead! Oh, has the sun gone down forever? Dead? Dead?

TIM. Yes! [*Pointing to* BILLY.] And there is her murderer.

JUDGE. Hang him to the cabin loft.

ALL. Hang him! Hang him! Hang him!

SANDY. No, you *shall not* hang him. [*Springs between as they attempt to seize* BILLY.] I promised that poor, poor, dead woman there to defend this boy, and I'll *do* it, or die right here.

CURTAIN

ACT IV

SCENE. *Old mining camp. Moss-grown cabin. Set tree. Sunrise on the Sierras. Lapse of three years.*

Enter LIMBER TIM, *with* JUDGE, *older and better dressed*

TIM. Warn't down to the saloon last night and don't know the news, eh?

JUDGE. No, no. Since I've come to be a family man, I'm sort of exclusive; got to set an example for my family. But what's this news?

TIM. The Parson's back.

JUDGE. What! Him that loved the widder so? No! Impossible! Why, he went away North to Frazer River; got smashed up in a mine there, I hear; washed through a flume and his limbs all broke up till he had as many joints as a sea crab. O, no, he can't never get back here.

TIM. But he *is* back. And the sorriest wreck, too, that ever you seed, I reckon. Ought to have seed him and Sandy meet. Cried like babies, both on 'em. Come back here to be buried up on the hill there, he says.

JUDGE. Well, well, well! The Parson wasn't bad, Tim; he was about the best of the old boys of forty-nine, 'ceptin' always Sandy. And Sandy, after the murder of the widder and his kid—well, he's all broke up, body and mind. Spec' he's 'bout as near gone up the flume as the Parson is. But I must get round and see how Billy Piper is this mornin'. The school master, what's boardin' 'round, came home by his cabin here, and didn't see him at all last night; but Tim, he seed a black cat a sittin' in the door a washin' of its face. It's a bad sign when you see a black cat, Capt. Tommy, my wife, Missus Judge, says. Guess that boy's pretty sick. [*Going.*]

TIM [*aside*]. That *boy*. 'Pears to me that varmint won't never grow to be a man. And he twists *his* wife and my wife right around his cussed little fingers, and makes 'em look after him. Well, Judge can look after him, cussed if I will. [*To* JUDGE.] O, I say, Judge; there was two others came to camp last night, too.

JUDGE. Two others? Who?

TIM. Don't know 'zactly. Quartz speculators, they say: Mormon elders, I say.

JUDGE. Mormon elders! Bet a dog skin they're Danites. But so long; must look after Billy and get back to my family. [*Going, meets* HICKMAN *and* CARTER *disguised. They shake hands and converse.*]

TIM [*solus*]. Hello! Here's them quartz speculators now, and Judge shakin' hands and jist a talkin'. 'Spec he's tryin' to impress them with the glorious climate of California. Guess I'll go back down to the "howlin' wilderness." Judge will be powerful dry time *he* gets there, if he keeps on talkin' like that. [*Exit.*

HICKMAN [*coming down stage*]. And so you are a family man and your wife was one of the first families of the Sierras?

JUDGE. Family man; yes, sir; and my wife is one of the very first families. The very first. That is, she and Mrs. Limber Tim. Mr. Limber Tim's member of the Legislature now, wife, family name Bunkerhill, of the Bunkerhills of Boston. Yes, my wife and his wife, too, trace family clean back to Boston, sir. Yes, proud to say I'm a family man, sir.

HICKMAN. But this widow the miners spoke of as one of the first settlers? She who came as a sort of missionary. She here yet?

JUDGE. Dead. Buried up yonder, sir, with her baby. First baby born in the Sierras, sir.

HICKMAN. Dead, eh? Fever? Natural death, or accident?

JUDGE. No, sir! Neither natural death nor accident. No, sir! But murder! Why, that was the pitifullest thing; and it was the meanest murder that ever happened, I reckon. The boys at first thought it might be Sandy; for he was angry because of Billy Piper, that night. And then the boys thought it might be Billy, because;—well, because they didn't like him, never did, and never will, I guess. But when they came to examine Sandy, there was no blood on the knife he had in his belt. And, as to Billy, well, he had no knife at all.

CARTER. Why, we heard about this last night.

JUDGE. Dare say; dare say; may be the miners talked about it last night. They don't forget it. You bet.

CARTER. Mother and child found murdered?

HICKMAN. And no trace of the murderers was ever found?

JUDGE. None. It's the queerest case that ever was, I reckon. For whatever beast or devil could murder a little baby like that, asleep and helpless? Why! Well, sir, since I've come to be a family man, sir—if I should ever find a man that murdered a baby—sir—as judge of this 'ere camp, I'd hang him first and try him afterwards.

HICKMAN. Yes, yes. That's all right. But this boy Billy; he here still?

JUDGE. There's his cabin. Same old cabin been in for years; the same one the Danites killed three fellers in. Pretty sick, too, I guess. Wife told me to drop in, see how he is. You'll excuse me. Must go in and see the boy and get back to my family.

[*Exit into cabin.*

HICKMAN [*to* CARTER]. That *boy* is Nancy Williams!

CARTER. Well, and if it is, she's dying, they say. Can't you wait till nature does the work for you?

HICKMAN. Though that boy should, by nature, die tomorrow, our duty is to slay today.

CARTER. You seem to thirst for blood. A wife and babe dead at our hands will cry for revenge yet. Make no more mistakes like that. If this should not be she—

HICKMAN. It *is* she! There shall be no second mistake. Look here. [*Takes out small Testament.*] Yesterday, I saw this boy's face, as he sat reading up yonder, by his mine; our eyes met as I stood over him. His lips trembled with fear, and his eyes fell. He remembered the time, on the Plains, years ago, when we were commissioned by the church to slay the last of the Williams'. I say that boy is the last of the family. I know it.

CARTER. Then, I say, you must do the murder yourself, if it is to be done on such slender evidence as your word.

HICKMAN. It is not to be done on slender evidence. Look here! Frightened, he let this fall and slunk away.

CARTER. A little, old Testament. Well?

HICKMAN. The boy was reading this as I appeared and spoke to him.

CARTER. Well, he might read something worse than a Testament.

HICKMAN. But, look here! On the fly leaf. Read this dim and faded dedication. "TO NANCY WILLIAMS, FROM HER AFFECTIONATE MOTHER, NANCY WILLIAMS, CARTHAGE, MISSOURI, 1850."

CARTER. Too true! Too true! He *must* die. But not here. Give him a chance to fly. It is not as safe as it was when we were here before. The Vigilantes!

HICKMAN. Ha! ha! I have thought of all that. The Vigilantes shall be for us. They will be made to accuse him of the widow's death. Did the Judge not say he is suspected?

CARTER. Yes, yes. Let them then accuse and hang him. But see, the door opens. He is coming from the cabin.

HICKMAN. I'll back till that man is gone, and you go stir up the Vigilantes. Tell them he murdered the widow and her child. I'll console him with this. [*Lifts Testament. Exit* CARTER. *Enter* BILLY *from cabin, supported by* JUDGE, *who seats him by the door.* HICKMAN *up stage, behind tree.*]

JUDGE. Now don't break up here, just as the birds begin to sing, and the leaves come out. I'll send my family 'round to cheer you.

BILLY. You are so kind. Do send her; and the children, too. And please, won't you let them stay? Let them stay all day. Yes, and all night. O, all the time, always.

JUDGE. Why, now, don't tremble like that. I'll—I'll send my family 'round. Why, it's the sweetest day that ever was in this glorious climate of California. [*Aside.*] O, I can't bear to see a body cry. I'll go and send 'round my family. [*Going.*]

BILLY. And you won't be long? You won't leave me long? You will not?

JUDGE. Why, no, Billy. I'll send my family right 'round.

BILLY. And Sandy. You will tell Sandy to come, will you not? I have kept away from him, and he from me, all this time; ever since she, and—and the baby died. But, now you will bring him. For I feel that the sands of my life are almost run. My feet touch the dark waters of death. I hear the ocean of Eternity before me.

JUDGE [*takes out handkerchief and going*]. Confound it! This bright sun on the snow hurts my eyes.

HICKMAN [*coming from behind tree, and speaking to* JUDGE *aside*]. Ah, going? I've been thinking, Judge, about that murder of the widow. A very remarkable case. And do you know, I have a theory? Yes. It's that boy. No, don't start. What's the matter with him now? Conscience! Conscience stricken! Of course it's very sad. The idea is not mine. I got it from the miners last night. If the boy wasn't sick, they'd *hang* him now. As for Sandy, poor man, he is certain the boy did it. My friend has gone down to lay his opinion before the camp. For my part, I am very sorry for the boy.

JUDGE. Well, now, 'tween you and me, I think —[*Aside.*] But if my family, Capt. Tommy, was to hear me—O Lord! [*To* HICKMAN.] But I'll go and send 'round my family.

HICKMAN. Yes. Meantime, while you are gone, I will offer him consolation. [*Exit* JUDGE. HICKMAN *approaches* BILLY *from behind, and taps shoulder.*] Beg pardon, but is this yours? A little Testament I picked up where you sat reading yesterday. Is it yours?

BILLY. Yes, yes. Oh, thank you. It is mine; given me by my mother—

HICKMAN. Yes. I thought it was yours; I saw your name on the fly leaf. No mistake about it, I suppose? That is your name!

BILLY [*looks up and sees face; starts*]. No, no, no! Not my name. No, no, no!

HICKMAN. Well, I think it is yours, and you had better keep it; and read it, too. You will not live long. [*Aside and going.*] Condemned out of your own mouth! Now to make them believe that this is the murderer, and the last seed of this cursed tree is uprooted. [*Exit.*

BILLY [*rising, and wildly*]. At last! My time has come at last! Over her grave they have reached me at last; and it no longer lifts between me and a dreadful death at these men's hands. Fly! Fly! But where? And how? [*Staggers and leans against cabin for support.*] I have no strength to fly! I have no heart or will. All, all, ends here! I must die here! Now! That knife! That knife that entered her heart, that pierced the baby's breast, dripping with its mother's blood! Oh! [*Falls at cabin door.*]

Enter PARSON, *dragging a leg, old and broken up.* BILLY *starts up and about to enter cabin*

BILLY. They come! They come! O, will not Sandy help me now?

PARSON. Billy Piper, no. Don't—don't go.

BILLY. Why, who are you? And what do you want here?

PARSON. Have a few years then made such a change in me?

BILLY. The Parson!

PARSON. Yes, the Parson. Come back to the Forks to die.

BILLY. To die?

PARSON. Yes. To die, and lay my bones by the side of hers, up yonder on the hill.

BILLY. And you loved her so?

PARSON [*half falls to seat on log*]. Loved her so? Can't you understand, that when a man like me loves, he loves but once, and but one thing in all this world?

BILLY. O, yes, I understand. For I, too, loved her, Parson.

PARSON [*starting up, and crosses*]. Yes, you loved her, too. But how? To put her to shame; to make her the mockery and shame of the camp; to hide away in her cabin like a spotted house-snake; to creep there like a reptile warmed to life by her hearth-stone in winter, and then sting her to death after she warmed you into life.

BILLY. And do you think I ever harmed her?

PARSON. Ever harmed her? Ever harmed her? She is dead and beyond the reach of word or deed. A few more days and I shall meet her. But here, standing here on the edge of the dark river, I tell you, you murdered her.

BILLY. I? Great heavens! What do you mean!

PARSON. I mean what they say down there, now, this morning. Yes, they are saying it now. No, don't start, or run away. I am powerless to harm or to help now. But I, when I heard that, that you murdered her that night, I hobbled up here; I wanted this revenge before they came. I wanted to see you, to tell you that while I gave her all I had, and climbed that mountain in the storm, and went forth to begin life over, a broken man, you stayed here, a Danite, to take, first, her good name, and then her life, her baby's life, and Sandy's life, and now my life, too.

BILLY [*starts, staggers forward, lifts hand with Testament*]. Parson, hear me! And look in my face! Do you not see the dark shadow of the Angel's wings that are to waft my soul away? Oh, I, too, am sadly broken. And today, tonight, maybe this very hour, from somewhere, a hand will strike to lay me low in death. We stand beside the dark river together.

PARSON. Why, boy, you tremble. Your hand is cold and helpless. And you are not guilty?

BILLY. Guilty? Do you see this? The last, the only gift of my poor murdered mother, who died by the Danites' hands.

PARSON. Why, you! You not a Danite? Then swear by the book; swear by the book that you never did her harm by word or deed.

BILLY [*falling on knees and lifting book*]. By the holy book and by my mother's memory, I swear!

PARSON. Why, what is this? The boy tells the truth! The boy is honest and true. Some devilish work is against him, and I will stand by him. I'll stand by you, boy. You are true as the stars in heaven. I know it—I know it. I'll meet them. I'll face and fight them all, all as I did—[*Half falls.*] no, no, not as I did. I'm on the down grade and can't reach the brake. But stand up, boy, and be strong. You are young yet, and the world is all before you. And while I live, you'll find a friend in me. Yes, in the old Parson, to the last drop of blood. Yes, yes. I'll die right here by your side when they come. Don't you be skeered, Billy. When they come, I'll come, too, and be your friend to the last bone and muscle in the old Parson's body. [*Leads* BILLY *to seat on log by cabin, and exit.*]

BILLY. A friend at last! O, then there *is* hope. I may at last escape from this and again be strong and well. O, thank Heaven for one friend at least. But I am so afraid!

Enter HICKMAN *and* CARTER

HICKMAN. You shall see and be satisfied. The Vigilantes are gathering and will be here. We have only to say that he has confessed the murder to us, and the work is done. [*Crosses, taps* BILLY *on shoulder.*] I have come back to console you. We will talk over the holy little book, which your mother gave you before she died. You see you will not live long. [*Half exposes knife.*]

BILLY. No, no, no! Not with the knife! No! Oh, no, no. See! I am but a woman, a poor weak girl.

HICKMAN [*to* CARTER]. *You* see. [*To* BILLY.]

Yes, we have come to offer you the consolation of religion.

BILLY. My God! My God! Why is this cup given me to drink?

CARTER. Here! Some one comes! [*Pulls* HICKMAN *aside.*] Quick. [*Both exit.*

Enter SANDY

SANDY. Why, Billy? Don't you know me? It's been a long time, Billy; but there's my hand. What! Got the fever, Billy?

BILLY. O, Sandy, Sandy! I'm so glad you have come at last, for my time to die has come.

SANDY. No, no. Now you look here. I'm goin' to take care of you after this, whether the camp likes it or not. Yes, I will; and just 'cause they make it too hard on you. I'll come to your cabin and stay right here.

BILLY. No, Sandy. But let the school children come, and not be frightened and run away. Let some one stay with me all the time. O, please, all the time, Sandy.

SANDY. I will stay with you all the time. Yes, I will. Why not? What else am I fit for now?

BILLY. No, Sandy, no. But when it's all, all over, Sandy, I want to be laid by her side, Sandy. She was so good to me; so unselfish; pure as the lily's inmost leaf; white and high as yonder snowy mountains in their crown of clouds. Yes, by her side. Promise me that, Sandy; by her side.

SANDY [*aside*]. By her side! [*Aloud.*] Well, yes. Yes, Billy, by her side.

BILLY. And, Sandy, you will set up a little granite stone, and you will place on that stone the name that you find in this book.

SANDY. The name I find in that book?

BILLY. Promise me. Trust me and promise me. It is a little thing I ask and the last, the last I shall ever ask of any one. A little stone by your own hand, and the name you find here, Sandy. Promise! O, promise me this last, last request. No, don't open the book now; don't look at the book now; but promise me.

SANDY. I promise.

BILLY. O, thank you; thank you. Why, what is that! O, Sandy, I tremble at every sound. It may be that it is death calling me now. Help me! Help!

Enter CAPT. TOMMY *and* BUNKERHILL, *running, and out of breath*

CAPT. TOMMY. Sandy! Sandy! [*Twisting up hair.*] Now, where's that bald-headed old mule of mine?

SANDY. Why, what's up in the Forks, now?

BUNKERHILL. What's up? Why, them strangers have called out the Vigilantes. They say that this boy, Billy Piper, has confessed he killed her; yes, her and the baby.

SANDY. Then *I'll* kill him. [*About to strike.*]

CAPT. TOMMY [*catching him*]. You're a fool! Come here! That boy is—well, that boy is—is—well, if you don't stand up and fight for him—O, a man never has no sense, nohow. [BUNKERHILL *and she roll up sleeves.*]

BUNKERHILL [*talking off*]. If you want to pitch in, just pitch into us.

SANDY. Well, if he's squar'.

CAPT. TOMMY. Squar'! In there, Billy. [*Pushes him into cabin and closes door.*] You just win this fight and swing them Danites! Yes, Danites! Nobody dares say it but me and Bunkerhill. I tell you they are Danites. Shoo, here they come!

Enter JUDGE, *puffing and blowing, and mopping face. Shouts heard.* CAPT. TOMMY *catches him and spins him round*

JUDGE. A hot mornin' for the glorious climate of—

CAPT. TOMMY. Now you fight on the right side, you old simpleton, or it'll be hotter. And I'll teach you suthin' about the glorious climate of California you never heard of before.

BUNKERHILL. And there's Tim a leadin' of the Vigilantes! [*Enter* TIM.] Here! [*Wheels him in place by* SANDY *and* JUDGE.] There's your place.

Enter mob of miners, led by HICKMAN *and* CARTER

TIM. But Billy's got to go, Bunker.

MINERS. Yes, run him out!

PARSON [*entering and drawing pistol*]. What's that? You run out Billy Piper? Poor, sickly little Billy, that never gets any bigger and never has a beard? Look here! When you run him out, you do it right here over my bones. [*Pistol at face of* HICKMAN.]

HICKMAN. But he is a murderer. He has confessed to us both that it was he who murdered that poor wife and babe. He is a murderer and must die.

PARSON. That voice! That face! Here! Didn't I tell you we should meet again? And didn't I tell you I should know you when we met? [*Tears off beard disguise from* HICKMAN'S *face.*] These are the men I saw at her cabin. These are the men that murdered her. Danites! Danites! Danites! Boys, what shall be their sentence?

Enter WASHEE WASHEE *brandishing razor*

JUDGE [*draws long pistol*]. Well, as I am the only Judge in this part of this glorious climate of California, I pronounce them guilty and sentence them to die with their boots on.

ALL. Hang them! Hang them! [HICKMAN *and* CARTER *are seized and hurried off.*]

CAPT. TOMMY. Well, I guess the Judge will look after them. And Bunker, we better look after Billy. Sandy, you stay here; we may need you. Billy's pretty sick. But he won't be half so sick, when they're dancin' in the air.

SANDY. I'll stop right here, and if I can help poor Billy, say so.

BUNKERHILL. You're right. Billy's the best friend you ever had. [*Exit with* CAPT. TOMMY *into cabin. Enter* TIM *and* JUDGE, *followed by miners.*]

TIM. Well, they're on their way, Sandy.

SANDY. To San Francisco?

JUDGE. To Kingdom Come!

SANDY. Good, good! Served 'em right. True, it don't bring her and the baby back to us boys: but we can be kind to Billy now. Poor little Billy. We've been mighty hard on him.

TIM. Well, I feel kind o' cheap about it, too. Let's go in and cheer him up.

JUDGE. And get him out in this glorious— [*About to lead into cabin. Is met by* CAPT. TOMMY.]

CAPT. TOMMY. Stop! Only women must enter that cabin now. For it is a woman who has lived there all these years. Billy Piper is no more.

ALL. What, dead?

BUNKERHILL [*leading out* BILLY *in woman's dress*]. Yes, Billy Piper is dead. But Nancy Williams lives!

ALL. Nancy Williams!

PARSON. Shake hands! Shake hands with the old Parson. [*Takes hand, shakes and kisses it.*] And Sandy, old pard, I know where this little hand, like a fluttered bird, wants to fly to. [*Gives hand to* SANDY.]

SANDY. And you give me your hand, to—to—to—keep always?

BILLY. To keep as the stars keep place in heaven, Sandy.

MINERS [*forward; hats in hand*]. We all begs your pardon, Miss.

SANDY. Yes, we all do. We don't mean bad; but it's a rough country, and we're rough, and we've not been good to you. But there is an old and beautiful story in the Bible— [*To audience.*]—You've all heard it before you learned to read, I reckon. It is of that other Eden. There the living God met man face to face, communed with him every day in his own form. And yet that man fell. Well, now, we don't claim to be better than they were in Eden, even in the heart ot the Sierras.

CURTAIN

NOTE: The Danites were members of a secret society founded originally in 1836 for the alleged purpose of combating the enemies of the Mormon Church. All the atrocities charged against the Mormons were attributed to the activities of this organization. The Mormons have generally asserted that no such organization ever had an existence in connection with their church.

Joaquin Miller himself made the following comment on the subject of his play: "The Mormons are not murderers. Some of their fanatics led the Mountain Meadows Massacre, but they were no worse and certainly not better than the Missouri mob that butchered Joseph Smith and his brother Hiram, founders of the Mormon Church."

See also Kelly, C., and Birney, H., *Holy Murder*. New York: 1934.

THE HENRIETTA

By Bronson Howard

BRONSON HOWARD

[1842–1908]

Bronson Crocker Howard has been referred to as the first professional dramatist in America to give his whole time to the writing of plays; he has also been credited with having initiated modern drama. There can be no doubt that his firmly-knit, fresh, vigorous plays, his solid, comprehensive thinking in the field of dramatic theory, and his vision in establishing a "school" of playwrights placed him in a commanding position in our theatre at the turn of the century. He was born October 7, 1842, in Detroit, where he later engaged in newspaper work and undertook the writing of his first play, *Fantine*. This was a dramatic trifle which saw production in Detroit. He subsequently moved to New York where he continued his newspaper and dramatic writing. In common with other playwrights he wrote several pieces which were rejected by producers, but he finally won recognition with his *Saratoga*, a brisk farce of contemporary manners, produced by Augustin Daly in 1870. The play had a long run in this country and was produced in England under the title, *Brighton*, and in Germany as *Seine Erste und Einzige Liebe*.

After *Diamonds* in 1872, Howard produced in Chicago *Lilian's Last Love* (1873), the theme of which concerns the danger in marrying for duty instead of love. This play is of especial interest because it is the first phase in a threefold revision, trenchantly analyzed in Howard's *Autobiography of a Play*.[1] The second stage of the play was produced as *The Banker's Daughter* in New York, September 30, 1878, and subsequently reached the London stage as *The Old Love and the New*. In his *Autobiography of a Play* Howard shows clearly how each version of the play was deliberately changed to meet certain theatrical conditions; one would have to read the whole treatise to gain a full and accurate understanding of each change and the motive underlying it, but in the main it may be noted that the death of the virtuous mother in the first version was replaced in the second by the killing of the lover in a duel, for "In England and America, the death of a pure woman on the stage is not 'satisfactory,' except when the play rises to the dignity of tragedy." [2] The next alteration of the play was made with British views of morality in mind. We have in the instance of this play's alterations an illustration of Howard's theory that the play, being a social art, should

[1] *The Autobiography of a Play*. Dramatic Museum of Columbia University. New York: 1914. Introduction by Augustus Thomas.

[2] *Ibid.* Quoted by permission of Columbia University Press.

be constructed with reference to the public's taste: "a play must be, in one way or another, 'satisfactory' to the audience."

Old Love Letters (a one-act play, 1878), *Wives* (1879), and the farcical *Fun in a Green Room* (1882) were followed by the important society play *Young Mrs. Winthrop*, which opened October 9, 1882. In this play Howard employed the theme of business and its tragic inroads upon family life, a theme he was to treat again in *The Henrietta* (1887). Between these two latter plays intervened two others, *One of Our Girls* and *Met by Chance*, both portraying international contrasts; such plays as these confirm William Archer's opinion that "Mr. Bronson Howard may be said to occupy a place among the English dramatists [Archer claimed Howard for England] similar to that occupied by Mr. Henry James among the English novelists." [1] In 1888–89 appeared one of Howard's finest plays, *Shenandoah*, dealing faithfully and vividly with the social schisms attendant upon the Civil War.

Aristocracy (1892) exposes the hunting of American heiresses by unscrupulous titled foreigners (cf. *Fashion*); *Peter Stuyvesant*, written in collaboration with Brander Matthews, pictures the Dutch governor in the role of an unsuccessful matchmaker; and *Kate*, Howard's last play (1906), is a comedy concerning an English country housewife.

In an article entitled "The American Drama" [2] Howard traces the growth of a school of dramatists (which he organized in 1891 as the American Dramatists Club); he points out the need of wise dramatic criticism; and he stresses the importance of heeding public taste. His activities in behalf of his fellow dramatists, as well as in the writing of plays, rendered his death in 1908 the occasion for widespread mourning.[3]

Howard's thinking on the subject of the drama led him to the conclusion that each country had its own master theme: in England it was caste, in France marital infidelity, and in America business. It is striking as artistic theory, though perhaps not as social discovery, that as far back as 1882 Howard directly stated the theme which Howells made use of three years later (*The Rise of Silas Lapham*, 1885) and which is centrally involved in so much present-day literature.[4] Carrying his theory into practice, Howard treated this theme with skill, humor, and penetration in *The Henrietta;* and foreshadowing the evaluation placed upon the great American occupation by many present-day writers,[5] Howard reveals the flat disregard of ethics fundamental to the practice of "high finance." Vanalstyne,

[1] Archer, William, *English Dramatists of To-day*. London: 1882, pp. 209–219.

[2] *Sunday Magazine*, October 7, 1906. Reprinted in Moses's introduction to *Shenandoah* in his *Representative Plays by American Dramatists, 1856–1911*.

[3] The most valuable data and criticisms regarding Howard are to be found in *In Memoriam, Bronson Howard. Addresses Delivered at the Memorial Meeting, October 18, 1908*. New York: 1910.

[4] Lewis's *Babbitt*, O'Neill's *Marco Millions, The Great God Brown*, Barry's *You and I*, Elmer Rice's *The Adding Machine* are but a few titles.

[5] See, for example, James Truslow Adams's *Our Business Civilization*.

for whom business is "health, religion, friendship, love," moralizes with a twinkle in his eye as he reproves his son for speculating: "But that's gambling, my son. Sell an option on Nebraska and Montana; I'm going to water that stock tomorrow. Never gamble, my son; it isn't right." "'Truth crushed to earth will rise again.' I know exactly when to let her rise; that's all." The ramifications of "high finance" are far-reaching; business undermines friendships, it cuts ruthlessly across family ties. The father will cheat his son-in-law to regain the cost of the wedding present, but the daughter has already forestalled her father; the wife has "double-crossed" her husband, and it is the son's sole ambition to ruin his sire. Vanalstyne, Jr., will also betray his wife and turn the suspicion on his innocent brother, whose quiet acceptance of guilt secures for him a warm place in the hearts of the audience. The stress of big business is ruinous to health, it forces love to wait upon the ticker tape, and it renders impossible aesthetic appreciation (Vanalstyne buys pictures by the square inch; he knows the dimensions of a canvas, but not its title). The final thrust against Wall Street lies in the success which Bertie, who doesn't even know what a security is, has in determining the value of an investment by the simple process of flipping a coin into the air: "That is the intellectual process, father. It takes brain to deal at the Stock Exchange."[1] Howard's satire acquires a certain poignancy when one realizes that at times veteran traders have done just the opposite of what their best judgment told them to do. Howard may often sacrifice verisimilitude to drama, but none can deny either the theatrical effectiveness nor the underlying truth of the disastrous social toll taken by the Wall Street machine that "kills more men than dynamite."[2]

The clergy is not free from the taint of "high finance": on Sunday the Rector preaches against materialism and insists on one's obligations to distribute his wealth to the poor; on Monday the Rector is in Vanalstyne's office in search of advantageous "tips," and the Wall Street general is induced to observe that "the leading pillars of our church are also pillars of the Stock Exchange."[3] The Rector later withdraws his protestations of love when he learns the widow has lost her fortune.

In politics it is the old story, hardly discovered by Howard, that money is power; but Vanalstyne is a super-operator: he will not contribute to election expenses until after the candidate has got to Washington, and he will buy a whole legislature at a time.

The grasping figures of Vanalstyne and his son, though dramatically heightened, are copied from life; their ruthless philosophy is the product of an age in which the Darwinian theory of the survival of the fittest, in conjunction with

[1] Act IV, sc. 1, p. 453.
[2] Act III, sc. 1, p. 444.
[3] Act I, p. 417.

the nation's vast physical resources, opened the way for the business giant to acquire immense material power at the expense of his fellow men (who, on the plan of natural selection, were conveniently nearer mechanisms than men). In Twain's *The Gilded Age* (1873) Colonel Sellers realizes the enormous natural wealth of the country and becomes ardently desirous of great riches; in *The Octopus* (1901) Norris represents Trade, in the form of a railroad, attempting to seize the wealth that Agriculture produces; in *The Financier* (1912) and *The Titan* (1914) Dreiser portrays the super-businessman who can fearlessly exploit his victims because they are little more than puppets in a mechanistic universe. It is at such soulless commercial aggrandizement that Howard aims his well-turned shafts of satire; for, though he writes to entertain, he also invests his plays with that criticism of life which Arnold believes is essential to literature. Augustus Thomas observes this when he says: "There is always dramatic conflict between interesting characters, of course, but behind them is always the background of some considerable social tendency—some comprehensive generalization—that includes and explains them all." [1]

Several of Howard's dramatic theories have already been referred to, and the relationships between his thought and his practice can be seen when one considers the following generalizations in the light of a play such as *The Henrietta:* the interest of a play must be universal, not partial (this can be reconciled with Howard's concept of business as the American theme only by construing universal as national or by thinking of business as simply one type of livelihood); the play must be "satisfactory" to the audience: it must have a plot which will be accepted as inevitable; that which has no integral part in the plot must be eliminated; drama should be divorced from literature (but Howard's "sincerity of purpose and honesty of presentation" are qualities the play readily shares with literature and other works of art); drama should have an "ennobling influence." In the main, Howard achieves a fairly close inter-relation between his plays and his dramatic theories. It is interesting to note, incidentally, Howard's prophecy that "the next great revival of literature in the English language will be in the theatre." The force of this remark may be tested in the light of such writers as Shaw and O'Neill.

Brander Matthews speaks of *The Henrietta* as "vibratingly American" and predicts that "with its virility, its hearty humor, and its ingenuity of stagecraft, will last the longest" of Howard's plays. He further states: "There is imagination, and imagination of a high order, in that scene of *The Henrietta* where the stricken stock speculator dies alone in his chair while the indicator behind him ticks off

[1] Introduction to *The Autobiography of a Play*, p. 5. For important background material about this era see Beard, C. A. and Mary R., *The Rise of American Civilization*, 2 vols., New York, 1927; Regier, C. C., *The Era of the Muckrakers*, Chapel Hill, N. C., 1932; Schlesinger, A. M., and Fox, D. R., editors, *A History of American Life*, 12 vols., New York, 1927–

the death-watch."[1] The graphic powers of *Shenandoah* are likewise notable. Howard shows a keen sense of dramatic values in setting the love between Kerchival West of the North and Gertrude Ellingham of the South against the dispelling force of the civil upheaval which sundered friendships and obliged West Point classmates to fight opposite one another on the battlefield. And it is in the final outcome of Gertrude's conflict that one finds an indication of Howard's attitude toward the power of love when countered by the urge of patriotism. Other plays have their individual excellences, but for Brander Matthews it is *The Henrietta* "which remains today his finest work, the truest and the deepest."[2]

The present text of *The Henrietta* is based on that of the first edition, printed in 1901.

[1] *In Memoriam, Bronson Howard*, p. 25.

[2] *Ibid.*, p. 41.

CHARACTERS

Nicholas Vanalstyne, Old Nick in the Street
Dr. Parke Wainwright
Nicholas Vanalstyne, Jr.
Bertie Vanalstyne, his Brother, a Lamb
Lord Arthur Trelawney, Another
The Rev. Dr. Murray Hilton, a Shepherd

"It was to combat and expose such as these, no doubt, that laughter was made."—Vanity Fair.

Watson Flint, a Broker
Musgrave, an old Clerk
Mrs. Cornelia Opdyke, a Widow
Mrs. Rose Vanalstyne, Wife of Vanalstyne, Jr.
Agnes, her Sister, in love with Bertie
Lady Mary Trelawney, old Vanalstyne's Daughter

SYNOPSIS OF SCENERY

Act I.—Residence of Nicholas Vanalstyne, in New York. A Giant and a Lamb.
Act II.—The Drawing-room. A Packet of Letters. Henrietta.
Act III.—Private office of Watson Flint & Co., Stock Exchange Brokers, Wall Street, New York. Bulls, Bears and the Tiger. (An interval of 18 months.)
Act IV.—Vanalstyne's residence.

THE HENRIETTA

ACT I

SCENE.—*Residence of* NICHOLAS VANALSTYNE, *in New York. Private office. Bay-window at back, mantel and fire at right, desks. A telephone on wall of this apartment, near the door. Revolving chair at desk, right, concealed at rise of curtain by screen, which can afterwards be folded back towards the mantel. Heavy curtains across bay-window. All appointments very rich. Mantel and woodwork carved or inlaid. General tone of scene deep in color, to contrast with brilliancy of drawing-room in next act.* NICHOLAS VANALSTYNE, JR., *sitting at desk.*

Enter MUSGRAVE, *inventory in hand.* VANALSTYNE, JR., *is opening letters from a pile of correspondence; glancing at some and putting them aside, reading others. He is in rich dressing-jacket, his face rather pale and slightly sunken.* MUSGRAVE *is an elderly man; he is running up columns of figures in a business paper as the curtain rises.*

MUSGRAVE [*footing up the columns*]. Five; eight; fifty-three. [*Speaks to* VANALSTYNE, JR.] The whole amount is fifty-three millions, eight hundred and fifty thousand dollars, sir. [*Comes down, lays inventory on young* NICK's *desk.*]

VANALSTYNE, JR. [*consulting a memorandum*]. I forgot to give you the Delaware, Lackawanna and Western first mortgage bonds in the Chemical Bank. Put them in at two millions; and unencumbered real estate—say five millions.

MUSGRAVE. Yes, sir. [*Speaking aside as he proceeds.*] I'm certain there's another great operation under weigh. I wonder if it *is* the Henrietta Mining and Land Company. But, Lord bless me, I know about as much of what old Nicholas Vanalstyne is doing as the body-servant of a general does about the plan of campaign. [*The telephone bell sounds.* MUSGRAVE *goes to it, putting the tube to his ear.*] Hello! [*Listens, and then speaks into telephone.*] The order was for five thousand shares at one forty-seven and an eighth. What? [*Listens, and then speaks to* VANALSTYNE, JR.] Watson Flint & Co. wish to know if they shall fill your order for Chicago and Northwestern preferred. It's a quarter higher this morning.

VANALSTYNE, JR. Yes.

MUSGRAVE [*in telephone*]. Yes; buy. Eh? Evansville and Terre Haute? [*Listens.*] Oh! [*To* VANALSTYNE, JR.] About that ninety-five thousand dollars, sir, in—

VANALSTYNE, JR. I don't care to be worried about trifles like that this morning. Tell them to use their own judgment.

MUSGRAVE [*in telephone*]. Do as you think best about the smaller matters today. Good-by.

VANALSTYNE, JR. I'm not well, Musgrave. Kindly tell the servant to show Dr. Wainwright directly to this room when he calls.

MUSGRAVE. Yes, sir. Trifles! In over thirty years I have laid by a little more than six thousand dollars by rigid economy, and the Vanalstynes made half a million by one little turn in the market last Friday. [*Exit.*

VANALSTYNE, JR. What's this? [*Suddenly looking at a letter.*] Gertrude's handwriting! Addressed to my real name!—and here! [*Breaks it open, and reads.*] "This letter will surprise you; but not so much, nor so terribly, as it surprised *me*, to learn, for the first time, tonight, your true name; and—I can hardly write the words—the fact—that you—have—a—wife! *I* have been your wife, and I am the mother of your child; the blessing of Heaven upon our union was never sought; but how little I knew that the *curse* of Heaven was hanging over me so darkly!" [*He reads a moment longer in silence, then sets his teeth, folds the letter deliberately, and tearing it up with a determined motion, throws the letter in waste-paper basket at foot of desk.*] Curse the woman!

Enter MUSGRAVE

MUSGRAVE. I have finished the inventory, sir, and struck the balance. [*Giving him paper.*]

VANALSTYNE, JR. [*taking it*]. Musgrave, tell Watson Flint & Co. to buy me an option. [MUSGRAVE *makes notes.*]—Chicago, Santa Fé and California—buy three—at current rates—five thousand shares.

NICHOLAS VANALSTYNE *appears above the screen, New York Herald in his hand*

VANALSTYNE. Here, here, what the devil are you doing that for? [*Crosses, smoking cigar.*]

VANALSTYNE, JR. I'm amusing myself, father. I *must* have something to think about.

[MUSGRAVE *crosses, folds screen, and places it behind desk.*]

VANALSTYNE. But that's gambling, my son. Sell an option on Nebraska and Montana; I'm going to water that stock tomorrow. Never gamble, my son; it isn't right. Squeeze the shorts, that's business. While you're about it, I may as well have a little fun with the boys on the street myself. Make it ten thousand for each of us, Musgrave.

MUSGRAVE. Yes, sir! [*Exit, closing door.*

VANALSTYNE. I see by the paper this morning that the Wall Street lambs are buying Nebraska and Montana very freely. [*Returns and sits at desk. Reads.*] "Nicholas Vanalstyne, the greatest operator now in the street, says that it is only a question of time when this stock will be a sure dividend at eight per cent." Did I say time? That was a slip of the tongue. I meant *eternity*. [*Reads.*] "The room-traders, who threw over Louisville and Nashville, were completely fooled by the fact that 'old Nick' Vanalstyne had been telling them the honest truth." The boys on the Stock Exchange will never understand the strictly truthful principles on which I conduct my business affairs. I never made a big haul yet, except by telling the honest truth. I only lie between times. "Truth crushed to earth will rise again." I know exactly when to let her rise; that's all. When I'm lying, I let 'em rob each other. The plaintive wail that goes up from Wall Street, whenever I corner it, is a touching tribute to the sincerity of my character. "Damn old Vanalstyne!—he's been telling us the truth again."

VANALSTYNE, JR. Here is the inventory of our securities, available and unavailable. [*Rises and crosses to* OLD NICK *at desk, and returns immediately to his desk.*]

VANALSTYNE. Ah! [*Taking it.*] Hello! Forty-eight millions already out as collaterals; balance available only twenty-two millions. My son. [*Turns in chair, and looks at* YOUNG NICK.] Some other big fish is swimming in these waters, and there aren't any signs of where he is yet. Some great operator is going against us in this Henrietta mine deal. I have felt his hand at every move in the game, but I can't see him. He's working in the dark. I did think it was my old enemy, John Van Brunt; but our lawyers have got him in Chancery. Whoever it is, we've got to move very carefully; my balance to work on is getting narrow. I got this infernal Henrietta mine on a three-hundred-dollar bluff, in a friendly game of poker. I incorporated the game—I mean the mine—for twenty millions capital; bought the whole town, including two newspapers and an opera house, and all the railways, running in that direction, not to mention the branch lines and a steamship company, to say nothing of six million acres of public land grants. The Henrietta Railway and Mining Company now pervades and ramifies the entire country—from Ohio to California. It has become the financial focus of the solar system. I only had ace, high and a Jack; drew to a bob-tail flush; fifty-cent ante.

VANALSTYNE, JR. A few of these letters need your personal attention. [*Crosses to his father, giving him letters.* OLD NICK *takes the letters, looking them over.* YOUNG NICK *recrosses to his desk, sits and speaks half over his shoulder.*] Butler, at Omaha, writes that two more competing lines of railroad—

VANALSTYNE [*incidentally, as he is looking at letters*]. Tell him to buy them both.

VANALSTYNE, JR. The Legislature of Nevada—

VANALSTYNE. Buy that, too.

VANALSTYNE, JR. The new Constitution of the State—

VANALSTYNE. Tell our agents to have it amended at once—same as Missouri.

VANALSTYNE, JR. Holliston has been nominated for Congress in Kansas. Shall we contribute to his election expenses?

VANALSTYNE. No; wait till he gets to Washington. [*Looks at a letter.*] "Poughkeepsie Bridge Bill—five votes short." [*Turns in chair, looks over glasses to* YOUNG NICK.] Telegraph to Holbrook at Albany. [VANALSTYNE, JR., *makes notes.*] "Buy six more country members, and charge to my account." [*Looks at another letter.*] Schauspil, the art dealer, has a new painting by Meissonier. Write to him for me, Nick. Tell him I'll give him thirty dollars a square inch. There's six per cent. in Meissonier at that; no sounder stock in the market.

VANALSTYNE, JR. [*making a note*]. What's the subject of the painting?

VANALSTYNE [*looks at letter intently*]. Eighteen inches by twenty-four. Hello! Ha—ha—ha—ha! [*Looking at another letter.*] Bill Jarvis lost his entire fortune in our twist on the Street last Friday. Ha—ha—ha! Bill Jarvis is my dearest old schoolmate. Ha—ha—ha—ha! Jarvis and I were brought up together. Ha—ha—ha! We let him in for two hundred thousand dollars. Ha—ha—ha! I was always getting jokes on Bill. We must give the old boy a chance to start again. Write to him that my bank account is at his service, Nick. Ah! He'll make another fortune in a year, and—ha—ha—ha!—I'll get that, too! [*Enter* MUSGRAVE *going towards small desk; stops.*] Oh, Musgrave! make a note for me. [MUSGRAVE *comes with writing-pad.*] The widow of Robert W. Worth—[*Then to* VANALSTYNE, JR.] How much did we make out of him on the last deal?

VANALSTYNE, JR. About ninety thousand.

VANALSTYNE. I see the poor devil died yesterday. We'll make that good to his widow.

MUSGRAVE. Yes, sir; I'll remind you of it. A telegram just come, sir. [*Gives* VANALSTYNE *a telegram and sits at desk making a note.*]

VANALSTYNE. A cable from your sister Mary in London. [*Reads.*] "I am going to marry Lord Arthur Fitzroy Waldegrave Rawdon Trelawney."

VANALSTYNE, JR. Indeed! [YOUNG NICK *turns in chair in surprise.*]

VANALSTYNE. How many men do you understand she's going to marry?

VANALSTYNE, JR. The usual number, I suppose.

VANALSTYNE. Ah! All those names belong to the same man. Musgrave, cable. [*Dictates.*] "Miss Mary Vanalstyne, Hotel Metropole, London:—Draw on me for whatever it costs you." [*Throws despatch on desk and is opening letter.*] Who *is* Lord Arthur—continued in our next—Trelawney?

VANALSTYNE, JR. [*writing at desk, paying no attention*]. Fourth son of the Marquis of Dorchester.

VANALSTYNE. Father's rich, isn't he?

VANALSTYNE, JR. I believe so.

VANALSTYNE [*to* MUSGRAVE]. Add to that cable. [*Dictates.*] "Tell the Marquis I can let him have a block of Northern Pacific Common at twenty-nine." I'll land the old man for all my girl's wedding expenses. [*Looks at letter.*] From the Rev. Dr. Murray Hilton; another subscription, I suppose. [*Long pause.*] By thunder! Our pastor has dropped on the Henrietta Mine deal, and he wants to know if I can let him in. I *thought* he'd been more than usually anxious about my spiritual welfare lately. But how the deuce did he learn anything about the Henrietta Mine? We *must* let him in for a few thousands. If we don't, he'll give us away to the whole congregation; and the leading pillars of our church are also pillars of the Stock Exchange. [*Turns half to* MUSGRAVE.] Write to the Rev. Dr. Murray Hilton. [*Dictates.*] "Will meet you at Friday evening prayers." [*Pause.*] That'll do, Musgrave. [*Turns to desk. Exit* MUSGRAVE *to apartments, closing door.*]

VANALSTYNE, JR. By the way, Governor, Mrs. Cornelia Opdyke—

VANALSTYNE. Mrs. Opdyke! I'm interested. [*Rises.*]

VANALSTYNE, JR. Interested?

VANALSTYNE. What about her?

VANALSTYNE, JR. Her property has been invested in government bonds; and nearly the whole amount has been called in. Watson Flint & Co. are her agents, you know. They asked me yesterday if I could suggest anything in the way of re-investment. She has about three hundred thousand dollars.

VANALSTYNE. Tell Watson Flint I'll let her have the entire amount in Louisville and West Tennessee preferred at par.

VANALSTYNE, JR. [*turns sharply in chair*]. But that is your pet gilt-edged stock. It's a sure ten per cent. dividend.

VANALSTYNE. The Reverend Dr. Murray Hilton is after the widow.

VANALSTYNE, JR. What has that to do with—

VANALSTYNE. My dear son! [*Puts his finger to his nose, winking at* VANALSTYNE, JR., *looks around; goes, hums to himself an air. Punches* VANALSTYNE, JR., *in the ribs.*] Have you any objection to a young and pretty stepmother?

VANALSTYNE, JR. None in the least.

VANALSTYNE. I control that railroad absolutely, and I'm going to freeze out the parson. This is a little flyer on my own account. Let her have the stock. I am buying an option. The Reverend Dr. Murray Hilton thinks he's got the inside track by having the widow's soul in charge; but if I can get control of her fortune, his chances of securing her person are not flattering. [*Goes to desk.*] It may cost me a million dollars but I'll get that [*Smacks lips.*] widow. [*Sits at desk.*]

VANALSTYNE, JR. Well, my dear father— [*Laughing slightly.*]—as I said before, I haven't the slightest objection to a young and pretty stepmother. Indeed, I think Mrs. Cornelia Opdyke would be a very charming addition to our family circle. [*Exits with papers in hand.*]

VANALSTYNE [*crosses legs and speaks, following deliberately*]. Hang the parson, anyhow! He's got all the unmarried ladies of the wealthiest congregation in New York to choose from. I'm his richest vestryman, too. I pay more for evangelical work and church decoration than any other man in the flock. When he told me our missionary in Shanghai was on the point of converting six more Chinamen and needed ten thousand dollars to do it, I gave him my check—sent the money by cable—we cornered the Presbyterian missionary on those six Chinamen in less than ten days from sight, and now he's after my widow.

MUSGRAVE [*appearing at door, an open letter in his hand*]. A letter from Forsdyke & Sharpe, our attorneys, sir; about the suit against Mr. John Van Brunt.

VANALSTYNE. Van Brunt?

MUSGRAVE. They say they can force him into bankruptcy.

VANALSTYNE [*savagely starting up*]. Tell them to do it. Put on the screws. Crush him to the earth. Exact the last cent and force him to ruin. At last! my bitterest enemy in the street. [MUSGRAVE *goes to small desk.*]

Enter AGNES

AGNES. Good-morning! [*Stops short, near entrance.*]

VANALSTYNE. Ah, Agnes, my little pet! [*Holding out his arms with a smile.* AGNES *runs to him, he kisses her.*]

AGNES [*patting both* VANALSTYNE'S *cheeks*]. I know we haven't any right in this room, but you can't keep me out. [*Laughing.*]

VANALSTYNE [*tenderly*]. I'd as soon drive out a bird that flew in at the window. [AGNES *sits at his knees on hassock.*] Tell me all about business, my pet. How are new bonnets quoted? Have you cornered all the other girls on those little high-heel shoes? You look very pretty on the pony I bought for you, the other day. Do you like him?

AGNES. Oh, yes, indeed; he's very nice. But I've been out with sister Rose on more important business. She took me with her on her charity calls this morning—and—oh—such a poor unhappy family we found all cuddled together in a single room—and the furniture sold to buy food with—and the baby with measles, and—

VANALSTYNE. Get 'em a comfortable flat, my darling; buy some new furniture—and a new baby—I mean get 'em a doctor to repair the old one. That's settled. What else?

AGNES. Then there was a poor old woman in another place and a—

VANALSTYNE [*looks at her tenderly*]. My little girl—when your sister Rose came here, I told my son he had chosen a good, true woman for a wife; and soon afterwards your poor father left you to us, also. I felt that another angel had come to stay with us. Go on with your little charities. [*Tapping her chin.*] Fix them all up to suit yourselves and send the bills to me. But the greatest charity of all—[*Stroking her head gently.*]—is to brighten the life and soften the heart of a poor old millionaire like me.

MUSGRAVE [*rises*]. The letter to your lawyers, sir. [VANALSTYNE *listens as* MUSGRAVE *reads:*] "You will proceed against Mr. Van Brunt as rigorously as possible; exacting every dollar, without compromise, and force him into bankruptcy."

VANALSTYNE [*savagely*]. Ah! ah! [AGNES *looks up in his face pleadingly and shakes her head; he looks around the room, swallows several times, looks at* AGNES *intently, changing his mind; looks up and speaks sharply to* MUSGRAVE, *with his hand resting on* AGNES' *head;* MUSGRAVE *returns to desk, and writes.*] Write another! [*An entire change of manner, softly.*]—Avoid all harsh measures. Treat Mr. Van Brunt as gently as possible, and give him every chance to recover. [*In lively manner.*] How is the canary doing, my girl? Is she a mother yet?

AGNES. Oh, yes! you must see them. Two little ones came out of their shells this morning. Come! [*Taking* VANALSTYNE'S *hand in hers and dragging him up to door.*]

MUSGRAVE [*rising and turning to* VANALSTYNE]. One moment, sir! About the two millions in bonds—St. Louis and San Francisco.

VANALSTYNE. Damn St. Louis! [AGNES *covers his mouth with her hand.*] I beg your pardon, my dear! [*With his hand to his mouth, to* MUSGRAVE.]—and San Francisco, too. [*Turns to* AGNES.] I've got more important business on hand. [*Kisses* AGNES.] We'll go and look at the canaries.

[MUSGRAVE *sits at desk;* VANALSTYNE *exits with* AGNES. VANALSTYNE, JR., *enters with paper in hand, as if to speak to* MUSGRAVE.]

Enter DR. PARKE WAINWRIGHT, *places hat on* MUSGRAVE'S *desk, and crosses to fireplace.* VANALSTYNE, JR., *sits at his desk.*

VANALSTYNE, JR. Ah, Dr. Wainwright, I instructed the servant to show you directly to this room.

WAINWRIGHT. And I instructed you not to be in this room until I gave you permission to return to business.

VANALSTYNE, JR. I must be here today.

[MUSGRAVE *retires to apartment, closing the door.*]

WAINWRIGHT. I am in the very headquarters of my great enemy, Death. [VANALSTYNE, JR., *glances at him suddenly.*] You start at his name. Let me feel your pulse. [*Crosses to* YOUNG NICK. *Takes his wrist.*] You have another Wall Street operation on hand. Your pulse hasn't been twice alike, two days in succession, for weeks. [*Crosses to fireplace.*] You New York business men have invited Death into your own houses. The telephone and the stock indicator have enabled His Sable Majesty to move up town with the rest of the fashionable world; he used to content himself with wearing out your souls and bodies at your offices.

VANALSTYNE, JR. I think you attribute my trouble to the wrong source, Doctor. My father, for instance; he is the largest operator in the street, but he is always in perfect health.

WAINWRIGHT. Your father was bred in the country. His nerves were as firm and as cold as steel before he ever came to the city. These Leviathans of the Money Market all come from quieter scenes of labor in their youth. Wall Street has never yet bred its own giants. The furnace-bred young men of New York are pigmies in the hands of such men; mere bundles of nerve, that burn themselves like the overcharged wires of a battery. Notice the electric lights at your club. Every now and then one of them fizzles convulsively and goes out.

VANALSTYNE, JR. I understand. Do you think that I am in any real danger?

WAINWRIGHT. You are doing what hundreds of young men are doing in this city today: Wearing your life out in the greatest gambling hell on earth. There is death in the street. Monaco is nothing. The gains and losses are settled every day. You dream on your chances night and day for weeks. Fighting the tiger!—bulls and bears are much fiercer animals; the tiger is an angel of mercy.

VANALSTYNE, JR. I shall take the rest I need as soon as I can find time.

WAINWRIGHT. You'll find plenty of time for rest, if you wait, in the grave. Epitaph for a New York man: "He has retired from business." [*Crosses to* YOUNG NICK *at desk and stands at back of chair.*] But I have another matter to talk about this morning; one that pertains neither to your health nor to my own profession—except in an accidental way. I was called to the bedside of a very sick woman last night. She was in a high fever and delirious. This morning she became conscious, though still very weak. Her name is Gertrude Reynolds.

VANALSTYNE, JR. Gertrude Reynolds! Well!

WAINWRIGHT. What I heard during her delirium and what she said to me afterwards is a professional confidence, and yet I—I—

VANALSTYNE, JR. I will relieve your embarrassment. [*Turns and looks up at* DOCTOR.] Gertrude Reynolds has discovered my real name, and the fact that I am a married man; she has letters in my handwriting, and she threatens to send those letters to my wife.

WAINWRIGHT. You have heard from her yourself. All I intended, all I could have done, was to put you on your guard. I have nothing whatever to do with your relations to this woman. That, of course, is your own affair and hers. But your wife loves you, Vanalstyne, with her whole heart; I know how deeply she loves you. Gertrude Reynolds is bitter, beyond all reason and control. I can hardly blame her, for she is herself a mother. But what she threatens to do would be a crime against a sincere and devoted woman. If anything can be done to protect your wife from the ruin of her domestic happiness, I shall assist you to the utmost of my ability. [*Crosses and goes to mantel.* AGNES *runs in suddenly.*] Agnes!

AGNES. Doctor Wainwright! H—s—h! [*Putting her finger to her lips, then aside.*] I was caught that time. Bertie saw me. [*Looks out of door.*]

VANALSTYNE, JR. I thank you, Doctor. We will see what can be done.

"Heaven hath no rage like love to hatred turned,
Nor hell a fury like a woman scorned."

AGNES [*aside*]. Bertie's coming this way. [*She dodges into the bay-window behind curtain.*]

MUSGRAVE *enters hurriedly, and remains in door*

MUSGRAVE. Watson Flint & Co. report a sudden turn in the market.

VANALSTYNE, JR. Ah! [*Starting to his feet.*] I thought there was danger today.

MUSGRAVE. There's a break to fifty-nine in Keokuk and New Mexico.

VANALSTYNE, JR. Watch the indicator, Musgrave! We have work before us. [MUSGRAVE *retires;* VANALSTYNE, JR., *starts up stage, stops, puts his hand to his heart, and staggers. The* DOCTOR *steps quickly to him and supports him. He recovers.*] It's all right, Doctor; these never last long. I—I am well now.

WAINWRIGHT. Nature adds her warning to mine. You *must* have rest. [*A signal on the telephone—loud.*]

VANALSTYNE, JR. Rest! There's a battle on hand today. Do you hear the musketry? [*Laughing and moving up stage to telephone, supported by* DR. WAINWRIGHT.] This is life! life! [*Signals at telephone; speaks into it.*] Hold the market at all hazards. Force the figures back to sixty-eight. Pardon me, Doctor; call again this afternoon. I have no time now. [*His hand on door.*] Business is business, you know; and what is rest with wealth and power within your grasp! [*Exits.*

WAINWRIGHT [*up stage, looking after* VANALSTYNE, JR.]. Business is business in New York. It *is* health, religion, friendship, love—everything. No; business isn't everything even in New York. [*Turns and looks off.*] Here is one exception. [BERTIE *walks in slowly; he is very neatly and elegantly dressed in morning home toilet, his hair parted in the middle, a single glass in his eye;*

he is smoking a cigarette. He stops; WAINWRIGHT *sees him.*] Good morning, Bertie!

BERTIE. Doctor—morning!

WAINWRIGHT. Just up?

BERTIE. No; breakfast.

WAINWRIGHT. Half-past eleven. [*Looking at watch.*] Out late last night?

BERTIE. Club—three o'clock.

WAINWRIGHT. What was going on?

BERTIE. Nothing. Nothing ever does go on—at our club—you know; it's a swell club.

WAINWRIGHT. Merely conversing together till that hour?

BERTIE. We never converse at our club.

WAINWRIGHT. Thinking?

BERTIE. No; just staying.

WAINWRIGHT. Does your head ache this morning?

BERTIE. No; only Apollinaris.

WAINWRIGHT. M-m. You mustn't smoke too many cigarettes.

BERTIE. Last night I smoked two whole ones.

WAINWRIGHT. You're a wild young dog. [*Crosses to chair.*]

BERTIE. All of us fellows at the club are wild young dogs.

WAINWRIGHT. Let me feel your pulse. [BERTIE *walks to him very quietly, putting out his hand slowly.* WAINWRIGHT *takes his wrist.*]

AGNES [*stepping out from the curtain and watching them*]. I hope Bertie hasn't over-exerted his system.

BERTIE. Is it beating too fast?

WAINWRIGHT. I haven't discovered it yet.

BERTIE. Try somewhere else.

WAINWRIGHT. You will never die of too much excitement, Bertie.

BERTIE. I was afraid I might. We fellows at the club lead such a fast life.

WAINWRIGHT [*puts his hand on* YOUNG NICK'S *chair*]. This chair has a quicker pulse. Your case puzzles me. I really don't see how you're going to die at all. You will never have energy enough to die a *natural* death. You'll find it very embarrassing one of these days. As to dying of love. [*Slight start.*] Good heavens! I felt a beat then! Two beats! Another! Bertie. [*Drops* BERTIE'S *hand, and shakes his finger at him slowly.*] You are in love.

BERTIE. You doctors are wonderful men. I *am* in love. Did Agnes come into this room a few minutes ago?

WAINWRIGHT. Yes, but she disappeared almost immediately.

BERTIE. I am in love with Agnes. [AGNES *gives a quick, joyous gasp. The* DOCTOR *turns suddenly, stepping back and looking from one to the other. She stands, hanging her head, abashed.*] I have declared my passion by accident.

WAINWRIGHT. I think I'd better leave you together.

BERTIE. Thank you. [*Walks to mantel.*]

MUSGRAVE *enters suddenly from apartment and moves down to the* DOCTOR

MUSGRAVE [*apart*]. Dr. Wainwright! Something very serious, I fear. Mr. Vanalstyne is lying upon the sofa within quite insensible.

WAINWRIGHT [*apart, goes, speaks speech as he goes*]. Bring some water! Summon a servant! Ask his wife to come to the room. [*Exits hurriedly.*

[MUSGRAVE *hurries out.* AGNES *walks down slowly across, her head drooping. She stops.*]

AGNES. Bertie!

BERTIE. Agnes!

AGNES. I—you—I—haven't you anything to say, Bertie?

BERTIE. I've said it. [*Crosses.*]

AGNES. You told Dr. Wainwright that—you—you loved me.

BERTIE. I've been trying to say that to you, instead of the doctor, for the last six weeks. I've said it to nearly everything else in the house, especially to the furniture in my room. If there'd been a parrot there, you'd a' heard it long ago. When I saw you in the hall a little while ago, I suddenly pulled myself together and determined to say it to you, at once. But you ran away and dodged into this room. What did you run away and dodge into this room for?

AGNES. Well, now that you've said you love me, I—I—don't mind telling you. I had just run out of *your* room.

BERTIE. Out of my room?

AGNES. Yes. Haven't you noticed a little bunch of rosebuds on your table, every morning, for the last few days?

BERTIE. Did *you* put them there? [AGNES *says* "Um—um."] I threw them all away.

AGNES. Oh!

BERTIE. I thought it was the new chambermaid.

AGNES. Bertie! [*Dropping her face into her hands.*]

BERTIE. I didn't want to encourage this one.

AGNES. *This* one? [*Sharply looking up.*]

BERTIE. She has cross eyes and red hair. I did what any young man of correct principles would have done.

AGNES. Albert! The last chambermaid was very pretty. Did you keep the rosebuds that she gave you?

BERTIE. No; I was equally particular in her case. She didn't give me any.

AGNES. Oh, Bertie! I'm afraid you're a very wicked young man.

BERTIE. That's what we fellows in the club all like the ladies to say about us.

AGNES. But you—you mustn't be wicked, for my sake.

BERTIE. Do you think that you can love me, Agnes, if I confess to you the whole truth?

AGNES. I—I will bear it. Tell me everything. It is best that I should know it now.

BERTIE. I am not wicked—a bit; and I say the prayers that mother taught me, every morning, before I go to bed.

AGNES. Bertie! Bertie! [*Running to him and throwing herself on his breast.*]

BERTIE [*looking directly over her head, blandly*]. I have confessed all to her, and she still loves me. Agnes, I will conceal nothing from you; I am as innocent as a lamb.

AGNES. My darling! [*Her head resting lovingly on his breast.*] I love you all the more for it.

BERTIE. Thank you. I was afraid you wouldn't; but I didn't want to deceive you. We'll get married, and we'll live in a little house together, all by ourselves. [*Walking across with her.*] We'll be as happy as your two canary birds in their cage.

AGNES. Dear Bertie!

BERTIE. *They've* got two little ones, haven't they?

AGNES [*simply*]. Yes, Bertie. [*Goes up, takes chair from* MUSGRAVE'S *desk, brings it down, and places it.*] But now I want to talk very seriously with you a few moments. Sit down. [*He sits in chair; she stands at his back, puts her arms around his neck; he pats her hands.*]

BERTIE. What is it, Agnes, dear?

AGNES. When I first ran into your room the other morning, to put the rosebuds on your table, I—I didn't intend to look at anything; but I—I couldn't help just—just glancing around, you know. There was a whole row of pictures on your mantelpiece, and—and others all over the room. They were pictures of actresses—and—and dancers, Bertie, dear.

BERTIE. Yes. We fellows at the club all have pictures like that in our rooms, and when we call to see each other we look at 'em, and then we wink at each other, and then each of us thinks that the other is a devil of a fellow—but he isn't.

AGNES. There was one picture there—I didn't like her face at all—and it had her name on, in a lady's handwriting—"Henrietta."

BERTIE. Henrietta is the most famous ballet-dancer in New York. All of us have her picture. We get them from the photographer for fifty cents apiece, but we have to pay her business manager five dollars apiece for her autograph. I suppose it's cheap enough, for no two of 'em are alike.

AGNES [*comes left of chair*]. Have you ever seen Henrietta off the stage?

BERTIE. Often. Nearly every night, about eleven o'clock, half a dozen of us fellows walk out of the club one by one, and we meet at the stage-door of the theatre. We stand there in a row till Henrietta passes out and gets into her carriage. Then we all go back to the club and sit there.

AGNES. I want you to send away all those pictures in your room, Bertie, Henrietta's particularly.

BERTIE. I'll burn 'em all up; Henrietta's particularly.

AGNES [*long pause; she looks around cautiously,*

as if making up her mind, then suddenly kisses him on top of his head]. Thank you.

BERTIE. Welcome.

AGNES. Now, there's one thing more I want to speak about. I'm to be your wife, you know, and I *can* talk seriously to you. Your father is very angry with you because you won't give your attention to business.

BERTIE. I know he is. He left word for me last night to meet him in this room as soon as I got up. Father says that I don't know any more about business than a kitten. I don't. A kitten that isn't more familiar with business principles than I am would starve.

AGNES. Business is very easy, Bertie. I can tell you all about it. You just speak through the telephone to a man in Wall Street. You say "sixty-five"—or any other number you choose—and a few weeks afterwards the man gives you a lot of money.

BERTIE. That does seem easy enough.

Enter NICHOLAS VANALSTYNE, *with bundles of bonds and written checks*

VANALSTYNE. Oh!—you are here.

BERTIE. Yes, father. [*Rising. Stands at chair.*] John said you wanted to see me this morning.

VANALSTYNE. Yes, I do; Agnes, my dear, I wish to speak with this young man alone.

AGNES. Mayn't I stay, if you please, Mr. Vanalstyne?

VANALSTYNE. Certainly, if you like; there's no secret about the matter. [*Begins looking over papers on desk.*]

AGNES. Bertie and I have been talking about business, sir.

VANALSTYNE. M—m. I dare say you could teach him a good deal more than he knows.

AGNES. Bertie would like to go into business. [*Exchanging nods with* BERTIE.]

BERTIE. Yes, sir. I have decided to go into business at once.

VANALSTYNE. Have you, young man! [*Turning towards* BERTIE, *with a folded paper in his hand.*] I have struggled with you in vain, and I am tired. You are a hopeless idiot. [AGNES *starts.*]

BERTIE. I cannot deny it, sir.

VANALSTYNE. The fact that many other fathers in New York have been blessed in a similar way is no consolation to me. Thank heaven! I have one son who is an honor to our family and to my name. The colossal fortune which I have accumulated shall be my monument, sir. I shall leave him my entire property, without exception, and he will continue the vast business interest which I have acquired. As for you, sir, your monthly allowance ceases from this date. I have made an arrangement with our business agents, Messrs. Watson Flint & Co., under which they will give you a certain amount in cash. You may do what you please with it; but it ought to last long enough for you to establish yourself in a decent position where you can make your own living. Beyond this, sir, you shall have no part or parcel of my property either while I am living or after my death.

BERTIE. Father!—I—[*Half choking.*]—I'm sure I'm—I'm—very grateful to you—for—for giving me anything; and for—for—all you've given me before. [*Dropping into chair.*]

AGNES [*crosses behind* BERTIE; *turns to* NICK, *with her back to* BERTIE, *remaining near his chair. Suddenly:*] And I say that you are a wicked, hard-hearted old man. I love Bertie, whether you do or not, and I'm going to be his wife. [*Turning to* BERTIE *and putting her arms about his neck.*]

VANALSTYNE. You! You are going to be his wife, Agnes? Are you in earnest?

AGNES. Yes, indeed, I'm in earnest. I just this moment told him I would. I've loved him for a long time, too; and I've been waiting for him to ask me. Bertie'll make a dear good husband; and I don't care whether he has any money or not.

VANALSTYNE. Well!—as you please, if you will insist on being a beggar's wife. [*Advancing and extending draft; stops and looks at it; extends it to* BERTIE, *who starts to take it; he draws it back again, looks at* AGNES, *then at* BERTIE, *as if undecided; looks again, offers it again; coughs.* AGNES *works slowly to left of* BERTIE.] But if you are going to be married —I—suppose you'll need a little more. [*Tears up the draft and returns to desk; sits writing another draft.*]

AGNES. Dear Bertie!

BERTIE [*holding her hand*]. Agnes.

DR. WAINWRIGHT *opens door from apartment, stepping in. Enter* ROSE VANALSTYNE, *in bonnet, etc. She comes in with an anxious quick motion, looks around a second, then hurries to the* DOCTOR, *speaking quickly in an undertone, apart.*

ROSE. Doctor! My husband! I was away. Tell me the worst.

WAINWRIGHT. Be calm. There is no danger now; he is sleeping quietly.

ROSE. Oh! [*She moves past him to door of apartment; turns; looks gratefully at the* DOCTOR.] *You* have saved his life. [*She takes his hand in her own to kiss it, he stops her, she looks up gratefully and says* "I thank you, I thank you," *then goes quietly into the apartment, looking earnestly before her.*]

WAINWRIGHT [*looks after her*]. His false and worthless life! I *have* saved it, for *her* sake; and I would have given my own life gladly—for one loving glance from her eyes. [*He turns up to window, where he stands with his back to the audience, looking out; his hand on the curtain.* VANALSTYNE *rises with the new draft.*]

VANALSTYNE [*gruffly, giving* BERTIE *the draft*]. There you are! sir. [BERTIE *looks up blankly at his father, and takes check mechanically, without looking at it, in his left hand and lets hand fall on his knee. Re-crosses to desk, sits and takes up the inventory.*] D—d young pauper! I'll turn him adrift on the world.

AGNES [*at back of* BERTIE'S *chair, her arms around his neck*]. We'll live in a little cottage together, Bertie. I'll do the work and you can help me. [*Comes down left of him.*] And we won't need any money.

BERTIE. Yes.

VANALSTYNE [*looking over inventory*]. Thirty-nine millions.

BERTIE. We'll live like two canary birds and we'll have just about as much to eat.

VANALSTYNE Fifty-five millions. [BERTIE *starts suddenly to his feet looking at the draft.*]

BERTIE. Agnes! [*Turns to* AGNES *and points at check.*] Five—hundred—thousand—dollars. [*They turn towards* VANALSTYNE *who is intent on inventory.*] Father!

VANALSTYNE. Not a cent more—not one cent. [*Turns savagely towards them and strikes desk heavily with right hand.*]

QUICK CURTAIN

SECOND PICTURE

BERTIE *goes behind* VANALSTYNE'S *chair.* AGNES *runs to* VANALSTYNE. *Kneels on ottoman.* VANALSTYNE *takes her face in his hands and kisses her.*

BERTIE. Father! Father! Father! [VANALSTYNE *shakes his head at him gruffly and pays no attention to him.*]

CURTAIN

ACT II

Drawing-room in VANALSTYNE'S *residence. Conservatory raised about two feet six inches, with opening and railing, and with steps up. Reception-room up left. Log-lighted. Sofa with two cushions. Cabinet with bric-a-brac. Ottomans and ornamental tables. Lamp lighted on cabinet and table.*

Enter WATSON FLINT, *as curtain rises, from reception-room. He is a man of about thirty, quick, firm and decisive in speech, gentlemanly in manner; evening dress.*

FLINT [*looking back as he enters*]. Do not disturb them at table! I will wait. [*Walks down. Enter* MUSGRAVE *from conservatory.*] Ah, Musgrave! The family are still at dinner, James tells me!

MUSGRAVE. I presume the gentlemen have got to their cigars, sir, if you care to join them.

FLINT. No. But I wish to have a few moments' chat with Mr. Vanalstyne, Junior. You might look into the smoking-room. If he's at liberty, kindly tell him that I am here.

MUSGRAVE. Yes, sir. [*Starting across; stops.*] Oh—Mr. Flint; I—I wish to—to—I—[*Hesitating.*]

FLINT. Well?

MUSGRAVE. I was merely going to say that I—I—this Henrietta Mine operation—I—I hope it is—doing well, sir—and—and—I trust it is perfectly safe, sir.

FLINT [*turns to* MUSGRAVE]. Musgrave, I have never known you before to take the slightest personal interest in any operation your employer was engaged in. I trust you haven't taken to *thinking;* a private secretary who *thinks* is a dangerous man.

MUSGRAVE. Believe me, I have always made it a rule *never* to think. I was only expressing the hope that—

FLINT. Never allow yourself to hope, Musgrave. That is another excellent rule for men in your position. It is so difficult to hope without thinking. [*Passing up to conservatory.*]

MUSGRAVE [*passing*]. You are quite right, sir. [FLINT *examines curios at cabinet.* MUSGRAVE *stops. Aside.*] I *have* allowed myself to hope a little. Fool! I have yielded to temptation at last, after withstanding it so many years. Every dollar that I have saved is invested in this Henrietta Mine speculation, and I haven't slept a night since I took the risk. [*At door.*] Not one hour of my old comfortable sleep! Not one hour! [*Exit.*

FLINT [*looks off after* MUSGRAVE, *with right foot on first step*]. The old private secretary has been speculating. My Uncle Vanalstyne ought to know about it, but he doesn't. That is his affair, not mine. I never allow anything to be an affair of mine that doesn't concern my own particular interest. It's an excellent rule. The interests of Watson Flint & Co. are quite enough for any one man to look after; and I have them in charge.

Enter VANALSTYNE, JR.

VANALSTYNE, JR. Anything new, cousin?

FLINT. I have something to say that will interest you.

VANALSTYNE, JR. What is it? [*Goes to mantel.*]

FLINT. The matter interests me also as the principal broker of your father and yourself. [YOUNG NICK *motions him to take chair, then sits on ottoman. Taking chair up and moving, sits.*] During the whole progress of this Henrietta Mining and Land Company operation there has been, as you know, a powerful enemy working in the dark and secretly obstructing the movements of your father at every point.

VANALSTYNE, JR. Yes. Father has frequently said that he felt the hand of such an enemy, but he has found it quite impossible as yet to discover who it is.

FLINT. *I* have discovered him.

VANALSTYNE, JR. Indeed! Who is it? [*Turns to* FLINT *quietly.*]

FLINT. Yourself. [VANALSTYNE, JR., *starts.* FLINT *watches him quietly.*]

VANALSTYNE, JR. May I ask *how* you have come to such a remarkable conclusion?

FLINT. You may. At a critical moment, about six weeks ago, you were struck insensible while directing me at the telephone. I was obliged to take matters into my own hands. From what I then learned and knowledge that has come to me since I have arrived at the exact truth. There was a sudden break in Keokuk and New Mexico on that day, but it was premature and would have exposed your plans. You are at the head of a powerful bear clique, bent on ruining your own father in this great Henrietta Mine scheme. With his own son as his secret enemy, even your father's enormous fortune may melt away. If the plot succeeds, you, not he, will be the Master of Wall Street.

VANALSTYNE, JR. [*aside*]. The Master of Wall Street! [*Aloud.*] Well! Business is business, cousin. What are you going to charge me for this knowledge? We will let you into the speculation. How much?

FLINT [*rises, with hand on back of chair*]. Pardon me. I never speculate under any circumstances whatever. I am simply a member of the New York Stock Exchange. I take my regular commission on all orders; nothing more, nothing less—one-eighth of one per cent.

VANALSTYNE, JR. I must pay you for your silence in solid cash. [*Looks at him inquisitively and rises.*]

FLINT. No. I have never yet done anything dishonorable as a business man, and I never shall.

VANALSTYNE, JR. Do you intend to inform my father?

FLINT. Certainly not. You are both my customers. It is quite immaterial to me whether you swindle each other or not. I shall continue to execute whatever orders either of you may give me at the usual commission—one-eighth of one per cent.

VANALSTYNE, JR. You didn't mention this to me for nothing.

FLINT [*puts chair back to place, and comes down*]. I have been intending to speak to you on another subject also this evening. Your wife's little sister, Agnes—

VANALSTYNE, JR. You are in love with her.

FLINT. Yes.

VANALSTYNE, JR. And I am her guardian.

FLINT. I once had hopes, as you know, that Agnes would consent to be my wife. But since your brother Bertie has returned from college—

VANALSTYNE, JR. They do seem to understand each other, though I don't know that it's a regular engagement, yet. I see what you mean. You are too honorable a business man to accept money, or a share, for your silence, but you will force me to use my influence as Agnes' guardian and as the husband of her elder sister, in your favor.

FLINT. Not at all. But if you are still afraid that I will betray you to your father, after my sincere assurance that I will not—that is your affair, not mine.

Enter ROSE, *goes down and turns to* FLINT

ROSE. Watson, you should have come in time for dinner.

FLINT [*bows to* ROSE]. I only dropped in on business.

VANALSTYNE, JR. Rose, my dear, we were just talking about Agnes.

FLINT. You know how deeply interested I am in that subject.

ROSE. I am afraid, Watson—[*Shaking her head.*]—that I must give up the hopes I once had; and you must give up your hopes, too. You know that you have been my choice from the first. I am sure you would have made Agnes a good, true husband; and I am very anxious for her future. But the dear little girl's heart has found another mate. [AGNES *runs in.*]

AGNES. Bertie! [*She stops suddenly. Abashed.*] Beg pardon. I—I thought Bertie was here. Good evening, Mr. Flint. [AGNES *and* FLINT *bow to each other.*]

ROSE. Agnes, dear! Show Watson the four new pictures that came today.

FLINT. I shall be delighted to go to the gallery with you.

AGNES. Very well; come. The prettiest is one by Meissonier. It's called "The Young Girl's Choice." [*Going out, followed by* FLINT. *Bows to* ROSE.]

ROSE [*looks after him*]. I wish for Agnes' sake that she had chosen your cousin Watson for her husband, instead of your brother Bertie. Bertie is kind and good-natured; but he has got among such a fast set of young men.

VANALSTYNE, JR. I've had some misgivings on that ground, myself, Rose. Bertie *is* a little wild.

Enter DR. PARKE WAINWRIGHT

ROSE [*turns and sees* DR. WAINWRIGHT]. Dr. Wainwright.

WAINWRIGHT. Mrs. Vanalstyne! [*Stopping and bowing to* ROSE *and* VANALSTYNE, JR.] I owe you an apology for not keeping my engagement.

VANALSTYNE, JR. There was an empty chair for you at the table.

ROSE. Professional duties, I suppose.

WAINWRIGHT. Yes; a very urgent case.

ROSE. A physician's time is never his own. By the way, Doctor, how is the poor sick woman that wrote to me—Gertrude Reynolds, I think her name was. [YOUNG NICK *starts, exchanges quick glance with* DOCTOR. *Then to* VANALSTYNE, JR.] She wrote, asking me to call upon her. She did not say why, though she is not in want, and we are perfect strangers. Dr. Wainwright insisted that I should not go to see her; he said it might be dangerous to the rest of our family. How is she today?

WAINWRIGHT. It was her case that kept me away. She died—[*Glancing at* VANALSTYNE, JR.]—about an hour ago.

ROSE. Poor woman! I wish I had seen her—in spite of your prohibition, Doctor.

VANALSTYNE, JR. [*aside*]. *That* danger is past. [*Turning to mantel and looking into the fire.*] Poor girl! She did love me.

Enter MUSGRAVE *with a note and a packet*

MUSGRAVE. Mrs. Vanalstyne, a woman just called [ROSE *comes down.*] with this packet and a letter. [*Hands packet and letter to* ROSE.] She said there was no answer, but a dying woman had made her promise to bring them. I assured her that I would give them to you personally. She has gone.

ROSE. They are for me?

MUSGRAVE. Yes, madam. [*Crosses and exits.* WAINWRIGHT *and* VANALSTYNE, JR., *turn and watch her.*]

ROSE. A dying woman! [*Goes up stage and lays the packet on the table and breaks the envelope of the letter, moving down.* VANALSTYNE, JR., *and* WAINWRIGHT *watch her intently as she takes out the letter. She turns a page reading signature.*] "Gertrude Reynolds." [WAINRIGHT *crosses up stage to the table, takes up the packet and places it in his breast-pocket.* VANALSTYNE, JR., *is still watching* ROSE *intently but quietly. She reads; staggering back as she does so, under emotion and in confusion; glances at* VANALSTYNE, JR., *and at the letter; then suddenly turns up stage to table.*] The packet! Dr. Wainwright!—that was lying on this table; you have it; give it to me.

WAINWRIGHT [*quietly*]. Will you let me read that letter?

ROSE. Yes. [*Giving it to him. Both come down room.* DOCTOR *above* ROSE. NICK *remains.*] You know the whole truth, whatever it may be.

WAINWRIGHT [*having glanced through the letter*]. Will you allow me to read this aloud? [*Looks at* NICK *intently.*] Your husband should know its contents as well as you.

ROSE. Yes; he should. [*Her glance fixed on* VANALSTYNE, JR., *who stands at mantel, immovable and impassive.*]

WAINWRIGHT [*aside*]. No name is mentioned; we may save her poor heart yet. He must think while I read. [*Aloud, reading.*] "I have had bitter and wicked thoughts; but they have all passed away in the shadows of approaching death. I think now only of my child, not of revenge on *him*, but *he* must be sacrificed for her. I know how good you are; Dr. Wainwright has told me; and he has tried to save you from this. But a dying mother appeals to you. It is my last desperate chance. Do all you can for my little one. The doctor will tell you where she is. The letters to me from her father, which I send with this, will tell you the rest. You know the handwriting well. Gertrude Reynolds."

ROSE. The packet of letters! [*Starts towards* DOCTOR *quickly. He makes a motion as if to give her the packet.*]

VANALSTYNE, JR. [*turns and speaks quickly*]. Will you kindly leave Rose and me together a few moments, Doctor?

WAINWRIGHT. It is your right to have the letters, madam. They were sent to you. If you insist upon it, after an interview with your husband, I will give them to you. [*Exit.* ROSE *drops upon the ottoman, her face in her hands, sobbing aloud.*]

VANALSTYNE, JR. [*looks around room, then at* ROSE]. Rose, I need hardly say that I am sorry this exposure has come at last. I would have concealed it from you entirely, but I may as well speak frankly to you now. I have known of this affair from the first. [ROSE *looks up suddenly.*] You are quite right. It will be better for Agnes' future for her to marry Watson Flint, instead of [*Turning full face to audience.*] my brother Bertie.

ROSE. Bertie?

VANALSTYNE, JR. I ought to have told you about it long ago, when Agnes was first becoming interested in him. But you'll forgive me, my dear old girl [*Moving toward her, extending arms.*], won't you?

ROSE. Forgive you! [*Springing up and falling into his arms, crying.*] Forgive you!

VANALSTYNE, JR. One doesn't like to stand in the way of his own brother's happiness, you know. But I should have told you, for your sister's sake. Come, come; don't cry; don't cry. [*Pats her on the back consolingly.*]

ROSE. I—I'm not crying, dear; I—I'm laughing. I don't know which I'm doing. [*Buries her head on his shoulder.*]

VANALSTYNE, JR. You *do* forgive me?

ROSE. Forgive *you?* It's you that must forgive me. [*Breaks away slightly.*] I—I thought—no—I won't speak it—my darling! [*Resumes position in his arms.*] I am so happy! so happy! But I haven't any right to be. It is very selfish of me. [*Turns away again.*] Poor Agnes! Oh, my darling! [*Rushing into his arms, conclusively. Enter* MRS. CORNELIA OPDYKE. *Laughs outside.*] I am so happy! so happy! [VANALSTYNE, JR., *kisses her.*]

CORNELIA. Oh! [*Stopping.*] I beg your pardon. [*Starts to go to conservatory.*]

ROSE. Cornelia! [*Starting up.*] Ha—ha—ha—ha—ha! You've caught us. I—I didn't intend to run away from you for so long a time. Oh, my dear Cornelia! [*Going to her.*] I've never felt so happy in all my life—I—I mean I'm miserable. I must go to my room for a moment. [*Laughs.*] Ha—ha—ha—ha—[*Drops her face into her hands, crying. Exit. Laughing and crying hysterically until well off.*]

CORNELIA [*looks off after her, then turns full to* NICK, *who stands with back to audience*]. What a scandal in New York society! I saw your wife in your arms. But you can trust me perfectly. I won't tell anybody. I'll tell 'em it was somebody else's wife.

VANALSTYNE, JR. Will you pardon me for leaving you alone, Mrs. Opdyke? [*Bows to* CORNELIA.] Rose is very nervous tonight.

CORNELIA. Certainly! Everybody knows how devoted you are to her—and other ladies. [*Goes down and bows sarcastically.*]

VANALSTYNE, JR. [*aside. Looks at her angrily*]. I'd better be with her for a while. She may need my advice—about my brother and Agnes. [*Bows to* CORNELIA. *Exit.*

CORNELIA [*goes up, looks off after* YOUNG NICK, *then comes down*]. What right has a man like that to kiss his wife? When *my* husband was alive, and he asked me for a kiss, I told him I didn't want him to be untrue to the rest. Heigho! [*Sighing and looking down.*] There are plenty of pretty women with him now. [*Goes to right, laughing heartily.*]

Enter NICHOLAS VANALSTYNE, *hurriedly. Sees* CORNELIA *and stops*

VANALSTYNE [*aside*]. The widow *is* alone.

CORNELIA [*seeing him*]. The gentlemen have finished their cigars.

VANALSTYNE [*comes down*]. The Reverend Dr. Hilton is still smoking with the young men. I gave him the biggest cigar in the house. It'll take him half an hour to smoke it. I took the smallest. [*Aside.*] Twist on the parson!

CORNELIA. Do you never smoke in the drawing-room?

VANALSTYNE. Oh, yes; I'm a widower. But I was afraid that *you* might—[*Bows to her.*]

CORNELIA. I like it exceedingly.

VANALSTYNE. Oh, thank you! Then *I'll* light a big one. [*Goes to mantel; takes match from match-safe; attempts to scratch it on mantel; it will not light; steals a glance at* CORNELIA, *then covertly scratches it on his trousers, and lights cigar, and puffs violently. Aside.*] Another twist on the parson. I get my smoke and the widow, too. [*Turns his back to fire.*]

CORNELIA [*comes and sits on ottoman*]. Mr. Vanalstyne, I feel that I ought to thank you, as well as my dear old friend Rose, for her kind invitation to visit here a few weeks, while my own house is undergoing repairs.

VANALSTYNE. Don't mention it. I gave her no rest till she—I would say—I was delighted when she told me she'd invited you. I trust there's a lot to do to your house—that is—I hope you won't have much trouble.

CORNELIA. About two weeks' work, the contractor tells me.

VANALSTYNE [*aside*]. I'll bribe him to make it ten. Her house is next door to the parsonage.

CORNELIA. I have settled down here already, as comfortable as if this were my own home.

VANALSTYNE. It *is*, madam! I mean—it ought to be; it must be—by Jove, madam, it shall be!

CORNELIA [*retiring before him, he following her*]. Sir!

VANALSTYNE [*still approaching her*]. Sell your own house! Rent it! Burn it! Blow it up!

Enter HILTON. *Comes down between* OLD NICK *and* CORNELIA

HILTON. A—h—e—m!

VANALSTYNE [*sees* HILTON. *Aside*]. I'd like to blow *him* up—with dynamite. [*Returning. Aloud.*] Have you finished that cigar already?

HILTON. It occurred to me, that if Mrs. Opdyke had no objection, I might venture to finish it here.

VANALSTYNE. She hates it. [*Notices his own cigar, and tosses it into fire.*]

CORNELIA. I just told Mr. Vanalstyne that I enjoy it.

HILTON. Then I'll retain my cigar. [OLD NICK *starts and looks in fire as if to recover his cigar.*]

VANALSTYNE. Twist on *Me!* [*Steps away from fire, and puts both hands in his pockets.*]

HILTON. All the ladies of my congregation know that I am fond of smoking. Dear creatures! My study is quite a museum of embroidered slippers and smoking caps. Kind, charitable souls! They are devoted to me—I mean—to the church. You must visit my study some day, Mrs. Opdyke. [*Turns to* CORNELIA.]

VANALSTYNE [*aside*]. Not after she becomes Mrs. Vanalstyne.

HILTON. But perhaps you will walk into the conservatory with me, Mrs. Opdyke. I can smoke there with a clearer conscience; and I should be glad to discuss the subject which we mentioned at dinner. You remarked [*Crosses to her.*] that you were deeply impressed with my sermon on the duty of distributing one's earthly possessions among the poor.

VANALSTYNE [*trying to attract his attention*]. Do you want me to buy some more of that stock for you, Hilton?

HILTON. Eh? Oh! Pardon me one moment. [*Bows to* CORNELIA *and crosses to* OLD NICK.]

VANALSTYNE [*aside*]. I suppose he's buying stock to distribute among the poor. [CORNELIA *goes up and looks in conservatory.*]

HILTON [*apart to* VANALSTYNE]. We were interrupted in the smoking-room. You received a note from me this afternoon about the Henrietta speculation?

VANALSTYNE [*feels for letter on outside of coat pocket*]. No—yes; the servant handed me a letter from you just before I went in to dinner. I haven't read it yet.

HILTON. It was delayed. Do you think you could place say ten thousand dollars more for me, to advantage?

VANALSTYNE. Oh, yes! I can place it—to advantage. [*Aside.*] In my own bank account, if he doesn't drop the widow.

HILTON. You are very kind. We'll talk about it later in the evening. [CORNELIA *comes down. Then to* CORNELIA, *returning.*] My remarks in the sermon [NICK *falls suddenly on ottoman.*] on the universal struggle in America for mere worldly fortune—especially the growing tendency in New York towards speculative gambling—impressed you particularly, you told me.

CORNELIA. Your sermons bring tears to the eyes of every woman in the congregation. [*They go up to conservatory.*]

VANALSTYNE [*aside*]. That's all he writes 'em for. They bring tears to *my* eyes. They cost us two hundred dollars apiece. [*Rises.*]

CORNELIA. Ah! [*Suddenly.*] Just a moment, please. [*She runs down across left.* HILTON *stands at cabinet, looking at a vase.* CORNELIA *speaks to* VANALSTYNE *apart.*] I want to ask you about something, Mr. Vanalstyne—something very odd. Do you know anything of a—a woman named "Henrietta"?

VANALSTYNE. "Henrietta"? [*Looking at her keenly; then aside.*] She's after a pointer on the Henrietta Mine deal. [*Aloud.*] No, I don't know any woman of that name.

CORNELIA. Oh, I thought you might. That's all. [OLD NICK *repeats*, "That's all." *Exchange glances between them, half laughingly. Turns back, stops, and looks from* HILTON *to* VANALSTYNE. *Then aside.*] *I* happen to be aware that they *both* know a young woman of that name. [*Aloud.*] Come, Doctor. [*Starts to go to conservatory.*] We will discuss the beauties of Henrietta—[*At the conservatory steps* HILTON *looks around sharply, dropping the vase, which is broken. Looks aghast at what he has done.*] I mean—of Christian charity—in the conservatory. [*She goes up the steps to conservatory, disappearing; laughing heartily.* HILTON *follows her; he stops at the top, looking back at* VANALSTYNE. *The latter walks up across right.*]

VANALSTYNE. She's dropped on the Henrietta Mine business. [*At foot of conservatory steps with* HILTON.] If we don't put a stop to that, all the women in New York will know about it, and the whole operation will be a failure. We must get her off the track some way. Meet me in my private office.

HILTON. I will leave the widow in about ten minutes—D. V. [*Exit.*

VANALSTYNE [*hands in his pockets*]. He'd better—D. Q. [*Looking at his watch.*] It'll be a serious thing if a woman gets hold of this big deal. Whenever Mary's mother read one of my business letters, I lost a railroad or two the next week. [*Comes down.*] She lifted forty thousand dollars out of me herself once, on a pointer she found in my pocket, while I was asleep. When I got the screws on old Van Brunt, for three million dollars, it was because he sent his broker's wife an order for stocks, and her husband a love-letter; he got 'em mixed. I'll read Hilton's letter to me now. [*Taking letter from pocket and opening it.*] He wants to go in deeper. [*Reads.*] "My dear Cornelia." Eh? [*Looking at envelope. Holds letter in one hand and envelope in other.*] "Nicholas Vanalstyne, Esq." They don't match. [*Sits on hassock.*] By thunder! he must have sent Mrs. Opdyke the letter about the Henrietta Mine. "My dear Cornelia." If he's got far enough along to address her that way, it looks rather blue for me. [*Reads.*] "My dear Cornelia—If this term, in addressing you, is more warmly affectionate than our short acquaintance would seem to justify, remember that I am your pastor." Now, let me see; Mrs. Opdyke has received his letter to me about Henrietta, and after reading it she thinks Henrietta is a woman. Hilton and I will agree on a story fitting that state of things, and I'll get him to tell it. [*Rises.*] I don't think I'd better let him know that she has read his letter; it might embarrass him. I'll tell him I mislaid it, and ask him what he wrote to me. I wonder if he said anything that would make it awkward for him, if Henrietta *were* a woman? If he did—so much the worse for the parson—and so much the better for me. [*Walking up, he looks out.*] There comes Mary, with my new son-in-law; just arrived today. How the devil that girl picked up that little English lord—all by herself, without a mother—is a mystery to me. Bertie is delighted. He can take him to the club, and set him up among his fellow Anglomaniacs. He's the original article. [*Starts to go off.*]

Enter LADY MARY

LADY MARY. Papa, dear! Here's Lord Arthur. [*Which stops* VANALSTYNE; *comes back.*]

Enter LORD ARTHUR TRELAWNEY. *The latter walks down. He is a little fellow, exquisitely dressed, with a single glass and hair parted in the middle. When* LORD ARTHUR *is well down:*

VANALSTYNE [*aside*]. I wonder if Mary smuggled that in or paid duty on it!

LADY MARY. Papa, dear! Lord Arthur was just asking me whether all the people in America are rich, or only some of them.

VANALSTYNE. There are occasional exceptions.

LADY MARY. I have been in Europe so long myself, I really can't tell Lord Arthur anything about America, you know.

VANALSTYNE. Oh, that girl's ears are longer than her memory. [*Walks. He stops abruptly before* LORD ARTHUR, *looking him up and down.* LORD ARTHUR *passes.* VANALSTYNE *watches him, then turns, speaking aside.*] I'll be stepping on that some day.

LADY MARY. Oh, papa, dear! [*Comes down to* VANALSTYNE.] I want to get your advice. You gave me fifty thousand dollars for my wedding present, you know; you cabled it with your blessing the day Lord Arthur and I were married. What would you advise me to put it into?—Is anything booming just now? How's the market?—bullish or bearish? Any chance to get a twist on the shorts? I don't want to salt it down, you know. I'd like to take a flyer on one of the fancy stocks. Can you give me a pointer? [*Note tablet and pencil, looking at* VANALSTYNE *out of the corner of her eyes.* VANALSTYNE *looks at her quizzingly.*]

VANALSTYNE [*aside*]. There's nothing European about that. She's her mother's own girl, after all. [*Aloud.*] Buy Salt Lake City and Denver—ten days—at forty-six.

LADY MARY [*making note on tablet*]. Thank you, papa. [*Looks up.*] Straight tip, governor? No larks, you know.

VANALSTYNE. Oh!—honor bright. [*Aside.*] It's worth thirty-six. I'll have Watson Flint sell it to her on my account, and I'll get back that wedding present.

LADY MARY. Some one has ruined one of my lovely vases that I brought from England. [*Running to cabinet and picking up the pieces.*]

VANALSTYNE [*looking at his watch*]. Hilton's ten minutes for refreshments are up. [*He crosses, stops abruptly before* LORD ARTHUR, *looks him up and down.* LORD ARTHUR *passes.* VANALSTYNE *looks at him over his shoulder, then turns to door. Aside.*] I wish Mary wouldn't let that run around on the carpet. [*Exit.*

LORD ARTHUR. Mary, my dear!

LADY MARY. Lord Arthur! [*Crossing to him.*]

LORD ARTHUR. Are all the girls' fathers in America like that one?

LADY MARY. I wish they were all such dear, good, kind fathers as he is.

LORD ARTHUR. Yes, he is very kind, only he's such a queer old chap. It's been the same way ever since I arrived. We've been passing each other every now and then all day, and I seem to take him by surprise every time.

LADY MARY [*laughing merrily*]. Ha! ha! ha! ha! You must remember that papa isn't accustomed to the British aristocracy yet. [*Going to him. Throws her arms around his neck.*] My own dear, sweet little English lord! *I* was astonished, too, when I first met you. But I love you now, darling, and so will papa; he's just as fond of pets as I am. But I want to talk to Alice a little. [*Places hands on his shoulders and forces him gently on ottoman. Places hands on each cheek and turns him towards fire.*] Sit down, Artie dear, and look into the fire until I get back.

Enter BERTIE

BERTIE. Tell Agnes I am here, please, Mary.

LADY MARY. I'll bring her back with me. [*Exit.* LORD ARTHUR *sits, looking into the fire.* BERTIE *walks down, looking at him with interest.*]

BERTIE [*aside*]. I am the brother-in-law of a real English lord. I will keep him six weeks before I take him to the club. I will study him carefully, and I will astonish all the other fellows. [*Sits on ottoman.*] We aren't like the real thing a bit. [*Aloud.*] Brother-in-law! [LORD ARTHUR *turns front quietly and looks at him.* BERTIE *looks at him a moment in silence. He looks at* LORD ARTHUR, *who still has his glass fixed on him, without the slightest movement of a finger or a foot.* BERTIE *looks at him and then away two or three times. Aside.*] If I don't think of something else to say pretty soon this will become embarrassing. [*Finally, aloud.*] Do you like America?

LORD ARTHUR. Yes. [*He still looks at* BERTIE *without a movement.* BERTIE *looks at him a moment, then away.*]

BERTIE [*aside*]. That's *one* thing we haven't got yet; we can't keep on looking at another fellow as if we didn't see anything in particular. I will practise that before a cigar-store Indian. [*Looks again at* LORD ARTHUR, *whose glass is still levelled at him.*] I feel as if I were sitting for my photograph. [*Aloud.*] Brother-in-law, did you think Fifth Avenue was pretty as you drove up in the carriage?

LORD ARTHUR. I didn't look out of the window.

BERTIE [*aside*]. He must have been looking at something. [*His face suddenly lights up. Aloud.*] How did you like the cushion on the front seat of the carriage?

LORD ARTHUR. Beautiful.

BERTIE. Awfully, isn't it? [*Aside.*] I've been waiting all day to hear how *he* says "awfully," and he hasn't said it once. [*Aloud.*] Brother-in-law, I would like to ask you, don't cher know—

LORD ARTHUR. Beg your pardon; that's an American word, I suppose.

BERTIE [*aside*]. I wonder what sort of an Englishman we've all been copying after anyway. If I shouldn't say "awfully" or "don't cher know" in the club for two days it would excite comment. If we drop both those expressions, we shall have nothing left but the eye-glass. [*Glances at* LORD ARTHUR, *who has not removed his gaze for a moment.*] He does wear an eye-glass. [*Aloud.*] Are you near-sighted?

LORD ARTHUR. No; what gave you that idea?

BERTIE [*swinging his own glass*]. Nothing.

LORD ARTHUR. Are you?

BERTIE. Only when I've got my glass in my eye.

LORD ARTHUR. Perhaps it isn't perfectly flat. [*Laughs.*]

BERTIE. I dare say it isn't quite accurate. [*He puts his glass in his eye; it drops. He glances at* LORD ARTHUR *and tries several times to keep the glass in; then aside.*] If I could wear a glass as he does I should paralyze New York. [*Aloud.*] Were you born so?

LORD ARTHUR. I suppose so.

BERTIE. Blood *will* tell. [*Rising, crosses to left, and sits on ottoman with* LORD ARTHUR. LORD ARTHUR *turns and looks into the fire again.*] My sister Mary—I would say Lady Mary;—she always was a lady; but we never before thought it necessary to call special attention to the fact every time we spoke of her; Lady Mary said this afternoon that you would tell me about your English clothes.

LORD ARTHUR. My valet will show them to you. He knows how they go on. I don't.

BERTIE. We fellows at the club all have our clothes made in London. [*Adjusts* LORD ARTHUR'S *trousers, then looks at them, and then at his own.*] Only we don't know when to wear the different kinds after they get to New York.

LORD ARTHUR. My valet always puts the right ones on me.

BERTIE. Your valet seems to be a remarkably gentlemanly man for his position.

LORD ARTHUR. He tries to imitate us.

BERTIE [*aside*]. That's it! I've got it! [*Rises quickly.*] He's the fellow we've been imitating. [*Walks.*]

LORD ARTHUR. You were speaking at dinner [*Turning front.*] of some races at St. Jerome Park.

BERTIE. Would you like to go with me tomorrow? [*Walking down to near* LORD ARTHUR.] The favorite at our club is a young mare from Kentucky named "Henrietta."

LORD ARTHUR. I can't, my dear boy, I haven't enough money with me. My father—

BERTIE. The Marquis.

LORD ARTHUR. He said he'd send me some more as soon as his bank account was all right. But he bought some railway shares from *your* father, about six weeks ago; and he lost a hundred thousand pounds on them.

BERTIE. Oh, that's all right. I've got it in *my* bank account. Father gave me exactly that amount about the same time. I believe that's what New York business men call "Foreign Exchange." I will put any amount you wish at your disposal. Then we will join our forces and lay our money on the favorite. [*Enter* LADY MARY *and* AGNES. *They stop, looking at gentlemen.*] We'll drive out to Jerome Park, tomorrow, in my new English dog-cart; I haven't any dogs, but I drive out my other friends in it. We'll go to the races together, and we will take Henrietta between us. [*The two ladies start with a scream.* BERTIE *turns toward them.* LORD ARTHUR *turns and looks quietly into the fire again.*]

LADY MARY. Take Henrietta between them!

AGNES. Oh, Bertie! [*Walking and covering her face with both hands.*]

BERTIE. Agnes, dear! [*Approaching her.*]

LADY MARY [*drawing up to her full height*]. Lord Arthur Fitzroy Waldegrave Rawdon Trelawney!

LORD ARTHUR. My full name. Lady Mary is serious. [*He rises and walks up towards her; she points out with stern dignity. He turns and walks straight out. She follows him out with an imperious air.*]

BERTIE. What is it, Agnes dear?

AGNES [*crying*]. That horrid woman.

BERTIE. Woman!

AGNES. Henrietta! You promised me you'd burn her photograph and have nothing to do with her, and now you're going to take her to the races with you.

BERTIE. Take her to the—Oh—I see. This is another Henrietta.

AGNES. Are there two? [*Turns quickly.*]

BERTIE. This one is a chestnut filly from Kentucky.

AGNES. Bertie! Look me straight in the face. How can you and Lord Arthur go in that little dog-cart of yours and take a chestnut filly from Kentucky between you?

BERTIE. We aren't. We are both going to *bet on* Henrietta, and divide what we win—or otherwise.

AGNES. Oh—Bertie! [*Resting her head on his breast with her back to audience.*] Forgive me!

BERTIE. I hope Lord Arthur will be able to explain the situation before Lady Mary divests him of any portion of his English wardrobe and chastises him.

Enter MRS. CORNELIA OPDYKE *in conservatory. She looks over railing*

CORNELIA. Bertie! You're just the one I wanted to see. [*Coming down steps.*] I've been dying of curiosity for the last three hours, [*Running.*] and the result will certainly be fatal if I don't get relief soon. Do you know anything about a woman named "Henrietta"?

AGNES. There's a chestnut filly called Henrietta; she's going to race at Jerome Park tomorrow.

CORNELIA. A chestnut filly! [*Takes a letter from her bosom, looks at it; then aside.*] The Rev. Dr. Murray Hilton has been betting on a horse race. [*Aloud.*] You don't know of any other female of that name?

BERTIE. There is a ballet dancer named Henrietta. [CORNELIA *suddenly opens the letter again and stares at it.*] Come, Agnes dear. [*Starts to go up to conservatory slowly.*] We will go into the conservatory and talk about something else. We haven't told each other how much we love each other since early this afternoon. [*They go up the steps into conservatory, disappearing in the shrubbery.*]

CORNELIA. The more I read this letter the more bewildered I am. "I would like another chat with you about Henrietta." [*Drops on the ottoman, still intent on the letter. Enter the* REV. DR. MURRAY HILTON, *followed by* NICHOLAS VANALSTYNE. CORNELIA *holds the letter in her right hand, which has fallen at her side.* HILTON *crosses to mantel.*] Now, is it the chestnut filly or the ballet-dancer?

VANALSTYNE [*aside*]. That's his letter to me about Henrietta in her hand now. [*Stops trying to read the letter, and at a slight sign from him,* CORNELIA *turns and sees him; looks surprised.* NICK *bows nervously. Aloud.*] I think you'd better tell Mrs. Opdyke about the matter we have been discussing, Hilton. Perhaps she can give you some good advice.

CORNELIA. If I can be of any service, I shall be very glad.

VANALSTYNE. If he knew that was his letter, he'd see me further first. [*Pays great attention to following scene.*]

HILTON. We have been—ah—consulting on the case of a—young woman—ah—named "Henrietta."

CORNELIA [*aside*]. It isn't the filly. [*Reads from letter, still aside.*]

VANALSTYNE [*aside*]. She's following every word he says with that letter.

HILTON [*leaning on mantel*]. I forget her last name, but she is known to the general public as the—"The Witch of Wall Street."

CORNELIA. Oh! I have heard of her.

HILTON. I—I regret to say, that—ah—Henrietta is a—very beautiful young woman. [VANALSTYNE *brings his hand to his mouth trying to suppress his laughter.*] And she is—ah—particularly fascinating to—ah—to members of my own sex. [VANALSTYNE *flops to one side and buries his face in the sofa-cushion*]. I am grieved to add, madam, that I have every reason to think that several members of my congregation have become interested in this woman. [VANALSTYNE *flops over to the other side and buries his head in the other cushion.*]

CORNELIA [*reading aside*]. "I am deeply interested in that direction, you know."

HILTON. My dear friend, Mr. Vanalstyne. [VANALSTYNE *suddenly sits up, trying to pull himself together and look serious.*] He—ha—he is the senior member of my vestry, and I have been discussing the subject with him. The woman's ostensible occupation is to give financial advice to gentlemen speculating in Wall Street; her ostensible occupation. You can understand my anxiety, as shepherd of a flock, which is largely composed of Wall Street lambs.

CORNELIA [*reading aside*]. "I trust that Henrietta is still booming."

HILTON. This woman's character is such that no gentleman can have the most distant association with her, without justly forfeiting the respect of his friends.

[VANALSTYNE *jumps around and smothers his face in the center of the sofa; seizing both cushions and bringing them to each side of his face; his heels describe circles in the air alternately.* MRS. OPDYKE *and* HILTON *see him.* CORNELIA *starts up. Both stare at him, and move up. They approach nearer.* VANALSTYNE *continues his struggles. The others appear alarmed.*]

CORNELIA. My dear Mr. Vanalstyne.

[VANALSTYNE *springs up and turns front, looking from one to the other, his face flushed and nearly choking. He finally bursts into laughter, coming down and dropping upon the ottoman.*]

VANALSTYNE. Ha—ha—ha—ha—ha. The—the parson has—ha—ha—ha—ha—landed himself—ha—ha—ha—high and dry with the widow—ha—ha—ha—ha—out of *my* way! Ha—ha—ha—ha—ha!

HILTON. I do not understand the cause of your mirth.

CORNELIA. Perhaps this will help you to understand it, Mr. Hilton. [*Holding up the letter.*] Your letter, intended for Mr. Vanalstyne, sent to me by mistake. [*Walks.*] "I trust that Henrietta is still booming." [VANALSTYNE *shouts with laughter.*]

HILTON [*recovering from his astonishment and moving down to* VANALSTYNE]. I will explain it all to her. [*Starts to go to* CORNELIA.]

VANALSTYNE [*stops him suddenly. Suddenly serious. Apart*]. If you do, you'll lose every dollar you've put in.

CORNELIA. But the postscript?

VANALSTYNE. Postscript!

CORNELIA. The postscript interests me even more than the letter itself.

VANALSTYNE [*rising suddenly*]. Postscript! [*To* HILTON.] You didn't tell me about any postscript.

CORNELIA [*reading*]. "I give you my entire confidence in this matter, my dear brother Vanalstyne, for I know that *you* are more deeply interested in Henrietta than anybody else." [HILTON *walks up, complacently.* VANALSTYNE *catches his breath, then turns up stage to go after* HILTON, *who has reached the door.* VANALSTYNE *stops him.*]

HILTON. If you explain it to her, you will lose every dollar you've put in. [*Walks out, with stately dignity.* VANALSTYNE *moves down, glances at* MRS. OPDYKE, *goes to door, looks to* CORNELIA, *turns to speak, she laughs, he bows awkwardly, looks at her again, she still continues laughing, he with a forced laugh.*]

VANALSTYNE. Down on both alleys! [*Exit.*

[CORNELIA *bursts into hearty laughter, and moves up stage.*]

CORNELIA. Ha—ha—ha—ha! [*Looking.*] Mary, Agnes—girls! [*Beckoning.*] Such fun! Ha—ha—ha—ha—ha! [*Enter* MARY; AGNES *runs in, in conservatory, moving down, still laughing,* MARY *on her left;* AGNES *runs down the steps.*] I have found out all about Henrietta.

LADY MARY. She's the favorite for the races tomorrow.

CORNELIA. No! Ha—ha—ha—ha! She's neither a chestnut filly nor a ballet-dancer. Ha—ha—ha—ha—ha! The Rev. Dr. Murray Hilton has just told me all about her, in the presence of Mr. Nicholas Vanalstyne, and they know Henrietta is a beautiful young woman, known as the Witch of Wall Street.

AGNES. Witch!

LADY MARY. Young woman.

CORNELIA. Her character is spotless—all black without a white spot on it. All the lambs of Dr. Hilton's flock are in love with her, and one, at least, that hasn't been a lamb in a great many years, not to mention the shepherd himself. Ha—ha—ha—ha! [CORNELIA *runs up stage into conservatory and disappears among the shrubbery; still continues laughing until it dies away in the distance. A slight pause before speaking.* BERTIE *appears in conservatory, looking back at* MRS. OPDYKE.]

AGNES. Mary!

LADY MARY [*drawing up to her full height*]. Lord Arthur Fitzroy Waldegrave Rawdon Trelawney has deceived me. [*She walks up with great dignity, stops, looking out.*] He is coming this way. [*She pauses a moment, looking sternly out, then points majestically away as if to a person approaching, and goes out.* AGNES *stands, choking slightly and touching her eyes with her handkerchief.*]

AGNES. There—there must be some mistake—somewhere. I—I am sure Bertie wouldn't tell me a story about it.

BERTIE. What's the matter. Agnes? [*Walks down the steps.*] Are you sobbing?

AGNES. Not exactly; almost. [*A slight sob.*]

BERTIE [*at her side*]. But why, Agnes, dear?

AGNES. There—there are so many different kinds of Henrietta.

BERTIE. Have you found another one?

Enter ROSE; *she stops up stage*

AGNES. Yes!

ROSE. Agnes.

BERTIE. Rose. [*Crosses;* AGNES *goes to* ROSE.]

ROSE. I was looking for you. Go to your room, my child. I have something to say to him [*Turns coldly to* BERTIE.] that is not right for you to hear.

AGNES [*looking at* ROSE, *and realizing it is something painful*]. No, there is nothing you can say to him that I have not the right to hear.

ROSE. Perhaps it may be better that you should hear. Bertie, you and my sister are engaged to be married.

BERTIE. Yes. [*Sits on ottoman.*]

ROSE. That engagement must be broken off.

BERTIE *and* AGNES [*together*]. Broken—off! [*Quickly rises and turns to* ROSE.]

ROSE. At once—

BERTIE. But—

ROSE. I insist upon it.

AGNES. Rose!

ROSE. I always knew that you were a *fool*, Bertie.

BERTIE. Agnes knew that before she said she loved me. [AGNES *nods her head approvingly.*]

ROSE. If she had known what I know now, she could *never* have loved you. I did not believe that you and your silly companions at the club were anything *worse* than fools.

BERTIE. We aren't. We only pretend to be. I told Agnes all about it. [AGNES *nods her head as before. Enter* VANALSTYNE, JR., *and* DR. WAINWRIGHT. *They stop.*] What have you heard?

ROSE. The worst that I could possibly hear. You have ruined and cruelly deserted a woman who loved and trusted you. [AGNES *drops on ottoman.*]

BERTIE. I—I have—what? [*Dazed.* MRS. OPDYKE *appears in conservatory.*]

WAINWRIGHT [*aside*]. He has thrown the blame on his brother, and made me a participant in his crime.

BERTIE [*suddenly*]. That must be the other Henrietta that Agnes was talking about. [*Turns to* ROSE.]

ROSE. You know her true name well enough, though I dare say you have been too careless to learn the whole sad truth. Dr. Wainwright can tell you that. He was at her side today, where you ought to have been also. Ask *him* what I have heard tonight.

BERTIE. Sister Rose, I declare to you, on the honor of a gentleman, that I know nothing whatever about the matter you are speaking of. [AGNES *turns hopefully.*]

WAINWRIGHT [*aside, glancing at* VANALSTYNE, JR.]. I will protect him no longer. [*Aloud.*] Mrs. Vanalstyne, here is the packet which was sent to you tonight. [*Hands her packet.* VANALSTYNE, JR., *starts in alarm, watching her intently.* CORNELIA *stands at rail, looking down.* VANALSTYNE, JR., *has taken a small chair and places it back to audience; sits.*]

ROSE. A packet of letters to the poor woman from the man who deserted her. [*Crosses to* BERTIE, *puts the letters in his hand, then recrosses to* AGNES. BERTIE *looks at the letters, bewildered, then slowly unwraps the packet, looks at the letters and starts.* VANALSTYNE, JR., *is watching him intently. He gives a slight start as he sees the letters. The others are looking at him deeply interested.* ROSE *turns to him.*] Do you recognize the handwriting? [*Music.*]

BERTIE. Yes, I—why? [*Turns sharply to* VANALSTYNE, JR., *who rises and looks at him appealingly.* BERTIE *turns to audience, looks at letters again, then looks to* AGNES.] Agnes!

AGNES. Bertie! [*Falls on ottoman, face in hands, sobbing.* ROSE *is consoling her.* BERTIE *turns again sharply to* VANALSTYNE, JR., *who points to* ROSE *appealingly and shakes his head.* ROSE *crosses to* VANALSTYNE, JR. BERTIE *turns again to audience, then slowly crosses to mantel, and drops letters quietly into fire. Music swells.* BERTIE *leans on mantel, head on hand.*]

CURTAIN

SECOND PICTURE

BERTIE *on ottoman, with elbow on knee.* DR. WAINWRIGHT *stands with his hand on his shoulder behind him.* AGNES *looking at*

BERTIE, ROSE *drawing her gently towards door;* VANALSTYNE, JR., *with one foot on conservatory steps.* MRS. OPDYKE *has picked letters out of fire and extinguished flame. Music kept up all through.*

CURTAIN

ACT III

SCENE I.—*Office of Watson Flint & Co., Stock Exchange Brokers. Double glass doors, up stage; corridor at back, door down left, door up right center, small hall beyond, desk down right, another up left, safe up right center, small table, revolving chair at each desk, two luxurious armchairs. Stock indicator, with basket; telephone. The decoration of the room as rich as possible, yet appropriate to a business office; the furniture and woodwork of polished hard woods, sofa ornamented to harmonize with the decorations, richly engraved glass in door. The indicator is working as the curtain rises.* WATSON FLINT *stands near indicator with the tape in his hand reading it.*

FLINT. New York Central down to one nine and three-eighths. Delaware and Hudson ninety-nine and a quarter; all the gilt edges giving way; and money locked up. The market is getting more and more excited. A flurry!—more than a flurry! "St. Paul & Omaha, preferred—one seven. Failure of Lapscomb & Co." The air is thick with failures today. Keokuk and New Mexico three points lower: that comes home to us. A danger signal! "Henrietta Mining and Land Company"—here we have it—"eighty-seven"—a drop of two points since ten o'clock—"eighty-five and a quarter." Aha! The squall has struck us suddenly. Henrietta is the center of attack. I suspected as much. "Eighty-four." It is going down with a rush. The enemy has chosen today for the final battle; and Old Nick is away on his yacht. [*A signal on the telephone; he goes up, speaks into it and listens alternately.*] Hello! Who is it? Oh!—Agnes! What? [*Repeats what he hears.*] "Mrs. Opdyke and Lady Mary have gone down to your office. They asked me to tell you they were coming." All right. [*Speaks in telephone.*] Is your brother Nicholas at home? [*Listens.*] "Bertie hasn't been at home for ten days." [*Speaks in telephone.*] Where is your brother Nicholas? [*Listens.*] "We haven't seen Bertie since a week ago last Tuesday." [*Speaks in telephone louder.*] Where is Nicholas? [*Listens.*] "If you see Bertie—" Bertie be—hanged! Good-bye. [*Rings off telephone, turns away.*] Bertie would be a valuable assistant at a crisis like this. [*Returns to indicator and reads tape.*] "A strong bear raid on Henrietta has developed itself. All the Vanalstyne's stocks are falling rapidly. A general panic is threatened. Intense excitement. Rumored suspension of two National Banks. Henrietta—seventy-nine!" [*The indicator stops.*] A break of ten points since the opening. [*Sits at desk.*] I must head off the enemy at once. If the old man were here, he'd toss the whole exchange on his horns. [*Writes.*] "Buy ten thousand shares Henrietta in one block." [*Enter* BERTIE; *he is dressed with exquisite neatness in the height of style, a glossy silk hat, gloves, etc.* BERTIE *coughs, which attracts* FLINT.] Ah, Bertie!

BERTIE. Cousin Watson!

FLINT [*writing*]. "If this does not check the fall, buy ten thousand more." [*Does not look up.*] Agnes was just speaking to me about you—through the telephone.

BERTIE. Agnes? Is Agnes well?

FLINT [*rising*]. She was not very well, when I last called; she couldn't see me. [*Stepping into passage and holding out his arm with note beyond door, and exits.*]

BERTIE. Agnes wasn't very well the last time I heard about her. Ah! Ah! Ah! [*Sighs; brings chair from table.*]

FLINT [*re-enter—comes down*]. Commission to us—one-half to the big operators—six hundred and twenty-five dollars. Whichever side loses, we brokers win. [*Sits; to indicator.*] Tick on, my friend, you entertain me. [*Turns to* BERTIE *and drops business tones.*] You left home very suddenly, and late at night, about ten days ago, Bertie.

BERTIE. Yes.

FLINT. We've all heard of you, now and then; though none of the family has seen you. You sent back word that you had taken apartments at Delmonico's. Are you still there?

BERTIE. Yes, Cousin Watson, I am launched upon a career of maddening dissipation.

FLINT. Indeed!

BERTIE. I have become a wild and desperate gambler. During the last ten nights I have been visiting faro-banks and other dens of iniquity. I have at last come down to Wall Street. I desire to encounter a tiger of a larger size and more savage nature. They tell me that I shall find such an animal here. The smaller ones have ceased to distract my thoughts. Will you teach me the game?

FLINT. You wish to buy a few shares of stock?

BERTIE. Yes, I will take a few dozen chips to begin with. What do you charge for them?

FLINT. Shares differ in value, like wall-paper, according to what is printed on them,

BERTIE. You may choose the pattern for yourself.

FLINT. How much margin do you want to put up?

BERTIE. Margin? They didn't say anything about that in the other places. What is a margin?

FLINT. Money—say ten thousand dollars—a check on your bank—or securities.

BERTIE. What do you mean by the word "securities"?

FLINT. Bonds—sound railway shares—anything that I can turn into money, at a moment's notice.

BERTIE. You never order stocks unless people give you money or securities first?

FLINT. Certainly not. That is my only protection. If stocks go up, you make a profit. If they go down—[*Turns to desk.*]

BERTIE. I lose the margin. I think I understand the game. I will try my luck. Where are the tables?

FLINT [*turns, looks at* BERTIE *in surprise*]. At the Stock Exchange, across the way.

BERTIE. I suppose I can go over there with safety. [*Rises and stands back of chair.*] About how often do the police pull it?

FLINT. Ha! Ha! Ha! Ha! You will be quite safe. [*Rises. The indicator ticks.*] This is the machine we play the game with.

BERTIE. I will give you my check for fifty thousand dollars. [*Walking to desk and sits.*]

FLINT. How does *Henrietta* suit you?

BERTIE [*turning suddenly*]. Henrietta does not suit me at all, sir. Henrietta has been the cause of all my troubles; and permit me to say this, sir, if any man mentions the name of Henrietta to me again, I will hit him.

FLINT. Oh, very well. Shall I buy Keokuk and—

BERTIE. Buy anything you like. [*At desk; writes check.*]

FLINT [*looking at tape*]. Ah! a rally of four points, from seventy-nine back to eighty-three. That last order has had its effects. [*Reads tape.*] "Henrietta is now holding its own. All the Vanalstyne stocks are stronger, *and the panic is checked.*" [*Indicator stops.*] The bear movement seems to be paralyzed. [*Turns to desk and writes.*]

Enter VANALSTYNE, JR., *with newspaper in his hand*

VANALSTYNE, JR. [*stopping near door*]. Bertie—here? Bertie! [BERTIE *rises,* VANALSTYNE, JR., *holds out hand and says* "Bertie!" BERTIE *turns suddenly, makes movement as if to take his hand, looks at him, then shakes his head and goes to* FLINT. VANALSTYNE, JR., *sighs and goes to desk and sits.*]

BERTIE. Here is the check.

FLINT [*turning in his chair*]. Oh, Nicholas! You've come at last. [*Takes* BERTIE'S *check and writes on a card, not looking up from desk.*] I will give you a card of introduction to my partner at the Exchange—the Broad Street entrance. There's a special place for private visitors. Be sure you don't get on the floor by mistake. No outsider has ever been on the floor of the New York Stock Exchange and come out alive. [*Looks up at* BERTIE.] We always kill them—and eat them for lunch. [*Giving a card.*]

BERTIE. It will entertain me. [FLINT *takes paper he has written on from desk and goes to door and exits.* BERTIE *crosses to table, takes hat and cane, turns to* VANALSTYNE, JR.] How did you leave Agnes this morning?

VANALSTYNE, JR. [*he does not look up from newspaper*]. She didn't come down to breakfast; a headache, Rose told me.

BERTIE [*half aside*]. *I* have a headache, too, nearly every morning now. [*Sighs.*] I wish that were the only pain. Perhaps the Stock Exchange is good for a headache. [*Exit.*

Re-enter FLINT, *goes to desk and sits*

VANALSTYNE, JR. [*throws down paper, rises suddenly*]. Flint!

FLINT. Well? [*At desk.*]

VANALSTYNE, JR. It was you, of course, that gave the order which checked the panic a few moments ago?

FLINT. Yes; I have general instructions to protect your father's stocks in case both of you are absent. Now that *you* are here, you can take charge of matters yourself.

VANALSTYNE, JR. You and I may as well understand each other today, Flint.

FLINT [*turns to* VANALSTYNE, JR]. I think we do understand each other. It was you that tried to bring about the panic this morning. Your father has sailed on his steam yacht for a day's excursion, leaving his affairs in your charge. You have been waiting for an opportunity like this to strike the final blow, after fighting against him in secret for more than three months. You have been working the market today from the private office of your father's bitterest enemy on the Street—Mr. John Van Brunt. If you succeed in beating down the price of Henrietta to sixty-five, before three o'clock, Nicholas Vanalstyne will be ruined, and you will be a millionaire many times over. We understand each other perfectly, you see.

VANALSTYNE, JR. Perfectly.

FLINT. But for the present you have failed. You forgot to instruct me not to protect the stocks. It was a serious oversight. I am a mere business machine.

VANALSTYNE, JR. It was, indeed, an oversight. [*Takes corner.*]

FLINT. The battle has been turned against you; you have exhausted all the money and securities within your reach, and it is after two o'clock already.

VANALSTYNE, JR. I have but one resource left.

FLINT [*rises*]. I see what you mean. Your father's own securities.

VANALSTYNE, JR. Yes.

FLINT. But even *you* cannot nerve yourself to take them from the safe deposit vaults and use them against him. It *would* be very much like robbery.

VANALSTYNE, JR. Father has his own keys with him, and I mislaid mine.

FLINT. I did you an injustice; I thought you had conscientious scruples. [*Returns to desk.*]

Enter MUSGRAVE, *nervous, anxious and out of breath; throws hat in chair, comes down*

MUSGRAVE. Ah, Mr. Vanalstyne! I hope the Henrietta mine is all right. I found your keys, sir—

VANALSTYNE, JR. Ah!

MUSGRAVE. After you left the house.

VANALSTYNE, JR. Quick! Give them to me. [*Comes to* MUSGRAVE *hurriedly.*]

MUSGRAVE [*searching his pockets*]. I saw how anxious you were about it, sir, and hurried right down. Where did I put them? I hope the delay hasn't been dangerous to your father's interests. Oh, here they are! [*Giving keys.*]

VANALSTYNE, JR. [*goes to corner, hurriedly turns, meets* OLD NICK *in door, starts back and goes to corner*]. Just in time! *Now*, watch the ticker, Flint.

VANALSTYNE. Hello, boys! The bears have been playing the devil with you this morning, haven't they? The old bull has come back. Just in from Bulltown. Stand from under, youngsters! [*Moving down.* FLINT *goes up and sits in armchair.*] Watch the blue Empyrean above my horns! You'll see a thousand bears pawing the air in about fifteen minutes. [*Looking at tape.*] My steam yacht broke her shaft while we were passing Staten Island. As we were landing at Stapleton, a friend called out to me from the dock, "There's an earthquake in Wall Street." I tumbled over the taffrail and caught the next ferry. I enjoy earthquakes. They *have* been hammering things down—a regular bear raid. Trying to catch me in a panic, eh? I've been through fifty panics before. Going to wipe out Old Nick, eh? I'll have a jollier excursion than I expected today. Things are safe for the present, I see. This is an ambuscade; they knew of my absence. [*Exit*

FLINT. *During the following* OLD NICK *rises into savage earnestness;* VANALSTYNE, JR., *half crouching as he proceeds*, FLINT'S *eyes fixed upon him.*] Strange!—that I can't find who my real enemy is. When I do find him, I'll crush him to the earth. I'll grind his life out. It will be a death struggle between us; but his heart will cease to beat. [*Stops suddenly, looking at* VANALSTYNE, JR., *who has staggered slightly with his hand at his heart.* OLD NICK *catches him.*] My boy, you're trembling. It's no time now to lose courage. The fight isn't over yet. How much ammunition have you left? What securities have you used up, so far?

VANALSTYNE, JR. I was about to go to the Safe Deposit, to get our securities.

VANALSTYNE. Just going!

MUSGRAVE. He mislaid the keys, sir.

VANALSTYNE. The devil he did!

MUSGRAVE. I have just brought them to him.

VANALSTYNE. Then hurry up! Bring all there are. We may need them today. [*Returning to indicator.*]

VANALSTYNE, JR. [*aside*]. I shall win the battle yet. [*Exit, hurriedly.*

VANALSTYNE. Musgrave, follow my son; he'll need your assistance. [*Exit* MUSGRAVE.] The bears have had everything their own way this morning. [*Looking at tape.*] But I'll toss 'em; the weather is changing; it will soon begin to rain bears. [*Stop ticker.*]

Re-enter FLINT, *goes to his desk, takes a paper and starts to go, sees the ladies as they enter. Enter* MRS. CORNELIA OPDYKE *and* LADY MARY; LORD ARTHUR *walks in quietly behind them.*

FLINT. Ladies! [*Takes chair from table, places it for* CORNELIA.]

VANALSTYNE. Mrs. Opdyke! Helloa, Mary!

CORNELIA. We have come down to Wall Street on business.

FLINT. You received my note. [*Then to* VANALSTYNE.] The Louisville and West Tennessee, preferred, which you instructed me to transfer to Mrs. Opdyke.

VANALSTYNE [*moving to* CORNELIA]. I signed the papers yesterday. [LORD ARTHUR *walks, the indicator begins to tick, he starts around and stands staring at it through his glass;* LADY MARY *has dropped into chair;* FLINT *has gone to safe, opening it and counting over a bundle of shares.*]

CORNELIA. I believe I am under great obligation to you, Mr. Vanalstyne, for letting me have these railway shares. Mr. Flint tells me they are the choicest now in the market. [*Ticker.*]

VANALSTYNE. Don't mention it, madam. I'm very glad to serve you. [*Aside.*] If the Rev. Dr. Hilton knew I had the widow's fortune in my control, the vestry meeting, next week, would be interesting. [*Returning he stops suddenly, looking at* LORD ARTHUR, *who is still staring at indicator. It stops ticking.* LORD ARTHUR *turns; glances up at* VANALSTYNE *a moment, then quietly crosses front.*] I wish that was a bear cub, instead of a British lion. I'd toss it so high, today, it'd never come down. [LORD ARTHUR *sits.*]

LADY MARY [*rising*]. *I* came down on business, too; my little flyer on Salt Lake City and Denver, at ten days! [*Going to indicator.*]

VANALSTYNE. *This* is the day. I'm sorry, old girl, but you've lost that little wedding present, [*Chuckling.*] and I've got it.

LADY MARY [*she has picked up the tape and is looking at it*]. Oh, no! Here it is now; just come, on the ticker. It's thirty-five today. [*Looks up slyly at* OLD NICK.] I saw a twinkle in your eye, governor, when you gave me that pointer. You advised me to buy at forty-six. I sold at that figure—*you* bought. [*Laughs.*]

VANALSTYNE. I!

FLINT [*during previous speech, he has come down to his desk, comes down to* OLD NICK]. Five thousand shares, sir!

VANALSTYNE. I! That rubbish!—at forty-six? Five thousand rat-traps!

FLINT. Here is your order to me, sir. [*Hands him order.*]

VANALSTYNE [*looking at order, then at* MARY]. Is this the order you wrote out and brought me to sign?

LADY MARY. I wrote two of them. You *read* one and *signed* the other.

FLINT. The difference due Lady Mary is fifty-five thousand dollars. [*Returning to safe.*] Commission to us from both sides.

VANALSTYNE [*bursting suddenly into hearty laughter*]. Ha! Ha! Ha! Ha! Kiss your dad! [*Goes to her; seizes her in his arms; kisses her.*] Exactly like her mother. I always tried to do Matilda out of her anniversary presents. [*Walking.*] But she doubled them on me every year. [*Stops suddenly before* LORD ARTHUR, *then turns to* CORNELIA.]

LORD ARTHUR. My American father-in-law hasn't got over being surprised every time he meets me, yet. [*The indicator ticks*, LADY MARY *looks at tape.*]

LADY MARY. Henrietta!

CORNELIA [*springing to her feet*]. The Witch of Wall Street! [LADY MARY *looks sternly across at* LORD ARTHUR; *he sits and speaks with all the injured dignity he can assume.*]

LORD ARTHUR. Lady Mary! I still insist that Henrietta is a chestnut filly from Kentuckissippiana, or some other damned American state, at the races at St. Jerome Park. [*The indicator stops.*]

LADY MARY [*looks sternly at* LORD ARTHUR]. I am surprised, Lord Arthur Trelawney, that you should persist so long in trying to deceive me. [*Turns and reads tape slowly.*] "Henrietta is now eighty-five." [*Slight pause.*]

CORNELIA [*rises suddenly*]. Dr. Hilton said she was a *young* woman.

VANALSTYNE [*at back of* CORNELIA, *trying to suppress laughs*]. Let me set you right, Mrs. Opdyke. Ten days ago, it was necessary to conceal matters; but it's an open fight now. Henrietta is not a woman. It is only the Henrietta Railway and Mining Company. There is a Witch of Wall Street and she is on the list of the Stock Exchange; but her name isn't Henrietta. Doctor Hilton and I made up that little story to put you off the track. Henrietta is not a woman. [*He takes chair up stage, and* CORNELIA *goes with him.*]

LADY MARY. O–h! Artie, *dear!* [*Crosses stage with arms extended and picks him up and stands him on his feet.*] My darling, sweet little English lord! And I haven't let you go outside the house, alone, since we arrived in New York. My poor, dear, little Artie! [*Patting him under the chin.*]

LORD ARTHUR. I always said it was only a chestnut filly.

LADY MARY. Ha! ha! ha! ha! My dear, innocent pet! [*Turns to* CORNELIA.] Cornelia, my love, there's another private room on the other side of the hall. Lord Arthur and I will wait there till you are ready. Come, Artie, dear! [*Apart.*] I owe you a thousand kisses. [*Goes up stage with her arm about* LORD ARTHUR. *Both go up stage rapidly, laughing and talking ad lib. until well off.*]

VANALSTYNE [*both* VANALSTYNE *and* CORNELIA *come down*]. I hope you will forgive me for deceiving you, Mrs. Opdyke.

CORNELIA. And I've been wronging our dear, good pastor all this time.

VANALSTYNE. Oh, by jove! [*Aside.*] It lets him out as well as me.

FLINT [*rises from desk with check and crosses to* CORNELIA]. Mrs. Opdyke, if you will sign this check for three hundred and sixteen thousand dollars, to the order of Mr. Vanalstyne, the transaction will be completed.

CORNELIA. Certainly. [*Both go to desk*, FLINT *hands her pen*, *she signs check*, *gives it to him*, *he crosses to* VANALSTYNE.]

FLINT. The railway shares are in my safe. [*The indicator ticks.*]

VANALSTYNE [*aside*]. I hope I shan't be obliged to ruin that railroad company to freeze out the parson. I'll propose to the widow before he has a chance to see her again.

FLINT [*the check in his hand*]. Where shall I deposit Mrs. Opdyke's check for you?

VANALSTYNE. What bank is it on?

FLINT. The Security.

VANALSTYNE. Transfer it to my own account in the same bank. [FLINT *goes to his desk.*] I may have to draw on it this afternoon. My other accounts are very low today. [*At indicator.*] Hello! What's this? [*Reads.*] "The bears have suddenly resumed their attack on the Vanalstyne stocks." Henrietta is going down again. Flint! What margin have you left for us?

FLINT. I can order ten thousand more shares.

VANALSTYNE. Do it—in Henriettas—at once.

FLINT. Yes, sir. [*Goes to door.*]

VANALSTYNE. It is time Nicholas returned.

FLINT. His worthy son has evidently got the securities in his own hands and is using them. [*Exits; indicator stops.*]

CORNELIA. Well! [*Rises from desk.*] We have completed this business matter. I will go. [*Starts to go.*]

VANALSTYNE [*turns to her*]. Don't you be in a hurry.

CORNELIA. Lady Mary is waiting.

VANALSTYNE. But *I* haven't completed my business with *you*, madam.

CORNELIA. Indeed!

VANALSTYNE. No! [*Holds tape in right hand, looks at her, then at tape several times undecidedly, then drops tape and goes to her.*] I'm in love with you.

CORNELIA. Eh?

VANALSTYNE. And I want you to be my wife.

CORNELIA. What!

VANALSTYNE. You heard what I said. I know I'm a rough, blunt man, and I can't describe my feelings as another man might, that didn't love you half as much.

CORNELIA [*turning away*]. At last!

VANALSTYNE. But my heart—[*The indicator ticks. He stops abruptly and goes back to it, watching tape.*]

CORNELIA [*aside, still looking away*]. I must not yield too easily, but I do like him. [*Aloud.*] Go on, sir. [*Aside.*] His tongue falters.

VANALSTYNE. Holy Moses!

CORNELIA. Eh? [*Turning.*]

VANALSTYNE. I've got to back out of this.

CORNELIA. Sir?

VANALSTYNE. Henrietta down to seventy-six. The old lady is getting me into a trap. Why the devil doesn't Nicholas return with those securities? [*Turns squarely towards her.*] They've got the old bull in a corner.

CORNELIA. Really, sir, I don't know what all this has to do with—with—[*Indicator stops.*]

VANALSTYNE. Oh, of course! As I was saying. [*Backs away from ticker.*] I've been in love with you since we first met. I have loved you more and more from that day to this. You *must* be my wife.

CORNELIA. *Must?* [*Looks away.*]

VANALSTYNE. Yes, madam—must! And if any man dares to come between us, I'll *choke* him—through his white cravat—*damn* him. [*Shakes his fist at audience.*]

CORNELIA. Oh, he is delightful!

VANALSTYNE. I *love* you, Cornelia, with all my strength—with a love that will not be denied. It *shall* not be denied—

CORNELIA. Do give me time.

VANALSTYNE. How much? [*Roughly.*]

CORNELIA. Time—to—say—"Yes."

VANALSTYNE. Yes! [*Throwing out his arms eagerly.*]

CORNELIA. Y-e-s. [*Spreading her arms and falling back towards him. The indicator ticks. He drops his arms and rushes to it, leaving her to totter back over her skirts and sit squarely on the floor. She springs up at once and stands like an enraged tigress, glaring at him. He is staring at the tape.*]

VANALSTYNE. The old girl is down again.

CORNELIA. Mr. Vanalstyne!

VANALSTYNE. That's the worst tumble I ever saw in so short a time.

CORNELIA. I say no—no—no—*no!*

VANALSTYNE. Sixty-nine!

CORNELIA. A thousand times—no! [*Sweeps up stage, throws open both doors with her hands, angrily, and exits rapidly.*]

VANALSTYNE. Cornelia! Cornelia! Cornelia! [*Has tape in right hand, half turning each time to see, as if undecided whether to follow or remain at ticker, but remains at ticker. The indicator ticks.*]

Enter FLINT, *hurriedly; comes down to* VANALSTYNE

FLINT. Bad news, Mr. Vanalstyne! My partner sends word that everything has gone by the board, and the whole Exchange is in full panic.

VANALSTYNE. "Sixty-eight." [*At ticker.*] Our margins are exhausted? [*Half turns to* FLINT.]

FLINT. Yes, sir.

VANALSTYNE [*looking at watch;* FLINT *takes his place at ticker*]. Half-past two. If Nicholas doesn't return within ten minutes, we shall be wiped out. Ah! The three hundred thousand just received from Mrs. Opdyke in the Security Bank. That'll keep us afloat till he gets here. I'll give you a check for it. [*Sits at desk.*] We'll get ahead of them yet. [*Writing check.*]

FLINT [*reading tape*]. "The chairman has just

announced the *failure* of the Security Bank." [*Indicator stops.*]

VANALSTYNE. Failed! The Security? [*Starting up and throwing down his pen. Enter* VANALSTYNE, JR.] Ah, you are here, my boy! [*Throws arms around his neck.*] The old bull is still alive. I'll toss them yet. The securities!

VANALSTYNE, JR. [*quietly*]. I am sorry to say, father, that I have not got them.

VANALSTYNE. You—you haven't brought them? [*Staggers back.*] And there's not a moment to lose. [FLINT *sits at his desk.*]

VANALSTYNE, JR. There are no securities belonging to us in the safe deposit vaults. Our safe there is quite empty.

VANALSTYNE. A robbery! You lost your keys this morning. It was Musgrave found them.

VANALSTYNE, JR. Yes, Musgrave found them.

VANALSTYNE. He has been bribed by the opposition. We can punish him, poor wretch! [*Indicator ticks.*]

FLINT [*business of reading tape from chair without rising*]. "Henrietta—*sixty*-five." [*Indicator stops.*]

VANALSTYNE [*hands extended, listening anxiously for report*]. We have lost the fight. [*Arms drop to his sides in despair.*] It has been a long battle and a hard one, and my entire fortune has been swept away. This is my Waterloo. [*Turns to* VANALSTYNE, JR.] Your fortune is gone also, my son. [*Crosses to* VANALSTYNE, JR., *and pats him on the back.*] But cheer up, Nick, old boy. You're still young, and I am only fifty-five. We'll begin life again together. The world's before us, and we'll enjoy the struggle. [*Enter* MUSGRAVE, *puts hat on chair as before.* VANALSTYNE *turns sharply, sees* MUSGRAVE, *motions for him to come down, which* MUSGRAVE *does.*] Musgrave, you have a wife and family; I'll do what I can for them, but *you* must go to prison. [*Then to* FLINT.] Send for an officer.

MUSGRAVE. To prison?

VANALSTYNE. Where are those securities?

MUSGRAVE. I accompanied your son to assist him, as you instructed me. He did not wish me to do that, but I watched him all the way—for fear he might be robbed—from the Safe Deposit Company to the very door of Mr. Van Brunt's office. [MUSGRAVE *bows his head.*]

VANALSTYNE. Van Brunt! [OLD NICK *puts his hand on his shoulder and* MUSGRAVE *raises his head, and they look at each other squarely in the face; then he turns slowly and looks at* VANALSTYNE, JR.]

FLINT [*aside*]. This is growing interesting.

VANALSTYNE, JR. My dear father! Let me explain matters. You have thought it to your own interest to increase the value of the Henrietta Mining and Land Company. I have found that my interests lay in the opposite direction.

VANALSTYNE [*removes hand from* MUSGRAVE'S *shoulder quickly, and starts back*]. Why, it is you, then, who have—[*Half starting forward with raised hands. He clinches his fists firmly and checks himself; puts his hands behind his back with an effort.*] Go on, sir!

VANALSTYNE, JR. I have done what seemed best for my own business interests. You have lost your fortune today, but *I* have gained one. I will settle upon you an allowance of ten thousand dollars a year. [*Turns squarely to* OLD NICK.]

VANALSTYNE. Scoundrel! [*Darting across and seizing* VANALSTYNE, JR., *by the throat; forces him down before him.*] You trembled when I said I would crush my enemy—tremble now! I told you it would be a death struggle between us; but his heart would cease to beat. Does yours beat now, you coward? By God! it will be the last time! [*Throws him savagely on the floor; starts forward as if to crush him.* VANALSTYNE, JR., *says appealingly,* "Father!" OLD NICK *stops suddenly, looks at him, staggers back, and says:*] My son! My loved and trusted son! My God! my own son! [*Staggers back feebly, with face to the audience, then turns, throws both hands above his head, says:*] My God! my own son! [*And staggers off. Slight pause until* NICK *well off; then* MUSGRAVE *takes his hat hurriedly and exits after him.* VANALSTYNE, JR., *rises to his feet, stands, wavering slightly and breathing heavily.*]

FLINT [*rises*]. Have you any orders at present for us?

VANALSTYNE, JR. [*stands with hand on heart, leaning heavily against desk*]. Not today.

FLINT. I hope that you will favor our firm in your future operations. [*Exit.*

VANALSTYNE, JR. I shall be master of Wall Street yet. [*Rushes over to ticker; takes tape and is looking at it eagerly.*] The master of Wall Street!

Enter DR. WAINWRIGHT; *puts hat on table, then crosses hurriedly to* VANALSTYNE, JR.; *puts hand on his shoulder.*

WAINWRIGHT. Vanalstyne, I have driven down from your house as rapidly as possible. Your wife told me you were here. I warned you yesterday that you should not leave your room for three days at the least.

VANALSTYNE, JR. Business is business.

WAINWRIGHT. Business—gambling—with the angel of death. I find the whole street in a furore of excitement. There are crowds surging to and fro, from Trinity Church to the Custom House. The newsboys are calling a suicide. I have come to meet my enemy Death on his own ground today. [*Drags him away from ticker.*] You need rest at once. Come! [*They exeunt.*

Enter BERTIE. *His hat is crushed and his clothes in general disorder; one side of his collar sticking up and his necktie askew on the other side, his gloves half torn off and cuff torn and hanging down, etc., etc.*

BERTIE. I have been introduced to the Stock Exchange. I shall never again refer in a light and profane way to the place of eternal punishment. The gentlemanly quiet that prevails at other gambling establishments in New York is Heaven. I got upon the floor at first, among the brokers, by accident. My hat was immediately jammed down over my eyes from behind. A policeman in the hall advised me to go the gallery. I had no sooner worked my way to the front rail, than I was recognized by every man on the floor below. They all suddenly began to howl: "Henrietta!" As I reached the street, a man ran up to me and cried out: "How is Henrietta?" I knocked him down and proceeded on my way. Half a dozen newsboys ran by me, yelling at the top of their voices: "All about Vanalstyne and Henrietta." My headache is cured. [*Sits despondently at desk.*]

Enter MUSGRAVE. *The following scenes must be played with great rapidity*

MUSGRAVE. Oh, Mr. Bertie, this is a sad day for all of us.

BERTIE. It is for *me.*

MUSGRAVE. Your father has lost his fortune.

BERTIE. Father! [*Turns suddenly.*]

MUSGRAVE. And I have lost all the little savings of a lifetime.

BERTIE. Father has lost his fortune? He gave me half a million dollars a few weeks ago. I'll give him back what there is left of it.

MUSGRAVE. How much have you? [*Turns sharply to* BERTIE.]

BERTIE. I've been getting rid of it as fast as I could, but there's more than four hundred thousand dollars left in the bank.

MUSGRAVE. In the bank? It is still there? Perhaps you can save him yet.

BERTIE. Where is he? I'll give it to him at once. [*Starts to go.*]

MUSGRAVE. No, no! It is too late for that. He is gone; and it is nearly three o'clock. Mr. Flint, make out a check to his order. [MUSGRAVE *hurries across;* BERTIE *goes to desk;* MUSGRAVE *calls out.*] Mr. Flint! [*Soliloquizes.*] He can order forty thousand shares with that margin and the enemy is unprepared. They think the victory is gained. The panic will set the opposite way like a torrent. [*Looks at watch.*] Ten minutes to three. The last moment. [*Turns up, calls.*] Mr. Flint! [*Moving to* BERTIE, *who is writing check.*]

Enter FLINT; *comes to ticker*

FLINT. What is it, Musgrave? Ah, Bertie, your fifty thousand dollars is gone.

MUSGRAVE. No, here—here! [*Crosses with check.*]

FLINT [*taking it*]. Four hundred thousand; what shall I buy with this?

BERTIE. Peanuts, if you like. Musgrave will tell you.

MUSGRAVE. Henrietta! Henrietta!!

BERTIE [*starting to his feet*]. What the devil do you mean by that?

FLINT. I'll go on the floor myself with this order. Forty thousand shares. It may turn the battle at the last moment. [*Takes hat from his desk and rushes off.*]

MUSGRAVE. It will. [*Goes to ticker, picks up tape and stands eagerly scanning it.*] The last sale was at sixty-five. It will soon be bouncing upwards.

BERTIE [*rolls up coat sleeves, buttons his coat, fixes his hat on straight, and crosses slowly to* MUSGRAVE, *and puts his hand on his shoulder*]. Musgrave! in speaking to Mr. Flint just now, you referred to a certain young woman. Permit me to say that I have great respect for your age, but I am a dangerous man.

MUSGRAVE. The last moment!

BERTIE. I have already knocked down one man today. I have not decided yet what I shall do to you, if you mention that lady's name again in my presence, but I'm prepared to knock down any number of men of suitable age, for that purpose. [*Returns to desk.*]

MUSGRAVE [*still looking at tape*]. Mr. Flint hasn't got there yet; but it will soon go up.

Enter VANALSTYNE, JR.; *hurriedly followed by* DR. WAINWRIGHT

VANALSTYNE, JR. Be patient, Doctor! I'll return in a moment; but I *must* see the closing quotation. [*Crosses hurriedly to indicator, throws* MUSGRAVE *aside roughly, seizes tape eagerly.* WAINWRIGHT *stands;* MUSGRAVE *drops back;* VANALSTYNE, JR., *looks at the tape.*] There is no further danger. Henrietta has gone to pieces. [*Indicator ticks.*]

BERTIE. She has gone to pieces. [*A broad smile, changing into a look of horror, then to a smile again.*] I am glad of it.

WAINWRIGHT. The infernal machine is still at work. It kills more men than dynamite.

VANALSTYNE, JR. [*with sudden interest, giving the words one by one as they come off the indicator*]. "Heavy and unexpected—orders—for—the Vanalstyne—Stocks."

MUSGRAVE [*aside*]. Flint is on the floor. He's carrying everything before him. There's a crowd of howling demons around him now. The panic is setting in the opposite way like a torrent.

VANALSTYNE, JR. Wild excitement! Prices bounding up—seventy-nine—eighty! [*He draws up, bringing his hand to his heart and stepping back; the* DOCTOR *starts, watching him;* MUSGRAVE *rushing down to indicator.*]

MUSGRAVE [*reading*]. Eighty-three, eighty-five. Ha—ha! [*Turning to* VANALSTYNE, JR.] You tried to ruin your father—it is you who are ruined. Henrietta is safe! [*Points exultantly to* VANALSTYNE, JR., *who has staggered and fallen into* WAINWRIGHT'S *arms.*]

BERTIE. Damn Henrietta! [*Rushes out of door.*]

MUSGRAVE. "Eighty-eight,—ninety." [*Indicator stops.*] One point higher than it was yesterday, and—and the Exchange is closed. [*Rushes up, wheels down armchair;* WAINWRIGHT *places* VANALSTYNE, JR., *in chair.*]

WAINWRIGHT [*looks up to* MUSGRAVE]. Water! water! [MUSGRAVE *goes out;* VANALSTYNE, JR., *sinks into the chair.*]

Enter the REV. DR. HILTON *hurriedly and comes down rapidly*

HILTON [*anxiously*]. Gentlemen, I—I have heard—is it true?—that Mr. Vanalstyne has been ruined? Believe me—I am deeply—very deeply—interested—I mean—concerned. [*Throws umbrella on* FLINT'S *desk. He suddenly moves down to the indicator and looks at tape, handling it nervously.*]

MUSGRAVE *enters with water; the* DOCTOR *waves him away*

WAINWRIGHT. It is useless now. [*Goes to back of chair.*]

MUSGRAVE. Useless! [*To* VANALSTYNE, JR.] Oh, sir, can you hear me? [VANALSTYNE, JR., *opens his eyes, looking at him.*] The last words your father said to me, as he tottered into his carriage, was this: "Look after my son, Musgrave, and—and tell him I forgive him."

VANALSTYNE, JR. Forgive! [*Weakly closing his eyes.* MUSGRAVE *goes up slowly to table, places glass on table, and stands with back to audience, head bowed.*]

WAINWRIGHT. Doctor Hilton?

HILTON. Eh! [*Turns to* WAINWRIGHT.]

WAINWRIGHT. My duty as a physician is ended. A dying man, sir! [*Takes off hat and stands with head bowed.*] You are his pastor. [*Moving a step back and to the other side of the chair;* HILTON *moves a few steps towards them, half cringing and bewildered.* VANALSTYNE, JR., *slowly opens his eyes and leans forward on the arm of the chair, looking at* HILTON.]

VANALSTYNE, JR. One of your rich parishioners! [*Looks at* HILTON as *he speaks, drawing up to his full height and raising his arm to its full length, pointing upwards.*] Show me the way to heaven! [HILTON *cringes before him.* VANALSTYNE, JR., *bursts into a laugh.*] Ha!—ha!—ha!—ha! You teach a man how to die! [*Then almost savagely, suddenly leaning forward and looking him straight in the face.*] Have you ever shown me how to *live?* You have robbed me of my hope. [HILTON *turns cringing and moves up, stands with his back to the audience; the indicator ticks;* VANALSTYNE, JR., *starts; it stops; he rises; starts forward.*] Seventy-one—sixty-eight. [*Ticker stops.* VANALSTYNE, JR., *staggers back into* DOCTOR'S *arms and sinks into chair; his head drops on his breast lifeless; the* DOCTOR *places his hand over his patient's heart; the indicator ticks a few times, and is silent.*]

WAINWRIGHT. Tick on! tick on! Bring fortune—and despair—to the living; the ear of a dead man cannot hear you. [*Indicator ticks till curtain is down.*]

SLOW CURTAIN

SECOND PICTURE

Everybody off stage except VANALSTYNE, JR. *Ticker ticks slowly and sharply until curtain is down.*

CURTAIN

ACT IV

SCENE I.—*An interval of eighteen months.* VANALSTYNE'S *residence. The drawing-room as in Act II. Furniture differently arranged. Sofa near mantel; table up center; table down right; on latter a small easel-frame, with cabinet photograph, facing up stage; an ottoman; armchair; sunlight through conservatory roof and sides; the plants in conservatory re-arranged; the curtains of the French window in reception-room drawn, showing balcony and street beyond; fire in grate—December. Discovered:* AGNES, *standing in the conservatory, half sitting on the railing against the further side of the arch. She has flowers in her hands, toying with them.*

AGNES. Almost a year and a half since I went away. It doesn't seem possible. Everything in the house looks so natural. It's over two hours since I got home, and I haven't seen Bertie yet. I—I'm very glad. I suppose I oughtn't to be, but I *am* glad that Bertie missed the steamer for Europe today.

Enter ROSE. *She walks in slowly, looking at the address of an unopened note. She pauses, still looking at it.*

ROSE. From Dr. Wainwright. [*Starts to tear it open; stops.*] I know what it must contain. His last words to me yesterday, and his last look, told me plainly enough. [*Sighs.*] He loves me. [*Pats her hand with the envelope irresolutely.*] I—I'm sure I—I have never said anything to—to encourage him. [*Sighs again; turning, stands before table.*] Dr. Wainwright has been a kind, dear friend, and I—I have always been glad to—to have him call—even when it was not absolutely necessary in the line of his professional duty, but I have never said one word to lead him to think that I—that I—but how foolish I am—I dare say it is only a prescription. I was threatened with a cold when he was here yesterday. [*She is opening the envelope. Her eyes rest on the portrait on the table. She stops suddenly, drops the note on the table, and sinks upon the ottoman, looking at the picture.*] My husband, the idol of my girlish dreams! Can I have a single thought that is not devoted to your memory? [AGNES *comes down the steps to* ROSE; *puts arm around her neck affectionately.*]

AGNES. Rose, darling! That's just the way I saw you sitting and looking at his picture, eighteen months ago, before I went away to Boston. I *wish* you could think of something else, dear. That's a note from Dr. Wainwright, isn't it?

ROSE. Yes! [*Snatching it up hastily.*] Some advice about my health—that is—I haven't read it yet—but—[*Thrusts note into her bosom; both rise;* ROSE *crosses;* AGNES *remains.*] Agnes, I have something very close to my heart, and I want to talk with you about a certain gentleman. I told him you were coming home from Boston today, and I asked him to call.

AGNES. Mr. Watson Flint?

ROSE. Yes, darling. He has loved you for a long time, and he has talked about you to me, every time we have met, since you first went away.

AGNES. Do you know where Bertie is?

ROSE. *Have you been* very unhappy in Boston, dear? [*Both cross and sit on sofa.*]

AGNES. I ought to have been happy, our dear old aunts in Charlestown were so kind.

ROSE. Some of your letters to me were very sad.

AGNES. How did Bertie happen to miss the steamer this morning? You said he was going to Europe to stay six months, in the same letter that you said that I might come back from Boston.

ROSE. I will be perfectly frank with you, Agnes. I did not wish you and Bertie to meet again.

AGNES. You have always been my mother, dear; the only mother I ever knew, and I know that my happiness is nearer to your heart than your own. After you told me that Bertie was so—so very wicked—I—I wouldn't have married him for the world. I am very glad you did send me away. [*Turning her face away and touching her eyes.*]

ROSE [*crosses to table and sits*]. I fear these eighteen months have not cured her dear little heart. Have *I* been as true to my first love as she? [*Looking at picture.*]

Enter BERTIE; *he stops as he sees* AGNES

BERTIE. Agnes! [*She looks around at him with a slight start, dropping her eyes. He steps forward, extending his hand; withdraws it, then extends it again, with another step towards her. She moves toward him with downcast eyes and timid manner, laying her hand in his.*] Thank you. I—I'm very glad to see you again.

AGNES. I—I'm sure, I'm—I—

BERTIE. I heard yesterday morning that you were coming home today. [*She suddenly withdraws her hand and runs to* ROSE, *who rises.*] That's the reason I missed the steamer this morning. I tried to tell the coachman to hurry, but I couldn't. [*Walking, puts hat on mantel and umbrella in corner.*]

Enter WATSON FLINT

FLINT. Agnes, I am delighted to see you again. [*Moving down and taking her hand.*]

AGNES. Thank you, Mr. Flint.

FLINT. I have come up from the office, expressly to meet you. A lively day at the Exchange. [*Looking across at* BERTIE, *and still holding* AGNES' *hand.*] Money at fifteen per cent., and stocks going down with a rattle. [*To* AGNES.] I have longed for this moment, Agnes, since you first left us.

ROSE. Agnes and I are going into the library. Won't you join us there?

FLINT. With pleasure, but I have a little business matter to talk over with Bertie. I'll be with you presently. [ROSE *inclines her head and goes with* AGNES. AGNES *goes out.* ROSE *looks back at* FLINT, *who joins* BERTIE.]

ROSE [*aside*]. I am not quite sure that Watson *would* make a woman happy. [*She takes the note from her bosom, opens it, and walks out, reading it.*]

FLINT. I came up at once, as soon as I heard you missed the steamer. An unexpected turn in the market in your favor, as usual. I thought you would lose in that last venture, but you have a large profit. I little thought two years ago, Bertie, that you would be known today as the Young Napoleon of Wall Street. Any further orders?

BERTIE. Yes, A. T. and S. F. I think those are the letters—but I don't care much what portion of the alphabet you use.

FLINT [*feels in all pockets for note-book and pencil; finding no book, he uses cuff and makes memorandum on it.*] Atchison, Topeka and Santa Fé.

BERTIE. Oh!—that's it. I never have the remotest idea what any particular combination of letters means, but I've got the list by heart. Five thousand shares on the red—[FLINT *looks at him in surprise.*] I mean—at thirty days.

FLINT. Current rates, I suppose. Buy or sell?

BERTIE. I will consider. [*He turns away, takes a coin from his pocket, and tosses it on his knee.*] Buy! [*Aside.*] I am the Young Napoleon of Wall Street.

FLINT [*during the following speech he continues writing on cuff, crosses, and exits without looking up*]. I'll send down the order at once by the telephone upstairs; then I'll join Agnes in the library. [*Aside.*] How I love that girl! Six hundred and twenty-five dollars more to us. [*Exit.*

BERTIE. If the right side of that fifty-cent piece continues to turn up, I shall be a Wall Street giant. [*Walking.*] Heigho! [*Sighs.*] I always win; it's getting monotonous. The old proverb is true, "Unlucky in love, lucky at cards." [*Looking at the picture on the table.*]

Enter DR. PARKE WAINWRIGHT; *he walks down and stands a second, looking over* BERTIE'S *shoulder.*

WAINWRIGHT. You are looking at your brother's picture, Bertie.

BERTIE [*looking up*]. Doctor!

WAINWRIGHT. I know what you are thinking about. Agnes has returned.

BERTIE. Yes.

WAINWRIGHT. And *his* crime still keeps you apart. I am the only man living who could clear your character and make you both happy.

BERTIE [*takes the* DOCTOR'S *hand*]. You have told me from the first that you would do so at any moment if I asked you.

WAINWRIGHT. I should be bound in justice to do that.

BERTIE. I do not ask you. [*Drops* DOCTOR'S *hand.*]

WAINWRIGHT. I am grateful to you for that, Bertie—it would pain her too deeply.

BERTIE. When Brother Nicholas died a black curtain was drawn over it all. Perhaps things will come right some day; but I can't open his grave, it would be too horrible. You have come to see Rose.

WAINWRIGHT. Yes.

BERTIE. I will go. I don't think it is a case which requires a consultation of physicians. I will go. [*Walking up stage. Exit.*

WAINWRIGHT. His memory stands between them like a solid wall. [*Looking at the picture.*] His *sacred* memory! The mere shadow of treachery and deceit. [*Walking.*]

Enter ROSE. *Her eyes are drooped and her hands folded. He turns and looks at her. They bow to each other gravely.*

ROSE. Dr. Wainwright.

WAINWRIGHT. I wrote to you less than half an hour ago, but I could not wait for your reply.

ROSE. I—I—was just writing a note to you when the servant brought me word that you wished to see me.

WAINWRIGHT. Forgive my impatience! What was your answer?

ROSE. I—I began—and tore it up—half a dozen times.

WAINWRIGHT. "Yes?"—or "No?"

ROSE. I forget which the last one was.

WAINWRIGHT. Ah! [*Springing towards her. She starts.*]

ROSE. I mean—

WAINWRIGHT. You mean "yes." I will give you no time to change it again.

ROSE. Oh, I have misled you. I did not intend to say what I did. I have hesitated—but I—I— [*Sees the picture.*]

WAINWRIGHT. Rose!

ROSE [*quietly*]. Dr. Wainwright!

WAINWRIGHT. I beg your pardon, Mrs. Vanalstyne.

ROSE. You may call me "Rose." We have been such sincere friends, and for so long a time. You seem like one of the family.

WAINWRIGHT. Heigho! [*Sighing.*] I have received your answer.

ROSE. I told you I tore them all up.

WAINWRIGHT. You were hesitating only to find the kindest words for a refusal; but we cannot be merely friends any longer.

ROSE. You will come to see me—to see us all—as heretofore?

WAINWRIGHT. If you are in pain or danger, Rose, [*Taking her hand gently in his.*] I will be at your side. [*Looking into her eyes.*] I shall count my skill as nothing, except when it brings relief to you. That is all I have valued it for in the past. My only prayer to heaven for myself is this: "When the inevitable time comes at last, that a physician's skill is useless, I pray that another may be at your bedside and I in the grave." [*Starts to go; then more lightly.*] In the meantime I hope you will not need my services often, but when you do, send for me. [*Presses her hand gently and goes up stage. She watches him and checks him with an* "Ah!" *He stops near door, looking back.*]

ROSE. You are not leaving so soon? Don't go, please—just now. I—I'm not feeling very well this afternoon. [*Crosses. She drops upon sofa quickly, turning her face away and looking down. He walks down and leans upon the back of sofa, looking down at her with a smile.*]

WAINWRIGHT. What are your symptoms?

ROSE. I—I hardly know. I—I have never felt exactly like this before. [*Drops her head.*]

WAINWRIGHT. Is your heart beating regularly? [*Takes her hand.*]

ROSE. Perhaps it *is* my heart; it hasn't been beating quite regularly since—since—

WAINWRIGHT. Since you have been in such distressing doubt as to how you should answer my note?

ROSE. For the last twenty minutes or so.

WAINWRIGHT. Your hand is warm. [*Raising it in his own.*] A trifle feverish, perhaps. Let me see your face. [*She looks up at him, her hand still resting in his.*] Your eyes look strange to me. No—not strange; for they remind me of the eyes that looked into mine six years ago, on the day we first met. Do you wonder, Rose, that I learned to love the sweet young girl I met so often in her rounds of charity, or that I love her now?

ROSE. The poor people all told me how generous and kind you were to them.

WAINWRIGHT. My charity was a selfish one, I fear; I visited those that you did twice as often as the rest.

ROSE [*turning back her head, looking up at him, and placing her other hand on his*]. You have loved me so long?

WAINWRIGHT. With a love that is all the stronger because—because it was once hopeless. Oh, the agony I suffered when I first saw those eyes turn with love upon another! [*Removing her hands from his quickly, she starts, sitting upright and looking before her.*]

ROSE. Leave me! leave me! They shall not turn away from him now. [*Dropping her face into her hands, weeping and rising; walks.*]

WAINWRIGHT. Your love is mine, Rose—not his! Mine by right! [*Passionately moving down.*] I loved you before he saw you, and when he gained your heart I suffered in silence. I bore the torture for months and years. I saved him from death, that you might not suffer as I had. But heaven itself decreed that you should be free; that you should return at last my long-tried love. You are mine, Rose—mine!

ROSE. No, no, no! I will not forget him—I cannot! [*Dropping on chair.*]

WAINWRIGHT [*almost fiercely*]. His memory shall not stand between us. I will tell you the truth—the whole truth. [*She looks up at him suddenly.*] That man to whom you gave your spotless life; that man to whom you brought the perfect faith of a young girl; that—[*She has risen to her feet and is looking at him in amazement. He stops abruptly, looks into her eyes, and moves back a step.*] What was I about to do? What have I been saying? I'm dreaming! I am wild! My words mean nothing—nothing! Cling to your memories, Rose; they are tender and pure, like the heart in which they grow. If a new love for me cannot grow among them, let it die. [*Starts to go.*]

Enter MRS. CORNELIA OPDYKE *in carriage dress and a cloak*

CORNELIA. Oh, I beg your pardon!

ROSE [*turns to her quickly*]. Cornelia!

CORNELIA. Sorry to interrupt you, but I *must* have a few moments' conversation with you, Rose—in private. Doctor—[*She comes down.*]

WAINWRIGHT. I have just finished my own call. [*Bowing to* ROSE, *she returns it. He turns up stage.*]

CORNELIA. Don't leave the house just yet. I shall have something to say to you also. I'll meet you in the—the little pink room at the end of the hall.

WAINWRIGHT. I will wait for you. [*Bows and exits.*]

CORNELIA [*stands, looking off after* DOCTOR]. Rose—I should be in love with that man, if you weren't.

ROSE. What nonsense, Cornelia.

CORNELIA. Not a bit of it; I really should. [*Comes down.*] My dear, I am a pauper!

ROSE. What!

CORNELIA. I have lost my entire fortune.

ROSE. Oh!

CORNELIA. Your father-in-law, Mr. Nicholas Vanalstyne, was the man that did it. It's what he calls "a turn in the street." *I* call it highway robbery in the street. My agent informs me this morning that the railway stock I bought of Mr. Vanalstyne, a year and a half ago, isn't worth a penny.

ROSE. My dear! [*Crosses to* CORNELIA.]

CORNELIA. I haven't a penny in the world; that is—there are a few pennies lying loose on my dressing table and a few thousand dollars in the bank. I owe that to my dress-maker. But that isn't what I came to see *you* about. It's quite a different matter. [*Sitting on sofa;* ROSE *sits on sofa.*] I've brought a little package of *dynamite* with me. [ROSE *starts slightly.* CORNELIA *takes a small packet from her bosom.*] Here it is. I'm going to explode it—right here—now!

ROSE. Dynamite.

CORNELIA. One doesn't like to interfere in family matters, you know; otherwise I should have taken the roof off this house long ago. I have hesitated; and this little packet of *nitro-glycerine* has lain all this time, in one of my jewel caskets. But when you told me, this morning, that Agnes was to come back today, and Mr. Watson Flint was still anxious to marry her, and Bertie was going to Europe, only he missed the steamer—and I do believe he did it on purpose—I took this little bundle of *gun-cotton* out of my dressing case, as soon as I got home. "Now is your time to go off," said I.

ROSE. Cornelia, what *are* you talking about?

CORNELIA. You are in love with Dr. Wainwright.

ROSE. As I have told you before, Cornelia—[*Turns away.*]

CORNELIA. It is nonsense. Of course it is—and very delightful nonsense, too. I've seen it coming on gradually for the last six months. I've been waiting for it.

ROSE. I will not allow [*Rises.*] you to speak so flippantly on a subject which ought to be sacred, even to you. No, Cornelia, I am still true—I shall always be true—to *his* memory. [*Crosses to table, looking at picture.* CORNELIA *rises, follows her and remains; bursts into hearty laughter.* ROSE *looks at her, startled and shocked.*]

CORNELIA. True to *his* memory! [*Points to picture.*]

ROSE. Cornelia, this is horrible! You are cruel—heartless! It is sacrilege!

CORNELIA. True to that miserable traitor and lying knave! [*Pointing at the picture.*] False alike to his father, to his brother, and to his wife!

ROSE. I will not listen to you—I will not believe you.

CORNELIA. No! Listen to *him;*—believe your own eyes. Do you remember, one night—I was visiting here, and happened to be looking over the railing, up there—you accused your husband's younger brother of ruining and deserting a woman who loved him? You gave him a packet of letters, that had been written to her by her lover and you asked him if he recognized the handwriting. [*She opens the packet, folding back the tissue paper covering deliberately and revealing a charred, half-burnt packet of letters. Extends it toward* ROSE.] Do *you* recognize the handwriting? [ROSE *takes letters, still looking at* CORNELIA, *turns face to audience, then looks at letters slowly, starts, exclaims* "Ah!" *drops letters at her feet, falls in chair, head on arm, sobbing on table.*] *I* picked that out of the fire, where Bertie had thrown it. I *thought* things were not quite as they appeared to be. I knew both of the brothers so well.

ROSE. Cornelia! Cornelia! [*Rises, dropping her head on* CORNELIA's *shoulder and weeping.* CORNELIA *pats her gently.*]

CORNELIA. Let the tears flow, my darling. [*Aside.*] They'll soon wash out all there is left of his memory in her heart.

ROSE. I am ill, Cornelia! I am ill!

CORNELIA. Yes, my dear! Shall I call Dr. Wainwright?

ROSE [*starting up, moving*]. Oh, don't do that!

CORNELIA. I'll send the Doctor to you.

ROSE. Not for the world.

CORNELIA. I'll send him away.

ROSE. O, no! You—you needn't do that. [*Goes, looks around at* CORNELIA. *Exits rapidly.*]

CORNELIA [*calling after her and laughing heartily*]. He's in the little pink room, at the end of the hall. I'll tell the Doctor to wait there till she comes to him for professional advice; but I must clear things up. [*Seeing the charred letters on the floor, she picks them up and lays them on the table, then draws the photograph from the frame, tears it up, placing the pieces on the pile, crosses and throws the whole into the fire; her eyes catch a photograph on the mantel, she takes it in her hands.*] What an excellent likeness of Dr. Wainwright. [*She starts to return picture to mantel, looks across at empty frame.*] My dynamite explosion has cleared the atmosphere. Now, for the Doctor. I will send him to her. [NICHOLAS VANALSTYNE *walks in. He stops, seeing her.*]

VANALSTYNE. Ahem! [*She stops; he bows.*] Mrs. Opdyke!

CORNELIA [*turns on him savagely*]. Monster! Robber! I will see you again presently. [*Sweeps out.*]

VANALSTYNE [*whistling softly*]. The recent earthquake in Wall Street has been brought to her attention. This is my last deal, but it's a lively one. The Fourth of July of our forefathers was painfully quiet to what this celebration will be. It has cost me twelve hundred thousand dollars so far to ruin the Louisville and West Tennessee Railway Company. But I'm certain the parson will back out as soon as he knows that Mrs. Opdyke has lost her fortune. She's been flirting with him ever since I let her drop on the floor that day instead of catching her in my arms. I've worn out the boiler of my fastest trotting horse—I mean of my steam yacht—and ruined my best trotter, trying to reconcile her. It's no use. [*Sitting on sofa.*] I've had to wreck that railway company after all. A woman never forgives a man for not hugging her when she expects him to.

Enter MUSGRAVE *with inventory. Comes down to* VANALSTYNE

MUSGRAVE. I've been over the books of the company and made all the necessary inquiries, Mr. Vanalstyne.

VANALSTYNE. M—m! Well? How many widows and orphans and helpless people generally have been struck by the failure of this company? [*Aside.*] I can't let them suffer, because I happen to be in love with a woman.

MUSGRAVE [*hands inventory to* VANALSTYNE, *who looks it over*]. The whole amount of stock held by such people, or in trust for them, is a little over two hundred and fifty thousand dollars, sir.

VANALSTYNE. Put 'em all down! [*Handing him the schedule. Aside.*] By jove!—widows aren't quoted at any such price in the market; but I want this particular widow, and I'm bidding against the church militant. [*Aloud.*] Did you get those bonds for me?

MUSGRAVE. Yes, sir. [*Taking bonds from pocket.*]

VANALSTYNE. Give them to me.

MUSGRAVE [*giving bonds*]. Mr. Bertie's last operation is a success, sir—like all the rest.

VANALSTYNE. Yes; I'm proud of him.

MUSGRAVE. He has a wonderful head for finance—a genius, sir! [*Walks.*] Great brains!—great brains! [*Exit.*

VANALSTYNE. Bertie is his father's own boy. I shall retire from business permanently and leave a worthy successor—after this little operation.

Enter the REV. DR. MURRAY HILTON

HILTON. Mr. Vanalstyne is here, James. [*Looking back as he enters; comes down.*] My dear and worthy friend. [*Extends hand effusively.*]

VANALSTYNE. Good morning, Hilton! [*Rising and placing the bonds in his pocket.*] I was just thinking of you. How are you getting on with Mrs. Opdyke?

HILTON. With—Mrs. Opdyke?

VANALSTYNE. You want to marry her?

HILTON. I did think at one time that *you*—

VANALSTYNE. She refused *me.*

HILTON. My dear friend! [*Grasping his hand.*] The Lord giveth and the Lord taketh away; but all things are for the best. I am convinced Mrs. Opdyke loves me, and your frankness reassures me. Our happy relations as shepherd and—and—

VANALSTYNE. Lamb—[*Aside.*]—with a fleece. [*Aloud.*] I'm rather old mutton, Doctor. But, go on!

HILTON. *Our* happy relations have led me

to hesitate somewhat in expressing my feelings to the lady. But—I will be as frank with you as you have been with me—I have also hesitated for—for another reason.

VANALSTYNE. Can I give you a pointer?

HILTON. You can, and no one but you could do it. I have made inquiries elsewhere in vain. Do you happen to know the—the actual amount of our dear sister's—of—the amount of her worldly possessions?

VANALSTYNE. Mrs. Opdyke gave me a check about eighteen months ago for three hundred and sixteen thousand dollars in exchange for railway shares drawing ten per cent. dividends.

HILTON. At par?

VANALSTYNE. At par. [*Walking.*]

HILTON. Ten per cent.! Something over thirty thousand dollars a year. [*Aside.*] I will hesitate no longer. My duty calls me, I will obey. [*Enter* MRS. OPDYKE; *comes down.*] She is here. [*Bows.*] Mrs. Opdyke!

CORNELIA. Dr. Hilton!

VANALSTYNE. I believe you wish to speak with me, madam [*Walking up.*], on matters of business.

CORNELIA [*coldly*]. I do, sir.

VANALSTYNE. I will see you again, presently. [*Imitating her previous exit, exits up steps and through conservatory.*]

CORNELIA. The wretch! [*Crossing angrily, walking down.*]

HILTON. Cornelia! I trust that—that I may call you by that name hereafter. Indeed, I hope that I may call you by no other. I have just learned—that is—I—I—

CORNELIA. You have learned the truth?

HILTON. I have learned what my true feelings are, and I cannot restrain them any longer. You know—you *know* that I love you. [*Taking her hands.*]

CORNELIA. Ah, Dr. Hilton, I feel now how deeply I have wronged you. I thought you were like some of the others who have sought my hand—that you were interested in my fortune.

HILTON. Cornelia, how could you!

CORNELIA. But you have come to me at a time when I have lost it all.

HILTON. I beg your pardon. What!

CORNELIA [*aside*]. So, so, a study in natural history. I'll watch a crab walk backwards. [*Aloud.*] I have lost every penny of my fortune, but it only proves how sincerely you love me. My hand is yours.

HILTON. Believe me, madam—I—[*She advances toward him, her hand still extended. Same business for* HILTON. VANALSTYNE *appears in conservatory.*] I assure you, Mrs. Opdyke—that while I—while I—[*She again advances.* HILTON *looks at her hand as before, gasps and retreats to door.* VANALSTYNE *appears at conservatory, and coughs to attract attention.*]

VANALSTYNE. The Lord giveth and the Lord taketh away! [CORNELIA *bursts into laughter and walks down.*] Wouldn't you like some stock in the Louisville and—

HILTON. No! You are utterly absorbed in worldly interests. I will return to my study and write a sermon. [CORNELIA *steps toward* HILTON *third time.* HILTON *gasps.*] No! [*Exits.*

CORNELIA. I'll hear that sermon. I'm sure he'll bring tears to my eyes. He certainly has today. [*Wiping her eyes and dropping upon the sofa.*]

VANALSTYNE [*aside*]. Now, it's my turn. [*On the steps. Aloud, coming down steps.*] My dear Mrs. Opdyke—

CORNELIA. Sir! [*Turning towards him savagely. He stops with a start.*]

VANALSTYNE [*aside*]. I'd as soon offer myself to a lioness in Central Africa that hadn't dined for a week. [*Aloud.*] One day, some months ago—the day you bought some railway shares of me—

CORNELIA [*fiercely*]. Well, sir!

VANALSTYNE [*starting, then aside*]. I'm afraid she'll accept me in about the same way the lioness would. [*Aloud.*] I asked you on that day—I—I asked you to be my wife.

CORNELIA [*angrily*]. You did, sir!

VANALSTYNE [*starting*]. I—see you remember the circumstance.

CORNELIA. Distinctly.

VANALSTYNE [*aside*]. She'll never forgive me for letting her tumble. [*Aloud.*] That was an accident, madam.

CORNELIA [*rising, angrily*]. We need not recall the incident.

VANALSTYNE. Of course, I ought to have

been there, when you—but you know—there was such a terrific fall—I mean, things went down so suddenly—that is—I would say—there was so much on the floor—the—so much on the floor of the Stock Exchange calling for my attention, that—well!—I ought to have been there when you fell into my arms, but I wasn't. We'll let that drop.

CORNELIA. Sir! [*Angrily.*]

VANALSTYNE. What I wanted to say to you was this: I loved you then, and I loved you before, and I've loved you ever since. I ruined your fortune on purpose [*She starts.*] to wipe out the parson. Will you marry me?

CORNELIA [*aside*]. He shall not compel me to be his wife through my poverty. [*Aloud, walking.*] I will *not* marry you.

VANALSTYNE [*looking down and blinking his eyes*]. Is that your final answer, Cornelia?

CORNELIA. It is my answer.

VANALSTYNE [*sighing*]. My last deal is a failure. I—prepared myself for it. [*Taking bonds from his pocket.*] I did not intend to rob you. [*She turns to him.*] Here are some bonds that cover the entire amount that I took from you. [*Going to her and extending his hand with the package. She looks at it, then at him.*]

CORNELIA. Keep the bonds—and take me.

VANALSTYNE. Eh? [*Throwing the package over his shoulder.*]

CORNELIA [*falling back*]. Be sure you're there this time. [*He catches her in his arms, brings her head to his breast, and is kissing her as* BERTIE *enters.*]

BERTIE. Father, what are you doing? [VANALSTYNE *looks up, still holding* CORNELIA *as if in a vise. She struggles to release herself.*]

VANALSTYNE [*turns to* BERTIE, *who comes down*]. If you don't know what I'm doing, the sooner you learn the better. [CORNELIA *frees herself, starting to her feet and catching her breath.*]

CORNELIA. He—he *was* there. I've been in the paws of a lion.

VANALSTYNE. That one kiss was worth every dollar it cost me. All the others will be profit, Cornelia! [*Extending his hand. She puts her own into it timidly.*] Oh, I've only just begun. [*He leads her and shows her up the steps; looks at* BERTIE, *pointing to the package on the floor.*] Young man! There's a wedding present for you. [*Goes up steps, following* CORNELIA. *They disappear in conservatory.* BERTIE *picks up the package and stands looking at it.* AGNES *runs in; stops and looks at him.*]

BERTIE. A wedding present. [*Sighs; looks up.*] Agnes!

AGNES. Rose says it was all a terrible mistake, Bertie, and we may—

BERTIE. My darling! [*Throws package of bonds on sofa, hurrying to her. She puts up her hands, checking him.*]

AGNES. *Rose* says it's all right—but—*I* want to know about all those Henriettas.

BERTIE. Oh! Henrietta is the name of a corporation.

AGNES. Which of 'em is the corporation—the ballet-dancer, the chestnut filly, or the witch?

BERTIE [*both sit on sofa*]. I will explain. You see—the—the corporation—it—it isn't the ballet dancer; neither is the filly; *she* isn't the corporation either and the witch isn't any of them—it's this way; the filly is one Henrietta—and so is the corporation; and the ballet girl, too; but the Witch of Wall Street—isn't. She's somebody else—also. Agnes!—I confessed to you at the very first, that I was as innocent as a new-born lamb, and you said you loved me in spite of it. I don't know anything more about Henrietta than you do and I never did.

AGNES. That's all *I* want to know. I don't care who she is. [*Resting her head quietly on his breast.* BERTIE *drops his arm over her gently.*]

BERTIE. I've been thinking of you all by myself, ever since you went away, Agnes. I've been very lonely.

AGNES. So have I, Bertie.

BERTIE. But I love you now more than I ever did before I had suffered so much. I would like to kiss you, please. [AGNES *looks up, offers her cheek;* BERTIE *makes movement to kiss her, hesitates, then raises her hand to his lips and kisses it, saying*—] Thank you.

AGNES [*sadly*]. You're welcome! [*Slight pause*—AGNES *looks away.*]

BERTIE. I would like to kiss you again.

[AGNES *draws her hand away and offers her cheek—he kisses her.*]

AGNES [*demurely*]. Thank you!

BERTIE. Don't mention it. We have been separated so long, Agnes, I will kiss you several times. [*He kisses her two or three times.* LADY MARY *enters in conservatory as he is doing so. She is looking back, stops at rail, sees* BERTIE.]

LADY MARY. Bertie, what are you doing? [BERTIE and AGNES look *up at her and cross, his arm about* AGNES.]

BERTIE. If you don't know what I'm doing, the sooner you learn, the better.

LADY MARY. I just caught the governor; we're going to have a new mother. [*Comes down, beckons.*] Come on, governor. Ha—ha—ha—ha! Lovers all over the house. The market is booming.

Enter DR. WAINWRIGHT *and* ROSE. *Her arm is in his and both are looking down demurely*

There's another pair! Where's Lord Arthur?

Enter LORD ARTHUR; *he is in knickerbockers, etc.; he strolls to table after all are on,* LADY MARY *crosses to him and stands by table at back.* ROSE *moves down to* BERTIE.

ROSE. Bertie! [*Taking his hand.*] I *know* you now.

BERTIE. Sister! [*Crosses to her. She presses his hand, then kisses* AGNES *and returns to the* DOCTOR, *who meets her.* WATSON FLINT *enters; he stops, and looks at* BERTIE, *who has his arm about* AGNES' *waist;* FLINT *moves across to him.*]

FLINT [*firmly*]. Bertie! [BERTIE *turns around.*] Have you any further orders for the Stock Exchange, today? [*Cuff business as before.*]

Enter VANALSTYNE *and* MRS. OPDYKE *from conservatory*

BERTIE. Yes, the C. R. of N. J. Ten thousand shares.

VANALSTYNE [*with pride*]. The Young Napoleon of Wall Street. [*Comes down and watches the following scene.*]

FLINT. Buy or sell?

BERTIE. I will consider. [*Tosses coin on his knee openly.* VANALSTYNE *starts forward, watching him.*] Sell.

VANALSTYNE. My son! [*Coming down and crossing to* BERTIE. CORNELIA *comes down.*]

FLINT. Twelve hundred and fifty dollars to us. [*Goes to sofa, picks up bonds, stands at back of sofa, examining bonds.*]

VANALSTYNE [*to* BERTIE]. Is that your regular modus operandi on the street?

BERTIE. That is the intellectual process, father. It takes brain to deal at the Stock Exchange.

VANALSTYNE. Let me congratulate you, young man. [*Shakes hands.*] You have discovered the system on which the leading financiers of this great country conduct their business interests. [*Crosses, encounters* LORD ARTHUR, *looks at him and goes up to* CORNELIA.]

LORD ARTHUR. I've been in this country nearly two years and I still continue to surprise him.

DR. WAINWRIGHT [*coming down with right arm around* ROSE]. The business interests of the country, these money transactions, these speculations in life and death, there are more sacred interests than those, and they lie deeper in our hearts.

[AGNES *and* BERTIE *extreme left,* VANALSTYNE *and* CORNELIA *on steps of conservatory.* FLINT *behind sofa,* LORD ARTHUR *and* LADY MARY *at table.* WAINWRIGHT *and* ROSE *center.*]

MUSIC

WEDDING MARCH

QUICK CURTAIN

THE NEW YORK IDEA

By Langdon Mitchell

LANGDON MITCHELL

[1862–]

LANGDON ELWYN MITCHELL was born February 17, 1862, in Philadelphia; he grew up amid the cultured circles of that city, an environment which was to train his sensibilities and provide him with materials later revealed in his most successful and important play, *The New York Idea*. After a period of foreign travel and education, he studied law at Harvard and Columbia, gaining his admission to the bar in 1886. In 1892 he was married to Marion Lea, of Philadelphia, who later played successfully in *The New York Idea*.

Mitchell has written seven plays, the majority of them being adaptations of novels. The most important of these is *Becky Sharp*, from Thackeray's *Vanity Fair;* it was a dramatization admirably adapted to the "hard, sharp playing of Mrs. Fiske," [1] who helped create the play's success; the dramatization also shows Mitchell's skill in employing the essentially dramatic episodes of the book.[2] Mitchell's first play was a romantic tragedy, *Sylvian* (1885). *The Adventures of François* (1900), from a novel by S. Weir Mitchell, was followed by *The Kreutzer Sonata* in 1906, adapted from the Yiddish of Jacob Gordin. Subsequent to *The New York Idea*, produced later in the same year, Mitchell wrote *The New Marriage* (1911), and *Major Pendennis* (1916), a dramatization of Thackeray's well-known novel.

The advent of *The New York Idea* has been recognized by historians of our drama as a highly significant event in American dramatic development. Montrose J. Moses concludes that "at last an American playwright had written a drama comparable with the very best European models, scintillating with clear, cold brilliancy, whose dialogue carried with it an exceptional literary style." [3] So universal are the implications in much of the play's satire that it has been translated into German, Hungarian, Danish, and Swedish.[4] Successful revivals of the play have revealed its modernity and its astute portrayal of characteristics that persist from generation to generation.

In *The New York Idea* we see the clash of social ideals relative to marriage and divorce; against the older, conservative concept of marriage as a more or less permanent union is set the newer view of it as a temporary arrangement for

[1] Moses, Montrose J., *Representative Plays by American Dramatists*, III, 599.

[2] For an able discussion of the artistic relation *Becky Sharp* bears to *Vanity Fair*, see William Winter's *Wallet of Time*, II, 273–286.

[3] *Op. cit.*, III, 599.

[4] The universality in Mitchell's plays is not accidental: "What gives us the most pleasure is to see a character, who, we can swear, is no infrequent occurrence." (See his "Comedy and the American Spirit," *American Mercury*, VII, 308, March, 1926.)

mutual pleasure, the provocative theme which Edith Wharton deals with some years later in *The Age of Innocence.* Although Philip Phillimore is one of the divorcees in the play, yet like his family he is temperamentally and philosophically conservative: "Sir, you cannot trifle with monogamy!" Judge that he is, he believes the head should direct the emotions, that marriage is "the rational coming together of two people." [1] When John Karslake proposes that he act as the best man at his former wife's marriage to Phillimore, the latter replies: ". . . gentlemen, there is a decorum which the stars in their courses do not violate." [2]

On the contrary, however, Karslake would create custom, rather than conform to it: ". . . of course it's not the custom, no. But we'll make it the custom." Commenting upon successive marriage and interpreting what he regards as the trend of social thought, Karslake affirms that "monogamy is just as extinct as knee-breeches. . . . Uncle Sam has established consecutive polyandry. . . ." Karslake will concede, however, that "there's got to be an interval between husbands." It is for Vida and her kind, it would seem, that the new plan is created: "Just think of the silly people, dear, that only have this sensation [getting married] once in a lifetime!" When Cynthia speculates upon the theory of marriage advanced by Sir Wilfrid, Philip characterizes it thus: "Marry for whim! That's the New York idea of marriage." Sir Wilfrid himself describes the attitude (though he is hardly the one to criticize): "That's what an American marriage is—a thank you, ma'am." And he is no doubt near a prophetic, if not a current, half-truth when he says that "New York is bounded on the North, South, East and West by the state of Divorce!" [3]

Cynthia's position is less clearly defined. To be sure, she is a divorcee apparently eager to re-marry and she seems to treat her change of status quite lightly, even sportively: e.g., when she wagers her wedding gown against her favorite horse that her former husband will not appear to act as best man at her impending marriage. But this gay contempt for Karslake, her plans to marry Phillimore, and her prenuptial escapade with Sir Wilfrid are perhaps only a pose, an acting out of the "huff" in which she parted from her husband. She finds that a "divorcee has no place in society," and that woman is, in a measure at least, spiritually monogamous: "It's just simply a fact, Karslake, and that's all there is to it—if a woman has once been married—that is, the first man she marries—then—she may quarrel, she may hate him—she may despise him—but she'll

[1] Act III, p. 493. Upon one occasion Philip reproves Cynthia because "some obscure, primitive, female *feeling* is at work corrupting" her "better judgment."

[2] That Mitchell was in some measure sympathetic with the premises of Phillimore's expressed attitude, though perhaps not going so far, is suggested by his theory that "essential comedy is the voice and expression of something purely rational." (*American Mercury,* VII, 305.) He is also of the opinion that "a slight degree of moderation, of prudence, a little ordinary and even cool kindness or good will . . ." are important factors in happiness. (*Ibid.,* 308.)

An able book dealing with ideas in the novel is Harry Hartwick's *The Foreground of American Fiction.* New York: 1934.

[3] Act I, p. 475.

always be jealous of him with other women. Always!" [1] The American woman is frequently depreciated in the play. Karslake has reason to be disturbed, of course, but he passes severe judgment: "I begin to understand our American women now. Fireflies—and the fire they gleam with is so cold that a midge couldn't warm his heart at it, let alone a man." Sudley is clear in his own mind about modern femininity: "The uncouth modern young woman, eight feet high, with a skin like a rhinoceros and manners like a cave dweller—an habitué of the race-track and the divorce court—" [2] Sir Wilfrid reflects the traditional European attitude which allows woman a place in the world—but keeps her in her place: "Friendship between the sexes is all fudge! . . . Might as well talk about being a friend to a whiskey and soda." Nor is the exposure of Vida's perfected technique in trapping man complimentary to her sex.

Certain other social evaluations are expressed in the play. Sudley will consider a young lady eligible if she comes from a "respectable family with some means," and Mrs. Phillimore doesn't "like common people any more than" she likes "common cats. . . ." To the youthful Grace "the nineteenth of May is ridiculously late to be in town," and it is Cynthia's contention that "if we cannot be decent, let us endeavor to be graceful. If we can't be moral, at least we can avoid being vulgar."

Langdon Mitchell's reading of life as illustrated in *The New York Idea* tends to censure the abuses of divorce arising from a lack of fundamental seriousness of character; the play seems to concede, however, the justice of wise separation. Thus Mitchell reflects the period at the turn of the century when people were beginning to view marriage critically rather than sentimentally. Mitchell himself states that he was not satirizing divorce itself, but an essential weakness of character that its recurrence indicated: "When I was writing the play, I had really no idea of satirizing divorce or a law or anything specially temperamental or local. What I wanted to satirize was a certain extreme frivolity in the American spirit and in our American life—frivolity in the deep sense—not just a girl's frivolity, but that profound, sterile, amazing frivolity which one observes and meets in our churches, in political life, in literature, in music; in short, in every department of American thought, feeling, and action. The old-fashioned, high-bred family in 'The New York Idea' are solemnly frivolous, and the fast, light-minded, highly-intelligent hero and heroine are frivolous in their own delightful way—frivolity, of course, to be used for tragedy or comedy. Our frivolity is, I feel, on the edge of the tragic." [3]

If Matthew Phillimore can be taken as representative, the church—at least the left wing—sanctions divorce: "I argued—that, as the grass withereth, and

[1] Act IV, pp. 506–7.

[2] Act I, p. 465.

[3] Quoted in the introduction to *The New York Idea* in Montrose J. Moses's *Representative Plays by American Dramatists*, III.

the flower fadeth,—there is nothing final in Nature; not even Death! And as there is nothing final in Nature, not even Death;—so then if Death is not final—why should marriage be final? And so the necessity of—eh—divorce! . . . All New York was there! And all New York went away happy!"

Whereas Phillimore opposes judgment to feeling, Sir Wilfrid believes in the natural man; warning Cynthia against her loveless match with the Judge, he says: "You're dying because you're ignorin' nature. . . . Can't ignore nature, Mrs. Karslake." The thing to do is "just throw the reins on nature's neck. . . ." It is this Cynthia feels she is doing when she decides against her marriage with Phillimore.

As one would naturally expect, Phillimore protests against a government that does not favor capitalism; he complains of the "shocking attack by the president on vested interests," and also of "the insanity of the United States Senate." Sudley is quite supercilious toward politics: "Very respectable family. Although I remember his father served a term in the senate."

The flippancy of dialogue and inconstancy of character in *The New York Idea* might suggest a farcical interpretation,[1] but such an approach is clearly beyond the intent of Mitchell. The author's statement quoted above indicates the indictment of frivolity in a comic vein, and his theory of dramatic art reveals the serious aspects of comedy: "The writer of comedy may, and often does verge upon the tragic. . . ."[2] Though comedy has its tragic elements, the effect of the whole is affirmative and optimistic: ". . . the comedic mind takes it that nothing is final, irretrievably wrong, hopelessly and helplessly bad. There is, it asserts, no despair, no death. . . ." "There is, in short, no possible posture of affairs but admits of a good outcome."[3] That Mitchell's theory of comedy coincides with his theory of life is suggested by his concept of higher realism as "a boundless delight in reality," and by his assertion that poets "are those men who are natively in love with life."[4]

The text of *The New York Idea* is from the first edition of 1908.

[1] It was produced in London as farce, but its performance was without Mitchell's permission.

[2] *American Mercury*, VII, 304.

[3] *Ibid.*, 305. Also: The drama's "natural activity is to warm, illuminate, enliven, vivify, and humanize." (From "The Drama: Can It Be Taught?" *Virginia Quarterly Review*, IV, 562, Oct., 1928.)

[4] *American Mercury*, VII, 310.

THE PEOPLE OF THE PLAY

(With the cast of the original production as given under the direction of Harrison Grey Fiske by Mrs. Fiske and The Manhattan Company at the Lyric Theatre, New York, on Monday evening, November 19, 1906.)

Philip Phillimore (*a Judge on the bench, age 50*)........................Charles Harbury
Grace Phillimore (*his sister, age 20*)....................................Emily Stevens
Mrs. Phillimore (*his mother, age 70*).....................................Ida Vernon
Miss Heneage (*his aunt, age 60*)..Blanche Weaver
Matthew Phillimore (*his brother—a bishop, age 45*)........................Dudley Clinton
William Sudley (*his cousin, age 50*)......................................William B. Mack
Mrs. Vida Phillimore (*his divorced wife, age 35*).........................Marion Lea
Sir Wilfrid Cates-Darby..George Arliss
John Karslake (*lawyer, politician and racing-man, age 35*)................John Mason
Mrs. Cynthia Karslake (*his divorced wife, age 25*)........................Mrs. Fiske
Brooks (*Mrs. Phillimore's footman*).......................................George Harcourt
Tim Fiddler (*Mr. Karslake's trainer*).....................................Robert V. Ferguson
Nogam (*his valet*)..Dudley Digges
Thomas (*the family servant of the Phillimores, age 45*)...................Richard Clarke
Benson (*Mrs. Vida Phillimore's maid, age 20*).............................Belle Bohn

SYNOPSIS

ACT I.—Drawing-Room in the Phillimore house, Washington Square.
Wednesday afternoon, at five o'clock.

ACT II.—Mrs. Vida Phillimore's Boudoir, Fifth Avenue.
Thursday morning, at eleven.

ACT III.—Same as Act I.
Thursday evening, at ten.

ACT IV.—John Karslake's House, Madison Avenue.
Thursday, at midnight.

Scene—*New York.* Time—*The Present.*

THE NEW YORK IDEA

THE FIRST ACT

SCENE.—*Living room in the house of* PHILIP PHILLIMORE. *Five* P.M. *of an afternoon of May. The general air and appearance of the room is that of an old-fashioned, decorous, comfortable interior. There are no electric lights and no electric bells. Two bell ropes as in old-fashioned houses. The room is in dark tones inclining to sombre and of old-fashioned elegance.*

At rise, discovered MISS HENEAGE, MRS. PHILLIMORE *and* THOMAS. MISS HENEAGE *is a solidly built, narrow minded woman in her sixties. She makes no effort to look younger than she is, and is expensively but quietly dressed, with heavy elegance. She commands her household and her family connection, and on the strength of a large and steady income feels that her opinion has its value.* MRS. PHILLIMORE *is a semi-professional invalid, refined and unintelligent. Her movements are weak and fatigued. Her voice is habitually plaintive and she is entirely a lady without a trace of being a woman of fashion.* THOMAS *is an easy-mannered, but entirely respectful family servant, un-English both in style and appearance. He has no deportment worthy of being so called, and takes an evident interest in the affairs of the family he serves.* MISS HENEAGE, *seated at the tea-table, faces footlights.* MRS. PHILLIMORE, *seated left of table.* THOMAS *stands near by. Tea things on table. Decanter of sherry in coaster. Bread and butter on plate. Vase with flowers. Silver match-box. Large old-fashioned tea urn. Guard for flame. "Evening Post" on tea-table.* MISS HENEAGE *and* MRS. PHILLIMORE *both have cups of tea.* MISS HENEAGE *sits up very straight, and pours tea for* GRACE, *who enters from door. She is a pretty and fashionably dressed girl of twenty. She speaks superciliously, coolly, and not too fast. She sits on the sofa, and does not lounge. She wears a gown suitable for spring visiting, hat, parasol, gloves, etc.*

GRACE [*crosses and sits*]. I never in my life walked so far and found so few people at home. [*Pauses. Takes off gloves. Somewhat querulously.*] The fact is the nineteenth of May is ridiculously late to be in town.

[*Pause.* THOMAS *comes down to table.*]

MISS HENEAGE. Thomas, Mr. Phillimore's sherry?

THOMAS. The sherry, ma'am. [THOMAS *nods and indicates table.*]

MISS HENEAGE. Mr. Phillimore's *Post?*

THOMAS [*same business. Pointing to "Evening Post" on tea-table*]. The *Post*, ma'am.

MISS HENEAGE [*indicates cup*]. Miss Phillimore.

[THOMAS *takes cup of tea to* GRACE. *Silence. They all sip tea.* THOMAS *goes back, fills sherry glass, remaining round and about the tea-table. They all drink tea during the following scene.*]

GRACE. The Dudleys were at home. They wished to know when my brother Philip was to be married, and where and how?

MISS HENEAGE. If the Dudleys were persons of breeding, they'd not intrude their curiosity upon you.

GRACE. I like Lena Dudley.

MRS. PHILLIMORE [*speaks slowly and gently*]. Do I know Miss Dudley?

GRACE. She knows Philip. She expects an announcement of the wedding.

MRS. PHILLIMORE. I trust you told her that my son, my sister and myself are all of the opinion that those who have been divorced should remarry with modesty and without parade.

GRACE. I told the Dudleys Philip's wedding was here, tomorrow.

[THOMAS *at back of table ready to be of use.*]

MISS HENEAGE [*to* MRS. PHILLIMORE, *picking up a sheet of paper which has lain on the table*]. I have spent the afternoon, Mary, in arranging and listing the wedding gifts, and in writing out the announcements of the wedding. I think I have attained a proper form of announcement. [*She takes the sheet of note paper and gives it to* THOMAS.] Of course the announcement Philip himself made was quite out of the question. [GRACE *smiles.*] However, there is mine.

[*Points to paper.* THOMAS *gives list to* MRS. PHILLIMORE *and moves up stage.*]

GRACE. I hope you'll send an announcement to the Dudleys.

MRS. PHILLIMORE [*reads plaintively, ready to make the best of things*]. "Mr. Philip Phillimore and Mrs. Cynthia Deane Karslake announce their marriage, May twentieth, at three o'clock, Nineteen A, Washington Square, New York." [*Replaces paper on* THOMAS'S *salver.*] It sounds very nice.

[THOMAS *hands paper to* MISS HENEAGE.]

MISS HENEAGE [THOMAS *up stage*]. In my opinion it barely escapes sounding nasty. However, it is correct. The only remaining question is—to whom the announcement should not be sent. [*Exit* THOMAS.] I consider an announcement of the wedding of two divorced persons to be in the nature of an intimate communication. It not only announces the wedding—it also announces the divorce. [*She returns to her teacup.*] The person I shall ask counsel of is cousin William Sudley. He promised to drop in this afternoon.

GRACE. Oh! We shall hear all about Cairo.

MRS. PHILLIMORE. William is judicious.

Re-enter THOMAS

MISS HENEAGE [*with finality*]. Cousin William will disapprove of the match unless a winter in Cairo has altered his moral tone.

THOMAS [*announces*]. Mr. Sudley.

[*Enter* WILLIAM SUDLEY, *a little oldish gentleman. He is and appears thoroughly insignificant. But his opinion of the place he occupies in the world is enormous. His manners, voice, presence are all those of a man of breeding and self-importance.*]

MRS. PHILLIMORE *and* MISS HENEAGE [*rise and greet* SUDLEY; *a little tremulously*]. My dear William! [*Exit* THOMAS.

SUDLEY [*shakes hands with* MRS. PHILLIMORE, *soberly glad to see them*]. How d'ye do, Mary? [*Same business with* MISS HENEAGE.] A very warm May you're having, Sarah.

GRACE [*comes to him*]. Dear Cousin William!

MISS HENEAGE. Wasn't it warm in Cairo when you left?

[*She will have the strict truth, or nothing; still, on account of* SUDLEY'S *impeccable respectability, she treats him with more than usual leniency.*]

SUDLEY [*sits*]. We left Cairo six weeks ago, Grace, so I've had no news since you wrote in February that Philip was engaged. [*Pause.*] I need not to say I consider Philip's engagement excessively regrettable. He is a judge upon the Supreme Court bench with a divorced wife—and such a divorced wife!

GRACE. Oh, but Philip has succeeded in keeping everything as quiet as possible.

SUDLEY [*acidly*]. No, my dear! He has not succeeded in keeping his former wife as quiet as possible. We had not been in Cairo a week when who should turn up but Vida Phillimore. She went everywhere and did everything no woman should!

GRACE [*unfeignedly interested*]. Oh, what did she do?

SUDLEY. She "did" Cleopatra at the tableaux at Lord Errington's! She "did" Cleopatra, and she did it robed only in some diaphanous material of a nature so transparent that—in fact she appeared to be draped in moonshine. [MISS HENEAGE *indicates the presence of* GRACE. *Rises.*] That was only the beginning. As soon as she heard of Philip's engagement, she gave a dinner in honor of it! Only divorcées were asked! And she had a dummy—yes, my dear, a dummy—at the head of the table. He stood for Philip—that is he sat for Philip!

[*Rises, and goes to table.*]

MISS HENEAGE [*irritated and disgusted*]. Ah!

MRS. PHILLIMORE [*with dismay and pain*]. Dear me!

MISS HENEAGE [*confident of the value of her opinion*]. I disapprove of Mrs. Phillimore.

SUDLEY [*takes cigarette*]. Of course you do, but has Philip taken to Egyptian cigarettes in order to celebrate my winter at Cairo?

GRACE. Those are Cynthia's.

SUDLEY [*thinking that no one is worth knowing

whom he does not know]. Who is "Cynthia"?

GRACE. Mrs. Karslake—She's staying here, Cousin William. She'll be down in a minute.

SUDLEY [*shocked*]. You don't mean to tell me—?—!

MISS HENEAGE. Yes, William, Cynthia is Mrs. Karslake—Mrs. Karslake has no New York house. I disliked the publicity of a hotel in the circumstances, and accordingly when she became engaged to Philip, I invited her here.

SUDLEY [*suspicious and distrustful*]. And may I ask *who* Mrs. Karslake is?

MISS HENEAGE [*with confidence*]. She was a Deane.

SUDLEY [*crosses up back of table, sorry to be obliged to concede good birth to any but his own blood*]. Oh, oh—well, the Deanes are extremely nice people. [*Goes to table.*] Was her father J. William Deane?

MISS HENEAGE [*still more secure; nods*]. Yes.

SUDLEY [*giving in with difficulty*]. The family is an old one. J. William Deane's daughter? Surely he left a very considerable—

MISS HENEAGE. Oh, fifteen or twenty millions.

SUDLEY [*determined not to be dazzled*]. If I remember rightly she was brought up abroad.

MISS HENEAGE. In France and England—and I fancy brought up with a very gay set in very gay places. In fact she is what is called a "sporty" woman.

SUDLEY [*always ready to think the worst*]. We might put up with that. But you don't mean to tell me Philip has the—the—the—assurance to marry a woman who has been divorced by—

MISS HENEAGE. Not at all. Cynthia Karslake divorced her husband.

SUDLEY [*gloomily, since he has less fault to find than he expected*]. She divorced him! Ah! [*Sips his tea.*]

MISS HENEAGE. The suit went by default. And, my dear William, there are many palliating circumstances. Cynthia was married to Karslake only seven months. There are no—[*Glances at* GRACE.] no hostages to Fortune! Ahem!

SUDLEY [*still unwilling to be pleased*]. Ah! What sort of a young woman is she?

GRACE [*with the superiority of one who is not too popular*]. Men admire her.

MISS HENEAGE. She's not conventional.

MRS. PHILLIMORE [*showing a faint sense of justice*]. I am bound to say she has behaved discreetly ever since she arrived in this house.

MISS HENEAGE. Yes, Mary—but I sometimes suspect that she exercises a degree of self-control—

SUDLEY [*glad to have something against some one*]. She claps on the lid, eh? And you think that perhaps some day she'll boil over? Well, of course fifteen or twenty millions—but who's Karslake?

GRACE [*very superciliously*]. He owns Cynthia K. She's the famous mare.

MISS HENEAGE. He's Henry Karslake's son.

SUDLEY [*beginning to make the best of fifteen millions-in-law*]. Oh!—Henry!—Very respectable family. Although I remember his father served a term in the senate. And so the wedding is to be tomorrow?

MRS. PHILLIMORE [*assents*]. Tomorrow.

SUDLEY [*bored, and his respectability to the front when he thinks of the ceremony; rises.* GRACE *rises*]. Tomorrow. Well, my dear Sarah, a respectable family with some means. We must accept her. But on the whole, I think it will be best for me not to see the young woman. My disapprobation would make itself apparent.

GRACE [*whispering to* SUDLEY]. Cynthia's coming. [*He doesn't hear.*]

[*Enter* CYNTHIA, *absorbed in reading a newspaper. She is a young creature in her twenties, small and high-bred, full of the love of excitement and sport. Her manner is wide awake and keen and she is evidently in no fear of the opinion of others. Her dress is exceedingly elegant, but with the elegance of a woman whose chief interests lie in life out of doors. There is nothing horsey in her style, and her expression is youthful and ingenuous.*]

SUDLEY [*sententious and determinately epigrammatic*]. The uncouth modern young woman, eight feet high, with a skin like a rhinoceros and manners like a cave dweller —an habitué of the race-track and the divorce court—

GRACE [*aside to* SUDLEY]. Cousin William!

SUDLEY. Eh, oh!

CYNTHIA [*comes down reading, immersed, excited, trembling. She lowers paper to catch the light*]. "Belmont favorite—six to one—Rockaway—Rosebud, and Flying Cloud. Slow track—raw wind—hm, hm, hm—At the half, Rockaway forged ahead, when Rosebud under the lash made a bold bid for victory—neck by neck—for a quarter—when Flying Cloud slipped by the pair and won on the post by a nose in one forty nine!" [*Speaks with the enthusiasm of a sport.*] Oh, I wish I'd seen the dear thing do it. Oh, it's Mr. Sudley! You must think me very rude. How do you do, Mr. Sudley? [*Goes to* SUDLEY.]

SUDLEY [*very respectable as he bows without cordiality*]. Mrs. Karslake.

[*Pause;* CYNTHIA *feels he should say something. As he says nothing, she speaks again.*]

CYNTHIA. I hope Cairo was delightful? Did you have a smooth voyage?

SUDLEY [*pompously*]. You must permit me, Mrs. Karslake—

CYNTHIA [*with good temper, somewhat embarrassed, and talking herself into ease*]. Oh, please don't welcome me to the family. All that formal part is over, if you don't mind. I'm one of the tribe now! You're coming to our wedding tomorrow?

SUDLEY. My dear Mrs. Karslake, I think it might be wiser—

CYNTHIA [*still with cordial good temper*]. Oh, but you must come! I mean to be a perfect wife to Philip and all his relations! That sounds rather miscellaneous, but you know what I mean.

SUDLEY [*very sententious*]. I am afraid—

CYNTHIA [*gay and still covering her embarrassment*]. If you don't come, it'll look as if you were not standing by Philip when he's in trouble! You'll come, won't you—but of course you will.

SUDLEY [*after a self-important pause*]. I will come, Mrs. Karslake. [*Pause.*] Good-afternoon. [*In a tone of sorrow and compassion.*] Good-bye, Mary. Good-afternoon, Sarah. [*Sighs.*] Grace, dear. [*To* MISS HENEAGE.] At what hour did you say the alimony commences?

MISS HENEAGE [*quickly and commandingly to cover his slip*]. The ceremony is at three P.M., William. [SUDLEY *goes up.*]

MRS. PHILLIMORE [*with fatigued voice and manner as she rises*]. I am going to my room to rest awhile. [MRS. PHILLIMORE *goes up.*]

MISS HENEAGE [*to* SUDLEY]. Oh, William, one moment—I entirely forgot! I've a most important social question to ask you [*She goes up slowly to the door with him.*] in regard to the announcements of the wedding—who they shall be sent to and who not. For instance—the Dudleys—

[*Exeunt* SUDLEY *and* MISS HENEAGE, *talking.*

CYNTHIA [*sitting on the sofa*]. So that's Cousin William?

GRACE [*near the tea-table*]. Don't you like him?

CYNTHIA [*calmly sarcastic*]. Like him? I love him. He's so generous. He couldn't have received me with more warmth if I'd been a mulatto.

[*Re-enter* THOMAS. *Enter* PHILLIMORE. PHILIP PHILLIMORE *is a self-centered, short-tempered, imperious member of the respectable fashionables of New York. He is well and solidly dressed and in manner and speech evidently a man of family. He is accustomed to being listened to in his home circle and from the bench, and it is practically impossible for him to believe that he can make a mistake.*]

GRACE [*outraged*]. Really you know—[CYNTHIA *crosses and sits at table.*] Philip!

[PHILIP *nods to her absent-mindedly. He is in his working suit and looks tired. He comes down silently, crosses to tea-table. Bends over and kisses* CYNTHIA *on forehead. Goes to his chair, which* THOMAS *has changed the position of for him. Sits, and sighs with satisfaction.*]

PHILIP [*as if exhausted by brain work*]. Ah, Grace! [*Exit* GRACE.] Well, my dear, I thought I should never extricate myself from the court room. You look very debonnair!

CYNTHIA. The tea's making. You'll have your glass of sherry?

PHILIP [*the strain of the day having evidently been severe*]. Thanks! [*Takes it from* THOMAS; *sighs.*] Ah!

CYNTHIA. I can see it's been a tiring day with you.

PHILIP [*as before*]. Hm! [*Sips.*]

CYNTHIA. Were the lawyers very long winded?

PHILIP [*almost too tired for speech*]. Prolix to the point of somnolence. It might be affirmed without inexactitude that the prolixity of counsel is the somnolence of the judiciary. I am fatigued, ah! [*A little suddenly, awaking to the fact that his orders have not been carried out to the letter.*] Thomas! My *Post* is not in its usual place!

CYNTHIA [*to* THOMAS]. It's here, Philip.

[THOMAS *gets it.*]

PHILIP. Thanks, my dear. [*Opens "Post."*] Ah! This hour with you—is—is really the —the—[*Absently.*] the one vivid moment of the day. [*Reading.*] Hm—shocking attack by the president on vested interests. Hm—too bad—but it's to be expected. The people insisted on electing a desperado to the presidential office—they must take the hold-up that follows. [*Pause; he reads.*] Hm! His English is lacking in idiom, his spelling in conservatism, his mind in balance, and his character in repose.

CYNTHIA [*amiable but not very sympathetic*]. You seem more fatigued than usual. Another glass of sherry, Philip?

PHILIP. Oh, I ought not to—

CYNTHIA. I think you seem a little more tired than usual.

PHILIP. Perhaps I am. [*She pours out sherry.* PHILIP *takes glass but does not sip.*] Ah, this hour is truly a grateful form of restful excitement. [*Pause.*] You, too, find it—eh?

[*Looks at* CYNTHIA.]

CYNTHIA [*with veiled sarcasm*]. Decidedly.

PHILIP. Decidedly what, my dear?

CYNTHIA [*as before*]. Restful.

PHILIP. Hm! Perhaps I need the calm more than you do. Over the case today I actually —eh—[*Sips.*] slumbered. I heard myself do it. That's how I know. A dressmaker sued on seven counts. [*Reads newspaper.*] Really, the insanity of the United States Senate—you seem restless, my dear. Ah—um—have you seen the evening paper? I see there has been a lightning change in the style or size of hats which ladies—

[*He sweeps a descriptive motion with his hand, gives paper to* CYNTHIA, *then moves his glass, reads, and sips.*]

CYNTHIA. The lamp, Thomas.

[THOMAS *blows out the alcohol lamp on the tea-table with difficulty. Blows twice. Movement of* PHILIP *each time. Blows again.*]

PHILIP [*irritably*]. Confound it, Thomas! What are you puffing and blowing at—?

THOMAS. It's out, ma'am—yes, sir.

PHILIP. You're excessively noisy, Thomas!

THOMAS [*in a fluster*]. Yes, sir—I am.

CYNTHIA [*soothing* THOMAS'S *wounded feelings*]. We don't need you, Thomas.

THOMAS. Yes, ma'am.

PHILIP. Puffing and blowing and shaking and quaking like an automobile in an ecstasy! [*Exit* THOMAS.

CYNTHIA [*not unsympathetically*]. Too bad, Philip! I hope my presence isn't too agitating?

PHILIP. Ah—it's just because I value this hour with you, Cynthia—this hour of tea and toast and tranquillity. It's quite as if we were married—happily married—already.

CYNTHIA [*admitting that married life is a blank, begins to look through paper*]. Yes, I feel as if we were married already.

PHILIP [*not recognizing her tone*]. Ah! It's the calm, you see.

CYNTHIA [*as before*]. The calm? Yes—yes, it's—it's the calm.

PHILIP [*sighs*]. Yes, the calm—the Halcyon calm of—of second choice. Hm! [*He reads and turns over leaves of paper.* CYNTHIA *reads. Pause.*] After all, my dear—the feeling which I have for you—is—is—eh—the market is in a shocking condition of plethora! Hm—hm—and what are you reading?

CYNTHIA [*embarrassed*]. Oh, eh—well—I—eh—I'm just running over the sporting news.

PHILIP. Oh! [*He looks thoughtful.*]

CYNTHIA [*beginning to forget* PHILIP *and to remember more interesting matters*]. I fancied Hermes would come in an easy winner. He came in nowhere. Nonpareil was ridden by Henslow—he's a rotten bad rider. He gets nervous.

PHILIP [*reading still*]. Does he? Hm! I suppose you do retain an interest in horses and races. Hm—I trust some day the—ah—law will attract— Oh [*Turning a page.*], here's the report of my opinion in that dressmaker's case—Haggerty *vs.* Phillimore.

CYNTHIA. Was the case brought against you? [*Puzzled.*]

PHILIP. Oh—no. The suit was brought by Haggerty, Miss Haggerty, a dressmaker, against the—in fact, my dear, against the former Mrs. Phillimore. [*Pause; he reads.*]

CYNTHIA [*curious about the matter*]. How did you decide it?

PHILIP. I was obliged to decide in Mrs. Phillimore's favor. Haggerty's plea was preposterous.

CYNTHIA. Did you—did you meet the—the—former—?

PHILIP. No.

CYNTHIA. I often see her at afternoon teas.

PHILIP. How did you recognize—

CYNTHIA. Why—[*Opens paper.*] because Mrs. Vida Phillimore's picture appears in every other issue of most of the evening papers. And I must confess I was curious. But, I'm sure you find it very painful to meet her again.

PHILIP [*slowly, considering*]. No,—would you find it so impossible to meet Mr.—

CYNTHIA [*much excited and aroused*]. Philip! Don't speak of him. He's nothing. He's a thing of the past. I never think of him. I forget him!

PHILIP [*somewhat sarcastic*]. That's extraordinarily original of you to forget him.

CYNTHIA [*gently, and wishing to drop the subject*]. We each of us have something to forget, Philip—and John Karslake is to me—Well, he's dead!

PHILIP. As a matter of fact, my dear, he *is* dead, or the next thing to it—for he's bankrupt. [*Pause.*]

CYNTHIA. Bankrupt? [*Excited and moved.*] Let's not speak of him. I mean never to see him or think about him or even hear of him!

[*He assents. She reads her paper. He sips his tea and reads his paper. She turns a page, starts and cries out.*]

PHILIP. God bless me!

CYNTHIA. It's a picture of—of—

PHILIP. John Karslake?

CYNTHIA. Picture of him, and one of me, and in the middle between us "Cynthia K!"

PHILIP. "Cynthia K?"

CYNTHIA [*excited*]. My pet riding mare! The best horse he has! She's an angel even in a photograph! Oh! [*Reading.*] "John Karslake drops a fortune at Saratoga."

[*Rises and goes up and down excitedly.* PHILIP *takes paper and reads.*]

PHILIP [*unconcerned, as the matter hardly touches him*]. Hem—ah—ah—Advertises country place for sale—stables, famous mare "Cynthia K"—favorite riding-mare of former Mrs. Karslake who is once again to enter the arena of matrimony with the well known and highly respected judge of—

CYNTHIA [*sensitive and much disturbed*]. Don't! Don't, Philip, please don't!

PHILIP. My dear Cynthia—take another paper—here's my *Post!* You'll find nothing disagreeable in the *Post!*

[CYNTHIA *takes paper.*]

CYNTHIA [*after reading, sits near table*]. It's much worse in the *Post.* "John Karslake sells the former Mrs. Karslake's jewels—the famous necklace now at Tiffany's, and the sporty ex-husband sells his wife's portrait by Sargent!" Philip, I can't stand this. [*Puts paper on table.*]

PHILIP. Really, my dear, Mr. Karslake is bound to appear occasionally in print—or even you may have to meet him.

Enter THOMAS

CYNTHIA [*determined and distressed*]. I won't meet him! I won't meet him. Every time I hear his name or "Cynthia K's" I'm so depressed.

THOMAS [*announcing with something like reluctance*]. Sir, Mr. Fiddler. Mr. Karslake's trainer.

[*Enter* FIDDLER. *He is an English horse trainer, a wide-awake stocky well-groomed little cockney. He knows his own mind and sees life altogether through a stable door. Well-dressed for his station, and not too young.*]

CYNTHIA [*excited and disturbed*]. Fiddler? Tim Fiddler? His coming is outrageous!

FIDDLER. A note for you, sir.

CYNTHIA [*impulsively*]. Oh, Fiddler—is that you?

FIDDLER. Yes'm!

CYNTHIA [*in a half whisper, still speaking on impulse*]. How is she! Cynthia K? How's

Planet II and the colt and Golden Rod? How's the whole stable? Are they well?

FIDDLER. No'm—we're all on the bum. [*Aside.*] Ever since you kicked us over!

CYNTHIA [*reproving him, though pleased*]. Fiddler!

FIDDLER. The horses is just simply gone to Egypt since you left, and so's the guv'nor.

CYNTHIA [*putting an end to* FIDDLER]. That will do, Fiddler.

FIDDLER. I'm waiting for an answer, sir.

CYNTHIA. What is it, Philip?

PHILIP [*uncomfortable*]. A mere matter of business. [*Aside to* FIDDLER.] The answer is, Mr. Karslake can come. The—the coast will be clear. [FIDDLER *exits.*

CYNTHIA [*amazed; rises*]. You're not going to see him?

PHILIP. But Karslake, my dear, is an old acquaintance of mine. He argues cases before me. I will see that you do not have to meet him.

[CYNTHIA *crosses in excited dejection.*]

[*Enter* MATTHEW. *He is a high church clergyman to a highly fashionable congregation. His success is partly due to his social position and partly to his elegance of speech, but chiefly to his inherent amiability, which leaves the sinner in happy peace and smiles on the just and unjust alike.*]

MATTHEW [*most amiably*]. Ah, my dear brother!

PHILIP. Matthew. [*Greets him.*]

MATTHEW [*nods to* PHILIP]. Good afternoon, my dear Cynthia. How charming you look! [CYNTHIA *sits at tea-table. To* CYNTHIA.] Ah, why weren't you in your pew yesterday? I preached a most original sermon.

[*Goes up and takes hat and cane to divan.*]

THOMAS [*aside to* PHILIP]. Sir, Mrs. Vida Phillimore's maid called you up on the telephone, and you're to expect Mrs. Phillimore on a matter of business.

PHILIP [*astonished and disgusted*]. Here, impossible! [*To* CYNTHIA.] Excuse me, my dear!

[*Exit* PHILIP, *much embarrassed, followed by* THOMAS.]

MATTHEW [*comes down to chair, happily and pleasantly self-important*]. No, really, it was a wonderful sermon, my dear. My text was from Paul—"It is better to marry than to burn." It was a strictly logical sermon. I argued—that, as the grass withereth, and the flower fadeth,—there is nothing final in Nature; not even Death! And, as there is nothing final in Nature, not even Death;—so then if Death is not final—why should marriage be final? [*Gently.*] And so the necessity of—eh—divorce! You see? It was an exquisite sermon! All New York was there! And all New York went away happy! Even the sinners—if there were any! I don't often meet sinners—do you?

CYNTHIA [*indulgently, in spite of his folly, because he is kind*]. You're such a dear, delightful Pagan! Here's your tea!

MATTHEW [*takes tea*]. Why, my dear—you have a very sad expression!

CYNTHIA [*a little bitterly*]. Why not?

MATTHEW [*with sentimental sweetness*]. I feel as if I were of no use in the world when I see sadness on a young face. Only sinners should feel sad. You have committed no sin!

CYNTHIA [*impulsively*]. Yes, I have!

MATTHEW. Eh?

CYNTHIA. I committed the unpardonable sin—whe—when I married for love!

MATTHEW. One must not marry for anything else, my dear!

CYNTHIA. Why am I marrying your brother?

MATTHEW. I often wonder why? I wonder why you didn't choose to remain a free woman.

CYNTHIA [*going over the ground she has often argued with herself*]. I meant to; but a divorcée has no place in society. I felt horridly lonely! I wanted a friend. Philip was ideal as a friend—for months. Isn't it nice to bind a friend to you?

MATTHEW. Yes—yes! [*Puts down teacup.*]

CYNTHIA [*growing more and more excited and moved as she speaks*]. To marry a friend—to marry on prudent, sensible grounds—a man—like Philip? That's what I should have done first, instead of rushing into marriage—because I had a wild, mad, sensitive, sympathetic—passion and pain and fury—of, I don't know what—that almost strangled me with happiness!

MATTHEW [*amiable and reminiscent*]. Ah—ah—in my youth—I,—I too!

CYNTHIA [*coming back to her manner of every day*]. And besides—the day Philip asked me I was in the dumps! And now—how about marrying only for love?

Re-enter PHILIP

MATTHEW. Ah, my dear, love is not the only thing in the world!

PHILIP [*half aside*]. I got there too late, she'd hung up.

CYNTHIA. Who, Philip?

PHILIP. Eh—a lady—eh—

Enter THOMAS, *flurried, with card on salver*

THOMAS. A card for you, sir. Ahem—ahem —Mrs. Phillimore—that was, sir.

PHILIP. Eh?

THOMAS. She's on the stairs, sir. [*Turns. Enter* VIDA. THOMAS *announces her as being the best way of meeting the difficulty.*] Mrs. Vida Phillimore!

[VIDA *comes in slowly, with the air of a spoiled beauty. She stops just inside the door and speaks in a very casual manner. Her voice is languorous and caressing. She is dressed in the excess of the French fashion and carries an outré parasol. She smiles and comes, undulating, down. Tableau. Exit* THOMAS.]

VIDA. How do you do, Philip. Don't tell me I'm a surprise! I had you called up on the 'phone and I sent up my card—and, besides, Philip dear, when you have the—the—habit of the house, as unfortunately I have, you can't treat yourself like a stranger in a strange land. At least, I can't—so here I am. My reason for coming was to ask you about that B. and O. stock we hold in common. [*To* MATTHEW, *condescendingly, the clergy being a class of unfortunates debarred by profession from the pleasures of the world.*] How do you do? [*Pause. She then goes to the real reason of her visit.*] Do be polite and present me to your wife-to-be.

PHILIP [*awkwardly*]. Cynthia—

CYNTHIA [*comes down to table. Cheerfully, with dash*]. We're delighted to see you, Mrs. Phillimore. I needn't ask you to make yourself at home, but will you have a cup of tea?

[MATTHEW *sits near little table.*]

VIDA [*to* PHILIP]. My dear, she's not in the least what I expected. I heard she was a dove! She's a very dashing kind of a dove! [*To* CYNTHIA; *comes to tea-table.*] My dear, I'm paying you compliments. Five lumps and quantities of cream. I find single life very thinning. [*To* PHILIP, *very calm and ready to be agreeable to any man.*] And how well you're looking! It must be the absence of matrimonial cares—or is it a new angel in the house?

CYNTHIA [*outraged at* VIDA'S *intrusion, but polite though delicately sarcastic*]. It's most amusing to sit in your place. And how at home you must feel here in this house where you have made so much trouble—I mean tea. [*Rises.*] Do you know it would be in much better taste if you would take the place you're accustomed to?

VIDA [*as calm as before*]. My dear, I'm an intruder only for a moment; I shan't give you a chance to score off me again! But I must thank you, dear Philip, for rendering that decision in my favor—

PHILIP. I assure you—

VIDA [*unable to resist a thrust at the close of this speech*]. Of course, you would like to have rendered it against me. It was your wonderful sense of justice, and that's why I'm so grateful—if not to you, to your Maker!

PHILIP [*he feels that this is no place for his future wife. Rises quickly, goes up. To* CYNTHIA]. Cynthia, I would prefer that you left us.

[MATTHEW *comes to sofa and sits.*]

CYNTHIA [*determined not to leave the field first, remains seated*]. Certainly, Philip!

PHILIP. I expect another visitor who—

VIDA [*with flattering insistence, to* CYNTHIA]. Oh, my dear—don't go! The truth is—I came to see you! I feel most cordially towards you—and really, you know, people in our position should meet on cordial terms.

CYNTHIA [*taking it with apparent calm, but pointing her remarks*]. Naturally. If people in our position couldn't meet, New York society would soon come to an end.

Enter THOMAS

VIDA [*calm, but getting her knife in too*]. Precisely. Society's no bigger than a band-box. Why, it's only a moment ago I saw Mr. Karslake walking—

CYNTHIA. Ah!

THOMAS [*announcing clearly. Every one changes place, in consternation, amusement or surprise.* CYNTHIA *moves to leave the stage, but stops for fear of attracting* KARSLAKE'S *attention*]. Mr. John Karslake!

[*Enter* KARSLAKE. *He is a powerful, generous personality, a man of affairs, breezy, gay and careless. He gives the impression of being game for any fate in store for him. His clothes indicate sporting propensities and his taste in waistcoats and ties is brilliant.* KARSLAKE *sees first* PHILIP *and then* MATTHEW. *Exit* THOMAS.]

PHILIP. How do you do?

JOHN [*very gay and no respecter of persons*]. Good-afternoon, Mr. Phillimore. Hello—here's the church! [*Crosses to* MATTHEW *and shakes hands. He slaps him on the back.*] I hadn't the least idea—how are you? By George, your reverence, that was a racy sermon of yours on Divorce! What was your text? [*Sees* VIDA *and bows, very politely.*] Galatians 4 : 2: "The more the merrier," or "Who next?" [*Smiles.*] As the whale said after Jonah!

[CYNTHIA *makes a sudden movement, turns, turns cup over.* JOHN *faces about quickly and they face each other.* JOHN *gives a frank start. Pause. Tableau.*]

JOHN [*astounded, in a low voice*]. Mrs. Karslake—[*Bows.*] I was not aware of the pleasure in store for me. I understood you were in the country. [*Recovers, crosses to chair.*] Perhaps you'll be good enough to make me a cup of tea?—that is if the teapot wasn't lost in the scrimmage. [*Pause.* CYNTHIA, *determined to equal him in coolness, returns to the tea-tray.*] Mr. Phillimore, I came to get your signature in that matter of Cox *vs.* Keely.

PHILIP. I shall be at your service, but pray be seated. [*He indicates chair up table.*]

JOHN [*sitting beyond but not far from the tea-table*]. And I also understood you to say you wanted a saddle horse. [*Sits.*]

PHILIP. You have a mare called—eh—"Cynthia K"?

JOHN [*promptly*]. Yes—she's not for sale.

PHILIP. Oh, but she's just the mare I had set my mind on.

JOHN [*with a touch of humor*]. You want her for yourself?

PHILIP [*a little flustered*]. I—eh—I sometimes ride.

JOHN [*he is sure of himself now*]. She's rather lively for you, Judge. Mrs. Karslake used to ride her.

PHILIP. You don't care to sell her to me?

JOHN. She's a dangerous mare, Judge, and she's as delicate and changeable as a girl. I'd hate to leave her in your charge!

CYNTHIA [*eagerly but in a low voice*]. Leave her in mine, Mr. Karslake!

JOHN [*after slight pause*]. Mrs. Karslake knows all about a horse, but—[*Turning to* CYNTHIA.] Cynthia K's got rather tricky of late.

CYNTHIA [*haughtily*]. You mean to say you think she'd chuck me?

JOHN [*with polite solicitude and still humorous. To* PHILIP]. I'd hate to have a mare of mine deprive you of a wife, Judge. [*Rises.* CYNTHIA, *business of anger.*] She goes to Saratoga next week, C. W.

VIDA [*who has been sitting and talking to* MATTHEW *for lack of a better man, comes to talk to* KARSLAKE]. C. W.?

JOHN [*rising as she rises*]. Creditors willing.

VIDA [*crossing and sitting left of tea-table*]. I'm sure your creditors are willing.

JOHN. Oh, they're a breezy lot, my creditors. They're giving me a dinner this evening.

VIDA [*more than usually anxious to please*]. I regret I'm not a breezy creditor, but I do think you owe it to me to let me see your Cynthia K! Can't you lead her around to my house?

JOHN. At what hour, Mrs. Phillimore?

VIDA. Say eleven? And you, too, might have a leading in my direction—771 Fifth Avenue.

[JOHN *bows.* CYNTHIA *hears and notes this.*]

CYNTHIA. Your cup of tea, Mr. Karslake.

JOHN. Thanks. [JOHN *gets tea and sips.*] I beg your pardon—you have forgotten, Mrs. Karslake—very naturally, it has slipped from your memory, but I don't take sugar.

[CYNTHIA, *furious with him and herself. He hands cup back. She makes a second cup.*]

CYNTHIA [*cheerfully; in a rage*]. Sorry!

JOHN [*also apparently cheerful*]. Yes, gout.

It gives me a twinge even to sit in the shadow of a sugar maple! First you riot, and then you diet!

VIDA [*calm and amused; aside to* MATTHEW]. My dear Matthew, he's a darling! But I feel as if we were all taking tea on the slope of a volcano! [MATTHEW *sits.*]

PHILIP. It occurred to me, Mr. Karslake, you might be glad to find a purchaser for your portrait by Sargent?

JOHN. It's not *my* portrait. It's a portrait of Mrs. Karslake, and to tell you the truth—Sargent's a good fellow—I've made up my mind to keep it—to remember the artist by. [CYNTHIA *is wounded by this.*]

PHILIP. Hm!

[CYNTHIA *hands second cup to* JOHN.]

CYNTHIA [*with careful politeness*]. Your cup of tea, Mr. Karslake.

JOHN [*rises; takes tea with courteous indifference*]. Thanks—sorry to trouble you.

[*He drinks the cup of tea standing by the tea-table.*]

PHILIP [*to make conversation*]. You're selling your country place?

JOHN. If I was long of hair—I'd sell that.

CYNTHIA [*excited. Taken out of herself by the news*]. You're not really selling your stable?

JOHN [*finishes his tea, places empty cup on tea-table and reseats himself*]. Every gelding I've got—seven foals and a donkey! I don't mean the owner.

CYNTHIA [*still interested and forgetting the discomfort of the situation*]. How did you ever manage to come such a cropper?

JOHN. Streak of blue luck!

CYNTHIA [*quickly*]. I don't see how it's possible—

JOHN. You would if you'd been there. You remember the head man? [*Sits.*] Bloke?

CYNTHIA. Of course!

JOHN. Well, his wife divorced him for beating her over the head with a bottle of Fowler's Solution, and it seemed to prey on his mind. He sold me—

CYNTHIA [*horrified*]. Sold a race?

JOHN. About ten races, I guess.

CYNTHIA [*incredulous*]. Just because he'd beaten his wife?

JOHN. No. Because she divorced him.

CYNTHIA. Well, I can't see why that should prey on his mind! [*Suddenly remembers.*]

JOHN. Well, I have known men that it stroked the wrong way. But he cost me eighty thousand. And then Urbanity ran third in the thousand dollar stakes for two-year-olds at Belmont.

CYNTHIA [*she throws this remark in*]. I never had faith in that horse.

JOHN. And, of course, it never rains monkeys but it pours gorillas! So when I was down at St. Louis on the fifth, I laid seven to three on Fraternity—

CYNTHIA. Crazy! Crazy!

JOHN [*ready to take the opposite view*]. I don't see it. With her record she ought to have romped it an easy winner.

CYNTHIA [*pure sport*]. She hasn't the stamina! Look at her barrel!

JOHN. Well, anyhow, Geranium finished me!

CYNTHIA. You didn't lay odds on Geranium!

JOHN. Why not? She's my own mare—

CYNTHIA. Oh!

JOHN. Streak o' bad luck—

CYNTHIA [*plainly anxious to say "I told you so"*]. Streak of poor judgment! Do you remember the day you rode Billy at a six foot stone wall, and he stopped and you didn't, and there was a hornet's nest [MATTHEW *rises.*] on the other side, and I remember you were hot just because I said you showed poor judgment? [*She laughs at the memory. A general movement of disapproval. She remembers the situation.*] I beg your pardon.

MATTHEW [*rises to meet* VIDA. *Hastily*]. It seems to me that horses are like the fourth gospel. Any conversation about them becomes animated almost beyond the limits of the urbane!

[VIDA *disgusted by such plainness of speech, rises and goes to* PHILIP *who waves her to a chair.*]

PHILIP [*formal*]. I regret that you have endured such reverses, Mr. Karslake.

[JOHN *quietly bows.*]

CYNTHIA [*concealing her interest; speaks casually*]. You haven't mentioned your new English horse—Pantomime. What did he do at St. Louis?

JOHN [*sits*]. Fell away and ran fifth.

CYNTHIA. Too bad. Was he fully acclimated? Ah, well—

JOHN. We always differed—you remember—on the time needed—

MATTHEW [*coming to* CYNTHIA, *speaking to carry off the situation as well as to get a tip*]. Isn't there a—eh—a race tomorrow at Belmont Park?

JOHN. Yes. I'm going down in my auto.

CYNTHIA [*evidently wishing she might be going too*]. Oh!

MATTHEW. And what animal shall you prefer? [*Covering his personal interest with amiable altruism.*]

JOHN. I'm backing Carmencita.

CYNTHIA [*gesture of despair*]. Carmencita! Carmencita! [MATTHEW *goes to* VIDA.]

JOHN. You may remember we always differed on Carmencita.

CYNTHIA [*disgusted at* JOHN'S *dunderheadedness*]. But there's no room for difference. She's a wild, headstrong, dissatisfied, foolish little filly. The deuce couldn't ride her—she'd shy at her own shadow—"Carmencita." Oh, very well then, I'll wager you—and I'll give you odds too—"Decorum" will come in first, and I'll lay three to one he'll beat Carmencita by five lengths! How's that for fair?

JOHN [*never forgetting the situation*]. Sorry I'm not flush enough to take you.

CYNTHIA [*impetuously*]. Philip, dear, you lend John enough for the wager.

MATTHEW [*as nearly horrified as so soft a soul can be*]. Ahem! Really—

JOHN. It's a sporty idea, Mrs. Karslake, but perhaps in the circumstances—

CYNTHIA [*her mind on her wager*]. In what circumstances?

PHILIP [*with a nervous laugh*]. It does seem to me there is a certain impropriety—

CYNTHIA [*remembering the conventions, which, for a moment, had actually escaped her*]. Oh, I forgot. When horses are in the air—

MATTHEW [*pouring oil on troubled waters. Crossing, he speaks to* VIDA *at back of armchair, where she sits*]. It's the fourth gospel, you see.

Enter THOMAS *with letter on salver, which he hands to* PHILIP

CYNTHIA [*meekly*]. You are quite right, Philip. [PHILIP *goes up.*] The fact is, seeing Mr. Karslake again [*Laying on her indifference with a trowel.*] he seems to me as much a stranger as if I were meeting him for the first time.

MATTHEW [*aside to* VIDA]. We are indeed taking tea on the slope of a volcano.

VIDA [*is about to go, but thinks she will have a last word with* JOHN]. I'm sorry your fortunes are so depressed, Mr. Karslake.

PHILIP [*looking at the card that* THOMAS *has just brought in*]. Who in the world is Sir Wilfrid Cates-Darby? [*General move.*]

JOHN. Oh—eh—Cates-Darby? [PHILIP *opens letter which* THOMAS *has brought with card.*] That's the English chap I bought Pantomime of.

PHILIP [*to* THOMAS]. Show Sir Wilfrid Cates-Darby in.

[*Exit* THOMAS. *The prospect of an Englishman with a handle to his name changes* VIDA'S *plans and instead of leaving the house, she goes to sofa and sits there.*]

JOHN. He's a good fellow, Judge. Place near Epsom. Breeder. Over here to take a shy at our races.

Enter THOMAS

THOMAS [*announcing*]. Sir Wilfrid Cates-Darby.

[*Enter* SIR WILFRID CATES-DARBY. *He is a high-bred, sporting Englishman. His manner, his dress and his diction are the perfection of English elegance. His movements are quick and graceful. He talks lightly and with ease. He is full of life and unsmiling good temper.*]

PHILIP [*to* SIR WILFRID *and referring to the letter of introduction in his hand*]. I am Mr. Phillimore. I am grateful to Stanhope for giving me the opportunity of knowing you, Sir Wilfrid. I fear you find it warm?

SIR WILFRID [*delicately mopping his forehead*]. Ah, well—ah—warm, no—hot, yes! Deuced extraordinary climate yours, you know, Mr. Phillimore.

PHILIP [*conventional*]. Permit me to present you to—[*The unconventional situation pulls him up short. It takes him a moment to decide how to meet it. He makes up his mind to pretend that everything is as usual, and presents* CYNTHIA *first.*] Mrs. Karslake.

[SIR WILFRID *bows, surprised and doubtful.*]

CYNTHIA. How do you do?

PHILIP. And to Mrs. Phillimore. [VIDA *bows nonchalantly, but with a view to catching* SIR WILFRID'S *attention.* SIR WILFRID *bows, and looks from her to* PHILIP.] My brother—and Mr. Karslake you know.

SIR WILFRID. How do, my boy. [*Half aside, to* JOHN.] No idea you had such a charming little wife—What?—Eh?

[KARSLAKE *goes up to speak to* MATTHEW *and* PHILIP *in the further room.*]

CYNTHIA. You'll have a cup of tea, Sir Wilfrid?

SIR WILFRID [*at table*]. Thanks, awfully. [*Very cheerfully.*] I'd no idea old John had a wife! The rascal never told me!

CYNTHIA [*pouring tea and facing the facts*]. I'm not Mr. Karslake's wife!

SIR WILFRID. Oh!—Eh?—I see—

[*Business of thinking it out.*]

VIDA [*who has been ready for some time to speak to him*]. Sir Wilfrid, I'm sure no one has asked you how you like our country?

SIR WILFRID [*goes to* VIDA *and speaks, standing by her at sofa*]. Oh, well, as to climate and horses, I say nothing. But I like your American humor. I'm acquiring it for home purposes.

VIDA [*getting down to love as the basis of conversation*]. Aren't you going to acquire an American girl for home purposes?

SIR WILFRID. The more narrowly I look the agreeable project in the face, the more I like it. Oughtn't to say that in the presence of your husband.

[*He casts a look at* PHILIP, *who has gone into the next room.*]

VIDA [*cheerful and unconstrained*]. He's not my husband!

SIR WILFRID [*completely confused*]. Oh—eh?—my brain must be boiled. You are—Mrs.—eh—ah—of course, now I see! I got the wrong names! I thought you were Mrs. Phillimore. [*He sits by her.*] And that nice girl Mrs. Karslake! You're deucedly lucky to be Mrs. Karslake. John's a prime sort. I say, have you and he got any kids? How many?

VIDA [*horrified at being suspected of maternity, but speaking very sweetly*]. He's not my husband.

SIR WILFRID [*his good spirits all gone, but determined to clear things up*]. Phew! Awfully hot in here! Who the deuce is John's wife?

VIDA. He hasn't any.

SIR WILFRID. Who's Phillimore's wife?

VIDA. He hasn't any.

SIR WILFRID. Thanks, fearfully! [*To* MATTHEW, *whom he approaches; suspecting himself of having lost his wits.*] Would you excuse me, my dear and Reverend Sir—you're a churchman and all that—would you mind straightening me out?

MATTHEW [*most gracious*]. Certainly, Sir Wilfrid. Is it a matter of doctrine?

SIR WILFRID. Oh, damme—beg your pardon,—no, it's not words, it's women.

MATTHEW [*ready to be outraged*]. Women!

SIR WILFRID. It's divorce. Now, the lady on the sofa—

MATTHEW. *Was* my brother's wife; he divorced her—incompatibility—Rhode Island. The lady at the tea-table *was* Mr. Karslake's wife; she divorced him—desertion—Sioux Falls. One moment—she is about to marry my brother.

SIR WILFRID [*cheerful again*]. I'm out! Thought I never would be! Thanks!

[VIDA *laughs.*]

VIDA [*not a whit discountenanced and ready to please*]. Have you got me straightened out yet?

SIR WILFRID. Straight as a die! I say, you had lots of fun, didn't you? [*Goes back to sofa; stands.*] And so *she's* Mrs. John Karslake?

VIDA [*calm, but secretly disappointed*]. Do you like her?

SIR WILFRID. My word!

VIDA [*fully expecting personal flattery*]. Eh?

SIR WILFRID. She's a box o' ginger!

VIDA. You haven't seen many American women!

SIR WILFRID. Oh, haven't I?

VIDA. If you'll pay me a visit tomorrow—at twelve, you shall meet a most charming young woman, who has seen you once, and who admires you—ah!

SIR WILFRID. I'm there—what!

VIDA. Seven hundred and seventy-one Fifth Avenue.

SIR WILFRID. Seven seventy-one Fifth Avenue—at twelve.

VIDA. At twelve.

SIR WILFRID. Thanks! [*Indicates* CYNTHIA.] She's a thoroughbred—you can see that with one eye shut. Twelve. [*Shakes hands.*] Awfully good of you to ask me. [*Joins* JOHN.] I say, my boy, your former's an absolute certainty. [*To* CYNTHIA.] I hear you're about to marry Mr. Phillimore, Mrs. Karslake?

[KARSLAKE *crosses to* VIDA; *they both go to sofa, where they sit.*]

CYNTHIA. Tomorrow, 3 P.M., Sir Wilfrid.

SIR WILFRID [*much taken with* CYNTHIA. *To her. Sits*]. Afraid I've run into a sort of family party, eh? [*Indicates* VIDA.] The Past and the Future—awfully chic way you Americans have of asking your divorced husbands and wives to drop in, you know—celebrate a christenin', or the new bride, or—

CYNTHIA. Do you like your tea strong?

SIR WILFRID. Middlin'.

CYNTHIA. Sugar?

SIR WILFRID. One!

CYNTHIA. Lemon?

SIR WILFRID. Just torture a lemon over it. [*He makes a gesture as of twisting a lemon peel. She gives tea.*] Thanks! So you do it tomorrow at three?

CYNTHIA. At three, Sir Wilfrid.

SIR WILFRID. Sorry!

CYNTHIA. Why are you sorry?

SIR WILFRID. Hate to see a pretty woman married. Might marry her myself.

CYNTHIA. Oh, but I'm sure you don't admire American women.

SIR WILFRID. Admire you, Mrs. Karslake—

CYNTHIA. Not enough to marry me, I hope.

SIR WILFRID. Marry you in a minute! Say the word. Marry you now—here.

CYNTHIA. You don't think you ought to know me a little before—

SIR WILFRID. Know you? Do know you.

[CYNTHIA *covering her hair with her handkerchief.*]

CYNTHIA. What color is my hair?

SIR WILFRID. Pshaw!

CYNTHIA. You see! You don't know whether I'm a chestnut or a strawberry roan! In the States we think a few months of friendship is quite necessary.

SIR WILFRID. Few months of moonshine! Never was a friend to a woman—thank God, in all my life.

CYNTHIA. Oh—oh, oh!

SIR WILFRID. Might as well talk about being a friend to a whiskey and soda.

CYNTHIA. A woman has a soul, Sir Wilfrid.

SIR WILFRID. Well, good whiskey is spirits—dozens o' souls!

CYNTHIA. You are so gross!

SIR WILFRID [*changes seat to above table*]. Gross? Not a bit! Friendship between the sexes is all fudge! I'm no friend to a rose in my garden. I don't call it friendship—eh—eh—a warm, starry night, moonbeams and ilex trees, "and a spirit who knows how" and all that—eh—[*Getting closer to her.*] You make me feel awfully poetical, you know—[PHILIP *comes down, glances nervously at* CYNTHIA *and* SIR WILFRID, *and walks up again.*] What's the matter? But, I say—poetry aside—do you, eh—[*Looks around to place* PHILIP.] Does he—y' know—is he—does he go to the head?

CYNTHIA. Sir Wilfrid, Mr. Phillimore is my sober second choice.

SIR WILFRID. Did you ever kiss him? I'll bet he fined you for contempt of court. Look here, Mrs. Karslake, if you're marryin' a man you don't care about—

CYNTHIA [*amused and excusing his audacity as a foreigner's eccentricity*]. Really!

SIR WILFRID. Well, I don't offer myself—

CYNTHIA. Oh!

SIR WILFRID. Not this instant—

CYNTHIA. Ah!

SIR WILFRID. But let me drop in tomorrow at ten.

CYNTHIA. What country and state of affairs do you think you have landed in?

SIR WILFRID. New York, by jove! Been to school, too. New York is bounded on the North, South, East and West by the state of Divorce! Come, come, Mrs. Karslake, I like your country. You've no fear and no respect—no can't and lots of can. Here you all are, you see—your former husband, and your new husband's former wife—sounds like Ollendoff! Eh? So there you are, you see! But, jokin' apart—why do you marry him? Oh, well, marry him if you must!

You can run around the corner and get a divorce afterwards—

CYNTHIA. I believe you think they throw one in with an ice-cream soda!

SIR WILFRID [*rises*]. Damme, my dear lady, a marriage in your country is no more than a—eh—eh—what do you call 'em? A thank you, ma'am. That's what an American marriage is—a thank you, ma'am. Bump—bump—you're over it and on to the next.

CYNTHIA. You're an odd fish! What? I believe I like you!

SIR WILFRID. 'Course you do! You'll see me when I call tomorrow—at ten? We'll run down to Belmont Park, eh?

CYNTHIA. Don't be absurd!

VIDA [*has finished her talk with* JOHN, *and breaks in on* SIR WILFRID, *who has hung about* CYNTHIA *too long to suit her*]. Tomorrow at twelve, Sir Wilfrid!

SIR WILFRID. Twelve!

VIDA [*shakes hands with* JOHN]. Don't forget, Mr. Karslake—eleven o'clock tomorrow.

JOHN [*bows assent*]. I won't!

VIDA [*comes to the middle of the stage and speaks to* CYNTHIA]. Oh, Mrs. Karslake, I've ordered Tiffany to send you something. It's a sugar bowl to sweeten the matrimonial lot! I suppose nothing would induce you to call?

CYNTHIA [*distant and careless of offending*]. Thanks, no—that is, is "Cynthia K" really to be there at eleven? I'd give a gold mine to see her again.

VIDA [*above chair*]. Do come!

CYNTHIA. If Mr. Karslake will accommodate me by his absence.

VIDA. Dear Mr. Karslake, you'll have to change your hour.

JOHN. Sorry, I'm not able to.

CYNTHIA. I can't come later for I'm to be married.

JOHN. It's not as bad as that with me, but I am to be sold up—Sheriff, you know. Can't come later than eleven.

VIDA [*to* CYNTHIA]. Any hour but eleven, dear.

CYNTHIA [*perfectly regardless of* VIDA, *and ready to vex* JOHN *if possible*]. Mrs. Phillimore, I shall call on you at eleven—to see Cynthia K. I thank you for the invitation. Good-afternoon.

VIDA [*aside to* JOHN, *crossing to speak quietly to him*]. It's mere bravado; she won't come.

JOHN. You don't know her.

[*Pause. General embarrassment.* SIR WILFRID *business with eye-glass.* JOHN *angry.* CYNTHIA *triumphant.* MATTHEW *embarrassed.* VIDA *irritated.* PHILIP *puzzled. Everybody at odds.*]

SIR WILFRID [*for the first time a witness to the pretty complications of divorce; to* MATTHEW]. Do you have it as warm as this ordinarily?

MATTHEW [*for whom these moments are more than usually painful, and wiping his brow*]. It's not so much the heat as the humidity.

JOHN [*looks at watch; glad to be off*]. I shall be late for my creditors' dinner.

SIR WILFRID [*comes down*]. Creditors' dinner.

JOHN [*reads note*]. Fifteen of my sporting creditors have arranged to give me a blowout at Sherry's, and I'm expected right away or sooner. And by the way, I was to bring my friends—if I had any. So now's the time to stand by me! Mrs. Phillimore?

VIDA. Of course!

JOHN [*ready to embarrass* CYNTHIA, *if possible, and speaking as if he had quite forgotten their former relations*]. Mrs. Karslake—I beg your pardon. Judge? [PHILIP *declines.*] No? Sir Wilfrid?

SIR WILFRID. I'm with you!

JOHN [*to* MATTHEW]. Your Grace?

MATTHEW. I regret—

SIR WILFRID. Is it the custom for creditors—

JOHN. Come on, Sir Wilfrid! [THOMAS *opens door.*] Good-night, Judge—Your Grace—

SIR WILFRID. Is it the custom—

JOHN. Hang the custom! Come on—I'll show you a gang of creditors worth having!

[*Exit* SIR WILFRID *with* JOHN, *arm in arm, preceded by* VIDA. MATTHEW *crosses, smiling, as if pleased, in a Christian way, with this display of generous gaiety. Looks at his watch.*]

MATTHEW. Good gracious! I had no idea the hour was so late. I've been asked to a meeting with Maryland and Iowa, to talk over the divorce situation. [*Exit. Voice heard off.*] Good-afternoon! Good-afternoon!

[CYNTHIA *evidently much excited. The outer*

door slams. PHILIP *comes down slowly.* CYNTHIA *stands, her eyes wide, her breathing visible, until* PHILIP *speaks, when she seems suddenly to realize her position. A long pause.*]

PHILIP [*superior*]. I have seldom witnessed a more amazing cataclysm of jocundity! Of course, my dear, this has all been most disagreeable for you.

CYNTHIA [*excitedly*]. Yes, yes, yes!

PHILIP. I saw how much it shocked your delicacy.

CYNTHIA [*distressed and moved*]. Outrageous. [PHILIP *sits.*]

PHILIP. Do be seated, Cynthia. [*Takes up paper. Quietly.*] Very odd sort of an Englishman—that Cates-Darby!

CYNTHIA. Sir Wilfrid?—Oh, yes! [PHILIP *settles down to paper. To herself.*] Outrageous! I've a great mind to go at eleven—just as I said I would!

PHILIP. Do sit down, Cynthia!

CYNTHIA. What? What?

PHILIP. You make me so nervous—

CYNTHIA. Sorry—sorry.

[*She sits, sees paper, takes it, looks at picture of* JOHN KARSLAKE.]

PHILIP [*sighs with content*]. Ah! now that I see him, I don't wonder you couldn't stand him. There's a kind of—ah—spontaneous inebriety about him. He is incomprehensible! If I might with reverence cross question the Creator, I would say to him: "Sir, to what end or purpose did you create Mr. John Karslake?" I believe I should obtain no adequate answer! However [*Sighs.*], at last we have peace—and the *Post!* [PHILIP *settles himself, reads paper;* CYNTHIA *looks at her paper, occasionally looks across at* PHILIP.] Forget the dust of the arena—the prolixity of counsel—the involuntary fatuity of things in general. [*Pause. He reads.*] Compose yourself!

[MISS HENEAGE, MRS. PHILLIMORE *and* GRACE *enter.* CYNTHIA *sighs without letting her sigh be heard. Tries to compose herself. Glances at paper and then hearing* MISS HENEAGE, *starts slightly.* MISS HENEAGE *and* MRS. PHILLIMORE *stop at table.*]

MISS HENEAGE [*she carries a sheet of paper*]. There, my dear Mary, is the announcement as I have now reworded it. I took William's suggestion. [MRS. PHILLIMORE *takes and casually reads it.*] I also put the case to him, and he was of the opinion that the announcement should be sent *only* to those people who are really *in* society.

[*Sits above table.* CYNTHIA *braces herself to bear the Phillimore conversation.*]

GRACE. I wish you'd make an exception of the Dudleys. [CYNTHIA *rises and crosses to chair by table.*]

MISS HENEAGE. And, of course, that excludes the Oppenheims—the Vance-Browns.

MRS. PHILLIMORE. It's just as well to be exclusive.

GRACE. I do wish you'd make an exception of Lena Dudley.

MISS HENEAGE. We might, of course, include those new Girardos, and possibly—possibly the Paddingtons.

GRACE. I do wish you would take in Lena Dudley. [*They are now sitting.*]

MRS. PHILLIMORE. The mother Dudley is as common as a charwoman, and not nearly as clean.

PHILIP [*sighs. His own feelings as usual to the fore*]. Ah! I certainly am fatigued!

[CYNTHIA *begins to slowly crush the newspaper she has been reading with both hands, as if the effort of self-repression were too much for her.*]

MISS HENEAGE [*making the best of a gloomy future*]. We shall have to ask the Dudleys sooner or later to dine, Mary—because of the elder girl's marriage to that dissolute French Marquis.

MRS. PHILLIMORE [*plaintively*]. I don't like common people any more than I like common cats, and of course in my time—

MISS HENEAGE. I think I shall include the Dudleys.

MRS. PHILLIMORE. You think you'll include the Dudleys?

MISS HENEAGE. Yes, I think I will include the Dudleys!

[*Here* CYNTHIA *gives up. Driven desperate by their chatter, she has slowly rolled her newspaper into a ball, and at this point tosses it violently to the floor and bursts into hysterical laughter.*]

MRS. PHILLIMORE. Why, my dear Cynthia—Compose yourself.

PHILIP [*hastily*]. What is the matter, Cynthia?

[*They speak together. General movement.*]

MISS HENEAGE. Why, Mrs. Karslake, what is the matter?

GRACE [*comes quickly forward*]. Mrs. Karslake!

CURTAIN

THE SECOND ACT

SCENE.—MRS. VIDA PHILLIMORE'S *boudoir. The room is furnished to please an empty-headed, pleasure-loving and fashionable woman. The furniture, the ornaments, what pictures there are, all witness to taste up-to-date. Two French windows open on to a balcony, from which the trees of Central Park can be seen. There is a table between them; a mirror, a scent bottle, etc., upon it. On the right, up stage, is a door; on the right, down stage, another door. A lady's writing table stands between the two, nearer centre of stage. There is another door up stage; below it an open fireplace, filled with potted plants, andirons, etc., not in use. Over it a tall mirror; on the mantelpiece a French clock, candelabra, vases, etc. On a line with the fireplace, a lounge, gay with silk pillows. A florist's box, large and long, filled with American Beauty roses, on a low table near the head of the lounge. Small tables and light chairs where needed.*

At rise, BENSON *is discovered up stage looking about her. She is a neat and pretty little English lady's maid in black silk and a thin apron. She comes down stage still looking about, sees flower box; then opens door and speaks off.*

BENSON. Yes, ma'am, the flowers have come. [*She holds the door open.* VIDA, *in a morning gown, enters slowly. She is smoking a cigarette in as æsthetic a manner as she can, and is evidently turned out in her best style for conquest.*]

VIDA [*back to audience, always calm and, though civil, a little disdainful of her servants*]. Terribly garish light, Benson. Pull down the —[BENSON *obeys.*] Lower still—that will do. [*As she speaks, she goes about the room, giving the furniture a push here and there, arranging vases, etc.*] Men hate a clutter of chairs and tables. [*Stops before table and takes up hand mirror, standing with back to audience.*] I really think I'm too pale for this light.

BENSON [*quickly, understanding what is implied*]. Yes, ma'am. [BENSON *exits.* VIDA *sits. Knock at door.*] Come!

Enter BROOKS

BROOKS [*an ultra English footman, in plush and calves*]. Any horders, m'lady?

VIDA [*incapable of remembering the last man, or of considering the new one*]. Oh,—of course! You're the new—

BROOKS. Footman, m'lady.

VIDA [*as a matter of form*]. Your name?

BROOKS. Brooks, m'lady.

Re-enter BENSON *with rouge*

VIDA [*carefully giving instructions while she keeps her eyes on the glass and is rouged by* BENSON]. Brooks, I am at home to Mr. Karslake at eleven, not to any one else till twelve, when I expect Sir Wilfrid Cates-Darby.

[BROOKS *is inattentive; watches* BENSON.]

BROOKS. Yes, m'lady.

VIDA [*calm, but wearied by the ignorance of the lower classes*]. And I regret to inform you, Brooks, that in America there are no ladies, except salesladies!

BROOKS [*without a trace of comprehension*]. Yes, m'lady.

VIDA. I am at home to no one but the two names I have mentioned. [BROOKS *bows and exits. She dabs on rouge while* BENSON *holds glass.*] Is the men's club room in order?

BENSON. Perfectly, ma'am.

VIDA. Whiskey and soda?

BENSON. Yes, ma'am, and the ticker's been mended. The British sporting papers arrived this morning.

VIDA [*looking at her watch which lies on the dressing table*]. My watch has stopped.

BENSON [*glancing at the French clock on the chimney-piece*]. Five to eleven, ma'am.

[*Comes down a little.*]

VIDA [*getting promptly to work*]. Hm, hm, I shall be caught. [*Rises and crosses.*] The box of roses, Benson! [BENSON *brings the box of roses, uncovers the flowers and places them at* VIDA'S *side.*] My gloves—the clippers, and the vase! [*Each of these things* BENSON *places in turn within* VIDA'S *range where she sits on the sofa. She has the long box of roses at her side on a small table, a vase of water on the floor by her side. She cuts the stems and places the roses in the vase. When she feels that she has reached a picturesque position, in which any onlooker would see in her a creature filled with the love of flowers and of her fellow man, she says:*] There!

[*The door opens and* BROOKS *enters;* VIDA *nods to* BENSON.]

BROOKS [*announcing stolidly*]. Sir John Karslake.

[*Enter* JOHN, *dressed in very nobby riding togs, crop, etc., and spurs. He comes in gaily and forcibly.* BENSON *gives way as he comes down. Exeunt* BROOKS *and* BENSON. JOHN *stops near table.* VIDA, *from this point on, is busied with her roses.*]

VIDA [*languorously, but with a faint suggestion of humor*]. Is that really you, Sir John?

JOHN [*lively and far from being impressed by* VIDA]. I see now where we Americans are going to get our titles. Good-morning! You look as fresh as paint. [*Takes chair.*]

VIDA [*facing the insinuation with gentle pain*]. I hope you don't mean that? I never flattered myself for a moment you'd come. You're riding Cynthia K?

JOHN [*who has laid his gloves and riding crop on table*]. Fiddler's going to lead her round here in ten minutes!

VIDA. Cigars and cigarettes! Scotch? [*She indicates that he will find them on a small table up stage.*]

JOHN. Scotch! [*Goes up quickly to table and helps himself to Scotch and seltzer.*]

VIDA. And now *do* tell me all about *her!*

[*Putting in her last roses; she keeps one rosebud in her hand, of a size suitable for a man's buttonhole.*]

JOHN [*as he drinks*]. Oh, she's an adorable creature—delicate, high-bred, sweet-tempered—

VIDA [*showing her claws for a moment*]. Sweet-tempered? Oh, you're describing the horse! By "her," I meant—

JOHN [*irritated by the remembrance of his wife*]. Cynthia Karslake? I'd rather talk about the last tornado. [*Sits.*]

VIDA [*soothing the savage beast*]. There is only one thing I want to talk about, and that is, *you!* Why were you unhappy?

JOHN [*still cross*]. Why does a dollar last such a short time?

VIDA [*curious*]. Why did you part?

JOHN. Did you ever see a schooner towed by a tug? Well, I parted from Cynthia for the same reason that the hawser parts from the tug—I couldn't stand the tug.

VIDA [*sympathizing*]. Ah! [*Pause.*]

JOHN [*still cross*]. Awful cheerful morning chat.

VIDA [*excusing her curiosity and coming back to love as the only subject for serious conversation*]. I must hear the story, for I'm anxious to know why I've taken such a fancy to you!

JOHN [*very nonchalantly*]. Why do *I* like you?

VIDA [*doing her best to charm*]. I won't tell you—it would flatter you too much.

JOHN [*not a bit impressed by* VIDA, *but as ready to flirt as another*]. Tell me!

VIDA. There's a rose for you.

[*Giving him the one she has in her hand.*]

JOHN [*saying what is plainly expected of him*]. I want more than a rose—

VIDA [*putting this insinuation by*]. You refuse to tell me—?

JOHN [*once more reminded of* CYNTHIA, *speaks with sudden feeling*]. There's nothing to tell. We met, we loved, we married, we parted; or at least we wrangled and jangled. [*Sighs.*] Ha! Why weren't we happy? Don't ask me, why! It may have been *partly* my fault!

VIDA [*with tenderness*]. Never!

JOHN [*his mind on* CYNTHIA]. But I believe it's all in the way a girl's brought up. Our girls are brought up to be ignorant of life —they're ignorant of life. Life is a joke, and marriage is a picnic and a man is a shawl-strap—'Pon my soul, Cynthia Deane— no, I can't tell you!

[*Rises and goes up. During the following, he walks about in his irritation.*]

VIDA [*gently*]. Please tell me!

JOHN. Well, she was an heiress, an American heiress—and she'd been taught to think marriage meant burnt almonds and moonshine and a yacht and three automobiles, and she thought—I don't know what she thought, but I tell you, Mrs. Phillimore, marriage is three parts love and seven parts forgiveness of sins.

VIDA [*flattering him as a matter of course*]. She never loved you.

JOHN [*on whom she has made no impression at all*]. Yes, she did. For six or seven months there was not a shadow between us. It was perfect, and then one day she went off like a pistol-shot! I had a piece of law work and couldn't take her to see Flashlight race the Maryland mare. The case meant a big fee, big Kudos, and in sails Cynthia, Flashlight mad! And will I put on my hat and take her? No—and bang she goes off like a stick o' dynamite—what did I marry her for?—and words—pretty high words, until she got mad, when she threw over a chair and said oh, well,—marriage was a failure, or it was with me, so I said she'd better try somebody else. She said she would, and marched out of the room.

VIDA [*gently sarcastic*]. But she came back!

JOHN. She came back, but not as you mean. She stood at the door and said, "Jack, I shall divorce you." Then she came over to my study-table, dropped her wedding ring on my law papers, and went out. The door shut, I laughed; the front door slammed, I damned. [*Pause; crosses to window.*] She never came back.

[*Goes up, then comes down to chair.* VIDA *catches his hands.*]

VIDA [*hoping for a contradiction*]. She's broken your heart.

JOHN. Oh, no! [*Crosses to chair by lounge.*]

VIDA [*encouraged, begins to play the game again*]. You'll never love again!

JOHN [*speaking to her from the foot of her sofa*]. Try me! Try me! Ah, no, Mrs. Phillimore, I shall laugh, live, love and make money again! And let me tell you one thing—I'm going to rap her one over the knuckles. She had a stick of a Connecticut lawyer, and he—well, to cut a legal story short, since Mrs. Karslake's been in Europe, I have been quietly testing the validity of the decree of divorce. Perhaps you don't understand?

VIDA [*letting her innate shrewdness appear*]. Oh, about a divorce, everything!

JOHN. I shall hear by this evening whether the divorce will stand or not.

VIDA. But it's today at three she marries—you won't let her commit bigamy?

JOHN [*shakes his head*]. I don't suppose I'd go as far as that. It may be the divorce will hold, but anyway I hope never to see her again. [*He sits beside her facing up stage as she faces down.*]

VIDA. Ah, my poor boy, she has broken your heart. [*Believing that this is her psychological moment, she lays her hand on his arm, but draws it back as soon as he attempts to take it.*] Now don't make love to me.

JOHN [*bold and amused, but never taken in*]. Why not?

VIDA [*with immense gentleness*]. Because I like you too much! [*More gaily.*] I might give in, and take a notion to like you still more!

JOHN. Please do!

VIDA [*with gush and determined to be womanly at all hazards*]. Jack, I believe you'd be a lovely lover!

JOHN [*as before*]. Try me!

VIDA [*not hoping much from his tone*]. You charming, tempting, delightful fellow, I could love you without the least effort in the world,—but, no!

JOHN [*playing the game*]. Ah, well, now *seriously!* Between two people who have *suffered* and made their own mistakes—

VIDA [*playing the game too, but not playing it well*]. But you see, you don't *really* love me!

JOHN [*still ready to say what is expected*]. Cynthia—Vida, no man can sit beside you and look into your eyes without feeling—

VIDA [*speaks the truth as she sees it, seeing that her methods don't succeed*]. Oh! That's not love! That's simply—well, my dear Jack, it's beginning at the wrong end. And the truth is you hate Cynthia Karslake with such a whole-hearted hate, that you haven't a moment to think of any other woman.

JOHN [*with sudden anger*]. I hate her!

VIDA [*very softly and most sweetly*]. Jack—Jack, I could be as foolish about you as—oh, as foolish as anything, my dear! And perhaps some day—perhaps some day you'll come to me and say, Vida, I am totally indifferent to Cynthia—and then—

JOHN. And then?

VIDA [*the ideal woman in mind*]. Then, perhaps, you and I may join hands and stroll together into the Garden of Eden. It takes two to find the Garden of Eden, you know —and once we're on the inside, we'll lock the gate.

JOHN [*gaily, and seeing straight through her veneer*]. And lose the key under a rose-bush!

VIDA [*agreeing very softly*]. Under a rose-bush! [*Very soft knock.*] Come!

[JOHN *rises quickly. Enter* BENSON *and* BROOKS.]

BROOKS [*stolid and announcing*]. My lady— Sir Wilf—

[BENSON *stops him with a sharp movement and turns toward* VIDA.]

BENSON [*with intention*]. Your dressmaker, ma'am.

[BENSON *waves* BROOKS *to go. Exit* BROOKS, *very haughtily.*]

VIDA [*wonderingly*]. My dressmaker, Benson? [*With quick intelligence.*] Oh, of course, show her up. Mr. Karslake, you won't mind for a few minutes using my men's club room? Benson will show you! You'll find cigars and the ticker, sporting papers, whiskey; and, if you want anything special, just 'phone down to my "chef."

JOHN [*looking at his watch*]. How long?

VIDA [*very anxious to please*]. Half a cigar! Benson will call you.

JOHN [*practical*]. Don't make it too long. You see, there's my sheriff's sale on at twelve, and those races this afternoon. Fiddler will be here in ten minutes, remember! [*Door opens.*]

VIDA [*to* JOHN]. Run along! [*Exit* JOHN. VIDA *suddenly practical, and with a broad gesture to* BENSON.] Everything just as it was, Benson! [BENSON *whisks the roses out of the vase and replaces them in the box. She gives* VIDA *scissors and empty vases, and when* VIDA *finds herself in precisely the same position which preceded* JOHN'S *entrance, she says:*] There!

Enter BROOKS, *as* VIDA *takes a rose from basket*

BROOKS [*stolidly*]. Your ladyship's dress-maker! M'lady!

Enter SIR WILFRID *in morning suit, boutonnière, etc.*

VIDA [*with tender surprise and busy with the roses*]. Is that really you, Sir Wilfrid! I never flattered myself for an instant that you'd remember to come.

SIR WILFRID [*coming to her above end of sofa*]. Come? 'Course I come! Keen to come see you. By jove, you know, you look as pink and white as a huntin' mornin'.

VIDA [*ready to make any man as happy as possible*]. You'll smoke?

SIR WILFRID. Thanks! [*He watches her as she trims and arranges the flowers.*] Awfully long fingers you have! Wish I was a rose, or a ring, or a pair of shears! I say, d' you ever notice what a devil of a fellow I am for originality, what? [*Comes down. Unlike* JOHN, *is evidently impressed by her.*] You've got a delicate little den up here! Not so much low livin' and high thinkin', as low lights and no thinkin' at all, I hope—eh?

[*By this time* VIDA *has filled a vase with roses and rises to sweep by him and if possible make another charming picture to his eyes.*]

VIDA. You don't mind my moving about?

SIR WILFRID [*impressed*]. Not if you don't mind my watchin'. [*Sits on sofa.*] And sayin' how well you do it.

VIDA. It's most original of you to come here this morning. I don't quite see why you did.

[*She places the roses here and there, as if to see their effect, and leaves them on a small table near the door through which her visitors entered.*]

SIR WILFRID. Admiration.

VIDA [*sauntering slowly toward the mirror as she speaks*]. Oh, I saw that you admired her! And of course, she did say she was coming here at eleven! But that was only bravado! She won't come, and besides, I've given orders to admit no one!

SIR WILFRID. May I ask you—

[*He throws this in in the middle of her speech, which flows gently and steadily on.*]

VIDA. And indeed, if she came now, Mr. Karslake has gone, and her sole object in coming was to make him uncomfortable. [*Goes up above table; stopping a half minute at the mirror to see that she looks as she wishes to look.*] Very dangerous symptom, too, that passionate desire to make one's former husband unhappy! But, I can't believe that your admiration for Cynthia Karslake is so warm that it led you to pay me this visit a half hour too early in the hope of seeing—

SIR WILFRID [*rises; most civil, but speaking his mind like a Briton*]. I say, would you mind stopping a moment! [*She smiles.*] I'm not an American, you know; I was brought up not to interrupt. But you Americans, it's different with you! If somebody didn't interrupt you, you'd go on forever.

VIDA [*she passes him to tantalize*]. My point is you come to see Cynthia—

SIR WILFRID [*he believes she means it*]. I came hopin' to see—

VIDA [*as before*]. Cynthia!

SIR WILFRID [*perfectly single-minded and entirely taken in*]. But I would have come even if I'd known—

VIDA [*crosses*]. I don't believe it!

SIR WILFRID [*as before*]. Give you my word I—

VIDA [*the same*]. You're here to see *her!* And of course—

SIR WILFRID [*determined to be heard because, after all, he's a man*]. May I have the—eh —the floor? [VIDA *sits in chair.*] I was jolly well bowled over with Mrs. Karslake, I admit that, and I hoped to see her here, but—

VIDA [*talking nonsense and knowing it*]. You had another object in coming. In fact, you came to see Cynthia, and you came to see me! What I really long to know, is why you wanted to see *me!* For, of course, Cynthia's to be married at three! And, if she wasn't she wouldn't have you!

SIR WILFRID [*not intending to wound; merely speaking the flat truth*]. Well, I mean to jolly well ask her.

VIDA [*indignant*]. To be your wife?

SIR WILFRID. Why not?

VIDA [*as before*]. And you came here, to my house—in order to ask her—

SIR WILFRID [*truthful even on a subtle point*]. Oh, but that's only my first reason for coming, you know.

VIDA [*concealing her hopes*]. Well, now I *am* curious—what is the second?

SIR WILFRID [*simply*]. Are you feelin' pretty robust?

VIDA. I don't know!

SIR WILFRID [*crosses to buffet*]. Will you have something, and then I'll tell you!

VIDA [*gaily*]. Can't I support the news without—

SIR WILFRID [*trying to explain his state of mind, a thing he has never been able to do*]. Mrs. Phillimore, you see it's this way. Whenever you're lucky, you're too lucky. Now, Mrs. Karslake is a nipper and no mistake, but as I told you, the very same evenin' and house where I saw her—

[*He attempts to take her hand.*]

VIDA [*gently rising and affecting a tender surprise*]. What!

SIR WILFRID [*rising with her*]. That's it!—You're over!

[*He suggests with his right hand the movement of a horse taking a hurdle.*]

VIDA [*very sweetly*]. You don't really mean—

SIR WILFRID [*carried away for the moment by so much true womanliness*]. I mean, I stayed awake for an hour last night, thinkin' about you.

VIDA [*speaking to be contradicted*]. But, you've just told me—that Cynthia—

SIR WILFRID [*admitting the fact*]. Well, she did—she did bowl my wicket, but so did you—

VIDA [*taking him very gently to task*]. Don't you think there's a limit to—[*Sits.*]

SIR WILFRID [*roused by so much loveliness of soul*]. Now, see here, Mrs. Phillimore! You and I are not bottle babies, eh, are we? You've been married and—I—I've knocked about, and we both know there's a lot of stuff talked about—eh, eh, well, you know: —the one and only—that a fellow can't be awfully well smashed by two at the same time, don't you know! All rubbish! You know it, and the proof of the puddin's in the eatin', I am!

VIDA [*as before*]. May I ask where I come in?

SIR WILFRID. Well, now, Mrs. Phillimore, I'll be frank with you, Cynthia's my favorite, but you're runnin' her a close second in the popular esteem!

VIDA [*laughs, determined not to take offense*]. What a delightful, original, fantastic person you are!

SIR WILFRID [*frankly happy that he has explained everything so neatly*]. I knew you'd take it that way!

VIDA. And what next, pray?

SIR WILFRID. Oh, just the usual,—eh,—thing,—the—eh—the same old question, don't you know. Will you have me if she don't?

VIDA [*a shade piqued, but determined not to risk showing it*]. And you call that the same old usual question?

SIR WILFRID. Yes, I know, but—but will you? I sail in a week; we can take the same boat. And—eh—eh—my dear Mrs.—mayn't I say Vida, I'd like to see you at the head of my table.

VIDA [*with velvet irony*]. With Cynthia at the foot?

SIR WILFRID [*practical, as before*]. Never mind Mrs. Karslake,—I admire her—she's—but you have your own points! And you're here, and so'm I!—damme, I offer myself, and my affections, and I'm no icicle, my dear, tell you that for a fact, and, in fact what's your answer!—[VIDA *sighs and shakes her head.*] Make it, yes! I say, you know, my dear Vida—

[*He catches her hands.*]

VIDA [*she slips them from him*]. Unhand me, dear villain! And sit further away from your second choice! What can I say? I'd rather have *you* for a lover than any man I know! You must be a lovely lover!

SIR WILFRID. I am!

[*He makes a second effort to catch her fingers.*]

VIDA. Will you kindly go further away and be good!

SIR WILFRID [*quite forgetting* CYNTHIA]. Look here, if you say yes, we'll be married—

VIDA. In a month!

SIR WILFRID. Oh, no—this evening!

VIDA [*incapable of leaving a situation unadorned*]. This evening! And sail in the same boat with *you?* And shall we sail to the Garden of Eden and stroll into it and lock the gate on the inside and then lose the key—under a rose-bush?

SIR WILFRID [*pauses, and after consideration, says:*] Yes; yes, I say—that's too clever for me!

[*He draws nearer to her to bring the understanding to a crisis.*]

VIDA [*soft knock*]. My maid—come!

SIR WILFRID [*swings out of his chair and goes to sofa*]. Eh?

Enter BENSON

BENSON [*to* VIDA]. The new footman, ma'am—he's made a mistake. He's told the lady you're at home.

VIDA. What lady?

BENSON. Mrs. Karslake; and she's on the stairs, ma'am.

VIDA. Show her in.

[SIR WILFRID *has been turning over the roses. On hearing this, he faces about with a long stemmed one in his hand. He uses it in the following scene to point his remarks.*]

SIR WILFRID [*to* BENSON, *who stops*]. One moment! [*To* VIDA.] I say, eh—I'd rather not see her!

VIDA [*very innocently*]. But you came here to see her.

SIR WILFRID [*a little flustered*]. I'd rather not. Eh,—I fancied I'd find you and her together—but her—[*Comes a step nearer.*] findin' me with you looks so dooced intimate,—no one else, d'ye see, I believe she'd—draw conclusions—

BENSON. Pardon me, ma'am—but I hear Brooks coming!

SIR WILFRID [*to* BENSON]. Hold the door!

VIDA. So you don't want her to know—?

SIR WILFRID [*to* VIDA]. Be a good girl now—run me off somewhere!

VIDA [*to* BENSON]. Show Sir Wilfrid the men's room.

Enter BROOKS

SIR WILFRID. The men's room! Ah! Oh! Eh!

VIDA [*beckons him to go at once*]. Sir Wil—

[*He hesitates, then as* BROOKS *comes on, he flings off with* BENSON.]

BROOKS. Lady Karslake, milady!

VIDA. Anything more inopportune! I never dreamed she'd come—[*Enter* CYNTHIA, *veiled. She comes down quickly. Languor-*

ously.] My dear Cynthia, you don't mean to say—

CYNTHIA [*rather short, and visibly agitated*]. Yes, I've come.

VIDA [*polite, but not urgent*]. Do take off your veil.

CYNTHIA [*doing as* VIDA *asks*]. Is no one here?

VIDA [*as before*]. Won't you sit down?

CYNTHIA [*agitated and suspicious*]. Thanks, no—That is, yes, thanks. Yes! You haven't answered my question?

[CYNTHIA *waves her hand through the smoke, looks at the smoke suspiciously, looks for the cigarette.*]

VIDA [*playing innocence in the first degree*]. My dear, what makes you imagine that any one's here!

CYNTHIA. You've been smoking.

VIDA. Oh, puffing away!

[CYNTHIA *sees the glasses.*]

CYNTHIA. And drinking—a pair of drinks? [*She sees* JOHN'S *gloves on the table at her elbow.*] Do they fit you, dear? [VIDA *smiles;* CYNTHIA *picks up crop and looks at it and reads her own name.*] "Jack, from Cynthia."

VIDA [*assured, and without taking the trouble to double for a mere woman*]. Yes, dear; it's Mr. Karslake's crop, but I'm happy to say he left me a few minutes ago.

CYNTHIA. He left the house? [VIDA *smiles.*] I wanted to see him.

VIDA [*with a shade of insolence*]. To quarrel?

CYNTHIA [*frank and curt*]. I wanted to see him.

VIDA [*determined to put* CYNTHIA *in the wrong*]. And I sent him away because I didn't want you to repeat the scene of last night in my house.

CYNTHIA [*looks at crop and is silent*]. Well, I can't stay. I'm to be married at three, and I had to play truant to get here!

Enter BENSON

BENSON [*to* VIDA]. There's a person, ma'am, on the sidewalk.

VIDA. What person, Benson?

BENSON. A person, ma'am, with a horse.

CYNTHIA [*happily agitated*]. It's Fiddler with Cynthia K!

[*She goes up rapidly and looks out back through window.*]

VIDA [*to* BENSON]. Tell the man I'll be down in five minutes.

CYNTHIA [*looking down from the balcony with delight*]. Oh, there she is!

VIDA [*aside to* BENSON]. Go to the club room, Benson, and say to the two gentlemen I can't see them at present—I'll send for them when—

BENSON [*listens*]. I hear some one coming.

VIDA. Quick!

[BENSON *crosses. Door opens, and* JOHN *enters.* JOHN *comes in slowly, carelessly.* VIDA *whispers to* BENSON.]

BENSON [*crosses, goes close to* JOHN *and whispers*]. Beg par—

VIDA [*under her breath*]. Go back!

JOHN [*not understanding*]. I beg pardon!

VIDA [*as before*]. Go back!

JOHN [*the same*]. Can't! I've a date! With the sheriff!

VIDA [*a little cross*]. Please use your eyes.

JOHN [*laughing and flattering* VIDA]. I am using my eyes.

VIDA [*fretted*]. Don't you see there's a lovely creature in the room?

JOHN [*again taking the loud upperhand*]. Of course there is.

VIDA. Hush!

JOHN [*teasingly*]. But what I want to know is—

VIDA. Hush!

JOHN [*delighted at getting a rise*]. —is when we're to stroll in the Garden of Eden—

VIDA. Hush!

JOHN. —and lose the key. [*To put a stop to this, she lightly tosses her handkerchief into his face.*] By George, talk about attar of roses!

CYNTHIA [*up at window, excited and moved at seeing her mare once more*]. Oh, she's a darling! [*She turns.*] A perfect darling! [JOHN *starts up; sees* CYNTHIA *at the same instant that she sees him.*] Oh! I didn't know you were here. [*Pause; then with "take-it-or-leave-it" frankness.*] I came to see *you!*

[JOHN *looks extremely dark and angry;* VIDA *rises.*]

VIDA [*to* CYNTHIA, *most gently, and seeing there's nothing to be made of* JOHN]. Oh, pray feel at home, Cynthia, dear! [*Stands by door; to* JOHN.] When I've a nice street frock on, I'll ask you to present me to Cynthia K.

[*Exit* VIDA. JOHN *and* CYNTHIA, *tableau.*

CYNTHIA [*agitated and frank*]. Of course, I told you yesterday I was coming here.

JOHN [*irritated*]. And I was to deny myself the privilege of being here?

CYNTHIA [*curt and agitated*]. Yes.

JOHN [*ready to fight*]. And you guessed I would do that?

CYNTHIA. No.

JOHN. What?

CYNTHIA [*above table. She speaks with agitation, frankness and good will*]. Jack—I mean, Mr. Karslake,—no, I mean, Jack! I came because—well, you see, it's my wedding day!—and—and—I—I—was rude to you last evening. I'd like to apologize and make peace with you before I go—

JOHN [*determined to be disagreeable*]. Before you go to your last, long home!

CYNTHIA. I came to apologize.

JOHN. But you'll remain to quarrel!

CYNTHIA [*still frank and kind*]. I will not quarrel. No!—and I'm only here for a moment. I'm to be married at three, and just look at the clock! Besides, I told Philip I was going to Louise's shop, and I did—on the way here; but, you see, if I stay too long he'll telephone Louise and find I'm not there, and he might guess I was here. So you see I'm risking a scandal. And now, Jack, see here, I lay my hand on the table, I'm here on the square, and,—what I want to say is, why—Jack, even if we have made a mess of our married life, let's put by anger and pride. It's all over now and can't be helped. So let's be human, let's be reasonable, and let's be kind to each other! Won't you give me your hand? [JOHN *refuses.*] I wish you every happiness!

JOHN [*turns away, the past rankling*]. I had a client once, a murderer; he told me he murdered the man, and he told me, too, that he never felt so kindly to anybody as he did to that man after he'd killed him!

CYNTHIA. Jack!

JOHN [*unforgiving*]. You murdered my happiness!

CYNTHIA. I won't recriminate!

JOHN. And now I must put by anger and pride! I do! But not self-respect, not a just indignation—not the facts and my clear memory of them!

CYNTHIA. Jack!

JOHN. No!

CYNTHIA [*with growing emotion, and holding out her hand*]. I give you one more chance! Yes, I'm determined to be generous. I forgive everything you ever did to me. I'm ready to be friends. I wish you every happiness and every—every—horse in the world! I can't do more than that! [*She offers it again.*] You refuse?

JOHN [*moved but surly*]. I like wildcats and I like Christians, but I don't like Christian wildcats! Now I'm close hauled, trot out your tornado! Let the Tiger loose! It's the tamer, the man in the cage that has to look lively and use the red hot crowbar! But by jove, I'm out of the cage! I'm a mere spectator of the married circus!

[*He puffs vigorously.*]

CYNTHIA. Be a game sport then! Our marriage was a wager; you wagered you could live with me. You lost; you paid with a divorce; and now is the time to show your sporting blood. Come on, shake hands and part friends.

JOHN. Not in this world! Friends with you, no! I have a proper pride. I don't propose to put my pride in my pocket.

CYNTHIA [*jealous and plain spoken*]. Oh, I wouldn't ask you to put your pride in your pocket while Vida's handkerchief is there. [JOHN *looks angered.*] Pretty little bijou of a handkerchief! [CYNTHIA *takes handkerchief out.*] And she is charming, and divorced, and reasonably well made up.

JOHN. Oh, well, Vida is a woman. [*Business with handkerchief.*] I'm a man, a handkerchief is a handkerchief, and as some old Aristotle or other said, whatever concerns a woman, concerns me!

CYNTHIA [*not oblivious of him, but in a low voice*]. Insufferable! Well, yes. [*She sits. She is too much wounded to make any further appeal.*] You're perfectly right. There's no possible harmony between divorced people! I withdraw my hand and all good feeling. No wonder I couldn't stand you. Eh? However, that's pleasantly past! But at least, my dear Karslake, let us have some sort of beauty of behavior! If we cannot be decent, let us endeavor to be graceful. If we can't be moral, at least we can avoid being vulgar.

JOHN. Well—

CYNTHIA. If there's to be no more marriage in the world—

JOHN [*cynical*]. Oh, but that's not it; there's to be more and more and more!

CYNTHIA [*with a touch of bitterness*]. Very well! I repeat then, if there's to be nothing but marriage and divorce, and remarriage, and redivorce, at least, at least, those who *are* divorced can avoid the vulgarity of meeting each other here, there, and everywhere!

JOHN. Oh, that's where you come out!

CYNTHIA. I thought so yesterday, and to-day I know it. It's an insufferable thing to a woman of any delicacy of feeling to find her husband—

JOHN. Ahem—former!

CYNTHIA. *Once* a husband always—

JOHN [*still cynical*]. Oh, no! Oh, dear, no.

CYNTHIA. To find her—to find the man she has once lived with—in the house of—making love to—to find you here! [JOHN *smiles; rises.*] You smile,—but I say, it should be a social axiom, no woman should have to meet her former husband.

JOHN [*cynical and cutting*]. Oh, I don't know; after I've served my term I don't mind meeting my jailor.

CYNTHIA [JOHN *takes chair near* CYNTHIA]. It's indecent—at the horse-show, the opera, at races and balls, to meet the man who once—It's not civilized! It's fantastic! It's half baked! Oh, I never should have come here! [*He sympathizes, and she grows irrational and furious.*] But it's entirely your fault!

JOHN. My fault?

CYNTHIA [*working herself into a rage*]. Of course. What business have you to be about —to be at large. To be at all!

JOHN. Gosh!

CYNTHIA [*as before*]. To be where I am! Yes, it's just as horrible for you to turn up in my life as it would be for a dead person to insist on coming back to life and dinner and bridge!

JOHN. Horrid idea!

CYNTHIA. Yes, but it's *you* who behave just as if you were not dead, just as if I'd not spent a fortune on your funeral. You do; you prepare to bob up at afternoon teas,—and dinners—and embarrass me to death with your extinct personality!

JOHN. Well, of course we *were* married, but it didn't quite kill me.

CYNTHIA [*angry and plain spoken*]. You killed yourself for me—I divorced you. I buried you out of my life. If any human soul was ever dead, you are! And there's nothing I so hate as a gibbering ghost.

JOHN. Oh, I say!

CYNTHIA [*with hot anger*]. Go gibber and squeak where gibbering and squeaking are the fashion!

JOHN [*laughs, pretending to a coldness he does not feel*]. And so, my dear child, I'm to abate myself as a nuisance! Well, as far as seeing you is concerned, for my part it's just like seeing a horse who's chucked you once. The bruises are O. K., and you see him with a sort of easy curiosity. Of course, you know, he'll jolly well chuck the next man!—Permit me! [JOHN *picks up gloves, handkerchief and parasol and gives her these as she drops them one by one in her agitation.*] There's pleasure in the thought.

CYNTHIA. Oh!

JOHN. And now, may I ask you a very simple question? Mere curiosity on my part, but, why did you come here this morning?

CYNTHIA. I have already explained that to you.

JOHN. Not your real motive. Permit me!

CYNTHIA. Oh!

JOHN. But I believe I have guessed your real —permit me—your real motive!

CYNTHIA. Oh!

JOHN [*with mock sympathy*]. Cynthia, I am sorry for you.

CYNTHIA. Hm?

JOHN. Of course we had a pretty lively case of the fever—the mutual attraction fever, and we *were* married a very short time. And I conclude that's what's the matter with *you!* You see, my dear, seven months of married life is too short a time to cure a bad case of the fancies.

CYNTHIA [*in angry surprise*]. What?

JOHN [*calm and triumphant*]. That's my diagnosis.

CYNTHIA [*slowly and gathering herself together*]. I don't think I understand.

JOHN. Oh, yes, you do; yes, you do.

CYNTHIA [*with blazing eyes*]. What do you mean?

JOHN. Would you mind not breaking my crop! Thank you! I mean [*With polite impertinence.*] that ours was a case of premature divorce, and, ahem, you're in love with me still.

[*Pause.* CYNTHIA *has one moment of fury, then she realizes at what a disadvantage this places her. She makes an immense effort, recovers her calm, thinks hard for a moment more, and then, has suddenly an inspiration.*]

CYNTHIA. Jack, some day you'll get the blind staggers from conceit. No, I'm not in love with you, Mr. Karslake, but I shouldn't be at all surprised if she were. She's just your sort, you know. She's a man-eating shark, and you'll be a toothsome mouthful. Oh, come now, Jack, what a silly you are! Oh, yes, you are, to get off a joke like that; me—in love with— [*Looks at him.*]

JOHN. Why are you here? [*She laughs and begins to play her game.*] Why are you here?

CYNTHIA. Guess! [*She laughs.*]

JOHN. Why are you—

CYNTHIA [*quickly*]. Why am I here! I'll tell you. I'm going to be married. I had a longing, an irresistible longing to see you make an ass of yourself just once more! It happened!

JOHN [*uncertain and discomfited*]. I know better!

CYNTHIA. But I came for a serious purpose, too. I came, my dear fellow, to make an experiment on myself. I've been with you thirty minutes; and—[*She sighs with content.*] It's all right!

JOHN. What's all right?

CYNTHIA [*calm and apparently at peace with the world*]. I'm immune.

JOHN. Immune?

CYNTHIA. You're not catching any more! Yes, you see, I said to myself, if I fly into a temper—

JOHN. You did!

CYNTHIA. If I fly into a temper when I see him, well that shows I'm not yet so entirely convalescent that I can afford to have Jack Karslake at my house. If I remain calm I shall ask him to dinner.

JOHN [*routed*]. Ask me if you dare! [*Rises.*]

CYNTHIA [*getting the whip hand for good*]. Ask you to dinner? Oh, my dear fellow. [JOHN *rises.*] I'm going to do much more than that. [*Rises.*] We must be friends, old man! We must meet, we must meet often, we must show New York the way the thing should be done, and, to show you I mean it—I want you to be my best man, and give me away when I'm married this afternoon.

JOHN [*incredulous and impatient*]. You don't mean that! [*Puts back chair.*]

CYNTHIA. There you are! Always suspicious!

JOHN. You don't mean that!

CYNTHIA [*hiding her emotion under a sportswoman's manner*]. Don't I? I ask you, come! And come as you are! And I'll lay my wedding gown to Cynthia K that you won't be there! If you're there, you get the gown, and if you're not, I get Cynthia K!—

JOHN [*determined not to be worsted*]. I take it!

CYNTHIA. Done! Now, then, we'll see which of us two is the real sporting goods! Shake! [*They shake hands on it.*] Would you mind letting me have a plain soda? [JOHN *goes to table, and, as he is rattled and does not regard what he is about, he fills the glass three-fourths full with whiskey. He comes to* CYNTHIA *and gives her this. She looks him in the eye with an air of triumph.*] Thanks. [*Maliciously, as* VIDA *enters.*] Your hand is a bit shaky. I think *you* need a little King William.

[JOHN *shrugs his shoulders, and as* VIDA *immediately speaks,* CYNTHIA *defers drinking.*]

VIDA [*to* CYNTHIA]. My dear, I'm sorry to tell you your husband—I mean, my husband—I mean Philip—he's asking for you over the 'phone. You must have said you were coming here. Of course, I told him you were not here, and hung up.

Enter BENSON

BENSON [*to* VIDA]. Ma'am, the new footman's been talking with Mr. Phillimore on the wire. [VIDA, *gesture of regret*]. He told

Mr. Phillimore that his lady was here, and if I can believe my ears, ma'am, he's got Sir Wilfrid on the 'phone now!

Enter SIR WILFRID

SIR WILFRID [*perplexed and annoyed*]. I say y' know—extraordinary country; that old chap, Phillimore, he's been damned impertinent over the wire! Says I've run off with Mrs. Karslake—talks about "Louise!" Now who the dooce is Louise? He's comin' round here, too—I said Mrs. Karslake wasn't here—[*Sees* CYNTHIA.] Hello! Good job! What a liar I am!

BENSON [*to* VIDA]. Mr. Fiddler, ma'am, says the mare is gettin' very restive.

[*Comes up to door.* JOHN *hears this and moves at once. Exit* BENSON.]

JOHN [*to* VIDA]. If that mare's restive, she'll break out in a rash.

VIDA [*to* JOHN]. Will you take me?

JOHN. Of course. [*They go up to exit.*]

CYNTHIA [*to* JOHN]. Tata, old man! Meet you at the altar! If I don't, the mare's mine! [SIR WILFRID *looks at her amazed.*]

VIDA [*to* CYNTHIA]. Do the honors, dear, in my absence!

JOHN. Come along, come along, never mind them! A horse is a horse!

[*Exeunt* JOHN *and* VIDA, *gaily and in haste. At the same moment* CYNTHIA *drinks what she supposes to be her glass of plain soda. As it is whiskey straight, she is seized with astonishment and a fit of coughing.* SIR WILFRID *relieves her of the glass.*]

SIR WILFRID [*indicating contents of glass*]. I say, do you ordinarily take it as high up—as seven fingers and two thumbs.

CYNTHIA [*coughs*]. Jack poured it out. Just shows how groggy he was! And now, Sir Wilfrid—[*Gets her things to go.*]

SIR WILFRID. Oh, you can't go!

Enter BROOKS

CYNTHIA. I am to be married at three.

SIR WILFRID. Let him wait. [*To* BROOKS, *whom he meets near the door; aside.*] If Mr. Phillimore comes, bring his card up.

BROOKS [*going*]. Yes, Sir Wilfrid.

SIR WILFRID [*to* BROOKS, *as before*]. To me! [*He tips him.*]

BROOKS [*bowing*]. To you, Sir Wilfrid. [*Exit* BROOKS.

SIR WILFRID [*returning to* CYNTHIA]. I've got to have my innings, y' know! [*He looks at her more closely.*] I say, you've been crying!—

CYNTHIA. King William!

SIR WILFRID. You *are* crying! Poor little gal!

CYNTHIA [*tears in her eyes*]. I feel all shaken and cold.

Enter BROOKS *with card*

SIR WILFRID [*astonished and sympathetic*]. Poor little gal.

CYNTHIA [*as before*]. I didn't sleep a wink last night. [*With disgust.*] Oh, what is the matter with me?

SIR WILFRID. Why, it's as plain as a pikestaff! You— [BROOKS *has brought salver to* SIR WILFRID. *A card lies upon it.* SIR WILFRID *takes it and says aside to* BROOKS.] Phillimore? [BROOKS *assents. Aloud to* CYNTHIA, *calmly deceitful.*] Who's Waldorf Smith? [CYNTHIA *shakes her head. To* BROOKS, *returning card to salver.*] Tell the gentleman Mrs. Karslake is not here! [*Exit* BROOKS.

CYNTHIA [*aware that she has no business where she is*]. I thought it was Philip!

SIR WILFRID [*telling the truth as if it were a lie*]. So did I! [*With cheerful confidence.*] And now, Mrs. Karslake, I'll tell you why you're cryin'. [*He sits beside her.*] You're marryin' the wrong man! I'm sorry for you, but you're such a goose. Here you are, marryin' this legal luminary. What for? You don't know! He don't know! But I do! You pretend you're marryin' him because it's the sensible thing; not a bit of it. You're marryin' Mr. Phillimore because of all the other men you ever saw he's the least like Jack Karslake.

CYNTHIA. That's a very good reason.

SIR WILFRID. There's only one good reason for marrying, and that is because you'll die if you don't!

CYNTHIA. Oh, I've tried that!

SIR WILFRID. The Scripture says: "Try! try! again!" I tell you, there's nothing like a w'im!

CYNTHIA. What's that? W'im? Oh, you mean a *whim!* Do please try and say W*h*im!

Sir Wilfrid [*for the first time emphasizing his H in the word*]. W*h*im. You must have a w'im—w'im for the chappie you marry.

Cynthia. I had—for Jack.

Sir Wilfrid. Your w'im wasn't wimmy enough, my dear! if you'd had more of it, and tougher, it would ha' stood, y' know! Now, I'm not proposin'!

Cynthia [*diverted at last from her own distress*]. I hope not!

Sir Wilfrid. Oh, I will later! It's not time yet! As I was saying—

Cynthia. And pray, Sir Wilfrid, when will it be time?

Sir Wilfrid. As soon as I see you have a w'im for me! [*Rising, looks at his watch.*] And now, I'll tell you what we'll do! We've got just an hour to get there in, my motor's on the corner, and in fifty minutes we'll be at Belmont Park.

Cynthia [*her sporting blood fired*]. Belmont Park!

Sir Wilfrid. We'll do the races, and dine at Martin's—

Cynthia [*tempted*]. Oh, if I only could! I can't! I've got to be married! You're awfully nice; I've almost got a "w'im" for you already.

Sir Wilfrid [*delighted*]. There you are! I'll send a telegram!

[*She shakes her head. He sits and writes at the table.*]

Cynthia. No, no, no!

Sir Wilfrid [*reads what he writes*]. "Off with Cates-Darby to races. Please postpone ceremony till seven-thirty."

Cynthia. Oh, no, it's impossible!

Sir Wilfrid [*accustomed to have things go his way*]. No more than breathin'! You can't get a w'im for me, you know, unless we're together, so together we'll be! [*Enter* John Karslake.] And tomorrow you'll wake up with a jolly little w'im—[*Reads.*] "Postpone ceremony till seven-thirty." There. [*He puts on her cloak. Sees* John.] Hello!

John [*surly*]. Hello! Sorry to disturb you.

Sir Wilfrid [*cheerful as possible*]. Just the man! [*Gives him the telegraph form.*] Just step round and send it, my boy. Thanks!

[John *reads it.*]

Cynthia. No, no, I can't go!

Sir Wilfrid. Cockety-coo-coo-can't. I say, you must!

Cynthia [*positively*]. *No!*

John [*astounded*]. Do you mean you're going—

Sir Wilfrid [*very gay*]. Off to the races, my boy!

John [*angry and outraged*]. Mrs. Karslake can't go with you there!

[Cynthia *starts, amazed at his assumption of marital authority, and delighted that she will have an opportunity of outraging his sensibilities.*]

Sir Wilfrid. Oho!

John. An hour before her wedding!

Sir Wilfrid [*gay and not angry*]. May I know if it's the custom—

John [*jealous and disgusted*]. It's worse than eloping—

Sir Wilfrid. Custom, y' know, for the husband, that was, to dictate—

John [*thoroughly vexed*]. By George, there's a limit!

Cynthia. What? What? What? [*Gathers up her things.*] What did I hear you say?

Sir Wilfrid. Ah!

John [*angry*]. I say there's a limit—

Cynthia [*more and more determined to arouse and excite* John]. Oh, there's a limit, is there?

John. There is! I bar the way! It means reputation—it means—

Cynthia [*enjoying her opportunity*]. We shall see what it means!

Sir Wilfrid. Aha!

John [*to* Cynthia]. I'm here to protect your reputation—

Sir Wilfrid [*to* Cynthia]. We've got to make haste, you know.

Cynthia. Now, I'm ready—

John [*to* Cynthia]. Be sensible. You're breaking off the match—

Cynthia [*excitedly*]. What's that to you?

Sir Wilfrid. It's boots and saddles!

John [*he takes his stand between them and the door*]. No thoroughfare!

Sir Wilfrid. Look here, my boy—!

Cynthia [*catching at the opportunity of putting* John *in an impossible position*]. Wait a moment, Sir Wilfrid! Give me the wire! [*Faces him.*] Thanks! [*She takes the telegraph *form from him and tears it up.*] There! Too rude to chuck him by wire! But you, Jack, you've taken on yourself to look after my interests, so I'll just ask you, old man, to run down to the Supreme Court and tell Philip—nicely, you know—I'm off with Sir Wilfrid and where! Say I'll be back by seven, if I'm not later! And make it clear, Jack, I'll marry him by eight-thirty or nine at the latest! And mind *you're* there, dear! And now, Sir Wilfrid, we're off.

JOHN [*staggered and furious, giving way as they pass him*]. I'm not the man to—to carry—

CYNTHIA [*quick and dashing*]. Oh, yes, you are.

JOHN. —a message from you.

CYNTHIA [*triumphant*]. Oh, yes, you are; you're just exactly the man!

[*Exeunt* CYNTHIA *and* SIR WILFRID.

JOHN. Great miracles of Moses!

CURTAIN

THE THIRD ACT

SCENE.—*The same as that of Act I, but the room has been cleared of too much furniture, and arranged for a wedding ceremony. The curtain rises on* MRS. PHILLIMORE *reclining on the sofa.* MISS HENEAGE *is seated left of table.* SUDLEY *is seated at the right of the table.* GRACE *is seated on sofa. There are cushions of flowers, alcove of flowers, flowers in vase, pink and white hangings, wedding bell of roses, calla lilies, orange blossoms, a ribbon of white stretched in front of an altar of flowers; two cushions for the couple to kneel on; two candelabra at each side of back of arch on pedestals.*

The curtain rises. There is a momentary silence, that the audience may take in these symbols of marriage, etc. Every member of the Phillimore family is irritable, with suppressed irritation.

SUDLEY [*impatiently*]. All very well, my dear Sarah. But you see the hour. Twenty to ten! We have been here since half-past two.

MISS HENEAGE. You had dinner?

SUDLEY. I did not come here at two to have dinner at eight, and be kept waiting until ten! And, my dear Sarah, when I ask where the bride is—

MISS HENEAGE [*with forced composure*]. I have told you all I know. Mr. John Karslake came to the house at lunch time, spoke to Philip, and they left the house together.

GRACE. Where is Philip?

MRS. PHILLIMORE [*feebly, irritated*]. I don't wish to be censorious or to express an actual opinion, but I must say it's a bold bride who keeps her future mother-in-law waiting for eight hours. However, I will not venture to—[MRS. PHILLIMORE *reclines again and fades away into silence.*]

GRACE [*sharply and decisively*]. I do! I'm sorry I went to the expense of a silver ice-pitcher.

[MRS. PHILLIMORE *sighs.* MISS HENEAGE *keeps her temper with an effort which is obvious.*]

Enter THOMAS

SUDLEY [*to* MRS. PHILLIMORE]. For my part, I don't believe Mrs. Karslake means to return here or to marry Philip at all!

THOMAS [*to* MISS HENEAGE]. Two telegrams for you, ma'am! The choir boys have had their supper.

[*Slight movement from every one;* THOMAS *steps back.*]

SUDLEY [*rises*]. At last we shall know!

MISS HENEAGE. From the lady! Probably!

[MISS HENEAGE *opens telegram; reads first one at a glance, lays it on salver again with a glance at* SUDLEY. THOMAS *passes salver to* SUDLEY, *who takes telegram.*]

GRACE. There's a toot now.

MRS. PHILLIMORE [*feebly, confused*]. I don't wish to intrude, but really I cannot imagine Philip marrying at midnight.

[*As* SUDLEY *reads,* MISS HENEAGE *opens the second telegram, but does not read it.*]

SUDLEY [*reads*]. "Accident, auto struck"—something! "Gasoline"—did something—illegible, ah! [*Reads.*] "Home by nine forty-five! Hold the church!"

[*General movement from all.*]

MISS HENEAGE [*profoundly shocked*]. "Hold the church!" William, she still means to marry Philip! and tonight, too!

SUDLEY. It's from Belmont Park.

GRACE [*making a great discovery*]. She went to the races!

MISS HENEAGE. This is from Philip! [MISS

HENEAGE *reads second telegram.*] "I arrive at ten o'clock. Have dinner ready." [MISS HENEAGE *motions to* THOMAS *to withdraw.* THOMAS *exits.* MISS HENEAGE *looks at her watch.*] They are both due now. [*Movement.*] What's to be done?

[*Rises.* SUDLEY *shrugs shoulders.*]

SUDLEY [*rises*]. After a young woman has spent her wedding day at the races? Why, I consider that she has broken the engagement,—and when she comes, tell her so.

MISS HENEAGE. I'll telephone Matthew. The choir boys can go home—her maid can pack her belongings—and when the lady arrives—

[*Very distant toot of an auto-horn is heard. Tableau. Auto-horn a little louder.* GRACE *flies up stage and looks out of door.* MRS. PHILLIMORE *does not know what to do, or where to go.* SUDLEY *crosses excitedly.* MISS HENEAGE *stands ready to make herself disagreeable.*]

GRACE [*speaking rapidly and with excitement*]. I hear a man's voice. Cates-Darby and brother Matthew.

[*Loud toot. Laughter and voices off back, faintly.* GRACE *looks out of door, and then comes rapidly down.*]

MISS HENEAGE. Outrageous!

SUDLEY. Disgraceful!

MRS. PHILLIMORE. Shocking! [*Voices and horn off; a little louder. Partly rising.*] I shall not take any part at all, in the—eh—

[*She fades away.*]

MISS HENEAGE [*interrupting her*]. Don't trouble yourself.

[*Voices and laughter, louder.* CYNTHIA'S *voice is heard off.* SIR WILFRID *appears back. He turns and waits for* CYNTHIA *and* MATTHEW. *He carries wraps. He speaks to* CYNTHIA, *who is still off.* MATTHEW'S *voice is heard and* CYNTHIA'S. CYNTHIA *appears at back, followed by* MATTHEW. *As they appear,* CYNTHIA *speaks to* MATTHEW, *on her right.* SIR WILFRID *carries a newspaper and parasol. The hat is the one she wore in Act II. She is in get-up for auto. Goggles, veil, an exquisite duster in latest Paris style. All three come down rapidly. As she appears,* SUDLEY *and* MISS HENEAGE *exclaim, and there is a general movement.*]

SUDLEY [*to table*]. 'Pon my word!

GRACE. Hah!

MISS HENEAGE [*rises*]. Shocking!

[GRACE *remains standing above sofa.* SUDLEY *moves toward her.* MISS HENEAGE *sits.* MRS. PHILLIMORE *reclines on sofa.* CYNTHIA *begins to speak as soon as she appears and speaks fluently to the end.*]

CYNTHIA. No! I never was so surprised in my life, as when I strolled into the paddock and they gave me a rousing reception—old Jimmy Withers, Debt Gollup, Jack Deal, Monty Spiffles, the Governor and Buckeye. All of my old admirers! They simply fell on my neck, and, dear Matthew, what do you think I did? I turned on the water main! [*Movements and murmurs of disapprobation from the family.* MATTHEW *indicates a desire to go.*] Oh, but you can't go!

MATTHEW. I'll return in no time!

CYNTHIA. I'm all ready to be married. Are they ready? [MATTHEW *waves a pious, polite gesture of recognition to the family.*] I beg everybody's pardon! [*She takes off her wrap and puts it on the back of a chair up stage.*] My goggles are so dusty, I can't see who's who! [*To* SIR WILFRID.] Thanks! You *have* carried it well! [*Parasol from* SIR WILFRID.]

SIR WILFRID [*aside to* CYNTHIA]. When may I—?

CYNTHIA. See you next Goodwood!

SIR WILFRID [*imperturbably*]. Oh, I'm coming back! [CYNTHIA *comes down.*]

CYNTHIA. Not a bit of use in coming back! I shall be married before you get here! Ta! Ta! Goodwood!

SIR WILFRID [*as before*]. I'm coming back.

[*He goes out quickly. More murmurs of disapprobation from family. Slight pause.*]

CYNTHIA [*begins to take off her goggles, and comes down slowly*]. I do awfully apologize for being so late!

MISS HENEAGE [*importantly*]. Mrs. Karslake—

SUDLEY [*importantly*]. Ahem!

[CYNTHIA *lays down goggles, and sees their severity.*]

CYNTHIA. Dear me! [*She surveys the flowers, and for a moment pauses.*] Oh, good heavens! Why, it looks like a smart funeral!

[MISS HENEAGE *moves; then speaks in a per-*

fectly ordinary natural tone, but her expression is severe. CYNTHIA *immediately realizes the state of affairs in its fullness.*]

MISS HENEAGE [*to* CYNTHIA]. After what has occurred, Mrs. Karslake—

[CYNTHIA *glances at table.*]

CYNTHIA [*sits at table, composed and good tempered*]. I see you got my wire—so you know where I have been.

MISS HENEAGE. To the race-course!

SUDLEY. With a rowdy Englishman.

[CYNTHIA *glances at* SUDLEY, *uncertain whether he means to be disagreeable, or whether he is only naturally so.*]

MISS HENEAGE. We concluded you desired to break the engagement!

CYNTHIA [*indifferently*]. No! No! Oh! No!

MISS HENEAGE. Do you intend, despite of our opinion of you—

CYNTHIA. The only opinion that would have any weight with me would be Mrs. Phillimore's. [*She turns expectantly to* MRS. PHILLIMORE.]

MRS. PHILLIMORE. I am generally asleep at this hour, and accordingly I will not venture to express any—eh—any—actual opinion. [*Fades away.* CYNTHIA *smiles.*]

MISS HENEAGE [*coldly*]. You smile. We simply inform you that as regards *us*, the alliance is not grateful.

CYNTHIA [*affecting gaiety and unconcern*]. And all this because the gasoline gave out.

SUDLEY. My patience has given out!

GRACE. So has mine. I'm going.

[*Exit* GRACE.

SUDLEY [*comes down, vexed beyond civility. To* CYNTHIA]. My dear young lady: You come here, to this sacred—eh—eh—spot—altar! —[*Gesture.*] odoriferous of the paddock! —speaking of Spiffles and Buckeye,—having practically eloped!—having created a scandal, and disgraced our family!

CYNTHIA [*as before*]. How does it disgrace you? Because I like to see a high-bred, clean, nervy, sweet little four-legged gee play the antelope over a hurdle!

MISS HENEAGE. Sister, it is high time that you—[*Turns to* CYNTHIA. *Gesture.*]

CYNTHIA [*with quiet irony*]. Mrs. Phillimore is generally asleep at this hour, and accordingly she will not venture to express—

SUDLEY [*spluttering with irritation*]. Enough, madam—I *venture* to—to—to—to say, you are leading a fast life.

CYNTHIA [*with powerful intention*]. Not in this house! For six heavy weeks have I been laid away in the grave, and I've found it very slow indeed trying to keep pace with the dead!

SUDLEY [*despairingly*]. This comes of horses!

CYNTHIA [*indignant*]. Of what?

SUDLEY. C-c-caring for horses!

MISS HENEAGE [*with sublime morality*]. What Mrs. Karslake cares for is—men.

CYNTHIA [*angry and gay*]. What would you have me care for? The Ornithorhyncus Paradoxus? or Pithecanthropus Erectus? Oh, I refuse to take you seriously.

[SUDLEY *begins to prepare to leave; he buttons himself into respectability and his coat.*]

SUDLEY. My dear madam, I take myself seriously—and madam, I—I retract what I have brought with me [*He feels in his waistcoat pocket.*] as a graceful gift,—an Egyptian scarab—a—a—sacred beetle, which once ornamented the person of a—eh—mummy.

CYNTHIA [*getting even with him*]. It should never be absent from your pocket, Mr. Sudley! [SUDLEY *goes up in a rage.*]

MISS HENEAGE [*rises. To* SUDLEY]. I've a vast mind to withdraw my—

[CYNTHIA *moves.*]

CYNTHIA [*interrupts; maliciously*]. Your wedding present? The little bronze cat!

MISS HENEAGE [*moves, angrily*]. Oh!

[*Even* MRS. PHILLIMORE *comes momentarily to life, and expresses silent indignation.*]

SUDLEY [*loftily*]. Sarah, I'm going.

[*Enter* PHILIP *at back with* GRACE. PHILIP *looks dusty and grim.* GRACE, *as they come in, speaks to him.* PHILIP *shakes his head. They pause up stage.*]

CYNTHIA [*emotionally*]. I shall go to my room! [MRS. PHILLIMORE *sees* PHILIP. PHILIP *represses* GRACE; *gives her a stern look and forceful gesture to be silent.* CYNTHIA *goes up, and* MISS HENEAGE *comes down.*] However, all I ask is that you repeat to Philip—

[*Comes suddenly on* PHILIP, *and speaks to him in a low tone.*]

SUDLEY [*to* MISS HENEAGE, *determined to win*]. As I go out, I shall do myself the pleasure of calling a hansom for Mrs. Karslake—

[PHILIP *comes down two or three steps.*]

PHILIP. As you go out, Sudley, have a hansom called, and when it comes, get into it.

SUDLEY [*furious, and speaking to* PHILIP]. Eh, —eh,—my dear sir, I leave you to your fate.

[PHILIP *angrily points him the door. Exit.*

MISS HENEAGE [*with weight*]. Philip, you've not heard—

PHILIP [*interrupts*]. Everything—from Grace! [CYNTHIA *goes down to table.*] My sister has repeated your words to me—and her own! I've told her what I think of *her*.

[PHILIP *looks witheringly at* GRACE.]

GRACE. I shan't wait to hear any more.

[*Exit* GRACE, *indignantly.*

PHILIP. Don't make it necessary for me to tell you what I think of you. [PHILIP *crosses;* MISS HENEAGE *crosses in fury.* PHILIP *gives his arm to his mother.* MISS HENEAGE *goes to door.*] Mother, with your permission, I desire to be alone. I expect both you and Grace, Sarah, to be dressed and ready for the ceremony a half hour from now.

[*As* PHILIP *and* MRS. PHILLIMORE *are about to cross,* MISS HENEAGE *speaks.*]

MISS HENEAGE. I shall come or not as I see fit. And let me add, my dear brother, that a fool at forty is a fool indeed.

[*Exit* MISS HENEAGE, *high and mighty, and much pleased with her quotation.*]

MRS. PHILLIMORE [*stupid and weary as usual, to* PHILIP, *as he leads her to the door.*] My dear son—I won't venture to express—

[CYNTHIA *crosses to table.*]

PHILIP [*soothing a silly mother*]. No, mother, don't! But I shall expect you, of course, at the ceremony. [MRS. PHILLIMORE *exits.* PHILIP *comes down.* PHILIP *takes the tone and assumes the attitude of the injured husband.*] It is proper for me to tell you that I followed you to Belmont. I am aware—I know with whom—in fact, *I know all!* [*Pauses. He indicates the whole censorious universe.*] And now let me assure you—I am the last man in the world to be jilted on the very eve of—of—everything with you. I won't be jilted. [CYNTHIA *is silent.*] You understand? I propose to marry you. I won't be made ridiculous.

CYNTHIA [*glancing at* PHILIP]. Philip, I didn't mean to make you—

PHILIP. Why, then, did you run off to Belmont Park with that fellow?

CYNTHIA. Philip, I—eh—

PHILIP [*sits right of table*]. What motive? What reason? On our wedding day? Why did you do it?

CYNTHIA. I'll tell you the truth. I was bored.

PHILIP. Bored? In my company?

[PHILIP, *in a gesture, gives up.*]

CYNTHIA. I was bored, and then—and besides, Sir Wilfrid asked me to go.

PHILIP. Exactly, and that was why you went. Cynthia, when you promised to marry me, you told me you had forever done with love. You agreed that marriage was the rational coming together of two people.

CYNTHIA. I know, I know!

PHILIP. Do you believe that now?

CYNTHIA. I don't know what I believe. My brain is in a whirl! But, Philip, I am beginning to be—I'm afraid—yes, I am afraid that one can't just select a great and good man [*She indicates him.*] and say: I will be happy with him.

PHILIP [*with dignity*]. I don't see why not. You must assuredly do one or the other: You must either let your heart choose or your head select.

CYNTHIA [*gravely*]. No, there's a third scheme; Sir Wilfrid explained the theory to me. A woman should marry whenever she has a whim for the man, and then leave the rest to the man. Do you see?

PHILIP [*furious*]. Do I see? Have I ever seen anything else? Marry for whim! That's the New York idea of marriage.

CYNTHIA [*giving a cynical opinion*]. New York ought to know.

PHILIP. Marry for whim and leave the rest to the divorce court! Marry for whim and leave the rest to the man. That was the former Mrs. Phillimore's idea. Only she spelled "whim" differently; she omitted the "w." [*He rises in his anger.*] And now you—*you* take up with this preposterous— [CYNTHIA *moves uneasily.*] But, nonsense! It's impossible! A woman of your mental calibre—No. Some obscure, primitive, female *feeling* is at work corrupting your better judgment! What is it you *feel?*

CYNTHIA. Philip, you never felt like a fool, did you?

PHILIP. No, never.

CYNTHIA [*politely*]. I thought not.

PHILIP. No, but whatever your feelings, I conclude you are ready to marry me.

CYNTHIA [*uneasy*]. Of course, I came back. I am here, am I not?

PHILIP. You are ready to marry me?

CYNTHIA [*twisting in the coils*]. But you haven't had your dinner.

PHILIP. Do I understand you refuse?

CYNTHIA. Couldn't we defer—?

PHILIP. You refuse?

CYNTHIA [*a slight pause; trapped and seeing no way out*]. No, I said I'd marry you. I'm a woman of my word. I will.

PHILIP [*triumphant*]. Ah! Very good, then. Run to your room. [CYNTHIA *turns to* PHILIP.] Throw something over you. In a half hour I'll expect you here! And Cynthia, my dear, remember! I cannot cuculate like a wood pigeon, but—I esteem you!

CYNTHIA [*hopelessly*]. I think I'll go, Philip.

PHILIP. I may not be fitted to play the love-bird, but—

CYNTHIA [*as before*]. I think I'll go, Philip.

PHILIP. I'll expect you,—in half an hour.

CYNTHIA [*with leaden despair*]. Yes.

PHILIP. And, Cynthia, don't think any more about that fellow, Cates-Darby.

CYNTHIA [*amazed and disgusted by his misapprehension*]. No. [*Exit* CYNTHIA.

THOMAS *enters*

PHILIP [*goes to table*]. And if I had that fellow, Cates-Darby, in the dock—!

THOMAS. Sir Wilfrid Cates-Darby.

PHILIP. Sir what—what—wh-who? [*Enter* SIR WILFRID, *in evening dress. Tableau.* PHILIP *looks* SIR WILFRID *in the face and speaks to* THOMAS.] Tell Sir Wilfrid Cates-Darby I am not at home to him.

[THOMAS *embarrassed.*]

SIR WILFRID [*undaunted*]. My dear Lord Eldon—

PHILIP [*to* THOMAS, *as before*]. Show the gentleman the door.

[*Pause.* SIR WILFRID *glances at door, and gesture.*]

SIR WILFRID [*goes to the door, examines it and returns to* PHILIP]. Eh,—I admire the door, my boy! Fine, old carved mahogany panel; but don't ask me to leave by it, for Mrs. Karslake made me promise I'd come, and that's why I'm here. [THOMAS *exits.*

PHILIP. Sir, you are—impudent—!

SIR WILFRID [*interrupting*]. Ah, you put it all in a nutshell, don't you?

PHILIP. To show your face here, after practically eloping with my wife!

SIR WILFRID [*pretending ignorance*]. When were you married?

PHILIP. We are as good as married.

SIR WILFRID. Oh, pooh, pooh! You can't tell me that grace before soup is as good as a dinner!

[*Takes cigar-case out; business of a dry smoke.*]

PHILIP. Sir—I—demand—

SIR WILFRID [*calmly carrying the situation*]. Mrs. Karslake is *not* married. *That's* why I'm here. I am here for the same purpose *you* are; to ask Mrs. Karslake to be my wife.

PHILIP. Are you in your senses?

SIR WILFRID [*touching up his American cousin in his pet vanity*]. Come, come, Judge—you Americans have no sense of humor. [*He takes a small jewel-case from his pocket.*] There's my regards for the lady—and [*Reasonably.*], if I must go, I will. Of course, I would like to see her, but—if it isn't your American custom—

Enter THOMAS

THOMAS. Mr. Karslake.

SIR WILFRID. Oh, well, I say; if he can come, I can!

[*Enter* JOHN KARSLAKE *in evening dress, carrying a large and very smart bride's bouquet which he hands to* PHILIP. PHILIP *takes it because he isn't up to dropping it, but gets it out of his hands as soon as he can.* PHILIP *is transfixed;* JOHN *comes down. Deep down he is feeling wounded and unhappy. But, as he knows his coming to the ceremony on whatever pretext is a social outrage, he carries it off by assuming an air of its being the most natural thing in the world. He controls the expression of his deeper emotion, but the pressure of this keeps his face grave, and he speaks with force.*]

JOHN. My compliments to the bride, Judge.

PHILIP [*angry*]. And you, too, have the effrontery?

SIR WILFRID. There you are!

JOHN [*pretending ease*]. Oh, call it friendship— [THOMAS *exits.*

PHILIP [*puts bouquet on table. Ironically*]. I suppose Mrs. Karslake—

JOHN. She wagered me I wouldn't give her away, and of course—

[*Throughout this scene* JOHN *hides the emotions he will not show behind a daring irony. He has* PHILIP *on his left, walking about in a fury;* SIR WILFRID *sits on the edge of the table, gay and undisturbed.*]

PHILIP [*a step toward* JOHN]. You will oblige me—both of you—by immediately leaving—

JOHN [*smiles and goes to* PHILIP]. Oh, come, come, Judge—suppose I *am* here? Who has a better right to attend his wife's obsequies! Certainly, I come as a mourner—for *you!*

SIR WILFRID. I say, is it the custom?

JOHN. No, no—of course it's not the custom, no. But we'll make it the custom. After all,—what's a divorced wife among friends?

PHILIP. Sir, your humor is strained!

JOHN. Humor,—Judge?

PHILIP. It is, sir, and I'll not be bantered! Your both being here is—it is—gentlemen, there is a decorum which the stars in their courses do not violate.

JOHN. Now, Judge, never you mind what the stars do in their divorces! Get down to earth of the present day. Rufus Choate and Daniel Webster are dead. You must be modern. You must let peroration and poetry alone! Come along now. Why shouldn't I give the lady away?

SIR WILFRID. Hear! Hear! Oh, I beg your pardon!

JOHN. And why shouldn't we both be here? American marriage is a new thing. We've got to strike the pace, and the only trouble is, Judge, that the judiciary have so messed the thing up that a man can't be sure he *is* married until he's divorced. It's a sort of marry-go-round, to be sure! But let it go at that! Here we all are, and we're ready to marry my wife to you, and start her on her way to him!

PHILIP [*brought to a standstill*]. Good Lord! Sir, you cannot trifle with monogamy!

JOHN. Now, now, Judge, monogamy is just as extinct as knee-breeches. The new woman has a new idea, and the new idea is—well, it's just the opposite of the old Mormon one. Their idea is one man, ten wives and a hundred children. Our idea is one woman, a hundred husbands and one child.

PHILIP. Sir, this is polyandry.

JOHN. Polyandry? A hundred to one it's polyandry; and that's it, Judge! Uncle Sam has established consecutive polyandry,—but there's got to be an interval between husbands! The fact is, Judge, the modern American marriage is like a wire fence. The woman's the wire—the posts are the husbands. [*He indicates himself, and then* SIR WILFRID *and* PHILIP.] One—two—three! And if you cast your eye over the future you can count them, post after post, up hill, down dale, all the way to Dakota!

PHILIP. All very amusing, sir, but the fact remains—

JOHN [*goes to* PHILIP. PHILIP *moves*]. Now, now, Judge, I like you. But you're asleep; you're living in the dark ages. You want to call up Central. "Hello, Central! Give me the present time, 1906, New York!"

SIR WILFRID. Of course you do, and—there you are!

PHILIP. There I am not, sir! And—[*To* JOHN.] as for Mr. Karslake's ill-timed jocosity,—sir, in the future—

SIR WILFRID. Oh, hang the future!

PHILIP. I begin to hope, Sir Wilfrid, that in the future I shall have the pleasure of hanging you! [*To* JOHN.] And as to you, sir, your insensate idea of giving away your own—your former—my—your—oh! Good Lord! This is a nightmare!

[*He turns to go in despair. Enter* MATTHEW, *who, seeing* PHILIP, *speaks as he comes in from door.*]

MATTHEW [*to* PHILIP]. My dear brother, Aunt Sarah Heneage refuses to give Mrs. Karslake away, unless you yourself,—eh—

PHILIP [*as he exits*]. No more! I'll attend to the matter!

[*Exit. The choir boys are heard practicing in the next room.*]

MATTHEW [*mopping his brow*]. How do you both do? My aunt has made me very warm. [*He rings the bell.*] You hear our choir practicing—sweet angel boys! Hm! Hm! Some of the family will not be present. I am very fond of you, Mr. Karslake, and I think it admirably Christian of you to have waived your—eh—your—eh—that is, now that I look at it more narrowly, let me say, that in the excitement of pleasurable anticipation, I forgot, Karslake, that your presence might occasion remark—

Enter THOMAS

Thomas! I left, in the hall, a small handbag or satchel containing my surplice.

THOMAS. Yes, sir. Ahem!

MATTHEW. You must really find the handbag at once.

[THOMAS *turns to go, when he stops startled.*]

THOMAS. Yes, sir. [*Announcing in consternation.*] Mrs. Vida Phillimore.

Enter VIDA PHILLIMORE, *in full evening dress. She steps gently to* MATTHEW

MATTHEW [*always piously serene*]. Ah, my dear child! Now this is just as it should be! That is, eh— [*He comes with her; she pointedly looks away from* SIR WILFRID.] That is, when I come to think of it—your presence might be deemed inauspicious.

VIDA. But, my dear Matthew,—I had to come. [*Aside to him.*] I have a reason for being here.

THOMAS *enters*

MATTHEW. But, my dear child—[*Gesture.*]

THOMAS [*with sympathetic intention*]. Sir, Mr. Phillimore wishes to have your assistance, sir—with Miss Heneage *immediately!*

MATTHEW. Ah! [*To* VIDA.] One moment! I'll return. [*To* THOMAS.] Have you found the bag with my surplice?

[*He goes out with* THOMAS, *speaking.* SIR WILFRID *comes to* VIDA. JOHN *crosses and comes down and watches door.*]

SIR WILFRID [*to* VIDA]. You're just the person I most want to see!

VIDA [*with affected iciness*]. Oh, no, Sir Wilfrid, Cynthia isn't here yet! [*Crosses to table.* JOHN *comes down right of table. To him with obvious sweetness.*] Jack, dear, I never was so ravished to see any one.

SIR WILFRID [*taken aback*]. By jove!

VIDA [*very sweet*]. I knew I should find you here!

JOHN [*annoyed but civil*]. Now don't do that!

VIDA [*as before*]. Jack! [*They sit.*]

JOHN [*civil but plain spoken*]. Don't do it!

VIDA [*in a voice dripping with honey*]. Do what, Jack?

JOHN. Touch me with your voice! I have troubles enough of my own.

[*He sits not far from her; the table between them.*]

VIDA. And I know *who* your troubles are! Cynthia!

[*From this moment* VIDA *gives up* JOHN *as an object of the chase and lets him into her other game.*]

JOHN. I hate her. I don't know why I came.

VIDA. You came, dear, because you couldn't stay away—you're in love with her.

JOHN. All right, Vida, what I feel may be *love*—but all I can say is, if I could get even with Cynthia Karslake—

VIDA. You can, dear—it's as easy as powdering one's face; all you have to do is to be too nice to me!

JOHN [*looks inquiringly at* VIDA]. Eh!

VIDA. Don't you realize she's jealous of you? Why did she come to my house this morning? She's jealous—and all you have to do—

JOHN. If I can make her wince, I'll make love to you till the Heavenly cows come home!

VIDA. Well, you see, my dear, if you make love to me it will [*She delicately indicates* SIR WILFRID.] cut both ways at once!

JOHN. Eh,—what! Not Cates-Darby? [*Starts.*] Is that Cynthia?

VIDA. Now don't get rattled and forget to make love to me.

JOHN. I've got the jumps. [*Trying to accept her instructions.*] Vida, I adore you.

VIDA. Oh, you must be more convincing; that won't do at all.

JOHN [*listens*]. Is that she now?

Enter MATTHEW, *who goes to the inner room*

VIDA. It's Matthew. And, Jack, dear, you'd best get the hang of it before Cynthia comes. You might tell me all about your divorce. That's a sympathetic subject. Were you able to undermine it?

JOHN. No. I've got a wire from my lawyer this morning. The divorce holds. She's a free woman. She can marry whom she likes. [*The organ is heard, very softly played.*] Is that Cynthia? [*Rises quickly.*]

VIDA. It's the organ!

JOHN [*overwhelmingly excited*]. By George! I should never have come! I think I'll go.

[*He crosses to go to the door.*]

VIDA [*she rises and follows him remonstratingly*]. When I need you?

JOHN. I can't stand it.

VIDA. Oh, but, Jack—

JOHN. Good-night!

VIDA. I feel quite ill. [*Seeing that she must play her last card to keep him, pretends to faintness; sways and falls into his arms.*] Oh!

JOHN [*in a rage, but beaten*]. I believe you're putting up a fake.

[*The organ swells as* CYNTHIA *enters sweepingly, dressed in full evening dress for the wedding ceremony. Tableau.* JOHN, *not knowing what to do, holds* VIDA *up as a horrid necessity.*]

CYNTHIA [*speaking as she comes on, to* MATTHEW]. Here I am. Ridiculous to make it a conventional thing, you know. Come in on the swell of the music, and all that, just as if I'd never been married before. Where's Philip?

[*She looks for* PHILIP *and sees* JOHN *with* VIDA *in his arms. She stops short.*]

JOHN [*uneasy and embarrassed*]. A glass of water! I beg your pardon, Mrs. Karslake—

[*The organ plays on.*]

CYNTHIA [*ironical and calm*]. Vida!

JOHN. She has fainted.

CYNTHIA [*as before*]. Fainted? [*Without pause.*] Dear, dear, dear, terrible! So she has. [SIR WILFRID *takes flowers from a vase and prepares to sprinkle* VIDA'S *forehead with the water it contains.*] No, no, not her forehead, Sir Wilfrid, her frock! Sprinkle her best Paquin! If it's a real faint, she will not come to!

VIDA [*as her Paris importation is about to suffer comes to her senses*]. I almost fainted.

CYNTHIA. Almost!

VIDA [*using the stock phrase as a matter of course, and reviving rapidly*]. Where am I? [JOHN *glances at* CYNTHIA *sharply.*] Oh, the bride! I beg every one's pardon. Cynthia, at a crisis like this, I simply couldn't stay away from Philip!

CYNTHIA. Stay away from Philip?

[JOHN *and* CYNTHIA *exchange glances.*]

VIDA. Your arm, Jack; and lead me where there is air.

[JOHN *and* VIDA *go into the further room;* JOHN *stands left of her. The organ stops.* SIR WILFRID *comes down. He and* CYNTHIA *are practically alone on the stage.* JOHN *and* VIDA *are barely within sight. You first see him take her fan and give her air; then he picks up a book and reads from it to her.*]

SIR WILFRID. I've come back.

CYNTHIA [*to* SIR WILFRID]. Asks for air and goes to the greenhouse. [CYNTHIA *crosses.* SIR WILFRID *offers her a seat.*] I know why you are here. It's that intoxicating little whim you suppose me to have for you. My regrets! But the whim's gone flat! Yes, yes, my gasoline days are over. I'm going to be garaged for good. However, I'm glad you're here; you take the edge off—

SIR WILFRID. Mr. Phillimore?

CYNTHIA [*sharply*]. No, Karslake. I'm just waiting to say the words [*Enter* THOMAS.] "love, honor and obey" to Phillimore—[*Looks up back.*] and *at* Karslake! [CYNTHIA *sees* THOMAS.] What is it? Mr. Phillimore?

THOMAS. Mr. Phillimore will be down in a few minutes, ma'am. He's very sorry, ma'am, [*Lowers his voice and comes nearer* CYNTHIA, *mindful of the respectabilities.*] but there's a button off his waistcoat.

CYNTHIA [*rises, crossing*]. Button off his waistcoat! [*Exit* THOMAS.

SIR WILFRID [*delightedly*]. Ah! So much the better for me. [CYNTHIA *looks up back.*] Now, then, never mind those two! [CYNTHIA *moves restlessly.*] Sit down.

CYNTHIA. I can't.

SIR WILFRID. You're as nervous as—

CYNTHIA. Nervous! Of course I'm nervous! So would you be nervous if you'd had a runaway and smash up, and you were going to try it again. [*Looks up back.* SIR WILFRID *uneasy.*] And if some one doesn't do away with those calla lilies—the odor makes me faint! [SIR WILFRID *moves.*] No, it's not the lilies! It's the orange blossoms!

SIR WILFRID. Orange blossoms.

CYNTHIA. The flowers that grow on the tree that hangs over the abyss! [SIR WILFRID *gets the vase of orange blossoms.*] They smell of six o'clock in the evening. When Philip's fallen asleep, and little boys are crying the winners outside, and I'm crying inside, and dying inside and outside and everywhere.

[SIR WILFRID *comes down.*]

SIR WILFRID. Sorry to disappoint you. They're artificial. [CYNTHIA *shrugs her shoulders.*] That's it! They're emblematic of artificial domesticity! And I'm here to help you balk it. [*He sits;* CYNTHIA *half rises and looks toward* JOHN *and* VIDA.] Keep still now, I've a lot to say to you. Stop looking—

CYNTHIA. Do you think I can listen to you make love to me when the man who—who—whom I most despise in all the world, is reading poetry to the woman who—who got me into the fix I'm in!

SIR WILFRID [*leaning over the chair in which she sits*]. What do you want to look at 'em for? [CYNTHIA *moves.*] Let 'em be and listen to me! Sit down; for damme, I'm determined. [CYNTHIA *sits right of table.*]

CYNTHIA [*half to herself*]. I won't look at them! I won't think of them. Beasts!

[SIR WILFRID *interposes between her and her view of* JOHN. *Enter* THOMAS, *who comes down.*]

SIR WILFRID. Now, then—[*He sits.*]

CYNTHIA. Those two *here!* It's just as if Adam and Eve should invite the snake to their golden wedding. [*She sees* THOMAS.] What is it, what's the matter?

THOMAS. Mr. Phillimore's excuses, ma'am. In a very short time— [THOMAS *exits.*

SIR WILFRID. I'm on to you! You hoped for more buttons!

CYNTHIA. I'm dying of the heat; fan me.

[SIR WILFRID *fans* CYNTHIA.]

SIR WILFRID. Heat! No! You're dying because you're ignorin' nature. Certainly you are! You're marryin' Phillimore! [CYNTHIA, *business; feels faint.*] Can't ignore nature, Mrs. Karslake. Yes, you are; you're forcin' your feelin's. [CYNTHIA *glances at him.*] And what you want to do is to let yourself go a bit—up anchor and sit tight! I'm no seaman, but that's the idea! [CYNTHIA *moves and shakes her head.*] So just throw the reins on nature's neck, jump this fellow Phillimore and marry me!

[*He leans over to* CYNTHIA.]

CYNTHIA [*naturally and irritably*]. You propose to me here, at a moment like this? When I'm on the last lap—just in sight of the goal—the gallows—the halter—the altar, I don't know what its name is! No, I won't have you! [*Looking toward* KARSLAKE *and* VIDA.] And I won't have you stand near me! I won't have you talking to me in a low tone! [*As before.*] Stand over there—stand where you are.

SIR WILFRID. I say—

CYNTHIA. I can hear you—I'm listening!

SIR WILFRID. Well, don't look so hurried and worried. You've got buttons and buttons of time. And now my offer. You haven't yet said you would—

CYNTHIA. Marry you? I don't even know you!

SIR WILFRID [*feeling sure of being accepted*]. Oh,—tell you all about myself. I'm no duke in a pickle o' debts, d'ye see? I can marry where I like. Some o' my countrymen are rotters, ye know. They'd marry a monkey, if poppa-up-the-tree had a corner in cocoanuts! And they do marry some queer ones, y' know.

[CYNTHIA *looks up, exclaims and turns.* SIR WILFRID *turns.*]

CYNTHIA. Do they?

SIR WILFRID. Oh, rather. That's what's giving your heiresses such a bad name lately. If a fellah's in debt he can't pick and choose, and then he swears that American gals are awfully fine lookers, but they're no good when it comes to continuin' the race! Fair dolls in the drawin'-room, but no good in the nursery.

CYNTHIA [*thinking of* JOHN *and* VIDA *and nothing else*]. I can see Vida in the nursery.

SIR WILFRID. You understand when you want a brood mare, you don't choose a Kentucky mule.

CYNTHIA. I think I see one.

SIR WILFRID. Well, that's what they're saying over there. They say your gals run to talk, [*He plainly remembers* VIDA'S *volubility.*] and I have seen gals here that would chat life into a wooden Indian! That's what you Americans call being clever.—All brains and no stuffin'! In fact, some of your American gals are the nicest boys I ever met.

CYNTHIA. So that's what you think?

SIR WILFRID. Not a bit what *I* think—what my countrymen think!

CYNTHIA. Why are you telling me?

SIR WILFRID. Oh, just explaining my character. I'm the sort that can pick and choose —and what I want is heart.

CYNTHIA [*always* VIDA *and* JOHN *in mind*]. No more heart than a dragon-fly!

[*The organ begins to play softly.*]

SIR WILFRID. That's it, dragon-fly. Cold as stone and never stops buzzing about and showin' off her colors. It's that American dragon-fly girl that I'm afraid of, because d'ye see, I don't know what an American expects when he marries; yes, but you're not listening!

CYNTHIA. I am listening. I am!

SIR WILFRID [*speaks directly to her*]. An Englishman, ye see, when he marries expects three things; love, obedience and five children.

CYNTHIA. Three things! I make it seven!

SIR WILFRID. Yes, my dear, but the point is, will you be mistress of Traynham?

CYNTHIA [*who has only half listened to him*]. No, Sir Wilfrid, thank you, I won't. [*She turns to see* JOHN *crossing the drawing-room at back, with* VIDA, *apparently absorbed in what she says.*] It's outrageous!

SIR WILFRID. Eh? Why you're cryin'?

CYNTHIA [*almost sobbing*]. I am not.

SIR WILFRID. You're not crying because you're in love with me?

CYNTHIA. I'm not crying—or if I am, I'm crying because I love my country. It's a disgrace to America—cast-off husbands and wives getting together in a parlor and playing tag under a palm-tree.

[JOHN *with intention and determined to stab* CYNTHIA, *kisses* VIDA'S *hand.*]

SIR WILFRID. Eh! Oh! I'm damned! [*To* CYNTHIA.] What do you think that means?

CYNTHIA. I don't doubt it means a wedding here, at once—after mine!

[VIDA *and* JOHN *come down.*]

VIDA [*affecting an impossible intimacy to wound* CYNTHIA *and tantalize* SIR WILFRID]. Hush, Jack—I'd much rather no one should know anything about it until it's all over!

CYNTHIA [*starts and looks at* SIR WILFRID]. What did I tell you?

VIDA [*to* CYNTHIA]. Oh, my dear, he's asked me to champagne and lobster at *your* house —his house! Matthew is coming! [CYNTHIA *starts, but controls herself.*] And you're to come, Sir Wilfrid. [VIDA *speaks, intending to convey the idea of a sudden marriage ceremony.*] Of course, my dear, I would like to wait for your wedding, but something rather—rather important to me is to take place, and I know you'll excuse me.

[*Organ stops.*]

SIR WILFRID [*piqued at being forgotten*]. All very neat, but you haven't given me a chance, even.

VIDA. Chance? You're not serious?

SIR WILFRID. I am!

VIDA [*striking while the iron is hot*]. I'll give you a minute to offer yourself.

SIR WILFRID. Eh?

VIDA. Sixty seconds from now.

SIR WILFRID [*uncertain*]. There's such a thing as bein' silly.

VIDA [*calm and determined*]. Fifty seconds left.

SIR WILFRID. I take you—count fair. [*He hands her his watch and goes to where* CYNTHIA *stands.*] I say, Mrs. Karslake—

CYNTHIA [*overwhelmed with grief and emotion*]. They're engaged; they're going to be married tonight, over champagne and lobster at my house!

SIR WILFRID. Will you consider your—

CYNTHIA [*hastily, to get rid of him*]. No, no, no, no! Thank you, Sir Wilfrid, I will not.

SIR WILFRID [*calm, and not to be laid low*]. Thanks awfully. [*Crosses to* VIDA. CYNTHIA *goes up.*] Mrs. Phillimore—

VIDA [*she gives him back his watch*]. Too late! [*To* KARSLAKE.] Jack, dear, we must be off.

SIR WILFRID [*standing and making a general appeal for information*]. I say, is it the custom for American girls—that sixty seconds or too late? Look here! Not a bit too late.

I'll take you around to Jack Karslake's, and I'm going to ask you the same old question again, you know. [*To* VIDA.] By jove, you know in your country it's the pace that kills.

[*Exeunt* SIR WILFRID *and* VIDA.

JOHN [*gravely to* CYNTHIA, *who comes down*]. Good-night, Mrs. Karslake, I'm going; I'm sorry I came.

CYNTHIA. Sorry? Why are you sorry? [JOHN *looks at her; she winces a little.*] You've got what you wanted. [*Pauses.*] I wouldn't mind your marrying Vida—

JOHN [*gravely*]. Oh, wouldn't you?

CYNTHIA. But I don't think you showed good taste in engaging yourselves *here*.

JOHN. Of course, I should have preferred a garden of roses and plenty of twilight.

CYNTHIA [*rushing into speech*]. I'll tell you what you *have* done—you've thrown yourself away! A woman like that! No head, no heart! All languor and loose—loose frocks—she's the typical, worst thing America can do! She's the regular American marriage worm!

JOHN. I have known others—

CYNTHIA [*quickly*]. Not me. I'm not a patch on that woman. Do you know anything about her life? Do you know the things she did to Philip? Kept him up every night of his life—forty days out of every thirty—and then, without his knowing it, put brandy in his coffee to make him lively at breakfast.

JOHN [*banteringly*]. I begin to think she is just the woman—

CYNTHIA [*unable to quiet her jealousy*]. She is *not* the woman for *you!* A man with your bad temper—your airs of authority—your assumption of—of—everything. What you need is a good, old-fashioned, bread poultice woman!

[CYNTHIA, *full stop; faces* JOHN.]

JOHN [*sharply*]. Can't say I've had any experience of the good old-fashioned bread poultice.

CYNTHIA. I don't care what you say! If you marry Vida Phillimore—you shan't do it. [*Tears of rage choking her.*] No, I liked your father and for *his* sake, I'll see that his son doesn't make a donkey of himself a second time.

JOHN [*too angry to be amused*]. Oh, I thought I was divorced. I begin to feel as if I had you on my hands still.

CYNTHIA. You have! You shall have! If you attempt to marry her, I'll follow you—and I'll find her—I'll tell Vida—[*He turns to her.*] I will. I'll tell Vida just what sort of a dance you led me.

JOHN [*quickly on her last word but speaking gravely*]. Indeed! Will you? And *why* do you care what happens to me?

CYNTHIA [*startled by his tone*]. I—I—ah—

JOHN [*insistently and with a faint hope*]. *Why* do you *care?*

CYNTHIA. I don't. Not in your sense—

JOHN. How dare you then pretend—

CYNTHIA. I don't pretend.

JOHN [*interrupting her; proud, serious and strong*]. How dare you look me in the face with the eyes that I once kissed, and pretend the least regard for me? [CYNTHIA *recoils and looks away. Her own feelings are revealed to her clearly for the first time.*] I begin to understand our American women now. Fire-flies—and the fire they gleam with is so cold that a midge couldn't warm his heart at it, let alone a man. You're not of the same race as a man! You married me for nothing, divorced me for nothing, because you *are* nothing!

CYNTHIA [*wounded to the heart*]. Jack! What are you saying?

JOHN [*with unrestrained emotion*]. What,—you feigning an interest in me, feigning a lie—and in five minutes—[*Gesture indicating altar.*] Oh, you've taught me the trick of your sex—you're the woman who's not a woman!

CYNTHIA [*weakly*]. You're saying terrible things to me.

JOHN [*low and with intensity*]. You haven't been divorced from me long enough to forget—what you should be ashamed to remember.

CYNTHIA [*unable to face him and pretending not to understand him*]. I don't know what you mean.

JOHN [*more forcibly and with manly emotion*]. You're not able to forget me? You know you're not able to forget me; ask yourself if you are able to forget me, and when your heart, such as it is, answers "no," then— [*The organ is plainly heard.*] Well, then, prance gaily up to the altar and marry that, if you can!

[*He exits quickly.* CYNTHIA *crosses to armchair and sinks into it. She trembles as if she were overdone. Voices are heard speaking in the next room. Enter* MATTHEW *and* MISS HENEAGE. *Enter* PHILIP. CYNTHIA *is so sunk in the chair they do not see her.* MISS HENEAGE *goes up to sofa back and waits. They all are dressed for an evening reception and* PHILIP *in the traditional bridegroom's rig—large buttonhole, etc.*]

MATTHEW [*as he enters*]. I am sure you will do your part, Sarah—in a spirit of Christian decorum. [*To* PHILIP.] It was impossible to find my surplice, Philip, but the more informal the better.

PHILIP [*with pompous responsibility*]. Where's Cynthia?

[MATTHEW *gives glance around room.*]

MATTHEW. Ah, here's the choir! [*Goes up stage. Choir boys come in very orderly; divide and take their places, an even number on each side of the altar of flowers.* MATTHEW *vaguely superintends.* PHILIP *gets in the way of the bell. Moves out of the way. Enter* THOMAS.] Thomas, I directed you—One moment if you please.

[*Indicates table and chairs.* THOMAS *hastens to move chairs and table against wall.* PHILIP *comes down.*]

PHILIP [*looking for her*]. Where's Cynthia?

[CYNTHIA *rises.* PHILIP *sees her when she moves and crosses toward her, but stops. Organ stops.*]

CYNTHIA [*faintly*]. Here I am.

[MATTHEW *comes down. Organ plays softly.*]

MATTHEW [*coming to* CYNTHIA]. Ah, my very dear Cynthia, I knew there was something. Let me tell you the words of the hymn I have chosen:

"Enduring love; sweet end of strife!
Oh, bless this happy man and wife!"

I'm afraid you feel—eh—eh!

CYNTHIA [*desperately calm*]. I feel awfully queer—I think I need a Scotch.

[*Organ stops.* PHILIP *remains uneasily.* MRS. PHILLIMORE *and* GRACE *enter back slowly, as cheerfully as if they were going to hear the funeral service read. They remain.*]

MATTHEW. Really, my dear, in the pomp and vanity—I mean—ceremony of this—this unique occasion, there should be sufficient exhilaration.

CYNTHIA [*as before*]. But there isn't!

[*She sits.*]

MATTHEW. I don't think my Bishop would approve of—eh—anything *before!*

CYNTHIA [*too agitated to know how much she is moved*]. I feel very queer.

MATTHEW [*piously sure that everything is for the best*]. My dear child—

CYNTHIA. However, I suppose there's nothing for it—now—but—to—to—

MATTHEW. Courage!

CYNTHIA [*desperate and with sudden explosion*]. Oh, don't speak to me. I feel as if I'd been eating gunpowder, and the very first word of the wedding service would set it off!

MATTHEW. My dear, your indisposition is the voice of nature.

[CYNTHIA *speaks more rapidly and with growing excitement.* MATTHEW *goes up near the choir boys.*]

CYNTHIA. Ah,—that's it—nature! [MATTHEW *shakes his head.*] I've a great mind to throw the reins on nature's neck.

PHILIP. Matthew! [*He moves to take his stand for the ceremony.*]

MATTHEW [*looks at* PHILIP. *To* CYNTHIA]. Philip is ready.

[PHILIP *comes down. The organ plays the wedding march.*]

CYNTHIA [*to herself, as if at bay*]. Ready? Ready? Ready?

MATTHEW. Cynthia, you will take Miss Heneage's arm. [MISS HENEAGE *comes down near table.*] Sarah! [MATTHEW *indicates to* MISS HENEAGE *where* CYNTHIA *is.* MISS HENEAGE *advances a step or two.* MATTHEW *goes up and speaks in a low voice to choir.*] Now please don't forget, my boys. When I raise my hands so, you begin, "Enduring love, sweet end of strife," etc. [CYNTHIA *has risen. On the table is her long lace cloak. She stands by this table.* MATTHEW *assumes sacerdotal importance and takes his position inside the altar of flowers.*] Ahem! Philip! [*He indicates to* PHILIP *to take his position.*] Sarah! [CYNTHIA *breathes fast, and supports herself on table.* MISS HENEAGE *goes down and stands for a moment looking at* CYNTHIA.] The ceremony will now begin.

[*The organ plays Mendelssohn's wedding march.* CYNTHIA *turns and faces* MISS HENEAGE. MISS HENEAGE *comes slowly, and extends her hand in her readiness to lead the bride to the altar.*]

MISS HENEAGE. Mrs. Karslake!

PHILIP. Ahem!

[MATTHEW *steps forward two or three steps.* CYNTHIA *stands turned to stone.*]

MATTHEW. My dear Cynthia. I request you—to take your place. [CYNTHIA *moves one or two steps across as if to go to the altar. She takes* MISS HENEAGE'S *hand and slowly they walk toward* MATTHEW.] Your husband to be—is ready, the ring is in my pocket. I have only to ask you the—eh—necessary questions,—and—eh—all will be blissfully over in a moment. [*The organ is louder.*]

CYNTHIA [*at this moment, just as she reaches* PHILIP, *she stops, faces round, looks him,* MATTHEW *and the rest in the face and cries out in despair*]. Thomas! Call a hansom! [THOMAS *exits and leaves door open.* MISS HENEAGE *crosses.* MRS. PHILLIMORE *rises.* CYNTHIA *grasps her cloak on table.* PHILIP *turns and* CYNTHIA *comes right and stops.*] I can't, Philip—I can't. [*Whistle of hansom is heard off; the organ stops.*] It is simply a case of throwing the reins on nature's neck—up anchor—and sit tight! [MATTHEW *crosses to* CYNTHIA.] Matthew, don't come near me! Yes, yes, I distrust you. It's your business, and you'd marry me if you could.

PHILIP [*watching her in dismay as she throws on her cloak*]. Where are you going?

CYNTHIA. I'm going to Jack.

PHILIP. What for?

CYNTHIA. To stop his marrying Vida. I'm blowing a hurricane inside, a horrible, happy hurricane! I know myself—I know what's the matter with me. If I married you and Miss Heneage—what's the use of talking about it—he mustn't marry that woman. He shan't. [CYNTHIA *has now all her wraps on; goes up rapidly. To* PHILIP.] Sorry! So long! Good-night and see you later.

CYNTHIA *goes to door, rapidly;* MATTHEW, *in absolute amazement, throws up his arms.* PHILIP *is rigid.* MRS. PHILLIMORE *sinks into a chair.* MISS HENEAGE *supercilious and unmoved.* GRACE *the same. The choir, at* MATTHEW'S *gesture, mistakes it for the concerted signal, and bursts lustily into the Epithalamis.*

"Enduring love—sweet end of strife!
Oh, bless this happy man and wife!"

CURTAIN

THE FOURTH ACT

SCENE.—JOHN KARSLAKE'S *study and smoking-room. Bay window. Door to stairs and the front door of house. Door, at back, leading to the dining-room. Fireplace and mantel. 'Phone. Bookcase containing law books and sporting books. Full-length portrait of* CYNTHIA *on the wall. Nothing of this portrait is seen by audience except the gilt frame and a space of canvas. A large table with writing materials is littered over with law books, sporting books, papers, pipes, crops, a pair of spurs, etc. A wedding ring lies on it. There are three very low easy-chairs. The general appearance of the room is extremely gay and garish in color. It has the easy confusion of a man's room. A small table. On this table is a woman's sewing-basket. The sewing-basket is open. A piece of rich fancy work lies on the table, as if a lady had just risen from sewing. On the corner are a lady's gloves. On a chair-back is a lady's hat. It is a half hour later than the close of Act III. Curtains are drawn over window. Lamp on table lighted. Electric lights about room also lighted. One chair is conspicuously standing on its head.*

Curtain rises on NOGAM, *who busies himself at table, back. Door at back is half open.*

SIR WILFRID [*comes in door, up*]. Eh—what did you say your name was?

NOGAM. Nogam, sir.

SIR WILFRID. Nogam? I've been here thirty minutes. Where are the cigars? [NOGAM *motions to a small table near the entrance door where the cigars are.*] Thank you. Nogam, Mr. Karslake was to have followed us here, immediately. [*He lights a cigar.*]

NOGAM. Mr. Karslake just now 'phoned from his club [SIR WILFRID *comes down.*], and he's on his way home, sir.

SIR WILFRID. Nogam, why is that chair upside down?

NOGAM. Our orders, sir.

VIDA [*speaking as she comes on*]. Oh, Wilfrid! [SIR WILFRID *turns*. VIDA *comes slowly down*.] I can't be left longer alone with the lobster! He reminds me too much of Phillimore!

SIR WILFRID. Karslake's coming; stopped at his club on the way! [*To* NOGAM.] You haven't heard anything of Mrs. Karslake—?

NOGAM [*surprised*]. No, sir!

SIR WILFRID [*in an aside to* VIDA, *as they move right to appear to be out of* NOGAM'S *hearing*]. Deucedly odd, ye know—for the Reverend Matthew declared she left Phillimore's house before *he* did,—and she told them she was coming here!

[NOGAM *evidently takes this in*.]

VIDA. Oh, she'll turn up.

SIR WILFRID. Yes, but I don't see how the Reverend Phillimore had the time to get here and make us man and wife, don't y' know—

VIDA. Oh, Matthew had a fast horse and Cynthia a slow one—or she's a woman and changed her mind! Perhaps she's gone back and married Phillimore. And besides, dear, Matthew wasn't in the house four minutes and a half; only just long enough to hoop the hoop. [*She twirls her new wedding ring gently about her finger*.] Wasn't it lucky he had a ring in his pocket?

SIR WILFRID. Rather.

VIDA. And are you aware, dear, that Phillimore bought and intended it for Cynthia? Do come [*She goes up to the door through which she entered*.], I'm desperately hungry! Whenever I'm married that's the effect it has!

[VIDA *goes out*. SIR WILFRID *sees her through door, but stops to speak to* NOGAM.]

SIR WILFRID. We'll give Mr. Karslake ten minutes, Nogam. If he does not come then, you might serve supper. [*He follows* VIDA.]

NOGAM [*to* SIR WILFRID]. Yes, sir.

Door opens. Enter FIDDLER

FIDDLER [*easy and business-like*]. Hello, Nogam, where's the guv'nor? That mare's off her oats, and I've got to see him.

NOGAM. He'll soon be here.

FIDDLER. Who was the parson I met leaving the house?

NOGAM [*whispers*]. Sir Wilfrid and Mrs. Phillimore have a date with the guv'nor in the dining-room, and the reverend gentleman—

[*Gesture as of giving an ecclesiastical blessing*.]

FIDDLER [*amazed*]. He hasn't spliced them? [NOGAM *assents*.] He has? They're married? Never saw a parson could resist it!

NOGAM. Yes, but I've got another piece of news for you. Who do you think the Rev. Phillimore expected to find *here?*

FIDDLER [*proud of being in the know*]. Mrs. Karslake? I saw her headed this way in a hansom with a balky horse only a minute ago. If she hoped to be in at the finish—

[FIDDLER *goes down and is about to set chair on its legs*.]

NOGAM [*quickly*]. Mr. Fiddler, sir, please to let it alone.

FIDDLER [*puts chair down in surprise*]. Does it live on its blooming head?

NOGAM. Don't you remember? *She* threw it on its head when she left here, and he won't have it up. Ah, that's it—hat, sewing-basket and all,—the whole rig is to remain as it was when she handed him his knock-out.

[*A bell rings outside*.]

FIDDLER. There's the guv'nor—I hear him!

NOGAM. I'll serve the supper. [*Takes letter from pocket and puts it on mantel*.] Mr. Fiddler, would you mind giving this to the guv'nor? It's from his lawyer—his lawyer couldn't find him and left it with me. He said it was very important. [*Goes up. Bell rings again. Speaking off to* SIR WILFRID.] I'm coming, sir!

[NOGAM *goes out back, and shuts door. Enter* JOHN KARSLAKE. *He looks downhearted, his hat is pushed over his eyes. His hands in his pockets. He enters slowly and heavily. Sees* FIDDLER, *who salutes, forgetting letter*. JOHN *comes and sits in armchair at study table*.]

JOHN [*speaking as he walks to his chair*]. Hello, Fiddler!

[*Pause*. JOHN *throws himself into a chair, keeps his hat on. Throws down gloves; sighs*.]

FIDDLER. Came in to see you, sir, about Cynthia K.

JOHN [*drearily*]. Damn Cynthia K!—

FIDDLER. Couldn't have a word with you?

JOHN [*grumpy*]. No!

FIDDLER. Yes, sir.

JOHN. Fiddler.

FIDDLER. Yes, sir.

JOHN. Mrs. Karslake—[FIDDLER *nods.*] You used to say she was our mascot?

FIDDLER. Yes, sir.

JOHN. Well, she's just married herself to a—a sort of a man!

FIDDLER. Sorry to hear it, sir.

JOHN. Well, Fiddler, between you and me, we're a pair of idiots.

FIDDLER. Yes, sir!

JOHN. And now it's too late!

FIDDLER. Yes, sir—oh, beg your pardon, sir—your lawyer left a letter.

[JOHN *takes letter; opens it and reads it, indifferently at first.*]

JOHN [*as he opens letter*]. What's he got to say, more than what his wire said?—Eh—[*As he reads, he is dumbfounded.*] what?—Will explain.—Error in wording of telegram.—Call me up.—[*Turns to telephone quickly.*] The man can't mean that she's still—Hello! Hello! [JOHN *listens.*]

FIDDLER. Would like to have a word with you, sir—

JOHN. Hello, Central!

FIDDLER. That mare—

JOHN [*looks at letter; speaks into 'phone*]. 33246a 38! Did you get it?

FIDDLER. That mare, sir, she's got a touch of malaria—

JOHN [*at the phone*]. Hello, Central—33246a—38!—Clayton Osgood—yes, yes, and say, Central—get a move on you!

FIDDLER. If you think well of it, sir, I'll give her a tonic—

JOHN [*still at the 'phone*]. Hello! Yes—yes—Jack Karslake. Is that you, Clayton? Yes—yes—well—

FIDDLER. Or if you like, sir, I'll give her—

JOHN [*turning on* FIDDLER]. Shut up! [*To 'phone.*] What was that? Not you—not you—a technical error? You mean to say that Mrs. Karslake is still—my—Hold the wire, Central—get off the wire! Get off the wire! Is that you, Clayton? Yes, yes—she and I are still—I got it! Good-bye!

[*Hangs up receiver; falls back in chair. For a moment he is overcome. Takes up telephone book.*]

FIDDLER. All very well, Mr. Karslake, but I must know if I'm to give her—

JOHN [*turning over the leaves of the telephone book in hot haste*]. What's Phillimore's number?

FIDDLER. If you've no objections, I think I'll give her a—

JOHN [*as before*]. L—M—N—O—P—It's too late! She's married by this! Married!—and—my God—I—I am the cause. Phillimore—

FIDDLER. I'll give her—

JOHN. Give her wheatina!—give her grape nuts—give her away! [FIDDLER *goes up.*] Only be quiet! Phillimore!

Enter SIR WILFRID, *back*

SIR WILFRID. Hello! We'd almost given you up!

JOHN [*still in his agitation unable to find Phillimore's number*]. Just a moment! I'm trying to get Phillimore on the 'phone to—to tell Mrs. Karslake—

SIR WILFRID. No good, my boy—she's on her way here! [JOHN *drops book and looks up dumbfounded.*] The Reverend Matthew was here, y' see—and he said—

JOHN [*rises; turns*]. Mrs. Karslake is coming here? [SIR WILFRID *nods.*] To this house? here?

SIR WILFRID. That's right.

JOHN. Coming here? You're sure? [SIR WILFRID *nods assent.*] Fiddler [*Crosses to* FIDDLER. FIDDLER *comes.*], I want you to stay here, and if Mrs. Karslake comes, don't fail to let me know! Now then, for Heaven's sake, what did Matthew say to you?

SIR WILFRID. Come along in and I'll tell you.

JOHN. On your life now, Fiddler, don't fail to let me—

[*Exeunt* JOHN *and* SIR WILFRID.

VIDA [*voice off*]. Ah, here you are!

FIDDLER. Phew!

[*A moment's pause, and* CYNTHIA *enters. She comes in very quietly, almost shyly, and as if she were uncertain of her welcome.*]

CYNTHIA. Fiddler! Where is he? Has he come? Is he here? Has he gone?

FIDDLER [*rattled*]. Nobody's gone, ma'am, except the Reverend Matthew Phillimore.

CYNTHIA. Matthew? He's been here and gone? [FIDDLER *nods assent.*] You don't mean I'm too late? He's married them already?

FIDDLER. Nogam says he married them!

CYNTHIA. He's married them! Married! Married before I could get here! [*Sits in armchair.*] Married in less time than it takes to pray for rain! Oh, well, the church—the church is a regular quick marriage counter. [*Voices of* VIDA *and* JOHN *heard off in light-hearted laughter.*] Oh!

FIDDLER. I'll tell Mr. Karslake—

CYNTHIA [*rising and going to the door through which* JOHN *left the stage; she turns the key in the lock and takes it out*]. No—I wouldn't see him for the world! [*She comes down with key to the work-table.*] If I'm too late, I'm too late! and that's the end of it! [*She lays key on table; remains standing near it.*] I've come, and now I'll go! [*Long pause.* CYNTHIA *looks about the room; changes her tone.*] Well, Fiddler, it's all a good deal as it used to be in my day.

FIDDLER. No, ma'am—everything changed, even the horses.

CYNTHIA [*same business; absent-mindedly*]. Horses—how are the horses?

[*Throughout this scene she gives the idea that she is saying good-bye to her life with* JOHN.]

FIDDLER. Ah, when husband and wife splits, ma'am, it's the horses that suffer. Oh, yes, ma'am, we're all changed since you give us the go-by,—even the guv'nor.

CYNTHIA. How's he changed?

FIDDLER. Lost his sharp for horses, and ladies, ma'am—gives 'em both the boiled eye.

CYNTHIA. I can't say I see any change; there's my portrait—I suppose he sits and pulls faces at me.

FIDDLER. Yes, ma'am, I think I'd better tell him of your bein' here.

CYNTHIA [*gently but decidedly*]. No, Fiddler, no! [*She again looks about her.*] The room's in a terrible state of disorder. However, your new mistress will attend to that. [*Pause.*] Why, that's not her hat!

FIDDLER. Yours, ma'am.

CYNTHIA. Mine? [*She goes to the table to look at it.*] Is that my work-basket? [*Pause.*] My gloves? [FIDDLER *assents.*] And I suppose—[*She hurriedly goes to the writing-table.*] My—yes, there it is: my wedding ring!—just where I dropped it! Oh, oh, oh, he keeps it like this—hat, gloves, basket and ring, everything just as it was that crazy, mad day when I—[*Glances at* FIDDLER *and breaks off.*] But for Heaven's sake, Fiddler, set that chair on its feet!

FIDDLER. Against orders, ma'am.

CYNTHIA. Against orders?

FIDDLER. You kicked it over, ma'am, the day you left us.

CYNTHIA. No wonder he hates me with the chair in that state! He nurses his wrath to keep it warm. So, after all, Fiddler, everything *is* changed, and that chair is the proof of it. I suppose Cynthia K is the only thing in the world that cares a whinney whether I'm alive or dead. [*She breaks down and sobs.*] How is she, Fiddler?

FIDDLER. Off her oats, ma'am, this evening.

CYNTHIA. Off her oats! Well, she loves me, so I suppose she will die, or change, or—or something. Oh, she'll die, there's no doubt about that—she'll die. [FIDDLER, *who has been watching his chance, takes the key off the table while she is sobbing, tiptoes up the stage, unlocks the door and goes out. After he has done so,* CYNTHIA *rises and dries her eyes.*] There—I'm a fool—I must go—before—before—he—

[*As she speaks her last word* JOHN *comes on.*]

JOHN. Mrs. Karslake!

CYNTHIA [*confused*]. I—I—I just heard Cynthia K was ill—[JOHN *assents.* CYNTHIA *tries to put on a cheerful and indifferent manner.*] I—I ran round—I—and—and—[*Pauses, turns, comes down.*] Well, I understand it's all over.

JOHN [*cheerfully*]. Yes, it's all over.

CYNTHIA. How is the bride?

JOHN. Oh, she's a wonder.

CYNTHIA. Indeed! Did she paw the ground like the war horse in the Bible? I'm sure when Vida sees a wedding ring she smells the battle afar off. As for you, my dear Karslake, I should have thought once bitten, twice shy! But, you know best.

Enter VIDA

VIDA. Oh, Cynthia, I've just been through it again, and I feel as if I were eighteen. There's no use talking about it, my dear, with a woman it's never the second time! And how nice you were, Jack,—he never even laughed at us! [*Enter* SIR WILFRID, *with hat and cane.* VIDA *kisses* JOHN.] That's the wages of virtue!

SIR WILFRID [*in time to see her kiss* JOHN]. I say, is it the custom? Every time she does that, my boy, you owe me a thousand pounds. [*Sees* CYNTHIA, *who comes down above chair; he looks at her and* JOHN *in turn.*] Mrs. Karslake. [*To* JOHN.] And then you say it's not an extraordinary country!

[CYNTHIA *is more and more puzzled.*]

VIDA [*to* JOHN]. See you next Derby, Jack! [*Crosses to door. To* SIR WILFRID.] Come along, Wilfrid! We really ought to be going. [*To* CYNTHIA.] I hope, dear, you haven't married him! Phillimore's a tomb! Good-bye, Cynthia—I'm so happy! [*As she goes.*] Just think of the silly people, dear, that only have this sensation once in a lifetime!

[*Exit* VIDA. JOHN *follows* VIDA *off.*

SIR WILFRID [*to* CYNTHIA]. Good-bye, Mrs. Karslake. And I say, ye know, if you have married that dull old Phillimore fellah, why, when you've divorced him, come over and stay at Traynham! I mean, of course, ye know, bring your new husband. There'll be lots o' horses to show you, and a whole covey of jolly little Cates-Darbys. Mind you come! [*With real delicacy of feeling and forgetting his wife.*] Never liked a woman as much in my life as I did you!

VIDA [*outside; calling him*]. Wilfrid, dear!

SIR WILFRID [*loyal to the woman who has caught him*]. Except the one that's calling me!

[*Re-enter* JOHN. SIR WILFRID *nods to him and goes off.* JOHN *shuts door and crosses. A pause.*]

CYNTHIA. So you're not married?

JOHN. No. But I know that you imagined I was. [*Pause.*]

CYNTHIA. I suppose you think a woman has no right to divorce a man—and still continue to feel a keen interest in his affairs?

JOHN. Well, I'm not so sure about that, but I don't quite see how—

CYNTHIA. A woman can be divorced—and still— [JOHN *assents; she hides her embarrassment.*] Well, my dear Karslake, you've a long life before you, in which to learn how such a state of mind is possible! So I won't stop to explain. Will you be kind enough to get me a cab? [*She moves to the door.*]

JOHN. Certainly. I was going to say I am not surprised at your feeling an interest in me. I'm only astonished that, having actually married Phillimore, you come here—

CYNTHIA [*indignantly*]. I'm not married to him! [*A pause.*]

JOHN. I left you on the brink—made me feel a little uncertain.

CYNTHIA [*in a matter of course tone*]. I changed my mind—that's all.

JOHN [*taking his tone from her*]. Of course. [*A pause.*] Are you going to marry him?

CYNTHIA. I don't know.

JOHN. Does he know you—

CYNTHIA. I told him I was coming here.

JOHN. Oh! He'll turn up here, then—eh? [CYNTHIA *is silent.*] And you'll go back with him, I suppose?

CYNTHIA [*talking at random*]. Oh—yes—I suppose so. I—I haven't thought much about it.

JOHN [*changes his tone*]. Well, sit down; do. Till he comes—talk it over. [*He places the armchair more comfortably for her.*] This is a more comfortable chair!

CYNTHIA [*shamefacedly*]. You never liked me to sit in that one!

JOHN. Oh, well—it's different now. [CYNTHIA *crosses and sits down near the upset chair. Long pause.* JOHN *crosses.*] You don't mind if I smoke?

CYNTHIA [*shakes her head*]. No.

JOHN [*business with pipe. Sits on arm of chair right of table*]. Of course, if you find my presence painful, I'll—skiddoo.

[*He indicates.* CYNTHIA *shakes her head.* JOHN *smokes pipe and remains seated.*]

CYNTHIA [*suddenly and quickly*]. It's just simply a fact, Karslake, and that's all there is to it—if a woman has once been married —that is, the first man she marries—then—she may quarrel, she may hate him—she may despise him—but she'll always be jealous of him with other women. Always!

[JOHN *takes this as if he were simply glad to have the information.*]

JOHN. Oh—Hm! ah—yes—yes. [*A pause.*]

CYNTHIA. You probably felt jealous of Phillimore.

JOHN [*reasonably, sweetly, and in doubt*]. N-o! I felt simply: Let him take his medicine. [*Apologetically.*]

CYNTHIA. Oh!

JOHN. I beg your pardon—I meant—

CYNTHIA. You meant what you said!

JOHN [*comes a step to her*]. Mrs. Karslake, I apologize—I won't do it again. But it's too late for you to be out alone—Philip will be here in a moment—and of course, then—

CYNTHIA. It isn't what you *say*—it's—it's—it's everything. It's the entire situation. Suppose by any chance I don't marry Phillimore! And suppose I were seen at two or three in the morning leaving my former husband's house! It's all wrong. I have no business to be here! I'm going! You're perfectly horrid to me, you know—and—the whole place—it's so familiar, and so—so associated with—with—

JOHN. Discord and misery—I know—

CYNTHIA. Not at all with discord and misery! With harmony and happiness—with—with first love, and infinite hope—and—and—Jack Karslake,—if you don't set that chair on its legs, I think I'll explode.

[JOHN *crosses rapidly, sets chair on its legs. Change of tone.*]

JOHN [*while setting on its legs*]. There! I beg your pardon.

CYNTHIA [*nervously*]. I believe I hear Philip. [*Rises.*]

JOHN [*goes up to window*]. N-o! That's the policeman trying the front door! And now, see here, Mrs. Karslake,—you're only here for a short minute, because you can't help yourself, but I want you to understand that I'm not trying to be disagreeable—I don't want to revive all the old unhappy—

CYNTHIA. Very well, if you don't—give me my hat. [JOHN *does so.*] And my sewing! And my gloves, please! [*She indicates the several articles which lie on the small table.*] Thanks! [CYNTHIA *throws the lot into the fireplace, and returns to the place she has left near table.*] There! I feel better! And now—all I ask is—

JOHN [*laughs*]. My stars, what a pleasure it is!

CYNTHIA. What is?

JOHN. Seeing you in a whirlwind!

CYNTHIA [*wounded by his seeming indifference*]. Oh!

JOHN. No, but I mean, a real pleasure! Why not? Time's passed since you and I were together—and—eh—

CYNTHIA. And you've forgotten what a vile temper I had!

JOHN [*reflectively*]. Well, you did kick the stuffing out of the matrimonial buggy—

CYNTHIA [*pointedly but with good temper*]. It wasn't a buggy; it was a break cart—[*She stands back of the armchair.*] It's all very well to blame me! But when you married me, I'd never had a bit in my mouth!

JOHN. Well, I guess I had a pretty hard hand. Do you remember the time you threw both your slippers out of the window?

CYNTHIA. Yes, and do you remember the time you took my fan from me by force?

JOHN. After you slapped my face with it!

CYNTHIA. Oh, oh! I hardly touched your face! And do you remember the day you held my wrists?

JOHN. You were going to bite me!

CYNTHIA. Jack! I never! I showed my teeth at you! And I said I would bite you!

JOHN. Cynthia, I never knew you to break your word! [*He laughs. Casually.*] And anyhow—they were awfully pretty teeth! [CYNTHIA, *though bolt upright, has ceased to seem pained.*] And I say—do you remember, Cyn—

[*Leans over the armchair to talk to her.*]

CYNTHIA [*after a pause*]. You oughtn't to call me "Cyn"—it's not nice of you. It's sort of cruel. I'm not—Cyn to you now.

JOHN. Awfully sorry; didn't mean to be beastly, Cyn. [CYNTHIA *turns quickly.* JOHN *stamps his foot.*] Cynthia! Sorry. I'll make it a commandment: thou shalt not Cyn!! [CYNTHIA *laughs and wipes her eyes.*]

CYNTHIA. How can you, Jack? How can you?

JOHN. Well, hang it, my dear child, I—I'm sorry, but you know I always got foolish with you. Your laugh'd make a horse laugh. Why, don't you remember that morning in the park before breakfast—when you laughed so hard your horse ran away with you!

CYNTHIA. I do, I do! [*Both laugh. The door opens.* NOGAM *enters.*] But what was it started me laughing? [*Laughs. Sits. Laughs again.*] That morning. Wasn't it somebody we met? [*Laughs.*] Wasn't it a man on a horse? [*Laughs.*]

JOHN [*laughing too*]. Of course! You didn't know him in those days! But I did! And he looked a sight in the saddle!

[NOGAM, *trying to catch their attention, comes down.*]

CYNTHIA. Who was it?

JOHN. Phillimore!

CYNTHIA. He's no laughing matter now. [*Sees* NOGAM.] Jack, he's here!

JOHN. Eh? Oh, Nogam?

NOGAM. Mr. Phillimore, sir—

JOHN. In the house?

NOGAM. On the street in a hansom, sir—and he requests Mrs. Karslake—

JOHN. That'll do, Nogam. [*Exit* NOGAM. *Pause.* JOHN *from near the window.* CYNTHIA *faces audience.*] Well, Cynthia?

[*He speaks almost gravely and with finality.*]

CYNTHIA [*trembling*]. Well?

JOHN. It's the hour of decision; are you going to marry him? [*Pause.*] Speak up!

CYNTHIA. Jack,—I—I—

JOHN. There he is—you can join him. [*He points to the street.*]

CYNTHIA. Join Phillimore—and go home—with him—to his house, and Miss Heneage and—

JOHN. The door's open. [*He points to the door.*]

CYNTHIA. No, no! It's mean of you to suggest it!

JOHN. You won't marry—

CYNTHIA. Phillimore—no; never. [*Runs to window.*] No; never, never, Jack.

JOHN [*goes up. He calls out of window, having opened it*]. It's all right, Judge. You needn't wait.

[*Pause.* JOHN *comes down. Tableau.* JOHN *bursts into laughter.* CYNTHIA *looks dazed. He closes door.*]

CYNTHIA. Jack! [JOHN *laughs.*] Yes, but I'm here, Jack.

JOHN. Why not?

CYNTHIA. You'll have to take me round to the Holland House!

JOHN. Of course, I will! But, I say, Cynthia, there's no hurry.

CYNTHIA. Why, I—I—can't stay here.

JOHN. No, of course you can't stay here. But you can have a bite, though. [CYNTHIA *shakes her head.* JOHN *places the small chair which was upset, next to table. Armchair above.*] Oh, I insist. Just look at yourself—you're as pale as a sheet and—here, here. Sit right down. I insist! By George, you must do it!

[CYNTHIA *crosses to chair beside table, left of it, and sits.*]

CYNTHIA [*faintly*]. I *am* hungry.

JOHN. Just wait a moment.

[JOHN *exits, upper door, leaving it open.*

CYNTHIA. I don't want more than a nibble! [*Pause.*] I am sorry to give you so much trouble.

JOHN. No trouble at all. [*He can be heard off, busied with glasses and a tray.*] A hansom of course, to take you round to your hotel?

[*Speaks as he comes down.*]

CYNTHIA [*to herself*]. I wonder how I ever dreamed I could marry that man.

JOHN [*above table by this time*]. Can't imagine! There!

CYNTHIA. I am hungry. Don't forget the hansom.

[*She eats; he waits on her, setting this and that before her.*]

JOHN [*goes to door, up; opens it and speaks off*]. Nogam, a hansom at once.

NOGAM [*off stage*]. Yes, sir.

JOHN [*back to above table; from here on he shows his feelings for her*]. How does it go?

CYNTHIA [*faintly*]. It goes all right. Thanks! [*Hardly eating at all.*]

JOHN. You always used to like anchovy. [CYNTHIA *nods and eats.*] Claret? [CYNTHIA *shakes her head.*] Oh, but you must!

CYNTHIA [*tremulously*]. Ever so little. [*He fills her glass and then his.*] Thanks! [*He pours out a glass for himself.*]

JOHN. Here's to old times! [*Raising glass.*]

CYNTHIA [*very tremulous*]. Please not!

JOHN. Well, here's to your next husband.

CYNTHIA [*very tenderly*]. Don't!

JOHN. Oh, well, then, what shall the toast be?

CYNTHIA. I'll tell you—[*Pause.*] you can drink to the relation I am to you!

JOHN [*laughing*]. Well—what relation are you?

CYNTHIA. I'm your first wife once removed!

JOHN [*laughs; drinks*]. I say, you're feeling better.

CYNTHIA. Lots.

JOHN [*reminiscent*]. It's a good deal like those mornings after the races—isn't it?

CYNTHIA [*nods*]. Yes. Is that the hansom? [*Half rises.*]

JOHN [*going up to the window*]. No.

CYNTHIA [*sits again*]. What is that sound?

JOHN. Don't you remember?

CYNTHIA. No.

JOHN. That's the rumbling of the early milk wagons.

CYNTHIA. Oh, Jack.

JOHN. Do you recognize it now?

CYNTHIA. Do I? We used to hear that—just at the hour, didn't we—when we came back from awfully jolly late suppers and things!

JOHN. Hm!

CYNTHIA. It must be fearfully late. I must go.

[*Rises, crosses to chair, where she has left cloak. She sees that* JOHN *will not help her and puts it on herself.*]

JOHN. Oh, don't go—why go?

CYNTHIA [*embarrassed and agitated*]. All good things come to an end, you know.

JOHN. They don't need to.

CYNTHIA. Oh, you don't mean that! And, you know, Jack, if I were caught—seen at this hour, leaving this house, you know—it's the most scandalous thing any one ever did—my being here at all. Good-bye, Jack! [*Pause; almost in tears.*] I'd like to say, I—I—I—well, I shan't be bitter about you hereafter, and—[*Pause.*] Thank you awfully, old man, for the fodder and all that! [*Turns to go out.*]

JOHN. Mrs. Karslake—wait—

CYNTHIA [*stopping to hear*]. Well?

JOHN [*serious*]. I've rather an ugly bit of news for you.

CYNTHIA. Yes?

JOHN. I don't believe you know that I have been testing the validity of the decree of divorce which you procured.

CYNTHIA. Oh, have you?

JOHN. Yes; you know I felt pretty warmly about it.

CYNTHIA. Well?

JOHN. Well, I've been successful. [*Pause.*] The decree's been declared invalid. Understand?

CYNTHIA [*looks at him a moment; then speaks*]. Not—precisely.

JOHN [*pause*]. I'm awfully sorry—I'm awfully sorry, Cynthia, but you're my wife still. [*Pause.*]

CYNTHIA [*with rapture*]. Honor bright? [*She sinks into the armchair.*]

JOHN [*nods. Half laughingly*]. Crazy country, isn't it?

CYNTHIA [*nods. Pause*]. Well, Jack—what's to be done?

JOHN [*gently*]. Whatever you say.

NOGAM [*quietly enters door*]. Hansom, sir.

[*Exits;* CYNTHIA *rises.*

JOHN. Why don't you finish your supper? [CYNTHIA *hesitates.*]

CYNTHIA. The—the—hansom—

JOHN. Why go to the Holland? After all—you know, Cyn, you're at home here.

CYNTHIA. No, Jack, I'm not—I'm not at home here—unless—unless—

JOHN. Out with it!

CYNTHIA [*bursting into tears*]. Unless I—unless I'm at home at your heart, Jack!

JOHN. What do you think?

CYNTHIA. I don't believe you want me to stay.

JOHN. Don't you?

CYNTHIA. No, no, you hate me still. You never can forgive me. I know you can't. For I can never forgive myself. Never, Jack, never, never! [*She sobs and he takes her in his arms.*]

JOHN [*very tenderly*]. Cyn! I love you! [*Strongly.*] And you've got to stay! And hereafter you can chuck chairs around till all's blue! Not a word now. [*He draws her gently to a chair.*]

CYNTHIA [*wiping her tears*]. Oh, Jack! Jack!

JOHN. I'm as hungry as a shark. We'll nibble together.

CYNTHIA. Well, all I can say is, I feel that of all the improprieties I ever committed this—this—

JOHN. This takes the claret, eh? Oh, Lord, how happy I am!

CYNTHIA. Now don't say that! You'll make me cry more.

[*She wipes her eyes.* JOHN *takes out wedding ring from his pocket; he lifts a wine glass, drops the ring into it and offers her the glass.*]

JOHN. Cynthia!

CYNTHIA [*looking at it and wiping her eyes*]. What is it?

JOHN. Benedictine!

CYNTHIA. Why, you know I never take it.

JOHN. Take this one for my sake.

CYNTHIA. That's not benedictine. [*With gentle curiosity.*] What is it?

JOHN [*he slides the ring out of the glass and puts his arm about* CYNTHIA. *He slips the ring on to her finger and, as he kisses her hand, says:*] Your wedding ring!

CURTAIN

MADAME SAND: A BIOGRAPHICAL COMEDY

By Philip Moeller

PHILIP MOELLER

[1880–   ]

PHILIP MOELLER is one of the significant forces in the current American theatre—"forces" here suggesting a certain anonymity and yet strong motivating power inherent in much of his work. As a director of the superior type of play, he has combined with an aesthetic sense and an imagination capable of grasping O'Neill in all his subtleties, a compelling knowledge of stagecraft which has given theatre-life to dramatic conceptions that in lesser hands would have suffered immeasurably. In addition to his distinguished abilities as a director, Mr. Moeller is a trained and competent playwright.

Mr. Moeller was born in New York City in 1880, and after graduating from Columbia University, he spent much time in foreign travel. He was active with the Washington Square Players (1914–1917), a "quality" theatre group which ultimately led to the development of the Theatre Guild, premier dramatic association in America at the present time. Mr. Moeller is one of the permanent directors of this organization.

An early play of Moeller's that attracted attention and is still frequently produced among amateur groups is *Helena's Husband* (1915). This is a clever one-act piece recounting, in a satiric vein, Helena's abduction by Paris. Tellingly ironic is the picture of Menelaus, the wife-hater and peace-lover, whose stratagem to rid himself of Helen has precipitated a war waged solely to recover the stolen queen. Then, too, Menelaus, who has defied fate, who will "never allow religion to interfere with life," is helpless in the hands of his counsellors urging the populace to war. Much of the sharp humor in *Helena's Husband* arises from placing a person with modern temperament and problems in an ancient character-setting.

After the production of another one-act play, *Two Blind Beggars and One Less Blind* (1915), Moeller wrote his first full-length play, *Madame Sand* (1917), which takes rank as a vitalized biographical play along with such others as Drinkwater's *Abraham Lincoln* and *Robert E. Lee*, Maxwell Anderson's *Elizabeth the Queen*, Eaton and Carb's *Queen Victoria*, and Sacha Guitry's *Pasteur*.

Equally skillful in bringing historical figures to life is *Molière* (1919), which portrays Molière's literary and social relations to Louis XIV. Moeller's next play, *Sophie* (1919), is a clever account of the opera singer, Sophie Arnold, in the time of Louis XV. In addition to other one-act plays, there are several adaptations to Moeller's credit: *Fata Morgana* (in collaboration with J. L. A. Burrell), from Ernst Vajda; *Caprice*, from Sil-Vara (pseudonym for Greza Silberer); and *Camel Through the Needle's Eye*, from Frantizek Langer.

Meredith's "comic spirit" of thoughtful laughter reveals itself in *Madame Sand* in the reflective smiles which play upon the characters and their foibles; we are here in the intellectual world Meredith postulates, and comedy good-naturedly pursues folly—good-naturedly by all means, for though George Sand's mutability comes to light, yet she is portrayed with sufficient sympathy and conviction to disarm the scorner. The philosophy of consistency perhaps forms the basis of the central commentary of the play: it is not George Sand's changeability itself that Moeller impales; it is her unfailing protestation that each new affair is her only real and abiding love—"As I have never loved before. . . ." The capacity of man, or perhaps woman, for emotional amnesia and deception is exemplified in George Sand's facility in forgetting former ecstasies and sweeping on to new ones, which will last, she believes, "to the world's end." A corollary to this emotional mutability is her intellectual inconsistency: fate is either all-powerful or impotent, according to the exigencies of the situation. When Pagello thanks God for the day he chanced to pass George's window, the impromptu philosopher apostrophizes chance: "And in that little word lies all the joy and sorrow of the world"; then again, when George is attempting to "abduct" Pagello, she urges that they cannot wait for anything, that "destiny has spoken." [1] Subsequently when George is attempting to console Alfred for her desertion, she points out that he can keep from being broken-hearted, that "our fate is what we make it." [2] "There is no such thing as fate. . . . Fate is the death cry of the coward." [3] An instance of another inconsistency: though practically the whole of George Sand's facultative being is absorbed in the production of books, though in the midst of life her pen is never dry (she calmly draws her pen when Lucrezia draws her dagger), yet upon Chopin's remark that he does not read much, the authoress suddenly affirms: "There are too many books. It is life that really matters." A moment later when she is rhapsodizing on their future in the Mediterranean, she is so impressed with one of her own remarks that she copies it down on her fan for future use.

With respect to George Sand's romantic qualities one feels that the playwright is tolerant, if not sympathetic. Her emphasis on feeling, especially love, is movingly presented; freedom and desire are important in her philosophy: "At least there shall be one free thing answering the winds of desire." ". . . Life is meant to be squandered." [4] A nympholeptic longing for the land of otherwhere descends upon her at the approach of each new love: when she is in Paris, she pines for Venice; when she is in Venice, she sighs for the Alpine hills. Social conventions are to yield to individual wants: "Need is the only tradition I acknowledge"; and instinct is to be the ethical guide: "A woman only feels

[1] Act II, p. 538.
[2] Act II, p. 547.
[3] Act II, p. 547.
[4] Act I, p. 529.

and knows she is right." Feebly opposed to this philosophy is Madame de Musset's protestation to Paul that she is not losing her temper: "I am calm, Paul. I've been trained to control myself. Only peasants and literary people give way to their emotions."[1]

What sympathy there may be for George Sand's position, however, appears to regard it as a way of pleasure rather than as a basis of a philosophy. For behind the Greek-chorus commentaries of Heine, and beneath the reflections of others, lie the present-day realism and skeptical estimate of life, derived in some measure from the scientific attitude stemming from Darwin, which explains man in the light of natural forces. It is this tendency to interpret man in terms of physico-chemical reactions, to regard him as a part of a mechanistic universe, that makes itself felt in Dreiser, Sherwood Anderson, and Lewis. Though determinism does not appear in *Madame Sand*, sub-rational fatalism seems to be accepted not only by Heine, but by others as well.[2] In the words of Alfred de Musset: "Fate is our enemy. We are born to defeat. . . . I am but a poor reed, broken in the wind of destiny." Or of Liszt: "Alas, we poor men are but threads between the shears." Or of Heine: "We jig at the end of the wires, poets and cooks, saints and grisettes —hung from the nimble fingers of the Gods." The figure of the puppets, implying basic indifferentism in the manipulator, is suggestive of the devil's heartlessness in Mark Twain's *The Mysterious Stranger*. There is no God according to Heine: "I'm a Jew by birth, a Christian by necessity and an atheist by conviction. . . . Pessimism is my spiritual purge." He is cynical about virtue and love: "Virtue is its own disappointment. . . . Beware of this love of ours. It is our enemy, most selfish, most subtle, and most sinister." Likewise Alfred: "Life lays the trap of love and we, poor human fools, are crowding, crowding and waiting to be caught." For Paul de Musset love does not go beyond the physical: "Love is only an affair of good evening, good morning—and good-bye."

Heine looks at society and finds its structure cruel: "Some must suffer that others may sup. Socially, spiritually, everywhere, always true—paying the toll to life—that others may sup." Fine lineage is not immune to failure: "Many of the best family trees bore the worst fruit." George Sand does not have great faith in the marriage tie, either practically or theoretically: "What does a husband matter? He is an incident all married women should forget."

The literary commentaries in the play naturally center about George Sand, the brilliant exponent of romanticism. Rousseau's theory of social and artistic freedom as essent al to true literary creation finds expression in her speech: "You must be free to realize yourself." She depreciates thinking: "Geniuses do not stop to think." It is feeling, especially love, that she values: "Love is all." Although it

[1] Act I, p. 520.

[2] Cf. also the helpless Menelaus in *Helena's Husband*. Heine had a strong influence on Howells; see the latter's *My Literary Passions*.

might appear that George Sand is the protagonist of realism when she says: "Life is my theme," yet she is nearer romantic individualism, for it is *her* life that she writes about: "My stories are the mirror of my life. Tho I write with my heart's blood, still I must write."

But the critical temper is evident in Heine's lance-thrusts into her expansive ebullitions: "She writes like water tumbling from a pump." The romantic Alfred is also skeptical—with good cause, to be sure—but he places a telling stroke: "She's like a noisy old clock that can't stop ticking." When Buloz states that George contemplates suicide, Heine pierces the romantic pretense: "Everybody does since 'Werther.' She'll probably live till ninety."

Madame Sand has received critical approbation in this country,[1] but it suffered strong adverse criticism in England, in many cases because of its allegedly false picture of George Sand. *The Athenaeum* finds the play not true to life, not "plausible for a single instant." [2] *The Saturday Review* (London) takes exception to the picture of George Sand and reprimands Moeller for his impertinence in bringing these historic personages upon the stage (a privilege, says *The Saturday Review*, reserved for Mr. Shaw).[3] *The Illustrated London News* likewise finds that the play does not give a satisfactory picture of the heroine.[4] Although none of the above critics has adduced any evidence in support of his view, together they challenge consideration of the issue they raise. Inquiry reveals that in a sense these English critics are justified in pointing out the discrepancy between Moeller's George Sand and the actual character. With respect to her behavior in company, Heine himself testifies:

> "She shines little in conversation. She has absolutely none of the sparkling wit characteristic of Frenchwomen, but also nothing of their endless chatter. With an amiable and sometimes singular smile, she listens when others speak, as if she sought to absorb into herself the best of your words." [5]

Madame de Musset agreed in this estimate, and George's mother referred to her daughter as "St. Tranquillity." Furthermore, with reference to her external methods of work, Elme Caro informs us:

[1] Quinn says the play reveals Moeller as "a master of the sophisticated romance of history." (*History of the American Drama from the Civil War to the Present Day*, II, 137.) In answer to an attack on the play for lack of unity, Quinn affirms: "But partly through the preservation of her personal background in the friends like Heine and Buloz, but more fundamentally through the co-ordinating motive of her remorseless demand as an artist that life should provide the novelist with experiences, the episodes fuse into a unity complete and satisfying." (*Ibid.*, p. 139.) S. Marion Tucker says of the play that it is "a brilliant piece of high comedy" and "one of the very few biographical plays that have actual dramatic vitality." (*Modern American and British Plays*, p. 457.)

[2] P. 776, June 11, 1920.

[3] CXXIX, 558–559.

[4] CLVI, 1024, June 12, 1920. One is inclined to discount the particular force of these comments when he realizes that there apparently exists a feeling against American plays in general. *The Saturday Review* asks: "When is this invasion of American plays to cease?" It ingenuously adds, after attacking Moeller's characters, that "their remarks ought to be translated into English."

[5] Elme Caro. *George Sand*. Trans. by Melville B. Anderson. Chicago: 1888, p. 182.

"Upon a very simple table, she showed me a pile of great sheets of blue paper cut in quarto size. 'After your departure this evening,' she said, 'I shall set to work, and I shall not sleep until I have filled twelve of those pages.' This was her daily stint, her labor being thus planned beforehand. . . ." [1]

"This was for me an almost unlooked-for opportunity of acquainting myself intimately with her method of work, the results of which had always surprised me by their abundance less than by their exact regularity." [2]

But the picture is changed when one realizes George Sand's inner nature:

". . . She passed by fits from the enthusiasm that confounds all to the enthusiasm attaching itself exclusively to a thought or to a name,—and all this at the beck of the present sensation or the caprice of the imagination." [3]

She had "an imagination unrestrained and self-excited"; her biographer speaks of "her whole restless, palpitating, and superb nature." [4] Relative to her method of composition we learn that

"it was the mere pleasure of writing that impelled her, almost without pre-meditation, to throw upon paper, in some confusion, but in concrete and living form, her dreams, her affections, her meditations, and her whimseys." [5]

We see, then, a certain twofold aspect of George Sand's character; Caro describes it as "an existence very active within, but very solitary and retired. . . ." [6] It would appear, perhaps, that the objection made by the English critics is answered if we regard Moeller's play as a dramatization of Madame Sand's inner character, rather than her outer; in other words, if we consider the dramatist resorting in some measure to the modern technique of expressionism. Whatever one's conclusion may be in the matter, few can deny that the play is eminently readable and sharply stimulating.[7]

The present text of *Madame Sand* is from the first edition of the play (1917).

[1] *Ibid.*, p. 205.
[2] *Ibid.*, p. 206.
[3] *Ibid.*, p. 28.
[4] *Ibid.*, p. 41.
[5] *Ibid.*, p. 207.
[6] *Ibid.*, p. 42.

[7] For George Sand's earlier vogue in America see Howard Mumford Jones, "American Comment on George Sand, 1837–1848," *American Literature*, III, 389–407 (Jan., 1932). Henry James was interested in George Sand; see his *French Poets and Novelists* (1888).

CHARACTERS

(With the cast of the original production as given, under the direction of Arthur Hopkins, at the Academy of Music, Baltimore, October 29, 1917.)

ROSALIE, *Maid at Mme. Sand's*.............Jean Robb
PAUL DE MUSSET, *Alfred's brother*.............Harold Hendee
MME. DE MUSSET, *Alfred's mother*.............Muriel Hope
CASIMIR DUDEVANT, *Mme. Sand's husband*.............Ben Lewin
BULOZ, *Editor of the Revue des Deux Mondes*.............Walter Kingsford
HEINRICH HEINE.............Ferdinand Gottschalk
ALFRED DE MUSSET.............Jose Ruben
MME. JULIE AURORE LUCILLE AMANDINE DUDEVANT—GEORGE SAND.............Mrs. Fiske
DR. GIUSEPPE PIETRO PAGELLO, *Mme.'s Italian Physician*.............John Davidson
LUCREZIA VIOLENTE, *His Mistress*.............Olin Field
MLLE. DE FLEURY.............Marjorie Hollis
MLLE. ROLANDE.............Imogen Fairchild
MLLE. DE LATOUR.............Caroline Kohl
FRANZ LISZT.............Owen Meech
FREDERICK CHOPIN.............Alfred Cross

and

GUESTS at the reception of Baron de Rothschild.

SYNOPSIS

ACT I. *Rosalie's Omelet*
The farewell supper at Mme. Sand's apartment in the Quartier, Paris, 1833.

ACT II. *Nothing but Time Lasts Forever*
Mme. Sand's apartment in Venice, 1834.

ACT III. . . . *and Liszt plays on*
The reception for Chopin at Baron de Rothschild's, Paris.

MADAME SAND: A BIOGRAPHICAL COMEDY

ACT I. ROSALIE'S OMELET

The Scene

MME. SAND'S *apartment in the Quartier, Paris, 1833. It is a large studio-like room. Through a long window in the rear one sees the roofs of the city and the streets beyond with the first lamps lit. In the far distance are the twin towers of Notre Dame. The room is a shrine of literary Bohemia. The furnishings are of bizarre incongruity. An ornate Japanese screen barely hides an old-fashioned rubber bathtub, an India chest shows its design of arabesque in the shadow of a bed couch near a piano of the period. In the window are several cages in which canaries are asleep. On the balcony is a sort of little conservatory enclosed in glass. About the place are trunks, half finished in the packing and clothes, hats and shawls are scattered about. Books are everywhere. In the center a table is set for supper. The place is dim with candle light and shadows. The atmosphere is confused, that of an impromptu feast on the brink of a sudden farewell.* ROSALIE, MME. SAND'S *servant, a pretty blunt country woman of about thirty, does not know that the curtain has risen. She is seated at* MADAME'S *writing desk and at the moment is deeply puzzled, attempting to read the fifth chapter of* MADAME'S *new novel which is piled in manuscript before her. She turns the leaves, one by one, and is bored. The bell of the concierge jangles. She reads on. Again the jangling of the bell. The girl is oblivious. The canaries wake to a little shower of song, then silence, then footsteps below in the streets.* ROSALIE *mystified, turns another page.* MADAME *doesn't write for such as she. A knock at the door. She jumps up, pushes the manuscript into the rear of the desk and opens the door to* PAUL *and* MME. DE MUSSET. MME. DE MUSSET *is an aristocrat, a mother of the old régime who never loses the quiet dignity of her manner even under the stress of intense emotion.* PAUL, *the elder brother of a more famous brother, exists only in his own estimation. He hopes he is something of a gallant and doesn't for a moment doubt that he is a wit.*

MME. DE MUSSET [*sinking into a chair*]. Those stairs! Ah, my poor heart!

PAUL. You took the four flights without stopping.

MME. DE MUSSET. Do you think a mother ever stops when her son is in peril?

ROSALIE [*to* PAUL]. Good evening, monsieur.

MME. DE MUSSET. I am Mme. de Musset. Is Mme. Sand in? [*She glances about the room.*]

ROSALIE. No. Madame is not at home.

MME. DE MUSSET [*to* PAUL]. Home! Why, there is actually a bed in the dining room!

PAUL. These artists think it is a waste of time to live in more than one room.

MME. DE MUSSET. You might spare me these disgusting details. [*Then to* ROSALIE.] What time will Mme. Sand return?

ROSALIE. I do not know, Madame.

MME. DE MUSSET. But you must know. I am Alfred de Musset's mother.

ROSALIE. He is kind to me. He gave me a hundred francs when my sister was careless—and—

MME. DE MUSSET. Alfred!

PAUL. Mother, Alfred is not the papa of every bambino in Paris. [*Then to* ROSALIE.] You don't know when they are coming back?

ROSALIE. These days I know nothing. Everything is up-side down now that Madame is leaving.

MME. DE MUSSET. Ah, my mother's instinct. I was right. So she is going when—when?

ROSALIE. I do not know, because Madame does not know. On Monday I pack because Madame is leaving on Wednesday. On Wednesday I unpack because Madame is staying till Friday. On Friday I pack because Madame leaves on Saturday and on Sunday I unpack because Madame isn't going at all.

PAUL. You see, mother, there is no need to worry.

ROSALIE. And while I pack and unpack Madame sits writing, writing all the time. She never stops. I go to bed. At four in the morning I hear a noise. Madame wishes me, I say to myself. I come in. Instead of writing she is mending furniture. And then she goes out. One night I followed her. She leans on the walls of quays watching the river till the washer women come out and the sun's up. She's a queer one. All that scribbling has gone to her head.

MME. DE MUSSET. Alone at five in the morning?

PAUL. Well, anyway, she is alone.

ROSALIE. Sometimes I try to read what she's written. I can't make it out. The words are too long. Sometimes she cries when she writes.

[MME. DE MUSSET *has been examining the room and at this moment she reaches the table.*]

MME. DE MUSSET. The table is set. At what time do they dine?

PAUL. They never dine in the Quartier. They only eat. [*He enjoys this immensely.*]

MME. DE MUSSET. Paul, how can you waste your time trying to be witty when Alfred is in danger? [*Then to* ROSALIE.] At what time is supper?

ROSALIE. Whenever Madame gets back. She orders dinner at six and it turns into supper at eleven. It makes no difference, nothing matters. Madame is busy writing. All the time writing, except when the gentlemen come. Dinner for breakfast, breakfast for lunch. She'll let her omelet cool while she scrawls her ten pages. Nothing matters as long as there's ink for Madame and plenty of cigars. It wasn't like this in the country.

MME. DE MUSSET [*amazed*]. Cigars!

ROSALIE. Black and long, twenty-five centimes. Now I must see to my tarts. Mons. Alfred likes them. Call if you want me. [*She goes out.*]

MME. DE MUSSET. Except when the gentlemen come! Cigars! Five o'clock in the morning! God help my boy.

[*She is walking in agitation about the room. She stops in front of the screen.*]

Heavens, isn't this a bathtub?

PAUL. What could be more innocent than an empty bathtub? Ha! Ha!

MME. DE MUSSET. So this is her lair.

[*She runs her fingers over the top of the desk and lifts them covered with dust.*]

She isn't very clean. So! In such a dusty place as this she snares men with her smiles. [*She has reached the window.*] And look! [*A tone of deep shame in her voice.*] In sight of Notre Dame. [*She grows more excited.*] God grant I'm in time.

PAUL. You must keep calm, mother.

MME. DE MUSSET. I am calm, Paul. I've been trained to control myself. Only peasants and literary people give way to their emotions.

PAUL. You shouldn't have come.

MME. DE MUSSET. I do not regret it, even after having seen the place. I'll do my duty. She sha'n't take him with her. God give me strength.

PAUL. Hasn't he promised you he wouldn't go?

MME. DE MUSSET. Yes, but he will, unless I am by to save him. She is his mistress—and I—am only his mother.

PAUL. If you had left it all to me.

MME. DE MUSSET. As I did from the beginning and what has happened? Were you blind? When I asked you what was going on, you told me Alfred was looking well—my poor Alfred—and that Madame was only more intelligent than charming.

PAUL. You might think so yourself if you knew her.

MME. DE MUSSET. Paul!

PAUL. Sometimes I envy Alfred.

MME. DE MUSSET. My son! Have you forgotten I'm your mother?

PAUL. I don't think you'd better stay.

MME. DE MUSSET. You were the elder. You should have known what would come of this. He was a most sensitive baby, a most fragile boy; and now at the beginning of his career, just when the great Hugo has praised his verses—she! she! My boy, my poor boy!

PAUL. Why, you've never even seen the lady.

MME. DE MUSSET. Yes, once in the Bois. She was driving with Alfred. I hid behind my sunshade. She's a dragon decked in ribbons. God help him!

PAUL. Well—er—do you think she is the first woman that Alfred has—shall I say known?

MME. DE MUSSET [*defending her darling*]. No, Paul. How could one expect that from Alfred? I can understand my son's having a mistress but let my son's mistress belong to my son. When my son belongs to his mistress it is time for his mother to descend from modesty and reticence.

PAUL. If you'd only given me a little longer.

MME. DE MUSSET. They might have been on their way to Egypt and those dreadful crocodiles. My poor boy! [*She weeps.*]

PAUL. What are you going to do?

MME. DE MUSSET. Plead with her as a mother. She is a mother, isn't she?

PAUL. Heine says she was born a mother and that her dolls were her lovers.

MME. DE MUSSET. Don't you ever bring that man to my house. These artists have been the ruin of Alfred. Are you to be the next?

PAUL. You can't understand their sort.

MME. DE MUSSET. Thank God for that.

PAUL. Mother, you're no match for her.

MME. DE MUSSET [*proudly*]. Why not, my son?

PAUL. Because you're a lady and she's a woman.

MME. DE MUSSET. I can descend. You think, don't you, that I know of nothing but my flowers and my old laces,—but life has taught me many things.

PAUL. A man must love, mother. Does it matter whom? Love is only an affair of good evening, good morning—and good-bye.

MME. DE MUSSET. Then he must say good-bye. [*She sits down.*]

PAUL. Do you find it so pleasant here?

MME. DE MUSSET. Pleasant! Why, the place reeks of Bohemia.

PAUL [*taking up his hat*]. Then let's drive in the Bois. It will calm you.

MME. DE MUSSET. For a little while. Perhaps the air will do me good.

[PAUL *gives her his arm. They turn towards the door. Suddenly she stops.*]

But if they leave before we get back—

PAUL. Don't you see the table is set for supper? They are spiritual but they still have stomachs.

[*They have reached the door. Suddenly it flies open and* CASIMIR DUDEVANT *bursts in. He is "fresh come" from Nohant and has been paying his respects to the Parisian cafés. He is rather handsome but not of an unusual sort, a mixture of the military and the country squire. At the moment he is a trifle unsteady.*]

CASIMIR [*politely but swayingly to* MME. DE MUSSET]. Good evening, Madame.

MME. DE MUSSET [*drawing back, half in dignity and half in fright*]. Another friend of Madame Sand?

CASIMIR [*with a deep tho tippling bow*]. No, Madame, not a friend. I am her husband.

[*And* PAUL *and* MADAME DE MUSSET *are gone and* CASIMIR *from the top of the landing is waving them farewells. Then* ROSALIE *enters from the kitchen with her dish of tarts. She doesn't see* DUDEVANT *who is now leaning against the wall in a corner near the door. A minute later and the girl is again engrossed in the manuscript of* MADAME'S *new book, "Valentine."*]

CASIMIR [*as he recognizes* ROSALIE]. Good evening, my girl.

ROSALIE. How did you get in without ringing the bell?

CASIMIR. I slipped by, my dear; because this morning when I asked below for Madame, my wife, he said no one was at home. And this afternoon again no one was at home, and when I said are you sure, he said he was sure, because Madame was never at home; and when I came again this evening [*He sways a little.*] I couldn't bear to hear him repeat himself, so I came right up. The door was open and here I am.

ROSALIE. Well, what do you want?

[*He has been eyeing her as he used to at Nohant.*]

CASIMIR. First, I want to sit down. [*And he does so.*] And now, have you a nice little glass of wine for my nice little stomach?

ROSALIE. Another drop and you might spill over.

CASIMIR. You haven't learned to talk like a Parisian. [*He leans against the table.*]

ROSALIE. No, and I never wish to. Don't lean on that table cloth. It was clean three days ago.

CASIMIR. So then I'm in time for dinner—Ah, my poor little stomach.

ROSALIE. Get away from there.

CASIMIR. If I weren't a gentleman, I mightn't like your tone. But I don't mind, I'm used to it. [ROSALIE *turns away from him.*] I always like the swing of your hips, so I came up from Berri to get you. You can tell a horse by its flanks and a woman by the swing of her hips. [*He comes nearer.*]

ROSALIE [*more hotly*]. Get away!

CASIMIR. So, so, and your hot little temper, too. Come here, my dear, I think I'd like to burn myself. [*He steps nearer.*]

ROSALIE. None of that, I wasn't born yesterday.

CASIMIR. Then thank God for today. Don't you like me?

ROSALIE. No, I don't, and I never did. I wouldn't come within ten feet of you by choice.

CASIMIR. Then I must take the first step. [*But he finds this difficult to do.*] Why don't you have sawdust on the floor? I can move much better in a stable. The city always makes me thirsty. [*He begins singing.*] "*How sweet are the fields, the fields of clover.*" Stop looking at me like that.

ROSALIE [*dodging him*]. What did you come here for?

CASIMIR. To tell Madame I don't like the way she's carrying on. Ain't I her husband? I've come to take the census of her lovers.

ROSALIE [*resenting this*]. Get out of here or I'll call the concierge.

CASIMIR. Is he one of them too? Ha! ha! Call until all the pretty angels listen, you can't budge me. [*He tries to take her in his arms. She runs from him.*]

CASIMIR [*reeling a little*]. Come over here and kiss me. [*He tries to get her into a corner.*] I've always wanted you. [*He has crossed the room and is in front of* GEORGE'S *desk.*] So here's where she scribbles. Fine, very fine. But she never thinks of me. [*He takes up some sheets of the new manuscript.*]

ROSALIE. Let that alone. [*She pushes him away from the desk and stands on guard.*] That cost Madame five sleepless nights.

CASIMIR. And how many sleepless nights do you think Madame has cost me? [*He sings* "*Your teeth are like dew in the roses.*"] I haven't forgotten you, my pet. [*He lurches towards her and slips his arm around her waist.*]

ROSALIE [*shoving him away*]. You'd better get out of here before the gentlemen come.

CASIMIR. Maybe I will and maybe I won't. I'll stay to see my darling. [*And then very maudlin.*] I'm the father of her children, she's the mother of mine. Nature, how wonderful is nature. She, me, then—they. One and one make—many. She is ill, she writes to her mother, and I come up to Paris to see her and you, my pet. If she's ill, she needs me. [*He weeps.*] Look at me, I'm a very worried husband. Kiss me, before my heart breaks.

ROSALIE. Get away, I'm too old for that sort of nonsense. I told you that long ago.

CASIMIR. How do you know, my darling, until you've tried? [*He hums.*] "*How innocent are the fields, the fields.*"

ROSALIE. Sh—be quiet! [*His voice grows louder.*] Sh—some of the guests are coming.

CASIMIR. Maybe they'll pity a poor wronged husband.

ROSALIE. They mustn't see you like this; get out.

CASIMIR. You want me to leave without seeing her? What gentleman would do that? [*He again bursts into melody.*] "*How sweet are the fields.*"

ROSALIE [*pushing him toward the kitchen*]. Sleep it off in my room, behind there.

CASIMIR. Sleep, gentle sleep, how sweet are the fields. [*He stops.*] But I must see Madame.

ROSALIE. Yes, yes, I'll tell her. She'll come in to you. Get out! Get out!

[*There is a sound of footsteps on the stairs and* CASIMIR *barely tumbles into the kitchen as* ROSALIE *opens the door for* BULOZ *and* HEINE. BULOZ *is a sort of sublimated journalist, terse, pat, with his eyes perpetually on the literary chance. He is editor of The Revue des Deux Mondes and finds* MADAME'S "*stuff*" *an attractive feature.* HEINE *is a tense, wandering soul who has drifted to the spiritual haven of Paris. Distinguished, keen,—he is dynamic even in unessentials.*]

BULOZ. I almost knocked you over, Heine.

HEINE. I was finishing this on the last landing. I've been half an hour coming up. Each floor I read a few pages. [*He looks at an open book in his hand.*] She writes like water tumbling from a pump. Some day her words will flood the boulevards and Paris will be drowned.

ROSALIE. Good evening, gentlemen, Madame will be back soon.

BULOZ. Good evening, Rosalie. [*Then to* HEINE.]. Whenever George finishes a new book, I kiss Rosalie and sometimes she kisses me. It's a sensible arrangement. [*Then to* ROSALIE.] When Madame leaves, would you like to come and cook for me?

ROSALIE. No, sir; I'm a respectable girl.

BULOZ [*anxiously*]. They're leaving tonight, aren't they?

ROSALIE. I don't know. One day she's going, the next she ain't.

[CASIMIR'S *voice is heard singing in the kitchen.*]

ROSALIE. Ah! I haven't washed the endive.

[*The voice becomes more distinct*—"*The fields of cl—o—ver.*"]

HEINE. How sweetly the salad sings.

[ROSALIE *exits.* HEINE *has reached the table.*]

HEINE. Seven candles. That's for luck, but I thought George was giving this farewell supper to commemorate her parting from Alfred.

BULOZ. The bulletins differ. But we'll surely know before morning.

HEINE. If his mother interferes it will be difficult for George. A woman can do what she wants with a man until another woman knocks at the door. Then the Gods bend down to listen, knowing the odds are even.

BULOZ. There's the real danger. Tho he doesn't know it, he still obeys his mother. She has written George threatening to prevent it.

HEINE. And George?

BULOZ. She's distracted with uncertainty. I've had five letters since noon. The first dark despair. Alfred has again given his word to his mother. He won't go. [*He takes a packet of letters from his pocket.*] The third is cryptic. What do you make of this? [*He reads.*] "*Night, Nubian night, but a skylark still soars in my heart.*"

HEINE. Rather confining for the skylark.

BULOZ. Then the fourth—again abject misery. Written on the back of a menu of the Café de Soleil. She contemplates suicide.

HEINE. Everybody does since "Werther." She'll probably live till ninety.

BULOZ [*glancing at the paper*]. She regrets the river is frozen near the quays. Every week, every hour, they decide to part—but the fire of hope burns eternal.

HEINE [*an echo of bitterness in his voice*]. Till fate chokes the flame with the douche of disillusion.

BULOZ. You're still young enough to be a pessimist?

HEINE. Pessimism is my spiritual purge. How else can I keep my soul clean in this filthy world? My faith is the faith of tomorrow. I'm a Jew by birth, a Christian by necessity and an atheist by conviction. [*He glances at the table.*] Changeably religious—but always hungry. When will they be back?

BULOZ. Here's her last note. They are going together to the top of Notre Dame, to say farewell in the sunset.

HEINE. Pinnacles are her obsessions. But she'll come down. Bed's the great leveler. Can't you see them, Buloz? Here's Madame preparing for the lover's leap. The last farewell has driven them to madness. There's de Musset peeping over the parapets,—wondering just where they'll bump first. And the gargoyles with their granite hearts,—hideous because they are doomed to grin forever,—leer in silence lest their laughter should shake the turrets when George again nobly renounces death. [*Then bitterly.*] Ah, Buloz, beware of this love of ours. It is our enemy, most selfish, most subtle, and most sinister. What time does the coach start for Lyons?

BULOZ. At nine from the Post Hotel.

HEINE [*looking at his watch*]. Nearly eight. They'll be here in ten minutes. Supper in fifteen. Haste may outwit his loving and too watchful mother. They've tasted love and drunken, they know not they are drunk. Then, Italy—Italy, where golden youth lies sleeping in the shadow of the centuries. Italy and dreams—and then some rainy morning,—the awakening.

BULOZ. They must go. Think what it means to me.

HEINE. You?

BULOZ. I've signed with her for five years. My subscriptions have been falling off. I needed just her sort of copy to boost them. Nothing sells like love.

HEINE. Except a liaison.

BULOZ. Exactly.

HEINE [*musingly*]. And if they should awake too soon and suffer—

BULOZ [*laconically*]. I count on that. Pathetic relief—the contrast of tears.

HEINE. There's a thought to make an essay.

BULOZ. Send it to me first. I'll print it in *The Revue*.

HEINE [*half to himself*]. Some must suffer that others may sup. Socially, spiritually, everywhere, always true—paying the toll to life—that others may sup.

BULOZ. That ought to make, say, seven thousand words. Large type that means, shall we say—er—twenty pages?

HEINE [*tempering his scorn with a smile*]. You journalistic Judas. For thirty new subscriptions you would sell your soul.

BULOZ [*oblivious*]. Or perhaps twenty-two pages. We can expect something from de Musset, too.

HEINE. Of course. He has a splendid past ahead of him, and besides he's a poet—a poet soaked in absinthe and dried in moonshine. But he needs more rust in his blood.

BULOZ [*dryly*]. And you?

HEINE. I'm perfect where I am, Buloz, but not quite finished. Don't misjudge me. I'm not as modest as I sound,—but hungrier.

[ROSALIE *rushes in from the kitchen.*]

ROSALIE. A cab has stopped in the courtyard. [*She begins lighting the candles. Then to* BULOZ.] Don't let her start writing again till dinner's served.

BULOZ [*anxiously*]. Not if we can help it.

HEINE. But if Calliope descends—

ROSALIE. Another of those actor people? Put her out and remember the omelet. [*She leans out of the window.*] Yes, it's them, it's them. Madame is helping Monsieur out. Madame is paying the driver. Monsieur Alfred is coming up. He'll be so tired and so hungry. She's most likely been telling him novels all day. He's been so good to me. [*And she runs into the kitchen.*]

HEINE. And how long do you think this affair will last, my friend?

BULOZ. How long? Does that matter if the copy is good?

[*And* ALFRED *stands in the doorway, a poet, an aristocrat and something of a dandy. His glance is firm, his red lips half open. He is fragile and fine with that exquisite delicacy of virility, so irresistible to women.*]

ALFRED [*in the doorway*]. My friends! My friends! So you have come to say good-bye and I have come to say good-bye. I am giving up forever [BULOZ *starts.*] the most beautiful companion that man has ever known. [ROSALIE *enters.*] Rosalie, a glass of wine. [*He drinks it and sinks into a chair.*] See my people for me. I can't face them now. I might curse my mother whom I would die to save from suffering. [*His head drops in his hands.*] Buloz, you see my brother and say good-bye for me, and you, Heine, because your style is rarer, you see my mother and tell her I bless her and will pray for her and will write her when my wound is healed.

BULOZ [*low, to* ROSALIE]. Bring the soup.

ALFRED. I'm so tired. George almost carried me up the last turn of the tower. Paris was like a fading print below us. Half-way up we saw two lovers embracing in a window.

HEINE. Life is a see-saw and love swings the plank. Up and down, up and down.

ALFRED. Till we slip, and the blind little worms are waiting. On the top of the tower verses came to me. I called them "The Blind." Where's the absinthe? Listen. [*He pulls out his cuff and begins reading the lines he has composed and which he has scrawled on his linen.*]

"The nightingale impassioned wounds his heart to sing,
Whilst in the perfumed shade of roses mating.
Love bursts to blossom each new bud of spring.
But death, dim death with scythe in hand stands waiting."

[ROSALIE, *enraptured in spite of herself, stands in the door to the kitchen.* HEINE *looks at* BULOZ, *who, on tiptoes, goes over to her.*]

BULOZ [*whispering aside to* ROSALIE]. I told you to bring the soup. [*And she goes out.*]

Alfred. That's death's victory and life's defeat. We are the blind.

Heine. We ostriches sticking our heads in the sands of hope.

[*And at this moment enters* George—*the brilliant, sumptuous, ridiculous but conquering* George. *She is never sentimental, never sententious, never conscious of her exuberance or her exaggerations; mistress of everything but her emotions which, tho she thinks she masters, master her. The men listening to* Alfred *do not see her.*]

Alfred [*turning over his cuff, goes on with his reading*].

"Upon the moon-white waters glides the lonely swan,
The willows bend—"

[*He stops, looks at the other side of his cuff, then back, then to the other cuff.*]

Alfred [*slightly embarrassed repeats the last line*].

"The willows bend"—ahem—eh—[*There is a pause.*] I must have stopped writing.

[*And then* George *steps forward and speaks very simply in spite of her emotion.*]

George. You did, Alfred, because at that very moment we said good-bye forever. [*Again* Buloz *starts.*] We were born but to say good-bye.

[*There is a danger that the moment may become unbearably sublime, but* Rosalie *opportunely arrives with the steaming tureen.*]

Rosalie. Here's the cream of onions, Madame.

Buloz [*sniffing*]. Supper at last.

George [*to* Buloz]. Is your stomach more important than our souls?

Heine. No! But emptier.

[*And the romantic spell is broken, and greetings are exchanged.*]

George [*to* Buloz]. Did you get all my letters? [*Then to* Heine.] Don't be too bitter tonight. I always mistrust you pessimists. Far down you're apt to be so sweet. Look deep enough in tears there's laughter, and deep enough in laughter, tears. Ah, well! Let's be gay. Tho we feast on the brink of a precipice I shall smile. One must either smile—or die.

[*During this speech they have taken their places at the table.*]

Alfred. Where's the absinthe?

George. Not too much, Freddo, you'll get drowsy and I can't let you sleep here tonight. I've got to unpack and finish five chapters.

Buloz [*eagerly*]. Five chapters tonight?

George. Perhaps six. I'm very tired. [*She looks lovingly at* Alfred.] My soul has been sapped today but I must work. That's the one way of forgetting. Six chapters—and I haven't yet planned the fourth. [*She sits for a moment in deep thought eating radishes.*] I'll bring in this farewell supper. Why not, why not, I ask you? My stories are the mirror of my life. Tho I write with my heart's blood, still I must write. This supper will make chapter five. [*She starts improvising.*] After the opera this little farewell feast. Bitter herbs and tears. [*She begins eating the onion soup as she talks.*] For weeks, Olivia has refused to see Raymond, but that night at the opera to the divine strains of Donizetti their eyes have met. [*She leans towards* Heine.] Have you ever tasted such superb onion soup? Where was I? [*A moment and then she recaptures her theme.*] Ah! yes! Raymond has left his box and come over to Olivia's. Her hair is dark as night in the Apennines. [*Then very sadly.*] We might have seen the Apennines, Freddo—if—

Alfred. "If" is the epitaph on the tomb of opportunity.

George [*patting his hand*]. Never mind, dear. We must be brave. [*Another loving glance and then she goes on with her story.*] There in the shadow of her box, whilst the melting music woos the stars. [*Suddenly she jumps up from the table and brings paper, ink and pen from her writing desk. Writing, she repeats.*] Whilst the melting music woos the stars—charming phrase, isn't it?—There is a hurried conversation. Yes, she will go to his apartments, that very night for their last supper together. Theirs and—ours, Freddo, —ours. [*She chokes back a sob.*]

Heine [*the tension getting on his nerves*]. You might open the window, Rosalie.

George [*continuing*]. She has ordered her coachman to drive thru the Bois. She must think, her brain pulses like Vesuvius. [*She gives a quick glance in* Alfred's *direction.*

He sits sadly examining the bottom of his empty glass. She goes on.] Vesuvius. Passion masters her. Where are the olives, Rosalie? [*She continues.*] It has begun to rain. She leans from the window. The great drops wound her brow. [*She makes a note of this.*] Yes, she will go to Raymond, but—to say farewell. That ought to be a good ending for chapter four.

HEINE. Yes, very. If it ends there.

GEORGE. Chapter five. Her husband has been hunting tigers in the Pyrenees.

BULOZ. But are there any tigers in the Pyrenees?

GEORGE. What difference does that make? Aren't there giraffes in the zoo?

[BULOZ *consoles himself with his fish.*]

GEORGE [*unruffled*]. Her husband, whilst hunting tigers—[*A glance at* BULOZ.] Is the salmon nice and fresh? [*Then she goes on.*] Whilst hunting tigers has been wounded. Chapter five brings him back to Paris. At an inn on the way he has seduced Carmella, a peasant girl.

BULOZ [*methodically*]. Of course!

HEINE. Is there a peasant girl in Europe that hasn't been seduced?

GEORGE [*undisturbed*]. He brings with him a Spanish dagger, bought at Burgos.

ALFRED [*catching her spirit*]. From a stall near the sunburnt cathedral.

GEORGE. Sunburnt cathedral—that's a charming phrase, Freddo. [*She jots it down.*]

ALFRED [*playfully*]. Plagiarist.

GEORGE [*patting his hand*]. Darling. He arrives at his home. It is past midnight. Madame is out. In her boudoir he finds Raymond's handkerchief. He recognizes the crest. Meanwhile, the lovers are at supper. How do you like it, Buloz?

BULOZ. That's just the place to announce the next instalment.

ALFRED. Why have we decided to part?

GEORGE. We?

ALFRED. I might have persuaded you to give up writing novels.

BULOZ. Nonsense!

ALFRED. Then think of the blissful life we might have led together philosophising under all the chestnut trees in Europe. [*He takes her hand.*]

GEORGE [*looking deep into his eyes*]. We must learn to live alone, Freddo—alone. [*She presses his hand to her lips.*]

[BULOZ *sits watching them.*]

HEINE [*aside to* BULOZ]. Don't worry, she won't stop writing. Every novel to George is a new love affair. She always sees them thru to the end.

GEORGE. But you mustn't interrupt me, Freddo. [*Then choking back her sobs.*] I call him Freddo because we were going to Italy together. Where was I? [*Recalling.*] The rain has ceased.

[*There is a slight disturbance in the kitchen.*]

BULOZ [*at the door*]. Sh—be quiet. Madame is composing.

ROSALIE [*sticking her head in, rather excited*]. I'm beating the eggs for the omelet. [*She closes the door.*]

GEORGE [*by mistake sprinkling her salmon with sugar*]. They are out on the veranda together in the moonlight.

ALFRED. What would the romantic movement do, if it weren't for the moonlight?

BULOZ. That's sugar, George, not salt.

GEORGE [*oblivious*]. She has come to say farewell, but poor, weak woman, she has forgotten the feud twixt flesh and spirit.—We are but marionettes hung from the nimble fingers of the Gods.

HEINE [*looking up quickly as he breaks his bread*]. Yes, all of us! We jig at the end of the wires, poets and cooks, saints and grisettes—hung from the nimble fingers of the Gods. All, all of us—even you, George, —even you!

GEORGE. You mustn't break in with your Germanic philosophies. [*Then as she turns to* ALFRED, *slightly wetting her lips with her tongue.*] There in the pungent odors of the night they melt into each other's arms. And Olivia turns only to see her husband standing in the room.

[*And this is only too true, for the noise outside has increased, and at the next moment,* CASIMIR *bursts in from the kitchen, bottle in hand. The men jump up.*]

GEORGE [*quite calmly*]. Oh, you! Wait a minute, please. [*Then unperturbed, she goes on with her story.*] Olivia, trembling like a lily in the wind [*She is writing this all down.*]

throws herself between the men as the Burgos blade [*A loving glance at* ALFRED.] bought from a stall near the sunburnt cathedral,—flashes in the moonlight. [*She dots the sentence and turns to* CASIMIR.]

GEORGE. And now, what do you want?

CASIMIR [*leering*]. You. I want you to come back to the country, my dear. I've no one to talk to, your mother's too old and the servants each has each.

[*He comes towards her.* ALFRED *intercepts him.*]

ALFRED. Don't you dare come near this lady.

CASIMIR. Eh?

[HEINE *goes over to the window and stands there calmly smoking. The others are all excited except* GEORGE, *who sits quietly finishing her salmon.* ROSALIE *peeps thru the door.*]

ALFRED. Get out of here, you're drunk.

CASIMIR [*lurching forward*]. Ain't I her broken-hearted husband? [*He begins to weep.*] She's mine by law.

GEORGE. Have you come up from Nohant to teach me the law?

CASIMIR. You still talk just like a man, Aurora. You haven't changed at all, but you're a wee bit fatter, my dear,—a wee bit fatter.

GEORGE [*really resenting this*]. Nonsense, Casimir. [*And then very significantly, as she glances towards the door.*] Good-evening, now. These three gentlemen are my friends.

CASIMIR. Friends, Aurora? Isn't that a fancy way of putting it?

[*He pats* ROSALIE *on the cheek and begins singing "How sweet are the fields."*]

ROSALIE [*to* GEORGE]. He was after me at Nohant, too. That's why I came with you. He was awful bad and tho you're kind of queer, I knew it would be better with you and anyhow I'd be safe in Paris.

CASIMIR [*lyrically*]. "The—fields—of—cl—oo—o—ver."

HEINE. So he was the singing salad!

ROSALIE. I tried to keep him in there till you'd gone, because you told me this morning you'd surely be leaving for Venice tonight.

[*There is a quick glance exchanged between* HEINE *and* BULOZ. *General consternation is imminent, but* GEORGE *is ready.*]

GEORGE [*sweetly and with a swooning look at* ALFRED]. But since then so much has happened.

[*Trustingly he takes her hand.* HEINE *comes down to* BULOZ.]

HEINE [*aside to* BULOZ]. I can't let these domestic scenes spoil my supper. [*He sits down and begins to eat.*]

CASIMIR [*to* ALFRED]. Let go that lady's hand.

ALFRED. Keep away or I'll throw you out of the window.

CASIMIR. You will? [*He roars with laughter.*] You will,—you, with your pale face and your hair like a woman's? I'm a soldier, young man, do you know I'm a soldier? [ALFRED *steps threateningly towards him.*]

GEORGE [*calmly*]. You'd better go now, Casimir,—[*And then pointing it with smiling delicacy.*] before these gentlemen show you the way. The stairs are very steep, my friend. [*Then she turns to* HEINE.] Have some more salmon, do.

CASIMIR [*nastily*]. Look here, I've had enough of your cooing voice! Ain't you my wife?

GEORGE. I have as much respect for our marriage contract as I have for you. The day you took the whip into your hands, I took the law into mine.

CASIMIR [*cowering*]. Wives don't talk that way.

GEORGE. Then it's time they did. I don't want you, I don't need you. [*And then ever so sweetly.*] Are you going now?

CASIMIR [*reaching the door and stopping*]. I can't leave, I can't.

[BULOZ *and* ALFRED *step forward.* GEORGE, *with a gentle smile on her face, sits watching the scene.*]

CASIMIR. You see—well—er—I—

GEORGE. Is it money, my dear?

CASIMIR [*brightening*]. Just like you, Lucy. Sooner or later you get to the point. The fact is—[*He reels.*] I lost a few francs at my inn. He had cross-eyes, Lucy. Never gamble with a cross-eyed man,—and now I've nothing to take me to Nohant.

GEORGE [*going to her desk*]. Here are twenty francs. [*And then to* BULOZ.] Advance me a hundred, Buloz. So,—a hundred and twenty and you—[*She turns to* HEINE.] What do you add to get rid of this nuisance? That makes nearly two hundred. Rosalie, lend me ten francs. [*Which the girl takes from her stocking.*]

ALFRED. And I?

GEORGE [*modestly*]. No, no; not that. Could I borrow from *you* to get rid of a husband?

ALFRED. If it means your happiness.

GEORGE [*melting*]. Well, since you put it so beautifully.

[*And unwillingly she takes the money and gives it to* CASIMIR.]

GEORGE. Good-bye. Don't stop to thank us.

[CASIMIR *takes the money, and stuffing it in his pocket, again reaches the door, and again stops.*]

CASIMIR. I might have forgotten, Aurora, if my hand hadn't got to my pocket. [*He takes out a crumpled piece of paper.*] Maurice sent you this. [*He gives her a little water-color drawing.*]

[GEORGE'S *whole manner changes. All the mother in her welling up at the thought of* MAURICE.]

GEORGE. My little darling. How is he, Casimir? Is he well? Does he blow his nose nicely? Is he kind to mother? Kiss him for me. [CASIMIR *steps towards her,* ALFRED *again threateningly intercepting him.*]

CASIMIR [*stumbling back*]. To think that I should live to see the day when my wife sits at table with murderers and long-haired swine. You've broken my heart, Aurora.

[*And singing "How fair are the fields," he reels down the stairs. There is an embarrassed silence.*]

GEORGE [*lifting the gloom*]. My friends, don't take this too seriously. What does a husband matter? He is an incident all married women should forget. [*Then reminiscently.*] My marriage began what might have ended happily. [*She smiles wanly at* ALFRED.] What might have ended happily, Freddo, if fate had willed it.

ALFRED. Fate is our enemy. We are born to defeat.

GEORGE [*fervidly*]. What have I now to live for, but my children and my dreams? To-day I have lacerated my soul on the altars of renunciations. [*A poignant glance at* ALFRED.] Life called us and we turned away.

ALFRED. How can I leave you to face the possibilities of such another scene? You have suffered and you have borne in silence. There are tears in your eyes.

GEORGE [*resignedly*]. My friend, do not hope to dry them. I must weep lest my heart break.

[*She looks imploringly thru the ceiling as tho trying to see God, then she rushes over to the piano, she begins to play a sad lament, in a desolate minor key. Then a few chords, arpeggios, and she begins chanting.*]

"The nightingale impassioned wounds his heart to sing,
Whilst in the perfumed shade of roses mating."

BULOZ [*to* ROSALIE, *who stands listening*]. Go and get the omelet.

ROSALIE. The eggs are beat.

HEINE [*with an apprehensive glance towards the piano as* ROSALIE *goes out*]. And put plenty of rum in it. [*And then to* BULOZ.] You shouldn't have brought me here. I can't stand music while I'm eating.

BULOZ. Honestly, I didn't count on this sort of thing.

ALFRED [*tenderly to* GEORGE]. You have remembered my poor verses.

GEORGE. Are they not seared in my soul?

[*More arpeggios. Then thru her sobs she continues her chant.*]

"Love burst to blossom each new bud of spring,
But death— [*A chord, two chords, three chords.*]
Dim death with scythe in hand stands——"

[*She can't finish the line. She throws herself into* ALFRED'S *arms. A passionate embrace. Then she rushes from him over to the window. It is nicely timed, the moon is rising. Swiftly she opens one of the bird cages and takes out one of the canaries.*]

GEORGE [*in an ecstasy*]. At least there shall be one free thing answering the winds of desire. [*She sets the bird free.*] Let him fly into the dawn.

BULOZ. Him? How does she know it's a him?

HEINE. In such matters she is infallible.

[*There is a tableau at the window. The music, the moonlight and the flight of the bird have been too much for* ALFRED. *He leans sobbing against the window frame.* GEORGE *is watching him. Then suddenly he reels about.*]

ALFRED. No! no! I shall not sacrifice two souls to duty.

HEINE [*dryly*]. As I thought. He is beginning to realize that virtue is its own disappointment.

[GEORGE *and* ALFRED *are in each other's arms. A passionate embrace thru which* HEINE *and* BULOZ *speak.*]

HEINE. Don't you think we had better go into the kitchen?

BULOZ. Why?

HEINE. I am being pushed into the corner. Nothing fills a room like love. [*A sigh from the lovers.*] When do you think it will be finished?

BULOZ [*with an apprehensive glance towards* GEORGE *and* ALFRED]. What? The kiss?

HEINE [*with an eager look in the direction of the kitchen*]. No. The omelette.

[*A moment later and* ALFRED *in a rapture swings* GEORGE *toward the open window.*]

ALFRED. Listen, over the rumble of the city love is calling! Beyond the roofs of Paris lie the radiant valleys of the south!

HEINE. Splendid eye-sight, hasn't he? The heart sees all.

ALFRED. You love me, George?

GEORGE [*mysteriously*]. As I have never loved before.

ALFRED [*lyrically*]. There is a higher right than duty, my adored one. Let us not hesitate. Love is calling. Italy and the waiting years. Italy, where one drinks oblivion in a moment's ecstasy.

GEORGE [*in a sort of vision*]. Italy!—The moon is rising in my heart. [*A trill of song from the canaries.*] Listen! That is the music of the serenata. The night is waiting. We are at the gates of Eden.

ALFRED. Then let us enter in.

HEINE. At the very gates. What if they should slip?

[*A sound comes up from the street. Voices, laughter. It is Paris, not Italy. Suddenly* GEORGE *awakes.*]

GEORGE [*her voice gone gray*]. And your mother?

ALFRED. She is dead to me. Let us escape from the shadow of her tomb.

GEORGE [*barely controlling her triumphant satisfaction*]. Alfred, my own, I have been waiting.

[*Again they are in each other's arms as* ROSALIE *arrives with the omelet.*]

GEORGE. Quick! My bags, my trunks, my shawls, my manuscripts!

[*Then follows a scene of intense confusion, all of them running about to get the traps ready while* HEINE, *undisturbed, sits eating.*]

GEORGE. Hurry, Rosalie, my bonnet!

ROSALIE. The new one with the broad brim which you bought for Italy?

GEORGE. Yes, hurry, hurry.

[BULOZ *is out of breath strapping the bags. Supper is forgotten.* ALFRED *is no help. He is in the way; every moment insisting on clasping* GEORGE *to his bosom. Soon, however, they are ready.*]

BULOZ. You go by way of Avignon?

GEORGE. Yes—but first a stop at Lyons to see Stendhal.

ALFRED [*remonstratingly*]. But he will talk to us all night.

GEORGE. No. He will dance for us in his Russian boots. And then the sea.

HEINE [*as he takes the last olive*]. Yes. We are all of us afloat.

GEORGE [*her voice aflame*]. Ah, my friends, life is meant to be squandered. Buloz, Heine, farewell, farewell. I'll write—I'll write.

[*Then general embracing. For a moment the lovers stand bathed in the moonlight that floods the room. Confused voices: "Good-bye, farewell, Italy, life, love, etc., etc." They turn to leave. Suddenly there is a knock at the door.* ROSALIE *looks up. She hesitates. Then she goes to the door. In a moment she is back.*]

ROSALIE [*furtively*]. There is a lady to see you, Madame.

GEORGE [*gayly*]. Tell her I am dying of love and can see no one.

ROSALIE. She's been here before.

GEORGE. I never turn a beggar from my doors. Buloz, give me twenty francs.

ROSALIE [*vainly trying to warn her*]. She came in a carriage.

GEORGE. I've no objection. Let her drive back in it.

[*The knock is repeated. Timidly* ROSALIE *opens*

the door and Mme. de Musset *and* Paul *enter.*]

Alfred. Mother!

Mme. de Musset [*who with quiet dignity has arisen to the occasion*]. Alfred!

Buloz [*under his breath*]. Mme. de Musset!

Mme. de Musset [*with gentle courtesy*]. Pardon this late intrusion, Madame. I see I disturb you at dinner. [*And then, pointing the facts with delicacy, but with a will behind it.*] I thought my son might be leaving and would care to drive home with me.

[*A tense moment. The literary history of France hangs in the balance, and then* Mme. de Musset *brilliantly comes to the rescue.*]

Mme. de Musset [*with sudden inspiration*]. Delightful weather for December?

Heine [*dryly*]. It always is.

Buloz [*clearing his throat*]. Hem!

Mme. de Musset [*quietly but firmly*]. Well, Alfred?

Alfred. Please, mother, let's avoid a scene.

Mme. de Musset. I've spent most of my life doing that, my son. [*She glances at* George.] Are you coming, Alfred?

Alfred. I—I must speak to you.

Mme. de Musset. It will be very quiet in the carriage. Paul can take a cab. [*And then, with a note of graceful condescension, she turns to* George.] Madame, I hope I find you well?

[*And then equally sweetly,* George, *who mentally has been aiding destiny, answers her.*]

George. I'm well, Madame, I thank you, very, but won't you and your son finish supper with us? We've but just begun.

Rosalie [*cheerily*]. Yes, the omelet just finished. Have some, Monsieur Paul. It's the kind you like.

[Paul *involuntarily steps towards the table.*]

Mme. de Musset. Paul! [*Then to* George]. Thank you, Madame, but I've already supped. But we are keeping you so long from table. Come, Alfred, have you forgotten that you promised to read your new verses to your sister's friends, this evening? [*She steps towards the door.*] A thousand apologies for my intrusion. Good-evening, Madame; good-evening, gentlemen. Come, my sons.

[Paul *is at his mother's side. All eyes are on* Alfred. *He steps towards the rack where he has hung his cape and hat. A pause. Then* George *takes the reins.*]

George. Madame, will you permit me to speak to you alone?

Mme. de Musset. I doubt, Madame, if there is anything that we have to say to each other.

George [*significantly*]. Butterflies are fragile. Shall we bruise them on the anvils of our rashness?

Mme. de Musset [*slightly mystified*]. Pardon me, Madame, but—

George. Gentlemen, you will excuse us. There are things that we women say to each other that you men can never know. Don't go into my bedroom, if you please. The bed is tossed.

[*And* Rosalie *and the gentlemen go off leaving the candle-lit battle-field to* George. *Throughout the following scene her tone varies. One moment she is soft and feminine, the next masculine and dominant!*]

George. And now we can have a nice cozy chat together. Do sit down.

Mme. de Musset [*stiffly*]. Thank you. [*But she remains standing.*]

George [*lightly*]. As you please.

[*And* George, *turning a chair about, seats herself at the table.*]

George [*offering* Mme. de Musset *a cigarette*]. Will you smoke?

Mme. de Musset. That is one of the things, Madame, that I leave to men.

George [*pleasantly*]. That's the mistake we women make. We leave too much to the men. We bury our souls in satin, and they take advantage of our weakness. Perhaps you would prefer a cigar, Madame.

Mme. de Musset [*a gasp*]. No, Madame.

George. After breakfast I cannot live without my cigar. The odor is so delicious mixed with my rose geraniums. [*She sniffs.*] Is there anything in the world so redolent as the odor of rose geraniums,—or perhaps you prefer jasmine? But it's too late for jasmine.

Mme. de Musset [*involuntarily sitting down*]. Madame, do you think I came here to talk botany?

George [*tensely*]. No, Madame. You came to do what God alone can do, to command two people to cease loving each other. Do you think you can do that, Madame? Since the beginning of time all nature has been preparing for this love of ours—Alfred's and mine. The stars are in their allotted places so that we might love.

MME. DE MUSSET. I know nothing about astronomy.

GEORGE [*oblivious*]. Eden first bloomed so that we might love. [*She has stretched across the table and has reached her ink and pen and paper, and in the shadow of the sugar bowl, is jotting down the phrases that particularly appeal to her.*] Abel slew Cain—er—er—so that we might love. Since the remotest hint of time, fate has willed it. Are you God, Madame? Can you toy with destiny?

MME. DE MUSSET. Pardon me, but I cannot understand this literature you speak.

GEORGE. You call my words literature? No, indeed, Madame, they are the burning truth,—a truth you cannot understand. You have lived too long in your damask-dusty world where the blinds are always drawn whilst I,—I have cut my flesh on the thorns. Do you know what my life has been?

MME. DE MUSSET. No, that I do not presume to know. I do not wish to know. It will not move me; my son shall not go with you. What would become of him?

GEORGE. He would enter the glorious kingdom hand in hand with the woman he loves. Do you dare deny him that? Can God,—God who is love be watching this?

MME. DE MUSSET. Madame, spare me this melodrama. You are right. I have lived a guarded and what you would call a narrow life, but in that old-fashioned, ridiculous seclusion at which you scoff I have learned to respect tradition.

GEORGE [*tensely*]. Need is the only tradition I acknowledge.

MME. DE MUSSET. Alfred will not go with you. He has given me his word. He is a gentleman.

GEORGE. Ah, yes. It takes generations to make a gentleman, but it takes only one man to make a generation. I am helping to make mine because I am free. He, too, must be free. Do not fetter a falcon lest he break his chains.

MME. DE MUSSET [*not quite sure that she understands George's elaborate simile*]. If you mean that I restrain Alfred, you are wrong.

GEORGE. Ah, that's what you would have him think. But you mothers have a way of holding on. I tell you he must be free to sing. I have bought my freedom with my heart's blood. I have suffered.

MME. DE MUSSET. And we mothers, do you think we mothers do not suffer?

[*This is a superb moment for* GEORGE. *She snatches from her bosom the little water-color drawing which* CASIMIR *has brought her.*]

GEORGE. I too am a mother, Madame! Look what my darling son has sent me! This poor little painting of roses. [*She is sobbing.*] Do you think I do not know a mother's heart?

MME. DE MUSSET. Then give my son back to me.

GEORGE. I have not taken him. God has sent him. Ah, my friend, he has made me so happy. Every day finds me more attached to him. Every day the beauty of life shines more brilliantly. Would you shatter this love of ours? He is my universe, my all.

MME. DE MUSSET [*slowly*]. Pardon me, Madame, but you force me to be cruel.

GEORGE. Go on, go on, life has not spared me, why should you?

MME. DE MUSSET. You say you are his universe, but, Madame, are you sure you are all of this to him?

GEORGE. Ask him and his tears will answer you. [*She jots this down.*] After the desolation of my past he has come like a new dawn into my life. I was a mere girl when I married, young, furtive, reticent, romantic. I adored my husband. I gave him my faith, my life. And what did he make of them?

MME. DE MUSSET. Spare me.

GEORGE [*leaning towards her*]. He tossed them to the first chambermaid that smiled on him. I suffered this because I still loved him. Men,—Madame, men never know what agony we women hush in our hearts.

MME. DE MUSSET [*in spite of herself*]. Yes—that is true.

GEORGE. I bore this. My baby came. I still preserve his first wee darling shoes.

MME. DE MUSSET [*off her guard*]. And I've kept Alfred's curls. There's still a glint of gold in them. [*Her voice softens.*]

GEORGE [*making the most of the moment*]. I bore this till the day he struck me.

MME. DE MUSSET [*more gently*]. Struck you?

GEORGE. Then I left him forever to find refuge in Paris and consolation in my work. Ah, Madame, do you begin to understand?

[*Then* MME. DE MUSSET *speaks very quickly attempting to cover a softening emotion which she can't suppress.*]

MME. DE MUSSET. But why,—why have you chosen my boy from all the men you—

[*She stops short.*]

GEORGE. Because he has come as my first love, when I thought that love was over forever. You must not, you cannot take him from me.

[MME. DE MUSSET *is half-consciously beginning to pity her and she fights against it.*]

MME. DE MUSSET. I am taking him away to save him.

GEORGE. Save him? Is he not a man? Would you fling him to the grisettes of the boulevard as the Philistines flung Daniel to the lions? [*Again the Bible. The Scriptures were ever her "present help in trouble."*] No! no! I will be a mother to him. A mother and a mistress. That combination is unique, Madame, unique, but none the less sublime.

MME. DE MUSSET. I—

GEORGE [*in a last beautiful effort*]. You are his mother. You gave him life. He drank in love at your breasts. You have reared and tendered him and in gratitude he would give back some of this love you have given him. He would pay heaven by loving in return. There are tears in your eyes. There are tears in the hearts of each of us. You have taught him love and now he would bring an offering of love to lay on the altar of my heart.

MME. DE MUSSET [*almost won*]. Your eloquence, Madame—

GEORGE. No! No! It is not my eloquence, it is your mother's love, understanding the love of an unfortunate sister.

[*She throws herself on her knees before her, then with dulcet sweetness.*]

May I call you mother?

MME. DE MUSSET. I have misjudged you, Madame. I ask your pardon. There is much good in your heart.

GEORGE. I have opened it to you. [*And then from a sublimated height of spirituality.*] You will tell him to go with me.

MME. DE MUSSET [*on the verge of a collapse*]. I—I—

GEORGE [*very gently*]. You will, mother?

MME. DE MUSSET [*slowly*]. Yes, he shall go with you.

[*And* GEORGE *springs up and rushes triumphantly to the door of the kitchen.*]

GEORGE [*calling*]. Alfred, Alfred. Madame, you have chosen well.

[*But the emotional strain has been too much for* MME. DE MUSSET *and she is weeping when* ALFRED *enters.*]

ALFRED. Mother, my mother, do not weep. If one of us must suffer, it shall not be you.

MME. DE MUSSET. My son, my son.

ALFRED. You have suffered agony to give me life, shall I not suffer agony to bring you peace? Come, mother, I renounce my love, and will go with you.

[*And* MME. DE MUSSET *is so swept away by her son's nobility that she forgets her words to* GEORGE.]

MME. DE MUSSET [*throwing her arms about him*]. Then come, my Alfred, and your mother will help you to forget.

[*They move towards the door. A pause.* GEORGE *is almost swooning. But a moment later and she is ready even for this seeming defeat on the brink of victory. She bars their way.*]

GEORGE [*darkly*]. He loves me with his life. [*And then very tragically.*] He will not hesitate if you come between us. He is a genius, and geniuses do not stop to think.

[*In horror* MME. DE MUSSET *looks at* ALFRED. *Dejectedly he turns away, his head fallen.*]

MME. DE MUSSET [*in terror*]. No! No! Not that! Not that!

[*The men crowd in at the doorway.*]

ALFRED. I am but a poor reed, broken in the wind of destiny.

[GEORGE *watches* MME. DE MUSSET. *Her last thrust has gone home.*]

HEINE [*with a quick glance at* GEORGE *as she puts on the new bonnet bought for Italy*]. The wind has changed.

ALFRED. I am ready, mother. I shall go with you, tho I leave my life behind me.

[*Candle-light and pathos crown the scene. Then* MME. DE MUSSET *speaks.*]

MME. DE MUSSET [*her voice trembling*]. No, Alfred, you shall go to Italy. I am your mother and I wish it. I have misjudged this lady. Her heart is noble. My blessings follow you.

[*She sinks into a chair at the table and* ALFRED *throws himself on his knees before her.*]

ALFRED. My mother, my noble mother.

[*Pause. Tableau, then* BULOZ *bustles in.*]

BULOZ [*briskly*]. You haven't much time, if you're leaving tonight. The diligence starts from the Post in ten minutes.

GEORGE. Quick, Rosalie, a cab, a cab. [ROSALIE *rushes out.*] Alfred, when Elysium beckons we'll not wait for baggage. Buloz, give Rosalie two hundred francs and send my trunks to Genoa and twenty reams of Weynan paper. My pen adores it. Alfred, Alfred, the world is kind.

[ALFRED *has got up and braced himself with half a bottle of claret.*]

ALFRED [*gayly*]. I'll write five comedies, a tragedy and three books of poems.

BULOZ. Hurry! Hurry!

[*One or two wraps and a few small bags are hustled into the hall.*]

HEINE. Good-bye, fond lovers, the Gods have made you artists.

[ROSALIE *comes rushing in.*]

GEORGE [*rapturously*]. And love will make us Gods!

ROSALIE. There was a cab in the courtyard. [*Then to* GEORGE.] He said you told him to wait all evening.

[GEORGE *from her pinnacle, disregarding this last blatant proof of her campaigning.*]

GEORGE. Good-bye,—farewell, my friends. [*And then beautifully to* MME. DE MUSSET.] Madame, God looks down on us. Love is all.

MME. DE MUSSET [*suddenly succumbing to the practical*]. Be sure that Alfred wears his heaviest flannels in that drafty diligence.

GEORGE. Trust me! Love is all!

[*And snatching her half-finished manuscript from the desk, she and* ALFRED *rush from the room, followed by* BULOZ *and* HEINE. MME. DE MUSSET *sits silently, quite overcome, as* PAUL *runs over to the window to watch the departure; and* ROSALIE *begins clearing the table. She sees the omelet.*]

ROSALIE [*laconically*]. And all those ten eggs wasted.

[*Voices sound up from the courtyard. The noise has again wakened the canaries. There is a shower of song and the curtain falls.*]

END OF ACT I

ACT II. NOTHING BUT TIME LASTS FOREVER

It is six months later. The scene is GEORGE'S *apartment in the Hotel Danieli, Venice. It is evening. Through a great Venetian window, back center, in the distance across the Grand Canal, can be seen the Island of San Giorgio with its Campanile silhouetted against the moon. The room is huge, tiled and gloomy. Deep shadows are everywhere. A few chairs are about.* MADAME'S *writing desk piled high with manuscripts is in a corner, and to the right a great four-poster bed with the curtains drawn. But the hand of the occupant hangs below them and is just visible in the dim light of a night lamp which stands on a little bottle-covered table near the bed. There is a suggestion of the atmosphere of a sick-room, but somehow the idea of gloom is not too pervasive.*

Outside on the Grand Canal a "serenata" is in full swing. One hears the call of the gondoliers, the bump of the boats, the chatter of voices, the beating of tambourines and the shrill laughter of women, like little rockets shooting up in the shifting hum of sound. A sudden stillness and then a man's voice sings, lusciously, meltingly, a Venetian love song with an accompaniment like a Barcarole of Mendelssohn.

Italy—night—and love—and this sick-room. But still the background is fitting for in the deep, dark embrasure of the Venetian window in the rear which opens on a balcony over the canal, two figures are leaning, listening to their hearts and the music. They are GEORGE *and her lover.*

GEORGE. No! No! Don't answer. The stillness is too eloquent. Listen! Listen!

[*The voice of the singer at the serenata, lifts in poignant ecstasy.*]

GEORGE. Listen, his voice has reached the

stars that bend down to hear. Ah, my beloved, love is the end and the beginning.

[*They are smoking in the shadows of the deep window. The fumes float out.*]

GEORGE. Do you know what my life has been until you came bearing a light in the darkness? Nights of despair and dawns of disillusionment. Life was but a sorry riddle whose answer was death. [*She is almost sobbing.*] That thought came to me yesterday in the Hebrew cemetery. All was over and now love again sings in my heart. Let silence be our prayer of thanksgiving.

[*A moment's attempt at this "silence," but the crowd outside do not understand its beautiful necessity and the next second the song is over and a tumultuous burst of applause lifts from the waters.*]

GEORGE. And now we'll have tea. How beautifully he sang. Music is perpetual passion yearning forever. Sh!—*you* mustn't speak so loudly or our patient may awake.

[*She comes from the window. Her lover stops in the shadow watching her as she glides about. She dips a taper into the night lamp and at the end of the room farthest from the bed lights a candle standing in a bracket hanging on the wall. The stage grows a little lighter. She is dressed in man's clothing and is smoking a huge cigar. She leans over a little brazier.*]

GEORGE. Yes—it's bubbling. I adore cooking. Even making tea fascinates me. That's why Dumas would never come to see me in Paris—ah, Paris—he was jealous of my sauces. [*She pours a little water into a teapot.*] Come, dear, it's ready.

[*And* DR. PAGELLO *steps out of the shadow of the window. He is* GEORGE'S *deep-eyed, hesitant, but none too brilliant Italian doctor. He has no mental distinction, no authority, no particular magnetism, but he is charmingly simple and* GEORGE *has discovered in him a latent talent for the tender one-syllabled sort of love which at the moment of the threatening "debacle" of her affair with* DE MUSSET, *her soul needs; and withal though he is not too masterful he is extraordinarily handsome.*]

GEORGE. Sh—You mustn't speak too loudly. He may awake. [*She glances toward the bed.*] Though he has outraged our love, still I pity him.

PAGELLO. He needs sleep badly.

GEORGE. Ah, my friend, we must heal him. France needs him. He is weak, weak—his imagination has sapped his will. [*And then rather mysteriously.*] But he must not pass beyond.

PAGELLO. No. He will live, but I do not see why you say pass beyond. It is very difficult for a physician to understand how you other people feel about that sort of thing.

GEORGE [*half playfully*]. You ponderous scientist. You wicked, wicked materialist, don't you believe the soul goes on forever? [*Then beautifully.*] Isn't love,—our love—an earthly symbol of the soul's eternity? Don't you understand that, Pietro?

PAGELLO. I—I used to understand only what I saw, but you somehow, you make me understand what I do not see. I cannot explain you to myself.

GEORGE. I thought nothing was hidden from you doctors.

PAGELLO. Most of the women I know are different from you. You are very unlike my mother.

GEORGE. No, no, Pietro, perhaps you misjudge me. I, too, am only a woman.

PAGELLO. I carry my mother's picture with me. See. [*He shows her a little locket, which hangs from a chain about his neck.*] She is very dear to me.

GEORGE [*looking at the miniature*]. Your eyes—your brow—and that look of trust. Some day you must tell me all about her. You will have a little rum? Yes—some day we'll go to her—you and I. [PAGELLO *starts slightly.*] I'll read her part of my latest novel. I wrote for six hours last night.

PAGELLO [*deeply concerned*]. That's too much.

GEORGE. And for seven again this morning before breakfast. I've gotten used to it. [*She glances toward the bed, and then with a note of genuine sadness in her voice.*] It helps me to forget.

PAGELLO [*professionally*]. Work like that is bad for you, you cannot keep it up,—or—

GEORGE. Is it can or cannot? I must live and to live I must write.

PAGELLO. Why, even we physicians—

GEORGE. Yes, yes, I know. [*She is smiling*

gently at him.] Your mother will like my book and you too, Pietro. It is written out of my heart.

PAGELLO. I think my father would care more to hear it. He is a scholar, you know. He has come up from Castelfranco to read some books in the library here. He is waiting for me in the Piazzetta; we are to have ices together. All day he is busy with his books, and in the evening I meet him.

GEORGE. You are a dutiful son. Do not believe the cynics, Pietro. The world is full of dutiful sons. [*A half glance towards the bed.*]

PAGELLO. He is writing a history of Castelfranco. He loves our home.

GEORGE. Yes, yes, I too love the scenes of my childhood. Dear, secluded Nohant—but lately I have been dreaming [*She leans a little toward him.*] of the Alpine hills. Why, even here in Venice I smell the scent of the almond flowers. [*Then very tenderly.*] You know the Alpine valleys, Pietro—it is spring [*And into the last word she crowds all the essence of the sweet beginning of things.*]—spring.

PAGELLO. I have seen very little. Venice and the country about my home.

GEORGE. Yes, we will go there some day.

PAGELLO. George! [*He leans towards her, then stops.*] George—

GEORGE. You have an adorable way of hesitating and then a lovely worried smile comes into your eyes. You must ever stay what I know you are rather than what you may be.

PAGELLO. What I am, what I have done, does that matter now?

GEORGE. You must tell me nothing. [*She glances towards the bed.*] Once before I thought I knew the heart of a man. Ah, well! [*She sadly shakes her head.*] But now—now—[*She leans towards him.*] You must remain a mystery.

PAGELLO. Why? Why?

GEORGE. Because my love for you is beyond understanding. It is part of myself. You have come to me [*Again a pathetic glance at the patient.*] when my heart was broken.

PAGELLO. Before I knew you nothing used to interest me so much as gall-stones. But now—

GEORGE. You droll darling. Sh—Sh—We mustn't talk so loud. [*There is a movement and a sigh from the sleeper behind the curtains.*] God grant he is quiet tonight. I cannot stand this terrible life much longer.

PAGELLO. I pity you, you have nursed him like a mother.

GEORGE. What has he not done to break my heart?

[*She steps towards the bed and mournfully looks in at the sleeper. Then she is back at the table.*]

GEORGE. May God—who is love—some day give me the strength to forgive him.

PAGELLO. He is better, almost well again—if he can give up this drinking—

GEORGE. If? Think of it, Pietro. The other night I had to call up two of the stoutest porters to hold him down. He wept and sang and without a stitch of clothing danced about the room shrieking that the place was full of demons with vipers in their hair. It was terrible.

PAGELLO [*attempting to quiet her*]. Don't speak of these things, George.

[*The memory of it is too much for her, but the old instinct conquers.*]

GEORGE. Some day I shall put that scene into a novel. Why not—life is my theme. He has come reeling home. He has squandered his money and mine, Pietro. He has lost thousands of francs at the tables. I sent to Paris, Buloz advanced me more.

PAGELLO. What? This money that you earn, writing day and night,—

GEORGE. Yes! Yes!—By the sweat of my soul—I should say brow. It is true, my friend. The French Consul has taken him to these gambling houses and other places—other places, Pietro.

PAGELLO. And all the while you sat there. [*He points to the desk.*]

GEORGE. Do you think he minded that? One night in the pocket of his coat I found a slipper—a slipper of a ballerina. It was soaked with champagne.

PAGELLO [*the extravagance rather than the impropriety getting the better of him*]. No! Champagne. That costs two lire a bottle!

GEORGE. The toe was stuffed. That's how these people seem to dance on nothing. Ah—I have borne much.

PAGELLO. Yes, yes.

George. Sh—he is awake.

[*A moment's pause, then again quiet. The hand below the curtain falls a little lower in exhausted relaxation.*]

Pagello. George, George, my noble friend, how you have suffered.

George. I have borne all. The gold he flung about him, that mattered little. I could write, write. The incessant drink—I forgave him that.

Pagello. And the ballet dancer?

George [*bitterly*]. That, too, my friend. Do you think that mattered? No. All that is nothing—nothing; but he has committed the one sin a woman cannot forgive. [*And then with a sincerity that sounds through the romance of it all.*] He has ceased to love me. [*She is weeping.*]

Pagello. And you, George, you no longer love him?

George. Pietro, how can you ask me that? No, that is over.

Pagello. No mother could have nursed him more tenderly than you.

George. No, no.

Pagello. I loved you for your care of him.

George [*getting up*]. Perhaps his pillow needs turning.

Pagello. No, do not disturb him.

George. I would give my life rather than see him suffer.

Pagello. The world will never know what you have done for him.

George [*for the moment forgetting her itching pen*]. Never, never, Pietro, but does that matter? [*She is over at the bedside, a symbol of sacrificial duty.*] I at least have kept my faith. [*Then reminiscently.*] How he urged me to go with him to Italy, when I hesitated.

[*Then she is back at the table, weeping and slicing a lemon as she speaks.*]

George [*with deep meaning*]. You came just in time, Pietro.

Pagello [*again with a tinge of professional pride*]. I hope I have helped him, the case wasn't easy.

George [*dramatically*]. It is me whom you have lifted from the grave.

Pagello. You?

George [*darkly*]. I had decided to die.

Pagello. You?

George. The day before you came into my life. I had planned to leap from the Campanile in the afternoon just when the band was playing so that all the world might know what he had done to me.

Pagello [*stirred*]. You must stop writing—you're tired, overstrained.

George [*tenderly*]. Ah! Pietro. Now I am better. God has sent you. Can you know what you mean to me? Help me to be strong.

Pagello. I too thank God for the day I chanced to pass your window.

George [*suddenly, her hand on his*]. Chance! Chance! And in that little word lies all the joy and sorrow of the world.

[*Pause. Farther in the distance can be heard the sound of the serenata.* Pagello *goes to the window.*]

Pagello [*pointing to the balcony*]. It was here you stood. De Musset was next you. There was something strange about you, as you flecked the ashes from your cigar. I looked up. [*He is back from the window.*]

George. I remember, Pietro. [*She gleams up at him.*]

Pagello. Was it a sort of mesmerism?

George. Older than Mesmer, Pietro, man calling unto woman. It began in Eden.

Pagello. It was as if we spoke.

George [*lyrically*]. Our hearts were answering one another.

[*The tenor's song lifts in the distance.*]

Pagello. All day I thought of the beauty of your sad eyes.

George [*gently*]. Beauty,—no, my friend. They were dim with weeping.

Pagello. All my visits seemed dull to me. Even my most serious case—a fat Turk dying of typhus—didn't interest me. Whilst I bled him, I thought of you.

George [*sweetly, accepting the compliment*]. Yes, Pietro?

Pagello. Back in my office, I could think of nothing but you.

[*There is a restless move from the sleeper behind the curtains, but* George,—*who for a long while has heard no such tenderness as this,—doesn't notice it.*]

Pagello. You—you.

George. And I, Pietro, I of you. As I leaned over my writing, I saw you. Do you remember Dante?—your Dante—Paolo, Francesca,—only I must change the words a little. [*She smiles faintly.*] I must say; that day I *wrote* no more. [*She drifts over to the window. She leans out.*] Ah! Pietro, the night is like a drawn sword. Listen, the very stars are singing.

PAGELLO [*a little confused*]. No, that's the tenor at the serenata. Ah, how I love you! That day even Dr. Ganetti's book on gall-stones couldn't interest me.

GEORGE. No, Pietro? [*She is back at the table, he follows her.*]

PAGELLO. Always across the page I saw the scarlet of the scarf that you wore about your head.

[*They are leaning across the table, their hands clasped together.*]

PAGELLO [*passionately*]. You love me, George?—

GEORGE [*sweetly, simply, all that is deepest in her welling up*]. I love you, Pietro. Why I do not know. I love you as I have never loved before. All my other love has been but as a preparation for this love of ours which shall last forever. [*Another sigh from the bed.*] Sh—he is awake.

PAGELLO. No, if he has taken the powder he will sleep till morning. [*He is around the table next to her.*] George, George, how grateful I am to God that so beautiful a soul as yours has bent down to me.

GEORGE. Bent, my darling? No! It is you who have lifted me from despair. [*They are about to embrace. The sleeper is again restless. She whispers.*] Sh—we are much too loud.

[*Love in the shadow of the patient's bed is too incongruous even for her artist's nature.*]

GEORGE [*with an attempt at readjustment*]. Let's finish our tea. It's from India. Alfred bought it in the Rialto. It cost four lire.

PAGELLO. What! That's a lot of money.

GEORGE. Nothing is too fine for Alfred. [*Then with a sad little laugh in her voice.*] It was my money.

[*She pours out the tea. There is only one cup.* PAGELLO *not noticing this, takes it up.*]

PAGELLO [*sipping his tea*]. It tastes strange.

GEORGE [*fantastically*]. Nude girls gathered it.

PAGELLO. It certainly does taste different.

GEORGE [*continuing*]. It's what the jeweled and drowsy nabobs sip whilst they loll in their hammocks of spun silk.

[*She goes over to her desk and makes a note on the back of one of the sheets of her manuscript paper.*]

GEORGE [*writing*]. That's a beautiful sentence. It has the odor of twilights in the East.

PAGELLO. The tea?

GEORGE. No, darling, my words. You mustn't be too literal. That's what too much science does.

[*As she passes him on her way back to the table, she lovingly taps his head.*]

GEORGE [*smiling*]. All the night is in your eyes.

PAGELLO [*slipping his arm about her*]. Let's go out on the balcony. By now the crowds are far beyond the Piazzetta. [*He takes a step towards her.*]

GEORGE [*admonishing him, as she glances toward the bed*]. No, no, Pietro, you are too impetuous. Our poor Alfred might need something.

PAGELLO. He is almost well, tomorrow he can get up. [*He takes up his tea-cup.*]

GEORGE. I am waiting till he is strong again. [*She glances at the doctor.*] Then he must be told.

PAGELLO. He has my pity. Sooner or later he would find out.

GEORGE. Yes—we are above subterfuge.

PAGELLO [*sipping his tea*]. But you aren't drinking. [*He looks down at the table to hand her the other cup.*] Why look,—there is only one.

GEORGE. Isn't one enough, Pietro? [*She is over next to him.*] I shall sup from yours.

PAGELLO [*tenderly*]. Then you must bend down.

[*And she does so, and his arm goes about her waist. And the next moment she is in his lap. And their mouths are almost touching as they press the cup to their lips. And at this moment* ALFRED'S *night-capped head pops out through the curtains of the bed behind them. Tableau. He chokes back an exclamation of amazement and the curtains hanging about him tremble.*]

GEORGE [*wistfully*]. There now—I have had my tea.

PAGELLO [*ardently*]. And I shall have my kiss.

GEORGE [*faintly*]. Pietro! Pietro!

[*And* ALFRED, *pale as the curtains about him, leans forward, watching them. And passionately they embrace and then suddenly she jumps up and as suddenly* ALFRED *drops back behind the curtains.*]

GEORGE [*the "éclaircissement" has come*]. Now I understand everything. I see it all clearly.

PAGELLO [*quite taken by surprise*]. What's the matter?

GEORGE. We must go away, and at once.

PAGELLO. What—

GEORGE. We cannot stay. It is a desecration, no, not here, not here. It is an insult to this love of ours. We dare not hesitate.

PAGELLO. I—George—

GEORGE. Life is calling us. This room stifles me.

PAGELLO [*practical as ever*]. Then let's go out on the balcony.

GEORGE. No, no, come, come away, away.

PAGELLO [*quite misunderstanding her dynamic impetuosity*]. Shall we go to the Lido? Shall I call a gondola?

GEORGE. No, no, to the Alpine valleys. I am dressed for climbing.

PAGELLO [*completely stupefied*]. What! George!

GEORGE. It is spring—spring. [*The thought gives a buoyant ring to her voice.*] We will wander hand in hand like innocent, laughing children, and we will love to the sound of the tumbling cascades.

[PAGELLO *stands looking at her in wonder.*]

GEORGE. And then—Paris. We've got to be in time, Pietro, to see my little darlings, Solange, Maurice, take their prizes at school.

PAGELLO [*who can scarcely gasp*]. To Paris—

GEORGE. And to freedom! Come!

[*She glances toward the bed.* ALFRED, *his head poked out on the other side, is listening.*]

Let us not hesitate. A moment may shatter—all.

PAGELLO [*completely at a loss*]. But—

GEORGE. For weeks, weeks I have known this would come. I have prophetic visions. Tomorrow, the day after, it will be the same. I cannot live in the shadow of these memories.

PAGELLO [*not quite keyed to such speed*]. And —de Musset—?

GEORGE. He shall be told. But now, now we cannot wait. We must leave together. Destiny has spoken.

[*She is in his arms, and* ALFRED *is leaning half out of bed. His intentions are patently to have something to do with this destiny, but as* GEORGE *sweeps forward, he involuntarily slips back.*]

GEORGE. Come, Pietro.

PAGELLO [*not knowing what to say*]. And leave Venice?—George—

GEORGE. I have been sent to save you, you must go lest your future sink in the mud of these languorous lagoons. The world is waiting to receive you.

PAGELLO. And my patients?

GEORGE [*inspirationally*]. Your patients—why, emperors shall call you in for gallstones.

PAGELLO [*still unpersuaded*]. And my mother?

GEORGE [*involuntarily*]. Mother, mother. No, no. That mustn't happen again. [*But in a moment she has recovered.*] You must be free to realize yourself. I have done that. I am free.

PAGELLO [*still doubtful*]. And my father?

GEORGE. Have you any aunts or uncles? Your father, what of him?

PAGELLO. He will never consent to this.

GEORGE. I shall persuade him.

PAGELLO [*in amazement*]. You?

GEORGE. He is eating ices in the Piazzetta. He is a scholar. You told me this. A scholar who is eating ices—the combination proves him gentle. He will understand. He will bless you and send you with me.

PAGELLO. But—

GEORGE. Again but—nothing but buts. Come, Pietro. Come.

[*They are at the door.*]

PAGELLO [*pointing to her trousers*]. Can you go like that?

GEORGE. Yes. Venice has got used to me.

PAGELLO. This is madness.

GEORGE. Love has spoken.

PAGELLO. But my father will never consent to this.

GEORGE [*undaunted*]. I know a parent's heart. [ALFRED *is about to call out.*] I have not lived my life for nothing. Come! The scent of the almond bloom is calling.

[*And half dragging him after her they are gone.* ALFRED *gazes after them in speechless astonishment. Then he tries to get up to follow. He is too weak. He falls back on the bed. Very far in the distance the noise of the serenata can be heard. Slowly he rouses himself. He pours out some brandy which stands on the little table near the bed. Half swooning he reaches the window. He tries to call out. His strength fails him. He leans against the window frame. Suddenly there is a knock at the door and he turns to see* PAUL *at the threshold.*]

ALFRED. Paul!

PAUL. Good God, Alfred, what's the matter? You look half dead.

ALFRED [*faintly*]. Help me back to bed.

PAUL. Where's George?

[ALFRED *leaning on him reaches the bed.*]

ALFRED. Eating ices on the Piazzetta.

PAUL. She leaves you alone like this?

ALFRED. She must have her ices. [*He pours out another glass of brandy.*] You didn't write you were coming. What brings you to Venice?

PAUL. Mother sent me. She was uneasy.

ALFRED. Uneasy?

PAUL. Yes. You and George. Your letters came less frequently.

ALFRED. I've been busy. I've started three tragedies, four comedies and a book of poems. How's mother?

PAUL. She sends her kindliest greetings to George.

ALFRED [*smiling faintly*]. Yes—

PAUL. When will George be back?

ALFRED. When?

PAUL. Mother is so grateful to her. Buloz says she's taken such good care of you.

ALFRED. And—

PAUL. But lately he's been silent. Mother drove to his office every day.

ALFRED. Poor Buloz—

PAUL. And all he would do was to sit there looking at her strangely thru his monocle.

ALFRED. And mother, I suppose, would stare back thru her lorgnon. Curious, isn't it, Paul? Sometimes the harder people look the less they see.

PAUL. Of course I told her everything was all right.

ALFRED [*on the verge of laughter*]. Of course.

PAUL. I saw Heine.

ALFRED. Yes?

PAUL. Said he knew nothing but he advised me to leave it all to George. Said that she would manage somehow.

ALFRED. She has managed,—somehow. [*He is laughing to himself.*]

PAUL. I told Heine I was going to Venice.

ALFRED. Yes.

PAUL. He sent you a message.

ALFRED. A blessing that sneers?

PAUL. No, he told me to tell you that Hell is the place where the satisfied compare disappointments.

ALFRED. He knows.

PAUL. You're so white, Alfred, what's the matter?

ALFRED. I've been ill. Sunstroke, lying on the beach at the Lido.

PAUL. You should have known better.

ALFRED. I couldn't get away. George insisted on reading me her last six chapters. Such rubbish! Perhaps it was the book and not the sun.

PAUL. You're better now?

ALFRED. Tomorrow I'll be about again.

PAUL. Mother sent you this. [*He hands him a letter.*]

ALFRED [*slipping it under his pillow*]. How much?

PAUL. A thousand francs.

ALFRED [*petulantly flinging himself back on the pillow*]. But I needed fifteen hundred. Has she forgiven my going?

PAUL. A week after and she was glad you'd gone.

ALFRED. Glad?

PAUL. Said it would do you good to see life.

ALFRED. Yes—Yes—It's done me good. Have a bit of brandy, Paul. [*He sits up and pours out a little in a glass.*]

PAUL. As I came by two men raced past me. They almost knocked me over.

ALFRED [*sipping his brandy*]. You're not easily bowled over, are you, Paul?

PAUL. These Italians have such brutal manners. But just the same I was amused.

ALFRED. Yes.

PAUL. One of them bore the strangest resemblance to George.

ALFRED. Naturally.

PAUL. What?

ALFRED. Have a bit of brandy.

PAUL. Why did you say naturally?

ALFRED [*speaking slowly and rather amused, watching the effect on* PAUL]. It was George.

PAUL. What? George? Running thru the streets with another man dressed like that!

ALFRED [*a twinkle in his voice*]. To hesitate is to hinder history.

PAUL. Can't you be serious? Where were they running to?

ALFRED. As far as their trousered legs can carry them.

PAUL. What?

ALFRED. If something doesn't stop them they'll reach the end of the earth and then drop off.

PAUL. You mean the Grand Canal?

ALFRED. Not exactly. But something will stop them.

PAUL. I hope so. Can she swim?

ALFRED. In any waters. But she'll be stopped unless I am mistaken and by something she doesn't quite expect. The old man's a scholar.

PAUL [*in the dark*]. What?

ALFRED. She'll bump into his papa.

PAUL [*mystified*]. Papa?

ALFRED. Yes. The papa of the other man who nearly knocked you over.

PAUL. I—

ALFRED [*shedding the light*]. She is planning to elope with him.

PAUL [*springing up*]. Then it's ended?

ALFRED. How swiftly you deduce. A great philosopher lies buried deep—very deep, in you.

PAUL. If ever again I believe in a woman I'll cease to believe in God. I've come just in time. Mother was right to send me. Perhaps I can patch it up.

ALFRED. No, leave it torn. That's how the light soaks thru.

PAUL [*sympathetically coming towards him*]. My poor, poor Alfred. Don't let it hurt too much. Paris is crowded with women. They mayn't all know literature but nearly all know love.

ALFRED. Yes, Paul.

PAUL. My poor, poor brother.

ALFRED. My poor, poor imbecile. Thank God it's over! I wish she were in Hell!

[*And* PAUL *flops back into his chair and then* ALFRED *lets loose what has been storing up in him for months.*]

ALFRED. I can't bear her about me. She's like a noisy old clock that can't stop ticking. Why, she actually had the indelicacy when I lay here recovering from my sunstroke [*He takes a gulp of brandy.*] to sit next to my bed scratching away all night at her endless novels. She writes as a cow gives milk. All she has to do is to jerk at her mind. Sometimes I drank a little to forget. [PAUL *in silent astonishment sits listening.*] There are two ways to get to know a person, Paul. Gambling with them or travelling with them. The first is better, it's over sooner. [*His pent-up vehemence comes pouring out.*] She has the soul of a bourgeoise. One day I sat there trying to write and what do you think I heard in the next room? She was telling the chambermaid—the chambermaid, Paul, how her mother was dancing at a ball a month before her marriage and how she stopped in the middle of the quadrille and five minutes afterwards gave birth to George.

PAUL. My God—no—

ALFRED. I called her in. I remonstrated with her and she sneered at my hypocritical breeding.

PAUL. And could you expect her to understand that?

ALFRED. She laughed at me and said that many of the best family trees bore the worst fruit. I rushed away and drank, drank, drank [*And he does so.*] to forget the vulgarity of it all.

PAUL [*commiseratingly*]. My poor Alfred!

ALFRED. And when I got back, there she sat scribbling. All my beautiful, glorious ideas deserted me. There she sat—scribbling, scribbling all the night long, scratching away like a rusty old file.

[*He is exhausted and falls weakly back on the bed.*]

PAUL [*leaning over him*]. My poor brother, what you have lived thru.

ALFRED. Think of it, Paul. Only a few minutes ago I caught them kissing, actually kissing, in the shadow of my bed,—my bed of torture.

PAUL [*slowly*]. What will mother say?

ALFRED. She must never know.

PAUL. Two weeks and the boulevards will be gabbing. George tells everything to Buloz.

ALFRED. She tells everything to everybody. [*Then half bitterly, half humorously.*] Copy—copy.

PAUL. But I'll defend you now that I know the truth.

ALFRED [*suddenly sitting up*]. What?

PAUL. I'll answer her. Leave it to me; wait and see.

ALFRED [*making the most of the moment by adding to the data*]. There she lay in his arms, Paul, drinking my tea from the one cup, both of them, whilst she mumbled something about haste and almond blossoms.

PAUL. And so George the untiring, weary of the de Musset doll, tosses the broken puppet into a corner.

ALFRED. God knows how kind, how gentle, I have been with her. [*And then he too begins thinking of the beginning of their love in Paris.*] How she urged me to go to Italy when I hesitated. I at least have been faithful.

PAUL. And now she's leaving you?

ALFRED. If fate is kind and the old father is a fool. If he can't stop her nothing will. Listen, they are coming back. [*He points to a door beyond the bed.*] Quick, wait in there.

[*And he is about to crawl back into bed but the next instant the door flies open and* LUCREZIA VIOLENTE, PAGELLO'S *mistress, rushes into the room. She is tense, dark, scented, a colorful combination of a languorous poppy when happy and an angry firecracker when stirred. She slams the door behind her and leans against it.*]

LUCREZIA [*panting*]. I must speak with you, you. [*She glares at* ALFRED.] You!

[*And* PAUL *with a sly, knowing glance at his brother, begins to whistle a sprightly snatch of a love song and then trips over to examine more closely the beautiful, though tempestuous* LUCREZIA.]

ALFRED [*to* PAUL]. What are you doing? What's the matter with you?

PAUL [*smiling significantly*]. So! So! My naughty, naughty brother. And this is why the George gets on your poor nerves. But I don't blame you, Alfred, really I don't.

[*Very intimately he begins ogling* LUCREZIA *and whistling even louder. He steps with a swaggering familiarity closer to her.*]

ALFRED [*coming between them*]. I tell you to wait in the next room.

PAUL [*laughing*]. All right. Two's company, three's a chaperon.

[*And he enjoys his wit immensely, to the intense discomfort of* ALFRED *and the astonishment of* LUCREZIA.]

ALFRED. Get out. I tell you I've never seen the girl before.

PAUL. Then thank the dear gods who sent her.

[*And* PAUL *backs out of the room, still whistling, with an intimate wave of his hand to* LUCREZIA.]

ALFRED. Who are you?

LUCREZIA [*with terrific speed as she speaks throughout*]. Lucrezia Maria Camilla Elvira Violente.

ALFRED [*rather gallantly but a bit uncertain*]. And what do you wish with me, my dear?

LUCREZIA [*resenting his tone*]. What do you think?

ALFRED [*taking her in*]. Well—er—er—

[LUCREZIA *with a slight swagger steps towards him.*]

LUCREZIA. Well!

ALFRED [*smiling at her*]. Did the French Consul send you to me?

LUCREZIA. No one has sent me.

ALFRED. I haven't seen you at the serenatas.

LUCREZIA. No.

ALFRED. Nor at the opera.

LUCREZIA. No.

ALFRED. Nor in the Piazzetta, watching the fireworks.

LUCREZIA [*as he steps a little nearer*]. No. No.

ALFRED [*not quite sure of his ground but he is* ALFRED *and she is beautiful*]. Well, you see [*And then very sweetly.*], my dear—[*He is closer to her.*]

LUCREZIA [*starting back*]. My dear! How dare you! How dare you! Dio Mio, Dio Mio, how dare you?

ALFRED. Forgive me, my dear, but you see I am a man—it is night—You come to my room—

LUCREZIA. Yes, yes, I come to your room. [*She looks about her.*]

ALFRED. Well, then, who are you?

LUCREZIA. Lucrezia, Maria—

ALFRED [*stemming the tide*]. Yes, yes—but where do you come from?

LUCREZIA. From Castelfranco.

ALFRED. And what do you want with me?

LUCREZIA [*not tempering her disdain*]. You—I want nothing with you.

ALFRED [*resenting this, his tone a mixture of surprise and disappointment*]. Then why do you come here?

LUCREZIA [*almost spitting the words in his face*]. It is your woman, your woman that I want.

ALFRED [*in the dark*]. What—why, I've never even seen you before.

LUCREZIA. You! Bah! [*With a gesture as though wiping him off her hands.*] I am an Italian. I want to see this George Sand. [*She has a curious way of sounding the "e" in George.*]

ALFRED [*backing into a chair at the table*]. Yes. I see that you're an Italian. And what do you want with Mme. Sand?

LUCREZIA [*mysteriously handling something which is in her belt under her shawl and speaking very simply like a wide-eyed child*]. I wish to kill her.

ALFRED [*darting back*]. Good God! Who are you? What are you?

LUCREZIA [*coming close to him and leaning in his face as she speaks the words slowly and with intense significance*]. I am a friend—a good friend—of Dr. Pietro Pagello. Do you understand me, you Frenchman?

ALFRED [*the light breaking*]. How did you get in here?

LUCREZIA. I said I had come to nurse the invalid. Bah! [*She glares at him in abject disgust.*] And now where is this Signora George Sand?

ALFRED. She has gone out with—[*He stops short*, LUCREZIA *watching him.*] With a friend—a friend. They have gone to—to [*And then with inspiration.*] to see the Punch and Judy show. Madame adores to watch the puppets dance.

LUCREZIA. So. Then they will soon be back. [*She steps towards a chair.*]

ALFRED [*fencing*]. No. No. That was last night. Tonight—tonight they—she—

LUCREZIA [*pointing it*]. *They*—Yes—

ALFRED [*a bit at a loss*]. She—they,—yes, they—have gone by moonlight to the open sea beyond Murano. Yes—yes. [*His imagination begins to work.*] Madame couldn't stand the noise of the serenata. Listen, it's coming back. [*The boats on the Canal have shifted and are coming nearer.*] Listen!

LUCREZIA. So! So! [*She draws a chair away from the table and sits watching* ALFRED.] Then I will wait till she comes back from this open sea beyond Murano with this friend. [*Her breath comes in little panting gasps.*] Madonna mia, this friend—this friend.

ALFRED [*at his wit's end*]. They may stay away all night.

LUCREZIA [*her eyes aflame*]. Madonna mia. So it has come to that,—all night.

ALFRED. That is—Madame sometimes waits to see the dawn rise over the sea—the Adriatic, you know.

LUCREZIA [*less imaginative perhaps but quite his match*]. Then I will stay till morning till Madame has seen this dawn rise over this Adriatic.

ALFRED. You can't do that, Madame. Can't you see I'm in my dressing gown?

LUCREZIA. If you are so modest, my little Frenchman, then go back to bed. I didn't come to talk with you.

ALFRED. But see here—people don't do that sort of thing. Stop and think.

LUCREZIA. My heart speaks. I do not stop to think.

ALFRED. No. I can see that.

LUCREZIA. What do I care what you see? I have come to save my Pietro. I shall take him from this George Sand.

[*This is too much for* ALFRED. *Suddenly he realizes how she may entangle the chances of his own happy and imminent release.*]

ALFRED [*with intense conviction*]. No, you mustn't, you mustn't do that.

LUCREZIA [*jumping up*]. What—you say that?

ALFRED [*rushing along*]. It will do him good. Let him see life. Madame will teach him much.

LUCREZIA. Madonna, Madonna. You tell me that. You dead little dove of a man! Are you not her lover?

ALFRED [*at a loss*]. Yes—was—that is—yes—yes, of course I am. [*His emotions are mixed.*] Now you just go away and I'll have a nice little talk with George and she'll send him back to you.

LUCREZIA [*the hand under her shawl nervously twitching*]. If—I—no, no—there is nothing but milk in your veins.

ALFRED [*vainly groping for a way out*]. Yes, yes, lots of milk. Goat's milk. I've been sick, sunstroke. He makes me take milk, gallons of milk. He's a wonderful doctor, this Dr. Pagello.

LUCREZIA [*her hand at her heart*]. My Pietro,—my Pietro. He gives you milk?

ALFRED [*grasping the straw*]. It's time for it now. You'll excuse me, good evening. I've got to go out for my milk.

[*He hopefully glances towards the door but* LUCREZIA *is unbudgeable. He tries to take a step but he is too weak and slips back into his chair.*]

LUCREZIA. Go back to your bed lest you faint like a woman.

ALFRED [*weakly*]. But you can't sit there all night long.

LUCREZIA [*firmly*]. No?

ALFRED. Look here. I'll—[*He turns to move towards her. He is exhausted.*]

LUCREZIA [*the hand under her shawl twitching*]. Yes—

[*The sound of the serenata comes up from the waters—tambourines, the laughter of women, the song of the tenor.*]

ALFRED. Listen! That's a song of love. [*He falters towards the bed.*]

LUCREZIA [*with a sneer*]. Love! What do you know of love, you little Frenchman?

ALFRED [*throwing himself down*]. This—only this. Life lays the trap of love and we, poor human fools, are crowding, crowding and waiting to be caught. [*He lies back a moment in thought. Then suddenly.*] Ah! No sooner is she out of the way than it comes back to me. [*Then to* LUCREZIA.] Bring me some paper, quick.

LUCREZIA [*marvelling*]. What?

ALFRED. From that desk. There in the corner.

[LUCREZIA *resents his sudden, shifting impetuosity. Her experience with poets has been limited.*]

LUCREZIA. What! You dare to order me—

ALFRED. Oh, don't mind that. Women always do what I ask them. My mother began it. [*He tries to get up but sinks back on the pillow.*] Quick! Some verses have come to me, beautiful verses. The first in months.

[*There is something pathetic in his voice.* LUCREZIA *goes towards the desk.*]

ALFRED. Yes. That's it. Several sheets.

LUCREZIA [*lifting up some of the pages of* GEORGE'*s latest romance*]. This?

ALFRED. Yes, yes. It's her new novel. But she'll never miss it. Never. [*Angrily* LUCREZIA *is about to crush the papers in her hand.*] And dip a pen for me. As soon as she's out. Of course, of course, I might have known. One room isn't big enough for two muses.

LUCREZIA [*bringing the paper and pen to his bedside*]. Here.

ALFRED [*propping himself up*]. Won't you go now?

LUCREZIA. What?

ALFRED. You mustn't stand there watching me when I write. It makes me nervous. [LUCREZIA *glares at him in astonishment.*] Go, please, please.

[*For a moment he forgets her. He begins writing whilst she backs to the table and sits watching him.*]

LUCREZIA [*under her breath*]. I cannot understand these Frenchmen. They are mad.

[*And in her deep disgust she goes to the window and stands looking out.*]

ALFRED [*fanning his inspiration*]. Yes—yes—yes—

[*His pen glides over the paper. Silence for a moment, only the scratching of the quill is heard. Then suddenly voices sound just outside the door.* LUCREZIA *leaps up like a smoldering flame that is hit by the wind, and instinctively glides into the deep embrasure of the window.*

The papers fall from ALFRED'S *hand to the floor as swiftly he draws the curtains together and slips back into the bed. A moment and* GEORGE *triumphantly enters smoking a huge cigar and at her heels is* PAGELLO, *his big eyes filled with love.*]

PAGELLO. Ah, my beloved, how you spoke to him. There were tears in his eyes. Such eloquence.

[LUCREZIA *is watching them. She is mystified.* PAGELLO *is* PAGELLO *but who is* GEORGE? *The man's costume baffles her, the room is but dimly lit. But then* GEORGE *speaks.*]

GEORGE. No, Pietro, it was not my eloquence.

[*Then the girl recognizes her. She is about to spring forward but* GEORGE *goes on.*]

GEORGE [*lyrically*]. He understood my sorrow. I will bless and remember him forever. His heart is gentle. There is only one wound that hurts my happiness.

PAGELLO. There is much perhaps that I should tell you.

GEORGE. No, no, not you. [*Then sadly she glances towards the bed.*] He must be told.

PAGELLO. Wait until tomorrow.

GEORGE. Tomorrow we may die. Life has spoken. What must be, must be.

[*She goes towards the bed. She draws back the curtains. Tenderly she leans over the patient.*]

GEORGE. Alfred! Alfred!

[*A moment's quiet. Then* ALFRED *stirs in his slumber. Then he awakes.*]

ALFRED [*with a far-away voice*]. Ah! You, George. What time is it? You've been gone so long. [*He leans out of bed and looks about him.*] Ah! She is gone.

[LUCREZIA *is too deep in the window for him to see her, but she too is leaning forward listening.*]

GEORGE [*at a loss*]. Who? Who?

ALFRED. That's well. That is well. She is gone.

GEORGE [*mystified*]. Who? Who?

ALFRED. Perhaps I've been dreaming. I'm so tired.

PAGELLO. Yes. Lie down. [*Then softly to* GEORGE.] He still is weak and imagines that he sees things. [*He draws her away from the bed.*] Wait until tomorrow.

GEORGE. Sooner or later we must tell him.

ALFRED [*trying to overhear them*]. What are you two whispering about? Don't tell me that I've got to take one of those nasty powders and more milk. I'll fling it out of the window.

GEORGE. Yes. He's better. Much better. It is time.

[*She goes towards the bed and stands for a moment looking at him. Her hesitancy worries him.*]

ALFRED [*encouragingly*]. I'm well again. Strong as a porter. [*He glances at* GEORGE.] Look. [*And expectantly he sits bolt upright in the bed.*] My sunstroke's over.

GEORGE. Ah, my friend, you must beware of this sun that comes in bottles.

ALFRED. Strong as two porters that I've seen somewheres.

GEORGE [*putting her hand on his shoulder. Her tone is simple but deeply fraught*]. Alfred, I have something to say to you.

ALFRED [*eagerly*]. Yes—yes—

GEORGE [*almost philosophically*]. Life is so different from literature.

ALFRED [*not expecting the digression*]. What?

GEORGE. Some day I must use this scene and I must be careful to keep it unelaborate.

ALFRED [*lest her commentary go on too long*]. Doctor, do you think I'm strong enough to talk literature?

GEORGE. No, my friend, I haven't come to speak of literature—but life. But I was thinking after all how very simple reality really is. Be brave, Alfred, I have something to say to you.

ALFRED. Yes?

GEORGE. We are at the cross-roads. Even as Ruth [*A puff at her cigar.*] and Naomi. [*As always God and the Bible are her refuge.*]

ALFRED [*impatiently*]. Yes—yes.

GEORGE [*very simply*]. I can no longer be your mistress, Alfred. I can only be your friend. I love Dr. Pagello.

[*A pause. Four hearts are for a moment still. From the water lifts the sound of the serenata. The girl in the window starts forward but the next instant out of the bed comes what is meant to be a heart-broken wail of despair.*]

ALFRED [*from among the pillows*]. George, George, why do you tell me this, George?

GEORGE [*beautifully*]. Be brave, be brave,

my friend. [PAGELLO *stands looking at her in rapture.*] I tell you this because I cannot let the shadow of a lie dim the fading memory of what once we were to one another. [*And she takes a long deep pull at her cigar.*]

ALFRED. George, George, how can I bear this?

GEORGE. We are but born to bear. We poor pilgrims. [*And she smiles tenderly at the doctor.*] Life is our cross. [*Then she turns to* ALFRED.] I shall remember that once I loved you.

ALFRED [*taking her hand and pressing it to his lips*]. Though I weep I shall remember [*He is perhaps sobbing a little.*] what you have done for me.

[LUCREZIA *in blank-eyed amazement leans forward listening to their beautiful pathos.*]

GEORGE. It is over, over. Our poor romance is ended. Time has written [*Then she turns graciously to* PAGELLO.] finito. Come, Pietro, this place is no longer holy. This shrine of love has been defiled. [*And then in mysterious metaphor.*] Something has entered in.

[*And the something in the window is almost convulsed with passionate hate.*]

GEORGE. Come, my beloved. [*And then she turns to* ALFRED, *speaking with childlike frankness.*] We must go from here. Out into the light. We are going high into the mountains where the air shall purify. There, there perhaps I shall be able to forget. [*She turns to the doctor.*] Come, my beloved.

[*She is almost in his arms but suddenly from the window there is a mad little yelp of rage and the next instant* LUCREZIA *springs forward confronting her, burning, indomitable.*]

ALFRED [*as the beautiful structure of similes tumbles*]. She! She! I thought she'd gone.

PAGELLO [*as tho shot*]. Lucrezia, you! You!

GEORGE [*quite calmly*]. Good evening, Madame. Did you climb up the columns to the balcony?

LUCREZIA. You shall not take him. You shall not.

GEORGE. What, Madame?

LUCREZIA. I shall kill you.

GEORGE [*oblivious*]. I can't see how you ever did it in those skirts.

LUCREZIA [*a mixture of temper and tears*]. Pietro, Pietroninni, caro mio, caro mio—you no longer love me—me. [*She is shrieking.*] Dio,—Madonna—you no longer love me.

GEORGE. I beg you, Madame, not to shout. My friend Monsieur de Musset is none too strong. Won't you be seated?

[*And* GEORGE *sits down at the table unbuttoning the lowest button of her vest.*]

LUCREZIA. Who are you? What are you? You crazy woman! [*Her fingers are twitching.*] You woman in breeches dressed like that.

PAGELLO. Lucrezia, be still, be still.

LUCREZIA [*poco fortissimo*]. No! No! She must listen. No! No!

GEORGE. I am trying to, Madame, but you make so much noise. I cannot hear you.

LUCREZIA [*piu forte*]. I make noise! No! No! I make no noise!

[*She is almost dancing in her rage.*]

GEORGE. What a fascinating personality!

[*And she goes over to her desk and brings over some manuscript paper and a pen.*]

LUCREZIA. I spit at you.

GEORGE. No, I wouldn't do that. It isn't nice.

LUCREZIA. Nice! Nice! I dig my nails in your heart.

GEORGE [*sweetly*]. My dear girl, save up all that energy and one of these days you'll bring beautiful children into this ugly world. I am a mother and I know.

[LUCREZIA *suddenly whips the stiletto from under her shawl and springs towards* GEORGE.]

LUCREZIA. You sneer, you short-haired French one.

[*And she makes a dash towards her.* PAGELLO *catches her by the wrist and the knife falls to the floor.*]

PAGELLO. For God's sake, what are you doing?

GEORGE [*calmly taking notes*]. Ah! What a place to end a chapter.

PAGELLO [*struggling with the girl*]. Do you know who she is?

LUCREZIA [*trying to get away*]. What do I care who, what she is.

PAGELLO [*with a sort of awe*]. She is the great George Sand.

[*And* GEORGE *glances up from her writing smilingly to accept the compliment.*]

PAGELLO. She is a famous woman. A great writer.

[ALFRED *is leaning far out of bed clutching one of the posts.*]

ALFRED. Have you no respect for literature?

LUCREZIA [*in blinding scorn, sizzling over like a miniature Vesuvius*]. Literature! What do I care—literature, lies, lies. I too know literature. [*And then in her rage she flings out all the names she can remember, mixing geography with letters to justify her claim.*] Dante, Dante, Alighieri, Tasso, Campanile, San Marco, Venezia, Ariosto, Petrarca, Laura. Literature, bah! bah!—lies, lies! I spit at them. I spit at you.

[*She is again going for* GEORGE *wildly gesticulating and* PAGELLO *again intercepts her. Suddenly in a wild paroxysm of passion she clutches him to her breast. By this time* ALFRED *is almost tumbling out of bed and* GEORGE *sits quietly writing.*]

LUCREZIA [*clinging to him, her voice hot with passion and rage*]. I love you. I hate you. I love you. I speak your name when I sleep; when I go to the well the water says, Pietro, and I drink, and drink, and drink.

GEORGE [*writing as quickly as she can*]. Charming, charming. Do you mind repeating that? How many times did you say drink? Alfred, what does fiction know of life?

[LUCREZIA *clings to* PAGELLO *as to a spar in this tossing sea of passion.*]

LUCREZIA. Pietro! Pietroninni!

ALFRED [*looking at* GEORGE *and speaking into the curtain of his bed*]. God! That woman, even now she can write.

GEORGE. Ah! What a scene this will make when I'm thru with it. Such fervor, such reality. Buloz will be delighted.

[PAGELLO *has forced* LUCREZIA *into a chair. In a frenzy her fists beat the table.*]

GEORGE. Don't do that, my dear, or I can't write.

[*And then* LUCREZIA, *her passion for the moment spent, goes forward, her head in her arms, shaken with convulsive weeping. And then* GEORGE *springs up and goes over to her. Her whole manner changes. She speaks to her as she would to an angry child.*]

GEORGE. You have my pity, Madame. I speak to you out of my soul. I too have loved and lost. [*Sorrowfully she glances at* ALFRED.] That is the lot of us poor women. We give our love only to be forsaken.

PAGELLO [*half in a whisper, half stupidly*]. I wanted to tell you, tell you all.

GEORGE. No, no, don't speak. I understand. [*And then with a tone of universal pity.*] We are but human. [*By a glance she even includes* ALFRED *in her deep love for humanity. Then sympathetically to* LUCREZIA.] Life has spoken and life must be answered. He has come to save me when my nature faltered and he shall go with me—eventually—to Paris.

[*And at this* LUCREZIA *springs up. This is the last straw. Again her rage begins to bubble.*]

LUCREZIA. No. No.

GEORGE. Not right away. After we have found love in the Alpine valleys. Ah, the scent of the almond blossoms.

LUCREZIA [*turning on* PAGELLO]. You have deceived me. Dio! Dio! You have lied to me. You have deserted me.

GEORGE [*gliding between them*]. Madame, you are wrong. He has not deserted you. God has sent him.

LUCREZIA. No! No!

GEORGE. Who can change the choice of love? It is as blind as we.

LUCREZIA [*by this time strident*]. No! No! You shall not take him. You shall not take him.

GEORGE. Love is our master. [*This is almost to herself. A sad little smile plays about her lips.*]

LUCREZIA [*glaring at her*]. You! You oil your words with lies.

[GEORGE *is standing in a sort of sublimated ecstasy lit by the light from the night lamp. The music sounds from the serenata.* ALFRED *on the bed's edge sits watching her in wonder.*]

GEORGE [*her head shaking slowly*]. Love gives us power—power but to obey.

LUCREZIA [*almost frightened*]. Pietro! Look! The devil's speaking to her. Come away. Her heart is black.

[*A moment's pause. They all look at her. Then she takes a deep pull at her cigar and goes* over to her desk to make a note of this power of love.]

GEORGE [*to* LUCREZIA. *From the farthest heights of sisterly sympathy*]. Madame, you have my love.

[LUCREZIA *makes another dash for the knife.* PAGELLO *stops her.*]

GEORGE. Take her to her gondola, Pietro. [ALFRED *starts.*] I shall watch from the window.

[*And* PAGELLO *attempts to lead the struggling* LUCREZIA *from the room.*]

LUCREZIA [*in a last wild frenzy*]. You shall not take him. No! No!

GEORGE [*quietly*]. Love has spoken.

[PAGELLO *and the girl have almost reached the door.*]

LUCREZIA. I'll follow him. I'll save him. He will come back to me.

ALFRED [*involuntarily*]. I wonder.

LUCREZIA. I will follow you to Paris or—to Hell.

[*She is half kissing, half beating the doctor as he leads her from the room.*]

GEORGE [*at her desk making a last note or so*]. What a wonderful girl. The most splendid type I have seen in Italy. Ah, I shall be sad to go.

[*And then she glides over to the window and leans out to see that no harm comes to* PIETRO.]

ALFRED [*lifting up the sheets of manuscript near the bed*]. Look, George, I have been reading your last few pages. They are wonderful. How you have moved me. If I could write as you—

GEORGE. I'll do even better after tonight. Ah! There they are! She is weeping. How gently he helps her into her gondola.

[ALFRED *braces himself with another swallow of brandy and steps towards her.*]

ALFRED. There is something besides farewell that I must say to you.

GEORGE [*oblivious*]. He shall be the hero of my next romance.

ALFRED [*with a strange note of seriousness in his voice*]. Some day, George, this love of yours will break your heart.

GEORGE [*almost tragically*]. You say that after what you have done to me. [*Then again at the window, her voice low and tender.*] Look, Freddo, they are weeping.

ALFRED [*for a moment succumbing to her mood*]. You will never know what you have meant to me.

GEORGE [*almost sobbing*]. Ah, my friend, do not let the sorrow of our parting break your heart. Some day you will forget me.

ALFRED [*sadly*]. If such is fate.

GEORGE [*almost sternly*]. Our fate is what we make it.

ALFRED [*with a note of bitterness*]. Do you remember that night in Paris? "We are but marionettes," you said.

GEORGE [*her voice soft again*]. Pietro—my Pietro—

ALFRED. "Hung from the fingers of the gods." Heine stopped you as he broke his bread.

GEORGE. He eats too much. Besides Heine is a German and I mistrust him.

ALFRED. That is true of all of us, he echoed.

GEORGE [*again leaning out*]. Look at his profile in the moonlight. Worthy of Giorgione. I shall love him forever.

ALFRED. You too, George—even you—must jig to this music of fate.

GEORGE [*lyric, dominant, speaking as a priestess with a prophecy*]. There is no such thing as fate. That is what life has still to teach you. Fate is the death cry of the coward. I at least am mistress of my destiny.

ALFRED [*with a touch of cynicism, perhaps of anger in his voice*]. We shall see.

GEORGE [*in glory*]. Look! He is coming back. Yes, we shall see.

[*And she rushes over to the door and stands anxiously waiting, and in a moment she is in* PIETRO'S *arms.*]

GEORGE. Ah! How noble you were, my Pietro, and she,—she will forget.

ALFRED [*sotto voce*]. Perhaps.

GEORGE [*sadly to* ALFRED]. It is time to say farewell. Once our love was noble. May our friendship still be beautiful.

[*And she gives him her hand.* ALFRED *bends over it.*]

PAGELLO [*catching the mood*]. Alfred, will we,—we still be friends?

ALFRED [*magnificently rising to the beauty of the moment*]. George,—Pagello,—my companions, my saviors, and my friends! [*Then to* PAGELLO.] You have given life back to me. [*And then to* GEORGE.] You have taught me the nobility of love. In my silence read my gratitude. How shall we seal our trinity of trust?

[*Their three hands are almost touching. Suddenly he sees* LUCREZIA'S *stiletto at their feet. He cannot resist the romantic effect. He takes it up.*]

ALFRED. On this let us pledge our faith!

GEORGE. Yes! On this symbol of death we shall pledge our love that shall survive the tomb.

PAGELLO [*not quite liking the sight of* LUCREZIA'S *stiletto*]. No! No! Not on that! On this. It has never known hate!

[*And he tears out from under his shirt his mother's picture. Their hands close about it. The light in the night lamp flickers.*]

GEORGE [*solemnly—lyrically*]. Forever friends.

ALFRED [*echoing*]. Friends.

PAGELLO [*on the verge of tears*]. Friends.

GEORGE. And now farewell. Come, we shall see the sun rise, Pietro, and then to Padua.

[*They are about to move. Then* PAGELLO *stops embarrassed.*]

PAGELLO. But—I—

GEORGE. What? What?

PAGELLO. I have but [*His hand comes out of his pocket.*]—I'm but a poor practitioner—look, seven lire. [*And he holds them out.*] I have a little money in my office but most of what I make goes to my mother.

[GEORGE *rushes over to her desk and flings the drawer open.*]

GEORGE [*on the brink of disaster*]. Only yesterday the bill was paid. There is no money.

[*A pause. Imminent tragedy.* PAGELLO *is in despair.* GEORGE *for the second time in six months is on the verge of swooning.* ALFRED *sees his freedom tumbling; but suddenly he jumps into the breach and to the rescue. He rushes over and snatches from under his pillow the money that his mother has sent him.*]

ALFRED. Here, my friends, go, go. Love must be obeyed. Here are a thousand francs.

[*He forces the money into* PAGELLO'S *hand.*]

GEORGE [*gazing at him in admiring wonder*]. Alfred! Alfred! You have redeemed our love.

[*And again their three hands are clasped, this time over the money.*]

GEORGE. Come, love has saved us. We will see the sun rise after all. And then to Padua. Alfred, see Pietro's papa and have his things and my other trousers sent there, poste restante.

[*And she snatches her new manuscript from her writing desk and they are gone, and the door slams behind them and in the reverberating echoes* ALFRED *is heard laughing softly. Then he calls.*]

ALFRED. Paul. Paul.

PAUL [*rushing in*]. You've kept me waiting.

ALFRED [*significantly*]. History was in the making.

PAUL. And?

ALFRED [*leaning against the bed post*]. They're gone.

PAUL. If you had only left it to me. [ALFRED *laughs.*] Aren't you laughing to hide something that hurts?

ALFRED. Hurts! I am healed. [*Gayly.*] I haven't felt better since Paris.

PAUL. And what will mother say to this?

ALFRED. God bless her. She has saved me.

PAUL. Mother?

ALFRED. Yes. The thousand francs she sent me. Her money pays their way. She's bought me back. [*But the emotional strain has been too much for him. Then weakly.*] God help Pagello. Who's next? History will complete the catalogue. Sandeau—Mérimée—De Musset—Pa—

[*The curtain is descending as he speaks. The list is incompleted, whilst from the Canal the tenor's voice again singing of love for a little moment, lifts in poignant ecstasy and then dies away in the starlit stillness of the night.*]

END OF ACT II

ACT III. . . . AND LISZT PLAYS ON

The scene is a reception at Baron de Rothschild's. The room is a typical drawing-room of the period, panelled, severe, dignified, with a sense of quiet spaciousness. The furniture does not clutter the stage. What there is should be exquisite in design and lend to the general air of distinction. Down left is a fireplace, and below this is a door with a smaller drawing-room beyond. Down right is the entrance to the conservatory. Towards the rear is the entrance from the hall of the house and to the right of this a great door beyond which is the music room. If practical throughout the act, the guests should be seen coming and going, because, while not absolutely necessary, this will add to the refinedly expectant atmosphere of this soirée of tuft-hunters and celebrities. Later on a charming effect could be realized if the people in the picturesque costumes of the period could be seen, rapt and ecstatic, listening to the playing of the virtuosi. I leave the possible arrangement of the room beyond to the genius of the scene designer. It is not inevitably essential to the action of the play. The lighting is candle light, low, soft, rather too little than too glaringly distinct. Throughout the act a sound of admiring murmurs and subdued applause should be heard from the music room.

The curtain lifts on three pretty chattering girls, quaint, beruffled, beribboned. Two are on a long sofa and one is opposite or vice versa, rearranged as best accords with the charm of the decoration. It is the first great reception for these three demoiselles and their hearts and tongues are aflutter; but now the curtain is lifted and you can see and hear for yourself. They are MLLE. DE LATOUR, MLLE. ROLANDE *and* MLLE. DE FLEURY.

MLLE. DE FLEURY. I think we are too early.

MLLE. ROLANDE. I am afraid I exasperated mamma. She's in the little drawing-room. I couldn't wait until we'd started.

MLLE. DE FLEURY. How adorable of the Baron to ask us.

MLLE. ROLANDE. It was surely the idea of the Baroness.

MLLE. DE FLEURY. What matter! We're here. And as every one is going to be so important, there may as well be a few who are pretty.

[*And they laugh like children.*]

Do you like my new gown?

MLLE. ROLANDE. Quite adorable but I think I like you in gray better.

MLLE. DE FLEURY. Nonsense! [*And she turns to* MLLE. DE LATOUR *to ask her opinion, but* MLLE. DE LATOUR *sits deep in thought.*] Elise, don't try to hide your excitement by attempting to look bored.

MLLE. DE LATOUR. I was just wondering how many pages of my diary I would need to write about everything tonight. [*She looks at a huge book she holds in her lap.*]

MLLE. DE FLEURY. A hundred at least. [*Then with ill-concealed excitement.*] Do you know who is coming?

MLLE. ROLANDE. De Musset and Heine.

THE OTHER GIRLS. Yes! Yes!

MLLE. ROLANDE. And the great Franz Liszt.

MLLE. DE FLEURY. And his rival Thalberg?

MLLE. ROLANDE. I do not think so. They are seldom seen together.

MLLE. DE FLEURY. Who else? Who else?

MLLE. ROLANDE. Surely the Italian, Pagello. I saw him in the Palais Royal leaning on her arm. [*She gives a quivering stress to the "her."*]

MLLE. DE FLEURY. Is he a blond? I think blonds are so wonderful.

MLLE. ROLANDE. No, he is more wonderful than any blond. He looks like Paris of Troy.

MLLE. DE LATOUR. How do you know that?

MLLE. DE FLEURY. Elise, you have the silliest way of asking things.

[*And again they laugh merrily.*]

MLLE. ROLANDE. And Chopin, imagine, Chopin!

MLLE. DE FLEURY. Will he play?

MLLE. ROLANDE. If the whim moves him. Of course the Baroness would never ask him.

MLLE. DE LATOUR. I don't see why not.

MLLE. DE FLEURY. Elise, you are too absurd. How could one have the atrocious taste to *ask* a guest to perform? These artists are not trained monkeys who will run up a stick when you want them to.

MLLE. ROLANDE. I do not suppose we can ever understand them. Ah! these artists—they are so different from us ordinary mortals.

MLLE. DE LATOUR. Yes?

MLLE. ROLANDE. They are not moved by human passions as you and I.

MLLE. DE FLEURY. No. No.

MLLE. ROLANDE. Their life is aloof,—removed—they do not suffer as we suffer.

MLLE. DE FLEURY. No. No.

MLLE. DE LATOUR [*quite unsentimentally*]. I do not suffer.

MLLE. ROLANDE. Wait till you are a little older, Elise. Ah, have you seen this Pagello? I have been dreaming of him every night.

MLLE. DE FLEURY. I would give all the world if I could be a great artist,—a writer. There are only four things I love: literature, art, music and nature. Ah!—imagine what it would mean to see one's name in the *Revue* of the great Buloz.

MLLE. ROLANDE. He's coming too.

MLLE. DE LATOUR. I am more anxious to see *her* than any of the others.

MLLE. ROLANDE [*with awed voice*]. Her!

MLLE. DE FLEURY [*as though addressing God*]. Her!

MLLE. ROLANDE. She is removed from earthly passions. She lives in a sphere apart.

MLLE. DE LATOUR. What do you mean by that?

MLLE. DE FLEURY. Elise, you ask as many questions as a hungry parrot.

[*And they all burst into ripples of laughter. Some guests pass through the room beyond.*]

MLLE. ROLANDE. She is the greatest woman in France.

MLLE. DE FLEURY [*in astonished contradiction*]. In France, Mathilde? Why, in the whole, whole world.

MLLE. DE LATOUR. I do not see how you can decide that.

MLLE. DE FLEURY [*to silence her forever*]. No? Have you ever read [*She lowers her voice.*] "Lelia"?

MLLE. DE LATOUR. No.

MLLE. ROLANDE. Mamma forbids me to read any books of *hers*. [*Again the religious intonation.*]

MLLE. FLEURY. So does mine but my maid bought "Lelia" for me. I sat up all night reading it and I wept and wept and wept. I never enjoyed myself so much.

MLLE. DE LATOUR. Because you wept?

MLLE. ROLANDE. Of course. Elise, you are too funny.

[*And the two girls laugh together.*]

MLLE. DE LATOUR. I shall ask her to write in my album. I brought it with me.

MLLE. DE FLEURY [*springing to her feet as though shot*]. Elise, my dear, you wouldn't do that! One can see that you went to school in the country. Why, I'd rather cut off my little finger than even dare speak to her.

MLLE. DE LATOUR. I can't see why not.

[*Some guests preceded by a lackey pass through the room.*]

MLLE. ROLANDE [*over at the door*]. Quick, my dears, quick, some one has arrived.

MLLE. DE FLEURY. We mustn't miss anything. Who? Who?

MLLE. DE LATOUR [*laconically*]. It oughtn't take more than three pages of my diary.

[*Some people pass into the conservatory and the three girls flutter after them. And then the door is opened by a lackey and* BULOZ *enters. He is somewhat nervous. With him is* PAGELLO *and at their heels is* HEINE.]

BULOZ [*to* PAGELLO, *pointing to the little room on the left*]. You can wait in there, Doctor, if you wish to.

PAGELLO. But I do not understand. What has happened? I was to meet Mme. Sand and she was to present me to the Baron.

BULOZ. I don't think she has arrived yet. The moment she comes I will send for you. You will excuse me—I should say us. I have something important to say to Heine.

PAGELLO. Of course. [*He steps towards the door.*]

BULOZ. Business, you know, literary business. It's terrible being the editor of a magazine. You will find some charming books on the table in there.

HEINE. Nothing medical, Doctor, I'm afraid, but perhaps something of Mme. Sand's.

[*And* BULOZ *almost pushes* PAGELLO *out of the room and quickly closes the door behind him. Then he turns very excitedly to* HEINE.]

BULOZ. But, good God, what are we to do?

HEINE. Don't talk so quickly. Give me a moment to think.

BULOZ. In a moment that girl will be up. Nothing will stop her. I asked her to wait. I told her I'd bring Pagello down. George will be here any second. She's dining with Liszt. He's bringing her here.

HEINE. We've a moment then. That means they'll talk late.

BULOZ. Yes—

HEINE. How did you prevent Pagello seeing this Italian?

BULOZ. Whilst he was leaving his cloak I managed to get her into the picture gallery. It was by the merest chance I was at the door. As soon as she asked for him I knew something was wrong.

HEINE. Who is she?

BULOZ. His mistress. She had a letter with her. Some enemy of George has sent the girl money to come from Venice.

HEINE. Our enemies are the price we pay for fame.

BULOZ. What shall we do?

HEINE [*is silent for a moment in thought and then*]. It would be best to wait until to-morrow.

BULOZ. By tomorrow they may be gone.

HEINE. She will be able to bear it better when he is no longer in Paris.

BULOZ. It will break her heart if she is separated from him.

HEINE. I wonder—

BULOZ. She has never loved like this before. There is something mysterious, something hidden about it.

HEINE. The hidden is not always the mysterious. But when you say hidden perhaps you are right.

BULOZ. It's not as it was with de Musset. It's deeper, more profound.

HEINE. How do you know that?

BULOZ. Because she doesn't find time to write me letters telling me about her heart.

HEINE [*slowly*]. Perhaps she's reading it and hasn't time to write.

BULOZ [*thinking it out*]. If we don't tell her the girl has come she'll never forgive us for not warning her and if we do it may kill her.

HEINE. Think of the *Revue.* Don't tell her.

BULOZ. I must.

HEINE. Why?

BULOZ. Because she's the one woman in Paris who would know how to find a way to prevent it. What shall we do?

HEINE. First find our chessman, if we're to play the game. I'll see if George is in the music room. Keep Pagello in there until I warn you. Then we must get him home.

[*And as he goes into the music room and* BULOZ *in to guard* PAGELLO *some guests cross the stage on their way to the conservatory. As they enter the chatter of voices is heard and a moment later a lackey opens the door and* FRANZ LISZT *comes in, and with him is* GEORGE. *She is in an elaborate evening gown. Perhaps it is a little unusual, the conventional might even say a bit bizarre, but nevertheless she looks extraordinarily handsome and though her soul is sad she has made the most of the beautiful shoulders which* HEINE *so much admired.* LISZT *is thin, pale, distinguished, aesthetic, but not of the exquisite fragility of* CHOPIN, *who is also on his way to the reception. He is a queer mixture of impetuosity and method. A surprising streak of practicality governs his pyrotechnic nature.* GEORGE'S *manner is fraught with melancholy and deep intentions.*]

LISZT. These Parisian dinners, George—

GEORGE. I'm telling you this, Franz, because you know the human heart.

LISZT. If I do it is because I do not try to. But why haven't you told Buloz?

GEORGE. Because he wouldn't understand.

LISZT. And Heine?

GEORGE. Because he would understand too well. It's you I may need as I did this morning. He has come. He wouldn't stay at home.

LISZT. Your Pagello is a fool.

GEORGE. Poor boy, he never wants to leave me. He's afraid of being alone. He's insensible.

LISZT. Quite! Quite!

GEORGE. Weeks ago it was over and he still stays on.

LISZT. Seeking the oasis in the desert of your heart.

GEORGE. I can still respect his simplicity, but I can no longer love his naïveté.

LISZT. He needed his background of lagoons.

GEORGE [*sadly, reminiscently*]. Perhaps, perhaps.

LISZT. Alas, "Lelia"—how circumstances alter love.

GEORGE. Can you expect me to be untrue to my soul?

LISZT [*subtly*]. If you mean by that your instincts—no, never!

GEORGE. I was blind. What I thought was his purity I have found to be his emptiness.

LISZT. Lelia, I too have learned from life that nothing is so unlovely as the thing one used to love. Some day I shall write, shall I call it a symphonic poem with that idea for theme? Three movements, hope,—love—disillusion. Disillusion in the violins struggling against love in the wood-winds. Write the program for me, Lelia.

GEORGE [*disregarding the digression*]. He has cost me dearly.

LISZT. Yes, spending emotion leaves one poor.

GEORGE. I have ceased to love him and [*With a tone like a funeral knell.*] ceasing to love him I have ceased to love forever.

LISZT. When one says forever one is apt to forget tomorrow. Something must be done. He can't spend the rest of his life going from hospital to hospital studying these diseases. It isn't healthy.

GEORGE. No, you are right.

LISZT. Heine hasn't decided which is dearer to Pagello, you or these gall-stones.

GEORGE. Do not speak unkindly of him, Franz.

LISZT. Why, all you had to do was to look at his perfect profile to realize his limitations.

GEORGE. That is the way a man reasons. A woman only feels and knows she is right.

LISZT. And when the feelings change?

GEORGE [*sadly*]. Life is calling us to school.

LISZT. Paris has soon wearied of this moony medico.

GEORGE. He was once dear to me. [*And then almost tenderly.*] He still imagines that he loves me.

LISZT. Poor Pagello! Why, any man knows that love is over the day the woman begins telling herself that it will last forever.

GEORGE [*very melancholy, thinking perhaps more of herself than* PAGELLO]. Yes, yes.

LISZT. And when will this be over?

GEORGE [*quite simply*]. If things happen as I plan, tonight.

LISZT. And how?

GEORGE [*as though she might be saying "good morning"*]. I am sending him back to Venice.

[*And* LISZT *looks up barely concealing his astonishment.*]

LISZT. What?

GEORGE [*in explanation*]. It breaks my heart to see the poor boy suffer.

LISZT [*with a smile*]. So, so,—and that is why you're out of mourning.

GEORGE [*in the dark*]. Mourning?

LISZT. Yes, this is the first time since Italy that Paris has seen your shoulders. And how does Lelia manage this with Pietro?

GEORGE. He will leave tonight for Lyons.

LISZT [*smiling ever so little*]. Poor Pagello! Poor poodle! He entered Paris a triumphant captive of love and now he goes back alone.

GEORGE. No, not alone. A month ago a letter arrived from Castelfranco and with that letter my salvation.

LISZT. Salvation by post?

GEORGE [*oblivious*]. Yes, yes.

LISZT. Why not, salvation is such a little thing. Just what one wants at the moment.

GEORGE [*continuing*]. Suddenly everything was clear to me. I got money from Buloz on my new book. Pagello is the hero. [*And then quite unconscious of the subtle truth she is speaking.*] The book is almost finished.

LISZT. So is Pagello.

GEORGE. Of this money I sent her enough to come to Paris.

LISZT. Ah! His mother?

GEORGE. No! No! I am done with fathers and with mothers.

LISZT. If not his mother, then—[*He looks at her questioningly.*]

GEORGE. Yes, you are right. His mistress. The letter came as from any anonymous sympathetic friend of Pietro's here in Paris.

LISZT [*in admiration*]. So?

GEORGE. Ah, I can tell you, Franz, that friend did not spare George Sand.

LISZT. Then his mistress is the woman I met at the coach this morning?

GEORGE. Yes, she will follow him here.

LISZT. Here?

GEORGE. I came tonight because my soul needed the consolation of the music. As I tell you, he would not stay at home; but I left word where he was going.

LISZT. Swift as my technic, Lelia. You act as quickly as I play my scales. [*And he runs his fingers through the air.*]

GEORGE. If I know her, and I think I do, she will come tonight and fetch him. I cannot stand the strain a moment longer. It must end at once. I am saving him, Franz. His sadness breaks my heart.

LISZT. Alas, we poor men are but threads between the shears. [*And he makes a snapping little movement as though cutting the thread in two. Then suddenly.*] Ah! That would make a splendid finger exercise. [*And he begins trying it over and over.*] Do you know that Chopin is going to play tonight?

GEORGE [*looking up*]. Why has he refused to meet me?

LISZT. Because being an artist he has little time for art. Besides I don't think he likes you. He's very shy.

GEORGE [*as though trying to explain it to herself*]. There is something in his music as of desire, chained.

LISZT. He is the greatest artist in the world, save one.

GEORGE. Thalberg?

LISZT [*angrily*]. No, no, one Liszt. Franz Liszt. If the women keep away long enough to allow him to practice the world will hear of him.

GEORGE. And what of Chopin? Do the women bother him? These Poles are so romantic.

LISZT. Poor Frederick, he has just recovered. He and the Wodzinska. They loved as children and because she was a woman she has married some one else. It nearly broke his heart.

GEORGE [*deeply*]. Life is cruel and the most sensitive to beauty are those who suffer most. The other night at de Custines when he was playing it was as though a soul were singing—seeking.

[*And at this moment the three girls appear in the doorway whispering together and trying not to seem too rudely interested in the celebrities.*]

GEORGE. Ah, we are early, Franz. But it is just as well. I shall come back here and sit alone to listen to the music. Sorrow is but unwelcome company. [*And she sighs deeply as she glances at the three girls.*] Come, Franz, where is the Baron? I must say good evening.

LISZT. They are receiving in the conservatory.

GEORGE. Come.

[*And she goes into the conservatory, followed by* LISZT.]

MLLE. ROLANDE. That was *she*.

MLLE. DE FLEURY [*breathless*]. Yes, yes!

MLLE. DE LATOUR. Was that Pagello?

MLLE. ROLANDE. Nonsense, that was Chopin.

MLLE. DE FLEURY. No, my dear, I'm sure it was de Musset. Chopin is taller.

MLLE. ROLANDE. Did you notice how she glanced at us? Let us follow them.

MLLE. DE FLEURY. Do you think we ought?

MLLE. DE LATOUR. Why not?

MLLE. ROLANDE. We can stay at the other side of the room and seem not to be watching them.

MLLE. DE FLEURY. Isn't it all just wonderful? Did you like her dress?

MLLE. ROLANDE. That certainly was last year's bodice.

MLLE. DE LATOUR. Let's go after them.

THE OTHER GIRLS. Yes! Yes!

[*And they follow* GEORGE *and* LISZT *into the conservatory as* HEINE *comes in from the music room. He goes over to the door of the little drawing-room and calls* BULOZ.]

BULOZ [*entering*]. Well?

HEINE. She's come. They are in the conservatory. Only a few are ahead of them. They'll be back in a second.

BULOZ. They mustn't see each other. God knows what'll happen to George if that woman takes Pagello away from her. She mustn't break down for my sake.

HEINE. Your sake?

BULOZ. She's promised me three chapters before morning. We go to press at ten. Did you see how that Italian woman looked?

HEINE. Silent as a pool before the storm.

BULOZ. If it were the old George she'd meet her match.

HEINE. George is unmatchable.

BULOZ [*at his wit's end*]. Well, what will come of it?

[*And indeed at this moment there is a sound of voices from the hall.*]

BULOZ. Chopin has arrived. Hear them buzz.

HEINE [*mischievously, with a sort of impish prophecy*]. The toy box is too crowded. Some of the dolls will be broken. Pagello—George—this girl—and Chopin come in the nick of time, perhaps, to play an obligato to their parting. [*He begins laughing quietly to himself.*] The gods are busy at the strings. Come, Buloz, let us dance, dance!

[*And at this moment from one side of the stage enters* CHOPIN *escorted by a lackey and from the conservatory opposite comes* GEORGE *followed by* LISZT. *And as they come forward* GEORGE *and* FREDERICK *stop and look at each other even as Tristan and Isolde and as all other mortals who are doomed to love have looked since the beginning of time when Adam—or was it Eve—looked and thus began the trouble.*]

LISZT [*rushing forward to* CHOPIN]. Frederick!

[*And* CHOPIN *speaks. He is fragile, exquisite, spiritual. There is something about him as of flame and sleep. He is simple and profound, childlike and dominant, his whims are emotional necessities. He is part reticent reserve and part sudden irritability. Withal he is a genius who in the words of Balzac was less a musician than a soul which makes itself audible.*]

CHOPIN. Good evening, Franz. Ah, Heine,—Buloz—

HEINE [*with elaborate and fantastic ceremony*]. May it be my privilege to present the matchless composer of the B Minor Scherzo to the peerless creator of the immortal Lelia.

[*And* GEORGE *gives* CHOPIN *her hand and he bends over to press it to his lips.*]

CHOPIN [*kissing her fingers*]. Madame.

GEORGE [*as their eyes meet as he straightens up*]. You have suffered, that is why you can sing. You must come some time with Franz to see me.

CHOPIN. Madame.

[*He again bows and she turns to* HEINE.]

LISZT [*to* CHOPIN]. Shall I present you to the Baron?

HEINE. I can hear Olympus rumbling with almighty laughter.

[*And as* LISZT *and* CHOPIN *cross to the right of the stage* HEINE *and* GEORGE *cross to the left.*]

LISZT [*low to* CHOPIN]. What do you think of her?

CHOPIN [*low to* LISZT]. Her eyes are too large but she is less impossible than I thought.

HEINE [*low to* GEORGE]. What do you think of him?

GEORGE [*low to* HEINE]. His chin is weak but he is more of a man than I had imagined.

[*And at this moment the three girls appear, still hunting the celebrities, and as* CHOPIN *and* LISZT *go in to the conservatory* LISZT *stops to chat with them and then he and the adoring girls exit to follow* CHOPIN.]

GEORGE [*sitting down*]. Chopin alone can make this party bearable. The Baron is a charming gentleman, but his guests are too wealthy to be anything but stupid.

BULOZ [*aside to* HEINE]. What shall I do?

HEINE. Tell her now.

BULOZ [*coming forward—nervously*]. Good evening, George.

GEORGE. Ah, Buloz. Now I know what you're going to say. [BULOZ *starts.*]

HEINE. Not this time, George.

GEORGE. Heine, please don't begin quoting Faust in that horrid guttural German, and you, Buloz, don't jump at my throat and shriek for those last two chapters. You shall have them by tomorrow.

HEINE [*trying to lead up*]. Perhaps you mayn't write tonight, George.

GEORGE. Nothing but death can stop me.

BULOZ [*desperately*]. Why should we beat about the bush?

GEORGE [*lightly*]. Why not? That's one way of stirring the birds to sing.

HEINE. To sing? First they may fly away.

GEORGE. Questing the eternal fires of the dawn. Ah, that's a fine phrase.

[*And she takes a tiny pencil from a little bag hanging at her waist and jots down the words on one of the panels of her fan.*]

BULOZ [*guardedly, darkly, attempting to begin*]. George, I believe in you.

GEORGE [*lightly*]. Of course you do. Don't you print me?

BULOZ [*lugubriously*]. George—

GEORGE. You sound as if you were reciting Corneille.

[*He hesitates and looks across the room for help from* HEINE, *but* HEINE *is deep in a book he has lifted from the table.*]

BULOZ [*clearing his throat and attempting to go on*]. You are strong, you can control—

[*Embarrassed, he stops short.*]

GEORGE. Are you writing my obituary?

BULOZ. Be brave. Remember you have children.

[*And* GEORGE *springs up and for a second goes white and leans half fainting against her chair.*]

GEORGE. My God! My children! Maurice, Solange. Have they fever? Are they dead?

BULOZ. No, George, it is not your children, but—

[*And the next second the light breaks in* GEORGE'S *face and she can hardly suppress an exclamation of long hoped for relief. And all the while* HEINE *stands scrutinizing her.*]

GEORGE. What is it? Tell me. Tell me.

BULOZ [*speaking very slowly. He is doing his stumbling best to keep from hurting her too suddenly*]. Remember, France, the world, has need of you.

GEORGE. Is it all preface? Begin—Begin.

BULOZ [*he stops and wipes his monocle*]. Well—

GEORGE. Yes.

BULOZ [*carefully, with deep pity for her, watching the effect*]. Pagello's mistress has come from Italy.

[*And to his amazement she takes the news quite calmly. Indeed in a way that puzzles him. But* HEINE'S *eyes never leave her face.*]

GEORGE. Lucrezia?

BULOZ. She is waiting in the hall for him.

GEORGE [*solemnly, as though she felt* HEINE'S *eyes*]. It is the hand of heaven. Fate doesn't mean that I should keep him from her any longer.

[*And a sound of voices is heard beyond in the hall—A lackey's and a woman's voice in remonstrance and the door is thrown open and* LUCREZIA *rushes in.*]

LUCREZIA. He is here, I tell you. I will wait no longer. [*Then she sees* GEORGE.] You! You! Where are your breeches?

BULOZ. Not so loud, Madame. The greatest pianist in the world is about to improvise in the music room.

HEINE. Whilst fate is improvising here. [*And then almost inaudibly.*] Fate—or George.

LUCREZIA [*threateningly to* GEORGE]. Once before you drove him dumb with your words. This time I shall speak.

GEORGE [*quite unflustered*]. Yes, apparently, apparently. And how is Venice? Do tame nightingales still sing on every balcony and are there still fresh oysters on every door-step?

LUCREZIA [*pointing to the letter in her hand*]. I know all, all.

HEINE. Rivalling the Omnipotent. Does she mean George or God?

LUCREZIA. Madonna, what have you done to him?

GEORGE. What have I done to him? Perhaps the greatest thing any woman can do for any man. I have given him his soul.

LUCREZIA. It is all written here. [*And she waves her letter in* GEORGE'S *face.*] This friend of Pietro's knows the lies your heart hides and has told me all. Caro mio Pietro. [*And to stifle back her tears her voice goes louder.*] Pietro!

[*And the door of the little drawing-room opens and* PAGELLO *enters, an open book in his hand.*]

PAGELLO [*on the threshold, not seeing* LUCREZIA]. Did some one call me?

HEINE. Yes, Doctor, a voice from beyond the Alps.

PAGELLO. I do not understand this poetical way you have of saying things. Ah, George, good evening.

GEORGE [*a bit mournfully but nevertheless leading in the right direction*]. "Good evening"?—No, my friend, not good evening but alas, good-bye.

PAGELLO [*as usual a bit mystified*]. What?

GEORGE [*unable to resist the cadence*]. Good-bye—forever.

[*And in a second all is clear because as he looks up for an explanation he sees* LUCREZIA *and he stumbles back against the sofa and the book falls from his hand.*]

PAGELLO. San Giovanni,—San Pietro,—San Paolo,—San Luichele—

HEINE [*low to* BULOZ]. This is a splendid chance to learn the Italian calendar.

BULOZ [*his eyes on* GEORGE]. Will she be strong enough to bear it?

PAGELLO. Santa Maria, you—you—Where have you come from?

GEORGE. From Italy, Pietro, moonlit Italy.

[*And in the next room* CHOPIN *can be heard improvising.*]

GEORGE. Ah, Madame, life has taught me much. I have wronged you, wronged you deeply.

LUCREZIA [*to* PAGELLO]. Come away, she is beginning to talk.

PAGELLO [*hardly recovered from the shock*]. How did you get here, Lucrezia?

LUCREZIA. You have a friend in Paris, Pietroninni. One who hates this George Sand. [*And she again points to the letter.*]

GEORGE. Madame, alas, there are many such. The rich because I would enrich the poor, the wise because I pity fools.

BULOZ [*aside to* HEINE]. She is magnificent.

HEINE. Yes, perhaps more so than you think.

GEORGE. In Venice, Madame, I wronged you. In Paris I ask your pardon. [*She steps toward* LUCREZIA *but the girl, protecting* PAGELLO, *backs into a corner.*] Ah, Madame, do not shrink from me. Love has taught me humility. Though it breaks my heart I give him back to you.

LUCREZIA [*shrieking*]. You do not give him. He comes. He comes.

[*And at this moment* LISZT'S *head pops in at the door.*]

LISZT. Shhh! my dears! If you are playing charades be a little quieter. You're disturbing the music Chopin is improvising. [*And then he lowers his voice to a whisper and hushes them with his lifted finger.*] Piano! Piano! [*Then he sees* LUCREZIA *and begins thoughtlessly to bubble over.*] Ah—so, George,—she—you—

[*But* GEORGE *is ready and suddenly she turns to him and speaks as though nothing but the answer to her question mattered.*]

GEORGE. Isn't that Thalberg playing? It's like his touch.

LISZT [*swiftly, almost angrily*]. No, no. Chopin. Only Chopin can play like that. Listen, ah, that phrasing—such delicacy, such nuance. Listen to that modulation.

GEORGE. And can you modulate so beautifully, my friend?

[*And the message has registered not unseen by* HEINE.]

LISZT [*his whole manner changing, looking at* LUCREZIA]. What a beautiful girl! Is she an artist come to dance the Tarantula?

HEINE. No, she is an avenging fury whose wings are clipped.

GEORGE [*peering through him*]. That is very cryptic, Heine.

HEINE [*smiling back*]. Perhaps, George, but not too deep for you to read.

[*There is a pause.* CHOPIN *has reached a brilliant passage and instinctively they all stop to listen.*]

LISZT. Ah! Beauty made audible. Singing starlight.

LUCREZIA [*in utter disgust*]. Monkey!

LISZT. Ah! [*His hand lifted in ecstatic admiration.*] The moment's inspiration—

GEORGE [*as the music swells and dies*]. The heritage of all the years.

[*And* LISZT, *softly closing the door behind him, goes back into the music room.*]

LUCREZIA [*to* PAGELLO]. Come away, Pietro, these people are all crazy. They rattle in their heads.

PAGELLO [*at a loss. It is all too much for him*]. George—

GEORGE. Go, Pietro, I shall be brave. My blessings follow you, my friend. Life must be answered—youth be heard. She is Sarah come from the South to call you. I am as Hagar cast without. But in the wilderness I shall find my peace. My little Ishmaels are calling me.

HEINE. She's a little mixed, but what difference does it make—they're Italians.

GEORGE. Under the trees at Nohant I shall find forgetfulness and rest. Do not forget me, Pietro. [*And she bends over to kiss him a last farewell.*]

LUCREZIA [*in a corner, her hands twitching*]. Madonna mia. She's a witch.

GEORGE. No, no, Pietro. [*Thru habit and not knowing what to do he is about to kiss her on the lips.*] No, no, not on the lips—the brow, my friend, the brow, as you would kiss a sister. [*And thus nobly and sadly they embrace.*] Good-bye, my brother.

[*And then* LUCREZIA *is over next to him, her arm thru his and they are moving towards the door.*]

PAGELLO [*suddenly stopping*]. But—[*And instinctively his hand goes to his pocket.*] I—I [*And at a loss just how to put it.*]—I am but a poor practitioner.

GEORGE [*thoughtfully*]. Pietro, it seems to me I've heard you say that same thing once before.

[*There is an embarrassed pause but in an instant she is ready.*]

GEORGE. Of course, of course. Buloz, advance me a thousand francs. They may need it. You shall have two books for it instead of one. The writing will help me to forget. Go with them, remember they are strangers in this whirling world of Paris.

HEINE [*with significance*]. Strange as two babies at a ball.

[*And as* PAGELLO *comes over tenderly to shake her hand in gratitude,* LUCREZIA *keeps hold of his other hand with a sort of instinctive feeling that he won't be safe until out of sight of* GEORGE.]

HEINE [*aside to* BULOZ]. Michael Angelo alone could do justice to that group.

GEORGE. Come, Buloz, see these two children on their way. You remember the coach for Lyons leaves the Post Hotel at nine.

[*And she is over at the door with* PAGELLO *and* LUCREZIA.]

HEINE [*sotto voce to* BULOZ *as he moves towards them*]. It was on this very coach that she started with de Musset.

BULOZ. Well, what of it?

HEINE. If this sort of thing goes on the people of the diligence should make her an allowance.

GEORGE. Good-bye, my brother. [*And then even more beautifully.*] Good-bye, my new-found sister.

[*And at this moment the* CHOPIN *improvisation is over and a burst of applause sounds from the next room.*]

GEORGE [*unperturbed*]. Love will protect you.

[*And she stretches out her hand to* PIETRO *and he bends over and kisses it. And she offers her hand to* LUCREZIA *but the girl refuses it and suddenly turns and faces her.*]

LUCREZIA [*all the passion in her spilling over*]. Corpo di Cristo, I will not take your hand. I am an Italian and I do not forget. Dio! And I do not forgive. What you have stolen I have taken back. Maladetta! What you have taught him I shall profit by.

[*And half dragging, half embracing her recaptured Doctor, they are gone and* BULOZ *with them.* GEORGE *for a moment stands looking after them, a sad little smile in her eyes. Then she turns to* HEINE.]

GEORGE. Ah, Heine, youth is the one thing worth having longest. She is glorious. Mark my words, my friend, the world shall yet be saved by women.

HEINE. Then as their first priestess let me tender you my homage. [*And he gallantly kisses her hand.*] If you ever cease writing, George, go on the stage. Melpomene herself could not have played it better.

GEORGE. Yes—I wrote that letter, Heine.

HEINE. Ah, my prophetic soul.

GEORGE. Poor Pietro could never have managed it alone.

HEINE [*seriously*]. George, I have ever loved you.

GEORGE [*lightly*]. Too late, too late, my German. My soul is turning gray.

HEINE. That is why my admiration for you means the more. Tell them to carve upon your tombstone: "Here lies George the indefatigable."

GEORGE. That doesn't interest me. I won't be there to read it.

HEINE. You'll probably outlive us all.

GEORGE. No, Heine, you are wrong. [*And then as irrefutable proof.*] I've just had my old mattresses recovered and I regret it. It wasn't worth while for the little time I still contemplate living. I am going to an island in the Mediterranean to die. Wait and see, time will tell.

HEINE. Time tells nothing. Leave it to your biographers.

GEORGE [*though a minute ago life was over*]. What! Never! I'll forestall their lies and some day, like Rousseau, I'll confess in twenty volumes. [*Then sadly.*] My heart is a graveyard.

HEINE. Don't you mean a cemetery, George?

[*And at this moment a lackey opens the door from the hall and* ALFRED DE MUSSET *enters, his mother leaning on his arm. It is their first meeting since Italy.*]

MME. DE MUSSET [*stepping forward and cordially taking* GEORGE'S *hand*]. Alfred has told me all. [*And* GEORGE *is as near hysterical surprise as she has ever come in her life.*]

MME. DE MUSSET. A mother's thanks for all that you have done for him. Yes, I know how patiently you nursed him thru his sunstroke and sat at his bedside bathing his brow and giving him his milk.

GEORGE [*equal even to this*]. I promised you that I would care for him.

MME. DE MUSSET. And you have, you have. A mother's gratitude goes out to you.

[*And in her enthusiasm she bends over and kisses* GEORGE, *and* HEINE, *who has been watching* ALFRED—*who stands like a monument trying to solve a riddle—comes to the rescue.*]

HEINE [*bowing to* MME. DE MUSSET]. May I have the honor of escorting you to the Baron?

MME. DE MUSSET [*taking his arm*]. We are very late.

[*Again the piano sounds from the music room.*]

GEORGE [*a little more enthusiastically than she realizes*]. Ah, that is Chopin. Liszt is to play later in the evening.

MME. DE MUSSET. Are you coming in, Madame?

GEORGE. No, I shall sit here alone to listen. I am not well, Madame. I do not like the crowd.

MME. DE MUSSET [*as she reaches the door*]. I shall see you later then, at supper?

HEINE. At supper,—of course.

GEORGE. If I stay, but alas, Madame, I am so spent. [*And she heaves a deep sigh.*] I do not know what will happen to me.

[*As indeed she doesn't. And* GEORGE *and* ALFRED *are left alone.*]

GEORGE [*sadly*]. That was kind of Heine. I wanted to see you, Alfred, once before I left Paris. I'm very tired.

ALFRED. You're overworking. You should break with Buloz. He expects too much of you.

GEORGE. No, it isn't that. [*And then slowly.*] I have just sent Pietro back to Venice.

ALFRED [*as the memories stir*]. Ah—

GEORGE. All is over. It is the end,—the end.

ALFRED. Go down to the country, you will rest there out in the open. It is quiet under the trees.

GEORGE [*wearily*]. It is a quiet deeper than the silence of Nohant that I seek.

ALFRED. You mean—

GEORGE. Yes, my friend. I welcome it as a long rest after a too long journey. I can no longer live with dignity.

ALFRED. You've been like this before. Why, by tomorrow—

GEORGE. No. No. That was long ago. [*A nocturne of exquisite melancholy sounds from the music room.*] Tomorrow bears but the same sad burden as today. I shall miss only the sound of my children's voices. Solange is so sweet—you should see her, Alfred. I can hardly keep from weeping when I kiss her. I shall miss my children and the feel of the wind in my face. I adore the wind. It is the symbol of perpetual energy.

ALFRED. Blowing nowhere and forever—but such is life.

GEORGE [*sadly. It is her tragic moment*]. And such is love. We are like leaves tossed in the wind of desire. Do you remember that night in Venice in the window? I laughed at you and your fear of fate. But you were right, Alfred. Destiny has piped and I have danced—and now I'm tired.

ALFRED. And love?

GEORGE [*and from her heart comes a cry of bitterness*]. Love, alas, I have called to love and it has answered me with lies. I am done with that delusion. It is nature's trick to make us fools. It is empty, empty. You remember you gave me a message at parting in Venice. Now I shall give you one. [*And she holds out her hand to him.*] Store up the gold of life in youth, my friend, whilst you can still believe this lie that men call love.

ALFRED [*bending over her hand and kissing it*]. Good-bye.

[*And he goes into the conservatory and as* GEORGE *is about to sit down on the long sofa near the fireplace she sees the book that* PIETRO *has dropped and she picks it up.*]

GEORGE [*perhaps she is weeping a little. She reads the title*]. "Lelia." Faithful to the last. Finis. Finis. [*And she glances toward the little room through which* PAGELLO *and* LUCREZIA *have gone.*] Adieu, Pagello! [*And she lets the little book fall to the table and then she looks toward the conservatory through which* DE MUSSET *has gone.*] Adieu, Freddo. [*And then she looks into the fire as though bidding a last farewell.*] Adieu, love!

[*And she sits gazing for a moment into the flame. A pause. And a little later a tremendous burst of applause sounds from the music room. The nocturne is finished. Another sound of voices, then more applause and then* CHOPIN *bursts in from the music room followed by* LISZT; *and the three young girls all aflutter are crowded in the doorway. From her deep seat next the fireplace* GEORGE *is almost invisible.*]

CHOPIN [*irritable, excited*]. No, no. No more. I'm tired.

LISZT. The humming fools. Give them the B Minor Scherzo, Frederick.

CHOPIN. No, no. No more. No more.

MLLE. DE ROLANDE *and* MLLE. DE FLEURY. Ah! Ah!

MLLE. DE LATOUR. He's probably tired. Look how white he is.

MLLE. DE FLEURY. Have you ever heard anything so divine?

MLLE. ROLANDE. Positively beguiling, my dear. I—

CHOPIN [*low to* LISZT]. Get them away. Get them away.

LISZT [*with exaggerated politeness*]. Ladies, your pardon.

[*And he slowly closes the door. And the three demoiselles sink back into the music room.*]

CHOPIN. It distresses me to play before a crowd like that.

LISZT. Do you know that in the middle of your most beautiful pianissimi one of those fat hyenas sneezed?

CHOPIN. I didn't notice it.

LISZT [*amazed*]. What, why I hear everything when I perform.

CHOPIN. I like best playing for my beloved Poles. They are breathless when an artist plays.

[*More applause from the next room. Then* MLLE. DE FLEURY *and* MLLE. ROLANDE *are back.*]

MLLE. DE FLEURY [*to* CHOPIN]. Monsieur, the people are clamoring for you.

CHOPIN. Ladies, you must excuse me.

MLLE. ROLANDE. But we beseech you.

CHOPIN. You must pardon me. I am sorry to refuse. [*And as he turns away he unknowingly drops his handkerchief. The applause sounds again.*] Franz, for God's sake go in and appease them. I want to be alone. Alone.

[*And the two girls flutter up to* LISZT *with exclamations of admiration. And as* CHOPIN *turns from them barely concealing his irritation,* MLLE. DE FLEURY *swiftly lifts his handkerchief from the floor and with a look as though she were robbing a shrine of the sacred "bambino," she stuffs the precious relic into her bodice and* GEORGE *who is watching smiles. This is unseen by all the others.* MLLE. ROLANDE *and* LISZT *are at the door. Then* MLLE. DE FLEURY *joins them, and as they enter the music room* LISZT *is greeted with a salvo of approval. The door is closed and then* CHOPIN *begins walking up and down. He is warm. He wants to mop his brow. He is nervous. He looks at a picture. Then again for his handkerchief. It is gone. This increases his irritation. He sits down, still feeling in his pockets; and then—and it sounds as if it came from nowheres—* GEORGE *speaks. And as she does so* CHOPIN *jumps up not knowing from whence it came.*]

GEORGE. Here, take mine. [*And she hands him her handkerchief.*]

CHOPIN [*taking it*]. Ah, you. Thank you, Madame.

GEORGE. Sit down, you must be very tired. Sit down and rest.

CHOPIN. Yes. Yes.

GEORGE. I can't imagine anything more frightful than having to face a room of people like that. It must be so much more wonderful to play for two or three.

CHOPIN. I like best to play for only one. That is when I can "speak."

GEORGE. Yes—

CHOPIN. I always choose some one to whom I play. Tonight there was no one in there who interested me.

GEORGE. Your art is the most fragile of all the arts. It is born of the moment and as it lives it dies.

CHOPIN. Yes. Yes. [*He begins walking about again.*]

GEORGE. Oh, don't be alarmed, I'm not going to talk music. Would you like some champagne? Shall I call a lackey?

CHOPIN. No. Let us sit quietly for a while.

[*And they do so, listening to the music.*]

CHOPIN [*after a moment*]. That is a beautiful melody but in a second he will spoil it with his fireworks.

[GEORGE *doesn't answer. Then after a little while he goes on.*]

CHOPIN. I have never read any of your books.

GEORGE [*unconcerned*]. No?

CHOPIN. No. Listen! Music should have more soul and less speed. [*A pause.*] You do not answer me. [*Another pause.*] You are so different from other women. You seem to know how to be still.

GEORGE [*smiling*]. I am listening to you.

CHOPIN. Some day I will come and play for you.

GEORGE [*unmoved*]. Yes?

CHOPIN [*a bit piqued at her lack of enthusiasm*]. I do not do that often.

GEORGE. No, I am sure of that.

[*There is another pause. Then* GEORGE *speaks. Something stirs in the ashes of her heart.*]

GEORGE. Why have you avoided me since you've been in Paris?

CHOPIN. I was afraid of you.

GEORGE. Afraid? If that is a compliment it is too roundabout.

CHOPIN. From a distance you seemed, shall I say—[*He hesitates for a word.*]

GEORGE [*lightly*]. Formidable.

CHOPIN. No—er—[*Then he gets it.*] complicated.

GEORGE. You have chosen badly. I am really very simple. [*Then with a shake of her head because she really means it.*] Too simple for my good.

[*And he looks at her and she turns away and gazes into the fire. Another pause.*]

CHOPIN. Weren't you at the Marquis de Custine's last Saturday?

GEORGE [*almost carelessly*]. Yes.

CHOPIN. I didn't meet you.

GEORGE. No, I left early.

CHOPIN. But women always want to meet me.

GEORGE. You're very shy.

CHOPIN. I thought I saw you looking at me when I was playing.

GEORGE. And so beautifully—

CHOPIN. I was dreaming of some one long ago.

GEORGE. Yes.

CHOPIN. Why did you leave so early?

GEORGE. I went home to work.

CHOPIN. At night?

GEORGE. Yes. Till four in the morning.

CHOPIN. My art too is exacting. Sometimes I practice ten hours a day.

GEORGE [*as she glances at him, she is thinking of her writing but, alas, how often people mean one thing and say another*]. I have been practicing all my life.

CHOPIN. One of these days I must read something you've written.

GEORGE. Why?

CHOPIN. I do not read much.

GEORGE. There are too many books. It is life that really matters. [*A note of sadness comes into her voice.*] Life!

CHOPIN. You are sad, Madame?

GEORGE. Alas, my friend, I have suffered.

[*She looks at him tenderly, then back into the flames.*]

CHOPIN [*slowly. It is to very few he would say this, but she is different*]. I understand, Madame. I too have lived.

GEORGE [*expectantly*]. Yes?

[*A pause. She waits for him to go on but he is silent.*]

GEORGE. Some day, perhaps, you will care to tell me?

CHOPIN [*perhaps he is a little embarrassed*]. Listen! Liszt is playing the "Liebestraum." Less than Beethoven—but 'twill serve. Listen!

GEORGE. Yes. You are right. I too cannot abide these people who are an Æolian harp thru which their grief is forever moaning. [*She is in danger. She is beginning to forget herself. She glances at him. He is listening to the music.*] It is a love that has lasted long, my friend? [*Her hand is on his.*]

CHOPIN. Since my boyhood. I do not know why I tell you this.

GEORGE [*very tenderly*]. That is the only love that matters. So you too have been lonely.

CHOPIN. I've been alone for all my life.

GEORGE. That is the sad melody that runs through life. We are forever seeking companionship whilst in reality we are forever alone, alone.

[*And her voice drifts away on the sweet sadness of the word.*]

CHOPIN. Yes. I must come and play for you.

GEORGE. I shall listen with my soul.

[*A little flame stirs in the ashes. Is it the spell of the music that moves her?*]

CHOPIN. You are not like what I thought.

GEORGE. No?

CHOPIN. I imagined you were always talking philosophy.

GEORGE. That's what the world thinks of literary people. The truth is I seldom mention books.

CHOPIN. Franz told me that you were the cleverest woman in Paris.

GEORGE. I thought he was my friend.

CHOPIN. There are days when I cannot abide Paris and these crowds of brilliant people. [*He looks towards the music room.*]

GEORGE. Yes, I know what you mean. I too have felt that. Why don't you go away?

CHOPIN. I would but though I dislike people, I don't like being all alone. It gives me a feeling of peace to know there is some one to whom I can go—some one who will understand.

GEORGE [*for the first time looking him straight in the eyes*]. Yes. That is the perfect companion. Some one you know is there and still never feel about you. I have tried many but all have failed, even Alfred.

CHOPIN. Does such a one exist?

GEORGE. In dreams perhaps.

[*And she is languorously fanning herself whilst in the music room* LISZT *plays "The Lorelei."*]

CHOPIN. What a delicious odor.

GEORGE. "Lily of Japan." Pagello bought it for me in the Palais Royal with his last two francs. But the odor was too strong for him. That's why he's run away to Venice.

CHOPIN [*looking at her*]. With such a person far away—

GEORGE [*lightly but still with a faint sense of suggestion*]. In a blue isle in the Mediterranean shall we say? I too have been dreaming of the South.

CHOPIN [*smiling back at her fantasy*]. Yes. Why not? The Mediterranean—

GEORGE [*leaning back a little, her tongue wetting her lips, goes on with the delicious nonsense*]. Where the tropic palms droop in the odorous shadows and the scarlet flamingoes sleep in the sun.

[*She likes this and begins jotting it down on her fan.*]

CHOPIN. What are you doing?

GEORGE [*almost sprightly*]. I just thought of what I must order for luncheon tomorrow. [*And she repeats as she writes.*]—Scarlet flamingoes.

CHOPIN. Flamingoes for lunch?

GEORGE. Why not? Perhaps you will come and dine with me.

CHOPIN. Perhaps. You are the one woman in Paris who doesn't bore me.

GEORGE [*laughing*]. What! Go back to your island, my friend.

CHOPIN. No. Do not think I am jesting. If for a while I could break away from all this cleverness. [*And again he waves his hand with a gesture of disgust towards the music room.*] There in this mythical island I could realize my dreams and give to the world all the music that struggles and mounts in my heart.

GEORGE [*whimsically*]. And if you go I shall follow you and lie quietly listening among the ferns. [*He looks at her. She looks back. There is a pause. Then jestingly, laughingly.*] Or perhaps we might go together.

CHOPIN [*slowly*]. Why not? Why not?

GEORGE [*her hand again touching his. Her voice low*]. Why not? [*The light of the fire shines about them.*] Some day, perhaps. [*Half prophetically, half in subconscious hope.*] Some day.

[*And* CHOPIN *sits looking at her and she leans back, her eyes slightly closed.*]

CHOPIN. I am so tired.

GEORGE [*leaning towards him*]. Shall I drive you home?

CHOPIN. Would you? [*And he smiles at her wanly, sweetly.*]

GEORGE. Poor boy, you are very tired, aren't you? [*A pause, she is closer to him.*] There is something about you so like my little son.

CHOPIN. Yes?

GEORGE. And do you know what I should do if you were he?

CHOPIN. No.

GEORGE. This, my poor tired child—this.

[*And like a mother—indeed love and the mother in her are mixed beyond comprehension—she takes him in her arms and kisses him and the next instant she awakes to the calamitous rashness of her deed.*]

GEORGE. What have I done? What have I done? Can you ever forgive me?

CHOPIN [*bending towards her*]. Why not?

GEORGE [*springing up as once before she has done in Venice*]. Now I realize it all. For weeks the ecstasy of your music has sustained my fainting spirit. All the while I have loved you, loved you as I have never loved before, loved when I thought that love was over forever—and I haven't known. And now that I have told you, good-bye. [*She rushes from him.*]

CHOPIN [*his voice low*]. Wait! Wait! You mustn't leave me now, now at the beginning.

GEORGE [*struggling with her heart*]. No, no. I am done with love. I have prayed to love and it has come to hurt me. No, no. Not again, not again. I am through with love forever.

CHOPIN [*his arm is about her*]. This is the beginning. We have found each other in our loneliness. You have brought peace to my heart. [*His lips are close to hers.*] George! George, nothing else matters. This is the beginning.

[*And he kisses her. A pause. And then she breaks from him. There are tears in her eyes. For a moment she stands watching him, the old wonder ever new breaks in her heart. He comes over to her. His voice is very gentle.*]

CHOPIN. You know you said that you would drive me home.

GEORGE [*and all that she has forgotten and all that she hopes are in the words*]. You mean?

CHOPIN. If you are willing—yes.

[*And again they are in each other's arms. Tableau! From beyond sounds the music. She has lost her head. This is rash. Some one may come in. She breaks away from him. He follows her.*]

GEORGE [*she looks about her*]. No, no. This is not the Mediterranean. There are too many lackeys. [*She steps towards the door.*]

CHOPIN. But aren't you going to drive me home?

GEORGE. And if I should tell the coachman to drive to this island in the sea?

CHOPIN. I should follow you. There is too much art in Paris. Come.

GEORGE [*swiftly*]. A moment. A word to Buloz lest he wait for me.

[*And impetuously she tears out the fly leaf from the copy of "Lelia" lying on the table and scrawls some words and then:*]

GEORGE. Chopin, we may be driving to the world's end.

CHOPIN. To the sound of music. Come.

[*And they rush out as very cautiously from the music room enters* MLLE. DE LATOUR *with her autograph album in her hand followed by* MLLE. ROLANDE.]

MLLE. DE LATOUR [*looking about*]. Why, I thought she was in here.

MLLE. ROLANDE. Probably they're in the supper room.

MLLE. DE LATOUR. I'm going to ask her. I may never see her again. I don't care what Agnès says.

[*And they run out through the little drawing-room to the applause which sounds from the music room as* HEINE *opens the door and comes in.*]

HEINE [*calling*]. Frederick! Where is he?

[*And* BULOZ *bustles in from the hall.*]

HEINE. Where's Chopin?

BULOZ. Gone!

HEINE. Gone! The Baroness was hoping he would play again. Liszt seems tied to the piano. Nothing can budge him.

BULOZ. No.

HEINE. I'll ask George to read a chapter of "Lelia" [*He takes the book from the table.*]; that will quiet him.

BULOZ. She's gone.

HEINE. What? She too.

BULOZ. I saw them leave together.

HEINE. Together? [*He looks surprised.*]

BULOZ. Yes. Why not? Can't a man and a woman drive from a party without the world coming to an end? She left me this. [*He points to the note in his hand.*] It's written on the half title of "Lelia."

HEINE. Perhaps you can print it in the *Revue.*

BULOZ [*with a quick look*]. Not yet. Read it, Heine.

[*And* HEINE *does so and in his amazement he lets the note flutter to the floor.*]

BULOZ. And how long this time, Heine?

HEINE. How long? How long? Does it matter? Think of the copy it will make and how the world will revel in it. And now—let's go in to supper.

[*And as they exit* MLLE. DE FLEURY *comes in from the music room on her way to join* MLLE. DE LATOUR *and* MLLE. ROLANDE. *Suddenly she sees the note which* HEINE *has let fall. She picks it up.*]

MLLE. DE FLEURY [*with swimming eyes as she reads it*]. "Good-night, Buloz, don't wait for me. Life is love. That's all that matters. I've taken Chopin home to put the poor, tired boy to bed."

[*And she clutches the note to her trembling heart.*]

MLLE. DE FLEURY [*tenderly, lit with the thrilling romance of it all*]. How beautiful! How beautiful!

[*And the curtain falls as* LISZT, *the untiring, thunders from the music room the beginning of a brilliant Polonaise.*]

THE END

YOU AND I

By Philip Barry

PHILIP BARRY

[1896–]

A skilled interpreter of modern temper and technique, Philip Barry has created several studies of character often as subtle, if not as profound, as those of O'Neill. After his graduation from Yale in 1919 he attended Baker's 47 Workshop at Harvard, out of which grew his first play, *You and I*, in 1923. In addition to his activities as a playwright, Barry was for a time with the Department of State at Washington and served in the American Embassy in London.

Following the "smart and substantial success" of *You and I*,[1] Barry wrote *The Youngest* (1924), which concerns the reaction of the youngest son against a socially conservative family in an Eastern town. The next year Barry's penetrating *In a Garden* revealed an interest in states of mind and their generative qualities if properly manipulated, an interest to reappear later in *Hotel Universe*. The theme of *In a Garden* concerns the stratagem of a playwright husband, who is a close student of human nature, to determine whether his wife has previously had a love affair with another man. The scheme is to arrange a meeting between the two in question amid the same surroundings, a certain garden, in which their romance is supposed to have occurred. The states of mind thus re-created by duplicate environment awaken the former love; the man's proposal of flight secures a favorable hearing, since the wife has become impatient with her husband who is so absorbed in observing life that he has forgotten how to live it. But the wife learns that the first garden scene was also prearranged and she is skeptical of both lover and husband. Here we see Barry delving into aspects of character and psychology after the fashion of many contemporary writers.

White Wings (1926) is a burlesque comedy depicting the vicissitudes of social position in a world subject to violent change; the ideas are humorously portrayed in the decline of a great family of street-cleaners and the rise of their social inferiors who invented the automobile. The following year *Paris Bound* continued Barry's discussion of the marriage problem; owing to an unforeseen stray kiss, the wife of an unfaithful husband learns how easy is the way of temptation and decides that one adventure on the part of her husband is not sufficient reason for wrecking a marriage. The question of the double standard is here involved by making the woman's kiss approximately equal to the greater fault in the man. *John*, also produced in 1927, concerns the Biblical Baptist who is an evangelist unable to understand the significance of the event he is foretelling.

[1] *Theatre Arts Monthly*, July, 1927.

The Aristotelian idea of tragedy is illustrated in the death of John at a moment of exaltation. In Barry's next play, *Holiday* (1928), is pictured a struggling youth who sees in his heiress-love an opportunity to escape from his economic shackles and to catch up with life. His desire to live life, however, is thwarted by the insistence of the "vested interests" that he make a living, with the consequence that he shifts his attentions to the sympathetic, wealth-spurning sister.

After *Cock Robin* (with Elmer Rice), a mystery-murder, Barry wrote *Hotel Universe* (1930), a drama dealing with states of mind, in which several people who are "fixed" by some emotional experience of the past achieve release through trances induced by a scientist. The marriage theme again occurs in *Tomorrow and Tomorrow;* the childless wife of a small-town college teacher has her desire for greater intellectual and emotional opportunities fulfilled in the person of a visiting professor; the resultant child creates for the woman a difficult choice among love, loyalty, pride, and motherhood. An involved problem is also presented in *The Animal Kingdom* (1932), in which a young publisher, after leaving an inspiriting artist for a conventional society marriage, finds he is retrogressing mentally and culturally. Barry shows sharp observation and understanding in his skillful analyses of these more subtle emotional and mental aspects of marriage; it is possible, perhaps, to observe that in certain of these society plays orthodox ethical evaluations yield to a more sophisticated philosophy. In a recent play, *The Joyous Season* (1934), Barry again concerns himself with religious drama, as he did in *John.*

The title theme of *You and I* is one discussed centuries ago by Francis Bacon in his essay *Of Marriage and Single Life:* "Certainly the best works, and of greatest merit for the public, have proceeded from the unmarried or childless men, which, both in affection and means, have married and endowed the public." In Barry's play the idea is worded dramatically: ". . . For a while you need absolute independence—freedom to think only 'I—I—I—I and my work'—After marriage that is no longer possible. From then on it's 'You and I'—with the 'You' first, every time."[1] Maitland White's advice, perhaps like that of Bacon, warns against the encroachment of marriage on self-development, for "the most important thing in a man's life is his work"; and White places himself in a delicate position when he exclaims: "In my opinion, any man who sacrifices his career for the sake of a girl, hasn't the backbone of—a cup-custard." Nancy, "good sport" that she is, adds her bit of contemporary skepticism: "And when you're forty or so, you may look on love as a kind of captivating robber—who chatted so sweetly, as he plucked your destiny out of your pocket. . . ."

But there are different kinds of work:—one would hardly sacrifice love and marriage for the sake of business, which has only "one dimension" and is a

[1] Act I, p. 579.

"dump for dreams." White believes that "every fourth man in business has something shut down in him. You can see it in their faces. . . . And now most of them will die in the traces, poor devils . . . die of market reports—Babsonitis—hardening of the soul. . . ." Barry is here treating the theme (from a different angle, of course) exploited by Howard in *The Henrietta* and dissected by O'Neill in *The Great God Brown;* in both *Main Street* and *Babbitt* Lewis reveals business as a dreary, hardening enterprise.

Important also is the concept of vocational discontent with its larger implication of perversity in human nature. When Maitland is in business, he is dreaming of the artist life and surreptitiously sketching and painting; when at last he openly takes the brush in hand, he is involuntarily mapping out advertising campaigns. It is not until the son is in business that he begins to draw and to purchase books on architecture. Nichols points out: "My gardener kept me occupied for twenty minutes this morning telling me what a splendid carpenter he would have made—and means to make still."[1] An ironical but persistent truth it is that most men carry to their compromise occupations the unvoiced conviction they were meant for better things; in the words of Nichols, quoting Thoreau, these men "lead lives of quiet desperation." According to Nancy, however, this circle of desire has its value as a Shelleyan quest after the unattained or unattainable: "—If you don't still think the bird in the bush worth any two in the hand, you might as well die." "I'm so glad contentment hasn't caught us—and wrapped us in cotton-wool."

But tragedy may lie in wait for the adventurous. The fervid artistic aspirations, long stifled in Matey and at last given liberation, reach up boldly, but are doomed to frustration by his own technical incompetence: "It's like the beating of clipped wings . . . longing for flight. . . ." The painting which to him is the creation of ideal feminine loveliness, comes to have no real value except as an advertisement for the soap he detests in his heart. The lightness of tone and touch prevailing throughout the play render all the more poignant Matey's quiet but bitter tragedy so deftly symbolized by his departure for the party disguised as an artist.[2]

How sharply Matey feels the whole problem is clearly evident in the tense scene with Ronny in which his desperation drives him to the grim assertion that "there's a very cruel law that rules most men's destinies." A higher selfishness may be the law hinted at; that it is a law at least within man is suggested by Matey's observation to Nancy: ". . . Habit has a way of changing destinies, don't you think?"

[1] Act II, p. 598.

[2] The tragic note of the play, however, was apparently lost upon the audiences as a whole. John Farrar points out that "the author has intended to write a tragi-comedy, and the public warmly accepted the product as comedy." The explanation seems to be that "So many people refuse to believe that Maitland White, facing the comfort of a thirty thousand a year job, is really facing defeat." (*The Bookman*, LVII, 318, May, 1923.)

The implication is also in Matey's advice to his son: "And don't underestimate, either, the suffering a flouted destiny can send you. There's a course you feel cut out to take—step off it now, and you'll regret it as long as you live."

Several pointed reflections relative to art appear, such as Matey's disputed theory that love is a weakness in an artist, or Nancy's assertion that an art career must be begun at once, not at a future date. Nichols contrasts the freedom, the "spiced and succulent" life of the single writer with the slavery of the married business man whose hours are from nine to five. Pertinent, too, is Nichols' belief that "there's no such hell on earth as that of the man who knows himself doomed to mediocrity in the work he loves."[1] Represented as effective to a certain degree is Matey's implanted inspiration in his Pygmalion-created model.

You and I is philosophically consonant with certain current views that men's destinies are not in their stars but in their own constitutional properties and bias; it is artistically significant in its treatment of the universal aspiration toward fields of other service; and it is dramatically effective in its rapid dialogue and pointed situation.

The present text is from the first edition (1923).

[1] Act I, p. 584.

CHARACTERS

(With the original cast as first presented in New York at the Belmont Theatre on February 19th, 1923.)

MAITLAND WHITE.......................................H. B. Warner
NANCY WHITE.......................................Lucile Watson
RODERICK WHITE.......................................Geoffrey Kerr
VERONICA DUANE.......................................Frieda Inescort
GEOFFREY NICHOLS.......................................Reginald Mason
G. T. WARREN.......................................Ferdinand Gottschalk
ETTA.......................................Beatrice Miles

SCENES

Act I.—The library of the Whites' country home in Mount Kisco, Westchester County, New York. A late September evening.

Act II.—"The Studio" in the attic, an afternoon the following May.

Act III.—"The Studio" later the same evening.

YOU AND I

ACT I

Here you are, in the library of the Whites' country home in Mount Kisco, Westchester County, New York.

The Whites' home is one of those rambling white houses that began as a farm house and has been added to year by year as the family grew, and the family's fortunes prospered. In architecture, it is nearer colonial than anything else. There was always plenty of land, but the orchard, of which MAITLAND WHITE *is so proud, he planted himself.*

When you come for your first week-end, he will delight in telling you that when NANCY *and he bought the place twenty years ago, the room in which you now stand was, with the exception of a tiny kitchen, the entire lower floor. The second beam from the left in the ceiling will show you where the partition came between living and dining rooms.*

The big hall, by which you entered, is the west wing—that came first—and the spacious dining room and study are the east wing, which was built four years later. The servants' wing was added at the same time. The little cottage down by the swimming-pool is of course quite new. That is to be Jean's, when she grows up and is ready to be married—fancy Jeanie married!

You will be awfully surprised and say What!—this enormous place grown out of a little old farm house? And MAITLAND *will chuckle and say Oh, Nanny and I have had no end of fun out of it, haven't we, Nanny? And like as not, the next time you come (as you will, if they like you) he will begin to tell you about it all over again. But* NANCY *will stop him, without in the least hurting his feelings.*

The Library—which is also the main living room—is a huge, uneven, motherly sort of a room that pats your hand as you come into it, and tells you to sit down and be comfortable with the rest of us. Out here we don't even know that there is *such a place as the City!*

There is a large white fireplace, with two ample chairs flanking it. A long table stands just away from the center of the room. There are a few more easy-chairs, and a writing-desk. A great sofa invites you to abandon yourself to its lethal depths. Wherever there is not a window or a door, there are built-in bookcases, filled with books. MAITLAND *will show you, among the really fine etchings upon the wall, two rare Whistlers, in which he takes a just pride. You enter—through glass doors at the right—a kind of sun-room, from which, if you are sufficiently enterprising, you may proceed through the garden into the orchard. The woodwork of the library is a soft ivory. There is no scheme of decoration, but the whole effect is one of warmth and light and color. It is what you would call, not a beautiful, but a charming room.*

The time is about seven o'clock of a late September evening and someone, someone whom you must wait a moment to see, is playing a frivolous tune on the piano in the sun-room. In the middle of a measure, the music stops abruptly. There is a short silence, followed by the bang of a discord. Then, with her head high, thoroughly angry, VERONICA DUANE *enters and traverses the library, nearly to the hall.*

She is about 19, slim, of medium height, with a decidedly pretty, high-bred face, lovely hair, lovely hands, and a soft, low-pitched voice—whatever she may be saying. Heredity, careful up-bringing, education and travel have combined to invest her with a poise far in advance of her years. She has attained the impossible—complete sophistication without the loss of bloom. Her self-confidence is, you will be happy to know, free from any taint of youthful cock-suredness.

RONNY *(as she is fortunately called) was made to wear clothes well, and she wears her present out-of-door ones superlatively so. There is something in the ensemble—it may be a scarf, the marking of a sweater, or the tongue of a shoe—that everyone will have next summer:* RONNY *adopted it at Deauville last Spring.*

Following her, comes RODERICK WHITE, *with the fireplace as his objective. There he stands leaning back against a chair, stuffing a pipe with tobacco, and looking just a little bit scared.*

He is a well set-up, thoroughly nice boy about 21, with high color, hair carefully brushed, a disarming smile. Although his expression is bright and animated, his countenance appears to be totally without guile. Only RICKY *knows the multitude of scrapes that has got him out of.*

If you come near enough, particularly on a rainy day, you will catch, as it hovers about his golf clothes, a thoroughly satisfactory aroma of peat-smoke. RICKY *has a proper regard for old clo'. His polo-shirt, though it may be a little frayed, has the merit of being clean. His brown-and-white shoes—genuine antiques—have not.*

RONNY [*with a rigid back to him*]. I think I'll be—going home.

RICKY [*amiability itself*]. Good idea—if you expect to dress and be back here in time for dinner. [*A pause.*] Well—you needn't be so darn snootey about it. [RONNY *wheels about and faces him.*]

RONNY. Ricky—I could kill you for doing that.

RICKY [*puffing on his pipe*]. I've been resisting the impulse all summer—and when you turned your head and looked up that way—well—it was rather pleasant.

RONNY. I don't see how you dared!

RICKY. Oh, come on, Ronny,—you can't get away with that. You loved it.

RONNY. Who said I didn't! For months you've had me literally quaking in my boots. Because I knew that if ever you did, I'd—I'd—

RICKY [*bearing in her direction*]. Ronny! Did you know that, too . . . ? [*She nods her head, dumbly.*]—And *do* you now—as much as I do . . . ?

RONNY. Hang it—of course I do!—On the fifteenth of October you're going abroad for three years. For the love of Pete, why couldn't you have held out just two weeks more?—Then you'd have gone, and I'd have forgotten you.—And that would have been all there was to it.

RICKY. —In a pig's eye.

RONNY. I tell you it would! And now—after this—[*She flings a magazine from table to sofa.*] Oh—a sweet winter I'll put in, getting over you!

RICKY [*genuinely dismayed*]. Getting *over* me . . . ? Gosh, I don't want you to do *that!*

RONNY. No—I'll sit around doing basket-work, while you and your little playmates at the Beaux-Arts scamper up and down Paris.

RICKY [*grandly*]. I am going abroad to study architecture—not to go on parties.

RONNY. Show *me* a student on the Left Bank who doesn't study life! Thanks, Rick. By Spring you will be but a memory.

RICKY. But—but Ronny—can't you get it into your silly head that I'm *really* in love with you? I'm—you've—oh damn it—*won't* you marry me?

[RONNY'S *hand, in a quick gesture, covers his. For one breathless moment their eyes hold them together.*]

RONNY. Ricky! [*Then she removes her hand, and shakes her head with conviction.*] Uh-uh. It's awfully nice of you—but I couldn't wait three years for the Prince of Wales.

RICKY [*moodily*]. Fat lot you love me.

RONNY. Oh—don't think I'm an absolute dud—[*With a trace of embarrassment.*] You—know how it is—with Father and Mother, don't you?

RICKY. Why—they don't hit it off too well, do they?

RONNY. Mother's never said a word to me—but of course she's simply sticking it out till I'm what-they-call "settled." I had it all planned to marry the next person I was honestly fond of. But now you—you egg—you've ruined it. I'll have to forget *you* first. It would be such a filthy trick—when I—when there was someone I actually—[*She shudders.*] Oh—I couldn't stand it!

RICKY. I can't imagine being—to anyone but you, really I can't.

RONNY [*softly*]. It would be too delightful, to be—to you. [*There is a pause.*]

RICKY [*a sudden idea*]. Listen, Ronny: there's no reason why we *shouldn't* be—I'll go into Father's factory, instead. Mr. Warren said he'd start me at two thousand a year, and if I was any good—

RONNY. But Rick—you've *always* meant to be an architect. I won't have you wash out on it for me.

RICKY. Oh—will you listen?—I'm not washing out on anything. I'll study on the side—and drift into it gradually. I can go to night school—

RONNY. "'Whom are you?' said Cyril."

RICKY. But why not? Other people have. Life shouldn't be all gravy, anyway. After ten years of school and college I feel like a burglar at the prospect of riding Dad for three years more. I know I could swing it every bit as well, right here on my own.

RONNY. But that sounds like such a makeshift. And supposing once you got into business you had to stay put?

RICKY. Well, that's no calamity. Father dished painting in order to marry Nanny. And do you suppose he's ever regretted it? Look at them!

RONNY. I know—they're so happy, it's painful. But—

RICKY. Ronny, it's simply that I want *you*—so much more than anything else, that it's silly even to talk about it.

RONNY. Are you sure you'll keep *on* wanting me more?

RICKY. Damn right, I will!

RONNY [*thoughtfully*]. There's a kink in it somewhere. . . .

RICKY. Oh—you're full of cold tea. Listen: I'll work like the very devil, and next summer we'll be married. What do you say?

RONNY [*after a troubled pause*]. Why—I've no really strong objections. . . .

RICKY [*in embarrassed delight*]. Oh Lord—this is wonderful. . . . [*She rises and faces him. They stand looking at each other, silently.* RICKY *finally ventures it.*] Dearest. . . .

RONNY. Angel. . . .

RICKY. Darling. . . .

RONNY. Lover. . . .

RICKY [*groping for it*]. Uh—uh—*Precious.*

RONNY [*dramatically*]. My tr-r-r-easure. [RICKY *presents a cheek, but* RONNY *edges away.*] Not on your life. . . . [RICKY *intrepidly kisses her on the cheek. She laughs.*] Gosh, Rick—you're poor!

RICKY. How do you know?

RONNY. I read a book.

[*At which* RICKY *takes her in his arms, as if she were made of spun-glass.*]

RICKY. "To Veronica from Roderick, with love."

[*He kisses her lightly, but unmistakably.*]

RONNY [*softly*]. Oh—how diverting.

RICKY. I'm going to tell Mother!

RONNY [*in consternation*]. She'll crown me!

RICKY. Rot, my child. She'll think what a clever lad her son is.

RONNY. I'm scared of her. . . .

RICKY [*pooh-poohing*]. Scared of Nanny?—Why, she's nothing but a kid.

RONNY. She appalls me. She knows so much. . . .

RICKY. She'll be all for it. Just you see—[*He starts toward the door, but comes back.*] Ronny—honestly—I simply adore you. . . .

RONNY [*with a faint smile*]. Dear—you've got nothing on me.

[*On this second expedition he reaches the door, and calls upstairs.*]

RICKY. Mother! [*Where can she be?*] Dearest! [*Can she have gone out?*] Oh, Nanny—stick out your neck!

NANCY [*an enchanting voice from above*]. What is it, you simpleton?

RICKY. What do you think?

NANCY. I think it's time you changed for dinner.

RICKY. Ronny and I are engaged. Can you beat it?

NANCY. Wh-a-a-t—?

RICKY. We have plighted our troth. Big news. C'mon down! [*He returns to* RONNY.] Beau'ful—I feel awfully sacred all of a sudden. Tell you what I'll do; I'll go to church with you in the morning.

RONNY. Check. The Maiden's Prayer.

RICKY. Then I'll take you on for nine fast holes before luncheon. Give you a stroke a hole—two, on the sixth—and beat the shoes off you!

RONNY. You lie, Dumbbell, you won't.

RICKY. A dollar a hole. Are you on?

RONNY [*scornfully*]. Am I on! For nine dollars, I'd—

[NANCY WHITE *appears in the hall doorway, carrying a half-written letter in her hand. She is a young forty, not-so-short, not-so-tall, but anyway with a slim, girlish figure, lively, humorous brown eyes, dark brown hair, and a manner as charming as her appearance. Despite her poise, one feels that her age is merely put on—youth dwells in her spirit, and no mere calendar can oust it.* RICKY *meets her at the door, and they enter together, his arm about her shoulder.*]

RICKY [*with a gesture toward* RONNY]. Behold!—My willing slave.

NANCY [*a brave attempt at severity*]. Veronica—is what Roderick tells me true?

RONNY. All but the "slave," Mrs. White.

[NANCY *looks from one to the other, goes to* RONNY, *takes her hand, gazes into her eyes for a moment, and then kisses her on the cheek.*]

NANCY [*emotionally*]. My dear! [*She brushes away a hypothetical tear, and reaches one hand out behind her, to* RICKY.] My first-born child!

RICKY [*for* RONNY'S *information*]. Nanny wanted to go on the stage once. She just eats a thing like this.

NANCY [*pointing an imperious finger toward the sofa*]. Ricky—sit down there! [RICKY *obeys, grinning.* NANCY *designates a place beside him.*] Veronica—[RONNY *sits at his side, a little frightened.* NANCY *pulls a large chair around, and sits facing them.*] Now, you two precious idiots, we'll talk this over.

RICKY [*to* RONNY]. Isn't she immense?

[*He affects a most solemn expression, and leans forward attentively, resting his chin upon his hand.*]

NANCY. I thought the fact of your living next door to each other for twelve summers would act as an anti-toxin.

RONNY. You could have knocked me over with a feather, Mrs. White.

NANCY. I dare say. But of course it's quite out of the question. You're nothing but children.

RICKY [*shaking his head reprovingly*]. Gosh, Nanny—that's awfully old stuff. . . .

NANCY [*with some acerbity*]. Roderick—be kind enough to reserve your infantile comments. [RICKY *subsides. She leans back with a sigh.*]—Nothing but children. It is beautiful, my dears, but quite, quite ridiculous.

RICKY. Pardon the interruption,—but how old were you, when *you* became a Married Maiden?

NANCY. That has nothing to do with it!

RICKY [*indulgently*]. I know—but just as a matter of record. . . .

NANCY [*the dignified mother of two children*]. I was—nineteen. But—

RICKY. You mean a couple of weeks past eighteen. What're you, Ronny?

RONNY. I'll be twenty in December. Big girl.

RICKY. Check. And how about Dad?

NANCY. He was a great deal older than you are!

RICKY. Your memory's failing! He had me just four months.

NANCY [*ironically*]. I don't want to be sordid—but what *do* you expect to live on?

RICKY. Query: What did *you* live on, Darling?

NANCY. Why—I had a little of my own, and your Father worked.

RICKY [*with a gesture*]. 'S a perfect equation!

RONNY. I've about two thousand a year from Aunt Isabel's estate. Dad's promised me a house. . . .

NANCY [*to* RICKY]. And may I ask what you intend doing about your architecture?

RONNY [*leaning forward*]. You and me both, Mrs. White. . . .

RICKY. Quiet, Child—let me manage this. I'm going like a breeze. [*To* NANCY.] Well, you see, I'm going to pass that up, and—

NANCY [*really troubled*]. But—

RICKY. Oh—maybe not for good. Maybe, by and by, when we get on our feet—

NANCY. "By and by!" Somehow, that sounds vaguely reminiscent to me. Unless you do it now, you'll never do it!—That's certain as death and my hay-fever.

RICKY. Well, really—what if I don't? I mean, you told me that Father wanted to paint, or something—but you and he were married at 21 and 18 respectively, and he went into business, and stayed there. What I mean is, it seems to me that you two have made a pretty good go of it.

NANCY [*proudly*]. We have made an uncommonly good go of it. But—[*She scrutinizes* RICKY'S *ankles in despair*.] Oh—your stockings again! Ronny—can't *you* make him wear garters?

RONNY. Isn't it awful?—Slippety-slop. . . .

NANCY. What you find attractive in him, I'm sure I can't see.—I was saying. . . ? Ah yes—my reminiscences—[*She hesitates. Then to* RONNY.] Of course, you look very charming as you are. But we dine at a quarter before eight. . . .

[RONNY *rises and moves toward the hall.*]

RONNY. Then I'd better shove off.

NANCY [*just as she is about to go out*]. Oh—uh—Veronica—

RONNY [*turning*]. Yes . . . ?

NANCY. Do you think you really love my Ricky?

[*A short pause.* RONNY *looks straight at* NANCY.]

RONNY [*simply*]. I've—never given a happy hang for anyone else. I'd—simply—lie down and die for him.

[RICKY *rises and makes for her, but a sweep of* NANCY'S *arm intercepts him.*]

NANCY. —A quarter before eight. And—I think it will be all right—somehow—

RONNY. Oh—you *are* a dear. . . .

RICKY [*calling after her*]. Make it seven-thirty, if you can. President of Dad's Company's coming, and we may rate a cocktail!

RONNY [*a voice from the hall*]. Right-o!

[NANCY *goes to the desk, with her unfinished letter.*]

NANCY. I'm writing to your sister. Your love . . . ?

RICKY. Sure. But don't say anything about Ronny and I—

NANCY [*automatically*]. "—about Ronny and *me*."

RICKY [*grammar is an affectation*]. —about Ronny and I. You know Jean—she'd have it all over the school in six minutes.

NANCY. Now—I want to talk to you sensibly.

RICKY. Shoot, Darling—

[NANCY *opens a drawer of the desk. It is filled to overflowing with small pieces of paper. Two fall upon the floor.* RICKY *picks them up and looks at them.*]

NANCY. You see these?

RICKY. Sketches!—Father's . . . ?

NANCY. Yes. Before I give Roberts his clothes to press, I always go through the pockets. Not more than twenty times in twenty years have I failed to find one or two of these, all nicely folded up and tucked away. He does murals, too. That's why the wall beside the telephone is repapered so often. . . . [*Looking at sketches, which* RICKY *gives her*.] Charming, aren't they . . . ?

[*She puts them back and closes the drawer. Taking* RICKY'S *arm, they return together to the sofa.*]

RICKY. But what's Dad's foolishness got to do with my—?

NANCY. There's something very sad in that folly, Rick. It's like the beating of clipped wings . . . longing for flight. . . .

[RICKY *stares at her.*]

RICKY [*disgustedly*]. Oh—if you're going to get deep on me—

NANCY. You've no idea how deep it goes. . . . [*She studies his face for a moment and then continues, matter-of-factedly.*] Now Ronny is a sweet, lovable girl. And if the truth must be known, I heartily approve of early marriages, when—

[RICKY *leans over and pecks her cheek.*]

RICKY. Great!

NANCY. Behave yourself, and listen to me!—*When* they are possible without too great sacrifices. Ricky—from the time you began to play with blocks, you've wanted to study architecture. Don't you still . . . ?

RICKY. Why of course I do. But I can't have both—and I want Ronny more.

NANCY. We might arrange—

RICKY. —To carry the two of us?—That's like you, Dear—but no, thanks. When I'm married, I've got to be on my own. Maybe I'm in the same place Father was. Well—I know what I want most, just the way he did. It's a simple question of values. . . .

NANCY. Your values may shift a little, later on.

RICKY [*by way of refutation*]. Did Father's?

NANCY. —And when you're forty or so, you may look on love as a kind of captivating robber—who chatted so sweetly, as he plucked your destiny out of your pocket. . . .

RICKY. There you go again! Ask Dad—*he* knows!

[*From the hall is heard a whistled refrain which, possibly, you will recognize as "Rodolfo's Narrative" from "La Bohème."*]

NANCY [*rapidly*]. —You may suddenly feel choked-off—thwarted—in the one really big thing you could have done. Then—though you love her dearly—you'll resent Ronny. You'll try not to let her see. If she loves you, she can't avoid it. Or even you yourself may not know quite what's wrong. You may simply find, all at once, that you are very empty, very unhappy. . . .

RICKY. But Nanny—look how happy Father is!

[*The whistle draws closer.*]

NANCY. You can't tell much by a whistle, son. . . .

[MAITLAND WHITE *comes in. He is 43, about five feet ten, and golf and squash have kept him in the pink of trim. He is not particularly handsome, but with a face and smile that—unless you be an incurable misanthrope—win you immediately. There are a few gray hairs, which* NANCY *or the barber will pull out at his next sitting. To look at him you might think him any one of a number of things. You guess that it is business, and you know that he is successful. His hands—long, slender and restless—and a kind of boyish whimsicality in him, are all that betray the artist. He wears a dinner-coat, and wears it well. He is unwrapping a large, flat package as he enters. He places it upon the center table, and carelessly drops the paper to the floor.*]

MATEY [*to* NANCY]. Do come here and see this Watteau print I've got for your room—

[*He sets it up against some books, and stands off to look at it, continuing his low whistling.* NANCY *goes to his side, picking up the paper en route, and slips her arm through his.*]

NANCY. Matey—you lamb—it's too enchanting!

MATEY. —How pensive, how reluctant, it is. The way that man combines grace and abandon is a miraculous thing. . . .

RICKY. Father—I'm going to marry Ronny Duane—

MATEY [*quite unimpressed by this momentous announcement*].—I call it at once a bubble, and a monument. See this lady, with her head turned, so. You know, my dear—I think she's extraordinarily like you. . . .

NANCY. Imbecile!—Look at her nose. . . .

[MATEY *does so. Then lifts* NANCY'S *chin and studies her face for a moment.*]

MATEY. I could fix that with one line.

[*Being so accessible, he kisses her.* NANCY *steals a furtive look at* RICKY, *who does not attempt to conceal his disgust.*]

RICKY. Aw—cut it out!—I say, Father, that I'm going to—

MATEY. —It's called "The Embarkation for Cythera"—hangs in the Louvre. [*Chuckles reminiscently.*]—Remember that night the summer before we were married—when *we* embarked for Greenwich in the sailboat from Long Island?—And got becalmed half way across? Lord! I'll never forget your Mother's face, as we tip-toed in at five-thirty!

RICKY [*compassionately*]. Poor Dad—middle age at last.

MATEY. What *is* that infant babbling about?

RICKY. It's the first time I've ever heard you brag of what a cut-up you were as a lad. Unmistakably, Dad,—you're *done*. . . .

MATEY. Done, eh—? Who beat you 6-love, 6-3, 6-2 this morning?

RICKY. Oh—you're *fit* enough. It's the mind that goes first.

MATEY [*scornfully*]. Middle age!

[*Nonetheless, he does look a little worried.*]

RICKY. I don't want to bore you—but I was breaking the news of my approaching nuptials with one Veronica Duane. . . .

MATEY. —And didn't I felicitate you? How careless. Congratulations, my boy—and upon the inheritance, too.

RICKY. The—what . . . ?

MATEY [*with a gesture*]. The—uh—legacy. . . .

RICKY. What do you mean?

MATEY. Why—er—haven't you come into a large fortune, as well?

RICKY. I haven't been advised of the fact.

MATEY. Then how do you expect to marry Ronny?

RICKY. She's got her own running-expenses, and I'm going to work.

MATEY. I sincerely trust that eventually you will.

RICKY. I want to begin right away. I'm not going abroad, Father.

[MATEY *looks to* NANCY *for an explanation. She makes a helpless gesture, as if to say, "I've done all I can." A pause.* MATEY *is dumbfounded. He turns to* RICKY, *drops his bantering air, and speaks kindly and sympathetically.*]

MATEY. Look here, old fellow, this is a little confusing. Would you mind telling me more about it?

RICKY. Why—there isn't a great deal to tell, Sir. It's just that we're—very much in love, and want to be married as soon as we possibly can. I figure that if I go to work now, by Spring everything will be rosy.

MATEY. What do you plan to do?

RICKY. Same as you—the Warren Company. —Caught you, Sir—you thought I'd say "sell bonds."

MATEY. And your architecture goes by the boards, eh?

RICKY. Why should it? I can study evenings, and Sundays, and finally—[*At this patent absurdity,* MATEY *laughs.* RICKY *is injured.*] Well—I can. . . .

MATEY [*gravely*]. Ricky—our method of upbringing for you and Jean has allowed room for very few "Thou-shalt-nots." I'm not going to start ordering you about now, but there are a few things, that—as an older man—I want to remind you of—

[NANCY *proceeds to examine the Watteau print more closely.*]

RICKY. Yes, Dad. . . .

MATEY. I have my own eyes, and the word of your masters at school and college, to tell me that you have a considerable gift for building-design. You love the work, and you're unusually well-suited to it. You need technique, and a background—and you need them badly. Three years at the Beaux-Arts will give you the best there are. . . .

RICKY. But Ronny—

MATEY [*a little exasperated*]. If Ronny won't wait for you, there'll be another girl just as charming, later on. . . .

[NANNY *puts down the picture and looks at them.*]

MATEY. I want to tell you, Son, that the most important thing in a man's life is his work—particularly when he has an equipment such as yours. It's hard to get going; for a while you need absolute independence—freedom to think only "I—I—I—I and my work"—After marriage that is no longer possible. From then on it's "You and I"—with the "You" first, every time. "*You* and I"—

RICKY. Sound grammar, anyway.

MATEY [*swiftly*]. I'm not speaking idly!—And don't underestimate, either, the suffering a flouted destiny can send you. There's a course you feel cut out to take—step off it now, and you'll regret it as long as you live.

[NANCY *aimlessly picks up a magazine.*]

RICKY. But—I simply can't give up Ronny—

[MATEY *stares at him, and then rises abruptly from his chair.*]

MATEY [*brutally*]. In my opinion, any man who sacrifices his career for the sake of a girl, hasn't the backbone of—a cup-custard. [NANCY'S *head drops a little, over her magazine.* RICKY *glances at her apprehensively.*]—And any girl selfish enough to permit—

RICKY. Dad—isn't this a bit rough on Mother?

MATEY. Rough on—? What do you mean . . . ?

NANCY [*very quietly*]. Don't be silly, Ricky.

[MATEY *looks from one to the other.*]

MATEY. But . . . ?

NANCY. I must go and dress. . . .[*To* RICKY.] You'd better come too. [*She starts to cross, toward the hall.*]

MATEY. Just a moment, dear—[*Again to* RICKY.] It's sheer nonsense to think you can manage two occupations—One or the other must go. You—

RICKY. I'm afraid it's no use, Father. I've thought it all out, and my mind's made up.

[MATEY *shakes his head sadly—pityingly, perhaps. Before* NANCY *reaches the door,* ETTA, *in maid's costume, enters. The kindest of all laws—that of compensations—has endowed her with lustrous hair, perfect coloring, a charming figure, and eyes to which the Blue Grot is a dirty gray. Who cares at what age the psychological tests will place her?*]

ETTA. Mr. Warren has arrived.

[*Yes, here is* G. T. WARREN *himself. He is about 55, and partially bald—a short, plump, gusty little man, with a ready smile. He has the conceit of most self-made men, but in his case, it is made amusing by his naïveté. He is, in the business vernacular, always "on his toes," and literally exudes prosperity and good nature. He speaks rapidly, and with conviction.* NANCY, MATEY *and* RICKY *rise to greet him.*]

MATEY. "—and seizing his golf-clubs, and the latest 'Cosmopolitan,' our Captain of Industry determined to relax."

WARREN [*briskly, as always*]. Hello, White. Relax, is the word. Never felt stiffer. [*Taking* NANCY'S *hand, and beaming upon her.*] And how's the little woman?

NANCY. Growing up, Mr. Warren. Delightful, having you here. I'd concluded you thought rest only for the dead. [*To* ETTA.] Have Mr. Warren's chauffeur take his car to the garage. He will stay in William's quarters. [*To* WARREN.] Do sit down. Would you like a pick-me-up?

WARREN [ETTA *is in the corner of his eye*]. I'll wait—. What a pretty girl!

[*The pretty one goes out.*]

NANCY. Better than that, she's one of the few mortals who can get on with my old Katie. She came as a temporary, but I think I'll perpetuate her.

[WARREN *advances deeper into the room, mopping his brow and adjusting his cuffs.*]

WARREN. Miserable trip, coming up. Brought that advertising man Davis, far as White Plains with me. He talked saturated markets and customer resistance till I had to ask him if he handled a hot-air furnace account!

[*At which he chuckles. And if you were one of his clerks, you may be certain you would roar with laughter. But*—]

NANCY [*with a grimace to* MATEY]. Mr. Warren says the quaintest things.

WARREN. Well—as I told that reporter fellow who interviewed me last week—"Smile through to success"—that's been my motto ever since I was a kid. [*To* RICKY.] Hello, Son—all through with college?

RICKY. —The youngest living graduate. . . .

WARREN. I must mind my who's and whom's. Let's see,—it was Harvard, wasn't it?

RICKY [*a gentle reproof*]. Mr. Warren—*please*—

WARREN. My mistake! Well—I got *my* education at the University of Hard Knocks, and—

RICKY [*an end to these wall-mottoes!*]. "—and began business without a nickel in my pocket—and look at me now!"

[WARREN *stares at him for a moment and then laughs.*]

WARREN. White—this is a fresh youngster of yours, but I like his spirit. Can't stand men who're afraid of me.

RICKY. You know—I like you, too. You look exactly like our old baseball trainer. If you don't mind, I think I'll come and work for you. I won't be like this in the office. At toil, I'll be very reserved. But *here—?* Well—both good fellows, wot?

WARREN [*I can be a hale fellow, as well met as any*]. Both good fellows! When can you start?

RICKY. A week from Monday. Are you on?

WARREN. Suits me. Given up your other plans?

MATEY [*quickly*]. I don't think he's quite decided, G. T.

NANCY. He's not himself today, Mr. Warren.

RICKY [*scowling at them*]. As a matter of fact, Sir, they're full of red ants. I have *quite* decided, and I've never been more myself.

WARREN. He couldn't do better than to come with us. This is an age of business. [*He picks up the Watteau print and glances at it.*] H'm—pretty. . . . [*Replaces it and turns again to* RICKY.] I'll put you through the production end in six months. Then the sales department. Then the—you see, we're entirely departmentalized. [*Takes pencil and paper from pocket, and sits beside* RICKY.] Look here. It's arranged like this. Here's the top: "G. T. Warren"—

RICKY. Himself!

WARREN. Then the vice-president—you know old Lawson. Then your father. Beneath us, come the—

[*Then—as people will—they all talk together. But unless you have an inordinate interest in business, you would better listen to* NANCY *and* MATEY.]

MATEY [*to* NANCY]. I nearly forgot. Who do you think is staying with the Carharts?

[WARREN *is saying, "I'll draw it like a line of*

descent, showing the complete unit." RICKY, *for want of something better, replies,* "*—The Warren genealogy, h'm?*"]

NANCY. —Someone swanky.—Who?

MATEY. Geoff Nichols. He just phoned me.—Got back from China last week.

NANCY [*puzzled*]. Nichols . . . ?

[WARREN *says,* "*—Might call it that. First—Administration; then Sales; next—Distribution—with that little arrow indicating our foreign business*"*—at which* RICKY *appreciatively murmurs,* "*Europe too!*"]

MATEY. You remember Geoffrey—he was one of our ushers.

NANCY. The writer person!

MATEY. Of course.—Haven't laid eyes on him for years. He's going to stop in for a moment before dinner.

[WARREN *has informed* RICKY *that* "*We cover the entire world*" *and gone on to explain:* "*Then Production—then finally the Purchasing Department—raw materials. There—you have it all—a three-million-dollar business. Simple, isn't it?*"]

NANCY. Must we talk literature to him?

MATEY [*laughing*]. Heavens—*no!*

[RICKY, *having told his future employer that* "*It depends on what you call simple,*" *brings the competitive conversation to a conclusion.*]

RICKY. You can count on young Roderick for the literary stuff. I've just gone another two inches on my Five-Foot-Shelf of Books.

WARREN [*giving* RICKY *the diagram*]. I'll leave this with you. And if you're half the man your father is—

RICKY [*laconically*]. Oh—I'll draw circles around Dad.

NANCY. Would you like to go to your room, Mr. Warren?—The gray room, Ricky. And remember—a *stiff* shirt!

RICKY. What! Is the dear Duchess coming? [*To* WARREN.] The gray room's usually reserved for ambassadors and bishops, Sir, but—[*With a deprecating gesture.*]—You see how you stand with us.

[WARREN *laughs, and puts his hand on* RICKY'S *shoulder, preparatory to going out.*]

WARREN [*to* MATEY]. White, you've been looking completely worn out. Why not pack up and forget business for a month or two?

MATEY. The Company would crack to pieces!

RICKY. Not with you and me there, would it, Chief?

WARREN. No indeed! We've got youth on our side. It's your poor old father, who's aging so fast. [*Slips his arm through* RICKY'S *as they cross.*]—Both good fellows, eh?

RICKY [*solemnly*]. The best there are! [*They go out, and their voices die away on the favorite theme.*] You know—I think I'm going to like business.

WARREN. We *need* young blood. I've always said—

MATEY [*a little annoyed*]. That amazing child!

NANCY. He's cleverer than you think. G. T. was pleased as Punch. [MATEY *seats himself in a chair.*] Oh—I've gone flat, from standing so long. [*She sinks down on the arm of* MATEY'S *chair.*] Why don't you make me go up and dress?

MATEY [*sternly*]. Go up and dress!

NANCY. I won't!

MATEY [*comfortably*]. You're an obstinate baggage.

NANCY. I am the wife of your bosom, and you adore me.

MATEY. —Which makes you none the less obstinate, and none the less a baggage.

NANCY. Matey—you're a grand old thing—do you know it?

MATEY. I do.

NANCY. —But it doesn't become you to admit it—[*A slight pause.*] I believe I'm in love with you.

MATEY [*impressively*]. It is my fatal fascination. [*Suddenly troubled.*] Nanny—have I been looking done in, lately—or done up—or done anyway?

NANCY. Why—*no!* [*She turns his head around and scrutinizes his face.*]—A little tired, perhaps. [*She finds a gray hair, and with squinting eye and set mouth, proceeds to separate it from the others.*] Here's another gray one. Out you come, false prophet! [MATEY *submits to the operation. The offending member is held up for his inspection.*] *Voilà!*—As the driven snow. . . .

[MATEY *laughs, a little nervously.*]

MATEY. Any other signs?

NANCY. Of what?

MATEY. Senility.

NANCY. None but the fact that you are being unusually childish.

MATEY. Well—G. T. and the infant both spoke of it.

NANCY. Of what?

MATEY. My premature decline.

NANCY [*lovingly*]. Matey—you idiot!

MATEY. Well, after all—here I am, forty odd—life's half over. . . .

NANCY. I never heard such nonsense! You're in the very prime of life. . . .

MATEY [*with a grimace*]. "Prime"—wretched word. Soon I'll be "spry."—What a week it's been! Went to the mat with G. T. again yesterday. He can't seem to get it into his head that if we're to keep up our expansion, we've got to advertise in a big way—like Colgate's. . . .

NANCY. Of course we have—

MATEY. I've been at him for years. Our appropriation is fifty thousand, where it ought to be five hundred. And he says he won't increase it a nickel until he finds a way to advertise the entire line as a unit. Which is simple rot.

NANCY. He's a tight-fisted old fool.

MATEY. No, he's not. He's merely obtuse.

NANCY. You put things so beautifully, my dear.

MATEY. Honestly, Nanny—I get so fed-up at times, I could throw over the whole works.

NANCY [*with genuine sympathy*]. Poor lamb. Seriously—what about a holiday? It's years since we've been abroad.

MATEY. The market's shot to pieces. We can't afford it—not if we're to send Ricky.

NANCY. But—you know—he's not going.

MATEY. You think he's actually in earnest about the factory?

NANCY. I'm almost certain he is. But perhaps—on the side—he can—

MATEY. "On the side"!—Heaven save him from it! His one hope for peace is to forget it entirely—[*Shaking his head sadly.*] Oh—it's criminal for that boy to give up his career. [*A slight pause.*]

NANCY. Was it—criminal—for *you* to, Matey?

[*Another pause. Then* MATEY *laughs easily.*]

MATEY. So *that's* what he meant! [*Reassuringly.*] It's quite different with us—quite.

NANCY. *Is* it?

MATEY [*with spirit*]. Of course!

NANCY [*dubiously*]. Well—I'm glad to know *that.* [*From the hall is heard a man's voice saying,* "*Well—if people* will *leave their doors open they can expect other people to walk in without ringing—so here I am!*"] I wonder if that's—

[*Quite right—it is* GEOFFREY NICHOLS. *He is* MATEY'S *age, taller, very slight and with a most engaging manner. In comparison with the other successful literary men of your acquaintance, his affectations are very few.*]

MATEY. Geoff! By Gad—this is fine!

NICHOLS [*taking his hand delightedly*]. Matey—you pig! If you don't look prosperous! And this is—Mrs. Matey—[*Crooking a speculative finger at* NANCY.] Your name is—don't tell me, now—your name is—Nancy! And you were the prettiest bride ever I saw. What a wedding! I was frightfully sorry about that punch-bowl—I should have known that I couldn't balance it on my nose. By Jove, you seem *two* years older, instead of—[*He covers his eyes with his hands, in mock dismay.*] Oh—I mustn't say it—I can feel my shroud as I do. . . .

NANCY. You delightful man.

NICHOLS [*to* MATEY]. I begged you not to marry. I eat my words. I behold the ideal wife.

NANCY. Can nothing induce you to stay and dine?

NICHOLS. It would be writing my doom with the Carharts.

NANCY. Then do come to us for next week-end.

NICHOLS. I'm so sorry. I sail Wednesday on the *Majestic.*

NANCY. Pity us.

NICHOLS. But Monday—join me in town for dinner and the theater—I've seats for the *Chauve Souris.*

NANCY [*to* MATEY]. Are you free?

MATEY. As these United States.

NANCY [*to* NICHOLS]. We should be charmed. Now I simply must re-drape myself for dinner. You want to talk, anyway. Don't go till I come down, will you?

[NICHOLS *bows, and with her most gracious smile* NANCY *goes out.* MATEY *offers* NICHOLS *a cigarette, which he accepts.*]

NICHOLS. Well—"home is the sailor, home from the sea"—and all that jolly rot.

MATEY. Geoff—it's been twenty years at least.

NICHOLS. I demand a recount!

MATEY. I last broke bread with you in the Spring of '99. . . .

NICHOLS. My Victorian Memoirs.

[*They seat themselves.*]

MATEY. Where *have* you been?

NICHOLS. Everywhere! I'm a veritable flea for travel. London is my old lady—Paris, my mistress—and Rome—ah, Rome—my saint in décolleté! [MATEY *laughs, a little enviously, and begins sketching, absently, on the back of a magazine.*]—and what have the long years held for you, as they say?

MATEY. Oh—here and New York—business as usual.

NICHOLS. What different lives we've had.

MATEY. Haven't we?

NICHOLS [*reflectively*]. —And yet at twenty we were much the same. Twenty—the incendiary age, Matey.—I was going to set the world on fire with my novels—your match was a paint-brush.

MATEY. And I gave up my painting to marry Nancy Lyon. . . .

NICHOLS. —While I forsook sweet Kitty Nash, to wed with an ink-pot! A pair of jilts, we two! Well—what do you think of *your* bargain?

MATEY. I've come out the winner, Geoff.

NICHOLS. And so have I!

MATEY. Impossible!—I've a happy home—sufficient leisure—a regular income—two fine, spoiled children—and a wife that's a simple miracle. Trump them, if you can!

NICHOLS [*gayly, with the gesture of laying cards on the table, one by one*]. The world's my home—every hour of my time is my own—I'll match my income with yours any day!—And as for your last three items, I say what Bacon said: "A man with wife and children has given hostages to Fortune!"

MATEY. But old lady Fortune has done me rather well.

NICHOLS. Oh—she has her favorite slaves. But freedom's the thing! As Shaw said to me one day last April—dash it—what *was* it he said?—At any rate, it was simply convulsing.

MATEY. But how on earth have you done any work?

NICHOLS. Work? Why, every new experience is material. Wherever I go, my typewriter follows. No worries, no responsibilities—just *life*,—the one life I have—spiced and succulent.

MATEY. While I—day after day—"Nine to five—nine to five."

NICHOLS. Those words are the business man's epitaph.

MATEY [*determined to be sprightly*]. Oh—one has one's moments. Even a business man.

[NICHOLS *glances at* MATEY'S *sketch.*]

NICHOLS. But as I remember, you showed amazing promise. I've known artists with wives—with children, even. Why didn't you go on with it?

[MATEY *returns the magazine to the table, and pockets the pencil.*]

MATEY. Well, you see, Nancy and I married ridiculously young—neither of us rich, but both accustomed to a certain standard of living.—A regular income became pretty much of a necessity.

NICHOLS. —And you put it off. Tsch—what a shame—

MATEY [*reluctantly*]. Perhaps—I don't know. Sometimes—when I think that I haven't yet done the thing I wanted to do—my forty-three years do seem rather futile and misspent. It's been particularly salty today. My boy Roderick, for whom I've expected great things—[*He shifts uneasily in his chair.*] Oh, well—it's the old story over again: Expediency's heel, on the neck of inclination.

NICHOLS. But some phases of your life must be very interesting. Now business is not without its—

MATEY. Geoff, business is a dump for dreams. I believe every fourth man in it has something shut down in him. You can see it in their faces. Some of them wanted to paint, like me,—some to write, to sing—to be doctors, lawyers—God bless me, even preachers! But expediency ordered it otherwise. And now most of them will die in the traces, poor devils . . . die of market reports—Babsonitis—hardening of the soul—

NICHOLS. Ah yes—as someone says, "Most men lead lives of quiet desperation."

MATEY [*softly*]. "Quiet desperation." [*He rises, sharply.*] By God—here's one who's fed-up with it! I've a good mind to chuck business *now*—and go to painting!

[NICHOLS *looks somewhat alarmed; this is being taken too literally.*]

NICHOLS. —You're not serious . . . ?

MATEY. So serious, that the turn of a hair would decide it.

NICHOLS [*rising after a helpless pause*]. You must realize that the—uh—artistic life—has its *dis*advantages, too. One's laurels are so insecure. Popularity is such a fickle thing . . .

MATEY. Who said anything about popularity?

NICHOLS [*shrugging*]. One might as well live, as not.

MATEY. If you do good work, you make quite enough.

NICHOLS. But my income isn't half what it's reputed to be! And the irregular hours! Lord, Matey—my nerves are chaos.

MATEY. Mine are paralyzed.

NICHOLS. —And look at me!—My age—and still flitting about from pillar to post like a gouty bumblebee . . .

MATEY. In motion, at any rate. I never leave the ground.

[NICHOLS, *with a profound sigh, sinks into a comfortable chair.*]

NICHOLS [*the fraud*]. What I wouldn't give for a home like this—and children—and a wife like your Nancy!

MATEY. You have your Art . . .

NICHOLS. She's not so sweet as Kitty Nash! —And if it weren't for her and her importunities, I might have Kitty now—and a home that *is* a home.

MATEY. You've compensations. . . .

NICHOLS. No, Matey. I suppose I should have, if I could honestly feel that art—true art—was the gainer for my sacrifice. But a popular novelist! Oh—don't you suppose *I* know what my stuff is worth? [*He continues with deep feeling.*] I give you my word—there's no such hell on earth as that of the man who knows himself doomed to mediocrity in the work he loves—whatever it may be. You love painting—you think you could paint great pictures.—Well—go on thinking—but don't try it. No! No!—You've done well in business—be wise, and stick to it.

MATEY. I am stuck.

NICHOLS. What are you, anyway?

MATEY. Why—uh—I'm a manufacturer . . .

NICHOLS. What do you make?

MATEY [*this is painful*]. Oh—uh—various things . . .

NICHOLS. But what's the—*pièce de résistance*, so to speak?

MATEY [*very painful indeed*]. Well—uh—I suppose one would say—uh—*soap*. . . .

NICHOLS. Soap! God!—You can get your *teeth* into soap!

MATEY [*cynically*]. You can into *ours*. It proclaims itself made of only the purest edible fats.

NICHOLS. Believe me, I envy you—

MATEY. But you've no idea of the—*hunger* I have, to be painting.

NICHOLS. Can't you find time to daub a bit on the side?

MATEY. Business life has no side. It's one dimension. Try it and see. Ah—if only I could get free of it—altogether free of it, for a while. To feel a brush in my hand again—to see a picture grow under my eyes—to create—good God!—something other than a cake of soap.

NICHOLS. By Jove—if it's *good* soap . . .

MATEY [*interrupting*]. —But this house—and the apartment in town—and the servants—and the children to educate! Of course it's impossible,—plainly impossible.

NICHOLS. And lucky for you that it is. Forget it, Matey, forget it—

MATEY. I wish to heaven I could!

NANCY'S *entrance—a vision in evening dress—brings the men to their feet*

NICHOLS. Ah—*vous êtes adorable!*

NANCY. *Mille fois merci, cher Monsieur.*

NICHOLS [*glancing at his watch*]. I'd no idea it was so late. [*Going to the door, followed by* MATEY.] I shall look forward to Monday night. Sherry's at 7.30?

NANCY. Me, and my man Matey; prompt, as always.

NICHOLS [*at door*]. *Dieu soit béni d'avoir conçu une aussi ravissante personne*—

NANCY [*which serves him right*]. The new slippers of my old grandmother are red. [NICHOLS *laughs, and he and* MATEY *go out.* NANCY *moves toward the desk, humming—and stops halfway with a perplexed frown. Continues to desk, again humming. Seats herself and begins to finish letter.* MATEY *re-enters, and, going to the table, stands there with his fingers resting upon it, staring down at the Watteau print, rapt in thought.* NANCY *speaks without turning.*]—Enjoy your talk?

MATEY [*absently*]. What—?—Oh—uh—*yes*—very much . . . [*His voice trails off.*] . . . very much . . . [*A pause.*] What a fascinating time Nichols has had of it!

NANCY [*a few more lines, and Jean's letter will be finished*]. M-m-m—I must read something of his. . . .

MATEY [*half to himself*]. "Hostages to Fortune." [*A pause; lower.*] "Most men lead lives of quiet desperation."

NANCY. What, dear . . . ?

[MATEY *looks a little startled.*]

MATEY. I said, "Most men lead lives of quiet desperation."

[NANCY, *puzzled, glances over her shoulder at him. Turns again, reflectively biting the end of her pen. Then cheerfully continues her writing.*]

NANCY. Well—so long as they're quiet about it—let's—let them go right ahead—shall we . . . ? [MATEY, *deep in thought, does not answer.* NANCY *seals the note, addresses it, stamps it with a bang, and goes to him. She puts her hands upon his shoulders, and faces him about.*] Matey—you sweet old thing—what *is* the matter?

MATEY [*with an attempt at a smile*]. Oh—nothing. . . . [*He cups her elbows in the palms of his hands for an instant and then leaves her.*]

NANCY [*after a thoughtful pause*]. Dear—it seems to me that you've about everything that a person could desire. We've—most of the good things of life—health—position—enough money—a happy family. [*She hesitates.*]—And we've—each other. Nor is ours the tame, settled love most people have at forty. Some blessed good fortune has kept the keen edge on it. I love my children—but compared to you—oh, Matey! [*A little laugh.*] I fancy—there's more woman in me, than mother. . . . [*A pause;* MATEY *says nothing.* NANCY *is chilled.*]—You have been unusually successful in your work. What more could any man ask—than *you have* . . . ?

MATEY [*impatiently, but with intense suffering*]. Nanny—*Nanny*—what *do you* know about it!

[NANCY *catches her breath sharply, holds it a moment, and then lets it go.*]

NANCY [*almost in a whisper*]. I suppose—you know—it—just about knocks the heart out of me, to hear you say that. . . . [*She waits for a response. None comes. She clenches her fists, half raises her arms, and throws back her head, in pain.*] Oh—this *can't* be you and I! [*Her arms drop again, lifelessly. A moment's silence. She regains her composure, and going to* MATEY, *speaks to him in a matter-of-fact voice.*] Maitland—as you love me—there's something I want you to do.

MATEY. What is it?

NANCY [*directly*]. —Leave business for a year. Get leave of absence, if possible. Otherwise, resign. . . .

MATEY [*affecting to be puzzled*]. But—my dear—*why . . . ?*

NANCY [*with an impatient gesture*]. Oh—*please!* Do you think I've had all these years of you—to be fooled by pretense now? I've known for a *long* time that you weren't happy—and why you weren't. But I've *not* known—quite how much it meant to you. I want you to devote the year to painting.

MATEY [*indulgently*]. It's a nice idea, Nanny, but—

[*His gesture includes the house, the cars, the servants.*]

NANCY [*rapidly*]. We'll give up the apartment. We'll stay out here over the winter. One car—and run it ourselves. We'll keep Katie and Etta—and let the others go. I'll do the upstairs myself. Ricky will be in business—no longer an expense. My own income will be enough to dress Jean and pay her school bills.

MATEY. You understand—I've very little outside of my salary?

NANCY. Little—but plenty for us. We'll economize in everything—[*She looks at the three lighted lamps with a smile.*]—We'll—begin with the electric lights. The front attic can be made into a studio. . . .

MATEY. People would think I'd lost my mind.

NANCY [*scornfully*]. People!

MATEY. I suppose they wouldn't have to know. But G. T.—

NANCY [*quickly*]. Tell him it's—personal research work.

MATEY. —And if the research finds nothing?

NANCY. Matey—if you don't still think the bird in the bush worth any two in the hand, you might as well die.

MATEY [*smiling*]. That's very deft, indeed. But I'm *not* going to be bullied into—

NANCY. Nobody's bullying you.

MATEY. Well—we'll think it over. Perhaps—by-and-by. . . .

NANCY. We'll do nothing of the sort. You must tell G. T. tonight. How long would it take you to wind up your affairs?

MATEY. Why, I always keep them arranged, so that if anything should happen to me—

NANCY. Splendid! Something *has* happened to you: You've decided to start painting the first of the month.

MATEY [*after a thoughtful pause*]. Nope. It's no use—the whole thing's too absurd.

NANCY. This isn't a whim. If you won't do it for your own happiness, perhaps you will for mine. . . . [MATEY *glances at her quickly.*]

MATEY [*in spite of himself*]. By Gad, Nanny—you *are* a brick!

NANCY [*enigmatically*]. Maybe I'm not a brick at all. Maybe I'm—just fighting for something I thought I had.

MATEY [*scoffing*]. *Thought* you had!

NANCY. At any rate, you've got to do it. . . . [*This should settle it.*]

MATEY [*but it doesn't*]. No, Nanny, *no.*—Think of the practical side—the expense.

NANCY. I did. My plans for economy quite astonished me!

MATEY. They might apply out here. Not in town.

NANCY. *Town . . . ?*

MATEY [*lamely*]. I'd—uh—I'd naturally do portraits, wouldn't I?—And that necessitates models, doesn't it?

NANCY. Well?

MATEY. Well—the countryside's not precisely dotted with them. [NANCY *amusedly shakes her head over him.*]—And that's only one objection.

NANCY. I've seldom heard a lamer one. If I can get servants to come to the country, why can't you get models?

MATEY. You don't realize that—

[NANCY *presses a button in the wall.*]

NANCY. Matey, I realize that the thing of main importance is for you to begin your painting at once.

MATEY. I never saw such a devil for speed.

NANCY. —Give yourself time to think up objections, and you won't start at all. If I can manage with a temporary maid, you can with a temporary model.

MATEY. Some pinched, painted relic, I suppose—

NANCY. Not at all.

ETTA *enters, the apotheosis of young, fresh beauty*

MATEY. It's impossible, Nanny. It's—

ETTA. You rang?

NANCY. Yes.—Etta—I—uh—I presume you never posed as a model?

[ETTA'S *mouth opens in astonishment. She looks from one to the other.*]

ETTA. Why, *Ma'am!* Of *course* I didn't! Who said that I—?

NANCY. There, Etta—no one. I merely—

ETTA [*is a pretty girl never safe from scandal?*]. Didn't I not bring the best of references? Wasn't I not three years in my last place?—And two in the—a *model!* Why I—

[MATEY *is studying her, crimson lake in his eye.*]

NANCY. You know—a model may be a model, and still be—er—*model.* . . .

ETTA [*desperately*]. But Mrs. White—really—I tell you that—

NANCY. Yes—I comprehend. You have never been a model—never, in the *slightest* degree. Now, what I am attempting to tell you, is that Mr. White expects to spend the next year painting—in the attic . . . [ETTA *regards* MATEY *as if he had gone insane. He is most uncomfortable under her scrutiny.*] . . . which will be made over into a studio. [*To

MATEY.] Do you think Etta would serve your purpose?

MATEY [*off his guard*]. Why, you know—it's quite extraordinary—[*Then, with attempted nonchalance.*] Oh—I dare say she might do to start with.

NANCY [*to* ETTA]. If you will consent to remain here in the country with us this winter, and pose for a few hours each day—

ETTA [*gently*]. I am sorry, Ma'am—

NANCY. Just a moment!—I shall increase your wages, and help you with your work.

ETTA [*firmly*]. No, Ma'am—I could not consider it. Not for all the money in the world.

NANCY [*frankly puzzled*]. But—I don't understand. Would you mind telling us why? [ETTA *hesitates, peering at* MATEY.]—You may be quite frank.

ETTA. Well—I do not like to say nothing, but the man of the house in the third last place I was in, made advances that was—advances that *were*—most unwelcome. You know how careful a girl has got to be—specially when Nature has blessed her with looks like mine. I can usually tell by their eyes—[*She tries to get a look at* MATEY'S, *but the clever man outwits her.*] I am not saying nothing against Mr. White. So far, he has behaved like a real gennulmun. But if I should ferget myself to the extent of—oh, you know what artists are—they, and sailors—

MATEY. I think I can practically assure you that my admirable conduct will continue indefinitely.

ETTA [*cannily*]. You cannot tell what'll happen, if you take to paintin'. I know all about artists; women to them, are as tinders to the flames. . . .

NANCY. There's the Hearst of it, Matey! [*To* ETTA.] I shall vouch for Mr. White. He is not at all—combustible. Come now, will you—or will you not?

ETTA. No Ma'am—I cannot do it. I would like to help you, but I simply dassent—do not dare to—do it.

NANCY. Very well. You are an extremely silly girl. That's all—[ETTA *turns to go out.*] Oh—by the way—in the morning please pack that old foulard of mine, and the gray crêpe de chine. I wish them sent to the C. O. S.

ETTA [*heartbroken at having to wear something less becoming next Thursday*]. But—didn't you say—?

NANCY. I was mistaken. I thought you were more obliging.

ETTA. But I *am* obliging—

NANCY. You have given me no indication of it.

[ETTA *looks searchingly at* MATEY. *He shifts uneasily in his chair.*]

ETTA. But Ma'am—I want to *improve* myself. I want to be a lady, Mrs. White. In all my spare time I read books. I study you and your friends, and seek to em-ulate you. . . .

NANCY [*kindly, after a disconcerted pause*]. Thank you, Etta. But surely every lady should know something about art. Now Mr. White is a very charming, cultivated man—[MATEY *rises abruptly.*]—Your hours with him would be a great opportunity for you.

ETTA [*with difficulty*]. Well—well, there is one thing we would have to have an understanding on: none of his gennulmun friends could come in while I—while I was—was—[*She is unable to go on.*]

NANCY [*puzzled*]. —While you were—? [*It suddenly dawns upon her, but she controls her mirth.*] But I cannot see your objection. I should think you would look very charming in your—[*To* MATEY.] Do you think one of my *dresses* will do—or shall we have one made?

[ETTA *looks first surprised, then considerably relieved as she echoes the wonderful word "dresses."*]

MATEY. Better have it made—[ETTA'S *face lights up.*]

NANCY [*smiling*]. Well, Etta—?

ETTA [*beaming*]. Oh, *yes*, Ma'am—I didn't understand. Yes, Ma'am—with pleasure.—And any of his friends that want to look on—

NANCY. Well—that's better.—You may bring the tray in now—five glasses. Mr. White will give you more explicit directions later. [ETTA *fixes* MATEY *with an appraising stare, borne with difficulty by him. She finally goes out.* NANCY *now laughs without con-*

straint.] Oh—Matey—I couldn't have stood it a minute longer! Virtue in jeopardy! What a brave fight she put up!

MATEY [*shaking himself*]. Whew!—I feel like the Seven Deadlies! I could do with a cocktail. . . .

NANCY. They're coming.—You know, I don't think she's at all certain about you yet.

MATEY. I hope she understands that I'm going to paint, and not conduct a finishing-school. Seriously though, Nanny—we're insane to rush into this thing as if—

NANCY [*her merriment gone at once*]. *Rush?*—After twenty *years?* My *dear!* [WARREN'S *voice is heard from the hall.*]

WARREN [*expounding it*]. —So you see, the entire organization is composed of interlocking units—

MATEY [*opening his hand to release them*]. All right! There they go—the two-in-the-hand! We're off for the bird-in-the-bush! [NANCY *exclaims in joy.*]

RICKY [*seriously*]. I think that cost-accounting system is a knock-out, Sir.

He and WARREN *come in, dressed for dinner*

NANCY. Mr. Warren, Maitland has something important to tell you—

ETTA *enters, with a tray of glasses and a cocktail-shaker*

WARREN [*to* MATEY]. What about? No business, I hope.

[ETTA *places the tray on the table.* MATEY *begins to shake the shaker.* ETTA *watches him like a hawk. He tries to cover his embarrassment.*]

MATEY [*giving shaker a final shake*]. I'll tell you later. Prepare for the worst! [*To* ETTA.] I'll serve them. . . . [*Still she watches him, transfixed. He loses patience.*] I say *I* will *serve* them!

[ETTA *goes out.* MATEY *fills glasses, and gives one to* NANCY *and one to* WARREN. RONNY *appears in hall. She is in evening dress and leaves her wrap in* ETTA'S *hands as she sails past her.*]

NANCY. We must hurry through these. The birds will be ruined. [*Nobody notices* RONNY.]

RONNY [*in self-defense*]. Good evening, Ronny—[RICKY *rapidly reaches her side.*]

NANCY. My dear—how sweet you look!

RONNY [*why not be honest?*]. I think I look pretty well, myself. . . .

RICKY. Plain face, but a nifty dresser.

RONNY. Hello, Handsome—I hardly knew you. Aren't you clean!

RICKY. Dad's in the business.

NANCY. This is our friend Miss Duane, Mr. Warren.

WARREN. Very glad to meet you, Miss Duane.

RONNY [*in her cool manner with strangers*]. How do you do? [RICKY *quickly whispers something to her. She goes to* WARREN, *smiling graciously. Extending a slim hand to him, she speaks as if she had not heard the name.*] Oh—Mr. *Warren!* How delightful! I hear you're to have a new laborer next week . . . ?

WARREN. Indeed I am—*Rocky!* [RICKY *scowls at the name.*] He begins in what we call "The Kitchen."

RONNY. How amusing! I should think he'd be simply priceless, mixing cold cream. He's such an oil-can as it is, that—

RICKY. Dad! Give her a cocktail—quick!

[*He takes one from* MATEY *and gives it to her.*]

RONNY [*accepting it*]. Good dog. . . .

[MATEY *gives* RICKY *another, and takes one for himself.*]

NANCY [*to* WARREN]. Will he need an apron?

WARREN. White overalls!

RONNY [*slowly sipping her cocktail*]. Little Purity—with a lily in his hair. . . .

RICKY [*disregarding her and raising his glass*]. Here's to bigger and better soap!

WARREN [*to* RONNY]. Never you mind—Rocky and I—[RONNY *all but chokes at the repetition of the name.*]

RICKY [*politely*]. The name is "Ricky," Sir.

WARREN. Ricky and I are going to smile through to success—aren't we, old fellow?

RICKY. Chief—we're going to laugh out loud!

MATEY [*from table*]. Here, G. T.—give me your glass.

[WARREN *shakes his head, and he and* NANCY *place their empty glasses upon the tray.*]

RICKY [*to* RONNY]. —That's Mr. Warren's motto: "Use our Pearly Paste, and Smile with Confidence."

RONNY [*over her cocktail*]. Gosh, you're coarse. . . .

RICKY [*aggrieved*]. I *must* say, I fail to see anything coarse about—

NANCY. Never mind, Ricky. [*To* WARREN *and* MATEY.] Are we ready . . . ?

[NANCY, WARREN *and* MATEY *go to the door.* RONNY *is finishing her cocktail.*]

RICKY. C'mon, Beau'ful—lap it up!

RONNY [*putting down her glass*]. M-m-m-m— I shall be charming at dinner.

[MATEY *stands at the door to let them all pass, and turns to follow.* NANCY *re-enters hurriedly, and in reply to his questioning glances says, "I'll come in a minute." He goes out and* NANCY *tours the room, turning out the lamps one by one.* RICKY *calls from the dining room.*]

RICKY [*imperatively*]. Dear-r-r-r-r-est—!

NANCY [*singing it out, with a falling inflection*]. Com-m-m-m-m-m-ing—!

[*She turns out the last lamp, and is rapidly crossing the darkened room to the lighted hall, as . . .*

THE CURTAIN FALLS

ACT II

You may be a little out of breath when you come into MATEY'S *Studio, for it is in the attic, and you must climb a flight of steep steps to get there. The stairway is in a small recess at the back, and we shall see your head first. The small door at the left—as you enter—is the entrance to the playroom.*

The Studio is a spacious, rectangular room with a large dormer window cut in the back wall, and in the right wall two smaller windows through which may be seen the tip of an apple branch, in bloom. The curtains at the windows show NANCY'S *touch—this room has been great fun for her, and she has been very successful in keeping out of it any suggestion of the "arty."*

At one side, there is a long refectory table, covered with a "runner" and bearing two wrought-iron sconces, each containing six white candles. By the large window there are book-shelves and a comfortable sofa. Chairs ad lib.—but space is the thing.

Being essentially a workroom, there is a dais with a throne-chair for the model, an easel (turned away from the front), a small work-table with brushes, paints, etc., and a life-sized lay-figure (a great family joke, by the way) which sprawls upon the floor in a thoroughly gauche manner.

With the exception of a bear-skin and a small rug, the floor is uncovered. On the walls you will see Hokusai's "Fujiyama" and "The Wave"—and very good prints they are. There are also two mounted heads of wild goats, upon the smaller of which a red Spanish béret is set at a rakish angle.

The fact that the studio was once an attic is still apparent, to the close observer, through the medium of only partially hidden trunks, and a dappled-gray hobby-horse.

It is late the following May—about four in the afternoon. MATEY, *in a smock, with a small daub of paint on his cheek, is busily painting at his easel.* ETTA *poses in the throne-chair. She wears a simple, exquisite afternoon-dress, and a small string of pearls at her throat. Her hands rest in her lap. Her hair is dressed most becomingly, and the transformation into a charming lady of unusual grace and beauty is quite complete. For a few moments* MATEY *paints silently. Gradually* ETTA'S *features lose their repose. An expression of acute suffering grows in her eyes. She wrinkles her nose and sets her teeth. Finally:*

ETTA [*at the end of her tether, poor dear*]. Mr. White—I have jest *got* to do it . . .

MATEY [*patiently ceasing his work*]. All right, Etta—go ahead—[ETTA *with a great sigh of relief, vigorously scratches her nose.*] Would you like to rest for a moment?

ETTA. Oh—may I . . . ? [MATEY *gestures acquiescence, lays brushes on work-table, and goes to the open windows, where the bees are humming among the apple blossoms.*] Sech a relief! [MATEY *picks a small sprig of blossoms and presents it to her.*]

MATEY. Here—this will refresh you.

[*For his own refreshment, he lights a cigarette.* ETTA *inhales the fragrance of the blossoms and regards the twig lovingly.*]

ETTA. Oh—thank you. M-m-m-m—I jest simply love apple blossoms.

MATEY. You have an unhappy knack of pronouncing "just" and "such" as if they were spelled with "e's" instead of "u's."

ETTA. "Just"—"Such."

MATEY. That's better. . . .

ETTA [*diffidently*]. It's nice, being a lady, Mr. White—[*Lest he misunderstand her.*]—Of course, I *am* a lady. But—[*Looking down at her dress and fingering her pearls.*]—I mean a de luxe one—like those that come to see Mrs. White. How I'd love to be like they are—and talk the way they do!

MATEY [*absently, as he studies the portrait*]. You should practise—in private.—It's only the mouth that bothers me now.—"'The Portrait of a Lady,' by an Unknown Artist"—[*Reflectively.*] When we've sold it to some great lover of art, *then* perhaps I'll sign it—[*Softly.*] *When*—[*He extinguishes his cigarette and picks up his brush and palette.*] Come on—are you ready?

ETTA. Jest—*just* a minute. . . . [*Once more she strikes her pose, and* MATEY *silently continues his painting.*] Is it really almost done?

MATEY [*engrossed*]. It may be two minutes—it may be two days.

ETTA. I could jest cry, I could—

MATEY. Please don't—I'm no good at marines. [*He paints rapidly for a few moments. Then stands off and regards her quizzically from several positions.*] Softer lines around the mouth—[*Just to make it sure, she grins.*] No! No!—You know better than that! *Soft*, I said. [*He studies her attempt.*] Bring your eyes into it. . . . [*He shakes his head hopelessly, but continues to paint. Suddenly a little laugh escapes her.*] What are you laughing at?

ETTA. It just struck me funny—here you've been trying for months to make that look like me, when with a camera you could get it perfect in a jiffy.

[MATEY *stares at her speechless.*]

MATEY [*softly*]. Oh my God. . . . [*With increased vehemence.*] You sit there prattling of cameras, when you ought to be thanking heaven for the dignity that's done you! Don't you see the chance you've got? Who was Helen of Troy, but a pretty thing with convenient morals? Who was—La Gioconda, but a woman with a smile? If there'd been no Homer to sing of Helen, no Leonardo to fix that smile forever with his brush, they'd both be dead and forgotten as—[*He picks up the twig of apple blossoms.*]—as this will be tomorrow! And—[*She is staring at him without a trace of comprehension in her face.*]—and you haven't the faintest idea what I'm talking about. [*He throws the twig out of the window, falls into thought for a moment, and then speaks again, with restrained but poignant feeling.*] Is there nothing that will make you understand what this means? [*He indicates the portrait.*] Can't you realize that what is here is more than merely you and my work? That in it, there's a—spirit that can strike life into—[*He holds the prostrate lay-figure up to view.*]—a lump of sawdust, like this? You?—Why, it can immortalize you! Let me see in your face—joy—wonder—consecration! [*A big order:* ETTA *bites her lip anxiously.*]

ETTA. All at once, or—one at a time?

[MATEY *shakes his head, as if to say "No use," and placing the lay-figure at the foot of the easel, again ponders a means whereby he may instill into his subject's spirit a something that will show in her face. Finally an idea strikes him, and bringing a high stool to a position directly in front of* ETTA, *he sits upon it, and proceeds to draw for her as alluring a verbal picture as he can.*]

MATEY. Now listen! You want to be a lady, don't you?—Well—I'll make you one. Think—up on Fifth Avenue, there's a palatial white edifice. There, in a long, high room lavishly embellished with palms and other potted plants, *you* sit, *you*, Etta—the hostess at a most de luxe reception. The room is filled with fashionable ladies in their jewels and furs and orchids. Their stylish escorts stand about with silk hats in their white-gloved hands. From everywhere, they've come thronging to pay you homage—earls and dukes and duchesses—ambassadors and their wives . . .

[*Can it be that he, too, has read "The Earl's Revenge"?*]

. . . And for all time, you will live in their memories. In the far capitals of the world exquisite women will sit before their glasses in costly boudoirs, and whisper sadly, "Ah—if I were as lovely as she!" Handsome men, on whose word the fates of empires hang, will pause in the middle of an important stroke of diplomacy, and sigh to themselves, "Ah—what would I not do, for the love of such a lady!" You will be with them at their rich dinners—their gorgeous balls. Books will be written about you, and elegantly bound in leather. And you will hold your queenly sway, not for a season or two, like other fine ladies—but for a hundred years, *two* hundred! You, Etta, *you*—the finest lady of them all! [*His voice sinks.*] Can you—see it?—*feel* it—? [*A look of wonderment has grown in her eyes. She sits entranced, her face transfigured with a kind of gracious, queenly joy.* MATEY *draws a deep and grateful breath and rising goes slowly to the easel, with his eyes still upon her, repeating softly.*] The—finest—lady—of—them—all—[*He paints rapidly, but with infinite care, looking from her to the portrait and back again. A few more strokes—and tossing his brush in the air, he exclaims jubilantly.*] There! By the Lord Harry, we've got it! Etta—you *Love*—we've *got* it! [ETTA *comes out of her trance and starts forward.* MATEY *seizes her hand and drags her to the portrait.*] Look—it's done!

[*She gazes at the marvel with widening eyes, while* MATEY *gleefully daubs a sign* "*Fresh Paint*" *on a piece of card-board.*]

ETTA. Oh—if that isn't simply the grandest thing!—And to think that it's me—a lady like that! Oh, *isn't* she lovely! [MATEY *places the sign on the corner of the easel, thereby eliciting a giggle from Etta—not a difficult achievement.*]—Jest as if it was a park bench! Mr. White—you do the *cutest* things. . . . [*In sheer jubilance,* MATEY *takes her hands and dances her around.*]

MATEY [*to the tune of* "*Round and Round the Mulberry Bush*"]. It's done! It's done! It's done—done—done—so early in the morning!

ETTA [*breathlessly*]. But it's *afternoon!*

MATEY. —So early in the *morning—!*

[ETTA, *at first a reluctant partner, at length abandons herself to the celebration.*]

MATEY *and* ETTA [*as they dance around*]. It's done! It's done, done, done—so early in the morning!

NANCY *enters, attired—heaven save us!—in a short black house dress, and a white apron*

NANCY. The ceilings may hold out downstairs. But the odds are against it. What is it all about?

MATEY [*ten years off his age*]. —History, my dear!—I've finished the portrait! We were celebrating the dawn of a new epoch in American Art—[*He performs a pirouette.*]—So early in the morning!

NANCY. Finished . . . ? Oh—wonderful—! [*She goes swiftly to the portrait and regards it with shining eyes.*] Matey—I could go on my knees to it. . . .

MATEY [*huskily*]. I'm—glad it pleases you, dear—

NANCY. *Pleases* me!—Can't you see what's in my silly eyes? [*She blinks back the tears, and laughs joyfully.*] There—I'm a fool. Oh! —Those pearls might be alive! You know, one feels awfully cocky, with a husband who can—[*She sees* ETTA *staring at her and trying to control her laughter.*]—What is it you find so diverting?

ETTA [*with the air of the lady* MATEY *has painted*]. Your appearance. It amuses one. —Chawming, though—really *quate* chawming. . . .

NANCY. You'd better go finish cleaning the silver. [ETTA, *somewhat diminished, goes out.*] Matey—you've simply ruined her. She'll serve the children's dinner-guests tonight like a queen throwing pence to the poor.

MATEY [*amused*]. Why not have a buffet supper up here, instead?

[NANCY *is struck by the idea.*]

NANCY. May we?—Splendid! They'd love it.—And incidentally, with all this—atmosphere, we can figure on less food.

MATEY. —How many are they?

NANCY. Sixteen, counting you and me—the prospective ushers and bridesmaids, you know. They've hit on rather a sweet way of announcing it at Ronny's dance. Ricky's to be a troubadour, and Ronny a Seventeenth Century lady. I've a costume for you. . . .

MATEY [*as he scrapes paint from the palette*]. Good.—How *are* the funds, dear?

NANCY. They haven't been lower since the day after our wedding-trip.

MATEY. Thank God there's a picture for sale—and a dividend due.

NANCY [*regarding the pile of mail on the table*]. You haven't touched your mail since Tuesday!

MATEY. Me and the Goddess has been talkin' confidential.

NANCY [*looking over the mail*]. Perhaps it's in this lot—no. . . .

MATEY. It'll come Monday.

NANCY. Here's one from your broker, dated May 24th. . . .

MATEY. A circular, probably. [*He takes the mail from* NANCY, *slitting the envelopes with his scalpel.*]

NANCY. Oh, I meant to ask you,—are these of any use? [*She takes two square slips of paper from the pocket of her apron.*] They were in the pocket of that smock you wanted washed. [*Giving him one of them, she studies the other.*] They're not sketches, are they?—I had one fearful moment when I thought you'd gone in for cubism.

MATEY. Not I!—This is merely a demonstration proving that if a National Advertising Campaign increased our sales—I mean Warren's sales—only four per cent, it would more than pay for itself.

NANCY [*dryly*]. What could be fairer than that? [*Proffering the second bit of paper.*] And this—?

MATEY [*more reluctantly*]. —It's a diagram showing that by running the raw mix from the vats direct to the ripeners by pipe, we'd save at least two and one-half per cent on our production costs. . . .

NANCY. Most ingenious of you. I suppose I'd best reserve a *separate* drawer for these.

[*She holds out her hand for them.* MATEY *stares at them dumbly for a moment, then tears them up and jams the pieces into his pocket.*]

MATEY. Habit again!—Must I ride two horses my whole life long?

NANCY [*calmly*]. That, I presume, is the question.

[MATEY *begins to read his mail.*]

MATEY. Remind me to pay my insurance policy Tuesday, will you? Here's another notice from them. And the infernal income-tax on the fifteenth. Otherwise, they'll double it. Hope the dividend's not late. . . .

[NANCY *takes a bill from his hands.*]

NANCY. Here—I'll take that. It's a bill for Jean's mumps. —Whew! They've gone up—fifty dollars a mump!

MATEY [*giving her another*]. What do you want done about this?

NANCY [*which she returns promptly*]. Nothing. By now those Armenians must be living on caviar.

MATEY [*reading a letter*]. Good Lord!

NANCY. What's the matter?

MATEY [*as he goes to the sofa*]. Is this a morning paper?

NANCY. —"The Times." Dear—what *is* it? [*She reads the letter which* MATEY *extends to her.*] Oh—how awful. . . .

[MATEY *opens the newspaper to the financial page.*]

MATEY. It may have been a false alarm. I don't see anything. Yes—here it is—. Here it is, all right—and worse than they prophesied, too.

NANCY [*in spite of herself*]. If you'd only got this letter in time!

MATEY [*ironically*]. Ah, no!—I was too busy with my brushes, to watch the market, and read my mail. [*He scans the letter again.*] Well—I've got to have cash by Tuesday, loss or no loss. You'd better take Hubbard's advice, and hold on to your stock. I'll go to town and see him right away. A fine mess I've got us into!—Matey and his money—they were soon parted, weren't they?

NANCY [*her comforting arms about him*]. Dear—*don't* say things bitterly, like that. We didn't expect this to be a bed of roses. . . .

[*Up from the stairs comes* RICKY, *golf-trousers—linen; coat—homespun, and over one ear a Troubadour cap, with flowing feather. He has a guitar tied around his neck by two long silk stockings, and thrums a chord as he enters.*]

RICKY. Say, Nanny—where's the rest of my costu—[*He discovers his parents once more unmindful of their dignity.*] Will you two *never* grow up? [NANCY *and* MATEY *part, looking a little sheepish, and* MATEY *goes to a chair at the window—reading the paper.*] I feel more like Chanticleer than a troubadour. Don't mind my freezing on to a pair of your stockings, do you? Lord! You must have long legs!

NANCY [*primly*]. I mind very much. There's a ribbon with the rest of it downstairs.

RICKY. I cannot relinquish the socks. [*He crosses to* MATEY, *thrumming and singing.*] "List to me, Lady Love, heark to my plea—" [*But stops suddenly at the sight of* MATEY'S *face.*] What's the matter, old Lad?—you look as though a mule had kicked you.

MATEY. *Two* mules, Rick—

NANCY. Your father has had bad news from his broker.

RICKY [*all bantering aside*]. Gosh, Dad—that's a rotten shame. I've got four hundred and sixty saved up, if that'll help any—

MATEY. The money for your wedding trip?

RICKY [*Chamber of Commerce, please note*]. What's Bermuda—compared to our own Niagara Falls?

MATEY. Thanks, Son—but I don't think I'll need it. [*With an attempt at jocosity.*] I may sell my picture over the week-end.

NANCY. It's finished. You haven't seen it yet. . . . [RICKY *examines the portrait admiringly.*]

RICKY. I call this painting! Say, how about my buying it?

MATEY. You haven't enough.

RICKY. I'll take it on installments. Listen, lady—[*He prepares to sing to the picture.*] "List to me, Lady Love—" [*But* MATEY *brings the serenade to a deservedly abrupt conclusion.*]

NANCY. What have you children been doing?

[RICKY *finds a comfortable place on the window-seat.*]

RICKY. Ronny's had the nag out—went home to change—coming right over. I've been shooting clay pigeons—only got twelve out of twenty-five—but I gave the others a nasty scare. [NANCY *laughs.*] Say Dad, G. T.'s up here with the Thompsons over Sunday. Said he might drop in to see you.

MATEY. I hope he does. Is he still handling most of my work?

RICKY. No—didn't I tell you?—new man came in three weeks ago. Name's Chadwick—

MATEY [*sharply*]. T. L. Chadwick—?

RICKY. Think so. He's famous as the Battle of the Marne—and acts it. They say he's dragging down forty-five thousand a year. He's taken over your job—*I* thought G. T.'d keep it open for a year, anyway.

[*This has all been a considerable shock for* MATEY. *For a moment he stares speechlessly at* RICKY, *then turns to* NANCY, *speaking in a changed voice.*]

MATEY. What time do you expect Geoff?

NANCY. About four-thirty.

MATEY. Good—I'll have time to see him before I leave.

[*He goes out by stairs.* RICKY *rises, and with a gesture of disgust with himself, goes to a chair near* NANCY.]

NANCY. Rick—you must learn tact. You couldn't have chosen a worse moment to speak of that new man at Warren's.

RICKY [*shamefacedly*]. I knew it as soon as I opened my face. I ought to be shot. But after all, Nancy, I can't say that I blame G. T. . . .

NANCY [*suddenly*]. Are you really happy there?

RICKY [*off hand*]. Sure. Why not?

NANCY. Tell me honestly!

RICKY [*confidentially*]. Well—you see it's this way: When I look at the men higher up in the office—men of about forty or so—and realize that if I barge through in really noble style that that's where *I'll* land at forty—I don't exactly jump up and down and clap my hands at the prospect. But after all—that's life, isn't it, darling?—You get some things, and some things you don't. And I've packed a *couple* of hearts full in Ronny and you—[*To prove it, he kisses her cheek.*] You're a wench after my own heart.

NANCY [*persisting*]. But *don't* you miss your architecture?

RICKY [*strumming*]. Rarely think of it.

RONNY *comes in, very fresh and sprightly, as the result of a ride, a tub and a pretty new dress*

RONNY [*however*]. I don't expect to sit down for several centuries.

RICKY. Serves you right for jumping that green mare. If I were her—

NANCY. "—if I were *she.*"

RICKY [*a proper rebuke to the purist*]. . . . If I were her—I'd have bounced you off on your nose.

RONNY [*so sweetly*]. No, precious one—if you'd been the mare, I'd have taken you over the roof. [*She sees the portrait, which occasions a deep breath of admiration.*] Oh, this is too beautiful.

NANCY [*who is putting* MATEY'S *paint table in order*]. I'm inclined to agree with you, Ronny.

[*But there is a sudden new interest, for* RONNY *sees the mannikin. She picks it up and hugs it passionately.*]

RONNY. Oh—I want her! I want her!

RICKY. —Name's "Genevieve." She's Dad's mistress.

NANCY. Ricky!

RICKY [*with a gesture*]. Art's his mistress. Genevieve is Art.

[RONNY *takes from a chair a piece of the same stuff as* ETTA'S *dress, and wraps it about the figure's shoulders. Henceforward, "Genevieve" remains gratefully near her.*]

NANCY [*as she moves toward the stairs*]. I'll be back in a few minutes. If Mr. Nichols comes, you entertain him, will you?

RICKY. Certainly shall! [NANCY *goes out, and* RICKY *turns to his* RONNY.] As studios go—not so nasty—wot? [*He lights a cigarette for her and one for himself.*]

RONNY. I love it.

RICKY. Nanny calls it the Zoo. [*He takes her hand and conducts her across the room.*] Here you see a mountain-goat, at the age of seven months. And here—[*Indicating another specimen on the opposite wall.*]—the same goat, several years later.

[RONNY *nods gravely.* RICKY, *before letting her hand go, raises it to his lips and kisses it. For a silent moment life's infinite fulfillment looks out to each, from the other's eyes.* RONNY *speaks softly.*]

RONNY. You dear—[*But, after all, one must be practical.*] Not *very* stiff!—Chuck us a cushion, will you, Dreadful?

[RICKY *procures a cushion from the window seat and another from the sofa.*]

RICKY [*preparing a place for them on the floor*]. Lord—three sets of tennis—and I'm fit for the ash-can! This working indoors all week takes it out of you, do you know it?

[*They seat themselves, back to back on the cushions.*]

RONNY [*sleepily*]. Um—. Now do you *really* like it there, Stupe?

RICKY. Child, I'm engrossed!

RONNY. Sure?

RICKY. Absolutely! I'd no idea soap and toothpaste could hand me such a thrill. Had a talk with G. T. this morning. Told me I'd rate three thousand as soon's I marched back down the aisle.

RONNY. He's a sweet old thing. We'll be filthy rich. [*Yawns.*] Umph!

RICKY. I regard that as a deliberately unfriendly act.

RONNY. I'm a dead bunny.

RICKY. Not too sprightly myself. Let's play shut-eye for a while.

RONNY [*closing her eyes*]. You're on. Night-O. . . .

RICKY [*hunching his shoulders*]. Move over. . . .

RONNY. Great Oaf!

[*They close their eyes, and there is a short pause.*]

RICKY. ". . . and God bless everybody in this house."

[*Another short pause.*]

RONNY. —Two minds without a single thought. . . . [*—And still another. Then* RONNY *begins to wriggle.*] Hell's bells—I'm being prodded in the spine. What is it?—something in your pocket, or just—anatomy . . . ? [RICKY *is wide-awake in a moment.*]

RICKY [*eagerly*]. Oh—I forgot. [*Rising, he puts out his cigarette, and extracting an old book from his pocket, again seats himself.*] Look here, Beau'ful—I picked this up in a bookstore this noon. Sixteen dollars. It's a first edition of Mossgrave's "Architecture, and ye Associated Artes"—published in 1611—illustrated with woodcuts—rare as hell.

RONNY [*regarding it sleepily*]. Priceless!

RICKY. You said it. And look—[*He opens the book to the flyleaf and proudly points to the signature thereon.*]

RONNY. "I. Jones—His Book."—Should I be impressed?

RICKY [*ironically*]. A little. Do you know who it is?

RONNY. I bite: Who?

RICKY [*impressively*]. This book belonged to—Inigo Jones!

RONNY. What a screaming name. [*To* GENEVIEVE.] Did you hear that, Genevieve?—"In-again Jones" [*To* RICKY.] She wants to know who he was?

RICKY [*witheringly*]. —Just one of the greatest architects that ever lived, that's all. Designed Whitehall, and Queen's House, and a few miserable little things like that. Not *very* famous.

RONNY [*somewhat abashed*]. I am the Indian Club among Dumbbells.

RICKY [*studying the pages*]. —And look at this—isn't it great? [*He becomes engrossed in the book.* RONNY *watches him quizzically.*] Honestly if I could design a façade like that, I'd die happy.—And this gargoyle—you see the vine-motif has been carried—

RONNY [*quietly*]. Put your arm around me, Ricky. [*Absently he does so.*]

RICKY [*going right on*]. —The vine-motif has been carried out even here. And I'll be blowed—this must be one of the very earliest developments of the rose window—

RONNY [*experimentally*]. Rick—I want to be kissed—[RICKY *kisses her. A piece of paper falls from the book to the floor.* RONNY *sighs.*] Oh—that's rather delightful. . . .

RICKY [*for the moment, genuinely moved*]. Damn right! [*But only for the moment, for he turns back to the book, almost immediately.*]—The facing shows that it's at a very primitive stage—

RONNY [*a certain heart-breaking realization is slowly tightening about her*]. Does it . . . ?

RICKY. Um. . . . [*He sees that she has picked up the piece of paper, and is studying it listlessly.*] Here—lay off!—That's not finished yet!

RONNY. What is it?

RICKY. It's a plan I was making for our new diggings. Now you know what made me late for your dinner last night. [RONNY'*s face lights up; here is hope.*]

RONNY [*eagerly—handing it to him*]. Tell me about it!

RICKY [*explaining*]. You see—I wanted something we could add on to—the way Dad and Nancy did to this. First comes the cellar—for the furnace and things. Downstairs: hall, living-room, dining-room—that little hole is the library, kitchen—out back, servants' quarters above it. Upstairs: four bedrooms—yours and mine, and two guests' rooms. Three baths. Top floor: small store room and playroom. . . .

RONNY. . . . For us . . . ?

RICKY [*solemnly*]. For our progeny.

RONNY. Isn't it big! How many do you think there ought to be?

RICKY. Oh—[*Conservatively.*]—three or four. . . .

RONNY [*thoughtfully*]. Well—I'll see what I can do. . . . [*She leans over to examine the plans more closely.*] What are these?

RICKY [*with additional enthusiasm*]. Ah—here's the real work! Look, Beau'ful—the stables—miniature reproduction of Charles the Second's at Windsor. And this is the kennels—just like some I once saw for St. Bernards at a monastery near St. Moritz.

RONNY [*regarding him oddly*]. They're more interesting than the house, aren't they?

RICKY. Ever so much!—You see it's one of my pet convictions that you can make any building beautiful—even a cow-shed,—without in the least contradicting its original charac—[*He regards her in surprise.*] Dearest!—What is the matter with you?—You look like the very devil—

RONNY [*confused*]. I—? Why—I—Don't be a fool, Rick—[*Her hand brushes across her eyes. She sighs, shakes her head, and laughs shortly.*] I'm—just simply in a fog over tonight. . . .

[RICKY *regards her dubiously, then becomes matter-of-fact once more.*]

RICKY. Oh say—I don't want to muff that troubadour stunt. Slip me the dope again, will you . . . ?

RONNY [*lifelessly*]. It's—not my idea, you know. It's Mother's: We're to have supper on the south terrace at twelve. When they're all seated, you amble up below the second story window, and begin—

[RICKY *begins thrumming and singing gayly. As he does so,* RONNY *frowns over the revelatory little slip of paper.*]

RICKY [*singing and strumming*].

"List to me, Lady Love, heark to my plea.
Love hold'th no bounty so precious as thee,
Flown my heart's gayety, lovelorn my life,
Sad and desolate I, save I have thee to wife."

—and then you press a red, red rose to your lips, and toss it lightly to me, and I catch it in my teeth, or something, and *voilà!*—[*He strikes a chord.*] The kitty is out of the bag!

RONNY [*slowly*]. And—suppose—instead—I just—turned away—and shut the window—*would* you be sad and desolate—?

RICKY. On the contrary I should execute a few choice clog steps and sing:

"Be she fairer than the day
Or the flow'ry meads in May—
What care I how fair she be
If she be not so to me?"

[*During the song* RONNY *has rolled the plans together into a small roll.*]

RONNY [*rising*]. Is that the way you'd really feel—do you think?

RICKY [*gayly*]. Sure!

RONNY [*quietly*]. I'm glad.—Because I—don't—

RICKY. Don't what . . . ?

[*His soft strumming continues, an ominous accompaniment to the words that follow.*]

RONNY. . . . Don't love you, Rick.

[*The mannikin is permitted to topple to the floor.* RICKY *looks at* RONNY, *appalled—and then laughs.*]

RICKY [*scoffing*]. No—that's why you're marrying me!

RONNY. It's—why I'm *not*. . . .

RICKY [*not to be taken in*]. Too late now.

RONNY. It's—just this side of—too late. . . . [*Pause,* RICKY *is trying bravely to smile.*] I—*mean* it, you know.

RICKY [*with difficulty; his smile comes and goes. He stands the guitar against a chair and goes to her*]. Ronny—please find some other way to—ride me. I'm—you're—I—you see, I'm such a fool about you, that I can't—play up to this.

RONNY [*speaking in a small voice*]. It—breaks me into little pieces—but I mean it. [*He takes her hand.*]

RICKY [*dazed and incredulous*]. Ronny—you—you simply *can't*. . . .

[RONNY *withdraws her hand.*]

RONNY. Do—you remember that day last Autumn—what I told you about Father and Mother—? [RICKY *tries to speak, but nods, instead.*]—How I said I was going to marry the next nice person I was—fond of?—You were the nice person, Ricky—[*Shakes her head, sorrowfully.*] Oh—the nicest one!—And I thought surely I'd love you. But—I don't. And I can't—just *can't* go through with it, without—

RICKY [*with effort*]. I—don't know what to do. I don't know what's expected of me. I—don't quite understand it. Nearly—but not quite. I can't believe that you—you've simply got to tell me some more about it. . . . [*There is a sound at the stairs.* RICKY *glances over his shoulder. His voice lowers.*] Hell—Nichols, I suppose. . . . The playroom—quick!

[*He holds the playroom door open and follows her through, closing it after them.* ETTA *comes up the stairs, dressed as a lady still, but carrying a sobering dust-cloth. She places the guitar upon a trunk and begins aimlessly to dust. Goes to the portrait, looks at it adoringly, turns about, as though posing before a mirror, the better to see her profile, then suddenly pirouettes to her first position. She picks up "Genevieve," and looking about to see that she is alone, places her upon a chair facing the dais. Then, draping herself in the throne-chair, she touches her hair lightly with the arched tips of her fingers, assumes a rather weary expression, and begins to talk to her inanimate companion.*]

ETTA [*affectedly*]. Yes—*such* weather! Just *too* dreadful! I've had no gulf for weeks. . . . [*Lowly, to herself.*] Gulf—golf—galf—gowf—guff—[*This satisfies her. Aloud.*]—I have had no guff for weeks. [*A pause. Then she smiles, and extends a properly limp hand to the air.*] Oh—ah—how-do-you-do?—So good of you to come. [*She waits for the inaudible answer.*] *No!* What a piddy! [*Lowly, to herself.*] Piddy—pity—pit-ty—[*This is quite satisfactory, so she tries it aloud.*] *What* a pitt-ty! [*Pause. To "Genevieve".*] But my deah—my bridge is *simply* deplorable! [*Pause. This has been a good one, and she is well pleased with herself. There is more than one person at this most de luxe of receptions, so she greets another.*] Oh—ah—how-do-you-do? [*The response is audible this time, for* GEOFFREY NICHOLS *has quietly mounted the stairs to the studio.*]

NICHOLS. How do you do?

[ETTA *has one very bad moment, but fortunately regains composure in time.*]

ETTA [*what's good for one, is good for another*]. So—good of you to come—

NICHOLS [*a little surprised*]. Thanks. Permit me to present myself: I am Geoffrey Nichols.

ETTA [*this, with effort*]. How do you do? I am—Miss—Henrietta Hone—[*With a gracious gesture.*] Won't you sit down?

NICHOLS. Thanks—[*He finds "Genevieve," however, the occupant of the logical chair. Tenderly, he places her upon the floor, and takes her place, facing* ETTA.] An extraordinary person at the door told me that Mrs. White would be up here—

ETTA. Oh, yes—that was Katie. What a piddy—[*Oh! She has muffed it!*]

NICHOLS. Not at all! I consider myself very fortunate. Are you staying with the Whites?

ETTA. Yes.

NICHOLS. Charming, aren't they?

ETTA [*a little less securely*]. Yes. [*Pause.* NICHOLS *is rather taken aback by her apparent aloofness.*]

NICHOLS [*at a loss*]. Er—

[ETTA *turns quickly.*]

ETTA. My deah—my bridge is *simply* deplorable.

NICHOLS [*sympathetically*]. I'm *so* sorry. Mine is, too. Will they expect us to play? [ETTA *looks away, not answering.*] I hope not. I've just gone two rounds of goff, and—

ETTA. Of *what . . . ?*

NICHOLS. —Of goff—and lost six balls, and most of my mind. [ETTA, *unnoticed by him, forms the word "goff" several times with her lips.*] I've been chanting the "Götterdämmerung," with variations, most of the afternoon—

[*It is not a distaste for Wagner that causes* ETTA *to flinch.*]

ETTA. Mr. Nichols—I do not consider such language at all refined.

[*For one appalled moment,* NICHOLS *stares at her. Then he realizes that she is, of course, purposely burlesquing. This guest of the Whites' has, indeed, both originality and charm! He laughs delightedly.*]

NICHOLS. Delicious! [*He settles himself more comfortably, and speaks with amused gravity.*] Of course, I ain't exactly what you'd call a *gent*—but I gotta hearta gold. . . . [ETTA *never changes expression.*] How long have you been here with the Whites?

ETTA. Oh—quite awhile—

NICHOLS. I must take Nancy to task for this. I'm a native now, you know. I've taken the Burton place for the Summer. I can't think why I haven't seen you. . . .

ETTA. Do you attend the dances at the Odd Fellows Hall?

NICHOLS [*not to be outdone*]. No—I'm of the Loyal Order of Moose. But I hear they're real tasty affairs.

ETTA [*soulfully*]. They are grand.

NICHOLS [*we are getting on*]. What a delightful person you are! Won't you lunch with me tomorrow?

ETTA [*slowly*]. Why—I *can't*—

NICHOLS. Then when *may* I see you?

ETTA [*hesitatingly*]. Uh—uh—Thursday afternoon?

NICHOLS. Splendid! We'll motor out to Waukubuc.

ETTA. That would be elegant.

NICHOLS [*mockingly*]. "Excuse our dust!" [*A silence; he finds nothing to top that mental image of a red and white pennant on the back of his car.*] Do you suppose Nancy knows I'm here?

[ETTA, *who has had enough practice for the present, rises and goes quickly to the stairs.*]

ETTA. I'll go tell her. . . .

NICHOLS [*protesting*]. Oh, please—I didn't mean—I'm enjoying myself so much, really. . . .

[ETTA *continues straight on, regardless. At the top of the stairs, she meets, coming up,* NANCY, *who has changed to an afternoon dress.*]

NANCY [*hastily to* ETTA.] The flowers for tonight have come. Bring them up here now. And you must change—*at once!* [ETTA *goes out.*] Geoffrey—do forgive me. I simply had to scrub up. Did you just arrive? [*She moves toward portrait.*] Look! The *chef d'œuvre* is finished! Now please tell me honestly what you think of it. Isn't it enchanting? Would you believe my Matey could do it?

[NICHOLS *is more than a little puzzled. He glances toward the stairs and proceeds to play safe.*]

NICHOLS [*enthusiastically*]. Such grace of line! What a flair for color! The flesh tints are exquisite. It's simply incredible!

NANCY. Yes. . . . There—we've done our duty! Now tell me what you *really* think.

[NICHOLS *permits himself the steadying influence of a cigarette.*]

NICHOLS. Well—upon my word, I don't know. It's such an extraordinary fine likeness, I suspect it's not great work. He may be merely—clever with a brush—as I'm clever with a typewriter.

NANCY [*feelingly*]. Oh—I *hope* it's not that! [*Realizes what she has said, and laughs.*] Geoffrey—you know what I mean—

NICHOLS. No—I am completely mashed.

[*They seat themselves upon the sofa.*]

NANCY [*in a business-like manner*]. Our really pressing problem now is how to sell it.

NICHOLS [*reflectively*]. If I only had a stationary home—

NANCY. That's very kind. But he wouldn't hear of it, anyway. How *does* one market pictures—do you know?

NICHOLS. Why—I suppose you get them exhibited. . . .

NANCY. You've a nice broad back. Will you walk up and down Fifth Avenue?

NICHOLS. That *was* helpful, wasn't it?

NANCY. If only someone would want it at once.

NICHOLS. Has he done anything else?

NANCY. Just a few sketches. It was difficult, getting under way.

NICHOLS. Such a different life—quite natural. Last Autumn, I did my best to dissuade him. Frankly—how do you think he likes it?

NANCY. Oh, underneath, I think he's been very—I think he's been *happier*—

NICHOLS. Good! You know, apart from my personal interest—to me Matey is Everyman.

NANCY. How do you mean, precisely?

NICHOLS. My gardener kept me occupied for twenty minutes this morning telling me what a splendid carpenter he would have made—and means to make still. [*He laughs shortly.*] He's sixty-three.

NANCY [*thoughtfully*]. I see. But is it the same?

NICHOLS. Maybe not.—How have you weathered the change?

NANCY. I've tried—Oh, I've tried so hard! [*With a little shudder.*] It's shameful, the way prosperity softens one.

NICHOLS [*incredulously*]. You—?

NANCY [*nodding*]. It's a little pathetic, you know, to find you're the sort of person whose conception of a real sacrifice consists in managing with two servants, instead of five.

NICHOLS [*nothing truer, you know*]. Nonsense! Sacrifice is relative. You suffer as much from lack of luxuries, as another woman from lack of meat.

NANCY. Maybe—but it's rather disconcerting, to reach down into your—depths, and touch bottom so quickly.

NICHOLS. Matey's not faltering, is he?

NANCY [*rising*]. No—only a trifle worried. The family budget does it—it's not precisely bulging. And today—poor dear—he's had such upsetting news—[*With a wry smile.*] Someone at a directors' table said, "Please pass the dividends."

NICHOLS. What a bore. [*Thoughtfully.*] I wonder if I couldn't—

NANCY [*with a grateful smile*]. No—he wouldn't let you. When it comes to taking help, he's the rankest of egotists!

NICHOLS. But—[*A thoughtful pause. He rises and looks at the portrait. His face lights up.*] Nancy—I've an idea! This portrait—it's really charming. Now Mrs. Carhart is having her usual drove of twenty or so up for the week-end. There are certain to be a few wealthy patrons of art among them, and—

NANCY [*excitedly*]. Geoffrey!

NICHOLS. —I'm sure that if I asked her, she'd hang it in her drawing room. One of them might want to buy it. At any rate, they'd talk—and it would be a fair test of its worth. The only difficulty is, that if they damned it, Matey would be so cast down that—

NANCY. You darling! Listen: he won't have to know anything about it! He's going into town on the 4.51—coming out again later in the evening. . . .

NICHOLS. Yes?

NANCY. Yes.—Can't we take it over right

after he goes—and have it back before 9.30? They'd have plenty of time to see it. . .

NICHOLS. I don't know why not. But—if it wasn't a go, some one of them might speak about it afterwards. . . .

NANCY. But they won't know who did it! You see—it isn't signed! Say it's the work of an unknown painter—a protégé of Matey's—just in case—[*Turns to portrait.*] Oh, it isn't dry yet. Suppose we had an accident with it?

NICHOLS. That's not likely—wrap it carefully. I'll drive over now and see her—come back for you about 5.30. Then we'll—

[*There is a sound on the stairs.* NANCY *murmurs "Sh-h-h!" and nods an excited assent.* MATEY *enters.*]

MATEY. What's to happen at 5.30? I shan't be here.

NICHOLS. That's just the point. Nancy and I are going to run away together.

MATEY. Good! She needs a change. [*He indicates the portrait.*] Have you seen the—ah—"White" . . . ?

NICHOLS. Rather!—I'm delighted with it.

MATEY. Isn't he nice, Nanny?

NANCY. No one has ever so endeared himself to me.

MATEY. I'm going to let the Metropolitan and the Luxembourg fight it out. Look here, Balzac—what do you think of this left arm?

NICHOLS. But my good Gainsborough—I find it a bit muscular!

MATEY. That, my dear Hawthorne, is light—not muscle.

NICHOLS. But I tell you, Sargent, that I know a muscle when I see one!

MATEY. The thing I want really to know, Chambers, is just how well *do* you see?

NICHOLS. Quite well enough, Mr. Christy, to know a tendon from a sunbeam.

MATEY. Harold Bell, I find you a very stuffy person. . . .

NICHOLS. Oh, Briggs!—Think what you'll suffer when the critics start to bark! [MATEY *throws up his hands in surrender.* NICHOLS *becomes serious.*] By the way, Matey—I've five or ten thousand that's simply mouldering away. Do you know of any trustworthy individual who'd be willing to take it on for a year or so at, say, six per cent . . . ?

MATEY. Why—[*He looks suspiciously to* NANCY, *who brazens it out.*]—There must be any number of them, old son. But I can't think of one just at the moment.

NICHOLS. If you hear of one, let me know. I'd consider it a favor.

MATEY [*slowly*]. Yes—I'll let you know. . . .

NICHOLS. Well—I must be rolling along. The Duane's dance ahead of me—and I haven't done a line all day.

MATEY [*amiably*]. We artists must think of posterity, mustn't we?—See you later, anyway!

NICHOLS. Right-O. . . .

NANCY. I'll go down with you. . . .

[NICHOLS *stands aside to let her pass, and is about to follow when* MATEY *stops him.*]

MATEY. Oh—Geoff—

NICHOLS. Yes?

MATEY. Thanks very much—but I really think I can manage without it. . . .

NICHOLS. Without what?

MATEY [*smiling*]. The five or ten thousand at six per cent.

NICHOLS [*impatiently*]. *Damn* the interest, Matey.

MATEY. It's bully of you—but I don't think I'll need it.

NICHOLS. Well—in case you do—

[*He turns to go.* MATEY *goes to the far window and stands there, looking out. Just as* NICHOLS *reaches the stairs,* ETTA *comes in. She is in her simple gray working-dress once more, and carries a box of flowers and a water-filled vase.* NICHOLS *stares at her—his incredible suspicion confirmed.*]

ETTA. Good-by, Mr. Nichols—

NICHOLS [*genially*]. *Good*-by! [*He glances at* MATEY, *who is apparently oblivious, and continues lowly.*] Oh,—uh—in case I can't come myself on Thursday, I'll send my chauffeur. He's a delightful chap—Odd Fellow, I believe—

[*With a gracious bow, he goes out.* ETTA *begins to arrange the flowers in the vases.* MATEY *comes over to the portrait.*]

MATEY [*absently*]. What did Mr. Nichols say?

ETTA. I'm going riding in his auto Thursday afternoon. It'll be wonderful practice. He's the funniest man!—I had a perfectly *lovely* talk with him before Mrs. White came in.

[MATEY *looks at her in frank amazement. Then his brow puckers reminiscently, and he suddenly sees the joke on* NICHOLS. *He laughs silently to himself, but* ETTA *is aware of nothing amiss.*] I can't imagine how anyone *could* be much pleasanter'n Mr. Nichols.

MATEY [*genuinely*]. Nor I! Friends are very nice things—and sons—and wives.—And money's a nice thing, too—you know that, when you haven't any. . . . [RICKY *enters from the playroom, looking very white and sick. He carries the roll of white paper—his "plans"—upon which he nervously twirls the engagement ring. At first* MATEY *does not see him.*] Job gone—income gone—Art's a hard mistress, Etta—she picks your bones dry—

ETTA [*the Champion*]. Oh, *no*, Mr. White! Art is lovely—jest lovely.

MATEY [*seeing* RICKY]. Hello, Rick!—Where did *you* blow from?

RICKY. Playroom. . . . [*There is a short pause.*] Father—you might as well know—it's all off between Ronny and me.

MATEY [*astounded*]. What's this?

RICKY [*with an attempt at a smile*]. Over—done—*fini*—. We aren't going to be married.

MATEY. But I don't understand. . . .

RICKY. It took *me* a long while too. It was all—bogus. She wants to see you—don't know why. Please don't cross-examine her —I think I've asked about all the questions there are—

MATEY [*impotently*]. But—tonight—?

RICKY [*turns to him*]. Too late to call off the dance, of course. We're going right ahead with it—just as if it were an—ordinary party. [*He laughs ironically.*] Not *very* different! [*He sees* ETTA, *who, you may be sure, is not missing a word.*] C'mon, Etta—finish those later. [ETTA *goes out and* RICKY *turns again to* MATEY.] Be decent to her, won't you?—She's feeling pretty sunk.

[*He picks up the guitar, but as he does so, a string twangs. With a scarcely perceptible shudder, he carefully replaces it upon the trunk.* RONNY *appears in the playroom doorway. Her color is high, and her eyes very bright. She holds her chin up, as if by effort. For a moment their eyes meet, and* RICKY *contrives to smile, before he goes out, leaving her with* MATEY.]

RONNY. Mr. White—

MATEY. Yes, Ronny. . . .

RONNY. Ricky—told you?

[MATEY *nods, unable completely to hide his scorn for this little jilt.*]

MATEY. You don't love him, h'm—?

RONNY [*passionately*]. Love him! Oh—if a year ago someone had told me that I'd ever love anyone as I love Rick now, I'd have—I'd have—[*She cannot go on.*]

MATEY. Then I fail to see why you've—

RONNY. I'll tell you why!—if I told *him*, he'd just laugh me out of it. Give me your word no one else shall know—no one at all. . . .

MATEY [*after a pause*]. Very well—my word.

RONNY. I'm between Ricky and the thing he wants to do. That's plain. If I don't marry him, he'll go abroad and study as he should. [*Her hand falls upon his arm.*] *You* know what it means to him. *You* know he *must* be what he's cut *out* to be!

MATEY. You dear child. . . .

[*He picks up her hand and touches his lips to it. She takes it from him at once.*]

RONNY [*in pain*]. Oh—please—that's Ricky's trick!

MATEY. You're very brave, Ronny, and very fine—[*She shakes her head violently.*]—but we can't afford to send him abroad, now.

[RONNY *straightens up, puzzled and shocked.*]

RONNY. Wha-a-a-t . . . ?

MATEY. I am not a rich man. I depended largely upon my salary. It stopped when I left business.

RONNY. But you've *something*—and I only need half of what I have a year. Take the other half—put it with whatever *you* can. I'd be happier—*much.*

MATEY. My dear. . . . But there's been bad news, you see. I've almost nothing, now—not even enough for Nancy and me.

RONNY [*cruelly*]. Then why don't you go back to business? [MATEY *flinches, in spite of himself.*]

MATEY. One has—certain obligations to oneself—you know. [RONNY *squares off—a cold fury.*]

RONNY. I've just taken my heart and [*With*

a gesture of breaking it between her hands.] done *that* with it. For him—for my Ricky! And you can stand there talking about yourself! Aren't you his father? Aren't you responsible for him?

MATEY [*genuinely moved, but smiling a little*]. You are telling me I've—given hostages to Fortune?

RONNY [*impatiently*]. I don't know anything about "hostages." I just know that there's something big in Ricky, that's got to come out. You can help him—and because you *can*, you *must*. He's your son—you've let yourself in for it!

[*This is too much;* MATEY'S *spirit is up at last.*]

MATEY. Listen to me: your reasoning's very bad. You say I'm responsible for Ricky. All right—I'm responsible for bringing him out of nowhere into a very lively, very interesting world—for giving him twenty-one years of every advantage a boy can have. Now why shouldn't I think of myself for awhile?

RONNY. When all that time you've been teaching him to love something, aren't you bound to stick by him till he shows what he can make of it?

MATEY. He had his chance.

RONNY. And now that it's gone, must he wait till he's—forty, or so—for another? [*This shot tells.*]

MATEY [*doggedly*]. Why not?—That's what *I* did.

RONNY. So—you want everything to be for him—just as it's been for you—

MATEY [*sharply*]. Please! Please!

RONNY. —Only *you* had Mrs. White in its place. He'd have nothing: I'd feel like a thief. You're *used* to doing what you don't want to do. He's not. He'd be just—empty. . . .

MATEY. He can quit now, and do what he wants on his own.

RONNY. —And so he would! But could he go abroad? Could he be all that he *might* be?

MATEY. That's up to him.

RONNY. It's up to—! Oh, we *can't* argue, can we? What makes my reasons right for me, is just what makes them wrong for you.

MATEY. That's the old and the young of it, Ronny.

RONNY [*swiftly*]. But there's one thing we jibe on! Both of us love Ricky. What you won't do for duty, you *will* do for love!

MATEY [*with a gesture toward his painting*]. Do you know how I love this?

RONNY. Not half so much as Ricky! He's your *son*. He'll come first!

MATEY [*whimsically*]. You haven't convinced me, Ronny. But you've reminded me that there's a very cruel law that rules most men's destinies.

RONNY [*an avalanche*]. Not only *men's!*

[*She shuts her eyes in pain, swallows hard, shakes her hand as if to shake something out of it, and then raises her chin sharply.* NANCY *appears at the top of the stairs, carrying a large piece of brown wrapping-paper and a ball of cord.*]

NANCY. Matey—your train. . . .

[RONNY *wheels about and confronts* NANCY. *For a moment, you feel that she is about to attack her as she attacked* MATEY. *But when her voice is heard it is the voice of a broken-hearted little girl, trying her best to be spunky to the end.*]

RONNY. Doing anything special Monday morning?

NANCY [*puzzled*]. Why, no.

RONNY. If I may, I want to come over—

NANCY. Do. . . .

RONNY. —and cry on your shoulder.

NANCY. But what has happened?

[RONNY *flings her last words over her shoulder as she goes down the stairs.*]

RONNY. I'll be in about eleven! [NANCY, *bewildered, looks after her for a moment and then turns to* MATEY.] Matey—what *is* it?

MATEY [*grimly*]. A joke on me—one of fate's funniest. [*He crosses toward the stairs, shaking his head and laughing softly and bitterly.*] Laugh, my dear—laugh at me.

[NANCY *is gazing after him intently, as*

THE CURTAIN FALLS

ACT III

It is shortly after nine, the same evening, and the studio is unlighted, save for the bright moonlight which flows through the great dormer-window upon the empty easel. Through this window a string of Japanese lanterns is seen, glowing in the dim distance.

There is a sound at the stairs. NANCY *enters, and crosses quickly to the long table, fumbles for a match, scratches it, and begins to light the half-burned candles in the sconces.*

The increasing light shows that the fifteen chairs at the table have been hastily pulled back, and that the table has not yet been entirely cleared. The dappled-gray hobby-horse has been brought from its hiding-place, and upon it sits "Genevieve," a paper cap upon her head.

NANCY *is dressed as a Spanish Lady. She wears a black dress, a lace mantilla of black shot through with jade green, earrings, beads, bracelets, and a jade comb in her hair, which is worn high, in the Spanish fashion.*

As she lights the candles, a heavy, halting step is heard upon the stairs. She seizes one of the sconces, and crossing to the stairway, holds it high above her head, to light the entrance.

NANCY. Geoff—do hurry. . . . [*Still the very slow, heavy steps continue.* NANCY *becomes impatient.*] . . . Do you want him to come in and *find* us? [*The steps continue at the same speed.*] Be careful at the corner! [*A silence. Then the steps begin again, slower than before.* NANCY *is vexed.*] Oh—I *know* you'll rip it to shreds! [*Pause. Then suddenly the steps begin to race.* NANCY *leaps back, and the tip of the portrait, wrapped in brown paper, appears, and behind it* NICHOLS, *who enters as if he had been hurled by a catapult. He wears a Pierrot costume of black and silver, a black skull-cap, and an enormous white ruff at his neck.*] Useless person—utterly. . . .

NICHOLS. Useless! Three flights of stairs without a mishap—and she calls me useless!

[*Together, they remove the paper and a protecting frame from the portrait, which* NICHOLS *replaces upon the easel.* NANCY *folds the paper, ties string around it, and conceals it and the frame.*]

NANCY. Do you really think there's a chance?

[NICHOLS *extracts a watch with great difficulty from somewhere within his clothes.*]

NICHOLS. Mrs. Carhart sent word that she'd phone me here before 9.30. [*He looks at the watch.*] Sixteen past. By a lightning calculation, fourteen minutes left.

NANCY [*seating herself at the table*]. I wonder who it could be.

NICHOLS. *I* haven't the slightest idee.

NANCY. But whom was she having up?

NICHOLS. She expected the Graysons, and the Hoyts—

NANCY. Wait a minute!

[*She takes down the names, writing with a crayon upon a piece of* MATEY'S *sketching-paper.*]

NICHOLS. —And the Crams, and Reggie de Courcy—

NANCY. Wretched little worm. Tony Cram must be blind.

NICHOLS. And the Webbs, and Gregory Kendall—

NANCY. It might be Kendall! Wouldn't that be luck?

NICHOLS. —Doubt if it's Greg. He once dined with Whistler. —And the Warrens—

NANCY. The G. T.'s—?

NICHOLS. Yes—not staying there. Just came in with some other people for dinner.

NANCY. Well—we can cross *them* out. Go on.

NICHOLS. And Mrs.—what's her name—Parkerson—

NANCY. The front-page Parkerson?

NICHOLS. Herself.

NANCY [*with a grimace*]. Me-aow! Who else?

NICHOLS. Burke McAllister, and the David Ewings. . . .

NANCY. Precious, fat old things! *They* might—

NICHOLS. It'd be a great feather for Matey, if he made their November Loan Exhibition.

NANCY. They're the ones!—It's come to me in a vision!—That all—?

NICHOLS. So far as I remember.

NANCY. Perhaps three or four of them will simply battle for it. You referee, Geoff—[*Thoughtfully.*]—And perhaps no one will want it at all. And what will my Matey do then, poor thing . . . ? [*Dropping her head upon her hand.*] Oh—I'm too old to be as excited as this over anything! What *can* be keeping him? [*She goes to the window and looks out.*] See the lanterns strung through the orchard at the Duanes. They look like plums and oranges, come suddenly to life. . . . Ricky—the lamb—he was such a corker at dinner. Kept them in perfect gales of laughter—just as if nothing had happened at all. Oh—that wretched girl.

NICHOLS. Odd—her tacking about this way, at the last minute. Simple funk, perhaps. . . .

NANCY. Nonsense! She dives twenty feet, without turning a hair!

NICHOLS. I could dive forty—before I could marry.

NANCY. What time is it now?—Come here—let's go over this again—

[NICHOLS *makes a movement to take out his watch. Then remembers what a task it is, and desists.*]

NICHOLS [*glibly*]. Just 9.21.

MATEY *comes in.* NANCY *conceals the list*

NANCY. Hello, Matey. Thought you'd never come.

MATEY. So did I. That train was more than usually local. My dear—how charming you look.

NANCY. I am a product of Southern Spain, where men are men—and women, minxes.

NICHOLS. Three guesses what I am.

ETTA *comes in*

ETTA [*to* NICHOLS]. There's a telephone call for you.

[NANCY *starts, and then sets about concealing her excitement.*]

NICHOLS. Thank you, Etta. . . .

ETTA [*shyly*]. You're welcome, Geoffrey. . . .

[NICHOLS *accelerates his exit, and* ETTA *turns to follow him.* NANCY, *with an effort, avoids the laughter that has overcome* MATEY, *and calls to her.*]

NANCY. Etta—

ETTA [*turning*]. Yes, Ma'am—

NANCY [*after a pause*]. Ah—never mind. . . . [ETTA *goes out.* NANCY *and* MATEY *seat themselves upon the sofa.* MATEY *still laughs.*] I can't rebuke the girl. Matey—you *shouldn't* fool with people's souls, that way. She's miles above domestic service now. We must do something about her.

MATEY [*seriously*]. Um. I know we must—

NANCY. It's a nice idea, though—

MATEY. What?

NANCY. —That in creating the portrait of a lady, you may have created a lady as well. [*She glances toward the stairs and continues nervously.*] How did you find things in town?

MATEY. Pretty bad. It took another slump today. I told Hubbard to sell four hundred shares at ten o'clock Monday. No use grousing over it, I suppose.

NANCY. Not the slightest. Let's forget it till we *have* to think—

MATEY. That's been our method with most disagreeable things, hasn't it?

NANCY. Um.

MATEY. —And we've marched along pretty damn splendidly, haven't we?

NANCY [*nodding*]. I'm so glad contentment hasn't caught us—and wrapped us in cotton-wool. We'll never be quite content, you and I.—So we'll never be dead until they shut our eyes, and fold our hands.

MATEY. And even then I dare say our spirits will go on poking about the heavenly shrubbery—looking for birds that may be there!

NANCY. Darling—it's the way to live—[*Another furtive glance at the stairs.*]—But it plays simple havoc with your nerves. . . . [*Suddenly.*] Matey—tell me you love me.

MATEY. Child! I abominate you.

NANCY. Ah—very satisfactory.

MATEY. I particularly like you in earrings.

[NANCY *taps one of the pendant earrings with her forefinger.*]

NANCY. "Waggle-waggle!" [*They laugh at their absurdity.*]

MATEY. I phoned Greg Kendall from the Club, but they said he was in the country. I've concluded that the thing to do with the portrait, is to get an exhibition.

NANCY [*keeping her voice steady*]. Kendall might even want it himself.

MATEY. I doubt it. But he often acts as an agent, you know.

NANCY [*airily*]. Would you like Mr. Ewing to have it?

MATEY. Oh, no—not at all! Be hung along with Goya and El Greco? My dear—such ignominy!—How did the supper go?

NANCY. Delightfully—for all but the three of us who knew. [*She shakes her head sadly.*] Ricky would have broken your heart.

MATEY. He didn't sulk?

NANCY. Matey!—Our boy *sulk?* He was splendid!

MATEY. I was certain of it.

NANCY. That girl! I don't see how she dares—

MATEY. Nanny—if only I could tell you.—Ronny—

[*He is interrupted by* NICHOLS' *entrance.* NANCY *goes to him quickly, and in the recess of the stairway, they whisper together excitedly.*]

NICHOLS. Ssss-s-s-s—pss-sssh—pscpssch—

NANCY. Not *really!?*—But I never *heard* of anything so remarkable!

MATEY [*approaching them*]. Here—what's this?—Why not include the smaller nations in the conference?

NANCY [*motioning to him behind her back*]. Go away!

[*They whisper more earnestly.* MATEY *returns to the sofa.*]

MATEY. What *have* you two got up your sleeves?

NICHOLS [*over* NANCY'S *shoulder.*] A white rabbit, now. It *was* a white elephant.

[MATEY *picks up a magazine and begins to look it over.* NANCY *and* NICHOLS *join hands, and keeping perfect step, march over to a position in front of* MATEY.]

MATEY [*speaks to them indulgently*]. Yes, my little ones—what can I do for you?

NANCY [*at once timid and exultant*]. Maitland—Geoff and I have something to tell you. . . .

MATEY [*quite unimpressed*]. Fancy that, now.

[NANCY *turns imploringly to* NICHOLS.]

NANCY. I *won't* have my biggest moment ruined by such crass stupidity.

NICHOLS. Really, old son—we've three columns of news.

MATEY. Um.—Newspapers bore me.

NANCY [*in desperation*]. Matey—we've sold your picture.

NICHOLS. Not quite *sold*, but—

NANCY. At any rate, we've got an offer for it.

MATEY. Well, well—isn't that nice? [*He sighs.*] Come on—we might as well get it over with: Who has made the offer?

[NANCY *appeals to* NICHOLS. *He laughs.*]

NICHOLS. The truth is, that we don't *know* who!

MATEY. I shouldn't have spoiled it. Make it a good one: The—uh—Corcoran gallery—or the Vatican—[*Yawning and settling back.*] What tiresome people. . . . [NANCY *determinedly takes him by both ears, shakes his head, and literally lifts him to his feet.*] Here!—Let go!

NANCY. Matey! Will you listen? I tell you we're serious!

[MATEY *looks at* NICHOLS, *who solemnly raises his right hand.*]

NICHOLS. By the bones of my ancestors!

[MATEY, *dumbfounded, looks from one to the other.*]

MATEY. Well, of—. I'll be—. *Tell* me about it—quick!

NANCY [*eagerly*]. It was Geoff's plan. He gets the credit.

NICHOLS. It was just as much yours as mine.

NANCY. But *Geoffrey*—you *know* you—

MATEY [*impatiently*]. Honors are even! Come *on—what . . . ?*

NANCY [*very rapidly*]. Well—we took the portrait over to Mrs. Carhart's. Geoff had arranged with her to hang it in her drawing room, and show it to everyone before dinner—said it was by a protégé of yours. Then, just before you arrived, her chauffeur brought it back, and with it a message saying that she'd phone before nine-thirty. That was Geoff's call, and—

MATEY [*confused*]. But—who—?

NICHOLS. That's what we don't know. It was her butler who phoned. Said she was sending the—prospective purchaser here to see me now.

NANCY. —And it's probably either Kendall or the Ewings! They were both there. And it's an out-and-out offer—

NICHOLS. A handsome one, Matey—four thousand dollars.

MATEY. Four thousand dollars—for the work of an unknown modern?

NICHOLS. I made him repeat it three times. Not, of course, that I doubted its worth. . . .

MATEY. Oh, no—certainly not—of course not. But—[*In sudden buoyancy.*] I say!—He must have *liked* it, h'm . . . ? [*He gathers* NANCY *to his side with one sweep of his arm, and grasps* NICHOLS' *hand.*] Oh—you bully good people! I wouldn't trade you for any other two on earth! [*He goes to the portrait.*] Geoff—bring those candles over, will you?

NANCY. No—let me!

[*She picks up the sconce, and holds it up to light the portrait.* MATEY *dips his brush.*]

MATEY. Now for the great ceremony. Anonymity—farewell!

NANCY [*reluctantly*]. I wonder if we aren't being—a little—previous . . . ?

MATEY [*with his brush poised*]. Why . . . ? [*To* NICHOLS.] Didn't you say it was definite?

NICHOLS. It seemed so to me.

NANCY. But—there might be a slip—'twixt the offer—and the check.

MATEY [*hesitating*]. I wonder—What do you think, Geoff?

NICHOLS. He'll be here in a moment. Why not wait?

MATEY. I bow to your good judgment. I'll sign it under his very nose.

NICHOLS [*suddenly*]. I'm going to give up my popular writing, and see if I can't do one thing I'm not ashamed of—

MATEY. Fine!—Of *course* you can. . . .

NICHOLS. I don't know. You jilted your art, but I did worse. I sent mine on the streets. She's not a forgiving lady.

MATEY [*in high spirits*]. Not forgiving?—When she came back to me after years of neglect? Try her! Try her!—Now tell me: who else saw it?

NANCY. I have a list right here—

NICHOLS. I cling doggedly to a belief that it may be Mrs. Parkerson.

MATEY. I hear she has some beautiful things.

NICHOLS. —And she likes new people.

NANCY. Matey—I *won't* let that woman have it!

MATEY [*good humoredly*]. Not even for four thousand dollars?

NANCY. Not for twenty! [MATEY *draws a line and wafts a kiss to the dreadful woman.*]

MATEY. *Au 'voir*, Mrs. Parkerson. We thank you for your kindly interest—but our prig of a wife objects to you. [*He reads over the names.*] Of course—it might be any one of these—with two or three exceptions. . . .

NANCY. How I do hope that—[*She hesitates, troubled.*] It's almost too ideal, to be altogether true.

MATEY. Nanny—you haven't been—pulling my leg?

NANCY. As if I could—in a thing like this! [*Again, apprehensively.*] But—I mean—it seems so adventitious—so—pat to our needs.

[*Enter* RICKY *in a Troubadour costume, but without the guitar.*]

MATEY. Still—if he definitely said—. Well, Rick, you look positively dashing.

RICKY. Keep your seats; the chorus will be right in. [*He sees "Genevieve" on the hobby-horse.*] I see the Lady Godiva still rides. Hi, Mr. Nichols!

NICHOLS. Hello, Ricky. [*To* MATEY.] Don't you think I'd better go down and wait for—whoever it is?

NANCY. By all means. I'll go with you.

RICKY. Stick around a minute, will you, Nanny?

NANCY. I'll be with you presently, Geoff.

NICHOLS [*going out*]. Right.

RICKY [*to* NANCY]. Ronny is downstairs. She wants to talk to you.

NANCY. I—don't think I care to see her now. . . .

RICKY. Off that, Dearest. If Ronny wants to change her mind, why, that's her privilege. I'll expect you to be just as nice to her as you possibly can be. And by that, I don't mean any of your well-known politeness at ten below zero. . . .

MATEY. I haven't yet told you how sorry I am about this.

RICKY [*smiling*]. Oh—it's not every one has *your* luck getting married.

NANCY. Come here, Rick—[*He goes to her and she takes his face between her hands and kisses him.*] Tell Ronny to come up—

[RICKY *hugs her, drops his head upon her shoulder for a moment, and then looks up, smiling brightly.*]

RICKY. Thanks, old Precious—thanks. [*He goes out.*]

NANCY. Matey—he makes me ache all over.

MATEY. Our own good fortune seems nothing when I think of it.

NANCY. He'll get over it, of course—they always do. But a thing like this takes the sweetness out of a boy. It hardens him—makes him shrewd—metallic—[*Exclaims in pain.*] Oh—the poor darling! [*Flaming into anger against* RONNY.]—And all along I've thought that Ronny's air of inconsequence was—merely an overlay—to many things fine, and true—

MATEY. My dear—it *is*—

NANCY. This looks it, doesn't it—this parody of love!

MATEY. —It's hardly that, Nanny.—And you must be very careful with her.

NANCY [*coldly*]. —And why should I be?

[RONNY *enters by the stairs. She wears a long dress of peacock-blue satin, brocaded with silver, a silver girdle and silver slippers. Binding her hair is a slim bandeau of pearls. It is the costume of a Seventeenth Century court. She looks considerably older—a charming woman of, say 26. She crosses a few steps from the top of the stairs, and stops.*]

MATEY. Van Dyck might have painted you.

RONNY. I wish he had. I'd like it better—if I were—just stuck up somewhere. . . . [*To* NANCY.] I hadn't a chance at dinner—I wanted to be sure that—you weren't hating me too much—

NANCY. I'm afraid I am very old-fashioned. Forgive me—but I find it difficult to regard jilting with anything but—distaste.

MATEY [*an entreaty*]. *Ronny—?*

RONNY. All right—only Ricky mustn't know.

MATEY [*to* NANCY]. Ronny told me something this afternoon—she told me a number of things. One of them was the motive for what she has done. She loves him very much. Rightly or wrongly, she felt that she was keeping him from the thing—from a perhaps notable career. So she broke her engagement, and gave him a trumped up reason for it.

NANCY [*incredulously*]. *She* could do *that?!*—When I—? Oh—

[*She stands with her head bowed, one hand resting upon the table.*]

MATEY [*he must say something*]. No doubt she's placed too much importance upon it. She's—[NANCY *turns to* RONNY.]

NANCY. Ronny—I think I am one of the few mothers who consider the girl their son loves, really good enough for him.

RONNY [*barely audible*]. You're very kind. But—

NANCY [*with a gesture asking her to come to her*]. Please—[RONNY *crosses, and* NANCY *takes her hand.*] You make me feel very little. You are doing something that I, years ago, hadn't the courage to do.

[RONNY *looks from her to* MATEY. *Then realizes what she means.*]

RONNY. Oh—it's not at all the same, you know.

NANCY. I think it is very much the same—[*Pause.*] But—I don't know what to advise you. I've—had a happy life, my dear. . . .

MATEY. —And so have I, Ronny—a very happy one.

[NANCY *glances at him, gratefully.*]

NANCY. It's—doubtful now, whether we *could* send Ricky abroad. . . . [RONNY *looks at* MATEY, *who looks away.*] . . . even if he would consent to go. And it may be that you and your love could mean—

MATEY. —Could mean—much more than anything else could, without them.

RONNY [*quietly*]. —As I see it, that's not the point—

MATEY. But the more I think of it, the more certain I am that—

RONNY. It's no good arguing, Mr. White. I'm sure I'm right.—And you know what a stubborn little mule I am. . . .

NANCY. You've told your mother?

RONNY. —That it was off? Yes. Told both of them. Father won't speak to me, and I left Mother eating aspirin tablets. [*She laughs shortly.*] It's a great life.

NANCY. I only hope you're not making a mistake.

RONNY. It's not a mistake. Not if Ricky is started right.

[*Again* MATEY *looks away.*]

NANCY. I'm afraid we couldn't afford—what do you think, Maitland?

[RONNY *holds* MATEY'S *eyes for a long instant. Slowly he shifts his gaze to* NANCY.]

MATEY [*with difficulty*]. It—doesn't seem likely—no.

RONNY [*after a pause*]. Then at least he can go into an architects' office—you must insist on that.

NANCY. —And perhaps turn out to be merely—clever with a ruler? No—he might better stay in business.

RONNY. Then—[*Almost breaking.*] Oh—just because last Autumn I was a selfish, shortsighted little fool, is this all to be useless now?

[*She looks at* MATEY, *and after a moment he turns and meets her gaze without flinching.*]

MATEY. —One thing's certain: If Ricky is to do it at all, he must have the best training possible.

RONNY [*with a wan, grateful smile*]. I knew you'd think that.

MATEY [*after a short pause*]. Happily, I've just had some rather good news about—my painting. And—

RONNY. Oh—I'm *so* glad!

[MATEY *smiles his thanks.*]

MATEY. —And it is possible that the success of this particular piece may make my future work even more profitable.

RONNY [*her eyes shining*]. Then—everything's all right for *both* of you, isn't it?

MATEY. That's what I'm hoping.—So I think you may be confident, that your very fine and generous sacrif—

RONNY [*swiftly*]. Please don't say "sacrifice." It's not one—not if Ricky comes through as I know he will.

MATEY. —At any rate, what you have done, will not—go for nothing.

RONNY [*lowly*]. That's good of you. Thanks —. I'm—satisfied now. [*She turns.*] I'd better go back—the people have started to dribble in.

MATEY. Will you tell Ricky I should like to see him here in about half an hour?

RONNY [*lifelessly*]. I'll tell him. [*She begins to move toward the stairs. Reaching* NANCY, *she turns impulsively, and buries her head in her shoulder.*]—And I thought love all just a happy lark!

NANCY [*tenderly, as she pats her head*]. Not all, Dear. [RONNY *smiles much as* RICKY *did and straightens up quickly.*]

RONNY. Not—*any*—

[*There is a sound from the stairs and* WARREN'S *voice is heard.*]

WARREN [*with difficulty*]. *Is* there any top?—Or—do we—just—keep going—?

NICHOLS [*cheerily*]. Push on, Brave Heart—push on!

MATEY [*lowly, to* NANCY]. Lord—I forgot Rick said G. T. was up here. I'll take him downstairs. Geoff should have known. [*He quickly moves the easel back into the shadow, and covers the paint table with a silk scarf, which he snatches from a chair. The sound draws closer, and* RONNY *steps back to let* WARREN *and* NICHOLS *enter.* WARREN *wears a dinner-coat, and looks quite exhausted.*] Hello, G. T. I heard you were somewhere in the neighborhood.

[*They shake hands, blocking* RONNY'S *exit.*]

WARREN [*breathlessly*]. H'lo—White—[*Looks around for a chair, and finding none near by, sits upon a trunk.*] I'd—no idea—your house—was so tall.

NANCY. How do you do, Mr. Warren. So long since we've had this pleasure.

WARREN. How-do-do, Mrs. White. I expected—Saint Peter.

MATEY. I think we'd be more comfortable downstairs.

WARREN. Maybe we would. But—now that—I'm up—here—[*Taking a deep breath.*]—I'm going—to sit down—long enough—to—make it pay.

[*He sees* RONNY, *and rises.*]

RONNY. How do you do?

[WARREN *looks puzzled at first, then beams and shakes hands with her.*]

WARREN. Why—bless my soul—it's Miss—Miss Duane, isn't it? My, how pretty you look—just like a picture. Your young man is doing very well for me. I—uh—understand the secret's coming out tonight. Let me be among the first to congratulate you—he's a fine boy.

RONNY [*glancing furtively at the stairs*]. Thank you very much.

MATEY [*to save the situation*]. G. T.—

WARREN [*going right on*]. —Yes, a wife's the best thing in the world for a young man, if he can afford one—[*He chuckles.*]—and I'll see to it that *you* two don't starve right away. [*And continues talking to her, while looking at* MATEY. RONNY *quietly slips out.*] Expect big things of Ricky. Don't doubt that some day he'll be more valuable to me than his father ever thought of being. And I once thought White indispensable! Well—I mustn't keep you too long. I wish you every happiness—[*Turning about slowly.*]—my dear. And I'm sure—[*He sees that she is not there, and laughs.*] Humph—that's one on me!

MATEY. G. T.—there are two or three things I'd like to mull over with you. Let's go down to the library. We can talk better there. I'm expecting a caller—but he won't keep me long.

[WARREN *goes to the sofa*, MATEY *watching him anxiously*. NICHOLS *goes to the window and stands there silently looking out*, *weaving his fingers in and out behind him*.]

WARREN. Don't see anything wrong with this. [*He seats himself and his long pent-up curiosity finally breaks through*.] White—what on earth've you been doing with yourself?

MATEY. Oh—resting—and indulging a few neglected tastes. [WARREN *looks to* NANCY *for corroboration*.]

NANCY. You said he needed a rest, you know.

WARREN. Eight months of it?—It's not resting after the first six weeks. It's rotting. . . . Well, I'm not here to talk vacations.

[NANCY'S *hand flies to her mouth. She bites her knuckle*, *drops her hand*, *turns quickly and looks at* NICHOLS. *He crosses to them*.]

NICHOLS. Oh, yes—Mr. Warren saw the portrait, Matey—

[*Dance music begins to be heard faintly*, *from the Duanes'*.]

MATEY [*easily*]. That's right—you were at the Carharts', weren't you? Amusing chap—this protégé of mine. A bit erratic, of course—you know painters. . . .

WARREN. Um.

MATEY. Oh—by the way—did you hear Ewing or Kendall say anything about coming over?

WARREN. —Here?—No. And listen—those fellows make me tired. You should have heard them pulling your friend's picture to pieces. All about "dim cherry-askuro" and "flat composition"—and all that highbrow rot. Blind as bats—both of 'em! Missing the greatest thing about it! [*Leaning forward*, *and tapping* MATEY'S *knee confidentially with his forefinger*.] White—I want to tell you that that picture has Human Interest Appeal!

MATEY [*bravely*]. You—found it interesting?

WARREN [*settling back*]. Enough to pay four thousand dollars for it!

NANCY [*quietly*]. You—are the prospective purchaser, Mr. Warren?

[NICHOLS *returns to the window*. MATEY *nods his head reflectively*, *staring at the floor*.]

MATEY. H'm—very generous offer, very—

WARREN. You bet I am!—Why, it's the sweetest face I ever saw! [*He rises and crosses to the easel*.] This it?—Ah—if that doesn't give trumps to all the Old Masters *I've* ever seen—

[*He gazes at the portrait with a rapt expression*. MATEY *brings himself heavily to his feet*. NANCY *edges closer to him*, *watching him*.]

MATEY. You say—Kendall and Ewing and the others—didn't think so much of it? [NANCY *is at his side*.]

WARREN [*snorting*]. Bah—they make me sick!

MATEY [*very softly*]. They make *me*—a little sick. . . .

[NANCY *grasps his hand behind his back*, *and presses it as tightly as she can*, *as* WARREN *moves the easel around to get the full light upon the face*.]

WARREN. But that didn't change *my* opinion. If you discovered this, I'm tremendously indebted to you.

MATEY [*dully*]. Oh—not at all—

WARREN. But I tell you it's just what I've been after for years! It's the most perfect type you could ask for!

MATEY. Type—? Perfect—? What *for—?*

WARREN [*triumphantly*]. Why—to personify the Warren Line, of course!

NANCY. Oh—this is unthinkable!

[WARREN *looks at her*, *surprised. He has not caught the words*, *but the tone was unmistakable*. MATEY *drops his hand upon her shoulder*, *removing it in an instant*.]

MATEY. Just a minute, Dear. [*To* WARREN.] Let me get this straight.—Precisely why is it that you want the picture?

WARREN. Advertising, man, advertising.—What did you think? [MATEY'S *head sinks*.]

MATEY. I—*didn't*—

WARREN. Why—you ought to be delighted. Haven't you been howling for years for a big national campaign? And haven't I been holding out till I could find a way of putting the whole line over as a unit? Well, your dream's coming true,—'n' so's mine—

[*Tapping the shoulder of the portrait.*]—And we owe it all to this little lady right here.

MATEY. Ah—this is Fame!

WARREN. You're right it is!

NICHOLS [*to* MATEY]. Millais once did a painting for Pears' Soap, you know. . . .

MATEY. Thanks, Geoff.

WARREN. Look!—Can't you just *see* it with "The Warren Line is Purity Itself" written in 9-point script across the bottom?

MATEY. —Instead of the painter's signature. Yes—I can see it. [*He turns and regards* WARREN *speculatively.*] G. T.—you're not aware of it—but in a way you're—uncannily like God.

[NANCY'S *head drops upon her breast.* NICHOLS *abruptly returns to the window. The music at the Duanes' stops, and the faint sound of laughter is heard.*]

WARREN [*after a pause. Surprised, then amused*]. Me—? God—? Ho! Ho!—Thanks for the compliment. [*Again contemplating the picture.*] Wonder if it wouldn't be better to put something in her hand. Art Department could retouch it in—a bunch of flowers . . . or a can of talcum—

NANCY [*quietly*]. I think, Mr. Warren, that its great charm is its—refreshing freedom from artifice—

WARREN. Well—you ought to know. You're a woman—and it's women we want to reach. [*To* MATEY.] Make the check out to you?

MATEY. You'd better wait. The—artist may not care to have it used for advertising purposes. I'll—let you know Monday. . . .

WARREN [*laughing*]. What? Temperament? [*He goes to the table and writes a check.*] Wave this under his nose. If he's as poor as most artists, he'll soon forget his highty-tighty notions.—And tell him I want to see him about doing two or three more, in different poses. Same price. . . .

MATEY [*directly*]. That, I am certain he will not consent to.

NANCY [*softly*]. Ah—you *brick!*

NICHOLS [*simultaneously*]. Bravo!

WARREN [*to* NANCY]. What's that?

NANCY. I was speaking to my husband.

WARREN. Oh. [ETTA *enters with a note for* MATEY. WARREN *leaves the check on the table, and rises.*] You watch—he'll come around. He'll—

MATEY. It is—the *face* you like, isn't it?

WARREN. Certainly. I don't know anything about the technique, or whatever you call it. [ETTA *passes* WARREN, *unnoticed by him.*]

MATEY. I think perhaps we—can find the model—and some proficient—commercial artist can do her in other poses.

WARREN. Suits me.—Say now—before I go—there's one more thing—

ETTA [*giving* MATEY *the envelope*]. A message for you, sir—and thank you, sir.

MATEY [*gravely*]. All right, Etta.

[ETTA *joyfully turns to go out.*]

WARREN [*continuing*]. I'm not too well pleased with the way the Chicago—[*As she passes* WARREN, ETTA *looks up at him. He stops speaking abruptly, and his mouth drops open in amazement. He turns and watches her as she goes out. He looks again at the portrait, then wheels about quickly, and explodes.*] White—there's something damn queer about this whole thing. Did *you* paint this picture?

MATEY [*smiling*]. G. T.!—Imagine me an artist!

WARREN [*suddenly* WARREN'S *face lights up in complete understanding*]. *Now* I see it! *That's* why you left! You knew we had to advertise. You knew I couldn't find what I wanted. So you got a big idea—worked it out by yourself—and then sprang it on me! What a fellow you are!

MATEY. It's a pretty explanation,—but quite erroneous, quite—

NICHOLS. Oh, agree with him, Matey—what's the odds?

MATEY. You're quite wrong—

WARREN. Dammit, right *or* wrong, I want you back. And now that I've O.K.'d your advertising plans, you ought to be on hand to manage 'em.—Well, what do you say?

MATEY. I don't know. I'll—tell you that on Monday, too. [*Thoughtfully.*] If I should come back—would you agree to my having Fridays and Saturdays free the entire year round—to devote to a—hobby of mine?

WARREN. Absolutely!

MATEY. I'll think it over, and let you know.

WARREN [*tapping the portrait*]. Have this sent to me, will you?

MATEY. If the artist agrees. Your house?

WARREN. No—right to the office.—And you ought to shake up that Chicago crowd, and shake 'em up good! You could leave Wednesday and be back by the first of the week. . . .

MATEY [*reflectively*]. I'd have a lot to tell those fellows.

WARREN. I bet you would!

NANCY [*alarmed*]. —But didn't you say that week-ends were to be free?

WARREN. Oh, occasionally it may be necessary to—[*With a gesture.*] Business is business, you know.

NANCY [*softly*]. So it is. . . .

WARREN. Well—I'll be going along. Good-night, Mrs. White.

NANCY. Good-night.

WARREN [*to* MATEY]. Expect to hear from you Monday. No need to come down with me.

NICHOLS [*crossing from window*]. No—let me—[*As he passes* MATEY, *he stops and looks at him searchingly.*]

WARREN [*on the stairs*]. Good-bye! Good-bye, Mr.—uh—uh—*Good*-bye! [*He goes out.*

MATEY [*with a smile*]. No, Geoff—not done yet!

NICHOLS. It's a rotten shame—*I* know what it's like—

[*He follows* WARREN *down the stairs.* MATEY *tears open the envelope and extracts the note.* NANCY *crosses to him.*]

MATEY. Something of a facer, isn't it?

NANCY. Oh, Matey—be careful, be careful! Don't do anything till you're sure that you're right.

MATEY. No, dear. . . . [*Turning to the signature of the note.*] H'm—from Greg Kendall—

NANCY [*eagerly*]. Oh—what does he say? [MATEY *frowns over the writing.*]

MATEY. "Ewing and I—home—a lovely—" [*He gives it to her.*] Can you make it out?

NANCY [*reading slowly*]. "Ewing and I have had a lively discussion concerning the portrait painted by your protégé. Ewing insists that—" [*She stops and looks at him fearfully.*]

MATEY [*grimly*]. Let's have it.

NANCY. "Ewing insists that it is of no consequence, but I cannot bring myself wholly to agree with him. . . ." [*Delightedly.*] Matey!

MATEY. Crumbs are good.

NANCY [*continuing*]. "I find the technique above average, and the brush-work distinctly promising. My main objections hang upon a certain inflexibility in treatment. We do not expect a painter's early work to be individual, but such rigidity is as ominous as it is uncommon. [*She turns the page.*] . . . Unless your young friend is content with a place in the ranks of the agreeably mediocre, he should devote the next three or four years to the most painstaking study under a good European master. This may, or may not, be his salvation."

MATEY [*staring straight in front of him*]. —And there's not a better judge than Kendall!

NANCY. No . . . ?

MATEY. —Nor a fairer one.—But it doesn't convince me—do you understand? Not by half! Ah—how I'd like to show them!

NANCY. You will—I'm sure you will.

MATEY [*grasping at the straw*]. —He did like my brush-work. You see?—That's very important.—Now if I should get someone in town to tutor me—

NANCY. You—who have just said "If he's to do it at all, he must have the best training possible"—? [*He looks at her oddly.*]

MATEY [*half to himself*]. Which of us—

NANCY. You're not one to do things by halves. Why not go abroad, as Kendall advises? *I* shan't mind—and it's no one else's business. Rick can support himself. I've still enough for Jean and me. And—[*She hesitates.*]—for *you*—why, we can sell the place, you know. It ought to bring enough —land's valuable up here.

MATEY. But Nanny—you love it so.

NANCY. So do I—love you.

MATEY. But it's yours—it's your own—

NANCY [*softly*]. Have I—anything—my *own . . . ?* [MATEY *draws her to him.*]

MATEY. Ah—my dear—[*A pause.*] I don't know what to do. I don't know—. This afternoon—I'll never admit that all Ronny said was right. But on one thing we were agreed—on a weakness of mine—[*There is a tinge of harshness in his forced gayety.*]—A *weakness*, Nanny—that's what love is, in an artist! [*From the stairs comes the sound of whistling.*]

NANCY. What was it she said?

[RICKY *comes in, softly continuing the tune the orchestra at the Duanes' has been playing.*]

MATEY [*with a gesture toward him*]. This—

RICKY. I am informed, O King, that you command my presence. Let the royal tongue wag—[*He sits on a trunk and begins to whistle again, lowly.* MATEY *looks at him speculatively.*]—or, in the vulgar parlance, shoot—

MATEY. Ricky—how do you feel?

RICKY [*with a short laugh*]. Well, Dad, if you really want to know, I feel like holy hell.

MATEY. I thought so.

RICKY. But I promised to act like a little soldier. And when a fellow lets himself in for something, he's got to see it through, hasn't he? So—[*He whistles a bar.*]—Cheero! [*And goes on whistling moodily.*]

MATEY. When—a fellow does *what?*

RICKY. Lets himself in for something—

[*He returns again to his whistling.* MATEY *is in a study. Suddenly his brow clears, and he speaks spiritedly.*]

MATEY. Rick, how'd you like to go abroad—as you planned? [RICKY *glances at him quickly.*]

RICKY. What? [*A thoughtful pause.*]—Take the wherewithal from you? No—thanks a lot—but it can't be done. I'll manage all right in some New York office.

NANCY. That's the *you* in him speaking, Matey.

[MATEY *thinks rapidly for a moment.*]

MATEY. —But I've good news for you.—When you were born, your grandfather took out an endowment policy in your name. You're supposed to get it when you're thirty—a yearly income of about two thousand, for a term of five years.

RICKY. But—I'm only—

MATEY. —Hubbard's the executor. This afternoon he told me that it can come to you now—provided I consider you old enough to expend it properly.

RICKY. Gosh, Dad—that's knockout news—

MATEY. —And if you and Ronny are careful, it's enough to take her with you. Together, you'll have four thousand a year. You'll do better work than you would if you had more—

RICKY. But Ronny doesn't—

MATEY. Let me finish! Son—the happiness of a man's family can mean a lot to him—a tremendous lot. So if you've something you feel it's your destiny to do—something out of the beaten track—unusual—difficult—you'd better begin your married life doing it.

NANCY [*quietly*]. And if you don't?

MATEY. The chances are it will never be done.

[RICKY *looks from one to the other, bewildered.*]

RICKY. But listen—

NANCY [*to* MATEY]. Then what—?

[*For a moment* MATEY'S *head sinks. He lifts it again, smiling.*]

MATEY. Why—then I suppose—you turn philosopher.

NANCY. —Philosophy—to fill an empty heart. It must be rather dreadful. . . .

MATEY. . . . It *would* be—if one's heart *were* empty. But when it's full already—well—habit has a way of changing destinies, don't you think? [*He laughs lightly.*]—How's that—for philosophy? [NANCY *turns away.*]

RICKY. Wait a minute, Dad—I'm in a perfect fog.—You're sure you don't need that money yourself?—It's yours, you know—[MATEY *shakes his head decisively.*] Then it—oh, it'd be—I mean, you simply couldn't beat it. Gosh, how I'd work—. But as for Ronny—[*He looks up, smiling.*]—She doesn't want me. . . .

MATEY. Tell her what I've told you—and see what she says. [RICKY *looks at him searchingly.*]

RICKY. Dad—*what do you know—?*

MATEY [*with sudden sharpness*]. Never mind what I know! Stop arguing, and try it—quickly—before your luck changes!

[RICKY *turns and starts for the stairs as fast as he can.* NANCY *picks up the guitar from the trunk.*]

NANCY. Ricky—! [*He stops, and she holds it out to him.*] Here—[*He comes back, and takes it.*]

RICKY [*breathlessly*]. Thanks, Dearest. . . .

[*He kisses her, hastily.*] I love you. . . . [*He makes the stairs in record time and goes out.*]

NANCY. His grandfather did nothing of the sort.

MATEY. I know he didn't. But he wouldn't have taken it from me—not for both of them.

NANCY. Are you certain—you're acting wisely?

MATEY. Wisdom has nothing to do with love, my dear.

NANCY [*a stilled voice*]. Matey—if this is failure, it's a kind I've never seen before.

MATEY [*brightly*]. Why—you talk as though I'd given it up entirely! Didn't you hear me arrange with G. T. for time to—

NANCY [*with a hopeless gesture*]. Week-ends . . . ?

MATEY. Um.—And by and by when Ricky's on his feet, and Jean is married—

[NANCY *buries her head in his shoulder.*]

NANCY [*pitying him with her whole heart*]. Oh —*Matey*—you'll be nearly fifty!

MATEY. You call that old!?

NANCY [*clinging to him*]. I don't like the look of this—at all. . . .

[MATEY *holds her to him, staring fixedly into space over her shoulder. The orchestra at the Duanes' begins to play a waltz. His face brightens.*]

MATEY [*as briskly as he can*]. Well—if we're going to the dance, I'd better get into costume. [*He blows out the candles, and* NANCY *turns out the lamps, leaving the room lighted only by the moonlight, which faintly illuminates the small windows, and flows strongly through the great dormer upon the portrait, and upon* NANCY. *A shaft of pale light lights the stairs from below.* MATEY *takes one last look at the portrait and then goes to* NANCY.] —What hideous disguise have you got for me?

NANCY. The usual—a matador.

MATEY. No!—Tonight I shall be something different.

NANCY. But there isn't anything!

MATEY. Yes, there is—[*He picks up his smock and holds it out for her to see.*] I am going, my love—[*The smock envelops him now, and he turns to give* NANCY *the full picture as he stands there, a parody of himself and his hopes.*]—as an artist!

[NANCY'S *hand goes out to him in a little vain protest. He takes the red Spanish béret from the animal's head on the wall and sets it jauntily upon his own. He lifts "Genevieve" from the hobby horse, and takes* NANCY'S *arm through his. The three cross toward the stairs,* MATEY *with his head high—"Genevieve" on one arm,* NANCY *a tragic figure on the other—whistling the waltz with the orchestra, as*

THE CURTAIN FALLS

ICEBOUND

By Owen Davis

OWEN DAVIS

[1874–]

OWEN DAVIS was born in Maine of "staid New England farmers and lawyers whose lives had been devoted to the stern necessity of grubbing an existence out of the rather stubborn soil of Maine and Vermont." [1] He early had a liking for the glamorous and romantic, a propensity which he attributes to his descent from bold Yankee sailors on his mother's side; he was not interested in the practical world, only in "drawing pictures on the wall," and to the present day he maintains he knows nothing beyond the theatre. At the age of nine he wrote a play which suggests the flavor of his later melodrama; it was entitled *Diamond Cut Diamond, or the Rival Detectives*. After graduating from Harvard in 1893, whence he secured a "solid and lasting technique" at draw poker, he was persuaded by his father to become a mining engineer; serving in this capacity for a short time, during which he still retained "a bland uncertainty as to how many times three went into nine," he later reverted to type and again took up playwriting. He at first depreciated melodrama, such as *The Great Train Robbery*, but he saw that it was successful and deliberately set about writing it. By studying the reactions of the audience, rather than the contents of the plays, he devised a "mechanical but really effective mold," which enabled him to write more than one hundred and fifty melodramas (from 1898 to 1921). There are three types into which these melodramas fall: (1) western thrillers; (2) New York comedy drama; (3) "sexy" plays in which the beautiful and unfortunate heroine is persecuted by the villain, as illustrated in *Nellie, the Beautiful Cloak Model*.

After the war Davis was sensitive to a changed spirit in the theatre as well as in the nation, and he felt that a more serious and truthful drama would come nearer expressing the particular temper of the times. Partly under the influence of Ibsen [2] and encouraged by the example of O'Neill, Davis entered the field of realistic native drama with *The Detour* in 1921. This is a sincere and moving study of a Long Island farm woman, who sacrificed a career for marriage,[3] in her efforts to secure opportunity for her daughter against the opposition of a land-ambitious father. The issue is decided when a critic reveals that the daughter has no talent for painting; the mother is then obliged to transfer her hopes to the prospect of the next generation. Though not a popular success, *The Detour*

[1] The biographical data here given are taken largely from Davis's autobiography, *I'd Like to Do It Again*. New York: 1931.

[2] See Quinn, *History of the American Drama from the Civil War to the Present Day*, II, 217.

[3] Cf. Barry's *You and I*.

was received by critics as "a sign of the deepening of native dramaturgic art" and "thus far one of our highest attainments in American realism for the stage."[1]

But the "more palpitant spirit, akin to mysticism" which was looked for from Davis was hardly forthcoming.[2] *Icebound* (1923) has come the nearest to fulfilling that hope; Davis's subsequent plays have not carried him any further. His later writings include: *The Nervous Wreck*, 1923; *Easy Come, Easy Go*, 1925; *Gentle Grafters*, 1926; *The Donovan Affair*, 1926; *The Great Gatsby* (adaptation of the novel by F. Scott Fitzgerald), 1926; and *The Good Earth* (adaptation of the novel by Pearl Buck), 1932.[3]

Literary realism in America, which took its impetus from Howells, has had a continued development, with interruptions and modifications, to be sure,[4] until very recent times, when it tended to dominate the approach to most forms of literary creation. Its manifestations vary appreciably, in some cases extending only to one phase of technique, while in others virtually constituting the artistic whole. Removed from the twentieth century in subject as Robinson's *Tristram* is, there yet remains an organic quality in the language which integrates it with the language of life; in John V. A. Weaver's *Drug Store*, on the other hand, there is a photographic (and phonographic) fidelity to life complete in every detail. This authentic rendering of life with a minimum of artistic alloy characterizes many recent American plays: the very title *Street Scene* suggests the direct and faithful observation which determines the portrayal, and in *What Price Glory* there is a dictation from life so cleaving that special apology for the language is required. Though not so extreme as the foregoing, Davis's *Icebound* properly belongs to the latter type of realism. In its representation of dialectical pronunciations and expressions,[5] in its inclusion of homely details, in its essential, as well as superficial, truth to character and situation, and in its persistent exclusion of "drama," *Icebound* is an extract from reality that has placed upon the stage Davis's "own people, the people of northern New England": "I am of their blood, born of generations of Northern Maine, small-town folk, and brought up among them."[6] This is not to say there is no selection in the play; otherwise it would hardly be art; but Davis's treatment of the tenser or more significant situations has little or none of that heightening so tempting to the dramatist. When Jane discovers that the supreme moment of her careful planning has been "stolen" by the trivial Nettie, she stifles her feelings and calls dinner; the reformation of Ben leaves much to be desired in the way of courtesy, generosity, and resolution; love-making hardly goes beyond quiet amusement over a spool of thread.

[1] Foreword by Montrose J. Moses to *The Detour*. Boston: 1922. [2] *Ibid*.

[3] For reviews of the latter play see Krutch, Joseph Wood, *The Nation*, CXXXV, 438 (Nov. 2, 1932); Young, Stark, *The New Republic*, LXXII, 330–331.

[4] See chapter VII in Foerster's *The Reinterpretation of American Literature*. New York: 1928.

[5] E.g., more'n, wa'n't; adopted her legal, died sudden, a body would think, down to Thomaston, etc.

[6] Foreword to *Icebound*. Boston: 1923.

According to Davis's portrayal, the New Englanders have a strong sense of family: there is pride in ancestry, and Henry points out that "there hasn't been a Jordan, before Ben, who's disgraced the name in more'n a hundred years. . . ."[1] And the Jordans, though bickering and wrangling among themselves, unite in their feeling against Jane, in whose veins "there ain't scarcely a drop of Jordan blood . . . ." Ironically, though plausibly enough, it is Ben who taps the well of universal truth. He sees the ingrowing tendencies of the New England family: "Just a family by itself, maybe. Just a few folks, good an' bad, month after month, with nothin' to think about but just the mean little things, that really don't amount to nothin', but get to be bigger than all the world outside." In contrast to the gaieties of the French families, whom Ben has visited, the Jordans are spiritually congealed: "Just a few folks together, day after day, and every little thing you don't like about the other raspin' on your nerves 'til it almost drives you crazy! Most folks quiet, because they've said all the things they've got to say a hundred times; other folks talkin', talkin', talkin' about nothing. Sometimes somebody sort of laughs, and it scares you; seems like laughter needs the sun, same as flowers do. Icebound, that's what we are, all of us, inside and out."[2] This rugged inarticulateness, so consistently portrayed by Davis, is like the "outcroppings of granite" in Edith Wharton's *Ethan Frome*. Though Ben is himself marked by this New England characteristic, yet it is Jane who embodies the trait more fully. Out of her silent love for Ben she furnishes his bond, teaches him the meaning of work and self-respect, secures the dismissal of his charges, and offers him her whole estate—her only comment is: "It doesn't matter what folks do, if you love 'em enough."

The universal element is to be observed in Mrs. Jordan's love for her youngest son which persists in spite of his ingratitude and wayward behavior. Some would be less willing to admit that a truth of human nature is hinted at in Ben's remark: "Let a man get miserable, and he *is* miserable. A woman ain't really happy no other way."

Davis's characters are no more voluble about theology than any other subject, but like the minister who was "against sin," they are a part of the New England Puritan tradition. Modern science has made no serious inroads on the faith of their fathers and they accept without questioning the existence of God: "Decent folks don't reason about religion; they just accept it."[3] Disrespect and doubt are to be suppressed; in answer to Orin's questions about God, Henry remonstrates: "Are you going to let him talk about God like that, like He was a real person?" There is the same joylessness that was a part of the early New England Puritanism: "A parlor's where a person's supposed to sit and think of God, and you couldn't

[1] Act I, p. 627.
[2] Act II, p. 637.
[3] Act I, p. 624.

expect it to be cheerful!" There is also the concept of judgment and penalty for transgression: according to Emma the exclusion from the will is "a judgment on all of yer," and the proverb-quoting Henry feels that "folks that plant the wind reap the whirlwind!" Modified and less severe by far than Jonathan Edwards's articles of faith, the religion of Davis's characters yet shows many traits of its parent theology.

Significant among other portrayals of New England life are Sarah Orne Jewett's careful, reverent pictures of the changes and disintegration gently taking place among the older social groups; more despairing than these are Mary E. Wilkins Freeman's coldly realistic studies of New England repression; still later, and likewise despairing, are O'Neill's *Beyond the Horizon*, *Desire Under the Elms*, and *Mourning Becomes Electra.*

Perhaps the reason we have had no more plays from Davis like *The Detour* and *Icebound* is that they were fundamentally uncongenial to his own theory of the drama. "*The Detour* and *Icebound* were true plays from my point of view, honest attempts to do the best work I knew how to do. But I had a feeling that the American drama should express a more optimistic note. . . ." [1] To be sure, his farces may in some measure fulfill this expectation, but his two native dramas are pre-eminent in truth and power.

The present text is the 1923 edition of the play published by Little, Brown and Company.

[1] *I'd Like to Do It Again*, p. 184.

CHARACTERS

Icebound was originally produced in New York, February 10, 1923, with the following cast:

HENRY JORDAN...John Westley
EMMA, his wife...Lotta Linthicum
NETTIE, her daughter by a former marriage.................................Boots Wooster
SADIE FELLOWS, once Sadie Jordan, a widow..................................Eva Condon
ORIN, her son...Andrew J. Lawlor, Jr.
ELLA JORDAN, the unmarried sister...Frances Neilson
DOCTOR CURTIS...Lawrence Eddinger
JANE CROSBY, a second cousin of the Jordans...............................Phyllis Povah
JUDGE BRADFORD..Willard Robertson
BEN JORDAN...Robert Ames
HANNAH...Edna May Oliver
JIM JAY..Charles Henderson

SYNOPSIS

Act I.—The parlor of the Jordan Homestead, 4 P.M., October, 1922.

Act II.—The sitting room of the Jordan Homestead, two months later. Afternoon.

Act III.—Same as Act I, late in the following March.

ICEBOUND

ACT ONE

SCENE. *The parlor of the Jordan Homestead at Veazie, Maine.*

It is late October, and through the two windows at the back one may see a bleak countryside, the grass brown and lifeless, and the bare limbs of the trees silhouetted against a gray sky. Here, in the room that for a hundred years has been the rallying point of the Jordan family, a group of relatives are gathered to await the death of the old woman who is the head of their clan. The room in which they wait is as dull and as drab as the lives of those who have lived within its walls. Here we have the cleanliness that is next to godliness, but no sign of either comfort or beauty, both of which are looked upon with suspicion as being signposts on the road to perdition.

In this group are the following characters: HENRY JORDAN, *a heavy-set man of fifty, worn by his business cares into a dull sort of hopeless resignation;* EMMA, *his wife, a stout and rather formidable woman of forty, with a look of chronic displeasure;* NETTIE, *her daughter by a former marriage, a vain and shallow little rustic beauty;* SADIE, *a thin, tight-lipped woman of forty, a widow and a gossip;* ORIN, *her son, a pasty-faced boy of ten with large spectacles;* ELLA, *a "Maiden lady" of thirty-six, restless and dissatisfied.*

ELLA *and* SADIE, *true Jordans by birth, are a degree above* EMMA *in social standing, at least they were until* HENRY'S *marriage to* EMMA *made her a somewhat resentful member of the family. In* EMMA'S *dialogue and in her reactions, I have attempted a rather nice distinction between the two grades of rural middle-class folk; the younger characters here, as in most other communities, have advanced one step.*

Rise: At rise there is a long silence; the occupants of the room are ill at ease. EMMA *is grim and frowning.* NETTIE *sits with a simper of youthful vanity, looking stealthily at herself from time to time in a small mirror set in the top of her cheap vanity case.* ELLA *and* SADIE *have been crying and dab at their eyes a bit ostentatiously.* HENRY *makes a thoughtful note with a pencil, then returns his notebook to his pocket and warms his hands at the stove.*

There is a low whistle of a cold autumn wind as some dead leaves are blown past the window. ORIN, *who has a cold in his head, sniffs viciously; the others, with the exception of his mother, look at him in remonstrance. An eight-day clock in sight, through the door to the hall, strikes four.*

EMMA [*sternly*]. Four o'clock.

HENRY [*looks at watch*]. Five minutes of. That clock's been fast for more'n thirty years.

NETTIE [*looks at wrist watch*]. My watch says two minutes after.

HENRY. Well, it's wrong!

EMMA [*acidly*]. You gave it to her yourself, didn't you?

SADIE [*sighs*]. Good land! What does it matter?

NETTIE [*offended*]. Oh! Doesn't it? Oh!

ELLA. Maybe it does to you. She ain't your blood relation.

EMMA. Nettie loves her grandma, don't you, dear?

NETTIE. Some folks not so far off may get fooled before long about how much grandma and I was to each other.

EMMA [*sternly*]. You hush!

[*Again there is a pause, and again it is broken by a loud sniff from* ORIN, *as the women look at him in disgust.* SADIE *speaks up in his defense.*]

SADIE. He's got kind of a cold in his head.

HENRY. The question is, ain't he got a handkerchief?

SADIE. Here, Orin! [*She hands him her handkerchief.*]

ELLA. The idea! No handkerchief when you've come expectin' some one to die!

ORIN. I had one, but I used it up. [*He blows his nose.*]

HENRY. After four. Well, I expect they'll have to close the store without me.

ELLA. I left everything just as soon as Jane sent me word!

SADIE. Why should Jane be with her instead of you or me, her own daughters?

HENRY. You girls always made her nervous, and I guess she's pretty low. [*He looks at his watch again.*] I said I'd be back before closin' time. I don't know as I dare to trust those boys.

EMMA. You can't tell about things, when Sadie's husband died we sat there most all night.

SADIE [*angrily*]. Yes, and you grudged it to him, I knew it then and it isn't likely I'm going to forget it.

ELLA. Will was a good man, but even you can't say he was ever very dependable.

EMMA. My first husband died sudden—[*She turns to* NETTIE.]—you can't remember it, dear.

ELLA. *You* didn't remember it very long, it wa'n't much more'n a year before you married Henry.

HENRY [*sighs*]. Well, he was as dead then as he's ever got to be. [*He turns and glances nervously out window.*] I don't know but what I could just run down to the store for a minute, then hurry right back.

SADIE. You're the oldest of her children, a body would think you'd be ashamed.

HENRY. Oh, I'll stay.

[*There is a silence.* ORIN *sniffs.* ELLA *glares at him.*]

ELLA. Of course he *could* sit somewheres else.

[SADIE *puts her arm about* ORIN *and looks spitefully at* ELLA. DOCTOR CURTIS, *an elderly country physician, comes down the stairs and enters the room, all turn to look at him.*]

DOCTOR. No change at all. I'm sendin' Jane to the drug store.

ELLA [*rises eagerly*]. I'll just run up and sit with mother.

[SADIE *jumps up and starts for door.*]

SADIE. It might be better if I went.

ELLA. Why might it?

[*They stand glaring at each other before either attempts to pass the* DOCTOR, *whose ample form almost blocks the doorway.*]

SADIE. *I've* been a wife and a mother.

DOCTOR. Hannah's with her, you know. I told you I didn't want anybody up there but Jane and Hannah.

ELLA. But we're her own daughters.

DOCTOR. You don't have to tell me, I brought both of you into the world. The right nursing might pull her through, even now; nothing else can, and I've got the two women I want. [*He crosses to* HENRY *at stove.*] Why don't you put a little wood on the fire?

HENRY. Why—I thought 'twas warm enough.

ELLA. Because you was standin' in front of it gettin' all the heat.

[HENRY *fills the stove from wood basket.*]

[JANE CROSBY *enters on stairs and crosses into the room.* JANE *is twenty-four, a plainly dressed girl of quiet manner. She has been "driven into herself" as one of our characters would describe it, by her lack of sympathy and affection and as a natural result she is not especially articulate; she speaks, as a rule, in short sentences, and has cultivated an outward coldness that in the course of time has become almost aggressive.*]

JANE. I'll go now, Doctor; you'd better go back to her. Hannah's frightened.

DOCTOR. Get it as quick as you can, Jane; I don't know as it's any use, but we've got to keep on tryin'.

JANE. Yes.

[*She exits;* DOCTOR *warms his hands.*]

DOCTOR. Jane's been up with her three nights. I don't know when I've seen a more dependable girl.

ELLA. She ought to be.

HENRY. If there's any gratitude in the world.

DOCTOR. Oh, I guess there is; maybe there'd be more if there was more reason for it. It's awful cold up there, but I guess I'll be gettin' back. [*He crosses toward door.*]

HENRY. Doctor! [*He looks at his watch.*]

DOCTOR [*stops in doorway*]. Well?

HENRY. It's quite a bit past four, I don't suppose—I don't suppose you can tell—

DOCTOR. No, I can't tell. [*He turns and exits up the stairs.*]

ELLA. There's no fool like an old fool.

SADIE. Did you hear him? "Didn't know when he'd seen a more dependable girl than her!"

EMMA. Makes a lot of difference who's goin' to depend on her. I ain't, for one.

NETTIE. If I set out to tell how she's treated me lots of times, when I've come over here to see grandma, nobody would believe a word of it.

SADIE. Mother took her in out of charity.

ELLA. And kept her out of spite.

HENRY. I don't know as you ought to say that, Ella.

ELLA. It's my place she took, in my own mother's house. I'd been here now, but for her. I ain't goin' to forget that. No! Me, all these years payin' board and slavin' my life out, makin' hats, like a nigger.

NETTIE [*smartly*]. Oh! So *that's* what they're like. I've often wondered!

ELLA [*rises*]. You'll keep that common little thing of your wife's from insultin' me, Henry Jordan, or I won't stay here another minute.

EMMA [*angry*]. Common!

NETTIE. Mother!

HENRY [*sternly*]. Hush up! All of yer!

SADIE. It's Jane we ought to be talkin' about.

EMMA. Just as soon as you're the head of the family, Henry, you've got to tell her she ain't wanted here!

HENRY. Well—I don't know as I'd want to do anything that wasn't right. She's been here quite a spell.

SADIE. Eight years!

ELLA. And just a step-cousin, once removed.

HENRY. I guess mother's made her earn her keep. I don't know as ever there was much love lost between 'em.

EMMA. As soon as your mother's dead, you'll send her packing.

HENRY. We'll see. I don't like countin' on mother's going; that way.

SADIE [*hopefully*]. Grandmother lived to eighty-four.

HENRY. All our folks was long-lived; nothin' lasts like it used to,—Poor mother!

ELLA. Of course she'll divide equal, between us three?

HENRY [*doubtfully*]. Well, I don't know!

SADIE. Orin is her only grandchild; she won't forget that.

HENRY. Nettie, there, is just the same as my own. I adopted her legal, when I married Emma.

EMMA. Of course you did. Your mother's too—just a woman to make distinctions!

NETTIE. Yes, and the funny part of it is grandma may leave me a whole lot, for all any of *you* know.

ELLA. Nonsense! She'll divide equally between us three; won't she, Henry?

HENRY [*sadly*]. She'll do as she pleases, I guess we all know that.

ELLA. She's a religious woman, she's *got* to be fair!

HENRY. Well, I guess it would be fair enough if she was to remember the trouble I've had with my business. I don't know what she's worth, she's as tight-mouthed as a bear trap, but I could use more'n a third of quite a little sum.

ELLA. Well, you won't get it. Not if I go to law.

EMMA. It's disgusting. Talking about money at a time like this.

HENRY. I like to see folks reasonable. I don't know what you'd want of a third of all mother's got, Ella.

SADIE [*to* ELLA]. You, all alone in the world!

ELLA. Maybe I won't be, when I get that money.

SADIE. You don't mean you'd get married?

EMMA. At your age!

ELLA. I mean I never had anything in all my life; now I'm going to. I'm the youngest of all of you, except Ben, and he never was a real Jordan. I've never had a chance; I've been stuck here till I'm most forty, worse than if I was dead, fifty times worse! Now I'm going to buy things—everything I want—I don't care what—I'll buy it, even if it's a man! Anything I want!

NETTIE. A *man!*

[NETTIE *looks at* ELLA *in cruel amazement and all but* ORIN *burst into a laugh*—ELLA *turns up and hides her face against the window as* ORIN *pulls at his mother's skirt.*]

ORIN. Mum! Mum! I thought you told me not to laugh, not once, while we was here!

HENRY. You're right, nephew, and we're wrong, all of us. I'm sorry, Ella, we're all sorry.

ELLA [*wipes her eyes*]. Laugh if you want to—maybe it won't be so long before I do some of it myself.

HENRY [*thoughtfully*]. Equally between us three? Well, poor mother knows best, of course. [*He sighs.*]

SADIE. She wouldn't leave *him* any, would she,—Ben?

ELLA [*shocked*]. Ben!

HENRY [*in cold anger*]. She's a woman of her word; no!

SADIE. If he was here he'd get around her; he always did!

HENRY. Not again!

SADIE. If she ever spoiled anybody it was him, and she's had to pay for it. Sometimes it looks like it was a sort of a judgment.

HENRY. There hasn't been a Jordan, before Ben, who's disgraced the name in more'n a hundred years; he stands indicted before the Grand Jury for some of his drunken deviltment. If he hadn't run away, like the criminal he is, he'd be in the State's Prison now, down to Thomaston. Don't talk *Ben* to me, after the way he broke mother's heart, and hurt my credit!

NETTIE. I don't remember him very well. Mother thought it better I shouldn't come around last time he was here; but he looked real nice in his uniform.

SADIE. It was his bein' born so long after us that made him seem like an outsider; father and mother hadn't had any children for years and years! Of course I never want to sit in judgment on my own parents, but I never approved of it; it never seemed quite —what I call proper.

NETTIE [*to* EMMA]. Mother, don't you think I'd better leave the room?

SADIE [*angrily*]. Not if half the stories I've heard about you are true, I don't.

HENRY. Come, come, no rows! Is this a time or place for spite? We've always been a united family, we've always got to be,—leavin' Ben out, of course. You can't make a silk purse out of a sow's ear.

ORIN. Mum! Say, Mum! [*He pulls at* SADIE's *dress.*] Why should anybody want to make a silk purse out of a sow's ear?

ELLA. Can't you stop that boy askin' such fool questions?

SADIE. Well, as far as that goes, why should they? It never sounded reasonable to me.

HENRY [*sternly*]. Decent folks don't reason about religion; they just accept it.

ORIN. You could make a skin purse out of a sow's ear, but I'll be darned if you could make a silk purse out of one. I'll bet God couldn't.

HENRY. Are you going to let him talk about God like that, like He was a real person?

ELLA. I don't know as a body could expect any better; his father was a Baptist!

SADIE [*angrily*]. His father was a good man, and if he talked about God different from what you do, it was because he knew more about him. And as for my being here at all —[*She rises with her arms about* ORIN.]—I wouldn't do it, not for anything less than my own mother's deathbed.

HENRY. This family don't ever agree on nothin' but just to differ.

EMMA. As far as I see, the only time you ever get together is when one of you is dead.

ELLA. Maybe that's the reason I got such a feelin' against funerals.

[*The outside door opens and* JANE *enters, a druggist's bottle in her hand; she is followed by* JOHN BRADFORD, *a man of about thirty-five. He is better dressed than any of the others and is a man of a more cosmopolitan type,—a New Englander, but a university man, the local judge and the leading lawyer of the town.*]

JANE. I met Judge Bradford on the way.

JUDGE [*John Bradford*]. Court set late. I couldn't get here before. Jane tells me that she's very low.

HENRY. Yes.

JUDGE. I can't realize it; she has always been so strong, so dominant.

ELLA. In the midst of life we are in death.

ORIN. Say, Mum, that's in the Bible too!

SADIE. Hush!

ORIN. Well, ain't it?

SADIE. Will you hush?

HENRY. It's our duty to hope so long as we can.

JUDGE. Yes, of course.

JANE. I'll take this right up. [*She exits up the stairs.*]

JUDGE [*removes his coat*]. I'll wait.

SADIE. She can't see you; she ain't really what a body could call in her right mind.

JUDGE. So Jane said. [*He crosses to stove and warms his hands.*]

ELLA [*sighs*]. It's a sad time for us, Judge!

JUDGE. She was always such a wonderful woman.

HENRY. An awful time for us. Did you come up Main Street, Judge?

JUDGE. Yes.

HENRY. Did you happen to notice if my store was open?

JUDGE. No.

HENRY. Not that it matters—

SADIE. Nothing matters now.

HENRY. No—Mother wasn't ever the kind to neglect things; if the worst does come she'll find herself prepared. Won't she? Won't she, Judge?

JUDGE. Her affairs are, as usual, in perfect order.

HENRY. In every way?

JUDGE [*looks at him coldly*]. Her will is drawn and is on deposit in my office, if that is what you mean.

HENRY. Well—that *is* what I mean—I'm no hypocrite.

EMMA. He's the oldest of the family. He's got a right to ask, hasn't he?

JUDGE. Yes.

HENRY [*honestly*]. If I could make her well by givin' up everything I've got in the world, or ever expect to git, I'd do it!

SADIE. All of us would.

HENRY. If it's in my mind at all, as I stand here, that she's a rich woman, it's because my mind's so worried, the way business has been, that I'm drove most frantic; it's because, well—because I'm human; because I can't help it.

ELLA [*bitterly*]. You're a man! What do you think it's been for me!

SADIE [*with arm about* ORIN]. His father didn't leave much, you all know that, and it's been scrimp and save till I'm all worn to skin and bone.

ELLA. Just to the three of us, that would be fair.

HENRY. Judge! My brother's name ain't in her will, is it? Tell me that? Ben's name ain't there!

JUDGE. I'd rather not talk about it, Henry.

ELLA. She'd cut him off, she said, the last time he disgraced us, and she's a woman of her word.

SADIE [*eagerly, to* JUDGE]. And the very next day she sent for you because I was here when she telephoned; and you came to her that very afternoon because I saw you from my front window cross right up to this door.

JUDGE. Possibly. I frequently drop in to discuss business matters with your mother for a moment on my way home.

SADIE. It was five minutes to four when you went in that day, and six minutes to five when you came out, by the clock on my mantel.

JUDGE. Your brother has been gone for almost two years; your memory is very clear.

ELLA. So's her window.

NETTIE. I know folks in this town that are scared to go past it.

SADIE [*to her*]. I know others that ought to be.

HENRY [*discouraged*]. Every time you folks meet there's trouble.

JANE *enters down the stairs and into the room*

JUDGE [*looks at her*]. Well, Jane?

JANE. No change. It's—it's pitiful, to see her like that. [SADIE *sobs and covers her face.*]

HENRY. It's best we should try to bear this without any fuss, she'd 'a' wanted it that way.

SADIE. She didn't even want me to cry when poor Will died, but I did; and somehow I don't know but it made things easier.

HENRY. When father died she didn't shed a tear; she's been a strong woman, always.

[*The early fall twilight has come on and the stage is rather dim, the hall at right is in deep shadow; at the end of* HENRY'S *speech the outside door supposedly out at right is opened, then shut rather violently.*]

ELLA [*startled*]. Someone's come in.

SADIE. Nobody's got any right—

[*She rises as someone is heard coming along the hall.*]

HENRY [*sternly*]. Who's that out there? Who is it?

ORIN. Mum! Who is it!

[*He clings to his mother afraid, as all turn to the door, and* BEN JORDAN *steps into the room and faces them with a smile of reckless contempt.* BEN *is the black sheep of the Jordan family, years younger than any of the others, a wild, selfish, arrogant fellow, handsome but sulky and defiant. His clothes are cheap and dirty and he is rather pale and looks dissipated. He doesn't speak but stands openly sneering at their look of astonishment.*]

JANE [*quietly*]. I'm glad you've come, Ben.

BEN [*contemptuously*]. *You* are?

JANE. Yes, your mother's awful sick.

BEN. She's alive?

JANE. Yes.

BEN. Well—[*He looks contemptuously about.*] Nobody missin'. The Jordans are gathered again, handkerchiefs and all.

HENRY. You'll be arrested soon as folks know you've come.

BEN [*scornfully*]. And I suppose you wouldn't bail me out, would you, Henry?

HENRY [*simply*]. No, I wouldn't.

BEN. God! You're still the same, all of you. You stink of the Ark, the whole tribe. It takes more than a few Edisons to change the Jordans!

ELLA. How'd you get here? How'd you know about mother?

BEN [*nods at* JANE]. She sent me word, to Bangor.

SADIE [*to* JANE]. How'd you get to know where he was?

JANE [*quietly*]. I knew.

HENRY. How'd you come; you don't look like you had much money?

BEN. She sent it. [*He nods toward* JANE.] God knows, it wasn't much.

ELLA [*to* JANE]. Did mother tell you to—?

BEN. Of course she did!

JANE [*quietly*]. No, she didn't.

HENRY. You sent your own money?

JANE. Yes, as he said it wasn't much, but I didn't have much.

BEN [*astonished*]. Why did you do it?

JANE. I knew she was going to die; twice I asked her if she wanted to see you, and she said no—

HENRY. And yet you sent for him?

JANE. Yes.

HENRY. Why?

JANE. He was the one she really wanted. I thought she'd die happier seeing him.

ELLA. You took a lot on yourself, didn't you?

JANE. Yes, she's been a lonely old woman. I hated to think of her there, in the churchyard, hungry for him.

BEN. I'll go to her.

JANE. It's too late; she wouldn't know you.

BEN. I'll go.

JANE. The doctor will call us when he thinks we ought to come.

BEN [*fiercely*]. I'm going now.

HENRY [*steps forward*]. No, you ain't.

BEN. Do you think I came here, standin' a chance of bein' sent to jail, to let *you* tell me what to do?

HENRY. If she's dyin' up there, it's more'n half from what you've made her suffer; you'll wait here till we go to her together.

EMMA. Henry's right.

SADIE. Of course he is.

ELLA. Nobody but Ben would have the impudence to show his face here, after what he's done.

BEN. I'm going just the same!

HENRY. No, you ain't. [*Their voices become loud.*]

EMMA. Henry! Don't let him go!

SADIE. Stop him.

ELLA [*grows shrill*]. He's a disgrace to us. He always was.

HENRY. You'll stay right where you are.

[*He puts his hand heavily on* BEN'S *shoulder—* BEN *throws him off fiercely.*]

BEN. Damn you! Keep your hands off me!

[HENRY *staggers back and strikes against a table that falls to the floor with a crash.* NETTIE *screams.*]

JANE. Stop it—stop! You must!

JUDGE. Are you crazy? Have you no sense of decency?

DOCTOR CURTIS *comes quickly downstairs*

DOCTOR. What's this noise? I forbid it. Your mother has heard you.

HENRY [*ashamed*]. I'm sorry.

BEN [*sulkily*]. I didn't mean to make a row.

HENRY. It's him. [*He looks bitterly at* BEN.] He brings out all the worst in us. He brought trouble into the world with him when he came, and ever since.

HANNAH, *a middle-aged servant, comes hastily half-way downstairs and calls out sharply*

HANNAH. Doctor! Come, Doctor!

[*She exits up the stairs, as the* DOCTOR *crosses through the hall and follows her.*]

ORIN [*afraid*]. Is she dead, Mum? Does Hannah mean she's dead?

[SADIE *hides her head on his shoulder and weeps.*]

JANE. I'll go to her. [*She exits.*

ELLA [*violently*]. She'll go. There ain't scarcely a drop of Jordan blood in her veins, and *she's* the one that goes to mother.

EMMA [*coldly*]. Light the lamp, Nettie; it's gettin' dark.

NETTIE. Yes, mother. [*She starts to light lamp.*]

HENRY. I'm ashamed of my part of it, makin' a row, with her on her deathbed.

BEN. You had it right, I guess. I've made trouble ever since I came into the world.

NETTIE. There! [*She lights lamp; footlights go up.*]

JUDGE [*sternly*]. You shouldn't have come here; you know that, Ben.

BEN. I've always known that, any place I've been, exceptin' only those two years in the Army. That's the only time I ever was in right.

JUDGE [*sternly*]. I would find it easier to pity you if you had anyone to blame besides yourself.

BEN. Pity? Do you think I want your pity?

[*There is a pause.* JANE *is seen on stairs, they all turn to her nervously as she comes down and crosses into room. She stops at the door looking at them.*]

HENRY [*slowly*]. Mother—mother's—gone!

JANE. Yes.

[*There is a moment's silence broken by the low sobs of the women who for a moment forget their selfishness in the presence of death.*]

HENRY. The Jordans won't ever be the same; she was the last of the old stock, mother was—No, the Jordans won't ever be the same.

DOCTOR CURTIS *comes downstairs and into the room*

DOCTOR. It's no use tryin' to tell you what I feel. I've known her since I was a boy. I did the best I could.

HENRY. The best anybody could, Doctor, we know that.

DOCTOR. I've got a call I'd better make—[*He looks at watch.*]—should have been there hours ago, but I hadn't the heart to leave her. Who's in charge here?

HENRY. I am, of course.

DOCTOR. I've made arrangements with Hannah; she'll tell you. I'll say good night now.

HENRY. Good night, Doctor.

JANE. And thank you.

DOCTOR. We did our best, Jane. [*He exits.*

SADIE. He's gettin' old. When Orin had the stomach trouble a month ago, I sent for Doctor Morris. I felt sort of guilty doin' it, but I thought it was my duty.

JUDGE. You will let me help you, Jane?

JANE. Hannah and I can attend to everything. Henry! [*She turns to him.*] You might come over for a minute this evening and we can talk things over. I'll make the bed up in your old room, Ben, if you want to stay.

EMMA [*rises and looks at* JANE *coldly*]. Now, Henry Jordan, if she's all through givin' orders, maybe you'll begin.

ELLA. Well, I should say so. Let's have an understandin'.

SADIE. You tell her the truth, Henry, or else one of us will do it for you.

HENRY [*hesitates*]. Maybe it might be best if I should wait until after the funeral.

ELLA. You tell her now, or I will.

JANE. Tell me what?

HENRY. We was thinkin' now that mother's dead, that there wasn't much use in your stayin' on here.

JANE. Yes? [*She looks at him intently.*]

HENRY. We don't aim to be hard, and we don't want it said we was mean about it; you can stay on here, if you want to, until after the funeral, maybe a little longer, and I don't know but what between us, we'd be willing to help you till you found a place somewheres.

JANE. You can't help me, any of you. Of course now she's dead, I'll go. I'll be glad to go.

ELLA. Glad!

JANE [*turns on them*]. I hate you, the whole raft of you. I'll be glad to get away from you. She was the only one of you worth loving, and she didn't want it.

EMMA. If that's how you feel, I say the sooner you went the better.

HENRY. Not till after the funeral. I don't want it said we was hard to her.

JUDGE [*quietly*]. Jane isn't going at all, Henry.

HENRY. What's that?

ELLA. Of course she's going.

JUDGE. No, she belongs here in this house.

HENRY. Not after I say she don't.

JUDGE. Even then, because it's hers.

SADIE. Hers?

JUDGE. From the moment of your mother's death, everything here belonged to Jane.

HENRY. Not everything.

JUDGE. Yes, everything—your mother's whole estate.

BEN. Ha! Ha! Ha! [*He sits at right laughing bitterly.*]

JANE. That can't be, Judge, you must be wrong. It's a mistake.

JUDGE. No.

HENRY. My mother did this?

JUDGE. Yes.

HENRY. Why? You've got to tell me why!

JUDGE. That isn't a part of my duties.

HENRY. She couldn't have done a thing like that without sayin' why. She said something, didn't she?

JUDGE. I don't know that I care to repeat it.

HENRY [*fiercely*]. You must repeat it!

JUDGE. Very well. The day that will was drawn she said to me, "The Jordans are all waiting for me to die, like carrion crows around a sick cow in a pasture, watchin' till the last twitch of life is out of me before they pounce. I'm going to fool them," she said, "I'm going to surprise them; they are all fools but Jane—Jane's no fool."

BEN [*bitterly*]. No—Ha! Ha! Ha! Jane's no fool!

JUDGE. And she went on—[*He turns to* JANE.] You'll forgive me, Jane; she said, "Jane is stubborn, and set, and wilful, but she's no fool. She'll do better by the Jordan money than any of them."

ELLA. We'll go to law, that's what we'll do!

SADIE. That's it, we'll go to law.

HENRY [*to* JUDGE]. We can break that will; you know we can!

JUDGE. It's possible.

HENRY. Possible! You *know*, don't yer! You're supposed to be a good lawyer.

JUDGE. Of course if I *am* a good lawyer you can't break that will, because you see I drew it.

ELLA. And we get nothing, not a dollar, after waitin' all these years?

JUDGE. There are small bequests left to each of you.

SADIE. How much?

JUDGE. One hundred dollars each.

ELLA [*shrilly*]. One hundred dollars.

JUDGE. I said that they were small.

BEN. You said a mouthful!

ELLA. Ha! Ha! Ha! Ha! Ha! [*She laughs wildly.*]

HENRY [*sternly*]. Stop your noise, Ella.

ELLA. I—Ha! Ha! Ha!—I told you I was going to have my laugh, didn't I? Ha! Ha! Ha!

ORIN [*pulls* SADIE'S *dress*]. Mum! What's she laughin' for?

SADIE. You hush!

EMMA [*faces them all in evil triumph*]. If anybody asked me, I'd say it was a judgment on all of yer. You Jordans was always stuck up, always thought you was better'n anybody else. I guess I ought to know, I married into yer!—You a rich family?—You the salt of the Earth—You Jordans! You paupers—Ha! Ha! Ha!

ORIN [*pulls* SADIE'S *skirt*]. Ain't she still dead, Mum! Ain't grandma still dead?

SADIE [*angrily*]. Of course she is.

ORIN. But I thought we was all goin' to cry!

SADIE. Cry then, you awful little brat.

[*She slaps his face and he roars loudly; she takes him by the arm and yanks him out of the room, followed by* HENRY, EMMA, NETTIE *and* ELLA*—through his roars, they all speak together as they go.*]

EMMA [*to* HENRY]. One hundred dollars! After all your blowin'.

HENRY. It's you, and that child of yourn; you turned her against me.

NETTIE. Well, I just won't spend my hundred dollars for mournin'. I'll wear my old black dress!

ELLA. And me makin' hats all the rest of my life—just makin' hats!

[*The front door is heard to shut behind them.* JANE, BEN *and* JUDGE *are alone.* JUDGE *stands by stove.* JANE *is up by window, looking out at the deepening twilight.* BEN *sits at right.*]

BEN. Ha! Ha! Ha! "Crow buzzards" mother called us—the last of the Jordans—crow buzzards—and that's what we are.

JUDGE. You can't stay here, Ben; you know that as well as I do. I signed the warrant for your arrest myself. It's been over a year since the Grand Jury indicted you for arson.

BEN. You mean you'll give me up?

JANE. You won't do that, Judge; you're here as her friend.

JUDGE. No, but if it's known he's here, I couldn't save him, and it's bound to be known.

JANE [*to* BEN]. Were you careful coming?

BEN. Yes.

JUDGE. It's bound to be known.

BEN. He means they'll tell on me. [*He nods his head toward door.*] My brother, or my sisters.

JUDGE. No, I don't think they'd do that.

BEN. Let 'em! What do I care? I'm sick of hiding out, half starved! Let 'em do what they please. All I know is one thing,—when they put her into her grave her sons and daughters are goin' to be standin' there, like the Jordans always do.

JANE [*quietly*]. Hannah will have your room ready by now. There are some clean shirts and things that was your father's; I'll bring them to you.

BEN [*uneasily*]. Can I go up there, just a minute?

JANE. To your mother?

BEN. Yes.

JANE. If you want to.

BEN. I do.

JANE. Yes, you can go.

[BEN *turns and exits up the stairs.* JANE *crosses and sits by stove, sinking wearily into the chair.*]

JUDGE. And she left him nothing, just that hundred dollars, and only that because I told her it was the safest way to do it. I thought he was her one weakness, but it seems she didn't have any.

JANE. No.

JUDGE. She was a grim old woman, Jane.

JANE. I think I could have loved her, but she didn't want it.

JUDGE. And yet she left you everything.

JANE. I don't understand.

JUDGE. She left a sealed letter for you. It's in my strong box; you may learn from it that she cared more about you than you think.

JANE. No.

JUDGE. There was more kindness in her heart than most people gave her credit for.

JANE. For her own, for Uncle Ned, who never did for her, for Ned, for the Jordan name. I don't understand, and I don't think I care so very much; it's been a hard week, Judge. [*She rests her head against the back of the chair.*]

JUDGE. I know, and you're all worn out.

JANE. Yes.

JUDGE. It's a lot of money, Jane.

JANE. I suppose so.

JUDGE. And so you're a rich woman. I am curious to know how you feel?

JANE. Just tired.

[*She shuts her eyes. For a moment he looks at her with a smile, then turns and quietly fills the stove with wood as* BEN *comes slowly downstairs and into the room.*]

BEN. If there was only something I could do for her.

JUDGE. Jane's asleep, Ben.

BEN. Did she look like that, unhappy, all the time?

JUDGE. Yes.

BEN. Crow buzzards! God damn the Jordans!

[*Front door bell rings sharply,* BEN *is startled.*]

JUDGE. Steady there! It's just one of the neighbors, I guess. [*Bell rings again as* HANNAH *crosses downstairs and to hall.*] Hannah knows enough not to let anyone in.

BEN [*slowly*]. When I got back, time before

this, from France, I tried to go straight, but it wasn't any good, I just don't belong—

HANNAH *enters frightened*

HANNAH. It's Jim Jay!

BEN [*to* JUDGE]. And you didn't think my own blood would sell me?

JIM JAY, *a large, kindly man of middle age, enters*

JIM. I'm sorry, Ben, I've come for you!

[JANE *wakes, startled, and springs up.*]

JANE. What is it?

JIM. I got to take him, Jane.

BEN [*turns fiercely*]. Have you!

JIM [*quietly*]. I'm armed, Ben—better not be foolish!

JANE. He'll go with you, Mr. Jay. He won't resist.

JIM [*quietly*]. He mustn't. You got a bad name, Ben, and I ain't a-goin' to take any chances.

BEN. I thought I'd get to go to her funeral, anyway, before they got me.

JIM. Well, you could, maybe, if you was to fix a bail bond. You'd take bail for him, wouldn't you, Judge?

JUDGE. It's a felony; I'd have to have good security.

JANE. I'm a rich woman, you said just now. Could I give bail for him?

JUDGE. Yes.

BEN [*to her*]. So the money ain't enough. You want all us Jordans fawnin' on you for favors. Well, all of 'em but me will; by mornin' the buzzards will be flocking round you thick! You're going to hear a lot about how much folks love you, but you ain't goin' to hear it from me.

JANE [*turns to him quietly*]. Why did you come here, Ben, when I wrote you she was dying?

BEN. Why did I come?

JANE. Was it because you loved her, because you wanted to ask her to forgive you, before she died—or was it because you wanted to get something for yourself?

BEN [*hesitates*]. How does a feller know why he does what he does?

JANE. I'm just curious. You've got so much contempt for the rest, I was just wondering? You were wild, Ben, and hard, but you were honest—what brought you here?

BEN [*sulkily*]. The money.

JANE. I thought so. Then when you saw her you were sorry, but even then the money was in your mind—well—it's mine now. And you've got to take your choice,—you can do what I tell you, or you'll go with Mr. Jay.

BEN. Is that so? Well, I guess there ain't much doubt about what I'll do. Come on, Jim!

JIM. All right. [*He takes a pair of handcuffs from his pocket.*] You'll have to slip these on, Ben.

BEN [*steps back*]. No—wait—[*He turns desperately to* JANE.] What is it you want?

JANE. I want you to do as I say.

BEN [*after a look at* JIM *and the handcuffs*]. I'll do it.

JANE. I thought so. [*She turns to* JUDGE.] Can you fix the bond up here?

JUDGE. Yes. [*He sits at table and takes pen, ink and paper from a drawer.*] I can hold court right here long enough for that.

JIM. This is my prisoner, Judge, and here's the warrant. [*He puts warrant on table.*]

JANE. First he's got to swear, before you, to my conditions.

BEN. What conditions?

JANE. When will his trial be, Judge?

JUDGE. Not before the spring term, I should think—say early April.

JANE. You'll stay here till then, Ben; you won't leave town! You'll work the farm,—there's plenty to be done.

BEN [*sulkily*]. I don't know how to work a farm.

JANE. I do. You'll just do what I tell you.

BEN. Be your slave? That's what you mean, ain't it?

JANE. I've been about that here for eight years.

BEN. And now it's your turn to get square on a Jordan!

JANE. You'll work for once, and work every day. The first day you don't I'll surrender you to the judge, and he'll jail you. The rest of the Jordans will live as I tell them to live, or for the first time in any of their lives, they'll live on what they earn. Don't forget,

Ben, that right now I'm the head of the family.

JUDGE [*to* BEN]. You heard the conditions? Shall I make out the bond?

BEN [*reluctantly*]. Yes.

[*He sits moodily at right, looking down at the floor.* JANE *looks at him for a moment, then turns up to window.*]

JANE. It's snowing!

JIM. Thought I smelled it. [*He buttons his coat.*] Well, nothin' to keep me, is there, Judge?

JUDGE. No. [*He starts to write out the bond with a rusty pen.*] This pen is rusty!

JIM. I was sorry to hear about the old lady. It's too bad, but that's the way of things.

JUDGE [*writes*]. Yes.

JIM. Well—It's early for snow, not but what it's a good thing for the winter wheat.

[*He exits.*

CURTAIN

ACT TWO

SCENE. *Sitting room of the Jordan Homestead some two months later.*

This room also shows some traces of a family's daily life, and to that extent is less desolate than the "parlor" of the first act, although the stern faith of the Puritan makes no concession to the thing we have learned to call "good taste." The old-fashioned simplicity seen in such a room as this has resulted from poverty, both of mind and of purse, and has nothing akin to the simplicity of the artist; as a matter of fact, your true descendants of the settlers of 1605 would be the first to resent such an implication; to them the arts are directly connected with heathen practices, and any incense burned before the altars of the Graces still smells to them of brimstone.

At back center folding doors, now partly open, lead to dining room. In this room may be seen the dining table, back of the table a window looking out on to the farm yard, now deep in midwinter snow. At right is an open fireplace with a log fire. Below fireplace a door to hall. Up left door to small vestibule in which is the outside door. Down left a window overlooking a snowbound countryside. The clock above the fireplace is set for quarter past four. Several straight-backed chairs and a woodbox by fireplace. A sewing table and lamp at center. A sewing machine near window at left. A wall cupboard on the wall right of the doors to the dining room. An old sofa down left, two chairs at right. When the door at left, in vestibule, is opened, one may see a path up to the door, between two walls of snow.

Discovered: ELLA *sits right at sewing machine, hemming some rough towels.* ORIN *and* NETTIE *are by fireplace.* SADIE *sits right of center.* SADIE *and* ORIN *are dressed for outdoors.* NETTIE'S *coat, hat and overshoes are on a hatrack by door at left.* ORIN, *as the curtain goes up, is putting a log on the fire.*

SADIE [*acidly to* ELLA]. Why shouldn't he put wood on the fire if he wants to?

ELLA [*at sewing machine*]. Because it ain't your wood.

SADIE. No, it's *hers!* Everything is hers!

ELLA. And maybe she just don't know it.

NETTIE [*at fireplace*]. Ah! [*She bends closer to the fire as the log blazes up.*] I do love a good fire! Oh it's nice to be warm!

SADIE. There's somethin' sensual about it.

NETTIE. Mother told me that the next time you started talkin' indecent I was to leave the room.

SADIE. Tell your mother I don't wonder she's sort of worried about you. I'd be if you was *my* daughter.

ELLA. I don't see why you can't let Nettie alone!

NETTIE. She's always picking on me, Aunt Ella! To hear her talk anybody would think I was terrible.

SADIE. I know more about what's going on than some folks think I do.

NETTIE. Then you know a lot. I heard Horace Bevins say a week ago that he didn't know as it was any use tryin' to have a Masonic Lodge in the same town as you.

SADIE. They never was a Bevins yet didn't have his tongue hung from the middle; the day his mother was married she answered both the responses.

ORIN. Mum! Mum! Shall I take my coat off; are we going to stay, Mum?

SADIE. No, we ain't going to stay. I just want to see Cousin Jane for a minute.

ELLA. She's in the kitchen with Hannah.

SADIE. Watchin' her, I bet! I wonder Hannah puts up with it.

ELLA. If you was to live with Jane for a spell, I guess you'd find you had a plenty to put up with.

SADIE. It's enough to make the Jordans turn in their graves, all of 'em at once.

ELLA. I guess all she'd say would be, "Let 'em if it seemed to make 'em any more comfortable."

JANE *enters. She has apron on and some towels over her arm*

JANE. Are those towels finished?

ELLA. Some is! Maybe I'd done all of 'em if I'd been a centipede.

JANE. Oh! I didn't see you, Sadie.

SADIE. Oh! Ha, ha! Well, I ain't surprised.

JANE [*with* ELLA, *selecting finished towels*]. Well, Orin, does the tooth still hurt you?

ORIN. Naw, it don't hurt me none now. I got it in a bottle. [*He takes small bottle from pocket.*]

NETTIE. Oh, you nasty thing. You get away!

SADIE [*angrily*]. What did I tell you about showin' that tooth to folks!

JANE. Never mind, Orin, just run out to the barn and tell your Uncle Ben we've got to have a path cleared under the clotheslines.

ORIN. All right. [*He crosses toward door.*]

JANE. Hannah's going to wash tomorrow, tell him. I'll expect a good wide path.

ORIN. I'll tell him. [*He exits.*

SADIE. I must say you keep Ben right at it, don't you?

JANE. Yes. [*She takes the last finished towel and speaks to* ELLA.] I'll come back for more.

SADIE [*as* JANE *crosses*]. First I thought he'd go to jail before he'd work, but he didn't, did he?

JANE. No. [*She exits right.*

SADIE. Yes. No! Yes. No! Folks that ain't got no more gift of gab ain't got much gift of intellect. I s'pose Hannah's out there.

ELLA. Yes, she keeps all of us just everlastingly at it.

SADIE. When Jane comes back, I wish you and Nettie would leave me alone with her, just for a minute.

ELLA [*as she works over sewing machine*]. It won't do you much good; she won't lend any more money.

SADIE. Mother always helped me. I've got a right to expect it.

ELLA [*as she bites off a thread*]. Expectin' ain't gettin'.

SADIE. I don't know what I'll do.

ELLA. You had money out of her; so has Henry.

SADIE [*shocked*]. You don't mean to say your father's been borrowin' from her. [*This to* NETTIE.]

NETTIE. He's always borrowin'. Didn't he borrow the hundred dollars grandma left me? I'm not going to stand it much longer.

ELLA. Henry's havin' trouble with his business.

SADIE. We're fools to put up with it. Everybody says so. We ought to contest the will.

ELLA. Everybody says so but the lawyers; they won't none of 'em touch the case without they get money in advance.

SADIE. How much money? Didn't your father find out, Nettie?

NETTIE. The least was five hundred dollars.

ELLA. Can you see us raisin' that?

SADIE. If we was short, we might borrow it from Jane.

ELLA. We'd have to be smarter'n I see any signs of; she's through lendin'.

SADIE. How do you know?

ELLA. I tried it myself.

SADIE. What do you want money for? Ain't she takin' you in to live with her?

ELLA. I don't call myself beholden for that. She had to have someone, with Ben here, and her unmarried, and next to no relation to him.

NETTIE. Everybody's callin' you the chaperon! [*She laughs.*] Not but what they ought to be one with *him* around; he's awful good lookin'.

SADIE. You keep away from him. He's no blood kin of yours, and he's a bad man, if he is a Jordan. Always makes up to everything he sees in petticoats, and always did.

NETTIE. Thanks for the compliment, but I'm not looking for any jailbirds.

ELLA. It will be awful, Ben in State's Prison, —and I guess he'll have to go, soon as he stands his trial.

SADIE. He got drunk and had a fight with the two Kimbal boys, and they licked him, and that night he burned down their barn; everybody knows it.

ELLA. He's bad, all through, Ben is.

NETTIE. He'll get about five years, father says. I guess that will take some of the spunk out of him.

[*A sound in the hall at right.*]

ELLA. Hush! I think he's coming.

BEN *enters at right with a big armful of firewood and crosses and drops it heavily into woodbox, then turns and looks at them in silence.*

SADIE. Seems kind of funny, your luggin' in the wood.

BEN [*bitterly*]. Does it?

SADIE. Did you see Orin out there?

BEN. Yes, he went along home.

SADIE. How do you like workin'?

BEN. How do you think I like it? Workin' a big farm in winter, tendin' the stock and milking ten cows. How do I like it?

[*As he stands by fire* NETTIE *looks up at him.*]

NETTIE. I think it's just a shame!

SADIE [*turns to* ELLA]. Are you going to make towels all the afternoon?

ELLA. I am 'til they're done, then I expect she'll find somethin' else for me to do.

NETTIE [*to* BEN]. Do you know I'm sorry for you, awful sorry?

[*She speaks low.* ELLA *and* SADIE *are at the other side of room.*]

BEN. Then you're the only one.

NETTIE. Maybe I am, but I'm like that.

BEN. Another month of it, then State's Prison, I guess. I don't know as I'll be sorry when the time comes.

NETTIE. Oh, Uncle Ben! No, I'm not goin' to call you *that*. After all, you're not really any relation, are you? I mean to me?

BEN. No.

NETTIE [*softly*]. I'm just going to call you Ben!

BEN. You're a good kid, Nettie.

NETTIE. Oh, it isn't that, Ben, but it does just seem too awful.

[*As she looks up at him, the outside door opens and* HENRY *and* EMMA *enter. They see* NETTIE *and* BEN *together by the fire.*]

EMMA [*sternly*]. Nettie!

NETTIE [*sweetly*]. Yes, mother?

EMMA. You come away from him.

BEN [*angrily*]. What do you mean by that?

EMMA. You tell him, Henry.

HENRY. I don't know as it's any use to—

EMMA [*sternly*]. Tell him what I mean.

HENRY [*to* BEN]. Emma thinks, considerin' everything, that it's best Nettie shouldn't talk to you.

BEN. Why don't you keep her at home then? You don't suppose I want to talk to her.

EMMA. Oh, we ain't wanted here, I guess. We know that, not by you, or by *her;*—and Henry's the oldest of the Jordans. All this would be his, if there was any justice in the world.

NETTIE. Father wouldn't have taken that hundred dollars grandma left me if there had been any justice in the world. That's what I came here for, not to talk to him. To tell Cousin Jane what father did, and to tell her about Nellie Namlin's Christmas party, and that I've got to have a new dress. I've just got to!

SADIE. A new dress, and my rent ain't paid. She's got to pay it. My Orin's got to have a roof over his head.

HENRY. I don't know as you've got any call to be pestering Jane all the time.

ELLA. She's always wantin' something.

SADIE. What about you? Didn't you tell me yourself you tried to borrow from her?

ELLA. I got a chance to set up in business, so as I can be independent. I can go in with Mary Stanton, dressmakin'. I can do it for two hundred dollars, and she's got to give it to me.

HENRY. You ought to be ashamed, all three of you, worryin' Jane all day long. It's more'n flesh and blood can stand!

NETTIE [*to him*]. Didn't you say at breakfast you was coming here today to make Cousin Jane endorse a note for you?Didn't you?

EMMA [*fiercely*]. You hush!

BEN [*at back by window*]. Ha! Ha! Ha! Crow buzzards.

HENRY. Endorsing a note ain't lending money, is it? It's a matter of business. I guess my note's good.

BEN. Take it to the bank without her name on it and see how good it is.

EMMA. You don't think we want to ask her favors, but Henry's in bad trouble and she'll just have to help us this time.

BEN. There's one way out of your troubles. One thing you could all do, for a change, instead of making Jane pay all your bills. I wonder you haven't any of you thought of it.

HENRY. What could we do?

BEN. Go to work and earn something for yourselves.

SADIE. Like you do, I suppose.

EMMA. The laughing-stock of all Veazie!

ELLA. Everybody's talkin' about it, anywhere you go.

NETTIE. Jane Crosby's White Slave, that's what they call you. Jane Crosby's White Slave.

BEN [*fiercely*]. They call me that, do they?

ELLA [*to* NETTIE]. Why can't you ever hold your tongue?

BEN [*in cold anger*]. I've been a damned fool. I'm through.

HANNAH *enters*

HANNAH. She wants you.

BEN. Jane?

HANNAH. Yes.

BEN. I won't come.

HANNAH. There'll be another row.

BEN. Tell her I said I wouldn't come.

[*He sits.*]

HANNAH. She's awful set, you know, when she wants anything.

BEN. You tell her I won't come.

HANNAH. Well, I don't say I hanker none to tell her, but I'd rather be in my shoes than yourn. [*She exits.*

SADIE. Well, I must say I don't blame you a mite.

EMMA. If the Jordans is a lot of slaves, I guess it's pretty near time we knew it.

HENRY [*worried*]. She'll turn you over to Judge Bradford, Ben; he'll lock you up. It ain't goin' to help me none with the bank, a brother of mine bein' in jail.

BEN. So they're laughing at me, are they, damn them!

NETTIE [*at door right*]. She's coming!

[*There is a moment's pause and* JANE *enters door right.* HANNAH *follows to door and looks on eagerly.*]

JANE. I sent for you, Ben.

BEN. I won't budge.

JANE [*wearily*]. Must we go through all this again?

BEN. I ain't going to move out of this chair today. You do what you damned please.

JANE. I am sorry, but you must.

BEN. Send for Jim Jay, have me locked up, do as you please. Oh, I've said it before, but this time I mean it.

JANE. And you won't come?

BEN. No.

JANE. Then I'll do the best I can alone.

[*She crosses up to wall closet and opens it and selects a large bottle, and turns.* BEN *rises quickly.*]

BEN. What do you want of that?

JANE. It's one of the horses. I don't know what's the matter with her. She's down in her stall, just breathing. She won't pay any attention to me.

BEN. Old Nellie?

JANE. Yes.

BEN. What you got? [*He steps to her and takes the bottle from her and looks at it.*] That stuff's no good. Here! [*He steps to cabinet and selects another bottle.*] If you hadn't spent five minutes stalling around, I might have had a better chance.

[*He exits quickly at left.*

HANNAH. I allers said 'twas easier to catch flies with honey than 'twas with vinegar.

HENRY. What's Ben know about horses?

JANE. A lot.

HENRY. I didn't know that.

JANE. Neither did Ben, six weeks ago.

[*She exits.*

HENRY. Mother was like that, about animals. I guess Ben sort of takes after her.

EMMA [*shocked*]. Ben! Like your mother!

HANNAH. Of course he is. He's the "spit and image of her." [*She exits.*

NETTIE. She made him go! It wouldn't surprise me a mite if she'd pushed that old horse over herself.

JANE *enters*

JANE. He wouldn't let me in the barn. [*For the first time in the play, she laughs lightly.*]

Well—[*She looks about at them.*] we have quite a family gathering here this afternoon. I am wondering if there is any—special reason for it?

HENRY. I wanted to talk with yer for just a minute, Jane.

SADIE. So do I.

JANE. Anybody else? [*She looks about.*]

ELLA. I do.

NETTIE. So do I.

JANE. I've a lot to do; suppose I answer you all at once. I'm sorry, but I won't lend you any money.

HENRY. Of course, I didn't think they'd call that note of mine; it's only five hundred, and you could just endorse it.

JANE. No!

SADIE. I was going to ask you—

JANE. No!

ELLA. I got a chance to be independent, Jane, and—

JANE. No. I haven't any money. I won't have before the first of the month.

EMMA. No money!

HENRY. I bet you're worth as much today as you was the day mother died.

JANE. To a penny. I've lived, and run this house, and half supported all of you on what I've made the place earn. Yesterday I spent the first dollar that I didn't have to spend. I mean, on myself. But that's no business of yours. I *am* worth just as much as the day I took the property, and I'm not going to run behind, so you see, after all, I'm a real Jordan.

EMMA. Seems so. I never knew one of 'em yet who didn't seem to think he could take it with him.

HENRY. Well, Jane, I don't know as it's any use tryin' to get you to change your mind?

JANE. I'm sorry.

EMMA. You can leave that for us to be. I guess it's about the only thing we've got a right to. Get your things on, Nettie!

NETTIE. I'm going to stay a while with Aunt Ella; I won't be late.

HENRY. I don't know what I'm goin' to do about that note. I s'pose I'll find some way out of it.

JANE. I hope so.

EMMA. Thank yer. Of course we know there's always the poorhouse. Come, Henry. [*She exits at left, leaving the outside door open.*]

HENRY. Emma is a little upset. I hope you won't mind her talk. I guess her part of it ain't any too easy. [*He exits, shutting the door.*]

ELLA [*to* JANE]. Poor Henry! Of course I s'pose you're right not to lend it to him. But I don't know as *I* could do it, but I'm sensitive.

JANE. Perhaps it's harder to say no than you think.

HANNAH *enters*

HANNAH. I got everything ready for tomorrow's wash, but the sheets off your bed, Miss Ella.

ELLA. Good Land! I forgot 'em. Nettie will bring 'em right down.

NETTIE [*to* JANE]. After that, I'm going to stay and help Aunt Ella. I was wondering if you'd be here all the afternoon.

JANE. Yes.

NETTIE [*charmingly*]. Nothing special, you know. I'd just like to have a little visit with you. [*She exits at left with* ELLA.

HANNAH [*looks after her*]. Every time I listen to that girl I get fur on my tongue.

JANE. Fur?

HANNAH. Like when my dyspepsia's coming. There's two things I can't abide, her and cucumbers. [*She crosses to door left.*]

JANE. Hannah!

HANNAH [*stops*]. Well?

JANE [*rather shyly*]. We are going to have rather a special supper tonight.

HANNAH [*doubtfully*]. We are?

JANE. Yes. That's why I had you roast that turkey yesterday.

HANNAH [*firmly*]. That's for Sunday!

JANE. No, it's for tonight.

HANNAH [*angrily*]. Why is it?

JANE. It's my birthday.

HANNAH. I didn't know that.

JANE. No, it isn't exactly a national holiday, but we'll have the turkey, and I'll get some preserves up, and I want you to bake a cake, a round one. We'll have candles on it. I got some at the store this morning.

HANNAH [*shocked*]. Candles?

JANE. Yes.

HANNAH. Who's going to be to this party?

JANE [*a little self-conscious*]. Why—just—just ourselves.

HANNAH. Just you and Mr. Ben and Miss Ella?

JANE. Yes.

HANNAH. You don't want candles on that cake, you want crape on it.

[*She exits door left.*

[JANE *crosses up and starts to clear the dining-room table of its red table cover, as* BEN *enters door left.*]

BEN [*cheerfully*]. Well, I fixed Old Nellie up. [*He puts his bottle back in its place in the wall cabinet.*] Just got her in time. Thought she was gone for a minute, but she's going to be all right.

JANE. That's good. [*She folds the tablecloth up and puts it away.*]

BEN [*in front of fire*]. She knew what I was doin' for her too; you could tell by the way she looked at me! She'll be all right, poor old critter. I remember her when she was a colt, year before I went to high school.

[JANE *crosses into room, shutting the dining-room door after her.*]

JANE. You like animals, don't you, Ben?

BEN [*surprised*]. I don't know. I don't like to see 'em suffer.

JANE. Why?

BEN. I guess it's mostly because they ain't to blame for it. I mean what comes to 'em ain't their fault. If a woman thinks she's sick, 'til she gets sick, that's her business. If a man gets drunk, or eats like a hog, he's got to pay for it, and he ought to. Animals live cleaner than we do anyhow—and when you do anything for 'em they've got gratitude. Folks haven't.

JANE. Hand me that sewing basket, Ben.

[*She has seated herself at left center by table.* BEN *at left of table, hands her the basket as she picks up some sewing.*]

BEN. It's funny, but except for a dog or two, I don't remember carin' nothin' for any of the live things, when I lived here I mean.

JANE. I guess that's because you didn't do much for them.

BEN. I guess so—Sometimes I kind of think I'd like to be here when spring comes—and see all the young critters coming into the world—I should think there'd be a lot a feller could do, to make it easier for 'em.

JANE. Yes.

BEN. Everybody's always makin' a fuss over women and their babies. I guess animals have got some feelings, too.

JANE [*sewing*]. Yes.

BEN. I *know* it—Yes, sometimes I sort of wish I could be here, in the spring.

JANE. You'll be a big help.

BEN. I'll be in prison. [*He looks at her. She drops her head and goes on sewing.*] You forgot that, didn't yer?

JANE. Yes.

BEN. What's the difference? A prison ain't just a place; it's bein' somewheres you don't want to be, and that's where I've always been.

JANE. You liked the Army?

BEN. I s'pose so.

JANE. Why?

BEN. I don't know, there was things to do, and you did 'em.

JANE. And some one to tell you what to do?

BEN. Maybe that's it, somebody that knew better'n I did. It galled me at first, but pretty soon we got over in France, an' I saw we was really doin' something, then I didn't mind. I just got to doin' what I was told, and it worked out all right.

JANE. You liked France, too?

BEN. Yes.

JANE. I'd like to hear you tell about it.

BEN. Maybe I'll go back there some time. I don't know as I'd mind farming a place over there. Most of their farms are awful little, but I don't know but what I'd like it.

JANE. Farming is farming. Why not try it here?

BEN. Look out there! [*He points out of the window at the drifted snow.*] It's like that half the year, froze up, everything, most of all the people. Just a family by itself, maybe. Just a few folks, good an' bad, month after month, with nothin' to think about but just the mean little things, that really don't amount to nothin', but get to be bigger than all the world outside.

JANE [*sewing*]. Somebody must do the farming, Ben.

BEN. Somebody like the Jordans, that's been doin' it generation after generation. Well, look at us. I heard a feller, in a Y. M. C. A. hut, tellin' how nature brought animals into the world, able to face what they had to face—

JANE. Yes, Ben?

BEN. That's what nature's done for us Jordans,—brought us into the world half froze before we was born. Brought us into the world mean, and hard, so's we could live the hard, mean life we have to live.

JANE. I don't know, Ben, but what you could live it different.

BEN. They *laugh* over there, and sing, and God knows when I was there they didn't have much to sing about. I was at a rest camp, near Nancy, after I got wounded. I told you about the French lady with all those children that I got billeted with.

JANE. Yes.

BEN. They used to *sing*, right at the table, and laugh! God! It brought a lump into my throat more'n once, lookin' at them, and rememberin' the Jordans!

JANE. I guess there wasn't much laughing at your family table.

BEN. Summers nobody had much time for it, and winters,—well, I guess you know.

JANE. Yes.

BEN. Just a few folks together, day after day, and every little thing you don't like about the other raspin' on your nerves 'til it almost drives you crazy! Most folks quiet, because they've said all the things they've got to say a hundred times; other folks talkin', talkin', talkin' about nothing. Sometimes somebody sort of laughs, and it scares you; seems like laughter needs the sun, same as flowers do. Icebound, that's what we are, all of us, inside and out. [*He stands looking grimly out window.*]

JANE. Not all. I laughed a lot before I came here to live.

BEN [*turns and looks at her*]. I remember, you were just a little girl.

JANE. I was fourteen. See if there's a spool of black sewing cotton in that drawer.

BEN [*looking in drawer*]. You mean thread?

JANE. Yes.

BEN. This it? [*He holds up a spool of white thread.*]

JANE. Would you call that black?

BEN [*looks it over*]. No—it ain't black. [*He searches and finds black thread.*] Maybe this is it!

JANE. Maybe it is! [*She takes it.*] You were with that French family quite a while, weren't you?

BEN. Most a month; they was well off, you know; I mean, they was, before the war. It was a nice house.

JANE [*sewing*]. How nice?

BEN [*hesitates*]. I don't know, things—well —useful, you know, but nice, not like this. [*He looks about.*]

JANE [*looks around with a sigh*]. It's not very pretty, but it could be. I could make it.

BEN. If you did, folks would be sayin' you wasn't respectable.

JANE. Tell me about the dinner they gave you the night before you went back to your company.

BEN. I told you.

JANE. Tell me again.

BEN [*smiles to himself at the remembrance*]. They was all dressed up, the whole family, and there I was with just my dirty old uniform.

JANE. Yes.

BEN [*lost in his recollections*]. It was a fine dinner, but it wasn't that. It was their doin' so much for me, folks like that—I've sort of pictured 'em lots of times since then.

JANE. Go on.

BEN. All of the young ones laughing and happy, and the mother too, laughing and tryin' to talk to me, and neither one of us knowing much about what the other one was sayin'. [*He and* JANE *both laugh.*]

JANE. And the oldest daughter? The one that was most grown up?

BEN. She was scared of me somehow, but I don't know as ever I've seen a girl like her, before or since.

JANE. Maybe 'twas that dress you told me about; seems to me you don't remember much else about her; not so much as what color her hair was, only just that that dress was blue.

BEN [*thoughtfully*]. Yes.

JANE [*sewing*]. Sometimes you say dark blue! [*She is watching him closely through half-shut eyes.*]

BEN [*absently*]. I guess so.

JANE. And then I say, dark as something I point out to you, that isn't dark at all, and you say, "No, lighter than that!"

BEN [*absently*]. Just—sort of blue.

JANE. Yes, sort of blue. It had lace on it, too, didn't it?

BEN. Lace? Maybe—yes, lace.

JANE. There's more than one blue dress in the world.

BEN. Like enough. Maybe there's more'n one family like that lady's, but I'll be damned if they live in Veazie. [*He crosses and opens cupboard and selects a bottle.*] I might as well run out and see how the old mare is getting on. [*He selects bottle from shelf.*]

JANE. And you've got to shovel those paths for the clothes-lines yet.

BEN. I know.

JANE. Well, don't forget.

BEN. It ain't likely you'll let me.

[*He exits at door right.* JANE *laughs softly to herself, and runs to closet and takes out a large cardboard box and putting it on the table, she cuts the string and removes the wrapping paper, then lifts the cover of the box and draws out a dainty light-blue gown with soft lace on the neck and sleeves. She holds it up joyfully, then, covering her own dress with it, she looks at herself in a mirror on wall. As she stands smiling at her reflection, there is a sharp knock on the outside door.* JANE *hastily returns dress to box and as the knock is repeated, she puts the box under the sofa at left and crosses and opens the outside door.*]

JUDGE BRADFORD *enters*

JANE. Oh, it's you, Judge! Come in.

JUDGE. I thought I'd stop on my way home and see how you were getting on, Jane.

JANE. I'll take your coat.

JUDGE. I'll just put it here. [*He puts coat on chair.*] Have you time to sit down a minute?

JANE. Of course. [*They sit.*]

JUDGE [*looks at her*]. That isn't a smile on your lips, is it, Jane?

JANE. Maybe—

JUDGE [*laughingly*]. I'm glad I came!

JANE. It's my birthday.

JUDGE. Why, Jane! [*He crosses to her and holds out his hand. She takes it.*] Many happy returns!

JANE [*thoughtfully*]. Many—happy returns—that's a lot to ask for.

JUDGE. You're about twenty-two, or twenty-three, aren't you?

JANE. Twenty-three.

JUDGE. Time enough ahead of you. [*His eye falls on the box, imperfectly hidden under the sofa; out of it a bit of the blue dress is sticking.*] Hello! What's all that?

JANE. My birthday present.

JUDGE. Who gave it to you?

JANE. I did.

JUDGE. Good! It's about time you started to blossom out.

JANE. I ordered a lot of things from Boston; they'll be here tomorrow.

JUDGE. I suppose that one's a dress?

JANE. Yes.

JUDGE [*bends over to look*]. Light blue, isn't it?

JANE [*smiles*]. Just sort of blue—with lace on it.

JUDGE. Oh, you're going to wear it, I suppose, in honor of your birthday?

JANE [*startled*]. Tonight—oh, no—soon maybe, but not tonight.

JUDGE [*smiles*]. How soon?

JANE. Soon as I dare to; not just yet.

JUDGE. You have plenty of money; you ought to have every comfort in the world, and some of the luxuries.

JANE [*gravely*]. Judge! I want you to do something for me.

JUDGE. And of course I'll do it.

JANE. I want you to get Ben off. I want you to fix it so he won't go to State's Prison.

JUDGE. But if he's guilty, Jane?

JANE. I want you to go to old Mr. Kimbal for me and offer to pay him for that barn of his that Ben burned down. Then I want you to fix it so he won't push the case, so's Ben gets off.

JUDGE. Do you know what you are asking of me?

JANE. To get Ben off.

JUDGE. To compound a felony.

JANE. Those are just words, Judge, and

words don't matter much to me. I might say I wasn't asking you to compound a felony, I was askin' you to save a sinner, but those would be just words too. There's nobody else; you've *got* to help me.

JUDGE [*thoughtfully*]. I've always thought a lot could be done for Ben, by a good lawyer.

JANE. It doesn't matter how, so long as it's done.

JUDGE. He was drinking, with a crowd of young men; the two Kimbal boys jumped on him and beat him up rather badly. That's about all we know, aside from the fact that Ben was drunk, and that that night the Kimbals' barn was set on fire.

JANE. Just so long as you can get him off, Judge.

JUDGE. I think a case of assault could be made against the Kimbal boys, and I think it would stand.

JANE. What of it?

JUDGE. It is quite possible that the old man, if he knew that action was to be taken against his sons, and if he could be tactfully assured of payment for his barn, say by Ben, in a year's time, might be persuaded to petition to have the indictment against Ben withdrawn. In that event, I think the chances would be very much in Ben's favor.

JANE. I don't care what names you call it, so long as it's done. Will you fix it?

JUDGE. Well, it's not exactly a proper proceeding for a Judge of the Circuit Court.

JANE. I knew you'd do it.

JUDGE. Yes, and I think you knew why, didn't you?

JANE. Ever since she's died, you've helped me about everything. Before she died you were just as good to me, and nobody else was.

JUDGE. I am glad you said that, because it clears me from the charge of being what poor Ben calls "one of the crow buzzards," and I don't want you to think me that.

JANE. No, you're not that.

JUDGE. I love you, Jane.

JANE. No!

JUDGE. Yes—I've done that for a long while. Don't you think you could get used to the thought of being my wife?

JANE [*gently*]. No.

JUDGE. I think I could make you happy.

JANE. No.

JUDGE. I am afraid being happy is something you don't know very much about.

JANE. No.

JUDGE. It isn't a thing that I am going to hurry you over, my dear, but neither is it a thing that I am going to give up hoping for.

JANE. When you told me, that day, that Mrs. Jordan had left me all her money, I couldn't understand; then, afterwards, you gave me the letter she left for me. I want you to read it.

JUDGE. What has her letter to do with us?

JANE. Maybe, reading it, you'll get to know something you've got a right to know, better than I could tell it to you.

JUDGE. Very well.

JANE. It's here. [*She opens drawer, and selects a letter in a woman's old-fashioned handwriting, from a large envelope of papers.*] She was a cold woman, Judge. She never let me get close to her, although I tried. She didn't love me. I was as sure of it then as I am now. [*She holds out the letter.*] Read it.

JUDGE. If it's about the thing I've been speaking of, I'd rather hear it in your voice.

JANE [*reads*]. "My dear Jane, the doctor tells me I haven't long to live, and so I'm doing this, the meanest thing I think I've ever done to you. I'm leaving you the Jordan money. Since my husband died, there has been just one person I could get to care about; that's Ben, who was my baby so long after all the others had forgotten how to love me. And Ben's a bad son, and a bad man. I can't leave him the money; he'd squander it, and the Jordans' money came hard."

JUDGE. Poor woman! It was a bitter thing for her to have to write like that.

JANE [*reads on*]. "If squandering the money would bring him happiness, I'd face all the Jordans in the other world and laugh at them, but I know there's only just one chance to save my boy,—through a woman who will hold out her heart to him and let him trample on it, as he has on mine."

JUDGE [*in sudden fear*]. Jane!

JANE [*reads on*]. "Who'd work, and pray, and live for him, until as age comes on, and maybe he gets a little tired, he'll turn to her. And you're that woman, Jane; you've loved him ever since you came to us. Although he doesn't even know it. The Jordan name is his, the money's yours, and maybe there'll be another life for you to guard. God knows it isn't much I'm leaving you, but you can't refuse it, because you love him, and when he knows the money is yours, he will want to marry you. I'm a wicked old woman. Maybe you'll learn to forgive me as time goes on—It takes a long time to make a Jordan." [JANE *drops her hand to her side.*] Then she just signed her name.

JUDGE. Is the damnable thing she says there true?

JANE. Yes, Judge.

JUDGE. And you're going to do this thing for her?

JANE. No, for him.

JUDGE [*bitterly*]. He isn't worth it.

JANE. I guess you don't understand.

JUDGE. No. [*He crosses and picks up his coat.*]

JANE. You can't go like that, angry. You have to pay a price for being a good man, Judge—I need your help.

JUDGE. You mean *he* needs my help?

JANE. Yes, and you'll have to give it to him, if what you said a little while ago was true.

JUDGE [*after a pause*]. It *was* true, Jane. I'll help him. [*He picks up his hat.*]

JANE. I've an errand at the store. I'll go with you. [*She takes hat and coat from rack and puts them on.*]

JUDGE. Is it anything I could have sent up for you?

JANE [*putting on coat*]. I guess not. You see, I've got to match a color.

JUDGE. Another new dress?

JANE [*they start toward door*]. Just a ribbon, for my hair.

JUDGE. I didn't know women still wore ribbons in their hair.

JANE. It seems they do—in France.

[*They exit together at left to the outside door and off.*]

NETTIE *and* ELLA *enter quickly, after a slight pause,* NETTIE *running in from right, followed more sedately by* ELLA

NETTIE. You see! I was right! She went with him. [*She has run to window left and is looking out.*]

ELLA. That's what money does. If mother hadn't left her everything, he wouldn't have touched her with a ten-foot pole.

NETTIE. Well, if she's fool enough to stay in this place, I guess he's about the best there is.

ELLA. Then trust her for gettin' him; by the time she gets through in Veazie, this town will be barer than Mother Hubbard's cupboard by the time the dog got there. [*Her eye falls on* JANE'S *box, partly under sofa.*] What's that? [*She bends over, looking at it.*]

NETTIE. What?

ELLA. I never saw it before. [*She draws it out.*] Looks like a dress. See! Blue silk!

NETTIE. Open it.

ELLA [*hesitates*]. Must be hers! Maybe she wouldn't like it.

NETTIE. Maybe she wouldn't know it.

ELLA. A cat can look at a king! [*She opens the box and holds up the blue dress.*]

NETTIE. Oh! Oh!

ELLA [*really moved*]. Some folks would say a dress like that wasn't decent, but I wouldn't care, not if it was mine, and it might have been mine—but for her.

NETTIE. Yours! Grandma wouldn't have left her money to you. She hated old people. Everybody does. She'd have left it to me, but for Jane Crosby!

ELLA [*looks at dress*]. I always wanted a dress like this; when I was young, I used to dream about one, but mother only laughed. For years I counted on gettin' me what I wanted, when she died; now I never will.

NETTIE [*fiercely*]. I will—somehow!

ELLA. Maybe, but not me. Oh, if I could have the feelin' of a dress like that on me, if I could wear it once, where folks could see me—Just once! Oh, I know how they'd laugh—I wouldn't care—

NETTIE [*almost in tears*]. I can't stand it if she's going to wear things like that.

ELLA. I'll put it back. [*She starts to do so.*]

NETTIE [*catches her hand*]. Not yet.

ELLA. I guess the less we look at it, the better off we'll be. [*There is a ring at the front door.*]

NETTIE. Who's that?

ELLA. Here! [*She hands the box to* NETTIE.] Shove it back under the sofa. I'll go and see. [*She turns and crosses to door left and out to the vestibule.* NETTIE, *with the box in her arms, hesitates for a moment then turns and exits at right taking the box with her.* ELLA *opens the outside door at left, showing* ORIN *on the doorstep.* ELLA *looks at him angrily.*] For time's sake, what are *you* ringing the bell for?

ORIN. Mum says for me not to act like I belonged here.

ELLA. Well, I'm goin' to shut the door. Git in or git out!

ORIN. I got a note. [*He enters room as* ELLA *shuts door.*] It's for her.

ELLA [*holds out hand*]. Let me see it.

ORIN. Mum said not to let on I had nothin' if you came nosin' around.

JANE *enters from left*

JANE. I just ran across to the store. I haven't been five minutes. [*She takes coat off.*]

ELLA. He's got a note for you, from Sadie.

JANE. Oh, let me see it, Orin.

ORIN [*gives her note*]. She said, if you said is they an answer, I was to say yes, they is.

JANE. Just a minute. [*She opens note and reads it.*]

ELLA. I must say she didn't lose much time.

JANE [*after reading note*]. Poor Sadie! Wait, Orin! [*She sits at table and takes checkbook from the drawer and writes.*] Just take this to your mother.

ELLA. You don't mean you're goin' to—

JANE. Be quiet, Ella. Here, Orin. [*She hands him check.*] Don't lose it, and run along.

ORIN. All right. Mum said we was goin' to have dinner early, and go to a movie! Good night.

JANE [*again writing in checkbook*]. Good night. [ORIN *exits.*

ELLA. So you sent her her rent money, after all?

JANE. Here! [*She rises and hands a check to* ELLA.]

ELLA. What's that?

JANE. Two hundred dollars. You can try that dressmaking business if you want to, Ella.

ELLA [*looks at check*]. Two hundred dollars!

JANE. You needn't thank me.

ELLA. That ain't it. I was just wonderin' what's come over you all of a sudden.

BEN *enters*

JANE. It's my birthday, that's all. Did you know it was my birthday, Ben?

BEN [*carelessly*]. Is it? I shoveled them damned paths! [*He crosses and sits by fire.*]

JANE. Ella's going into the dressmaking business, Ben.

BEN [*moodily*]. What of it?

ELLA. That's what I say. It ain't much of a business. [*She exits at right; outside it grows to dusk.*]

JANE. Are you tired?

BEN. Maybe. [*He stretches his feet out toward fire.*]

JANE. You've done a lot of work today.

BEN. And every day.

JANE. I don't suppose you know how much good it's done you, how well you look!

BEN. Beauty's only skin deep.

JANE. Folks change, even in a few weeks, outside and in. Hard work don't hurt anybody.

BEN. I got chilblains on my feet. The damned shoes are stiffer than they ever was.

JANE. Icebound, you said. Maybe it don't have to be like that. Sometimes, just lately, it's seemed to me that if folks would try, things needn't be so bad. All of 'em try, I mean, for themselves, and for everybody else.

BEN. If I was you, I'd go out somewheres and hire a hall.

JANE. If you'd put some pork fat on those shoes tonight, your feet wouldn't hurt so bad.

BEN. Maybe.

[*He sits looking moodily into the fire. After a moment's hesitation,* JANE *crosses and sits in the chair beside his. The evening shadows deepen around them but the glow from the fire lights their faces.*]

JANE. I'm lonesome tonight. We always made a lot of birthdays when I was a girl.

BEN. Some do.

JANE. Your mother didn't. She found me once trying, the day I was fifteen. I remember how she laughed at me.

BEN. All the Jordans have got a sense of humor.

JANE. She wasn't a Jordan, not until she married your father.

BEN. When a woman marries into a family, she mostly shuts her eyes and jumps in all over.

JANE. Your mother was the best of the whole lot of you. Anyway, I think so.

BEN. I *know* it. I always thought a lot of her, in spite of our being relations.

JANE. She loved you, Ben.

BEN. She left me without a dollar, knowin' I was going to State's Prison, and what I'd be by the time I get out.

JANE. Maybe some day you'll understand why she did it.

BEN. Because she thought you'd take better care of the money than any of the rest of us.

JANE. And you hate me because of that, the way all the rest of the Jordans do?

BEN. Sometimes.

JANE [*sadly*]. I suppose it's natural.

BEN. But I ain't such a fool as Henry, and the women folks. They think you took advantage and fooled her into what she did. I thought so at first, now I don't.

JANE. What do you think now, Ben?

BEN. She'd watched you; she knew you were worth more'n all of us in a lump. I know it, too, but some way it riles me worse than if you wasn't.

JANE. That's silly!

BEN [*with growing resentment*]. Don't you suppose I know what you've been doin' to me? Tryin' to make a man of me. Tryin' to help me. Standing up to me and fightin' me every day, tryin' to teach me to be decent. Workin' over me like I was a baby, or somethin', and you was tryin' to teach me how to walk. Gettin' me so upset that every time I don't do what I ought to do, I get all het up inside; I never was so damned uncomfortable in all my life.

JANE. And I never was so happy.

BEN. I s'pose God knew what he was about when he made women.

JANE. Of course he did.

BEN. Anyhow, he gave 'em the best of it, all right.

JANE. You don't mean that! You *can't!*

BEN. I do. Let a man get miserable, and he *is* miserable. A woman ain't really happy no other way.

JANE. Maybe you think I'm having an easier time right now than you are.

BEN. I know it.

JANE. They all hate me, and they all want something, all the time. I can't say yes, and it's hard to always say no. Then there's the farm, big, and poor, and all worked out. The Jordans have been taking their living out of this soil for more than a hundred years, and never putting anything back.

BEN. Just themselves, that's all.

JANE. Worked right, like they do out West, this place could be what it ought to be. How can I do that? It needs a man.

BEN. I been thinkin' lately things could be done a whole lot different.

JANE. By a man, if he loved the old place—You Jordans robbed this soil always. Suppose one of you tried to pay it back—it would mean work and money, for a couple of years maybe, then I guess you'd see what gratitude meant.

BEN. It could be done; it ought to be.

JANE. By you, Ben!

BEN. No—I guess I ain't got the judgment.

JANE. You've got it, if you'd learn to use it.

BEN. Anyhow, I've got just a month, that's all.

JANE. Maybe you'll have more.

BEN. I'm as good as convicted as I sit here. I've only got a month.

JANE. Then help me for that month. We could plan how to start out in the spring. I've got books that will help us, and I can get more. We could do a lot!

BEN. I don't know but what we could!

JANE [*bends toward him*]. Will you shake hands on it? [*She offers her hand.*]

BEN [*surprised*]. What for?

JANE. Oh, just because we never have.

BEN. We ain't goin' to change *everything*, are we?

JANE. One thing. We're going to be friends.

BEN [*takes her hand awkwardly*]. You're a good sport, game as a man, gamer maybe.

JANE. And now for the surprise.

BEN. The what!

JANE [*draws her hand away and rises*]. You'll see. I want you to sit right here, until I open those doors. [*She points to doors to dining room.*]

BEN. I wasn't thinkin' of movin'.

JANE. Just sit right there.

BEN. And do what?

JANE. Think.

BEN. What of?

JANE. Oh, anything—so long as it's pleasant —of the spring that's coming—

BEN. In the prison down at Thomaston.

JANE. Of France then, of the family that was so good to you—of the beautiful lady—of the daughter, if you want to, the one that was most grown up—and of the wonderful blue dress. Just shut your eyes and think, 'til I come back!

[*She exits through doors to dining room and closes the doors after her.* BEN *sits in glow from the fire, his eyes closed. In a moment the door at right is thrown open and* NETTIE *stands in the doorway, the light from the hall falling on her. She has on* JANE'S *blue dress and is radiant with youth and excitement.*]

NETTIE. Ben! Look at me! Look, Ben!

BEN. What?

NETTIE. Look, Ben! [*He looks at her and for a moment sits in stupid wonder, then rises slowly to his feet.*]

BEN. It's—It's Nettie!

NETTIE. Did you ever see anything so lovely, did you?

BEN. You're—you're a woman, Nettie!

NETTIE. Of course I am, you stupid!

BEN [*crosses down to her*]. God! How I've starved for somethin' pretty to look at! God! How I've starved for it!

NETTIE. That's why I came down, I wanted you to see! I waited there in the hall till she went out.

BEN. And you've been here all the time, and I haven't so much as looked at you!

NETTIE [*softly*]. You've been in trouble, Ben!

BEN. I'll get out of that somehow! I'm going to make a fight. I ain't goin' to let 'em take me now.

NETTIE. Honest, Ben?

BEN. Not now. Oh, you pretty kid! You pretty little thing! [*He catches her fiercely in his arms.*]

NETTIE. You mustn't, Ben!

BEN [*triumphant*]. Mustn't! You don't know me!

NETTIE. Just one then! [*She holds up her lips, and as he kisses her ardently, the dining-room doors back of them open and* JANE *stands in the doorway, looking at them. She has removed her apron and has made some poor attempt at dressing up. Back of her we see the table bravely spread for the festive birthday party. There is a large turkey and other special dishes, and a round cake on which blaze twenty-three tiny candles. They turn their heads, startled, as* JANE *looks at them, and* BEN *tightens his arms defiantly about* NETTIE.] Let me go!

BEN [*holding her and looking past her to* JANE]. No! [*Then to* JANE.] Why are you looking at me like that?

NETTIE. Let me go.

BEN [*to* JANE]. To hell with your dream of grubbing in the dirt. Now I know what I want, and I'm going to get it.

NETTIE. Let go, dear. [*She draws away.*] I'm ashamed about wearin' your dress, Cousin Jane. I'll take it right off.

JANE. You needn't. I guess I don't want it any more. [*For the first time her eyes leave* BEN'S *face. She turns and steps past them to the door at right and calls.*] Supper's ready, Ella!

HANNAH *enters at back in dining room with a plate of hot biscuits*

CURTAIN

ACT THREE

SCENE. *Same as Act One. Parlor at the Jordans', two months later.*

At rise the characters are grouped exactly as they were at the opening of the play. The white slip covers, however, have been removed from the chairs, and the backing through the window shows partly melted snowdrifts. HENRY *sighs; the clock strikes two.* HENRY *looks at his watch.*

There is a pause. The outside door slams and BEN *enters and looks about.*

BEN. Well—here we all are again.

SADIE [*sadly*]. Yes.

HENRY. I ain't been in this room before since the funeral.

SADIE. And I ain't, and the last time before that was when father died.

EMMA. I sat right here, in the same chair I'm settin' in now, but to your grandfather's funeral, right after I married Henry, I was treated like one of the poor relations! I had to stand up.

HENRY. I remember; it made considerable trouble.

ELLA. I don't know as it was ever what I called a cheerful room.

HENRY [*severely*]. A parlor's where a person's supposed to sit and think of God, and you couldn't expect it to be cheerful!

ELLA [*looks about*]. Seems like we'd had trouble and disgrace enough in this family without her takin' all the slip covers off of the chairs and sofa!

EMMA. It ain't *right!*

SADIE. That Boston woman that's building the house over on Elm Street ain't so much as goin' to have a parlor. I stopped her right on the street and asked her what she was plannin' to do soon as the first of 'em died.

EMMA. What did she say?

SADIE. Said she tried not to think about such things.

HENRY [*sternly*]. We got Atheists enough in this town right now.

BEN. Well, if Jane's coming I wish she'd come; this ain't exactly my idea of pleasant company.

ELLA. She says we're all to wait in here for Judge Bradford.

SADIE. What did she send for us for?

ELLA. I don't know.

EMMA. Why didn't you ask her?

ELLA. I did, and she most bit my head off.

BEN. She most bites mine off every time I see her. I must say she's changed, Jane has; she ain't the same girl at all she was a few weeks ago.

NETTIE. She's actin' just awful, especially to me!

SADIE. Of course, I'd be the last one to say anything against her, but—

BEN. But nothin'! There ain't one of you here fit to tie her shoes!

SADIE. *We* ain't?

BEN. And I ain't! The only difference between us is I ain't worth much and I know it, and you ain't worth nothin' and you don't.

EMMA. I guess you'd better be careful how you talk!

NETTIE. If anybody says anything about Jane lately, that's the way he always talks! The worse she treats him the better he seems to like it.

SADIE. Well, I don't know as I'm surprised more about his insultin' the rest of us, but it's sort of comical his talkin' that way about you, Nettie.

EMMA. Nettie! What's Nettie got to do with him?

SADIE. Oh! Excuse me! I didn't know 'twas supposed to be a secret.

EMMA. What is?

SADIE. About the way those two have been carryin' on together!

HENRY. What!

ELLA. Ben and Nettie!

NETTIE [*afraid*]. Stop her, Ben, can't you?

BEN. If I knew a way to stop women like her I'd patent it and get rich!

EMMA [*sternly*]. Him and Nettie?

SADIE. They passed my house together *once* a week ago Wednesday, *once* the Tuesday before that, and *twice* the Sunday after New Year's.

HENRY. Together!

SADIE. And Eben Tilden's boy told Abbie Palsey that Tilly Hickson heard Aaron Hamlin say he'd seen 'em together at the picture show!

HENRY [*to* BEN]. Is it true?

EMMA. You've been with him after all I told you!

BEN. It ain't going to hurt her none just to talk to me, is it?

EMMA. Them that touches pitch gets defiled!

HENRY [*to* NETTIE]. I want you to tell me everything that's took place between you two.

SADIE. Wait!

HENRY. What?

SADIE. Orin! Leave the room!

NETTIE. He don't have to leave the room. I don't care who knows what happened!

HENRY. Go on then.

NETTIE. Well—Ben and I—We—Just for a few days—anyway, it was all his fault.

BEN. She threw me down because I was going to prison.

NETTIE. He said he'd get out of it somehow, but he can't, and I just won't have folks laughing at me!

BEN. It's all right, it never meant nothin' to her, and I guess it didn't mean much to me. It's just as well it's over.

NETTIE. It's a whole lot better.

HENRY. Well—what's passed is passed. Folks that plant the wind reap the whirlwind! There's no use cryin' over spilled milk.

ORIN. Say, Mum! What do you s'pose Uncle Henry thinks he means when he says things?

HENRY. Somehow I can't help wishin' you was my son for just about five minutes.

HANNAH *and* JUDGE BRADFORD *enter*

HANNAH. They're all in here, Judge.

JUDGE. Good afternoon.

HENRY. How are you, Judge?

SADIE. It's a mild day; winter's most over. Stop scratching yourself. [*This last to* ORIN *who seems to be uneasy and frequently scratches himself.*]

HANNAH [*at door*]. I'll tell her you're here, Judge. She'll be right down.

[HANNAH *exits.*

ELLA. Won't you sit?

JUDGE. Thanks. [*He sits by table.*]

HENRY. What's it about? Why did she say we was to all be here at two o'clock?

JUDGE. She will probably be able to answer that question herself, Ben.

SADIE [*to* ORIN]. Don't.

ORIN. What?

SADIE. Scratch!

ORIN. Oh.

JANE *enters. The* JUDGE *rises*

JUDGE. Well, Jane?

JANE. Don't get up, Judge.

JUDGE. Will you sit here?

[JUDGE *turns to get a chair for* JANE. ORIN *scratches himself.* ELLA *rises.*]

ELLA. What is the matter with this brat?

ORIN. I itch!

SADIE. It's warm, and he's got on his heavy flannels! He's as clean as you are!

[JANE *and* JUDGE *sit.*]

BEN. You said to heat this room up and wait here for you and the Judge. Why? I got my stock to tend.

HENRY. It's a bad time for me to get away from the store; what was it you wanted of us?

JANE. I'm afraid it isn't going to be easy to tell you.

JUDGE. Won't you let me do it, Jane?

JANE. No. I've come to know that your mother didn't really want that I should have the Jordan money.

SADIE. What's that?

JANE. I put it as simply as I could.

BEN. You mean a later will's been found?

JUDGE. No.

JANE. In a way, Judge, it's like there had. Your mother left me a letter dated later than the will.

ELLA. Leavin' the money different?

JANE. Tellin' what she really wanted.

BEN. Well, what did she want?

JANE. It was like she left me all her money in trust, so I could keep it safe until the time she was hopin' for come, and in a way it did come, not quite like she wanted it, but near enough so I can give up a burden I haven't strength enough to carry any more. [*She stops.*]

JUDGE. Let me finish, Jane. Jane has asked me to draw a deed of gift, making the Jordan property over to Ben.

BEN. Why?

JANE. She wanted you to have it.

BEN. Why didn't she will it to me, then?

JANE. She was afraid to trust you.

BEN. Well?

JANE. You've learned to work; you'll keep on working.

HENRY. You mean to say my mother wanted him to have it all?

JANE. Yes.

HENRY. I am a religious man, but there was a time when even Job gave up! So—all our money goes to Ben—and he can't even buy himself out of prison!

JANE [*after a pause*]. Ben isn't going to prison.

BEN. Why? Who's to stop it?

JUDGE [*after a look from* JANE]. Kimbal agreed not to press the charge against you. It seems that there were certain extenuating circumstances. A motion has been made for the dismissal of the indictment, and it won't be opposed.

BEN. Why did he? Who fixed this thing?

JANE. Judge Bradford did. [*She looks at* JUDGE.]

BEN [*slowly*]. It means a lot to me. There's things I'd like to do. I haven't dared to think about 'em lately—now I'll do 'em. [*There is a pause.*]

HENRY. Well, Ben, so you've got the money! I guess maybe it's better than her havin' it; after all blood's thicker than water! We'll help you any way we can and—er—of course you'll help us.

BEN. Why will I?

HENRY. We're brothers, Ben! We're old Jordans!

BEN. What was we when I got back from France? There was a band met us boys at the station. I was your brother all right that day, only somehow, in just a little while you forgot about it. I was a Jordan when I was hidin' out from the police, and all that kept me from starvin' was the money Jane sent me! I was your brother the night mother died, and you said you wouldn't go my bail.

ELLA. You ain't going to be hard, Ben!

BEN. I'm the head of the family now, ain't I, and you can bet all you've got I'm going to be a real Jordan.

HENRY. I think, Ben—

BEN. From now on, there ain't nobody got any right to think in this house but just me! So run along home, the whole pack of you, and after this, when you feel like you must come here—come separate.

ELLA. Turn us out, Ben?

BEN. Sure, why not?

NETTIE [*crosses to him. Sweetly*]. There ain't any reason why *we* can't be friends, is there?

BEN. Well, I don't know. There's only one way I could ever get to trust you.

NETTIE. What way, Ben?

BEN. I'd have to go to jail for five years and see if you'd wait for me!

EMMA. It's an awful thing for a mother to have a fool for a child.

ELLA [*goes upstage with* NETTIE]. Well, I must say you made a nice mess of things!

NETTIE [*exits with* ELLA]. Well, I don't care! I don't see how anybody would expect me to be a mind reader!

SADIE. Come, Orin—say good-by to your Uncle Ben.

ORIN. What will I do that for?

SADIE. Because I tell you to!

ORIN. Yesterday you told me he wasn't worth speakin' to!

SADIE. Are you going to move, you stupid little idiot? [*She drags him out.*]

ORIN [*as they go*]. What did I say? You let me alone!

HENRY. I was wonderin', Ben, how you'd feel about endorsing that note of mine.

BEN. You was?

HENRY. Yes, I don't know what I'm going to do about it.

BEN. As far as I care, you can go nail it on a door. [HENRY *and* EMMA *start to exit.*] No, hold on, I'll pay it.

HENRY. You will!

BEN. Yes, I don't know as it would do me much good at the bank, havin' a brother of mine in the poorhouse. [BEN *laughs as* HENRY *and* EMMA *exit.*]

JUDGE. Well, Ben? "Uneasy lies the head that wears a crown."

BEN [*down to stove*]. Depends on the head. Mine's thick, I guess. Anyhow, none of them is going to bother it. I'm boss here now.

JUDGE. You'll find a copy here of the inventory of the estate, and other legal papers. Everything is in order.

JANE. And my accounts, Ben; you'll find the exact amount your mother left. I spent some money about six weeks ago, on myself, but I've been careful ever since and I've made up for it.

BEN. You said, Judge, she didn't have to go by that letter of my mother's, if she didn't want to? She didn't have to give anything back at all?

JUDGE. No, she didn't.

BEN. Then if I was you—[*To* JANE.] I wouldn't talk so much about the little you spent on yourself. I guess to look at you it wasn't much.

JANE. Yes, it was.

BEN. Well, we'll fix things so you can keep on spendin'. Only let's see somethin' come of it. I never was so damned sick of anything in my life as I am of that old black dress of yours! [*Crosses stage up and over right.*]

JANE. I've got plenty of clothes upstairs. I'm sorry now I ever bought them, but I'll take them with me when I go.

BEN. Go? Go where?

JANE. To Old Town. I've got a place there, clerking in the Pulp Mill.

BEN. You!

JANE. Yes.

BEN. But what about me?

JUDGE. Don't you think Jane has done about enough for you?

BEN. She's done a lot, she's given up the money. I don't know as I like that; 'course I like gettin' it, but not if she's going away.

JANE. I couldn't stay now, and I wouldn't want to.

BEN. I don't suppose you remember about plannin' what you and me was to do with this old farm?

JANE. I remember.

BEN. Well—then what are you going away for?

JANE. Because I couldn't be happy here, Ben —It's been harder than anything I ever thought could come to anybody, the last few weeks here—and so I'm going. [*She turns to* JUDGE.] I'll go upstairs and get my things. I'll stop at your office, Judge, on the way to the station.

JUDGE. Thank you, Jane.

BEN. You're goin' today? Before I order my new farm machinery or anything? You're goin' to leave me with all this work on my hands?

JANE. Yes, Ben. [*She exits.*

BEN. Well—that's a lesson to me! Oh, she's a good woman! I ain't denyin' that—but she's fickle!

JUDGE. You're a fool, Ben!

BEN. I been doin' kitchen police around this town for quite a spell now, Judge, but from this day on I ain't goin' to take that sort of talk from anybody.

JUDGE. I assure you that you won't have to take any sort of talk at all from me. [*He starts for the door.*]

BEN. I didn't mean that. I don't want you to think I ain't grateful for all you've done for me.

JUDGE [*coldly*]. I have done nothing for you.

BEN. If it wasn't for you, I'd want to die; that's what I did want. I was afraid of that prison, just a coward about it. Now I'm a free man, with a big life openin' out ahead of me—I got everything in the world right here in my two hands, everything—and I owe it to you!

JUDGE. I am very glad to say that you don't owe me anything. I don't like you, I haven't forgiven you for what you did to your mother's life. Nor for a worse thing, one you haven't brains enough to even know you've done. Don't be grateful to me, Ben, please. I think nothing could distress me more than that.

BEN. You've been a good friend to me.

JUDGE. I haven't meant to be; as I said, I don't like you. I haven't any faith in you. I don't believe in this new life of yours. You made a mess of the old one, and I think you will of the new.

BEN. No matter what you say, you can't get away from me. I'll be grateful till I die. But for you I'd have gone to that damned prison!

JUDGE. But for Jane.

BEN. How Jane?

JUDGE. How Jane? Jane went your bond the day your mother died. Jane took you in and taught you how to work, made you work, taught you through the one decent spot in you something of a thing you'd never known, self-respect. Worked over you, petted you, coaxed you—held you up— Then you hurt her—but she kept on—She went herself to Kimbal, after he had refused me, and got his help to keep you out of prison—then, against my will, against the best that I could do to stop her, she turns over all this to you—and goes out with nothing—and you ask "How Jane?"

BEN. Why? Why has she done this, all this, for me?

[*The* JUDGE *looks at* BEN *with contempt and turns and exits.* BEN *is left in deep thought.* JANE *comes downstairs dressed for a journey with a handbag, etc. She enters.*]

JANE. Good-by, Ben. [*She crosses to him, her hand out.*] Good-by. Won't you say good-by?

BEN. First, there's some things I got to know about.

JANE [*smiles*]. I guess there's not much left for us to say, Ben.

BEN [*she crosses to door, but he gets ahead of her*]. There's things I got to know. [*She looks at him but does not speak.*] The Judge tells me 'twas you got Kimbal to let me go free. [*He looks at her—she half turns away.*] Answer me. [*Pause.*] The Judge tells me you gave up what was yours—to me—without no other reason than because you wanted me to have it. That's true, ain't it? [*Pause.*] You sent me every cent you had, when you knew mother was dying, then you went bail for me, like he said—and did all them other things. I don't know as any woman ever did any more—. I want to know why!

JANE. Why do you think?

BEN. I don't know—I sort of thought—sort of hoped—

JANE [*bravely*]. It was because I loved her, Ben—

BEN. Oh. [*He turns away disappointed.*]

JANE. You're forgetting, I guess, how long we was alone here—when you was in France—then the months we didn't know where you was, when the police was looking for you—She used to make me promise if ever I could I'd help you.

BEN. Well—all I've got to say is you're no liar.

JANE. Good-by. [*She turns to go.*]

BEN. Wait. [*Closes door.*] Let's see that letter you said she left for you.

JANE. No. I won't do that. I've done enough; you're free, you've got the money and the farm.

BEN [*crosses in front of table and sits left of table*]. They ain't worth a damn with you gone—I didn't know that till just now, but they ain't.

JANE. It's sort of sudden, the way you found that out.

BEN. Oh, it don't take long for a man to get hungry—it only takes just a minute for a man to die; you can burn down a barn quick enough, or do a murder; it's just living and getting old that takes a lot of time—Can't you stay here, Jane?

JANE. There's Nettie.

BEN. Nettie—that couldn't stand the gaff—that run out on me when I was in trouble.

JANE. It doesn't matter what folks do, if you love 'em enough.

BEN. What do you know about it? I suppose you've been in love a lot of times?

JANE. No.

BEN. Then you be quiet and let an expert talk. I was lonesome and I wanted a woman; she was pretty and I wanted to kiss her—that ain't what I call love.

JANE. You. You don't even know the meaning of the word.

BEN. That don't worry me none—I guess the feller that wrote the dictionary was a whole lot older'n I am before he got down to the L's.

JANE. You've got good in you, Ben, deep down, if you'd only try. [BEN *turns.*] I know, it's always been that way! You've never tried for long; you've never had a real ambition.

BEN. When I was a kid I wanted to spit farther than anybody.

JANE. Good-by. [*She starts up to door.*]

BEN. And so you're going to break your word? [JANE *turns, hurt.*]

BEN. I don't know what 'twas you promised mother, but you've broke your word. No man ever needed a woman more'n I need you, and you're leaving me.

JANE. That isn't fair.

BEN. It's true, ain't it; truth ain't always fair—You ain't helped me none, you've hurt me—worse than being broke, worse than bein' in jail.

JANE. It don't seem like I could stand to have you talk like that.

BEN. What you done you done for her. I didn't count, I never have, not with you.

JANE. When you've been trying to do a thing as long as I have, it gets to be a part of you.

BEN. You done it all for her—well—she's dead—you'd better go.

JANE. Maybe I had, but if I do it will be with the truth between us. Here's the letter she left for me, Ben—I got a feeling somehow like she was here with us now, like she wanted you to read it. [*She holds it out.*] It's like she was guiding us from the grave—Read it. [*Crosses up to window.*]

BEN [*reads*]. "My dear Jane: The doctor tells me I haven't long to live and so I am doing this, the meanest thing I think I've ever done to you. I'm leaving you the Jordan money. Since my husband died there has been just one person I could get to care about, that's Ben, who was my baby so long after all the others had forgotten how to love me. [*He mumbles the letter to himself, then brings out the words.*] Hold out her heart and let him trample on it, as he has on mine." [*Slowly he breaks down, sobbing bitterly.*]

JANE. Don't, Ben—

BEN. Look what I done to her. Look what I done.

JANE [*hand on his shoulder*]. Oh, my dear—my dear!

BEN. I did love her, more'n she thought, more'n I ever knew how to tell her!

JANE [*kneels beside him*]. It wasn't all your fault—you were a lonely boy—she never said much—she was like you, Ben, ashamed to show the best that's in you.

BEN [*bitterly*]. The best in me. I ain't fit that you should touch me, Jane—you'd better go.

JANE. Not if you need me, Ben, and I think you do.

BEN. I love you—more'n I ever thought I could—tenderer—truer—but I'm no good—You couldn't trust me—I couldn't trust myself.

JANE. Spring's coming, Ben, everywhere, to you and me, if you would only try.

BEN. Can a feller change—just 'cause he wants to?

JANE. I don't want you changed. I want you what you are, the best of you—just a man that loves me—if you do love me, Ben.

BEN. Can't you help me to be fit?

JANE. I'm going to do the thing I always meant to do—good times and bad, Ben, I'm going to share with you.

BEN. God knows I—

JANE. Hush, Ben—I don't want another promise.

BEN. What do you want?

JANE. You said I was a good sport once—You shook hands on what we'd do to bring this old place back—there's plenty to be done. I'll stay and help you if you want me.

BEN. A good sport? [*He takes her hand.*] I'll say you're all of that.

HANNAH *enters*

HANNAH. If you ain't careful you'll miss that train.

JANE. That's just what I want to do.

HANNAH. You ain't going?

JANE. I'm never going, Hannah.

HANNAH. You going to marry him?

BEN. You bet your life she is!

HANNAH. I guess you'll be mighty happy—marriage changes folks—and any change in him will be a big improvement.

[*She picks up* JANE'S *bag and exits*—JANE *and* BEN *laugh.*]

CURTAIN

THE GREAT GOD BROWN

By Eugene O'Neill

EUGENE O'NEILL

[1888–]

EUGENE GLADSTONE O'NEILL was born October 16, 1888, of a strong Celtic strain, which has left its mark on much of his work.[1] His youth was spent in the environment of the stage, his father being an actor; after an intermittent schooling O'Neill entered Princeton in 1906, where he remained only one year. For five years he led an irregular life, variously employed on or near the high seas, unthinkingly gathering the material of life he was later to draw upon in his plays. It was during a period of enforced rest in 1912–1913, owing to poor health, that O'Neill first began "thinking it over," digesting his colorful experiences, and initiating his career as a playwright. His subsequent activities included: wide reading, "the Greeks, the Elizabethans—practically all the classics—and of course all the moderns"; a year in English 47 at Harvard; life in Greenwich Village, New York, among I. W. W.'s, anarchists, Negroes, and Italians; residence in Provincetown with contemporary artists, such as George Cram Cook and Susan Glaspell; and perhaps most important of all, extensive work with the Provincetown Players.

Out of an apprenticeship group of short plays, the first to be produced, *Bound East for Cardiff*, gave promise of the future in its realistic treatment of the mysteries of life and in its symbolism of the fog. O'Neill's first long play to survive (he knew the wisdom of the wastebasket) is *Beyond the Horizon*, produced in 1920; it concerns two New England brothers, one being lured by "what lies beyond," the other drawn to his native farm; by reason of a tangled love affair, the first brother remains at home and the second travels, with the resultant tragedy that neither finds what he thinks he desires. The play makes little use of the devices O'Neill later exploited so effectively, but it reveals his power of realistic delineation and profound sense of tragedy. *The Emperor Jones* (1920), with its novel monologue form and crescendo drum beat, depicts the emotional fears and mental hallucinations of a Negro fleeing from those whom he has oppressed in a period of personal arrogance. *Anna Christie* portrays the regeneration of a woman under the power of the sea and the influence of genuine love. *The Hairy Ape* is a "symbol of man, who has lost his old harmony with nature, the harmony which he used to have as an animal and has not yet acquired in a spiritual way." [2] *All God's Chillun Got Wings* reveals the beauty that can exist in interracial love and depicts the tragedy of a Negro fighting against unseen forces to raise himself above his

[1] The data for this biographical sketch are taken from Barrett H. Clark's *Eugene O'Neill: the Man and His Plays*. New York: 1929; 1933.

[2] New York *Herald Tribune*, Nov. 16, 1924.

present position. In *Desire Under the Elms* the bold and tragic themes, such as infanticide committed in proof of a woman's love for a man (her stepson), provoked much discussion; but critical opinion has insisted on the essential exaltation of the play and its purging effect upon the spectator.

Following *The Great God Brown* (1926) came the brilliant satire on commercialism, *Marco Millions*, in which the "go-getting" American business man, disguised as Marco Polo "so that no one can fail to recognize him," makes himself and his enterprising materialism a bit ridiculous against the background of Eastern dignity and culture. The monumental *Strange Interlude* is a provocative account of a temperamental woman's endeavor to fulfill her psychiatric love aspirations which a memory-ideal and three men are hardly enough to satisfy; the play is also significant because of the brilliant use of asides in a trenchant analysis of character and motive. O'Neill once said: "Sure, I'll write about happiness if I ever happen to meet up with that luxury, and find it sufficiently dramatic and in harmony with any deep rhythm of life." [1] Considering O'Neill's idea of happiness as the exaltation found in tragic plays, not the pleasantness of happy-ending plays, we might find in *Lazarus Laughed* reason to suppose that the playwright had "met up with that luxury." In its defiance of gloom and death, the play asserts the triumph of life and proclaims the immortality of Man, though not of men.[2]

The religious theme becomes the center of interest in O'Neill's next play, *Dynamo;* in the words of the playwright, this first part of a contemplated trilogy symbolizes the "death of an old God and the failure of science and materialism to give any satisfying new one for the surviving primitive religious instinct to find a meaning for life in, and to comfort its fears of death with." The story is of a youth who breaks away from Fundamentalism to Atheism and subsequently turns to the worship of science as embodied in a dynamo. It is interesting to note the near identity of this concept with that expounded over a quarter of a century ago by Henry Adams in "The Dynamo and the Virgin (1900)" in *The Education of Henry Adams*. The second part of the trilogy above referred to (at first entitled *Without Ending of Days*) had its première in New York, January 8, 1934; a "modern miracle play," *Days Without End* recounts the spiritual wanderings of its central figure (perhaps a continuation of Reuben Light in *Dynamo*), who finally returns to faith in a successful effort to save his wife from the death his own evil has threatened her with.[3]

Mourning Becomes Electra is derived from O'Neill's study of Greek tragedy;

[1] Interview with Malcolm Mollan, "Making Plays with a Tragic End." Magazine section, *Philadelphia Public Ledger*, Jan. 22, 1922.

[2] Elizabeth Shepley Sergeant says of *Lazarus:* "And one sees at last, reflected on the page, the look of happy serenity that transforms the face of the swimmer as he strikes out into that blue sustaining sea." (*Fire under the Andes.* New York: 1927, p. 102.)

[3] For a review of this play by Brooks Atkinson, see *The New York Times*, Jan. 14, 1934.

it concerns an involved situation in an American family, resembling the story of Agamemnon, Clytemnestra, Orestes, and Electra. The expressionistic technique was dropped in favor of direct dialogue presentation. O'Neill's latest play, *Ah, Wilderness!* deals with the cleavage between the older and younger generations in an average American family, the struggle between surviving Victorianism and approaching modernism at the turn of the century.

Complex, subtle, baffling, *The Great God Brown* grapples with the profundities and mysteries of life; being a play readily capable of divergent interpretation, it is fortunate that O'Neill has been willing to give us his own. It follows:

"I realize that when a playwright takes to explaining he thereby automatically places himself 'in the dock.' But where an open-faced avowal by the play itself of the abstract theme underlying it is made impossible by the very nature of that hidden theme, then perhaps it is justifiable for the author to confess the mystical pattern which manifests itself as an overtone in *The Great God Brown*, dimly behind and beyond the words and actions of the characters.

"I had hoped the names chosen for my people would give a strong hint of this. (An old scheme, admitted—Shakespeare and multitudes since.) Dion Anthony—Dionysus and St. Anthony—the creative pagan acceptance of life, fighting eternal war with the masochistic, life-denying spirit of Christianity as represented by St. Anthony—the whole struggle resulting in this modern day in mutual exhaustion—creative joy in life for life's sake frustrated, rendered abortive, distorted by morality from Pan into Satan, into a Mephistopheles mocking himself in order to feel alive; Christianity, once heroic in martyrs for its intense faith now pleading weakly for intense belief in anything, even Godhead itself. (In the play it is Cybele, the pagan Earth Mother, who makes the assertion with authority: 'Our Father Who Art!' to the dying Brown, as it is she who tries to inspire Dion Anthony with her certainty in life for its own sake.)

"Margaret is my image of the modern direct descendant of the Marguerite of *Faust*—the eternal girl-woman with a virtuous simplicity of instinct, properly oblivious to everything but the means to her end of maintaining the race.

"Cybel is an incarnation of Cybele, the Earth Mother doomed to segregation as a pariah in a world of unnatural laws but patronized by her segregators who are thus themselves the first victims of their laws.

"Brown is the visionless demi-god of our new materialistic myth—a Success—building his life of exterior things, inwardly empty and resourceless, an uncreative creature of superficial preordained social grooves, a by-product forced aside into slack waters by the deep main current of life-desire.

"Dion's mask of Pan which he puts on as a boy is not only a defense against the world for the supersensitive painter-poet underneath it but also an integral part of his character as the artist. The world is not only blind to the man beneath but it also sneers at and condemns the Pan-mask it sees. After that Dion's inner self retrogresses along the line of Christian resignation until it partakes of the nature of the Saint while at the same time the outer Pan is slowly transformed by his struggle with reality into Mephistopheles. It is as Mephistopheles he falls stricken at Brown's feet after having condemned Brown to destruction by willing him his mask, but, this mask falling off as he dies, it is the Saint who kisses Brown's feet in abject contrition and pleads as a little boy to a big brother to tell him a prayer.

"Brown has always envied the creative life force in Dion—what he himself lacks. When he steals Dion's mask of Mephistopheles he thinks he is gaining the power to live creatively while in reality he is only stealing that creative power made self-destructive by complete frustration. The devil of mocking doubt makes short work of him. It enters him, rending him apart, torturing and transfiguring him until he is even forced to wear a mask of his Success, William A. Brown, before the world, as well as Dion's mask toward wife and children. Thus Billy Brown becomes not himself to anyone. And thus he partakes of Dion's anguish—more poignantly, for Dion had the Mother, Cybele—and in the end out of this anguish his soul is born, a tortured Christian soul such as the dying Dion's, begging for belief, and at the last finding it on the lips of Cybel.

"And now for an explanation regarding this explanation. It was far from my idea in writing *Brown* that this background pattern of conflicting tides in the soul of Man should ever overshadow and thus throw out of proportion the living drama of the recognizable human beings, Dion, Brown, Margaret and Cybel. I meant it always to be mystically within and behind them, giving them a significance beyond themselves, forcing itself through them to expression in mysterious words, symbols, actions they do not themselves comprehend. And that is as clearly as I wish an audience to comprehend it. It is Mystery—the mystery any one man or woman can feel but not understand as the meaning of any event—or accident—in any life on earth. And it is this mystery I want to realize in the theatre. The solution, if there ever be any, will probably have to be produced in a test tube and turn out to be discouragingly undramatic." [1]

No one can doubt the finality of the above explanation, but there are several questions that arise in one's mind as he reflects upon it. In the first part of the explanation Pan is made synonymous with Dionysus and "the creative joy in life," all of which are put in opposition with Christianity. But in the play itself the following account is given:

"The mask is a fixed forcing of his own face—dark, spiritual, poetic, passionately supersensitive, helplessly unprotected in its childlike, religious faith in life—into the expression of a mocking, reckless, defiant, gayly scoffing and sensual young Pan."

In the play it appears that the poetic and spiritual natures are linked in opposition to the Pan character, whereas in the former explanation it is Christianity that is set against the creative Pan nature. Also, if Dion's inner self "retrogresses along the line of Christian resignation," can his death as "the Saint" be achievement (which it seems to be since his fall as Mephistopheles is destruction)?

It is interesting to note that though the concept of multiplicity in character is brought into prominence and dealt with scientifically by modern psychology and psychoanalysis,[2] yet it is an idea by no means new. Among the literary treatments of the concept are Stevenson's *Dr. Jekyll and Mr. Hyde* and Hazlitt's essay *On Going a Journey*. The approach in each of these differs, to be sure, the first being a dramatic projection of character duality into two persons, and the second a quiet commentary on varied reactions; but the underlying idea of

[1] "Eugene O'Neill Writes about His Latest Play, *The Great God Brown*." New York *Evening Post*, Feb. 13, 1926.

[2] A brief discussion of this subject may be found in Robert S. Woodworth's *Psychology*. New York: rev. ed. 1929, pp. 571–574. Though Woodworth's illustrations differ somewhat from Dion's character, yet there are parallels to be observed. Dion's self and Pan mask are in a sense complementary characters: the defiance-mask may be regarded as a "defense reaction" induced by the sharp realization of meekness and asceticism. In discussing multiple personality, or "*dissociation* of the personality," Woodworth describes the primary as the "more lasting state" and the secondary state as "a sort of complement to the first. . . ." Faintly parallel to Dion is the case Woodworth cites in which the individual in the primary state "may be excessively quiet, while in the secondary state he is excessively mischievous."

each is similar. Exponent of twentieth-century thought that O'Neill is, there is little wonder that he seized upon and fruitfully developed so provocative a theme as man's potential, and actual, multiple self. With respect to Brown's supernatural assumption of Dion's life and dual personality, by proxy of the latter's bequeathed strength, there may be symbolized man's dissatisfaction with self, his desire to lead another's life and to adopt that person's identity.[1]

In a satirical mood in *The Great God Brown* is presented a criticism of the average man—or perhaps more particularly, the American businessman. We see the supersensitive, imaginative artist dominated, exploited, and finally crushed, in spite of a Nietzschean pride, by the crude and successful man of business. In the colloquial and slang-ridden speech of Brown, in his blindness to art, and in the mob-psychology of Anthony Senior, there is held up to scorn the unimaginative and unthinking "go-getter" graphically impaled in Lewis's *Babbitt* and humorously taunted in O'Neill's own *Marco Millions*.

Arthur H. Quinn speaks of the "final note of exaltation" in the play, quoting Cybel's hymn to the recurrence of spring and life; [2] Barrett H. Clark points out that in the play "man's road passes through the vale of tragedy, but it emerges triumphant." [3] However, it must not be overlooked that there is much in the play to suggest a cynical view of life as a whole, and it will be recalled that upon completion of the play O'Neill wrote: "I've just finished a devastating, crucifying new one called 'The Great God Brown'. . . ." [4]

Though O'Neill has not written extensively about playwriting in general or his own plays in particular, yet he has revealed enough of his dramatic thought, by means of articles, letters, and interviews, to give one an understanding of the theory behind his plays. Perhaps the central concept of this theory is that suggested in his interpretation of *The Great God Brown:* the "conflicting tides in the soul of Man" should always be "mystically within and behind them [the characters], giving them a significance beyond themselves, forcing itself through them to expression in mysterious words, symbols, actions they do not themselves comprehend." "And it is this mystery I want to realize in the theatre." [5] A sympathetic reading of O'Neill reveals how abundantly he invests many of his characters with this mystery whence they came; to be sure, certain of his plays refract it more than others, but perhaps here is one source of the power that marks nearly all of O'Neill's work.

In an interview with Malcolm Mollan, O'Neill gave a concise and revealing

[1] Conspicuous among the studies of confused identity are Pirandello's provocative plays, especially *Right You Are, If You Think You Are; As You Desire Me;* and *Six Characters in Search of An Author*.

[2] *A History of the American Drama from the Civil War to the Present Day*, II, 192.

[3] *Eugene O'Neill*. New York: 1926, p. 95.

[4] Isaac Goldberg, *The Theatre of George Jean Nathan*. New York: 1926, p. 159.

[5] This same idea is also set forth in a letter O'Neill wrote to Arthur H. Quinn; see Quinn, *op. cit.*, II, 199.

account of his reflections on the drama; though coming early in the career of O'Neill, they throw much light on the depth, freedom, and originality of the playwright's later productions. Extracts from this interview follow:

"Sure, I'll write about happiness if I ever happen to meet up with that luxury, and find it sufficiently dramatic and in harmony with any deep rhythm of life."

"A work of art is always happy; all else is unhappy."

"Tragedy not native to our soil? Why, we are tragedy—the most appalling yet written or unwritten!"

"I love life, I always have. . . . But I don't love life because it is pretty. Prettiness is only clothes deep. I am a truer lover than that. I love it naked. There is beauty to me even in its ugliness. In fact, I deny the ugliness entirely, for its vices are often nobler than its virtues, and nearly always closer to revelation. . . . To me there are no good people or bad people, just people. The same with deeds. 'Good' and 'evil' are stupidities, as misleading and outworn fetiches as Brutus Jones' silver bullet."

"I intend to use whatever I can make my own, to write about anything under the sun, in any manner that fits or can be invented to fit the subject. And I shall never be influenced by any consideration but one: Is it truth as I know it—or, better still, feel it? If so, shoot, and let the splinters fly where they may. If not, not.

"This sounds brave and bold—but it isn't. It simply means that I want to do what gives me pleasure and worth in my own eyes, and don't care to do what doesn't. I don't deserve any credit for this 'noble' stand because there is no temptation for me."

"It is just life that interests me as a thing in itself. The why and wherefore I haven't attempted to touch on yet." [1]

The important literary influences on O'Neill include Strindberg, Ibsen, and Aeschylus. It is Strindberg that O'Neill himself most particularly acknowledges: "Strindberg still remains among the most modern of moderns, the greatest interpreter in our theatre of the characteristic spiritual conflicts which constitute the drama. . . ." [2] In contrast to Ibsen's "daring aspirations toward self-recognition by holding the family kodak up to ill-nature," O'Neill points out the more significant "behind-life play, which is directly traceable to Strindberg." [3] The skill and effectiveness with which Strindberg employed the technique of expressionism (the use of dialogue, and other devices, to reveal the inner reality) had its influence on O'Neill.[4] Though Ibsen occupies a less important position in O'Neill's mind than Strindberg, there is no doubt that the Norwegian dramatist, "the father of the modernity of twenty years or so ago," helped pave the way for

[1] "Making Plays with a Tragic End, an Intimate Interview with Eugene O'Neill, Who Tells Why He Does It." *Philadelphia Public Ledger*, January 22, 1922.

[2] "Strindberg and Our Theatre." *Provincetown Playbill*, No. 1, Season 1923–24.

[3] *Ibid.*

[4] Perhaps the most extended study of Strindberg and O'Neill is Ira N. Hayward's "Strindberg's Influence on Eugene O'Neill." (*Poet-Lore*, XXXIX, 596–604, Winter, 1928.) Hayward concludes that the Swedish playwright influenced O'Neill: (1) In philosophy and choice of material: supernaturalism, self-obsession, spiritual conflicts; effect of the past and the subconscious; insanity as a pivotal point; "seamy side of life"; character under stress. (2) In form: expressionism to portray inner thought and feeling. (3) In the use of poetic and imaginative language.

the American playwright. Brooks Atkinson finds striking similarities in philosophy and technique between Ibsen and O'Neill,[1] and Elizabeth Shepley Sergeant states that Ibsen and Strindberg "have influenced him more than any other moderns." [2] For a study of the Greek influences on O'Neill see Barrett H. Clark's "Aeschylus and O'Neill." [3]

A central aspect of O'Neill's work that may strike the reader is its almost universal note of frustration and despair: one has the feeling that man is living in a universe inimical to his desires, his aspirations, his life. It has been pointed out that in *Beyond the Horizon* we see the value of striving, unsuccessful though it be; but it is a striving that has little attendant charm: a pall of mocking gloom hangs over the whole scene. It is as if a malignant force surrounded the characters and held them fast in its grip, ready at any moment to destroy without reference to human values. The universe appears inimical to man: it manifests its hostility in terms of betrayal, disease, frustration, misunderstanding, frenzy, death. Emperor Jones is a victim of his thirst for showy, tyrannical power and as a result is relentlessly pursued by terror-awakened visions of individual and racial crimes. The hostile universe appears as constitutional weakness: man's capacity for arrogance and fear. According to *The Great God Brown*, in worldly ambition and in love expectancy, in artistic enterprise and in aesthetic creation, in poetic-spiritual aspiration and in life-desire—in the subtlest and deepest reaches of man's soul, we are doomed to utter and irrevocable frustration. To be sure, Cybel does chant a hymn to ever-recurrent life, but it is a depersonalized recurrence of life on earth, and it is sung by one in whom life appears to be decayed.

Strange Interlude has its rise in love-frustration, and the frenzied victim pursues her violent way through life trying in vain to make the fragments of reality piece out the ideal that has been cruelly snatched away. In *Mourning Becomes Electra* a cosmos-structure unfriendly to man is seen in the implacable hate that motivates its principal characters: the loathing of wife for husband, the mutual hate between mother and daughter, the subsequent self-hatred of the brother; to this may be added the love-defeat of the husband, the degradation of the daughter, and the perversion of the son. Over the Mannon family hangs an accursed atmosphere, bitter, frenzied, violent. It may be suggested that a transgression of the moral code must be atoned for by succeeding generations, as it is, for example, in *The House of the Seven Gables*. In Hawthorne's novel the powers finally relent; in *Mourning Becomes Electra* they are unsatisfied to the end.

Of *Lazarus Laughed* it has been asserted that O'Neill proclaims the triumph

[1] "Ibsen and O'Neill," *New York Times*, Dramatic Section, Jan. 31, 1926.

[2] "Eugene O'Neill: Man with a Mask," in *Fire Under the Andes*. New York: 1927, pp. 81–104.

[3] *English Journal*, XXI, 699–710 (Nov., 1932). See also John Corbin, "O'Neill and Aeschylus," *Saturday Review of Literature*, VIII, 693–694 (Apr. 30, 1932). For a list of O'Neill's writings about the drama, see Clark's *Eugene O'Neill: the Man and His Plays*. New York: 1933, pp. 217–218.

of life over death, that by the affirmation of laughter we conquer the destructive forces in life. In a sense this cannot be denied, and we have here one of O'Neill's positive plays; yet the laughter is not joyous: there is implicit in its insistence a note of calculation and even mockery. Perhaps the most affirmative of O'Neill's plays is *The Fountain*, in which Ponce de Leon, searcher for the fountain of youth, ultimately triumphs over bitterness and disappointment to learn at the close of life that eternal youth is to "accept, absorb, give back," and that

"Death is a mist
Veiling sunrise."

There is also triumph in *Days Without End*, when John at last kills his disbelieving self and affirms that "Life laughs with God's love again." But the mocking, denying self has the better of the argument at every turn and it has, no doubt, tortured its opponent beyond the capacity for enjoying life; it is a victory whose fruits seem wizened and bitter. In an earlier religious play, *Dynamo*, Reuben Light embraces a faith in electricity, after abandoning Puritanism, only to find that his new object of worship betrays his love and himself to death. In one of O'Neill's most recent plays, *Ah, Wilderness!* the fates appear somewhat milder: Richard Miller, though of "advanced" ideas for 1906, is an essentially fine character, and one waits in vain for his idyllic romance to be dissipated by personal flaw or hostile circumstance.

Almost without exception O'Neill deals with significant and compelling themes; his characterization is sharp and faithful; his expression is graphic and rhythmic; and his dramaturgy is sound, trenchant, original. His mysticism lies in his desire to find what is behind and beneath human feeling, motivation, thought; the clue to his cynicism may lie in his probing intellect which rigorously dissects, and at times dispels, the organic entity which is the object of its search. The ultra-edged intellect may disintegrate the emotional and spiritual realities it is seeking, and as a consequence be obliged to report negative findings. Add to this the powerful and poetic imagination that is O'Neill's and you have a partial explanation of those magnificent tapestries of despair that are his most characteristic work.

O'Neill's final evaluations are in many respects consonant with those reflected in recent or contemporary writers, such as Henry Adams, Stephen Crane, Frank Norris, Theodore Dreiser, Sherwood Anderson, Sinclair Lewis, Edgar Lee Masters; the currency of these views is further indicated by the renewed interest in Melville and the vogue of Hardy and Conrad. The ultimate correspondence of O'Neill's evaluations with the nature of life may be questioned by those who find the universe less hostile or indifferent than it appears to nonrational fatalism.

The present text is from the edition of 1926.

CHARACTERS

William A. Brown
His Father, *a contractor*
His Mother
Dion Anthony
His Father, *a builder*
His Mother
Margaret
Her Three Sons
Cybel
Two Draftsmen } *in Brown's office*
A Stenographer }

SCENES

PROLOGUE. The Pier of the Casino. Moonlight in middle June.

ACT ONE

Scene 1: Sitting room, Margaret Anthony's apartment. Afternoon, seven years later.
Scene 2: Billy Brown's office. The same afternoon.
Scene 3: Cybel's parlor. That night.

ACT TWO

Scene 1: Cybel's parlor. Seven years later. Dusk.
Scene 2: Drafting room, William A. Brown's office. That evening.
Scene 3: Library, William A. Brown's home. That night.

ACT THREE

Scene 1: Brown's office, a month later. Morning.
Scene 2: Library, Brown's home. That evening.
Scene 3: Sitting room, Margaret's home. That night.

ACT FOUR

Scene 1: Brown's office, weeks later. Late afternoon.
Scene 2: Library, Brown's house, hours later. The same night.

EPILOGUE. The Pier of the Casino. Four years later.

THE GREAT GOD BROWN

PROLOGUE

SCENE. *A cross section of the pier of the Casino. In the rear, built out beyond the edge, is a rectangular space with benches on the three sides. A rail encloses the entire wharf at the back.*

It is a moonlight night in mid-June. From the Casino comes the sound of the school quartet rendering "Sweet Adeline" with many ultra-sentimental barber-shop quavers. There is a faint echo of the ensuing hand-clapping—then nothing but the lapping of ripples against the piles and their swishing on the beach—then footsteps on the boards and BILLY BROWN *walks along from right with his* MOTHER *and* FATHER. *The* MOTHER *is a dumpy woman of forty-five, overdressed in black lace and spangles. The* FATHER *is fifty or more, the type of bustling, genial, successful, provincial businessman, stout and hearty in his evening dress.*

BILLY BROWN *is a handsome, tall and athletic boy of nearly eighteen. He is blond and blue-eyed, with a likeable smile and a frank good-humored face, its expression already indicating a disciplined restraint. His manner has the easy self-assurance of a normal intelligence. He is in evening dress.*

They walk arm in arm, the MOTHER *between.*

MOTHER [*always addressing the* FATHER]. This Commencement dance is badly managed. Such singing! Such poor voices! Why doesn't Billy sing?

BILLY [*to her*]. Mine is a regular fog horn! [*He laughs.*]

MOTHER [*to the air*]. I had a pretty voice, when I was a girl. [*Then, to the* FATHER, *caustically.*] Did you see young Anthony strutting around the ballroom in dirty flannel pants?

FATHER. He's just showing off.

MOTHER. Such impudence! He's as ignorant as his father.

FATHER. The old man's all right. My only kick against him is he's been too damned conservative to let me branch out.

MOTHER [*bitterly*]. He has kept you down to his level—out of pure jealousy.

FATHER. But he took me into partnership, don't forget—

MOTHER [*sharply*]. Because you were the brains! Because he was afraid of losing you! [*A pause.*]

BILLY [*admiringly*]. Dion came in his old clothes on a bet with me. He's a real sport. He wouldn't have been afraid to appear in his pajamas! [*He grins with appreciation.*]

MOTHER. Isn't the moonlight clear! [*She goes and sits on the center bench.* BILLY *stands at the left corner, forward, his hand on the rail, like a prisoner at the bar, facing the judge. His* FATHER *stands in front of the bench on right. The* MOTHER *announces, with finality.*] After he's through college, Billy must study for a profession of some sort, I'm determined on that! [*She turns to her husband, defiantly, as if expecting opposition.*]

FATHER [*eagerly and placatingly*]. Just what I've been thinking, my dear. Architecture! How's that? Billy a first-rate, number-one architect! That's my proposition! What I've always wished I could have been myself! Only I never had the opportunity. But Billy—we'll make him a partner in the firm after. Anthony, Brown *and Son, architects* and builders—instead of *contractors* and builders!

MOTHER [*yearning for the realization of a dream*]. And we won't lay sidewalks—or dig sewers—ever again?

FATHER [*a bit ruffled*]. I and Anthony can build anything your pet can draw—even if it's a church! [*Then, selling his idea.*] It's a great chance for him! He'll design—expand us—make the firm famous.

MOTHER [*to the air—musingly*]. When you proposed, I thought your future promised success—my future—[*With a sigh.*]—Well,

I suppose we've been comfortable. Now, it's his future. How would Billy like to be an architect? [*She does not look at him.*]

BILLY [*to her*]. All right, Mother. [*Then sheepishly.*] I guess I've never bothered much about what I'd like to do after college —but architecture sounds all right to me, I guess.

MOTHER [*to the air—proudly*]. Billy used to draw houses when he was little.

FATHER [*jubilantly*]. Billy's got the stuff in him to win, if he'll only work hard enough.

BILLY [*dutifully*]. I'll work hard, Dad.

MOTHER. Billy can do anything!

BILLY [*embarrassed*]. I'll try, Mother. [*There is a pause.*]

MOTHER [*with a sudden shiver*]. The nights are so much colder than they used to be! Think of it, I once went moonlight bathing in June when I was a girl—but the moonlight was so warm and beautiful in those days, do you remember, Father?

FATHER [*puts his arm around her affectionately*]. You bet I do, Mother. [*He kisses her. The orchestra at the Casino strikes up a waltz.*] There's the music. Let's go back and watch the young folks dance. [*They start off, leaving* BILLY *standing there.*]

MOTHER [*suddenly calls back over her shoulder*]. I want to watch Billy dance.

BILLY [*dutifully*]. Yes, Mother! [*He follows them. For a moment the faint sound of the music and the lapping of waves is heard. Then footsteps again and the three* ANTHONYS *come in. First come the* FATHER *and* MOTHER, *who are not masked. The* FATHER *is a tall lean man of fifty-five or sixty with a grim, defensive face, obstinate to the point of stupid weakness. The* MOTHER *is a thin, frail, faded woman, her manner perpetually nervous and distraught, but with a sweet and gentle face that had once been beautiful. The* FATHER *wears an ill-fitting black suit, like a mourner. The* MOTHER *wears a cheap, plain, black dress. Following them, as if he were a stranger, walking alone, is their son,* DION. *He is about the same height as young* BROWN *but lean and wiry, without repose, continually in restless nervous movement. His face is masked. The mask is a fixed forcing of his own face—dark, spiritual, poetic, passionately supersensitive, helplessly unprotected in its childlike, religious faith in life—into the expression of a mocking, reckless, defiant, gayly scoffing and sensual young Pan. He is dressed in a gray flannel shirt, open at the neck, sneakers over bare feet, and soiled white flannel trousers. The* FATHER *strides to the center bench and sits down. The* MOTHER, *who has been holding to his arm, lets go and stands by the bench at the right. They both stare at* DION, *who, with a studied carelessness, takes his place at the rail, where young* BROWN *had stood. They watch him, with queer, puzzled eyes.*]

MOTHER [*suddenly—pleading*]. You simply must send him to college!

FATHER. I won't. I don't believe in it. Colleges turn out lazy loafers to sponge on their poor old fathers! Let him slave like I had to! That'll teach him the value of a dollar! College'll only make him a bigger fool than he is already! I never got above grammar school but I've made money and established a sound business. Let him make a man out of himself like I made of myself!

DION [*mockingly—to the air*]. This Mr. Anthony is my father, but he only imagines he is God the Father. [*They both stare at him.*]

FATHER [*with angry bewilderment*]. What—what—what's that?

MOTHER [*gently remonstrating to her son*]. Dion, dear! [*Then to her husband—tauntingly.*] Brown takes all the credit! He tells everyone the success is all due to his energy—that you're only an old stick-in-the-mud!

FATHER [*stung, harshly*]. The damn fool! He knows better'n anyone if I hadn't held him down to common sense, with his crazy wildcat notions, he'd have had us ruined long ago!

MOTHER. He's sending Billy to college—Mrs. Brown just told me—going to have him study architecture afterwards, too, so's he can help expand your firm!

FATHER [*angrily*]. What's that? [*Suddenly turns on* DION *furiously.*] Then you can make up your mind to go, too! And you'll learn to be a better architect than Brown's boy or I'll turn you out in the gutter without a penny! You hear?

DION [*mockingly—to the air*]. It's difficult to

choose—but architecture sounds less laborious.

MOTHER [*fondly*]. You ought to make a wonderful architect, Dion. You've always painted pictures so well—

DION [*with a start—resentfully*]. Why must she lie? Is it my fault? She knows I only try to paint. [*Passionately.*] But I will, some day! [*Then quickly, mocking again.*] On to college! Well, it won't be home, anyway, will it? [*He laughs queerly and approaches them. His* FATHER *gets up defensively.* DION *bows to him.*] I thank Mr. Anthony for this splendid opportunity to create myself—[*He kisses his mother, who bows with a strange humility as if she were a servant being saluted by the young master—then adds lightly.*]—in my mother's image, so she may feel her life comfortably concluded. [*He sits in his* FATHER'S *place at center and his mask stares with a frozen mockery before him. They stand on each side, looking dumbly at him.*]

MOTHER [*at last, with a shiver*]. It's cold. June didn't use to be cold. I remember the June when I was carrying you, Dion—three months before you were born. [*She stares up at the sky.*] The moonlight was warm, then. I could feel the night wrapped around me like a gray velvet gown lined with warm sky and trimmed with silver leaves!

FATHER [*gruffly—but with a certain awe*]. My mother used to believe the full of the moon was the time to sow. She was terrible old-fashioned. [*With a grunt.*] I can feel it's bringing on my rheumatism. Let's go back indoors.

DION [*with intense bitterness*]. Hide! Be ashamed! [*They both start and stare at him.*]

FATHER [*with bitter hopelessness. To his wife—indicating their son*]. Who is he? You bore him!

MOTHER [*proudly*]. He's my boy! He's Dion!

DION [*bitterly resentful*]. What else, indeed! The identical son! [*Then mockingly.*] Are Mr. Anthony and his wife going in to dance? The nights grow cold! The days are dimmer than they used to be! Let's play hide-and-seek! Seek the monkey in the moon! [*He suddenly cuts a grotesque caper, like a harlequin and darts off, laughing with forced abandon. They stare after him—then slowly follow. Again there is silence except for the sound of the lapping waves. Then* MARGARET *comes in, followed by the humbly worshiping* BILLY BROWN. *She is almost seventeen, pretty and vivacious, blonde, with big romantic eyes, her figure lithe and strong, her facial expression intelligent but youthfully dreamy, especially now in the moonlight. She is in a simple white dress. On her entrance, her face is masked with an exact, almost transparent reproduction of her own features, but giving her the abstract quality of a Girl instead of the individual,* MARGARET.]

MARGARET [*looking upward at the moon and singing in low tone as they enter*]. "Ah, moon of my delight that knowest no wane!"

BILLY [*eagerly*]. I've got that record—John McCormack. It's a peach! Sing some more. [*She looks upward in silence. He keeps standing respectfully in back of her, glancing embarrassedly toward her averted face. He tries to make conversation.*] I think the *Rubáiyát's* great stuff, don't you? I never could memorize poetry worth a darn. Dion can recite lots of Shelley's poems by heart.

MARGARET [*slowly takes off her mask—to the moon*]. Dion! [*A pause.*]

BILLY [*fidgeting*]. Margaret!

MARGARET [*to the moon*]. Dion is so wonderful!

BILLY [*blunderingly*]. I asked you to come out here because I wanted to tell you something.

MARGARET [*to the moon*]. Why did Dion look at me like that? It made me feel so crazy!

BILLY. I wanted to ask you something, too.

MARGARET. That one time he kissed me—I can't forget it! He was only joking—but I felt—and he saw and just laughed!

BILLY. Because that's the uncertain part. My end of it is a sure thing, and has been for a long time, and I guess everybody in town knows it—they're always kidding me—so it's a cinch you must know—how I feel about you.

MARGARET. Dion's so different from all the others. He can paint beautifully and write poetry and he plays and sings and dances so marvelously. But he's sad and shy, too, just like a baby sometimes, and he understands what I'm really like inside—and—and I'd love to run my fingers through his hair—and I love him! Yes, I love him! [*She stretches out her arms to the moon.*] Oh, Dion, I love you!

BILLY. I love you, Margaret.

MARGARET. I wonder if Dion—I saw him looking at me again tonight—Oh, I wonder . . . !

BILLY [*takes her hand and blurts out*]. Can't you love me? Won't you marry me—after college—

MARGARET. Where is Dion now, I wonder?

BILLY [*shaking her hand in an agony of uncertainty*]. Margaret! Please answer me!

MARGARET [*her dream broken, puts on her mask and turns to him—matter-of-factly*]. It's getting chilly. Let's go back and dance, Billy.

BILLY [*desperately*]. I love you! [*He tries clumsily to kiss her.*]

MARGARET [*with an amused laugh*]. Like a brother! You can kiss me if you like. [*She kisses him.*] A big-brother kiss. It doesn't count. [*He steps back crushed, with head bowed. She turns away and takes off her mask—to the moon.*] I wish Dion would kiss me again!

BILLY [*painfully*]. I'm a poor boob. I ought to know better. I'll bet I know. You're in love with Dion. I've seen you look at him. Isn't that it?

MARGARET. Dion! I love the sound of it!

BILLY [*huskily*]. Well—he's always been my best friend—I'm glad it's him—and I guess I know how to lose—[*He takes her hand and shakes it.*]—so here's wishing you all the success and happiness in the world, Margaret—and remember I'll always be your best friend! [*He gives her hand a final shake—swallows hard—then manfully.*] Let's go back in!

MARGARET [*to the moon—faintly annoyed*]. What is Billy Brown doing here? I'll go down to the end of the dock and wait. Dion is the moon and I'm the sea. I want to feel the moon kissing the sea. I want Dion to leave the sky to me. I want the tides of my blood to leave my heart and follow him! [*She whispers like a little girl.*] Dion! Margaret! Peggy! Peggy is Dion's girl—Peggy is Dion's little girl—[*She sings laughingly, elfishly.*] Dion is my Daddy-O! [*She is walking toward the end of the dock, off left.*]

BILLY [*who has turned away*]. I'm going. I'll tell Dion you're here.

MARGARET [*more and more strongly and assertively, until at the end she is a wife and a mother*]. And I'll be Mrs. Dion—Dion's wife—and he'll be my Dion—my own Dion—my little boy—my baby! The moon is drowned in the tides of my heart, and peace sinks deep through the sea! [*She disappears off left, her upturned unmasked face like that of a rapturous visionary. There is silence again, in which the dance music is heard. Then this stops and* DION *comes in. He walks quickly to the bench at center and throws himself on it, hiding his masked face in his hands. After a moment, he lifts his head, peers about, listens huntedly, then slowly takes off his mask. His real face is revealed in the bright moonlight, shrinking, shy and gentle, full of a deep sadness.*]

DION [*with a suffering bewilderment*]. Why am I afraid to dance, I who love music and rhythm and grace and song and laughter? Why am I afraid to live, I who love life and the beauty of flesh and the living colors of earth and sky and sea? Why am I afraid of love, I who love love? Why am I afraid, I who am not afraid? Why must I pretend to scorn in order to pity? Why must I hide myself in self-contempt in order to understand? Why must I be so ashamed of my strength, so proud of my weakness? Why must I live in a cage like a criminal, defying and hating, I who love peace and friendship? [*Clasping his hands above in supplication.*] Why was I born without a skin, O God, that I must wear armor in order to touch or to be touched? [*A second's pause of waiting silence—then he suddenly claps his mask over his face again, with a gesture of despair and his voice becomes bitter and sardonic.*] Or rather, Old Graybeard, why the devil was I ever born at all? [*Steps are heard from the right.* DION *stiffens and his mask stares straight ahead.* BILLY *comes in from the right. He is shuffling along disconsolately. When he sees* DION, *he stops abruptly and glowers resent-*

fully—but at once the "good loser" in him conquers this.]

BILLY [*embarrassedly*]. Hello, Dion. I've been looking all over for you. [*He sits down on the bench at right, forcing a joking tone.*] What are you sitting here for, you nut—trying to get more moonstruck? [*A pause—awkwardly.*] I just left Margaret—

DION [*gives a start—immediately defensively mocking*]. Bless you, my children!

BILLY [*gruffly and slangily*]. I'm out of it—she gave me the gate. You're the original white-haired boy. Go on in and win! We've been chums ever since we were kids, haven't we?—and—I'm glad it's you, Dion. [*This huskily—he fumbles for* DION'S *hand and gives it a shake.*]

DION [*letting his hand fall back—bitterly*]. Chums? Oh no, Billy Brown would despise me!

BILLY. She's waiting for you now, down at the end of the dock.

DION. For me? Which? Who? Oh no, girls only allow themselves to look at what is seen!

BILLY. She's in love with you.

DION [*moved—a pause—stammers*]. Miracle? I'm afraid! [*He chants flippantly.*] I love, thou lovest, he loves, she loves! She loves, she loves—what?

BILLY. And I know damn well, underneath your nuttiness, you're gone on her.

DION [*moved*]. Underneath? I love love! I'd love to be loved! But I'm afraid! [*Then aggressively.*] *Was* afraid! Not now! Now I can make love—to anyone! Yes, I love Peggy! Why not? Who is she? Who am I? We love, you love, they love, one loves! No one loves! All the world loves a lover, God loves us all and we love Him! Love is a word—a shameless ragged ghost of a word—begging at all doors for life at any price!

BILLY [*always as if he hadn't listened to what the other said*]. Say, let's you and me room together at college—

DION. Billy wants to remain by her side!

BILLY. It's a bet, then! [*Forcing a grin.*] You can tell her I'll see that you behave! [*Turns away.*] So long. Remember she's waiting. [*He goes.*]

DION [*dazedly, to himself*]. Waiting—waiting for me! [*He slowly removes his mask. His face is torn and transfigured by joy. He stares at the sky raptly.*] O God in the moon, did you hear? She loves me! I am not afraid! I am strong! I can love! She protects me! Her arms are softly around me! She is warmly around me! She is my skin! She is my armor! Now I am born—I—the I!—one and indivisible—I who love Margaret! [*He glances at his mask triumphantly—in tones of deliverance.*] You are outgrown! I am beyond you! [*He stretches out his arms to the sky.*] O God, now I believe! [*From the end of the wharf, her voice is heard.*]

MARGARET. Dion!

DION [*raptly*]. Margaret!

MARGARET [*nearer*]. Dion!

DION. Margaret!

MARGARET. Dion! [*She comes running in, her mask in her hands. He springs toward her with outstretched arms but she shrinks away with a frightened shriek and hastily puts on her mask.* DION *starts back. She speaks coldly and angrily.*] Who are you? Why are you calling me? I don't know you!

DION [*heart-brokenly*]. I love you!

MARGARET [*freezingly*]. Is this a joke—or are you drunk?

DION [*with a final pleading whisper*]. Margaret! [*But she only glares at him contemptuously. Then with a sudden gesture he claps his mask on and laughs wildly and bitterly.*] Ha-ha-ha! That's one on you, Peg!

MARGARET [*with delight, pulling off her mask*]. Dion! How did you ever— Why, I never knew you!

DION [*puts his arm around her boldly*]. How? It's the moon—the crazy moon—the monkey in the moon—playing jokes on us! [*He kisses her with his masked face with a romantic actor's passion again and again.*] You love me! You know you do! Say it! Tell me! I want to hear! I want to feel! I want to know! I want to want! To want you as you want me!

MARGARET [*in ecstasy*]. Oh, Dion, I do! I do love you!

DION [*with ironic mastery—rhetorically*]. And I love you! Oh, madly! Oh, forever and ever, amen! You are my evening star and all my Pleiades! Your eyes are blue pools in which gold dreams glide, your body is a young white birch leaning backward beneath the lips of spring. So! [*He has bent her back, his arms supporting her, his face above hers.*] So! [*He kisses her.*]

MARGARET [*with overpowering passionate languor*]. Oh, Dion! Dion! I love you!

DION [*with more and more mastery in his tone*]. I love, you love, we love! Come! Rest! Relax! Let go your clutch on the world! Dim and dimmer! Fading out in the past behind! Gone! Death! Now! Be born! Awake! Live! Dissolve into dew—into silence—into night—into earth—into space—into peace—into meaning—into joy—into God—into the Great God Pan! [*While he has been speaking, the moon has passed gradually behind a black cloud, its light fading out. There is a moment of intense blackness and silence. Then the light gradually comes on again.* DION'S *voice, at first in a whisper, then increasing in volume with the light, is heard.*] Wake up! Time to get up! Time to exist! Time for school! Time to learn! Learn to pretend! Cover your nakedness! Learn to lie! Learn to keep step! Join the procession! Great Pan is dead! Be ashamed!

MARGARET [*with a sob*]. Oh, Dion, I am ashamed!

DION [*mockingly*]. Sssshh! Watch the monkey in the moon! See him dance! His tail is a piece of string that was left when he broke loose from Jehovah and ran away to join Charley Darwin's circus!

MARGARET. I know you must hate me now! [*She throws her arms around him and hides her head on his shoulder.*]

DION [*deeply moved*]. Don't cry! Don't—! [*He suddenly tears off his mask—in a passionate agony.*] Hate you? I love you with all my soul! Love me! Why can't you love me, Margaret? [*He tries to kiss her but she jumps to her feet with a frightened cry holding up her mask before her face protectingly.*]

MARGARET. Don't! Please! I don't know you! You frighten me!

DION [*puts on his mask again—quietly and bitterly*]. All's well. I'll never let you see again. [*He puts his arm around her—gently mocking.*] By proxy, I love you. There! Don't cry! Don't be afraid! Dion Anthony will marry you some day. [*He kisses her.*] "I take this woman—" [*Tenderly joking.*] Hello, woman! Do you feel older by æons? Mrs. Dion Anthony, shall we go in and may I have the next dance?

MARGARET [*tenderly*]. You crazy child! [*Then, laughing with joy.*] Mrs. Dion Anthony! It sounds wonderful, doesn't it? [*They go out as*

THE CURTAIN FALLS

ACT ONE

SCENE ONE

SCENE. *Seven years later.*

The sitting room of MRS. DION ANTHONY'S *half of a two-family house in the homes section of the town—one of those one-design districts that daze the eye with multiplied ugliness. The four pieces of furniture shown are in keeping—an armchair at left, a table with a chair in back of it at center, a sofa at right. The same court-room effect of the arrangement of benches in Act One is held to here. The background is a backdrop on which the rear wall is painted with the intolerable lifeless realistic detail of the stereotyped paintings which usually adorn the sitting rooms of such houses. It is late afternoon of a gray day in winter.*

DION *is sitting behind the table, staring before him. The mask hangs on his breast below his neck, giving the effect of two faces. His real face has aged greatly, grown more strained and tortured, but at the same time, in some queer way, more selfless and ascetic, more fixed in its resolute withdrawal from life. The mask, too, has changed. It is older, more defiant and mocking, its sneer more forced and bitter, its Pan quality becoming Mephistophelean. It has already begun to show the ravages of dissipation.*

DION [*suddenly reaches out and takes up a copy of the New Testament which is on the table and, putting a finger in at random, opens and reads aloud the text at which it points*]. "Come unto me all ye who are heavy laden and I will give you rest." [*He stares before him in a sort of trance, his face lighted up from within but painfully confused—in an uncertain whisper.*] I will come—but where are you, Savior? [*The noise of the outer door shutting is heard.* DION *starts and claps the mocking mask on his face again. He tosses the Testament aside contemptuously.*] Blah! Fixation on old Mama Christianity! You infant blubbering in the dark, you! [*He laughs, with a bitter self-contempt. Footsteps approach. He picks up a newspaper and hides behind it hurriedly.* MARGARET *enters. She is dressed in stylish, expensive clothes and a fur coat, which look as if they had been remodeled and seen service. She has grown mature and maternal, in spite of her youth. Her pretty face is still fresh and healthy but there is the beginning of a permanently worried, apprehensive expression about the nose and mouth—an uncomprehending hurt in her eyes.* DION *pretends to be engrossed in his paper. She bends down and kisses him.*]

MARGARET [*with a forced gayety*]. Good morning—at four in the afternoon! You were snoring when I left!

DION [*puts his arms around her with a negligent, accustomed gesture—mockingly*]. The Ideal Husband!

MARGARET [*already preoccupied with another thought—comes and sits in chair*]. I was afraid the children would disturb you, so I took them over to Mrs. Young's to play. [*A pause. He picks up the paper again. She asks anxiously.*] I suppose they'll be all right over there, don't you? [*He doesn't answer. She is more hurt than offended.*] I wish you'd try to take more interest in the children, Dion.

DION [*mockingly*]. Become a father—before breakfast? I'm in too delicate a condition. [*She turns away, hurt. Penitently he pats her hand—vaguely.*] All right. I'll try.

MARGARET [*squeezing his hand—with possessive tenderness*]. Play with them. You're a bigger kid than they are—underneath.

DION [*self-mockingly—flipping the Bible*]. Underneath—I'm becoming downright infantile! "Suffer these little ones!"

MARGARET [*keeping to her certainty*]. You're my oldest.

DION [*with mocking appreciation*]. She puts the Kingdom of Heaven in its place!

MARGARET [*withdrawing her hand*]. I was serious.

DION. So was I—about something or other. [*He laughs.*] This domestic diplomacy! We communicate in code—when neither has the other's key!

MARGARET [*frowns confusedly—then forcing a playful tone*]. I want to have a serious talk with you, young man! In spite of your promises, you've kept up the hard drinking and gambling you started the last year abroad.

DION. From the time I realized it wasn't in me to be an artist—except in living—and not even in that! [*He laughs bitterly.*]

MARGARET [*with conviction*]. But you *can* paint, Dion—beautifully!

DION [*with deep pain*]. No! [*He suddenly takes her hand and kisses it gratefully.*] I love Margaret! Her blindness surpasseth all understanding! [*Then bitterly.*]—or is it pity?

MARGARET. We've only got about one hundred dollars left in the bank.

DION [*with dazed surprise*]. What! Is all the money from the sale of the house gone?

MARGARET [*wearily*]. Every day or so you've been cashing checks. You've been drinking—you haven't counted—

DION [*irritably*]. I know! [*A pause—soberly.*] No more estate to fall back on, eh? Well, for five years it kept us living abroad in peace. It bought us a little happiness—of a kind—didn't it?—living and loving and having children—[*A slight pause—bitterly.*]—thinking one was creating before one discovered one couldn't!

MARGARET [*this time with forced conviction*]. But you *can* paint—beautifully!

DION [*angrily*]. Shut up! [*A pause—then jeeringly.*] So my wife thinks it behooves me to settle down and support my family in the meager style to which they'll have to become accustomed?

MARGARET [*shamefacedly*]. I didn't say—still—something's got to be done.

DION [*harshly*]. Will Mrs. Anthony helpfully suggest what?

MARGARET. I met Billy Brown on the street.

He said you'd have made a good architect, if you'd stuck to it.

DION. Flatterer! Instead of leaving college when my Old Man died? Instead of marrying Peggy and going abroad and being happy?

MARGARET [*as if she hadn't heard*]. He spoke of how well you used to draw.

DION. Billy was in love with Margaret at one time.

MARGARET. He wanted to know why you've never been in to see him.

DION. He's bound heaven-bent for success. It's the will of Mammon! Anthony and Brown, contractors and builders—death subtracts Anthony and I sell out—Billy graduates—Brown and Son, architects and builders—old man Brown perishes of paternal pride—and now we have William A. Brown, architect! Why, his career itself already has an architectural design! One of God's mud pies!

MARGARET. He particularly told me to ask you to drop in.

DION [*springs to his feet—assertively*]. No! Pride! I have been alive!

MARGARET. Why don't you have a talk with him?

DION. Pride in my failure!

MARGARET. You were always such close friends.

DION [*more and more desperately*]. The pride which came after man's fall—by which he laughs as a creator at his self-defeats!

MARGARET. Not for my sake—but for your own—and, above all, for the children's!

DION [*with terrible despair*]. Pride! Pride without which the Gods are worms!

MARGARET [*after a pause, meekly and humbly*]. You don't want to? It would hurt you? All right, dear. Never mind. We'll manage somehow—you mustn't worry—you must start your beautiful painting again—and I can get that position in the library—it would be such fun for me working there! . . . [*She reaches out and takes his hand—tenderly.*] I love you, dear. I understand.

DION [*slumps down into his chair, crushed, his face averted from hers, as hers is from him, although their hands are still clasped—in a trembling, expiring voice*]. Pride is dying! [*As if he were suffocating, he pulls the mask from his resigned, pale, suffering face. He prays like a Saint in the desert, exorcizing a demon.*] Pride is dead! Blessed are the meek! Blessed are the poor in spirit!

MARGARET [*without looking at him—in a comforting, motherly tone*]. My poor boy!

DION [*resentfully—clapping on his mask again and springing to his feet—derisively*]. Blessed are the meek for they shall inherit graves! Blessed are the poor in spirit for they are blind! [*Then with tortured bitterness.*] All right! Then I ask my wife to go and ask Billy Brown—that's more deadly than if I went myself! [*With wild mockery.*] Ask him if he can't find an opening for a talented young man who is only honest when he isn't sober—implore him, beg him in the name of old love, old friendship—to be a generous hero and save the woman and her children! [*He laughs with a sort of diabolical, ironical glee now, and starts to go out.*]

MARGARET [*meekly*]. Are you going up street, Dion?

DION. Yes.

MARGARET. Will you stop at the butchers' and have them send two pounds of pork chops?

DION. Yes.

MARGARET. And stop at Mrs. Young's and ask the children to hurry right home?

DION. Yes.

MARGARET. Will you be back for dinner, Dion?

DION. No. [*He goes, the outer door slams.* MARGARET *sighs with a tired incomprehension and goes to the window and stares out.*]

MARGARET [*worriedly*]. I hope they'll watch out, crossing the street.

CURTAIN

SCENE TWO

SCENE. BILLY BROWN'S *Office, at five in the afternoon. At center, a fine mahogany desk with a swivel chair in back of it. To the left of desk, an office armchair. To the right of desk, an office lounge. The background is a backdrop of an office wall, treated similarly to that of Scene One in its over-meticulous representation of detail.*

Billy Brown is seated at the desk looking over a blueprint by the light of a desk lamp. He has grown into a fine-looking, well-dressed, capable, college-bred American business man, boyish still and with the same engaging personality.

The telephone rings.

BROWN [*answering it*]. Yes? Who? [*This in surprise—then with eager pleasure.*] Let her come right in. [*He gets up and goes to the door, expectant and curious.* MARGARET *enters. Her face is concealed behind the mask of the pretty young matron, still hardly a woman, who cultivates a naïvely innocent and bravely hopeful attitude toward things and acknowledges no wound to the world. She is dressed as in Scene One but with an added touch of effective primping here and there.*]

MARGARET [*very gayly*]. Hello, Billy Brown!

BROWN [*awkward in her presence, shakes her hand*]. Come in. Sit down. This is a pleasant surprise, Margaret. [*She sits down on the lounge. He sits in his chair behind the desk, as before.*]

MARGARET [*looking around*]. What lovely offices! My, but Billy Brown is getting grand!

BROWN [*pleased*]. I've just moved in. The old place was too stuffy.

MARGARET. It looks so prosperous—but then, Billy is doing so wonderfully well, everyone says.

BROWN [*modestly*]. Well, to be frank, it's been mostly luck. Things have come my way without my doing much about it. [*Then, with an abashed pride.*] Still—I have done a little something myself. [*He picks the plan from the desk.*] See this? It's my design for the new Municipal Building. It's just been accepted—provisionally—by the Committee.

MARGARET [*taking it—vaguely*]. Oh? [*She looks at it abstractedly. There is a pause. Suddenly.*] You mentioned the other day how well Dion used to draw—

BROWN [*a bit stiffly*]. Yes, he certainly did. [*He takes the drawing from her and at once becomes interested and squints at it frowningly.*] Did you notice that anything seemed lacking in this?

MARGARET [*indifferently*]. Not at all.

BROWN [*with a cheerful grin*]. The Committee want it made a little more American. It's too much of a conventional Greco-Roman tomb, they say. [*Laughs.*] They want an original touch of modern novelty stuck in to liven it up and make it look different from other town halls. [*Putting the drawing back on his desk.*] And I've been figuring out how to give it to them but my mind doesn't seem to run that way. Have you any suggestion?

MARGARET [*as if she hadn't heard*]. Dion certainly draws well, Billy Brown was saying?

BROWN [*trying not to show his annoyance*]. Why, yes—he did—and still can, I expect. [*A pause. He masters what he feels to be an unworthy pique and turns to her generously.*] Dion would have made a cracking good architect.

MARGARET [*proudly*]. I know. He could be anything he wanted to.

BROWN [*a pause—embarrassedly*]. Is he working at anything these days?

MARGARET [*defensively*]. Oh, yes! He's painting wonderfully! But he's just like a child, he's so impractical. He doesn't try to have an exhibition anywhere, or anything.

BROWN [*surprised*]. The one time I ran into him, I thought he told me he'd destroyed all his pictures—that he'd gotten sick of painting and completely given it up.

MARGARET [*quickly*]. He always tells people that. He doesn't want anyone even to look at his things, imagine! He keeps saying they're rotten—when they're really too beautiful! He's too modest for his own good, don't you think? But it is true he hasn't done so much lately since we've been back. You see the children take up such a lot of his time. He just worships them! I'm afraid he's becoming a hopeless family man, just the opposite of what anyone would expect who knew him in the old days.

BROWN [*painfully embarrassed by her loyalty and his knowledge of the facts*]. Yes, I know. [*He coughs self-consciously.*]

MARGARET [*aroused by something in his manner*]. But I suppose the gossips are telling the same silly stories about him they always did. [*She forces a laugh.*] Poor Dion! Give a dog a bad name! [*Her voice breaks a little in spite of herself.*]

BROWN [*hastily*]. I haven't heard any stories —[*He stops uncertainly, then decides to plunge in.*]—except about money matters.

MARGARET [*forcing a laugh*]. Oh, perhaps they're true enough. Dion is such a generous fool with his money, like all artists.

BROWN [*with a certain doggedness*]. There's a rumor that you've applied for a position at the library.

MARGARET [*forcing a gay tone*]. Yes, indeed! Won't it be fun! Maybe it'll improve my mind! And one of us has got to be practical, so why not me? [*She forces a gay, girlish laugh.*]

BROWN [*impulsively reaches out and takes her hand—awkwardly*]. Listen, Margaret. Let's be perfectly frank, will you? I'm such an old friend, and I want like the deuce to. . . . You know darn well I'd do anything in the world to help you—or Dion.

MARGARET [*withdrawing her hand, coldly*]. I'm afraid I—don't understand, Billy Brown.

BROWN [*acutely embarrassed*]. Well, I—I just meant—you know, if you needed— [*A pause. He looks questioningly at her averted face—then ventures on another tack, matter-of-factly.*] I've got a proposition to make to Dion—if I could ever get hold of him. It's this way: business has been piling up on me—a run of luck—but I'm short-handed. I need a crack chief draftsman darn badly—or I'm liable to lose out. Do you think Dion would consider it—as a temporary stop-gap—until he felt in the painting mood again?

MARGARET [*striving to conceal her eagerness and relief—judicially*]. Yes—I really do. He's such a good sport and Billy and he were such pals once. I know he'd be only too tickled to help him out.

BROWN [*diffidently*]. I thought he might be sensitive about working for—I mean, with me—when, if he hadn't sold out to Dad he'd be my partner now—[*Earnestly.*]—and, by jingo, I wish he was! [*Then, abruptly.*] Let's try to nail him down right away, Margaret. Is he home now? [*He reaches for the phone.*]

MARGARET [*hurriedly*]. No, he—he went out for a long walk.

BROWN. Perhaps I can locate him later around town somewhere.

MARGARET [*with a note of pleading*]. Please don't trouble. It isn't necessary. I'm sure when I talk to him—he's coming home to dinner—[*Getting up.*] Then it's all settled, isn't it? Dion will be so glad to be able to help an old friend—he's so terribly loyal, and he's always liked Billy Brown so much! [*Holding out her hand.*] I really must go now!

BROWN [*shakes her hand*]. Good-by, Margaret. I hope you'll be dropping in on us a lot when Dion gets here.

MARGARET. Yes. [*She goes.*]

BROWN [*sits at his desk again, looking ahead in a not unsatisfying melancholy reverie. He mutters admiringly but pityingly*]. Poor Margaret! She's a game sport, but it's pretty damn tough on her! [*Indignantly.*] By God, I'm going to give Dion a good talking-to one of these days!

CURTAIN

SCENE THREE

SCENE. *Cybel's parlor. An automatic, nickel-in-the-slot player-piano is at center, rear. On its right is a dirty gilt second-hand sofa. At the left is a bald-spotted crimson plush chair. The backdrop for the rear wall is cheap wall-paper of a dull yellow-brown, resembling a blurred impression of a fallow field in early spring. There is a cheap alarm clock on top of the piano. Beside it her mask is lying.*

DION *is sprawled on his back, fast asleep on the sofa. His mask has fallen down on his chest. His pale face is singularly pure, spiritual and sad.*

The player-piano is groggily banging out a sentimental medley of "Mother—Mammy" tunes.

CYBEL *is seated on the stool in front of the piano. She is a strong, calm, sensual, blonde girl of twenty or so, her complexion fresh and healthy, her figure full-breasted and wide-hipped, her movements slow and solidly languorous like an animal's, her large eyes dreamy with the reflected stirring of profound instincts. She chews gum like a sacred cow forgetting time with an eternal end. Her eyes are fixed, incuriously, on* DION'S *pale face.*

CYBEL [*as the tune runs out, glances at the clock, which indicates midnight, then goes slowly over to* DION *and puts her hand gently on his forehead*]. Wake up!

DION [*stirs, sighs and murmurs dreamily*]. "And He laid his hands on them and healed them." [*Then with a start he opens his eyes and, half sitting up, stares at her bewilderedly.*] What—where—who are you? [*He reaches for his mask and claps it on defensively.*]

CYBEL [*placidly*]. Only another female. You was camping on my steps, sound asleep. I didn't want to run any risk getting into more trouble with the cops pinching you there and blaming me, so I took you in to sleep it off.

DION [*mockingly*]. Blessed are the pitiful, Sister! I'm broke—but you will be rewarded in Heaven!

CYBEL [*calmly*]. I wasn't wasting my pity. Why should I? You were happy, weren't you?

DION [*approvingly*]. Excellent! You're not a moralist, I see.

CYBEL [*going on*]. And you look like a good boy, too—when you're asleep. Say, you better beat it home to bed or you'll be locked out.

DION [*mockingly*]. Now you're becoming maternal, Miss Earth. Is that the only answer—to pin my soul into every vacant diaper? [*She stares down at his mask, her face growing hard. He laughs.*] But please don't stop stroking my aching brow. Your hand is a cool mud poultice on the sting of thought!

CYBEL [*calmly*]. Stop acting. I hate ham fats. [*She looks at him as if waiting for him to remove his mask—then turns her back indifferently and goes to the piano.*] Well, if you simply got to be a regular devil like all the other visiting sports, I s'pose I got to play with you. [*She takes her mask and puts it on—then turns. The mask is the rouged and eye-blackened countenance of the hardened prostitute. In a coarse, harsh voice.*] Kindly state your dishonorable intentions, if any! I can't sit up all night keeping company! Let's have some music! [*She puts a plug in the machine. The same sentimental medley begins to play. The two masks stare at each other. She laughs.*] Shoot! I'm all set! It's your play, Kid Lucifer!

DION [*slowly removes his mask. She stops the music with a jerk. His face is gentle and sad—humbly*]. I'm sorry. It has always been such agony for me to be touched!

CYBEL [*taking off her mask—sympathetically as she comes back and sits down on her stool*]. Poor kid! I've never had one, but I can guess. They hug and kiss you and take you on their laps and pinch you and want to see you getting dressed and undressed—as if they owned you—I bet you I'd never let them treat one of mine that way!

DION [*turning to her*]. You're lost in blind alleys, too. [*Suddenly holding out his hand to her.*] But you're strong. Let's be friends.

CYBEL [*with a strange sternness, searches his face*]. And never nothing more?

DION [*with a strange smile*]. Let's say, never anything less! [*She takes his hand. There is a ring at the outside door bell. They stare at each other. There is another ring.*]

CYBEL [*puts on her mask,* DION *does likewise. Mockingly*]. When you got to love to live it's hard to love living. I better join the A. F. of L. and soap-box for the eight-hour night! Got a nickel, baby? Play a tune. [*She goes out.* DION *puts a nickel in. The same sentimental tune starts.* CYBEL *returns, followed by* BILLY BROWN. *His face is rigidly composed, but his superior disgust for* DION *can be seen.* DION *jerks off the music and he and* BILLY *look at each other for a moment,* CYBEL *watching them both—then, bored, she yawns.*] He's hunting for you. Put out the lights when you go. I'm going to sleep. [*She starts to go—then, as if reminded of something—to* DION.] Life's all right, if you let it alone. [*Then mechanically flashing a trade smile at* BILLY.] Now you know the way, Handsome, call again! [*She goes.*]

BROWN [*after an awkward pause*]. Hello, Dion! I've been looking all over town for you. This place was the very last chance. . . . [*Another pause—embarrassedly.*] Let's take a walk.

DION [*mockingly*]. I've given up exercise. They claim it lengthens your life.

BROWN [*persuasively*]. Come on, Dion, be a good fellow. You're certainly not staying here—

DION. Billy would like to think me taken in *flagrante delicto*, eh?

BROWN. Don't be a damn fool! Listen to me! I've been looking you up for purely selfish reasons. I need your help.

DION [*astonished*]. What?

BROWN. I've a proposition to make that I hope you'll consider favorably out of old friendship. To be frank, Dion, I need you to lend me a hand down at the office.

DION [*with a harsh laugh*]. So it's the job, is it? Then my poor wife did a-begging go!

BROWN [*repelled—sharply*]. On the contrary, I had to beg her to beg you to take it! [*More angrily.*] Look here, Dion! I won't listen to you talk that way about Margaret! And you wouldn't if you weren't drunk! [*Suddenly shaking him.*] What in hell has come over you, anyway! You didn't use to be like this! What the devil are you going to do with yourself—sink into the gutter and drag Margaret with you? If you'd heard her defend you, lie about you, tell me how hard you were working, what beautiful things you were painting, how you stayed at home and idolized the children!—when everyone knows you've been out every night sousing and gambling away the last of your estate. . . [*He stops, ashamed, controlling himself.*]

DION [*wearily*]. She was lying about her husband, not me, you fool! But it's no use explaining. [*Then, in a sudden, excitable passion.*] What do you want? I agree to anything—except the humiliation of yelling secrets at the deaf!

BROWN [*trying a bullying tone—roughly*]. Bunk! Don't try to crawl out! There's no excuse and you know it. [*Then as* DION *doesn't reply—penitently.*] But I know I shouldn't talk this way, old man! It's only because we're such old pals—and I hate to see you wasting yourself—you who had more brains than any of us! But, damn it, I suppose you're too much of a rotten cynic to believe I mean what I've just said!

DION [*touched*]. I know Billy was always Dion Anthony's friend.

BROWN. You're damn right I am—and I'd have proved it long ago if you'd only given me half a chance! After all, I couldn't keep chasing after you and be snubbed every time. A man has some pride!

DION [*bitterly mocking*]. Dead wrong! Never more! None whatever! It's unmoral! Blessed are the poor in spirit, Brother! When shall I report?

BROWN [*eagerly*]. Then you'll take the—you'll help me?

DION [*wearily bitter*]. I'll take the job. One must do something to pass away the time, while one is waiting—for one's next incarnation.

BROWN [*jokingly*]. I'd say it was a bit early to be worrying about that. [*Trying to get* DION *started.*] Come along, now. It's pretty late.

DION [*shakes his hand off his shoulder and walks away from him—after a pause*]. Is my father's chair still there?

BROWN [*turns away—embarrassed*]. I—I don't really remember, Dion—I'll look it up.

DION [*taking off his mask—slowly*]. I'd like to sit where he spun what I have spent. What aliens we were to each other! When he lay dead, his face looked so familiar that I wondered where I had met that man before. Only at the second of my conception. After that, we grew hostile with concealed shame. And my mother? I remember a sweet, strange girl, with affectionate, bewildered eyes as if God had locked her in a dark closet without any explanation. I was the sole doll our ogre, her husband, allowed her and she played mother and child with me for many years in that house until at last through two tears I watched her die with the shy pride of one who has lengthened her dress and put up her hair. And I felt like a forsaken toy and cried to be buried with her, because her hands alone had caressed without clawing. She lived long and aged greatly in the two days before they closed her coffin. The last time I looked, her purity had forgotten me, she was stainless and imperishable, and I knew my sobs were ugly and meaningless to her virginity; so I shrank away, back into life, with naked nerves jumping like fleas, and in due course of nature another girl called me her boy in the moon and married me and became three mothers in one person, while I got paint on my paws in an endeavor to see God! [*He laughs wildly—claps on his mask.*] But that Ancient Humorist had given me weak eyes, so now I'll have to foreswear my quest for Him and go in for the Omnipresent Successful Serious One, the Great God Mr. Brown, instead! [*He makes him a sweeping, mocking bow.*]

BROWN [*repelled but cajolingly*]. Shut up, you nut! You're still drunk. Come on! Let's start! [*He grabs* DION *by the arm and switches off the light.*]

DION [*from the darkness—mockingly*]. I am thy shorn, bald, nude sheep! Lead on, Almighty Brown, thou Kindly Light!

CURTAIN

ACT TWO

SCENE ONE

SCENE. CYBEL'S *parlor—about sunset in spring seven years later. The arrangement of furniture is the same but the chair and sofa are new, bright-colored, costly pieces. The old automatic piano at center looks exactly the same. The cheap alarm clock is still on top of it. On either side of the clock, the masks of* DION *and* CYBEL *are lying. The background backdrop is brilliant, stunning wall-paper, on which crimson and purple flowers and fruits tumble over one another in a riotously profane lack of any apparent design.*

DION *sits in the chair on left,* CYBEL *on the sofa. A card-table is between them. Both are playing solitaire.* DION *is now prematurely gray. His face is that of an ascetic, a martyr, furrowed by pain and self-torture, yet lighted from within by a spiritual calm and human kindliness.*

CYBEL *has grown stouter and more voluptuous, but her face is still unmarked and fresh, her calm more profound. She is like an unmoved idol of Mother Earth.*

The piano is whining out its same old sentimental medley. They play their cards intently and contentedly. The music stops.

CYBEL [*musingly*]. I love those rotten old sob tunes. They make me wise to people. That's what's inside them—what makes them love and murder their neighbor—crying jags set to music!

DION [*compassionately*]. Every song is a hymn. They keep trying to find the Word in the Beginning.

CYBEL. They try to know too much. It makes them weak. I never puzzled them with myself. I gave them a Tart. They understood her and knew their parts and acted naturally. And on both sides we were able to keep our real virtue, if you get me. [*She plays her last card—indifferently.*] I've made it again.

DION [*smiling*]. Your luck is uncanny. It never comes out for me.

CYBEL. You keep getting closer, but it knows you still want to win—a little bit—and it's wise all I care about is playing. [*She lays out another game.*] Speaking of my canned music, our Mr. Brown hates that old box. [*At the mention of* BROWN, DION *trembles as if suddenly possessed, has a terrible struggle with himself, then while she continues to speak, gets up like an automaton and puts on his mask. The mask is now terribly ravaged. All of its Pan quality has changed into a diabolical Mephistophelean cruelty and irony.*] He doesn't mind the music inside. That gets him somehow. But he thinks the case looks shabby and he wants it junked. But I told him that just because he's been keeping me so long, he needn't start bossing like a husband or I'll—[*She looks up and sees the masked* DION *standing by the piano—calmly.*] Hello! Getting jealous again?

DION [*jeeringly*]. Are you falling in love with your keeper, old Sacred Cow?

CYBEL [*without taking offense*]. Cut it! You've been asking me that for years. Be yourself! He's healthy and handsome—but he's too guilty. What makes you pretend you think love is so important, anyway? It's just one of a lot of things you do to keep life living.

DION [*in same tone*]. Then you've lied when you've said you loved me, have you, Old Filth?

CYBEL [*affectionately*]. You'll never grow up! We've been friends, haven't we, for seven years? I've never let myself want you nor you me. Yes, I love you. It takes all kinds of love to make a world! Ours is the living cream, I say, living rich and high! [*A pause. Coaxingly.*] Stop hiding. I know you.

DION [*taking off his mask, wearily comes and sits down at her feet and lays his head in her lap—with a grateful smile*]. You're strong. You always give. You've given my weakness strength to live.

CYBEL [*tenderly, stroking his hair maternally*]. You're not weak. You were born with ghosts in your eyes and you were brave enough to go looking into your own dark—and you got afraid. [*After a pause.*] I don't blame your being jealous of Mr. Brown sometimes. I'm jealous of your wife, even though I know you do love her.

DION [*slowly*]. I love Margaret. I don't know who my wife is.

CYBEL [*after a pause—with a queer broken laugh*]. Oh, God, sometimes the truth hits me such a sock between the eyes I can see the stars!—and then I'm so damn sorry for the lot of you, every damn mother's son-of-a-gun of you, that I'd like to run out naked into the street and love the whole mob to death like I was bringing you all a new brand of dope that'd make you forget everything that ever was for good! [*Then, with a twisted smile.*] But they wouldn't see me, any more than they see each other. And they keep right on moving along and dying without my help anyway.

DION [*sadly*]. You've given me strength to die.

CYBEL. You may be important but your life's not. There's millions of it born every second. Life can cost too much even for a sucker to afford it—like everything else. And it's not sacred—only the you inside is. The rest is earth.

DION [*gets to his knees and with clasped hands looks up raptly and prays with an ascetic fervor*]. "Into thy hands, O Lord," ... [*Then suddenly, with a look of horror.*] Nothing! To feel one's life blown out like the flame of a cheap match ... ! [*He claps on his mask and laughs harshly.*] To fall asleep and know you'll never, never be called to get on the job of existence again! "Swift be thine approaching flight! Come soon—soon!" [*He quotes this last with a mocking longing.*]

CYBEL [*pats his head maternally*]. There, don't be scared. It's born in the blood. When the time comes, you'll find it's easy.

DION [*jumps to his feet and walks about excitedly*]. It won't be long. My wife dragged in a doctor the day before yesterday. He says my heart is gone—booze—He warned me, never another drop or—[*Mockingly.*] What say? Shall we have a drink?

CYBEL [*like an idol*]. Suit yourself. It's in the pantry. [*Then, as he hesitates.*] What set you off on this bat? You were raving on about some cathedral plans. . . .

DION [*wildly mocking*]. They've been accepted—Mr. Brown's designs! My designs really! You don't need to be told that. He hands me one mathematically correct barn after another and I doctor them up with cute allurements so that fools will desire to buy, sell, breed, sleep, love, hate, curse and pray in them! I do this with devilish cleverness to their entire delight! Once I dreamed of painting wind on the sea and the skimming flight of cloud shadows over the tops of trees! Now ... [*He laughs.*] But pride is a sin—even in a memory of the long deceased! Blessed are the poor in spirit! [*He subsides weakly on his chair, his hand pressed to his heart.*]

CYBEL [*like an idol*]. Go home and sleep. Your wife'll be worried.

DION. She knows—but she'll never admit to herself that her husband ever entered your door. [*Mocking.*] Aren't women loyal—to their vanity and their other things!

CYBEL. Brown is coming soon, don't forget.

DION. He knows too and can't admit. Perhaps he needs me here—unknown. What first aroused his passion to possess you exclusively, do you think? Because he knew you loved me and he felt himself cheated. He wanted what he thought was my love of the flesh! He feels I have no right to love.

He'd like to steal it as he steals my ideas—complacently—righteously. Oh, the good Brown!

CYBEL. But you like him, too! You're brothers, I guess, somehow. Well, remember he's paying, he'll pay—in some way or other.

DION [*raises his head as if starting to remove the mask*]. I know. Poor Billy! God forgive me the evil I've done him!

CYBEL [*reaches out and takes his hand*]. Poor boy!

DION [*presses her convulsively—then with forced harshness*]. Well, homeward Christian Soldier! I'm off! By-bye, Mother Earth! [*He starts to go off right. She seems about to let him go.*]

CYBEL [*suddenly starts and calls with deep grief*]. Dion! [*He looks at her. A pause. He comes slowly back. She speaks strangely in a deep, far-off voice—and yet like a mother talking to her little son.*] You mustn't forget to kiss me before you go, Dion. [*She removes his mask.*] Haven't I told you to take off your mask in the house? Look at me, Dion. I've—just—seen—something. I'm afraid you're going away a long, long ways. I'm afraid I won't see you again for a long, long time. So it's good-by, dear. [*She kisses him gently. He begins to sob. She hands him back his mask.*] Here you are. Don't get hurt. Remember, it's all a game, and after you're asleep I'll tuck you in.

DION [*in a choking, heart-broken cry*]. Mother! [*Then he claps on his mask with a terrible effort of will—mockingly.*] Go to the devil, you sentimental old pig! See you tomorrow! [*He goes, whistling, slamming the door.*]

CYBEL [*like an idol again*]. What's the good of bearing children? What's the use of giving birth to death? [*She sighs wearily, turns, puts a plug in the piano, which starts up its old sentimental tune. At the same moment* BROWN *enters quietly from the left. He is the ideal of the still youthful, good-looking, well-groomed, successful provincial American of forty. Just now, he is plainly perturbed. He is not able to see either* CYBEL'S *face or her mask.*]

BROWN. Cybel! [*She starts, jams off the music and reaches for her mask but has no time to put it on.*] Wasn't that Dion I just saw going out—after all your promises never to see him! [*She turns like an idol, holding the mask behind her. He stares, bewildered—stammers.*] I—I beg your pardon—I thought—

CYBEL [*in her strange voice*]. Cybel's gone out to dig in the earth and pray.

BROWN [*with more assurance*]. But—aren't those her clothes?

CYBEL. Cybel doesn't want people to see me naked. I'm her sister. Dion came to see me.

BROWN [*relieved*]. So that's what he's up to, is it? [*Then with a pitying sigh.*] Poor Margaret! [*Then with playful reproof.*] You really shouldn't encourage him. He's married and got three big sons.

CYBEL. And you haven't.

BROWN [*stung*]. No, I'm not married.

CYBEL. He and I were friends.

BROWN [*with a playful wink*]. Yes, I can imagine how the platonic must appeal to Dion's pure, innocent type! It's no good your kidding me about Dion. We've been friends since we were kids. I know him in and out. I've always stood up for him whatever he's done—so you can be perfectly frank. I only spoke as I did on account of Margaret—his wife—it's pretty tough on her.

CYBEL. You love his wife.

BROWN [*scandalized*]. What? What are you talking about? [*Then uncertainly.*] Don't be a fool! [*A pause—then as if impelled by an intense curiosity.*] So Dion is your lover, eh? That's very interesting. [*He pulls his chair closer to hers.*] Sit down. Let's talk. [*She continues to stand, the mask held behind her.*] Tell me—I've always been curious—what is it that makes Dion so attractive to women—especially certain types of women, if you'll pardon me? He always has been and yet I never could see exactly what they saw in him. Is it his looks—or because he's such a violent sensualist—or because he poses as artistic and temperamental—or because he's so wild—or just what is it?

CYBEL. He's alive!

BROWN [*suddenly takes one of her hands and kisses it—insinuatingly*]. Well, don't you think I'm alive, too? [*Eagerly.*] Listen.

Would you consider giving up Dion—and letting me take care of you under a similar arrangement to the one I've made with Cybel? I like you, you can see that. I won't bother you much—I'm much too busy—you can do what you like—lead your own life—except for seeing him. [*He stops. A pause. She stares ahead unmoved as if she hadn't heard. He pleads.*] Well—what do you say? Please do!

CYBEL [*her voice very weary*]. Cybel said to tell you she'd be back next week, Mr. Brown.

BROWN [*with queer agony*]. You mean you won't? Don't be so cruel! I love you! [*She walks away. He clutches at her pleadingly.*] At least—I'll give you anything you ask!—please promise me you won't see Dion Anthony again!

CYBEL [*with deep grief*]. He will never see me again, I promise you. Good-by!

BROWN [*jubilantly, kissing her hand—politely*]. Thank you! Thank you! I'm exceedingly grateful. [*Tactfully.*] I won't disturb you any further. Please forgive my intrusion, and remember me to Cybel when you write. [*He bows, turns, and goes off left.*]

CURTAIN

SCENE TWO

SCENE. *The drafting room in* BROWN'S *office.* DION'S *drafting table with a high stool in front is at center. Another stool is to the left of it. At the right is a bench. It is in the evening of the same day. The black wall drop has windows painted on it with a dim, street-lighted view of black houses across the way.*

DION *is sitting on the stool in back of the table, reading aloud from the "Imitation of Christ" by Thomas à Kempis to his mask, which is on the table before him. His own face is gentler, more spiritual, more saintlike and ascetic than ever before.*

DION [*like a priest, offering up prayers for the dying*]. "Quickly must thou be gone from hence, see then how matters stand with thee. Ah, fool—learn now to die to the world that thou mayst begin to live with Christ! Do now, beloved, do now all thou canst because thou knowst not when thou shalt die; nor dost thou know what shall befall thee after death. Keep thyself as a pilgrim, and a stranger upon earth, to whom the affairs of this world do not—belong! Keep thy heart free and raised upwards to God because thou hast not here a lasting abode. 'Because at what hour you know not the Son of Man will come!'" Amen. [*He raises his hand over the mask as if he were blessing it, closes the book and puts it back in his pocket. He raises the mask in his hands and stares at it with a pitying tenderness.*] Peace, poor tortured one, brave pitiful pride of man, the hour of our deliverance comes. Tomorrow we may be with Him in Paradise! [*He kisses it on the lips and sets it down again. There is the noise of footsteps climbing the stairs in the hallway. He grabs up the mask in a sudden panic and, as a knock comes on the door, he claps it on and calls mockingly.*] Come in, Mrs. Anthony, come in! [MARGARET *enters. In one hand behind her, hidden from him, is the mask of the brave face she puts on before the world to hide her suffering and disillusionment, and which she has just taken off. Her own face is still sweet and pretty but lined, drawn and careworn for its years, sad, resigned, but a bit querulous.*]

MARGARET [*wearily reproving*]. Thank goodness I've found you! Why haven't you been home the last two days? It's bad enough your drinking again without your staying away and worrying us to death!

DION [*bitterly*]. My ears knew her footsteps. One gets to recognize everything—and to see nothing!

MARGARET. I finally sent the boys out looking for you and came myself. [*With tired solicitude.*] I suppose you haven't eaten a thing, as usual. Won't you come home and let me fry you a chop?

DION [*wonderingly*]. Can Margaret still love Dion Anthony? Is it possible she does?

MARGARET [*forcing a tired smile*]. I suppose so, Dion. I certainly oughtn't to, had I?

DION [*in same tone*]. And I love Margaret! What haunted, haunting ghosts we are! We dimly remember so much it will take us so many million years to forget! [*He comes forward, putting one arm around her bowed shoulders, and they kiss.*]

MARGARET [*patting his hand affectionately*]. No, you certainly don't deserve it. When I stop to think of all you've made me go through in the years since we settled down here . . . ! I really don't believe I could ever have stood it if it weren't for the boys! [*Forcing a smile.*] But perhaps I would, I've always been such a big fool about you.

DION [*a bit mockingly*]. The boys! Three strong sons! Margaret can afford to be magnanimous!

MARGARET. If they didn't find you, they were coming to meet me here.

DION [*with sudden wildness—torturedly, sinking on his knees beside her*]. Margaret! Margaret! I'm lonely! I'm frightened! I'm going away! I've got to say good-by!

MARGARET [*patting his hair*]. Poor boy! Poor Dion! Come home and sleep.

DION [*springs up frantically*]. No! I'm a man! I'm a lonely man! I can't go back! I have conceived myself! [*Then with desperate mockery.*] Look at me, Mrs. Anthony! It's the last chance! Tomorrow I'll have moved on to the next hell! Behold your man—the sniveling, cringing, life-denying Christian slave you have so nobly ignored in the father of your sons! Look! [*He tears the mask from his face, which is radiant with a great pure love for her and a great sympathy and tenderness.*] O woman—my love—that I have sinned against in my sick pride and cruelty—forgive my sins—forgive my solitude—forgive my sickness—forgive me! [*He kneels and kisses the hem of her dress.*]

MARGARET [*who has been staring at him with terror, raising her mask to ward off his face*]. Dion! Don't! I can't bear it! You're like a ghost! You're dead! Oh, my God! Help! Help! [*She falls back fainting on the bench. He looks at her—then takes her hand which holds her mask and looks at that face—gently.*]

DION. And now I am permitted to understand and love you, too! [*He kisses the mask first—then kisses her face, murmuring.*] And you, sweetheart! Blessed, thrice blessed are the meek! [*There is a sound of heavy, hurrying footsteps on the stairs. He puts on his mask in haste. The* THREE SONS *rush into the room. The* ELDEST *is about fourteen, the two others thirteen and twelve. They look healthy, normal likeable boys, with much the same quality as* BILLY BROWN'S *in Act One, Scene One. They stop short and stiffen all in a row, staring from the woman on the bench to their father, accusingly.*]

ELDEST. We heard someone yell. It sounded like Mother.

DION [*defensively*]. No. It was this lady—my wife.

ELDEST. But hasn't Mother come yet?

DION [*going to* MARGARET]. Yes. Your Mother is here. [*He stands between them and puts her mask over* MARGARET'S *face—then steps back.*] She has fainted. You'd better bring her to.

BOYS. Mother! [*They run to her side, kneel and rub her wrists. The* ELDEST *smooths back her hair.*]

DION [*watching them*]. At least I am leaving her well provided for. [*He addresses them directly.*] Tell your mother she'll get word from Mr. Brown's house. I must pay him a farewell call. I am going. Good-by. [*They stop, staring at him fixedly, with eyes a mixture of bewilderment, distrust and hurt.*]

ELDEST [*awkwardly and shamefacedly*]. Honest, I think you ought to have . . .

SECOND. Yes, honest you ought . . .

YOUNGEST. Yes, honest . . .

DION [*in a friendly tone*]. I know. But I couldn't. That's for you who can. You must inherit the earth for her. Don't forget now, boys. Good-by.

BOYS [*in the same awkward, self-conscious tone, one after another*]. Good-by—good-by—good-by. [DION *goes.*]

CURTAIN

SCENE THREE

SCENE. *The library of* WILLIAM BROWN'S *home—night of the same day. A backdrop of carefully painted, prosperous, bourgeois culture, bookcases filled with sets, etc. The heavy table at center is expensive. The leather armchair at left of it and the couch at right are opulently comfortable. The reading lamp on the table is the only light.*

BROWN *sits in the chair at left reading an architectural periodical. His expression is com-*

posed and gravely receptive. In outline, his face suggests a Roman consul on an old coin. There is an incongruous distinction about it, the quality of unquestioning faith in the finality of its achievement.

There is a sudden loud thumping on the front door and the ringing of the bell. BROWN *frowns and listens as a servant answers.* DION'S *voice can be heard, raised mockingly.*

DION. Tell him it's the devil come to conclude a bargain.

BROWN [*suppressing annoyance, calls out with forced good nature*]. Come on in, Dion. [DION *enters. He is in a wild state. His clothes are disheveled, his masked face has a terrible deathlike intensity, its mocking irony becomes so cruelly malignant as to give him the appearance of a real demon, tortured into torturing others.*] Sit down.

DION [*stands and sings*]. William Brown's soul lies moldering in the crib but his body goes marching on!

BROWN [*maintaining the same indulgent, big-brotherly tone, which he tries to hold throughout the scene*]. Not so loud, for Pete's sake! I don't mind—but I've got neighbors.

DION. Hate them! Fear thy neighbor as thyself! That's the leaden rule for the safe and sane. [*Then advancing to the table with a sort of deadly calm.*] Listen! One day when I was four years old, a boy sneaked up behind when I was drawing a picture in the sand he couldn't draw and hit me on the head with a stick and kicked out my picture and laughed when I cried. It wasn't what he'd done that made me cry, but him! I had loved and trusted him and suddenly the good God was disproved in his person and the evil and injustice of Man was born! Everyone called me cry-baby, so I became silent for life and designed a mask of the Bad Boy Pan in which to live and rebel against that other boy's God and protect myself from His cruelty. And that other boy, secretly he felt ashamed but he couldn't acknowledge it; so from that day he instinctively developed into the good boy, the good friend, the good man, William Brown!

BROWN [*shamefacedly*]. I remember now. It was a dirty trick. [*Then with a trace of resentment.*] Sit down. You know where the booze is. Have a drink, if you like. But I guess you've had enough already.

DION [*looks at him fixedly for a moment—then strangely*]. Thanks be to Brown for reminding me. I must drink. [*He goes and gets a bottle of whisky and a glass.*]

BROWN [*with a good-humored shrug*]. All right. It's your funeral.

DION [*returning and pouring out a big drink in the tumbler*]. And William Brown's! When I die, he goes to hell! Skoal! [*He drinks and stares malevolently. In spite of himself,* BROWN *is uneasy. A pause.*]

BROWN [*with forced casualness*]. You've been on this toot for a week now.

DION [*tauntingly*]. I've been celebrating the acceptance of *my* design for the cathedral.

BROWN [*humorously*]. You certainly helped me a lot on it.

DION [*with a harsh laugh*]. O perfect Brown! Never mind! I'll make him look in my mirror yet—and drown in it! [*He pours out another big drink.*]

BROWN [*rather tauntingly*]. Go easy. I don't want your corpse on my hands.

DION. But I do. [*He drinks.*] Brown will still need me—to reassure him he's alive! I've loved, lusted, won and lost, sang and wept! I've been life's lover! I've fulfilled her will and if she's through with me now it's only because I was too weak to dominate her in turn. It isn't enough to be her creature, you've got to create her or she requests you to destroy yourself.

BROWN [*good-naturedly*]. Nonsense. Go home and get some sleep.

DION [*as if he hadn't heard—bitingly*]. But to be neither creature nor creator! To exit only in her indifference! To be unloved by life! [BROWN *stirs uneasily.*] To be merely a successful freak, the result of some snide neutralizing of life forces—a spineless cactus—a wild boar of the mountains altered into a packer's hog eating to become food—a Don Juan inspired to romance by a monkey's glands—and to have Life not even think you funny enough to see!

BROWN [*stung—angrily*]. Bosh!

DION. Consider Mr. Brown. His parents bore him on earth as if they were thereby entering him in a baby parade with prizes for the fattest—and he's still being wheeled along in the procession, too fat now to learn to walk, let alone to dance or run, and he'll never live until his liberated dust quickens into earth!

BROWN [*gruffly*]. Rave on! [*Then with forced good-nature.*] Well, Dion, at any rate, I'm satisfied.

DION [*quickly and malevolently*]. No! Brown isn't satisfied! He's piled on layers of protective fat, but vaguely, deeply he feels at his heart the gnawing of a doubt! And I'm interested in that germ which wriggles like a question mark of insecurity in his blood, because it's part of the creative life Brown's stolen from me!

BROWN [*forcing a sour grin*]. Steal germs? I thought you caught them.

DION [*as if he hadn't heard*]. It's mine—and I'm interested in seeing it thrive and breed and become multitudes and eat until Brown is consumed!

BROWN [*cannot restrain a shudder*]. Sometimes when you're drunk, you're positively evil, do you know it?

DION [*somberly*]. When Pan was forbidden the light and warmth of the sun he grew sensitive and self-conscious and proud and revengeful—and became Prince of Darkness.

BROWN [*jocularly*]. You don't fit the rôle of Pan, Dion. It sounds to me like Bacchus, alias the Demon Rum, doing the talking. [DION *recovers from his spasm with a start and stares at* BROWN *with terrible hatred. There is a pause. In spite of himself,* BROWN *squirms and adopts a placating tone.*] Go home. Be a good scout. It's all well enough celebrating our design being accepted but—

DION [*in a steely voice*]. I've been the brains! I've been the design! I've designed even his success—drunk and laughing at him—laughing at his career! Not proud! Sick! Sick of myself and him! Designing and getting drunk! Saving my woman and children! [*He laughs.*] Ha! And this cathedral is my masterpiece! It will make Brown the most eminent architect in this state of God's Country. I put a lot into it—what was left of my life! It's one vivid blasphemy from sidewalk to the tips of its spires!—but so concealed that the fools will never know. They'll kneel and worship the ironic Silenus who tells them the best good is never to be born! [*He laughs triumphantly.*] Well, blasphemy is faith, isn't it? In self-preservation the devil must believe! But Mr. Brown, the Great Brown, has no faith! He couldn't design a cathedral without it looking like the First Supernatural Bank! He only believes in the immortality of the moral belly! [*He laughs wildly—then sinks down in his chair, gasping, his hands pressed to his heart. Then suddenly becomes deadly calm and pronounces like a cruel malignant condemnation.*] From now on, Brown will never design anything. He will devote his life to renovating the house of my Cybel into a home for my Margaret!

BROWN [*springing to his feet, his face convulsed with strange agony*]. I've stood enough! How dare you . . . !

DION [*his voice like a probe*]. Why has no woman ever loved him? Why has he always been the Big Brother, the Friend? Isn't their trust—a contempt?

BROWN. You lie!

DION. Why has he never been able to love—since my Margaret? Why has he never married? Why has he tried to steal Cybel, as he once tried to steal Margaret? Isn't it out of revenge—and envy?

BROWN [*violently*]. Rot! I wanted Cybel, and I bought her!

DION. Brown bought her for me! She has loved me more than he will ever know!

BROWN. You lie! [*Then furiously.*] I'll throw her back on the street!

DION. To me! To her fellow creature! Why hasn't Brown had children—he who loves children—he who loves *my* children—he who envies me *my* children?

BROWN [*brokenly*]. I'm not ashamed to envy you them!

DION. They like Brown, too—as a friend—as an equal—as Margaret has always liked him—

BROWN [*brokenly*]. And as I've liked her!

DION. How many million times Brown has thought how much better for her it would have been if she'd chosen him instead!

BROWN [*torturedly*]. You lie! [*Then with sudden frenzied defiance.*] All right! If you force me to say it, I do love Margaret! I always have loved her and you've always known I did!

DION [*with a terrible composure*]. No! That is merely the appearance, not the truth! Brown loves me! He loves me because I have always possessed the power he needed for love, because I am love!

BROWN [*frenziedly*]. You drunken bum! [*He leaps on* DION *and grabs him by the throat.*]

DION [*triumphantly, staring into his eyes*]. Ah! Now he looks into the mirror! Now he sees his face! [BROWN *lets go of him and staggers back to his chair, pale and trembling.*]

BROWN [*humbly*]. Stop, for God's sake! You're mad!

DION [*sinking in his chair, more and more weakly*]. I'm done. My heart, not Brown—[*Mockingly.*] My last will and testament! I leave Dion Anthony to William Brown—for him to love and obey—for him to become me—then my Margaret will love me—my children will love me—Mr. and Mrs. Brown and sons, happily ever after! [*Staggering to his full height and looking upward defiantly.*] Nothing more—but Man's last gesture—by which he conquers—to laugh! Ha—[*He begins, stops as if paralyzed, and drops on his knees by* BROWN'S *chair, his mask falling off, his Christian Martyr's face at the point of death.*] Forgive me, Billy. Bury me, hide me, forget me for your own happiness! May Margaret love you! May you design the Temple of Man's Soul! Blessed are the meek and the poor in spirit! [*He kisses* BROWN'S *feet—then more and more weakly and childishly.*] What was the prayer, Billy? I'm getting so sleepy. . . .

BROWN [*in a trancelike tone*]. "Our Father who art in Heaven."

DION [*drowsily*]. "Our Father." . . . [*He dies. A pause.* BROWN *remains in a stupor for a moment—then stirs himself, puts his hand on* DION'S *breast.*]

BROWN [*dully*]. He's dead—at last. [*He says this mechanically but the last two words awaken him—wonderingly.*] At last? [*Then with triumph.*] At last! [*He stares at* DION'S *real face contemptuously.*] So that's the poor weakling you really were! No wonder you hid! And I've always been afraid of you—yes, I'll confess it now, in awe of you! Paugh! [*He picks up the mask from the floor.*] No, not of you! Of this! Say what you like, it's strong if it is bad! And this is what Margaret loved, not you! Not you! This man!—this man who willed himself to me! [*Struck by an idea, he jumps to his feet.*] By God! [*He slowly starts to put the mask on. A knocking comes on the street door. He starts guiltily, laying the mask on the table. Then he picks it up again quickly, takes the dead body and carries it off left. He reappears immediately and goes to the front door as the knocking recommences—gruffly.*] Hello! Who's there?

MARGARET. It's Margaret, Billy. I'm looking for Dion.

BROWN [*uncertainly*]. Oh—all right—[*Unfastening door.*] Come in. Hello, Margaret. Hello, Boys! He's here. He's asleep. I—I was just dozing off too. [MARGARET *enters. She is wearing her mask. The* THREE SONS *are with her.*]

MARGARET [*seeing the bottle, forcing a laugh*]. Has he been celebrating?

BROWN [*with strange glibness now*]. No. I was. He wasn't. He said he'd sworn off tonight—forever—for your sake—and the kids!

MARGARET [*with amazed joy*]. Dion said that? [*Then hastily defensive.*] But of course he never does drink much. Where is he?

BROWN. Upstairs. I'll wake him. He felt bad. He took off his clothes to take a bath before he lay down. You just wait here. [*She sits in the chair where* DION *had sat and stares straight before her. The* SONS *group around her, as if for a family photo.* BROWN *hurries out left.*]

MARGARET. It's late to keep you boys up. Aren't you sleepy?

BOYS. No, Mother.

MARGARET [*proudly*]. I'm glad to have three such strong boys to protect me.

ELDEST [*boastingly*]. We'd kill anyone that touched you, wouldn't we?

NEXT. You bet! We'd make him wish he hadn't!

YOUNGEST. You bet!

MARGARET. You're Mother's brave boys!

[*She laughs fondly—then curiously.*] Do you like Mr. Brown?

ELDEST. Sure thing! He's a regular fellow.

NEXT. He's all right!

YOUNGEST. Sure thing!

MARGARET [*half to herself*]. Your father claims he steals his ideas.

ELDEST [*with a sheepish grin*]. I'll bet father said that when he was—just talking.

NEXT. Mr. Brown doesn't have to steal, does he?

YOUNGEST. I should say not! He's awful rich.

MARGARET. Do you love your father?

ELDEST [*scuffling—embarrassed*]. Why—of course—

NEXT [*ditto*]. Sure thing!

YOUNGEST. Sure I do.

MARGARET [*with a sigh*]. I think you'd better start on before—right now—before your father comes—He'll be very sick and nervous and he'll want to be quiet. So run along!

BOYS. All right. [*They file out and close the front door as* BROWN, *dressed in* DION'S *clothes and wearing his mask, appears at left.*]

MARGARET [*taking off her mask, gladly*]. Dion! [*She stares wonderingly at him and he at her; goes to him and puts an arm around him.*] Poor dear, do you feel sick? [*He nods.*] But you look—[*Squeezing his arms.*]—why, you actually feel stronger and better already! Is it true what Billy told me—about your swearing off forever? [*He nods. She exclaims intensely.*] Oh, if you'll only—and get well —we can still be so happy! Give Mother a kiss. [*They kiss. A shudder passes through both of them. She breaks away laughing with aroused desire.*] Why, Dion! Aren't you ashamed? You haven't kissed me like that in ages!

BROWN [*his voice imitating* DION'S *and muffled by the mask*]. I've wanted to, Margaret!

MARGARET [*gayly and coquettishly now*]. Were you afraid I'd spurn you? Why, Dion, something has happened. It's like a miracle! Even your voice is changed! It actually sounds younger, do you know it? [*Then, solicitously.*] But you must be worn out. Let's go home. [*With an impulsive movement she flings her arms wide open, throwing her mask away from her as if suddenly no longer needing it.*] Oh, I'm beginning to feel so happy, Dion—so happy!

BROWN [*stifledly*]. Let's go home. [*She puts her arm around him. They walk to the door.*]

CURTAIN

ACT THREE

SCENE ONE

SCENE. *The drafting room and private office of* BROWN *are both shown. The former is at left, the latter at right of a dividing wall at center. The arrangement of furniture in each room is the same as in previous scenes. It is ten in the morning of a day about a month later. The backdrop for both rooms is of plain wall with a few tacked-up designs and blueprints painted on it.*

TWO DRAFTSMEN, *a middle-aged and a young man, both stoop-shouldered, are sitting on stools behind what was formerly* DION'S *table. They are tracing plans. They talk as they work.*

OLDER DRAFTSMAN. W. B. is late again.

YOUNGER DRAFTSMAN. Wonder what's got into him the last month? [*A pause. They work silently.*]

OLDER DRAFTSMAN. Yes, ever since he fired Dion. . . .

YOUNGER DRAFTSMAN. Funny his firing him all of a sudden like that. [*A pause. They work.*]

OLDER DRAFTSMAN. I haven't seen Dion around town since then. Have you?

YOUNGER DRAFTSMAN. No, not since Brown told us he'd canned him. I suppose he's off drowning his sorrow!

OLDER DRAFTSMAN. I heard someone had seen him at home and he was sober and looking fine. [*A pause. They work.*]

YOUNGER DRAFTSMAN. What got into Brown? They say he fired all his old servants that same day and only uses his house to sleep in.

OLDER DRAFTSMAN [*with a sneer*]. Artistic temperament, maybe—the real name of which is swelled head! [*There is a noise of footsteps from the hall. Warningly.*] Ssstt! [*They bend over their table.* MARGARET *enters. She does not need to wear a mask now. Her face has regained the self-confident spirit of its youth, her eyes shine with happiness.*]

MARGARET [*heartily*]. Good morning! What a lovely day!

BOTH [*perfunctorily*]. Good morning, Mrs. Anthony.

MARGARET [*looking around*]. You've been changing around in here, haven't you? Where is Dion? [*They stare at her.*] I forgot to tell him something important this morning and our phone's out of order. So if you'll tell him I'm here—[*They don't move. A pause.* MARGARET *says stiffly:*] Oh, I realize Mr. Brown has given strict orders Dion is not to be disturbed, but surely. . . . [*Sharply.*] Where is my husband, please?

OLDER DRAFTSMAN. We don't know.

MARGARET. You don't know?

YOUNGER DRAFTSMAN. We haven't seen him.

MARGARET. Why, he left home at eight-thirty!

OLDER DRAFTSMAN. To come here?

YOUNGER DRAFTSMAN. This morning?

MARGARET [*provoked*]. Why, of course, to come here—as he does every day! [*They stare at her. A pause.*]

OLDER DRAFTSMAN [*evasively*]. We haven't seen him.

MARGARET [*with asperity*]. Where is Mr. Brown?

YOUNGER DRAFTSMAN [*at a noise of footsteps from the hall—sulkily*]. Coming now. [BROWN *enters. He is now wearing a mask which is an exact likeness of his face as it was in the last scene—the self-assured success. When he sees* MARGARET, *he starts back apprehensively.*]

BROWN [*immediately controlling himself—breezily*]. Hello, Margaret! This is a pleasant surprise! [*He holds out his hand.*]

MARGARET [*hardly taking it—reservedly*]. Good morning.

BROWN [*turning quickly to the* DRAFTSMEN]. I hope you explained to Mrs. Anthony how busy Dion . . .

MARGARET [*interrupting him—stiffly*]. I certainly can't understand—

BROWN [*hastily*]. I'll explain. Come in here and be comfortable. [*He throws open the door and ushers her into his private office.*]

OLDER DRAFTSMAN. Dion must be putting over some bluff on her.

YOUNGER DRAFTSMAN. Pretending he's still here—and Brown's helping him. . . .

OLDER DRAFTSMAN. But why should Brown, after he . . . ?

YOUNGER DRAFTSMAN. Well, I suppose—Search me. [*They work.*]

BROWN. Have a chair, Margaret. [*She sits on the chair stiffly. He sits behind the desk.*]

MARGARET [*coldly*]. I'd like some explanation. . . .

BROWN [*coaxingly*]. Now, don't get angry, Margaret! Dion is hard at work on his design for the new State Capitol, and I don't want him disturbed, not even by you! So be a good sport! It's for his own good, remember! I asked him to explain to you.

MARGARET [*relenting*]. He told me you'd agreed to ask me and the boys not to come here—but then, we hardly ever did.

BROWN. But you might! [*Then with confidential friendliness.*] This is for his sake, Margaret. I know Dion. He's got to be able to work without distractions. He's not the ordinary man, you appreciate that. And this design means his whole future! He's to get full credit for it, and as soon as it's accepted, I take him into partnership. It's all agreed. And after that I'm going to take a long vacation—go to Europe for a couple of years—and leave everything here in Dion's hands! Hasn't he told you all this?

MARGARET [*jubilant now*]. Yes—but I could hardly believe . . . [*Proudly.*] I'm sure he can do it. He's been like a new man lately, so full of ambition and energy! It's made me so happy! [*She stops in confusion.*]

BROWN [*deeply moved, takes her hand impulsively*]. And it has made me happy, too!

MARGARET [*confused—with an amused laugh*]. Why, Billy Brown! For a moment, I thought it was Dion, your voice sounded so much . . . !

BROWN [*with sudden desperation*]. Margaret, I've got to tell you! I can't go on like this any longer! I've got to confess . . . ! There's something . . . !

MARGARET [*alarmed*]. Not—not about Dion?

BROWN [*harshly*]. To hell with Dion! To hell with Billy Brown! [*He tears off his *mask and reveals a suffering face that is ravaged and haggard, his own face tortured and distorted by the demon of* DION'S *mask.*] Think of me! I love you, Margaret! Leave him! I've always loved you! Come away with me! I'll sell out here! We'll go abroad and be happy!

MARGARET [*amazed*]. Billy Brown, do you realize what you're saying? [*With a shudder.*] Are you crazy? Your face—is terrible. You're sick! Shall I phone for a doctor?

BROWN [*turning away slowly and putting on his mask—dully*]. No. I've been on the verge—of a breakdown—for some time. I get spells. . . . I'm better now. [*He turns back to her.*] Forgive me! Forget what I said! But, for all our sakes, don't come here again.

MARGARET [*coldly*]. After this—I assure you. . . ! [*Then looking at him with pained incredulity.*] Why, Billy—I simply won't believe—after all these years . . . !

BROWN. It will never happen again. Good-by.

MARGARET. Good-by. [*Then, wishing to leave on a pleasant change of subject—forcing a smile.*] Don't work Dion to death! He's never home for dinner any more. [*She goes out past the* DRAFTSMEN *and off right, rear.* BROWN *sits down at his desk, taking off the mask again. He stares at it with bitter, cynical amusement.*]

BROWN. You're dead, William Brown, dead beyond hope of resurrection! It's the Dion you buried in your garden who killed you, not you him! It's Margaret's husband who . . . [*He laughs harshly.*] Paradise by proxy! Love by mistaken identity! God! [*This is almost a prayer—then fiercely defiant.*] But it *is* paradise! I *do* love! [*As he is speaking, a well-dressed, important, stout man enters the drafting room. He is carrying a rolled-up plan in his hand. He nods condescendingly and goes directly to* BROWN'S *door, on which he raps sharply, and, without waiting for an answer, turns the knob.* BROWN *has just time to turn his head and get his mask on.*]

MAN [*briskly*]. Ah, good morning! I came right in. Hope I didn't disturb . . . ?

BROWN [*the successful architect now—urbanely*]. Not at all, sir. How are you? [*They shake hands.*] Sit down. Have a cigar. And now what can I do for you this morning?

MAN [*unrolling his plan*]. It's your plan. My wife and I have been going over it again. We like it—and we don't—and when a man plans to lay out half a million, why, he wants everything exactly right, eh? [BROWN *nods.*] It's too cold, too spare, too like a tomb, if you'll pardon me, for a liveable home. Can't you liven it up, put in some decorations, make it fancier and warmer—you know what I mean. [*Looks at him a bit doubtfully.*] People tell me you had an assistant, Anthony, who was a real shark on these details but that you've fired him—

BROWN [*suavely*]. Gossip! He's still with me but, for reasons of his own, doesn't wish it known. Yes, I trained him and he's very ingenious. I'll turn this right over to him and instruct him to carry out your wishes. . . .

CURTAIN

SCENE TWO

SCENE. *The same as Act Two, Scene Three—the library of* BROWN'S *home about eight the same night. He can be heard feeling his way in through the dark. He switches on the reading lamp on the table. Directly under it on a sort of stand is the mask of* DION, *its empty eyes staring front.*

BROWN *takes off his own mask and lays it on the table before* DION'S. *He flings himself down in the chair and stares without moving into the eyes of* DION'S *mask. Finally, he begins to talk to it in a bitter, mocking tone.*

BROWN. Listen! Today was a narrow escape—for us! We can't avoid discovery much longer. We must get our plot to working! We've already made William Brown's will, leaving you his money and business. We must hustle off to Europe now—and murder him there! [*A bit tauntingly.*] Then you—the I in you—*I* will live with Margaret happily ever after. [*More tauntingly.*] She will have children by me! [*He seems to hear some mocking denial from the mask. He bends toward it.*] What? [*Then with a sneer.*] Anyway, that doesn't matter! Your children already love me more than they ever loved you! And Margaret loves me more! You think you've won, do you—that I've got to vanish into you in order to live? Not yet, my friend! Never! Wait! Gradually Margaret will love what is beneath—me! Little by little I'll teach her to know me, and then finally I'll reveal myself to her, and confess that I stole your place out of love for her, and she'll understand and forgive and love me! And you'll be forgotten! Ha! [*Again he bends down to the mask as if listening—torturedly.*] What's that? She'll never believe? She'll never see? She'll never understand? You lie, devil! [*He reaches out his hands as if to take the mask by the throat, then shrinks back with a shudder of hopeless despair.*] God have mercy! Let me believe! Blessed are the merciful! Let me obtain mercy! [*He waits, his face upturned—pleadingly.*] Not yet? [*Despairingly.*] Never? [*A pause. Then, in a sudden panic of dread, he reaches out for the mask of* DION *like a dope fiend after a drug. As soon as he holds it, he seems to gain strength and is able to force a sad laugh.*] Now I am drinking your strength, Dion—strength to love in this world and die and sleep and become fertile earth, as you are becoming now in my garden—your weakness the strength of my flowers, your failure as an artist painting their petals with life! [*Then, with bravado.*] Come with me while Margaret's bridegroom dresses in your clothes, Mr. Anthony! I need the devil when I'm in the dark! [*He goes off left, but can be heard talking.*] Your clothes begin to fit me better than my own! Hurry, Brother! It's time we were home. Our wife is waiting! [*He reappears, having changed his coat and trousers.*] Come with me and tell her again I love her! Come and hear her tell me how she loves you! [*He suddenly cannot help kissing the mask.*] I love you because she loves you! My kisses on your lips are for her! [*He puts the mask over his face and stands for a moment, seeming to grow tall and proud—then with a laugh of bold self-assurance.*] Out by the back way! I mustn't forget I'm a desperate criminal, pursued by God, and by myself! [*He goes out right, laughing with amused satisfaction.*]

CURTAIN

SCENE THREE

SCENE. *Is the same as Scene One of Act One—the sitting-room of* MARGARET'S *home. It is about half an hour after the last scene.* MARGARET *sits on the sofa, waiting with the anxious, impatient expectancy of one deeply in love. She is dressed with a careful, subtle extra touch to attract the eye. She looks young and happy. She is trying to read a book. The front door is heard opening and closing. She leaps up and runs back to throw her arms around* BROWN *as he enters from right, rear. She kisses him passionately.*

MARGARET [*as he recoils with a sort of guilt—laughingly*]. Why, you hateful old thing, you! I really believe you were trying to avoid kissing me! Well, just for that, I'll never . . .

BROWN [*with fierce, defiant passion, kisses her again and again*]. Margaret!

MARGARET. Call me Peggy again. You used to when you really loved me. [*Softly.*] Remember the school commencement dance—you and I on the dock in the moonlight?

BROWN [*with pain*]. No. [*He takes his arms from around her.*]

MARGARET [*still holding him—with a laugh*]. Well, I like that! You old bear, you! Why not?

BROWN [*sadly*]. It was so long ago.

MARGARET [*a bit melancholy*]. You mean you don't want to be reminded that we're getting old?

BROWN. Yes. [*He kisses her gently.*] I'm tired. Let's sit down. [*They sit on the sofa, his arm about her, her head on his shoulder.*]

MARGARET [*with a happy sigh*]. I don't mind remembering—now I'm happy. It's only when I'm unhappy that it hurts—and I've been so happy lately, dear—and so grateful to you! [*He stirs uneasily. She goes on joyfully.*] Everything's changed! I'd gotten pretty resigned to—and sad and hopeless, too—and then all at once you turn right around and everything is the same as when we were first married—much better even, for I was never sure of you then. You were always so strange and aloof and alone, it seemed I was never really touching you.

But now I feel you've become quite human —like me—and I'm so happy, dear! [*She kisses him.*]

BROWN [*his voice trembling*]. Then I have made you happy—happier than ever before —no matter what happens? [*She nods.*] Then—that justifies everything! [*He forces a laugh.*]

MARGARET. Of course it does! I've always known that. But you—you wouldn't be— or you couldn't be—and I could never help you—and all the time I knew you were so lonely! I could always hear you calling to me that you were lost, but I couldn't find the path to you because I was lost, too! That's an awful way for a wife to feel! [*She laughs—joyfully.*] But now you're here! You're mine! You're my long-lost lover, and my husband, and my big boy, too!

BROWN [*with a trace of jealousy*]. Where are your other big boys tonight?

MARGARET. Out to a dance. They've all acquired girls, I'll have you know.

BROWN [*mockingly*]. Aren't you jealous?

MARGARET [*gayly*]. Of course! Terribly! But I'm diplomatic. I don't let them see. [*Changing the subject.*] Believe me, they've noticed the change in you! The eldest was saying to me today: "It's great not to have Father so nervous, any more. Why, he's a regular sport when he gets started!" And the other two said very solemnly: "You bet!" [*She laughs.*]

BROWN [*brokenly*]. I—I'm glad.

MARGARET. Dion! You're crying!

BROWN [*stung by the name, gets up—harshly*]. Nonsense! Did you ever know Dion to cry about anyone?

MARGARET [*sadly*]. You couldn't—then. You were too lonely. You had no one to cry to.

BROWN [*goes and takes a rolled-up plan from the table drawer—dully*]. I've got to do some work.

MARGARET [*disappointedly*]. What, has that old Billy Brown got you to work at home again, too?

BROWN [*ironically*]. It's for Dion's good, you know—and yours.

MARGARET [*making the best of it—cheerfully*]. All right. I won't be selfish. It really makes me proud to have you so ambitious. Let me help. [*She brings his drawing-board, which he puts on the table and pins his plan upon. She sits on sofa and picks up her book.*]

BROWN [*carefully casual*]. I hear you were in to see me today?

MARGARET. Yes, and Billy wouldn't hear of it! I was quite furious until he convinced me it was all for the best. When is he going to take you into partnership?

BROWN. Very soon now.

MARGARET. And will he really give you full charge when he goes abroad?

BROWN. Yes.

MARGARET [*practically*]. I'd pin him down if I could. Promises are all right, but—[*She hesitates.*] I don't trust him.

BROWN [*with a start, sharply*]. What makes you say that?

MARGARET. Oh, something that happened today.

BROWN. What?

MARGARET. I don't mean I blame him, but— to be frank, I think the Great God Brown, as you call him, is getting a bit queer and it's time he took a vacation. Don't you?

BROWN [*his voice a bit excited—but guardedly*]. But why? What did he do?

MARGARET [*hesitatingly*]. Well—it's really too silly—he suddenly got awfully strange. His face scared me. It was like a corpse. Then he raved on some nonsense about he'd always loved me. He went on like a perfect fool! [*She looks at* BROWN, *who is staring at her. She becomes uneasy.*] Maybe I shouldn't tell you this. He simply wasn't responsible. Then he came to himself and was all right and begged my pardon and seemed dreadfully sorry, and I felt sorry for him. [*Then with a shudder.*] But honestly, Dion, it was just too disgusting for words to hear him! [*With kind, devastating contempt.*] Poor Billy!

BROWN [*with a show of tortured derision*]. Poor Billy! Poor Billy the Goat! [*With mocking frenzy.*] I'll kill him for you! I'll serve you his heart for breakfast!

MARGARET [*jumping up—frightenedly*]. Dion!

BROWN [*waving his pencil knife with grotesque flourishes*]. I tell you I'll murder this God-damned disgusting Great God Brown who stands like a fatted calf in the way of our health and wealth and happiness!

MARGARET [*bewilderedly, not knowing how much is pretending, puts an arm about him*]. Don't, dear! You're being horrid and strange again. It makes me afraid you haven't really changed, after all.

BROWN [*unheeding*]. And then my wife can be happy! Ha! [*He laughs. She begins to cry. He controls himself—pats her head—gently.*] All right, dear. Mr. Brown is now safely in hell. Forget him!

MARGARET [*stops crying—but still worriedly*]. I should never have told you—but I never imagined you'd take it seriously. I've never thought of Billy Brown except as a friend, and lately not even that! He's just a stupid old fool!

BROWN. Ha-ha! Didn't I say he was in hell? They're torturing him! [*Then controlling himself again—exhaustedly.*] Please leave me alone now. I've got to work.

MARGARET. All right, dear. I'll go into the next room and anything you want, just call. [*She pats his face—cajolingly.*] Is it all forgotten?

BROWN. Will you be happy?

MARGARET. Yes.

BROWN. Then it's dead, I promise! [*She kisses him and goes out. He stares ahead, then shakes off his thoughts and concentrates on his work—mockingly.*] Our beautiful new Capitol calls you, Mr. Dion! To work! We'll adroitly hide old Silenus on the cupola! Let him dance over their law-making with his eternal leer! [*He bends over his work.*]

CURTAIN

ACT FOUR

SCENE ONE

SCENE. *Same as Scene One of Act Three—the drafting room and* BROWN'S *office. It is dusk of a day about a month later.*

The TWO DRAFTSMEN *are bent over their table, working.*

BROWN *at his desk, is working feverishly over a plan. He is wearing the mask of* DION. *The mask of* WILLIAM BROWN *rests on the desk beside him. As he works, he chuckles with malicious glee—finally flings down his pencil with a flourish.*

BROWN. Done! In the name of the Almighty Brown, amen, amen! Here's a wondrous fair capitol! The design would do just as well for a Home for Criminal Imbeciles! Yet to them, such is my art, it will appear to possess a pure common-sense, a fat-bellied finality, as dignified as the suspenders of an assemblyman! Only to me will that pompous façade reveal itself as the wearily ironic grin of Pan as, his ears drowsy with the crumbling hum of past and future civilizations, he half-listens to the laws passed by his fleas to enslave him! Ha-ha-ha! [*He leaps grotesquely from behind his desk and cuts a few goatish capers, laughing with lustful merriment.*] Long live Chief of Police Brown! District Attorney Brown! Alderman Brown! Assemblyman Brown! Mayor Brown! Congressman Brown! Governor Brown! Senator Brown! President Brown! [*He chants.*] Oh, how many persons in one God make up the good God Brown? Hahahaha! [*The* TWO DRAFTSMEN *in the next room have stopped work and are listening.*]

YOUNGER DRAFTSMAN. Drunk as a fool!

OLDER DRAFTSMAN. At least Dion used to have the decency to stay away from the office—

YOUNGER DRAFTSMAN. Funny how it's got hold of Brown so quick!

OLDER DRAFTSMAN. He was probably hitting it up on the Q. T. all the time.

BROWN [*has come back to his desk, laughing to himself and out of breath*]. Time to become respectable again! [*He takes off the* DION *mask and reaches out for the* WILLIAM BROWN *one—then stops, with a hand on each, staring down on the plan with fascinated loathing. His real face is now sick, ghastly, tortured, hollow-cheeked and feverish-eyed.*] Ugly! Hideous! Despicable! Why must the demon in me pander to cheapness—then punish me with self-loathing and life-hatred? Why am I not strong enough to perish—or blind enough to be content? [*To heaven, bitterly but pleadingly.*] Give me the strength to destroy this!—and myself!—and him!—and I will believe in Thee! [*While he has been speaking there has been a noise from the stairs. The* TWO DRAFTSMEN *have bent over their work.* MARGARET *enters, closing the door behind her. At this sound,* BROWN *starts. He immediately senses who it is—with alarm.*] Margaret! [*He grabs up both masks and goes into room off right.*]

MARGARET [*she looks healthy and happy, but her face wears a worried, solicitous expression —pleasantly to the staring* DRAFTSMEN]. Good morning. Oh, you needn't look worried, it's Mr. Brown I want to see, not my husband.

YOUNGER DRAFTSMAN [*hesitatingly*]. He's locked himself in—but maybe if you'll knock—

MARGARET [*knocks—somewhat embarrassedly*]. Mr. Brown! [BROWN *enters his office, wearing the* WILLIAM BROWN *mask. He comes quickly to the other door and unlocks it.*]

BROWN [*with a hectic cordiality*]. Come on, Margaret! Enter! This is delightful! Sit down! What can I do for you?

MARGARET [*taken aback—a bit stiffly*]. Nothing much.

BROWN. Something about Dion, of course. Well, your darling pet is all right—never better!

MARGARET [*coldly*]. That's a matter of opinion. I think you're working him to death.

BROWN. Oh, no, not him. It's Brown who is to die. We've agreed on that.

MARGARET [*giving him a queer look*]. I'm serious.

BROWN. So am I. Deadly serious! Hahaha!

MARGARET [*checking her indignation*]. That's what I came to see you about. Really, Dion has acted so hectic and on edge lately I'm sure he's on the verge of a breakdown.

BROWN. Well, it certainly isn't drink. He hasn't had a drop. He doesn't need it! Haha! And I haven't either, although the gossips are beginning to say I'm soused all the time! It's because I've started to laugh! Hahaha! They can't believe in joy in this town except by the bottle! What funny little people! Hahaha! When you're the Great God Brown, eh, Margaret? Hahaha!

MARGARET [*getting up—uneasily*]. I'm afraid I—

BROWN. Don't be afraid, my dear! I won't make love to you again! Honor bright! I'm too near the grave for such folly! But it must have been funny for you when you came here the last time—watching a disgusting old fool like me, eh?—too funny for words! Hahaha! [*Then with a sudden movement he flourishes the design before her.*] Look! We've finished it! Dion has finished it! His fame is made!

MARGARET [*tartly*]. Really, Billy, I believe you are drunk!

BROWN. Nobody kisses me—so you can all believe the worst! Hahaha!

MARGARET [*chillingly*]. Then if Dion is through, why can't I see him?

BROWN [*crazily*]. See Dion? See Dion? Well, why not? It's an age of miracles. The streets are full of Lazaruses. Pray! I mean—wait a moment, if you please.

[BROWN *disappears into the room off right. A moment later he reappears in the mask of* DION. *He holds out his arms and* MARGARET *rushes into them. They kiss passionately. Finally he sits with her on the lounge.*]

MARGARET. So you've finished it!

BROWN. Yes. The Committee is coming to see it soon. I've made all the changes they'll like, the fools!

MARGARET [*lovingly*]. And can we go on that second honeymoon, right away now?

BROWN. In a week or so, I hope—as soon as I've gotten Brown off to Europe.

MARGARET. Tell me—isn't he drinking hard?

BROWN [*laughing as* BROWN *did*]. Haha! Soused to the ears all the time! Soused on life! He can't stand it! It's burning his insides out!

MARGARET [*alarmed*]. Dear! I'm worried about you. You sound as crazy as he did—when you laugh! You must rest!

BROWN [*controlling himself*]. I'll rest in peace—when he's gone!

MARGARET [*with a queer look*]. Why, Dion, that isn't your suit. It's just like—

BROWN. It's his! We're getting to be like twins. I'm inheriting his clothes already! [*Then calming himself as he sees how frightened she is.*] Don't be worried, dear. I'm just a trifle elated, now the job's done. I guess I'm a bit soused on life, too! [*The*

COMMITTEE, *three important-looking, average personages, come into the drafting room.*]

MARGARET [*forcing a smile*]. Well, don't let it burn *your* insides out!

BROWN. No danger! Mine were tempered in hell! Hahaha!

MARGARET [*kissing him, coaxingly*]. Come home, dear—please!

OLDER DRAFTSMAN [*knocks on the door*]. The Committee is here, Mr. Brown.

BROWN [*hurriedly to* MARGARET]. You receive them. Hand them the design. I'll get Brown. [*He raises his voice.*] Come right in, gentlemen. [*He goes off right, as the* COMMITTEE *enter the office. When they see* MARGARET, *they stop in surprise.*]

MARGARET [*embarrassedly*]. Good afternoon. Mr. Brown will be right with you. [*They bow.* MARGARET *holds out the design to them.*] This is my husband's design. He finished it today.

COMMITTEE. Ah! [*They crowd around to look at it—with enthusiasm.*] Perfect! Splendid! Couldn't be better! Exactly what we suggested!

MARGARET [*joyfully*]. Then you accept it? Mr. Anthony will be so pleased!

MEMBER. Mr. Anthony?

ANOTHER. Is he working here again?

THIRD. Did I understand you to say this was your husband's design?

MARGARET [*excitedly*]. Yes! Entirely his! He's worked like a dog—[*Appalled.*] You don't mean to say—Mr. Brown never told you? [*They shake their heads in solemn surprise.*] Oh, the contemptible cad! I hate him!

BROWN [*appearing at right—mockingly*]. Hate me, Margaret? Hate Brown? How superfluous! [*Oratorically.*] Gentlemen, I have been keeping a secret from you in order that you might be the more impressed when I revealed it. That design is entirely the inspiration of Mr. Dion Anthony's genius. I had nothing to do with it.

MARGARET [*contritely*]. Oh, Billy! I'm sorry! Forgive me!

BROWN [*ignoring her, takes the plan from the* COMMITTEE *and begins unpinning it from the board—mockingly*]. I can see by your faces you have approved this. You are delighted, aren't you? And why not, my dear sirs? Look at it, and look at you! Hahaha! It'll immortalize you, my good men! You'll be as death-defying a joke as any in Joe Miller! [*Then with a sudden complete change of tone—angrily.*] You damn fools! Can't you see this is an insult—a terrible, blasphemous insult!—that this embittered failure Anthony is hurling in the teeth of our success—an insult to you, to me, to you, Margaret—and to Almighty God! [*In a frenzy of fury.*] And if you are weak and cowardly enough to stand for it, I'm not! [*He tears the plan into four pieces. The* COMMITTEE *stands aghast.* MARGARET *runs forward.*]

MARGARET [*in a scream*]. You coward! Dion! Dion! [*She picks up the plan and hugs it to her bosom.*]

BROWN [*with a sudden goatish caper*]. I'll tell him you're here. [*He disappears, but reappears almost immediately in the mask of* DION. *He is imposing a terrible discipline on himself to avoid dancing and laughing. He speaks suavely.*] Everything is all right—all for the best—you mustn't get excited! A little paste, Margaret! A little paste, gentlemen! And all will be well! Life is imperfect, Brothers! Men have their faults, Sister! But with a few drops of glue much may be done! A little dab of pasty resignation here and there—and even broken hearts may be repaired to do yeoman service! [*He has edged toward the door. They are all staring at him with petrified bewilderment. He puts his finger to his lips.*] Ssssh! This is Daddy's bedtime secret for today: Man is born broken. He lives by mending. The grace of God is glue! [*With a quick prancing movement, he has opened the door, gone through, and closed it after him silently, shaking with suppressed laughter. He springs lightly to the side of the petrified* DRAFTSMEN*—in a whisper.*] They will find him in the little room. Mr. William Brown is dead! [*With light leaps he vanishes, his head thrown back, shaking with silent laughter. The sound of his feet leaping down the stairs, five at a time, can be heard. Then a pause of silence. The people in the two rooms stare. The* YOUNGER DRAFTSMAN *is the first to recover.*]

YOUNGER DRAFTSMAN [*rushing into the next

room, shouts in terrified tones]. Mr. Brown is dead!

COMMITTEE. He murdered him! [*They all run into the little room off right.* MARGARET *remains, stunned with horror. They return in a moment, carrying the mask of* WILLIAM BROWN, *two on each side, as if they were carrying a body by the legs and shoulders. They solemnly lay him down on the couch and stand looking down at him.*]

FIRST COMMITTEEMAN [*with a frightened awe*]. I can't believe he's gone.

SECOND COMMITTEEMAN [*in same tone*]. I can almost hear him talking. [*As if impelled, he clears his throat and addresses the mask importantly.*] Mr. Brown—[*Then stops short.*]

THIRD COMMITTEEMAN [*shrinking back*]. No. Dead, all right! [*Then suddenly, hysterically angry and terrified.*] We must take steps at once to run Anthony to earth!

MARGARET [*with a heart-broken cry*]. Dion's innocent!

YOUNGER DRAFTSMAN. I'll phone for the police, sir! [*He rushes to the phone.*]

CURTAIN

SCENE TWO

SCENE. *The same as Scene Two of Act Three —the library of* WILLIAM BROWN'S *home. The mask of* DION *stands on the table beneath the light, facing front.*

On his knees beside the table, facing front, stripped naked except for a white cloth around his loins, is BROWN. *The clothes he has torn off in his agony are scattered on the floor. His eyes, his arms, his whole body strain upward, his muscles writhe with his lips as they pray silently in their agonized supplication. Finally a voice seems torn out of him.*

BROWN. Mercy, Compassionate Savior of Man! Out of my depths I cry to you! Mercy on thy poor clod, thy clot of unhallowed earth, thy clay, the Great God Brown! Mercy, Savior! [*He seems to wait for an answer—then leaping to his feet he puts out one hand to touch the mask like a frightened child reaching out for its nurse's hand—then with immediate mocking despair.*] Bah! I am sorry, little children, but your kingdom is empty. God has become disgusted and moved away to some far ecstatic star where life is a dancing flame! We must die without him. [*Then—addressing the mask—harshly.*] Together, my friend! You, too! Let Margaret suffer! Let the whole world suffer as I am suffering! [*There is a sound of a door being pushed violently open, padding feet in slippers, and* CYBEL, *wearing her mask, runs into the room. She stops short on seeing* BROWN *and the mask, and stares from one to the other for a second in confusion. She is dressed in a black kimono robe and wears slippers over her bare feet. Her yellow hair hangs down in a great mane over her shoulders. She has grown stouter, has more of the deep objective calm of an idol.*]

BROWN [*staring at her—fascinated—with great peace as if her presence comforted him*]. Cybel! I was coming to you! How did you know?

CYBEL [*takes off her mask and looks from* BROWN *to the* DION *mask, now with a great understanding*]. So that's why you never came to me again! You are Dion Brown!

BROWN [*bitterly*]. I am the remains of William Brown! [*He points to the mask of* DION.] I am his murderer and his murdered!

CYBEL [*with a laugh of exasperated pity*]. Oh, why can't you ever learn to leave yourselves alone and leave me alone!

BROWN [*boyishly and naïvely*]. I am Billy.

CYBEL [*immediately, with a motherly solicitude*]. Then run, Billy, run! They are hunting for someone! They came to my place, hunting for a murderer, Dion! They must find a victim! They've got to quiet their fears, to cast out their devils, or they'll never sleep soundly again! They've got to absolve themselves by finding a guilty one! They've got to kill someone now, to live! You're naked! You must be Satan! Run, Billy, run! They'll come here! I ran here to warn—someone! So run away if you want to live!

BROWN [*like a sulky child*]. I'm too tired. I don't want to.

CYBEL [*with motherly calm*]. All right, you needn't, Billy. Don't sulk. [*As a noise comes from outside.*] Anyway, it's too late. I hear them in the garden now.

BROWN [*listening, puts out his hand and takes the mask of* DION—*as he gains strength, mockingly*]. Thanks for this one last favor, Dion! Listen! Your avengers! Standing on your grave in the garden! Hahaha! [*He puts on the mask and springs to the left and makes a gesture as if flinging French windows open. Gayly mocking.*] Welcome, dumb worshippers! I am your great God Brown! I have been advised to run from you but it is my almighty whim to dance into escape over your prostrate souls! [*Shouts from the garden and a volley of shots.* BROWN *staggers back and falls on the floor by the couch, mortally wounded.*]

CYBEL [*runs to his side, lifts him on to the couch and takes off the mask of* DION]. You can't take this to bed with you. You've got to go to sleep alone. [*She places the mask of* DION *back on its stand under the light and puts on her own, just as, after a banging of doors, crashing of glass, trampling of feet, a Squad of Police with drawn revolvers, led by a grizzly, brutal-faced* CAPTAIN, *run into the room. They are followed by* MARGARET, *still distractedly clutching the pieces of the plan to her breast.*]

CAPTAIN [*pointing to the mask of* DION—*triumphantly*]. Got him! He's dead!

MARGARET [*throws herself on her knees, takes the mask and kisses it—heart-brokenly*]. Dion! Dion! [*Her face hidden in her arms, the mask in her hands above her bowed head, she remains, sobbing with deep, silent grief.*]

CAPTAIN [*noticing* CYBEL *and* BROWN—*startled*]. Hey! Look at this! What're you doin' here? Who's he?

CYBEL. You ought to know. You croaked him!

CAPTAIN [*with a defensive snarl—hastily*]. It was Anthony! I saw his mug! This feller's an accomplice, I bet yuh! Serves him right! Who is he? Friend o' yours! Crook! What's his name? Tell me or I'll fix yuh!

CYBEL. Billy.

CAPTAIN. Billy what?

CYBEL. I don't know. He's dying. [*Then suddenly.*] Leave me alone with him and maybe I'll get him to squeal it.

CAPTAIN. Yuh better! I got to have a clean report. I'll give yuh a couple o' minutes. [*He motions to the Policemen, who follow him off left.* CYBEL *takes off her mask and sits down by* BROWN'S *head. He makes an effort to raise himself toward her and she helps him, throwing her kimono over his bare body, drawing his head on to her shoulder.*]

BROWN [*snuggling against her—gratefully*]. The earth is warm.

CYBEL [*soothingly, looking before her like an idol*]. Ssshh! Go to sleep, Billy.

BROWN. Yes, Mother. [*Then explainingly.*] It was dark and I couldn't see where I was going and they all picked on me.

CYBEL. I know. You're tired.

BROWN. And when I wake up . . . ?

CYBEL. The sun will be rising again.

BROWN. To judge the living and the dead! [*Frightenedly.*] I don't want justice. I want love.

CYBEL. There is only love.

BROWN. Thank you, Mother. [*Then feebly.*] I'm getting sleepy. What's the prayer you taught me—Our Father—?

CYBEL [*with calm exultance*]. Our Father Who Art!

BROWN [*taking her tone—exultantly*]. Who art! Who art! [*Suddenly—with ecstasy.*] I know! I have found Him! I hear Him speak! "Blessed are they that weep, for they shall laugh!" Only he that has wept can laugh! The laughter of Heaven sows earth with a rain of tears, and out of Earth's transfigured birth-pain the laughter of Man returns to bless and play again in innumerable dancing gales of flame upon the knees of God! [*He dies.*]

CYBEL [*gets up and fixes his body on the couch. She bends down and kisses him gently—she straightens up and looks into space—with a profound pain*]. Always spring comes again bearing life! Always again! Always, always forever again!—Spring again!—life again!—summer and fall and death and peace again!—[*With agonized sorrow.*]—but always, always, love and conception and birth and pain again—spring bearing the intolerable chalice of life again!—[*Then with agonized exultance.*]—bearing the glorious, blazing crown of life again! [*She stands like an idol of Earth, her eyes staring out over the world.*]

MARGARET [*lifting her head adoringly to the mask—triumphant tenderness mingled with her grief*]. My lover! My husband! My boy! [*She kisses the mask.*] Good-by. Thank you for happiness! And you're not dead, sweetheart! You can never die till my heart dies! You will live forever! You will sleep under my heart! I will feel you stirring in your sleep, forever under my heart! [*She kisses the mask again. There is a pause.*]

CAPTAIN [*comes just into sight at left and speaks front without looking at them—gruffly*]. Well, what's his name?

CYBEL. Man!

CAPTAIN [*taking a grimy notebook and an inch-long pencil from his pocket*]. How d'yuh spell it?

CURTAIN

EPILOGUE

SCENE. *Four years later.*

The same spot on the same dock as in Prologue on another moonlight night in June. The sound of the waves and of distant dance music.

MARGARET *and her* THREE SONS *appear from the right. The eldest is now eighteen. All are dressed in the height of correct Prep-school elegance. They are all tall, athletic, strong and handsome-looking. They loom up around the slight figure of their mother like protecting giants, giving her a strange aspect of lonely, detached, small femininity. She wears her mask of the proud, indulgent Mother. She has grown appreciably older. Her hair is now a beautiful gray. There is about her manner and voice the sad but contented feeling of one who knows her life-purpose well accomplished but is at the same time a bit empty and comfortless with the finality of it. She is wrapped in a gray cloak.*

ELDEST. Doesn't Bee look beautiful tonight, Mother?

NEXT. Don't you think Mabel's the best dancer in there, Mother?

YOUNGEST. Aw, Alice has them both beat, hasn't she, Mother?

MARGARET [*with a sad little laugh*]. Each of you is right. [*Then, with strange finality.*] Good-by, boys.

BOYS [*surprised*]. Good-by.

MARGARET. It was here on a night just like this your father first—proposed to me. Did you ever know that?

BOYS [*embarrassedly*]. No.

MARGARET [*yearningly*]. But the nights now are so much colder than they used to be. Think of it, I went in moonlight-bathing in June when I was a girl. It was so warm and beautiful in those days. I remember the Junes when I was carrying you boys—[*A pause. They fidget uneasily. She asks pleadingly.*] Promise me faithfully never to forget your father!

BOYS [*uncomfortably*]. Yes, Mother.

MARGARET [*forcing a joking tone*]. But you mustn't waste June on an old woman like me! Go in and dance. [*As they hesitate dutifully.*] Go on. I really want to be alone—with my Junes.

BOYS [*unable to conceal their eagerness*]. Yes, Mother. [*They go away.*]

MARGARET [*slowly removes her mask, laying it on the bench, and stares up at the moon with a wistful, resigned sweetness*]. So long ago! And yet I'm still the same Margaret. It's only our lives that grow old. We *are* where centuries only count as seconds and after a thousand lives our eyes begin to open—[*She looks around her with a rapt smile.*]—and the moon rests in the sea! I want to feel the moon at peace in the sea! I want Dion to leave the sky for me! I want him to sleep in the tides of my heart! [*She slowly takes from under her cloak, from her bosom, as if from her heart, the mask of* DION *as it was at the last and holds it before her face.*] My lover! My husband! My boy! You can never die till my heart dies! You will live forever! You are sleeping under my heart! I feel you stirring in your sleep, forever under my heart. [*She kisses him on the lips with a timeless kiss.*]

CURTAIN

THE FIELD GOD

By Paul Green

PAUL GREEN

[1894–]

Paul Green was born and bred amid the life he describes in *The Field God* and *In Abraham's Bosom*. He gives a terse account of his own career:

"Born on a farm near Lillington, N. C., March 17, 1894. Farmed in the spring and summer and went to country school a few months in the winter. Later went to Buie's Creek Academy, from which he was graduated in 1914. Taught country school two years. Entered the University of North Carolina in 1916. Enlisted in the army in 1917. Served as private, corporal, sergeant and sergeant-major with the 105th Engineers, 30th Division. Later as second lieutenant with the Chief of Engineers at Paris. Served four months on the Western front. Returned to the University of North Carolina in 1919. Was graduated from there in 1921. Did graduate work at his alma mater and at Cornell University. At present is a member of the faculty at the University of North Carolina." [1]

He was devoted to books, but surprisingly enough he had read only one play and part of another (*Hamlet* and part of *Julius Caesar*) when he submitted his first production in a college contest and won the prize with *Surrender to the Enemy*. After several other plays dealing with the white people and Negroes of the Carolinas, Green wrote *The Prayer Meeting*, which portrays the Negro as the "victim of the white man's laws, prejudices, and cruelties." This latter play, though dealing with the relationships of the Negro to the white man, is not a "sociological document," but a work of art concerned "first with human beings as individuals. . . ." [2]

Green's method of rewriting and expanding plays is illustrated in the composition of one of his most important dramas, *In Abraham's Bosom*. A one-act play, *Sam Tucker*, was rewritten in 1923 as *Your Fiery Furnace;* then another one-act play, *In Abraham's Bosom*, together with additional material, was combined with the foregoing to make the full-length play *In Abraham's Bosom*. This piece represents the tragic frustration of a Negro in his repeated attempts to answer the flickering intellectual aspirations within him. He is one who "wanter rise him up wid eddication"; he feels himself the messiah "foh all de black in de world, to lead 'em up out'n ignorance." Had Abraham's frustration resulted chiefly from racial barrier, the play might have been local or sociological, but it springs largely from a weakness in his own character—an uncontrollable temper. In a fit of fury he beats the son of his master and as a consequence suffers deferment of his educational undertaking; when at last he gains a post, he whips his pupils

[1] Reprinted by permission of the author from *Paul Green*, by Barrett H. Clark. New York: 1928, pp. 5–6.

[2] *Ibid.*, p. 12.

and loses his school; he fights at a subsequent meeting and defeats a new enterprise. To this defeat is added the universal tragedy of a son who is pitifully incapable of fulfilling the character imaged in the mind of the father: "I name you foh a great man, a man what stand high lak de sun, and you turn out to be de lowest of de low!" A one-act play, *The End of the Row*, has a similar theme: a negro woman is defeated in her desire for education by the advances of a white man upon whose aid she was counting.

Following *The Field God* in 1927 came *The House of Connelly*, produced in 1931; it pictures the disintegration of the old southern plantation life under the influence of changing conditions; with the passing of this aristocratic life, there has departed at once something ugly and charming. As in the case of O'Neill's widening scope of subject, we have here a movement toward a larger field for the employment of the playwright's gifts. *The House of Connelly* was received favorably and spoken of as the "accomplishment" of which his earlier plays had given promise.[1] Barrett Clark defines the aim of *Tread the Green Grass* as the endeavor "to shadow forth a somewhat fantastic interpretation of a young and delicately attuned country girl going mad through dreams and fears."[2] This play could also be thought of as picturing the struggle between Puritanism and naturalism. The task of staging this difficult piece was undertaken by the University of Iowa in 1932. Of *Potter's Field* (produced as *Roll, Sweet Chariot*), Green says the aim is "to give an absolutely true picture of the spirit and philosophy of a certain type of negro life. The play verges towards a sort of opera, and I hope it will be done somewhere by a producer with a feeling for the tragic life that lives in the place called Potter's Field."[3]

The third decade of the present century in America witnessed many discussions between "fundamentalism" and "modernism," and *The Field God* embodies in a measure this cleavage between divine and human philosophies—a question, to be sure, which has disturbed man probably since the emergence of thought.[4] The rural community of eastern North Carolina, as depicted in the play, reflects

[1] This is the opinion of Joseph Wood Krutch, who further adds that it is "the most interesting presented this season on Broadway." (*Nation*, CXXXIII, 408, Oct. 14, 1931.) Stark Young speaks of its "profound source" and "richness in texture," but he detects traces of unconvincing characterization. (*New Republic*, LXVIII, 234–6, Oct. 14, 1931.)

[2] *Op. cit.*, p. 20.

[3] Quoted in Barrett H. Clark's *An Hour of American Drama*. Philadelphia: 1930, p. 140.

[4] "The struggle between the two opposing points of view in religion, the sharp and bitter conflict that results from such opposition when the death fight is on, makes the play powerful and essential drama. And all this is embodied in Hardy Gilchrist." (Tucker, S. Marion, *Modern American and British Plays*. Introduction to *The Field God*.) The struggle is appropriately stated, but to say it is all embodied in Hardy Gilchrist is hardly tenable: he is one of the protagonists in the struggle, and his temporary wavering at the end is induced largely by the stress of the situation, not by his own inner struggle.

For important background materials in these fields see: Riley, Woodbridge, *American Thought: From Puritanism to Pragmatism and Beyond*, New York, 1923; Couch, W. T., editor, *Culture in the South*, Chapel Hill, N. C., 1933; Strong, Augustus, *American Poets and their Theology*, Philadelphia, 1916; Townsend, Harvey G., *Philosophical Ideas in the United States*, New York, 1934.

almost to a man orthodox American Protestantism, which contains so much of Calvin. A compelled belief in God: "I've got to believe in him. I couldn't live without it"; a feeling of complete dependence: "We are nothing in our own strength . . ."—these plus a sense of God's omnipotence are central to Mrs. Gilchrist's theology; she has a strong conviction of sin and the punishment that inevitably follows: "Lonie and Mag both have a lot to answer to before their God. They've been bad women in their young days." ". . . Now she's paying for her living in sin." It is the mental sin of unbelief which, in the eyes of the preacher, has caused the death of Mrs. Gilchrist and Neill and is killing Rhoda. God is wrathful, like the Puritan God of earlier days: "The lightning came in the summer and struck his barns as a message of thy wrath. His crops begun to fail him and disease has come among his cattle and his stock. Yea, thou art God of all things and there's none beside thee. Crucify him, Lord, until he sees the light. . . . Yea, thou wilt continue to persecute him. . . ." The Almighty has decreed that some can reach Him only through pain: "Stretch him [Gilchrist] on the rack, for it is the way to his salvation" and the way to save him "from the burning pit." This is a theology strongly reminiscent of Jonathan Edwards's Puritanism.

The reality of conscience is attested by the play. The haunting memories of the woman she has wronged have created in Rhoda's mind Macbeth-like images that disturb her peace: "She's never left us, Mag. She stays in there. I hear her at night moving about, slipping around. I know it's her. I got her locked in, but she can get out, Mag, she comes through the keyhole. She wants to steal the baby, wants to kill him. . . . I heard the bedsprings pop in there about dark and she got up and opened her trunk for something. I heard her plain. And I run and locked the door tight. But she can get out." Even Gilchrist feels inner reproach: ". . . it's been eating in me—here. . . . I know there's something wrong somewhere."

But the standards against which Gilchrist measures his wrong are different from those of the community in which he lives; and these standards in turn are derived from basic attitudes profoundly at variance with those which motivate his associates. Briefly, Gilchrist is an atheist with respect to the supernatural concept of God: "He won't answer me, and he won't answer you . . . for this God of yours don't exist. He ain't nowhere." What immortality there is concerns only love between man and woman. A human, not a religious, universality pervades mankind: "Deep down they ain't Christian, Jew or Gentile, black or white, but just people."

At one point, under the stress of the situation, Gilchrist seems to embrace repentantly the orthodox God, but subsequently he affirms, "I know I'm crazy, and yet I can't seem to stop. . . . Something driving me on." And later in reply to the preacher's invocation, "Blessed be the name of the Lord forever," Gilchrist says, "Cursed be his name forever." Gilchrist's atheism, however, comes not from scientific uncertainty, intellectual pride, aesthetic preoccupation, or emotional revolt; it comes more from experiential reflection, a sober "common sense" questioning of the unfair and unreasonable things that happen in life. "Poor old Lonie. She's suffered and been hurt till the pore soul's petrified. And asking about Old Moster out there in the stars!" "But he won't answer. He won't come in the night. He won't come in the day, for this God of yours don't exist. He ain't nowhere."

At the core of Gilchrist's philosophy is man's ability to help himself: "Pore Aunt Marg'ret has trusted in him all the days of her life and she's never known nothing but suffering. If she'd gone to work trusting in her own might. . . . Ah, it would have been different." "My strength and my good name is all I've had." But this self-trust is obviously not Emerson's self-reliance which is grounded "in the lap of an immense intelligence," "that inspiration of man which cannot be denied without impiety and atheism." Like Whitman's philosophy in *Song of Myself*, Gilchrist's is the apotheosis of man: "We are God—Man is God. That's the light, that's the truth." "The God—the God who is in us. The one and only God."

Despite his excellent qualities as a man and his New Testament humanitarianism, Gilchrist is viewed as a cursed sinner; perhaps herein lies the irony of the play and is suggested the clue to Green's commentary on God and man. This interpretation of the dramatist's position, though asserted to be otherwise by Mantle and Clark,[1] seems to be indicated by Gilchrist's concluding emphasis on the powers of earth rather than those of heaven, by Rhoda's loyalty to human love rather than to divine religion,[2] and by the unfavorable light in which the frenzied attempts at conversion, with their shouting and pounding, place the minister and his religion.

It is interesting to note a similarity in the outlines of the character situation in *The Field God* and that in *Ethan Frome:* in both a weary, worn, and complaining farm wife and her active husband are estranged by the advent of a gay and attractive girl relative who comes to assist with the farm work; the husband's love for the young girl is discovered by the wife and she orders the intruder to depart. In both the play and the novel are also found realistic, authentic portrayals of rural scenes, characters, occupations, and language of the respective locales.

In their preoccupation with life rather than the theatre, in their simple and

[1] According to Burns Mantle, Gilchrist is "a defiant religionist who runs second in a contest with the representatives of God in his somewhat benighted Southern community." (*American Playwrights of To-day*, p. 41.) Barrett Clark speaks of Green as still "toiling in the vineyard of the Lord." (*An Hour of American Drama*, p. 140.)

[2] In her struggle with the church members Rhoda concludes: "He's a thousand times better than you all, better than anybody, better than God is . . . ." In spite of death and afflictions she clings to him at the end: "You are my God."

powerful delineation of elemental characters, and in their profound understanding of the tragic frustration in life, O'Neill and Green suggest points of comparison. But there is a vein of bitterness and sardonic irony in the elder dramatist that is lacking in the younger; then, too, as is only natural, O'Neill has gone further in range, complexity, and technique. But it is pertinent to remember with Burns Mantle in his terse commentary on Green: "Being a philosopher with the soul of a poet he represents the perfect type of progressive playwright."

The present text is reprinted from the edition of 1927.

CHARACTERS

HARDY GILCHRIST, *a farmer*
ETTA GILCHRIST, *his wife*
RHODA CAMPBELL, *Mrs. Gilchrist's niece*
NEILL SYKES, *a young farm-hand to Gilchrist*
MAG } *two old farm women, day laborers*
LONIE }
JACOB ALFORD, *an old farm helper*
SION ALFORD, *his son*
OLD MARGARET, *a neighbor*
TWO WOMEN, *neighbors*
A PREACHER

ACTS AND SCENES

ACT I

The yard and rear part of the Gilchrist house. A summer evening.

ACT II

SCENE 1. *Same as Act I. A day in the following winter.*
SCENE 2. *The sitting-room in the Gilchrist house. Night of the same day.*

ACT III

SCENE 1. *Same as Act I. An afternoon the following June.*
SCENE 2. *Same as Scene 2, Act II. Nearly a year later.*
(During this scene the curtain will be lowered to denote the passing of several hours)

TIME: *Within the first decade of the twentieth century.*

PLACE: *A farm in eastern North Carolina.*

THE FIELD GOD

ACT I

THE *scene is the back-yard and rear-part of the* GILCHRIST *farmhouse.*

The one-storey house with a chimney at the end projects into the yard from the right rear. A narrow porch, about eighteen inches above the ground, with small two-by-four posts for columns, runs the length of it. Near the left end is a door opening back into the kitchen, and about ten feet farther up the porch to the right a door leads back into the dining-room. Over to the left front a small outhouse with a door in the center projects into the yard. A short log drum before it serves as a step. A clothes-line stretches from the outhouse across the yard to the column at the end of the porch where a water-shelf with a basin and bucket is built. A soap gourd is nailed to the column, and higher up a towel hangs on a nail. A farm-bell caps the top of a pole by the water-shelf, a wire hanging down for ringing. Farther to the front of the outhouse is a clumpy china tree with a wash-bench and two wooden tubs beneath it. In the yard at the center front are two large iron wash-pots with a pile of brown ashes and charred pieces of wood around them. And to the right of these is a well, boarded up to the height of a man's waist, a bucket and chain hanging from a wheel and cross-piece above. The yard is bare save for a few straggling bunches of footworn grass here and there. Between the end of the outhouse and the house an open space gives a view of GILCHRIST'S *wide cottonfields.*

A summer evening is coming down over the GILCHRIST *farm. The sun has set, and beyond the rim of pines that enclose the level fields to the west the sky burns with a great smouldering flame, and the evening star hangs up above the circle of the sky's glow. From behind the house come the sounds of flapping wings and cackling of chickens going to roost, and somewhere down the lane the muffled bark of a dog is heard. In this immensity of silent fields a Negro on his way home gives his quavering lonely yodel, bursting now and then into a high snatch of song*—"You kin bury me in de east, you kin bury me in de west . . ." *reaches his cabin and is silent. A wagon passes on the road before the house, off to the right, the teamster cracking his whip and complaining to his team.*

The GILCHRIST *household is at supper in the dining-room. The door is open and the room is lighted by a lamp on the table.* HARDY GILCHRIST *sits at the end of the table with his back to the door.* MRS. GILCHRIST, *a pale, dark-eyed elderly woman, is at the opposite end facing* GILCHRIST. NEILL SYKES, *at* GILCHRIST'S *right, is eating in huge mouthfuls and washing down his food with buttermilk. He is a heavy-set muscular young fellow of twenty-six or seven.* MAG *and* LONIE, *two scarred and weatherbeaten old creatures, sit at the left.* MAG *is stout and talkative;* LONIE, *her sister, is a little silent, bent old woman with a wizened drawn face.*

GILCHRIST. Have something else, Neill.

NEILL [*crossing his knife and fork on his plate and pushing back his chair*]. No-a-thanky. I ain't et so much in I don't know when. Them was good biscuits, Mis' Etta.

MRS. GILCHRIST [*with a look out of her great gaunt eyes*]. Thanky, Neill.

MAG [*passing her cup*]. I'd choose a little more coffee, please ma'am. Takes a lot of moist to run a hoe-hand this hot weather. [*She pulls up her apron and wipes her streaming brow.*]

MRS. GILCHRIST. Have some more, Lonie? [LONIE *is picking timidly at a bone and only shakes her gray head without looking up.*] You, Hardy?

GILCHRIST. Got all I want, thanky. [*He crosses his knife and fork, clears his throat and wipes his lips with his handkerchief.*] Like you, Neill, I've overdone it tonight. But if you want a steam-engine to run you've got to fire it, hanh?

NEILL [*rising and coming out on the porch*]. Right. And I've done more work today than any steam-engine I knows of.

[*He sits down on the edge of the porch, picking his teeth with a goose-quill pick, and gazing across the fields.*]

GILCHRIST [*breaking into a loud boyish laugh, and looking around*]. You have that. You've slayed the crab-grass this day, my boy. That bottom corn's a-r'aring this very minute.

NEILL [*taking a plug of tobacco from his pocket and biting off a chew*]. I bet so.

GILCHRIST. Grow! It'll grow if we have rain. [*Teasingly.*] In a few years, Neill, maybe you'll be able to keep sight of me in the field. [*Laughing again.*] You're a little young and tender yet. [*Bringing his hand down on the table so that the dishes rattle and* LONIE *drops her bone.*] Go to it, you Mag and Lonie! Tomorrow's another day, and you'll need all you can hold.

MAG. Lord, Mr. Hardy, looks like you'd be tired adder your day's work. You're spry as a spring gander.

GILCHRIST. Tired! Take all the mules in Black River township to plow me down. Mag, you're getting old, old like a frost-bit 'simmon.

MAG. G'wan, Mr. Hardy, allus a-teasing. Old? Muh lived to be ninety. I got forty year to go yit.

GILCHRIST. I hope you got fifty of 'em, sixty—yea, seventy for that matter, Mag. I wisht you could live forever, wisht all of us could. [*He lapses into silence and sits drumming on the table.* MRS. GILCHRIST *glances sharply at him. He looks up.*] How you feeling tonight, Etta?

MRS. GILCHRIST. About as common, I reckon.

GILCHRIST [*kindly*]. That hurting in your breast eased off any?

MRS. GILCHRIST. A little, not much.

GILCHRIST [*moodily*]. Ah, that's bad, bad. But that Rhody of yours coming down from Durham will take some of the work off'n you.

MAG. Mr. Hardy, you better go up to Raleigh and git Mis' Etta one o' old Miss Smith's plasters. That'll bring whatever it is gnawing in there to a head.

GILCHRIST. Don't reckon Miss Smith can do much if the doctors can't.

[*As if stung by some untoward remembrance he stands up and walks out on the porch. In the lamplight his face and figure are visible. He is a tall well-built man of thirty-five or forty, broad-shouldered and powerfully muscled. His face is etched and lined with the marks of exposure to rain and wind and sun. From beneath the grimness of his manner and the will that shows in his countenance a sort of irrepressible boyishness now and then breaks through. He goes to the water-shelf at the end of the porch and takes a drink of water. With the dipper in his hand he stares at the west and then up at the sky above.*]

NEILL. Looks right nice—out there.

GILCHRIST. Looks dry though. No sign of falling weather.

NEILL [*spitting in the yard*]. Hanh, not much, Mr. Hardy. But that snake I hung up in the bottom may fetch it.

GILCHRIST [*going into the kitchen and returning with a cheroot which he lights*]. I'd like to see them cotton rows out there standing full of water, Neill. . . . Have a smoke?

[*He sits down on the edge of the porch before the kitchen door.*]

NEILL. 'Twould be fine, shore. We need it. . . . No a-thanky. [*In the dining-room* MAG *and* LONIE *continue their eating.* MRS. GILCHRIST *sits with her chin resting on her hand gazing vacantly before her.*]

GILCHRIST. I heard raincrows hollering this morning too.

NEILL. Mought a-been a' old turkle-dove.

GILCHRIST. A raincrow. I've heard too many of 'em not to know.

NEILL. Yeh. [*He leans his head wearily against a porch column.* GILCHRIST *looks at him slyly.*]

GILCHRIST [*chuckling*]. Tired, Neill?

NEILL [*jerking up his head*]. Hunh—me? No sir-ee.

GILCHRIST. Tired.

NEILL. Well, a fellow do get sorter sleepy-like adder a heavy meal like what I et.

GILCHRIST. Come on now, you're broke down, ain't you?

NEILL. This here has been a hard day. Hot, Lord, you could cook a' egg in the furrow about two o'clock. Yeh, I'll give in, Mr. Hardy, you just about plowed me to death today.

GILCHRIST [*gleefully*]. That so? Come on, come on, a great big fellow like you let an old man kill you at work. And I'd already sided half a' acre when you got to the fields this morning.

NEILL. "Old fellow," the dog's foot! You ain't old.

GILCHRIST [*mockingly*]. Old, old I am. Why, I can remember back and 'way, 'way back.

NEILL. You ain't forty yit.

GILCHRIST. Don't lack but a year of it, Neill. And you ain't but twenty-five.

NEILL. Twenty-six 'cording to Muh's Bible.

GILCHRIST. Just a boy. [*Reaching playfully over and touching* NEILL's *cheek.*] Hunh, he ain't never stropped his razor yet.

NEILL [*grinning*]. Pshaw, my beard's grow worse'n a turkey gobbler's.

[GILCHRIST *suddenly tumbles over from the porch in a handspring. He jumps to his feet shuffling a jig.*]

MAG [*who has pushed herself back from the table along with* LONIE]. Lord, Lord, listen to Mr. Hardy out there.

MRS. GILCHRIST [*still looking before her*]. Mag, I wish you wouldn't use the Lord's name that-a-way.

MAG. But he's jest sich a case.

GILCHRIST. Can you do that, Neill?

NEILL. I ain't no good at tricks.

GILCHRIST [*spitting*]. Tricks! [*Exercising his arms.*] Muscle power, Neill. [*Slapping himself.*] In here and here and here. I hope it'll be a hundred year giving out. [*Soberly.*] But threescore and ten is all we're promised, Neill, and most of the time them promises don't hold good at that. [*Rising suddenly and going to the dining-room door.*] Mag, you and Lonie clean up the dishes, Mis' Etta's wore out tonight.

MRS. GILCHRIST. No, no, they've chopped cotton hard all day. I'll wash the dishes.

GILCHRIST. No, let them wash 'em. I'll add a little extry to your day's work, Mag. [*Gently.*] Come and sit out on the porch awhile, Etta. That dining-room's hot as a furnace. [*He takes a chair out for her.*]

MAG. Yeh, we'll wash the dishes, Mis' Etta.

[MRS. GILCHRIST *rises and lights a lamp from a table in the corner and passes through a partition door into the kitchen. Through the open kitchen porch door a cupboard, stove and cooking utensils are seen.* MAG *and* LONIE *begin clearing away the dishes and passing into the kitchen with them.* MRS. GILCHRIST *throws a shawl over her shoulders, comes out on the porch and sits down. She takes out her snuff brush and box and begins dipping.*]

GILCHRIST. Etta, I've told you about working at that hot stove the way you do. Wisht you'd quit it.

MRS. GILCHRIST. Nobody else to.

GILCHRIST. I can get Sandy's gal back if you'd let me.

MRS. GILCHRIST. I don't want that Negro girl in the same house with me.

GILCHRIST. Why?

MRS. GILCHRIST. I believe she steals—and —and—she's low-down—

GILCHRIST. The first I've ever heard—well—

NEILL. I never heard nothing ag'in' her as a nigger.

MRS. GILCHRIST. I don't want her around.

GILCHRIST [*looking at her sharply*]. What you mean, Etta?

MRS. GILCHRIST [*nervously*]. I—I couldn't stand her uppity ways.

NEILL [*whistling through his teeth*]. Mebbe her good looks made her uppity.

MRS. GILCHRIST. I've seen things about her I didn't like, I tell you.

GILCHRIST [*suddenly*]. Anh!

MRS. GILCHRIST. What is it, Hardy?

GILCHRIST. Nothing.

MRS. GILCHRIST. But now that Rhoda's coming from Durham to live with us, I won't need any help. I can get along.

NEILL. When's she coming, Mis' Etta?

MRS. GILCHRIST. Any time now.

GILCHRIST [*striking his thigh with his fist*]. Great goodness!

MRS. GILCHRIST. Hardy!

GILCHRIST [*standing up and walking back and forth in the yard*]. Nothing, Etta. [*He goes to the left at the end of the house and stands gazing out at his growing cotton.*] Be having blooms out there, Neill, before the nineteenth of June. Grown squares on it now.

NEILL. Boll weevils'll be stirring soon too.

MRS. GILCHRIST [*who has been watching* GILCHRIST]. We got a letter in the mail yesterday from Rhoda and she said she'd come soon's she could git her pore muh's things straightened out. She may come tomorrow or next day or she may not come till next week. I wouldn't have been surprised to see her come today.

NEILL. Wonder how she'll take to the farm?

GILCHRIST [*turning back into the yard*]. Nohow, that's how. Anybody's been living in a town all their life ain't no use out here, I guess.

NEILL. Bet it'll be lonesome for her here.

GILCHRIST. She won't find no bathtubs and shining lights here and great crowds jostling and jamming. No, she won't by a long sight. I give her just a week to learn there's just one place she hates worse'n a farm and that's the place the good preachers talk so much about.

NEILL. What place is that, Mr. Hardy? Hahhah.

GILCHRIST. It's the place Etta and the good folks around here say I'm going to. I ain't baptized and I don't go to church.

NEILL. Reckon I'll be right there trying to far the b'ilers fast as you can. 'Twouldn't seem natural if we weren't trying to outdo each other.

MRS. GILCHRIST. Neill!

NEILL. Course, Mis' Etta, we hadn't ort to joke about scripture matters, I reckon.

GILCHRIST [*sitting again on the edge of the porch and puffing his cheroot*]. According to the Book I guess I'll go there all right, me being an infidel and all, but I ain't done nothing particular wrong as I know of. [*Thumping his chest.*] I'm not condemned in here.

MRS. GILCHRIST. Hardy!

GILCHRIST [*turning and looking directly at* MRS. GILCHRIST]. From people's talk I know they suspicion things about me. [*Smiling grimly.*] Anh, it worries 'em because they can't find nothing against me.

MRS. GILCHRIST [*agitated*]. No, Hardy, it don't neither. People respect you everywhere, all but your religious notions.

NEILL. That they do. They swear by you up and down the country.

GILCHRIST [*fixing* NEILL *with his eye*]. Neill, people are quare. They look up to me around here, do they? I'm honest, I work hard, I've accumulated property—some. And yet half this neighborhood would be glad tomorrow to hear I'd done something awful. It's not because I don't join in with 'em at the church and sing, and shout at meeting and be like the rest of 'em. You know what's in folks, Neill, that makes 'em like that?

NEILL [*shaking his head*]. No sir-ee. Cain't make heads or tails of it when you git to talking deep.

GILCHRIST. You don't know what it was in old man Jacob Alford made him start a little tale on me, do you?

NEILL. What tale?

GILCHRIST. Tell him, Etta.

MRS. GILCHRIST. What in the world is he talking about?

NEILL. Search me, Mis' Etta.

GILCHRIST. Now old Jacob is a good soul. He prays in the church, he shouts at revivals and a few times has dropped into trances praying over sinners. And he's a good man and still he tells a little lie about me and Sandy's colored gal.

MAG [*coming to the kitchen door*]. Course none of us didn't believe it, Mr. Hardy!

NEILL [*snorting*]. Hunh, that tale! Nobody believed it.

GILCHRIST. Somebody believed it a little bit, didn't they, Etta?

MRS. GILCHRIST [*hurriedly*]. Let's quit talking about that! Old Jacob Alford's weakminded.

GILCHRIST. You see, Neill, people like such stuff; it's excitement, something to interest 'em. Deep down they ain't Christian, Jew or Gentile, black or white, but just people. [*Spitting on the ground.*] And people are quare, Neill, quare. They want something to talk about, something to interest 'em, I say.

MAG [*going back to her dishes*]. You hear that, Lonie? [LONIE *nods her head.*]

NEILL. I reckon you're right, Mr. Hardy.

GILCHRIST [*picking up a stick and beginning to mark on the ground*]. That's how I've figgered it out. . . . Ah, funny!

NEILL [*after a long silence*]. I saw something that interested me once.

GILCHRIST [*teasing*]. You know you didn't, Neill.

NEILL. I did too. [MAG *comes to the door and listens.* LONIE *washes away automaton-like at the dishes inside.*] That time I carried a load of tobacco up to Durham for the old man. Talking about Rhody and her coming from Durham made me think of it. Adder I sold my tobacco that day it was late at night and I was coming out late from town. Just as I got clost to the Malbourne Hotel I never heard sich a racket of music and horns a-blowing and drums a-going it inside. It was music to beat the band. Never heard nothing fine as that before. Tell you what, it made the natchel hair quile up on the back of my neck. What'd I do but drive off in a side street and hitch my mules and go back there and ast a man all dressed up in a uniform at the door if I could git inside. He didn't say nary a word, jest motioned me in. I went inside a big waiting room and stood, Lord, I don't know how long, looking through a glass door at the goings-ons in another big room, bigger'n the whole end of this house here. And there was men and women cutting up in there, kicking their heels, sashaying and promenading up and down same as they was wild. And dresses! A plumb millionaire's fortune was walking on that floor. The men was all diked out in white shirts as stiff as a' arning board down to their belly-band and shoes you could see yourself in. And their claw-hammer coats hung 'way, 'way down behind.

GILCHRIST. And the women, how were they dressed, Neill?

NEILL [*waving his hand*]. I'm jest gitting to them. The women—some of 'em had gray hair, but they looked young like girls—they was dressed like a wedding, and they didn't have much on above their waists but little strips over their shoulders and enough to hide things. Behind they was as bare as the pa'm of my hand—down, well, low down.

MRS. GILCHRIST. Neill!

NEILL. I'm telling what happened, Mis' Etta. It ain't my fault how they dressed. Some of 'em had on little gold shoes Mag there couldn't git her big toe in, and silver shoes and satin and I don't know what all. And most every one of 'em had a bunch of flowers at their waist big as a slop-bucket. Their cheeks was red and their teeth white as snow, and they was plumb purty as angels.

MRS. GILCHRIST [*shrilly*]. They were painted hussies, every one of 'em!

NEILL [*staring at her*]. I'm sorry, Mis' Etta.

MRS. GILCHRIST [*twisting her shawl around her*]. The sin in such places!

GILCHRIST. Pleasure ain't sin to everybody, Etta.

[MRS. GILCHRIST *is silent. Presently* NEILL *goes on.*]

NEILL. Well, I reckon I'd a-been there yit if the thing hadn't busted up. And I couldn't git that music out'n my head for a month or two. Fact is, it ain't out even to this day. [*He hums reminiscently.*] Ta-ta, ta-ta.

MAG [*from the door*]. Wonder if Miss Rhody'll be like one of them painted women. [*She bursts into a loud laugh.*]

MRS. GILCHRIST. That she won't. Sister Minnie knew how to raise her child. I'll give her credit for that.

GILCHRIST. Didn't look much like it when Rhody was down here years ago—and mischievous!—my—into everything. And as thin as a rail. She'll be too weak to help much in the house.

MRS. GILCHRIST [*suddenly crying out*]. She'll at least be company in this lonesome place, company.

[NEILL *lowers his head and* GILCHRIST *is silent.*]

GILCHRIST [*presently*]. I hope she will, Etta. Yeh, I hope she'll be able to play the organ in there and help you sing your hymns.

MRS. GILCHRIST [*shyly*]. That'd be fine.

NEILL. I reckon she's about grown now, ain't she?

MRS. GILCHRIST. She was twelve or thirteen when she was down here visiting and that's been ten years ago.

GILCHRIST. Has? Goodness, don't seem more'n four or five at the most.

MRS. GILCHRIST. Time seems longer to some folks, Hardy, than it does to you.

GILCHRIST [*looking at her kindly*]. Yeh, yeh, I reckon it does, Etta. [*Turning towards the kitchen and calling.*] Mag, bring that lamp out'n the dining room, if you don't mind, getting a little dark out here. [*He goes to the tree in the front of the yard and gets a tub and takes it to the well. He then draws a bucket of water, pours it in and takes it back to the porch.* MAG *brings the lamp out and sets it on the water-shelf. By this time dusk has come on and the fields have become filled with a blue nebulous shade.* GILCHRIST *sets his tub down and begins taking off his shoes.* MAG *and* LONIE *come from the kitchen wearing their slat bonnets, and sit farther up the porch dipping their snuff. They are barefooted.* GILCHRIST *pours dirt out of his shoes and stares at the sky.*] See that, Neill?

NEILL [*jerking his head again from the post*]. I didn't see nothing.

GILCHRIST. A little wink of lightning right below the North Star.

NEILL. Where?

GILCHRIST. To the north. [*Pointing.*] Look, there it goes again. That means rain, Neill, rain in forty-eight hours. That'll hit us just right—cotton and corn!—According to the old saying.

MAG [*to* LONIE]. Look, Lonie, there goes the lightning again. Rainy weather coming on and you can rest.

GILCHRIST [*taking off his other shoe and pouring out the dirt*]. The moon quarters day after tomorrow. [*Suddenly in the trees behind the house the katydids burst into a floody chattering.*] And there goes them June bugs singing their heads off in them maples. Hot nights and June bugs and rain, what more can crops want? [*Pointing up into the sky at an angle of about forty degrees.*] See there, Neill, how the Great Dipper is tipped up on its edge? [*With a childlike smugness in his voice.*] It'll be pouring out water soon. You'n me better clean out that bottom corn on the creek tomorrow.

NEILL. Thought you laughed at me yistiddy for talking o' signs.

GILCHRIST. I don't especially believe 'em [*Laughing.*]—but then they used to work for my daddy.

NEILL. Is that Dipper the one old man Jacob says fell out of the north the year of the earthquake? [*Softly.*] Oh, ho, I believe in 'em myself.

GILCHRIST. The same, except it didn't fall.

LONIE [*in a sudden sharp husky little voice*]. Reckon Ol' Moster lives out there 'mongst them stars?

MRS. GILCHRIST. God's power is everywhere, Lonie, in you and me and in them fields out there—everywhere. [GILCHRIST *pulls off his socks, rolls up his trouser legs and begins washing his feet in the tub.*] He made everything that creepeth, everything that flies, everything to glorify his holy name. Yea, he's there among the stars and beyond.

GILCHRIST. Did he make old Jacob's Sion, Etta?

MRS. GILCHRIST. You and Lonie mustn't forget to say your prayers, Mag. Do you?

MAG. I dunno hardly—mebbe so. I dunno. Ask Lonie.

LONIE [*with a dry cough*]. Did he make the pore and the rich, Mis' Etta, some to live easy, some to live hard?

MRS. GILCHRIST. He made all things, Lonie.

LONIE [*her voice dying in a wheezy sigh*]. I reckon he did. Sump'n' made it.

[*She bows her head under her bonnet and says no more.* GILCHRIST *finishes rinsing his feet and props them up on the side of the tub to dry.*]

GILCHRIST. Neill, when you go down the road, I wish you'd give the mules some more water. A hot night like this they need it.

NEILL. All right, sir.

MAG [*standing up*]. Time for you'n me to be gitting up the road along home, Lonie.

[LONIE *gets to her feet and they go across the yard to the left.*]

GILCHRIST. See you all tomorrow bright and early. We'll have breakfast on the dot, Mag. [LONIE *suddenly stubs her foot against a plank as she goes across the yard.*] Look out, Lonie, you hurt your foot. [*He rises quickly.*] Here, let me help you. [*But she limps on off around the house without a word.*]

MAG. She ain't hurt, Mr. Hardy. See you all tomorrow if nothing happens.

GILCHRIST. Yea.

NEILL [*getting up*]. Believe I'll mosey along too, Mr. Hardy.

GILCHRIST. All right, Neill. Catch a good

night's sleep. [*Laughing.*] You'll need it tomorrow. I want you to work my tongue out down on that creek.

NEILL [*going around the end of the house*]. Cain't be done. I give up. Good night. Good night, Mis' Etta.

MRS. GILCHRIST. Good night.

GILCHRIST. See you in the morning. [*He sits down on the porch again.*] Poor old Lonie! [*He suddenly strikes the porch floor with his clenched fist.*] God A'mighty, she's suffered and been hurt till the pore soul's petrified. And asking about Old Moster out there in the stars!

MRS. GILCHRIST. Why you want to swear so much, Hardy? Lonie and Mag both have a lot to answer to before their God. They've been bad women in their young days.

GILCHRIST [*a sudden savagery in his voice*]. Both man and God have wiped their feet upon 'em. Etta, sometimes I think you got too much religion.

MRS. GILCHRIST. Hardy, don't take the Lord's name in vain.

GILCHRIST. Well, I'm right. The old Squire Morgan et up Lonie's looks and strength all the years of his life and then dies without leaving her a brownie. He threw her off like a nigger's shoe in a fence-jamb. Why did God Almighty make such a man, tell me, if he made everything?

MRS. GILCHRIST. His ways are beyond us. Judge not.

GILCHRIST. Yeh, I hadn't ought to talk so, I reckon. Anyhow it's most over now. Lonie won't be good for many more summers' work.

MRS. GILCHRIST. Yes, she'd better get ready to go.

GILCHRIST [*sharply*]. God better get ready to receive her.

MRS. GILCHRIST [*crying out*]. Hardy! Don't talk like that, I tell you.

GILCHRIST [*brushing the dirt from his feet*]. All right, I'm done. Yeh, maybe you and the preachers are right. I am a blaspheming man—I'm an infidel, I'm lost. But the things in this world are enough to make a man cuss out the Holy Ghost, whatever that is.

MRS. GILCHRIST [*sadly*]. Some day, Hardy, it'll come to you in a great light. You see through a glass darkly now, then as face to face. [*Bowing her head in her shawl.*] I've prayed and prayed it would.

GILCHRIST. Now, Etta, never mind me.

MRS. GILCHRIST [*drying her eyes*]. Still, let's don't fall out, Hardy.

GILCHRIST [*reassuringly*]. Sure we won't. [*Buoyantly.*] We have our ups and downs like other folks, but as long as we pull together we'll get along. Don't get down in the mouth, Etta, everything'll come out somehow.

MRS. GILCHRIST. Yes, everything'll come out for the best. It's promised to us in the Bible.

GILCHRIST. Them promises—[*He bites his lip and refrains.*] I tell you what, Etta, I was a-thinking as I plowed along today that if something happened to me before Mag and Lonie passed out, I'd want 'em provided for so's they wouldn't suffer. As long as I live I'll see to 'em and give 'em work to do.

MRS. GILCHRIST. You'll be here many a day after they've gone to the churchyard.

GILCHRIST. You never can tell. Yes, I'd want you to see to 'em. I'll do for 'em what that cussed old Morgan ought to have done.

MRS. GILCHRIST. Yes, yes.

GILCHRIST. I've worked and saved to accumulate something and—well, there's nobody to leave it to after we're gone—[MRS. GILCHRIST *makes no reply, and they sit for a moment in silence. Presently he turns and looks toward the west.*] Look at the evening star there, Etta, shining through them pines, big as a young moon. I've heard it said that the evening star is the same as the morning star. [MRS. GILCHRIST *suddenly breaks into low sobs.*] What's the matter? [*He rises and comes over to her.*] Stop it now. Don't cry.

MRS. GILCHRIST. Oh, I keep thinking and thinking about it. I've ruined your life. I ought never to have married you.

GILCHRIST. Now you feel bad. Go on to bed, tomorrow you'll be all right.

MRS. GILCHRIST. No, no. I'll never be all right any more. [*She catches his hand and holds it.*] I was sitting there at the table and hearing you talk and laugh and play out here and it come all over me of a sudden how old I am and you so young.

GILCHRIST. Why, we're the same age, Etta.

MRS. GILCHRIST. No, I'm old, old enough for your mother.

[*There is the noise of a buggy on the road before the house.*]

GILCHRIST. Now that's all right. [*He pats her shoulder.*] I think that was a buggy stopped out there. Somebody's talking. [*He listens. Presently hoof-beats are heard going up the lane.*] No, I guess they've gone on, whoever it is. You've got nothing to feel bad about, Etta. Fifteen years you've been a faithful wife. I'd never been able to make what I have without you.

MRS. GILCHRIST [*raising her head*]. What's to be will be anyhow. But I've ruined your life.

GILCHRIST. Stop it, Etta.

MRS. GILCHRIST. I've been worthless to you. I've been a barren fig tree, fit only for casting in the fire.

GILCHRIST [*jerking his hand from her and walking up and down the porch*]. You can't help it.

MRS. GILCHRIST. With the right sort of woman you'd have boys of your own now going with you in the fields—

GILCHRIST. I tell you to hush it! [*He sits suddenly down on the porch, running his hands through his thick hair and patting his foot nervously on the ground. In a moment he goes on quietly.*] And still you go on believing in this God of yours, praying to him, trusting in him, and what does he do for you? [*Bitterly.*] It's all for the best, it'll all come out right! Yes, it will, and when? Where is this God? Show him to me—[*Stretching out his palm and closing it as if strangling something.*] Him who mashes us in the hollow of his hand like a worm! Is he up there in the sky? Is he down there in the earth? [*Spitting scornfully.*] No, he ain't. He won't answer me and he won't answer you till the judgment day, and what good will it do then?

MRS. GILCHRIST. Hardy, Hardy, that's blasphemy to talk like that.

GILCHRIST [*standing up*]. Sometimes I think on it till I'll go crazy. Yea, your God, he boasts and brags in his great Book about making the sun and the moon and the stars and the light of the firmament above. And he made man, he says, in his own image and set him a king among all things. Then tell me why he persecutes people so? Look at Lonie—ground down to the bottom like the dirt I plow in. And you ain't seen them four idiot women over at the porehouse, have you? Where is he? Let him show hisself, and I'd match muscle with him like Jacob of old. [*Throwing out his hands helplessly.*] But he won't answer. He won't come in the night. He won't come in the day, for this God of yours don't exist. He ain't nowhere. I'm right and you and the preachers are wrong.

MRS. GILCHRIST [*vehemently*]. I know that my Redeemer liveth and I'll trust him though he slay me. There's the word for it.

GILCHRIST. Go ahead and trust him then, for he'll slay you all right. Pore Aunt Marg'ret has trusted in him all the days of her life and she's never known nothing but suffering. If she'd gone to work trusting in her own might. . . . Ah, it would have been different.

MRS. GILCHRIST. I've got to believe in him. I couldn't live without it, and Aunt Margaret couldn't live without it.

GILCHRIST. Well, let's stop. Talking won't change it either way.

[*They are both silent. Suddenly out of the darkness at the left a young girl appears carrying a cheap suitcase. She speaks in a soft voice.*]

GIRL. Good evening, you all.

GILCHRIST [*looking up in astonishment*]. Good evening, ma'am.

[*The girl comes forward into the light. She is about twenty-three or -four years old, strong and well-made. Under a wide hat her brown hair clusters around her pale tired face and soft eyes. About her is a queer combination of innocence and wisdom. Her drooping weariness only partly conceals a sort of richness in her—a richness of living around her lips and in her eyes and full-breasted figure. Her movements and speech betray a kind of matronliness engrafted in her, giving along with her girlishness an air of decisiveness and strength as of one who had known the hard responsibility of bread and meat for others. She sets her suitcase heavily down.*]

GIRL. You all don't know me, do you?

[GILCHRIST *rises to his feet and in embarrassment rolls down his trousers.* NEILL *comes in with a small trunk under his arm.*]

GILCHRIST. I can't say we do.

MRS. GILCHRIST. It ain't Rhody, is it?

GIRL [*laughing*]. That's who it is, Aunt Etta. [*She hurries over to* MRS. GILCHRIST *and kisses her.*] How are you all? [*Turning to* GILCHRIST.] You didn't know me, did you, Uncle Hardy—I haven't seen you in so long.

GILCHRIST [*fumbling with his shoes as he puts them on*]. You don't mean you're the little girl who was down here visiting once?

RHODA [*shaking hands with him*]. I've grown up, you see. Anybody will grow up in ten years.

MRS. GILCHRIST. Well, I do declare. I'm glad to see you, Rhoda.

[GILCHRIST *hurries into the dining-room and fetches a chair.*]

GILCHRIST. Sit down, I bet you're tired out.

[NEILL *sets the trunk on the porch, takes off his hat and remains respectfully standing.*]

RHODA. No, I'll sit right here on the edge of the porch the way I did a long, long time ago when you would sit over there making hawk-callers for me.

GILCHRIST. Did I? I be dog!

[*She pulls out her hat-pin and takes off her hat.*]

MRS. GILCHRIST. You sure have changed, Rhoda. I wouldn't a-known you anywhere.

GILCHRIST. How'd you get here?

RHODA. I came over from the station with Mr. Matthews. He brought my trunk by—if you can call it a trunk—and everything. We met Neill—your name is Neill, isn't it?—as we came by the barn.

NEILL. Yes, ma'am, that's my name. Yeh, I met 'em out there in the lane. Where you want me to put the trunk, Mis' Etta?

MRS. GILCHRIST. Put it in the upper room, Neill. [NEILL *takes the trunk and goes along the porch and into the house at the right.* MRS. GILCHRIST *gets to her feet and follows him.*] You just sit still, Rhoda, and I'll go in and see that the room is all straight. We've had it fixed for you several days.

RHODA. Oh, Hardy, I can hardly realize I'm going to live here with you and Aunt Etta the rest of my life.

GILCHRIST [*mumbling*]. Won't take you long to get tired of this place.

RHODA. Tired? I'll never get tired. For ten long years I've wanted to come back. And now I'm here—[*She stands listening.*] What's that?

GILCHRIST. What?

RHODA. That singing in the trees?

GILCHRIST. That's June bugs, we call 'em. The right name is katydids.

RHODA. They sound happy enough. And look up there in the sky at the stars shining. I never saw 'em much in Durham. I could lie right down here and sleep forever.

GILCHRIST [*mumbling again*]. Yeh, yeh.

RHODA. There was always a crowd going and coming up there, such a stir nobody could rest. And out here there's room, plenty of room and so quiet you can hear yourself think. And everything smells so sweet too. [*She gets up and goes over to the left and stands straining her eyes in the darkness.*] Is that cotton growing out there?

GILCHRIST. The best in the neighborhood.

RHODA. I know you'd raise the best. I know you would. Tomorrow I'll get me a hoe and chop along with the others.

[NEILL *and* MRS. GILCHRIST *come down the porch.*]

GILCHRIST. You'd blister your hands the first thing.

RHODA [*without looking around*]. I want to blister them. My granddaddy and grandmother on both sides were farmers and I've inherited it. I've always felt it so. Mother had no business in a town. [*She looks up at the sky with shining eyes.*] This is my home.

MRS. GILCHRIST. I reckon you'll want some supper.

RHODA. I've already had my supper, thank you, Aunt Etta.

MRS. GILCHRIST. Maybe you'll want to go straight to bed, Rhoda. . . . Your room is ready.

RHODA [*pointing to the tree in the yard*]. Yes. . . . What kind of tree is that?

GILCHRIST. That's a common china tree.

NEILL. They're common everywhere.

RHODA. Sure. It was nothing but a sprout

when I was here a long time ago. [*Turning.*] All right, Aunt Etta. I am purty tired. [*She goes up the porch.*] Good night, you all. See you in the morning, I'm sorry I got here so late.

GILCHRIST. Good night.

NEILL. Good night, Miss Rhody.

RHODA [*turning back*]. And won't I just eat you out of house and home though! Eggs and potatoes and sausage and ham and collards and cracklings and all the garden "sass" you could haul in a cart, and buttermilk by the gallon! [*With a sudden look at* MRS. GILCHRIST.] But, Aunt Etta, I'm so glad to be here!

[*She and* MRS. GILCHRIST *go up into the house at the right.* NEILL *leans against a post looking up the porch and slapping his leg idly with his hat.*]

NEILL. Well, sir—I declare!

GILCHRIST. What'd you say, Neill?

NEILL. Nothing, nothing.

[GILCHRIST *picks up his cheroot from the floor and lights it. He rises and walks in the yard.*]

GILCHRIST. That lightning's quit in the north, Neill.

NEILL. Yeh.

GILCHRIST [*walking back and forth*]. Quit!

NEILL. No rain after all mebbe.

GILCHRIST. Dry weather, and it'll rain when it will rain. No, I don't believe in signs, Neill.

NEILL. Well, I believe I'll mosey on down the road.

GILCHRIST. Water the mules, Neill?

NEILL [*chagrined*]. I be blamed, I forgot it!

GILCHRIST. I thought so.

NEILL. Sir?

GILCHRIST. Nothing. . . .

NEILL. Then ag'in I didn't have time. Good night. [*He goes off and immediately comes back.*] Reckon she can play the organ, Mr. Hardy?

GILCHRIST. Don't know. [NEILL *starts off again.*] Neill!

NEILL. Sir?

GILCHRIST [*lightly*]. She ain't painted.

NEILL. That's right, she ain't. [*He goes off chuckling.* GILCHRIST *sits again on the porch, leaning his head between his hands and smoking.*]

ACT II

SCENE I

Several months later, the same setting as before. It is a cold December day near noon, and a big fire is roaring around the pots in the middle of the yard. A pile of firewood is near by. Off to the left rear stretch the fields of brown cotton stalks, dull and dead in the sickly light of the winter sun. The empty burrs rattle in the freezing wind, and the smoke rising out of the kitchen chimney is swept away in its breath. The china tree to the left front is bare. HARDY GILCHRIST *is killing hogs, and off to the left by the outhouse the sound of voices, shouts, singing and grunting is heard.* MAG'S *voice is raised in a song:*

Ta-ra-ra-ra-boom-da-ree—
I got bumps all over me.

SION ALFORD, *old man* JACOB'S *boy of sixteen, thin and snaggle-toothed, is squatted near the fire broiling hog milts on the coals. He makes some pretensions to being dressed up, with a dirty collar and tie. And now and then he carefully takes off his cap, pulls out a small pocket mirror and arranges his hair which is shining with grease and parted in the middle, with two little rolls of twisted curls on either side. A battered auto-harp is lying on the bench close by. Presently he takes up a milt, squints, blows on it, and carefully lays it back to cook. Then after diligently cleaning his fingers with his dirty handkerchief, he sits on the bench and begins twanging the harp.*

SION [*watching the kitchen door and singing in a high contralto voice*].

I wisht I was a snowbird
With nothing else to do,
I'd set in the top of the apple-tree
And make sweet music fer you—
Good-by, my lover, oh, tell me good-by.

[*Old* LONIE *comes in at the left with a bucket. She wears heavy brogan shoes, an old slat bonnet, and a man's ragged coat. She dips the bucket into one of the pots and returns the way she came.*]

MAG [*calling*]. Hurry up, Lonie, and help ketch me these hyuh chit'lings!

GILCHRIST [*shouting outside*]. Now everybody pull together! Pull there, Neill, don't let the hair set on that hog! That's it, scrape him, boys! Get it off him while he's hot.

OLD JACOB [*grunting and laboring*]. Don't be afraid of him, folkses. He's dead and cain't bite you. Shuck him. I tell you, shuck that hog!

GILCHRIST [*presently shouting again*]. Spit on your hands and turn him! [*In a moment* GILCHRIST *with his sleeves rolled up rushes in carrying a bucket. He dips it in the pot.*] Look out, everybody, here I come! This boiling stuff'll bring that hair. [*He rushes out. Presently he shouts again.*] Mag, bring us a pan of hot water to work on this head!

[SION *takes out a bottle of perfume and anoints himself and goes on singing.*]

SION.

If all the trees was silver
And the blooms was diamonts too,
I'd take me my ax and cut 'em all down
And bring the sweet blossoms to you—
Good-by, my lover, oh, tell me good-by.

MAG [*sniffing the air as she comes in*]. The Lord help my life, such a scent!

SION. Hanh?

MAG. You stink worse'n a goat.

SION [*sullenly*]. It smells sweet. She uses it.

MAG. She don't wallow in it. Reckon she puts lard on her hair too, don't she?

SION. Hern's purty and'll lay without it.

MAG. He's plumb crazy with love. . . . Setting hyuh all roached up, greased and perfumed and singing like the cherrybims in heaven. You'd better be out there helping your pore old daddy scrape them hogs.

SION. I ain't able to work.

MAG. I'd like to git me a stick and blister your hide, you'd work.

SION. Mammy and Pappy says I'm weakly, I tell you. [*He seizes a milt and begins eating it.*]

MAG. Your belly ain't weakly. I can tell you that. [*Going out with her steaming pan.*] If you was my young'un I'd break me a hick'ry and beat some o' that love and mess out'n you.

[SION *stares after her, puckering his forehead thoughtfully. He giggles gleefully and gobbles down the milt. The kitchen door opens and* RHODA *comes to the well with a pail. She is neatly dressed and wears a bright red sweater. Her eyes sparkle and her cheeks are glowing in the cold.*]

SION [*cleaning his fingers and jumping up*]. Lemme git your water fer you, Miss Rhody.

RHODA. Help yourself.

[*He draws the water for her as she stands looking out at the workers, and takes it to the kitchen. At the porch he relinquishes the bucket and stares open-mouthed at the door that closes behind her.* OLD JACOB, *a little bent man of sixty-five with a gray ragged mustache, comes in and drags up the wash-bench before the fire. His old coat is pinned across his breast with wooden pegs. He sits down, blows upon his fingers and stretches his heavy shoes to the fire, laying a whet-stone and butcher-knife beside him.*]

JACOB [*in a piping voice*]. Sion, your milt hyuh is a-burning up. [*With a bound* SION *is back to the pot. He grabs his broil from the coals and begins eating it.*] Gimme a leetle piece of it, Sion.

SION. Nunh-unh. They's plenty of 'em out there in the tub, Pa.

JACOB [*musing*]. Sech a hog killing, sech a hog killing. He's got enough meat to stock the county. Anh, that's the way it is, Sion, them that has gits more and them that ain't got nothing it's tuk away.

SION [*irritably*]. That's it mebbe.

JACOB [*looking at him fondly*]. Course you don't understand it, pore fellow. You know you'll be keered fer. The Laord pervides fer babes and sech.

SION [*licking his fingers*]. Hee-hee.

[MAG *comes in and bends over the fire warming her hands.*]

MAG. It's a cold day and his meat'll shore keep. [*Shivering.*] That wind jest cuts through you.

JACOB [*punching the fire*]. It do. [*Cocking his eye towards the northeast.*] Bad weather a-coming. Wild geese was flying south last night. [*Holding up his hand.*] The feel in the air 'minds me of the winter of 'ninety-four. Laord, Laord, that was a cold 'un. The Cape Fair froze over so you could drive acrost it with a mule and wagon. Mis' Kivette did, and her baby with her. [SION *goes out and gets another milt and begins broiling it.* OLD JACOB *looks at him and chuckles.*] Jest look at that there boy. He ain't never had a bait of them things in his life, and don't he smell good?

MAG. If I was Mr. Hardy I wouldn't let him eat up my fresh meat that-a-way, and he not earning his salt.

SION. He don't keer.

JACOB. That he don't, Mag. Hardy's sorry for the pore boy and him afflicted. Sion's pleasures is few in this vale below.

MAG. Hunh!

JACOB [*changing the subject*]. Don't seem lak a r'al hawg-killing and Aunt Marg'ret not hyuh.

MAG. She's a-nussing that dying boy o' hern.

JACOB. I reckon.

GILCHRIST [*off at the left*]. Step back, Neill, and let me hang him!

JACOB. Jest look a-there at Hardy lifting that hawg up by hisself. He'll weight three hundred if a pound.

GILCHRIST [*outside*]. Hanh, there you are. All right, Neill, bring me fresh water and the tub and I'll gut him in a pair o' minutes.

[NEILL *comes in and gets a bucket of water from the pot.*]

NEILL. Jacob, you better fill up this here pot. [*He goes out as old* JACOB *creaks to his feet and begins drawing water at the well.*]

MAG. Sion, git some wood and put on the fire.

SION. This hyuh melt is jest a-cooking fine.

MAG [*cutting the wood herself and replenishing the fire*]. You make me mad enough to kill.

[LONIE *comes in and sits on the bench. Old* JACOB *empties his bucket into the pot and sits down by her. He begins whetting his knife.* MRS. GILCHRIST, *wrapped in a heavy cloak, walks unsteadily down the porch from the right and stands leaning against a post looking out.*]

MRS. GILCHRIST. How you all getting on, Jacob?

JACOB. Got 'em all killed and hanging up now, Mis' Etta, and a mighty fine chanct of meat you got out there too.

MRS. GILCHRIST. How much you reckon it'll make, Jacob?

JACOB. Three thousand pounds, no less. I'd stake them two haslets Hardy give me on it.

MRS. GILCHRIST. Two?

JACOB [*with a touch of gleeful malice*]. Two and a backbone. Me'n my raft o' young'uns 'll feed Sunday.

MRS. GILCHRIST. Yes.

[*Her eyes roam wearily over the fields and sky. She turns and goes slowly up the porch into the house again. Presently there is the weak labored sound of an organ inside, and a thin shrill voice singing* "There is a fountain filled with blood."]

JACOB. Pore thing. . . . Ah, clost and stingy right up to the grave.

MAG. Hanh! . . . Getting most too weak to play her organ now.

[LONIE *gives a little nodding jerk with her head.*]

JACOB. 'Twon't be long and she'll be to that bo'rne from whence no traveler returns, as the scripture says.

LONIE [*with a gasp*]. Sump'n's killing her.

JACOB. Aye, it is. She's wasting fast. [*Sighing.*] We've all got to come to it.

MAG. She's a good woman too—better'n most people know.

JACOB. She is that. She don't talk much, but she's good. I ain't never hearn her say a harm word 'bout nobody. Anh, she's good . . . [*With afterthought.*] and a lonesome woman too.

MAG [*laughing and jerking her thumb towards the kitchen*]. That 'un she's got in the house with her ain't lonesome. She talks, she's lively.

JACOB [*with an admiring chuckle*]. Ain't that young critter a wheel-hoss though? Laord, Laord. She's same as Neill and Hardy for work.

MAG. I didn't think it when she come here from Durham. But she were made fer the farm if anybody were.

JACOB [*his eyes narrowing introspectively as he appears to forget the subject*]. Where does the scriptures say the spirits of hogs go when they die, Mag?

MAG [*popping her lips*]. They don't go nowhere. They're just dead, that's all.

JACOB. In the ground, that's where. It says the animal spirits return in the earth and the heavenly spirits go upward. Hah, hah.

MAG. Hogs ain't got no souls.

JACOB. That's what the scriptures says.

[*They are silent. Presently* RHODA *comes to the*

kitchen door. JACOB *watches her meaningly as he whistles to himself.*]

RHODA. Sion, bring me some more water, please!

[SION *springs up and hurries to do her bidding.*]

JACOB. Jest look at that boy. He'll work fer her, plumb crazy about her.

MAG [*nodding as she spits*]. They's others crazy about her if I'm any judge.

JACOB [*looking at her slyly*]. Heh—heh—heh, ain't they though? [*Jerking his knife behind him and lowering his voice.*] How's Neill gitting on with her?

MAG. Worships the ground she walks on. He goes around like a man asleep.

JACOB [*quickly*]. Sho', sho'. . . . And her?

MAG. Cain't make out whe'r she takes to him or not. [JACOB *chuckles wisely again.*]

JACOB [*looking back over the top of the house at the sun*]. Well, I reckon it's 'bout dinner time fer us.

MAG. Yeh. Me'n Lonie's going to leave the rest of the chit'lings to rid till after dinner.

JACOB. Heigh, Miss Rhody, ain't it time to stop and feed!

SION [*coming out of the kitchen*]. She told me to. [*He rings the bell and returns to his broil.*]

GILCHRIST [*outside*]. Yeh, we're just coming. [*Presently he and* NEILL *enter at the left. They come to the fire and warm themselves. Their hands are greasy and stained with blood.* GILCHRIST *turns and stands surveying the scene of his handiwork.*] How's that for pork, Jacob?

JACOB. A sight fer sore eyes sartain.

GILCHRIST. Every one of them hogs hanging up there is less'n two years old. Purty good for piney-woods rooters, anh?

JACOB. You got the neighborhood beat in everything, Hardy. You're the luckiest man!

GILCHRIST. Ain't luck, Jacob, it's hard work and a little use of my head. Sion, run there to the hog barrel and bring them two pans.

SION. My melt'll burn, Mr.—

GILCHRIST [*reaching down with a laugh and lifting him up by the collar*]. Get the pans, Sion. [SION *with a terrified scamper dashes out and brings the pans.*] That's a good boy. You all wash and get ready for dinner. I'll get some soap. [*He goes to the water-shelf and takes a cake of home-made soap from the soap-gourd, calling.*] Is dinner ready, Rhody?

RHODA [*opening the kitchen door and looking out*]. It'll be ready in a few minutes, Hardy.

GILCHRIST. Well, bring a little of your blackberry wine out here and warm up Jacob and the rest of 'em a bit, if you don't mind. [MRS. GILCHRIST *suddenly begins playing the organ again and singing.* GILCHRIST *stands listening a moment and then turns abruptly back to the group in the yard. He dips water from a pot and begins washing his hands in a basin.*] You all excuse me and I'll wash this grease off'n my hands first. I want to step down to the barn and get a bag of salt. [*He pulls out a checkered handkerchief and wipes his hands.* RHODA *comes out with a pitcher of wine and a glass. As* GILCHRIST *goes off around the house, he calls back over his shoulder.*] Help yourself, folks. It'll make you feel young.

JACOB. Yes, and Neill needs it. He's down in the dumps today.

[NEILL *savagely stirs the fire around the pots.*]

RHODA [*pouring out the wine*]. Here, Lonie, drink a little. You must be frozen.

[LONIE *takes it in her trembling clawlike hands and drinks. Old* JACOB *eyes her closely.*]

JACOB. You'll git high if you don't mind out, Lonie, heh-heh.

RHODA. And here's some for you, Mag.

MAG. Thanky, ma'm. [*She drinks and hands the glass back.*]

RHODA. How much, Jacob?

JACOB. Heh-heh-heh, I leave that to you.

[*She pours him out a large glass. With a preparatory smacking of his lips and a clearing of his throat he takes the glass and drains it down. He screws up his cheeks till they close his eyes, washing the wine around over his toothless gums.*]

MAG. You're a-gitting all there is out'n it, Jacob.

JACOB. I am that, heh-heh, I am that, Mag.

RHODA [*pouring out another glass*]. Here, Neill.

NEILL [*without looking up*]. I don't want none.

RHODA. Come on and drink some.

NEILL [*sharply*]. I don't want none, I tell you.

JACOB. What ails you, Neill, got the mulligrubs?

RHODA. Here, drink it, Sion.

JACOB. Hyuh, that boy'll be down drunk if he swallows all that. [*He reaches out and drinks the glass nearly to the bottom and hands it to* SION.] Mebbe that won't hurt you. Don't know though, the smell of a rotten apple makes him drunk.

[SION *drinks his swallow and hands the glass back to* RHODA.]

SION [*shyly*]. That was shore good, Miss Rhoda.

RHODA. Glad it was, Sion. Anybody have any more?

JACOB. No, no, a little snitch later on in the evening when the cold gits blue.

MAG. No'm, I got enough now.

[LONIE *shakes her head too and* RHODA *returns into the kitchen.*]

JACOB. Wonder Mis' Etta would let 'em have wine around. [*Hastily.*] Not that there's any harm in it, of course.

MAG. Mebbe she cain't help herself.

JACOB. They's gospel fer drinking it though. God the Saviour hisself made wine at a wedding onct. [*Suddenly he pops his hands together and rubs his thighs.*] That stuff shore goes to the right spot. Now a good dinner of collards and backbone and sweet 'taters and I'll be ready to ride. How 'bout you, Neill?

NEILL. What?

JACOB [*cackling*]. By gums, he didn't even hear me. Anh, he's studying, wropped up in sump'n'. What is it, Neill?

NEILL. Cain't a man keep his mouth shet if he wants to?

JACOB. Heh-heh-heh, I reckon he kin. More mouths than one's been shet up—some of 'em forever—by a bright piece o' calico.

NEILL [*turning his burning eyes upon him*]. What'd you say?

JACOB [*starting back*]. Oh, nothing, Neill, nothing. [*Suddenly reaching down and grabbing a pan.*] Le's wash, everybody.

[*He dips water out of a pot and begins washing his hands.* MAG *and* LONIE *do likewise;* NEILL *stands staring at the fire. Old* JACOB *throws the water from his pan and gets the towel from the porch. He wipes his hands and passes it on to* MAG. SION, *now that* RHODA *is in the house, sits contentedly on his haunches gnawing his meat.*]

RHODA [*opening the dining-room door*]. Mag, could you and Lonie come help me set the table and get the things on? We'll have dinner in a jiffy. And you'll be a lot warmer in here out of that wind.

[*They hang the towel on a limb of the tree and go in, closing the door behind them. Old* JACOB *sits down on the bench whetting his butcher knife.*]

JACOB. Neill, I didn't mean to make you mad with my talk. You know I will talk, my tongue jest will.

NEILL [*turning himself about*]. Oh, that's all right. I ain't feeling well.

JACOB. Ain't? I'll declare that's bad. Where do you hurt, Neill?

NEILL. Jest feel bad.

JACOB [*slyly*]. Pneumony?

NEILL. I dunno, I tell you.

JACOB [*mournfully*]. Anh, pore fellow. [*Again he pops his hands together and slaps his thighs.*] Laord, that stuff warmed me up. [*He gets up from the bench, brandishes his knife in the air and cuts a step or two.*] Here I am eighteen ag'in, ready to go to old man Ransom Pate's dance. [*He turns and pokes his face up by* NEILL'S *shoulder.*] Ain't she a purty thing, Neill?

NEILL. Who's purty?

JACOB [*cackling and gesturing towards the house*]. Her in there. She's like one o' them big red apples you buy at the store.

NEILL [*spitting with a distasteful grimace*]. I've seed better looking many a time.

JACOB. No, you ain't, Neill. They don't make 'em no purtier. And I ain't never seed a smarter one. Wisht I could call back about thirty year, I'd go fer her.

NEILL [*breaking into a bitter laugh*]. You!

JACOB. Yeh, me. Oh, yes, I had a way with 'em, Neill, I had a way. [*Stepping before him and looking significantly up in his face.*] Oh, my boy, you don't know your business. The way to do is to walk in and take 'em. Laord, with your strength you don't have to wait. Why, if I was you, when she comes out to this here pot, I'd jest up and say, "Rhody, we'll git married tomorrow," perviding that was the date you'd sot, and tomorrow we'd be married.

NEILL. Hunh, you don't know Rhody. [*Quickly.*] I ain't planning to git married to nobody nohow.

JACOB. Heh-heh-heh, I know you, Neill, I see through you. Anh, she'd make a match fer you, she would. [*Smacking his lips, his eyes shining.*] Anh, blackberries and strawberries, Neill, they ain't nothing to her. . . . Boy, she's ripe and ready to pick. I hate to see her going to waste and you'd better retch and pick her or somebody will.

NEILL [*angrily*]. I don't want to hear no more of it.

JACOB [*throwing out his arms*]. I'm giving you good advice all right. [*Stretching his hands out towards the fire.*] Don't she keer nothing fer you a-tall, Neill?

NEILL. She likes me all right, but nothing more'n that, I reckon.

JACOB. Mebbe they's somebody else.

NEILL. Ain't nobody else to be.

JACOB. Heh-heh-heh. Yeh, you're mebbe blind. You see the sporrer 'way, 'way yander, and miss the turkey clost by.

NEILL [*grasping his arm*]. Have you seed her with anybody else? [*Casting* JACOB *from him.*] Naw, they ain't nobody in the neighborhood she'd think of going with, though plenty of 'em wants to.

JACOB [*winking his eye*]. Look clost by, Neill, clost by.

NEILL [*staring at him*]. What you mean?

JACOB [*rubbing his hands in delight*]. I'm too deep for you, ain't I? They do accuse me o' that at times. [*Casually.*] Well, jest to be talking, say a man marries a woman like Mis' Etta in there—no harm meant to her, pore critter—Say he's a big strong fellow like Hardy. Well, sech a fellow sleeping in a cold bed every night fer fifteen year is gonna have some thoughts, ain't he?

NEILL [*looking at him puzzled*]. Yeh, you're too deep fer me.

JACOB. You ain't never been married. That gal'd warm Hardy's bed proper, wouldn't she? Mebbe she already has, heh, heh! Yeh, them two'd make a fine match to see, wouldn't they? . . . And the pore woman in there can't live much longer.

NEILL. Great God! Air you crazy?

[GILCHRIST *comes in at the left with a bag of salt on his shoulder. He throws it in the outhouse at the left. Unseen by them* MRS. GILCHRIST *comes out on the porch and stands leaning against a post at the extreme right.*]

JACOB [*watching* GILCHRIST *and chuckling*]. Aye, boy, she's a rich 'un, ripe and ready. And I've seed looks going between 'em. And I've seed other things.

[MRS. GILCHRIST *draws herself up rigid, listening.* NEILL'S *long arm shoots out and knocks old* JACOB *behind him.*]

NEILL [*in a strained voice*]. You old—you old dirty b'ar hog!

GILCHRIST. What's the matter, Neill?

JACOB. Nothing, nothing, we're playing, fer I'm feeling young ag'in. [*Drawing back in alarm.*] Why, Mis' Etta, I didn't know you was out here.

MRS. GILCHRIST [*faintly*]. I just this second stepped out for a breath.

RHODA [*opening the dining-room door*]. Come on to dinner, you all.

[MAG *and* LONIE *are seen taking their seats at the table inside.*]

GILCHRIST [*going towards the house*]. Come on, Jacob. Come on, Neill. Sion, get up and see if you can eat a little more.

JACOB. Coming with my mouth open.

[SION *looks in his mirror and follows him, polishing his fingernails as he goes.*]

GILCHRIST [*stopping at the porch*]. What's the matter, Etta?

MRS. GILCHRIST. Nothing, nothing. [*Shivering.*] I'm cold.

RHODA. You want me to bring your dinner up to the fire, Aunt Etta?

MRS. GILCHRIST [*creeping weakly up the porch*]. Yes, bring it up there.

[*She goes off to the sitting-room.* GILCHRIST *looks sharply after her a moment and then goes into the dining-room and seats himself at the table. Old* JACOB *and* SION *troop in after him.*]

GILCHRIST [*looking out through the door*]. Come on in to dinner, Neill.

NEILL. Go ahead and eat, I'll be in in a minute.

RHODA [*coming out with a bucket*]. You all go ahead and wait on yourselves. I've got to put some water on to heat. [*She comes to the well and begins filling her bucket.* GILCHRIST, *inside, reaches behind him, glances out, hesitates, and then closes the dining-room door.*]

NEILL [*suddenly clenching his hands*]. Great God Almighty! Blind, blind, I been blind as a bat!

RHODA. You better go on in and eat your dinner, Neill.

NEILL. Come here a minute, Rhody.

RHODA [*leaving the well and moving uncertainly towards him*]. What is it?

NEILL [*snatching her hand*]. Are you going with me to that party tonight?

RHODA [*struggling to free herself*]. I told you once I would, Neill.

NEILL. Do you *want* to go with me?

RHODA. If I didn't I wouldn't a-promised. [*Angrily.*] You better turn me loose or I won't go with you anywhere.

[MRS. GILCHRIST *begins playing the organ again and singing* "How Firm a Foundation."]

NEILL. Oh, Rhody, I cain't eat nor sleep for thinking of you. Cain't you think a little bit of me, cain't you?

RHODA. Behave yourself, Neill. Now let me go on back, somebody might see you.

NEILL. I don't care who sees us. [*Wildly, as he puts his arm around her, holding her to him and pointing to the house.*] It's him in there, ain't it? Swear to God you don't love him in there at that table!

RHODA. I won't swear nothing. Let me go, I tell you.

NEILL. I won't let you loose. I'm gonna find out something.

RHODA. I'll scream so Hardy will come out here. . . . No, no, I won't either. I'm not afraid of you.

NEILL [*wild with anger*]. You do and I'll cut his rotten heart out with that there butcher-knife. Tell me, is it him?

RHODA. I won't tell you. I won't.

[NEILL *snatches her to him and kisses her. She fights against him and finally breaks into low sobs.*]

NEILL. By God, it is him; it is him! And I'll git him!

[*The dining-room door suddenly opens and* GILCHRIST *stands on the porch.*]

GILCHRIST [*yelling*]. Neill! [*There is a scramble inside as old* JACOB *rushes to the door to look out.* NEILL *releases* RHODA *and she drops down on the wash-bench weeping.* GILCHRIST *turns back towards the dining-room.*] You all go right on eating your dinner and don't none of you open this here door! [*He closes the door and steps out into the yard.*] Neill, what you mean treating Rhody like that?

NEILL. Nothing. I ain't hurt her. Let me alone now, I'm going in to dinner. [*He starts by* GILCHRIST.]

GILCHRIST [*grasping him by the shoulder*]. No, you're not till you explain yourself.

NEILL [*springing back and seizing old* JACOB's *butcher-knife from the bench*]. Get out of my way now. The first man lays hands on me I'll kill him.

GILCHRIST. What'n the name of God ails you, boy! Neill, wake up, have you gone crazy?

RHODA [*running to* GILCHRIST]. Go back, Hardy, go back in the house. He'll hurt you.

GILCHRIST [*looking down at her*]. No, no, he won't. [*He pushes her gently behind him.*]

NEILL [*whining with rage*]. I see it all now. Yeh, it's you been standing in between us. [*Stepping forward with the knife in his hand.*] Git out'n my way now.

[GILCHRIST *hesitates a moment and then suddenly kicks the knife out of his hand.* NEILL *doubles up, nursing his hand against his stomach.* GILCHRIST *picks up the knife and throws it out into the field.*]

GILCHRIST. Now, Neill, go on and eat your dinner and behave yourself. [*Old* JACOB's *inquisitive face is seen peering through the half-opened door.* MRS. GILCHRIST *is heard singing within*—GILCHRIST *sees* JACOB's *face.*] Shut that door, Jacob, and eat your dinner. [JACOB *bangs the door.*]

NEILL [*half sobbing*]. Oh, I couldn't see it and it all going on under my nose. Look at you there with your arm around her!

GILCHRIST [*dropping his arm, his mouth twitching and his fists clenched*]. Neill, you and me've been together too many days on this old farm to fight like cats and dogs. But if you say another word like that I'll break your neck.

NEILL [*springing at him*]. Try it then, you sneaking devil!

[GILCHRIST *grapples with him and as they scuffle back and forth over the yard,* RHODA *stands wringing her hands and moaning. The dining-room door is opened cautiously and old* JACOB *comes out followed by* SION, LONIE *and* MAG. *They are gnawing potatoes and meaty bones which they carry in their hands.* SION *looks on a moment and then clings to his father in fear.*]

RHODA. Stop it! Please stop it!

GILCHRIST [*trying to hold* NEILL'S *hands*]. Behave yourself now, Neill. Le's stop it!

JACOB. Laord a-mercy, what's up?

[MRS. GILCHRIST *comes down the porch.*]

MRS. GILCHRIST [*dropping weakly to the edge of the porch and calling in a low voice*]. Hardy, Hardy!

[*As they struggle,* GILCHRIST *casts his eyes over* NEILL'S *shoulder at her.*]

NEILL [*gasping*]. I'll kill you. I know about you two dirty dogs!

GILCHRIST [*snarling*]. Now, Neill, I'll fix you!

NEILL. Yeh, and I'll knock your teeth down your damn throat!

[GILCHRIST *with a wrench frees his hand and strikes* NEILL *full in the face. He falls flat in the yard, the blood running from his mouth.*]

MRS. GILCHRIST. Let me get away from it all, let me get away! [*She totters up the porch again.*]

GILCHRIST [*bending over* NEILL]. Bring me some water, Rhoda, and a towel. [*She snatches the towel hanging in the tree and brings the bucket from the pump.* GILCHRIST *bathes* NEILL'S *face.*] He'll be all right in a minute.

[MRS. GILCHRIST *is heard praying in the house.*]

MAG. Lord, he ain't dead, is he?

GILCHRIST [*sharply*]. No.

JACOB [*slobbering with excitement*]. A mule couldn't a-kicked him no harder. Laord, that was a blow!

GILCHRIST [*looking up*]. Go on back to your dinner. [*Shouting.*] Every one of you!

[*He waves them off before him. With backward glances they all finally return to their meal and close the door.*]

RHODA. He's getting better now.

NEILL [*suddenly sitting up and speaking in a low hard voice*]. Let me alone now, I'm all right. [*He sits quietly a moment and then springs to his feet sobbing.*] Damn you both. [*Raising his hands above his head.*] May I bust hell wide open if I don't git even. [*Whirling upon them.*] You God-damn dirty hawgs, that's what you are!

[RHODA *shrinks back with her fingers to her ears, and* NEILL *rushes off around the house sobbing and cursing, leaving* GILCHRIST *bent on his knees. He leans forward, balancing himself with his hand on the ground.* RHODA *comes up to him and stretches out her hand, touching his hair.*]

RHODA. Oh, Hardy, Hardy!

GILCHRIST [*standing up and looking at her with a queer smile*]. Such things happen, they just seem to happen all of a sudden sometimes.

RHODA [*twisting her hands in her apron*]. What's to come? And poor Aunt Etta saw it all. [*Suddenly clutching his arm.*] I'm afraid he'll hurt you!

GILCHRIST [*taking her hands from him*]. Well, let him. I'll never lift my hands against him again. [*With a sharp sigh.*] Anh, I've loved him like my own boy!

RHODA. It's all because of me. I ought never to have come here. I've felt it before.

[*He suddenly looks at her intently and then turns away.*]

GILCHRIST. You belong here. Come on, let's go in now. I've got to get back to my work.

RHODA [*shuddering*]. What he said!

GILCHRIST. Ah, don't remember it. [*Helplessly.*] Still people will believe whatever he tells.

[*He shakes his shoulders and opens the door for her.*]

RHODA [*looking up at him as she passes*]. I don't know what to do. [*They go in.*]

SCENE 2

The scene is the GILCHRIST *sitting-room and parlor, the night of the same day. At the center back is a fireplace with a log fire going, and to the right of this is a door which opens into the* GILCHRISTS' *bedroom. At the right is a neatly curtained window, and farther up at the right front an organ at which* MRS. GIL-

CHRIST *sits playing feebly. A lighted lamp is on the table in the center of the room. In the left center a door opens into* RHODA'S *room, and farther back at the left rear is a door which opens to the back porch. By the door is a wooden box piled high with firewood. The room is carpeted with straw matting, and here and there cheap prim chairs are placed about the room. On the walls hang several crayon portraits, distorted likenesses of relatives dead and gone. A rocking chair with a quilt draped over it is before the fire. The wind whistles and whines around the eaves of the house and drums like a brood of swallows in the chimney.*

MRS. GILCHRIST [*singing and playing slowly*].

What a friend we have in Jesus
All our sins and griefs to bear!
What a privilege to carry
Everything to God in prayer!

[*Her voice dies away and she leans her face over the keys, sobbing softly in her shawl. Steps are heard coming up the porch, and she rises hurriedly and sits in the rocking chair.* MAG *comes in through the door at the left rear.*]

MAG. Mr. Hardy told me to come in here and warm, Mis' Etta. The fire's gone out in the kitchen.

MRS. GILCHRIST. That's all right. Come in. [MAG *stands to the fire warming herself.*] Where's Mr. Gilchrist?

MAG. He's out in the smoke-house salting down the meat.

MRS. GILCHRIST. When will he be done?

MAG. He and Lonie's jest finishing up trimming the hams now. He'll be hyuh in a minute. [*Punching the fire.*] Lonie don't feel the cold the way I do. My toes is like tags of ice.

MRS. GILCHRIST. Listen to that wind, Mag, how it cries!

MAG [*looking at her closely and shivering*]. Like sump'n' lost. Well, it's got cause to moan adder the doings around here this day.

MRS. GILCHRIST. Ugh!

MAG. I've knowed Mr. Hardy all my life and I ain't knowed nothing but good of him before.

MRS. GILCHRIST. We're all poor erring creatures, Mag. We are nothing in our own strength, even Hardy ain't, though, poor man, he thinks he is.

MAG [*embarrassed*]. Yeh, yes, ma'm, I know. Lord. . . . [*Hastily.*] Well, I ain't never seed such a come-off in my born days.

MRS. GILCHRIST. Let me forget it, Mag.

MAG. And it's jest about to kill Mr. Hardy. He looks like his best friend had died.

MRS. GILCHRIST. Have you heard where Neill is?

MAG. Jacob come by about dark and said he'd gone and hired to old man Turner.

MRS. GILCHRIST [*bowing her head suddenly in her hands*]. He's young and headstrong, and maybe he'll come back. But it'll be a sad day for him if he goes back to drinking the way he useter.

MAG. Hunh, Neill Sykes'll not come back. I know him and I know th' Sykeses. They never fergit nor forgive, and he cain't fergit that lick he got in the face. It's that gal, Mis' Etta!

MRS. GILCHRIST [*quietly*]. What do you mean?

MAG. She's run him out'n his senses. He wouldn't a-done what he done today fer a million dollars, but now that he's done it he'll harbor it up till it eats his insides out like box-lye.

MRS. GILCHRIST [*in a gentle voice*]. Mebbe they'll make up tonight at the party.

MAG. Quare—her driving over there in the cold by herself.

MRS. GILCHRIST. Hardy told her to go.

MAG [*shaking her head*]. I don't understand it all, not me. Mebbe we're all crazy.

MRS. GILCHRIST [*wildly as she suddenly seizes her by the hand*]. Yes, you do understand it, Mag. You know what's up.

MAG [*trying to pull away*]. Lord, Mis' Etta, what's the matter?

MRS. GILCHRIST [*beseechingly*]. Ain't you seen something, Mag?

MAG. I ain't seed nothing, whatever you mean, Mis' Etta.

MRS. GILCHRIST. Ain't she loving somebody else in the place of Neill? Ain't you seen looks going between 'em?

MAG [*getting free and staring at the ceiling*]. I don't know nothing about all that you're saying, Mis' Etta. [*Backing towards the door at the left rear.*] Miss Rhody'll come to her senses and take Neill adder all, she will. Don't you worry. Neill's the very one cut out fer her. He'll be her husband yit. [*Hurriedly.*] I got to go back now and help 'em finish. [*As she catches hold of the door it opens and* LONIE *comes creeping in and draws up a chair by the fire.* MAG, *somewhat reassured, moves up again.*] You git done, Lonie?

[LONIE *nods her head, bends down and takes off her shoes and warms her feet.* MRS. GILCHRIST *looks into the fire and says nothing. Presently* GILCHRIST *comes up the porch and enters. He sits down and stretches out his legs. For several minutes no one says anything.* MAG *turns herself about by the fire.*]

GILCHRIST. Well, Mag, you and Lonie done fine today. I appreciate it.

MAG. That's all right. We're glad to do it, Mr. Hardy.

GILCHRIST. I didn't mean to keep you so late. [*Pulling out his watch and winding it.*] Going on ten o'clock. Well, you all sleep late tomorrow. Needn't come till dinner time if you don't want to.

MAG. All right, sir. [*They sit in silence, embarrassed.*] . . . I reckon we better be going, Lonie.

[LONIE *begins to put on her shoes.* GILCHRIST *takes out his pocketbook and pulls a bill from it.*]

GILCHRIST. Here, Mag, is pay for today.

MAG [*taking it*]. That's too much, Mr. Hardy.

GILCHRIST. No, it's not. And there's a couple of backbones wrapped up out there on the porch for you to boil of a-Sunday.

MAG. Thanky, thanky. Come on, Lonie. [LONIE *gets up and follows* MAG.] Good night, you all.

GILCHRIST. See you tomorrow some time.

MRS. GILCHRIST. Good night.

GILCHRIST. Oh, Lord! [*He drops his head wearily on his breast.* MRS. GILCHRIST *looks at him searchingly.*] This has been a hard day for you, Etta. How you feeling?

MRS. GILCHRIST. Now, Hardy, it's come upon you at the last.

GILCHRIST. What?

MRS. GILCHRIST. Now you see what can happen to a man who's proud in his own heart.

GILCHRIST. I know I done wrong to hit him. [*Looking at his hand.*] If I could just get the feeling of his face from my hand. [*Growling.*] Stop, don't bring it up to me no more.

MRS. GILCHRIST. All these years you've stood out and matched your strength against God, and now he's brought you down low to the ground. I been setting here by the fire since supper running it all through my mind. It's God's work.

GILCHRIST. What's God got to do with it?

MRS. GILCHRIST [*breathing heavily*]. He's got everything to do with it. He can keep your heart purified and save you from strange women.

GILCHRIST [*in amazement*]. Etta!

MRS. GILCHRIST. He can keep you from temptation. He can open your eyes and show you the gin of the adversary set for your unwary feet.

GILCHRIST. Well, you pray for me then.

MRS. GILCHRIST [*with a sob*]. I've prayed and prayed and prayed. And all this time you've hardened your heart, and now you've brought a curse down upon you and your household.

GILCHRIST. Don't talk no more, Etta. You've had enough excitement for one day.

MRS. GILCHRIST. You've got to reach in your heart and tear this sin out by the roots.

GILCHRIST. What sin, Etta?

MRS. GILCHRIST [*panting*]. You know what sin. [*With a sort of chant.*] And if thine eye offend thee pluck it out. [*Raising her clasped hands above her.*] This house must be purified.

GILCHRIST. Oh, God.

MRS. GILCHRIST [*weeping*]. Hardy, Hardy, can't you see where you are going? Whoever looketh on a woman—as the Saviour said—[*Crying out.*] Thou shalt not—

GILCHRIST [*jumping up and walking across the room*]. Stop, stop! [*He goes through the door at the rear. In a moment he returns with a stone churn in his hands and sets it near the fire.* MRS. GILCHRIST *dries her eyes and sits up cold and straight. With an effort he retains control of himself. He turns to her kindly.*]

She told me to set her milk to turn and I was about to forget it.

MRS. GILCHRIST [*softly*]. Her milk.

GILCHRIST [*angrily*]. That's just a way of speaking, Etta.

MRS. GILCHRIST. Yes, yes, her milk, her broom, her chairs, her everything. I'm a burden to the earth, I'm in the way, but I'll live to save you from yourself. I've prayed to God and he's promised me that.

GILCHRIST [*bitterly*]. Promised. If you're going to save me, then wipe out what happened between me and Neill today. Wipe out his black and bitter words about Rhody and send him back here where he belongs.

MRS. GILCHRIST. They can't be wiped out. They were the truth.

GILCHRIST [*shouting*]. It's a lie! You know it! She's as pure as an angel!

MRS. GILCHRIST [*putting out a weak hand*]. Don't talk that way, Hardy. If I die the next minute I know it ain't no lie. You've looked on her, yes, you have . . . [*Hoarsely.*] . . . And it's a horrible sin against me and against God. [*She closes her eyes and leans back in her chair.*] There ain't no difference between the thought and the deed. And for all I know—[*Her voice dies away.*]

GILCHRIST [*dropping down in his chair, thunderstruck*]. Well, by God in heaven!

MRS. GILCHRIST. You love her.

GILCHRIST. I won't say no more to you.

MRS. GILCHRIST. And she loves you. I've known it a long time from the way she sews for you and fixes things and can't never get enough of slaving for you. Oh, God above, this house is accursed! She's tried to hide it, but I've seen it and today I've heard more of it from other lips.

GILCHRIST. Who's been talking again—Jacob?

MRS. GILCHRIST. If it was him he knew something of what he said.

GILCHRIST. The poor God-damned old crook! But he can't help it, I reckon.

MRS. GILCHRIST. It's the truth.

GILCHRIST. Etta, listen to me.

MRS. GILCHRIST. There's nothing you can say, Hardy. Tomorrow Rhoda gets her things and leaves here.

GILCHRIST. We'll come to that later. Listen to me now.

MRS. GILCHRIST. Speak then.

GILCHRIST. They ain't no use in what we're doing and saying. Let's get at the truth. I'll tell you everything that's passed between Rhody and me. Last summer, it was August and about sunset down there in the bottom, she was helping me pile up the hay and there by her something come over me and I kissed her. You can call it what you want. Since then I ain't looked at her and that's the God's truth. It was wrong to kiss her and I know it, but there's no use denying it. I done it.

MRS. GILCHRIST. What you going to do now?

GILCHRIST. Ah!

MRS. GILCHRIST. After what happened between you and Neill today she can't stay here no more. People are going to be talking, Hardy.

GILCHRIST. Let 'em talk. They'll talk more if she goes away. We'll think of something to do. Stop fretting now, you'll worry yourself into your grave.

MRS. GILCHRIST. And that's what you want me to do. You and her both would be glad to see me carried out through that door feet foremost to the tomb.

GILCHRIST [*helplessly*]. Etta.

MRS. GILCHRIST. But you won't see it. I'll live and save you yet. . . . Now you listen to me, Hardy. We're going to settle things tonight. I've told you Rhoda's got to leave.

GILCHRIST [*shaking his head*]. You needn't say that.

MRS. GILCHRIST. She's got to leave, I tell you, and that tomorrow.

GILCHRIST. And I tell you she ain't going. She come here for us to take care of and we're going to do it.

MRS. GILCHRIST. If she stays here you're both lost and ruined. I'm the one that had her to come. You didn't want her.

GILCHRIST. They ain't no place for her to go and let's say no more about it.

MRS. GILCHRIST [*struggling for breath*]. If she stays here I'll go out afflicted as I am and shame you before the world.

GILCHRIST. You and her stay, I'll go. Yeh,

I'll go out as a harling somewhere for wages and you can let the land lie out and grow up in sheep-burrs and wire-grass. [*Savagely.*] And turn out the hogs in the fields and let the cows and mules into the barn and devour all I've made like the locusts of Egypt.

MRS. GILCHRIST. It's come to the last stand between us, Hardy. I've never stood against you before, but I will now. If I am sickly and half dead, I won't give in. She's got to leave. If she stays here it'll be over my dead body and the curse of the Almighty I'll put on you and her. [*Light footsteps are heard coming up the porch.* MRS. GILCHRIST *rises out of her seat and clings to the back of her chair.*] That's her now, and I won't stay and look upon her face. Tomorrow—[*Going across the room to the door at the left rear.*] It's your immortal soul, Hardy, and her soul I'm thinking of. I'm going to bed now.

[*She goes into her room and closes the door.* GILCHRIST, *as if awed at her manner, sits staring intently after her. The door at the left rear opens and* RHODA *comes in. She is dressed in a becoming hat, dark coat-suit, and trim shoes. Her eyes are red with weeping.*]

RHODA [*going to the fire*]. What you looking at?

GILCHRIST [*starting*]. Nothing. [*She goes into her room at the left and takes off her hat and gloves. When she returns,* GILCHRIST *stands up and gets her a chair.*] Warm yourself, I'll go out and put up the horse.

RHODA. I stopped by the barn and put him up.

GILCHRIST. Come back by yourself?

RHODA. I came back like I went—by myself.

GILCHRIST. You hadn't ought to have stopped out there in the cold and took out the horse.

RHODA [*sitting down*]. I thought you'd be working at the meat still. Did you get it all fixed?

GILCHRIST. Yes, Mag and Lonie stayed and helped.

RHODA [*leaning over and looking at the churn*]. The milk's turned. I believe it'll churn now.

GILCHRIST. You've done enough for one day. Have a good time?

RHODA [*with a strained little laugh*]. Not much.

GILCHRIST. Was Neill there?

RHODA. Yes.

GILCHRIST [*after a moment*]. What all did you play?

RHODA. "Fruit-basket" and "Put a bird in my cup" and "Going to Jerusalem," and that's about all.

GILCHRIST [*a smile hovering around his lips*]. Wisht I'd a-been there. We used to play another good game called "Weaving the Thimble."

RHODA. I'm glad you wa'n't, myself. If you could have seen Neill.

GILCHRIST. Still I hoped you could get him to come to his senses.

RHODA. Where's Aunt Etta?

GILCHRIST. Gone to bed.

RHODA [*bowing her head*]. Oh, Hardy!

GILCHRIST. I know. [*Presently.*] What you been crying about?

RHODA. Neill was there at the party, drunk, and he stood up in the middle of the floor and made a speech about me. [*She hides her face in her hands.*]

GILCHRIST. Not you by yourself, Rhody?

RHODA. No, about you and me together—yes.

GILCHRIST. He's rushing on to ruin. I hate to think of what'll happen when he gets sober. He'll want to kill hisself. I know him.

RHODA. I couldn't stand it, and I run away and come home.

GILCHRIST. What'd he say?

RHODA. He told everything he knew and more, and he hinted and winked about a whole lot of things. [*Twisting her hands nervously.*] Hardy, Jacob saw us in the hay-field that evening. He was passing along by the hedgerow.

GILCHRIST [*throwing out his hands*]. There you are—

RHODA. Neill told all that right before the crowd. Jacob let him on to it this evening when you sent him down the road to see Neill.

GILCHRIST [*sitting down*]. Now, it's getting too much, Rhody. Neill got drunk because he's kinder lost faith in you and me, that's it too.

RHODA. I know it, and there ain't a thing we can do to convince him different.

GILCHRIST. Tomorrow it'll be all over the neighborhood. [*Raising his voice as if imitating some one.*] There goes Hardy Gilchrist whose word has been his bond, a man among men, one I wanted my boys to pattern after. All the time I trusted him he was rotten as a wormy apple. Him running after a young girl before his wife—[*Groaning.*] Ah, Rhody, I've lived on my good name. My strength and my good name is all I've had. I've thrown it away.

RHODA [*convulsively catching his hand*]. And it's all on account of me. I've done it. [*He gestures.*] Now don't, it's true.

GILCHRIST. It's not your fault. We both have been weak. Etta says no man can make it alone. He's got to have an everlasting arm around him. Mebbe she's right, I don't know. . . . Reckon she's right? [*He pulls his hand from hers.*]

RHODA. I don't know.

GILCHRIST. Nor I. . . .

RHODA. If we could just call back that one time.

GILCHRIST. You wish it hadn't happened?

RHODA [*in a low voice*]. I'll always remember it and be glad just the same. But it's you I hate it for.

GILCHRIST. I'll always carry it with me, Rhody—the—the kiss you give me and—and—the words you said. [*Striking his knee with his fist.*] I don't care if all the angels in the sky said it was wrong I'd know it wa'n't.

RHODA. And I'd know it wa'n't.

GILCHRIST [*straightening himself up*]. So le's put it behind us, child. Let that day stand there like a pillar in our minds.

RHODA [*in a hushed voice*]. The fields and the sweet hay and the sunset there—and—oh, it will be with me till I die.

GILCHRIST [*leaning towards her*]. Hush! Hush! [*He puts his hand on her shoulder and then suddenly draws it away.*] Tomorrow I'll go down and talk to Neill and tell him everything. Mebbe he'll understand.

RHODA. And tomorrow I'm going away never to come back.

GILCHRIST. No, no, you can't. That won't settle it, Rhody. The only thing you can do is—to marry Neill.

RHODA. I don't love him. I can't marry him.

GILCHRIST. We've got to live among people and we've got to do what we don't want to—sometimes.

RHODA. I'd do anything you said for me to do but that. Marrying wouldn't fix it. Let me go away and folks will forget, and all can be like it was before I come. [*She stands up.*]

GILCHRIST. Where'd you go?

RHODA [*the tears running down her cheeks*]. I'll go back to town or somewhere and work, and I'll leave all these fields and things behind. [*She stifles her sobs in her handkerchief.*] But I won't be able to get 'em out of my mind to save my soul.

GILCHRIST. A-ah, child, all could have been different for you and me. [*Abruptly.*] I don't see no way but for you to marry him. I'll build you and him any sort of house you want, and you can stay here on the farm where you want to be.

RHODA. If you just knew how I feel and will to the grave, Hardy, you'd see what a sin it is to talk of Neill.

GILCHRIST [*brokenly*]. Yes, yes, and I love you. It's you that I was made for. [*Suddenly he takes her in his arms and falls to kissing her. In a moment she pushes his face away and with her head against his breast stands clinging to him.* GILCHRIST *looks out before him.*] I don't care what they do, they shan't take you away from me. Let 'em talk and let 'em laugh and mock me, I'll keep you before the whole world.

RHODA [*moaning and pushing him away*]. No, no. I've got to go. Let this be the last, Hardy, forever. [*She looks up at him and, catching his face in her hands, rises on her tiptoes and kisses him.*] That's for good-by now.

GILCHRIST [*recklessly*]. Then I'll go too. I'll go where you go and be with you.

RHODA. No, no, let me loose. I'll pack my trunk now.

GILCHRIST [*following her to the door of her room, his arm still around her*]. I'll go with you, and we'll leave it all to her in there.

RHODA [*opening the door*]. Aunt Etta.

GILCHRIST. We'll leave her to her God and her Bible.

RHODA [*shivering*]. After tonight I won't see you any more. Now leave me. [*She pushes him from her and moves into her room.*]

GILCHRIST. Oh, Rhody!

RHODA [*suddenly turning back and throwing her arms around his neck*]. I can't go from you. I'll die without you. You're my man, my god—everything to me. [*She kisses him in an abandonment of love and grief.*]

GILCHRIST [*hoarsely*]. You're mine tonight, Rhody.

RHODA [*holding him by the hand*]. Yes, yes. [*Her face aflame.*] This night is mine; it's all I'll have. [*She moves within the door, her eyes closed and her head bent down.*]

GILCHRIST [*softly*]. Rhody—

RHODA [*looking about her in the room and whispering*]. The nights and nights I've laid on that bed and thought of you. Oh, Hardy, Hardy. [*She leans against him and he bends over her stroking her hair.* MRS. GILCHRIST *opens her door and sees them. With a low cry she falls upon her knees.*]

MRS. GILCHRIST. God have mercy upon their pore souls. [*She sinks moaning to the floor.*]

GILCHRIST [*springing around*]. Etta!

MRS. GILCHRIST [*raising her head*]. Don't touch me. [*Screaming.*] Keep your hands off of me! [*Her head falls back against the floor.*]

GILCHRIST [*hurrying to her and picking her up in his arms*]. Are you hurt? What is it, Etta? [*He carries her into the bedroom and is heard laying her on the bed.*]

RHODA [*standing alone in the room*]. Oh, my Lord, what have we done?

MRS. GILCHRIST [*moaning, within*]. You cursed and defiled—you black of heart, God will—Vengeance is mine saith the Lord. . . . Ye are cursed with a curse. . . .

GILCHRIST [*sharply*]. Come here, Rhody, quick!

RHODA [*horror-stricken*]. Aunt Etta.

GILCHRIST [*in a moment* GILCHRIST *comes back and takes the lamp from the table*]. Come on in, Rhody. [*Huskily.*] Did you hear her? Did you hear her? She went with a curse on her lips, a curse for you and me, Rhody. [*He looks heavily around him.*]

RHODA [*bursting into sobs*]. We killed her, you and me!

[*Terror-stricken, they go into the room and stand by the bedside of the dead woman.*]

ACT III

SCENE I

The scene is the same as Act One, several months later. It is a late afternoon in summer. The china tree is in full leaf and the green cotton-fields stretch away to the left. Morning-glories have been planted along the porch, winding up the columns in leafy thickness, and the well has been replaced by a pump. MAG *is at the tub washing. The wire running from the outhouse to the porch is hung with freshly washed clothes.*

MAG [*singing to herself with mournful introspection*].

Get up in the morning,
  Trouble bothers my mind,
I go to bed at evening,
  It's trouble all the time.
    Oh, I wisht I'd heeded what my mammy said.
    Oh,—and now I wisht that I was lying dead.

He come by my window,
  All in the sweet springtime,
I rose up to listen,
  Nothing to bother my mind.
    Oh, I wisht I'd heeded what my mammy said.
    Oh,—and now I wisht that I was lying dead.

[LONIE *comes quietly in from the left rear and stands by the wash-bench.*]

MAG [*starting*]. Lord, you skeered me, Lonie!

LONIE. I thought I'd come down and maybe help you.

MAG. I'm shore glad you did for I was lonesome as a graveyard here by myself. You can start washing in that tub.

LONIE [*holding a garment up from her tub*]. Mis' Etta's dress, pore soul, ain't it?

MAG. Yeh, I found it back in the closet this morning. That dress brings it all back to me. It was a fair day when she put it on. She come out on the porch there and called to me and said look at it. And she had a little bit of lace on the collar or something. But, Lord, I couldn't help seeing her pale face and hollow eyes like a body looking in the tomb.

LONIE [*soaping the dress on the board*]. Reckon she sees me washing out her dress from up there?

MAG. No doubt she does while she's a-singing with her harp. It's good they got music up there, for she did like to play and sing here below.

LONIE. Yeh, she did. [*After a moment.*] Seems quare, jest like I mought any minute feel her flesh inside this here dress.

MAG. Pime-blank the way I've felt seeing her shoes setting about and her specs and snuff-box on the mantelpiece by the clock. And yistiddy I found a ball of her knitting with the needle stuck in it.

LONIE [*wheezily*]. Anh, everybody has to give up what they're a-doing some day and stop it.

MAG. That they do. And dying won't keep things from going right on and on. They'll be marrying and giving in marriage still.

LONIE. Yeh, they will.

MAG. If I ain't mistook they's a wedding going on some'er's now.

LONIE. Is it them two?

MAG. They dressed up and drove off this morning about ten o'clock—Miss Rhody all dolled up in finery and looking like a queen and he with his black suit and starched collar and shirt on. [*Shaking her head.*] Well, let 'em, pore things, fer if two souls ever loved one another them two does. But Hardy ain't so happy though at times. Sump'n's weighing down on him.

LONIE. I see she was a-loving him a month adder she come down hyuh from Durham.

MAG. And Mis' Etta seed it too, pore thing. That's what holp put her in her grave, 'twixt you and me.

LONIE. Yeh, yeh.

MAG. Still she hadn't ort to mind now fer she's dead and gone and nothing cain't hurt her there.

LONIE. Hardy needs a wife like Miss Rhody.

MAG. Well, I hope they're gitting married for I don't want to stay here another night. [*Looking intently at* LONIE.] I tell you I don't.

LONIE. I wouldn't sleep in that there house for nothing.

MAG. And I ain't gonna stay in there nary another 'un—listen! Last night, Lonie, some time 'way in the night I woke up and couldn't hardly breathe. They was somebody in the room; I felt it.

LONIE. Nanh, nanh!

MAG. I struck a light, but they warn't nobody there. Then I heard sump'n' in the wall trying to git out. I couldn't sleep another wink. And this morning the new plaster was cracked clean acrost.

LONIE [*holding up the dead woman's dress fearfully*]. Lordy!

[*They wash away in silence.* LONIE *wrings out* MRS. GILCHRIST'S *dress and hangs it carefully on the line, the two sleeves stretched widely out and caught to the wire by clothespins. Presently old* JACOB *and his boy* SION *come around the house at the rear and sit down on the pump platform.* JACOB *carries a trowel and level in his hand and* SION *carries a shovel.*]

JACOB [*taking off his hat and wiping his face with his sleeve*]. How you all come on?

MAG. Well as common. You well?

JACOB. Right well fer sich stirring times and it so hot. [*Gazing at the morning-glories.*] Anh, them flowers shore do grow. Makes everything look purty around hyuh.

SION. Mis' Rhody planted 'em.

JACOB. Aye, reckon she did. I'll declare this place has changed the most. Coming up the road there I got to thinking how fine everything looked. New posts on the front porch and window shutters, an' a new pump hyuh too.

MAG. Yeh, he shore has fixed up things the last few months.

JACOB. Heh-heh, he has. [*Winking.*] That whole front yard looks pime-blank like a flower garden.

SION. Mis' Rhody likes flowers. Mis' Etta didn't never keer nothing fer 'em.

JACOB. And them new lightning rods on top of the house shore do shine fine in the sun, heh-heh. Now since Mis' Etta ain't hyuh to pray for him Hardy must be afraid the Upper Powers is going to strak him dead with some o' their fire.

MAG [*sharply*]. He mought.

JACOB [*winking again and spitting profusely*]. Heh-heh, he mought be fearful of it.

SION. That there's Mis' Etta's dress dripping there on the line.

JACOB [*mournfully*]. And I seed her a-wearing it onct.

MAG. Lonie's jest this minute hung it out.

JACOB. What's become of all her things, pore critter?

MAG. They're all washed and arned and laid in her trunk.

JACOB. Looks like the young 'un would wear 'em.

MAG. She wouldn't put one of 'em on fer the wide world.

JACOB. Heh-heh, no, I reckon she wouldn't. Well, they's a lot o' good clothes going to waste, I betcha.

MAG. They's a whole trunk full o' things. Miss Rhody put 'em away one morning, crying like her heart would break.

JACOB. That there's a good gal fer you, Mag, if I do say it myself.

MAG [*dipping clothes from the pot and carrying them to the tub on a stick*]. You've said a lot of hard words about her, Jacob.

JACOB. Nanh-nanh, I've jest said what the others said. I ain't never wished her a grain o' harm, not me. [*Excitedly.*] But you jest wait till I tell you all the news, folkses.

MAG [*angrily*]. I've talked about 'em myself some, but not like you. [*Thinking.*] News—still a news-toter—I've hearn you at church laying Hardy out fer being a' infidel, and you used to talk about pore Mis' Etta, too, and both of 'em was as good to you as they could be.

JACOB. But I've done her a good turn today. ain't we, Sion? And that'll help her to rest.

SION. We have, I reckon.

JACOB. We jest finished putting up her tombstone at the church.

MAG. You have?

JACOB. Yeh.

SION. It shore is a purty 'un.

JACOB. With two hands a-shaking on it and a verse out under it saying "Asleep in Jesus." So she's fixed and complete now and can rest till the judgment day. When we was done I said a little bit of a prayer over her, didn't I, Sion?

SION [*slicking down his hair*]. He stood up and prayed out loud.

JACOB [*wiping his eyes*]. And the pure tears come up in my eyes a-thinking on her, pore thing.

MAG. I bet they did and I bet Sion bellowed like a calf.

SION [*sullenly*]. Not me. I ain't no calf—I tell you.

MAG. Hardy didn't know the tombstone had come.

JACOB. That he didn't and he off—off—But I'm a-coming to that, folkses. The man brung it over from the depot this morning. Hardy'd told me he wanted me to put it up when it did come. And I went and got Sandy and his two boys and we sot it. [*He suddenly breaks into a long toothless laugh.*]

MAG. A tombstone's a quare thing to be laughing about.

JACOB [*wiping his eyes*]. It ain't that, no sir-ee, it ain't that. I've got a piece of news fer ye. What you reckon that depot man told me while he was unloading Mis' Etta's stone? Heh-heh. He told me he saw Hardy and the gal driving the fine new horse out o' town a-flying towards Dunn. And, folkses, they was married at the courthouse this morning. [*He slaps his leg with his hat.*] And here I set waiting to welcome the bride and groom, and Sion too.

SION [*polishing his nails*]. Me too.

JACOB [*sadly*]. Bad fer pore Sion to lose his sweetheart that-a-way. But you'll git you another 'un, boy. You and Neill kin go out courting together now.

MAG. Has Neill heard about 'em marrying?

JACOB. I told him.

MAG [*scornfully*]. Course you did.

JACOB. And he's coming up to welcome 'em home. Now if you got a leetle o' that good wine in the house fer Neill, we'll all git ready to celebrate.

MAG. You better go down that road and tell Neill Sykes not to come up here. There's been enough trouble 'twixt him and Mr. Hardy. Apt as not he'll come drunk ag'in like he's been half the summer.

JACOB. A-ah, he's lost faith in man and

woman too, Mag. Who wouldn't drink in sich a fix?

MAG. If you'd a-kept your long tongue out of it, him and Mr. Hardy would a-been friends ag'in long ago.

JACOB [*angrily*]. Why, I've talked to him and Hardy's talked to him and it don't do no good. He's done quit old man Turner and don't do nothin' but lie in his daddy's house and eat and sleep. He's ruint fer good!

MAG. And you helped ruin him, you and him off together drunk every two weeks.

JACOB. Not me, Mag. He tempts me no doubt, and I'd ort not to give in to him.

MAG. Next month the preachers'll be after you at big meeting and you'll be up testifying and praising God.

JACOB. We all are weak and empty vessels, Mag.

[NEILL *comes in around the house, unshaven and haggard. He has been drinking.*]

NEILL [*shouting*]. Hooray for the bride and groom!

[*He sits down on the porch before the kitchen door.* MAG *and* LONIE *hang out their last garment.*]

JACOB. Hooray!

MAG. You'd better stop that hooraying and go back home if you know what's good fer you.

NEILL. The happy couple come yet?

JACOB. Not yit. We'll jest set and wait fer 'em.

[LONIE *sits down on the wash-bench.*]

MAG. I'm going in, Lonie, and tie up my clothes. I won't be needed hyuh tonight.

JACOB [*chuckling*]. That you won't, Mag. Hardy and the gal will be enough—heh-heh.

[MAG *goes up the porch and into the house.*]

NEILL [*with a magnanimous wave of his arm*]. Come over hyuh, Jacob! Come over, I got sump'n' purty for you. And you too, Sion!

JACOB. Nanh-nanh, Neill, I'd jest as leave set hyuh.

SION [*sullenly*]. I don't want nothing.

NEILL. Come on over, I tell you. [*They move over to him and sit down on the porch.* NEILL *pulls a large flask of whiskey from his pocket.*] How's that for joy and singing at a wedding!

JACOB [*looking at* LONIE]. No, no, Neill, I cain't now. I've quit.

NEILL. Quit! When, this morning? Hyuh, if you don't drink you ain't my friend. [*He hands it to* JACOB.]

JACOB. Well, what kin a-body do? We are commanded to be friends one with another. [*Spitting out his tobacco and uncorking the bottle.*] They was spirits at the wedding in Canaan, and here's to everybody. [*He takes a deep drink.*] A-n-h!

NEILL [*taking it from him and drinking*]. Here's to him and to her, by God! [*He pushes the bottle into* SION'*s hands.*]

JACOB. Heh-heh—I be danged, Neill. Yeh, hyuh's to 'em.

NEILL. Drink some o' this far and git some color in your cheeks.

[SION *raises the bottle and drinks, his face crawling in pain under the burning liquor.*]

JACOB. Hyuh, hyuh, that's enough.

[*He lifts the bottle from him and drinks again.* MAG *suddenly bursts out of the house carrying a bundle of clothes in her hand.*]

MAG. Lord-a-mercy!

JACOB. What'n the world has happened?

MAG [*dropping down on the pump platform*]. I seed a sight that chilled me to the bone.

JACOB. Was it a ghost or what?

MAG. When I come out of her room with my clothes, there sot Mis' Etta playing the orgin.

JACOB [*giving a squeak*]. Nanh, nanh, you couldn't.

MAG. And when I looked ag'in she was gone.

LONIE [*in a low throaty voice*]. She cain't rest in her grave.

JACOB [*drinking from the bottle and appealing to* NEILL]. It ain't so, don't you know t'ain't so?

NEILL [*springing up and waving his hat*]. Hooray fer the wedding! Now we'll have a grand reception. The old woman's come back from her grave to help welcome 'em to her bed. [*The hoof-beats of a trotting horse are heard down the lane.* NEILL *staggers to the left of the house and stands looking off around behind it. He comes back into the yard.*] Yonder they come burning the wind. A-ah, but they're in a hurry. [*Brandishing his bottle.*] It's love, love burning 'em up and driving 'em on.

[*The buggy draws up and stops before the house.*

SION *suddenly begins to cry.* JACOB *gives him a drunken punch.*]

JACOB. Stop it, boy, there comes Miss Rhody. You don't want to let her see you.

[SION *snuffles in his sleeve. They listen and* RHODA *is heard entering the house at the front.*]

MAG. Come on, Lonie, le's leave hyuh. [LONIE *gets up and follows her across the yard.*] Neill, you and Jacob better go on away from hyuh.

[RHODA *comes down the porch at the right wearing a long gray clinging dress and a pale green scarf thrown over her shoulders. She starts back on seeing* NEILL.]

NEILL [*bowing low*]. Greetings to the bride.

RHODA. Are you going, Mag?

MAG. I've got all my things tied up here and I'm going. You won't need me tonight, will you?

[JACOB *bursts into a guffaw.*]

RHODA [*looking at him sharply*]. All right. Did you get through the wash?

MAG. Yes'm. [*Hurriedly.*] Come on, Lonie, le's git away.

[*They go quickly off at the left.* RHODA *stands looking after them perplexed.*]

NEILL. Where's the happy groom?

RHODA [*brushing her hand across her face*]. Hardy's putting up the horse, Neill. Is there anything I can do for you and Jacob?

NEILL. Not by a damn sight!

JACOB [*winking*]. No'm, Neill and me and Sion jest want to bid you welcome into the holy state of matrimony. Don't we, Sion?

SION [*giggling drunkenly through his tears*]. Merry Christmas to you, Miss Rhody.

[*He leans against a post slobbering and his tongue hanging out.*]

RHODA. You've been giving him liquor, Neill?

NEILL [*waving his bottle*]. We're all drinking to your honor. [*Holding out the flask.*] And won't you join with us to celebrate?

JACOB. Wedding and love—heh-heh.

RHODA [*shrinking back against the wall*]. Stop it, please. Oh, Neill, please go away before Hardy comes in.

NEILL [*clinging to the porch post*]. What's wrong with me? Ain't I sober as a judge, sober as that damned Hardy Gilchrist you'll sleep with tonight?

[RHODA *covers her face with her hands and moves up the porch.*]

JACOB. Course he's sober, we're all sober. And they ain't no harm in tasting a drap to you.

NEILL. And this is my farewell party to everybody. I've joined Uncle Sam's men and tomorrow I'm going to the army. And I got my gatling gun with me. [*He pulls out a pistol and brandishes it in the air.*]

JACOB. Gonna be a soldier, Neill? Hooray—fight fer your country. [*He eyes* NEILL *foolishly.*]

NEILL [*putting the pistol back in his pocket*]. I signed up yistiddy in Dunn. In a week I'll be on the border killing Mexicans. [*He suddenly waves his bottle like a saber and marches up and down the yard singing.*]

Tramp, tramp, tramp, the boys are marching.

[*He makes a drunken salute and then waves his hands unsteadily over the fields.*] What's in this farming and sweating your insides out? Nothing. It's war for me in the service of the flag. I hate them fields out there. I hate everybody. I hate Hardy Gilchrist and all he's done to me. I hope to God trouble comes on him like hail out'n the sky till it beats him to the earth as low-down as me. [*His voice breaking in drunken sobs.*] He's laid awake at night and hatched his plans and sot his steel-trap to ketch me in. Jacob knows he has. And he's caught me all right. I'm down hyuh lower'n a nigger and he's up there with his woman like God A'mighty on the throne.

RHODA [*moaning*]. Oh, Neill, don't, don't. . . .

NEILL [*throwing his bottle from him and breaking it to pieces against the side of the outhouse*]. He's plowed me in the fields like a damned old steer, night and day he's drove me on in a yoke with him. I've dug in his bottoms, and rooted up stumps a' engine couldn't budge and dug in his ditches and cut away his briars and hedges for him. And all the time he's sot back and smiled at his eating me up in his hopper. Look at his hogs and mules and corn and his hay piled up higher'n a barn and his money rusting in a bank—I helped make it, these hyuh two arms piled it up for him. [*Spitting.*] A-ah, he takes all and leaves me nothing. [*Singing.*]

Tramp, tramp, tramp, the boys are marching,
Cheer up, comrades, they will come. . . .

[*Old* JACOB *takes up the song and begins marching with him.* RHODA *runs into the house and shuts the door behind her. Presently* NEILL *stops and puts his hands to his head, swaying from side to side.*]

JACOB [*belching and looking out at the fields*]. He's done me the same way, Neill, the same way. Hyuh I've lived on his land fer ten long year and what have I got? Durn his black soul. Me'n Nancy ain't got nothing, nothing. Sion there'll be left a pore boy without a cent in the world. A-ah, he's et the fat of the land and fed us the husks and crumbs. God is hard on the pore harlings and tenants.

[GILCHRIST *is heard entering the house.*]

NEILL. Come on, there's the bridegroom coming in to the bride. [*He pulls* SION *up and starts across the yard towards the rear.*]

JACOB. Leave 'em alone—heh-heh.

[NEILL *stops and looks around him. He points to the outhouse door.*]

NEILL. Le's git in there. I ain't gonna leave him yit. We'll come out and serenade the devil torectly.

JACOB. We'll watch 'em—heh-heh.

[*After much clambering and pushing they succeed in getting over the door-sill. Presently* GILCHRIST *and* RHODA *come down the porch.*]

GILCHRIST. Where is he?

RHODA. Don't say anything to him, Hardy. He's drunk and out of his head almost and he's got a pistol.

GILCHRIST. Never mind that. [*Looking around.*] They all must have gone. [*He steps down in the yard and walks to the end of the house.*] Jacob.

RHODA. They've gone, thank the Lord. [RHODA *comes down into the yard and stands beside* GILCHRIST.] I'd give anything if he was back our friend again. [*Clinging to* GILCHRIST.] Oh, it just makes me feel awful to think of him. . . . If he could just forgive us and be at peace!

GILCHRIST. Aye, I'd like for everybody to be at peace today, tonight. [*They stand looking out over the cotton-fields towards the red of the sunset. From behind a small cloud that hangs above the pines to the west the light from the hidden sun spreads up across the sky like the spangles of a great exploded rocket.* GILCHRIST *puts his arm around* RHODA.] Yes, I'd like for all the hard words and the bitterness to be wiped out everywhere. It's like ashes in my mouth to think of Neill.

RHODA. Maybe he'll come back from the army with it all forgot.

GILCHRIST. The army!

RHODA. He's going off tomorrow.

GILCHRIST. Anh, worse and worse. The army. I'll miss him and them fields'll miss him. And as for him he can't never forget 'em. Still, maybe it's for the best. Now let's go in, go into our house, your house and mine.

RHODA. Our house.

[*They step up on the porch and* GILCHRIST *turns and looks out at the fields and sky,* RHODA *leaning against him.*]

GILCHRIST. Try to forget all the trouble now. I'll take care of you.

RHODA. I ought not to feel afraid. But every now and then I feel like a cold breath of wind comes over me—feel afraid somehow.

GILCHRIST. You just imagine a lot. Rest against me and put it all out of your mind.

RHODA. I'll try. I will, Hardy.

GILCHRIST. Somehow I feel almost like believing in Etta's God tonight, Rhody.

RHODA. I do, I do too.

GILCHRIST. Look at that sky full of glory over there, Rhody, and the trees reaching around the fields like shutting off all the world for you and me.

RHODA. Yes, yes.

GILCHRIST [*looking up at the sky*]. If they's any place up there beyond the stars like Etta believed, I know she sees us and is satisfied.

RHODA. She can't hold it against us any longer. I know she can't.

GILCHRIST. No. For now she understands and knows we've never meant no harm. She sees how hard it's been for you and me, what we've suffered and gone through with all these months.

RHODA. And we'll still have to suffer, Hardy.

GILCHRIST. Ah, that we will. People will go on talking, but we'll live it down. We'll make 'em believe in us. We'll give to the poor and the afflicted and this house shall be like a well of kindness in a weary land.

RHODA. It will, Hardy, we'll make it so.

GILCHRIST [*exultantly*]. And in these fields we'll toil and labor and bring forth a hundredfold and more, [*With a wide gesture of his arm.*] toiling and sweating and happy for the joy and the life that's in us, Rhody.

RHODA [*with a broken sob*]. I could die with you now just about, and not be sorry.

GILCHRIST [*holding her tightly to him*]. And we'll raise up sons and daughters, Rhody, many of 'em, as strong and solid as that dirt out there. And we'll go down into the grave, them blessing us. [*He bends his head over her, and then bows down brokenly, clasping his arms around her knees.*] Oh, God, or spirit—if there is one up there or anywhere—look down on us and hear our prayer. Remember not our transgressions, we are the weak and erring ones, maybe thy children—in the image of the Most High. And—oh, Etta, Etta, be at peace and be merciful, for now we are happy . . . [*His voice dying out.*] happy at last. [*He bends his head and kisses the hem of* RHODA'S *dress.*]

RHODA [*leaning over him, her body shaken with sobs*]. Don't . . . don't . . . not that . . . oh, you are great and wonderful and I am nothing. . . .

[*A little gale of mocking laughter trickles out of the outhouse. In a moment it sounds again.*]

GILCHRIST [*standing up in horror*]. What's that? Who's out there? [*In the silence the chickens are heard flapping their wings and making muffled noises on the roost.*]

RHODA. It was the chickens going to roost.

GILCHRIST [*looking about*]. I thought I heard somebody. Maybe it was nothing. [*Bending tenderly over her.*] Le's go in now, honey. [*With his arm around her they go up the porch. Again the laughter breaks across the yard.* GILCHRIST *starts back as if struck.*] Who's that!

[*As he turns again down the porch, the outhouse door opens and* NEILL, *old* JACOB *and* SION *tumble out.* NEILL *has a guano trumpet in his hand and old* JACOB *carries the joint of a stovepipe. They are drunker than ever.*]

NEILL. Hooray for the bride and groom!

JACOB. Hooray.

[NEILL *blows a blast upon his trumpet, old* JACOB *beats the stovepipe, and* SION *claps his hands.*]

NEILL. We've come to serenade you.

[*They stagger up and down the yard blowing and beating.* SION *makes his way over to the bell-post and leans against it slobbering.*]

GILCHRIST [*shouting above the din*]. Neill, stop that foolishness!

NEILL [*lowering his trumpet and leering up at them*]. My best wishes to you. I hope you have a warm bed and great joy.

[GILCHRIST *starts out of the porch, but* RHODA *clings to him.*]

JACOB. The same here, Hardy, with all my heart.

NEILL. May God A'mighty set a burning mark on you and give you no peace and send you a gang of children with the head of calves. A brood of goats and cows and stinging adders, by God! Yea, I hope they'll be snake-headed, for you're both snakes in the grass!

JACOB [*beating on his stovepipe*]. Heh-heh-heh, and die without a roof over they heads.

GILCHRIST [*groaning and throwing out his hands*]. So be it. I won't hit you, for I know it's tearing in your liver, Neill, and you're drunk. . . . A-ah, Jacob. Le's go in, Rhody.

[*He bows his head and he and* RHODA *go up the porch and into the house.* NEILL *and his companions fall to their blowing and beating again.*]

NEILL [*shouting*]. You two dirty whores! [GILCHRIST *rushes out through the door and down the porch, and then stops again, staring at them. Shouting.*] You two dirty whores! Hawgs and whores, God damn you! [*He marches up and down the yard singing.*]

Tramp, tramp, tramp, the boys are marching . . .

[*He pulls out his pistol and suddenly shoots himself in the breast, falling heavily in the yard.* JACOB *stands looking at him crazily, beating abstractedly upon his stovepipe and* SION *begins tolling the bell.*]

JACOB. Heh-heh—what you doing like that fer, Neill?

GILCHRIST [*rushing down the porch*]. What—Great God! Rhody, Rhody, Neill's shot hisself! [*He hurries into the yard and bends down beside him. In a moment he turns away and stares at the ground.* JACOB *stands looking on in amazement, his mouth open and slobbering, tapping with his stick as if in a dream.* RHODA *comes slowly down the porch, her face hid in her scarf.* GILCHRIST *looks at her in anguish.*] Rhody, he's gone.

RHODA [*sitting suddenly down on the edge of the porch*]. Oh, I can't look at it. [*She bows her head in her lap, weeping and moaning.*]

GILCHRIST [*screaming at* JACOB]. Stop that beating. . . . Sion!

[SION *stands looking at him terrified. Presently he begins to sob.* JACOB *comprehends what has happened, and with a howl of terror scrambles out at the left rear.* GILCHRIST *raises his head and looks at* ETTA'S *dress hanging on the wire like something crucified.* RHODA *rises and moves blindly towards him.*]

SCENE 2

The scene is the GILCHRIST *sitting-room nearly a year later. The room is furnished much as before except that a center table with a vase of flowers takes the place of the organ, a new bureau with a mirror has been placed at the left, and a few sprays of budding branches are placed decoratively in pots in the corners of the room. It is a cold Sunday in Spring, and a log fire is smoldering in the fireplace.* RHODA GILCHRIST, *dressed in a loose wrapper, her hair hanging down in two shining braids, sits leaning over a baby's cradle before the fire. Her face is drawn and pale. After a moment she rises and stares about her uncertainly. Finally she moves over to the door at the right rear, stands as if listening and then turns and takes up the Bible from the table with a touch of furtiveness, opens it and sits down reading. Every now and then she leans sorrowfully over the crib. Once or twice her words are audible as she reads.*

RHODA. ". . . and said . . . Suffer little children to come unto me and forbid them not. . . ." Ah, me! [*She clutches at her brow and goes on reading.*] "Whosoever shall not receive the Kingdom of God as a little child . . ." [*Her voice dies into a mumble. Presently* HARDY GILCHRIST *comes quietly in at the rear. He is dressed in his Sunday best, his hair combed back, his dark clothes pressed and neat save for splotches of mud on his shoes. The passing months have deepened certain lines of grimness in his face. As he enters,* RHODA *looks up startled and lets the Bible slide to the floor.*] You've come back soon, Hardy.

GILCHRIST [*his face softening as he glances at her*]. Yes. . . . [*He looks down at the baby in the crib a moment and sighs.*] Poor little fellow. [*He bends down to listen and then lifts his head and stares in the distance.*] Ah—well. . . . [*Reaching in the crib and taking up a bottle filled with milk.*] Won't he drink any of it yet? [RHODA *shakes her head and looks hungrily at him.* GILCHRIST *sets the bottle up on the mantelpiece and comes over behind her chair and smoothes her forehead gently.*] Don't worry, honey child.

RHODA [*clutching his hand*]. He's not had an ounce of food in two days. . . . You didn't go.

GILCHRIST. You do like the doctor said and quit worrying, and in a little bit you'll be so you can nurse him.

RHODA. I wish so.

GILCHRIST. I don't worry; you mustn't.

RHODA. Hardy.

GILCHRIST. Maybe some but not much. Forget it now. Come and rest yourself.

[*He sits down in a rocking chair and takes her in his arms, soothing her. She closes her eyes and as he looks down at her a haggard restless look comes over his face. He begins abstractedly pushing his hand through his hair.*]

RHODA [*looking up*]. Something—now, look, you're worrying again. [*She watches him intently.*] And you just told me not to.

GILCHRIST. I was thinking—

RHODA [*sitting up straight in his lap*]. Sometimes it seems you ought to hate me.

GILCHRIST [*smiling at her*]. Don't be foolish, child, rest yourself against me.

RHODA. All the time we were planning about him, strong and healthy, and then he comes so little and weak. It was my fault.

GILCHRIST [*soberly*]. It's not that, hush. . . .

Oh, then so many things kept worrying you.

RHODA. And I couldn't help it, I love you so.

GILCHRIST [*restlessly*]. We both worried too much.

RHODA [*catching his face between her hands*]. Reckon we'll ever get things straightened out the way we thought?

GILCHRIST. Sure we will.

RHODA [*staring at him searchingly*]. Are you keeping something from me again, Hardy?

GILCHRIST. Why should I?

RHODA. You talk strong that way every time something happens. Has anything else happened?

GILCHRIST [*caressing her*]. And every time I go out you think something bad has happened or is going to happen.

RHODA. And I have reason to.

GILCHRIST. Hanh?—Yes, yes, in a way.

RHODA. Why'd you come back from church so soon?

GILCHRIST. I haven't been to church, Rhody.

RHODA. Why . . . you said you'd go.

GILCHRIST. I started, but I didn't go.

RHODA. It was to be a big day for you, Hardy, all the people there to pray and try to help you, help you and me.

GILCHRIST. Did you want me to go and be prayed over?

RHODA. I don't know. . . . I don't know what I want. [*Timidly.*] Maybe it'd help some. . . . Oh, I don't know.

GILCHRIST [*decisively*]. No, I decided not to go. Let them go on and follow after their God and I'll follow mine.

RHODA [*leaning against him*]. Somehow I wanted you to go, maybe for the baby's sake, I don't know.

GILCHRIST. What you mean?

RHODA. After what the preacher said yesterday I wanted you to go over there, I think I did.

GILCHRIST. And I'd a-been weak if I had gone.

RHODA. Maybe it don't pay to be too strong.

GILCHRIST. Don't, Rhody. Only with strength can we make it clean right on to the end.

RHODA. I hope we can make it.

GILCHRIST [*buoyantly*]. Sure, poor child. Reading the Bible?

RHODA. I'm always lonesome when you're away. I picked it up.

GILCHRIST. Well—yes, I might a-gone to church, but I went by the pasture to see about the big hog.

RHODA. Is he better?

GILCHRIST. I suppose so. [*Grimly.*] He was lying in the pen dead as a door-knob.

RHODA. Oh, Hardy. [*She looks at him a long while. Whispering.*] It keeps being that way.

GILCHRIST [*with a faint touch of anger*]. I've had cholera to kill my hogs off before. [*He pulls her tight in his arms.*] Lay your head on my shoulder and go to sleep. Everything is quiet and just us here, forget everything. . . .

RHODA [*starting up*]. I felt something sharp in your pocket. [*She reaches into his pocket and pulls out a butcher-knife.*]

GILCHRIST [*taking it quickly from her*]. And would I go to church? I saw it lying there where I throwed it in the field that day—it all come back to me—and would I go to church? . . .

RHODA [*uncertainly*]. Maybe.

GILCHRIST. My mind was so full of things I had no mind for their God, I tell you.

[RHODA *gets up from his lap and sits in a chair. Soon* GILCHRIST *rises, lays the knife on the mantel, and reseats himself in his chair. Again for a moment his face is filled with a somber brooding.*]

RHODA [*watching the knife*]. I don't like for it to be up there.

GILCHRIST [*starting*]. All right. [*He gets the knife down and holds it undecidedly in his hand.*]

RHODA. Burn it up.

[*He looks at her sharply and then throws the knife into the fire.*]

GILCHRIST. You can't burn it up, nothing but the handle. The blade is steel. [*Looking at the baby.*] He never cries, poor little man.

RHODA. He's never had the strength.

GILCHRIST [*taking off his coat*]. I got to go up and bury that hog.

[*He goes into the room at the left and reappears with his work-clothes in his hands.*]

RHODA. I wish you wouldn't go.

GILCHRIST. I'll be back purty soon. Mag'll keep you company.

RHODA. She's gone home a minute to look after Lonie.

GILCHRIST [*dropping his clothes again in the room at the left*]. All right.

[*He stands a moment thinking. Abstractedly he rolls up his sleeve and runs his hand back and forth along his forearm. His face darkens again with shaggy introspection.*]

RHODA [*smiling with mournful teasingness*]. You're just about the strongest man in the world, I bet.

GILCHRIST [*quickly*]. And the weakest, like today, for instance.

RHODA [*coming over to him and putting her arms around his neck*]. That was my fault. I'm sorry. You're strong, stronger than any man . . . almost as strong as God himself.

GILCHRIST [*kissing her*]. You make me strong.

[*He hugs her to him and puts his face against her hair. The door at the left rear opens cautiously and old* JACOB *sticks his head in.*]

JACOB. Kin a pore soul come in?

GILCHRIST [*releasing* RHODA]. Come on in.

[*Old* JACOB *comes in, followed by* SION. *They are both dressed in their preaching clothes.* JACOB *with an old seedy brown suit, a collar without a tie and a brown derby.* SION *wears the same clothes as before, and his hair still keeps its greasy curls. They respectfully sit down near the fire, and* HARDY *reseats himself.* SION *at once begins to polish his fingernails and arrange his hair with his little looking-glass.*]

JACOB. How's little Hardy coming on?

RHODA. No better.

JACOB. Ah, that's bad.

GILCHRIST. Oh, yes.

JACOB. Hanh?

GILCHRIST. It's bad, of course.

JACOB. Oh, yeh, as I said.

[HARDY *stands up, turns moodily about the room, and sits down again. The eyes of* JACOB *and* RHODA *follow him.*]

GILCHRIST. You gonna be here long, Jacob?

JACOB. I dunno, I mought.

GILCHRIST. I got to go up and bury my big hog and I wish you'd keep Rhody company a bit.

JACOB. Great goodness, is your prize hog dead, too?

GILCHRIST. Yes, dead . . . [*Echoing.*] "too."

JACOB [*with a groan*]. Anh!

GILCHRIST. And "anh."

JACOB. Warnings on top o' warnings.

GILCHRIST [*snapping his fingers*]. Yes, yes, all the time warnings!

JACOB [*studying*]. When'd you find him dead?

GILCHRIST. 'Bout half a' hour ago.

JACOB [*raising his eyes sanctimoniously aloft*]. And I know what's behind it.

GILCHRIST. Yes, you do.

RHODA. There's nothing behind it.

JACOB. You don't go to church, and a sign comes.

RHODA. Stop now, Jacob.

JACOB. And why didn't you come to church? Everybody was there and we waited fer you and they all said you'd come fer they knowed you was a man of your promise.

GILCHRIST [*suddenly striking his thigh*]. There again!

JACOB. And then you didn't and we sent up a hundred prayers for your soul, didn't we, Sion?

SION [*morosely*]. They prayed and prayed.

GILCHRIST. Thank 'ee.

JACOB. And we prayed for the whole neighborhood to be delivered from the curse of yer transgression.

GILCHRIST. Jacob, I'd be much obliged if you'd go on now and leave us.

JACOB. I'm going then, but they's others'll not go so easy. If you'd a-heard that preacher it'd a-melted yer heart.

GILCHRIST. He come here yesterday to melt my heart.

JACOB. Yeh, and he jest about had ye marching to the house of God.

GILCHRIST. Not him—mebbe.

RHODA. I asked him to go.

JACOB. You?—Thank the Lord.

RHODA. I knew he'd go over there and stand up to you all.

JACOB [*watching her*]. Ah, it was enough to break down a heart of stone to see the brethren and sistern weeping over yer lost estate. My own eyes still burn from they tears. [GILCHRIST *stares at the floor saying nothing.*] And the preacher is on his way here with a committee to wrastle with yer unforgiving sperit, Hardy.

GILCHRIST. Here?

JACOB. They're coming up the road.

GILCHRIST [*nervously*]. I'm going now to bury my hog. [*He stands up.*]

RHODA [*her face hardening*]. Let them come on. Show them who you are. [*Suddenly fighting back the tears.*] It's not right for them to worry you so. They don't know you. It's a sin for them to torment you, and you the best man in the world. [*Turning to* JACOB, *the tears beginning to pour down her face.*] Why, he is, Jacob. You know he is. Look how much good he does for people. And God himself could be no better to me. [*Hotly.*] It's because he's got more sense than all of them put together, and is better. [*She finally controls herself and stares at old* JACOB *malignantly.*]

JACOB [*stirring uneasily*]. Oh, yes, good in a world'y way. But that won't save yer soul—plenty o' heathens is good, Mis' Rhody.

GILCHRIST [*suddenly shaking himself*]. I ought to've gone to church.

RHODA. And I ought not to've asked you.

GILCHRIST. They had my promise. I could have stood and answered 'em word for word, argument for argument, they couldn't a-beat me down. [*Broodingly.*] I don't know, Rhody, maybe I—[*She looks at him, saying nothing.*]

JACOB [*angrily*]. You can throw off on us pore folks, Mis' Rhody, but the preacher's got plenty of sense and he'll speak fer us.

GILCHRIST. Yes, let 'em come on and talk to me.

[MAG *comes in suddenly from the rear, wearing an old cape over her head.*]

MAG. They's some folks coming up the lane there—My, it's beginning to rain outside. . . .

RHODA. Mag, roll him in the other room.

MAG [*rolling the baby into the room at the left*]. Come on, precious. He sleeps and sleeps.

RHODA [*shivering and drawing a cloak up from the depths of her chair around her shoulders*]. It's cold to be in April.

[GILCHRIST *starts and stirs the fire.*]

GILCHRIST. Jacob, I'd be much obliged if you'd leave us now.

JACOB [*testily*]. All right. I ain't a hand to be where I ain't wanted. Come on, Sion. [SION *puts away his mirror and follows him. At the rear door* JACOB *turns and looks back.*] They ain't nobody prayed fer ye harder'n me, Hardy.

GILCHRIST [*impassively*]. Much obliged. [JACOB *and* SION *go out.* GILCHRIST *stands punching the fire with the toe of his shoe, leaning his elbow on the mantel.*] Look, Rhody, that knife-blade's red-hot.

RHODA. Yes.

GILCHRIST [*tapping his lips*]. It looks like a long finger stuck out—even like a body lying straight in the fires o' hell.

RHODA [*as* MAG *returns*]. You can go on and cook dinner now, Mag.

MAG. All right'm.

[*She picks up a straw broom from the chimney corner and sweeps the hearth.*]

GILCHRIST. How's Lonie today?

MAG. She sets looking at the fire, that's all.

GILCHRIST. Ah!

MAG. Yes, that's all. [*She goes out at the rear.*]

GILCHRIST. I ought to've gone to the church. Then you wouldn't have to stand this. Go on into the other room and let 'em talk to me alone.

RHODA. A long time ago you said my place was with you.

GILCHRIST [*kissing her with sudden fervor*]. And it is . . . Ah, I don't know how I lived them years without you.

RHODA [*putting her hands on his head*]. And don't let me ever fail you.

GILCHRIST [*flinging out his hands suddenly*]. I could stand anything, have stood it. When it comes to people like them out there—good and kind and wanting to help us—then—well—I don't know, I don't know, I tell you. [*Intensively.*] Why, Rhody, they're my own people, my folks. They love me and I love them. We know one another. All the year and last year a kind of wall has been growing up between us. [*Half to himself.*] I got to break it down somehow.

RHODA. If they loved you would they hurt you so?

GILCHRIST [*smiling and shaking his head*]. You already know the answer, honey.

RHODA [*wonderingly*]. Because they love us they hurt us? [*Running the words over.*]

Love and suffering, love and suffering . . . so we know it well.

GILCHRIST. We're all alike down deep. I used to say so. Something in our heads we got, something different, God's maybe . . . principles we follow after—I've thought about it a heap.

RHODA [*uncertainly*]. Theirs is in heaven, ours nearer with us, like we prayed on the porch that evening. And a great gulf as far as to the sky divides them.

GILCHRIST. Yes, here with us . . . Wisht we could go on believing.

RHODA. We can.

GILCHRIST [*abruptly*]. I don't know.

RHODA. Hardy.

GILCHRIST [*going to the window at their right*]. Old Aunt Margaret comes there tramping in the rain. She nursed my mother the night I was born and come and help lay her out when she died. And every meeting year after year she's sent up a prayer for my soul. She's put her own boys away in the graveyard and loves me like a son in their place. And there's old Mis' Jones and Mis' Jernigan with her. They've all suffered and followed their God to the tomb. And the preacher leads 'em, the preacher coming here to gather my soul into heaven. And he's a good man, a thousand times better than me. He'd lay down his life for our little boy in there even and I wouldn't. [*Turning back into the room with a despairing gesture.*] Ah, there you are.

RHODA. Push it back from you.

GILCHRIST. Who could fight against 'em when they've suffered so? Like me they've suffered. Yea, more, and I feel for 'em and they feel for me. [*Steps are heard coming up the porch at the left front. A knock sounds on the door and* GILCHRIST *calls:*] Come in!

[*Three old women enter at the left front dressed in their crude Sunday clothes, their faces hid under big black slat-bonnets. The preacher, a thin middle-aged man with a pale, gentle face, follows them. He is dressed in cheap baggy clothes and carries a Bible in his hands. Without a word the women pass by* GILCHRIST, *clasp his hand a moment and look beseechingly up into his face with eyes red from weeping. Then they move on to* RHODA, *kiss her on the forehead, and get down on their knees in different parts of the room, bending their heads over on the seats of chairs and praying silently.* GILCHRIST *looks about him in consternation, makes a gesture of supplication towards them and then turns to* RHODA, *but she suddenly hides her face in her hands, crushed under their gentleness. He motions the preacher to a chair and sits down holding his head in his hand.*]

PREACHER [*quietly*]. We've been moved to come to ye, Brother Gilchrist.

GILCHRIST. I'm sorry.

PREACHER. We've had a great outpouring of the spirit at the church today. God said come. [*He smiles at* GILCHRIST *wanly.*]

GILCHRIST [*kindly*]. Thank you, we both thank you.

OLD MARGARET [*at her chair, whispering*]. Lord, hear our prayer.

[GILCHRIST *flinches at her words.*]

PREACHER. We want to read a word of scripture and have a prayer with ye. [*He looks at* GILCHRIST *pleadingly.*]

GILCHRIST. I don't know—

RHODA. Yes, let him, Hardy.

[GILCHRIST *bows his head in acquiescence, and the* PREACHER *opens his Bible.*]

PREACHER [*pulling at his collar*]. These are the words of God, not my words, brother. Though his words be like goads to the flesh, blessed be his holy name, they are just and full of mercy. For he hath said again and again that the proud heart goeth before destruction and the haughty spirit before a fall. [*Reading.*] "A man hath joy by the answer of his mouth. And a word spoken in due season, how good it is. The way of life is above to the wise, that he may depart from hell beneath. [*More loudly.*] The Lord will destroy the house of the proud; but he will establish the border of the widow. [*His voice breaking in the room clear and bell-like.*] The thoughts of the weeked are an abomination to the Lord; but the words of the pure are pleasant words. He that is greedy of gain troubleth his own house; but he that hateth gifts shall live. The heart of the righteous studieth to answer; but the mouth of the weeked poureth out evil things. The Lord is far from the weeked; but he heareth the prayer of the righteous. The light of the eyes rejoiceth the heart; and a good report maketh the bones fat. The ear that heareth the reproof of life abideth among the wise. He that refuseth instruction despiseth his own soul; but he that heareth reproof getteth understanding. The fear of the Lord is the instruction of wisdom; and before honor is humility." [JACOB *and* SION *have crept in at the rear. The* PREACHER *closes the Bible.*] Let us pray.

[*He gets down on his knees and* JACOB *does likewise.* SION *looks on with his mouth agape and finally he bows down.* RHODA *and* GILCHRIST *sit bent over in their seats.*]

GILCHRIST [*softly*]. Go in your room, Rhody, and shut the door.

[*She makes no reply as the* PREACHER *begins to pray.*]

PREACHER. O Lord, come down now and be close to us and hear our prayer, give us strength, give our word strength, let it bring forth fruit from the heart of this man and this woman.

OLD MARGARET [*twisting her head against her chair*]. O Lord, do, Lord, adder these hyuh many years!

PREACHER. Day in and day out, night after night, we have called upon thee to bring these erring children, man and woman, man and wife in thy sight, towards thy holy throne. Thy ways are past understanding and we needs must continue to pray, holding on to thy promise, beseeching thee to save these for whom our hearts do ache and bleed. [*Old* JACOB *and the women answer with deep groans.*] Thou sawest the tears of thy children shed for them today, thou sendest thy holy spirit down to seal our hearts and give the message unto us. And we have obeyed thee, we have come to the threshold of this home to do thy will. And it please thy blessed name we shall not go away until thou hast sentest thy blessing to this afflicted house. Yea, Lord! Yea, Lord!

OLD MARGARET. Amen. [*The others answer her.*] Hardy, can't ye see how we love ye and her!

GILCHRIST. Rhody, please don't stay in here.

PREACHER [*his voice gathering strength*]. And thou hast promised thy wrath to them who sit in the seat of the scornful. Listen, Lord.

OLD MARGARET. Do, Lord. Save my boy.

THE OTHERS. Do, Lord.

PREACHER. Listen to our prayer, to the voice of thy children crying out of this dark world towards the gates of the New Jerusalem. Answer us and send thy power on this man. Touch him with thy finger that he may know thee as God, the very God, the Most High, the ruler of the firmament, the Alpha and Omega and the Great I Am. For thou art all good, all kind, and lovest all. This man and woman art precious in thy sight. You love them the way they love their little boy!

OLD MARGARET [*with a low moan*]. Yea, Lord.

[*The two women and* JACOB *groan and mumble after her.*]

PREACHER [*beginning to beat on the floor with his hands*]. Thou hast sentest warning and warning to him and he heeded them not. And woe, woe, woe, when thy wrath is loosed in the judgment day. For it is all prophesied and promised to them that forget God. Thou gavest him a saintly wife for ten years and five and she wrestled with his soul to bring it to the fold of thy salvation. And on her dying bed she warned him and he heeded her not. Yea, his proud spirit sent her to her grave. [GILCHRIST *jerks up his head.*] And who knows why he heeded her not? Yea, even so, she died so suddenly! The neighbors came and found her dead and another woman beside him. Lord, if there's evil hid away there make him confess and bring it to the light.

RHODA [*moaning*]. Stop it! Stop it!

GILCHRIST [*standing up and then sitting again*]. Great God!

JACOB. Lord, thou wilt bring all that is hid away to light.

PREACHER [*slashing his arms around him*]. Thou canst see into his heart, whe'r it's all black and vile there, what thoughts he's had, what he's planned in the night, for thou seest all.

OLD MARGARET [*turning and embracing* GILCHRIST'S *feet*]. Confess it all, Hardy, clean out yer heart and save yer pore soul.

[*He stares at her uncomprehendingly, shaking his head now and then as if trying to rid himself of a dream.*]

PREACHER. And thou hast seen it all and marked it all. Thou hast set a curse upon him since the day Sister Etta, a saint of God, died in this house. And yet thou lovest him, we all do. Thou sentest a young man, pore soul, who took his own life as a warning and still this man heeded thee not.

GILCHRIST [*hoarsely*]. Spare me something.

PREACHER. He heeded thee not. And thou hast marked him down in thy book and we thy children see thy wrath breaking upon him and breaking upon us. [*He wrings his hands and twists about the floor, his voice rising into a croon now and then, and the tears wetting his cheeks.*] The lightning came in the summer and struck his barns as a message of thy wrath. His crops begun to fail him and disease has come among his cattle and his stock. [*Wildly.*] Yea, thou art God of all things and there's none beside thee. Crucify him, Lord, until he sees the light. I would I could be crucified in his stead, but he must save himself and die unto salvation. [*He hesitates a moment as if listening for a message, and then his voice breaks forth jubilantly.*] I hear you, Lord, and receive thy word. Yea, thou wilt continue to persecute him, thou sendest me thy promise. Stretch him on the rack, for it is the way to his salvation. Already thou hast laid hand on his little son—keep it on him—take him away to make his proud heart yield. For he's a murderer, murderer! [*His voice sharp as a knife.*] And we know it, his neighbors know it!

THE WOMEN. Oh, Lord, ha' mercy!

PREACHER. Yea, he stands condemned as a murderer, a destroyer of life. So is he in the minds of his people. And so he will stand until he do confess and humble himself before Almighty God. As thou hast said, "Will a man rob God? Yet ye have robbed me." [*In a hollow voice.*] "Ye are cursed with a curse; for ye have robbed me, even—"

RHODA. Have mercy on us, have mercy.

[*She rises from her seat, turns helplessly about and then flees into the room at the left.* GILCHRIST *pays no attention to her, but sits rocking his head from side to side. The women suddenly burst forth in a frenzy of lamentation and prayer: "Lordy, Lord, keep thy hand on him, bow down his will—save him, Jesus, save him. Let us have the light—the light for the darkness—tear the scales from his eyes—have mercy!" The preacher leans his head over on the floor shivering.*]

JACOB [*beginning to clap his hands*]. Thy will, Holy Father, thy will be done. [*His voice choking with sobs.*] Save him, Our Father, save Hardy Gilchrist from the burning pit.

[MAG *comes in from the rear, watches a moment wide-eyed and then goes quickly out.* SION *sits back on his heels looking on, and now and then he wipes the tears from his eyes with his dirty handkerchief. The* PREACHER *on his knees feels blankly around him, touches a chair and leans weakly against it, mopping his face with trembling hands.* OLD MARGARET *breaks forth into loud screams, and rising to her feet, throws her arms ecstatically around* GILCHRIST, *hugging him to her breast.*]

OLD MARGARET. Glory to God! Glory to God! Hardy, boy, cain't ye confess yer sins fer me and save yourself in heaven? Yer pore mother is up there, Etta's up there watching for ye to come to God. [*She falls on his neck weeping piteously. The other women come and crouch down at his feet.* OLD MARGARET *raises* GILCHRIST'S *head and looks him in the face.*] Look at me, Hardy, look at the tears all of us is shedding fer ye. You're my little boy and my pore old heart aches fer ye.

GILCHRIST [*brokenly*]. Don't, Aunt Margaret. [*Catching her hands hungrily and staring at them.*] Pore hands that worked for me, cared for me—Oh, God!

OLD MARGARET. And they will to the end. [*Sobbing.*] They ain't nothing I wouldn't do fer ye, boy. I love ye better'n my own, that's dead and gone. I'm a mother to ye.

GILCHRIST [*convulsively*]. Mother!

OLD MARGARET [*falling on her knees and laying her head in his lap*]. Son! My son, my boy!

[*Her bonnet is pushed back and* GILCHRIST *gently touches her gray wispy hair. At his touch she throws her hands over her head, feverishly clasping his.*]

PREACHER [*turning and crying out*]. A man who mought be a prophet among us. Purify him, Lord, and let him lead!

THE OTHERS. Let him go before us.

PREACHER. And we will stand with him in that great day. [*Shouting.*] In that great day that's coming.

[*Standing up and beginning to sing:*]

There's a great day a-coming, a great day a-coming,
There's a great day a-coming by and by.

[*The women climb to their feet singing and clapping their hands.*]

When the saints and the sinners shall be parted right and left—
Are you ready for that day to come?

[*Old* JACOB *rises to his feet singing.* SION *clambers up after him, his fresh voice rising beautiful and clear. The song mounts into a high mournful harmony as the singers draw up and encircle* GILCHRIST.]

Are you ready? Are you ready?
Are you ready for that day to come?
Are you ready? Are you ready?
Are you ready for the judgment day?

[GILCHRIST *suddenly stands up and looms above them.*]

There's a sad day a-coming, a sad day a-coming,
There's a sad day a-coming by and by,
When the sinner shall hear his doom,
"Depart, I know ye not!"
Are you ready for that day to come?

GILCHRIST [*his face pale and drawn*]. Stop it, let me say something—[*His words piling out, low and vehement.*] I don't want her to know it, I don't want Rhody to hear. But it's been eating in me—here—[*Striking his breast.*] I been trying to get away from it. I don't know what to do about it. I've tried to pray—

PREACHER. Bless the Lord!

GILCHRIST. It won't come right—I know there's something wrong somewhere. I don't let her know—don't let her know. I hold up strong before her—I keep fighting —fighting without the light seems like—and things keep going against me. Maybe you're right—don't try me no more, leave me to myself. I got to see it for myself—

[OLD MARGARET *watches him happily, her toothless jaws trembling with eagerness.*]

PREACHER. God can clear it up.

GILCHRIST [*going on monotonously*]. Everything is all mixed up, my head seems all dead and cold—I keep lying awake at night—I don't tell her—I don't let her know—I keep trying and saying we'll make it—I got to think it out, there's a way out—Last night I saw a thousand faces looking at me. [*Half whining as he turns upon them.*] You come digging in my heart, you make me say things, you cut me in here like a knife—[*To himself.*] The preacher said you killed Etta—Murderer! Murderer!—He says God knows all the blackness in my heart—I'll see about it, I'll see. . . . "Ye are cursed with a curse . . ." Ah! . . . [*Pushing his way through them.*] Hardy Gilchrist never killed anybody, never hurt anybody—Didn't he? There's been death all around me—Etta, Neill—Something's all mixed up—[SION *continues singing, caught in the spell of the music, his face rapt and lifted towards the sky.* GILCHRIST *suddenly throws his arms around those nearest him.*] You are my own people, born with me in these fields, and I feel humbled down before you, you break my heart in two. Yea, the low and the high, the strong and the weak, all are one. I know nothing but that. [*Lifting up his voice.*] Where is this God? Let him speak to me and I would answer him. He knows my heart! Proud! I'm not proud! [*He drops on his knees before* SION *and bends his head to the floor.* SION *sings on unconscious of him.*]

THE OTHERS [*in a burst of fervor*]. Glory hallelujah! He'll see the light! God have mercy!

GILCHRIST [*standing up*]. Let me alone! [*Raising his head.*] All right. You use my people to crush me! Let it be you and me, man to man. I'll go talk to you, and you answer me!

[*He turns quickly and dashes out at the rear. They watch him go wonderingly, and then one by one they raise their illumined faces in song.*]

Are you ready? Are you ready?
Are you ready for that day to come?

[*The music swells into a high fervid harmony. In the midst of the singing* RHODA *bursts in from the room at the left.*]

RHODA [*screaming at them*]. You stop that and leave this house! Where's Hardy? You're trying to kill him. He's a thousand times better than you all, better than anybody, better than God is. . . . He loves all of you and that's why you . . . [*They sing on, paying no attention to her, their faces set in ecstasy.*] Hardy! Hardy!

[*She rushes through the door at the left rear after him. Presently* MAG *comes in leading her. She goes up to the* PREACHER, *starts to strike him, and then flings herself down on the floor sobbing. The music rises triumphant above her and* MAG *comes softly forward and bends down by her prostrate form.*]

Are you ready? Are you ready?
Are you ready for the judgment day?

[*The curtain is lowered and the music dies away. When it comes up again, several hours have elapsed. It is late at night of the same day. A fire is blazing in the fireplace and outside the wind and the rain drive through the trees and against the house in great droning gusts.* RHODA *sits by the baby's cradle as before. Now and then as the wind and rain swoop down in sudden violence, she lifts a pale anguished face to listen. Presently* MAG *comes in from the rear porch carrying an unlighted lamp and a coffee pot. She sets the lamp on the bureau, lights it and begins to heat the pot on a bed of coals at the hearth.*]

RHODA. Have you heard anything—anybody shouting?

MAG. No'm, nothing yit.

RHODA. I thought I heard his voice a while ago—in the wind, far-off like.

MAG. It was them trees out there bending and squeaking. Don't you worry, he'll be shore to come in a minute.

RHODA. Something's happened to him, something terrible.

MAG. I've told you a hundred times, Mis' Rhody, he'd come back in a little bit. [*She puts wood on the fire and sweeps the hearth.*]

RHODA. Ah, but the clock's struck 'leven and he's not here.

MAG. Cain't nothing happen to a big well man like him.

RHODA. He's sick. They did it with their preaching. They just about broke his heart and mine too.

MAG. He's off hunting the sow that's found pigs in the pasture, that's what I bet.

RHODA. Oh, me!

MAG. Have you fed the baby?

RHODA. Fed him?

MAG. Ah . . . Jacob'll soon be hyuh and give us news. Mebbe they're coming back together.

RHODA. If he could a-found him in the field he'd been back long ago.

MAG. I'll have you some coffee in a bit. It'll warm you up and make you feel better.

RHODA. I can't drink a drop.

MAG. But you ain't et a bite all day. You got to eat, Mis' Rhody, and git your strength back.

RHODA. I don't want my strength back. Oh, I don't want to live any more, Mag. Can't we have any peace?

MAG [*wiping her eyes with her apron*]. Now, now, in a week you'll be up a-singing about the house. You must stop worrying so for the baby's sake. [*She sets a chair with hanging clothes to the fire to dry.* RHODA *rises and makes her way to the window and stands staring out.*] You'd better come back to the fire, Mis' Rhody, you'll ketch your death o' cold there.

RHODA. Listen to that wind and that rain, rain, rain, day and night, day and night. Won't it ever stop? [*Turning to* MAG *and clutching her feverishly.*] Get somebody to make it stop, Mag! I can't stand it any more. [*Crying out.*] Somebody make it stop pouring down, and Hardy out there lost in it! [*She turns and stares abstractedly in the fire as if fascinated with some inner absorption. Her voice rises husky and level.*] I know now. Hardy's dead!

MAG. Nanh—nanh—he's as much alive as you or me.

RHODA. I don't believe it. I can't believe it. I can't believe nothing except he's dead. I've prayed and prayed to God; Mag, I prayed all the evening, but God won't hear me. Ah, he's set his curse on us forever.

MAG. You better go lie back down now. It'll fair off tomorrow and the sun'll be out again, and Mr. Hardy'll be back and all'll be fine.

[*She starts leading her across the room to the left. Suddenly the raindrops burst on the roof like a patter of gravel thrown, and a sharp gust of wind sucks the flame out of the lamp.*]

RHODA [*shrieking*]. Somebody blowed out the lamp!

MAG [*hurriedly getting a match from the mantel-piece and striking it*]. It was the wind. It blew suddent under the door there. [*She lights it again.*]

RHODA [*shivering and speaking in a throaty whisper*]. It's her, Mag. She's back here. Don't you reckon so?

MAG [*starting with terror*]. Anh?

RHODA. She's never left us, Mag. [*Pointing to the bedroom at the rear.*] She stays in there. I hear her at night moving about, slipping around. I know it's her. [*She tiptoes across the room to the door at the right rear and tries the knob.*] I got her locked in, but she can get out, Mag, she comes through the key-hole. She wants to steal the baby, wants to kill him. Don't you tell Hardy when he comes. He don't know. I heard the bed-springs pop in there about dark and she got up and opened her trunk for something. I heard her plain. And I run and locked the door tight. [*Moaning.*] But she can get out.

MAG. Lord a-mercy!

RHODA. And at night I'd wake up and hear her playing her organ in there and singing.

MAG [*nervously*]. Come on to bed now. [*She puts her arm around her and leads her across the room.*]

RHODA. You saw her once too, Mag. Jacob said you did.

MAG. No, no, I didn't. It was more of Jacob's lies.

RHODA [*drawing back from her bedroom door*]. I'm a-scared to go in there.

MAG. There's your bed in there.

RHODA. Hardy's in there. He'll hurt me.

MAG [*staring at her*]. What's the matter, Mis' Rhody?

RHODA [*shaking her head and brushing her hand across her face*]. I'm kinder lost or some-thing. Let me lie down now.

[MAG *helps her in to bed, comes out and closes the door. She takes the poker and stirs the fire into crackling flames.*]

MAG [*crouching down by the hearth*]. A-ah, the end of the world's coming on us. [*The door at the left rear opens gently and* JACOB *comes in with a lantern. His old rain-coat and felt hat are streaming with water, and a blast of rainy wind blows in behind him.* MAG *starts up at the suddenness of his entrance.*] Jacob, I didn't hear you.

JACOB [*softly*]. I didn't want to skeer her. Where is she?

MAG [*lowering her voice*]. Laid down a minute.

RHODA [*inside*]. Jacob, Jacob! [*The door opens and she bursts in.*]

JACOB. I was hoping mebbe he'd come while I was gone. I ain't found him.

RHODA [*staring before her*]. He's in the creek drowned!

MAG [*coming to her and leading her back into her room*]. We'll find him, we will.

JACOB. Yes'm, I'm going to git Sandy and we'll find him. Don't you worry.

MAG [*coming out of the room and closing the door*]. Pore thing!

JACOB. Aye, pitiful!

MAG. Didn't you see no sign?

JACOB. His tracks led off 'crost the bottom to the woods, and then I couldn't follow him.

MAG. No telling what's happened. Why'd you all come hyuh and try to run him out'n his senses?

JACOB [*warming himself*]. The sperit led us and you oughta helped. Laord in heaven, sich a sorrowful house—a-ah! [*He takes off his coat and sits down.*]

MAG. I'm going on home now and I want you to stay.

JACOB [*starting up*]. Nanh, nanh, I ain't gonna stay hyuh by myself.

MAG. They ain't nothing to hurt you, Jacob. I got to see about Lonie.

JACOB. This house's accursed, Mag, you said so.

MAG [*resignedly*]. Aye, it is, I reckon.

JACOB. If you go and leave, I'm going too.

MAG. I ain't slept in it a night since they was married and I don't 'spec' to. When I stayed I sot up.

JACOB. Aye.

MAG. I did.

JACOB [*taking up his lantern*]. I'm going to

find Hardy and bring him home if he's to be found.

MAG [*stepping before him*]. No, you ain't. You got to stay with me. She makes me skeered saying Mis' Etta's in the house.

JACOB. Hanh?—It's her being sick so long makes her think it, you reckon?

MAG. I reckon. She ain't well by no means. She hadn't ort to be out'n that bed, fer she give birth the hardest I've ever seed fer a healthy woman. [*Going over to the crib.*] And any minute now it'll die.

JACOB [*setting down his lantern*]. Anh! You've been faithful to 'em, Mag.

MAG. Lord, listen at that wind and rain!

JACOB. The whole world'll be washed away yit. They'll be a second Noey's flood.

[*A heavy step sounds on the rear porch.* JACOB *and* MAG *stand fearfully away from the left rear door.*]

MAG. That's him, that's him at last, Jacob!

JACOB. I knowed he'd come. [*The door opens and* GILCHRIST *enters. He is hatless and drenched to the skin, his face haggard. He comes in and sits by the fire without a word.*] Is that you, Hardy, safe at last?

GILCHRIST [*softly*]. Is Rhody asleep?

JACOB. Where've you been? We've scoured the country for you.

MAG. She's in there.

RHODA [*with a scream of joy within*]. Hardy!

[*As he goes into her room, she springs forward to meet him and throws her arms around him sobbing.* MAG *goes over and closes the door, and* RHODA'S *voice comes mumbling and broken from the room.*]

JACOB [*picking up his lantern*]. Anh, I don't understand it.

MAG. Air you going now?

JACOB. Adder I walk my legs off—a-hunting him, in he comes. He'd ort to be carried to Raleigh and put in the 'sylum. I'm going on now.

MAG [*getting her cape and bonnet from the corner and putting them on*]. I'm going with you.

JACOB. I'll be dead with a cold from this. [*They start out.*]

MAG. Mebbe we'd better not leave 'em, Jacob, what you say?

JACOB. I'm a-going, I tell you.

MAG. I don't like—[*She stands a moment undecided.*]

RHODA [*coming suddenly into the room*]. Don't go, Mag, don't go. Stay with me, you and Jacob!

MAG. You'll be all right now, Mis' Rhody. He's back. . . . You and him go to sleep. I'll come down in the morning, God willing.

RHODA [*beseechingly*]. No, no, you mustn't go, I'm afraid. . . .

MAG. I cain't. I cain't stay another minute, Mis' Rhoda. [*She and* JACOB *go out quickly.*]

RHODA [*going to the bedroom door*]. Come on, dry yourself. [*Fearfully.*] What you hunting for, Hardy?

GILCHRIST [*within*]. I can't find it nowhere. [*There is a sound of closing drawers and* GILCHRIST *comes into the room.*] Have you seen it, Etta?

RHODA [*starting*]. What you want?

GILCHRIST [*with a queer smile*]. I'd always put it where I couldn't find it, and when I'd want to shave I'd ask Etta where it was.

RHODA [*throwing her arms around him*]. Hardy, you've scared us all to death. I've cried and prayed for you all the evening.

GILCHRIST [*pushing her from him*]. Yeh, yeh, sorrow and tears is our lot.

[*He rummages in the drawers of the bureau.* RHODA *moves unsteadily over to him and clings to him.*]

RHODA. Hardy, you're scaring me again. Come to the fire; you're wringing wet.

GILCHRIST [*suddenly shouting out and striking her*]. Keep your hands away from me, you sinful woman! [*She staggers back from him and falls weakly into the rocking chair, staring at him terrified. For a moment he stands gazing back at her and then with a cry he runs to her and buries his face in her lap.*] No, no, honey, I didn't mean it. I'm crazy, crazy! [*His voice rising high in pain.*] Why won't they let me alone! [*He hugs her to him convulsively, his shoulders rocking and heaving.*]

RHODA. Don't worry, don't think of it any more. I'll take care of you. [*Stroking his head.*] Nothing can't bother you now.

GILCHRIST [*raising his head*]. There's somebody hammering and beating in my head, beating on an anvil with a sledge-hammer. [*Hitting his breast with his fists.*] And I'm stifling in here. [*Suddenly he stands up and his face hardens into its former cold and haggard look.*] I hear something like a voice talking to me in a field a thousand miles from here.

[*He moves away from her and begins searching through the drawers, on the mantel, and around the room.*]

RHODA. Hardy!

GILCHRIST. Somebody's hid it.

RHODA [*gasping*]. Come back, come back, you're sick.

GILCHRIST [*turning quickly towards her*]. Sick—you and me—sick unto death and they ain't enough doctors in the world to cure us. I know it now.

RHODA [*stretching out her hands*]. Come back to my arms, Hardy. I'll save you!

GILCHRIST [*starting back*]. Look, look, there's blood on your hands. [*Holding out his hands.*] And there's blood on mine. Blood everywhere. You and me killed her and we killed him.

RHODA [*shuddering*]. Ah.

GILCHRIST. And blood must pay for blood. [*He feels in the lower drawer of the bureau and takes out something.*] You thought I wouldn't find it, did you?

RHODA [*staring at him in horror*]. I didn't know it was there.

GILCHRIST. I've got it now.

RHODA [*staggering across the room to the door at the rear and pulling it open*]. Help, help!

GILCHRIST [*sitting down by the fire and looking before him*]. Don't cry and scream. I'm not going to hurt you.

[RHODA *creeps back to her chair and sits down, watching him with wide eyes.*]

RHODA. Hardy, don't look like that. What's happened?

GILCHRIST. That's a good fire there. Dry oak wood burns fine, a red flame in front and a blue one behind—hot as hell—and red as blood. . . . There's a plenty of wood under the shelter to last you till warm weather, ain't there?

RHODA. Yes, yes, but it don't matter now.

GILCHRIST. A good farmer is always prepared for anything that happens—a woodpile full of wood for bad weather and plenty of corn for his stock, ain't he?

RHODA. Yes, yes.

GILCHRIST [*bitterly*]. Is he? Hanh, no man knows what's liable to come upon him, no man knows what a fix his mind can get in, does he?

RHODA. Maybe not, maybe he can't know. But forget it, forget it all.

GILCHRIST. Nobody but God knows what's going to happen, and he won't tell no man. I went out in the rain there to talk with their God, to match muscle with him—to get at the truth. Oh—we are blind and scared like chickens before a hawk. A sparrow sets on the ditch bank and a snake raises his head and swallows him, and with my briar-hook I come along and kill that snake. Aye, God mebbe is lying in wait with his hook same as if I was a snake. That's what Neill called me—called me a snake, a snake in the grass. You heard him that day.

RHODA. That's all done been forgot long, long ago, Hardy. Rest your poor mind from it.

GILCHRIST. It's fresh with me now same as yesterday. [*Stretching out his arms.*] When my grandmammy died it was a cold winter day and I was a little boy no higher'n this chair I'm setting in. I was out in the yard playing marbles, and before she died I heard a sweet cheeping sound and I looked up and a little bird as white as snow was setting on the comb of the house. And it was singing so pitiful-like it made me want to cry. I run in the house to tell Muh and there they was all sitting around still as death and Grandmuh was stretched out long and stiff under a sheet. There come a whirring sound in the room and that little bird went flying around and around over the bed cheeping like its heart was broke. Then it flew out of the door and across the field. At the burying that day, after they put flowers on the grave, it come up out of the woods and perched itself on the headboard singing its song. When they weren't nobody looking I took my bean-shooter and shot at it and scared it away. They said after it was Grandmuh's soul.

RHODA [*trembling*]. What is it?

GILCHRIST. I saw that little bird again today setting on the fence in the graveyard. But I didn't have my bean-shooter with me, I'm too old.

RHODA. Was that where you've been, Hardy?

GILCHRIST [*suddenly standing up with a bitter laugh*]. When you and me die there won't be no little snow-white bird singing for us, will there? There'll be a buzzard setting on the roof of this house and his'll be the only mourning. [RHODA *stares at him in amazement.*] I'm going out to the barn now. Yeh, I went out to meet him and he was too much—

RHODA. No, no! You mustn't leave me!

GILCHRIST. I won't be long. I heard a plank flopping in the wind there and it's got to be nailed up and the mules ain't been fed, poor things. [*As he starts out* RHODA *springs up and clings to him. He throws her from him into the rocking chair and stands gazing at her cowering in her seat.*] Look at that hair and eyes and breast I've felt against my face night after night. I've drunk 'em down like a man perished and starved for a cool spring and they've et up my vitals. All the time it was a harlot sucking my soul out'n me . . . maybe so.

RHODA. O God, have mercy upon me!

GILCHRIST. Ah, it was.

[*He turns and strides out at the left rear, leaving the door open. The wind and the rain blow in scattering the sparks through the room.* RHODA *bends over in her chair rocking and moaning with her head in her arms. Then she springs up and starts after him. Presently the child emits a thin high wail in its crib, gasps once or twice and is silent.* RHODA *turns and snatches it frantically up in her arms, walking back and forth across the room, feeling its feet, rubbing its body and crooning over it. After a moment she runs to the door at the rear.*]

RHODA [*shrieking*]. Hardy! Hardy! [*She starts to dash out through the door, but a rush of wind and water breaks across her and the baby. Looking down at the bundle in her arms, she wraps it protectingly from the storm and then turns helplessly back into the room. Presently she goes over to* MRS. GILCHRIST'S *bedroom door and stands before it cold and straight.*] And you could get out. . . . You've had your way and taken him at last. You had no heart. . . . A good woman! . . . Ah, cold and dark as the grave itself. Death, bloody and cruel death, reaching out and taking life. . . . Now you can rest and be satisfied. . . . Aunt Etta, I never bothered you, I never hurt you. Still you won't let us be . . . Jesus! Jesus! . . . [*Sobbing, she lays the baby back in its crib and bows over it in heartbroken grief. And for a long while she bends her head crushed and stupefied. Then she moves uncertainly over before the fire and gradually raises her head and looks before her, her face settling into a cold impassive mask.*] Take all I've got then and drive me from the face of the earth. . . . Aunt Etta! God! [*Clenching her fist.*] And you can kill me, but I hate you for it all. Kill me, crucify me and I'll not bow my knee now. My tongue will not confess you. [GILCHRIST *opens the door and comes in. He sits down as before. A gasp breaks from her.*] Thank the Lord!

GILCHRIST. I heard a voice calling seemed like. A long ways off.

RHODA. It was me calling for you.

GILCHRIST. Aye. [*He sits staring abstractedly at the fire.*]

RHODA. I was calling for you.

GILCHRIST [*starting*]. He stuck his nose out of the stall and whickered at me and rubbed my shoulder. [*Shuddering.*] And that plank ain't nailed. [*Raising his head.*] I hear it banging.

RHODA. Yes. . . .

GILCHRIST. The cow was breathing soft and the pigs grunting and rubbing by the well-post. [*Shivering.*] It was all so plain, like I've heard them all my days.

RHODA [*to herself*]. And it said woe to them that strive with the maker of heaven and earth.

GILCHRIST [*watching her*]. Yea, woe! Woe here and woe hereafter in hell where you and me'll maybe burn forever and ever.

RHODA [*starting and turning toward him*]. It must be easier there.

GILCHRIST. She put a curse on us and we fed our lust on top of her grave.

RHODA. Let God judge.

GILCHRIST [*suddenly striking his breast and crying out in a loud voice*]. He set his mark on me and branded me and hunted me down like Cain of old. And he branded you along with me and our children would a-been born hewers of wood and drawers of water like the black men from the land of Nod. Him there in the crib'd be if he lives.

RHODA. Ah—God is a sneaking coward, their God! I hate him!

GILCHRIST. No, no! A just and righteous God, the Lord our God, like he says in the book. I was condemned here in my heart and I know now. Tonight my soul testifies it unto me.

RHODA. Hurry and kill me then if you believe it.

GILCHRIST [*standing up and staring before him*]. I was blinded in my own strength. And now I see things clearer. Etta said I would. He sent signs to me and I wouldn't heed 'em. He sent Etta on the way with me to pray for me and bring me to the fold and I wouldn't heed him. I kept piling up the goods of this world and bragging in my own might. And then he sent death on her and a curse in her mouth to drive me from my evil ways and still I wouldn't heed him.

RHODA. He. He! who is he! Ah, a thief that kills, that steals the first-born!

GILCHRIST [*sitting down again*]. Hush, hush. Look how he's sent his warnings to me. He stayed hid back behind his sky somewhere and let me go on my way. He let me stand up in the morning of life with you and taste of the joys of sin and when I was wropped away in it all he said to hisself, "Now I am the Great I Am and there's none beside me and I'll put forth my power and destroy him." And he sent fire from heaven to fall upon me and a drought to come in the summer and parch up my crops. That preacher he knew it all. The cholera come and killed off my hogs and he cursed the whole neighborhood because of me. And he says I got to answer to him, render up my account. I been out there under that pine where his lightning struck three times. I went and prayed to him and tried to get answer. And at last he heard me there with the wind and rain blowing. [*Calmly.*] He says death. [*Shouting.*] Death! And what was to be will be. . . . The God of these fields, the God of the whole universe says I got to make sacrifice unto Him. . . . Oh, Etta, Etta, hear me, speak to me and tell me you hear me now.

RHODA [*whispering*]. Their God, not our God.

GILCHRIST. Yes, the God of all. [*With a loud drunken-like cry.*] I hear you—yes—yes— [*He moves awkwardly across the room towards the door at the right rear.*] Come up out of that wide field—too far—too far away. [*Whispering.*] Yes, yes, we are nothing. [RHODA *pushes herself in front of him.*] He is everything. Like a breath we are gone. He abideth and remaineth like the hills—from generation to generation. Man is a flower soon cut down.

RHODA. She's gone away from in there.

GILCHRIST. Death must wipe out death. I'm going to her.

RHODA. No, no, not you.

GILCHRIST. Me, me. It's got to be paid somehow. Death for death, an eye for an eye—

RHODA. If it's death, then he's paid. Look.

GILCHRIST [*clasping his head in his hands and staring at her*]. I'm crazy, crazy. I know I'm crazy, and yet I can't seem to stop. . . . Something driving me on. [*His voice sharp with pain.*] But he's beat me down. I'm tired now and I give in under his hand. . . . Ah, me, I don' know what to do.

RHODA [*pushing him toward the crib*]. Look now. It was to be him and not you.

[GILCHRIST *gradually turns and stares down into the crib and then starts forward and puts his hand upon the dead child. He turns and blinks at* RHODA *uncomprehendingly.*]

GILCHRIST [*dully*]. Took him and spared me.

RHODA [*bitterly*]. The Great I Am that comes in the night! . . . A righteous God.

GILCHRIST [*starting back*]. Who done that?

RHODA. Him—her, God and Aunt Etta.

GILCHRIST. We didn't, did we? Not you and me? We didn't kill him too?

RHODA [*vehemently*]. She was here in the house and kept me afraid. Deep down I felt her stealing about, her spirit waiting to kill him.

GILCHRIST. Ha! She could never forget and

never forgive. Fifteen year she said she loved me, and I don't know. Maybe she hated me.

RHODA. She did. She loved nobody.

GILCHRIST. Her God, he done it?

RHODA. A God of hate.

GILCHRIST [*as if stung to sudden awareness*]. The innocent—I'm the guilty. [*Whining in sudden fury.*] Who would do that? [*Mumbling over and over.*] The innocent—the defenseless. [*His voice breaking in a bitter laugh.*] It wa'n't her, it was him behind her, principles, Gods—maybe something behind that, the way of things. [*Bending over the crib.*] He wants all. Whatever it is, that'll take all, will it? Take him and me and you and wipe us out . . . sweep us away like dust in a wind. [*The windows rattle in their sockets, and the wind booms around the house.*] Hah, listen at him there in the night. [*Beating the back of his hand fiercely in his palm.*] Same like he was trying to get in here at us —that wind is like God after us, like the world turned against us.

RHODA [*huskily, as she comes up and stands beside him*]. And we are not afraid.

GILCHRIST [*monotonously*]. Not afraid. [*Angrily.*] He comes when I'm gone and takes away my child.

RHODA. And spares you.

GILCHRIST [*savagely*]. To make me suffer more.

RHODA. Let it be, and we can bear it.

GILCHRIST. Now he's mashed us down to the bottom. The world wipes its feet on us. There's nothing else can happen to us, we're down, down at the bottom now.

RHODA [*weakly*]. But we can rise again.

GILCHRIST [*repeating childishly*]. Rise up and fight again. [*His hand wanders vaguely in the air before him, strengthening gradually into a clenched fist.*]

RHODA [*catching his arm*]. We both can. There's bound to be pleasure, joy somewhere for us.

GILCHRIST [*clutching her to him*]. Oh, Rhody, a little more—a little more.

RHODA. That can be the way—you and me in our love—together, going together.

GILCHRIST [*hungrily*]. Yes, yes. . . .

RHODA. Nothing can touch that—our love will remain, you and me together every day, you and me to the end. See all this sorrow, like a purpose to it, and still it didn't touch our love.

GILCHRIST [*tenderly*]. They can't touch that. Nothing ever has and nothing ever will. That's so, nothing can keep me from loving you. [*Triumphantly.*] And nothing can keep you from loving me. Ah, I feel now maybe death couldn't. [*Feverishly.*] Rhody, Rhody, help me now. Let that lead us towards rest, towards peace, peace. . . .

RHODA [*whispering*]. Peace . . . salvation and mercy . . . in our love.

GILCHRIST [*to himself*]. God can't kill that, nothing can. Yea, it is stronger than him, than all the world. It comes to me clearer now like a light—[*Wrinkling his forehead.*] like a great light.

RHODA. It is. And my love will never die.

GILCHRIST. Nor mine. . . . It lives. . . . It is life . . . life. . . . Life is—you—me—[*Lifting up his face.*] Let the dead pass behind us —like a dream and leave us forever. Their way is the way of death. Ours the way of love and that is life. It is, ain't it, honey?

RHODA. Yes, yes.

GILCHRIST [*as if seeing a vision*]. Love and life, love—life. It lives beyond death. [*His face crinkling into a smile.*] That's it, that's it. Life and more abundant life. You are my life, the one I love . . . my wife and I'm not afraid now with you here. [*Mumbling.*] Somehow all I can think of is you here with me now, so close to me there's nothing else in the world for me to think of hardly.

RHODA [*almost dreamily*]. And never be afraid, never any more.

GILCHRIST. Not afraid of God even, their God that sets on his golden throne. No, not that. God, their God—They are their god. But he's outside, up there in the sky—[*Loudly.*] They put him up there. [*Striking his heart.*] In here is where he belongs. [*Loudly.*] Rhody, Rhody, up there he is death and destruction, in here he is peace, life. [*His voice dies out and he stands gazing at her with burning intensity.* RHODA *leans her head against his breast and they stand locked in each other's embrace. Presently there is a loud knock on the door at the rear. They pay no attention to it. It sounds again.* GILCHRIST *calls.*] Who's knocking there?

[*The door opens and the* PREACHER *comes in dripping wet.*]

PREACHER [*timidly*]. Brother Hardy, I left 'em praying. I had to come and speak with you again. [*They make no reply. The* PREACHER *moves further into the room.*] Aunt Margaret's still praying for ye, and she won't sleep till you're saved and tonight's the night you must be saved. [*He stops by the crib, hesitates and looks down. After a moment he draws back in awe.*] Lord ha' mercy on these pore children! [*He watches them in sorrowful anguish.*] I'm sorry, sorry. [*Mournfully.*] From them that hath not it shall be taken even that which they hath.

GILCHRIST [*without looking around*]. Your God giveth and your God taketh away. Go tell Aunt Marg'ret we're saved.

PREACHER [*gazing at him hopefully*]. Blessed be the name of the Lord forever.

GILCHRIST. Cursed be his name forever.

PREACHER. Lord ha' mercy on him!

GILCHRIST. Still there's something never can be taken away. Amen!

PREACHER. The blessed light of God's love. Amen.

GILCHRIST. The light of our love.

RHODA. Yes, yes.

GILCHRIST. The light of life. Not the light up there, not the light from heaven.

RHODA [*dreamily*]. The light of our love that shall burn forever.

GILCHRIST. The light here in my breast and in your breast. The light of human beings that lighteth every man into this world. [*His face broken with a queer grieving happiness.*] And it will give us strength to go forth again in the morning. Now again I'm strong and will be to the end. I was dreaming and now I am awake. [*The* PREACHER *stares at him in perplexity.*] Now again we'll go into the fields and sow and reap and bring forth the fruits of life.

RHODA. Me with you.

GILCHRIST. And me with you—both together. For the joy that's in us. [*His voice rising fresh and triumphant.*] And we'll raise up sons and daughters unto—unto—the light—our God. Yea, and I'll go into the church and call my people and tell them the way of our salvation, the way of truth, the way of—of—our God. [*Stammering.*] The God—the God who is in us. The one and only God. [*The* PREACHER *watches them in amazement.* GILCHRIST *waves his hand at him.*] Go and leave us alone, now we are saved and you can stop your prayers! [*Loudly.*] Leave us! [*The* PREACHER *backs away from them in distress and goes wonderingly out at the rear.* GILCHRIST *falls on his knees and embraces* RHODA.] We are God—Man is God. That's the light, that's the truth. It will set them free. And love shall abide among us to the end.

[*He kisses the hem of* RHODA'S *skirt, his face touched again with a queer and indefinable sadness.*]

RHODA [*her face shining through her tears*]. You are my God.

APPENDIX I

BIBLIOGRAPHIES

INDEX TO THE BIBLIOGRAPHIES

INDIVIDUAL BIBLIOGRAPHIES

The following bibliographies, though by no means exhaustive, are intended to be adequate for the student who wishes to make a further study of the plays and their authors. An attempt has been made in the individual bibliographies to give some clue to the contents or nature of the entry.

The first date following the play (listed in the author's works) ordinarily indicates date of first production; the date in parentheses indicates the time of first publication. Where the play has been neither produced nor printed, the date of composition has sometimes been given.

ROYALL TYLER

PLAYS:

The Contrast, 1787 (1790). *May-Day in Town, or New York in an Uproar*, 1787. *A Georgia Spec, or Land in the Moon*, 1797. *The Farm House, or The Female Duellists. The Doctor in Spite of Himself. The Island of Barrataria. The Origin of the Feast of Purim, or The Destinies of Haman and Mordecai. Joseph and His Brethren. The Judgment of Solomon.*

BIOGRAPHY AND CRITICISM:

Balch, Marston. "Jonathan the First," *Modern Language Notes*, XLVI, 281–288 (May, 1931). (Brings to light an Irish play that might have served as a model for Tyler; produced before *The Contrast*, but not printed until after; Tyler's debt problematical.)

Brown, Helen Tyler, and Tupper, Frederick. *Grandmother Tyler's Book: the Recollections of Mary Palmer Tyler* (Mrs. Royall Tyler), *1775–1866*. New York: 1925. (Authentic source containing much material about the playwright and judge. See also Wilbur, J. B., below.)

Brown, Herbert R. "Sensibility in Eighteenth-Century American Drama," *American Literature*, IV, 47–60 (March, 1932). (Indicates the conspicuous strain of sentimentalism in *The Contrast*.)

Buckingham, J. T. *Personal Memoirs and Recollections*. New York: 1852.

Buckingham, J. T. *Specimens of Newspaper Literature*. New York: 1850. (Contains commentary on Tyler's political writings.)

Burnham, Henry. *Brattleboro, Vermont, Early History, with Biographical Sketches of Some of its Citizens*. Brattleboro: 1880. (Biographical account based on material by T. P. Tyler.)

Clark, Harry Hayden. "Nationalism in American Literature," *University of Toronto Quarterly*, II, 492–519 (July, 1933). (Excellent account of the nationalistic currents in American literature; mention of Tyler, p. 495.)

Dunlap, William. *A History of the American Theatre*. New York: 1832. (Earliest adequate account of *The Contrast*. Appendix contains list of American dramatists and plays, pp. 407–410.)

Ellis, Harold Milton. "Joseph Dennie and His Circle: a Study in American Literature from 1792 to 1812," *Bulletin of the University of Texas*, No. 40. Studies in English, No. 3 (July 15, 1915). (Tyler's literary relationship to this group.)

Ford, Paul Leicester. "The Beginnings of American Dramatic Literature," *New England Magazine*, N.S. IX, 673–687 (1894). (Brief survey, in popular form, of early drama to Dunlap.)

Hall, Benjamin H. *History of Eastern Vermont, from its Earliest Settlement, to the Close of the Eighteenth Century*. New York: 1858; repr. Albany: 1865. (Contains biography of Tyler.)

Matthews, Brander. "The American on the Stage," *Scribner's Monthly*, XVIII, 321–333 (July,

1879). (Quotes Dunlap's account of Jonathan in Tyler's *The Contrast;* traces other native characters of the American stage; concludes that more subtle delineations are needed at present.)

McKee, Thomas J. Introduction to *The Contrast*, in Dunlap Society Publications, Series 1, Vol. I. New York: 1887.

Moses, Montrose J. *Representative Plays by American Dramatists.* New York: 1918. (Reprints *The Contrast* in Vol. I, with introduction.)

Quinn, Arthur Hobson. *A History of the American Drama from the Beginning to the Civil War.* New York: 1923, pp. 64–73. (This work is by far the finest and most extensive account of the history of American drama.)

Quinn, Arthur Hobson. *Representative American Plays.* New York: 1917; rev. 1930. (Reprints *The Contrast* with short introduction.)

Seilhamer, George O. *History of the American Theatre.* 3 vols. Philadelphia: 1888–1891. II, 225–239. (Reliable.)

Wilbur, James B., editor. *The Contrast.* Boston: 1920. With introduction and bibliography by Helen Tyler Brown.

WILLIAM DUNLAP

Plays:

The Modest Soldier; or, Love in New York (wr. 1787). *The Father; or, American Shandyism*, 1789 (1789). *The Father of an Only Child* (a revision of *The Father*) (1806). *Darby's Return*, 1789 (1789). *The Miser's Wedding*, 1793. *The Fatal Deception; or, The Progress of Guilt*, 1794 (printed as *Leicester*, 1806). *Shelty's Travels*, 1794. *Fontainville Abbey*, 1795 (1806). *The Archers; or, Mountaineers of Switzerland*, 1796 (1796). *The Mysterious Monk*, 1796 (printed as *Ribbemont; or, The Feudal Baron*, 1803). *The Knight's Adventure* (revised by John Hodgkinson as *The Man of Fortitude; or, The Knight's Adventure*), 1797 (1807). *André*, 1798 (1798). *Sterne's Maria, or, The Vintage*, 1799. *The Natural Daughter*, 1799. *The Temple of Independence*, 1799. *The Italian Father*, 1799 (1810). *The Knight of Guadalquiver*, 1800. *The Soldier of '76*, 1801. *The Retrospect; or, The American Revolution*, 1802. *Liberal Opinions*, 1803. *The Glory of Columbia—Her Yeomanry!* 1803 (1817). *Bonaparte in England*, 1803. *The Proverb; or, Conceit Can Cure, Conceit Can Kill*, 1804. *Lewis of Monte Blanco; or, The Transplanted Irishman*, 1804. *The Battle of New Orleans*, 1816(?). *The Flying Dutchman*, 1827. *A Trip to Niagara; or, Travellers in America*, 1828 (1830).

(For a list of Dunlap's dramatic translations, see Coad, Oral Sumner, *William Dunlap*, pp. 289–293.)

Biography and Criticism:

Anonymous. Review of *The Father of an Only Child*, *American Quarterly Review*, I, 331–357 (June, 1827). (Incorrectly says it is the first American play presented on the stage; calls it "one of the best in all our collection.")

Benson, Adolph B. "Scandinavian Influences in the Works of William Dunlap and Richard Alsop," *Scandinavian Studies and Notes*, IX, 239–257 (November, 1927).

Bowman, Mary Rives. "Dunlap and the 'Theatrical Register' of the *New-York Magazine*," *Studies in Philology*, XXIV, 413–425 (July, 1921). (Contends that the able dramatic articles in the *New-York Magazine* may well have been by Dunlap.)

Coad, Oral Sumner. "The Dunlap Diaries at Yale," *Studies in Philology*, XXIV, 403–412 (July, 1927). (Digest of unpublished diary, which does not alter materially Coad's *William Dunlap*.)

Coad, Oral Sumner. "The Gothic Element in American Literature before 1835," *Journal of English and Germanic Philology*, XXIV, 72–93 (January, 1925). (Authentic and able survey.)

Coad, Oral Sumner. *William Dunlap*. The Dunlap Society, New York: 1917. (The standard work on Dunlap; extensive and thorough, although his thought is not emphasized.)

Dunlap, William. *A History of the American Theatre*. New York: 1832. (A remarkably able and comprehensive treatment of the pioneer history of our drama.)

Dunlap, William. *A History of the Rise and Progress of the Arts of Design in the United States*. 2 vols. New York: 1834.

Dunlap, William. *Manuscript Memoirs of Wm. Dunlap, or Daily Occurrences*. (The following volumes are in the Library of the New York Historical Society: Vols. 14, 15, 24, 30. See above, Coad, Oral S., "The Dunlap Diaries at Yale.")

Matthews, Brander. Introduction to *André*, in Dunlap Society Publications. New York: 1887. (States it was Dunlap's intention to portray *André* sympathetically. Appendix contains historical data regarding *André*.)

Moses, Montrose J. *Representative Plays by American Dramatists*. New York: 1918. Vol. I. (Reprints *André* with introduction.)

Quinn, Arthur Hobson. *A History of the American Drama from the Beginning to the Civil War*. New York: 1923, pp. 74–112. (Excellent account of Dunlap.)

Quinn, Arthur Hobson, and Baugh, A. C. Bibliography in *Cambridge History of American Literature*. New York: 1917. I, 496–499.

Wegelin, Oscar. *A Bibliographical Checklist of the Plays and Miscellaneous Writings of William Dunlap, Bibliographica Americana*, Vol. I. New York: 1916.

Wegelin, Oscar. *William Dunlap and His Writings*. Privately reprinted from *The Literary Collector* (January, 1904).

JAMES KIRKE PAULDING

PLAYS:

The Lion of the West, 1830. *The Bucktails; or, Americans in England* (1847).

BIOGRAPHY AND CRITICISM:

Adkins, N. F. "James K. Paulding's 'Lion of the West' (1830)," *American Literature*, III, 249–258 (November, 1931). (An account of Paulding's lost frontier play, together with Paulding's outline of the plot.)

Cairns, William B. *British Criticisms of American Writings, 1783–1815* and *British Criticisms of American Writings, 1815–1833*. In *University of Wisconsin Studies in Language and Literature*, Madison, Nos. 1 (1918) and 14 (1922) respectively. (Good background in literary relations between England and America during period indicated.)

Herold, Amos. *James Kirke Paulding, Versatile American*. New York: 1926.

New York Mirror, IX, 102 (1831). (Plot of *The Lion of the West*. See Adkins, N. F., above.)

Parrington, Vernon L. *The Romantic Revolution in America*. New York: 1927, pp. 212–221. (Traces the growth of Paulding's nationalism and anti-Federalism.)

Paulding, James Kirke. *The Merry Tales of the Three Wise Men of Gotham*. New York: 1839. (The three divisions are: "The Man Machine," "The Perfection of Reason," and "The Perfection of Science." Important in connection with a study of *The Bucktails*.)

Paulding, William Irving. *The Literary Life of James K. Paulding*. New York: 1867. (Definitive account of Paulding's life and work; contains index of all writings; largely an aptly-chosen and well-arranged selection of Paulding's writings, with the missing data supplied by the biographer.)

Quinn, Arthur Hobson. *A History of the American Drama from the Beginning to the Civil War*. New York: 1923. (Has a brief account of Paulding.)

JAMES NELSON BARKER

PLAYS:

The Spanish Rover (wr. 1804), only one act finished. *America* (wr. 1805), one-act masque. *Attila* (wr. 1805). *Tears and Smiles*, 1807 (1808). *The Embargo; or, What News?* 1808. *The Indian Princess; or, La Belle Sauvage*, 1808 (1808). *Marmion; or, The Battle of Flodden Field*, 1812 (1816). *The Armourer's Escape; or, Three Years at Nootka Sound*, 1817. *How to Try a Lover*, 1836 (under title *A Court of Love*), (1817). *Superstition; or, The Fanatic Father*, 1824 (1826).

BIOGRAPHY AND CRITICISM:

Anonymous. *American Quarterly Review*, I, 331–357 (June, 1827). (Review of *Marmion* and *Superstition*, both of which are "deserving of far more attention than they have hitherto met with, from the American public." General survey of theatrical conditions; laments public ignorance of sixty American dramas. Not an accurate or well-informed account of American drama.)

Anonymous. *National Cyclopædia of American Biography*. New York: 1904. XII, 276.

Anonymous. *Pennsylvania Magazine of History and Biography*, XVII, 131, 143 (1893); XLIX, 91–92 (1925). (Brief biographical account reprinted from *National Cyclopædia of American Biography*.)

Barker, James Nelson. *Democratic Press*, Philadelphia, December 18, 1816, to February 19, 1817. (Dramatic articles by Barker.)

Dunlap, William. *A History of the American Theatre*. New York: 1832, pp. 376–380. (Contains letter from Barker giving an account of his own work.)

Kittredge, G. L. *Witchcraft in Old and New England*. Cambridge, Mass.: 1929.

Moses, Montrose J. *The American Dramatist*. Boston: 1911; rev. 1925. (Brief commentary.)

Moses, Montrose J. *Representative Plays by American Dramatists*. New York: 1918. I, 567–571. (Reprints *The Indian Princess* with able introduction.)

Musser, Paul H. *James Nelson Barker, 1784–1858*. With a reprint of his comedy *Tears and Smiles*. Philadelphia: 1929. (Lengthiest, most important work on Barker; authoritative, comprehensive, thoughtful; full bibliography, pp. 211–223.)

Quinn, Arthur Hobson. *A History of the American Drama from the Beginning to the Civil War*. New York: 1923, pp. 136–151; short bibliography, p. 406. (Excellent.)

Quinn, Arthur Hobson. *Representative American Plays*. New York: rev. 1930. (Contains *Superstition*, with a brief introduction.)

Rees, James. *The Dramatic Authors of America*. Philadelphia: 1845, pp. 21–24.

Simpson, Henry. *The Lives of Eminent Philadelphians Now Deceased*. Philadelphia: 1859, pp. 26–28. (Short biographical account.)

Spiller, Robert E. Review of Musser's *James Nelson Barker*, *Modern Language Notes*, XLV, 407–409 (June, 1930). (Spiller states that this volume adds little to the claims for Barker already made by Quinn; a careful study of Barker's use of sources, increasing our admiration of Barker's originality; but Musser's book lacks the "larger view.")

ROBERT MONTGOMERY BIRD

PLAYS:

The Cowled Lover, 1827. *Caridorf, or The Avenger*, 1827. *News of the Night*, 1827. *'Twas All for the Best* (incomplete), 1827. *The City Looking Glass*, 1828. *The Volunteers*, 1828. *Giannone* (incomplete), *The Fanatick* (incomplete), 1828. *Isadora, or the Three Dukes* (incomplete), 1828. *Pelopidas, or The Fall of the Polemarchs*, 1830. *The Gladiator*, 1831. *Oralloossa*, 1832. *The Broker of Bogota*, 1834. *Metamora* (revision), 1836.

Biography and Criticism:

Alger, William R. *Life of Edwin Forrest*. 2 vols. Philadelphia: 1877. (Lengthy, appreciative account, especially of Forrest's acting in *The Gladiator;* extracts from contemporary opinion; digressive argumentation and moralizing.)

Barrett, Lawrence. *Edwin Forrest*. Boston: 1882, pp. 53–56, 131, 135. (Contains British commentary on *The Gladiator*.)

Clarence, Reginald T. "*The Stage*" *Cyclopedia*. London: 1909. (Merely a list of plays, but extensive.)

Conrad, Henry Clay. *History of the State of Delaware*. 3 vols. Wilmington: 1908. III, 1071. (Brief biographical sketch of Bird.)

Foust, Clement E. *The Life and Dramatic Works of Robert Montgomery Bird*. New York: 1919. (Definitive life of Bird, adequate account of plays; the lengthiest and most important work that has been done on Bird; contains the following plays: *Pelopidas*, *The Gladiator*, *Oralloossa*, *The Broker of Bogota;* also lists of Bird's other writings.)

Griswold, Rufus Wilmot. *The Prose Writers of America*. Philadelphia: 1851, pp. 434–439. (Contains biographical and critical sketch of Bird, together with three prose selections.)

Moses, Montrose J. *The American Dramatist*. Boston: 1911; rev. 1925. (Accounts of the early dramatists inadequate.)

Moses, Montrose J. *The Fabulous Forrest*. Boston: 1929, pp. 92–112. (Deals with Bird's relation to Forrest; brief account of *The Gladiator*.)

Oberholtzer, Ellis Paxson. *The Literary History of Philadelphia*. Philadelphia: 1906, pp. 242–244; 249–251. (Data regarding *The Gladiator* mostly taken from Alger's *Life of Edwin Forrest*.)

Oberholtzer, Ellis Paxson. *Philadelphia; a History of the City and Its People, a Record of 225 Years*. Philadelphia: 1911. II, 196. (Brief biographical and critical commentary; speaks of *The Gladiator* as "a work with some vital quality.")

Quinn, Arthur Hobson. "The Early Drama, 1756–1860," in *Cambridge History of American Literature*. New York: 1917. I, 221–222. (Short account of Bird's plays.)

Quinn, Arthur Hobson. *A History of the American Drama from the Beginning to the Civil War*. New York: 1923, pp. 220–248. (Extremely able and authoritative account of Bird and his writings.)

Rees, James. *The Life of Edwin Forrest*. Philadelphia: n.d. [1874], pp. 421–431. (Brief sketch of life and writings; inadequate account of plays; says of *The Gladiator:* ". . . Although written exclusively with a view to the stage, it abounds with poetic passages, and possesses no ordinary share of literary merit.")

Smyth, A. H. *The Philadelphia Magazines and Their Contributors, 1741–1850*. Philadelphia: 1892. (Bird mentioned as one of the "brilliant associates" of Mr. Peterson, editor of *Graham's Magazine*.)

Turner, Lorenzo Dow. *Anti-Slavery Sentiment in American Literature Prior to 1865*. Abstracts of Theses, University of Chicago Humanistic Series, V, 499–507 (1926–1927).

Winter, William. *The Wallet of Time*. 2 vols. New York: 1913. (Personal reminiscences and other data relative to the stage.)

NATHANIEL PARKER WILLIS

Plays:

Bianca Visconti; or, The Heart Overtasked, 1837 (1839). *The Betrothal*, 1837. *Imei, the Jew* (incomplete). *Tortesa; or, the Usurer Matched*, 1839 (1839).

Biography and Criticism:

Adkins, N. F. *Fitz-Greene Halleck. An Early Knickerbocker Wit and Poet*. New Haven: 1930. (See index of Adkins for references to Willis.)

Beers, Henry Augustin. *Nathaniel Parker Willis.* American Men of Letters series. Boston: 1885. (Authentic biography, but deals almost wholly with people and places; does not stress enough the intellectual aspects of Willis's life. Contains bibliography of Willis's writings, pp. 353–356.)

Felton, C. C. Review of *Two Ways of Dying for a Husband: Tortesa the Usurer; Bianca Visconti*, *North American Review*, LI, 141–158 (July, 1840). (Appreciative review; places *Bianca Visconti* above *Tortesa* in the manifestation of "rare poetic and dramatic powers.")

Poe, Edgar Allan. *Works.* (Virginia Edition.) New York: 1902. V, 27–30; XIII, 33–54.

MRS. ANNA CORA MOWATT

PLAYS:

Gulzara; or, the Persian Slave (1840). *Fashion*, 1845 (1850). *Armand; or, the Peer and the Peasant*, 1847 (1849).

BIOGRAPHY AND CRITICISM:

Anonymous. *The Athenaeum* (London), April 1, 1854, pp. 175–177. (Reviews Mrs. Mowatt's *Autobiography* as a "butterfly production," but gives a lengthy résumé of it. Reprinted in *Living Age*, XLI, 33–35.)

Anonymous. *North American Review*, LXXVIII, 544 (April, 1854). (A paragraph review of *Autobiography;* partially sympathetic.)

Anonymous. *North American Review*, XXCII, 580 (April, 1856). (A favorable review of *Mimic Life.*)

Duyckinck, Evert A. and George L. *The Cyclopædia of American Literature: From the Earliest Period to the Present Day.* 2 vols. New York: 1856; Philadelphia: 1877. (A brief biographical sketch of Mrs. Mowatt and a reprint of her poem "Time.")

Harland, Marion. "Personal Recollections of a Christian Actress," *Our Continent*, I, 73–74 (March 15, 1882). (Brief reminiscence emphasizing the religious side of Mrs. Mowatt's character.)

Hutton, Laurence, and Matthews, Brander. *Actors and Actresses of Great Britain and the United States.* New York: 1886. IV, 155–170. (Sketch of life; played many roles for a novice, merited praise.)

Ludlow, Noah Miller. *Dramatic Life as I Found It.* St. Louis: 1880. (A record of the western and southern performances of Mrs. Mowatt and of *Fashion;* brief biographical sketch.)

Matthews, Brander. See Hutton, Laurence, above.

Moses, Montrose J. *The American Dramatist.* Boston: 1911; rev. 1925. (Slighted treatment of earlier period; account of Mrs. Mowatt inadequate.)

Moses, Montrose J. *Representative Plays by American Dramatists, 1815–1858.* New York: 1925, pp. 523–601. (Reprints *Fashion;* adequate data relative to its production.)

Mowatt, Mrs. Anna Cora. *Autobiography of an Actress; or, Eight Years on the Stage.* Boston: 1854. (Readable, reflective; indispensable to the full understanding of Mrs. Mowatt.)

Mowatt, Mrs. Anna Cora. *Mimic Life; or, Before and Behind the Curtain.* Boston: 1856. (Experiences and stories concerning the stage.)

Poe, Edgar Allan. *The Works of Edgar Allan Poe.* New York: 1914. VIII, 34–40.

Quinn, Arthur Hobson. *A History of the American Drama from the Beginning to the Civil War.* New York: 1923, pp. 310–319. (Invaluable.)

Quinn, Arthur Hobson. *Representative American Plays.* New York: 1917; rev. 1930. (Reprints *Fashion*, with brief introduction.)

Winter, William. *Brief Chronicles.* Dunlap Society Publications. New York: 1889, pp. 221–222. (Merely a paragraph account of Mrs. Mowatt.)

GEORGE HENRY BOKER

PLAYS:

Calaynos, 1849 (1848). *Anne Boleyn* (1850). *The Betrothal*, 1850 (included in *Plays and Poems*, 1856). *The World a Mask*, 1851. *The Podesta's Daughter; A Dramatic Sketch* (in *The Podesta's Daughter and Other Miscellaneous Poems*, 1852). *The Widow's Marriage* (included in *Plays and Poems*, Vol. II, 1856). *Leonor de Guzman*, 1853 (included in *Plays and Poems*, Vol. I, 1856). *Don Pedro of Castile* (unfinished). *Francesca da Rimini*, 1855 (included in *Plays and Poems*, Vol. I, 1856). *The Bankrupt*, 1855 (1854). *Nydia* (wr. 1885, pub. 1929). *Glaucus* (wr. 1886).

BIOGRAPHY AND CRITICISM:

Boccaccio, Giovanni. *Il Comento Alla Divina Commedia*. Bari: 1918. Volume Secondo, pp. 137–146. (Appears in Longfellow's translation of *The Divine Comedy*. Boston: 1913, p. 127.)

Boker, George H. Essay in *The Book of the Sonnet*, ed. by Leigh Hunt and S. Adams Lee. 2 vols. Boston: 1867. (Helped write essay in Vol. I, 95–131; discusses Hayne's sonnets; objects to immorality of Swinburne.)

Boker, George H. *Plays and Poems*. Boston: 1856.

Bradley, Edward Sculley. *George Henry Boker: Poet and Patriot*. Philadelphia: 1927. (The definitive account of Boker's life and work; accurate, sympathetic, very readable; full bibliographies.)

Bradley, Edward Sculley, editor. *Nydia: a Tragic Play*. Philadelphia: 1929.

Bradley, Edward Sculley, editor. *Sonnets: a Sequence on Profane Love*. Philadelphia: 1929. (Bradley's recovery of this series is a significant literary event; places Boker next to Longfellow as a sonnet writer.)

Brewer, E. "Boker's Francesca da Rimini," *The American*, V, 363 (1883).

Hubbell, Jay B. "George Henry Boker, Paul Hamilton Hayne, and Charles Warren Stoddard: Some Unpublished Letters," *American Literature*, V, 146 ff. (May, 1933).

Metcalf, J. C. "An Old Romantic Triangle, Francesca da Rimini in Three Dramas," *Sewanee Review*, XXIX, 45–58 (1921).

Quinn, Arthur Hobson. *A History of the American Drama from the Beginning to the Civil War*. New York: 1923, pp. 337–364. (Able survey of Boker's work.)

Urban, Gertrude. "Paolo and Francesca in History and Literature," *Critic*, XL, 425–438 (1902).

AUGUSTIN DALY

PLAYS:

Leah the Forsaken, 1862. *Judith*, 1864. *Under the Gaslight*, 1867 (1867). *Pickwick Papers*, 1868. *A Flash of Lightning*, 1868 (1885). *The Red Scarf*, 1869. *Frou-Frou*, 1870. *Horizon*, 1871 (1885). *Delmonico's; or, Larks up the Hudson*, 1871. *Divorce*, 1871 (1884). *Roughing It*, 1873. *Madeleine Morel*, 1873 (1885). *Monsieur Alphonse*, 1874 (1886). *The Big Bonanza*, 1875 (1884). *Pique*, 1875 (1884). *The Princess Royal*, 1877. *The Dark City*, 1877. *Needles and Pins*, 1880 (1884). *Nancy and Company*, 1886 (1884). *An International Match*, 1889 (1890). *A Test Case*, 1892 (1893). *The Countess Gucki*, 1896 (1895).

(The above is a partial list of Daly's plays and adaptations; for a full list see A. H. Quinn's *A History of the American Drama from the Civil War to the Present Day*. New York: 1927. II, 278–283.)

BIOGRAPHY AND CRITICISM:

Anonymous. "Mr. Augustin Daly's Views," *Harper's Weekly*, Supplement, February 2, 1889.

Coleman, A. I. du P. "Augustin Daly: An Appreciation," *Critic*, XXXV, 712–720 (August, 1899). (Memorial in praise of Daly's character and work.)

Daly, Augustin. "The American Dramatist," *North American Review*, CXLII, 485–492 (May, 1886). (Contends that there have been native dramatists during the whole national existence, despite assertions to the contrary.)

Daly, Joseph Francis. *The Life of Augustin Daly*. New York: 1917.

Hazard, Lucy Lockwood. *The Frontier in American Literature*. New York: 1927. (Able, though not exhaustive.)

Hubbell, Jay B. "The Frontier," Ch. III in Foerster's *The Reinterpretation of American Literature*. New York: 1928.

Keiser, Albert. *The Indian in American Literature*. New York: 1933.

Kobbe, Gustav. "Augustin Daly and His Life Work," *Cosmopolitan*, XXVII, 405–418 (1899). (Highly popularized and pictorial account of Daly's theatrical career.)

Moses, Montrose J. *The American Dramatist*. Boston: 1911; rev. 1925.

Quinn, Arthur Hobson. *A History of the American Drama from the Civil War to the Present Day*. New York: 1927. I, 1–38.

Ryan, W. P. "The Augustin Daly Library," *The Athenaeum*, pp. 371–372 (March 24, 1900). (Account of Daly's extensive library.)

Shipman, Carolyn. "Some Treasures of the Daly Library," *Critic*, XXXVI, 213–219 (March, 1900). (Data relative to general contents of library.)

Winter, William. *Vagrant Memories*. New York: 1915.

JOAQUIN MILLER

PLAYS:

The Danites in the Sierras, 1877 (1882). *Forty-nine*, 1881 (1882). *Tally Ho!* (1910). *An Oregon Idyll* (1910).

BIOGRAPHY AND CRITICISM:

Allen, Merritt Parmelee. *Joaquin Miller, Frontier Poet*. New York: 1932.

Birney, H., and Kelly, C. *Holy Murder*. New York: 1934. (Treats the Danites.)

Gettmann, Royal A. "A Note on Columbia College," *American Literature*, III, 480–482 (January, 1932).

Hubbell, Jay B. "The Frontier," Ch. III in Foerster's *The Reinterpretation of American Literature*. New York: 1928.

Keiser, Albert. *The Indian in American Literature*. New York: 1933. (Contains a long chapter on Miller.)

Miller, Joaquin. "How I Came to Be a Writer of Books," *Lippincott's Magazine*, XXXVIII, 106–110 (July, 1886). (Leisurely account of Miller's literary life.)

Miller, Joaquin. Preface to *The Complete Poetical Works of Joaquin Miller*. San Francisco: 1904. (Discusses the career of a poet and general aspects of poetry; brief account of his literary life.)

Quinn, Arthur Hobson. *A History of the American Drama from the Civil War to the Present Day*. New York: 1927. I, 116–118.

Sherman, Stuart P. Introduction to *The Poetical Works of Joaquin Miller*. New York: 1923. (A solid critical account of Miller and his poetry.)

Vedder, Henry C. *American Writers of Today*. New York: 1899, pp. 301–313. (Brief account of Miller, the "American Byron," and his writings; but omits drama.)

Wagner, Harr. *Joaquin Miller and His Other Self*. San Francisco: 1929. (The standard and most extensive biography of Miller, by one who knew him for twenty-five years as "friend, publisher, and financial manager." Aim has been to "give to Joaquin a living reality." The biography is enthusiastic, uneven; good account of Miller's conversations with the Pre-Raphaelites.)

BRONSON HOWARD

PLAYS:

Fantine, 1864. *Saratoga*, 1870 (1870). *Diamonds*, 1872. *Lilian's Last Love*, 1873. *Moorcroft*, 1874. *Hurricanes*, 1878. *Old Love Letters*, 1878 (1897). *The Banker's Daughter* (revision of *Lilian's Last Love*), 1878 (1878). *The Old Love and the New* (revision of *The Banker's Daughter*), 1879. *Wives*, 1879. *Baron Rudolph* (revision of *Only a Tramp*), 1881. *Fun in a Green Room*, 1882. *Young Mrs. Winthrop*, 1882 (1899). *One of Our Girls*, 1885 (1897). *Met by Chance*, 1887. *The Henrietta*, 1887 (1901). *Shenandoah*, 1888 (1897). *Aristocracy*, 1892 (1898). *Peter Stuyvesant* (in collaboration with Brander Matthews), 1899. *Kate* (1906).

BIOGRAPHY AND CRITICISM:

Anonymous. "Mr. Bronson Howard Illustrates and Defines," *Harper's Weekly*, Supplement, February 2, 1889.

Anonymous. "The Plays of Bronson Howard," *Century Magazine*, III, 465–466 (January, 1883). (Hails Howard's success, especially in face of difficult conditions; points out originality in material, skill in construction, humor, and wholesome dialogue.)

Anonymous. "The Works of Bronson Howard," *Bookman*, X, 195 (November, 1899). (Paragraph account of his plays and method of composition; speaks of *The Henrietta* as his best, which grew out of an actual case, according to the article.)

Archer, William. *English Dramatists of To-day*. London: 1882, pp. 209–219. (Commendatory account of Howard, claiming him for the English drama.)

Briscoe, Johnson. "The Pioneer American Dramatist," *Green Book*, XI, 749–756 (May, 1914).

Clapp, J. B., and Edgett, E. F. *Plays of the Present*. Dunlap Society Publications. New York: 1902. (Theatrical notices of *Aristocracy*, *The Henrietta*, *Saratoga*, and *Shenandoah*.)

Clark, Barrett H. *The British and American Drama of To-day*. New York: 1915, pp. 219–227.

Clark, Barrett H. *A Study of the Modern Drama*. New York: 1925, pp. 362–368.

Edgett, E. F. See Clapp, J. B., above.

Ford, James L. "The Banker's Daughter," *Munsey's Magazine*, XXXIV, 199–202 (November, 1905). (Favorable review of this play; sketch of Howard's career.)

Frohman, Daniel, and Marcosson, I. *Charles Frohman: Manager and Man*. New York: 1916. (Ch. VI.)

Howard, Bronson. "The American Drama," *Sunday Magazine*, October 7, 1906. Reprinted in Montrose J. Moses's *Representative Plays by American Dramatists, 1856–1911*. (Traces the growth from 1890 of an American "school" of dramatists and dramatic criticism; indicates influence of Ibsen; stresses importance of heeding public taste.)

Howard, Bronson. *The Autobiography of a Play*. Dramatic Museum of Columbia University, New York: 1914. Introduction by Augustus Thomas. (Character and contents of this indicated in Howard introduction of the present volume.)

Howard, Bronson. "Our Schools for the Stage," *Century Magazine*, o.s. LXI, 28–37 (November, 1900). (Defends the theatre as a vocation and discusses the "art of acting.")

In Memoriam, Bronson Howard. Addresses Delivered at the Memorial Meeting, October 18, 1908, at the Lyceum Theatre. New York: 1910. (Contains important material by Howard and others; authentic biographical account; the personality of the man emerges vividly in these pages. Among the contents are: "An Appreciation," by Brander Matthews; "A Brief Biography," by Harry P. Mawson; "Among His Books," by John Ernest Warren; "The Autobiography of a Play," by Bronson Howard; "Trash on the Stage and the Lost Dramatists of America," by Bronson Howard. Includes bibliography of plays.)

Mabie, Hamilton Wright. "American Plays Old and New," *Outlook*, CII, 945–955 (December 28, 1912). (Discusses Howard's idea of business as the American theme; "business is in fact, the one thing from which art has the least to fear"; provocative survey of contemporary dramatists.)

Marcosson, I. See Frohman, Daniel, above.

Matthews, Brander. "An Appreciation," in *In Memoriam;* also *North American Review*, CLXXXVIII, 504–513 (October, 1908). (A sagacious, revealing survey of Howard's work by one who collaborated with him.)

Matthews, Brander. "Bronson Howard," in *Gateways to Literature*. New York: 1912.

Matthews, Brander. *These Many Years*. New York: 1917. (Scattered commentary relative to Howard.)

Montgomery, G. E. "Bronson Howard," *The Theatre*, I, 469–470 (August 2, 1886).

Morris, Clara. *Life on the Stage*. New York: 1901. (Chapter on *Saratoga*.)

Moses, Montrose J. *The American Dramatist*. Boston: rev. 1925.

Moses, Montrose J. Introduction to *Shenandoah*, in *Representative Plays by American Dramatists, 1856–1911*. New York: 1921. (Discusses Howard's Americanism, his theories of drama, the artisan character of his work, the genesis of *Shenandoah*.)

Quinn, Arthur Hobson. *A History of the American Drama from the Civil War to the Present Day*. New York: 1927. I, 39–65.

Quinn, Arthur Hobson. *Representative American Plays*. New York: rev. 1930. (Reprints *Shenandoah* with brief introduction.)

Regier, C. C. *The Era of the Muckrakers*. Chapel Hill, N. C.: 1932.

Thomas, Augustus. Introduction to *The Autobiography of a Play*. See Howard, Bronson, above.

Towse, J. Rankin. "Bronson Howard," *Book Buyer*, XVI, 113–117 (March, 1898). (Emphasizes his growth in dramatic powers; some inaccurate biographical data; unfavorable to *The Henrietta*.)

Winter, William. *The Life of David Belasco*. 2 vols. New York: 1918.

LANGDON MITCHELL

Plays:

Sylvian (1885). *Becky Sharp*, 1899. *The Adventures of François*, 1900. *The Kreutzer Sonata*, 1906. *The New York Idea*, 1906 (1908). *The New Marriage*, 1911. *Major Pendennis*, 1916.

Biography and Criticism:

Archer, William. Commentary on *The New York Idea* in London *Tribune*, May 27, 1907. (Appears as preface to *The New York Idea*. Baker, Boston: 1908. Refers to Mitchell's play as "a social satire so largely conceived and so vigorously executed that it might take an honorable place in any dramatic literature.")

Clapp, J. B., and Edgett, E. F. *Plays of the Present*. Dunlap Society Publications. New York: 1902. (Theatrical notice of *Becky Sharp*.)

Hapgood, Norman. *The Stage in America, 1897–1900*. New York: 1901. (Brief account of *Becky Sharp*.)

Mitchell, Langdon. "Comedy and the American Spirit," *American Mercury*, VII, 304–310 (March, 1926). (Contends that the Americans *do* respond to the poetic spirit in drama.)

Mitchell, Langdon. "The Drama: Can It Be Taught?" *Virginia Quarterly Review*, IV, 561–580 (October, 1928). (Emphasizes the fact that the drama is a social art; concludes that the externals can be learned, but that "the invisible art" comes only to those who are gifted. Appeared also as "Substance and Art in the Drama," in *The Art of Playwriting*, Philadelphia: 1928.)

Moses, Montrose J. *The American Dramatist*. Boston: rev. 1925.

Moses, Montrose J. *Representative Plays by American Dramatists, 1856–1911*. New York: 1921. (Reprints *The New York Idea*. Able introduction, pp. 599–604.)

Quinn, Arthur Hobson. *A History of the American Drama from the Civil War to the Present Day*. New York: 1927. II, 62–68.

Quinn, Arthur Hobson. *Representative American Plays*. New York: rev. 1930. (Reprints *The New York Idea* with introduction.)

Watson, E. B. *Contemporary Drama: American Plays*. New York: 1931. (Includes *The New York Idea* in Vol. I.)

Winter, William. *The Wallet of Time*. New York: 1913. II, 273–286. (Digressive analysis of *Henry Esmond* and *Vanity Fair;* detailed comparison of *Becky Sharp* with *Vanity Fair;* acting of Mrs. Fiske in *Becky Sharp*.)

PHILIP MOELLER

PLAYS:

Helena's Husband (one act), 1915 (1915). *Two Blind Beggars and One Less Blind* (one act), 1915 (1918). *Madame Sand*, 1917 (1917). *Five Somewhat Historical Plays* (1918. Contains: *Helena's Husband*, *The Little Supper*, *Sisters of Susannah*, *The Roadhouse in Arden*, *Pokey, or The Beautiful Legend of the Amorous Indian*). *Molière*, 1919 (1919). *Sophie*, 1919 (1919). *Caprice* (adaptation from Sil-Vara), 1928 (1929). *Camel Through the Needle's Eye*, 1929 (1929). *Fata Morgana* (adaptation from Ernst Vajda) in collaboration with J. L. A. Burrell, 1931 (1931).

BIOGRAPHY AND CRITICISM:

Anonymous. *The Athenaeum*, p. 776 (June 11, 1920). (Adverse criticism of *Madame Sand*, stating that Mr. Moeller "finds most inferior comedy in the business from the very start and pursues it to the length of his three acts.")

Anonymous. *Current Opinion*, LXIII, 390 (December, 1917). (Praises intellectual quality of *Madame Sand*, but points out lack of unity.)

Anonymous. *The Illustrated London News*, CLVI, 1024 (June 12, 1920). (Commentary on *Madame Sand*.)

Anonymous. *The Saturday Review* (London), CXXIX, 558–559 (June 19, 1920). (Commentary on *Madame Sand*.)

Hopkins, Arthur. Introduction to *Madame Sand*. New York: 1917. (Moeller's "resurrection of famous characters is worked with a touch that brings them really to life.")

Jones, Howard Mumford. "American Comment on George Sand, 1837–1848," *American Literature*, III, 389–407 (January, 1932).

Moeller, Philip. "The Guild and Production," in *The Theatre Guild: the First Ten Years*, ed. by W. P. Eaton. New York: 1929.

Quinn, Arthur Hobson. *A History of the American Drama from the Civil War to the Present Day*. New York: 1927. II, 137–140.

Tucker, S. Marion. *Modern American and British Plays*. New York: 1931. (Reprints *Madame Sand;* good introduction, though brief.)

PHILIP BARRY

PLAYS:

You and I, 1923 (1925). *The Youngest*, 1924 (1925). *In a Garden*, 1925 (1926). *White Wings*, 1926 (1927). *Paris Bound*, 1927 (1929). *John*, 1927 (1929). *Holiday*, 1928 (1929). *Cock Robin* (with Elmer Rice), 1928 (1929). *Hotel Universe*, 1930 (1930). *Tomorrow and Tomorrow*, 1931 (1931). *The Animal Kingdom*, 1932 (1932). *The Joyous Season*, 1934.

BIOGRAPHY AND CRITICISM:

Anonymous. *Current Opinion*, LXXIV, 702–707, 713–715 (June, 1923). (Extract-résumé of *You and I* with a few contemporary views of the play.)

Anonymous. "Some Playwright Biographies," *Theatre Arts Monthly*, XI, 532–533 (July, 1927). (Brief biographical account.)

Bellamy, Francis T. *Outlook*, CLI, 11 (January 2, 1929). (Fails to answer questions he asks; names Barry the "Lightning Bug" for lack of depth.)

Carmer, Carl. "Philip Barry," *Theatre Arts Monthly*, XIII, 819–826 (November, 1929). (Brief survey of Barry's plays, maintaining that he has not fulfilled his early promise.)

Clark, Barrett H. *An Hour of American Drama*. Philadelphia: 1930. (Excellent, brief account.)

Clark, Barrett H. "New Plays by Barry and Kelly," *Drama*, XVIII, 18–19, 139 (February, 1928). (*Paris Bound* is "a suavely poisonous shaft aimed at the heart of the marriage problem.")

Clark, Barrett H. "Philip Barry," *Theatre Guild Magazine*, May, 1930.

Farrar, John. Review of *You and I*, *Bookman*, LVII, 318 (May, 1923). (Points out the tragic aspect of *You and I*.)

Krutch, Joseph Wood. Review of *Paris Bound*, *Nation*, CXXVI, 75–76 (January 18, 1928). (Favorable.) Review of *Hotel Universe*, *Nation*, CXXX, 525–526 (April 30, 1930). (Unfavorable.)

Mantle, Burns. *American Playwrights of Today*. New York: 1929. (Emphasizes theatre.)

Parker, Robert Allerton. Review of *You and I*, *Independent*, CX, 205–207 (March 17, 1923). ("Slices of life" plays lack "a definite, sharply crystallized point of view . . . ." This criticism hardly applies to *You and I*.)

Quinn, Arthur Hobson. *A History of the American Drama from the Civil War to the Present Day*. New York: 1927. II, 81–84.

Quinn, Arthur Hobson. *Representative American Plays*. New York: rev. 1930. (Reprints *Paris Bound*.)

Skinner, Richard Dana. Review of *Hotel Universe*, *Commonweal*, XI, 741 (April 30, 1930). (Regards *Hotel Universe* as the finest of Barry's plays to date.)

Wilson, Edmund. Review in *Dial*, LXXV, 100–101 (July, 1923). (Finds fault with *You and I* as "silly-clever wit" and with its theatricality; not a convincing attack.)

Young, Stark. *Hotel Universe*, *New Republic*, CXII, 326–328 (May 7, 1930); *Holiday*, *ibid.*, LVII, 96–97 (December 12, 1928); *Paris Bound*, *ibid.*, LIII, 272–273 (January 25, 1928). (Reviews.)

OWEN DAVIS

Plays:

Through the Breakers, 1899. *At Yale*, 1907. *An Old Sweetheart of Mine*, 1911. *Robin Hood; or, the Merry Outlaws of Sherwood Forest*, 1915. *The Detour*, 1921 (1922). *Icebound*, 1923 (1923). *Home Fires*, 1923. *The Nervous Wreck*, 1923 (1926). *The Haunted House*, 1924. *Easy Come, Easy Go*, 1925. *Gentle Grafters*, 1926. *The Donovan Affair*, 1926. *The Great Gatsby*, 1926. *The Good Earth*, 1932. *The Ninth Guest*, 1932. *Jezebel*, 1934.

(The above is a partial list.)

Biography and Criticism:

Davis, Owen. *I'd Like to Do It Again*. New York: 1931. (Chiefly a humorous and popular account, in a strongly colloquial and colorful vein; reminiscent, uneven, but entertaining; contains practical suggestions for playwrights.)

Farrar, John. Review of *Icebound*, *Bookman*, LVII, 317–318 (May, 1923). ("He departs from the path of honesty and truth seldom." Speaks of the play's "essential fineness"; "as definite a contribution to the American theatre as Eugene O'Neill's 'Beyond the Horizon' or Lewis Beach's 'A Square Peg.'")

Moses, Montrose J. Foreword to *The Detour*. Boston: 1922. ("It is one of those studies in realism which—whether seen or read—impresses by reason of its tremendous sincerity," "it exudes a flavor born of struggle against environment," it is "a supreme picture of farm life.")

Parker, Robert Allerton. Review of *Icebound*, *Independent*, CX, 205–207 (March 17, 1923). (Objects to the "slice of life drama" on the ground that these plays "revel in mean motives, petty characterization, a pervasive atmosphere of chilly gloom.")

Quinn, Arthur Hobson. *A History of the American Drama from the Civil War to the Present Day*. New York: 1927. II, 217–220.

EUGENE O'NEILL

Long Plays:

Beyond the Horizon, 1920 (1920). *Diff'rent*, 1920 (1921). *Chris Christopherson* (later rewritten as *Anna Christie*), 1920. *The Emperor Jones*, 1920 (1921). *The Straw*, 1921 (1921). *Gold*, 1921 (1920). *Anna Christie*, 1921 (1922). *The First Man*, 1922 (1922). *The Hairy Ape*, 1922 (1922). *All God's Chillun Got Wings*, 1924 (1924). *Welded*, 1924 (1924). *Desire under the Elms*, 1924 (1924). *S. S. Glencairn* (a combination of *The Moon of the Caribbees*, *The Long Voyage Home*, *In the Zone*, and *Bound East for Cardiff*), 1924. *The Ancient Mariner*, 1924. *The Fountain*, 1925 (1926). *The Great God Brown*, 1926 (1926). *Strange Interlude*, 1928 (1928). *Marco Millions*, 1928 (1927). *Lazarus Laughed*, 1928 (1927). *Dynamo*, 1929 (1929). *Mourning Becomes Electra*, 1931 (1931). *Days Without End*, 1934 (1934). *Ah, Wilderness*, 1934 (1934).

One-Act Plays:

Recklessness (1914). *The Web* (1914). *Warnings* (1914). *Before Breakfast*, 1916 (1916). *Bound East for Cardiff*, 1916 (1916). *Thirst*, 1916 (1914). *Fog*, 1917 (1914). *Ile*, 1917 (1918.) *In the Zone*, 1917 (1919). *The Long Voyage Home*, 1917 (1917). *The Sniper*, 1917. *The Moon of the Caribbees*, 1918 (1919). *The Rope*, 1918 (1919). *Where the Cross is Made* (later rewritten as *Gold*), 1918 (1919). *The Dreamy Kid*, 1919 (1920). *Exorcism*, 1920.

Biography and Criticism:

Agate, James. *The Contemporary Theatre*. London: 1924. ("Anna Christie," pp. 165–170. Commends O'Neill for the happy ending.)

Anderson, John. "Eugene O'Neill," *Theatre Arts Monthly*, XV, pt. II, 938–942 (November, 1931). (Discusses the demands O'Neill makes on the facilities of the theatre; in his later plays he "began to rationalize futility into a sort of lyric ecstasy . . ." or "rapturous frustration.")

Atkinson, Brooks. "Ibsen and O'Neill," *New York Times*, Dramatic Section, January 31, 1926. (Points out the parallels in philosophy and technique.)

Atkinson, Brooks. "On 'Days Without End,'" *New York Times*, Dramatic Section, January 14, 1934.

Baker, George P. "O'Neill's First Decade," *Yale Review*, N.S. XV, 789–792 (July, 1926). (Restrained and concise appreciation by a former teacher.)

Baughan, E. A. "The Plays of Eugene O'Neill," *Fortnightly Review*, CXIX, 852–860 (May, 1923). ("Eugene O'Neill is a poet and not a realist at all"; one of the most understanding of the English reviews, but doesn't quite reach the O'Neill subtlety.)

Clark, Barrett H. "Aeschylus and O'Neill," *English Journal*, XXI, 699–710 (November, 1932).

Clark, Barrett H. *An Hour of American Drama*. Philadelphia: 1930. (Brief extracts from his *Eugene O'Neill*.)

Clark, Barrett H. *A Study of the Modern Drama*. New York: 1925. (A handbook of data regarding modern dramatists.)

Clark, Barrett H. *Eugene O'Neill.* New York: 1926.
Eugene O'Neill: the Man and His Plays. New York: 1929.
Eugene O'Neill: the Man and His Plays. New York: 1933.
(These volumes on O'Neill's life and work constitute the most extended and authentic critical survey of the dramatist.)

Clark, Barrett H., and Sanborn, Ralph. *A Bibliography of the Works of Eugene O'Neill.* New York: 1931.

Corbin, John. "O'Neill and Aeschylus," *Saturday Review of Literature*, VIII, 693–694 (April 30, 1932).

Dahlström, Carl Enoch William Leonard. *Strindberg's Dramatic Expressionism.* University of Michigan Publications of Language and Literature. Ann Arbor: 1930.

Dickinson, Thomas H. "The Playwright Unbound: Eugene O'Neill," in *Playwrights of the New American Theater.* New York: 1925, pp. 56–126. (One of the most penetrating analyses of O'Neill's plays; says O'Neill's teaching is to live deeply, to feel profoundly; states that O'Neill is not stage-struck, but world-struck.)

Eaton, Walter Prichard. *The Drama in English.* New York: 1930, pp. 331–343. (Brief, but inclusive, well-balanced and impersonal account of O'Neill and his work; designed for the novitiate.)

Fergusson, Francis. "Eugene O'Neill," *Hound and Horn*, III, 145–160 (January–March, 1930). (Discusses O'Neill in comparison with George Kelly and E. E. Cummings; lacks penetration.)

Geddes, Virgil. "Eugene O'Neill," *Theatre Arts Monthly*, XV, pt. II, 943–946 (November, 1931). (Asserts that O'Neill is overpraised, that he is not a great artist; discounts his reputation as a dramatist and an innovator; says he is unconvincing.)

Goldberg, Isaac. *The Theatre of George Jean Nathan.* New York: 1926, pp. 143 ff. (Reprints letters from O'Neill to Nathan; illuminating commentary on a number of his own plays.)

Hamilton, Clayton. *Conversations on Contemporary Drama.* New York: 1924, pp. 198–218. (A college lecture; résumé by one who knows the author; racy, personalized style.)

Hayward, Ira N. "Strindberg's Influence on Eugene O'Neill," *Poet-Lore*, XXXIX, 596–604 (Winter, 1928). (Account of this article given in O'Neill introduction, this volume.)

Hofmannsthal, Hugo von. "Eugene O'Neill," *Freeman*, VII, 39–41 (March 21, 1923). Trans. by Barrett H. Clark. (O'Neill's characters "not sufficiently drenched in the atmosphere of their own individual past" chiefly through inadequacy of dialogue which should be impregnated with the proper "movement.")

Katzin, Winifred. "The Great God O'Neill," *Bookman*, LXVIII, 61–66 (September, 1928). (Revealing the European idea that America's drama is not literature, nor its literature drama; the French critic in the dialogue accepts the one-act plays, but dismisses the others. Entertaining and brilliant article.)

Kemelman, H. G. "Eugene O'Neill and the Highbrow Melodrama," *Bookman*, LXXV, 482–491 (September, 1932). (O'Neill's "'highbrow melodrama' embodies intellectual and emotional romanticism." The "dark-eyed and sensitive" protagonist appearing throughout the plays is O'Neill. Attacks O'Neill for abnormality in women characters, for extravagant diction, for non-dramatic plots, for use of insanity; frustration "so artificially perfect that it loses all suspense." Most spirited and hostile of the attacks on O'Neill.)

Lewisohn, Ludwig. "The Development of Eugene O'Neill," *Nation*, CXIV, 349–350 (March 22, 1922). (Flagging of his imagination may be due to his isolation from the central movements in European literature; acclaims *The Hairy Ape.*)

Loving, Pierre. "Eugene O'Neill," *Bookman*, LIII, 511–520 (August, 1921). (Anecdotal; brief account of career and writings; resemblances to Conrad.)

Macgowan, Kenneth. "The O'Neill Soliloquy," *Theatre Guild Magazine*, February, 1929.

Macgowan, Kenneth. *The Theatre of Tomorrow*. New York: 1921. (Slight discussion of O'Neill in his relation to realism.)

Malone, Andrew E. "The Plays of Eugene O'Neill," *Contemporary Review*, CXXIX, 363–372 (March, 1926). (States the British view; points out preoccupation with the sea; plays "do not contain all the truth of human experience"; emphasizes Synge's influence; objects to O'Neill's language.)

Malone, Kemp. "The Diction of *Strange Interlude*," *American Speech*, VI, 19–28 (October, 1930). (A detailed study showing that though O'Neill's language in *Strange Interlude* is largely realistic, it does not attain perfection of realistic technique.)

Mantle, Burns. *American Playwrights of Today*, New York: 1929, pp. 3–21. (Familiar, lightly humorous treatment of biographical data; no discussion of plays; some miscellaneous facts regarding performances.)

Mickle, Alan D. *Six Plays of Eugene O'Neill*. New York: 1929. (The plays are: *Anna Christie*, *The Hairy Ape*, *The Great God Brown*, *The Fountain*, *Strange Interlude*, *Marco Millions*. Discursive theorizing about drama in general, not enough about O'Neill in particular; why plays have not had favor in England: coarse characters. Discerning analysis of masks, but doesn't quite reach the subtlety of O'Neill.)

Mollan, Malcolm. "Making Plays with a Tragic End, An Intimate Interview with Eugene O'Neill, Who Tells Why He Does It," *Philadelphia Public Ledger*, January 22, 1922. (Extracts from this interview given in O'Neill introduction of the present volume.)

Moses, Montrose J. *The American Dramatist*. Boston: 1911; rev. 1925.

Mullett, Mary B. "The Extraordinary Story of Eugene O'Neill," *American Magazine* (November, 1922).

Nathan, George Jean. "The Case of O'Neill," *American Mercury*, XIII, 500–502 (April, 1928). (Attacks the critics who praised O'Neill's novitiate and now turn upon his accomplishment; defends the length of and the asides in *Strange Interlude*.)

Nathan, George Jean. "O'Neill's Finest Play," *American Mercury*, XI, 499–506 (August, 1927).

Nathan, George Jean. *The Testament of a Critic*. New York: 1931. (Scattered comments on O'Neill.)

Nethercot, Arthur H. "O'Neill on Freudianism," *Saturday Review of Literature*, VIII, 759 (May 28, 1932); VIII, 807 (June 25, 1932).

O'Neill, Eugene. "Eugene O'Neill Writes About His Latest Play, *The Great God Brown*," *New York Evening Post*, February 13, 1926.

O'Neill, Eugene. Foreword to *Anathema! Litanies of Negation*, by Benjamin De Casseres. New York: 1928.

O'Neill, Eugene. "A Letter from O'Neill," *New York Times*, April 11, 1920.

O'Neill, Eugene. Letters to George Jean Nathan; see Goldberg, Isaac, above.

O'Neill, Eugene. "O'Neill Talks About 'Beyond the Horizon,'" *New York Evening Post*, November 27, 1926.

O'Neill, Eugene. "Strindberg and Our Theatre," *Provincetown Playbill*, No. 1, Season 1923–24.

Quinn, Arthur Hobson. "Eugene O'Neill, Poet and Mystic," *Scribner's Magazine*, LXXX, 368–372 (October, 1926).

Quinn, Arthur Hobson. *A History of the American Drama from the Civil War to the Present Day*. New York: 1927. II, 165–206. (Reprints significant letter from O'Neill regarding his dramatic theory.)

Quinn, Arthur Hobson. *Representative American Plays*. New York: rev. 1930. (Reprints *Beyond the Horizon* with short introduction.)

Ratcliffe, S. K. "An American Dramatist, and Some Players," *New Statesman*, XVII, 386 (July 9, 1921). (Chiefly about the Provincetown Players and the staging of *The Emperor Jones*.)

Schelling, Felix E. *Appraisements and Asperities*. Philadelphia: 1922, pp. 144–149. (Brief résumés of *Diff'rent*, *The Straw* and *The Emperor Jones;* lacks penetration as criticism.)

Sergeant, Elizabeth Shepley. "Eugene O'Neill: the Man with a Mask," in *Fire Under the Andes*. New York: 1927. Reprinted from *New Republic*, L, 91–95 (March 16, 1927). (Crisp, revealing picture of O'Neill the man; personalized evaluations; sharp, figurative style. Says O'Neill is "an agnostic in search of redemption.")

Shipley, Joseph T. *The Art of Eugene O'Neill*. Seattle: 1928.

Sutton, Graham. *Some Contemporary Dramatists*. London: 1924, pp. 167–183. ("Nearly all of Mr. O'Neill's plays are about the sea." Graham misses much of the significance in O'Neill.)

Thompson, Alan Reynolds. "The Dilemma of Modern Tragedy," in *Humanism and America*. New York: 1930, pp. 137–143. (Shows O'Neill's weaknesses from the humanist point of view; indicates especially the playwright's abnormality, inconclusiveness, and lack of unity.)

Waton, Harry. *The Historic Significance of Eugene O'Neill's "Strange Interlude."* New York: 1928.

Whipple, T. K. *Spokesmen: Modern Writers and American Life*. New York: 1928, pp. 230–253. First appeared in briefer form in *New Republic*, XLI, 222–225 (January 21, 1925). (The most able attack on O'Neill, who is limited to the tragedy of frustration, whose characters are the disinherited; O'Neill gives the "effect of narrowness and scantness" and does not "project a fully-imagined . . . three-dimensional" world [Thomas H. Dickinson gives O'Neill four dimensions]; he has "never given us subtly complex characterization" and we find in him an "emaciated skeleton world" hostile to life. But it must be pointed out that these comments apply to the period before *The Great God Brown*. Of this play Whipple says: "Intuitively, he has dived into the lowest and most secret of man's soul and has dredged up wonders from depths so profound that neither he nor we know what to make of these strange sea-children in the common light of day. He has penetrated far into the heart of the mystery, only to find the mystery grown more mysterious.")

White, Arthur Franklin. *The Plays of Eugene O'Neill*. Cleveland: 1923.

Winther, Sophus Keith. *Eugene O'Neill, a Critical Study*. New York: 1934. (Treats of the subject matter and philosophy of the plays.)

Woolf, S. J. "O'Neill Plots a Course for the Drama," *New York Times*, Magazine Section, October 4, 1931. (Personal interview after O'Neill's return from Europe; O'Neill suggests collaboration of American theatrical facilities.)

Young, Stark. "Eugene O'Neill," *New Republic*, XXXII, 307–308 (November 15, 1922). ("But the most significant thing that can be said about Mr. O'Neill's plays at this stage of the game is that his qualities are fundamental theatre." Forecasts growth.)

PAUL GREEN

Long Plays:

In Abraham's Bosom: the Biography of a Negro, in Seven Scenes, 1926 (1927). *The Field God*, 1927 (1927). *The House of Connelly*, 1931 (1931). *Tread the Green Grass*, 1932. *Roll, Sweet Chariot* (based on *Potter's Field*), 1934.

One-Act Plays:

Surrender to the Enemy, 1917. *The Long Night* (1920). *The Last of the Lowries*, 1920 (1922). *Old Wash Lucas*, 1920 (under title of *The Miser*) (1924). *The Old Man of Edenton*, 1920 (1925). *Wrack P'int*, 1923. *The Lord's Will*, 1921 (1922). *Blackbeard* (with Elizabeth Lay Green), 1921 (1922). *White Dresses* (1922). *Granny Boling* (1921). *Sam Tucker* (1923). Rewritten as *Your Fiery Furnace*, 1923. *Day by Day* (mimeographed, 1923). *The No 'Count Boy*, 1924 (1924). *The Man Who Died at Twelve O'clock* (1925). *The Hot Iron* (1924). *The End of the Row* (1924). *The Prayer-Meeting*, a rewritten version of *Granny Boling* (1924). *Your Fiery Furnace*, a rewritten version of *Sam Tucker*, later incorporated into the full-length play *In Abraham's Bosom* (1926). *In Aunt Mahalay's Cabin* (1924). *In Abraham's Bosom* became first act of full-length play of the same name (1926). *Fixin's* (with Erma Greene), 1924 (1924). *Quare Medicine*, 1925 (1928). *The Picnic* (1928). *The Man on the House* (1926). *Unto Such Glory* (1927). *Supper for the Dead* (1926). *In the Valley* (1928). *Saturday Night* (1928). *The Goodbye* (1928). *Old Christmas* (1928). *Bread and Butter Come to Supper* (1928). *Blue Thunder* (1928).

BIOGRAPHY AND CRITICISM:

Clark, Barrett H. *An Hour of American Drama*. Philadelphia: 1930.

Clark, Barrett H. "Notes on Paul Green," *Drama*, XVI, 137, 155 (January, 1926).

Clark, Barrett H. "Paul Green," *Theatre Arts Monthly*, XII, 730–736 (October, 1928).

Clark, Barrett H. *Paul Green*. New York: 1928. (Solid, authoritative, understanding; most extensive work on Green.)

Couch, W. T., editor. *Culture in the South*. A Symposium by Thirty-one Authors. Chapel Hill, N. C.: 1934.

Eaton, Walter Prichard. *The Drama in English*. New York: 1930. (Discusses Green largely from the point of sectional culture.)

Green, Paul. "A Playwright's Notes on Drama and the Screen," *New York Times*, February 4, 1924. (Argument for an imaginative cinema.)

Green, Paul. "The New Theatre." Preface to *One-Act Plays for Stage and Study*. Fourth Series. New York: 1928. ("The New York stage is an industry and not an art"; depreciates the "Art Theatres"; the "New Theatre" is the published play; "beauty has to maintain itself despite the world.")

Krutch, Joseph Wood. Review of *The House of Connelly*, *Nation*, CXXXIII, 408 (October 14, 1931).

Mantle, Burns. *American Playwrights of Today*. New York: 1929. (Emphasizes the stage careers of *In Abraham's Bosom* and *The Field God*.)

Quinn, Arthur Hobson. *A History of the American Drama from the Civil War to the Present Day*. New York: 1927. II. 242–245.

Riley, Woodbridge. *American Thought from Puritanism to Pragmatism and Beyond*. New York: 1927.

Strong, Augustus. *American Poets and their Theology*. Philadelphia: 1916.

Tucker, S. Marion. *Modern American and British Plays*. New York: 1931. (Reprints *The Field God* with introduction.)

Young, Stark. Review of *The House of Connelly*, *New Republic*, LXVIII, 234–236 (October 14, 1931).

THOUGHT BACKGROUNDS OF THE AMERICAN DRAMA

Social and Political

Beard, C. A. and Mary R. *The Rise of American Civilization.* 2 vols. New York: 1927.

Couch, W. T., editor. *Culture in the South.* A Symposium by Thirty-one Authors. Chapel Hill, N. C.: 1934.

Dondore, Dorothy A. *The Prairie and the Making of Middle America: Four Centuries of Description.* Cedar Rapids, Iowa: 1926.

Faust, Albert Bernhardt. *The German Element in the United States.* 2 vols. Boston: 1909.

Gettell, Raymond G. *History of American Political Thought.* New York: 1928. (Contains bibliographies.)

Hart, A. B., editor. *The American Nation: A History.* 28 vols. New York: 1904–1918.

Jones, Howard Mumford. *America and French Culture, 1750–1848.* Chapel Hill, N. C.: 1927.

Mesick, Jane L. *The English Traveller in America, 1785–1835.* New York: 1922.

Nevins, Allan. *American Social History as Recorded by British Travelers.* New York: 1923.

Paxson, F. L. *The History of the American Frontier, 1763–1893.* Boston: 1924.

Regier, C. C. *The Era of the Muckrakers.* Chapel Hill, N. C.: 1932.

Schlesinger, A. M., and Fox, D. R., editors. *A History of American Life.* 12 vols. New York: 1927– . (Admirable social history, with full critical bibliographies.)

Turner, F. J. *The Frontier in American History.* New York: 1921.

Religious and Philosophical

Adams, George P., and Montague, William Pepperell. *American Philosophy; Personal Statements.* New York: 1930.

Bailey, E. J. *Religious Thought in the Greater American Poets.* Boston: 1922.

Cohen, Morris. "Later Philosophy," in *Cambridge History of American Literature.* New York: 1921. III, 226–265.

Cooke, George W. *Unitarianism in America. A History of Its Origin and Development.* Boston: 1902.

Frothingham, O. B. *Transcendentalism in New England. A History.* New York: 1876.

Goddard, H. C. *Studies in New England Transcendentalism.* New York: 1908.

Koch, G. A. *Republican Religion: The American Revolution and the Cult of Reason.* New York: 1933.

Luccock, H. E. *Contemporary American Literature and Religion.* Chicago: 1934.

Morais, H. M. *Deism in Eighteenth Century America.* New York: 1934.

Parrington, V. L. (See below.)

Randall, H. M. *The Making of the Modern Mind.* Boston: 1926.

Riley, Woodbridge. *American Thought. The Early Schools.* New York: 1907.

Riley, Woodbridge. *American Thought from Puritanism to Pragmatism and Beyond.* New York: 1927.

Rowe, H. K. *The History of Religion in the United States.* New York: 1924.

Strong, Augustus. *American Poets and Their Theology.* Philadelphia: 1916.

Townsend, H. G. *Philosophical Ideas in the United States.* New York: 1934. (With bibliography.)

Widgery, Alban G. *Contemporary Thought of Great Britain.* New York: 1927.

Literary

American Writers Series. New York: 1934– . (Volumes of selections from the major American writers, edited with scholarly introductions and extensive critically-annotated bibliographies; H. H. Clark, general editor.)

Boynton, P. H. *Some Contemporary Americans*. Chicago: 1924.

Boynton, P. H. *More Contemporary Americans*. Chicago: 1927.

Brownell, W. C. *American Prose Masters*. New York: 1909.

The Cambridge History of American Literature. Edited by W. P. Trent, John Erskine, Stuart P. Sherman, and Carl Van Doren. 4 vols. New York: 1917–1921.

Canby, H. S. *Classic Americans*. New York: 1931.

Clark, H. H. "Nationalism in American Literature," *University of Toronto Quarterly*, II, 492–519 (July, 1933).

Foerster, Norman. *American Criticism: A Study in Literary Theory from Poe to the Present*. Boston: 1928.

Foerster, Norman. *Nature in American Literature*. New York: 1923.

Foerster, Norman, editor. *The Reinterpretation of American Literature*. New York: 1928. (With bibliographies.)

Foerster, Norman, editor. *Humanism and America*. New York: 1930.

Hartwick, Harry. *The Foreground of American Fiction*. New York: 1934. (With bibliographies.)

Hazard, Lucy L. *The Frontier in American Literature*. New York: 1927.

Hicks, Granville. *The Great Tradition; An Interpretation of American Literature since the Civil War*. New York: 1933.

Loshe, L. D. *The Early American Novel*. New York: 1907.

Nettleton, George H. *English Drama of the Restoration and Eighteenth Century, 1642–1780*. New York: 1914.

Parrington, V. L. *Main Currents in American Thought: An Interpretation of American Literature from the Beginnings to 1920*. 3 vols. New York: 1927–1930. I, *The Colonial Mind, 1620–1800;* II, *The Romantic Revolution in America, 1800–1860;* III, *The Beginnings of Critical Realism in America, 1860–1920*.

Pattee, F. L. *The Development of the American Short Story*. New York: 1923.

Pattee, F. L. *A History of American Literature Since 1870*. New York: 1915.

Pattee, F. L. *The New American Literature, 1890–1930*. New York: 1930.

Rusk, R. L. *The Literature of the Middle Western Frontier*. 2 vols. New York: 1925.

Sherman, Stuart P. *Americans*. New York: 1922.

Sherman, Stuart P. *Critical Woodcuts*. New York: 1926.

Sherman, Stuart P. *The Genius of America*. New York: 1923.

Sherman, Stuart P. *Points of View*. New York: 1924.

Tyler, Moses Coit. *The Literary History of the American Revolution, 1763–1783*. 2 vols. New York: 1897.

Van Doren, Carl. *The American Novel*. New York: 1921.

Van Doren, Carl. *The Contemporary American Novelists*. New York: 1931.

Van Doren, Carl, and Van Doren, Mark. *American and British Literature Since 1890*. New York: 1925. (Sketchy, conventional.)

Ward, A. C. *American Literature, 1880–1930*. New York: 1932.

Wendell, Barrett. *A Literary History of America*. New York: 1901.

AMERICAN DRAMA: HISTORICAL AND GENERAL

Adams, W. Davenport. *A Dictionary of the Drama*. Philadelphia: 1904.

"American Playwrights on the American Drama," *Harper's Weekly*, Supplement, February 2, 1889.

Andrews, Charlton. *The Drama To-day*. Philadelphia: 1913.

Archer, William. "The Development of American Drama," *Harper's Magazine*, CXLII, 75–86 (1920).

Arnold, R. F., editor. *Das deutsche Drama*. Munich: 1925.

Bellinger, Mrs. Martha Idell (Fletcher). *A Short History of the Drama*. New York: 1927.

Burton, Richard E. *The New American Drama*. New York: 1913.

Chandler, Frank W. *Aspects of Modern Drama*. New York: 1914.

Cheney, Sheldon. *The Art Theater*. New York: 1917; rev. 1925.

Cheney, Sheldon. *The New Movement in the Theatre*. New York: 1914.

Clapp, Henry Austin. *Reminiscences of a Dramatic Critic*. Boston: 1902.

Clark, Barrett H. "American Drama in Its Second Decade," *English Journal*, XXI, 1–11 (January, 1932).

Clark, Barrett H. *The British and American Drama of To-day*. New York: 1915.

Clark, Barrett H. *The Continental Drama of Today*. New York: 1914. (With bibliographies and suggestions for study.)

Clark, Barrett H. *An Hour of American Drama*. Philadelphia: 1930.

Clark, Barrett H. *The Modern Drama*. Reading with a Purpose series. Chicago: 1927.

Clark, Barrett H. *A Study of the Modern Drama*. New York: 1928.

Daly, Hon. Charles P. "The First Theatre in America: When Was the Drama First Introduced into America? An Inquiry." Dunlap Society Publications, N.S. 1, New York: 1896.

Dickinson, Thomas H. *The Case of American Drama*. Boston: 1915.

Dickinson, Thomas H. "The Dawn of a New Dramatic Era," *Virginia Quarterly Review*, V, 411–431 (July, 1929).

Dickinson, Thomas H. *The Insurgent Theatre*. New York: 1917.

Dickinson, Thomas H. *An Outline of Contemporary Drama*. New York: 1927.

Dickinson, Thomas H. *Playwrights of the New American Theater*. New York: 1925.

Dunlap, William. *A History of the American Theatre*. New York: 1832.

Eaton, Walter Prichard. *At the New Theatre and Others*. Boston: c. 1910.

Eaton, Walter Prichard. *The American Stage of To-day*. Boston: c. 1908.

Eaton, Walter Prichard. *The Drama in English*. New York: 1930.

Eaton, Walter Prichard. *Plays and Players: Leaves from a Critic's Scrapbook*. Cincinnati: 1916.

Ford, Paul Leicester. "The Beginnings of American Dramatic Literature," *New England Magazine*, N.S. IX, 673–687 (February, 1894).

Ford, Paul Leicester. "Washington and the Theatre," in Dunlap Society Publications, N.S. 8. New York: 1899.

Goldberg, Isaac. *The Drama of Transition*. Cincinnati: 1922.

Goldberg, Isaac. *The Theatre of George Jean Nathan*. New York: 1926.

Hamilton, Clayton. *Conversations on Contemporary Drama*. New York: 1924.

Hamilton, Clayton. *Problems of the Playwright*. New York: 1917.

Hamilton, Clayton. *Studies in Stagecraft*. New York: 1914.

Hamilton, Clayton. *The Theory of the Theatre*. New York: 1910.

Hapgood, Norman. *The Stage in America, 1897–1900*. New York: 1901.

Henderson, Archibald. *The Changing Drama*. New York: 1919.

Henderson, Archibald. "Early Drama and Professional Entertainment," *Reviewer*, V, 47–57 (1925).

Henry, David D. *William Vaughn Moody*. Boston: 1934. (A scholarly, comprehensive study.)
Hutton, Laurence. *Curiosities of the American Stage*. New York: 1891.
Hutton, Laurence. *Plays and Players*. New York: 1875.
Law, Robert A. "Notes on Some Early American Dramas," *University of Texas Studies in English*, No. 5, 96–100.
Lewisohn, Ludwig. *The Drama and the Stage*. New York: 1922.
Lewisohn, Ludwig. *The Modern Drama*. New York: 1915.
Macgowan, Kenneth. *The Theatre of Tomorrow*. New York: 1921.
MacKaye, Percy. *The Civic Theatre*. New York: 1912.
MacKaye, Percy. *The Playhouse and the Play*. New York: 1909.
Mantle, Burns. *American Playwrights of Today*. New York: 1929.
Matthews, Brander. *The American of the Future and Other Essays*. New York: 1909.
Matthews, Brander. "The American on the Stage," *Scribner's Monthly*, XVIII, 321–333 (July, 1879).
Matthews, Brander. *A Book about the Theater*. New York: 1916.
Matthews, Brander. *The Development of the Drama*. New York: 1903.
Matthews, Brander. *The Historical Novel, and Other Essays*. New York: 1901.
Matthews, Brander. *Inquiries and Opinions*. New York: 1907.
Matthews, Brander. *Playwrights on Playmaking*. New York: 1923.
Matthews, Brander. *Principles of Playmaking*. New York: 1919.
Matthews, Brander. *Rip Van Winkle Goes to the Play, and Other Essays on Plays and Players*. New York: 1926.
Matthews, Brander. *A Study of the Drama*. Boston: 1910.
Matthews, Brander. *These Many Years*. New York: 1917.
Mayorga, Margaret G. *A Short History of the American Drama: Commentaries on Plays Prior to 1920*. New York: 1932.
Moderwell, Hiram K. *The Theatre of To-day*. New York: 1927.
Moses, Montrose J. *The American Dramatist*. Boston: 1911; rev. 1925.
Moses, Montrose J. "The Drama, 1860–1918," in *Cambridge History of American Literature*. New York: 1917–1921. III, 266–298.
Moses, Montrose J., and Brown, John M. *The American Theatre, as Seen by Its Critics, 1752–1934*. New York: 1934.
Nathan, George Jean. *Another Book on the Theatre*. New York: 1915.
Nathan, George Jean. *Art of the Night*. New York: 1928.
Nathan, George Jean. *Intimate Notebooks*. New York: 1932.
Nathan, George Jean. *Materia Critica*. New York: 1924.
Nathan, George Jean. *Mr. George Jean Nathan Presents*. New York: 1917.
Nathan, George Jean. *The Popular Theatre*. New York: 1918.
Nathan, George Jean. *Testament of a Critic*. New York: 1931.
Nicoll, Allardyce. *British Drama; an Historical Survey from the Beginning to the Present Time*. 3rd ed., revised. London: 1932. (Bibliographies, pp. 495–511.)
Nicoll, Allardyce. "The Decline of Realism in the Theatre," *New York Times*, Dramatic Section, January 28, 1934.
Nicoll, Allardyce. *The Development of the Theatre; a Study of Theatrical Art from the Beginnings to the Present Day*. London: 1927. (Bibliographies, pp. 229–238.)
Nicoll, Allardyce. *A History of Early Nineteenth Century Drama, 1800–1850*. Cambridge, England: 1930.
Parrington, V. L. (See above.)
Pence, James Harry. *The Magazine and the Drama*. Dunlap Society Publications, Vol. 17. New York: 1896.
Phelps, William Lyon. *The Twentieth Century Theatre*. New York: 1918.

Quinn, Arthur Hobson. *A History of the American Drama from the Beginning to the Civil War*. New York: 1923.

Quinn, Arthur Hobson. *A History of the American Drama from the Civil War to the Present Day*. 2 vols. New York: 1927. (The standard treatment.)

Quinn, Arthur Hobson. Preface to *Lectures Delivered at the University of Pennsylvania on the Mask and Wig Foundation*. Philadelphia: 1928.

Quinn, Arthur Hobson. "The Significance of Recent American Drama," *Scribner's Magazine*, LXXII, 97–108 (July, 1922). (Reprinted in *Contemporary American Plays*.)

Reed, Perley Isaac. *The Realistic Presentation of American Characters in Native American Plays Prior to Eighteen Seventy*. Ohio State University Bulletin, XXII, No. 26, 5–168 (May, 1918). (Bibliography I: A list of representative American plays written prior to 1870. Bibliography II: Historical and critical works.)

Rockwell, Ethel Theodora. *American Life as Represented in Native One-Act Plays*. Bulletin of the University of Wisconsin. Madison: 1932.

Rockwell, Ethel Theodora. *Study Course in American One-Act Plays*. Chapel Hill, N. C.: 1924.

Ruhl, Arthur. *Second Nights*. New York: 1914.

Sayler, Oliver M. *Our American Theatre*. New York: 1923.

Seilhamer, George O. *History of the American Theatre*. 3 vols. Philadelphia: 1888–1891. I, 1749–1774; II, 1774–1792; III, 1792–1797.

Shipman, Louis Evan. *The True Adventures of a Play*. New York: 1914.

Smith, Hugh H. *Main Currents of Modern French Drama*. New York: 1925.

Sonneck, Oscar George Theodore. *Early Opera in America*. New York: 1915.

Stöeckins, Alfred. *Naturalism in the Recent German Drama, with Special Reference to Gerhart Hauptmann*. New York: 1903.

Strang, L. C. *Players and Plays of the Last Quarter Century*. 2 vols. Boston: c. 1902.

Tyler, Moses Coit. *The Literary History of the American Revolution, 1763–1783*. 2 vols. New York: 1897.

Watson, John F. *Annals of Philadelphia and Pennsylvania in the Olden Times*. Philadelphia: 1879.

Wegelin, Oscar. "The Beginnings of the Drama in America," *Literary Collector*, IX, 177–181 (1905).

Winter, William. *The Wallet of Time*. 2 vols. New York: 1913.

Witkowski, Georg. *The German Drama of the Nineteenth Century*. (Transl. Horning.) New York: 1909.

Young, Stark. *The Flower in Drama*. New York: 1923.

Young, Stark. *The Theater*. New York: 1927.

HISTORY OF THE AMERICAN STAGE

Blake, Charles. *An Historical Account of the Providence Stage.* Providence: 1868.

Brown, T. A. *A History of the New York Stage from the First Performance in 1732 to 1901.* 3 vols. New York: 1903.

Carson, William Glasgow Bruce. *The Theatre on the Frontier; the Early Years of the St. Louis Stage.* Chicago: 1932.

Clapp, William W., Jr. *A Record of the Boston Stage.* Boston: 1853.

Coad, Oral Sumner, and Mims, Edwin, Jr. *The American Stage.* New Haven: 1929.

Crawford, M. C. *The Romance of the American Theatre.* Boston: 1913.

Deutsch, Helen, and Hanau, Stella. *The Provincetown; a Story of the Theatre.* New York: 1931.

Dunlap, William. *A History of the American Theatre.* New York: 1832.

Durang, Charles. *The Philadelphia Stage. From the Year 1749 to the Year 1855.* Published in the *Sunday Despatch* in three series: 1749–1821, beginning in issue of May 7, 1854; 1822–1830, beginning in issue of June 29, 1856; 1830–1855, beginning in issue of July 8, 1860.

Eaton, Walter Prichard, editor. *The Theatre Guild: the First Ten Years.* New York: 1929. (Contains articles by the Directors.)

Hornblow, Arthur. *A History of the Theatre in America from its Beginnings to the Present Time.* 2 vols. Philadelphia: 1919.

Hunter, Alexander, and Polkinhorn, J. H. *The New National Theatre, Washington, D. C.; A Record of Fifty Years.* Washington: 1885.

Ireland, Joseph N. *Records of the New York Stage from 1750 to 1860.* 2 vols. New York: 1866.

James, Reese D. *Old Drury of Philadelphia. A History of the Philadelphia Stage, 1800–1835.* Philadelphia: 1932. (Contains the *Diary or Daily Account Book* of William Burke Wood.)

Macgowan, Kenneth. *Footlights Across America; towards a National Theatre.* New York: 1929.

Moses, Montrose J., and Brown, John M. *The American Theatre, as Seen by Its Critics, 1752–1934.* New York: 1934.

Odell, George C. D. *Annals of the New York Stage.* 7 vols. New York: 1927–1931. I, Beginning to 1798; II, 1798–1821; III, 1821–1834; IV, 1834–1843; V–VII, 1843–1865.

Phelps, H. P. *Players of a Century. A Record of the Albany Stage.* Albany: 1880; reprinted, 1890.

Pollock, Thomas Clark. *The Philadelphia Theatre in the Eighteenth Century.* Together with the *Day Book* of the same period. Philadelphia: 1933.

Seilhamer, G. O. *History of the American Theatre.* 3 vols. Philadelphia: 1888–1891. (Account to 1797.)

Tompkins, Eugene, and Kilby, Quincy. *The History of the Boston Theatre, 1854–1901.* Boston: 1908.

Wemyss, F. C. *The Chronology of the American Stage from 1752 to 1852.* New York: [1852].

Wemyss, F. C. *Twenty-six Years of the Life of an Actor and Manager.* 2 vols. New York: 1847.

Willard, George. *History of the Providence Stage, 1762–1891.* Providence: 1891.

Willis, Eola. *The Charleston Stage in the XVIII Century: with Social Settings of the Time.* Columbia, S. C.: 1924.

Wood, W. B. *Personal Recollections of the Stage.* Philadelphia: 1855. (For Wood's *Diary or Daily Account Book* see James, Reese D., above.)

BIBLIOGRAPHIES AND LISTS

Atkinson, F. W. *American Plays.* Private Catalogue. Brooklyn, N. Y.

Baker, Blanch M. *Dramatic Bibliography.* New York: 1933. (An annotated list of books on the history and criticism of the drama and stage and on the allied arts of the theatre.)

Carson, Lionel, editor. *The Stage Year Book*. London: 1908– . (Gives American plays after 1909.)

Catalogue of the Dramas and Dramatic Poems contained in the Public Library of Cincinnati. Cincinnati: 1879.

Clapp, J. B., and Edgett, E. F. *Plays of the Present*. Dunlap Society Publications, extra vol. New York: 1902.

Dramatic Compositions Copyrighted in the United States. Copyright Office, Washington, D. C. (Issued annually since 1870.)

Faxon, Frederick W., editor. *The Bulletin of Bibliography and Dramatic Index*. Boston: Quarterly.

Faxon, Frederick W. *The Dramatic Index*. Boston: Annual. (Since 1909 it has formed part 2 of *The Annual Magazine Subject Index*.)

Firkins, Ina Ten Eyck. *Index to Plays, 1880–1926*. New York: 1927.

Gilder, Rosamond. *A Theatre Library; a Bibliography of One Hundred Books Relating to the Theatre*. New York: 1932.

Harris, C. Fiske. *Index to American Poetry and Plays in the Collection of C. Fiske Harris*. Providence: 1874.

Haskell, Daniel C. *A List of American Dramas in the New York Public Library*. New York: 1916.

Logasa, Hannah, and Ver Nooy, Winifred. *An Index to One-Act Plays*. Boston: 1924.

Logasa, Hannah, and Ver Nooy, Winifred. *An Index to One-Act Plays. Supplement, 1924–1931*. Boston: 1932.

Moses, Montrose J. Bibliography in *Cambridge History of American Literature*, IV, 760–774 (1921). See also bibliographies in *Representative Plays by American Dramatists* (3 vols.).

Quinn, Arthur Hobson. Extended bibliographies in: *A History of the American Drama from the Beginning to the Civil War*, pp. 395–462; *A History of the American Drama from the Civil War to the Present Day*, II, 255–335.

Reed, Perley Isaac. See Reed, p. 772 above.

Roden, Robert F. *Later American Plays, 1831–1900*. Dunlap Society Publications, N.S., 1900.

Shay, Frank. *A Guide to Longer Plays*. New York: 1925.

Wegelin, Oscar. *Early American Plays, 1714–1830*. Dunlap Society Publications. New York: 1900 (revised and enlarged, 1905).

For indexes to current material see, in addition to *The Dramatic Index* above, "American Bibliography," in *Publications of the Modern Language Association of America*, in *American Literature*, and in *Annual Bibliography of English Language and Literature* (published by the Modern Humanities Research Association).

ANTHOLOGIES OF AMERICAN PLAYS

Baker, George Pierce. *Modern American Plays*. New York: 1920. Contains: Anspacher's *The Unchastened Woman;* Belasco's *The Return of Peter Grimm;* Massey's *Plots and Playwrights;* Sheldon's *Romance;* Thomas's *As a Man Thinks*.

Baker, George Pierce. *Plays of the 47 Workshop*. 4 vols. New York: 1918–1925.

Bates, Alfred. *The Drama*, Vols. XIX and XX. London: 1903. Contains: Anonymous, *The Wept of Wish-Ton-Wish;* Brougham's *Po-Ca-Hon-Tas;* Hanshew's *The Forty-Niners;* Jones's *Solon Shingle;* Longfellow's *The Spanish Student;* Payne's *Thérèse, the Orphan of Geneva*.

Cohen, Helen Louise. *Longer Plays by Modern Authors*. New York: 1922. Contains: Fitch's *Beau Brummel;* Kaufman and Connelly's *Dulcy;* Tarkington's *The Intimate Strangers;* Thomas's *The Copperhead*.

Cordell, Richard A. *Representative Modern Plays*. New York: 1929. Contains: Ade's *The College Widow;* Crothers's *Expressing Willie;* Fitch's *The Climbers;* Hughes's *Hell Bent for Heaven;* Kaufman and Connelly's *Beggar on Horseback;* O'Neill's *Diff'rent*.

Dickinson, Thomas H. *Chief Contemporary Dramatists*. Boston: 1915. Vol. I contains: Fitch's *The Truth;* Percy MacKaye's *The Scarecrow;* Moody's *The Great Divide;* Thomas's *The Witching Hour*. Vol. II contains: Hazleton and Benrimo's *The Yellow Jacket;* Peabody's *The Piper;* Walter's *The Easiest Way*.

Dickinson, Thomas H. *Wisconsin Plays*. New York: 1914. Contains: Dickinson's *In Hospital;* Gale's *The Neighbors;* Leonard's *Glory of the Morning*. Second Series (1918) contains: Gilman's *We Live Again;* Ilsley's *Feast of the Holy Innocents;* Jones's *The Shadow;* Sherry's *On the Pier*.

Dickinson, Thomas H. *Contemporary Drama: English and American*. Boston: 1925. Contains: Anspacher's *The Unchastened Woman;* Crothers's *Mary the Third;* Davis's *Icebound;* Kenyon's *Kindling;* O'Neill's *The Hairy Ape;* Rice's *The Adding Machine*.

Mantle, Burns. *Best Plays of 1919–1920;* and annual series to date. Extract-résumés.

Mayorga, Margaret G. *Representative One-Act Plays by American Authors*. New York: 1919. Contains twenty-four plays.

Moses, Montrose J. *Dramas of Modernism and Their Forerunners*. Boston: 1931. Contains: Howard's *The Silver Cord;* Kelly's *Craig's Wife;* Nichols and Browne's *Wings Over Europe;* O'Neill's *Desire Under the Elms*.

Moses, Montrose J. *Representative American Dramas. National and Local*. Boston: 1925. Contains: Belasco's *The Girl of the Golden West;* Crothers's *Nice People;* Davis's *The Detour;* Fitch's *The City;* Forbes's *The Famous Mrs. Fair;* Hoyt's *A Texas Steer;* Kaufman and Connelly's *Dulcy;* Kelly's *The Show-Off;* Percy MacKaye's *The Scarecrow;* Megrue and Hackett's *It Pays to Advertise;* O'Neill's *The Emperor Jones;* Peabody's *The Piper;* Rice's *The Adding Machine;* Smith's *Mrs. Bumpstead-Leigh*. In the 1933 edition the following plays are added: Barry's *Holiday;* Behrman's *The Second Man;* Connelly's *The Green Pastures;* Sidney Howard's *Lucky Sam McCarver;* Thomas's *The Witching Hour*.

Moses, Montrose J. *Representative Plays by American Dramatists*. New York. Vol. I (1918) contains: Barker's *The Indian Princess;* Brackenridge's *The Battle of Bunker's Hill;* Dunlap's *André;* Godfrey's *The Prince of Parthia;* Leacock's *The Fall of British Tyranny;* Low's *The Politician Outwitted;* Noah's *She Would Be a Soldier;* Rogers's *Ponteach;* Tyler's *The Contrast;* Mrs. Warren's *The Group*. Vol. II (1925) contains: Aiken's *Uncle Tom's Cabin;* Mrs. Bateman's *Self;* Brown's *Sertorius;* Conrad's *Jack Cade;* Hutton's *Fashionable Follies;* Jones's *The People's Lawyer;* Mrs. Mowatt's *Fashion;* Payne's *Brutus;* Tayleure's *Horseshoe Robinson;* Willis's *Bianca Visconti* and *Tortesa the Usurer*. Vol. III (1921) contains: Belasco's *The Return of Peter Grimm;* Boker's *Francesca da Rimini;* Bunce's *Love in '76;* Burke's *Rip Van Winkle;* Fitch's *The Moth and the Flame;* Howard's *Shenandoah;* Steele MacKaye's *Paul Kauvar;* Mitchell's *The New York Idea;* Thomas's *In Mizzoura;* Walter's *The Easiest Way*.

Quinn, Arthur Hobson. *Contemporary American Plays*. New York: 1923. Contains: Crothers's *Nice People;* Emery's *The Hero;* Kaufman and Connelly's *To the Ladies!* O'Neill's *The Emperor Jones;* Williams's *Why Marry?*

Quinn, Arthur Hobson. *Representative American Plays*. New York: 1917; rev. 1925. Contains: Barker's *Superstition;* Belasco and Long's *Madame Butterfly;* Bird's *The Broker of Bogota;* Boker's *Francesca da Rimini;* Boucicault's *The Octoroon;* Crothers's *He and She;* Custis's *Pocahontas;* Dunlap's *André;* Fitch's *Her Great Match;* Gillette's *Secret Service;* Godfrey's *The Prince of Parthia;* Howard's *Shenandoah;* Howe's *Leonora;* Jefferson's *Rip Van Winkle;* Percy MacKaye's *The Scarecrow;* Steele MacKaye's *Hazel Kirke;* Mitchell's *The New York Idea;* Moody's *The Faith Healer;* O'Neill's *Beyond the Horizon;* Payne and Irving's *Charles the Second;* Mrs. Mowatt's *Fashion;* Sheldon's *The Boss;* Smith's *The Triumph at Plattsburg;* Thomas's *The Witching Hour;* Tyler's *The Contrast;* Vollmer's *Sun-Up;* Willis's

Tortesa the Usurer. The 1930 copyright of *Representative American Plays* adds Barry's *Paris Bound*, Fitch's *The Girl with the Green Eyes* (for *Her Great Match*), Herne's *Margaret Fleming*, Howard's *The Silver Cord;* omits: Fitch's *Her Great Match* (as indicated), Howe's *Leonora*, and Smith's *The Triumph at Plattsburg*.

Quinn, Arthur Hobson. *Representative American Plays from 1880 to the Present Day*. New York: 1928. (Contains plays in foregoing volume from Steele MacKaye on.)

Shay, Frank. *Provincetown Plays*. 6 vols. New York: 1916–1918.

Shay, Frank. *Twenty Contemporary One-Act Plays*. New York: 1921; rev. 1922.

Tucker, S. Marion. *Modern American and British Plays*. New York: 1931. Contains: Anderson's *Saturday's Children;* Barry's *In a Garden;* Crothers's *Mary the Third;* Emery's *The Hero;* Green's *The Field God;* Howard's *The Silver Cord;* Kaufman and Connelly's *To the Ladies!* Millay's *The King's Henchman;* Moeller's *Madame Sand;* O'Neill's *The Great God Brown;* Vollmer's *Sun-Up*.

APPENDIX II

CHRONOLOGICAL TABLES

AMERICAN DRAMA
AMERICAN LITERATURE
ENGLISH AND EUROPEAN DRAMA AND LITERATURE

American Drama

PURITANISM · Colonial period: very little activity in drama.

1606	First dramatic production in America. French masque given in Acadia.
1665	First play in English. *Ye Bare and Ye Cubb* given in Virginia. Producers brought to court; acquitted.
1736	A few British plays given by the "Young Gentlemen" of William and Mary College.
1749	The first American acting company was organized in Philadelphia under the direction of Thomas Kean and Walter Murray. Staged Addison's *Cato.* Later removed to New York where they produced twenty-four plays, many from the Restoration era.
1752	Permission granted to Lewis Hallam's Company to open in Williamsburg, Virginia, September 15, with *The Merchant of Venice.* First important acting company in America, having a repertoire of over forty plays, chiefly from Elizabethan and Restoration dramatists.

NATIONALISM

1766	*Ponteach; or, The Savages of America*, Major Robert Rogers. First tragedy written on a native subject. Unproduced.
1767	*The Prince of Parthia*, Thomas Godfrey (1736–1763). Produced at Southwark Theatre, Philadelphia. The first native American play to be professionally staged. A five-act tragedy making use of Parthian names and laid in Parthia about the beginning of the Christian period; plot and events largely Godfrey's own creation. Influenced by Shakespeare.
1773	*The Adulateur*, Mrs. Mercy Otis Warren. Unproduced. Satire on corrupt Thomas Hutchinson, Governor of the Massachusetts Colony.
1775	*The Group*, Mrs. Mercy Otis Warren. Unproduced. Satire on those who violated the Massachusetts Charter.
1776	Publication of *The Fall of British Tyranny, or American Liberty Triumphant.* Ascribed to J. Leacock. Traces source of Revolution to Parliamentary rivalries. Publication of *The Battle of Bunker's Hill*, Hugh Henry Brackenridge (1748–1816). Drama of patriotism.
1787	*The Contrast*, Royall Tyler (1757–1826). (For an account of Tyler and his plays see introduction to *The Contrast*, this volume.)
1789	Publication of *The Politician Outwitted*, Samuel Low. Clever political satire; Federalistic. *The Father, or American Shandyism*, William Dunlap (1766–1839). Derived from Sterne's *Tristram Shandy.*
1795	*Fontainville Abbey*, William Dunlap. Gothic drama.
1797	*Bunker Hill*, John Burk. Patriotic drama.
1798	*André*, William Dunlap. (See introduction and play, in this volume.)
1807	*Tears and Smiles*, James Nelson Barker (1784–1858). Resemblances to Tyler's *The Contrast.*
1808	*The Indian Princess; or, La Belle Sauvage*, James Nelson Barker. One of the earliest Indian plays.

American Literature	English and European
Captain John Smith (1580–1631). Controversial account of the Pocahontas episode.	Close of Elizabethan period of drama. Death of Shakespeare, 1616.
Cotton Mather (1663–1728). *The Wonders of the Invisible World*, 1693. Advocates persecution of witches.	Inactivity of theatre during the Puritan Commonwealth, 1642–1660.
Jonathan Edwards (1703–1758). *God Glorified in Man's Dependence*, 1731. Orthodox statement of rigid Puritanism.	Corneille (1606–1684).
	Molière (1622–1673).
John Woolman (1720–1772). Quaker.	Racine (1639–1699).
Benjamin Franklin (1706–1790). Humanitarian; moralist; scientist.	Restoration and early Eighteenth-Century drama: Dryden, Congreve, Wycherley, Vanbrugh, Farquhar, Etherege, Otway, Rowe, Addison.
St. Jean de Crèvecœur (1735–1813). *Letters from an American Farmer*, 1782. Nationalistic; sets forth concept of ideal American.	Pope (1688–1744).
Thomas Paine (1737–1809). Revolution advocated in *Common Sense* and *The Crisis.* Philosophy of *Rights of Man* derived from Deistic thought. *The Age of Reason.*	Richardson (1689–1761).
	Johnson (1709–1784). Sterne (1713–1768). Burke (1729–1797).
Thomas Jefferson (1743–1826). Declaration of Independence. Faith in common man.	Voltaire (1694–1778).
Alexander Hamilton (1757–1804). *The Federalist.* Strong central government; distrust of common man.	Rousseau (1712–1778).
	Diderot (1713–1784).
Philip Freneau (1752–1832). Many partisan tracts and nationalistic poems. Jeffersonian *National Gazette*, founded in 1791.	Burns (1759–1796).
John Trumbull (1750–1831). Timothy Dwight (1752–1817). Joel Barlow (1754–1812). Nationalistic and patriotic writers.	Goldsmith (1728–1774). *The Good-Natured Man*, 1768. *She Stoops to Conquer*, 1773.
	Sheridan (1751–1816). *The Rivals*, 1775. *The School for Scandal*, 1777.
Charles Brockden Brown (1771–1810). Novels of horror and mystery; Gothicism.	Lessing (1729–1781). Kant (1724–1804). Schiller (1759–1805). Kotzebue (1761–1819). Source of many Dunlap plays.
Washington Irving (1783–1859). *Salmagundi*, 1807. Addisonian papers in collaboration with James K. Paulding. *Knickerbocker's History of New York*, 1809. *Sketch Book*, 1819. *The Alhambra*, 1832. Romantic stories and essays.	Wordsworth (1770–1850), Coleridge (1772–1834). *Lyrical Ballads*, 1798.

American Drama

ROMANTICISM

1812 *Marmion*, James Nelson Barker. Based on Scott's poem.

1818 *Brutus, or The Fall of Tarquin*, John Howard Payne (1791–1852). Produced first in London.

1824 *Superstition*, James Nelson Barker. (See introduction and play, this volume.)
Charles the Second; or, the Merry Monarch, John Howard Payne. Clever comedy, written in collaboration with Washington Irving. Based on *La Jeunesse de Henri V*, Alexandre Duval.

1829 John Kerr's version of *Rip Van Winkle*. Anonymous version of 1828 has not survived. Many later dramatizations of Irving's story based on Kerr's play. Joseph Jefferson the third (1829–1905) famous in the title role.
James H. Hackett (1800–1871). Prominent actor. Successful portrayal of Yankee characters.
Edwin Forrest (1806–1872). Leading actor of his day. Stimulated playwrights, particularly Robert Montgomery Bird.
Metamora, or the Last of the Wampanoags, John Augustus Stone. Indian drama.

1830 *Pocahontas, or the Settlers of Virginia*, G. W. P. Custis. The Pocahontas-John Smith episode.
The Triumph at Plattsburg, Richard Penn Smith. Recounts McDonough's naval victory at Plattsburg Bay in 1814.

1831 *The Gladiator*, Robert Montgomery Bird. (See introduction and the play, this volume.)

1832 William Dunlap's *A History of the American Theatre*. Invaluable account of American drama to time of publication.

1834 *The Broker of Bogota*, Robert Montgomery Bird.

1835 *Jack Cade*, Robert T. Conrad. Play deals with Kentish peasant uprising in 1450.

1837 *Bianca Visconti*, Nathaniel Parker Willis (1806–1867). (See introduction and play, this volume.)

1839 *Tortesa the Usurer*, Nathaniel Parker Willis. From an Italian story.
The People's Lawyer, J. S. Jones.

1845 *Fashion*, Mrs. Anna Cora Mowatt (1819–1870). (See introduction and play, this volume.)

1846 *Witchcraft, or the Martyrs of Salem*, Cornelius Mathews (1817–1889). Theme of Puritan persecution.

1847 Publication of *The Bucktails; or, Americans in England*, James Kirke Paulding. (See introduction and play, this volume.)

1848 *A Glance at New York*, Benjamin A. Baker. One of the first of the highly-localized "city" plays.

1849 *Calaynos*, George Henry Boker (1823–1890). Title character a Spaniard with a Moorish strain.

1850 *The Betrothal*, George Henry Boker. Comedy.

American Literature	English and European
James Fenimore Cooper (1789–1851). *The Spy*, 1821. *The Pilot*, 1823. *The Pioneers*, 1823. *The Pathfinder*, 1840. *The Deerslayer*, 1841. The romantic novel of the American forest and the sea.	Scott (1771–1832). Byron (1788–1824).
William Cullen Bryant (1794–1878). "Thanatopsis," 1817. *Poems*, 1821. *Poems*, 1832. Romantic naturalism in poetry.	Shelley (1792–1822). Keats (1795–1821).
Edgar Allan Poe (1809–1849). *Tamerlane and Other Poems*, 1827. *Al Aaraaf, Tamerlane, and Minor Poems*, 1829. *Poems*, 1831. "The Fall of the House of Usher," 1839. "The Murders in the Rue Morgue," 1841. *The Raven and Other Poems*, 1845. Lyric poems; short stories of horror, mystery, ratiocination.	Alexandre Duval (1760–1838). His *La Jeunesse de Henri V* is the basis of John Howard Payne's *Charles the Second; or, the Merry Monarch*.
Nathaniel Hawthorne (1804–1864). *Fanshawe*, 1828. *Twice-Told Tales*, first series, 1837. *Twice-Told Tales*, second series, 1842. *Mosses from an Old Manse*, 1846. *The Scarlet Letter*, 1850. *The House of the Seven Gables*, 1851. *The Blithedale Romance*, 1852. *The Marble Faun*, 1860. Romanticized short stories and novels.	Madame de Staël (1766–1817). Goethe (1749–1832). Heine (1797–1856). Balzac (1799–1850).
John Greenleaf Whittier (1807–1892). "To William Lloyd Garrison," 1831. "Massachusetts to Virginia," 1842. Editor of *The Pennsylvania Freeman*, 1838–1840. *Voices of Freedom*, 1846. *Poems*, 1849. *Songs of Labor*, 1850. *Snow-Bound*, 1866.	
Ralph Waldo Emerson (1803–1882). *Nature*, 1836. "The American Scholar," 1837. *Essays*, 1841, 1844. *Poems*, 1847. *Representative Men*, 1850. *English Traits*, 1856. *The Conduct of Life*, 1860. Transcendentalism.	Macaulay (1800–1859).
Henry David Thoreau (1817–1862). *A Week on the Concord and Merrimack Rivers*, 1849. *Walden*, 1854. *Excursions*, 1863. *The Maine Woods*, 1864. *Cape Cod*, 1865.	Carlyle (1795–1881). *Sartor Resartus*, 1833–1834. Ruskin (1819–1900).
Henry Wadsworth Longfellow (1807–1882). *Outre-Mer*, 1835. *Hyperion*, 1839. *Voices of the Night*, 1839. *Ballads and Other Poems*, 1841. *Evangeline*, 1847. *The Song of Hiawatha*, 1855. *The Courtship of Miles Standish*, 1858. *Tales of a Wayside Inn*, 1863.	Dickens (1812–1870). Thackeray (1811–1863).

American Drama

ROMANTICISM

1852 *Uncle Tom's Cabin*, George L. Aiken's version of Mrs. Stowe's epoch-making novel of the same year.

1853 *Leonor de Guzman*, George Henry Boker.

1855 *Francesca da Rimini*, George Henry Boker. (See introduction and play, this volume.)

1856 *Self*, Mrs. Sidney F. Bateman. Social satire in the vein of *Fashion.*
First copyright law passed protecting dramatists against literary piracy, which had been the practice up to this time.

1857 *Love in '76*, Oliver Bell Bunce (1828–1890). Clever Revolutionary comedy.
Leonora, or the World's Own, Julia Ward Howe. Romantic play set in Italy.
The Poor of New York, Dion Boucicault (1820–1890). Local drama.

1859 *The Octoroon*, Dion Boucicault. Nonpartisan slavery play based on Reid's *The Quadroon.*

1860 *The Colleen Bawn*, Dion Boucicault. Taken from Gerald Griffin's novel, *The Collegians.* Irish theme.
Organization of the "road show" by Boucicault, which led to the elevation in importance of the play over the actor, thus militating against the "star" system.

Beginnings of Realism

1862 *Leah the Forsaken*, Augustin Daly's (1838–1899) first play.

1867 Organization of the Daly stock company.
Under the Gaslight, Augustin Daly. Localized New York drama. Realism of setting and treatment.

1870 *Frou-Frou*, adaptation from the French, by Augustin Daly.
Saratoga, Bronson Howard (1842–1908). Produced by Daly.

1871 *Horizon*, Augustin Daly. Frontier drama. (See introduction and play, this volume.)

1872 *Davy Crockett*, Frank Hitchcock Murdoch. Early frontier drama; based on life of subject.

The Frontier

1874 *The Shaughraun*, Dion Boucicault. Irish theme.

1875 *The Big Bonanza*, Augustin Daly. Satire on speculation.

1876 *The Two Men of Sandy Bar*, Bret Harte. Frontier drama.

1877 *Ah Sin*, Bret Harte and Mark Twain. Frontier drama.
The Danites in the Sierras, Joaquin Miller. (See introduction and play, this volume.)

1878 *The Banker's Daughter*, Bronson Howard. Analyzed by the author in *The Autobiography of a Play.*

1879 *My Partner*, Bartley Campbell. Frontier drama.

1880 *Hearts of Oak*, James A. Herne (1839–1901). Realistic treatment of character.

1881 *Forty-Nine*, Joaquin Miller. Frontier drama.

1882 *Young Mrs. Winthrop*, Bronson Howard.

1887 *The Henrietta*, Bronson Howard. (See introduction and play, this volume.)

American Literature	English and European
James Russell Lowell (1819–1891). *Poems*, 1843. Contributions to the *Anti-Slavery Standard*, 1846–1850. *Poems*, second series, 1847. *Biglow Papers*, first series, 1848. *A Fable for Critics*, 1848. *Biglow Papers*, second series, 1867. *Among My Books*, 1870. *My Study Windows*, 1871.	Scribe (1791–1861). Mérimée (1803–1870). Dumas, *père* (1802–1870).
Oliver Wendell Holmes (1809–1894). *Poems*, 1833. *The Autocrat of the Breakfast-Table*, 1858. *The Professor at the Breakfast-Table*, 1859. *Elsie Venner*, 1861. *The Poet at the Breakfast-Table*, 1872.	George Sand (1804–1876). Victor Hugo (1802–1885). Alfred de Musset (1810–1857).
Walt Whitman (1819–1892). *Leaves of Grass*, 1855 (2nd edition, 1856). *Drum-Taps*, 1865. *Democratic Vistas*, 1871. *Specimen Days and Collect*, 1882.	
Herman Melville (1819–1891). *Typee*, 1846. *Omoo*, 1847. *Redburn*, 1849. *White-Jacket*, 1850. *Mardi*, 1849. *Moby Dick*, 1851. *Pierre*, 1852.	Bulwer-Lytton (1803–1873).
Joaquin Miller (1841–1913). *Songs of the Sierras*, 1871.	
Bret Harte (1836–1902). "The Luck of Roaring Camp," 1868. "The Outcasts of Poker Flat," 1869.	
Mark Twain (1835–1910). *The Jumping Frog and Other Sketches*, 1867. *The Innocents Abroad*, 1869. *Roughing It*, 1872. *The Adventures of Tom Sawyer*, 1876. *Life on the Mississippi*, 1883. *The Adventures of Huckleberry Finn*, 1884. *The Mysterious Stranger*, 1916.	
William Dean Howells (1837–1920). *A Modern Instance*, 1882. *The Rise of Silas Lapham*, 1885. Realism.	Renan (1823–1892). Taine (1828–1893).
Henry James (1843–1916). *The American*, 1876. *The Portrait of a Lady*, 1881. *The Bostonians*, 1886. *The Wings of the Dove*, 1902. *The Ambassadors*, 1903. *The Golden Bowl*, 1904.	Tennyson (1809–1892). Browning (1812–1889).
Sidney Lanier (1842–1881). *Poems*, 1877. *The Science of English Verse*, 1880.	Arnold (1822–1888). Meredith (1828–1909). Swinburne (1837–1909). Hardy (1840–1928).

American Drama

REALISM

1888 *Shenandoah*, Bronson Howard. Civil War theme.

1889 *Five O'Clock Tea*, William Dean Howells (1837–1920). Realistic social comedy.

1890 *A Texas Steer*, Charles Hale Hoyt (1860–1900). Comedy of western characters.
Margaret Fleming, James A. Herne. Realistic study of character.

1891 *Alabama*, Augustus Thomas (1857–1934). Localized realistic drama.

1892 *Shore Acres*, James A. Herne. Character study.

1893 *In Mizzoura*, Augustus Thomas. Localized drama.

1895 *Secret Service*, William Gillette (1855–). Civil War theme; southern sympathy.

1899 *Griffith Davenport*, James A. Herne. Civil War theme.
Sherlock Holmes, William Gillette.

1900 *Madame Butterfly*, David Belasco (1853–1931).

1901 *The Climbers*, Clyde Fitch (1865–1909). Society drama.

1902 *The Girl with the Green Eyes*, Clyde Fitch. Society drama.

1903 *Major André*, Clyde Fitch. Historical drama.

1904 *Adrea*, David Belasco in collaboration with John Luther Long.
The Girl of the Golden West, David Belasco.

1905 *The Woman in the Case*, Clyde Fitch.
Clarice, William Gillette. South Carolina drama.
Her Great Match, Clyde Fitch.

1906 *The Truth*, Clyde Fitch. Reflective social drama.
The New York Idea, Langdon Mitchell. (See play and introduction, this volume.)

1907 *The Great Divide*, William Vaughn Moody (1865–1910). Eastern vs. Western culture.
The Witching Hour, Augustus Thomas. Mental telepathy.

1909 *The City*, Clyde Fitch. Effects of city life.
The Easiest Way, Eugene Walter.
The Nigger, Edward Sheldon. Southern problem.

1910 *The Faith Healer*, William Vaughn Moody.
A Man's World, Rachel Crothers.

Impressionism

1911 *The Return of Peter Grimm*, David Belasco. Deals with the presence of the dead.
The Scarecrow, Percy MacKaye. Based on Hawthorne.
As a Man Thinks, Augustus Thomas. The double standard and mental healing.
The Boss, Edward Sheldon. Political play.
The Herfords (*He and She*), Rachel Crothers.

1912 *The Yellow Jacket*, George Hazleton and J. H. Benrimo.

1913 *Romance*, Edward Sheldon.

1915 *The Unchastened Woman*, Louis K. Anspacher.

1917 *Madame Sand*, Philip Moeller. (See play and introduction, this volume.)
Why Marry? Jesse Lynch Williams (1871–1929). Society comedy.

American Literature	English and European
Hamlin Garland (1860–). *Main-Travelled Roads*, 1891. *Crumbling Idols*, 1894. *A Son of the Middle Border*, 1917.	Oscar Wilde (1856–1900). Ibsen (1828–1906). Strindberg (1849–1912).
Stephen Crane (1871–1900). *The Red Badge of Courage*, 1895. *Maggie, a Girl of the Streets*, 1896. *War Is Kind*, 1899.	Tchekhov (1860–1904). Tolstoy (1828–1910). Björnson (1832–1910).
Frank Norris (1870–1902). *The Octopus*, 1901. *The Pit*, 1902.	Rostand (1868–1918). Maeterlinck (1862–).
Theodore Dreiser (1871–). *Sister Carrie*, 1900. *Jennie Gerhardt*, 1911. *The Financier*, 1912. *The Titan*, 1914. *The Genius*, 1915. *An American Tragedy*, 1925.	Stephen Phillips (1868–1915). *Paolo and Francesca*, 1899. Gabriele D'Annunzio (1863–). *Francesca da Rimini*, 1900.
Edwin Arlington Robinson (1869–). *The Torrent and the Night Before*, 1896. *The Children of the Night*, 1897. *The Man against the Sky*, 1916. *Tristram*, 1927.	Sir Arthur Wing Pinero (1855–1934). H. Granville Barker (1877–).
Edith Wharton (1862–). *The House of Mirth*, 1905. *Ethan Frome*, 1911. *The Age of Innocence*, 1920.	Eugène Brieux (1858–1932).
Amy Lowell (1874–1925). *Sword Blades and Poppy Seed*, 1914. *Men, Women and Ghosts*, 1916. *John Keats*, 1925.	John Millington Synge (1871–1909).
Sherwood Anderson (1876–). *Marching Men*, 1917. *Winesburg, Ohio*, 1919. *Poor White*, 1920. *The Triumph of the Egg*, 1921. *Dark Laughter*, 1925.	Hermann Sudermann (1857–1928). Gerhart Hauptmann (1862–).
Edgar Lee Masters (1869–). *Spoon River Anthology*, 1915.	Henry Arthur Jones (1851–1929).
Carl Sandburg (1878–). *Chicago Poems*, 1916. *Cornhuskers*, 1918. *Smoke and Steel*, 1920. *Slabs of the Sunburnt West*, 1922.	Lady Gregory (1859–1932).

American Drama

Modern Romanticism — REALISM — Satire — Expressionism

1919 *Molière*, *Sophie*, Philip Moeller.

1920 *Beyond the Horizon*, Eugene O'Neill (1888–). (See introduction to *The Great God Brown*, this volume.)
The Emperor Jones, Eugene O'Neill.
Miss Lulu Bett, Zona Gale (1874–).

1921 *Anna Christie*, Eugene O'Neill.
The Detour, Owen Davis (1874–). Realistic "folk" drama.
Dulcy, Marc Connelly (1890–) and George S. Kaufman (1889–). Satire on the conventionalized mind.

1922 *To the Ladies!* Marc Connelly and George S. Kaufman.

1923 *You and I*, Philip Barry (1896–). (See play and introduction, this volume.)
Icebound, Owen Davis. (See play and introduction, this volume.)
The Show-Off, George E. Kelly (1887–). Satire on exhibitionism.

1924 *What Price Glory*, Maxwell Anderson (1888–) and Laurence Stallings (1894–). Stark realism in war drama.
Desire Under the Elms, Eugene O'Neill.
Beggar on Horseback, Marc Connelly and George S. Kaufman. Satire on American commercialism.
They Knew What They Wanted, Sidney Howard (1891–). Pulitzer Prize play.

1925 *In a Garden*, Philip Barry.
Craig's Wife, George E. Kelly. Pulitzer Prize play.

1926 *The Great God Brown*, Eugene O'Neill. (See play and introduction, this volume.)
White Wings, Philip Barry.
Ned McCobb's Daughter, Sidney Howard.
In Abraham's Bosom; the Biography of a Negro, in Seven Scenes, Paul Green (1894–). (See introduction to *The Field God*, this volume.)

1927 *The Field God*, Paul Green. (See introduction and play, this volume.)
Paris Bound, Philip Barry.

1928 *Marco Millions*, *Strange Interlude*, *Lazarus Laughed*, Eugene O'Neill.

1929 *Dynamo*, Eugene O'Neill.

1930 *Hotel Universe*, Philip Barry.
The Green Pastures, Marc Connelly. Pulitzer Prize play.

1931 *Mourning Becomes Electra*, Eugene O'Neill.
The House of Connelly, Paul Green.

1932 *Tread the Green Grass*, Paul Green.
The Animal Kingdom, Philip Barry.

1933 *Ah, Wilderness!* Eugene O'Neill.

1934 *Days Without End*, Eugene O'Neill.
The Joyous Season, Philip Barry.
Roll, Sweet Chariot, Paul Green.

American Literature	English and European
Sinclair Lewis (1885–). *Main Street*, 1920. *Babbitt*, 1922. *Arrowsmith*, 1925. *Elmer Gantry*, 1927. *Dodsworth*, 1929. *Ann Vickers*, 1933. *Work of Art*, 1934.	Joseph Conrad (1857–1924). John Galsworthy (1867–1933).
Willa Cather (1876–). *O Pioneers*, 1913. *My Antonia*, 1918. *The Professor's House*, 1925. *Death Comes for the Archbishop*, 1927. *Shadows on the Rock*, 1931.	
James Branch Cabell (1879–). *Jurgen*, 1919. *Figures of Earth*, 1921. *The High Place*, 1923. *Straws and Prayer-Books*, 1924. *The Silver Stallion*, 1926. *Something About Eve*, 1927.	Leonid Andreyev (1871–1919). Maxim Gorki (1868–).
Zona Gale (1874–). *Friendship Village*, 1908. *Mothers to Men*, 1911. *Birth*, 1918 (dramatized as *Mister Pitt*, 1925). *Miss Lulu Bett*, 1920 (dramatized, 1920). *Faint Perfume*, 1923. *Preface to a Life*, 1926.	Karel Capek (1890–). Luigi Pirandello (1867–). Anatole France (1844–1924). Sacha Guitry (1885–).
Dorothy Canfield Fisher (1879–). *The Bent Twig*, 1915. *The Brimming Cup*, 1921. *Rough-Hewn*, 1922. *The Home-Maker*, 1924. *Deepening Stream*, 1930.	Ferenc Molnár (1878–). George Bernard Shaw (1856–). William Butler Yeats (1865–).
Robert Frost (1875–). *A Boy's Will*, 1913. *North of Boston*, 1914. *Selected Poems*, 1923. *West-Running Brook*, 1928.	Sir James M. Barrie (1860–). H. G. Wells (1866–).
H. L. Mencken (1880–). *A Book of Burlesques*, 1916. *A Book of Prefaces*, 1917. *The American Language*, 1919. *Prejudices*, 1919.	Arnold Bennett (1867–1931). John Drinkwater (1882–). Lord Dunsany (1878–).
George Jean Nathan (1882–). *Mr. George Jean Nathan Presents*, 1917. *Materia Critica*, 1924. *Testament of a Critic*, 1931.	John Masefield (1875–). A. A. Milne (1882–). W. Somerset Maugham (1874–).
Irving Babbitt (1865–1933). *The New Laokoön*, 1910. *The Masters of Modern French Criticism*, 1912. *Rousseau and Romanticism*, 1919. *Democracy and Leadership*, 1924.